Handbook of Child Language Disorders

Handbook of Child Language Disorders

Edited by
Richard G. Schwartz

Psychology Press
Taylor & Francis Group

NEW YORK AND HOVE

Published in 2009
by Psychology Press
270 Madison Avenue
New York, NY 10016
www.psypress.com

Published in Great Britain
by Psychology Press
27 Church Road
Hove, East Sussex BN3 2FA
www.psypress.com

Copyright © 2009 by Psychology Press

Psychology Press is an imprint of the Taylor & Francis Group, an Informa business

Typeset by RefineCatch Limited, Bungay, Suffolk, UK
Printed and bound by Sheridan Books, Inc. in the USA on acid-free paper
Cover design by Lisa Dynan

10 9 8 7 6 5 4 3

Library of Congress Cataloging in Publication Data
A catalog record for this book is available from the Library of Congress

ISBN: 978–1 –84169–433–7 (hbk)

This book is dedicated to my daughters Lindsay, Brandi, and Helene

Contents

About the Editor

Richard G. Schwartz is a Presidential Professor in the Ph.D. Program in Speech-Language-Hearing Sciences at the Graduate Center of the City University of New York. He has published widely in the areas of phonological acquisition, working memory, and language processing in SLI. Dr. Schwartz's research has been supported by grants from the National Institute on Deafness and Other Communication Disorders of the National Institutes of Health since 1979. He has served as an editor of the *Journal of Speech, Language, and Hearing Science*.

Contributors

Leonard Abbeduto
Department of Educational Psychology
Waisman Center
University of Wisconsin
Madison, WI, USA

Lisa M. Bedore
Department of Communication
    Sciences and Disorders
The University of Texas
Austin, TX, USA

Irena Botwinik-Rotem
Department of Linguistics
Tel Aviv University
Tel Aviv
Israel

Bonnie Brinton
Department of Communication Disorders
Brigham Young University
Provo, UT, USA

Miranda Cleary
Ph.D. Program in Speech and
    Hearing Sciences
The Graduate Center of the City of
    New York
New York, NY, USA

Patricia Deevy
Department of Speech, Language, and
    Hearing Sciences
Purdue University
West Lafayette, IN, USA

Jan Edwards
Department of Communicative Disorders
University of Wisconsin
Madison, WI, USA

Marc E. Fey
Department of Hearing and Speech
University of Kansas Medical Center
Kansas City, KS, USA

Lizbeth H. Finestack
Waisman Center
University of Wisconsin-Madison
Madison, WI, USA

Paul Fletcher
Speech and Hearing Sciences
University College Cork
Cork
Ireland

Naama Friedmann
School of Education
Tel Aviv University
Tel Aviv
Israel

Martin Fujiki
Department of Communication Disorders
Brigham Young University
Provo, UT, USA

Joanne Gerenser
Eden II Programs
Staten Island, NY, USA

Ronald B. Gillam
Communicative Disorders and
    Deaf Education
Utah State University
Logan, UT, USA

Sandra L. Gillam
Communicative Disorders and Deaf
    Education
Utah State University
Logan, UT, USA

Jeffrey R. Gruen
Section of Neonatology
Department of Pediatrics
Yale University School of Medicine
New Haven, CT, USA

Pamela A. Hadley
Department of Speech and Hearing
  Science
University of Illinois
Champaign, IL, USA

Charles W. Haynes
Graduate Program in Communication
  Sciences and Disorders
Institute of Health Professions
MGH
Boston, MA, USA

Pamela E. Hook
Graduate Program in Communication
  Sciences and Disorders
Institute of Health Professions
MGH
Boston, MA, USA

Marc F. Joanisse
Department of Psychology
The University of Western Ontario
London, Ontario, Canada

Kathryn Kohnert
Department of Speech-Language-
  Hearing Sciences
University of Minnesota
Minneapolis, MN, USA

Laurence B. Leonard
Department of Speech, Language,
  and Hearing Sciences
Purdue University
West Lafayette, IN, USA

Nathan D. Maxfield
Department of Communication Sciences
  and Disorders
University of South Florida
Tampa, FL, USA

Andrea McDuffie
Waisman Center
University of Wisconsin-Madison
Madison, WI, USA

Karla K. McGregor
Department of Communication Sciences
  and Disorders
University of Iowa
Iowa City, IA, USA

Maria Mody
Athinoula A. Martinos Center for
  Biomedical Imaging
Massachusetts General Hospital
Harvard Medical School
Boston, MA, USA

James W. Montgomery
School of Hearing, Speech, and
  Language Sciences
Ohio University
Athens, OH, USA

Benjamin Munson
Department of Speech-Language-
  Hearing Sciences
University of Minnesota
Minneapolis, MN, USA

Janna B. Oetting
Department of Communication Sciences
  and Disorders
Louisiana State University
Baton Rouge, LA, USA

Elizabeth D. Peña
Department of Communication Sciences
  and Disorders
The University of Texas
Austin, TX, USA

Richard G. Schwartz
Ph.D. Program in Speech-Language-Hearing
  Sciences
The Graduate Center
City University of New York
New York, NY, USA

Liat Seiger-Gardner
Department of Speech, Language, and
  Hearing Sciences
Lehman College
City University of New York
Bronx, NY, USA

Valerie L. Shafer
Ph.D. Program in Speech-Language-Hearing
 Sciences
The Graduate Center
City University of New York
New York, NY, USA

Bennett A. Shaywitz
Center for the Study of Learning,
 Reading, and Attention
Department of Pediatrics
Yale University School of Medicine
New Haven, CT, USA

Sally E. Shaywitz
Center for the Study of Learning,
 Reading, and Attention
Department of Pediatrics
Yale University School of Medicine
New Haven, CT, USA

J. Bruce Tomblin
Department of Communication Sciences
 and Disorders
University of Iowa
Iowa City, IA, USA

Baila Tropper
Ph.D. Program in Speech-Language-
 Hearing Sciences
The Graduate Center
City University of New York
New York, NY, USA

Julie A. Washington
Department of Communicative Disorders
University of Wisconsin
Madison, WI, USA

Jennifer Windsor
Department of Speech-Language-Hearing
 Sciences
University of Minnesota
Minneapolis, MN, USA

Preface

My own interests in developmental processes and what can go awry began in high school with a focus on biology. Although my specific focus changed somewhat through undergraduate and graduate studies, this core interest remained the same. I became interested in language and, ultimately, in the mechanisms of language acquisition and disorders of that process. Although I suspect the authors of the following chapters came to this interest along various paths, we all have arrived at the same destination in our focus on language impairments that affect children. This handbook is intended to bring our interests in these different groups of children together, for the first time, in a single volume.

As has often been noted, the acquisition of language is one of the most remarkable human achievements. It is achieved without effort or direct teaching for the vast majority of children, a remarkable interaction of biology and environment that occurs with seemingly wide individual variation, yet with remarkable consistency. Besides its intimate relationship with human cognition, it is also the thread that binds our social lives.

When language acquisition fails to occur as expected, the impact can be far-reaching. The consequences may be more significant than many other developmental challenges. Impairments in language affect social development, academic performance, and, ultimately, employment and quality of life. Research into the nature, causes, and remediation of children's language disorders provides important insights into the nature of language acquisition and its underlying bases and leads to innovative clinical approaches to these disorders.

The book is organized in five sections: Typology of Child Language Disorders; Bases of Child Language Disorders; Language Contexts of Child Language Disorders; Deficits, Assessment, and Intervention in Child Language Disorders; and Research Methods in Child Language Disorders. In Typology, we introduce some of the general diagnostic categories of children's language disorders. In Bases, the authors provide overviews of linguistics, cognitive science, neurobiology, memory and attention, speech perception and production, genetics, and cognitive science. The Language Contexts section considers the implications of language characteristics for children's language disorders when children acquire more than one language, across languages, and in other dialects. The chapters in Deficits, Assessment, and Intervention examine the deficits in areas such as pragmatics, syntax, semantics, morphosyntax, reading, and writing, as well as in processing speed, attention, and perception. The final section explores the research methods used in the study of production, comprehension, intervention, and neuroscience in children with language disorders.

Determining the most appropriate level for the book was a challenge. We wanted to bring state-of-the-art information in child language disorders together in a single volume for advanced undergraduate students and graduate students in speech language pathology, special education, and neuropsychology as well as for clinicians and active researchers in these disciplines. We believe we have accomplished this balancing act by including introductory-level information as well as advanced state-of-the-art reviews of current theories and research.

I want to acknowledge the generous and outstanding contributions of my fellow chapter authors, who all took time from their busy research and writing lives to contribute to this volume. I also want to thank my teachers, colleagues, students, and the children from whom I first learned about language disorders and from whom I continue to learn about the nature and impact of these disorders. Baila Tropper, Elizabeth Rodriguez, Rebecca Marcadis, and Micaela Wire provided valuable assistance in the final editing. The National Institutes of Health, particularly the National Institute on Deafness and Other Communicative Disorders, has funded my research for 30 years. Other authors in the volume have received support from the National Institute on Child Health and Development. The preparation of this volume was supported by grant DC03558 from NIDCD.

New York City
2008

Part I

Typology of Child Language Disorders

1

Specific Language Impairment

RICHARD G. SCHWARTZ

S tudies of specific language impairment (SLI) have become ubiquitous (Bishop, 1997; Leonard, 1998). The modern era of research in specific language learning disabilities began in the 1970s with a handful of studies that differentiated these children from children with autism, with developmental delays, with hearing impairments, and with seizures or other neurological conditions. This now large body of research has significantly enhanced our general understanding these impairments, while leaving us still uncertain about important aspects of their exact nature. We still do not know their cause(s), their range of manifestation, the course of their development, or the most effective remediation approaches. Our knowledge base has increased exponentially, allowing investigators to propose better informed models of SLI, links to other childhood language disorders, and approaches to assessment and intervention.

SLI affects approximately 7% of the population, with boys affected slightly more often than girls (Tomblin et al., 1997). SLI may occur at the same rate in other populations of children with language disorders. If this is true, subgroups of children with autism, children with genetic syndromes, and children with hearing impairments may have SLI. There is mounting evidence that it is genetically transmitted, and thus we expect to see familial patterns (see chapter 10 by Tomblin). Siblings of children who have already been diagnosed with SLI are approximately four times as likely to have SLI as children without a family history.

The definition is primarily one of exclusion. SLI is an impairment of language comprehension, language production, or both in the absence of hearing impairment, the absence of a general developmental delay (i.e., a normal performance IQ), the absence of any neurological impairment (e.g., perinatal bleeds, seizure disorders), and no diagnosis of autism. It is only in this singular sense that this language impairment is specific.

Children with SLI have various limitations in general auditory and speech perception; limitations in central cognitive domains such as memory, attention, and executive functions; deficits in other cognitive functions such as problem solving, mental rotation, mathematics; and deviations in neurological structure and function. They also have a relatively high incidence of dyslexia and other more global reading and writing disabilities. The nature of these limitations and their relation to SLI remain controversial.

In this chapter, I provide a review of theoretical proposals concerning the bases of SLI, an overview of the language and related cognitive deficits common to SLI, and the relation of SLI to other language disorders in children. The threads that runs through the chapter are the identification and subcategorization of SLI; the biology of SLI; and the role that underlying cognitive deficits may play in the origins and maintenance of language deficits.

THEORIES OF SLI

Theories of SLI can be divided into two general groups: those that explain SLI as a result of deficits in linguistic knowledge, typically attributed to delayed maturation or a deficient representation of language, and those that explain SLI in terms of domain-general (with respect to language) or domain-specific cognitive or cognitive–linguistic processes. A number of proposals have emerged over the last several decades. The greatest limitation of many of these theories is that they are not sufficiently comprehensive to account for all the deficits associated with SLI. Other proposals are, as yet, too vague. Finally, others still lack convincing evidence or have been demonstrated to not be true. Accurate or not, these proposals are important for the research direction they provide and for their potential implications for assessment and intervention.

Linguistic Knowledge and Computational Explanations

Among the earliest proposals of linguistic knowledge deficits in children with SLI is the extended optional infinitive (EOI) account (Rice & Wexler, 1996a, 1996b; Rice, Wexler, & Cleave, 1995). This proposal maintains that children with SLI extend a period that occurs in typically developing children during which tense is optionally marked on verbs that occur in main clauses. The result is that finite verbs are produced without markers such as tense and number. The extended unique checking constraint (EUCC) account is an elaboration of the EOI account (Wexler, 1998, 2003). In the required linguistic operation of checking, a feature in a phrase must check all of the relevant functional categories in order for an element to be produced. According to this proposal, children with SLI experience an extended period in which they are limited to checking a single functional category. For example, for the third person singular and for auxiliary and copula forms both tense (TNS) and agreement (AGRS) must be checked, but a child with SLI can check only one of these functional categories, and thus production is blocked (see chapter 13 by Leonard for a detailed discussion of this proposal). Although this proposal better accounts for morphosyntactic deficits in SLI across languages than the original EOI proposal, other, processing-based explanations (described below) have also been offered for these deficits (e.g., see chapter 13 by Leonard and chapter 11 by Joanisse).

The Representational Deficit for Dependent Relations (RDDR) proposal (van der Lely, 1998; van der Lely & Stollwerck, 1997), suggests that children with SLI have a limitation in building long-distance dependencies that include any kind of syntactic movement affecting passives, wh-questions, or object relative clauses and pronoun or reflexive antecedent relations (referred to as anaphoric dependencies), as they are governed by binding principles. Movement is characterized as optional, which leads to deficient production of sentences with these structures as well as their interpretation. Simply put, the various versions of RDDR propose are that children with SLI lack the linguistic structural knowledge necessary to establish anaphoric relations between pronouns and their antecedents, or long-distance relations between nouns or pronouns, or as gaps in relative clauses and in wh-questions.

Van der Lely (2005) has revised this proposal and renamed it the computational grammatical complexity (CGC) hypothesis. According to this view, children with SLI are impaired in the linguistic representation or computations that underlie hierarchical, structurally complex forms in one or more components of language (i.e., syntax, morphology, phonology). Specifically in syntax, the proposal implicates the optionality of an obligatory linguistic operation called *Move* that increases complexity with each application. Complexity is the result of one or more applications of this operation, each of which add to the complexity of the sentence. Although the same level of detail is not provided for morphology and phonology, this makes the proposal more general, and thus it is more capable of explaining deficits in language domains other than syntax. The notion of optionality and the distinction between a representation versus linguistic operation deficits have yet to be specified.

A related proposal provides additional focus to this notion that children with SLI have a deficient grammar affecting certain complex sentences with long-distance grammatical relations (e.g., Friedmann & Novogrodsky, 2004, 2007; Novogrodsky & Friedmann, 2006; see also chapter 6 by Botwinik-Rotem & Friedmann and chapter 17 by Fletcher). Although children with SLI appear to have the same general structural linguistic knowledge as their typically developing peers, their grammar seems to be deficient in the syntactic process of phrasal movement affecting reversible passives (Adams, 1990; Bishop, 1997; Leonard, Wong, Deevy, Stokes, & Fletcher, 2006; van der Lely & Harris, 1990; van der Lely & Stollwerck, 1996); relative clauses (Adams, 1990; Friedmann & Novogrodsky, 2004, 2007; Novogrodsky & Friedmann, 2006); and wh-questions (Deevy & Leonard, 2004; Ebbels & van der Lely, 2001; van der Lely & Battell, 2003). Notably, these same deficits have been reported in children with hearing impairment (see chapter 6 by Botwinik-Rotem & Friedmann and chapter 4 by Cleary). According to this proposal, the challenge presented by these sentences does not lie in establishing long-distance dependencies but, rather, in the underlying phrasal movement and, even more specifically, in the assignment of thematic roles (e.g., agent, patient) to noun phrases that appear in noncanonical or atypical locations because of phrasal movement (Friedmann & Novogrodsky, 2007; Novogrodsky & Friedmann, 2006).

These latter proposals and the studies on which they were based focused on children with SLI who exclusively have grammatical deficits, a subgroup I discuss later. The strength of these proposals lies in their detailed theoretical underpinnings (Fletcher, 1999; chapter 17 by Fletcher) and their focus on the language deficits of a narrowly defined and infrequently occurring subgroup of children with SLI. Their overall weakness is that they are not intended to address the full range of language deficits in children with SLI.

Process-based Explanations

As mentioned earlier, a large body of evidence has revealed limitations in speech perception, working memory, and slowed reaction times, as well as suggestions that children with SLI have deficits in attention and various executive functions. These deficits in psychological processes have formed the basis for several accounts of SLI. One central question concerning these accounts is whether these deficits are general (domain-general), affecting the linguistic and nonlinguistic cognitive processing, or whether they are specific to language (domain-specific). *Domain-specific* and *domain-general* (e.g., Marinis & van der Lely, 2007) have been used to differentiate views that propose underlying deficits in linguistic knowledge or operations such as movement from those that propose deficits in general or language-specific related cognitive processes (e.g., general auditory perception, speech perception, phonological working memory, processing speed, etc.). Here, these terms are used to distinguish general deficits in language-related cognitive processes (e.g., working memory, auditory perception) and deficits in these same processes that are specific to language (e.g., phonological working memory, speech perception).

Speech Perception   Beginning with a series of seminal studies in the 1970s (e.g., Tallal & Piercy, 1973, 1974), Tallal and her colleagues found that children with language impairments (some children in the initial studies had mild hearing impairments) exhibited poorer performance on temporal order judgments, discrimination, and categorization of tones and speech. These deficits have been varyingly characterized over years and across a number of studies as impairments in the ability to perceive stimuli that are presented rapidly, stimuli that are brief in duration, and stimuli that have components (e.g., formant transitions) that change rapidly. This deficit has also been characterized more generally as a deficit in temporal processing. The interpretation of this deficit has varied over the years from being a general processing deficit affecting all modalities to a general auditory deficit and to a deficit specific to speech processing. It has led to the development of an intervention program, *Fast ForWord*, designed to improve the speech perception and, consequently, the language abilities of children with SLI. Several findings (e.g., Bishop et al., 1999; Rosen & Eva, 2001) argued against a direct causal relationship between auditory perception deficits and the language deficits seen in these children. Furthermore, the identical deficits Tallal and her colleagues (Tallal, 1984) had reported in children who were poor readers were more aptly characterized (Mody, Studdert-Kennedy, & Brady, 1997; Studdert-Kennedy & Mody, 1995) as impairments in differentiating less discriminable sounds (e.g., fricatives such as /f/ and /th/). Other studies (e.g., Sussman, 1993) have indicated that children with SLI discriminate accurately (e.g., /ba/ vs. /da/) but have different boundaries in categorization tasks and appear to have more uncertainty at the category boundary than their age-matched peers. More recently, a study (Burlingame, Sussman, Gillam, & Hay, 2005) directly examined sensitivity to formant transition durations along two continua (/ba/ to /wa/ and /da/ to /ja/). On the first continuum, the children with SLI were less sensitive to phonetic changes and made more identification errors, whereas on the second continuum, the children with SLI were similar to their typically developing peers in identification at the longer formant transitions, but poorer on the short transitions. Some investigators have suggested that task effects such as the stimuli employed or the memory demands may affect the performance of children with SLI. For example, in a series of tasks involving categorical perception of words (e.g., *bowl/pole*) and nonword syllables (*ba/pa*), children with SLI performed comparably to age-matched peers on word perception but more poorly on identification for syllables, whether they were synthetic or natural speech (Coady, Evans, Mainela-Arnold, & Kluender, 2007; Coady, Kluender, & Evans, 2005).

A recent study (Scheffler & Schwartz, 2008) relying on the Ganong effect (Ganong, 1980) sheds some light on the relation between speech perception and language processes. This effect occurs when a continuum of a phonemic contrast (e.g. [d] vs. [t]) is embedded in a word–nonword pair (e.g., *dish* vs. *tish*). Listeners identify more of the tokens as having a "d" because of the influence of lexical knowledge. The *t–d* category boundary shifts from the one found with nonmeaningful syllables. Children with SLI differed from their age-matched peers in that they exhibited a great deal of uncertainty at category boundaries, and some children never actually established a clear boundary. Children with SLI relied more heavily on their lexical knowledge, perhaps attempting to compensate for a deficit in categorical perception. Thus, deficits in categorical perception appear to alter the overall process of lexical access, forcing children with SLI to place greater reliance on existing phonological representations in making categorical decisions. Coupled with evidence of weaker phonological representations of lexical items (see below), deficits in perception may affect lexical access both directly and indirectly.

Event-related potentials (ERPs) measuring electrical brain responses (see chapter 7 by Tropper & Schwartz and chapter 24 by Shafer & Maxfield) have revealed more detailed information about the nature of these perceptual deficits. Two of these studies used ERP and behavioral methods to study vowel perception in children with and without SLI. Children with SLI exhibited poor categorization of long (250-msec) and short (50-msec) vowels. Their discrimination of short vowels was also less accurate than that of their peers, and ERP data revealed the absence of mismatch negativity (MMN). A follow-up study reanalyzing these data provided further evidence that these perceptual deficits distinguish children with SLI from their age-matched peers on the basis of their overall brain response to these vowel distinctions (Shafer, Ponton, Datta, Morr, & Schwartz, 2007). Importantly, there were two conditions in the ERP study: one in which the child's attention was directed toward the auditory stimulus by asking them to report embedded tones and a second in which their attention was directed toward a silent condition. In the latter condition, the children without SLI exhibited an ERP attentional component (Nd) that was not seen in the children with SLI. These findings suggest that typically developing children continue to process speech automatically even when their attention is focused elsewhere, whereas this is not true for children with SLI. Another pair of studies examined brain responses in a backward masking task to tones differing in frequency and followed up with the same subjects 18 months later (Bishop & McArthur, 2005; McArthur & Bishop, 2004). A third of the individuals with SLI had poorer behavioral frequency discrimination thresholds, but the majority had age-inappropriate late ERP components. At follow-up, these individuals exhibited ERPs that were improved but were still outside the range of those of their typical language controls. In some cases, the ERPs were simply immature, whereas in other cases ERPs were unlike those of younger typically developing individuals. Although these latter studies are limited by the wide age range of a relatively small number of subjects, most of the children with SLI had immature brain responses to tones differing in frequency. Thus, although there is sufficient evidence to conclude that children with SLI have a deficit in the underlying neurophysiology of perception, the nature of this deficit and its relation to the language impairments in these children remains undetermined.

One of the more controversial aspects of the perceptual account of SLI is the relation between the presumed perceptual deficits and the various language deficits exhibited by these children. One view is that of Tallal and her colleagues (e.g., Merzenich et al., 1996; Tallal, Miller, Bedi, Wang, & Nagarajan, 1996), who have fashioned an intervention approach called *Fast ForWord*, in which children are exposed to speech and language stimuli that have been altered temporally and spectrally in a variety of tasks with feedback. Although the initial reports suggested that this approach was effective in improving language performance on several standardized measures, subsequent research questioned the effectiveness of this method in improving language performance.

An important proposal growing out of this research that relates perceptual deficits to language acquisition is the Surface Account of the morphosyntactic deficits in SLI (Leonard, 1989, 1998; see also chapter 15 by Oetting & Hadley and chapter 13 by Leonard). It suggests that these deficits result from the relative (to surrounding syllables) lack of perceptual salience of morphological markers (Leonard, McGregor, & Allen, 1992), in combination with the processing demands of establishing morphological paradigms. Specifically, for children with SLI, markers that have low phonetic substance require more exposure to become established because of the processing demands required by their poor perception. This view is supported by extensive evidence from English and by the varying patterns of morphosyntactic deficits in children across languages, reflecting the variations in the phonetic substance of certain morphosyntactic markers (see chapter 13 by Leonard). One specific characterization of these deficits is that children have particular difficulty perceiving brief syllables when they are embedded between two longer syllables (Leonard, et al., 1992).

In summary, it seems clear that children with SLI have deficits in speech perception. The specific nature of these deficits and, more critically, their relation to the language deficits observed remain unresolved. One promising suggestion is that these deficits may be related to some more general deficit in attention that may also affect other aspects of language. Their perceptual deficits may also reflect more general task demands (Coady et al., 2005), including attention, working memory, and the control or selectivity of attention.

Working Memory   Children with SLI have deficits in working memory that may underlie their language deficits (see chapter 8 by Gillam, Montgomery, & Gillam). A large body of evidence comes from a task called nonword repetition, which is the most widely used means of assessing phonological working memory. In this task, children are asked to repeat nonwords of increasing syllable length. Typically, there are four or five nonwords at each of four or five syllable lengths (Dollaghan, Biber, & Campbell, 1995; Dollaghan & Campbell, 1998; Gathercole & Baddeley, 1990; Weismer et al., 2000). These productions are typically scored as the number of nonwords produced correctly and, in some studies, the number of consonants and vowels produced correctly. Children with SLI diverge from their typically developing peers (age-matched and younger) once the nonwords reach three syllables in length (Archibald & Gathercole, 2006; Botting & Conti-Ramsden, 2001; Dollaghan & Campbell, 1998; Gathercole & Baddeley, 1990; Montgomery, 1995). This is true for children with SLI ranging from preschool age through adolescence. It holds true across languages, as well as in bilingual children. This deficit also notably appears to occur more frequently across monozygotic than across dizygotic twins (Bishop et al., 1999). Although the deficit is characterized as severe (Gathercole, 2006), because age-matched children typically perform at or near ceiling, the quantitative differences between the groups are quite small when the scores are the number of nonwords repeated correctly. The quantitative differences are magnified somewhat when the number of consonants or segments correct is compared. The groups do not differ in the production of one- and two-syllable nonwords. Several of these studies have demonstrated clearly that this task very successfully distinguishes children with SLI from their typically developing peers. Nonword repetition is, thus, a potentially useful clinical marker for SLI. Furthermore, it appears to be culturally unbiased in that it is unrelated to maternal education level (Alloway, Gathercole, Willis, & Adams, 2004) or race (Campbell, Dollaghan, Needleman, & Janosky, 1997). Although still controversial, evidence suggests that this difference reflects a deficit in the capacity of working memory that is most closely related to vocabulary growth and development. It is not clear that the working memory capacity deficit revealed by children's partially inaccurate repetition of nonwords of three, four, and five syllables could feasibly account for the range of language deficits of these children. To some extent, this deficit may reflect their familiarity with less frequent, multisyllabic words. Some evidence comes from a recent study (Kohnert, 2002) in which bilingual Spanish–English children with SLI did not exhibit poorer performance than their typically developing peers on longer nonwords. Multisyllabic words are much more frequent in Spanish than in English.

A number of other tasks have been used to examine working memory in children with SLI. They are similarly impaired on tasks such as scanning, which involves deciding whether a target item was heard in a previous list; serial list recall; and listening span tasks in which children are asked to repeat the sentence-final words for a series of sentences (Gillam, Cowan, & Day, 1995; Marton & Schwartz, 2003; Montgomery, 2000; Sininger, Klatzky, & Kirchner, 1989; Weismer & Evans, 1999). One particularly interesting set of findings has emerged from a series of listening span studies by Marton and her colleagues. In English, memory limitations were a function of syntactic complexity in the sets of sentences, not the sheer amount of material being held in working memory. The listening span task was also administered to Hungarian-speaking children with SLI. Because, in contrast to English, Hungarian is a very highly inflected language with relatively free word order, language complexity resides in the morphemes, not in the syntax. The children with SLI performed more poorly when the sentences were morphologically complex than when they were longer. Thus, one way of characterizing the working memory limitations of these children is that their working memory is less well able to deal with linguistic complexity, regardless of how it is reflected in a given language, in comparison to their typically developing peers.

Phonological working memory seems most closely related to vocabulary acquisition, whereas other measures of working memory may be more closely related to language comprehension and syntactic processing. Working memory plays an important role in language acquisition because it allows the child to analyze and to determine the structural properties of the language to which they are exposed. Early in development a short working memory span may be developmentally adaptive because it enables a child to focus on short-distance grammatical relations (e.g., subject–verb in canonical sentences). As memory span increases, children are increasingly able to determine and establish longer distance relations such as pronouns and antecedents, or displaced elements such as object relative clauses. Once language has been acquired, working memory is critical for processing language because the building of syntactic and discourse structures requires relating linguistic units across a number of intervening words and syllables and a lengthy time-span. The direct relationship between working memory and syntactic processing has not been extensively studied in children with SLI. Most of the studies (e.g., Deevy & Leonard, 2004) examined off-line sentence comprehension and, thus, do not reveal how children manage working memory demands while language is being processed. In studies of adults, alternative views of memory (e.g., content addressable memory) seem better suited to explaining the relation between language processing and memory (e.g., McElree, Foraker, & Dyer, 2003)

Another, markedly different, proposal concerning a causal underlying memory deficit in children with SLI as well as deficits in other populations (agrammatic aphasia, Parkinson's disease) relies on a distinction between two types of memory: procedural and declarative (Ullman & Pierpont, 2005). Procedural memory includes motor and cognitive abilities that involve a series of steps generated by a set of rules (i.e., procedures) that govern these steps (e.g., playing solitaire, folding origami, forming the regular past tense of verbs). Declarative memory includes facts or items that are stored and recalled individually and cannot be generated by rule (e.g., Mickey Mantle's jersey number, words in vocabulary, irregular past tense forms of verbs, etc.). It should be noted that this view of regular and irregular past tense is not uncontroversial (see chapter 11 by Joanisse), and the same is true for the general distinction between procedural and declarative knowledge. That said, this proposal maintains that children with SLI (and other clinical populations) have deficits in procedural memory that affect their linguistic and nonlinguistic abilities to form and execute such rule-based behavior. The proposal offers a detailed description of the neurobiology of the proposed deficit and cites supporting evidence from structural brain studies of SLI. When procedural memory is deficient, the declarative memory system is believed to compensate. This means that aspects of language typically generated by rules (e.g., regular past tense) will, in children with SLI, be learned and produced instead on an instance-by-instance basis. To date, the behavioral evidence for this deficit comes from reports of regular past tense deficits in children with SLI. There is, as yet, no strong evidence from syntax or phonology that suggests the same type of deficit.

Processing Speed   There is a long history of using reaction time (RT) to measure cognitive processing globally, and, when complex cognitive tasks can be subdivided into additive processes, the component operations can be inferred from the additive relation among the time each takes (Donders, 1969). RT decreases with age, particularly during adolescence and through early adulthood (Kail, 1991; Kail & Miller, 2006), and then begins to increase again later in the life span, reflecting a gradually decline in processing efficiency (e.g., Cerella & Hale, 1994). A meta-analysis revealed slower RTs across a number of studies on a variety of tasks (Kail, 1994), leading to the claim that children with SLI have cognitive slowing and that this cognitive slowing might account for their language impairments (see chapter 20 by Windsor & Kohnert). The slowing hypothesis posits that children with SLI differ from their age-matched and even language-matched peers in their overall speed of processing. Subsequent meta-analyses (Windsor, 1999; Windsor & Hwang, 1999; Windsor, Milbrath, Carney, & Rakowski, 2001) also found evidence of slowing in children with SLI but raised issues concerning the way in which RT data are analyzed. Although one analysis supported the slowing hypothesis, the other indicated slower RTs in children with SLI that were not significantly from typically developing peers and were highly variable. A more extensive study of RT in children with SLI across a number of linguistic and non-linguistic tasks generally supported the slowing hypothesis (Leonard, Weismer, et al., 2007; Miller, Kail, Leonard, & Tomblin, 2001). Taken as groups of tasks, the linguistic and nonlinguistic tasks each yielded slower reaction times for the SLI children than for their age-matched typically developing peers. However, when the tasks were further subdivided, motor and lexical tasks did not yield slower RTs for the children with SLI. Furthermore, individual analyses revealed that not all children with SLI exhibited slowing. A follow-up study five years later at age 14 (Miller, Leonard, & Kail, 2006) revealed similar findings. In general, children with SLI were slower than their age-matched peers, but some of these children did not exhibit slowing. Reaction times (RTs) at age 9 did not predict their RTs at age 14, and although the children with SLI were consistent across domains as a group, individual children were not. The investigators concluded that other factors may play a role in RT. If processing speed were a causal factor in SLI, it should be related to the severity of the impairment, but that does not seem to be the case (Lahey, Edwards, & Munson, 2001). A more recent study (Leonard, Weismer, et al., 2007) paints a different and more complex picture in which predictive models suggest that working memory and speed measures separately are related to language performance scores, accounting for almost two-thirds of the variance in these scores.

Reaction time may reflect global cognitive developments such as speed of processing, speed of response generation, or derivative developments such as automaticity or linguistic complexity. Although the slowing hypothesis is intriguing and seems to fit well with the notion that children with SLI have deficits in processing and in their processing resource capacity, it has some limitations. For example, reaction time on linguistic versus non-linguistic tasks may reflect very different cognitive processes. Even within the language domain, detection tasks (e.g., monitoring, match-to-sample or same-different, simple lexical decision or word/nonword tasks) and on-line language processing tasks (lexical priming, cross-modal word interference, sentence processing with cross-modal priming) tap, at best, some overlapping low-level processes, but otherwise a very different set of cognitive-linguistic processes and knowledge.

A novel perspective concerning processing speed has emerged from some recent, but as yet unpublished, work (Swinney, personal communication, 2000) and receives some support from several studies of children with SLI as well as with adults who have agrammatic aphasia. According to this view, the "slowing" in SLI directly reflects an impairment in the rate at which language can be processed. Thus, by slowing the rate of presentation, performance improves in clinical populations (see also Montgomery, 2005; Weismer & Hesketh, 1996), yet the slowed rate of presentation impairs sentence processing nonclinical populations. For example, in two studies, children with SLI did not exhibit priming for the filler (first) noun in the "gap" (*) of an object relative sentence (e.g., *The zebra that the hippo kissed* *ran far away) or for antecedents at pronouns or reflexives(*) (e.g., *The* *leopard that chased the tiger washed himself* *) at a normal rate, but did exhibit priming when these sentences were presented at a slower rate (Love et al., 2007). The typically developing, age-matched children exhibited priming at normal rates but did not when the rate was slowed. The specific mechanism underlying these findings has yet to be explicated.

Attention and Executive Functions   Attention is a basic component of cognitive and perceptual processing (see chapter 20 by Windsor & Kohnert). It is often treated as a unitary phenomenon when, in fact, it can be subdivided into at least orienting, selective attention, divided attention, and sustained attention. Executive functions refer to control of attention and other cognitive processes such as shifting attention, inhibition, and planning. Attention and executive processes are closely intertwined with working memory. Individual and developmental differences and variations in working memory and executive functions within and across groups of children have led to controversy concerning the control and allocation of processing resources. A variety of models (e.g., Conway & Engle, 1996; Cowan, 1997; Just, Carpenter, & Keller, 1996) have challenged Baddeley's (1986) model in which a phonological memory store does not directly interact with the central executive. In these alternative models, working memory capacity is tied more directly to attentional control in explaining performance on tasks that involve distraction or interference (Barrett, Tugade, & Engle, 2004). Individual differences in working memory capacity appear to be related to performance reflecting more general executive functions (e.g., Conway & Engle, 1994). Working memory span reflects attentional control (Engle, Kane, & Tuholski, 1999) by task switching ability (Towse, Hitch, & Hutton, 1998) and by the ability to inhibit irrelevant information (Hasher, Stoltzfus, Zacks, & Rypma, 1991). Working memory performance improves with greater abilities to control attention, to suppress irrelevant information, to avoid distraction, to focus on task-relevant thoughts, and to coordinate simultaneous processing and storage (Engle et al., 1999; Lustig, May, & Hasher, 2001; Miyake, 2001).

To date, only one study has examined attention in children with SLI (Hanson & Montgomery, 2002) using the *Auditory Continuous Performance Test* (Keith, 1994). The children listened to 600 monosyllabic words and indicated when they heard the word *dog*. The children with SLI did not differ from their typically developing peers in their identification accuracy (hits). Although this task is characterized as examining sustained selective attention, it actually confounds sustained and selective attention. Armstrong (1997) found that an auditory version of the *Continuous Performance Test* (Mirsky & Cardon, 1962) failed to differentiate sustained from selective attention. Therefore, this task may not have been sensitive to the attentional deficits that may occur in children with SLI. Limiting the dependent measure to accuracy may also have concealed deficits in attentional processes.

Several studies of working memory have incidentally revealed that children with SLI have poor cognitive control. Children with SLI have exaggerated (i.e., better recall) recency effects compared to their typically developing peers in the recall of one-syllable words following a set of digits (Gillam & McFadden, 1994). In working memory studies that require the recall of words and sentences, these children frequently provide irrelevant items from other sentence positions when the required response is the final word or from previous items (Marton & Schwartz, 2003; Weismer & Evans, 1999). These findings suggest that children with SLI have difficulty inhibiting linguistic information that is not relevant to the required response.

Despite these findings, few studies have directly examined attentional control in children with SLI. In a sentence processing and memory task, these children had greater difficulty than typically developing peers in inhibiting irrelevant information (Lorsbach,

Wilson, & Reimer, 1996). Similarly, Norbury (2005) found that children with SLI had slower reaction times and made more errors than did typically developing children in inhibiting secondary word meanings in ambiguous contexts (e.g., John stole from the *bank*—picture of a *river*). However, this finding was influenced by more limited knowledge of secondary word meanings in the children with SLI. There is a similarly limited finding concerning the nonverbal control abilities of children with SLI (Noterdaeme, Amorosa, Mildenberger, Sitter, & Minow, 2001). Their inhibition of predominant responses (interference task) and motor responses when presented with irrelevant stimuli (go/no-go task) was similar to that of typically developing peers. Both of these tasks had low levels of cognitive conflict, because there were equal numbers of the compatible/incompatible and go/no-go stimuli. In such tasks, the goal is generally to provide a higher level of conflict by manipulating the relative percentage of the two stimulus types. Bishop and Norbury (2005) provided clearer evidence of cognitive verbal and nonverbal control deficits in children with SLI on a task requiring inhibition of a verbal response and on an inhibition task requiring sustained attention but no verbal response. A large battery of verbal and nonverbal tasks (Im-Bolter, Johnson, & Pascual-Leone, 2006) revealed that children with SLI perform more poorly than typically developing children on verbal and nonverbal tasks requiring the activation or inhibition of task-relevant information and in working memory updating. These studies provide evidence of domain-general executive function deficits. Such deficits may be related to findings concerning processing speed, speech perception, working memory, and the deficits in language acquisition and processing that have been identified in children with SLI. These cognitive control abilities must be directly examined in language comprehension or production tasks before we can conclude that they are directly related to the language deficits associated with SLI.

Emergentist Perspective

A final proposal concerning the nature, origins, and maintenance of SLI is perhaps the broadest of those discussed so far. It is in the general category of an emergentist view, as discussed in chapter 11 by Joanisse. According to this view, typical language development depends heavily on the regularities of language input, and patterns such as morphosyntax and syntax, along with phonology and the lexicon, can be extracted from the input by the child. Thus, what are typically characterized as linguistic rules and representations emerge from an interaction of the child's general cognitive mechanisms or processes with the input. Proposals in this framework are often instantiated in connectionist models (see chapter 11 by Joanisse). Briefly, these computer models consist of multiple levels of units that are fully connected with adjustable weights reflecting the strength of connection and are sometimes presented as metaphors for neural networks. These networks take input of various sorts (e.g., a present tense verb) and produce outputs (e.g., past tense verb form). One of their most interesting characteristics is that they are capable of learning (i.e., becoming more accurate) with feedback. Connectionist models have been developed for lexical access in word production, subject–verb agreement, and past tense formation, among other aspects of language and language learning. Another interesting aspect of these models and of an emergentist view is that it offers a different perspective of SLI and other childhood language disorders related to dynamical systems or general systems theory. Many views of childhood language impairments entail an assumption that there is an impaired or deficient underlying developmental mechanism (e.g., general or specific linguistic knowledge, working memory, etc.). In this framework, a disorder arises from more peripheral deficits (e.g., speech perception, attention), which may, downstream, manifest themselves as broader deficits (Thomas & Karmiloff-Smith, 2003).

SUBGROUPS OF CHILDREN WITH SLI

Although the definition of children with SLI is relatively specific and can be quantified, the specific profiles of language deficits vary widely. This variation magnifies the typical variation we encounter in the course of normal language acquisition. In typically developing children, production performance typically seems to lag behind comprehension performance—though comprehension is often more difficult to test, and even production may not always fully reflect the child's underlying knowledge—and components of language develop at different rates across and within children. When we consider variations across children or groups of children with SLI, it is important to recognize the limitations of our measurements, the variation that occurs in and across typically developing children, and the extent to which these variations fit an explanatory framework.

One of the first groupings of children with SLI was a distinction between children who have expressive deficits only and those who have expressive and receptive deficits (Edwards & Lahey, 1996). Such a distinction should be viewed with some caution because of the limitations of our comprehension instruments. These standardized tasks typically ask children to point to one of four pictures in response to a word or a sentence containing critical contrastive elements. Most language comprehension tests do not examine the semantics of lexical comprehension in depth, the comprehension of contrastive morphosyntactic features in detail, or the comprehension of sentences with complex syntactic structures. The pointing response occurs at the end of comprehension; thus, the tests reveal little about the processes leading to the pointing response. Even the production data we obtain may have some limitations. Although some of the data in the literature come from systematically elicited productions, particularly focusing on morphosyntax, most production data come from spontaneous language samples. A number of studies have revealed that typically developing children's syntactic knowledge may be revealed through production priming and more sensitive elicitation tasks (Crain & Thornton, 1998; Shimpi, Gámez, Huttenlocher, & Vasilyeva, 2007). In light of these issues, we need additional research before we can conclude that these are different groups of children with SLI rather than a continuum of comprehension deficits.

Another approach to subgrouping children with SLI recognizes that some children have deficits across language components whereas other children have deficits focused primarily in a single component (Bishop, 1997; Leonard, 1998). One such group appears to have deficits that are specific to syntax, grammatical SLI (GSLI). This is an outgrowth of a proposal mentioned earlier (van der Lely, 2005), in which these children were first characterized as having difficulty establishing long-distance grammatical relations and subsequently as having a broader structural deficit in knowledge or processes that affect hierarchical syntactic, morphosyntactic, and structural knowledge or processes. Although this is an interesting proposal, there are some reasons to question the status of this subgroup. In a rather large-scale study of children with SLI, only a very small number met the criteria for GSLI (Bishop, Bright, James, Bishop, & van der Lely, 2000). Specifically, out of 37 same-sex twin pairs with at least one member identified as SLI, and of 104 pairs selected generally, there were only 2 children who met all five criteria, and 9 who met four criteria for GSLI. Most of the children who made grammatical errors exhibited deficits in other areas of language. The small number of children with GSLI is not surprising, given that studies involving these children typically span a very wide age range. The speed of response and the priming effects may be highly variable in these groups because of age-related changes. Even if these chronologically heterogeneous children with SLI are individually age-matched to controls, both groups will have high variability. A more critical limitation is the fact that some of the tasks that have been employed may not accurately reflect the deficit. The assumptions that these children fail to establish these grammatical relations at a distance or in complex sentences or that may do so inconsistently may not be completely accurate. Experimental tasks that involve answering questions about pictures or pointing to pictures in comprehension tasks provide valuable information, but they do not provide information about the automatic processes of sentence processing for production or comprehension. Adults with agrammatic aphasia exhibit slower activation and slower decay of information during sentence processing in online tasks (Prather, Shapiro, Zurif, & Swinney, 1991). Even when online sentence processing methods are applied, they need to be designed to permit the observation of processes that may be delayed compared to typically developing controls. In an online study with GLSI children, Marinis and van der Lely (2007) examined question processing to determine whether the filler noun (*Who/Matt*) is reactivated at the gap (*) (*Lindsay gives Matt a thick book in the office. Who did Lindsay give a thick book to** in the class?) using a crossmodal picture priming task. Children with SLI did not reactivate at the gap; but it is possible that they may do so later. There is evidence from a study of pronouns, reflexives, and antecedents that children with SLI do activate such information later (Schwartz et al., 2005). When presentation rate is slowed, children with SLI show normal reactivation at gaps (Love et al., 2007). It is not that they fail to establish these long-distance grammatical relations, but, rather, that they fail to do so in a timely fashion and that their brains process this linguistic information atypically (Hestvik, Tropper, Schwartz, & Shafer, 2007).

Despite these concerns, Friedmann and Novodgrodsky (2004; Novogrodsky & Friedmann, 2006) have provided supporting evidence for a subgroup of syntactically impaired children with SLI (S–SLI) who have been identified in greater numbers by a relative clause probe. Similarly, investigators including Friedman and her colleagues have identified groups of children with SLI who seem to have lexical deficits as their primary impairment (German & Newman, 2004; Dockrell & Messer, 2007; McGregor & Waxman, 1998; Messer & Dockrell, 2006).

A final subgroup of children with SLI are characterized as having pragmatic impairments (Bishop, 2000; Botting & Conti-Ramsden, 2003). These are children who exhibit atypical social behaviors, irrelevant utterances, atypical interests (e.g., obsessive focus on a particular topic), atypical conversational behaviors (e.g., misses nonverbal facial or intonational cues, poor coherence), poor use of conversation context (e.g., misses social cues such as politeness), and other communication limitations. This characterization is based on the *Children's Communication List* (Bishop, 1998). It is clear that some children with SLI exhibit these characteristics. Most of the items that identify these children address nonlinguistic issues in social interaction and the use of language for social purposes (see chapter 18 by Fujiki & Brinton), but some of the items address the ability to produce and comprehend structural and prosodic aspects of discourse. Many of the former characteristics define children with pervasive developmental disability, autism, or Asperger's syndrome (see chapter 3 by Gerenser). Typically, such children are excluded from research studies of SLI. The question remains whether at least some of these children might be better characterized as children with autism who have SLI. Bishop's (1998) solution to this issue was to distinguish between children with primary pragmatic language impairment (PLI) without autistic-like behaviors (PLI pure) and those with such behaviors (PLI plus). A battery of standardized and nonstandardized tasks successfully discriminates with a high degree of accuracy among PLI pure, PLI plus, autism spectrum disorders, and SLI (Botting & Conti-Ramsden, 2003). It would be useful to distinguish further among pragmatic deficits associated with autism, those that involve the structure and prosody of discourse, and those that represent the proficient use of language in social interaction.

Although the profiles and severity of language impairments vary across subjects, we have yet to identify, with certainty, subgroups of children with SLI that have clear implications for theories or for differential approaches to intervention. Even in the subgroups defined thus far, no one claims that children have exclusive deficits in a given component of language. Instead, claims are made regarding primary deficits. Clinicians can certainly respond to varying profiles in how they select and prioritize goals in intervention, but researchers continue to face a challenge in the heterogeneity of children with SLI. One solution in research may be to abandon group-driven statistical analyses in favor of analyses that permit the examination of multiple factors nested within subjects in relation to the outcome of experimental tasks. Hierarchical logistical modeling (Bryk & Raudenbush, 1992; Schonfeld & Rindskopf, 2007) is one approach that has been frequently used for growth curve monitoring, but it has not yet been widely used for this purpose (e.g., Jacobson & Schwartz, 2002, 2005). With the use of this and other related approaches, we may be better able to determine how varying profiles of linguistic and nonlinguistic abilities are related to a child's classification as SLI.

LANGUAGE DEFICITS

The various areas of language deficits that characterize SLI are summarized briefly here; they are discussed in great detail in other chapters in this volume. These deficits may be more prominent in some language domains than in others; the profiles of deficits vary across children with SLI, and in given children all domains may be affected.

Lexical and Semantic Deficits

Children with SLI are delayed in the emergence of first words; exhibit limited vocabularies, appear to have incomplete or underspecified phonological representations of words, have limited elaboration of the semantic information underlying words, and atypical organization or access to their mental lexicon (see chapter 16 by McGregor). Verbs seem to present particular problems for these children.

The general course and speed of lexical development is delayed in children with SLI. Their first words emerge much later than in their typically developing peers, and their word comprehension is also delayed (e.g., Clarke & Leonard, 1996). Children who are late talkers are variously identified as having fewer than 50 words and no word combinations at 24 months (Rescorla, 1989), as children who, on the MacArthur–Bates Communicative Development Inventory (Fenson et al., 1996), score below the 10th percentile at 24 and 30 months of age (e.g., Irwin, Carter, & Briggs-Gowan, 2002; Moyle, Weismer, Evans, & Lindstrom, 2007; Weismer & Evans, 2002), or below the 15th percentile (Thal, Reilly, Seibert, Jeffries, & Fenson, 2004). Late talkers who exhibit receptive delays are more often identified as having SLI than are late talkers who seem to have normal receptive vocabulary development (Thal et al., 2004). The outcomes for these children in language abilities at age 13 are predicted by their language abilities at age 2 (Rescorla, 2005). Those children who appear to catch up may actually have an *illusory recovery* in that they reach a plateau that masks continued deficits not apparent in standardized testing (Scarborough & Dobrich, 1990). Preschool children with SLI continue to exhibit delays in receptive (e.g., Clarke & Leonard, 1996) and expressive vocabulary (Thal, O'Hanlon, Clemmons, & Fralin, 1999; Watkins, Kelly, Harbers, & Hollis, 1995). Older school-aged children with SLI may have even more apparent deficits in vocabulary (Haynes, 1992; Stothard, Snowling, Bishop, Chipchase, & Kaplan, 1998). These children seem to have sparse lexical semantic representations (McGregor,

Friedman, & Reilly, 2002) and deficits in semantic category knowledge (Kail & Leonard, 1986).

Some measures of lexical diversity in language samples (number of different words, total number of words) suggest that children with SLI have less lexical diversity than the age-matched peers, but may be similar to MLU-matched peers (Goffman & Leonard, 2000; Klee, 1992; Leonard, Miller, & Gerber, 1999; Watkins et al., 1995). A more recently developed lexical diversity measure, D (Malvern & Richards, 2002), is a repeated calculation of the type–token ratio (TTR) over a range of tokens (35–50) related to sample size that is then compared to a mathematical model of TTR. It may provide a more accurate picture of lexical diversity in SLI. Owen and Leonard (Owen & Leonard, 2002) found no difference in D between children with SLI and their age-matched peers, although within both groups, older children had higher scores than younger children. This is a topic that warrants additional investigation.

Some children have apparent word-finding problems not unlike those associated with adult acquired anomia (Dockrell & Messer, 2007; German & Newman, 2004; Lahey & Edwards, 1999; Leonard, Nippold, Kail, & Hale, 1983; McGregor et al., 2002; Seiger-Gardner & Schwartz, in press). These children have difficulty in naming-on-demand tasks, use circumlocutions, exhibit pauses and hesitations, and have limitations in production vocabulary.

Vocabulary skills and the growth of vocabulary appear to be the aspects of language development that are most closely correlated with phonological working memory (Gathercole, 2006). However, as noted above, when the measure D is used, children with SLI do not differ from their age-matched peers (Owen & Leonard, 2002). Furthermore, children with SLI rarely have difficulty with phonological working memory when the nonwords to be repeated are one or two syllables in length. In English and in a number of other languages the vast majority of words are no more than two syllables in length.

A number of experimental studies conducted by Leonard and Schwartz and colleagues (e.g., Leonard, 1982; Schwartz, 1988; Schwartz, Leonard, Messick, & Chapman, 1987) have examined word learning in young children with SLI. These were novel or unfamiliar real words for objects and actions that were presented in 10 sessions over a month or so with comprehension and production testing. In general, the groups were similar, but children with SLI were less likely to extend the learned words to novel exemplars in a comprehension test. Furthermore, children with SLI were much more likely to produce novel words containing sounds that they attempted (in a language sample) in adult targets with errors that were not the same as the errors they made producing real words in their language sample. This suggests that children with SLI do not relate novel words to existing phonological representations of word production.

Several studies have used fast mapping (short-term limited exposure word learning) to examine early lexical abilities (Dollaghan, 1987; Rice, Buhr, & Nemeth, 1990; Rice, Buhr, & Oetting, 1992; Rice, Oetting, Marquis, & Bode, 1994). Although the findings vary somewhat, but children with SLI acquired a novel object word in comprehension but not in production with a single presentation; with five presentations embedded in a video story, children with SLI did more poorly than their peers; children with SLI did not learn object and action names with only three presentations; and even after 10 presentations they did not maintain their word learning. A more recent fast mapping study (Alt & Plante, 2006) revealed that children with SLI perform more poorly overall and that their performance is particularly impaired when they only receive visual information, when the task complexity increases, and when they are asked to learn words with low phonotactic (sound and sound sequence) probability.

It is difficult to dissociate the syntactic and semantic (argument structure vs. thematic role) bases for these children's difficulties with verbs (Conti-Ramsden & Jones, 1997;

Ingham, Fletcher, Schelleter, & Sinka, 1998; Loeb, Pye, Richardson, & Redmond, 1998; Oetting, Rice, & Swank, 1995; Watkins & Rice, 1991). However, it is clear that verbs pose a significant challenge for these children, in particular a special category of verbs—those that encode mental states (Johnston, Miller, & Tallal, 2001).

Morphosyntactic Deficits

The morphosyntactic deficits associated with SLI have been studied extensively in English (see chapter 15 by Oetting & Hadley) and in other languages (see chapter 13 by Leonard). It is the most studied language deficit in children with SLI. In English, children with SLI have particular difficulty with verb morphology, functional morphemes that mark finiteness (i.e., tense, agreement), often producing bare stem verbs (e.g., *jump*) without third person singular or past tense endings. These deficits are part of a more general pattern of morphosyntactic deficits in English during the preschool years, with deficits in finite verb morphology becoming more pronounced when MLU reaches 3.50 and continuing to be prominent up to 8 years of age. Notably, measures of finite verb morphology are remarkably sensitive (97% accuracy) in distinguishing children with and without SLI. In general, children with SLI perform more poorly than age-matched and language (MLU)-matched typically developing peers and exhibit distinct growth curves in development of these morphosyntactic markers. The patterns hold true across regional dialects of English and for children who speak African American English (see chapter 14 by Washington). There is behavioral evidence from twins (Bishop, Adams, & Norbury, 2006) that these specific deficits are heritable. In older children with SLI, morphosyntactic deficits may persist (e.g., Marshall & van der Lely, 2006), but they are no longer a reliable an indicator of the language status (Conti-Ramsden, Botting, Simkin, & Knox, 2001).

Studies of other verb-related morphological forms such as past participles have yielded mixed findings. Some indicated that children with SLI produce participles comparably to language-matched controls (e.g., Redmond & Rice, 2001), whereas others (Leonard et al., 2003) revealed deficits. Children with SLI were more likely to correctly mark participles than simple past tense.

The extent to which these deficits affect noun-related morphology (i.e., plurals, articles) is still unknown. Although some studies revealed deficits in noun plurals (Leonard, Bortolini, Caselli, & McGregor, 1992; Leonard, Eyer, Bedore, & Grela, 1997), others revealed minimal deficits (Oetting & Rice, 1993; Rice & Wexler, 1996b). McGregor and Leonard (1994) and Rice and Wexler (1996b) found lower degrees of article use by children with SLI than by TD-MLU-matched children, but another study (le Normand, Leonard, & McGregor, 1993) did not find a difference.

Case marking (subject versus object) for pronouns in English is also impaired in children with SLI compared to language-matched controls (Loeb & Leonard, 1991; Loeb et al., 1998). However, not all children with SLI make these errors, and the error rates differ between *he* and *she* (Pine, Joseph, & Conti-Ramsden, 2004; Wexler, Schütze, & Rice, 1998). Thus, the nature or underlying cause of this particular deficit remains unknown.

Similar patterns have been observed in bilingual children with SLI. Bilingual French–English children with SLI omitted tense markings in both languages (Paradis, Crago, Genesee, & Rice, 2003). Sequential Spanish–English bilinguals perform more poorly than typically developing bilingual children on past tense marking in English (Jacobson & Schwartz, 2005). Young typically developing children produced these forms correctly or, at least, demonstrated knowledge of rules for regular past tense in overregularizations (e.g., *goed* for *went*). The children with SLI overregularized infrequently, but more frequently they produced bare stem infinitive forms (e.g., *jump* for *jumped*). In Spanish, bilingual children exhibited verb tense errors as well as article and clitic errors in number and gender (Bedore & Leonard, 2001; Gutiérrez-Clellen, Restrepo, & Simón-Cereijido, 2006; Gutiérrez-Clellen & Simon-Cereijido, 2007).

Patterns of morphological deficits in languages reflect the prosodic and structural characteristics of the given language (see chapter 13 by Leonard). Whereas English-speaking children with SLI omit past tense markers and produce a bare stem infinitive form, in many other languages infinitives are different forms of the verb, not bare stems, and thus the specific errors manifest themselves differently. Even in languages that are similar, the error patterns seem to differ. For example, Italian-speaking children with SLI tend to omit object clitic pronouns, whereas Spanish-speaking children with SLI tend to produce substitute forms that have errors in gender or number. The nature of SLI in languages other than English is critical to our understanding of the underlying deficits characteristic of SLI.

Phonological Deficits

Children with phonological disorders are routinely excluded from studies of SLI in order to avoid including children whose speech production limitations might be the result of apparent nonlinguistic limitations in language production. However, a significant number of children with SLI have phonological impairments in production, perception, and phonological awareness. Furthermore, deficits in other areas of language, such as morphosyntax, may be conditioned by phonological factors. There are several ways to consider phonological deficits in children. One is the extent to which children with phonological disorders and children with language impairments overlap. One-third of the children with speech delays of unknown origin had significant deficits in language comprehension, and language-production abilities were deficient in almost 80% of these children (Shriberg & Kwiatkowski, 1994). Furthermore, cognitive–linguistic status is strongly associated with short-term and long-term normalization of phonological disorders (Shriberg, Gruber, & Kwiatkowski, 1994; Shriberg, Kwiatkowski, & Gruber, 1994). An additional study revealed that 11–15% of 6-year old children with speech delay had SLI, and 5–8% of children with SLI had speech delay (Shriberg, Tomblin, & McSweeny, 1999).

There are a number of other ways to consider phonological deficits in children. As discussed earlier, children with SLI have deficits in speech perception—notably, in categorical perception. Nonword repetition may also reflect phonological deficits and may, in some respects, be a more accurate measure of phonological abilities than working memory. Findings from a lexical decision task (Edwards & Lahey, 1996) have been interpreted as indicating deficits in phonological representations. In contrast, a crossmodal interference task requiring children to name pictures while they heard phonologically related and unrelated words revealed a similar time course for the availability of phonological information in naming for children with SLI and their peers for highly familiar words (Seiger-Gardner & Schwartz, in press). Less familiar words may have revealed group differences.

There is substantial evidence that deficits in the production of morphosyntax and function words may be attributed to phonological factors (see chapter 11 by Joanisse; see also Gallon, Harris, & van der Lely, 2007; Leonard, Davis, & Deevy, 2007; Marshall & van der Lely, 2006, 2007). Children with SLI are less likely to produce past tense –ed overall in novel words but were even less likely to do so when the word stem was low in its phonotactic (sound sequence) probability, whereas typically developing MLU-matched peers were not influenced by phonotactic probability (Leonard, Davis, & Deevy, 2007). Children with SLI were also less likely to produce the past tense when the addition of –ed formed a consonant cluster that does not occur in uninflected English words (Marshall & van der Lely, 2006). The production of inflections and function words also may be influenced by the prosodic structure of words and phrases (McGregor & Leonard, 1994). For example, unstressed syllables are more likely be omitted when they don't fit the trochaic (strong–weak) syllable pattern of English.

A final aspect of phonological deficits concerns phonological awareness. This includes a variety of metalinguistic abilities that have been related to dyslexia and reading disabilities (see chapter 5 by Shaywitz et al. and chapter 19 by Hook & Haynes). It includes tasks such as identifying the number of syllables or identifying the word that is formed when a segment is omitted (e.g., *bat/at*) or added, providing rhymes. Children with SLI exhibit mild deficits in phonological awareness, whereas children with dyslexia and SLI exhibit more severe deficits (Catts, Adlof, Hogan, & Weismer, 2005).

Syntactic Deficits

Early in development, children with SLI exhibit delayed growth in the syntactic complexity, beginning as early as the onset of syntactic comprehension and production. They also exhibit persistent difficulty producing and comprehending syntactically complex sentences. We now know a great deal about specific syntactic deficits of children with SLI (see chapter 17 by Fletcher). The vast majority of what we know comes from studies of language samples, although some more recent studies have used targeted elicitation, and a small number of studies have tested comprehension using offline and online tasks. Children with SLI have difficulties comprehending and producing sentences that involve long-distance dependencies, such as wh-questions (Deevy & Leonard, 2004; Hansson & Nettelbladt, 2006; Marinis & van der Lely, 2007; Stavrakaki, 2006) or relative clauses (Friedmann & Novogrodsky, 2004, 2007; Håkansson & Hansson, 2000; Novogrodsky & Friedmann, 2006; Schuele & Tolbert, 2001). It should be noted that some of these studies included children with SLI who speak languages other than English, and thus it appears to be a more global deficit. One view is that children with SLI construct grammars in acquisition where long-distance dependencies are optionally represented. Thus, in a sentence with a relative clause (e.g., *The zebra* that the hippo kissed $_t$ on the nose ran far away), the relationship between *the zebra* and its trace position ($_t$) may not be established. The deficit is in establishing long-distance relations or, in a more recent view, is specific to a grammatical operation called *Move*. A related proposal from Friedmann and her colleagues is that children with SLI have a problem in movement, which, in turn, causes a problem with the assignment of thematic roles.

An alternative view is that for children with SLI, the challenge of these complex syntactic structures lies in the processing of these sentences for comprehension affecting acquisition and the continuing comprehension of these structures and, perhaps, in production as well. Among the candidate deficits that might explain these difficulties are working memory (Deevy & Leonard, 2004; Marton, Schwartz, Farkas, & Katsnelson, 2006; Montgomery, 2000, 2003), attention, control of attention, and processing speed (Leonard, Weismer, et al., 2007). As discussed earlier in the chapter, deficits in these cognitive processes may be general, affecting domains other than language, or specific to language processing.

There is also evidence of deficits in other structures with complex syntax such as passives (Leonard et al., 2006; Marshall, Marinis, & van der Lely, 2007) that may be due to factors other than syntactic complexity. Sentences with finite complement clauses also seem to pose problems for children with SLI (Owen & Leonard, 2006). Finally, children with SLI have syntactic deficits in argument structure that affect production and comprehension (Grela & Leonard, 2000; Loeb et al., 1998; Thordardottir & Weismer, 2002). Processing studies of these and the preceding deficits are still limited in number and need to be the subject of future research.

Pragmatics

Children with SLI have deficits in the social use of language, overlapping to some degree and apart from the deficits seen in other populations of children with language disorders (see chapter 18 by Fujiki & Brinton and chapter 3 by Gerenser). Pragmatics is a heterogeneous category of language abilities including presuppositions about the knowledge and social status of the listener, the communicative intent or function or utterances, the structure of narratives and discourse and conversation, as well as the more global use of language and nonlinguistic means of communication (e.g., tone of voice, facial expression, and gesture for and in social interaction). One of the challenges posed by this category is that it combines social behavior with aspects of language that are truly structural. In the heyday of pragmatics, investigators initially focused on identifying and categorizing the communicative functions of children's utterances. Children with SLI performed similarly to their language-matched peers in the communication functions expressed and in their relative frequencies (Fey, 2006; Leonard, 1986), but they may do so less appropriately or efficiently (Brinton, Fujiki, & Sonnenberg, 1988; Conti-Ramsden & Friel-Patti, 1983). These deficits have been taken as indications of structural language deficits rather than a lack of pragmatic knowledge (Craig, 1985).

Children with SLI also have deficits in conversation that may reflect either social deficits or structural language deficits. Children SLI produced fewer adequate responses to adult requests for information (Bishop, Chan, Adams, Hartley, & Weir, 2000). Within the group of children with SLI, those defined as having pragmatic SLI were more likely to give no response (not even nonverbal) to such requests. A child who does not even acknowledge the obligation to respond clearly has a more general deficit with conversational turn-taking and social interaction than a child who gives an inadequate response due, perhaps, to a comprehension deficit. Brinton and her colleagues (Brinton, Fujiki, & Powell, 1997) reported a similar observation.

There is further evidence that children with SLI have structural deficits in conversational interaction, particularly as it affects the contingency and coherence (structural or semantic relatedness) of successive utterances (e.g., Craig & Evans, 1993). Children with expressive and receptive deficits exhibited fewer conversational interruptions and relied more on lexical ties than on conjunction connective, and more on incomplete cohesive ties that were ambiguous or incorrect, than children with just expressive deficits. There were a small number of children in this study, and it would be worthwhile to have more information on this structural aspect of pragmatics.

Several studies have revealed deficits in the narratives of children with SLI. In general, children with SLI produce narratives that are less structurally complex and less cohesive, include morphosyntactic errors, are syntactically less complex, have omitted information, and exhibit poor event sequencing (e.g., Botting, 2002; Liles, 1993; Norbury & Bishop, 2003; Reilly, Losh, Bellugi, & Wulfeck, 2004). A recent study examined story-telling and conversation in adolescents with SLI (Wetherell, Botting, & Conti-Ramsden, 2007). The children with SLI performed more poorly than their typically developing peers on both narrative types, with story-telling being more difficult in terms of productivity (total number of morphemes and number of different words), syntactic complexity (number of different syntactic units and number of complex sentences), syntactic errors, and performance (amount of examiner support and prompts, total number of fillers, and total number of dysfluencies). This confirms previous findings concerning these kinds of deficits and indicates that these deficits continue into adolescence.

Although there is a large body of literature on discourse processing and comprehension, including the establishment of inferences across sentences, this has not yet been applied to children with SLI. It seems likely to be a significant area of deficit for older children and may reveal deficits that have not been apparent in studies of narrative production.

The area of social interaction and its use have also received relatively limited attention, even though it is apparent that language deficits pose social problems for these children as well as for other groups of children with language impairments. Children with SLI have early difficulties in establishing peer relationships that extend into adolescence (e.g., Conti-Ramsden & Botting, 2004; Conti-Ramsden et al., 2001). Pragmatic abilities such as initiating conversations, contributing to conversations, communicating intentions clearly, addressing each child as part of joining a group, and adjusting to listeners' needs are critical to establishing positive peer interactions (Brinton & Fujiki, 1999; McCabe, 2005). Children with SLI have deficits in social initiation (e.g., Craig & Washington, 1993), in participation in social interactions (Hadley & Rice, 1991; Rice, Sell, & Hadley, 1991), in conflict resolution (Brinton, Fujiki, & McKee, 1998), and with appropriate responses to social bids (Brinton & Fujiki, 1982). Besides observations of these deficits, parent responses to questionnaires such as the *Child Behavior Checklist* reveal deficits across all social skills and in some internalizing behaviors, but not in externalizing behaviors (Stanton-Chapman, Justice, Skibbe, & Grant, 2007). These questionnaires revealed clinically significant problems in socialization, but not in behavior. A broad range of pragmatic deficits, including structural discourse deficits, deficits in the use of language for social interaction, and deficits social skills affect children with SLI.

GENETICS

The first hint that SLI might be genetically transmitted (see chapter 10 by Tomblin) came from interview studies of families with affected children. These were followed by studies in which family members were evaluated directly. As a whole, these studies provided convincing evidence that SLI is a heritable disorder (Beitchman, Hood, & Inglis, 1992; Choudhury, Leppänen, Leevers, & Benasich, 2007; Neils & Aram, 1986; Rice, Haney, & Wexler, 1998; Tallal, Ross, & Curtiss, 1989; Tomblin, 1989; Whitehurst, Arnold, Smith, & Fischel, 1991). With the exception of one, in all of these studies some increased rates of speech, language, or reading problems were reported for family members of children with SLI in comparison to children without SLI. The frequency of this varied because of the fact that these were reports and because the history questions were asked in widely different ways. Tomblin (chapter 10) indicates that having a first-degree relative with SLI increases your chances of being affected by approximately four times (the typical rate of occurrence is approximately 7% in the general population). This has strong implications for early assessment and intervention for children of parents who are affected and for children with affected siblings. Of course, family patterns do not conclusively demonstrate heritability. The next step in the accumulation of evidence for heritability was a series of twin studies (e.g., Bishop, North, & Donlan, 1995; Bishop et al., 2006; Lewis & Thompson, 1992; Tomblin & Buckwalter, 1998). Comparing monozygotic (100% shared genes) to dizygotic (50% shared genes) twins provided further evidence for those aspects of development that are heritable versus those that are attributable to environmental factors. These studies have revealed a greater degree of occurrence for SLI in general, and an increased likelihood of phonological working memory deficits in monozygotic twins. Some studies have also revealed some more specific information about the relation between heritability and the discrepancy between IQ and language scores; there is greater heritability of SLI when no discrepancy is required (Bishop et al., 1995; Eley, Bishop, Dale, Price, & Plomin, 2001;

Hayiou-Thomas, Oliver, & Plomin, 2005; Newbury, Bishop, & Monaco, 2005). More recently, Bishop and her colleagues (2006) found that both grammar and grammar deficits are heritable and some evidence that these deficits arise from different genes.

The greatest leap in our understanding of the genetics of SLI has come from the study of a single family in the United Kingdom, known as the KE family, with 15 family members who have severe speech and language impairments across three generations and 37 living members (Vargha-Khadem et al., 1998). It is important to note that although these affected family members do have expressive and receptive language deficits, they have apraxia of speech or oral facial apraxia (Hurst, Baraitser, Auger, Graham, & Norell, 1990; Vargha-Khadem et al., 1998). Crago and her colleagues (Crago & Gopnik, 1994; Gopnik, 1990; Gopnik & Crago, 1991) omitted any description of the apraxia and described these individuals as having a morphosyntactic deficit that reflected missing underlying features of morphosyntax. Because of the apraxia, these individuals would not fit the commonly used definitions of SLI. Nevertheless, this family has revealed a great deal about the genetic bases of language impairments. Molecular geneticists have identified the *FOXP2* as a location of anomaly that was consistent across the 15 affected members and a single case study of speech and language impairment (Lai et al., 2000; Lai, Fisher, Hurst, Vargha-Khadem, & Monaco, 2001). Follow-up studies revealed that the affected family members were differentiated from unimpaired members in intelligence, language, and limb and oral facial findings (Watkins, Dronkers, & Vargha-Khadem, 2002). Nonword repetition was the strongest predictor for being affected. These deficits were then associated with brain structure (Watkins, Vargha-Khadem et al., 2002) and functional imaging findings (Liégeois et al., 2003). Among the structural findings were abnormalities in the caudate nucleus, putamen, cerebellum, temporal cortex, inferior frontal gyrus, motor cortex, and the inferior frontal gyrus. Functionally, affected individuals exhibited lower activation during language tasks in Broca's area, the right inferior frontal gyri, and the putamen. They exhibited higher activation in traditionally nonlanguage areas such as posterior parietal, occipital, and postcentral regions. These findings were interpreted as indicating that the genetic abnormality interfered with the caudate development and results in procedural learning deficits, consistent with a proposal by Ullman and Pierpont (2005), as mentioned earlier.

Despite the KE family findings, several research groups (Meaburn, Dale, Craig, & Plomin, 2002; Newbury et al., 2002; O'Brien, Xuyang, Nishimura, Tomblin, & Murray, 2003) have not found *FOXP2* abnormalities in children with SLI. But suggestions of other gene associations have emerged (see chapter 10 by Tomblin). Nevertheless, the progress in this area has been substantial, and the rate at which new discoveries are made seems to increase each year.

NEUROBIOLOGY

Developmental cognitive neuroscience is still very much in its infancy, particularly as it has been applied to children with SLI, but new research is now emerging at a rapid pace (see chapter 7 by Tropper & Schwartz). Some of the reasons this research has emerged more slowly than behavioral research is the challenge of employing these methods with children (see chapter 24 by Shafer & Maxfield). The research to date has examined the underlying neurobiology of SLI using magnetic resonance imaging (MRI), functional magnetic resonance imaging (fMRI), and electrophysiology (ERPs). These studies have revealed structural and functional differences between the brains of children with SLI and their typically developing peers.

The characterization of the neurobiology underlying SLI begins with autopsy studies of adults who had histories of reading disabilities and a girl who had a history of a language disorder (e.g., Cohen, Campbell, & Yaghmai, 1989; Galaburda, 1985; Humphreys, Kaufmann, & Galaburda, 1990). The primary finding of interest was that these individuals seemed to lack hemispheric asymmetry in an area called the planum temporale (PT). The PT is an area defined by landmarks on the inferior portion of the Sylvian fissure. It is considered to be an area involved in receptive language that roughly corresponds to Wernicke's area. In previous studies, autopsies revealed that in adults with a history of normal language status the planum temporale was larger in the left hemisphere than in the right (e.g., Geschwind & Levitsky 1968).

MRI has been used to examine the relative size and volume of various brain areas and structures in living subjects. Plante and her colleagues have reported findings from a pair of dizygotic twins involving a boy with SLI and his twin sister with typical language development (Plante, Swisher, & Vance, 1989), a group of boys with SLI (4;2 to 9;6), and controls with typical language development (Plante, Swisher, Vance, & Rapcsak, 1991), as well as the parents and siblings of a subset of these children (Plante, 1991). Overall, these studies suggest that children with SLI, their siblings, and their parents tend to lack asymmetry or have atypical asymmetry (right hemisphere larger than left) in the perisylvian area, which includes the planum temporale. All of these findings should be considered against the finding that the presence of this asymmetry may vary with gender, with males being more likely to show asymmetry (Lane, Foundas, & Leonard, 2001). A more extensive MRI study (Jernigan, Hesselink, Sowell, & Tallal, 1991) was conducted of 20 children (8;0–10;0) with substantial receptive and expressive language delays and severe learning disabilities, along with 12 age-matched children with typical language development. The language-impaired children had leftward asymmetry in the superior parietal region and rightward asymmetry of the inferior frontal region, whereas symmetry was reversed in the typically developing children. The language-impaired children had lower volumes for most of the structures measured and for their overall left hemispheres, particularly for posterior perisylvian regions, which include the planum temporale. Subcortical structures, including the caudate nucleus, had bilaterally smaller volumes. Similar findings regarding subcortical structural abnormalities have been reported in studies of the KE family discussed above (Belton, Salmond, Watkins, Vargha-Khadem, & Gadian, 2003; Liégeois et al., 2003; Watkins, Vargha-Khadem et al., 2002). Such findings are consistent with the proposal that deficits in procedural memory underlie SLI and that motor deficits may be related. A final MRI study (Gauger, Lombardino, & Leonard, 1997) focused on the planum temporale (in Wernicke's area) and the pars triangularis (in Broca's area). In the children with SLI, there was atypical rightward asymmetry of the planum temporale and the poster ascending ramus, a smaller left pars triangularis, and a narrower right hemisphere.

To date only two studies have employed fMRI to investigate SLI. In the first, Weismer and her colleagues (Weismer, Plante, Jones, & Tomblin, 2005) examined brain differences during a modified listening span task focusing on sentence encoding and final word recognition for previous sentence sets. The adolescents with SLI exhibited lower activation during encoding in the left parietal region, associated with attentional control, and in the precentral sulcus, a region associated with memory processes, and lower activation during recognition in language processing regions, compared to their typically developing peers. They also exhibited different patterns of coordinating activation among brain regions during encoding and recognition compared to the typically developing adolescents, suggesting that their brains have a less well-established function network for such tasks. A second fMRI study (Niemi, Gundersen, Leppäsaari, & Hugdahl, K., 2003) compared the brain response of five family members with SLI and 6 control subjects to isolated vowel sounds, pseudowords, and real words. The family members with SLI exhibited reduced brain activation in areas associated with speech processing and phonological awareness located in the temporal and frontal lobes, most notably in the middle temporal gyrus bordering the superior temporal sulcus.

Electrophysiology is the most widely used method that has been applied to children with SLI. Event-related potentials (ERPs) have been used to examine speech perception, lexical-semantic processing, and syntactic processing in these children and in family members of these children (see chapter 7 by Tropper & Schwartz). ERP studies have revealed that children with SLI exhibit atypical responses, such as immature N1-P2-N2 responses, on a backward masking frequency discrimination task (Bishop & McArthur, 2005; McArthur & Bishop, 2004, 2005); smaller MisMatched Negativity discrimination responses to syllables and vowels (e.g., Shafer, Morr, Datta, Kurtzberg, & Schwartz, 2005; Uwer, Albrecht, & von Suchodoletz, 2002); absent left hemisphere responses or rightward asymmetry to speech, tones, and the word *the* in discourse (Bishop, Hardiman, Uwer, & von Suchodoletz, 2007; Shafer, Schwartz, Morr, Kessler, & Kurtzberg, 2000; Shafer et al., 2005); larger N400 to semantic anomalies (Neville, Coffey, Holcomb, & Tallal, 1993); lack of the typical leftward asymmetrical response to function words (Neville et al., 1993); and very delayed responses to gaps in sentences with relative clauses (Hestvik, Tropper, Schwartz, Shafer, & Tornyova, 2007). Some of the most interesting ERP findings regarding SLI involve the absence of N400 responses at 19 months of age in children who at 2;6 exhibited poor expressive language abilities (Friedrich & Friederici, 2006), as well as delayed positive mismatch response in 2-month-old infants from families with a history of SLI (Friedrich, Weber, & Friederici, 2004). Recently, Shafer and her colleagues (2007) used a global field power analysis to determine attention allocation in speech perception tasks where the child had to attend to a visual stimulus and ignore the speech or attend to the speech. The children with SLI reached an attentional peak later than their peers with typical language development (TLD), and when attention was directed towards the visual stimuli, the children with TLD still directed some attention resources to the speech, whereas the children with SLI did not. Evidence of deficits in selectional attention during story processing not apparent in a behavioral task was revealed by ERPs (Stevens, Sanders, & Neville, 2006). We are only beginning to tap the potential of this method in examining the neurobiology of SLI.

The great challenges remaining in the study of the neurobiology of SLI include the continuing establishment of relations between neurological findings and behavior, determining the specific cognitive and linguistic implications of anatomical and functional differences between children with SLI and their typically developing peers, the use of these methods to provide early identification of children at risk for SLI, as well as their use to measure changes following intervention.

ASSESSMENT

Clinical assessment of SLI predominantly relies on the use of standardized tests of syntax, morphosyntax, semantics, vocabulary, and phonology. These can be supplemented by tests of cognitive abilities, including performance IQ and working memory. The same tools are used by researchers in identifying children for research studies.

Many of these standardized language tests have limitations in sensitivity, specificity, reliability, and validity and are not amenable to examinations of language use in context (pragmatics) or of language processing. Furthermore, they often do not provide sufficient information to plan therapy because they are designed to survey various language abilities rather than to provide in-depth testing on any given aspect of language. Despite these limitations, standard tests remain the pillar of language assessment for SLI.

Language samples have been an important supplement to standardized testing. They have the advantage of permitting assessment of some pragmatic features and providing data about children's use of language structure (syntax and morphosyntax) and vocabulary in a more natural, communicative context. Several computer programs are available to analyze language samples. The programs that are most widely used are Systematic Analysis of Language Transcripts (SALT, Miller, & Iglesias, 2008), Computerized Language Analysis (CLAN, MacWhinney, 2000) and Computerized Profiling (Long, Fey, & Channell, 2004). All permit calculation of mean length of utterance (MLU) and provide other syntactic, morphosyntactic, and lexical analyses.

One issue that has been addressed by a number of investigators and clinicians is whether children are judged to be SLI by reference to their performance IQ (MA referencing) or to the mean language score(s) for their chronological age (CA referencing). Each of these approaches has advantages and disadvantages. MA referencing ensures that there is a language impairment rather than a more general developmental delay. CA referencing compares children to their age-matched peers, assuming that the normative data have been collected from a representative sample. Most research studies use a single omnibus language test with supplemental tasks (performance IQ, working memory, etc.) and set a criterion (e.g., 1.25 SD below the mean on two or more subtests of a standardized language test). The children must also have performance IQs within normal limits, generally intact speech production abilities, normal hearing, an absence of neurological issues (e.g., no perinatal bleeds, seizure activity, etc.), and no evidence of autism spectrum disorders. However, despite the seeming clarity of these definitions, researchers and clinicians encounter some difficulties identifying these children, especially across ages, when the specific deficits associated with SLI may vary in severity and the available tests may vary in their sensitivity to more subtle deficits in complex language. For children until approximately 8 years of age, some alternative measures such as nonword repetition and verb morphosyntax may be more sensitive (identifying all or most children with SLI) and specific (accurately labeling a child as SLI) than omnibus language tests.

Clinical definitions used to determine eligibility for services also vary widely. Many school districts or government regulations permit some latitude in the means for identifying children with SLI. Generally standardized tests are required, but language samples and, particularly for younger children, other observational and structured measures may be used. These alternatives to published omnibus tests include published and standardized tests that focus on a single language domain (i.e., morphosyntax) such as (Rice & Wexler, 2001), language samples (Miller, 1981), and nonstandardized language probes (Leonard, Prutting, Perozzi, & Berkley, 1978; Miller, 1981). Each has great potential to add to the assessment information for identifying SLI and for planning intervention.

One challenge that faces researchers and clinicians is the identification of SLI in children who speak African American English (AAE) and in children who are bilingual. Children who are speakers of AAE are overidentified as having language impairments because some dialect and SLI features overlap (see chapter 14 by Washington). Some language tests include procedures for distinguishing dialect features from SLI patterns. Only one test, the DELV (Seymour, Roeper, & de Villiers, 2004), provides information on dialect use in children. Analyses of language samples and nonstandardized probes may be more useful in identifying SLI in these children (e.g., Craig & Washington, 2006). Some alternative approaches such as nonword repetition (Campbell et al., 1997) or reaction-time-based tasks (see chapter 20 by Windsor & Kohnert) are less affected by cultural, linguistic, or dialect factors and, thus, may serve as useful approaches to the identification of children with SLI from these groups. Behavioral computer-based tasks, eye tracking, and event-related potentials (see chapter 21 by Seiger-Gardner, chapter 22 by Deevy, and chapter 24 by Shafer & Maxfield) have become increasingly well established as methods for measuring language production and language comprehension in research studies and may have a future role in the clinical assessment of language.

INTERVENTION

Intervention remains among the least studied aspects of SLI. Fewer intervention studies have been published to date than other types of investigations, in part because of publication limitations and because of the general challenges of intervention research (see chapter 23 by Fey & Finestack). There has been sufficient research published to demonstrate that language intervention is effective and has the best outcome when it begins early in development. Intervention for SLI can be described by the specific method, by the activity, physical context, and by the social context using a framework initially proposed by Fey (1986). The specific methods were divided into trainer-oriented, child-oriented, and hybrid approaches. The activity, physical, and social contexts can be characterized on continua of naturalness (e.g., drill to organized games to daily activities; clinic to school to home; clinician to teacher to parents). This brief overview of research on intervention for SLI focuses on some selected methods of intervention and some of the variables that have examined to determine their effect on outcomes of intervention.

Trainer-oriented approaches include methods such as operant procedures (e.g., Gray & Ryan, 1973) and social learning approaches (Leonard, 1975). Although these procedures are effective in establishing the production of new language forms, the extent to which these gains are maintained and generalized to communicative situations is limited (Fey, 1986).

Child-oriented approaches include facilitative play involving self-talk (the adult talks about her activities) and parallel-talk (the adult describes the child's activities) without requiring a response from the child (Van Riper, 1947). Expansions (the adult repeats the child's preceding utterance, adding additional grammatical and semantic information). Recasting is a form of expansion in which the adult takes the child's utterance and changes it into a different form (e.g., *I'm a scary monster. You're a scary monster, aren't you?*). Recasting has been extensively researched by Camarata, Nelson, and their colleagues (e.g., Camarata & Nelson, 2006; Camarata, Nelson, & Camarata, 1994; Nelson, Camarata, Welsh, & Butkovsky, 1996) as well as other investigators (e.g., Proctor-Williams, Fey, & Loeb, 2001). Across these studies, recasting was demonstrated to be a successful procedure for establishing new syntactic structures in children with language impairments that generalize to language samples. Recently, Proctor-Williams and Fey (2007) examined the effects of recast density in teaching novel irregular verbs over five sessions to children with SLI and to a younger group of children with TLD. They presented recasts at three frequency levels: none, conversational level, and intervention level. The children with TLD were more successful at producing the novel verbs presented with conversational density than those presented without recasting, but this was not true for the children with SLI. The children with SLI did not produce the verbs more accurately at the intervention-density level, and the children with TLD also performed more poorly in this condition. The authors suggested that one explanation for the findings is that the short period of intervention with high recast density is not efficient for word learning. In typically developing children, there is evidence that distributed presentations (over sessions) of novel words leads to greater acquisition than the same number of presentations condensed into a small number of sessions (Childers & Tomasello, 2002; Schwartz & Terrell, 1983).

Hybrid approaches include planned activities that modify the environment to motivate the use of certain linguistic forms (Lucas, 1980), focused stimulation (Fey, 1986), and incidental milieu teaching (e.g., Finestack, Fey, & Catts, 2006; Hancock & Kaiser, 2006; Hart & Risley, 1980). The latter two have been studied extensively. Fey, Cleave, Long, and Hughes (1993) employed focused stimulation in which the intervention agents—clinicians or parents—frequently modeled grammatical targets, provided recasts that included the target forms, and created activities designed to maximize opportunities and obligate the production of these forms. One purpose of this study was to examine whether the less costly approach using parents as primary intervention agents with support from clinicians would be as effective in establishing language target structures in spontaneous speech as an approach that only involved clinicians as intervention agents. The more costly clinician-only approach appeared to be more effective. A follow-up study (Fey, Cleave, & Long, 1997) with 18 of the participants confirmed the results and led to fewer gains than the first five-month intervention. It was successful in establishing recasting in the parents, especially for the younger children. This does not mean that parents are not effective intervention agents alone or in conjunction with clinicians, particularly for younger children (e.g., Girolametto, Weitzman, & Greenberg, 2006; Kaiser & Hancock, 2003).

Most of the preceding research has focused on preschool and young school-aged children. Two recent studies have examined intervention for more complex syntax in older children with SLI. The first study examined intervention for argument structure deficits using syntactic–semantic, semantic, and a control therapy to which they were randomly assigned. The semantic–syntactic therapy used shapes and positions to illustrate constructing syntactic structures and provided semantic information in terms of the category/function of verbs (change of location vs. change of state) along with unique associations to question words (*where* vs. *how*). Based on video probes, both approaches led to improvements, but the syntactic–semantic therapy led to increased use of optional arguments. In a single-subject study, Levy and Friedmann (in press) taught syntactic movement to a 12-year-old child with SLI who had deficits in this area using targeted comprehension, repetition, and elicitation of semantically reversible sentences. Performance improved on a probe compared to baseline and in some cases reached that of age-matched typically developing children. Generalization was noted, and the performance was maintained when reassessed 10 months later. Together these studies demonstrate that complex sentence structures can be taught to older children with SLI. Very often such children are no longer enrolled in speech-language therapy in public schools. The outcome of these syntactic interventions also has a role in evaluating theories of the syntactic deficits in SLI.

Two other disparate but widely used intervention methods warrant some attention: *Fast ForWord* and sensory integration. *Fast ForWord* is a commercially available program (Scientific Learning Corporation, 1998) based on the notions that perceptual deficits underlie SLI and that the brain is sufficiently plastic to be changed by relatively short-term participation in a computer-based intervention administered at a clinic or at home (Merzenich et al., 1996, 1999; Tallal et al., 1996). There are seven components: three sound tasks involving discrimination and identification and four word tasks in isolation or in sentence contexts. The sounds, words, and sentences used are lengthened, and selective frequencies are amplified in a way that is assumed to facilitate the child's perception of speech. These modifications are reduced adaptively as the child successfully proceeds through the program. Merzenich, Tallal, and their colleagues (Merzenich et al., 1996; Tallal et al., 1996) provided initial evidence for the effectiveness of this approach. The claim is that children's language age scores may increase by as much as three years. These initial studies were conducted by researchers who are the founders or are connected with the Scientific Learning Corporation (SLC). A more recent review by individuals associated with SLC (Agocs, Burns, De Ley, Miller, & Calhoun, 2006) presented data that have been collected from a national field trial, a school pilot study, and more recent users, all of which suggest a positive outcome. There were a number of methodological limitations in these initial studies, including a rather mixed group of subjects and measurement instruments that mirrored the intervention tasks too closely. Studies by independent investigators have revealed a much more mixed efficacy story. For example, a randomized control trial of children with severe receptive–expressive language disorder found no difference in outcome among children who received *Fast ForWord*, children who received other commercially available programs to enhance language, and children who received no treatment (Cohen et al., 2005). All the children made gains, but there was no difference among the groups, suggesting that this approach is not effective for these children. Similar concerns have been raised in case studies about the lack of or inconsistent outcomes from this approach (e.g., Friel-Patti, DesBarres, & Thibodeau, 2001; Loeb, Stoke, & Fey, 2001; Troia & Whitney, 2003). Very recently, a large-scale randomized controlled trial revealed that children with poor backward masking scores assigned to a *Fast ForWord Language* condition did not make any more improvement in language or temporal processing than children assigned to a general academic enrichment program or to a language intervention program without acoustically modified speech (Gillam et al., 2008).

Sensory integration was initially proposed to explain the relationship between learning disabilities and motor learning deficits in children who exhibit sensory processing disorders (Ayers, 1979). Clinical observations suggest that children with language impairments may also have motor planning deficits, poor attention, or difficulties with emotional or behavior regulation that are characterized as sensory processing deficits. Although sensory integration approaches do not directly address language, it appears to have some positive impact on reading scores for children with auditory-language learning disabilities (Ayers, 1979). As yet, there is no direct evidence of the effectiveness of this approach in facilitating language development in children with SLI. Given the proposal (Ullman & Pierpont, 2005) concerning the relationship between procedural learning (in motor and other domains) and SLI, such an approach may be worth investigating further. Given the current emphasis on evidence-based practice, it seems critical that we continue to evaluate our current approaches to intervention as well as novel approaches before they are widely adopted.

SLI AND OTHER LANGUAGE DISORDERS

With a still relatively small number of exceptions, there has been a tendency to focus on single clinical groups in given studies. However, it is apparent that groups of children with language impairments share certain deficits. This is even true in comparing deficits for children with developmental language disorders and adults with acquired language disorders. For example, adults with agrammatism appear to share deficits in morphosyntax and syntax with children who have SLI. Some of these apparently shared deficits may simply reflect weak points in the language that are affected by any general limitation in language production or comprehension or by deficits in related cognitive abilities. Another consideration is that SLI may occur in children from other groups with language disorders at the same rate as it does in the general population. For example, one proposal has suggested that the relationship between dyslexia and SLI can be characterized as quadrants: children with normal language and nondyslexia, children with dyslexia only, children with SLI only, and children with dyslexia and SLI (Bishop & Snowling, 2004). Yet even with this association/disassociation, there may be commonalities across these groups in language deficits and language-related deficits such as working memory, processing speed, neurobiological findings, and genetics. The same may hold true for autism (Rice, Warren, & Betz, 2005; Warren et al., 2006). The challenge of further defining these commonalities and differences will certainly engage researchers in the coming decade.

FUTURE DIRECTIONS

Clearly, we know far more about the nature of SLI, its origins, as well as the scope and details of the deficits seen in these children than we did in the 1970s, when the modern era of this research began. Although we now know something about the neurobiology and genetics of SLI, the next decade will bring us many more details. We still know relatively little about some basic cognitive processes such as procedural memory, attention and executive functions, and the role they play in SLI. There is a clear need for further research concerning the relative efficacy of various approaches to interventions and the variables that may facilitate language learning in these children. Finally, we need additional information about the relationships between SLI and other groups of childhood language disorders and possible subgroups of these children, so we have a fully integrated picture of childhood language disorders. The following chapters are one step in this direction.

REFERENCES

Adams, C. (1990). Syntactic comprehension in children with expressive language impairment. *British Journal of Disorders of Communication*, 25(2), 149–171.

Agocs, M. M., Burns, M. S., De Ley, L. E., Miller, S. L., & Calhoun, B. M. (2006). Fast ForWord language. In R. J. McCauley & M. E. Fey (Eds.), *Treatment of language disorders in children* (pp. 471–508). Baltimore: Paul H. Brookes.

Alloway, T. P., Gathercole, S. E., Willis, C., & Adams, A. (2004). A structural analysis of working memory and related cognitive skills in young children. *Journal of Experimental Child Psychology*, 87(2), 85–106.

Alt, M., & Plante, E. (2006). Factors that influence lexical and semantic fast mapping of young children with specific language impairment. *Journal of Speech, Language, and Hearing Research*, 49(5), 941–954.

Archibald, L. M. D., & Gathercole, S. E. (2006). Short-term memory and working memory in specific language impairment. In T. P. Alloway & S. E. Gathercole (Eds.), *Working memory and neurodevelopmental disorders* (pp. 139–160). New York: Psychology Press.

Armstrong, C. (1997). Selective versus sustained attention: A continuous performance test revisited. *Clinical Neuropsychologist*, 11(1), 18–33.

Ayers, A. J. (1979). *Sensory integration and the child*. Los Angeles, CA: Western Psychological Services.

Baddeley, A. (1986). *Working memory*. New York: Clarendon/Oxford University Press.

Barrett, L. F., Tugade, M. M., & Engle, R. W. (2004). Individual differences in working memory capacity and dual-process theories of the mind. *Psychological Bulletin*, 130(4), 553–573.

Bedore, L. M., & Leonard, L. B. (2001). Grammatical morphology deficits in Spanish-speaking children with specific language impairment. *Journal of Speech, Language, and Hearing Research*, 44(4), 905–924.

Beitchman, J. H., Hood, J., & Inglis, A. (1992). Familial transmission of speech and language impairment: A preliminary investigation. *Canadian Journal of Psychiatry*, 37(3), 151–156.

Belton, E., Salmond, C. H., Watkins, K. E., Vargha-Khadem, F., & Gadian, D. G. (2003). Bilateral brain abnormalities associated with dominantly inherited verbal and orofacial dyspraxia. *Human Brain Mapping*, 18(3), 194–200.

Bishop, D. V. M. (1997). *Uncommon understanding: Development and disorders of language comprehension in children*. Hove, UK: Psychology Press.

Bishop, D. V. M. (1998). Development of the Children's Communication Checklist (CCC): A method for assessing qualitative aspects of communicative impairment in children. *Journal of Child Psychology and Psychiatry*, 39(6), 879–891.

Bishop, D. V. M. (2000). Pragmatic language impairment: A correlate of SLI, a distinct subgroup, or part of the autistic continuum? In D. V. M. Bishop, & L. B. Leonard (Eds.), *Speech and language impairments in children: Causes, characteristics, intervention, and outcome* (pp. 99–113). New York: Psychology Press.

Bishop, D. V. M., Adams, C. V., & Norbury, C. F. (2006). Distinct genetic influences on grammar and phonological short-term memory deficits: Evidence from 6-year-old twins. *Genes, Brain and Behavior*, 5(2), 158–169.

Bishop, D. V. M., Bishop, S. J., Bright, P., James, C., Delaney, T., & Tallal, P. (1999). Different origin of auditory and phonological processing problems in children with language impairment: Evidence from a twin study. *Journal of Speech, Language, and Hearing Research*, 42(1), 155–168.

Bishop, D. V. M., Bright, P., James, C., Bishop, S. J., & van der Lely, H. K. J. (2000). Grammatical SLI: A distinct subtype of developmental language impairment? *Applied Psycholinguistics*, 21(2), 159–181.

Bishop, D. V. M., Chan, J., Adams, C., Hartley, J., & Weir, F. (2000). Conversational responsiveness in specific language impairment: Evidence of disproportionate pragmatic difficulties in a subset of children. *Development and Psychopathology*, 12(2), 177–199.

Bishop, D. V. M., Hardiman, M., Uwer, R., & von Suchodoletz, W. (2007). Atypical long-latency auditory event-related potentials in a subset of children with specific language impairment. *Developmental Science*, 10(5), 576–587.

Bishop, D. V. M., & McArthur, G. M. (2005). Individual differences in auditory processing in specific language impairment: A follow-up study using event-related potentials and behavioural thresholds. *Cortex*, 47, 327–341.

Bishop, D. V. M., & Norbury, C. F. (2005). Executive functions in children with communication impairments, in relation to autistic symptomatology, II: Response inhibition. *Autism: The International Journal of Research and Practice*, 9(1), 29–43.

Bishop, D. V. M., North, T., & Donlan, C. (1995). Genetic basis of specific language impairment: Evidence from a twin study. *Developmental Medicine and Child Neurology*, 37(1), 56–71.

Bishop, D. V. M., & Snowling, M. J. (2004). Developmental dyslexia and specific language impairment: Same or different? *Psychological Bulletin*, 130(6), 858–886.

Botting, N. (2002). Narrative as a tool for the assessment of linguistic and pragmatic impairments. *Child Language Teaching and Therapy*, 18(1), 1–22.

Botting, N., & Conti-Ramsden, G. (2001). Non-word repetition and language development in children with specific language impairment (SLI). *International Journal of Language and Communication Disorders*, 36(4), 421–432.

Botting, N., & Conti-Ramsden, G. (2003). Autism, primary pragmatic difficulties, and specific language impairment: Can we distinguish them using psycholinguistic markers? *Developmental Medicine and Child Neurology*, 45(8), 515–524.

Brinton, B., & Fujiki, M. (1982). A comparison of request-response sequences in the discourse of normal and language-disordered children. *Journal of Speech and Hearing Disorders*, 47(1), 57–62.

Brinton, B., & Fujiki, M. (1999). Social interactional behaviors of children with specific language impairment. *Topics in Language Disorders*, 19(2), 49–69.

Brinton, B., Fujiki, M., & McKee, L. (1998). Negotiation skills of children with specific language impairment. *Journal of Speech, Language, and Hearing Research*, 41(4), 927–940.

Brinton, B., Fujiki, M., & Powell, J. M. (1997). The ability of children with language impairment to manipulate topic in a structured task. *Language, Speech and Hearing Services in Schools*, 28(1), 3–11.

Brinton, B., Fujiki, M., & Sonnenberg, E. A. (1988). Responses to requests for clarification by linguistically normal and language-impaired children in conversation. *Journal of Speech and Hearing Disorders*, 53(4), 383–391.

Bryk, A. S., & Raudenbush, S. W. (1992). *Hierarchical linear models: Applications and data analysis methods*. Thousand Oaks, CA: Sage.

Burlingame, E., Sussman, H. M., Gillam, R. B., & Hay, J. F. (2005). An investigation of speech perception in children with specific language impairment on a continuum of formant transition duration. *Journal of Speech, Language, and Hearing Research, 48*(4), 805–816.

Camarata, S. M., & Nelson, K. E. (2006). Conversational recast intervention with preschool and older children. In R. J. McCauley & M. E. Fey (Eds.), *Treatment of language disorders in children* (pp. 237–264). Baltimore: Paul H. Brookes.

Camarata, S. M., Nelson, K. E., & Camarata, M. N. (1994). Comparison of conversational-recasting and imitative procedures for training grammatical structures in children with specific language impairment. *Journal of Speech and Hearing Research, 37*(6), 1414–1423.

Campbell, T., Dollaghan, C., Needleman, H., & Janosky, J. (1997). Reducing bias in language assessment: Processing-dependent measures. *Journal of Speech and Hearing Research, 40*(3), 519–525.

Catts, H. W., Adlof, S. M., Hogan, T. P., & Weismer, S. E. (2005). Are specific language impairment and dyslexia distinct disorders? *Journal of Speech, Language, and Hearing Research, 48*(6), 1378–1396.

Cerella, J., & Hale, S. (1994). The rise and fall in information-processing rates over the life span. *Acta Psychologica, 86*(2), 109–197.

Childers, J. B., & Tomasello, M. (2002). Two-year-olds learn novel nouns, verbs, and conventional actions from massed or distributed exposures. *Developmental Psychology, 38*(6), 967–978.

Choudhury, N., Leppänen, P. H. T., Leevers, H. J., & Benasich, A. A. (2007). Infant information processing and family history of specific language impairment: Converging evidence for RAP deficits from two paradigms. *Developmental Science, 10*(2), 213–236.

Clarke, M. G., & Leonard, L. B. (1996). Lexical comprehension and grammatical deficits in children with specific language impairment. *Journal of Communication Disorders, 29*(2), 95–105.

Coady, J. A., Evans, J. L., Mainela-Arnold, E., & Kluender, K. R. (2007). Children with specific language impairments perceive speech most categorically when tokens are natural and meaningful. *Journal of Speech, Language, and Hearing Research, 50*(1), 41–57.

Coady, J. A., Kluender, K. R., & Evans, J. L. (2005). Categorical perception of speech by children with specific language impairments. *Journal of Speech, Language, and Hearing Research, 48*(4), 944–959.

Cohen, M., Campbell, R., & Yaghmai, F. (1989). Neuropathological abnormalities in developmental dysphasia. *Annals of Neurology, 25*(6), 567–570.

Cohen, W., Hodson, A., O'Hare, A., Boyle, J., Durrani, T., McCartney, E., et al. (2005). Effects of computer-based intervention through acoustically modified speech (Fast ForWord) in severe mixed receptive–expressive language impairment: Outcomes from a randomized controlled trial. *Journal of Speech, Language, and Hearing Research, 48*(3), 715–729.

Conti-Ramsden, G., & Botting, N. (2004). Social difficulties and victimization in children with SLI at 11 years of age. *Journal of Speech, Language, and Hearing Research, 47*(1), 145–161.

Conti-Ramsden, G., Botting, N., Simkin, Z., & Knox, E. (2001). Follow-up of children attending infant language units: Outcomes at 11 years of age. *International Journal of Language and Communication Disorders, 36*(2), 207–219.

Conti-Ramsden, G., & Friel-Patti, S. (1983). Mothers' discourse adjustments to language-impaired and non-language-impaired children. *Journal of Speech and Hearing Disorders, 48*(4), 360–367.

Conti-Ramsden, G., & Jones, M. (1997). Verb use in specific language impairment. *Journal of Speech and Hearing Research, 40*(6), 1298–1313.

Conway, A. R. A., & Engle, R. W. (1994). Working memory and retrieval: A resource-dependent inhibition model. *Journal of Experimental Psychology: General, 123*(4), 354–373.

Conway, A. R. A., & Engle, R. W. (1996). Individual differences in working memory capacity: More evidence for a general capacity theory. *Memory, 4*(6), 577–590.

Cowan, N. (1997). The development of working memory. In N. Cowan (Ed.), *The development of memory in childhood* (pp. 163–199). Hove, UK: Psychology Press.

Crago, M. B., & Gopnik, M. (1994). From families to phenotypes: Theoretical and clinical implications of research into the genetic basis of specific language impairment. In R. V. Watkins & M. L. Rice (Eds.), *Specific language impairments in children* (pp. 35–51). Baltimore: Paul H. Brookes.

Craig, H. K. (1985). Pragmatic impairments. In P. Fletcher & B. MacWhinney (Eds.), *The handbook of child language* (pp. 623–640). Cambridge, MA: Blackwell.

Craig, H. K., & Evans, J. L. (1993). Pragmatics and SLI: Within-group variations in discourse behaviors. *Journal of Speech and Hearing Research, 36*(4), 777–789.

Craig, H. K., & Washington, J. A. (1993). Access behaviors of children with specific language impairment. *Journal of Speech and Hearing Research, 36*(2), 322–337.

Craig, H. K., & Washington, J. A. (2006). *Malik goes to school: Examining the language skills of African American students from preschool–5th grade.* Mahwah, NJ: Lawrence Erlbaum Associates.

Crain, S., & Thornton, R. (1998). *Investigations in universal grammar: A guide to experiments on the acquisition of syntax and semantics.* Cambridge, MA: MIT Press.

Deevy, P., & Leonard, L. B. (2004). The comprehension of wh-questions in children with specific language impairment. *Journal of Speech, Language, and Hearing Research, 47*(4), 802–815.

Dockrell, J. E., & Messer, D. (2007). Language profiles and naming in children with word finding difficulties. *Folia Phoniatrica et Logopaedica, 59*(6), 318–323.

Dollaghan, C. A. (1987). Fast mapping in normal and language-impaired children. *Journal of Speech and Hearing Disorders, 52*(3), 218–222.

Dollaghan, C. A., Biber, M. E., & Campbell, T. F. (1995). Lexical influences on nonword repetition. *Applied Psycholinguistics, 16*(2), 211–222.

Dollaghan, C., & Campbell, T. F. (1998). Nonword repetition and child language impairment. *Journal of Speech, Language, and Hearing Research, 41*(5), 1136–1146.

Donders, F. C. (1969). On the speed of mental processes. *Acta Psychologica, 30,* 412–431.

Ebbels, S., & van der Lely, H. (2001). Meta-syntactic therapy using visual coding for children with severe persistent SLI. *International Journal of Language and Communication Disorders, 36,* 345.

Edwards, J., & Lahey, M. (1996). Auditory lexical decisions of children with specific language impairment. *Journal of Speech and Hearing Research, 39*(6), 1263–1273.

Eley, T. C., Bishop, D., Dale, P., Price, T. S., & Plomin, R. (2001). Longitudinal analysis of the genetic and environmental influences on components of cognitive. *Journal of Educational Psychology, 93*(4), 698.

Engle, R. W., Kane, M. J., & Tuholski, S. W. (1999). Individual differences in working memory capacity and what they tell us about controlled attention, general fluid intelligence, and functions of the prefrontal cortex. In A. Miyake & P. Shah (Eds.), *Models of working memory: Mechanisms of active maintenance and executive control* (pp. 102–134). New York: Cambridge University Press.

Fenson, L., Marchman, V., Thal, D. J., Dale, P. S., Reznick, J. S., & Bates, E. (1996). *The MacArthur–Bates Communicative Development Inventories: User's guide and technical manual* (2nd ed.). Baltimore: Paul H. Brookes.

Fey, M. E. (1986). *Language intervention with young children.* San Diego, CA: College Hill Press.

Fey, M. E. (2006). Clinical forum. Commentary on "Making evidence-based decisions about child language intervention in schools" by Gillam and Gillam. *Language, Speech and Hearing Services in Schools, 37*(4), 316–319.

Fey, M. E., Cleave, P. L., & Long, S. H. (1997). Two models of grammar facilitation in children with language impairments: Phase 2. *Journal of Speech, Language, and Hearing Research, 40*(1), 5–19.

Fey, M. E., Cleave, P. L., Long, S. H., & Hughes, D. L. (1993). Two approaches to the facilitation of grammar in children with language impairment: An experimental evaluation. *Journal of Speech and Hearing Research, 36*(1), 141–157.

Finestack, L. H., Fey, M. E., & Catts, H. W. (2006). Pronominal reference skills of second and fourth grade children with language impairment. *Journal of Communication Disorders, 39*(3), 232–248.

Fletcher, P. (1999). Specific language impairment. In M. Barrett (Ed.), *The development of language* (pp. 349–371). New York: Psychology Press.

Friedmann, N., & Novogrodsky, R. (2004). The acquisition of relative clause comprehension in Hebrew: A study of SLI and normal development. *Journal of Child Language, 31*(3), 661–681.

Friedmann, N., & Novogrodsky, R. (2007). Is the movement deficit in syntactic SLI related to traces or to thematic role transfer? *Brain and Language, 101*(1), 50–63.

Friedrich, M., & Friederici, A. D. (2006). Early N400 development and later language acquisition. *Psychophysiology, 43*(1), 1–12.

Friedrich, M., Weber, C., & Friederici, A. D. (2004). Electrophysiological evidence for delayed mismatch response in infants at-risk for specific language impairment. *Psychophysiology, 41*(5), 180–187.

Friel-Patti, S., DesBarres, K., & Thibodeau, L. (2001). Case studies of children using Fast ForWord. *American Journal of Speech-Language Pathology, 10*(3), 203.

Galaburda, A. M. (1985). Developmental dyslexia: A review of biological interactions. *Annals of Dyslexia, 35,* 21–33.

Gallon, N., Harris, J., & van der Lely, H. (2007). Non-word repetition: An investigation of phonological complexity in children with grammatical SLI. *Clinical Linguistics and Phonetics, 21*(6), 435–455.

Ganong, W. F. (1980). Phonetic categorization in auditory word perception. *Journal of Experimental Psychology: Human Perception and Performance, 6*(1), 110–125.

Gathercole, S. E. (2006). Nonword repetition and word learning: The nature of the relationship. *Applied Psycholinguistics, 27*(4), 513–543.

Gathercole, S. E., & Baddeley, A. D. (1990). Phonological memory deficits in language disordered children: Is there a causal connection? *Journal of Memory and Language, 29*(3), 336–360.

Gauger, L. M., Lombardino, L. J., & Leonard, C. M. (1997). Brain morphology in children with specific language impairment. *Journal of Speech and Hearing Research, 40*(6), 1272–1284.

German, D. J., & Newman, R. S. (2004). The impact of lexical factors on children's word-finding errors. *Journal of Speech, Language, and Hearing Research, 47*(3), 624–636.

Geschwind, N., & Levitsky, W. (1968). Human brain: Left–right asymmetries in temporal speech region. *Science, 161*(3837), 186–187.

Gillam, R. B., Cowan, N., & Day, L. S. (1995). Sequential memory in children with and without language impairment. *Journal of Speech and Hearing Research, 38*(2), 393–402.

Gillam, R. B., Loeb, D. F., Hoffman, L. M., Bohman, T., Champlin, C. A., Thibodeau, L., et al. (2008). The efficacy of Fast ForWord language intervention in school-age children with language impairment: A randomized controlled trial. *Journal of Speech, Language, and Hearing Research, 51*(1), 97–119.

Gillam, R., & McFadden, T. U. (1994). Redefining assessment as a holistic discovery process. *Journal of Childhood Communication Disorders, 16*(1), 36–40.

Girolametto, L., Weitzman, E., & Greenberg, J. (2006). Facilitating language skills. *Infants and Young Children: An Interdisciplinary Journal of Special Care Practices, 19*(1), 36–49.

Goffman, L., & Leonard, J. (2000). Growth of language skills in preschool children with specific language impairment: Implications for assessment and intervention. *American Journal of Speech-Language Pathology, 9*(2), 151–161.

Gopnik, M. (1990). Feature-blind grammar and dysphagia. *Nature, 344*(6268), 139–164.

Gopnik, M., & Crago, M. B. (1991). Familial aggregation of a developmental language disorder. *Cognition, 39*(1), 1–50.

Gray, B. B., & Ryan, B. P. (1973). *A language program for the nonlanguage child.* Champaign, IL: Research Press.

Grela, B. G., & Leonard, L. B. (2000). The influence of argument-structure complexity on the use of auxiliary verbs by children with SLI. *Journal of Speech, Language, and Hearing Research, 43*(5), 362–378.

Gutiérrez-Clellen, V. F., Restrepo, M. A., & Simón-Cereijido, G. (2006). Evaluating the discriminant accuracy of a grammatical measure with Spanish-speaking children. *Journal of Speech, Language, and Hearing Research, 49*(6), 1209–1223.

Gutiérrez-Clellen, V. F., & Simon-Cereijido, G. (2007). The discriminant accuracy of a grammatical measure with Latino English-speaking children. *Journal of Speech, Language, and Hearing Research, 50*(4), 968–981.

Hadley, P. A., & Rice, M. L. (1991). Conversational responsiveness of speech- and language-impaired preschoolers. *Journal of Speech and Hearing Research, 34*(6), 1308–1317.

Håkansson, G., & Hansson, K. (2000). Comprehension and production of relative clauses: A comparison between Swedish impaired and unimpaired children. *Journal of Child Language, 27*(2), 313–333.

Hancock, T. B., & Kaiser, A. P. (2006). Enhanced milieu teaching. In R. J. McCauley, & M. E. Fey (Eds.), *Treatment of language disorders in children* (pp. 203–236). Baltimore, MD: Paul H. Brookes.

Hanson, R. A., & Montgomery, J. W. (2002). Effects of general processing capacity and sustained selective attention on temporal processing performance of children with specific language impairment. *Applied Psycholinguistics, 23*(1), 75–93.

Hansson, K., & Nettelbladt, U. (2006). Wh-questions in Swedish children with SLI. *Advances in Speech Language Pathology, 8*(4), 376–383.

Hart, B., & Risley, T. R. (1980). In vivo language intervention. *Journal of Applied Behavioral Analysis, 13*(3), 407–432.

Hasher, L., Stoltzfus, E. R., Zacks, R. T., & Rypma, B. (1991). Age and inhibition. *Journal of Experimental Psychology: Learning, Memory and Cognition, 17*(1), 163–169.

Hayiou-Thomas, M. E., Oliver, B., & Plomin, R. (2005). Genetic influences on specific versus nonspecific language impairment in 4-year-old twins. *Journal of Learning Disabilities, 38*(3), 222–232.

Haynes, C. (1992). Vocabulary deficit: One problem or many? *Child Language Teaching and Therapy, 8*(1), 1–17.

Hestvik, A., Tropper, B., Schwartz, R., Shafer, V., & Tornyova, L. (2007). *ERP measure of gap-filling in children with and without specific language impairment.* Paper presented at the CUNY Sentence Processing Conference, La Jolla, CA.

Humphreys, P., Kaufmann, W. E., Galaburda, A. M. (1990). Developmental dyslexia in women: Neuropathological findings in three patients. *Annals of Neurology, 28*(6), 727–738.

Hurst, J. A., Baraitser, M., Auger, E., Graham, F., & Norell, S. (1990). An extended family with a dominantly inherited speech disorder. *Developmental Medicine and Child Neurology, 32*(4), 352–355.

Im-Bolter, N., Johnson, J., & Pascual-Leone, J. (2006). Processing limitations in children with specific language impairment: The role of executive function. *Child Development, 77*(6), 1822–1841.

Ingham, R., Fletcher, P., Schelleter, C., & Sinka, I. (1998). Resultative VPs and specific language impairment. *Language Acquisition, 7*(2–4), 87–111.

Irwin, J. R., Carter, A. S., & Briggs-Gowan, M. J. (2002). The social–emotional development of "late-talking" toddlers. *Journal of the American Academy of Child and Adolescent Psychiatry, 41*(11), 1324.

Jacobson, P. F., & Schwartz, R. G. (2002). Morphology in incipient bilingual Spanish-speaking preschool children with specific language impairment. *Applied Psycholinguistics, 23*(1), 23–41.

Jacobson, P. F., & Schwartz, R. G. (2005). English past tense use in bilingual children with language impairment. *American Journal of Speech-Language Pathology, 14*(4), 313–323.

Jernigan, T. L., Hesselink, J. R., Sowell, E., & Tallal, P. A. (1991). Cerebral structure on magnetic resonance imaging in language- and learning-impaired children. *Archives of Neurology, 48*(5), 539–545.

Johnston, J. R., Miller, J., & Tallal, P. (2001). Use of cognitive state predicates by language-impaired children. *International Journal of Language and Communication Disorders, 36*(3), 349–370.

Just, M. A., Carpenter, P. A., & Keller, T. A. (1996). The capacity theory of comprehension: New frontiers of evidence and arguments. *Psychological Review, 103*(4), 773–780.

Kail, R. (1991). Developmental change in speed of processing during childhood and adolescence. *Psychological Bulletin, 109*(3), 490–501.

Kail, R. (1994). A method for studying the generalized slowing hypothesis in children with specific language impairment. *Journal of Speech and Hearing Research, 37*(2), 418–421.

Kail, R., & Leonard, L. B. (1986). Word-finding abilities in language-impaired children. *ASHA Monographs, 25*.

Kail, R., & Miller, C. A. (2006). Developmental change in processing speed: Domain specificity and stability during childhood and adolescence. *Journal of Cognition and Development, 7*(1), 119–137.

Kaiser, A. P., & Hancock, T. B. (2003). Teaching parents new skills to support their young children's development. *Infants and Young Children: An Interdisciplinary Journal of Special Care Practices, 16*(1), 9.

Keith, R. W. (1994). *Auditory Continuous Performance Test*. San Antonio, TX: Psychological Corporation.

Klee, T. (1992). Developmental and diagnostic characteristics of quantitative measures of children's language production. *Topics in Language Disorders, 12*(2), 28–41.

Kohnert, K. (2002). Picture naming in early sequential bilinguals: A 1-year follow-up. *Journal of Speech, Language, and Hearing Research, 45*(4), 759.

Lahey, M., & Edwards, J. (1999). Naming errors of children with specific language impairment. *Journal of Speech, Language, and Hearing Research, 42*(1), 195–205.

Lahey, M., Edwards, J., & Munson, B. (2001). Is processing speed related to severity of language impairment? *Journal of Speech, Language, and Hearing Research, 44*(6), 1354–1361.

Lai, C. S. L., Fisher, S. E., Hurst, J. A., Levy, E. R., Hodgson, S., Fox, M., et al. (2000). The SPCH1 region on human 7q31: Genomic characterization of the critical interval and localization of translocations associated with speech and language disorder. *American Journal of Human Genetics, 67*(2), 357–368.

Lai, C. S. L., Fisher, S. E., Hurst, J. A., Vargha-Khadem, F., & Monaco, A. P. (2001). A forkhead-domain gene is mutated in a severe speech and language disorder. *Nature, 413*(6855), 519–523.

Lane, A. B., Foundas, A. L., & Leonard, C. M. (2001). The evolution of neuroimaging research and developmental language disorders. *Topics in Language Disorders, 21*(3), 20–41.

le Normand, M., Leonard, L. B., & McGregor, K. K. (1993). A cross-linguistic study of article use by children with specific language impairment. *European Journal of Disorders of Communication, 28*(2), 153–163.

Leonard, L. B. (1975). Modeling as a clinical procedure in language training. *Language, Speech and Hearing Services in Schools, 6*(2), 72–85.

Leonard, L. B. (1982). Early lexical acquisition in children with specific language impairment. *Journal of Speech and Hearing Research, 25*(4), 554–564.

Leonard, L. B. (1986). Conversational replies of children with specific language impairment. *Journal of Speech and Hearing Research, 29*(1), 114–119.

Leonard, L. B. (1989). Language learnability and specific language impairment in children. *Applied Psycholinguistics, 10*(2), 179–202.

Leonard, L. B. (1998). *Children with specific language impairment*. Cambridge, MA: MIT Press.

Leonard, L. B., Bortolini, U., Caselli, M. C., & McGregor, K. K. (1992). Morphological deficits in children with specific language impairment: The status of features in the underlying grammar. *Language Acquisition: A Journal of Developmental Linguistics, 2*(2), 151–179.

Leonard, L. B., Davis, J., & Deevy, P. (2007). Phonotactic probability and past tense use by children with specific language impairment and their typically developing peers. *Clinical Linguistics and Phonetics, 21*(10), 747–758.

Leonard, L. B., Deevy, P., Miller, C. A., Rauf, L., Charest, M., & Robert, K. (2003). Surface forms and grammatical functions: Past tense and passive participle use by children with specific language impairment. *Journal of Speech, Language, and Hearing Research, 46*(1), 43–55.

Leonard, L. B., Eyer, J. A., Bedore, L. M., & Grela, B. G. (1997). Three accounts of the grammatical morpheme difficulties of English-speaking children with specific language impairment. *Journal of Speech, Language, and Hearing Research, 40*(4), 741–753.

Leonard, L. B., McGregor, K. K., & Allen, G. D. (1992). Grammatical morphology and speech perception in children with specific language impairment. *Journal of Speech and Hearing Research, 35*(5), 1076–1085.

Leonard, L. B., Miller, C., & Gerber, E. (1999). Grammatical morphology and the lexicon in children with specific language impairment. *Journal of Speech, Language, and Hearing Research, 42*(3), 678.

Leonard, L. B., Nippold, M. A., Kail, R., & Hale, C. A. (1983). Picture naming in language-impaired children. *Journal of Speech and Hearing Research, 26*(4), 609–615.

Leonard, L. B., Prutting, C., Perozzi, J., & Berkley, R. (1978). Nonstandardized approaches to the assessment of language behaviors. *American Speech and Hearing Association, 20*, 371–379.

Leonard, L. B., Weismer, S. E., Miller, C. A., Francis, D. J., & Tomblin, J. B., Kail, R. V. (2007). Speed of processing, working memory, and language impairment in children. *Journal of Speech, Language, and Hearing Research, 50*(2), 408–428.

Leonard, L. B., Wong, A. M., Deevy, P., Stokes, S. F., & Fletcher, P. (2006). The production of passives by children with specific language impairment: Acquiring English or Cantonese. *Applied Psycholinguistics, 27*(2), 267–299.

Levy, H., & Friedmann, N. (in press). Treatment of syntactic movement in syntactic SLI. *First Language,*

Lewis, B. A., & Thompson, L. A. (1992). A study of developmental speech and language disorders in twins. *Journal of Speech and Hearing Research, 35*(5), 1086–1094.

Liégeois, F., Baldeweg, T., Connelly, A., Gadian, D. G., Mishkin, M., & Vargha-Khadem, F. (2003). Language fMRI abnormalities associated with *FOXP2* gene mutation. *Nature Neuroscience, 6*(11), 1230–1237.

Liles, B. Z. (1993). Narrative discourse in children with language disorders and children with normal language: A critical review of the literature. *Journal of Speech and Hearing Research, 36*(5), 868–882.

Loeb, D. F., & Leonard, L. B. (1991). Subject case marking and verb morphology in normally developing and specifically language-impaired children. *Journal of Speech and Hearing Research, 34*(2), 340–346.

Loeb, D. F., Pye, C., Richardson, L. Z., & Redmond, S. (1998). Causative alternations of children with specific language impairment. *Journal of Speech, Language, and Hearing Research, 41*(5), 1103–1114.

Loeb, D. F., Stoke, C., & Fey, M. E. (2001). Language changes associated with Fast ForWord-language: Evidence from case studies. *American Journal of Speech-Language Pathology, 10*(3), 216.

Long, S., Fey, M., & Channell, R. (2004). Computerized profiling (Version 9.7.0) [Computer software]. Retrieved from http://www.computerizedprofiling.org/

Lorsbach, T. C., Wilson, S., & Reimer, J. F. (1996). Memory for relevant and irrelevant information: Evidence for deficient inhibitory processes in language/learning disabled children *Contemporary Educational Psychology, 21*(4), 447–466.

Love, T., Swinney, D., Sawyer, C., Bricker, B., Schwartz, R., & Vignati, D. (2007). *Rate of speech effects sentence processing in children with and without language impairments.* Paper presented to the CUNY Sentence Processing Conference, La Jolla, CA.

Lucas, E. (1980). A response to Prutting. *Journal of Speech and Hearing Disorders, 45*(1), 136–138.

Lustig, C., May, C. P., & Hasher, L. (2001). Working memory span and the role of proactive interference. *Journal of Experimental Psychology: General, 130*(2), 199–207.

MacWhinney, B. (2000). *The CHILDES project: Tools for analyzing talk: Vol. 1. Transcription format and programs* (3rd ed.). Mahwah, NJ: Lawrence Erlbaum Associates.

Malvern, D., & Richards, B. (2002). Investigating accommodation in language proficiency interviews using a new measure of lexical diversity. *Language Testing, 19*(1), 85.

Marinis, T., & van der Lely, H. (2007). On-line processing of wh-questions in children with G-SLI and typically developing children. *International Journal of Language and Communication Disorders, 42*(5), 557–582.

Marshall, C., Marinis, T., & van der Lely, H. (2007). Passive verb morphology: The effect of phonotactics on passive comprehension in typically developing and grammatical-SLI children. *Lingua, 117*(8), 1434–1447.

Marshall, C. R., & van der Lely, H. (2006). A challenge to current models of past tense inflection: The impact of phonotactics. *Cognition, 100*(2), 302–320.

Marshall, C. R., & van der Lely, H. (2007). The impact of phonological complexity on past tense inflection in children with grammatical-SLI. *Advances in Speech Language Pathology, 9*(3), 191–203.

Marton, K., & Schwartz, R. G. (2003). Working memory capacity and language processes in children with specific language impairment. *Journal of Speech, Language, and Hearing Research, 46*(5), 1138–1153.

Marton, K., Schwartz, R. G., Farkas, L., & Katsnelson, V. (2006). Effect of sentence length and complexity on working memory performance in Hungarian children with specific language impairment (SLI): A cross-linguistic comparison. *International Journal of Language and Communication Disorders, 41*(6), 653–673.

McArthur, G. M., & Bishop, D. V. M. (2004). Frequency discrimination deficits in people with specific language impairment: Reliability, validity, and linguistic correlates. *Journal of Speech, Language, and Hearing Research, 47*(3), 527–541.

McArthur, G. M., & Bishop, D. V. M. (2005). Speech and non-speech processing in people with specific language impairment: A behavioural and electrophysiological study. *Brain and Language, 94*(3), 260–273.

McCabe, P. C. (2005). Social and behavioral correlates of preschoolers with specific language impairment. *Psychology in the Schools, 42*(4), 373–387.

McElree, B., Foraker, S., & Dyer, L. (2003). Memory structures that subserve sentence comprehension. *Journal of Memory and Language, 48*(1), 67.

McGregor, K. K., Friedman, R. M., & Reilly, R. M. (2002). Semantic representation and naming in children with specific language impairment. *Journal of Speech, Language, and Hearing Research, 45*(5), 998–1014.

McGregor, K. K., & Leonard, L. B. (1994). Subject pronoun and article omissions in the speech of children with specific language impairment: A phonological interpretation. *Journal of Speech and Hearing Research, 37*(1), 171–181.

McGregor, K. K., & Waxman, S. R. (1998). Object naming at multiple hierarchical levels: A comparison of preschoolers with and without word-finding deficits. *Journal of Child Language, 25*(2), 419.

Meaburn, E., Dale, P. S., Craig, I. W., & Plomin, R. (2002). Language-impaired children: No sign of the *FOXP2* mutation. *NeuroReport, 13*(8), 1075–1077.

Merzenich, M. M., Jenkins, W. M., Johnston, P., Schreiner, C., Miller, S. L., & Tallal, P. (1996). Temporal processing deficits of language-learning impaired children ameliorated by training. *Science, 271*(5245), 77–81.

Merzenich, M. M., Saunders, G., Jenkins, W. M., Miller, S., Peterson, B., & Tallal, P. (1999). Pervasive developmental disorders: Listening training and language abilities. In S. H. Broman & J. M. Fletcher (Eds.), *The changing nervous system: Neurobehavioral consequences of early brain disorders* (pp. 365–385). New York: Oxford University Press.

Messer, D., & Dockrell, J. E. (2006). Children's naming and word-finding difficulties: Descriptions and explanations. *Journal of Speech, Language, and Hearing Research, 49*(2), 309.

Miller, C. A., Kail, R., Leonard, L. B., & Tomblin, J. B. (2001). Speed of processing in children with specific language impairment. *Journal of Speech, Language, and Hearing Research, 44*(2), 416–433.

Miller, J. F. (1981). *Assessing language production in children: Experimental procedures.* Baltimore: University Park Press.

Miller, J., & Iglesias, A. (2008). Systematic Analysis of Language Transcripts (SALT) (Research Version 2008) [Computer Software]. Madison, WI: SALT Software.

Miller, C., Leonard, L. B., & Kail, R. V. (2006). Response time in 14-year-olds with language impairment. *Journal of Speech, Language, and Hearing Research, 49*(4), 712–728.

Mirsky, A. F., & Cardon, P. V. (1962). A comparison of the behavioral and physiological changes accompanying sleep deprivation and chlorpromazine administration in man. *Electro-encephalography and Clinical Neurophysiology, 14*, 1–10.

Miyake, A. (2001). Individual differences in working memory: Introduction to the special section. *Journal of Experimental Psychology: General, 130*(2), 163–168.

Mody, M., Studdert-Kennedy, M., & Brady, S. (1997). Speech perception deficits in poor readers: Auditory processing or phonological coding? *Journal of Experimental Child Psychology, 64*(2), 199–231.

Montgomery, J. W. (1995). Sentence comprehension in children with specific language impairment: The role of phonological working memory. *Journal of Speech and Hearing Research, 38*(1), 187–199.

Montgomery, J. W. (2000). Verbal working memory and sentence comprehension in children with specific language impairment. *Journal of Speech, Language, and Hearing Research, 43*(2), 293–308.

Montgomery, J. W. (2003). Working memory and comprehension in children with specific language impairment: What we know so far. *Journal of Communication Disorders, 36*(3), 221–231.

Montgomery, J. W. (2005). Effects of input rate and age on the real-time language processing of children with specific language impairment. *International Journal of Language and Communication Disorders, 40*(2), 171–188.

Moyle, M. J., Weismer, S. E., Evans, J. L., & Lindstrom, M. J. (2007). Longitudinal relationships between lexical and grammatical development in typical and late-talking children. *Focus on Autism and Other Developmental Disabilities, 50*(2), 508–528.

Neils, J., & Aram, D. M. (1986). Family history of children with developmental language disorders. *Perceptual and Motor Skills, 63*(2), 655–658.

Nelson, K. E., Camarata, S. M., Welsh, J., & Butkovsky, L. (1996). Effects of imitative and conversational recasting treatment on the acquisition of grammar in children with specific language impairment and younger language-normal children. *Journal of Speech and Hearing Research, 39*(4), 850–859.

Neville, H. J., Coffey, S. A., Holcomb, P. J., & Tallal, P. (1993). The neurobiology of sensory and language processing in language-impaired children. *Journal of Cognitive Neuroscience, 5*(2), 235–253.

Newbury, D. F., Bishop, D. V. M., & Monaco, A. P. (2005). Genetic influences on language impairment and phonological short-term memory. *Trends in Cognitive Sciences, 9*(11), 528–534.

Newbury, D. F., Bonora, E., Lamb, J. A., Fisher, S. E., Lai, C. S. L., Baird, G., et al. (2002). *FOXP2* is not a major susceptibility gene for autism or specific language impairment. *American Journal of Human Genetics, 70*(5), 1318–1327.

Niemi, J., Gundersen, H., Leppäsaari, T., & Hugdahl, K. (2003). Speech lateralization and attention/executive functions in a Finnish family with specific language impairment (SLI). *Journal of Clinical and Experimental Neuropsychology, 25*(4), 457–464.

Norbury, C. F. (2005). Barking up the wrong tree? Lexical ambiguity resolution in children with language impairments and autistic spectrum disorders. *Journal of Experimental Child Psychology, 90*(2), 142–171.

Norbury, C. F., & Bishop, D. V. M. (2003). Narrative skills of children with communication impairments. *International Journal of Language and Communication Disorders, 38*(3), 287–313.

Noterdaeme, M., Amorosa, H., Mildenberger, K., Sitter, S., & Minow, F. (2001). Evaluation of attention problems in children with autism and children with a specific language disorder. *European Child and Adolescent Psychiatry, 10*(1), 58–66.

Novogrodsky, R., & Friedmann, N. (2006). The production of relative clauses in syntactic SLI: A window to the nature of the impairment. *Advances in Speech Language Pathology, 8*(4), 364–375.

O'Brien, E. K., Xuyang, Z., Nishimura, C., Tomblin, J. B., & Murray, J. C. (2003). Association of specific language impairment (SLI) to the region of 7q31. *American Journal of Human Genetics, 72*(6), 1536.

Oetting, J. B., & Rice, M. L. (1993). Plural acquisition in children with specific language impairment. *Journal of Speech and Hearing Research, 36*(6), 1236–1248.

Oetting, J. B., Rice, M. L., & Swank, L. K. (1995). Quick incidental learning (QUIL) of words by school-age children with and without SLI. *Journal of Speech and Hearing Research, 38*(2), 434–445.

Owen, A. J., & Leonard, L. B. (2002). Lexical diversity in the spontaneous speech of children with specific language impairment: Application of D. *Journal of Speech, Language, and Hearing Research, 45*(5), 927–937.

Owen, A. J., & Leonard, L. B. (2006). The production of finite and nonfinite complement clauses by children with specific language impairment and their typically developing peers. *Journal of Speech, Language, and Hearing Research, 49*(3), 548–571.

Paradis, J., Crago, M., Genesee, F., & Rice, M. (2003). French–English bilingual children with SLI: How do they compare with their monolingual peers? *Journal of Speech, Language, and Hearing Research, 46*(1), 113–127.

Pine, J. M., Joseph, K. L., & Conti-Ramsden, G. (2004). Do data from children with specific language impairment support the agreement/tense omission model? *Journal of Speech, Language, and Hearing Research, 47*(4), 913–923.

Plante, E. (1991). MRI findings in the parents and siblings of specifically language-impaired boys. *Brain and Language, 41*(1), 67–80.

Plante, E., Swisher, L., & Vance, R. (1989). Anatomical correlates of normal and impaired language in a set of dizygotic twins. *Brain and Language, 37*(4), 643–655.

Plante, E., Swisher, L., Vance, R., & Rapcsak, S. (1991). MRI findings in boys with specific language impairment. *Brain and Language, 41*(7), 52–66.

Prather, P., Shapiro, L., Zurif, E., & Swinney, D. (1991). Real-time examinations of lexical processing in aphasics. *Journal of Psycholinguistic Research, 20*(3), 271–281.

Proctor-Williams, K., & Fey, M. E. (2007). Recast density and acquisition of novel irregular past tense verbs. *Journal of Speech, Language, and Hearing Research, 50*(4), 1029–1047.

Proctor-Williams, K., Fey, M. E., & Loeb, D. F. (2001). Parental recasts and production of copulas and articles by children with specific language. *American Journal of Speech-Language Pathology, 10*(2), 155–168.

Redmond, S. M., & Rice, M. L. (2001). Detection of irregular verb violations by children with and without SLI. *Journal of Speech, Language, and Hearing Research, 44*(3), 655–669.

Reilly, J., Losh, M., Bellugi, U., & Wulfeck, B. (2004). "Frog, where are you?" Narratives in children with specific language impairment, early focal brain injury, and Williams syndrome. *Brain and Language, 88*(2), 229–247.

Rescorla, L. (1989). The language development survey: A screening tool for delayed language in toddlers. *Journal of Speech and Hearing Disorders, 54*(4), 587–599.

Rescorla, L. (2005). Age 13 language and reading outcomes in late-talking toddlers. *Journal of Speech, Language, and Hearing Research, 48*(2), 459–472.

Rice, M. L., Buhr, J. C., & Nemeth, M. (1990). Fast mapping word-learning abilities of language-delayed preschoolers. *Journal of Speech and Hearing Disorders, 55*(1), 33–42.

Rice, M. L., Buhr, J. C., & Oetting, J. B. (1992). Specific-language-impaired children's quick incidental learning of words: The effect of a pause. *Journal of Speech and Hearing Research, 35*(5), 1040–1048.

Rice, M. L., Haney, K. R., & Wexler, K. (1998). Family histories of children with SLI who show extended optional infinitives. *Journal of Speech, Language, and Hearing Research, 41*(2), 419–432.

Rice, M. L., Oetting, J. B., Marquis, J., & Bode, J. (1994). Frequency of input effects on word comprehension of children with specific language impairment. *Journal of Speech and Hearing Research, 37*(1), 106–121.

Rice, M. L., Sell, M. A., & Hadley, P. A. (1991). Social interactions of speech- and language-impaired children. *Journal of Speech and Hearing Research, 34*(6), 1299–1307.

Rice, M. L., Warren, S. F., & Betz, S. K. (2005). Language symptoms of developmental language disorders: An overview of autism, Down syndrome, fragile X, specific language impairment, and Williams syndrome. *Applied Psycholinguistics, 26*(1), 7–27.

Rice, M. L., & Wexler, K. (1996a). A phenotype of specific language impairment: Extended optional infinitives. In M. L. Rice (Ed.), *Toward a genetics of language* (pp. 215–237). Mahwah, NJ: Lawrence Erlbaum Associates.

Rice, M. L., & Wexler, K. (1996b). Toward tense as a clinical marker of specific language impairment in English-speaking children. *Journal of Speech and Hearing Research, 39*(6), 1239–1257.

Rice, M. L., & Wexler, K. (2001). *Rice/Wexler Test of Early Grammatical Impairment.* San Antonio, TX: Psychological Corporation.

Rice, M. L., Wexler, K., & Cleave, P. L. (1995). Specific language impairment as a period of extended optional infinitive. *Journal of Speech and Hearing Research, 38*(4), 850–863.

Rosen, S., & Eva, M. (2001). Is there a relationship between speech and nonspeech auditory processing in children with dyslexia? *Journal of Speech, Language, and Hearing Research, 44*(4), 720–736.

Scarborough, H. S., & Dobrich, W. (1990). Development of children with early language delay. *Journal of Speech and Hearing Research, 33*(1), 70–83.

Scheffler, F. L. V., & Schwartz, R. G. (2008). *Speech perception and lexical effects in specific language impairment.* Unpublished manuscript, The Graduate Center of the City University of New York, New York.

Schonfeld, I. S., & Rindskopf, D. (2007). Hierarchical linear modeling in organizational research: Longitudinal data outside the context of growth modeling. *Organizational Research Methods, 10*(3), 417–429.

Schuele, C. M., & Tolbert, L. (2001). Omissions of obligatory relative markers in children with specific language impairment. *Clinical Linguistics and Phonetics, 15*(4), 257–274.

Schwartz, R. G. (1988). Phonological factors in early lexical acquisition. In J. L. Locke & M. Smith (Eds.), *The emergent lexicon* (pp. 185–222). New York: Academic Press.

Schwartz, R. G., Hestvik, A., Swinney, D., Seiger, L., Almodovar, D., & Asay, S. (2005). *Anaphoric processing in children with specific language impairment.* Paper presented to IASCL, Berlin.

Schwartz, R. G., Leonard, L. B., Messick, C., & Chapman, K. (1987). The acquisition of object names in children with specific language impairment: Action context and word extension. *Applied Psycholinguistics, 8*(3), 233–244.

Schwartz, R. G., & Terrell, B. Y. (1983). The role of input frequency in lexical acquisition. *Journal of Child Language, 10*(1), 57–64.

Scientific Learning Corporation. (1998). Fast ForWord Language [Computer software]. Berkeley, CA: Author.

Seiger-Gardner, L., & Schwartz, R. G. (in press). Lexical access in children with and without specific language impairment: A cross-modal picture-word interference study. *International Journal of Language and Communication Disorders,*

Seymour, H. N., Roeper, T. W., & de Villiers, J. (2004). *Diagnostic evaluation of language variation.* San Antonio, TX: Harcourt Assessment.

Shafer, V. L., Morr, M. L., Datta, H., Kurtzberg, D., & Schwartz, R. G. (2005). Neurophysiological indexes of speech processing deficits in children with specific language impairment. *Journal of Cognitive Neuroscience, 17*(7), 1168–1180.

Shafer, V. L., Ponton, C., Datta, H., Morr, M. L., & Schwartz, R. G. (2007). Neurophysiological indices of attention to speech in children with specific language impairment. *Clinical Neurophysiology, 118*(6), 1230–1243.

Shafer, V. L., Schwartz, R. G., Morr, M. L., Kessler, K. L., & Kurtzberg, D. (2000). Deviant neuro-physiological asymmetry in children with language impairment. *NeuroReport: For Rapid Communication of Neuroscience Research, 11*(17), 3715–3718.

Shimpi, P. M., Gámez, P. B., Huttenlocher, J., & Vasilyeva, M. (2007). Syntactic priming in 3- and 4-year-old children: Evidence for abstract representations of transitive and dative forms. *Developmental Psychology, 43*(6), 1334–1346.

Shriberg, L. D., Gruber, F. A., & Kwiatkowski, J. (1994). Developmental phonological disorders: III. Long-term speech-sound normalization. *Journal of Speech and Hearing Research, 37*(5), 1151–1177.

Shriberg, L. D., & Kwiatkowski, J. (1994). Developmental phonological disorders: I. A clinical profile. *Journal of Speech and Hearing Research, 37*(5), 1100–1126.

Shriberg, L. D., Kwiatkowski, J., & Gruber, F. A. (1994). Developmental phonological disorders: II. Short-term speech-sound normalization. *Journal of Speech and Hearing Research*, 37(5), 1127–1150.

Shriberg, L. D., Tomblin, J. B., & McSweeny, J. L. (1999). Prevalence of speech delay in 6-year-old children and comorbidity with language impairment. *Journal of Speech, Language, and Hearing Research*, 42(6), 1461–1481.

Sininger, Y. S., Klatzky, R. L., & Kirchner, D. M. (1989). Memory scanning speed in language-disordered children. *Journal of Speech and Hearing Research*, 32(2), 289–297.

Stanton-Chapman, T. L., Justice, L. M., Skibbe, L. E., & Grant, S. L. (2007). Social and behavioral characteristics of preschoolers with specific language impairment. *Topics in Early Childhood Special Education*, 27(2), 98–109.

Stavrakaki, S. (2006). Developmental perspectives on specific language impairment: Evidence from the production of wh-questions by Greek SLI children over time. *Advances in Speech Language Pathology*, 8(4), 384–396.

Stevens, C., Sanders, L., & Neville, H. (2006). Neurophysiological evidence for selective auditory attention deficits in children with specific language impairment. *Brain Research*, 1111(1), 143–152.

Stothard, S. E., Snowling, M. J., Bishop, D. V., Chipchase, B. B., & Kaplan, C. A. (1998). Language-impaired preschoolers: A follow-up into adolescence. *Journal of Speech, Language, and Hearing Research*, 41(2), 407–418.

Studdert-Kennedy, M., & Mody, M. (1995). Auditory temporal perception deficits in the reading-impaired: A critical review of the evidence. *Psychonomic Bulletin and Review*, 2(4), 508–514.

Sussman, J. E. (1993). Perception of formant transition cues to place of articulation in children with language impairments. *Journal of Speech and Hearing Research*, 36(6), 1286–1299.

Tallal, P. (1984). Temporal or phonetic processing deficit in dyslexia? That is the question. *Applied Psycholinguistics*, 5(2), 167–169.

Tallal, P., Miller, S. L., Bedi, G., Wang, X., & Nagarajan, S. S. (1996). Language comprehension in language-learning impaired children improved with acoustically modified speech. *Science*, 271(5245), 81–84.

Tallal, P., & Piercy, M. (1973). Developmental aphasia: Impaired rate of non-verbal processing as a function of sensory modality. *Neuropsychologia*, 11(4), 389–398.

Tallal, P., & Piercy, M. (1974). Developmental aphasia: Rate of auditory processing and selective impairment of consonant perception. *Neuropsychologia*, 12(1), 83–93.

Tallal, P., Ross, R., & Curtiss, S. (1989). Familial aggregation in specific language impairment. *Journal of Speech and Hearing Disorders*, 54(2), 167–173.

Thal, D. J., O'Hanlon, L., Clemmons, M., & Fralin, L. (1999). Validity of a parent report measure of vocabulary and syntax for preschool children with language impairment. *Journal of Speech, Language, and Hearing Research*, 42(2), 482–496.

Thal, D. J., Reilly, J., Seibert, L., Jeffries, R., & Fenson, J. (2004). Language development in children at risk for language impairment: Cross-population comparisons. *Brain and Language*, 88(2), 167–179.

Thomas, M. S. C., & Karmiloff-Smith, A. (2003). Modeling language acquisition in atypical phenotypes. *Psychological Review*, 110(4), 647–682.

Thordardottir, E. T., & Weismer, S. E. (2002). Verb argument structure weakness in specific language impairment in relation to age and utterance length. *Clinical Linguistics and Phonetics*, 16(4), 233–250.

Tomblin, J. B. (1989). Familial concentration of developmental language impairment. *Journal of Speech and Hearing Disorders*, 54(2), 287–295.

Tomblin, J. B., & Buckwalter, P. R. (1998). Heritability of poor language achievement among twins. *Journal of Speech, Language, and Hearing Research*, 41(1), 188–199.

Tomblin, J. B., Records, N. L., Buckwalter, P., Zhang, X., Smith, E., & O'Brien, M. (1997). Prevalence of specific language impairment in kindergarten children. *Journal of Speech and Hearing Research*, 40(6), 1245–1260.

Towse, J. N., Hitch, G. J., & Hutton, U. (1998). A reevaluation of working memory capacity in children. *Journal of Memory and Language*, 39(2), 195.

Troia, G. A., & Whitney, S. D. (2003). A close look at the efficacy of Fast ForWord language for children with academic weaknesses. *Contemporary Educational Psychology*, 28(4), 465–494.

Ullman, M. T., & Pierpont, E. I. (2005). Specific language impairment is not specific to language: The procedural deficit hypothesis. *Cortex*, 41(3), 399–433.

Uwer, R., Albrecht, R., & von Suchodoletz, W. (2002). Automatic processing of tones and speech stimuli in children with specific language impairment. *Developmental Medicine and Child Neurology*, 44(8), 527–532.

van der Lely, H. K. J. (1998). SLI in children: Movement, economy, and deficits in the computational-syntactic system. *Language Acquisition*, 7(2–4), 161.

van der Lely, H. K. J. (2005). Domain-specific cognitive systems: Insight from grammatical-SLI. *Trends in Cognitive Sciences*, 9(2), 53–59.

van der Lely, H. K. J., & Battell, J. (2003). Wh-movement in children with grammatical SLI: A test of the RDDR hypothesis. *Language*, 79(1), 153–181.

van der Lely, H. K. J., & Harris, M. (1990). Comprehension of reversible sentences in specifically language-impaired children. *Journal of Speech and Hearing Disorders*, 55(1), 101–117.

van der Lely, H. K. J., & Stollwerck, L. (1996). A grammatical specific language impairment in children: An autosomal dominant inheritance? *Brain and Language*, 52(3), 484–504.

van der Lely, H. K. J., & Stollwerck, L. (1997). Binding theory and grammatical specific language impairment in children. *Cognition*, 62(3), 245–290.

Van Riper, C. (1947). *Speech correction: Principles and methods* (2nd ed.). Oxford, UK: Prentice-Hall.

Vargha-Khadem, F., Watkins, K. E., Price, C. J., Ashburner, J., Alcock, K. J., Connelly, A., et al. (1998). Neural basis of an inherited speech and language disorder. *Proceedings of the National Academy of Sciences U.S.A.*, 95(21), 12695–12700.

Warren, S. F., Bredin-Oja, S. L., Fairchild, M., Finestack, L. H., Fey, M. E., & Brady, N. C. (2006). Responsivity education/prelinguistic milieu teaching. In R. J. McCauley & M. E. Fey (Eds.), *Treatment of language disorders in children*. (pp. 47–75). Baltimore: Paul H. Brookes.

Watkins, K. E., Dronkers, N. F., & Vargha-Khadem, F. (2002). Behavioural analysis of an inherited speech and language disorder: Comparison with acquired aphasia. *Brain: A Journal of Neurology*, 125, 452–464.

Watkins, K. E., Vargha-Khadem, F., Ashburner, J., Passingham, R. E., Connelly, A., Friston, K. J., et al. (2002). MRI analysis of an inherited speech and language disorder: Structural brain abnormalities. *Brain: A Journal of Neurology*, 125(3), 465–478.

Watkins, R. V., Kelly, D. J., Harbers, H. M., & Hollis, W. (1995). Measuring children's lexical diversity: Differentiating typical and impaired language learners. *Journal of Speech and Hearing Research*, 38(6), 1349–1355.

Watkins, R. V., & Rice, M. L. (1991). Verb particle and preposition acquisition in language-impaired preschoolers. *Journal of Speech and Hearing Research*, 34(5), 1130–1141.

Weismer, S. E., & Evans, J. (1999). An examination of verbal working memory capacity in children with specific language impairment. *Journal of Speech, Language, and Hearing Research*, 42(5), 1249–1260.

Weismer, S. E., & Evans, J. L. (2002). The role of processing limitations in early identification of specific language impairment. *Topics in Language Disorders*, 22(3), 15–29.

Weismer, S. E., & Hesketh, L. J. (1996). Lexical learning by children with specific language impairment: Effects of linguistic input presented at varying speaking rates. *Journal of Speech and Hearing Research*, 39(1), 177–190.

Weismer, S. E., Plante, E., Jones, M., & Tomblin, J. B. (2005). A functional magnetic resonance imaging investigation of verbal working memory in adolescents with specific language impairment. *Journal of Speech, Language, and Hearing Research*, 48(2), 405–425.

Weismer, S. E., Tomblin, J. B., Zhang, X., Buckwalter, P., Chynoweth, J. G., & Jones, M. (2000). Nonword repetition performance in school-age children with and without language impairment. *Journal of Speech, Language, and Hearing Research*, 43(4), 865–878.

Wetherell, D., Botting, N., & Conti-Ramsden, G. (2007). Narrative in adolescent specific language impairment (SLI): A comparison with peers across two different narrative genres. *International Journal of Language and Communication Disorders, 42*(5), 583–605.

Wexler, K. (1998). Very early parameter setting and the unique checking constraint. *Lingua, 106,* 23–79.

Wexler, K. (2003). Lenneberg's dream: Learning, normal language development, and specific language impairment. In Y. Levy & J. Schaeffer (Eds.), *Language competence across populations: Toward a definition of specific language impairment* (pp. 11–61). Mahwah, NJ: Lawrence Erlbaum Associates.

Wexler, K., Schütze, C. T., & Rice, M. (1998). Subject case in children with SLI and unaffected controls: Evidence for the Agr/Tns omission model. *Language Acquisition: A Journal of Developmental Linguistics, 7*(2), 317–344.

Whitehurst, G. J., Arnold, D. S., Smith, M., & Fischel, J. E. (1991). Family history in developmental expressive language delay. *Journal of Speech and Hearing Research, 34*(5), 1150–1157.

Windsor, J. (1999). Testing the generalized slowing hypothesis in specific language impairment. *Journal of Speech, Language, and Hearing Research, 42*(5), 1205–1218.

Windsor, J., & Hwang, M. (1999). Children's auditory lexical decisions: A limited processing capacity account of language impairment. *Journal of Speech, Language, and Hearing Research, 42*(4), 990–1002.

Windsor, J., Milbrath, R. L., Carney, E. J., & Rakowski, S. E. (2001). General slowing in language impairment: Methodological considerations in testing the hypothesis. *Journal of Speech, Language, and Hearing Research, 44*(2), 446–461.

2

Language Disorders in Children with Mental Retardation of Genetic Origin: Down Syndrome, Fragile X Syndrome, and Williams Syndrome

ANDREA MCDUFFIE and LEONARD ABBEDUTO

*E*xamining language development in syndromes with identifiable genetic causes is particularly helpful for identifying the ways in which language and cognition can influence one another. By examining relationships between various aspects of language ability and other domains of psychological and behavioral functioning within a particular syndrome, we can learn about the behavioral consequences of particular genetic variations. In addition, cross-syndrome comparisons can help us to determine whether challenges to language development are due to mental retardation and cognitive delay, more generally, or are syndrome-specific (i.e., a direct or indirect consequence of the genetic anomalies in question). This type of comparison is particularly interesting for the three genetic syndromes that we consider in the current chapter: Down syndrome (DS), fragile X syndrome (FXS), and Williams syndrome (WS).

In the 1970s, WS was advanced as the prototypical example of modularity in the organization of the brain, as demonstrated by the reported independence of language from cognition (Bellugi, Bihrle, Jernigan, Trauner, & Doherty, 1990). More specifically, the common characterization of WS was that of excellent language skills in the presence of severe mental retardation (Mervis, Robinson, Rowe, Becerra, & Klein-Tasman, 2003). As is described in the following paragraphs, more recent characterizations have revealed substantial links between the language and cognitive profiles of individuals with WS, in direct opposition to modularity proposals. Just as specific associations between cognition and language have been identified for WS, so these associations are different or of different magnitudes for individuals with DS and FXS. Overall, current research supports, not the notion of modularity of brain organization, but the interdependence of language and its acquisition with patterns of strengths and weaknesses in other cognitive domains. In the next section we provide a brief overview of the cognitive and behavioral characteristics of each syndrome. The chapter then considers the language profiles of the three genetic disorders that provide our focus. We review research findings relevant to the development of language comprehension and production and highlight the ways in which the relationships between language and cognition differ across the three syndromes. We conclude by summarizing the overarching themes that emerge during the review.

SYNDROME-SPECIFIC PROFILES OF COGNITION AND BEHAVIOR

Down Syndrome

DS has a prevalence of 1 in 700–1,000 births and is the leading genetic cause of mental retardation (Hagerman, 1999; Roizen, 1997). Most cases (95%) are caused by nondisjunction, an error during meiotic cell division prior to fertilization, resulting in three copies of all or part of chromosome 21. As the embryo with trisomy 21 develops, the extra chromosome is replicated in virtually every cell of the body. Thus, the genetic abnormality in DS is quantitative, as the genes involved are normal, and involves the increased production of the gene products of chromosome 21 (Antonarakis & Epstein, 2006). Recent genomic sequencing has identified over 300 genes on the long arm of chromosome 21, and scientists are now working to identify specific characteristics of the DS cognitive and behavioral phenotype that are the result of particular gene dosage effects (Gardiner & Costa, 2006).

Advanced maternal age is the most common risk factor for DS caused by nondisjunction (Roizen, 1997). The likelihood of having a child with DS rises from less than 1 in 1,000 in mothers under age 30 to 1 in 12 by age 40. An additional 2% of cases of DS are caused when nondisjunction of chromosome 21 takes place in one of the early cell divisions after fertilization. In this condition, termed *mosaicism*, there is a mixture of cells, some containing 46 and some containing 47 chromosomes. Individuals with mosaic DS are less impaired cognitively, on average, although the degree of affectedness in any individual depends on the proportion of affected cells within the nervous system. Finally, the remaining 2% of cases of DS are caused by translocation, in which part of chromosome 21 breaks off during cell division and attaches to another chromosome, usually chromosome 14. Although the total number of chromosomes in the cells of an individual with a translocation is 46, extra genetic material is present. This is due to the extra segment of chromosome 21, resulting in the characteristic features of DS.

As is the case for all genetic syndromes, DS produces both structural and functional abnormalities in multiple organ systems, and a characteristic phenotype emerges across the lifespan of the individual (Antonarakis & Epstein, 2006). The physical features of DS include dysmorphologies of the face, hands, and feet, congenital heart disease and duodenal stenosis, hearing loss, and vision problems. Most individuals with DS function in the mild to moderate range of mental retardation, displaying average IQs of 50, with a range between 30 and 70 (Chapman, 1999). Individuals with DS often experience a loss of cognitive ability across the lifespan; DS confers 100% risk of developing early Alzheimer's disease (AD), with the full pathology of AD present by age 35 (Rumble et al., 1989).

Learning impairments in DS are thought to be related to cognitive processes that rely on the hippocampus (Pennington, Moon, Edgin, Stedron, & Nadel, 2003), although evidence also exists for involvement of the prefrontal cortex and cerebellum (Nadel, 2003). Brains of Ts65Dn strain of mice, providing a mouse model of DS, exhibit problems with long-term potentiation and long-term depression in hippocampal neurons (Siarey et al., 2006). Several genes have been suggested as associated with the behavioral and psychological features of DS. These genes, located on chromosome 21, include superoxide dismutase (SOD-1), associated with oxidative stress and rapid aging (Gullesarian, Seidel, Hardmeier, Cairns, & Lubec, 2001; Harman, 2006), and the beta-amyloid precursor protein gene (*APP*), associated with Alzheimer's disease (Golaz, Charnay, Vallet, & Bouras, 1991). Recent work has shown that one deleterious effect of APP, in the mouse model of DS, is to decrease neural growth factor (NGF) resulting in degeneration of the cholinergic neurons of the basal forebrain (Salehi et al., 2006). Findings such as these contribute to a growing understanding of the genetic pathways influencing the cognitive and behavioral phenotype of DS.

The cognitive profile of individuals with DS is characterized predominately by a weakness in auditory short-term memory relative to both visual short-term memory and nonverbal mental age (MA) (Chapman, 2003; Jarrold, Baddeley, & Phillips, 2002; Merrill, Lookadoo, & Rilea, 2003). Backward memory for both verbal and visual information is also impaired (Vicari, Carlesimo, & Caltagirone, 1995). By adolescence, a dissociation is observed within the domain of nonverbal visual cognition. Visual short-term memory, as measured with the Bead Memory subtest of the Stanford–Binet Intelligence Test (SB-IV, Thorndike, Hagen, & Sattler, 1986), falls behind visual ability, as measured with the Pattern Analysis subtest of the Stanford–Binet (Chapman, Hesketh, & Kistler, 2002). Hearing is mildly impaired in 60% of individuals with DS (Chapman, Seung, Schwartz, & Kay-Raining Bird, 2000). Finally, symptoms of Alzheimer's-related dementia may be observed in approximately 50% of individuals with DS over the age of 50 (Menendez, 2005). The result of this phenotypical pattern of skills is that individuals with DS often have better comprehension and problem-solving behavior than their spoken communication would indicate (Chapman, 2003). Individual differences in hearing status, auditory short-term memory, and visual short-term memory may contribute to the levels of language development achieved.

Fragile X Syndrome

FXS is less prevalent than DS, affecting 1 in 4,000 females and 1 in 8,000 males (Sherman, 1996). As the leading inherited form of mental retardation, FXS accounts for 40% of all X-linked mental retardation (Hagerman, 1999). FXS results from the mutation of a single gene (*FMR1*) on the X chromosome (Brown, 2002). In the full mutation, a repetitive sequence of trinucleotides (i.e., the CGG repeats), which in typically developing individuals consists of 54 or fewer repeats, expands to 200 or more. This expansion leads to methylation and subsequent transcriptional silencing of the *FMR1* gene, reducing or completely eliminating the production of its associated protein, FMRP (Oostra & Willemson, 2003). FMRP has been shown, in both animal and human studies, to be critical for experience-dependent neural development, affecting both the maturation and pruning of synapses (Klintsova & Greenough, 1999). The behavioral phenotype in DS arises from too much genetic material and consequent gene overexpression, but the phenotype in FXS results from gene underexpression (Abbeduto & Chapman, 2005).

Although the range of cognitive impairment is broader in FXS relative to DS, much of this variability is related to gender and the fact that females have two X chromosomes. Only one X chromosome in a female individual contains the CGG expansion and X inactivation determines the proportion of cells contributing to the phenotype (Brown, 2002). As with other X-linked disorders, males with FXS are more likely to be affected and to be affected more severely than females (Hagerman, 1999; Keysor & Mazzocco, 2002). Nearly all males with the FXS full mutation meet diagnostic criteria for mental retardation, with an IQ range similar to that observed for DS (Dykens, Hodapp, & Finucane, 2000). In contrast, females with the FXS full mutation may have mental retardation, a learning disability, or social adjustment difficulties with normal-range IQs. However, subtle impairments in cognition may still exist for females with FXS (Keysor & Mazzocco, 2002).

Whereas individuals with DS and WS, as a group, are highly sociable (Bellugi, Lichtenberger, Mills, Galaburda, & Korenberg, 1999; Kasari & Bauminger, 1998), the behavioral profile of FXS is characterized by problems with social avoidance or anxiety. Other defining characteristics of the FXS behavioral phenotype include eye gaze aversion, inattention, hyperactivity, and abnormal responses to sensory stimulation (Abbeduto & Murphy, 2004; Bailey, Hatton, & Skinner, 1998; Belser & Sudhalter, 1995, 2001; Cornish, Sudhalter, & Turk, 2004; Dykens et al., 2000; Ferrier, Bashir, Meryash, Johnston, & Wolff, 1991; Keysor & Mazzocco, 2002; Murphy & Abbeduto, 2003; Murphy, Abbeduto, Schroeder, & Serlin, in press; Sudhalter, Cohen, Silverman, & Wolf-Schein, 1990; Wisbeck et al., 2000). Many behaviors observed in individuals with FXS resemble the characteristics of individuals with diagnoses on the autism spectrum. Conservative estimates place the prevalence of autism in individuals with FXS at 25%; however, recent studies utilizing standardized diagnostic criteria representing the broader autism spectrum (i.e., inclusive of PDD-NOS) have documented prevalence rates as high as 47% in young children with FXS (Demark, Feldman, & Holden, 2003; Kaufmann et al., 2004; Rogers, Wehner, & Hagerman, 2001; Philofsky, Hepburn, Hayes, Hagerman, & Rogers, 2004). Autistic-like behaviors observed in individuals with FXS include avoidance of eye gaze, unusual reactions to sensory stimuli, hand and finger stereotypies, hand biting, and spinning and repetitive object use (Levitas et al., 1983). Poor social use of language and other expressive language characteristics, such as unusual prosody and tangential and repetitive speech, add to the clinical impression of autism in FXS.

Williams Syndrome

With an incidence of 1 in 20,000 live births, Williams syndrome is less common in occurrence than either DS or FXS. WS is caused by a microdeletion of 17 genes, including the genes coding for elastin and LIM Kinase, located on the long arm of chromosome 7 (Meyer-Lindenberg, Mervis, & Berman, 2006). More than 98% of individuals with WS have the same deletion breakpoints, referred to as *classic* Williams syndrome (Morris & Mervis, 2000). WS affects multiple organ systems and is characterized by a distinctive pattern of dysmorphic facial features, cardiovascular disease, growth deficiency, connective tissue abnormalities, and mental retardation (Mervis et al., 2003; Morris, 2004). Mean full-scale IQ in individuals with WS averages 58, with ability levels ranging from severe mental retardation to average intelligence (Mervis et al., 1999, 2003; Udwin, Yule, & Martin, 1987; Volterra, Capirci, Pezzini, Sabbadini, & Vicari, 1996). There is less variability in the range of performance noted on standardized tests of visual spatial ability, with most individuals with WS scoring at floor levels (Mervis et al., 2003). Individuals with WS typically demonstrate overfriendliness and a strong drive for social contact (Bellugi et al., 1999), complicated by generalized anxiety (Klein-Tasman & Mervis, 2003; Morris, 2004). The WS cognitive profile (Mervis et al., 2000) is characterized by a relative weakness in visual spatial construction ability and relative strengths in language and auditory memory (e.g., digit recall). This cognitive profile differs from the profile of individuals with DS who show weaknesses in auditory memory and language relative to nonverbal visual cognition (Miolo, Chapman, & Sindberg, 2005), as well as from the relatively flat profile of individuals with FXS (Abbeduto et al., 2003). Individuals with WS also demonstrate relative strengths in face processing (Donnai & Karmiloff-Smith, 2000). Weaknesses in visual-spatial abilities characteristic of WS may be the consequence of the absence of the LIM-Kinase 1 gene, rather than of the absence of the Elastin gene (Frangiskakis et al., 1996).

SYNDROME-SPECIFIC PROFILES OF LANGUAGE ABILITY

Down Syndrome

Language Comprehension Language, including both comprehension and production, may be the most affected domain of development for individuals with DS (Chapman & Hesketh, 2000; Roberts, Price, & Malkin, 2007). In general, language comprehension is less problematic than production, with most children with DS displaying levels of receptive language that are commensurate with levels of nonverbal cognition (Miller, 1999). By adolescence, syntax comprehension lags behind nonverbal MA (Chapman, Schwartz, & Kay-Raining Bird, 1991; Rosin, Swift, Bless, & Vetter, 1988). Vocabulary comprehension, in contrast, continues to keep pace with or exceed nonverbal cognition during adolescence (Chapman et al., 1991; Rosin et al., 1988). The uneven profile of performance observed among vocabulary, syntax comprehension, and nonverbal cognition depends to some extent on the measures used to assess these domains. When measured with the Peabody Picture Vocabulary Test–Revised (PPVT–R; Dunn & Dunn, 1981), vocabulary comprehension has a stronger relationship to chronological than to mental age.

Miolo et al. (2005) examined whether a discrepancy between vocabulary and syntax comprehension continued to be observed when a more conceptual measure was used to assess vocabulary comprehension. Participants were 19 adolescents and young adults matched pairwise for syntax comprehension with a group of typically developing 3- to 5-year-olds. The group with DS, but not the comparison group, achieved a significantly higher score on the PPVT than they did in response to the Vocabulary subtest of the Test of Auditory Comprehension of Language-3 (TACL–3; Carrow-Woolfolk, 1999). This pattern of performance may be attributable to the cumulative age-related experiences of the individual with DS (Facon, Facon-Bollengier, & Grubar, 2002; Fazio, Johnston, & Brandl, 1993), which have a positive impact on a frequency-based measure of vocabulary ability (Miolo et al., 2005). Thus, when tested with a measure based on frequency of occurrence, vocabulary comprehension appears in advance of mental age for adolescents with DS. When tested with a measure based on conceptual difficulty, vocabulary comprehension is commensurate with nonverbal mental age estimates (Miolo et al., 2005).

In contrast to vocabulary comprehension, syntax comprehension represents a domain of greater challenge for individuals with DS. Chapman, Hesketh, and Kistler (2002) used hierarchical linear modeling to identify longitudinal predictors of syntax comprehension, across a 6-year period, in 31 participants with DS. Participants were between 5 and 20 years of age at the onset of the study. Syntax comprehension, as measured by the TACL–R, was best predicted by three variables at the start of the study: auditory verbal short-term memory, visual short-term memory, and chronological age. Age at study start also predicted the change in slope for growth in comprehension. For a child of 7.5 years at study start, the change in comprehension growth rate was positive; for a child of 12.5 years, the slope was shallower, while the predicted growth rate actually became negative for participants who entered the study at age 17.5 years.

Miolo et al. (2005) also examined predictors of performance on different components of a sentence comprehension task requiring participants to act out the intended meaning of each tested sentence by manipulating objects. The experimental task, composed of information-dense sentences, was designed to place greater demands on auditory short-term memory than does a traditional comprehension measure (e.g., the TACL), which requires a picture-pointing response. The two Syntax Comprehension subtests of the TACL–3 were also used to provide a more traditional measure of sentence comprehension. The group with DS showed a larger discrepancy, relative to a syntax comprehension-matched, typically developing group, between nonverbal visual cognition and auditory memory (as measured by number recall and nonword repetition), as well as between syntax comprehension and production. For the DS group, auditory short-term memory accounted for a significant portion of the variance in performance on both the TACL–3 and the experimental comprehension task. Hearing status accounted for 23% of the variance in performance on the Grammatical Morphemes subtest of the TACL–3. In contrast to previous findings (Chapman et al., 2002), visual short-term memory did not contribute significant variance to any of the outcome measures. The results of Miolo et al. (2005) reveal the contribution of auditory memory to the syntax comprehension skills and provide evidence for the interdependence of language with other areas of cognitive development in adolescents and young adults with DS.

Abbeduto and colleagues (Abbeduto et al., 2003) examined associations between syntax comprehension, vocabulary comprehension, and nonverbal MA in 25 adolescents and young adults with DS, matched groupwise for nonverbal MA with 19 adolescent and young adult participants with FXS, and 24 typically developing 3- to 6-year-olds. Participants with DS and FXS were also matched groupwise for IQ and CA. Nonverbal cognition was assessed using an average of the Bead Memory, Pattern Analysis, and Copying subtests of the Stanford–Binet, 4th edition (SB; Thorndike et al., 1986). Language comprehension was measured using the three subtests of the TACL–R (Carrow-Woolfolk, 1985). On average, age-equivalent scores for overall comprehension were found to be significantly lower for participants with DS than for the MA-matched participants with FXS. In addition, participants with DS demonstrated a significant difference among TACL–R subtest scores, attributable to a significantly higher score for vocabulary relative to syntax comprehension. In comparison, the MA-matched FXS and TD groups demonstrated a relatively flat performance profile for the TACL–R subtests. All three participant groups demonstrated significant associations between nonverbal MA and each of the TACL–R subtests, consistent with theory proposing the importance of cognitive contributions to language development.

Language Production   Chapman et al. (1998) suggested that children and adolescents with DS demonstrate a specific expressive language impairment; expressive language skills are more delayed than would be expected based on levels of nonverbal visual cognition. This phenotypic profile of expressive language delay emerges early in development for children with DS. Prelinguistic communicative gestures are less likely to be accompanied by vocalizations (Greenwald & Leonard, 1979), and delays are observed in the emergence of nonverbal requesting behaviors (Mundy, Kasari, Sigman, & Ruskin, 1995). A delay in nonverbal requesting is a concurrent correlate of goal-directed problem-solving in toddlers with DS, relative to MA-matched typically developing children and CA- and MA-matched children with developmental delays (Fidler, Philofsky, Hepburn, & Rogers, 2005). Prelinguistic requesting also serves as a longitudinal predictor of subsequent expressive language development (Mundy et al., 1995).

The appearance of first words is substantially delayed in young children with DS (Berg-land, Eriksson, & Johansson, 2001), varying from 8 to 45 months (Berry, Gunn, Andrews, & Price, 1981; Miller, Leddy, Miolo, & Sedey, 1995). On average, both first words and multiword combinations emerge at the same mental ages as reported for typically developing children (Cardoso-Martins & Mervis, 1985; Miller et al., 1995), with early spoken vocabulary displaying a slower than typical rate of development (Beeghly & Cicchetti, 1987). Dykens, Hodapp, and Evans (1994) examined profiles of language development in 80 children with DS aged 1–11 years. Expressive language, as measured by the Vineland Adaptive Behavior Scales, was delayed relative to receptive language by the time overall communication performance exceeded a 24-month level (Dykens et al., 1994).

By adolescence, expressive language in individuals with DS is characterized by deficits in syntax, vocabulary, and speech intelligibility (Chapman & Hesketh, 2000). Language production is delayed relative to language comprehension as well as in comparison to the production skills of typically developing children matched on nonverbal mental age (Chapman, Seung, Schwartz, & Kay-Raining Bird, 1998). Problems with speech intelligibility are widespread and frequently reported as an area of parental concern (Kumin, 1994). Chapman et al. (1998) examined a variety of measures of language production in 47 children and adolescents with DS, ranging in age from 5 to 20 years. Participants were matched groupwise for nonverbal mental age with 47 typically developing children, 2 to 6 years of age. Measures of production, including mean length of utterance (MLU), total words, and number of different words, were significantly lower in the group with DS relative to the MA-matched comparison group, whereas rate of speaking (i.e., utterances per minute) was higher. For both groups, all three measures of language production were higher in narration than in conversation. However, participants with DS had poorer intelligibility in narration, whereas this pattern was not observed for the typically developing group. It is possible that individuals with DS may self-select more familiar words when speaking in a conversational context, whereas the vocabulary used in narration is determined, in large part, by the stimuli used to elicit the narrative sample (e.g., film, book, or pictures).

Chapman et al. (2000) examined predictors of language production, using the same participant group as Chapman et al. (1998). Number of different word roots and MLU in morphemes (both derived from a narrative sample), as well as intelligibility were used as criterion measures of production. Hearing status, chronological age, and nonverbal cognition emerged as significant predictors of the number of different words, accounting for 8%, 35%, and 13% of the variance in narrative production, respectively, for participants with DS. Hearing status, chronological age, and nonverbal cognition were also significant predictors of MLU, accounting for 7%, 35%, and 24% of the variance, respectively. Hearing status was a unique predictor of MLU, accounting for unique variance over and above the variance accounted for by language comprehension. Finally, hearing status and chronological age accounted for 8% and 24% of the variance in predicting speech intelligibility, with comprehension failing to contribute significant additional variance to the regression model. Although these findings emphasize the importance of language comprehension for the prediction of expressive vocabulary and syntax, they also confirm the contribution of hearing status to the ability of individuals with DS to produce utterances that are intelligible and syntactically complete.

An important developmental issue is whether language learning plateaus at the level of simple syntax for individuals with DS. Chapman and colleagues (2002) investigated this issue by conducting a longitudinal study of 31 individuals with DS, ages 5–20. Hierarchical linear modeling was used to predict change in MLU for spontaneous utterances over the course of 6 years. Results demonstrated that individuals with DS continued to make progress in expressive language, with average spontaneous MLU increasing from 3.48 words (SD 1.76) to 4.93 words (SD 2.14) across the 6-year observation period. In contrast to improvement in expressive language, slopes for growth in syntax comprehension, as measured by age-equivalent scores on the TACL–R, actually slowed and became negative for the older adolescents studied. Syntax production improved most for those individuals who demonstrated the least decline in syntax comprehension.

There is broad consensus that sampling context has an important influence on the characteristics of productive language (Abbeduto, Benton, Short, & Dolish, 1995; Evans & Craig, 1992; Miller, 1996). Narrative performance, in particular, is believed to rely upon the integration of both linguistic and cognitive abilities (Hemphill, Picardi, & Tager-Flusberg, 1991). Given their discrepancy between expressive language and nonverbal cognition, examination of narrative samples may be especially informative of the way these two domains contribute to the ability of individuals with DS to produce a narrative account. To this end, Chapman and colleagues examined the narrative performance of 31 individuals with DS, in response to a wordless film (Boudreau & Chapman, 2000) and a wordless picture book (Miles & Chapman, 2002). These studies included the same individuals as participated in the longitudinal study reported by Chapman et al. (1991, 1998), in which participants with DS were matched with three different groups of typically developing children, based on either nonverbal MA, syntax comprehension, or MLU.

When recounting the wordless film, *The Pear Story*, Boudreau and Chapman (2000) found that participants with DS produced longer narratives, recalled more events overall, and expressed more inferential relationships than did MLU-matched comparison participants. Thus, despite their deficits in expressive syntax, individuals with DS mentioned more of the content of the film than did typically developing children with the same MLU. Presumably, participants with DS compensated for challenges in the area of syntax by using more utterances to tell their stories. As expected, the MA-matched comparison group produced a greater number of different words in their narratives, and both the MA-matched and comprehension-matched comparison groups had longer average utterances than the group with DS. Participants with DS also produced more mazes in their narratives than did the MLU-matched group.

In response to the wordless picture book, *Frog, Where Are You?*, individuals with DS produced significantly more plot line components and made more mentions of both the search theme and the dog's misadventures than the MLU-matched comparison group (Miles & Chapman, 2002). However, they produced fewer mentions of the search theme than did the MA-matched comparison group. Overall, the group with DS performed most like the comparison group matched for syntax comprehension. In summary, both of these studies (Boudreau & Chapman, 2000; Miles & Chapman, 2002) suggest that narrative performance of individuals with DS is more similar to that of comparison participants matched for nonverbal cognition or syntax comprehension, than to those matched for expressive language ability. This finding, once again, emphasizes the interdependence of language and cognition and the ways in which individuals with DS may compensate for their specific impairment in expressive language.

Summary   Individuals with DS show a phenotypic pattern of greater impairment in expressive language relative to nonverbal cognition, social skills, and comprehension of vocabulary and syntax. Within the domain of comprehension, vocabulary skills are commensurate with, or in advance of, levels of nonverbal cognition, depending on the measures used to assess both domains. In addition, vocabulary is in advance of syntax, and individual differences in syntax comprehension predict individual differences in the complexity of expressive utterances. Levels of syntax comprehension are predicted by auditory, but not visual, short-term working memory and are likely to decline across adolescence for individuals with DS. Higher levels of expressive language are revealed when expressive language measures are based on lexical content rather than on lexical diversity or utterance length. Hearing status seems particularly important for understanding and productive use of morphological endings. Finally, chronological age and hearing status predict the intelligibility of expressive utterances for individuals with DS.

Fragile X Syndrome

Language Comprehension   Existing data indicate that males with FXS achieve well below chronological age expectations on measures of vocabulary and syntax comprehension

(Abbeduto, Brady, & Kover, 2007; Madison, George, & Moeschler, 1986; Paul et al., 1987; Sudhalter, Maranion, & Brooks, 1992). However, both aspects of comprehension appear to keep pace with nonverbal cognition in affected males, at least in adolescence and young adulthood (Abbeduto et al., 2003; Paul et al., 1987). Abbeduto and colleagues (2003) used the TACL–R (Carrow-Woolfolk, 1985) to examine patterns of receptive language in participants with FXS, relative to participants with either DS or typical development. Participants with FXS and DS were matched groupwise based on chronological age and nonverbal IQ, and all three participant groups were matched on nonverbal mental age. Participants with FXS, who included both males and females, achieved significantly higher total age-equivalent scores on the TACL–R than did participants with DS. In addition, females with FXS achieved higher total scores than did males with FXS, but this gender difference was not significant after controlling for differences in nonverbal mental age. A significant difference in total age-equivalent scores was not observed between participants with FXS and MA-matched typically developing children. It should be noted, however, that receptive language may pose more of a challenge for individuals with FXS during early childhood (Price, Roberts, Vandergrift, & Martin, 2007) and thus, receptive language may only "catch up" with nonverbal cognition during adolescence.

A closer look at performance for the individual TACL–R subtests in the Abbeduto et al. (2003) study reveals additional differences among the groups. All three groups achieved vocabulary comprehension scores commensurate with their nonverbal mental ages, replicating previous findings for individuals with DS. However, participants with FXS and MA-matched, typically developing children achieved vocabulary scores commensurate with their scores on the two TACL–R subtests measuring grammar and syntax. This contrasts with the profile for participants with DS, who performed less well on the subtests measuring syntactical skills. In contrast with individuals with DS, therefore, adolescents and young adults with FXS demonstrate neither an asynchrony in individual domains of language comprehension nor an asynchrony between language comprehension and nonverbal cognition. Price et al. (2007) have also found greater impairments in receptive language for DS than for FXS in early childhood.

Language Production   Most studies of language in FXS have focused on males, given the potential causal links between the behavioral characteristics of males with FXS syndrome (e.g., overarousal and inattention) and the ability to use language for interpersonal communication (Abbeduto et al., 2007). Existing data indicate that males with FXS achieve well below chronological-age expectations on measures of expressive vocabulary (Madison et al., 1986; Paul et al., 1987; Sudhalter, Maranion, & Brooks, 1992). Studies using summary measures that collapse across vocabulary and other domains of language also have reported more difficulty with expressive than receptive language skills for males with FXS (Roberts, Mirrett, & Burchinal, 2001). However, there is little consensus as to whether receptive and expressive vocabularies are delayed to a similar extent in males with FXS.

Few studies have provided data on expressive syntax for individuals with FXS. Madison et al. (1986) examined conversational samples of male participants from a single extended family and found that they generally displayed MLUs that were at or above nonverbal mental age expectations. In contrast, Paul, Cohen, Breg, Watson, and Herman (1984) found no differences on several measures of expressive syntax in conversational language between institutionalized adult males with FXS and age- and IQ-matched individuals with other etiologies of mental retardation. Similarly, Ferrier, Bashir, Meryash, Johnston, and Wolf (1991) found that males with FXS did not differ from cognitively matched individuals with DS or younger typically developing children on measures of syntax derived from conversational samples. It is difficult to generalize from studies such as these, however, given methodological and sampling limitations.

Using the Oral Expression subtest of the Oral and Written Language Scales (OWLS; Carrow-Woolfolk, 1995), Abbeduto et al. (2001) demonstrated that adolescents and young adults with FXS did not differ in age-equivalent scores from typically developing 3- to 6-year-olds matched groupwise on nonverbal MA and did not show a discrepancy between receptive language (as measured by the TACL–R) and expressive language as measured by the OWLS. Finally, participants with FXS demonstrated significantly better expressive language performance than did individuals with DS who were matched on nonverbal cognition. These findings add support to the notion of a specific expressive language impairment in individuals with DS.

Studies of language production in FXS typically have derived measures of expressive syntax (e.g., MLU) from conversational language samples (Murphy & Abbeduto, 2003). As is the case for individuals with DS and other etiologies of mental retardation, however, there is evidence that variations in sampling context can impact the length and complexity of expressive language (Abbeduto et al., 1995; Chapman et al., 1998). Abbeduto et al. (2001) found differences in MLU between individuals with DS and FXS in a task requiring narration of a wordless picture book, but not in a conversational context, with the narrative data showing a significant advantage for participants with FXS. The expectation would be for individuals with FXS to outperform MA-matched participants with DS in both sampling contexts. Given their characteristic inattention and hyperactivity, it is possible that the more structured narrative context facilitated performance for individuals with FXS such that an MLU advantage, relative to DS, became obvious. Indeed, comparison with a typically developing group, matched on nonverbal MA, revealed that the MLU of participants with FXS was commensurate with their nonverbal mental ages in the narrative context.

There are numerous ways in which the behavioral phenotype of FXS may affect the use of language in social interactions. Perseverative language, which is considered a unique and defining feature of the expressive language of males with FXS (Abbeduto & Hagerman, 1997; Bennetto & Pennington, 1996), may result directly from the hyperarousal and social anxiety characteristic of this syndrome (Cornish et al., 2004). In particular, males with FXS display especially high rates of both self-repetition and off-topic or tangential utterances (Belser & Sudhalter, 2001; Ferrier et al., 1991; Sudhalter & Belser, 2001; Sudhalter et al., 1990). Both strategies may allow males with FXS to escape the linguistic, social, and cognitive demands of participating in a conversational interaction.

Abbeduto et al. (2006) used a laboratory-based barrier task to examine the ability of adolescents and young adults with FXS to make the intended referents of their expressive utterances clear to other people. In this task, the participant assumed the role of speaker, with a researcher taking the role of listener. The task required the speaker to describe a novel target shape so that the listener could select the corresponding shape from a set of potential referents. Participants with FXS were less likely than nonverbal MA-matched typically developing children to create unique mappings between their descriptions and the target shapes; instead, they often extended the same description to multiple shapes. Participants with FXS were also less likely to use the same description each time a shape appeared as a target, even if the previous description of that shape had been comprehended by the listener. Thus, individuals with FXS produced talk that was less comprehensible than expected based on their nonverbal mental ages.

Although there has been little study of the pragmatic skills of females with FXS, Simon, Keenan, Pennington, Taylor, and Hagerman (2001) did examine the ability of high-functioning females with the full FXS mutation to complete a discourse task in a coherent manner. These participants had difficulty, relative to IQ-matched comparison females, in selecting humorous endings for stories that they read. Their inability to select cohesive endings to stories, while possibly attributable to memory constraints, is suggestive of a need to conduct more thorough investigations into the pragmatic ability of females with FXS.

Gender Difference in Language in FXS

Direct comparisons of males and females with FXS within the same study, using the same measures, or under the same experimental conditions have been surprisingly rare in the literature, making it difficult to understand the role that gender plays in shaping the language characteristics of individuals with FXS (Abbeduto et al., 2007; Murphy & Abbeduto, 2003; Pavetto & Abbeduto, 2002). Dykens et al. (2000) have suggested that, despite differences in the severity of affectedness, the profile of strengths and weaknesses associated with FXS does not vary by gender. This conclusion, however, is based largely on a synthesis of results from studies employing different methodologies with samples differing along many dimensions in addition to gender. Nevertheless, preliminary data collected by Abbeduto and colleagues support this conclusion, at least with respect to language comprehension. Abbeduto et al. (2003) examined gender differences in receptive vocabulary and syntax using age-equivalent scores from the three subtests of the TACL–R administered to adolescents and young adults with FXS. Although female participants with FXS had higher TACL–R scores than the males, on average, the magnitude of the male–female differences was constant across the three TACL–R subtests. In addition to these flat profiles of language comprehension, both males and females achieved language scores commensurate with a measure of nonverbal cognition. These results are consistent with a pattern of quantitative, but not qualitative, differences in receptive language ability between males and females with FXS.

Pavetto and Abbeduto (2002) compared the language produced by males and females in conversation and narration on talkativeness, fluency, lexical diversity, and syntactic complexity. Although no gender differences were observed for fluency or lexical diversity, two aspects of production were influenced by gender: males were more talkative than females, but females produced utterances of greater syntactic complexity. In addition, both males and females produced utterances of longer MLU in narration than in conversation; however, the magnitude of the gender difference in syntactic complexity was greater for narration than for conversation. This is consistent with previous findings demonstrating that narration elicits language with greater syntactic complexity than conversation (Abbeduto et al., 1995) and suggests that the language characteristics of males and females are influenced in fairly similar ways by sampling context.

Recently, Murphy and Abbeduto (2006) examined the relationship between perseverative language and both gender and sampling context in a group of adolescent males and females with FXS. Language samples were coded for utterance-level repetitions, topic repetitions, and conversational device repetitions (i.e., repetition of rote phrases or expressions used to manage the interaction). Males produced more conversational device repetitions than did females, and these gender differences were not explained by differences in nonverbal cognitive or expressive language ability. In addition, more topic repetitions occurred in conversation than in narration, regardless of gender. The use of utterance-level repetition also was marginally greater during conversation. The observed gender differences in verbal perseveration among adolescents with FXS suggest that, relative to females, males with FXS may rely more heavily on rote phrases in expressive language and that speakers of both genders are influenced by the context of the talk, with less structure leading to an increase in maladaptive verbal behavior.

Language in Individuals with Comorbid FXS and Autism

An association between FXS and autism is well documented (Bailey, Hatton, Skinner, & Mesibov, 2001), but a number of critical issues remain to be clarified. There is not yet agreement on the exact proportion of individuals with FXS who are likely to be diagnosed with an autism spectrum disorder. It is not clear whether the characteristics of autism are distributed on a continuum throughout the population of individuals with FXS or whether the comorbid diagnosis of an autism spectrum disorder represents a qualitatively distinct subtype of the FXS behavioral phenotype. Finally, it has yet to be determined whether autism within FXS has a different etiology compared with idiopathic autism (e.g., social anxiety versus social indifference).

Lewis and colleagues recently examined language profiles of adolescents and young adults with comorbid FXS and autism (Lewis et al., 2006). As expected from previous research, adolescents with comorbid FXS and autism ($N = 10$) scored significantly lower than adolescents with FXS only ($N = 44$) on a measure of nonverbal cognition; all 10 participants with both FXS and autism achieved the lowest possible standard score on the Stanford–Binet, 4th edition, in contrast to 48% of participants with FXS only. When participants with both FXS and autism were compared to age-matched participants with FXS only ($N = 21$) who had also achieved the lowest standard score on the Stanford–Binet, there were no significant between-group differences in expressive language as measured with the expressive subscale of the OWLS (Carrow-Woolfolk, 1995). With regard to receptive language, however, the group with comorbid FXS and autism performed more poorly on all three subtests of the TACL–R or TACL–3 (i.e., vocabulary, grammatical morphemes, and elaborated phrases) than did participants with FXS only. This study replicates the greater impairment in cognitive ability observed in younger children with comorbid FXS and autism (Rogers et al., 2001; but see Price et al., 2007, for contrary evidence) and suggests that this impairment persists into adolescence. In addition, the findings suggest that, while youth with FXS only typically display a flat profile of language and nonverbal cognitive skills, those with comorbid FXS and autism display an asynchronous profile, with receptive language more impaired than either expressive language or nonverbal cognition.

Summary   In contrast to individuals with DS, individuals with FXS demonstrate a relatively flat profile of language comprehension and production skills, and these language abilities are, on average, commensurate with levels of nonverbal cognition. The language of males and females with FXS is affected similarly, with quantitative differences that are related to differences in nonverbal cognition. The language produced within a naturalistic context may be more revealing of the syndrome-specific behavioral challenges faced by individuals with FXS (e.g., social anxiety, hyperarousal, and inattention). A significant proportion of individuals with FXS also meet diagnostic criteria for an autism spectrum disorder, and these individuals have comprehension and cognitive abilities that are challenged to a greater extent than individuals with FXS only.

Williams Syndrome

Language Comprehension   Comprehension of vocabulary is a relative strength for individuals with WS (Mervis & Beccera, 2007). Mervis et al. (2003) reported that individuals with WS demonstrate higher levels of performance on the PPVT (Dunn & Dunn, 1997) than on virtually any other standardized language measure. Of those tested, approximately three-quarters of individuals with WS score within the normal range (70 or above), and 10% score above the average standard score of 100. Mervis and colleagues compared vocabulary comprehension, as measured by the PPVT, with comprehension of abstract relational vocabulary, as measured with the Test of Relational Concepts (TRC; Edmonston & Litchfield Thane, 1988), in a group of 5- to 7-year-olds with WS (mean CA 6–3) (Mervis et al., 2003). A group of typically developing 4- to 7-year-olds, matched on PPVT raw scores, provided the comparison group. The typically developing group demonstrated a significantly larger abstract vocabulary size than did the group with WS (i.e., an average raw score of 31 words compared with 22 words). However, the typically developing group did not display a significant difference in standard scores on the PPVT relative to the TRC, while the WS group showed a difference of almost two standard deviations between the two measures. The same type of discrepancy between measures of concrete and abstract vocabulary comprehension has been reported for individuals with DS (Miolo et al., 2005).

In contrast to individuals with DS, comprehension of syntax is at a level similar to comprehension of concrete vocabulary for individuals with WS. Mean performance on the Test for Reception of Grammar (TROG; Bishop, 2003) is in the borderline normal range (with an average standard score of 74), comparable to performance on the PPVT (with an average score of 78) (Mervis et al., 2003). Grant and colleagues found that performance on the TROG was significantly correlated with nonword repetition performance for a group of participants with WS ranging in age from 8 to 35 years (Grant et al., 1997). These findings support the view that auditory working memory is a characteristic strength for individuals with WS and contributes to relatively strong levels of performance in the areas of vocabulary and syntax.

Language Production   Administration of the Mullen Scales of Early Learning (MSEL; Mullen, 1995) confirms that the Williams syndrome cognitive profile has already emerged in preschoolers and toddlers with WS, with performance weakest in the fine motor domain and considerably stronger for receptive and expressive language (Mervis & Beccera, 2007; Mervis et al., 2003). In addition, a group of 2-year-olds with WS, while scoring below the 10th percentile in vocabulary acquisition on the Words and Sentences version of the MacArthur Communicative Development Inventory (CDI: Fenson et al., 1994), displayed larger average expressive vocabulary sizes relative to a matched group of 2-year-olds with DS; mean vocabulary size was 133 words (range 3–391) for the toddlers with WS compared with 66 words (range 0–324) for the toddlers with DS (Mervis & Robinson, 2000). Mervis and Bertrand (1997) followed 10 children with WS longitudinally from 3–5 years beginning when the children ranged in age from 4 to 26 months. Of these 10 children, 9 began to produce words several months before they first understood or produced a referential pointing gesture, in contrast to the pattern observed for children with either typical development or DS. This delay in the emergence of referential pointing may be the consequence of a deficit in fine motor skill development for toddlers with WS and suggests a different pattern in the emergence of early language skills for these children.

In contrast to vocabulary comprehension scores as measured by the PPVT, with average scores approaching 80, scores in response to the Expressive Vocabulary Test (EVT; Williams, 1997) are lower for individuals with WS, with average scores below 65. Mervis et al. (2003) attribute this discrepancy to the response structure of the EVT. The task of providing a synonym for some of the EVT test items may be more challenging conceptually than simply pointing to a picture in response to PPVT items.

Individuals with WS are characterized in the literature as having a particular strength in grammatical abilities. This generalization forms the primary basis for Bellugi's controversial claim that the case of WS provides evidence for the independence, or modularity, of language from cognition (Bellugi, Poizner, & Klima, 1989; Bellugi et al., 1990, 1999). On average, the spontaneous language of individuals with WS is more syntactically complex than is that of CA- and IQ-matched individuals with DS (Klein & Mervis, 1999). Children with WS are also more proficient at tense marking than are younger children with specific language impairment who are matched for MLU (Mervis & Klein-Tasman, 2000; Rice, 1999). However, as Mervis et al. (2003) pointed out, these two comparison groups have deficits in morphosyntax relative to their levels of nonverbal cognition.

A more nuanced picture emerges when individuals with WS are matched with typically developing children based on chronological age or mental age. Volterra et al. (1996) compared the spontaneous expressive language of Italian children with WS to that of younger MA-matched typically developing children and found that MLU and other measures of syntax were similar for the two groups. In addition, Zukowski (2001) found that the ability of older children and adolescents with WS to produce complex sentence constructions (e.g., embedded relative clauses) was similar to that of a typically developing comparison group matched for MA. These findings suggest that, on average, the grammatical abilities of children with WS are commensurate with, rather than in advance of, their level of cognitive development.

Mervis and colleagues conducted an extensive examination of the associations among MLU, cognitive ability, and grammatical complexity in children with WS (Mervis & Klein-Tasman, 2000; Mervis et al., 1999). These investigators collected spontaneous language samples during play from 39 participants with WS, ranging in age from 2 to 12 years. Two measures of grammatical complexity—MLU in morphemes and Index of Productive Syntax (IPSyn) scores (Scarborough, 1990)—were lower than scores reported for typically developing children at ages 3 to 6 years in Scarborough's (1990) sample. Thus, rather than being advanced in grammatical development, children with WS were substantially delayed in the development of both syntax and grammar when compared to CA-matched children with typical development, rather than to children with other types of language delay. Moreover, for the children with WS, both MLU and IPSyn scores were commensurate with cognitive ability, but lower than expected based on auditory short-term memory and vocabulary comprehension.

Morris and Mervis (2000) compared the morphological abilities of this sample of children with WS to a group of younger typically developing 3-year-olds matched for MLU in morphemes. Use of noun plurals, determiners, and verb tense was similar for the two groups, indicating that the morphological abilities of the children with WS were at the level expected for the length of their productive utterances. However, the children with WS had larger receptive vocabularies than the MLU-matched, typically developing children, suggesting that utterance length and grammatical complexity are lower than expected relative to vocabulary size. This discrepancy between vocabulary and morphology was observed despite the fact that English is a relatively uninflected language. Children with WS learning languages that are morphologically more complex than English (e.g., French, Italian, and Hebrew) perform less well than do younger, MA-matched, typically developing children (Karmiloff-Smith et al., 1997; Levy & Hermon, 2003; Volterra et al., 1996). Thus, these studies support the notion that grammatical morphology is not advanced in individuals with WS relative to their levels of cognitive ability or vocabulary comprehension. Similarly, studies such as these refute the notion that language is "intact", or even advanced, for individuals with WS and do not support claims that language in WS is independent of other cognitive domains.

In contrast to DS, auditory short-term or working memory is a relative strength for individuals with WS and may provide an important mechanism for language learning in this population (Mervis et al., 1999). Individuals with WS perform at age-appropriate levels on tasks involving forward and backward digit span (Mervis et al., 1999), as well as nonword repetition (Grant et al., 1997). Individuals with DS, in contrast, show exceptional difficulty on tests of backward memory for both verbal and visual information (Vicari, Caselli, & Tonucci, 2000). It has been proposed that speech in individuals with WS may appear to be intact due to the use of unanalyzed, stereotyped phrases and sentences learned by rote memorization (Gosch, Stading, & Pankau, 1994; Udwin & Yule, 1990).

Robinson, Mervis, and Robinson (2003) examined the association between verbal short-term memory and language in 39 children with WS, aged 4 to 16 years. Participants with WS were matched to a comparison group of younger typically developing children based on performance on the TROG. After controlling for chronological age, measures of forward digit span, backward digit span, and nonword repetition showed significant associations with TROG performance for the children with WS. After controlling for CA and forward digit span, nonword repetition and backward digit span both accounted for unique variance in TROG performance, Robinson et al. (2003) proposed that phonological working memory, represented by nonword repetition performance, and verbal working memory, represented by backward digit span, probably make a strong contribution to the ability of individuals with WS to comprehend and produce vocabulary and grammar. In fact, the group with WS showed a significantly stronger association between backward digit span and TROG performance than did children with typical development. These findings suggest that individuals with WS may use a basic cognitive strength, in the form of verbal working memory, to overcome challenges to language learning that result from relative weaknesses in nonverbal cognitive ability (Mervis et al., 2003).

In a direct comparison between the two syndrome groups, Klein and Mervis (1999) examined a group of 9- and 10-year-olds with WS matched on chronological age with a group of children with DS. Of the 23 WS participants, 19 spoke in complete and grammatical sentences, whereas only 4 of the 25 participants with DS did so. The children with WS outperformed the CA-matched children with DS on the McCarthy Scales of Children's Abilities (McCarthy, 1972), on the PPVT, and on a test of verbal working memory. When a subset of each group was individually matched for both CA and MA, the DS group performed better on measures of visual spatial skills (i.e., block building, draw-a-person, and draw-a-design), while the WS group performed better on measures of verbal working memory. There were no significant between-group differences for the PPVT or for the McCarthy subtests measuring verbal ability.

Summary   In contrast to initial descriptions of language in WS as being unaffected by the syndrome, and even advanced, few individuals with WS have language skills at levels commensurate with their chronological ages. Instead, mean levels of performance on standardized tests of language ability are consistently in the borderline to mildly impaired range, commensurate with the language skills of cognitively matched, but younger, typically developing children. Both vocabulary and grammar are more advanced than nonverbal cognition. Visual spatial ability is an area of particular weakness for individuals with WS. In contrast, verbal working memory is an area of particular strength and may account for the ability of individuals with WS to acquire vocabulary and syntax. This syndrome-specific profile is in direct contrast to individuals with DS who show a relative strength in visual-spatial skills, a relative weakness in verbal working memory (especially for backward information), and a specific expressive language impairment.

CONCLUDING REMARKS

Four general themes emerge from the literature on language in DS, FXS, and WS. First, the profile of language development and strengths and weaknesses varies dramatically across syndromes, not only in terms of degree of impairment, but also in the profile or character of the impairments. Broadly speaking, language is most challenging for DS and least challenging for WS, although even the latter individuals do less well in language, on average, than do their typically developing chronological age peers. In WS and DS, vocabulary acquisition appears to be especially strong relative to other language domains, although this appears true more for comprehension of concrete than abstract or relational vocabulary. In DS, syntax, especially expressive syntax, is more impaired than is vocabulary, whereas the two domains are more synchronous and more highly developed in WS and FXS relative to DS. In FXS, the form and content of language (i.e., syntax and vocabulary) are less impaired, on average, than are the skills involved in using language for social ends. Approaches to assessment and intervention will need to be informed by and tailored to these syndrome-specific profiles (Fidler, Philofsky, & Hepburn, 2007). Moreover, it is important to recognize that language does not represent a unitary ability or set of skills but, rather, a set of separate but interrelated skills and domains of knowledge.

The profile of linguistic impairments associated with each syndrome emerges gradually and, thus, changes with age. In DS, for example, positive growth in expressive syntax continues, whereas syntax comprehension becomes increasingly delayed during adolescence and may even be characterized by regression in young adulthood. In FXS, the use of language for social ends appears to lag further behind age expectation during adolescence. In WS, the sequence of achievements in language and communication does not consistently follow the typical path, suggesting that there are various routes to language competence. From a clinical perspective, it is important to recognize the dynamic nature of the syndrome-specific phenotype and of the need to anchor assessment and interpretation of language and neurocognitive profiles to specific points in development.

These syndrome-related differences in language appear to reflect not a direct effect of the genes on behavior but the influence of nonlanguage dimensions of the behavioral phenotypes and, thus, the indirect effects of individual—or combinations of—genes. In FXS, for example, problems in attention and arousal regulation may account for the verbal perseveration that places limits on social interaction. The overlay of autistic-like symptoms in FXS has rather dramatic effects on language in general, but impacts especially on receptive language. The contextual variation in the expressive of language skills (e.g., higher MLU in narration than in conversation) is also likely to be attributable to the interaction of context with language skills, nonlanguage skills, and profiles of impairment. From a clinical perspective, such variations suggest the need to embed language assessment and intervention within a more integrated framework that recognizes the profile defining the "whole" child. Social-interactionist theories of language development are likely to be useful in this regard.

The linguistic profile of each syndrome is closely tied to its cognitive profile. Thus, all of the syndromes, even WS, are associated with language delays relative to chronological age peers. Indeed, correlations between summary measures of broad language domains (e.g., receptive syntax) and of nonverbal cognitive domains (e.g., nonverbal problem-solving) are substantial. Moreover, more subtle variations across cognitive domains appear to have a dramatic impact on the course of language development. For example, the relatively weak auditory short-term memory skills of individuals with DS contribute in important ways to their delays in syntax, whereas the relative strength in auditory short-term memory evidenced by individuals with WS appears to account, at least in part, for their stronger (relative to DS) syntactic skills. Such findings are difficult to reconcile with the modularity claims of Chomsky, Pinker, and others suggesting, instead, a model in which language learning and use are embedded in, and intimately connected to, all aspects of the psychological and behavioral life of the child.

ACKNOWLEDGMENTS

Preparation of this chapter was supported by NIH grants R01 HD24356 and T32 HD007489 awarded to L. Abbeduto and by NIH grant P30 HD03352 awarded to the Waisman Center.

REFERENCES

Abbeduto, L., Benton, G., Short, K., & Dolish, J. (1995). Effects of sampling context on the expressive language of children and adolescents with mental retardation. *Mental Retardation, 33,* 279–288.

Abbeduto, L., Brady, N., & Kover, S. (2007). Language development and fragile X syndrome: Profiles, syndrome specificity, and within-syndrome differences. *Mental Retardation and Developmental Disabilities Research Reviews, 13,* 36–46.

Abbeduto, L., & Chapman, R. (2005). Language and communication skills in children with DS and Fragile X. In P. Fletcher & J. Miller (Eds.), *Trends in language acquisition research: Vol. 4. Developmental theory and language disorders* (pp. 53–72). Amsterdam: John Benjamins.

Abbeduto, L., & Hagerman, R. (1997). Language and communication in fragile X syndrome. *Mental Retardation and Developmental Disabilities Research Reviews, 3,* 313–322.

Abbeduto, L., & Murphy, M. (2004). Language, social cognition, maladaptive behavior, and communication in Down syndrome and fragile X syndrome. In S. Warren & M. Rice (Eds.), *Developmental language disorders: From phenotypes to etiologies* (pp. 77–97). Mahwah, NJ: Lawrence Erlbaum Associates.

Abbeduto, L., Murphy, M., Cawthon, S., Richmond, E., Weissman, M., Karadottir, S., & O'Brien, A. (2003). Receptive language skills of adolescents and young adults with mental retardation: A comparison of Down syndrome and fragile X syndrome. *American Journal on Mental Retardation, 108,* 149–160.

Abbeduto, L., Murphy, M., Richmond, E., Amman, A., Beth, P., Weissman, M., Kim, J., Cawthon, S., & Karadottir, S. (2006). Collaboration in referential communication: Comparison of youth with Down syndrome or fragile X syndrome. *American Journal on Mental Retardation, 111,* 170–183.

Abbeduto, L., Pavetto, M., Kesin, E., Weissman, M., Karadottir, S., O'Brien, A., & Cawthon, S. (2001). The linguistic and cognitive profile of DS: Evidence from a comparison with fragile X syndrome. *Down Syndrome Research and Practice, 7,* 9–16.

Antonarakis, S. E., & Epstein, C. J. (2006). The challenge of Down syndrome. *Trends in Molecular Medicine, 12,* 473–479.

Bailey, D., Hatton, D., & Skinner, M. (1998). Early developmental trajectories of males with fragile X syndrome. *American Journal on Mental Retardation, 103,* 29–39.

Bailey, D., Hatton, D., Skinner, M., & Mesibov, G. (2001). Autistic behavior, FMR-1 protein, and developmental trajectories in young males with fragile X syndrome. *Journal of Autism and Developmental Disorders, 31,* 165–174.

Beeghly, M., & Cicchetti, D. (1987). An organizational approach to symbolic development in children with Down syndrome. In D. Cicchetti & M. Beeghly (Eds.), *Symbolic development in atypical children: New directions for child development* (No. 36, pp. 5–29). San Francisco: Jossey-Bass.

Bellugi, U., Bihrle, A., Jernigan, T, Trauner, D., & Doherty, S. (1990). Neurospychological and neuranatomical profile of Williams syndrome. *American Journal of Medical Genetics, 6,* 115–125.

Bellugi, U., Lichtenberger, L., Mills, D., Galaburda, A., & Korenberg, J. (1999). Bridging cognition, the brain, and molecular genetics: Evidence from Williams syndrome. *Trends in Neurosciences, 22,* 197–207.

Bellugi, U., Poizner, H., & Klima, E. (1989). Language, modality, and the brain. *Trends in Neurosciences, 12,* 380–388.

Belser, R., & Sudhalter, V. (1995). Arousal difficulties in males with fragile X syndrome: A preliminary report. *Developmental Brain Dysfunction, 8,* 270–279.

Belser, R., & Sudhalter, V. (2001). Conversational characteristics of children with fragile X syndrome: Repetitive speech. *American Journal on Mental Retardation, 106,* 28–38.

Bennetto, L., & Pennington, B. (1996). The neuropsychology of fragile X syndrome. In R. J. Hagerman & A. Cronister (Eds.), *Fragile X syndrome: Diagnosis, treatment, and research* (pp. 210–243). Baltimore: Johns Hopkins University Press.

Bergland, E., Eriksson, M., & Johansson, I. (2001). Parental reports of spoken language skills in children with Down syndrome. *Journal of Speech and Hearing Research, 44,* 179–191.

Berry, P., Gunn, P., Andrews, R., & Price, C. (1981). Characteristics of Down syndrome infants and their families. *Australian Paediatrics Journal, 17,* 40–43.

Bishop, D. V. M. (2003). *Test for Reception of Grammar, Version 2.* London: Psychological Corporation.

Boudreau, D., & Chapman, R. (2000). The relationship between event representation and linguistic skill in narratives of children and adolescents with Down syndrome. *Journal of Speech, Language, and Hearing Research, 43,* 1146–1159.

Brown, W. (2002). The molecular biology of the fragile X mutation. In R. Hagerman & P. Hagerman (Eds.), *Fragile X syndrome: Diagnosis, treatment and research* (3rd ed., pp. 110–135). Baltimore: Johns Hopkins University Press.

Cardoso-Martins, C., & Mervis, C. B. (1985). Maternal speech to prelinguistic children with Down syndrome. *American Journal of Mental Deficiency, 89,* 451–458.

Carrow-Woolfolk, E. (1985). *Test for Auditory Comprehension of Language—Revised.* Allen, TX: DLM Teaching Resources.

Carrow-Woolfolk, E. (1995). *Oral and Written Language Scales.* Circle Pines, MN: American Guidance Services.

Carrow-Woolfolk, E. (1999). *Test for Auditory Comprehension of Language* (3rd ed.). Circle Pines, MN: American Guidance Services.

Chafe, W. (Ed.). (1980). *The pear stories: Cognitive, cultural, and linguistic aspects of narrative production.* Norwood, NJ: Ablex.

Chapman, R. (1999). Language and cognitive development in children and adolescents with DS. In J. F. Miller, L. A. Leavitt, & M. Leddy (Eds.), *Improving the communication of people with DS* (pp. 41–60). Baltimore: Paul H. Brookes.

Chapman, R. (2003). Language and communication in individuals with Down syndrome. In L. Abbeduto (Ed.), *International Review of Research in Mental Retardation: Language and Communication* (Vol. 27, pp. 1–34). New York: Academic Press.

Chapman, R., & Hesketh, L. (2000). Behavioral phenotype of individuals with Down syndrome. *Mental Retardation and Developmental Disability Research Reviews, 6,* 84–95.

Chapman, R., Hesketh, L., & Kistler, D. (2002). Predicting longitudinal change in language production and comprehension in individuals with Down syndrome: Hierarchical linear modeling. *Journal of Speech, Language, and Hearing Research, 45,* 902–915.

Chapman, R., Schwartz, S., & Kay-Raining Bird, E. (1991). Language skills of children and adolescents with Down syndrome: I. Comprehension. *Journal of Speech and Hearing Research, 34,* 1106–1120.

Chapman, R., Seung, H.-K., Schwartz, S., & Kay-Raining Bird, E. (1998). Language skills of children and adolescents with Down syndrome: II. Production deficits. *Journal of Speech, Language, and Hearing Research, 41,* 861–873.

Chapman, R., Seung, H.-K., Schwartz, S., & Kay-Raining Bird, E. (2000). Predicting language development in children and adolescents with Down syndrome: The role of comprehension. *Journal of Speech, Language, and Hearing Research, 43,* 340–350.

Cornish, K., Sudhalter, V., & Turk, J. (2004). Attention and language in Fragile X. *Mental Retardation and Developmental Disabilities Research Reviews, 10,* 11–16.

Demark, J., Feldman, M., & Holden, J. (2003). Behavioral relationship between autism and fragile X syndrome. *American Journal on Mental Retardation, 108,* 314–326.

Donnai, D., & Karmiloff-Smith, A. (2000). Williams syndrome: From genotype through to the cognitive phenotype. *American Journal of Medical Genetics*, 97, 164–171.

Dunn, L., & Dunn, L. (1981). *Peabody Picture Vocabulary Test–Revised*. Circle Pines, MN: American Guidance Service.

Dunn, L., & Dunn, L. (1997). *Peabody Picture Vocabulary Test* (3rd ed.). Circle Pines, MN: American Guidance Service.

Dykens, E., Hodapp, R., & Evans, D. (1994). Profiles and development of adaptive behavior in children with Down syndrome. *American Journal on Mental Retardation*, 98, 580–587.

Dykens, E., Hodapp, R., & Finucane, B. (2000). *Genetics and mental retardation syndromes: A new look at behavior and interventions*. Baltimore: Paul H. Brookes.

Edmonston N., & Litchfield Thane, N. (1988). *TRC: Test of Relational Concepts*. Austin, TX: PRO-ED.

Evans, J., & Craig, H. (1992). Language sample collection and analysis: Interview compared to freeplay assessment context. *Journal of Speech and Hearing Research*, 35, 343–353.

Facon, B., Facon-Bollengier, T., & Grubar, J. (2002). Chronological age, receptive vocabulary, and syntax comprehension in children and adolescents with mental retardation. *American Journal on Mental Retardation*, 107, 91–98.

Fazio, B., Johnston, J., & Brandl, L. (1993). Relation between mental age and vocabulary development among children with mild mental retardation. *American Journal on Mental Retardation*, 97, 541–546.

Fenson, L., Dale, P., Reznick, J. S., Bates, E., Thal, D., & Pethnick, S. J. (1994). Variability in early communicative development. *Monographs of the Society for Research in Child Development*, 59, 5.

Ferrier, L., Bashir, A., Meryash, D., Johnston, J., & Wolff, P. (1991). Conversational skill of individuals with fragile X syndrome: A comparison with autism and DS. *Developmental Medicine and Child Neurology*, 33, 776–788.

Fidler, D. J., Philofsky, A., & Hepburn, S. L. (2007). Language phenotypes and intervention planning: Bridging research and practice. *Mental Retardation and Developmental Disabilities Research Reviews*, 13, 47–57.

Fidler, D., Philofsky, A., Hepburn, S., & Rogers, S. (2005). Nonverbal requesting and problem-solving by toddlers with Down syndrome. *American Journal on Mental Retardation*, 110, 312–322.

Fidler, D., Philofsky, A., Hepburn, S., & Rogers, S. (2007). Language phenotypes and intervention planning: Bridging research and practice. *Mental Retardation and Developmental Disabilities Research Reviews*, 13, 47–57.

Frangiskakis, J., Ewart, A., Morris, C., Mervis, C., Bertrand, J., Robinson, B. et al. (1996). LIM-kinase 1 hemizygosity implicated in impaired visuospatial constructive cognition. *Cell*, 86, 59–69.

Gardiner, K., & Costa, A. (2006). The proteins of human chromosome 21. *American Journal of Medical Genetics: Part C. Seminars in Medical Genetics*, 142, 196–205.

Golaz, J., Charnay, Y., Vallet, P., & Bouras, C. (1991). Alzheimer's disease and Down's syndrome: Some recent etiopathogenic data. *Encephale*, 17, 29–31.

Gosch, A., Stading, G., & Pankau, R. (1994). Linguistic abilities in children with Williams-Beuren syndrome. *American Journal of Medical Genetics*, 52, 291–296.

Grant, J., Karmiloff-Smith, A., Gathercole, S., Paterson, S., Howlin, P., Davies, M., & Udwin, O. (1997). Phonological short-term memory and its relationship to language in Williams syndrome. *Cognitive Neuropsychiatry*, 2, 81–99.

Greenwald, C., & Leonard, L. (1979). Communicative and sensorimotor development of Down's syndrome children. *American Journal of Mental Deficiency*, 84, 296–303.

Gulesserian, T., Seidl, R., Hardmeier, R., Cairns, N., & Lubec, G. (2001). Superoxide dismutase SOD1, encoded on chromosome 21, but not SOD2 is overexpressed in brains of patients with Down syndrome. *Journal of Investigational Medicine*, 49, 41–46.

Hagerman, R. (1999). *Neurodevelopmental disorders*. Oxford, UK: Oxford University Press.

Harman, D. (2006). Alzheimer's disease pathogenesis: Role of aging. *Annals of the New York Academy of Sciences, 1067*, 454–460.

Hemphill, L., Picardi, N., & Tager-Flusberg, H. (1991). Narrative as an index of communicative competence in mildly mentally-retarded children. *Applied Psycholinguistics, 12*, 263–279.

Jarrold, C., Baddeley, A., & Phillips, C. (2002). Verbal short-term memory in Down syndrome: A problem of memory, audition, or speech? *Journal of Speech, Language, and Hearing Research, 45*, 531–544.

Karmiloff-Smith, A., Grant, J., Berthoud, I., Davies, M., Howlin, P., & Udwin, O. (1997). Language and Williams syndrome: How intact is "intact"? *Child Development, 68*, 246–262.

Kasari, C., & Bauminger, N. (1998). Social and emotional development in children with mental retardation. In J. Burack, R. Hodapp, & E. Zigler (Eds.), *Handbook of mental retardation and development* (pp. 411–433). New York: Cambridge University Press.

Kaufmann, W., Cortell, R., Kau, A., Bukelis, I., Tierney, E., Gray, R. et al. (2004). Autism spectrum disorder in fragile X syndrome. *American Journal of Medical Genetics, 129*, 225–234.

Keysor, C., & Mazzocco, M. (2002). Physiological arousal in females with fragile X or Turner syndrome. *Developmental Psychobiology, 41*, 133–146.

Klein, B., & Mervis, C. (1999). Contrasting patterns of cognitive abilities of 9- and 10-year olds with Williams syndrome or Down syndrome. *Developmental Neuropsychology, 16*, 177–196.

Klein-Tasman, B., & Mervis, C. (2003). Distinctive personality characteristics of 8-, 9-, 10-year-olds with Williams syndrome. *Developmental Neuropsychology, 23*, 269–290.

Klintsova, A., & Greenough, W. (1999). Synaptic plasticity in cortical systems. *Current Opinion in Neurobiology, 9*, 203–208.

Kumin, L. (1994). Intelligibility of speech in children with Down syndrome in natural settings: Parents' perspective. *Perception and Motor Skills, 78*, 307–314.

Levitas, A., Hagerman, R., Braden, M., Rimland, B., McBogg, P., & Matus, I. (1983). Autism and fragile X syndrome. *Journal of Developmental Behavioral Pediatrics, 4*, 151–158.

Levy, Y., & Hermon, S. (2003). Morphological abilities of Hebrew-speaking adolescents with Williams syndrome. *Developmental Neuropsychology. Special Issue: Williams syndrome, 23*, 59–83.

Lewis, P., Abbeduto, L., Murphy, M., Richmond, E., Giles, N., Bruno, L., & Schroeder, S. (2006). Cognitive language and social-cognitive skills of individuals with fragile X syndrome with and without autism. *Journal of Intellectual Disability Research, 50*, 532–545.

Madison, L., George, C., & Moeschler, J. (1986). Cognitive functioning in the fragile X syndrome: A study of intellectual, memory, and communication skills. *Journal of Mental Deficiency Research, 30*, 129–148.

Mayer, M. (1969). *Frog, where are you?* New York: Dial Press.

McCarthy, D. (1972). *McCarthy Scales of Children's Abilities.* New York: Psychological Corp.

Menendez, M. (2005). Down syndrome, Alzheimer's disease and seizures. *Brain Development, 27*, 246–252.

Merrill, E., Lookadoo, R., & Rilea, S. (2003). Memory, language comprehension, and mental retardation. In L. Abbeduto (Ed.), *International review of research in mental retardation* (Vol., 26, pp. 151–189). New York: Academic Press.

Mervis, C., & Beccera, A. M. (2007). Language and communicative development in Williams syndrome. *Mental Retardation and Developmental Disabilities Research Reviews, 13*, 3–15.

Mervis, C., & Bertrand, J. (1997). Developmental relations between cognition and language: Evidence from Williams syndrome. In L. Adamson & M. A. Romski (Eds.), *Communication and language acquisition: Discoveries from atypical development* (pp. 75–106). New York: Paul H. Brookes.

Mervis, C., & Klein-Tasman, B. (2000). Williams syndrome: Cognition, personality, and adaptive behavior. *Mental Retardation and Developmental Disabilities Research Reviews, 6*, 148–158.

Mervis, C., Morris, C., Bertrand, J., & Robinson, B. (1999). Williams syndrome: Findings on an integrated program of research. In H. Tager-Flusberg (Ed.), *Neurodevelopmental disorders: Developmental cognitive neuroscience* (pp. 65–110). Cambridge, MA: MIT Press.

Mervis, C., & Robinson, B. (2000). Expressive vocabulary ability of toddlers with Williams syndrome or Down syndrome: A comparison. *Developmental Neuropsychology, 17*, 111–126.

Mervis, C., Robinson, B., Bertrand, J., Morris, C., Klein-Tasman, B., & Armstrong, S. (2000). The Williams syndrome cognitive profile. *Brain and Cognition, 44,* 604–628.

Mervis, C., Robinson, B., Rowe, M., Becerra, A., & Klein-Tasman, F. (2003). Language abilities of individuals with Williams syndrome. In L. Abbeduto (Ed.), *International Review of Research in Mental Retardation: Vol. 27. Language and communication in mental retardation* (pp. 35–82). New York: Academic Press.

Meyer-Lindenberg, A., Mervis, C., & Berman, K. (2006). Neural mechanisms in Williams syndrome: A unique window to genetic influences on cognition and behaviour. *Nature Reviews: Neuroscience, 7,* 380–393.

Miles, S., & Chapman, R. (2002). Narrative content as described by individuals with DS and typically-developing children. *Journal of Speech, Language, and Hearing Research, 45,* 175–189.

Miller, J. (1996). Progress in assessing, describing, and defining child language disorder. In K. Cole, P. Dale, & D. Thal (Eds.), *Assessment of communication and language* (6th ed., pp. 309–324). Baltimore: Paul H. Brookes.

Miller, J. (1999). Profiles of language development in children with Down syndrome. In J. Miller, M. Leddy, & L. Leavitt (Eds.), *Improving the communication of people with Down syndrome* (pp. 11–40). Baltimore: Paul H. Brookes.

Miller, J., Leddy, M., Miolo, G., & Sedey, A. (1995). The development of early language skills in children with Down syndrome. In L. Nadel & D. Rosenthal (Eds.), *Down syndrome: Living and learning in the community* (pp. 115–120). New York: Wiley-Liss.

Miolo, G., Chapman, R., & Sindberg, H. (2005). Sentence comprehension in adolescents with DS and typically-developing children: Role of sentence voice, visual context, and auditory–verbal short-term memory. *Journal of Speech, Language, and Hearing Research, 48,* 172–188.

Morris, C. (2004). Genotype–phenotype correlations: Lessons from Williams syndrome. In M. L. Rice & S. F. Warren (Eds.), *Developmental language disorders: From phenotypes to etiologies* (pp. 355–369). Mahwah, NJ: Lawrence Erlbaum Associates.

Morris, C., & Mervis, C. (2000). Williams syndrome and related disorders. *Annual Review of Genomics and Human Genetics, 1,* 461–484.

Mullen, E. M. (1995). *Mullen Scales of Early Learning* (AGS ed.). Circle Pines, MN: American Guidance Service.

Mundy, P., Kasari, C., Sigman, M., & Ruskin, E. (1995). Nonverbal communication and early language acquisition in children with Down syndrome and in normally developing children. *Journal of Speech and Hearing Research, 38,* 157–167.

Murphy, M., & Abbeduto, L. (2003). Language and communication in fragile X syndrome. In L. Abbeduto (Ed.), *International Review of Research in Mental Retardation* (Vol. 26, pp. 83–119). New York: Academic Press.

Murphy, M. M., & Abbeduto, L. (2006). Gender differences in repetitive language in fragile X syndrome. *Journal of Intellectual Disability Research, 15,* 387–400.

Murphy, M. M., Abbeduto, L., Schroeder, S., & Serlin, R. C. (2006). Contribution of social and information processing factors to eye gaze avoidance in fragile X syndrome. *American Journal on Mental Retardation, 112,* 349–360.

Nadel, L. (2003). Down's syndrome: A genetic disorder in biobehavioral perspective. *Genes, Brain, and Behavior, 2,* 156–166.

Oostra, B., & Willemsen, R. (2003). A fragile balance: fMRI expression levels. *Human Molecular Genetics, 12,* 249–257.

Paul, R., Cohen, D., Breg, R., Watson, M., & Herman, S. (1984). Fragile X syndrome: Its relations to speech and language disorders. *Journal of Speech and Hearing Disorders, 49,* 326–336.

Paul, R., Dykens, E., Leckman, F., Watson, M., Breg, W., & Cohen, D. (1987). A comparison of language characteristics of mentally retarded adults with fragile X syndrome and those with nonspecific mental retardation and autism. *Journal of Autism and Developmental Disorders, 17,* 457–468.

Pavetto, M. M., & Abbeduto, L. (2002, June). *Characteristics of expressive language among males and females with fragile X syndrome.* Poster session presented at the annual meeting of the Academy of Mental Retardation, Orlando, FL.

Pennington, B., Moon, J., Edgin, J., Stedron, J., & Nadel, L. (2003). The neuropsychology of Down syndrome: Evidence for hippocampal dysfunction. *Child Development, 74*, 75–93.

Philofsky, A., Hepburn, S., Hayes, A., Hagerman, R., & Rogers, S. (2004). Linguistic and cognitive functioning and autism symptoms in young children with Fragile X syndrome. *American Journal on Mental Retardation, 109*, 208–218.

Price, J., Roberts, J., Vandergift, N., & Martin, G. (2007). Language comprehension in boys with fragile X syndrome and boys with Down syndrome. *Journal of Intellectual Disability Research, 51*, 318–326.

Rice, M. (1999). Specific grammatical limitations in children with specific language impairment. In H. Tager-Flusberg (Ed.), *Neurodevelopmental disorders: Developmental cognitive neuroscience* (pp. 331–359). Cambridge, MA: MIT Press.

Roberts, J., Mirrett, P., & Burchinal, M. (2001). Receptive and expressive communication development of young males with fragile X syndrome. *American Journal on Mental Retardation, 106*, 216–230.

Roberts, J. E., Price, J., & Malkin, C. (2007). Language and communication development in Down syndrome. *Mental Retardation and Developmental Disabilities Research Reviews, 13*, 26–35.

Robinson, B., Mervis, C., & Robinson, B. (2003). The roles of verbal short-term memory and working memory in the acquisition of grammar by children with Williams syndrome. *Developmental Neuropsychology, 23*, 13–31.

Rogers, S., Wehner, E., & Hagerman, R. (2001). The behavioral phenotype in fragile X: Symptoms of autism in very young children with fragile X syndrome, idiopathic autism, and other developmental disorders. *Journal of Developmental and Behavioral Pediatrics, 22*, 409–418.

Roizen, N. (1997). Down syndrome. In M. Batshaw (Ed.), *Children with disabilities* (4th ed., pp. 361–376). Baltimore: Paul H. Brookes.

Rosin, M., Swift, E., Bless, D., & Vetter, D. (1988). Communication profiles of adolescents with Down syndrome. *Journal of Childhood Communication Disorders, 12*, 49–64.

Rumble, B., Retallack, R., Hilbich, C., Simms, G., Multhaup, G., Martins, R., et al. (1989). Amyloid A4 protein and its precursor in Down's syndrome and Alzheimer's disease. *New England Journal of Medicine, 320*, 1446–1452.

Salehi, A., Delcroix, J., Belichenko, P., Zhan, K., Wu, C., Valleta, J., et al. (2006). Increased *app* expression in a mouse model of Down's syndrome disrupts NGF transport and causes cholinergic neuron degeneration. *Neuron, 51*, 29–42.

Scarborough, H. (1990). Index of Productive Syntax. *Applied Psycholinguistics, 11*, 1–22.

Sherman, S. (1996). Epidemiology. In R. Hagerman & A. Cronister (Eds.), *Fragile X syndrome: Diagnosis, treatment, and research* (pp. 165–192). Baltimore: Johns Hopkins University Press.

Siarey, R., Kline-Burgess, A., Cho, M., Balbo, A., Best, T., Harashima, C., et al. (2006). Altered signaling pathways underlying abnormal hippocampal synaptic plasticity in the Ts65Dn mouse model of Down syndrome. *Journal of Neurochemistry, 98*, 1266–1277.

Simon, J., Keenan, J., Pennington, B., Taylor, A., & Hagerman, R. (2001). Discourse processing in women with fragile X syndrome: Evidence for a deficit establishing coherence. *Cognitive Neuropsychology, 18*, 1–18.

Sudhalter, V., & Belser, R. C. (2001). Conversational characteristics of children with Fragile X syndrome: Tangential language. *American Journal on Mental Retardation, 106*, 389–400.

Sudhalter, V., Cohen, I., Silverman, W., & Wolf-Schein, E. (1990). Conversational analysis of males with fragile X, Down syndrome, and autism: Comparison of the emergence of deviant language. *American Journal on Mental Retardation, 94*, 431–441.

Sudhalter, V., Maranion, M., & Brooks, P. (1992). Expressive semantic deficit in the productive language of males with fragile X syndrome. *American Journal of Medical Genetics, 43*, 65–71.

Thorndike, R., Hagen, E., & Sattler, J. (1986). *Stanford–Binet Intelligence Scale* (4th ed.). Chicago: Riverside Publishing Company.

Udwin, O., & Yule, W. (1990). Expressive language of children with Williams syndrome. *American Journal of Medical Genetics Supplement, 6*, 108–114.

Udwin, O., Yule, W., & Martin, N. (1987). Cognitive abilities and behavioral characteristics of children with idiopathic hypercalcaemia. *Journal of Child Psychology and Psychiatry, 28,* 297–309.

Vicari, S., Carlesimo, A., & Caltagirone, C. (1995). Short-term memory in persons with intellectual disabilities and Down's syndrome. *Journal of Intellectual Disability Research, 39,* 532–537.

Vicari, S., Caselli, M., & Tonucci, F. (2000). Asynchrony of lexical and morphosyntactic development in children with Down syndrome. *Neuropsychology, 38,* 634–644.

Volterra, V., Capirci, O., Pezzini, G., Sabbadini, L., & Vicari, S. (1996). Linguistic abilities in Italian children with Williams syndrome. *Cortex, 32,* 663–677.

Williams, K. (1997). *EVT: Expressive Vocabulary Test.* Bloomington, MN: Pearson Assessments.

Wisbeck, J., Huffman, L., Freund, L., Gunnar, M., Davis, E., & Reiss, A. (2000). Cortisol and social stressors in children with fragile X: A pilot study. *Journal of Developmental and Behavioral Pediatrics, 21,* 278–282.

Zukowski, A. (2001). *Uncovering grammatical competence in children with Williams syndrome.* Unpublished doctoral dissertation, Boston University.

3

Language Disorders in Children with Autism

JOANNE GERENSER

A utism spectrum disorders (ASD) are a group of severe developmental disorders that are characterized by deficits in social interaction and communication as well as restricted or repetitive patterns of behaviors or interests (American Psychiatric Association, 2000). There are five specific diagnoses within the autism spectrum disorders (see Table 3.1). Two of the disorders—Rett's disorder and childhood disintegrative disorder—are defined by a regression in skills (Corsello, 2005). The remaining three autism spectrum disorders include autism, Asperger's disorder (AD) and pervasive developmental disorder—not otherwise specified (PDD-NOS). PDD-NOS is sometimes referred to as "atypical autism" (Towbin, 1997). There is considerable overlap in the diagnostic criteria for the categories of autism, AD and PDD-NOS.

The Diagnostic and Statistical Manual of Mental Disorders, Fourth Edition, Text Revision (*DSM-IV-TR*: American Psychiatric Association, 2000), provides the criteria for the diagnosis of ASD (see Table 3.1). Until recently, a diagnosis of an ASD was generally not made until a child was 2½ to 3 years of age. Recent advances in early indicators of autism have, however, revealed behaviors that can distinguish infants with autism from typically developing infants as early as 1 year of age (Dawson, Osterling, Meltzoff, & Kuhl, 2000; Osterling & Dawson, 1994). The two behaviors most frequently noted in very young children that later received a diagnosis of autism were failure to participate in joint attention routines and failure to orient to name (Baranek, 1999; Werner, Dawson, Osterling, & Dinno, 2000).

Instruments used to diagnose autism have evolved and developed over the past 20 years, contributing to more effective differential diagnosis. The most used instruments today include the Autism Diagnostic Interview–Revised (ADI–R: Lord, Rutter, & Le Couteur, 1994), the Autism Diagnostic Observation Schedule–Generic (Lord et al., 2000), and the Diagnostic Interview for Social and Communication Disorders (Wing, Leekam, Libby, Gould, & Larcombe, 2002). In addition, there are several screening tools that are available for use. The Checklist for Autism in Toddlers (CHAT: Baron-Cohen, Allen, & Gillberg, 1992) has been the most rigorously researched and validated of the available screening instruments (Chakrabarti, Haubus, Dugmore, Orgill, & Devine, 2005).

Despite advances in early identifying behaviors and the development of sophisticated diagnostic and screening instruments, accurate differential diagnosis of ASD remains difficult and is often delayed. Many children continue to go undiagnosed or misdiagnosed until they are 3 or 4 years old (Brogan & Knussen, 2003). Some clinicians are hesitant to

TABLE 3.1 Overview of Diagnostic Criteria

Diagnosis	Characteristics
Autistic Disorder	1. *Qualitative impairment in social interaction* A. Impairment in use of nonverbal behaviors to regulate behavior B. Failure to develop age appropriate peer relationships C. Lack of spontaneous seeking to share enjoyment D. Lack of social or emotional reciprocity 2. *Qualitative impairment in communication* A. Delay or total lack of the development of spoken language B. Marked inability to initiate or sustain conversation, even with adequate speech C. Stereotyped or repetitive use of language D. Lack of spontaneous make-believe play 3. *Restrictive, repetitive, and stereotyped patterns of behaviors, interests, and activities* A. Preoccupation with one or more patterns of interests B. Inflexible adherence to nonfunctional routines C. Stereotyped and repetitive motor mannerisms D. Persistent preoccupation with parts of objects 4. *Onset of abnormal functioning prior to 3 years of age*
Rett's Disorder	1. *All of the following:* A. Apparently normal prenatal and perinatal development B. Apparently normal psychomotor development through the first 5 months after birth C. Normal head circumference at birth 2. *Onset of all of the following after the period of normal development:* A. Deceleration of head growth at 5–48 months of age B. Loss of previously acquired purposeful hand skills between 5 and 30 months, with subsequent development of stereotyped hand movements C. Early loss of social engagement D. Appearance of poorly coordinated gait or trunk movements E. Severely impaired expressive and receptive language development with severe psychomotor retardation
Childhood Disintegrative Disorder	1. *Apparently normal development for at least the first 2 years after birth*, as manifested by age-appropriate verbal and nonverbal communication, social relationships, play, and adaptive behavior 2. *Clinically significant loss of previously acquired skills* before 10 years of age in at least two of the following areas: A. Expressive or receptive language B. Social skills or adaptive behavior C. Bowel or bladder control D. Play E. Motor skills 3. *Abnormal functioning in at least two of the following areas:* A. Qualitative impairment in social interaction (see Autistic Disorder) B. Qualitative impairment in communication (see Autistic Disorder) C. Restricted, repetitive, and stereotyped patterns of behavior, interests, and activities
Asperger's disorder	1. *Qualitative impairment in social interaction* A. Impairment in use of nonverbal behaviors to regulate behavior B. Failure to develop age-appropriate peer relationships C. Lack of spontaneous seeking to share enjoyment D. Lack of social or emotional reciprocity 2. *Restrictive, repetitive, and stereotyped patterns of behaviors, interests, and activities* A. Preoccupation with one or more patterns of interests

B. Inflexible adherence to nonfunctional routines

C. Stereotyped and repetitive motor mannerisms

D. Persistent preoccupation with parts of objects

3. The disturbance causes *a clinically significant impairment in social, occupational, or other important areas of functioning*

4. There is *no clinically significant general delay of language*

5. There is *no clinically significant delay in cognitive development or in the development of age-appropriate self-help skills or adaptive behavior*

Pervasive Developmental Disorder—Not Otherwise Specified (PDD-NOS)	This category is used *when there is a severe and pervasive impairment in the development of reciprocal social interaction or verbal and nonverbal communication; or when stereotyped behavior, interests, and activities are present, but the criteria are not met for specific pervasive developmental disorder, schizophrenia, schizotypal personality disorder, or avoidant personality disorder.*

Note. Adapted from *DSM IV* (American Psychiatric Association, 1994).

discuss the possibility of autism because they anticipate family distress and assume adverse side effects of labeling the child (Filipek et al., 1999). However, families universally prefer to be informed about a diagnosis of autism as early as possible (Marcus & Stone, 1993). Furthermore, it has been well established that early intervention yields the most successful outcomes (Dawson & Osterling, 1997; Filipek et al., 2000).

Currently, the best estimate of the prevalence of ASD in children under the age of 8 years is approximately 60 in 10,000, or 1 in every 166 children (Fombonne, 2005). It is clear that the prevalence of ASD has increased in the past 15 years. What is not clear is the reason for this increase. Expanded diagnostic criteria, improved diagnostic tools and instruments, better awareness, and possible environmental and genetic factors have all been discussed as possible contributing factors (Rutter, 2005; Blaxill, 2004).

ASD can occur at all levels of intelligence, although 40% of people with ASD function in the range of mental retardation (Fombonne, 2005). It is four times more common in boys than in girls (Fombonne, 2005). There is a higher incidence of autism in siblings and family members, suggesting a strong genetic component (Bailey et al., 1995; Rutter, 2005). ASD is commonly associated with other developmental disabilities such as fragile X syndrome and tuberous sclerosis (Rutter, Silberg, O'Connor, & Simonoff, 1999; Wiznitzer, 2004). Almost one third of people with autism will develop epilepsy by adolescence (McDermott et al., 2005).

EARLY DEVELOPMENT

Joint Attention

Joint attention is the ability to use eye contact and pointing for the social purpose of sharing experiences with others. Typical infants demonstrate, from very early in life, a predisposition for focusing on eye gaze, facial expression, gestures, and caregivers' voice (Bushnell, Sai, & Mullin, 1989; Hains & Muir, 1996; Mundy & Neal, 2001).

Joint attention begins with face-to-face affective exchanges between the infant and caregiver. By 6 months of age, the infant becomes interested in objects in the environment. This is followed shortly by the coordination of the child's and caregiver's attention to a third object or event. These early triadic exchanges characterize communication between 6 and 18 months of age (Bakeman & Adamson, 1986).

A typical infant is able to follow a caregiver's point or eye gaze by 9 months of age. By

1 year, a child will begin to demonstrate protoimperative pointing (pointing to get an object). Protodeclarative pointing follows a few months later. The goal of protodeclarative pointing is to direct an adult's attention to an object or event of interest simply for the purpose of sharing this interest (Corkum & Moore, 1998).

Joint attention plays a critical role in the development of language, communication, and social interaction (Baldwin, 1991). Reading facial expressions and intonation in others helps the young child perceive emotional states, which, in turn, allows the child to perceive new events with fear or happiness. More importantly, it contributes to the development of social communication such as sharing experiences and expressing empathy (Vander Zanden, 1993).

Joint attention is important for appreciating a speaker's intention and perspective. By 16–19 months of age, a typical child is sensitive to a caregiver's nonverbal cues such as eye gaze or gestures as a source of information about the reference of novel objects (Baldwin, 1991). This is critical to allow the young language learner to accurately map words on to novel objects, given the infinite possibilities in the environment.

There is an abundance of research demonstrating a breakdown or failure to develop joint attention skills in children with ASD (Mundy et al., 1994; Osterling & Dawson, 1994; Werner, Dawson, Osterling, & Dinno, 2000). Differences in early joint attention behaviors become apparent in young children with ASD by approximately 1 year of age. Children with ASD fail to attend to attentional cues such as eye gaze, pointing, and gestures (Klin, Chawarska, Ruben, & Volkmar, 2004). They do not respond preferentially to a caregiver's voice (Lord, 1995; Dawson, Meltzoff, Osterling, & Rinaldi, 1998). Children with ASD have difficulty shifting gaze between people and objects and demonstrate little or no proto-declarative pointing (Werner et al., 2000). In a study examining word learning, Baron-Cohen, Baldwin, and Crowson (1997) found that children with autism made frequent mapping errors because of their inability to follow the eye gaze or pointing of others.

Research suggests that joint attention skills can serve as predictors of later language abilities (Baldwin, 1991; Mundy & Crowson, 1997). Measures of joint attention behaviors now serve as powerful prognostic indicators, allowing for earlier identification of children with ASD (Baron-Cohen, Cox, Baird, Swettenham, & Nightingale, 1996).

Early Regression vs. Nonregression

When Leo Kanner first described autism, he suggested that it was a disorder present from birth (Kanner, 1943). Until recently, however, little was actually known about the early development, as diagnosis was usually not made until the 3rd or 4th year of life. Clinicians and researchers were forced to rely upon parent recall of the course of development during the first two years of life. Many parents reported being aware of differences from the beginning and noted that these problems gradually became more severe (Hoshino et al., 1987). Others, however, described onset as occurring almost overnight; there was normal or even precocious development, followed by a sudden and dramatic loss of skills (Hoshino et al., 1987; Rogers & DiLalla, 1990).

These two distinct patterns of development have been validated using detailed parent interview protocols and tools, review of early home videos, as well as tracking from birth infants who were at risk of autism based on to familial history (Osterling & Dawson, 1994; Werner, Dawson, Munson, & Osterling, 2005). It has been estimated that anywhere between 20% and 47% of individuals with autism exhibit late-onset patterns (Davidovitch, Glick, Holtzman, Tirosh, & Safir, 2000; Lord, 1995). Furthermore, following regression, these children rarely regain skills immediately, and few, if any, demonstrate full recovery (Rapin & Katzman, 1998).

These two groups of children may represent distinct subgroups of autism with potentially very different underlying etiologies. Of significant interest to parents and clinicians
is the question of whether these two subgroups of children experience different outcomes (Werner et al., 2005). To date, studies have resulted in inconsistent findings with
respect to outcomes in relation to early versus late onset. Some studies found that the
late-onset or regression group was more severely impaired in speech and language as well
as in social skills compared to the early-onset or nonregression group (Brown & Prelock,
1995; Rogers & DiLalla, 1990). Davidovitch et al. (2000) found that more of the children
in the regression group developed verbal communication skills when compared to the
nonregression group. Still others found no differences between the groups (Werner et al.,
2005).

SPEECH, LANGUAGE, AND COMMUNICATION SKILLS

Although the behavioral characteristics of autism and related disorders vary considerably,
one consistent problem area is in the acquisition and use of language (Lord & Paul, 1997;
Rutter & Schopler, 1987). Many individuals with autism perform within normal limits on
nonverbal intelligence tests yet demonstrate severely impaired or restricted use of language
(Gluer & Pagin, 2003; Wetherby, Prizant, & Schuler, 2000). The unique speech and language problems present in children with autism have attracted significant attention developmental psycholinguists. However, the precise nature of these deficits has not yet been
delineated.

There is great heterogeneity across cognitive, linguistic, and behavioral functioning
within and across individuals with autism. Estimates indicate that approximately 35% of
children with autism may not develop functional speech (Mesibov, Adams, & Klinger,
1997). Anywhere from 40% to 75% of individuals diagnosed with autism have IQ scores
consistent with a diagnosis of mental retardation (Frith, 1989; Zelazo, 2001). The variability
and nature of the language deficits remain present, however, even in children with an IQ
that is within normal limits. Therefore, the language deficits cannot be simply accounted
for by deficits in general intelligence (Chan, Cheung, Leung, Cheung, & Cheung, 2005).
The best approach for determining cognitive and linguistic deficits specific to autism is to
focus on the higher functioning subgroup of individuals with autism spectrum disorders
(Lord & Paul, 1997; Rutter, 1983; Tager-Flusberg, 1985a, 1985b). This subgroup of individuals provides researchers with an opportunity to identify those characteristic deficits
that are unique to autism and are not the result of more general cognitive impairments.
Although these findings may not be generalizable to the entire population of individuals
diagnosed with autism and related disorders, this may be a starting point for research with
the other more severely impaired subgroups.

Articulation and Prosody

Delayed onset of speech is typical in children with autism. Despite this delay, children with
autism seem to demonstrate normal speech acquisition patterns and typical phonological
errors (Bartak, Rutter, & Cox, 1975; Gluer & Pagin, 2003; Kjelgaard & Tager-Flusberg,
2001). Thus, the phonological development of children with autism is appropriate for their
developmental levels. These findings, however, have been questioned with more recent
research. Flipsen (1999) found that 33% of high-functioning adolescents and adults with
autism and Asperger syndrome exhibited distortion errors. This is compared to estimates of
1–2% in the typical adult population. One of the problems with the earlier findings was that

researchers focused exclusively on children in preschool and elementary school (Flipsen, 1999; Shriberg et al., 2001).

Verbal individuals with autism demonstrate deficits in the comprehension and use of prosody (Shriberg, et al., 2001). These deficits typically persist over time, despite improvements in other aspects of speech and language (Simmons & Baltaxe, 1975).

Abnormal prosody has been shown to negatively affect the perception of social and communicative competence of a speaker (Paul et al., 2004; Shriberg et al., 2001). Furthermore, it has been reported that the atypical prosody of individuals with autism is the factor that most immediately creates an impression of oddness (Mesibov, 1992).

Prosody can be examined in three general categories: grammatical prosody, marking syntactic information within a sentence; pragmatic prosody, used to carry social information beyond what is conveyed in the sentence; and affective prosody, the change in register conveying speaker's general feelings. Paul, Augustyn, Klin, and Volkmar (2005) examined 30 individuals with autism who ranged in age from 10 to 49 years. They found that all of the speakers with ASD demonstrated significant problems with pragmatic and affective prosody. Problems with grammatical prosody were also noted.

Semantics

Semantic problems have been noted in children with autism at the earliest stages of language acquisition. The first words acquired by children with autism are generally names for concrete objects, such as "cookie" and "car." Noticeably absent from early vocabularies of children with autism are words such as "up," "more," or "all gone" (Menyuk & Quill, 1985).

Although it is clear that children with autism demonstrate semantic deficits, there are conflicting views as to the nature of these deficits. In a series of experiments examining naming and categorization skills, children with autism performed similarly to mental-age-matched control groups (Tager-Flusberg, 1985a; Ungerer & Sigman, 1987). These results suggest that the semantic deficits present in children with autism are a result of cognitive deficits and are not unique to autism.

Other findings, however, indicate that children with autism demonstrate semantic deficits that cannot be accounted for by cognitive deficits. Children with autism fail to use semantic information to aid in encoding verbal information and to recall information (Bowler, Matthews, & Gardiner, 1997; Tager-Flusberg, 1991). They are not able to recall words from a list of related words any better than from a list of unrelated word in free recall tasks (Tager-Flusberg, 1991). In addition, they rely on syntactic word order as opposed to semantic comprehension strategies when interpreting sentences (Paul, Fischer, & Cohen, 1988).

Although many children with autism demonstrate age-appropriate vocabulary skills as measured by standardized tests, there is compelling evidence that the underlying organization of the lexicon may be atypical and impoverished (Dunn & Bates, 2005; Gerenser, 2004; Kjelgaard & Tager-Flusberg, 2001). Dunn, Gomes, and Sebastian (1996) found that children with autism provided significantly fewer prototypical exemplars of categories in a word-fluency task when compared with typical developing children and language-impaired children matched on mental age. This apparent lack of organization within lexical categories could inhibit access to more prototypical exemplars.

Findings from more controlled online tasks also provide evidence of atypical lexical organization in children with autism. Gerenser (2004) used an online priming task to examine the lexical organization of children with autism. More specifically, naming reaction time was measured within a picture-naming task that included association primes (e.g., hat–head), category primes (e.g., nose–head) and identity primes (e.g., head–head). The results revealed significant differences within the association prime condition between the children with autism and the typically developing control group. Children with autism did not demonstrate the robust priming effect that is found in the typical population within association tasks. Differences have also been noted in semantic priming tasks. Kamio, Robins, Kelley, Swainson, and Fein (2007) examined naming reaction times in teens with autism and typically developing age-matched peers. The typical control group demonstrated significant priming effects for semantically related words, where as no effects were noted for the participants with autism.

Recent advances in electrophysiological research provide neurophysiologic support for these behavioral findings. Dunn and Bates (2005) found significant event-related potential (ERP) differences in responses by children with autism when compared to typically developing children. More specifically, the children with autism consistently failed to show a differentiation response to context-dependent words in a single-word semantic classification task.

Children with autism appear to rely on inflexible rule-based strategies to form novel categories (Klinger & Dawson, 1995, 2001). Children with autism and typically developing peers were given pictures of nonsense objects to sort into categories. In one condition, the children were given the rules for membership (e.g., big head; three eyes; yellow); in the other condition, they were not given any rules. When given the rules for category membership, both groups of children were able to categorize novel items. Typical children were also able to form novel categories using a prototype strategy in the "no rule" condition. The children with autism were unable to extract the common features of novel items to form prototypes.

Semantic development and processing is a complex and critical aspect of language (see chapter 16 by McGregor). Anecdotal information as well as recent research suggest that children with autism demonstrate unique deficits in semantic development and lexical processing. Further behavioral and electrophysiological research will be essential in the future in order to delineate the specific aspects of these deficits and guide future intervention.

Syntax

There are conflicting findings in the area of syntactic development. Some researchers have concluded that children with autism have no specific deficits in the comprehension and production of syntax (Gluer & Pagin, 2003; Tager-Flusberg, 1994; Waterhouse & Fein, 1982). The length and overall complexity of utterances seemed comparable to individuals with similar cognitive developmental levels.

A longitudinal study, spanning 2 years, compared six 3- to 6-year-old high-functioning children with autism with six mental-age-matched children with Down syndrome. The findings revealed similar syntactic development across the two groups (Tager-Flusberg et al., 1990). Furthermore, the development across the two groups did not differ from typical development.

Others, however, propose that there may be specific deficits in syntactic processing and development in children with autism (Boucher, 2003; Kjelgaard & Tager-Flusberg, 2001). For example, typically developing children are significantly better at recalling syntactically well-formed utterances, regardless of degree of semantic relatedness, than are children with autism (Ramando & Milech, 1984). In addition, children with autism use fewer grammatical morphemes than do typically developing children (Bartolucci, Pierce, & Streiner, 1980). Even when IQ scores and vocabulary scores are within normal limits, many children with autism demonstrate specific deficits in syntax on standardized language tests (Kjelgaard & Tager-Flusberg, 2001).

There remain many unresolved questions regarding the development and use of syntax in children with autism. In the past most of the research has examined only the most basic aspects of syntax, and findings have been mixed (see chapter 17 by Fletcher). The more recent findings demonstrating deficits in syntax and morphology that could not be accounted for by cognitive deficits have led to speculation about a possible link between specific language impairment (SLI) (see chapter 1 by Schwartz) and autism (Kjelgaard, & Tager-Flusberg, 2001). More research is necessary to determine whether similar linguistic profiles between some children with ASD and children with SLI demonstrate a superficial parallel or a specific subgroup of autism. It may be that the gene or genes involved in SLI are also involved in this subgroup of children with ASD (Kjelgaard & Tager-Flusberg, 2001).

Pragmatics

Deficits in social skills are one of the hallmark features defining autism. Thus, it is not surprising that individuals with ASD demonstrate significant problems in pragmatics. Pragmatics can be defined as the appropriate use of language in context (see chapter 18 by Fujiki & Brinton). More specifically, pragmatics refers to the conventions that govern language within social interactions (Prutting & Kirchner, 1987).

Deficits in pragmatics are seen across the entire autism spectrum. Even those individuals who develop advanced vocabulary skills and sophisticated grammar will have problems with the use of language in social situations (Klin & Volkmar, 1997). These social communication deficits often create a discrepancy between IQ and adaptive behavior (Volkmar, Klin, Schultz, Rubin, & Bronen, 2000). For example, an individual may have a score within normal limits on an IQ test but be unable to participate appropriately in a social conversation, or may get a college degree but not be able to keep a job due to the inability to respond to social cues.

Deficits in nonverbal communication skills are prominent in ASD. These deficits include problems with comprehension and use of gestures and intonation, an inability to read facial expressions, as well as qualitative issues with the use of eye contact (Lewy & Dawson, 1992; Mundy & Crowson, 1997). Eye contact issues typically involve a failure to make appropriate eye contact during conversations and in other social situations. In some cases, the individual overcompensates for a lack of eye contact by staring intently during a conversation. Much of what is communicated in social situations is done nonverbally. Thus, individuals on the autism spectrum often miss key information within social interactions.

Individuals with ASD have significant deficits in conversational skills (Loveland & Tunali, 1993). They demonstrate fewer initiations, frequent empty turns, as well as an inability to follow the topic or content of a conversation. This often leads to noncontextual or socially inappropriate comments (Klin & Volkmar, 1997). In addition, many individuals with ASD have problems with turntaking and perseveration of topics. They often have a difficult time recognizing and repairing breakdowns in communicative exchanges (Prizant & Rydell, 1993).

There is little debate as to the presence of a significant pragmatic language disorder in autism. One area that is under debate is the idea that there is a specific subgroup of children with ASD referred to as pragmatic language-impaired (PLI). PLI, previously referred to as semantic-pragmatic disorder, refers to a subgroup of children who demonstrate fluent expressive language skills with clear articulation but fail to use their language appropriately (Bishop, 2000). The question today involves the relationship between ASD, PLI, and SLI (Bishop & Norbury, 2002). There may be a closer relationship between

PLI and autism than between PLI and SLI; PLI may be a subgroup of autism, typically described as high-functioning autism (Shields, Varley, Broks, & Simpson, 1996).

An alternative to this concept is that some children with PLI may actually fall between the classifications of SLI and ASD (Bishop, 1998, 2000)—that is, these children demonstrate some aspects of SLI and some symptoms of autism, but they fail to reach diagnostic criteria for an autism spectrum disorder. The actual research exploring the relationship between SLI, PLI, and ASD is quite limited. Bishop and Norbury (2002) conducted the most extensive study to date. They examined 12 language-impaired children (ages 8–9 years) and found that some children met the criteria for PLI but did not meet the criteria for autism. This therefore contradicts the assumption that PLI is a subgroup of autism. Rather, they suggest that SLI, PLI, and ASD are on a continuum with no clear boundaries. It is likely that future research will reveal pragmatic deficits in language-impaired children with very different underlying causes (Bishop & Norbury, 2002).

Regardless of the specific diagnosis, any comprehensive language intervention program for individuals with ASD must address the challenges of social communication. In addition, careful evaluation of the child must involve the whole clinical picture, not just the communication impairment alone (Bishop & Norbury, 2002).

RELATED ISSUES

Echolalia

It has been estimated that more than 75% of verbal children with autism demonstrate echolalia, the repetition of what has been said by someone else (Prizant, 1983). This is a significantly higher incidence than in any other population of people who also demonstrate echolalia (e.g., mental retardation, schizophrenia). Echolalia can be immediate, or it can be delayed by hours or even days. As the child with autism develops more language, there is typically a reduction in the use of echolalia (McEvoy, Loveland, & Landry, 1988). Echolalia was once seen as nonfunctional and problematic (Lovaas, 1977). More recently, however, some aspects of echolalia have been shown to be quite functional and can actually play an important role in language and communication development (Prizant & Duchan, 1981; Prizant & Rydell, 1984). Echolalic utterances may actually be used with communicative intent (e.g., to request) before the individual with autism has learned the more appropriate words to use.

Even if some of the child's echolalic utterances may be functional and communicative, however, others may be nonfunctional and self-stimulatory in nature (Frith, 1998). It is essential, especially as the child grows older, to distinguish between echolalic utterances that are functional and communicative and those that are self-stimulatory and nonfunctional. There is an inverse relationship between the presence of high rates of self-stimulatory behavior and learning (Lovaas & Smith, 1989). Therefore, those behaviors determined to be self-stimulatory, including immediate and delayed echolalia, must be addressed programmatically to ensure the learning and development of more appropriate behaviors.

Deixis

Another unique aspect of the language of verbal individuals with autism is the difficulty with deictic terms. Deictic terms refer to places, times, or other participants in a conversation from the speaker's point of view. Deixis is the aspect of language that codes shifting reference. Personal or demonstrative pronouns, such as "I" and "you" or "this" and "that," depend on whether a person is a speaker or a listener. Other examples of deictic terms include terms such as here/there as well as temporal terms such as now and then. Typically developing children as young as 2 and 3 years of age are sensitive to deixis (Wales, 1986). There is evidence that speakers with autism have a great deal of difficulty with deictic terms from very early in development on through adulthood (Le Couteur et al., 1989; Lee, Hobson, & Chiat, 1994). One of the most frequently noted problems with deixis in autism is pronoun reversal. In the 1960s and 1970s the erroneous use of "I" and "you" was viewed as a problem in the identification of self (Bettelheim, 1967; Mahler, 1968). More recently, however, deficits in joint attention and perspective taking have been identified as the major factors that contribute to the problems with deixis in autism (Hemphill, Picardi, & Tager-Flusberg, 1991).

Play Skills

Play can be defined as an activity that is pleasurable, intrinsically motivational, flexible, nonliteral, and voluntary, and that involves active engagement (Wolfberg, 1999). Play skills in children with autism vary widely and appear to be influenced by the severity of autism and the degree of cognitive deficits. For some children, even the most basic object manipulation is severely impaired. Toys often occasion repetitive, nonfunctional, and concrete behaviors involving little or no imagination (Thomas & Smith, 2004; Stone et al., 1990). Children with ASD also demonstrate reduced frequency and complexity of pretend play (Rogers, Cook, & Meryl, 2005). In addition, they are more frequently engaged in solitary play activities as opposed to social play activities (Pierce-Jordan & Lifter, 2005).

Although the majority of the evidence suggests a wide array of play deficits in ASD, there are some conflicting findings. Most notably, there is some disagreement as to the extent of the deficits in pretend play. Some researchers have found that when controlling for cognitive abilities, children with ASD engaged in the same amount of pretend play as do their peers (Morgan, Maybery, & Durkin, 2003). Other conflicting results can be accounted for by variations in the definition of pretend play.

Despite some conflicting findings, play skills in most children with autism are qualitatively different from their age-matched and IQ-matched peers. These differences cannot be solely attributed to developmental delays (Rogers, Cook, & Meryl, 2005), and thus the underlying etiology of these deficits remains unclear. Deficits in joint attention, executive functioning, and theory of mind have all been proposed to underlie the play deficits in autism (Tager-Flusberg, 1999). However, there is no direct evidence for the relation of play deficits and each of these factors.

Jarrold, Boucher, and Smith (1993) suggested that executive functioning deficits were insufficient to account for play deficits in ASD. They argued that deficits in executive functioning would mean that the child would be less likely to rely on internal plans and to be more dependent on the investigation of external objects. Therefore, the children should be less likely to use objects in imaginative ways (e.g., using a banana as a telephone). Their results, however, indicated that children with autism were as skilled in using objects in imaginative ways as cognitively controlled peer groups. Furthermore, play skills in the children with ASD did not correlate with measures of theory of mind or of joint attention (Morgan et al., 2003). Specifically, many of the children (3 to 6 years of age) were able to demonstrate pretend play but unable to demonstrate theory of mind, as opposed to the age-matched control group, who were able to do both.

Deficits in play are frequently presented as a core diagnostic feature in autism. However, we still know relatively little about the nature of play in ASD, the severity and range of deficits across the spectrum, and the possible factors contributing to these deficits.

Hyperlexia

Hyperlexia has been defined as having word-recognition skills that are far above reading comprehension skills (Nation, 1999; Silberberg & Silberberg, 1967). The observation of exceptional reading skills in autism was first made by Kanner (1943). Even after 60 years, however, there remain more questions than answers about hyperlexia (for an excellent review, refer to Grigorenko, Klin, & Volkmar, 2003). Some investigators have proposed that hyperlexia is a subtype of dyslexia (Benton, 1978; Cohen, Campbell, & Gelardo, 1987). Others, however, believe it to be a subtype of a language impairment, not specific to ASD (Healy, Aram, Horowitz, & Kessler, 1982; Seymor & Evans, 1992).

Although hyperlexia is not exclusive to autism, it does occur at a higher frequency than in other groups (Grigorenko et al., 2003). The prevalence of hyperlexia in ASD is estimated to be between 5% and 10% (Burd & Kerkeshian, 1985). Children with ASD who have hyperlexia demonstrate an early and often obsessive interest in letters and in printed material in general (Nation, 1999). There is, however, a significant gap between the decoding abilities and comprehension.

One hypothesis concerning hyperlexia is that it is just one of many obsessive interests and is not tied directly to cognitive or linguistic factors (Klin et al., 2004). Instead, its maintenance reflects a reduced ability to make sense of social stimuli and a preference for unchanging, constantly interpretable stimuli, such as print. As the child develops better social skills and a capacity for social stimuli, the obsessive interest in letters and print diminishes.

THEORIES UNDERLYING CORE DEFICITS IN AUTISM

Extensive research has been conducted over the past three decades examining the genetic, neurological, behavioral, and cognitive foundations of autism. Genetic research to date suggests a polygenetic mode of inheritance with as many as 10–20 autism susceptibility genes involved (Minshew, Sweeney, Bauman, & Webb, 2005; Rutter, 2005; see also chapter 10 by Tomblin). Neurological research in autism has been greatly advanced in the past decade through the use of structural imaging, FMRI, and autopsy studies. Some of the most significant findings include evidence of early abnormalities in brain growth, which coincide with the onset of many clinical symptoms as well as evidence of underconnectivity of neocortical neural systems involved in social, communication, and reasoning abilities (Minshew et al., 2005).

There are four important cognitive theories that are prominent in the autism literature and attempt to explain the speech, language, and communication deficits in individuals with ASD.

One of the best-known perspectives, referred to as the mindblindness theory or theory of mind model (TOM model) was first described by Baron-Cohen and colleagues (Baron-Cohen, Leslie, & Frith, 1985). (For a comprehensive overview of this model, refer to Baron-Cohen et al., 2005.) This model suggests that the social communication deficits in autism reflect a fundamental impairment in the ability to understand the thoughts or intentions of others (Tager-Flusberg, 1999). By 4–5 years of age, typically developing children demonstrate theory of mind or the ability to understand the complex mental states of others (Leslie, 1987). There is considerable experimental evidence that children with autism fail to develop theory of mind, even at the most basic level (Baron-Cohen et al., 1985; Holroyd & Baron-Cohen, 1993). This failure to develop theory of mind is, in turn, thought to lead to the social and language impairments present in autism (Tager-Flusberg, 1999).

Although the model is compelling, there are some problems that must be considered. Some children with autism demonstrate language deficits that go beyond the inability to use language in social contexts. The theory of mind hypothesis fails to account for the grammatical, phonological, and semantic problems found in many individuals with autism (Tager-Flusberg, 1999). Furthermore, the theory of mind model does not provide an adequate explanation for some of the other deficits present in children with autism, such as executive function or perceptual processing difficulties (Burnette et al., 2005; Frith, 1989; Pennington & Ozonoff, 1991). Despite the limitations, the TOM account has provided both theoretical as well as practical benefits in understanding and treating the social and communication deficits in people with ASD (Happe, 2005).

The executive functions theory (EF) (Ozonoff, South, & Provencal, 2005) proposes that a general cognitive disturbance in executive function is central to autism (Pennington & Ozonoff, 1996). Specific executive functions include the ability to initiate behaviors while inhibiting competing responses that may interfere, the ability to regulate attention and filter distraction, and the ability to shift attention across relevant stimuli (Ozonoff, 1995). The primary EF deficit hypothesis argues that the symptoms observed in autism are consistent with breakdowns in EF related to frontal lobe damage (Hill, 2004; Pennington & Ozonoff, 1996). The research supporting the primary EF deficit hypothesis was, however, conducted primarily with school-aged children and adults. More recent research with young preschool children with autism failed to support the presence of specific EF deficits when compared with both chronological-age-matched and mental-age-matched peers (Dawson et al., 2002; Yerys, Hepburn, Pennington, & Rogers, 2007). These findings suggest that the EF deficits found in older children and adults may be secondary to the autism. It has been proposed that the delay in EF deficits may be the result of limitations of the social experiences needed to develop and refine EF skills (Dawson et al., 2002). Another perspective suggested that the deficits present in older individuals are primarily due to challenges in processing complex information, which would not be observable in young children due to the types of tasks employed with this population (Minshew & Goldstein, 2001; Williams, Goldstein, & Minshew, 2005).

Researchers propose that children fail theory of mind tasks because of a more general executive function deficit as opposed to a disturbance in theory of mind (Frye, Zelazo, & Palfai, 1995; Pennington & Ozonoff, 1996). There are a few problems with this conclusion. The first is that it fails to explain the individual with autism's ability to understand false photographs and maps while being unable to perform similar false belief tasks (Leslie & Thaiss, 1992). Deficits in executive functions should result in similar performance across both tasks. Second, it fails to offer an account for why some children with ASD demonstrate significant executive function deficits yet perform well on TOM tasks (Ozonoff, 1995).

Although the EF theory does not appear to be sufficient to account for all of the core deficits in autism, it is an important area of research that does effectively address some of the complex behaviors in autism. Future research in areas such as cognitive flexibility, working memory, and inhibition, as well as strategies for addressing these areas clinically, is already underway (Ozonoff et al., 2005).

The central coherence theory (Happe, 2005) is a third model that attempts to account for the core deficits present in autism (Frith, 1989; Frith & Happe, 1994). Typically developing children are able to interpret information rapidly because of automatic and implicit coherent processing (Frith, 1989). This model proposes that children with autism demonstrate weak central coherence. Thus, these children tend to focus on individual pieces of information as opposed to more holistic processing. There is considerable evidence for piecemeal processing in this population (Plaisted, Swettenham, & Rees, 1999; Jolliffe & Baron-Cohen, 2001). For example, children with autism demonstrate superior performance on block design or embedded figure tasks—two tasks that favor piecemeal processing—when compared to mental-age-matched peers (Morgan, Maybery, & Durkin, 2003). In addition, children with autism do poorly on tasks that require more holistic processing, such as disambiguation tasks or drawing inferences (Happe, 1997; Jolliffe & Baron-Cohen, 1999).

The central coherence theory provides insight into the learning styles of individuals with autism and could, in turn, help to inform teachers and clinicians working with this population. As with each of the theories presented, the central coherence theory is insufficient to account of all of the core deficits present in ASD. For example, there are some individuals with autism who appear to have theory of mind, pretend play skills, and joint attention skills, yet demonstrate the inability to process information holistically (Happe, 2005). It is very likely that the central coherence theory explains one component of a complex set of cognitive neural mechanisms or systems working together.

The social orienting model (Mundy & Burnette, 2005), is based on two key assumptions regarding early development. The first primary assumption is that typically developing children are predisposed to attend preferentially to social stimuli over nonsocial stimuli (Blass, 1999). The second assumption is that the early and pervasive deficits in joint attention in children with autism reflect a basic disturbance in this preference for social information (Mundy & Burnette, 2005; Mundy & Neal, 2001). There is considerable evidence of joint attention deficits in young children with autism (Baron-Cohen et al., 1996; Mundy, 1995; Osterling & Dawson, 1994).

In addition to the deficits in joint attention, there is evidence that children with autism do not attend preferentially to social information. For example, children with autism do not show a preference for speech over nonspeech (Klin, 1991). Dawson, Meltzoff, Osterling, Rinaldi, and Brown (1998) found that children with autism failed to orient preferentially to social stimuli such as clapping versus nonsocial stimuli such as shaking a rattle.

The social orienting and joint attention deficits in young children with autism deprive them of the social information necessary for typical neurodevelopment (Mundy & Burnette, 2005; Mundy & Neal, 2001). The loss of critical social input distorts or disrupts typical symbolic and social cognitive development (Mundy, 1995). The social orienting and joint attention deficits lead to secondary neurological disturbances. Over time, the child moves further and further off the path of normal development.

As with the first three theories, this proposal provides a compelling explanation for the language and social deficits in autism. However, it fails to account for some of the more unique learning characteristics described within the central coherence model. It seems clear from this review that the answers we are looking for to explain the complex and multifaceted disorder of autism will not fall within one single cognitive theory. Several independent cognitive deficits may collectively account for the core deficits present in individuals with autism, and the answer probably lies somewhere in all of these models. Future research should continue to examine these different models as well as the relationships among them to derive a more comprehensive picture of the autism spectrum disorders.

INTERVENTION

There has been a great deal written over the past decade regarding the treatment of speech and language skills of individuals with autism (for an in-depth review of communication intervention, see Corsello, 2005; Goldstein, 2002). Interventions range from behavioral approaches to developmental and social pragmatic models. A thorough review of the underlying theoretical foundations, as well as in-depth overview of the actual approaches, is beyond the scope of this chapter. The reader is referred to the following sources for reviews: for the traditional behavior approach (Lovaas, 2002); natural behavior approach (Koegel, 1995); developmental approach (Gerber, 2003), and social-pragmatic approach (Prizant, Wetherby, & Rydell, 2000).

There is evidence that supports the use of more traditional behavioral approaches, such as discrete trial instruction, and the more naturalistic behavioral interventions, such as natural learning paradigm, to successfully address the speech language deficits in individuals with autism (Buffington, Krantz, McClannahan, & Poulson, 1998; Koegel, O'Dell, & Dunlap, 1988; Lasky, Charlop, & Schreibman, 1988; Lovaas, 1987). The developmental model, known as DIR (developmental, individual difference, relationship-based) or "floor-time" (Greenspan, 1997; Greenspan & Wieder, 1998), and the SCERTS (social communication, emotional regulation, and transactional support) model (Prizant, Wetherby, & Rydell, 2000) are frequently discussed in the literature as interventions for the communication deficits in individuals with autism. Both intervention models are comprehensive and focus on the range of challenges present in learners on the autism spectrum. Although there is little scientific evidence available for either model, both have anecdotal support. Greenspan and Wieder (1997) reviewed charts of a large number of children who had received DIR and found progress across the majority of participants. The SCERTS model has evolved over the years in response to ongoing research focusing on the learning characteristics children with autism. However, as with the DIR approach, support for this SCERTS remains anecdotal in nature.

The use of augmentative/alternative communication (AAC) to support speech–language development in autism has also been found effective. There is evidence that the use of the Picture Exchange Communication System (PECS; Bondy & Frost, 1994), sign language, and other visual systems can enhance the speech, language, and communication of individuals with autism (Charlop-Christy, Carpenter, Le, LeBanc, & Keller, 2003; Konstantantareas, 1984; Layton & Baker, 1981).

Facilitated communication (FC) is not a form of AAC that has any empirical support. FC, first identified in Australia and later popularized in the United States (Biklen, 1990; Crossley, 1992), involves a facilitator providing physical support on the hand, arm, or shoulder of a person with autism as he types on a keyboard. Proponents of FC have made remarkable claims of extraordinary literacy and cognitive abilities in people with ASD and that their failure to express themselves was due largely to motor limitations (Biklen, Morton, & Gold, 1992; Biklen & Schubert, 1991). Due to the widespread and controversial claims made by the FC community, as well as the weak theoretical underpinnings (Hudson, 1995), there has been considerable experimental evaluation. More than 15 well-controlled evaluations conducted over the past decade have failed to find any support for the efficacy of FC (Mostert, 2001). Nevertheless, despite the lack of any credible evidence, FC continues to find support in the autism community.

Due to the great variability in the language profiles within ASD, careful evaluation of each individual is essential. In addition, understanding the variables that may underlie some of the unique deficits is critical. For example, many individuals with ASD have difficulty processing transient input such as speech (Frith, 1989, Quill, 1997). This can play a significant role in the development of both receptive and expressive language. Problems with the development of joint attention adversely affect language development (Baron-Cohen et al., 1997; Mundy & Crowson, 1997). Other learning characteristics that must be considered include issues of stimulus overselectivity (Lovaas, Koegel, & Schreibman, 1979), problems with motivational variables and social contingencies (Lovaas & Smith, 1989), as well as reduced observation learning and imitation skills (Rogers & Pennington, 1991).

There remains considerable debate and controversy over which interventions should be used for individuals with autism. Although some models of intervention have more empirical evidence supporting their efficacy, to date there is no evidence that indicates one approach is superior (Corsello, 2005). No one treatment is appropriate for all individuals. The individual's strengths, deficits, and unique learning profile should guide the practitioner to select the intervention strategies. The only two consistent findings regarding intervention and the attainment of the best outcomes are that the intervention must begin early and it must be intensive (Dawson & Osterling, 1997).

CONCLUSION

Speech and language, communication, and social deficits are the defining characteristics of individuals with ASD. As we make progress in understanding these deficits, we will also make progress in treatment and intervention. Many questions remain about the relative effectiveness of the current intervention models. As we enter the era of evidence-based practice, it will be critical that interventions with little formal empirical support be critically evaluated. It is very probable that specific interventions will work better with specific types of children with autism. It will be important that applied research in treatment efficacy delineate or identify the specific types of children and their cognitive and behavioral profiles that benefit from the intervention. The one aspect of intervention that we do know with certainty is that it must begin as early as possible and must be delivered with a high level of intensity.

Another important area for future research will be to better understand the exact nature of the core deficits in autism. Although there are at least four compelling cognitive theories that attempt to account for the core deficits, none is yet sufficient to account for the complex behaviors in autism. In fact, it is much more likely these theories are interrelated, and all contribute in some way to the multifaceted disorder of autism.

Understanding early-appearing markers of autism, especially in the area of joint attention, will be critical to early identification and intervention. Since we know that early intervention is essential to achieving the best outcomes for this population, any research that would allow earlier identification would be important. To date, most children are not identified until at least 18–24 months of age, allowing valuable time to pass before intervention can be initiated.

Individuals with autism spectrum disorders represent a diverse and heterogeneous group. It is quite likely that there are distinct subgroups with different etiologies and behavioral characteristics (Kjelgaard & Tager-Flusberg, 2001), and research into identifying the possible subgroups of ASD will be very important. In addition to helping delineate possible genetic and neurological influences, defining clear subgroups would contribute to subject definition within research and possibly provide insights into intervention strategies.

Individuals with ASD will continue to challenge researchers and clinicians with their complex profiles and diverse characteristics. It will only be through continued investigation of this population that we will gain the knowledge needed to provide optimal and effective interventions for all individuals on the autism spectrum.

REFERENCES

American Psychiatric Association (1994). *Diagnostic and statistical manual of mental disorders* (4th ed.). Washington, DC: Author.

American Psychiatric Association (2000). *Diagnostic and statistical manual of mental disorders* (4th ed.–text revision). Washington, DC: Author.

Bailey, A., Le Couteur, A., Gottesman, J., Bolton, P., Simonoff, E., Yuzda, F. Y., et al. (1995). Autism as a strong genetic disorder: Evidence from a British twin study. *Psychological Medicine, 25,* 63–77.

Baldwin, D. A. (1991). Infants' contribution to the achievement of joint reference. *Child Development, 62,* 875–890.

Bakeman, R., & Adamson, L. B. (1986). Infants' conventionalized acts: Gestures and words with mothers and peers. *Infant Behavior and Development, 9,* 215–230.

Baranek, G. T. (1999). Autism during infancy: A retrospective video analysis of sensory-motor and social behavior at 9–12 months of age. *Journal of Autism and Developmental Disorders, 29,* 213–224.

Baron-Cohen, S., Allen, J., & Gillberg, C. (1992). Can autism be detected at 18 months of age? The needle, the haystack and the CHAT. *British Journal of Psychiatry, 161,* 839–843.

Baron-Cohen, S., Baldwin, D. A., & Crowson, M. (1997). Do children with autism use the speaker's direction of gaze strategy to crack the code of language? *Child Development, 69,* 49–57.

Baron-Cohen, S., Cox, A., Baird, G., Swettenham, J., & Nightingale, N. (1996). Psychological markers in the detection of autism in infancy in a large population. *British Journal of Psychiatry, 168,* 158–163.

Baron-Cohen, S., Leslie, A. M., & Frith, U. (1985). Does the autistic child have a "theory of mind"? *Cognition, 21,* 37–46.

Baron-Cohen, S., Wheelwright, S., Lawson, J., Griffin, R., Ashwin, C., Billington, J., & Chakrabarti, B. (2005). Empathizing and systemizing in autism spectrum conditions. In F. R. Volkmar, R. Paul, A. Klin, & D. Cohen (Eds.), *Handbook of autism and pervasive developmental disorders.* Hoboken, NJ: Wiley.

Bartak, L., Rutter, M., & Cox, A. (1975). A comparative study of infantile autism and specific developmental receptive disorders: I: The children. *British Journal of Psychiatry, 126,* 127–145.

Bartolucci, G., Pierce, S., & Streiner, D. (1980). Cross-sectional studies of grammatical morphemes in autistic and mentally retarded children. *Journal of Autism and Developmental Disorders, 10,* 39–50.

Benton, A. L. (1978). Some conclusions about dyslexia. In A. L. Benton & D. Pearl (Eds.), *Dyslexia: An appraisal of current knowledge.* New York: Oxford University Press.

Bettelheim, B. (1967). *The empty fortress.* New York: Free Press.

Biklen, D. (1990). Communication unbound: Autism and praxis. *Harvard Educational Review, 60,* 291–314.

Biklen, D., Morton, M., & Gold, D. (1992). Facilitated communication: Implications for individuals with autism. *Topics in Language Disorders, 12,* 1–28.

Biklen, D., & Schubert, A. (1991). New words: The communication of students with autism. *RASE: Remedial and Special Education, 12,* 46–57.

Bishop, D. V. M. (1998). Development of the Children's Communication Checklist (CCC): A method for assessing qualitative aspects of communicative impairment in children. *Journal of Child Psychology and Psychiatry, 39,* 879–891.

Bishop, D. V. M. (2000). Pragmatic language impairment: A correlate of SLI, a distinct subgroup, or part of the autistic continuum. In D. V. M. Bishop & L. B. Leonard (Eds.), *Speech and language impairment in children: Causes, characteristics, intervention, and outcome.* Hove, UK: Psychology Press.

Bishop, D. V. M., & Norbury, C. F. (2002). Exploring the borderlands of autistic disorder and specific language impairment: A study using standardized diagnostic instrument. *Journal of Child Psychology and Psychiatry, 43,* 917–929.

Blass, E. (1999). The ontogeny of human infant face recognition: Orogustatory, visual, and social influences. In P. Rochat (Ed.), *Early social cognition: Understanding others in the first months of life.* Mahwah, NJ: Lawrence Erlbaum Associates.

Blaxill, M. F. (2004). What's going on? The question of time trends in autism. *Public Health Reports, 119,* 536–551.

Bondy, A. S., & Frost, L. A. (1994). *The picture exchange communication system: Training manual.* Cherry Hill, NJ: Pyramid.

Boucher, J. (2003). Language development in autism. *International Journal of Pediatric Otorhino-laryngology, 67,* 159–163.

Bowler, D. M., Matthews, N. J., & Gardiner, J. M. (1997). Asperger's syndrome and memory: Similarity to autism but not amnesia. *Neuropsychologia, 35,* 65–70.

Brogan, C. A., & Knussen, C. (2003). The disclosure of a diagnosis of an autistic spectrum disorder. *Autism: The International Journal of Research and Practice, 7,* 31–48.

Brown, J., & Prelock, P. A. (1995). Brief report: The impact of regression on language development in autism. *Journal of Autism and Developmental Disorders, 25,* 305–309.

Buffington, D. M., Krantz, P. J., McClannahan, L. E., & Poulson, C. L. (1998). Procedures for teaching appropriate gestural communication skills to children with autism. *Journal of Autism and Developmental Disorders, 38,* 535–545.

Burd, L., & Kerkeshian, J. (1985). Inquiry into the incidence of hyperlexia in a statewide population of children with Pervasive Developmental Disorder. *Psychological Reports, 57,* 236–238.

Burnette, C. P., Mundy, P. C., Meyer, J. A., Sutton, S. K., Vaughan, A. E., & Charak, D. (2005). Weak central coherence and its relations to theory of mind and anxiety in autism. *Journal of Autism and Developmental Disorders, 35,* 63–73.

Bushnell, I. W. R., Sai, F., & Mullin, J. T. (1989). Neonatal recognition of the mother's face. *British Journal of Developmental Psychology, 7,* 3–15.

Chakrabarti, S., Haubus, C., Dugmore, S., Orgill, G., & Devine, F. (2005). A model of early detection and diagnosis of autism spectrum disorder in young children. *Infants and Young Children, 18,* 200–211.

Chan, A. S., Cheung, J., Leung, W. W. M., Cheung, R., & Cheung, M. (2005). Verbal expression and comprehension deficits in young children with autism. *Focus on Autism and Other Developmental Disabilities, 20,* 117–124.

Charlop-Christy, M. H., Carpenter, M., Le, L., LeBanc, L. A., & Keller, K. (2003). Using the picture exchange communication system (PECS) with children with autism: Assessment of PECS acquisition, speech, social-communicative behavior, and problem behavior. *Journal of Applied Behavior Analysis, 35,* 213–231.

Cohen, M., Campbell, R., & Gelardo, M. (1987). Hyperlexia: A variant of aphasia or dyslexia. *Pediatric Neurology, 3,* 22–28.

Corkum, V., & Moore, C. (1998). The origins of joint visual attention in infants. *Developmental Psychology, 34,* 28–38.

Corsello, C. M. (2005). Early intervention in autism. *Infants and Young Children, 18,* 74–85.

Crossley, R. (1992). Getting the words out: Case studies in facilitated communication training. *Topics in Language Disorders, 12,* 46–59.

Davidovitch, M., Glick, L., Holtzman, G., Tirosh, E., & Safir, M. P. (2000). Developmental regression in autism: Maternal perception. *Journal of Autism and Developmental Disorders, 30,* 113–119.

Dawson, G., Meltzoff, A., Osterling, J., & Rinaldi, J. (1998). Neuropsychological correlates of early symptoms of autism. *Child Development, 69,* 1276–1285.

Dawson, G., Meltzoff, A. N., Osterling, J., Rinaldi, J., & Brown, E. (1998). Children with autism fail to orient to naturally occurring social stimuli. *Journal of Autism and Developmental Disorders, 28,* 479–485.

Dawson, G., Munson, J., Estes, A., Osterling, J., McPartland, J., Toth, K., Carver, L., & Abbott, R. (2002). Neurocognitive function and joint attention abilities in young children with autism spectrum disorders versus developmental delay. *Child Development, 73,* 345–358.

Dawson, G., & Osterling, J. (1997). Early intervention in autism. In M. J. Guralnick (Ed.), *The effectiveness of early intervention.* Baltimore: Paul H. Brookes.

Dawson, G., Osterling, J., Meltzoff, A. M., & Kuhl, P. (2000). Case study of the development of an infant with autism from birth to two years of age. *Journal of Applied Developmental Psychology, 21,* 299–313.

Dunn, M. A., & Bates, J. C. (2005). Developmental change in neutral processing of words by children with autism. *Journal of Autism and Developmental Disorders, 35,* 361–376.

Dunn, M., Gomes, H., & Sebastian, M. (1996). Prototypicality of autistic and language disordered children in a word fluency task. *Child Neuropsychology, 2,* 98–108.

Filipek, P. A., Accardo, P. J., Ashwai, S., Baranek, G. T., Cook, E. H., Jr., Dawson, G. G., et al. (2000). Practice parameter: Screening and diagnosis of autism. Report of the Quality Standards Subcommittee of the American Academy of Neurology and the Child Neurology Society. *Neurology, 55*, 468–479.

Filipek, P. A., Accardo, P. J., Baranek, G. T., Cook, E. H., Jr., Dawson, G., Gordon, B., et al. (1999). The screening and diagnosis of autistic spectrum disorders. *Journal of Autism and Developmental Disorders, 29*, 439–484.

Flipsen, P., Jr. (1999). *Articulation rate and speech-sound normalization following speech delay.* Unpublished doctoral dissertation, University of Wisconsin-Madison.

Fombonne, E. (2005). Epidemiological studies of pervasive developmental disorders. In F. R. Volkmar, R. Paul, A. Klin, & D. Cohen (Eds.) *Handbook of autism and pervasive developmental disorders.* Hoboken, NJ: Wiley.

Frith, U. (1989). A new look at language and communication in autism. *British Journal of Disorders of Communication, 24*, 123–150.

Frith, U. (1998). What autism teaches us about communication. *Logopedics and Phoniatrics Vocology, 23*, 51–58.

Frith, U., & Happe, F. (1994). Autism: Beyond "theory of mind." *Cognition, 50*, 115–132.

Frye, D., Zelazo, P. D., & Palfai, T. (1995). Theory of mind and rule-based reasoning. *Cognitive Development, 10*, 483–527.

Gerber, S. (2003). A developmental perspective on language assessment and intervention for children on the autism spectrum. *Topics in Language Disorders, 23*, 72–95.

Gerenser, J. E. (2004). Lexical organization in children with autism. *Dissertation Abstracts International, 65*, 04B

Gluer, K., & Pagin, P. (2003). Meaning theory and autistic speakers. *Mind and Language, 18*, 23–51.

Goldstein, H. (2002). Communication intervention for children with autism: A review of treatment efficacy. *Journal of Autism and Developmental Disorders, 32*, 373–396.

Greenspan, S. (1997). *The growth of the mind and the endangered origins of intelligence.* Reading, MA: Addison Wesley Longman.

Greenspan, S. I., & Wieder, S. (1997). Developmental patterns and outcomes in infants and children with disorders in relating and communicating: A chart review of 200 cases of children with autistic spectrum diagnoses. *Journal of Developmental and Learning Disorders, 1*, 87–141.

Greenspan, S., & Wieder, S. (1998). *The child with special needs: Encouraging intellectual and emotional growth.* Reading, MA: Addison Wesley Longman.

Grigorenko, E. L., Klin, A., & Volkmar, F. (2003). Annotation: Hyperlexia: Disability or superability? *Journal of Child Psychology and Psychiatry and Allied Disciplines, 4*, 1079–1091.

Hains, S. M. J., & Muir, D. W. (1996). Infant sensitivity to adult eye direction. *Child Development, 67*, 1940–1951.

Happe, F. (1997). Central coherence and theory of mind in autism: Reading homographs in context. *British Journal of Developmental Psychology, 15*, 1–12.

Happe, F. (2005). The weak central coherence account of autism. In F. R. Volkmar, R. Paul, A. Klin, & D. Cohen (Eds.), *Handbook of autism and pervasive developmental disorders: Vol. 1.* Hoboken, NJ: Wiley.

Healy, J. M., Aram, D. M., Horowitz, S. J., & Kessler, J. W. (1982). A study of hyperlexia. *Brain and Language, 9*, 1–23.

Hemphill, L., Picardi, M., & Tager-Flusberg, H. (1991). Narrative as an index of communicative competence in mildly mentally retarded children. *Applied Psycholinguistics, 12*, 263–279.

Hill, E. L. (2004). Evaluating the theory of executive dysfunction in autism. *Developmental Review, 24*, 189–233.

Holroyd, S., & Baron-Cohen, S. (1993). Added Brief report: How far can people with autism go in developing a theory of mind? *Journal of Autism and Developmental Disorders, 23*, 379–385.

Hoshino, Y., Yokoyama, F., Watanabe, M., Murata, S., Kaneko, M., & Kumashiro, H. (1987). The diurnal variation and response to dexamethasone suppression test of saliva cortisol level in autistic children. *Japanese Journal of Psychiatry and Neurology, 41*, 227–235.

Hudson, A. (1995). Disability and facilitated communication: A critique. *Advances in Clinical Child Psychology*, *17*, 197–232.

Jarrold, C., Boucher, J., & Smith, P. (1993). Symbolic play in autism: A review. *Journal of Autism and Developmental Disorders*, *23*, 281–307.

Jolliffe, T., & Baron-Cohen, S. (1999). The strange stories: A replication of high functioning adults with autism or Asperger syndrome. *Journal of Autism and Developmental Disorders*, *29*, 395–406.

Jolliffe, T., & Baron-Cohen, S. (2001). A test of central coherence theory: Can adults with high-functioning autism or Asperger syndrome integrate fragments of an object. *Cognitive Neuropsychology*, *6*, 193–216.

Kamio, Y., Robins, D., Kelley, E., Swainson, B., & Fein, D. (2007). Atypical lexical/semantic processing in high-functioning autism spectrum disorders without early language delay. *Journal of Autism and Developmental Disorders*, *37*, 1116–1122.

Kanner, L. (1943). Autistic disturbance of affective contact. *Nervous Child*, *2*, 213–250.

Kjelgaard, M. M., & Tager-Flusberg, H. (2001). An investigation of language impairment in autism: Implications for genetic subgroups. *Language and Cognitive Processes*, *16*, 287–308.

Klin, A. (1991). Young autistic children's listening preferences in regard to speech: A possible characterization of the symptoms of social withdrawal. *Journal of Autism and Developmental Disorders*, *21*, 29–42.

Klin, A., Chawarska, K., Ruben, E., & Volkmar, F. R. (2004). Clinical assessment of toddlers at risk of autism. In R. Del Carmen-Wiggens & A. Carter (Eds.), *Handbook of infant and toddler mental health assessment*. Oxford, UK: Oxford University Press.

Klin, A. & Volkmar, F. R. (1997). Asperger's syndrome. In D. Cohen & F. R. Volkmar (Eds.), *Handbook of autism and pervasive developmental disorders*. New York: Wiley.

Klinger, L. G., & Dawson, G. (1995). A fresh look at categorization abilities in children with autism. In E. Schopler & G. Mesibov (Eds.), *Learning, memory, and cognition in autism*. New York: Plenum Press.

Klinger, L. G., & Dawson, G. (2001). Prototype formation in autism. *Developmental Psychopathology*, *13*, 111–124.

Koegel, L. K. (1995). Communication and language intervention. In R. L. Koegel & L. K. Koegel (Eds.), *Teaching children with autism: Strategies for initiating positive interactions and improving learning opportunities*. Baltimore: Paul H. Brookes.

Koegel, R. L., O'Dell, M. C., & Dunlop, G. (1988). Producing speech use in nonverbal autistic children by reinforcing attempts. *Journal of Autism and Developmental Disorders*, *18*, 525–538.

Konstantantareas, M. M. (1984). Sign language as a communication prosthesis with language impaired children. *Journal of Autism and Developmental Disorders*, *14*, 9–25.

Lasky, K., Charlop, M., & Schreibman, L. (1988). Training parents to use the natural learning paradigm to increase their autistic children's speech. *Journal of Applied Behavior Analysis*, *21*, 391–400.

Layton, T. L., & Baker, P. S. (1981). Development of semantic-syntactic relations in an autistic child. *Journal of Autism and Developmental Disorders*, *11*, 345–399.

Le Couteur, A., Rutter, M. L., Lord, C., Rios, P., Robertson, S., Holdgrafer, M., & McLennan, J. D. (1989). A standardized investigator-based instrument. *Journal of Autism and Developmental Disorders*, *19*, 363–387.

Lee, A., Hobson, R. P., & Chiat, S. (1994). I, you, me, and autism: An experimental study. *Journal of Autism and Developmental Disorders*, *24*, 155–176.

Leslie, A. (1987). Pretence and representation: The origins of "theory of mind." *Psychological Review*, *94*, 412–426.

Leslie, A. M., & Thaiss, L. (1992). Domain specificities in conceptual development: Neuropsychological evidence from autism. *Cognition*, *43*, 225–251.

Lewy, A. L., & Dawson, G. (1992). Social stimulation and joint attention in young autistic children. *Journal of Abnormal Child Psychology*, *20*, 555–566.

Lord, C. (1995). Follow up of two year olds referred for possible autism. *Journal of Child Psychology and Psychiatry and Allied Disciplines*, *36*, 1365–1382.

Lord, C., & Paul, R. (1997). Language and communication in autism. In D. J. Cohen, & F. R. Volkmar (Eds.), *Handbook of autism and pervasive developmental disorders* (2nd ed.). New York: Wiley.

Lord, C., Risi, S., Lambrecht, L., Cook, E. H., Leventhal, B. L., DiLavore, P. C., et al. (2000). The autism diagnostic observation scale-generic: A standard measure of the social and communication deficits associated with the spectrum of autism. *Journal of Autism and Developmental Disorders, 30,* 205–223.

Lord, C., Rutter, M. L., & Le Couteur, A. (1994). The Autism Diagnostic Interview–Revised: A revised version of a diagnostic interview for caregivers of individuals with possible pervasive developmental disorders. *Journal of Autism and Developmental Disorders, 24,* 659–685.

Lovaas, O. I. (1977). *The autistic child: Language development through behavior modification.* New York: Irvington Press.

Lovaas, O. I. (1987). Behavioral treatment and normal educational and intellectual functioning in young autistic children. *Journal of Consulting and Clinical Psychology, 55,* 3–9.

Lovaas, O. I. (2002). *Teaching individuals with developmental delays: Basic intervention techniques.* Austin, TX: PRO-ED.

Lovaas, O. I., Koegel, R. L., & Schreibman, L. (1979). Stimulus overselectivity: A review of the research. *Psychological Bulletin, 86,* 1236–1254.

Lovaas, O. I., & Smith, T. (1989). A comprehensive behavioral theory of autistic children: Paradigm for research and treatment. *Journal of Behavior Therapy and Experimental Psychiatry, 20,* 17–29.

Loveland, K. A., & Tunali, B. (1993). Narrative language in autism and the theory of mind hypothesis: A wider perspective. In S. Baron-Cohen, H. Tager-Flusberg, & D. Cohen (Eds.), *Understanding other minds: Perspectives from autism.* Oxford, UK: Oxford University Press.

Mahler, M. S. (1968). *On human symbolism and the vicissitudes of individualization: Infantile Psychosis.* New York: International Universities Press.

Marcus, L. M., & Stone, W. L. (1993). Assessment of the young autistic child. In E. Schopler & G. Mesibov (Eds.), *Preschool issues in autism.* New York: Plenum Press.

McDermott, S., Moran, R., Platt, T., Wood, H., Isaac, T., & Dasari, S. (2005). Prevalence of epilepsy in adults with mental retardation and related disabilities in primary care. *American Journal of Mental Retardation, 110,* 48–56.

McEvoy, R. E., Loveland, K. A., & Landry, S. H. (1988). Functions of immediate echolalia in autistic children. *Journal of Autism and Developmental Disorders, 18,* 657–688.

Menyuk, P., & Quill, K. (1985). Semantic problems in children with autistic children. In E. Schopler & G. Mesibov (Eds.), *Communication problems in children with autism.* New York: Plenum Press.

Mesibov, G. (1992). Treatment issues with high functioning adolescents with autism. In E. Schopler & G. Mesibov (Eds.), *High functioning individuals with autism.* New York: Plenum Press.

Mesibov, G. B., Adams, L. W., & Klinger, L. G. (1997). *Autism: Understanding the disorder.* New York: Plenum Press.

Minshew, N. J., & Goldstein, J. G. (2001). The pattern of impaired and intact memory functions in autism. *Journal of Child Psychology and Psychiatry, 42,* 1095–1101.

Minshew, N. J., Sweeney, J. A., Bauman, M. C., & Webb, S. S. (2005). Neurologic aspects of autism. In F. R. Volkmar, R. Paul, A. Klin, & D. Cohen (Eds.), *Handbook of autism and pervasive developmental disorders* (Vol. 1). Hoboken, NJ: Wiley.

Morgan, B., Maybery, M., & Durkin, K. (2003). Weak central coherence, poor joint attention, and low verbal ability: Independent deficits in early autism. *Developmental Psychology, 39,* 646–656.

Mostert, M. (2001). Facilitated communication since 1995: A review of published studies. *Journal of Autism and Developmental Disorders, 31,* 287–313.

Mundy, P. (1995). Joint attention and social-emotional approach behavior in children with autism. *Development and Psychopathology, 7,* 63–82.

Mundy, P., & Burnette, C. (2005). Joint attention and neurodevelopmental models of autism. In

F. R. Volkmar, R. Paul, A. Klin, & D. Cohen (Eds.), *Handbook of autism and pervasive developmental disorders* (Vol. 1). Hoboken, NJ: Wiley.

Mundy, P., & Crowson, M. (1997). Joint attention and early social communication: Implications for research on intervention with autism. *Journal of Autism and Developmental Disorders, 27,* 653–676.

Mundy, P., & Neal, A. R. (2001). Neural plasticity, joint attention, and a transactional social-orienting model of autism. In L. M. Glidden (Ed.), *International review of research in mental retardation.* San Diego, CA: Academic Press.

Mundy, P., Sigman, M., & Kasari, C. (1994). Joint attention, developmental level, and symptom presentation in autism. *Development and Psychopathology, 6,* 389–401.

Nation, K. (1999). Reading skills in hyperlexia: A developmental perspective. *Psychological Bulletin, 125,* 338–355.

Osterling, J., & Dawson, G. (1994). Early recognition of children with autism: A study of first birthday home video tapes. *Journal of Autism and Developmental Disorders, 24,* 247–257.

Ozonoff, S. (1995). Executive functions in autism. In E. Schopler & G. B. Mesibov (Eds.), *Learning and cognition in autism.* New York: Plenum Press.

Ozonoff, S., South, M., & Provencal, S. (2005). Executive functions. In F. R. Volkmar, R. Paul, A. Klin, & D. Cohen (Eds.), *Handbook of autism and pervasive developmental disorders* (Vol. 1). Hoboken, NJ: Wiley.

Paul, R., Augustyn, A., Klin, A., & Volkmar, F. R. (2005). Perception and production of prosody by speakers with autism spectrum disorders, *Journal of Autism and Developmental Disorders, 35,* 205–220.

Paul, R., Fischer, M. L., & Cohen, D. J. (1988). Brief report: Sentence comprehension strategies in children with autism and specific language disorders. *Journal of Autism and Developmental Disorders, 18,* 669–679.

Paul, R., Miles, S., Cicchetti, D., Sparrow, S., Klin, A., Volkmar, F., et al. (2004). Adaptive behavior in autism and pervasive developmental disorder—not otherwise specified: Microanalysis of scores on the Vineland Adaptive Behavior Scale. *Journal of Autism and Developmental Disorders, 34,* 223–228.

Pennington, B. F., & Ozonoff, S. (1991). A neuro-scientific perspective on continuity and discontinuity in developmental psychopathology. In D. Cicchetti & S. L. Toth (Eds.), *Rochester symposium on developmental psychopathology: Vol. 3. Models and integrations.* Rochester, NY: University of Rochester Press.

Pennington, B. F., & Ozonoff, S. (1996). Executive functions and developmental psychopathology. *Journal of Child Psychology and Psychiatry, 37,* 51–87.

Pierce-Jordon, S., & Lifter, K. (2005). Interaction of social and play behaviors in preschoolers with and without pervasive developmental disorder. *Topics in Early Childhood Special Education, 25,* 34–47.

Plaisted, K. C., Swettenham, J., & Rees, L. (1999). Children with autism show local precedence in a divided attention task and global precedence in a selective attention task. *Journal of Child Psychology and Psychiatry, 40,* 733–742.

Prizant, B. M. (1983). Echolalia in autism: Assessment and intervention. *Seminars in Speech and Language, 4,* 63–67.

Prizant, B. M., & Duchan, J. F. (1981). The function of immediate echolalia in autistic children. *Journal of Speech and Hearing Disorders, 46,* 241–249.

Prizant, B. M., & Rydell, P. J. (1984). An analysis of the function of delayed echolalia in autistic children. *Journal of Speech and Hearing Research, 27,* 183–192.

Prizant, B. M., & Rydell, P. J. (1993). Assessment and intervention considerations for unconventional verbal behavior. In J. Reichle & D. Wacker (Eds.), *Communicative alternatives to challenging behavior: Integrating functional assessment and intervention strategies.* Baltimore: Paul H. Brookes.

Prizant, B. M., Wetherby, A. M., & Rydell, P. J. (2000). Communication intervention issues for children with autism spectrum disorders. In A. Wetherby & B. Prizant (Eds.) *Autism spectrum disorders: A transactional developmental perspective.* Baltimore: Paul H. Brookes.

Prutting, C., & Kirchner, D. M. (1987). A clinical appraisal of pragmatic aspects of language. *Journal of Speech and Hearing Disorders, 52,* 105–119.

Quill, K. A. (1997). Instructional considerations for young children with autism: The rationale for visually cued instruction. *Journal of Autism and Developmental Disorders, 27,* 697–714.

Ramando, N., & Milech, D. (1984). The nature and specificity of the language coding deficit in autistic children. *British Journal of Psychology, 75,* 95–103.

Rapin, I., & Katzman R. (1998). Neurobiology of autism. *Annals of Neurology, 43,* 7–14.

Rogers, S. J., Cook, I., & Meryl, A. (2005). Imitation and play in autism. In F. R. Volkmar, R. Paul, A. Klin, & D. Cohen (Eds.), *Handbook of autism and pervasive developmental disorders* (Vol. 1). Hoboken, NJ: Wiley.

Rogers, S. J., & DiLalla, D. L. (1990). Age of symptom onset in young children with pervasive developmental disorders. *Journal of the American Academy of Child and Adolescent Psychiatry, 29,* 863–872.

Rogers, S. J., & Pennington, B. F. (1991). A theoretical approach to the deficits in infantile autism. *Development and Psychopathology, 3,* 137–162.

Rutter, M. (1983). Cognitive deficits in the pathogenesis of autism. *Journal of Child Psychology and Psychiatry, 24,* 513–531.

Rutter, M. (2005). Genetic influences and autism. In F. R. Volkmar, R. Paul, A. Klin, & D. Cohen (Eds.), *Handbook of autism and pervasive developmental disorders* (Vol. 1). Hoboken, NJ: Wiley.

Rutter, M., & Schopler, E. (1987). Autism and pervasive developmental disorders: Concepts and diagnostic issues. *Journal of Autism and Developmental Disorder, 17,* 159–183.

Rutter, M., Silberg, J., O'Connor, T., & Simonoff, E. (1999). Genetics and child psychiatry: II. Empirical research findings. *Journal of Child Psychology and Psychiatry, 40,* 19–55.

Seymor, P. H., & Evans, H. M. (1992). Beginning reading without semantics: A cognitive study of hyperlexia. *Cognitive Neuropsychology, 9,* 89–122.

Shields, J., Varley, R., Broks, P., & Simpson, A. (1996). Social cognition in developmental language disorders and high-level autism. *Developmental Medicine and Child Neurology, 38,* 487–495.

Shriberg, L. D., Paul, R., McSweeny, J. L., Klin, A., Cohen, D. J., & Volkmar, F. R. (2001). Speech and prosody characteristics of adolescents and adults with high functioning autism and Asperger syndrome. *Journal of Speech and Hearing Research, 44,* 1087–1115.

Silberberg, N. E., & Silberberg, M. C. (1967). Hyperlexia: Specific word recognition skills in young children. *Exceptional Child, 34,* 41–42.

Simmons, J., & Baltaxe, C. (1975). Language pattern in adolescent autistics. *Journal of Autism and Childhood Schizophrenia, 5,* 331–351.

Stone, W. L., Lemanek, K. L., Fishel, P. T., Fernández, M. C., & Altemeier, W. A. (1990). Play and imitation skills in the diagnosis of autism in young children, *Pediatrics, 86,* 267–272,

Tager-Flusberg, H. (1985a). Basic level and superordinate level categorization by autistic, mentally retarded, and normal children. *Journal of Experimental Psychology, 40,* 450–469.

Tager-Flusberg, H. (1985b). The conceptual basis for referential word meaning in children with autism. *Child Development, 56,* 1167–1178.

Tager-Flusberg, H. (1991). Semantic processing in the free recall of autistic children: Further evidence of a cognitive deficit. *Journal of Developmental Psychology, 9,* 413–430.

Tager-Flusberg, H. (1994). Dissociations in form and function in the acquisition of language by autistic children. In H. Tager-Flusberg (Ed.), *Constraints on language acquisition: Studies of atypical children.* Hillsdale, NJ: Lawrence Erlbaum Associates.

Tager-Flusberg, H. (1999). A psychological approach to understanding the social and language impairment in autism. *International Review of Psychiatry, 11,* 325–334.

Tager-Flusberg, H., Calkins, S., Nolin, T., Baumberger, T., Anderson, M., & Chadwick-Dias, A. (1990). A longitudinal study of language acquisition in autistic and Down syndrome children. *Journal of Autism and Developmental Disorders, 20,* 1–21.

Thomas, N., & Smith, C. (2004). Developing play skills in children with autistic spectrum disorders. *Educational Psychology in Practice, 20,* 195–206.

Towbin, K. E. (1997). Autism and Asperger's syndrome. *Current Opinion in Pediatrics, 9,* 361–366.

Ungerer, J. A., & Sigman, M. (1987). Categorization skills and receptive language development in autistic children. *Journal of Autism and Developmental Disorders, 17*, 3–16.

Vander Zanden, J. W. (1993). *Human development* (5th ed.). New York: McGraw-Hill.

Volkmar, F. R., Klin, A., Schultz, R., Rubin, E., & Bronen, R. (2000). Clinical case conference: Asperger's disorder, *American Journal of Psychiatry, 2*, 262–267.

Wales, R. (1986). Deixis. In P. Fletcher & G. Gorman (Eds.), *Language acquisition*. Cambridge: Cambridge University Press.

Waterhouse, L., & Fein, D. (1982). Language skills in developmentally disabled children. *Brain and Language, 15*, 307–333.

Werner, E., Dawson, G., Munson, J., & Osterling, J. (2005). Variation in early developmental course in autism and its relation with behavioral outcome at 3–4 years of age. *Journal of Autism and Developmental Disorders, 35*, 337–350.

Werner, E., Dawson, G., Osterling, J., & Dinno, N. (2000). Recognition of autism spectrum disorder before one year of age: A retrospective study based on home videotapes [Brief report]. *Journal of Autism and Developmental Disorders, 30*, 157–162.

Wetherby, A. M., Prizant, B. M., & Schuler, A. L. (2000). Understanding the nature of communication and language impairments. In A. M. Wetherby & B. M. Prizant (Eds.), *Autism spectrum disorders: A transactional developmental perspective*. Baltimore: Paul H. Brookes.

Williams, D. L., Goldstein, G., & Minshew, N. J. (2005). Impaired memory for faces and social scenes in autism: Clinical implications of the memory disorder. *Archives of Clinical Neuropsychology, 20*, 1015.

Wing, L., Leekam, S. R., Libby, S. J., Gould, J., & Larcombe, M. (2002). The Diagnostic Interview for Social and Communication Disorders: Background, inter-rater reliability and clinical use. *Journal of Child Psychology and Psychiatry and Allied Disciplines, 43*, 307–325.

Wiznitzer, M. (2004). Autism and tuberous sclerosis. *Journal of Child Neurology, 19*, 675–679.

Wolfberg, P. (1999). *Play and imagination in children with autism*. New York: Teachers College Press.

Yerys, B. E., Hepburn, S. I., Pennington, B. F., & Rogers, S. J. (2007). Executive function in preschoolers with autism: Evidence consistent with a secondary deficit. *Journal of Autism and Developmental Disorder, 37*, 1068–1079.

Zelazo, P. R. (2001). A developmental perspective on early autism: Affective, behavioral, and cognitive factors. In J. A. Burack, T. Charman, N. Yirmiya, & P. R. Zelazo (Eds.), *The development of autism: Perspectives from theory and research*. Mahwah, NJ: Lawrence Erlbaum Associates.

4

Language Disorders in Children with Hearing Impairment

MIRANDA CLEARY

FACTORS IN LANGUAGE DEVELOPMENT

*M*ajor factors contributing to the course of language development in children with hearing impairment include: the age at which the hearing loss was identified, the severity of the hearing loss, in some cases etiology of the hearing loss, when and how hearing amplification devices are used, the presence of other medical conditions, and the nature of the communication environment provided. We first review the nature of these factors. Remaining sections then characterize specific aspects of spoken language acquisition, focusing primarily on hearing-impaired (HI) children with very early-acquired or congenital severe to profound hearing losses.

Age at Hearing Loss Identification

The age at which the hearing loss is identified can play a major role in shaping the rest of the child's development. In the past it was not uncommon in the United States for hearing losses in otherwise healthy children to remain undiagnosed until 2 years of age or later (Mace, Wallace, Whan, & Stelmachowicz, 1991). Since the mid- to late 1990s, however, the implementation of state-regulated newborn hearing screening requirements has led to a drop in the average age at hearing-loss identification (e.g., Connolly, Carron, & Roark, 2005). As of 2007, at least 40 US States have adopted laws establishing newborn and infant hearing screening programs (ASHA, 2007). This screening generally consists of measuring otoacoustic emissions (OAEs) or the auditory brainstem response (ABR). Although these methods are quite effective, they may miss some configurations of hearing loss.

Newborn hearing screenings do not, of course, catch postnatal onset hearing losses or progressive losses that cause hearing to deteriorate over months and years of early childhood. Hearing screenings following events for which hearing loss might be a secondary consequence are, therefore, particularly important. During children's school-age years, school systems in many industrialized nations require hearing screenings at regular intervals (Northern & Downs, 2002). Recent advances in the identification of genes associated with hearing losses, including typically progressive losses, have also helped identify children at risk for hearing impairments (Nance, 2003).

The age at identification typically drives the age at which both audiological and language-related intervention begins. Early amplification and oral/aural training are widely believed to have profound effects on later levels of spoken language attainment, although the timeline for this is still a matter of debate. Later identification does not necessarily preclude a child from developing good spoken language; however, the probability of such success is reduced. In many countries, infants as young as a few months of age are now routinely fitted with conventional hearing aids, and infants as young as 6 to 12 months of age with severe to profound bilateral sensorineural hearing loss are receiving cochlear implants.

Degree of Hearing Impairment

Hearing impairments can be quite varied in nature. The most general means by which to classify severity of hearing loss is through a pure tone average (PTA) threshold, usually defined as the average of the threshold for pure tones at 500, 1,000, and 2,000 Hz presented through headphones. This range of frequencies is particularly crucial for speech perception as many of the acoustic cues to speech sound identity lie within this range. The reference point for the degree of loss is typically taken as the average intensity threshold of detection under normal hearing, labeled as 0 dB HL. Thresholds between −10 and +15 dB HL are considered normal.

PTA hearing losses greater than 90 dB HL are typically classified as *profound*, losses of 90–70 dB HL as *severe*, of 70–55 dB HL as *moderately severe*, of 55–40 dB HL as *moderate*, and of 40–15 dB HL as *mild to slight*. Usage of this terminology has not been entirely uniform over time or across disciplines. This summarized description can also obscure whether the loss is fairly uniform or more variable across frequencies.

Hearing losses are also characterized in terms of their physiological origin. Conductive losses involve problems in the outer and middle ear, whereas sensorineural hearing loss typically involves dysfunction of the hair cells in the cochlea, which normally convert sound information from fluid-mechanical motion to electrical signals. Partial degeneration of the auditory nerve may also be associated with sensorineural hearing loss. Damage exclusively to the auditory pathways beyond the auditory nerve has not typically been classified as *hearing impairment* and is not dealt with here.

Hearing losses may be bilateral or unilateral, involving just one ear. Bilateral losses may be relatively symmetrical across the two ears in terms of the sound frequencies affected, or asymmetrical. The impact of unilateral hearing losses on language and behavior as a function of degree of loss has been an area of debate (e.g., Bess & Tharpe, 1986; Kiese-Himmel, 2002). Although current data suggest increased probability of academic difficulties and behavioral problems in children with more severe unilateral hearing losses, the true incidence of speech and language delays relative to degree of loss, amplification usage, and other concomitant risk factors remains under investigation (Lieu, 2004).

The buildup of extraneous fluid with or without infection in the middle ear cavity, referred to as otitis media with effusion (OME), can result in a transient (or often chronically recurring or fluctuating) mild conductive hearing loss. The effects of OME on language development have been controversial. The most recent research with large epidemiological samples indicates that contrary to earlier suggestion, a history of OME in the first 2 years of life (in otherwise healthy children) does not correlate strongly with speech and language development later in childhood (Roberts, Rosenfeld, & Zeisel, 2004). In recent years, evidence favoring a more conservative approach to typanostomy tube insertion in otherwise healthy children has also emerged (Paradise et al., 2005). As Roberts, Hunter, and colleagues (2004) suggest, however, additional research specifically considering resulting hearing levels, other risk factors, and involving special clinical populations of children may be needed. Additionally, only a subset of language behaviors has been assessed, with areas such as morphological and syntactic processing having received less study.

Etiology and Issues of Syndromic Conditions

For many HI children, expectations for language acquisition cannot be based on the hearing loss considered in isolation. It has been estimated that about 30% of children with moderate to profound hearing losses have additional disabilities (e.g., Fortnum, Marshall, & Summerfield, 2002). Some medical conditions and hearing loss etiologies—viral infections such as cytomegalovirus, for example—have been associated with lower than average performance on tests of nonverbal intelligence and developmental motor-skill milestones. In many cases, the hearing loss may be a situation for which at least partial corrective measures can be implemented, unlike other aspects of the child's medical condition that may be more difficult to address but which may also affect language acquisition.

Use of Amplification

Conventional amplification in the form of externally worn analog or, more commonly, digital hearing aids (HAs) is routinely used with children with mild to severe hearing losses. The fitting process is important, often requiring a series of refinements made over time, in order to provide sufficient amplification without exceeding comfort thresholds. Most sensorineural hearing losses of cochlear origin involve reduced dynamic range and abnormal increases in perceived loudness as signal intensity is increased. Thus, "ceilings" for amplified levels must be carefully selected. Ideally, aided hearing thresholds should be within or close to the normal range. Fitting usually involves verifying that the amplified signal is as desired as measured near the tympanic membrane, followed by validation of the fitting through testing in free-field conditions using standardized auditory materials. Programmable digital HAs allow for different device settings under different listening situations (Dillon, 2001).

Easily wearable transistor-based HAs were introduced in the 1950s. By the 1980s, it was becoming clear that many profoundly deaf children did not receive enough benefit even from the most modern high-powered conventional HAs to make fluent spoken language development a reasonable expectation (Geers & Moog, 1994; Levitt, 1987; Quigley & Paul, 1984). Cochlear implants were subsequently approved by the US FDA in 1992 for children with bilateral sensorineural hearing loss who fail to demonstrate benefit from conventional HAs, usually assessed through a trial period of several months. A cochlear implant (CI) consists, in part, of an externally worn microphone and electronic signal processing system that analyzes the energy content of the acoustic signal across a series of frequency bandwidths. This information is then sent via radio-range frequencies across the scalp to a surgically implanted receiver, which passes the information to a series of electrical contacts contained in an electrode array threaded into and along the scala tympani of the tonotopically arranged cochlea. High-frequency information is coded through minute electrical pulses transmitted to the base of the cochlea and progressively lower frequency information to more apical regions of the cochlea. Over the years, small variations made to the electronic strategies by which the acoustic signal is converted to electrical pulses have steadily improved average expected speech perception performance.

Open-set monosyllabic word-recognition scores for pediatric CI users (auditory-only at ~70 dB SPL in quiet) averaged around 10% of words correct in the early 1990s (Staller, Beiter, Brimacombe, Mecklenberg, & Arndt, 1991) which, while better than expected with conventional HAs, was still admittedly poor. Ten years later, the average score for an implanted child was more like 40% of words correct (ASHA, 2004). The current generation can expect even somewhat better scores, in the range of 40–60% of words correct, with enormous individual differences possible. Some children even achieve scores in quiet listening conditions comparable to those of normal-hearing (NH) children.

Although HA and CI technologies have become increasingly sophisticated, currently available devices continue to have some marked limitations. The issue of abnormal growth of loudness with increased signal level (be it amplified acoustic energy or electrical pulse characteristics), continues to be a challenging issue in sensorineural hearing loss. Various mechanisms that the normal human auditory system has evolved to deal with background noise and localizing sound are also not fully accessible using currently available HAs and CIs.

A growing number of children use a combination of a CI in one ear and a more traditional HA in the other ear. In recent years, bilateral CIs have also become an option. The best way to fit such patients is an active area of research. It is also the case, however, that many children around the world still do not have access to facilities and systems that will allow them to obtain HAs or CIs at early ages or even to be identified with hearing loss within the first few years of life.

Communication Methods

The issue of choosing a communication method through which a HI child will be exposed to language has historically been a contentious issue. From the point of view of developing a language system that can be used with the child's immediate caregivers, what is important is the availability of a sophisticated language model (or models) in the child's environment at home and at school. By sophisticated, what is meant is that the system be fully developed, with consistent use of syntactic and morphological patterns.

A variety of communication approaches currently exists in the United States. In general, the auditory/oral approach involves having a child learn to listen and speak while using HAs/CIs. Some traditional *oral* approaches emphasize the use of lipreading. Other oral methods, such as the *auditory–verbal* approach, encourage using only the auditory signal and argue that nonreliance on lip-reading cues should be taught. "Cued speech," though not very widely used today, encourages use of spoken language and lipreading but incorporates a set of manual gestures to disambiguate certain sound contrasts that are difficult to distinguish through lip-reading alone.

A number of other systems incorporate elements of both manual and spoken language and are sometimes referred to as *total communication* or *simultaneous communication* systems. In their strict form, combination systems that place emphasis on correspondence with spoken English require that gestures follow spoken English word order and that obligatory markings for the grammatical and morphological conventions of spoken English be included. Variants on these methods include *signed exact English, signed English, signing exact English*, and *manually coded English*. Such systems are argued to be appropriate for individuals who do not receive much benefit from amplification or lipreading, but who aim to be linked to the ambient spoken language. Phonics, spelling, and literacy skills can be emphasized through such systems. Concerns have been raised, however, regarding the ease with which such systems can be accurately learned and efficiently used by HI children and their parents (e.g., Crandall, 1978; Luetke-Stahlman, 1988, 1991; Moeller & Luetke-Stahlman, 1990; Schick & Moeller, 1992).

In contrast to combination systems, true sign languages, such as American Sign Language, do not operate with reference to the conventions of a particular spoken language. Sign languages display their own grammatical and morphological conventions and utilize space and action to code information that spoken languages code through the speech signal. Signed languages in different regions can differ from each other in their structure as dramatically as do spoken languages. The lexical equivalent of a vocabulary word in the ambient spoken language may or may not exist in the signed language.

Bilingualism involving manual and spoken languages is quite possible under the right circumstances. Hearing children of HI parents who sign, for example, are an interesting population that routinely demonstrate native fluency in both a signed and a spoken language. Although fostering bilingualism across modalities in HI children continues to be a contentious issue, it is the logistics of providing a truly adequate language model in more than one language that are debatable, not whether bilingual fluency is theoretically possible.

Most HI children are born to hearing parents and thus, assuming that good audiological and language support services are available, oral language methods are often most appropriate. For children in other circumstances who may not be benefiting from audiological or language services, combination or manual-only systems may be preferable. Tightly controlled studies of communication method effects are nearly impossible to conduct, as they pose obvious ethical problems. Another complicating factor is that it is common for HI children to move between different educational environments, depending on their perceived progress. Many children, for example, if they are progressing in the auditory modality, move from environments where both speech and sign are used to environments where no sign is used. The skills of a child prior to the onset of hearing impairment or prior to HA use can also serve to influence choice of communication method. Thus, assessing causal, as opposed to correlational, relationships between communication method and language development is extremely difficult.

The above section has reviewed several major variables believed to influence spoken language outcomes in HI children. The impact of these variables typically must be assessed in combination, not in isolation. It should also be kept in mind that many of the factors believed to contribute in part to individual differences in some measures of language among NH children (such as gender and socioeconomic status) also contribute to the language skills displayed by HI children.

SPOKEN LANGUAGE DEVELOPMENT

The following sections discuss spoken language development in HI children who use HAs and CIs, focusing on various aspects of language roughly in order of emergence. A selection of classic and recent findings is reviewed, discussing receptive and expressive skills in tandem. Gaps in the literature and prominent methodological issues are discussed.

Early Vocal Development, Babbling, First Words, and Early Vocabulary

Normal-hearing infants display a series of prelexical vocal production behaviors prior to the onset of first words at around the age of 12 months. From about 2 months of age, NH infants begin experimenting with interrupted phonation and vocal exploration, and between 6 to 12 months of age, babbling with the production of recognizably consonant + vowel sequences becomes apparent. For NH children the average age at onset of canonical babbling involving (reduplicated) CV syllables is at around 7 months.

Children with severe to profound hearing impairments typically begin babbling later than do NH children (e.g., Koopmans-van Beinum, Clement, & van den Dikkenberg-Pot, 2001; Oller & Eilers, 1988). Although considerable individual variability exists, an average

age of 18 months at onset of canonical babbling appears typical for infants who are receiving little if any auditory input. Oller and Eilers (1988), for example, found nonoverlapping distributions for age at onset of canonical babbling in 21 NH infants, as compared to 9 infants with severe to profound hearing losses fitted with HAs. Unlike the NH infants, who all began to babble canonically by 6–10 months of age, the HI infants displayed an onset of canonical babbling that ranged from 11 to 25 months of age. Furthermore, even once they began to produce these sounds, the HI infants' well-formed canonical babblings did not represent a high proportion of all their vocalizations, unlike those of the NH children.

Recent studies of small groups of not-yet-babbling infants receiving CIs before the age of 2 years have reported an onset of canonical babbling within several months following implant activation (e.g., Ertmer & Mellon, 2001; Schauwers, Gillis, Daemers, De Beukelaer, & Govaerts, 2004; Sharma et al., 2004). In these studies, because unimplanted deaf children also typically eventually show an onset of canonical babbling, it is difficult to know for certain whether implantation hastened this onset. Examination of whether the quality/quantity of the babble changes dramatically pre- versus postactivation in infants who may have been babbling preimplantation might be useful in this regard.

Although some research has documented structural differences in the prebabbling vocalizations of deaf versus NH infants, differences between groups become especially marked once HI children reach the age at which NH infants would be expanding their consonantal inventories in canonical babbling and first-word stages. Atypical sound inventories (limited, non-native sounds), atypical distributions of sound and syllable types (such as a higher proportion of glottal sequences involving a glottal stop or fricative), restricted formant frequency ranges, inappropriate nasality, and atypically elongated utterances have all been reported for HI toddlers beginning to babble between 14 and 18 months of age (e.g., Oller & Eilers, 1988; Stoel-Gammon, 1988). HI children's babbling may also decrease in complexity over time. Stoel-Gammon and Otono (1986), for example, reported gradual reductions in the number of different consonant-like sounds in the babble of severe-to-profoundly HI children as compared to consistent increases in NH children.

Some early researchers (e.g., Lenneberg, 1967; see discussion in Gilbert, 1982) suggested that the onset of babbling occurred at the same age for hearing and HI infants but did not progress in the usual manner for HI children. The empirical evidence, however, suggests that this is not the case; the onset of "canonical" babbling is typically delayed in HI infants. The earlier confusion is likely to be related to the definition of babbling adopted (e.g., precanonical babbling).

Following the onset of first words at about 12 months, NH children, by parental report, typically reach the 50-word productive stage around 15–17 months (1;3–1;5), and the 100-word stage at 17–19 months of age (1;5–1;7) (Fenson et al., 1993). Although studies of HI children that span the time period between onset of canonical babbling and the point at which the child has 50 to 100 words in his/her productive vocabulary are few and far between, available data suggest that children with moderate to profound losses exhibit substantial delays in reaching these milestones (Gregory & Mogford, 1981; Shafer & Lynch, 1981).

Gregory and Mogford (1981), for example, longitudinally examined the early productions of eight HI toddlers with moderate to profound hearing losses using conventional amplification and born to hearing parents. The authors found that two of the eight, with profound losses, had not reached the 10-word stage by 4 years, typically seen in NH children at around 12–14 months. The children with lesser degrees of hearing loss reached the 10-word stage at a mean age of 23 months and the 50-word stage at 29 months (2;5). On average, the children reached the 100-word stage at 2;10 as compared to 1;8 for a NH comparison group, thus displaying a delay of over a year, as well as a larger interval between the 50- and 100-word milestones. These results are in close agreement with data reported for implanted children (e.g., Ertmer & Mellon, 2001).

Gregory and Mogford also found that although their subjects reached the 50-word milestone quite late, the appearance of two-word combinations followed this milestone closely, as is the case with NH children. There was also some tendency for the HI group to produce a greater proportion of words with social and request functions (as compared to other functions, such as labeling objects) than in NH children, when comparing the groups at the 50-word and 100-word stages. This finding, together with other features of their vocabularies, suggests that HI children's lexicons are shaped by their developmental level and chronological age—their social and motor skills may put them into situations where they want to use language to accomplish goals that would be foreign to a younger child.

Phonetics and Phonology

Although variability across children is typically quite large even among NH toddlers and preschoolers, some general phonological acquisition patterns do exist. For the vast majority of English-speaking American children, for example, the labial sounds /p/, /m/, /b/, as well as /n/, /h/, /w/, emerge in adult-like forms early and well before age 3, followed by the other stop/plosive sounds. The /r/, /l/ sounds, and the fricatives (other than /h/), emerge in their mature form relatively late (Sander, 1972; Goldman & Fristoe, 2000). By age 8 or 9, however, the vast majority of NH American children are producing all of these sounds as well as the affricates, and even consonant clusters, in an adult-like manner. The frequency of the individual sounds in the ambient language, articulatory complexity in terms of motor coordination, location within an utterance, and perceptual audibility and confusability (both auditorily and visually), have all been argued to contribute to order of emergence.

These general patterns of acquisition are also roughly characteristic of HI children who are getting auditory benefit from well-fit HAs or CIs, although the rate of acquisition is typically slower on average (e.g., Osberger & McGarr, 1982; Serry & Blamey, 1999). Much of the research on the acoustic and phonetic characteristics of the speech of the HI has studied individuals older than 8 years of age, partly so as to be able to ascribe observed differences to the hearing impairment rather than to normal maturational issues. An early and often cited monograph by Hudgins and Numbers (1942) reported on the speech production of 192 students in oral schools for the HI, ranging in age from 8 to 20 years. They reported that although children with various degrees of loss were likely to exhibit cluster reductions, consonant substitutions, and syllable-final consonant deletions, children with profound losses were also likely to produce consonants that evidenced voicing errors and extra nasality and to omit syllable-initial consonants. These latter students also tended to display loss of vowel quality, atypical diphthongizations, and extra nasality in their vowel sounds. Substitution of nasal sounds with stops was another reported common error atypical of a hearing child.

These findings have generally stood the test of time for children using HAs (e.g., Levitt, Stromberg, Smith, & Gold, 1980; see discussion in Osberger & McGarr, 1982). Studies of younger HI children have, additionally, noted large proportions of omitted segments and relatively better production of consonants produced with frontal and more visible places of articulation even when nonimitative tasks are used (e.g., Geffner, 1980). Recent research has also noted that the speech of HI children often contains sounds that are not part of the usual sound system of the ambient language. For example, Chin (2003), in examining the phonological systems of 12 school-age American children using CIs, found that in addition to missing ambient phonemes, many children produced "additional" nonambient stop consonants, which in some cases replaced native fricative sounds.

Why do these particular errors arise, as opposed to others? Some of the atypical sound productions are related to an overall slowing in speech rate often observed in HI individuals. Other errors appear closely related to speech sound acoustics, and acoustic and lip-read similarity patterns among speech sounds. Sounds susceptible to being misidentified by NH listeners also tend to be misidentified by HI listeners. Interestingly, however, among the phonemes of Australian English, frequency of occurrence in the language predicts the order of acquisition in children using CIs better than do rankings of relative acoustic intensity or estimated visibility of place of articulation (Blamey, 2003). Some late-emerging but common sounds, such as [s], however, do not fit this generalization (Blamey, Barry, & Jacq, 2001).

Historically, enormous differences in articulatory development between HI and NH children led to the development of articulation tests specific to each group, thus making comparisons difficult. With the advent of more efficacious audiological interventions, however, such comparisons are becoming possible. Chin and Kaiser (2002), for example, examined performance on the Goldman–Fristoe Test of Articulation subtest for Sounds-In-Words (Goldman & Fristoe, 1986) in 20 CI users ranging from 4 to 9 years of age (with very-early-onset hearing losses) implanted before age 6. Performance was evaluated relative to age-norms for NH children and also relative to the "hearing-age" of the children expressed as years of implant use. Of the CI sample, 90% scored below the 8th percentile for their age, and 70% of total communication users and 20% of oral language users scored below the 1st percentile. When these scores were reevaluated in terms of the number of errors expected for their hearing age, 25% of the sample still scored below the 1st percentile, but 35% scored above the 25th percentile. Thus, there is some indication that with auditory experience, substantial progress can be made; however the constraints on this are not yet well understood.

The main goal in producing speech is to be understood. Intelligibility often depends on circumstances, but an approximate characterization for NH children is that by age 2;0 up to about 50% of a child's words will tend to be understood by an unfamiliar listener (Coplan & Gleason, 1988). By 3;0, this proportion will rise to about 75%, and by age 4, it can be expected that a NH child will be mostly intelligible, even though many sounds may still be in immature forms. These figures contrast markedly with estimates of the speech intelligibility of HI children using HAs or CIs, even those immersed in oral-language environments. For older school-age children with hearing losses greater than 90 dB HL, estimates of about 20–40% of words intelligible in sentences have been repeatedly reported (Markides, 1970; McGarr, 1983; Smith, 1975; Svirsky, Chin, Miyamoto, Sloan, & Caldwell, 2000), with some variability associated with other factors, such as listener experience and sentence content. Somewhat more encouraging results have been reported in recent studies of children receiving CIs early in life. Tobey, Geers, Brenner, Altuna, and Gabbert (2003), for example, in studying 181 8- and 9-year-old children implanted before age 5, reported that approximately 64% of familiar keywords produced in simple sentences were intelligible to naïve listeners.

Although productive speech skills do not necessarily fully reflect a child's receptive skills, these abilities are rarely dissociable in children with early-onset hearing impairment. Issues of articulation and intelligibility also bear heavily on how other higher-level productive language skills are assessed and interpreted for HI children.

Lexical Development

One of the most compelling aspects of language acquisition in NH children is the apparent ease with which new words are added to their vocabularies. This process has been studied using structured experimental situations in which children are exposed to novel words labeling new objects, actions, or attributes, and memory for these novel words is then tested. A small number of analogous studies have been carried out with HI school-age children (though not with the toddler and preschool ages studied in much of the normal developmental literature).

Gilbertson and Kamhi (1995), for example, compared the word-learning performance of 7- to 10-year-old children with mild-to-moderate hearing losses using amplification to that of younger NH children matched on receptive vocabulary. The HI children tended less often to correctly label trained referents after an initial exposure, and they took more trials to attain exactly correct novel word production. The HI children were also less likely than the NH children to correctly recognize correct and incorrect labelings using the new words, particularly for multisyllabic novel words.

Gilbertson and Kamhi also found that word-learning scores were related to receptive vocabulary scores for the HI group. About half of the HI children performed like the vocabulary-matched NH group. The remaining HI children, however, did particularly poorly, both on the word-learning and on the receptive vocabulary tasks. Because this poorer performing group actually had better unaided hearing thresholds than did the better performing group, the authors concluded that they had identified a subset of HI children with deficits specifically in spoken word learning.

Although the HI children in this study were reported to have normal articulation for their chronological age, defining word learning as exactly correct labeling remains problematic, as the phonemic composition and length of the novel words appears to have contributed to group differences. Additionally, the relationship between aided thresholds and performance was not reported on, and few details were provided regarding the children's early hearing and language history.

Noting these limitations, Stelmachowicz, Pittman, Hoover, and Lewis (2004) employed a rather different methodology to study the retention of novel nouns and verbs by HI children in the context of a short recorded narrative story shown with visual animation. Their participants ranged in age from 6 to 9 years, exhibited a mean hearing loss of approximately 50 dB HL (wide range within group), and used conventional amplification with known levels of auditory benefit. Stelmachowicz and colleagues found that the HI children found the word-learning task more difficult, on average, than did a group of age-matched (not language-matched) NH children. Unlike Gilbertson and Kamhi (1995), however, these researchers did not find a subgroup of HI children with greater than expected word-learning difficulties.

In novel word-learning tasks, children are typically dealing with unfamiliar labels, unfamiliar objects, and the task of mapping one to the other. In order to specifically study the mapping skill, Houston, Carter, Pisoni, Kirk, and Ying (2005) assessed the ability of children 2 to 5 years of age using CIs, to learn associations between already-familiar adjectives/attribute words used as proper names, and small stuffed animal toys (e.g., "Fuzzy" the Bear). After a play session used to train the associations, children were tested on their ability to select the correct referent when given the name, and to produce the name, given the referent. The children with CIs did more poorly on average than NH children of the same age.

An interesting and complementary study by Lederberg, Prezbindowski, and Spencer (2000) examined whether moderate-to-profoundly HI children ($M = 84$ dB HL) aged 3–6 years could make the inference that a novel spoken and signed label is more likely to refer to a novel object than to a familiar one that already possesses a known label. Normal-hearing children generally exhibit this inferential behavior by age 2. Lederberg and colleagues found that the majority of HI children demonstrated this inferential behavior. The remaining children who required explicit linking of the novel word and novel object to learn the label demonstrated the inferential behavior one year later.

The studies above highlight several methodological challenges in using behavioral word-learning tasks with HI children—ensuring stimulus audibility, retaining the child's attention, and assessing misarticulated responses, for example. These concerns permeate nearly all study of spoken language processing in HI children. Exercising control over such factors through study design and/or partial statistical control is important.

Morphology, Morphosyntax, and Syntax

Language is typically thought of as the ability to comprehend and produce sequences of morphemes, words, and phrases, where these sequences exhibit structurally predictable forms. In normal language acquisition, children begin to combine words into multiword utterances around or after 18 months of age, although there is wide variation among children.

Early MLU   Mean length of utterance (MLU) is a primary measure used to study early grammatical development. At early stages in development, MLU, typically measured in morpheme units, and based on a spontaneous language sample, relates closely with attained levels of grammatical complexity. Once the average utterance length is greater than 4 morphemes, MLU is no longer as good a summary measure of the child's grammatical level, and successful comprehension and production of individual morphemes and structures become the main measures of interest.

Several studies have looked at changes in MLU in HI children as a function of age. Although individual differences among NH children are large, one point of reference is that NH children take, on average, about a year to progress from an MLU of 1.0 to an MLU of 3.0 (Miller & Chapman, 1981). On average, an MLU of 3.0 is reached by a NH child by 2½–3 years of age. Hearing-impaired toddlers and preschoolers acquiring spoken language tend to display shorter MLUs and make slower gains in MLU, on average, than do NH age-mates (e.g., Geffner, 1987; Ramkalawan & Davis, 1992). Geffner (1987), for example, in a study of 50 6-year-old children with losses of greater than 80 dB, reported that the mean MLU of the group was approximately 2 words in length, and that only 14% of the sample displayed MLUs (in words) greater than 3.0. These results indicate several years of delay relative to NH children.

Studies of young preschool-age children using CIs have yielded analogous results. Much recent research in this area has used MLU as a measure along which to match groups of HI and NH children and has then longitudinally compared their progress. Although this method of matching by MLU provides an interesting perspective, it can be problematic (Plante, Swisher, Kiernan, & Restrepo, 1993). As data such as those reported by Brown (1984) demonstrate, such procedures can sometimes result in comparing the language of HI teenagers with that of NH toddlers.

Several nevertheless interesting studies adopting this methodology have been conducted with toddlers and preschoolers acquiring spoken German via a CI. Implanted children were found by Szagun (2001) to progress from an MLU of 1.0 to an MLU of approximately 2.4 in 18 months. MLU-matched NH 16-month-olds progressed from an MLU of 1.0 to an MLU of approximately 4.5 in the same time period. The CI group therefore showed markedly slower gain in MLU on average than did the NH group. Interestingly, however, nearly half the CI group displayed gains in MLU that fell within the range of gains seen in the NH group. The remaining children showed much slower rates of progress. Earlier-implanted children and children with some residual hearing performed more like NH children. Analogous findings showing slower gains in MLU compared to NH children initially matched for MLU have been reported for implanted children acquiring spoken French (LeNormand, Ouellet, & Cohen, 2003).

Lyon and Gallaway (1990), among others, have noted the additional complexities in calculating MLU for HI children. A higher proportion of unintelligible utterances is commonly encountered, and the coding of these productions is an issue. Collecting a sufficiently large amount of spontaneously produced speech for analysis can also be much more difficult for HI children.

Morphology   It has long been clear that the acquisition of spoken-language syntax and morphology poses a particular challenge for HI children with severe and profound hearing impairments. It can generally be said that although HI children learning spoken English show patterns similar to NH children in terms of order of emergence of inflectional morphemes, age at emergence is typically substantially later. As is the case for NH children, patterns of acquisition appear to be related to the structure of the individual language (emphasis on word order versus morphological markers, for example), the frequency of word/morpheme usage in the environment, and issues of perceptual salience and semantic/conceptual complexity. Frequency and perceptual robustness have been most studied in the case of HI children.

Many researchers have noted that the predominance of content words relative to function words characterizing the earliest multiword utterances of children learning English, is also found in the speech of HI children, but at much older ages. Others have noted that once some function words are expressed by HI children, a disproportionate number are determiners produced before nouns. The appropriate choice between definite and indefinite determiner has additionally been noted as difficult for HI children (e.g., Levitt, 1987; McAfee, Kelly, & Samar, 1990; Wilbur, 1977).

Although some of the earliest studies may have underestimated the basic skills of HI children due to their methodological reliance on reading and composition tasks (e.g., Cooper, 1967; Quigley & King, 1980), the bleak outlook for language development under all-oral methods for profoundly HI children contributed to the drive, peaking in the mid-1980s in the United States, to encourage communication systems that used signed gestures designed to reflect the sound, spelling conventions, and morphology of English. A number of studies then attempted to chart the emergence of various English morphemes in HI children using these combination systems, building on early work in normal child language acquisition establishing a relative ordering for the emergence of spoken English morphemes. It was known, for example, that bound inflectional morphemes such as the present progressive –*ing* and the regular plural +*s* are typically produced quite early by NH children—usually at around age 2.5 years (e.g., Brown, 1973). The bound morphemes (in their various phonological forms) used to mark the English regular past tense +*d* and third person regular present tense –*s* tend to emerge somewhat later, roughly at around 3.5+ years. Use of the various forms of auxiliary verbs (e.g., *are*, *is*) appears still later in NH children, but by the age of 4;0 most NH children are using a variety of auxiliary verb formations.

Results for HI children were decidedly mixed. Gaustad (1986), for example, tracked morphological acquisition in 40 children 5 to 7 years of age with losses greater than 75 dB. In addition to finding that the progress of the HI children was markedly slower than that of a comparison group of younger NH children, Gaustad noted a tendency for HI children to replace typical grammatical elements with other devices to convey the same meaning. For example, some children were observed using a numerical descriptor like *two* or the ASL-like device of duplicating the noun (or even the verb) to indicate plurality, instead of the appropriate form of the plural morpheme element "+s." Other perhaps ASL-exposure related errors included placing the gestural markers for grammatical bound morphemes such as "+ing," at the end of the utterance, rather than after the verb. ASL uses different strategies than spoken English to indicate tense or relative time of occurrence and typically does not "conjugate" the verb sign in the way many spoken languages do the spoken verb stem.

Somewhat more promisingly, Bornstein, Saulnier, and Hamilton (1980) reported that the majority of young school-age HI children followed over a number of years of exposure to Signed English demonstrated a grasp of productions using the signed markers for the regular plural, possessive "+'s," and present progressive "+ing." Few children, however, mastered the markers indicating past tense, an irregular plural, and irregular past participle. The difficulty of irregular past participle forms was also highlighted by Bamford and Mentz (1979), who reported that HI children tended to overuse simple past tense forms, often replacing irregular past participle forms with an incorrect regularized form.

The limited success of combined communication systems provided additional impetus for the development of CIs in the hopes that improving the "front-end" input signal would improve language skills. A handful of studies have compared the morphological acquisition of children using CIs to that of children with similar audiological profiles using conventional HAs. Spencer, Tye-Murray, and Tomblin (1998), for example, analyzed the inflectional morphology of spontaneous language from children ranging in age from 5 to 16 years. Inclusion of bound morphemes where required was more common for the CI users than for the HA users for all five common inflectional morphemes examined. Spencer and colleagues found that both groups of HI children were most accurate on the present progressive *–ing* and regular plural *–s* markers, mirroring NH children's earliest acquisition of these forms. The regular past tense form "+d," on the other hand, posed a problem for both groups of HI children. No child using a HA produced the regular past tense marker correctly in the samples collected, and the implant users did so only half of the time.

Not all research suggests that morphological acquisition is simply delayed. A recent study designed to examine whether children using CIs follow an atypical course of morphological acquisition employed a sentence completion task to test production of uncontracted copulas, noun plurals, and the regular past tense in children with CIs (Svirsky, Stallings, Lento, Ying, & Leonard, 2002). The children performed best with the uncontracted copulas (forms of the verb *to be* such as *is* or *are* as the sole verb), next best on regular noun plural forms, and worst on forms of the acoustically fragile regular past tense. This ordering matches the argued perceptual prominence of these particular morphemes (Leonard, Eyer, Bedore, & Grela, 1997) but does not match the order of acquisition found for NH children, which would predict acquisition of the regular plural and regular past tense markers before the uncontracted copula.

Data reported by Szagun (2000) and Ruder (2004) for CI users further suggests that the role of semantic/conceptual complexity can be assessed by comparing acquisition of phonologically equivalent but grammatically separate morphological forms. Ruder's data for English-speaking children with CIs, for example, suggest better acquisition of the uncontracted copular *is* than for *is* used as an auxiliary verb, and more difficulty producing *–s* as indicating a third person singular verb form than as indicating a regular plural. In German, where forms such as *der* can appear as an article preceding a noun or can appear alone as a (typically stressed) pronoun, usage as the arguably more perceptually prominent pronoun has been found to precede usage as an article (Szagun, 2000).

Studies that focus on the acquisition of particular inflectional morphemes are typical of English-language acquisition studies. Data across many different languages are now acknowledged as key to theoretical accounts of how morphosyntactic acquisition is affected by hearing impairment. Because it is not a heavily inflected language, English is, however, not ideal for making generalizations about HI children's acquisition of grammatical agreement systems. The few existing studies of other languages (reported in English) suggest that such systems pose significant difficulty for HI children in acquisition. For HI children acquiring spoken Hebrew, Tur-Kaspa and Dromi (1999, 2001) reported that grammatical agreement of the verb form with the head noun and between adjectives and the nouns they modify was highly prone to error. Similarly, German HI children ages 1–7 years, who began using CIs between 1 and 4 years of age, have been reported to omit case and gender markings more often than did NH children matched on MLU (Szagun, 2004). German HI children also made substitution errors of gender, unlike NH children, whose "more developmentally advanced" errors mainly involved case markings.

In addition to the inflectional morphology system, many languages, including English, use a derivational morphology system to create new words from existing words (such as adding –er to a verb stem to indicate an individual who performs that action). Although NH children become attuned to this derivational system relatively late, it is a key tool for dealing with novel vocabulary and more advanced reading-related academic skills. An early study by Cooper (1967) found that derivational morphology exercises posed more of a challenge than did inflectional morphology exercises, for both school-age HI children acquiring spoken English and NH children of similar age, but that in addition to lower scores overall, the HI group showed a larger difference between inflectional and derivational morphology scores.

Syntax   Morphological and syntactic development are closely intertwined during language acquisition. In many cases, specific syntactic forms require specific morphemes to be acquired. (The formation of many English passive constructions requires, for example, use of auxiliary verb and past-participle morphological forms.) The wide body of research on the syntactic development of typical children and NH children with language disorders has provided useful comparison points against which to assess the progress of HI children.

At a gross level, many researchers have commented on a tendency on the part of HI children, unlike NH children, to omit major obligatory syntactic elements of sentences even after many years of exposure to spoken language. Tur-Kaspa and Dromi (1999, 2001), for example, reported that HI children with severe-to-profound HI acquiring spoken Hebrew using HAs or a CI omitted the subject or main verb in ~15% of their spoken clauses. Levitt (1987) pointed out that in the case of main verb omission, such omissions were associated with environments such as preceding a prepositional phrase, and situations in which the main verb is a high-frequency irregular, like *to be*. Levitt also reported that main verb deletion is an error that is typically gradually corrected over the middle-school years.

Accounts of syntactic development in English-speaking NH children typically cite the early acquisition of negation. The formation of negative statements has been argued to involve first using an external or isolated negative marker, followed by use of the negative marker internally, but with no auxiliary verb. Finally the adult form with internal negative marker and preceding auxiliary verb is acquired. Formation of negative constructions has been found to be a relative strength for HI children but still quite prone to errors, even in the earlier acquired forms (Levitt, 1987).

Other well-studied syntactic advances include the formation of questions. The earliest structures in NH children generally involve yes/no question forms marked by rising intonation contours. In English, wh-questions then emerge, gradually incorporating an auxiliary verb in the correct location. The progress of HI children, both in terms of production and comprehension, has been found to parallel this pattern of emergence, but, on average, with much later ages of acquisition. The precise type of wh-question (who regarding a subject, vs. who regarding an object, vs. where, vs. when, etc.) has also been found to affect ease of processing in ways analogous to young NH children (Levitt, 1987; Quigley, Wilbur, & Montanelli, 1974).

Forms that involve combining clauses are some of the later acquired structures. These structures have attracted a great deal of research in typical and atypical populations as their processing appears key to abstract formalist theories of syntactic acquisition and because their level of complexity seems to tap nonlanguage-specific cognitive limits related to memory and attention. The relative clause formation, for example, has been studied in some depth in HI children (e.g., Quigley, Smith, & Wilbur, 1974). One reliable finding in this area is that while relative clauses can be located at different places within the main sentence, medially embedded relative clauses are particularly difficult for both NH and HI children to process (e.g., Levitt, 1987). Tur-Kaspa and Dromi (1999, 2001) have further reported for HI children acquiring spoken Hebrew that among instances of embedded clauses, HI children tended to produce more complement-type clauses (clauses that satisfy the argument structure of a predicate/verb: "I know [*that*] *you are visiting*," than relative clauses (which modify nouns "You are reading the book [*that*] *I bought.*"), whereas NH children of similar age produced more relative clauses than complement clauses. Interestingly, but perhaps not surprisingly, these researchers also reported that the number of different clause types was significantly higher in spoken language samples examined than in written language samples from the same HI children, suggesting that methodological reliance on written language samples to assess syntactic competence has limited generalizability.

Passive voice constructions are also acquired particularly late by NH children, and use of such structures has pragmatic purposes that seem not to be refined until late childhood. Particularly challenging, even for young NH children, are passive forms where the subject and object are logically reversible (such as in *The bear was chased by the moose* vs. *The moose chased the bear*). Comprehension errors have been reported for NH children even into early school-age years, with characteristics of the verb playing a large role.

The hypothesis that a default agent-action-object form is imposed in the early years was initially proposed by Bever (1970) with respect to English-speaking NH children. An interesting set of large-scale studies by Quigley and colleagues (Power & Quigley, 1973; see review in Quigley & King, 1980) focused on a tendency for HI schoolchildren (losses > 90 dB HL) to also impose a subject-verb-object interpretation on read sentences. This often involved treating the noun most closely preceding the verb as the subject and the noun most closely following the verb as the object. Quigley argued that this problem could underlie the children's poor comprehension of passive voice sentence structures and embedded relative clauses, among other structures.

A related recent investigation by Friedmann and Szterman (2006) found that moderate to severely HI children acquiring spoken Hebrew using HAs or a CI demonstrated poor comprehension and production of sentence structures argued to involve syntactic movement of a noun phrase. The structures studied included object-relative sentences (*This is the girl that the woman is drawing*) and sentences involving deviations from the basic Hebrew word order [S(ubject)V(erb)O(bject)] by topicalizing—that is, focusing attention on the object, through the use of object-initial ordering (OSV or OVS). Friedmann and Szterman argued that a simple account suggesting that a default linear word order structure is erroneously applied to all less-canonical structures is insufficient, as they found chance levels of performance for many individual HI children, rather than a consistent preference for canonical-form-based interpretations.

Global Measures of Language Processing

Performance on individual aspects of language structure is potentially the most revealing type of data for understanding the effects of HI on language acquisition, but it is useful also to have a more general feel for the overall level of spoken language skills attained. This information can be gleaned through studies that directly compare measures of general language competence for HI children relative to normative data from age-matched NH children. Many studies of this kind have reported results for both a general language measure and a receptive vocabulary measure. Although these measures are typically highly correlated in children with typical language development, in the case of HI children for whom vocabulary acquisition tends to be an area of strength relative to morphological and syntactic processing, comparing these two types of scores is informative.

Recent data suggest that children who receive effective audiological intervention early in life (i.e., in the infant, toddler, and preschool-age years) exhibit early language gains that approach 100% of those expected of NH children over the same number of months. For example, Svirsky, Chute, Green, Bollard, and Miyamoto (2000) have reported that children younger than 7 years implanted, on average, at age 3 years showed about 100% of the gain in early expressive and receptive language as measured by the Reynell Developmental Language Scales, expected from young NH children in a single year (see also Bollard, Chute, Popp, & Parisier, 1999). Somewhat older data reported by Blamey and colleagues for children implanted also by age 3 on average, but using standardized language tests geared toward more advanced language skills with all-oral administration, has, however, shown poorer rates on the order of 55–60% of the gains made by NH children in a single year. These more modest gains are comparable to the progress observed for HI children with severe hearing losses using conventional HAs (Blamey et al., 2001) and imply that the language "gap" will widen rather than stay uniform as the child enters the middle-school years.

Although the general language gain data remain somewhat controversial, results specifically regarding vocabulary have been more uniform. Tests of receptive vocabulary growth suggest that children with the most profound losses can advance from making gains of only about 40% of normal per year prior to implantation, to making gains of 100% or even somewhat more per year after implantation, on average, even under speech-only administration conditions (Bollard et al., 1999; Boothroyd, Geers, & Moog, 1991; Dawson, Blamey, Dettman, Barker, & Clark, 1995). A few studies (e.g., Blamey et al., 2001) have arrived at lower values of 60–65% of normal gain after implantation given oral-only testing conditions.

Although these postintervention data seem promising, even gains per year comparable to those of NH children will still result in significant language delays for children experiencing appreciable durations of no auditory input. Several recent smaller scale studies of children implanted under the age of 2.5 years and tested at early-school-age have reported language scores of 50–75% of that expected for their chronological age, and receptive vocabulary scores of about 55–60% of normal (Spencer, 2004; Eisenberg, Kirk, Martinez, Ying, & Miyamoto, 2004). Furthermore, although full matching and control procedures have not been implemented in any of the studies published to date, current data suggest that children at the high end of the profound range using CIs tend to do about as well in terms of spoken language and vocabulary scores as do children with PTA losses of approximately 78 dB HL using well-fitted conventional HAs (Blamey et al., 2001; Eisenberg et al., 2004).

Larger studies with slightly later implanted children provide additional perspective. For a large sample of congenitally and early-deafened children 8 and 9 years of age implanted by age 5, Geers, Nicholas, and Sedey (2003) reported that about 30% of the children scored within limits for their chronological age on a standardized measure of receptive language. Within this test, the children with CIs were found, on average, to score 3 standard deviations (*SD*) below NH subtest norms both for comprehension of bound morphemes and more complex syntactic forms, but only a half standard deviation below norms on a subtest for receptive vocabulary. Similarly, Nikolopoulos, Dyar, Archbold, and O'Donoghue (2004) reported that among a sample of British children with profound losses who received a CI before the age of 7 years, only 1 of 44 (2%) scored above the 1st percentile for their age, preimplantation, on a test of receptive grammar administered under speech-only conditions. At 3 years postimplantation, however, the number of children scoring above the 1st percentile jumped to 40%, and at 5 years to 67%. By 5 years postimplantation, 20% were scoring above the 25th percentile for their age. Taken together, these data suggest that about 1 in every 4 profoundly deaf children fitted with a CI early in life will obtain age-appropriate language scores on such standardized tests after 4–5 years of use.

Earlier and more effective device fitting also appears to affect language-related skills such as reading. For many years, an oft-cited statistic was that profoundly HI individuals frequently reached adulthood without exceeding a 4th-grade (a 9-year-old's) reading level (e.g., Trybus & Karchmer, 1977). With the advent of more effective audiological interventions, the picture is beginning to look more promising. Geers (2003), for example, reported that although average reading performance was nearly 1 *SD* lower, 52% of a large sample of 8- and 9-year-old children implanted by age 5 were reading words and sentences at levels considered acceptable for a NH child of the same age ($\geq -1\ SD$).

As emphasized by these recent findings, the speech and language performance of HI children varies widely. Many studies have attempted to account for this wide variability. For children with profound losses using a CI, approximately 35–75% of the variance, depending on the sample and language measures used, can be accounted for by known patient and device factors (e.g., Geers, Nicholas, & Sedey, 2003). A portion of the remaining variability may be due to individual differences in central cognitive functions. Certain facets of language acquisition in NH children seem to relate to individual differences in cognition, and it has been reasoned that such relationships may therefore also obtain in HI populations.

Cognition and Language

The literature on cognition in HI individuals is substantial. The topics of memory and attention will be focused on here because these aspects appear most closely intertwined with language use. Memory (in its various forms) refers to the brain mechanisms that allow new configurations of information to remain available after the stimulus is removed. Attention allows organisms to direct awareness to particular information and to ignore other potential inputs. The study of HI populations provides insight into the degree to which the human memory and attention systems engage in sensory modality-specific processing.

Although the most interesting issues concern specific domains of cognition, it is hard to avoid the controversial construct of the intelligence quotient, or IQ, in discussing cognitive processes. IQ scores, it has been argued, reflect an individual's capacity to learn. Measures of IQ have been specifically designed to predict educational achievement in hearing children by creating a single composite score out of scores on various tests designed to assess individual differences in skills such as memory, attention, pattern recognition, conceptual relations, and so on. It is therefore hardly surprising that such scores also correlate with HI children's educational attainment (e.g., Paal, Skinner, & Reddig, 1988).

On average, there is no difference in nonverbal IQ based on the most widely used assessment tools between HI children with no additional handicaps and NH children (e.g., Maller & Braden, 1993; Schildroth, 1976; see Mayberry, 1992; Vernon, 1968). Within this distribution, HI children with higher nonverbal (or "performance") IQ scores tend to demonstrate better spoken language skills for their age (e.g., Dawson, Busby, McKay, & Clark, 2002; Geers, Nicholas, & Sedey, 2003; Watson, Sullivan, Moeller, & Jensen, 1982), as is also found with NH children. In contrast to nonverbal IQ measures, many verbal IQ tests are inappropriate for use with HI children and are rarely administered due to difficulties in interpretation. When verbal IQ tests are administered, not surprisingly, group means for HI children tend to be lower than means for NH children, even among the highest-achieving HI children (Geers & Moog, 1989). Measures of verbal IQ can, on occasion, be informative, when adequate norms for HI children are available, or for individual children whose academic progress seems unexpectedly slow relative to their perceptual and spoken language skills.

Considerable research suggests that spoken language is more closely tied to certain skills involved in human intelligence than to others. Short-term memory is one area that has received considerable study. HI children tend to display poorer immediate recall for lists of auditory items than do NH children of matched chronological age, even when the items to be recalled are reliably identified when presented in isolation or when initial identification during list presentation is assured to be correct (Burkholder & Pisoni, 2003; Cleary, Schwartz, Wechsler-Kashi, & Madell, 2006; Conrad, 1972, 1979; Dawson et al., 2002; Pintner & Paterson, 1917). Additionally, poorer recall performance is typically also observed for lists of stimuli composed of familiar readily labeled images, and even for familiar shapes or sequences of colored lights (Cleary, Pisoni, & Geers, 2001; Dawson et al., 2002). Equivalent performance across groups is usually only seen with stimuli such as irregular shapes that are not readily named (Furth, 1966).

These results for namable visual stimuli underscore the fact that the human species has a strong tendency to use linguistically based information-encoding strategies whenever possible. Studies of children's behaviors during list recall demonstrate the ubiquity of simple strategies such as verbal repetition to aid short-term memory in the school-age years. HI children often exhibit different memory maintenance strategies from NH children of comparable age—in some cases strategies resembling those of younger NH children (Bebko & McKinnon, 1990).

In short-term memory tasks, one of the main constraints on performance for all children is the lapsing of time, and thus, processing speed is a key issue. Attempts are being made to dissect the time needed for stimulus identification from intervals needed for item rehearsal, retrieval, and response generation. Speed also emerges as an issue in discussing HI children's performance on tasks believed to involve "working" memory. Working memory tasks involve shifting attention across more than one task (in addition to disregarding irrelevant information) over relatively short periods of time.

Child language researchers have become interested in whether the processing of complex syntactic constructions, pronoun reference relations, and general comprehension of language passages relates in a measurable way to individual differences in working memory in NH children (e.g., Montgomery, 2003). This notion emerged in part from data suggesting that individual differences in working memory performance among adults were related to language processing skills (e.g., Just & Carpenter, 1992; MacDonald, Just, & Carpenter, 1992), although other recent research disputes this (e.g., Waters & Caplan, 2005). In the case of HI children, working memory tasks that require reordering of verbal elements before recall seem to correlate only weakly, if at all, with spoken language processing skills (perhaps due to the use of spatially based processing to effect the reversal). Tasks that involve judgments about a series of statements while also holding the final word of each statement in memory for later recall have, in contrast, yielded more suggestive findings.

Only preliminary research on working memory has been carried out with HI children. Daneman, Nemeth, Stainton, and Huelsmann (1995), for example, reported that performance on verbal and visual working memory tasks (but not level of hearing loss) was correlated with reading skills among school-age HI children in oral-education environments. Lyxell and Holmberg (2000) found that a text-based working memory task was correlated with lip-reading accuracy for sentences in children with moderate hearing losses. More recently, Willstedt-Svensson, Lofqvist, Almqvist, and Sahlén (2004) reported that performance on an all-auditory working memory task in a small heterogeneous sample of children with CIs was correlated with receptive and expressive grammar skills. None of these findings implies, necessarily a causal relationship, but taken together they are indicative of a role for general cognition in language processing.

There is also a small amount of data reported for individual subtests of popular language assessment measures that suggests that subtests believed to draw most heavily on auditory–verbal short-term/working memory pose a particular problem for HI children. Average scores for HI samples on subtests that require accurate recall of increasingly long spoken sentences or those that require following a set of spoken directions after a brief delay appear to reflect these particular weaknesses (e.g., Spencer, Barker, & Tomblin, 2003; Young & Killen, 2002).

Some argue that the apparent differences in short-term and working memory function between HI and NH populations can be accounted for in part in terms of differences in lexical long-term memory. List recall tends to be more accurate for more familiar spoken words and pictured items, and sheer amount of spoken language input and experience tends to be less extensive in HI children than in NH children of the same age, presumably resulting in less-well-established long-term memory representations either for the phonological representation of individual words or perhaps even the representation of individual concepts. Recent data suggesting that simple identification times for pictures of highly familiar objects are slower in HI children than in age-matched controls support this notion (e.g., Wechsler-Kashi, Schwartz, Cleary, & Madell, 2007).

An understudied but promising area of research concerns the organization of long-term lexical memory for word-sound forms and meanings in HI children (e.g., Eisenberg, Martinez, Holowecky, & Pogorelsky, 2002; Jerger, Lai, & Marchman, 2002a, 2002b; Marschark, Convertino, McEvoy, & Masteller, 2004). Research in NH individuals has shown that spoken words are identified through a process of discriminating the target word from other similar-sounding words. The relative probability and perceptual robustness of the phonemes contained in the target word and in the alternatives play a role in determining the outcome of identification. Similar principles have been shown to operate in HI children (Kirk, Pisoni, & Osberger, 1995), and the impact of HI on the discriminability of words in a child's vocabulary continues to be investigated.

CONCLUSION

The last two decades have seen strides made in understanding phonological development and vocabulary acquisition in HI children. Advances with regard to morphology and syntax have been more modest. More remains to be done also in the area of cognition. In pursuing these remaining issues, it will continue to be vital to take into account the heterogeneity of the population of HI children. In a sense, HI children are also a moving target in that their background characteristics continually undergo shifts due to medical, audiological, educational, social, and political changes. To aid in future attempts at a synthesis of the literature, language researchers should be conscientious about describing their participant samples in detail with respect to the variables discussed in the first third of this chapter.

Due to technological and political developments, more HI children than ever before are being educated in mainstream classrooms and rely primarily on oral language. Nevertheless, there are still a substantial number of children who do far more poorly than expected given their circumstances. A number of researchers have raised the issue of whether a subgroup of HI children exists who have language-learning deficits beyond those expected for their hearing impairment alone (e.g., Bunch & Melnyk, 1989; Gilbertson & Kamhi, 1995; Young & Killen, 2002). Such a group may indeed exist, but identifying these children represents a formidable challenge, as the identification of language-specific learning disorders even in NH children is fraught with methodological issues (Leonard, 1998).

There is clearly room for improvement in the spoken language skills attained by HI children. Nevertheless, current expectations are substantially higher than they were 20 years ago, particularly for children with severe to profound losses. No longer, for example, are we talking about HI children who need a separate test of grammatical competence designed for deaf children; rather, some children are starting to score in the range expected for NH children of the same chronological age. This represents a significant advance.

REFERENCES

ASHA (2004). *Technical report: Cochlear implants—ASHA Supplement 24.* Rockville, MD: American Speech-Language-Hearing Association.

ASHA (2007). American Speech-Language-Hearing Association Early Hearing Detection & Intervention Action Center (http://www.asha.org/about/legislation-advocacy/federal/ehdi/). Rockville, MD: American Speech-Language-Hearing Association.

Bamford, J., & Mentz, L. (1979). The spoken language of hearing-impaired children: Grammar. In J. Bench & J. Bamford (Eds.), *Speech-hearing tests and the spoken language of hearing-impaired children* (pp. 381–471). London: Academic Press.

Bebko, J. M., & McKinnon, E. E. (1990). The language experience of deaf children: Its relation to spontaneous rehearsal in a memory task. *Child Development, 61,* 1744–1752.

Bess, F. H., & Tharpe, A. M. (1986). An introduction to unilateral sensorineural hearing loss in children. *Ear and Hearing, 7,* 3–13.

Bever, T. G. (1970). The cognitive basis for linguistic structures. In J. R. Hayes (Ed.), *Cognition and development of language* (pp. 279–362). New York: Wiley.

Blamey, P. (2003). Development of spoken language by deaf children. In M. Marschark, & P. E. Spencer (Eds.), *Deaf studies, language, and education* (pp. 232–246). Oxford, UK: Oxford University Press.

Blamey, P. J., Barry, J. G., & Jacq, P. (2001). Phonetic inventory development in young cochlear implant users 6 years postoperation. *Journal of Speech, Language, and Hearing Research, 44,* 73–79.

Blamey, P. J., Sarant, J. Z., Paatsch, L. E., Barry, J. G., Bow, C. P., Wales, R. J., et al. (2001). Relationships among speech perception, production, language, hearing loss, and age in children with impaired hearing. *Journal of Speech, Language, and Hearing Research, 44,* 264–285.

Bollard, P. M., Chute, P. M., Popp, A., & Parisier, S. C. (1999). Specific language growth in young children using the CLARION cochlear implant. *Annals of Otology, Rhinology, and Laryngology, 177*(Suppl.), 119–123.

Boothroyd, A., Geers, A. E., & Moog, J. S. (1991). Practical implications of cochlear implants in children. *Ear and Hearing, 12*(Suppl.), 81S–89S.

Bornstein, H., Saulnier, K. L., & Hamilton, L. B. (1980). Signed English: A first evaluation. *American Annals of the Deaf, 125,* 467–481.

Brown, J. B. (1984). Examination of grammatical morphemes in the language of hard-of-hearing children. *Volta Review, 86,* 229–238.

Brown, R. (1973). *A first language.* Cambridge, MA: Harvard University Press.

Bunch, G. O., & Melnyk, T. L. (1989). A review of the evidence for a learning-disabled, hearing-impaired sub-group. *American Annals of the Deaf, 134,* 297–300.

Burkholder, R. A., & Pisoni, D. B. (2003). Speech timing and working memory in profoundly deaf children after cochlear implantation. *Journal of Experimental Child Psychology, 85,* 63–88.

Chin, S. B. (2003). Children's consonant inventories after extended cochlear implant use. *Journal of Speech, Language, and Hearing Research, 46,* 849–862.

Chin, S. B., & Kaiser, C. L. (2002). Measurement of articulation in pediatric users of cochlear implants. *Volta Review, 102,* 145–156.

Cleary, M., Pisoni, D. B., & Geers, A. E. (2001). Some measures of verbal and spatial working memory in eight- and nine-year-old hearing-impaired children with cochlear implants. *Ear and Hearing, 22,* 395–411.

Cleary, M., Schwartz, R. G., Wechsler-Kashi, D., & Madell, J. R. (2006). *Hearing impairment in children associated with slower retrieval from memory during recall.* Poster presented at the Association for Psychological Science 18th Annual Convention. New York, NY, May 25–28.

Connolly, J. L., Carron, J. D., & Roark, S. D. (2005). Universal newborn hearing screening: Are we achieving the Joint Committee on Infant Hearing (JCIH) objectives? *Laryngoscope, 115,* 232–236.

Conrad, R. (1972). Short-term memory in the deaf: A test for speech coding. *British Journal of Psychology, 63,* 173–180.

Conrad, R. (1979). *The deaf schoolchild.* London: Harper & Row.

Cooper, R. L. (1967). The ability of deaf and hearing children to apply morphological rules. *Journal of Speech and Hearing Research, 10,* 77–86.

Coplan, J., & Gleason, J. (1988). Unclear speech: Recognition and significance of unintelligible speech in preschool children. *Pediatrics, 82,* 447–452.

Crandall, K. E. (1978). Inflectional morphemes in the manual English of young hearing impaired children and their mothers. *Journal of Speech and Hearing Research, 21,* 372–386.

Daneman, M., Nemeth, S., Stainton, M., & Huelsmann, K. (1995). Working memory as a predictor of reading achievement in orally educated hearing-impaired children. *Volta Review, 97,* 225–241.

Dawson, P. W., Blamey, P. J., Dettman, S. J., Barker, E. J., & Clark, G. M. (1995). A clinical report on receptive vocabulary skills in cochlear implant users. *Ear and Hearing, 16,* 287–294.

Dawson, P. W., Busby, P. A., McKay, C. M., & Clark, G. M. (2002). Short-term auditory memory in children using cochlear implants and its relevance to receptive language. *Journal of Speech, Language, and Hearing Research, 45,* 789–801.

Dillon, H. (2001). *Hearing aids.* New York: Theime.

Eisenberg, L. S., Kirk, K. I., Martinez, A. S., Ying, E. A., & Miyamoto, R. T. (2004). Communication abilities of children with aided residual hearing: Comparison with cochlear implant users. *Archives of Otolaryngology—Head and Neck Surgery, 130,* 563–569.

Eisenberg, L. S., Martinez, A. S., Holowecky, S. R., & Pogorelsky, S. (2002). Recognition of lexically controlled words and sentences by children with normal hearing and children with cochlear implants. *Ear and Hearing, 23,* 450–462.

Ertmer, D. J., & Mellon, J. A. (2001). Beginning to talk at 20 months: Early vocal development in a young cochlear implant recipient. *Journal of Speech, Language, and Hearing Research, 44,* 192–206.

Fenson, L., Dale, P., Reznick, J. S., Thal, D., Bates, E., Hartung, J. P., et al. (1993). *The MacArthur Communicative Development Inventories: User's guide and technical manual.* San Diego, CA: Singular Press.

Fortnum, H. M., Marshall, D. H., & Summerfield. A. Q. (2002). Epidemiology of the UK population of hearing-impaired children, including characteristics of those with and without cochlear implants: Audiology, aetiology, comorbidity and affluence. *International Journal of Audiology, 41,* 170–179.

Friedmann, N., & Szterman, R. (2006). Syntactic movement in orally trained children with hearing impairment. *Journal of Deaf Studies and Deaf Education, 11,* 56–75.

Furth, H. G. (1966). *Thinking without language: Psychological Implications of deafness.* New York: Free Press.

Gaustad, M. A. G. (1986). Longitudinal effects of manual English instruction on deaf children's morphological skills. *Applied Psycholinguistics, 7,* 101–128.

Geers, A., & Moog, J. (1989). Factors predictive of the development of literacy in profoundly hearing-impaired adolescents. *Volta Review, 91,* 69–86.

Geers, A., & Moog, J. (1994). Spoken language results: Vocabulary, syntax and communication. *Volta Review, 96,* 131–150.

Geers, A. E. (2003). Predictors of reading skill development in children with early cochlear implantation. *Ear and Hearing, 24*(Suppl.), 59S–68S.

Geers A. E., Nicholas, J. G., & Sedey, A. L. (2003). Language skills of children with early cochlear implantation. *Ear and Hearing, 24*(Suppl.), 46S–58S.

Geffner, D. (1980). Feature characteristics of spontaneous speech production in young deaf children. *Journal of Communication Disorders, 13,* 443–454.

Geffner, D. S. (1987). The development of language in young hearing-impaired children. In H. Levitt, N. McGarr, & D. Geffner (Eds.), *Development of language and communication skills in hearing-impaired children—ASHA Monograph No. 26* (pp. 25–35). Rockville, MD: American Speech-Language-Hearing Association.

Gilbert, J. H. V. (1982). Babbling and the deaf child: A commentary on Lenneberg et al. (1965) and Lenneberg (1967). *Journal of Child Language, 9,* 511–515.

Gilbertson, M., & Kamhi A. G. (1995). Novel word learning in children with hearing impairment. *Journal of Speech and Hearing Research, 38,* 630–642.

Goldman, R., & Fristoe, M. (1986). *Goldman–Fristoe Test of Articulation.* Circle Pines, MN: American Guidance Service.

Goldman, R., & Fristoe, M. (2000). *Goldman Fristoe 2 Test of Articulation Manual.* Circle Pines, MN: American Guidance Service.

Gregory, S., & Mogford, K. (1981). Early language development in deaf children. In B. Woll & M. Deuchar (Eds.), *Perspectives on British sign language and deafness* (pp. 218–237). London: Croom Helm.

Houston, D. M., Carter, A. K., Pisoni, D. B., Kirk, K., & Ying, E. (2005). Word learning in children following cochlear implantation. *Volta Review, 105,* 41–72.

Hudgins, C., & Numbers, F. (1942). An investigation of the intelligibility of the speech of the deaf. *Genetic Psychology Monographs, 25,* 289–392.

Jerger, S., Lai, L., & Marchman, V. A. (2002a). Picture naming by children with hearing loss: I. Effect of semantically related auditory distractors. *Journal of the American Academy of Audiology, 13,* 463–477.

Jerger, S., Lai, L., & Marchman, V. A. (2002b). Picture naming by children with hearing loss: II. Effect of phonologically related auditory distractors. *Journal of the American Academy of Audiology, 13,* 478–492.

Just, M., & Carpenter, P. A. (1992). A capacity theory of comprehension: Individual differences in working memory. *Psychological Review, 99,* 122–149.

Kiese-Himmel, C. (2002). Unilateral sensorineural hearing impairment in childhood: Analysis of 31 consecutive cases. *International Journal of Audiology, 41,* 57–63.

Kirk, K. I., Pisoni, D. B., & Osberger, M. J. (1995). Lexical effects on spoken word recognition by pediatric cochlear implant users. *Ear and Hearing, 16,* 470–481.

Koopmans-van Beinum, F. J., Clement, C. J., & van den Dikkenberg-Pot, I. (2001). Babbling and the lack of auditory speech perception: A matter of coordination? *Developmental Science, 4,* 61–70.

Lederberg, A. R., Prezbindowski, A. K., & Spencer, P. E. (2000). Word-learning skills of deaf preschoolers: The development of novel mapping and rapid word-learning strategies. *Child Development, 71,* 1571–1585.

Lenneberg, E. (1967). *Biological foundations of language.* New York: Wiley.

LeNormand, M. T., Ouellet, C., & Cohen, H. (2003). Productivity of lexical categories in French-speaking children with cochlear implants. *Brain and Cognition*, 53, 257–262.

Leonard, L. B. (1998). *Children with specific language impairment*. Cambridge, MA: MIT Press.

Leonard, L. B., Eyer, J. A., Bedore, L. M., & Grela, B. G. (1997). Three accounts of the grammatical morpheme difficulties of English-speaking children with specific language impairment. *Journal of Speech, Language, and Hearing Research*, 40, 741–753.

Levitt, H. (1987). Development of syntactic comprehension. In H. Levitt, N. McGarr, & D. Geffner (Eds.), *Development of language and communication skills in hearing-impaired children—ASHA Monograph #26* (pp. 47–78). Rockville, MD: American Speech-Language-Hearing Association.

Levitt, H., Stromberg, H., Smith, C., & Gold, T. (1980). The structure of segmental errors in the speech of deaf children. *Journal of Communication Disorders*, 13, 419–441.

Lieu, J. E. (2004). Speech-language and educational consequences of unilateral hearing loss in children. *Archives of Otolaryngology—Head and Neck Surgery*, 130, 524–530.

Luetke-Stahlman, B. (1988). Documenting syntactically and semantically incomplete bimodal input to hearing-impaired subjects. *American Annals of the Deaf*, 133, 230–234.

Luetke-Stahlman, B. (1991). Following the rules: Consistency in sign. *Journal of Speech and Hearing Research*, 34, 1293–1298.

Lyon, M., & Gallaway, C. (1990). Measuring the spontaneous language of hearing-impaired children. *Clinical Linguistics and Phonetics*, 4, 183–195.

Lyxell, B., & Holmberg, I. (2000). Visual speechreading and cognitive performance in hearing-impaired and normal hearing children (11–14 years). *British Journal of Educational Psychology*, 70, 505–518.

MacDonald, M. C., Just, M. A., & Carpenter, P. A. (1992). Working memory constraints on the processing of syntactic ambiguity. *Cognitive Psychology*, 24, 56–98.

Mace, A. L., Wallace, K. L., Whan, M. Q., & Stelmachowicz, P. G. (1991). Relevant factors in the identification of hearing loss. *Ear and Hearing*, 12, 287–293.

Maller, S. J., & Braden, J. P. (1993). The construct and criterion-related validity of the WISC-III with deaf adolescents. *Journal of Psychoeducational Assessment—Monograph Series: WISC-III*, 105–113.

Markides, A. (1970). The speech of deaf and partially hearing children with special reference to factors affecting intelligibility. *British Journal of Disorders of Communication*, 5, 126–140.

Marschark, M., Convertino, C., McEvoy, C., & Masteller, A. (2004). Organization and use of the mental lexicon by deaf and hearing individuals. *American Annals of the Deaf*, 149, 51–61.

Mayberry, R. I. (1992). The cognitive development of deaf children: Recent insights. In S. J. Segalowitz & I. Rapin (Eds.), *Handbook of neuropsychology: Vol. 7. Child neuropsychology* (pp. 51–68). New York: Elsevier.

McAfee, M. C., Kelly, J. F., & Samar, V. J. (1990). Spoken and written English errors of postsecondary students with severe hearing impairment. *Journal of Speech and Hearing Disorders*, 55, 628–634.

McGarr, N. S. (1983). The intelligibility of deaf speech to experienced and inexperienced listeners. *Journal of Speech and Hearing Research*, 26, 451–458.

Miller, J. F., & Chapman, R. S. (1981). The relation between age and mean length of utterance in morphemes. *Journal of Speech and Hearing Research*, 24, 154–161.

Moeller, M. P., & Luetke-Stahlman, B. (1990). Parents' use of Signing Exact English: A descriptive analysis. *Journal of Speech and Hearing Disorders*, 55, 327–337.

Montgomery, J. W. (2003). Working memory and comprehension in children with specific language impairment: What we know so far. *Journal of Communication Disorders*, 36, 221–231.

Nance, W. E. (2003). The genetics of deafness. *Mental retardation and developmental disabilities research reviews*, 9, 109–119.

Nikolopoulos, T. P., Dyar, D., Archbold, S., & O'Donoghue, G. M. (2004). Development of spoken language grammar following cochlear implantation in prelingually deaf children. *Archives of Otolaryngology—Head and Neck Surgery*, 130, 629–633.

Northern, J. L., & Downs, M. P. (2002). *Hearing in children* (5th ed.). Philadelphia: Lippincott Williams & Wilkins.

Oller, D. K., & Eilers, R. E. (1988). The role of audition in infant babbling. *Child Development, 59,* 441–449.

Osberger, M. J., & McGarr, N. (1982). Speech production characteristics of the hearing impaired. In N. Lass (Ed.), *Speech and language: Advances in basic research and practice* (Vol. 8, pp. 221–283). New York: Academic Press.

Paal, N., Skinner, S., & Reddig, C. (1988). The relationship of non-verbal intelligence measures to academic achievement among deaf adolescents. *Journal of Rehabilitation of the Deaf, 21,* 8–11.

Paradise, J. L., Campbell, T. F., Dollaghan, C. A., Feldman, H. M., Bernard, B. S., Colborn, D. K., et al. (2005). Developmental outcomes after early or delayed insertion of tympanostomy tubes. *New England Journal of Medicine, 353,* 576–586.

Pintner, R., & Patterson, D. (1917). A comparison of deaf and hearing children in visual memory for digits. *Journal of Experimental Psychology, 2,* 76–88.

Plante, E., Swisher, L., Kiernan, B., & Restrepo, M. A. (1993). Language matches: Illuminating or confounding? *Journal of Speech and Hearing Research, 36,* 772–776.

Power, D. J., & Quigley, S. P. (1973). Deaf children's acquisition of the passive voice. *Journal of Speech and Hearing Research, 16,* 5–11.

Quigley, S. P., & King, C. M. (1980). An invited article: Syntactic performance of hearing impaired and normal hearing individuals. *Applied Psycholinguistics, 1,* 329–356.

Quigley, S. P., & Paul, P. V. (1984). *Language and deafness.* San Diego, CA: College Hill Press.

Quigley, S. P., Smith, N. L., & Wilbur, R. B. (1974). Comprehension of relativized sentences by deaf children. *Journal of Speech and Hearing Research, 17,* 325–341.

Quigley, S. P., Wilbur, R. B., & Montanelli, D. S. (1974). Question formation in the language of deaf students. *Journal of Speech and Hearing Research, 17,* 699–713.

Ramkalawan, T. W., & Davis, A. C. (1992). The effects of hearing loss and age of intervention on some language metrics in young hearing-impaired children. *British Journal of Audiology, 26,* 97–107.

Roberts, J., Hunter, L., Gravel, J., Rosenfeld, R., Berman, S., Haggard, M., et al. (2004). Otitis media, hearing loss, and language learning: Controversies and current research. *Journal of Developmental and Behavioral Pediatrics, 25,* 110–122.

Roberts, J. E., Rosenfeld, R. M., & Zeisel, S. A. (2004). Otitis media and speech and language: A meta-analysis of prospective studies. *Pediatrics, 113,* 238–248.

Ruder, C. C. (2004). Grammatical morpheme development in young cochlear implant users. *International Congress Series, 1273,* 320–323.

Sander, E. (1972). When are speech sounds learned? *Journal of Speech and Hearing Disorders, 37,* 55–63.

Schauwers, K., Gillis, S., Daemers, K., De Beukelaer, C., & Govaerts, P. J. (2004). Cochlear implantation between 5 and 20 months of age: The onset of babbling and the audiologic outcome. *Otology and Neurotology, 25,* 263–270.

Schick, B., & Moeller, M. P. (1992). What is learnable in manually coded English sign systems? *Applied Psycholinguistics, 13,* 313–340.

Schildroth, A (1976). *The relationship of nonverbal intelligence test scores to selected characteristics of hearing impaired students.* Washington, DC: Gallaudet College, Office of Demographic Studies.

Serry, T. A., & Blamey, P. J. (1999). A 4-year investigation into phonetic inventory development in young cochlear implant users. *Journal of Speech, Language, and Hearing Research, 42,* 141–154.

Shafer, D., & Lynch, J. (1981). Emergent language of six prelingually deaf children. *Journal of the British Association of Teachers of the Deaf, 4,* 94–111.

Sharma, A., Tobey, E., Dorman, M., Bharadwaj, S., Martin, K., Gilley, P., & Kunkel, F. (2004). Central auditory maturation and babbling development in infants with cochlear implants. *Archives of Otolaryngology—Head and Neck Surgery, 130,* 511–516.

Smith, C. R. (1975). Residual hearing and speech production in deaf children. *Journal of Speech and Hearing Research, 18*, 795–811.

Spencer, L. J., Barker, B. A., & Tomblin, J. B. (2003). Exploring the language and literacy outcomes of pediatric cochlear implant users. *Ear and Hearing, 24*, 236–247.

Spencer, L. J., Tye-Murray, N., & Tomblin, J. B. (1998). The production of English inflectional morphology, speech production and listening performance in children with cochlear implants. *Ear and Hearing, 19*, 310–318.

Spencer, P. E. (2004). Individual differences in language performance after cochlear implantation at one to three years of age: Child, family, and linguistic factors. *Journal of Deaf Studies and Deaf Education, 9*, 395–412.

Staller, S. J., Beiter, A. L., Brimacombe, J. A., Mecklenberg, D., & Arndt, P. (1991). Pediatric performance with the Nucleus 22-channel cochlear implant system. *American Journal of Otology, 12*, 126–136.

Stelmachowicz, P. G., Pittman, A. L., Hoover, B. M., & Lewis, D. E. (2004). Novel-word learning in children with normal hearing and hearing loss. *Ear and Hearing, 25*, 47–56.

Stoel-Gammon, C. (1988). Prelinguistic vocalizations of hearing-impaired and normally hearing subjects: A comparison of consonantal inventories. *Journal of Speech and Hearing Disorders, 53*, 302–315.

Stoel-Gammon, C., & Otomo, K. (1986). Babbling development of hearing-impaired and normally hearing subjects. *Journal of Speech and Hearing Disorders, 51*, 33–41.

Svirsky, M. A., Chin, S. B., Miyamoto, R. T., Sloan, R. B., & Caldwell, M. D. (2000). Speech intelligibility of profoundly deaf pediatric hearing aid users. *Volta Review, 102*, 175–198.

Svirsky, M. A., Chute, P. M., Green, J., Bollard, P., & Miyamoto, R. T. (2000). Language development in children who are prelingually deaf who have used the SPEAK or CIS stimulation strategies since initial stimulation. *Volta Review, 102*, 199–213.

Svirsky, M. A., Stallings, L. M., Lento, C. L., Ying, E., & Leonard, L. B. (2002). Grammatical morphologic development in pediatric cochlear implant users may be affected by the perceptual prominence of the relevant markers. *Annals of Otology, Rhinology, and Laryngology, 189*(Suppl.), 109–112.

Szagun, G. (2000). The acquisition of grammatical and lexical structures in children with cochlear implants: A developmental psycholinguistic approach. *Audiology and Neurotology, 5*, 39–47.

Szagun, G. (2001). Language acquisition in young German-speaking children with cochlear implants: Individual differences and implications for conceptions of a "sensitive phase." *Audiology and Neuro-Otology, 6*, 288–297.

Szagun, G. (2004). Learning by ear: On the acquisition of case and gender marking by German-speaking children with normal hearing and with cochlear implants. *Journal of Child Language, 31*, 1–30.

Tobey, E. A., Geers, A. E., Brenner, C., Altuna, D., & Gabbert, G. (2003). Factors associated with development of speech production skills in children implanted by age five. *Ear and Hearing, 24*(Suppl.), 36S–45S.

Trybus, R. J., & Karchmer, M. A. (1977). School achievement scores of hearing impaired children: National data on achievement status and growth patterns. *American Annals of the Deaf Directory of Programs and Services, 122*, 62–69.

Tur-Kaspa, H., & Dromi, E. (1999). Spoken and written language assessment of orally trained children with hearing loss: Syntactic structures and deviations. *Volta Review, 100*, 186–202.

Tur-Kaspa, H., & Dromi, E. (2001). Grammatical deviations in the spoken and written language of Hebrew-speaking children with hearing impairment. *Language, Speech, and Hearing Services in Schools, 32*, 79–89.

Vernon, M. (1968). Fifty years of research on the intelligence of deaf and hard-of-hearing children: A review of literature and discussion of implications. *Journal of Rehabilitation of the Deaf, 1*, 1–11.

Waters, G., & Caplan, D. (2005). The relationship between age, processing speed, working memory capacity, and language comprehension. *Memory, 13*, 403–413.

Watson, B. U., Sullivan, P. M., Moeller, M. P., & Jensen, J. K. (1982). Nonverbal intelligence and English language ability in deaf children. *Journal of Speech and Hearing Disorders, 47,* 199–204.

Wechsler-Kashi, D., Schwartz, R. G., Cleary, M., & Madell, J. R. (2007). *Lexical processing in hearing impaired children with cochlear implants.* Manuscript in preparation.

Wilbur, R. (1977). An explanation of deaf children's difficulty with certain syntactic structures in English. *Volta Review, 79,* 85–92.

Willstedt-Svensson, U., Lofqvist, A., Almqvist, B., & Sahlén B. (2004). Is age at implant the only factor that counts? The influence of working memory on lexical and grammatical development in children with cochlear implants. *International Journal of Audiology, 43,* 506–515.

Young, G. A., & Killen, D. H. (2002). Receptive and expressive language skills of children with five years of experience using a cochlear implant. *Annals of Otology, Rhinology, and Laryngology, 111,* 802–810.

5

Dyslexia

SALLY E. SHAYWITZ, JEFFREY R. GRUEN, MARIA MODY,
and BENNETT A. SHAYWITZ

Developmental dyslexia is characterized by an unexpected difficulty in reading in children and adults who otherwise possess the intelligence and motivation considered necessary for accurate and fluent reading, and who also have had reasonable reading instruction. More formally,

> Dyslexia is a specific learning disability that is neurobiological in origin. It is characterized by difficulties with accurate and/or fluent word recognition and by poor spelling and decoding abilities. These difficulties typically result from a deficit in the phonological component of language that is often unexpected in relation to other cognitive abilities and the provision of effective classroom instruction (Lyon, Shaywitz, & Shaywitz, 2003, p. 1).

Dyslexia (or specific reading disability) is the most common and most carefully studied of the learning disabilities, affecting 80% of all individuals identified as learning disabled. This chapter reviews recent advances in our knowledge of the epidemiology, etiology, cognitive influences, clinical manifestations, and neurobiology of reading and dyslexia in children and adults. We begin with a historical perspective.

Developmental dyslexia in children was first noted in the latter part of the nineteenth century. At that time, physicians began to take note of a puzzling group of children who seemed to have all the factors present to be good readers: they were bright and motivated, their parents were caring and concerned, they had received intensive reading instruction and tutoring, and yet they continued to struggle to learn to read. This paradox was captured by Dr. W. Pringle Morgan in his report about 14-year-old Percy F. in the *British Medical Journal* on 7 November 1896 (Morgan, 1896, p. 1378): "He has always been a bright and intelligent boy, quick at games, and in no way inferior to others his age. His great difficulty has been—and is now—his inability to read."

Morgan labeled this condition congenital word-blindness (the term word-blindness—*Wortblindheit*—was originated by the German neurologist Adolf Kussmaul). In his report, Morgan (p. 1378) emphasizes the lack of obvious contributing factors, such as a previous head injury or illness, to the reading difficulty; concludes the disorder is congenital; and, in a highly prescient statement, ascribes the problem to a malfunction in the brain, specifically to a region in the left angular gyrus (see discussion of neurobiology below). He comments that the boy has good vision ("His eyes are normal . . . and his eyesight is good") and is intelligent ("The schoolmaster who has taught him for some years says that he would be the smartest lad in the school if the instruction were entirely oral").

Although Morgan is credited with the first description of a developmental reading problem, the observation that otherwise seemingly healthy men and women could lose the ability to read had already been made by other physicians. These instances all seemed to occur under similar circumstances: educated adults suddenly find themselves unable to read, a condition referred to as "acquired alexia." Invariably these individuals had suffered a brain insult, typically a stroke. What is perhaps the first recorded case of acquired alexia dates back to Johann Schmidt's description in 1676 of his 65-year-old patient, Nicholas Cambier. Two centuries later, in 1877, Adolf Kussmaul took an important step forward with his observation that the inability to read the print on the page may exist in the context of good eyesight, intelligence, and with spoken language intact—a condition he termed word-blindness (*Wortblindheit*). He was the first to suggest that the origins of the reading difficulties were due to a lesion in the left angular gyrus in right-handed people (reviewed by S. Shaywitz, 2003). Another decade would elapse before Professor Berlin in Germany would make the next seminal contribution to our understanding of acquired alexia. In a monograph published in 1887, Berlin, for the first time, used the term dyslexia to refer to this specific group of men and women who lose their ability to read as a result of a brain lesion.

> If the lesion was complete there would follow an absolute inability to read, what is referred to as acquired alexia; however, if the disruption was only partial, there may be very great difficulty in interpreting written or printed symbols (dyslexia). He conceptualizes dyslexia as a member of the larger family of language disorders called aphasias in which there is difficulty in either understanding or producing spoken language, or both (S. Shaywitz, 2003, p. 15).

General physicians, puzzled by their patient's seeming inability to see the words on the page, frequently referred affected individuals to ophthalmologists for further evaluation. It was a report in 1895 (Hinshelwood, 1895) of an adult with acquired dyslexia by Dr. James Hinshelwood, an ophthalmologist in Glasgow, Scotland, that served as the impetus for Morgan's report of his pediatric patient, Percy F., the following year in the *British Medical Journal*: He could read figures printed on the same scale as Jaeger No. 1, the smallest of the test types, and from other tests it was evident that there was no lowering of his visual acuity. His inability to read was thus manifestly not due to any failure of visual power. . . . No other mental defect could be ascertained on the most careful examination (Morgan, 1896, p. 1378).

Morgan noted the similarities of symptoms in the adult patient reported by Hinshelwood to the adolescent he was asked to evaluate: neither could read print, even though neither had visual problems and each was intelligent. In the case of the adult the reading difficulty is acquired, occurring in an individual who had been a competent reader; in the child, the condition is present from birth—it is congenital.

Not surprisingly, following Hinshelwood's and Morgan's reports, there were many reports of similar cases of unexpected reading difficulties, some acquired in adults, others in children, reflecting a reading difficulty present presumably since birth. These reports came not only from Britain, but from Europe, South America, and later, the United States (S. Shaywitz, 2003). Hinshelwood's (1912) descriptions of dyslexic children, living in a different time and in a different place, give proof of the universality of the condition. For example, he comments that one of the children, a little boy, learns very well if the lessons are oral; he observes the child is, at times, able to conceal his reading difficulty by memorizing his lessons; he relates that classmates tease him; he notes that his reading worsens when he is anxious; and he then shares the child's mother's observation that he is, in many ways, brighter than her other children, except for his inability to learn to read. Hinshelwood further notes that these children tend to subvocalize during reading and experience most difficulty with longer, multisyllabic words. Hinshelwood and others at the time also emphasized the unexpected nature of the reading difficulty: it was not due to a generalized deficit in intelligence, but to a "localized" problem affecting reading, so that affected children also manifest strengths as well as the weakness in reading. He also observes that the disorder occurs in gradations rather than as an all-or-none phenomenon—a finding that our research group has validated (S. E. Shaywitz, Escobar, Shaywitz, Fletcher, & Makuch, 1992). Consistent, too, with current experience, he notes that the disorder tends to go unrecognized and is no doubt more common than generally appreciated. Germane to clinical care today, Hinshelwood emphasized the importance of the history and observations in identifying a reading problem. It is worth noting that Hinshelwood and his colleagues were able to diagnose dyslexia on the basis of its clinical presentation: there were no standardized tests (The Binet–Simon Intelligence Scale, the first standardized test, was not published until 1905). Also pertinent to a current clinical issue, accommodations for students with dyslexia, is the observation, made over a century ago, that children with congenital word-blindness continue to be slow readers later in life. Hinshelwood approached congenital word-blindness from the perspective of a concerned clinician, recognizing the need for early identification, even noting greater neural plasticity in younger children; he cautioned schools not to ascribe the reading difficulty to lack of intelligence or motivation; he called for the screening of schoolchildren for signs of reading difficulties; and he urged schools to use systematic, scientifically based approaches to reading instruction.

We have included this historical review because, as one of us has often noted, "these case reports represent a valuable legacy: they provide indisputable evidence of the unchanging and enduring nature of the characteristics of dyslexia in children" (S. Shaywitz, 2003, p. 24).

EPIDEMIOLOGY

Epidemiological data indicate that, like hypertension and obesity, dyslexia occurs in gradations and fits a dimensional model. In other words, within the population, reading ability and reading disability occur along a continuum, with reading disability representing the lower tail of a normal distribution of reading ability (Gilger, Borecki, Smith, DeFries, & Pennington, 1996; S. Shaywitz et al., 1992). Dyslexia is perhaps the most common neurobehavioral disorder affecting children, with prevalence rates ranging from 5% to 17.5% (Interagency Committee on Learning Disabilities, 1987; S. Shaywitz, 1998). Data from the 2005 National Assessment of Educational Progress (Perie, Grigg, & Donahue, 2005) indicate that only 31% of fourth graders are performing at or above proficient levels. Longitudinal studies, both prospective (Francis, Shaywitz, Stuebing, Shaywitz, & Fletcher, 1996; B. Shaywitz, Fletcher et al., 1995) and retrospective (Bruck, 1992; Felton, Naylor, & Wood, 1990; Scarborough, 1990), indicate that dyslexia is a persistent, chronic condition; it does not represent a transient developmental lag (Figure 5.1). Over time, poor readers and good readers tend to maintain their relative positions along the spectrum of reading ability (Francis et al., 1996; B. A. Shaywitz, Holford et al., 1995); children who early on function at the 10th percentile for reading and those who function at the 90% percentile and all those in-between tend to maintain their positions.

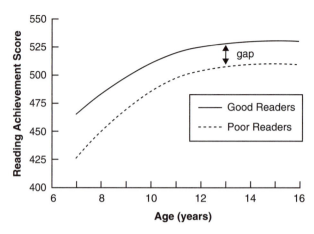

FIGURE 5.1   Trajectory of reading skills over time in nonimpaired and dyslexic readers. Ordinate is Rasch scores (W scores) from the Woodcock–Johnson reading test (Woodcock & Johnson, 1989), and abscissa is age in years. Both dyslexic and nonimpaired readers improve their reading scores as they get older, but the gap between the dyslexic and nonimpaired readers remains. Thus, dyslexia is a deficit and not a developmental lag. (Figure derived from data in Francis et al., 1996, and reprinted from S. Shaywitz, 2003, with permission.)

ETIOLOGY

Dyslexia is both familial and heritable (Pennington & Gilger, 1996). Family history is one of the most important risk factors, with 23% to as much as 65% of children who have a parent with dyslexia reported to have the disorder (Scarborough, 1990). A rate among siblings of affected persons of approximately 40% and among parents ranging from 27% to 49% (Pennington & Gilger, 1996) implies that it should be possible to identify affected siblings early and also to identify affected adults, such as a parent of the child known to be dyslexic. Yet despite the strong familial nature, within a single family both recessive and dominant transmission is frequently observed. These data are consistent with a complex etiology: studies of heritability show that between 44% and 75% of the variance is explained by genetic factors and the remaining by environmental factors (DeFries, Olson, Pennington, & Smith, 1991). These genetic factors are variations (i.e., alleles) of several genes (i.e., poly-genic) that act in concert to produce the dyslexia phenotype, and because of the polygenic nature, create confusing transmission patterns that do not follow traditional Mendelian rules governing recessive, dominant, or sex-linked single-gene disorders. Regardless of these complexities, contemporary methods have evolved, aided in large part by the strides of the Human Genome Project that enabled the identification of broad locations on human chromosomes, called loci, where candidate genes that contribute to the dyslexia phenotype were encoded. These loci, called "DYX1" through "DYX9" for the order in which they were recognized, were identified by genetic linkage studies of dyslexia transmission patterns and chromosome recombination events within families.

Of the nine described dyslexia loci, the most widely reproduced has been DYX2 located on the "p" or short arm of chromosome 6 in band "22" (6p22), spanning nearly 20 million bases. Recently, we reported association of the *DCDC2* gene encoded on 6p22 with several reading-related phenotypes suggesting a specific effect on reading performance (Meng et al., 2005). Furthermore, in the human brain, *DCDC2* expression correlated with the location of reading-related brain systems (see below), and we found that *DCDC2* in rats modulated neuronal migration. The association between *DCDC2* and dyslexia was subsequently and independently confirmed by Schumacheç et al. (2006) in a two-tiered study of 137 and 239 families with dyslexia from Germany, thereby validating our findings and the universality of the genetic effect across languages and cultures.

Other candidate genes for dyslexia have been described as well. Encoded just 500,000 bases away from *DCDC2*, Cope et al. (2005) described a second candidate gene for DYX2, called *KIAA0319*, which, in 143 families from the United Kingdom, also contributed to dyslexia. Two other candidates, *EKN1* (DYX1) and *ROBO1* (DYX5), were identified by cloning rare translocation breakpoints in single families from Finland, but validation in additional populations would make for more convincing evidence (Hannula-Jouppi et al., 2005; Taipale et al., 2003). Gene discovery for all the dyslexia loci remains an active area of study (see chapter 10 by Tomblin).

COGNITIVE INFLUENCES: THEORIES OF DEVELOPMENTAL DYSLEXIA

A number of theories of dyslexia have been proposed, including the phonological theory (Liberman, Shankweiler, & Liberman, 1989; Ramus et al., 2003); the rapid auditory processing theory (Tallal, 1980, 2000; Tallal, Miller, & Fitch, 1993); the visual theory (Livingstone, Rosen, Drislane, & Galaburda, 1991; Lovegrove, Bowling, Badcock, & Blackwood, 1980); the cerebellar theory (Nicolson & Fawcett, 1990; Nicolson, Fawcett, & Dean, 2001); and the magnocellular theory (Galaburda, Menard, & Rosen, 1994; Livingstone et al., 1991; Stein, 2003; Stein & Walsh, 1997). The reader is referred to Ramus et al. (2003) for a review and critique of the various theories. Among investigators in the field, there is now a strong consensus supporting the phonological theory. This theory recognizes that speech and language are acquired naturally, whereas reading must be taught. To read, the beginning reader must recognize that the letters and letter strings (the orthography) represent the sounds of spoken language. In order to read, a child has to develop the insight that spoken words can be pulled apart into the elemental particles of speech (phonemes) and that the letters in a written word represent these sounds (S. Shaywitz, 2003); such awareness is largely missing in dyslexic children and adults (Bruck, 1992; Fletcher et al., 1994; Liberman & Shankweiler, 1991; Shankweiler, Liberman, Mark, Fowler, & Fischer, 1979; S. Shaywitz, 2003; Torgesen & Wagner, 1995; Wagner & Torgesen, 1987). Results from large and well-studied populations with reading disability confirm that in young school-age children (Fletcher et al., 1994; Stanovich & Siegel, 1994) as well as in adolescents (S. Shaywitz et al., 1999) a deficit in phonology represents the most robust and specific correlate of reading disability (Mody, 2003; Morris et al., 1998; Ramus et al., 2003). Such findings form the basis for the most successful and evidence-based interventions designed to improve reading (Report of the National Reading Panel, 2000).

IMPLICATIONS OF THE PHONOLOGICAL MODEL OF DYSLEXIA

Reading is composed of two main processes: decoding and comprehension (Gough & Tunmer, 1986). In dyslexia, a deficit at the level of the phonological module impairs the ability to segment the spoken word into its underlying phonological elements and then link each letter(s) to its corresponding sound(s). As a result, the reader experiences difficulty, first in decoding the word and then in identifying it. The phonological deficit is domain-specific; it is independent of other, nonphonological, abilities. In particular, the higher order cognitive and linguistic functions involved in comprehension, such as general intelligence and reasoning, vocabulary (Share & Stanovich, 1995), and syntax (Shankweiler et al., 1995), are generally intact. This pattern—a deficit in phonological analysis contrasted with intact higher order cognitive abilities—offers an explanation for the paradox of otherwise intelligent, often gifted, creative people who experience great difficulty in reading (S. Shaywitz, 1996, 2003). According to the model, a circumscribed deficit in a lower order linguistic function (phonology) blocks access to higher order language processes. The affected reader cannot use his or her higher order linguistic skills to access the meaning until the printed word has first been decoded and identified.

NEUROBIOLOGICAL STUDIES OF DISABLED READERS

Though brain imaging studies of dyslexia are relatively recent, neural systems influencing reading were first proposed over a century ago by Dejerine in studies of adults who suffered a stroke with subsequent acquired alexia, the sudden loss of the ability to read (Dejerine, 1891). Dejerine proposed at least two brain regions in the left hemisphere, one in the parietotemporal region, the other more inferior in the occipitotemporal region. Since that time a large literature on acquired inability to read (acquired alexia) describes neuroanatomic lesions most prominently centered about the angular gyrus as a region considered pivotal in mapping the visual percept of the print onto the phonological structures of the language system (Damasio & Damasio, 1983; Friedman, Ween, & Albert, 1993; Geschwind, 1965). Other studies using postmortem brain specimens (Galaburda, Sherman, Rosen, Aboitiz, & Geschwind, 1985) and, more recently, brain morphometry (Brown et al., 2001; Eliez et al., 2000) and diffusion tensor MRI imaging (Klingberg et al., 2000) suggests that there are differences in the temporoparieto-occipital brain regions between dyslexic and nonimpaired readers. It has only been within the last two decades that neuroscientists have been able to determine the neural systems that influence reading and reading disability. This explosion in understanding the neural bases of reading and dyslexia has been driven by the development of functional neuroimaging, a technique that measures changes in metabolic activity and blood flow in specific brain regions while subjects are engaged in cognitive tasks. These technologies include positron emission tomography (PET) and functional magnetic resonance imaging (fMRI; chapter 7 by Tropper & Schwartz and chapter 24 by Shafer & Maxfield); both depend on the principle of autoregulation of cerebral blood flow (see Anderson & Gore, 1997; Frackowiak et al., 2004; and Jezzard, Matthews, & Smith, 2001 for a detailed description of fMRI).

A number of research groups, including our own, have used PET or fMRI to examine the functional organization of the brain for reading in nonimpaired and dyslexic readers, and generally have validated these two left hemisphere posterior systems as critical to reading. For example, in studies of adults (S. Shaywitz et al., 1998) and in a study of 144 children, half of whom were struggling readers and half nonimpaired readers, we (B. Shaywitz et al., 2002) found significant differences in brain activation patterns during phonological analysis between dyslexic and nonimpaired children. Specifically, nonimpaired children demonstrate significantly greater activation than do dyslexic children in predominantly left hemisphere sites (including the inferior frontal, superior temporal, parietotemporal, and middle temporal–middle occipital gyri). These data converge with reports that show a failure of left hemisphere posterior brain systems to function properly during reading and indicate that dysfunction in left hemisphere posterior reading circuits is already present in dyslexic children and cannot be ascribed simply to a lifetime of poor reading (reviewed in Price & Mechelli, 2005; S. Shaywitz & Shaywitz, 2005). Although dyslexic readers exhibit a dysfunction in posterior reading systems, they appear to develop compensatory systems involving areas around the inferior frontal gyrus in both hemispheres as well as the right hemisphere homologue of the left occipitotemporal word-form area (B. Shaywitz et al., 2002).

There are a number of interrelated neural networks used in reading, at least two in posterior brain regions as well as a distinct and related network in anterior regions. The anterior network in the inferior frontal gyrus (Broca's area) has long been associated with articulation and also serves an important function in silent reading and naming (Fiez & Peterson, 1998; Frackowiak et al., 2004). The two posterior regions appear to parallel the two systems proposed by Logan (1988, 1997) as critical in the development of skilled, automatic reading. One system involves word analysis, operates on individual units of words such as phonemes, requires attentional resources, and processes information relatively slowly. It is reasonable to propose that this system involves the parietotemporal posterior reading network (S. Shaywitz, 2003) (Figure 5.2). Considerable research in the last five years has converged to indicate that the second posterior network, localized to a region termed the visual word-form area (McCandliss, Cohen, & Dehaene, 2003) influences skilled, fluent reading. Dehaene and his associates (Cohen, Jobert, Le Bihan, & Dehaene, 2004; Dehaene, Cohen, Sigman, & Vinckier, 2005; Nakamura et al., 2005) have suggested a systematic sensitivity to coding within the left occipitotemporal region, with more posterior regions coding for letters and letter fragments and more anterior regions coding for bigrams and words. Furthermore, recent evidence indicates that the disruption in the left occipitotemporal word-form area in dyslexic individuals is found not only for reading words, but for naming the pictures of the words, suggesting that the disruption in this region "reflects a more general impairment in retrieving phonology from visual input. In other words, reduced activation in the same occipitotemporal region may underlie the reading and naming deficits observed in developmental dyslexia." (McCrory, Mechelli, Frith, & Price, 2005, p. 265).

Functional magnetic resonance imaging has been helpful in clarifying potentially different types of reading disability. The Connecticut Longitudinal Study (reviewed in S. Shaywitz, 2003, pp. 26–35, and Ferrer et al., 2007) includes a representative sample of now young adults who have been prospectively followed since 1983, when they were aged 5 years, and who have had their reading performance assessed yearly throughout their

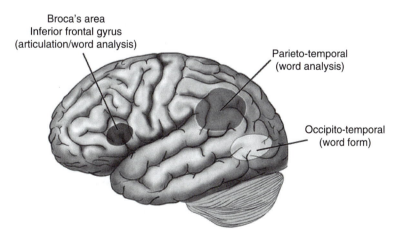

FIGURE 5.2 Neural systems for reading. (Reprinted from S. Shaywitz, 2003, with permission.)

primary and secondary schooling. We examined three groups of young adults, ages 18.5–22.5 years, who were classified as: (1) persistently poor readers (PPR: poor accuracy and poor fluency); (2) accuracy (but not fluency) improved (compensated) readers (AIR); and (3) nonimpaired readers (NI) (S. Shaywitz et al., 2003). During real word reading, brain activation patterns in the two groups of disabled readers (PPR and AIR) diverged, with AIR demonstrating the typical disruption of posterior systems and with PPR activating posterior systems, similar to that observed in NI readers, despite the significantly better reading performance in NI compared to PPR on every reading task administered. Connectivity patterns between the left occipitotemporal word-form area and other brain regions differed considerably between PPR and NI readers: for NI readers, these connectivity patterns from the left occipitotemporal word-form area occurred via what has come to be thought of as traditional reading-related brain areas—for example, the left inferior frontal gyrus (Broca's area). In contrast, for PPR readers, connectivity patterns from the left occipitotemporal word-form area were aberrant—occurring via right frontal regions that have come to be associated with memory systems.

A more recent fMRI study (B. Shaywitz et al., 2007) also demonstrates the importance of memory systems in dyslexic readers. This study found that brain regions developing with age in dyslexic readers differ from those in nonimpaired readers, primarily in being localized to a more left posterior and medial, rather than to a more left anterior and lateral occipitotemporal region. This difference in activation patterns between dyslexic and nonimpaired readers has parallels to reported brain activation differences observed during reading of two Japanese writing systems: Kana and Kanji. Kana script employs symbols that are linked to the sound (comparable to English and other alphabetic scripts), whereas Kanji script uses ideographs where each character must be memorized. In the imaging study of these writing systems, activation similar to that seen in nonimpaired readers occurred during reading Kana. In contrast, activation comparable to that observed in dyslexic readers was noted during reading of Kanji script, suggesting that the portion of the word-form region developing in dyslexic readers functions as part of a memory-based system.

Data from as early as kindergarten and first grade indicated that the two groups of disabled readers (PPR and AIR) began school with comparable reading skills but with PPRs having poorer cognitive ability (as measured by first-grade IQ scores) and tending to attend more disadvantaged schools (as measured by the percentage of children in school receiving free lunches) than AIRs. These findings suggest that the PPRs may be doubly disadvantaged in being exposed to a less rich language environment at home (including less reading experience) and then less effective reading instruction at school (reflected in the percentage of children receiving free lunches). The presence of compensatory factors such as stronger cognitive ability allowed the AIRs to minimize the consequences of their phonological deficit so that, as adults, AIRs were indistinguishable from NIs on a measure of reading comprehension. These findings of differences, neurobiologically, cognitively, and educationally, suggest that the two types of reading disability we observed in the Connecticut Longitudinal Study sample may represent different etiologies. The compensated group (AIR), with early higher cognitive ability and a disruption in posterior systems during pseudo word reading, may represent a primarily genetic type of reading disability, consistent with studies showing genetic reading difficulties tend to be associated with higher IQs (Olson, Forsberg, Gayan, & DeFries, 1999). We postulate that such children represent the classic dyslexic reader. Alternatively, the reading difficulties in the persistent group (PPR) may arise from environmental factors. Genetic studies should be helpful in differentiating these two types at an early age.

Functional imaging has been helpful, too, in examining the obvious question of whether the neural systems for reading are malleable and whether the disruption in these systems in struggling readers can be changed by an effective reading intervention that focuses on the five components of effective reading programs (see Management section for review). We (B. Shaywitz et al., 2004) examined this question in second- and third-grade dyslexic readers. Compared to dyslexic readers who received other types of intervention, children who received the experimental intervention not only improved their reading accuracy, reading fluency, and reading comprehension but, compared to preintervention brain imaging, demonstrated increased activation both in left anterior (inferior frontal gyrus) and left posterior (middle temporal gyrus) brain regions. Other investigators, too, have found that an effective reading intervention influences neural systems in brain in very much the same fashion (Aylward et al., 2003; Eden et al., 2004; Simos et al., 2002; Temple et al., 2000, 2003). These data have important implications for public policy regarding teaching children to read. The provision of an evidence-based reading intervention at an early age improves reading fluency and facilitates the development of those neural systems that underlie skilled reading.

Reading and Dyslexia in Languages Other than English

Phonological deficits also characterize dyslexia in individuals whose native language is not English, but who still use an alphabetic script in reading. Thus, Paulesu and colleagues (Paulesu et al., 2001) noted a comparable disruption to native English speakers in posterior reading systems in Italian- and French-speaking college students with dyslexia. Recent studies have begun to examine dyslexia in Chinese readers using fMRI tasks requiring subjects to judge whether two Chinese characters were homophones and whether two Chinese characters shared the same initial consonant. In nonimpaired readers, Siok and his associates suggested that the left middle frontal gyrus is critical for skilled Chinese reading (Siok, Jin, Fletcher, & Tan, 2003). This region appears critical in processing syllables, whereas the left inferior frontal gyrus mediates the processing of phonemes. This pattern of findings offers compelling evidence for distinct cortical areas relevant to the representation of syllables and phonemes. In a recent report, Siok et al. (Siok, Perfetti, Jin, & Tan, 2004) found that dyslexic Chinese children demonstrated reduction in activation of the left middle frontal gyrus with increased activation in the left inferior frontal gyrus—presumably a compensatory activation. Brain imaging during a word-recognition task indicated that dyslexic Chinese children showed reduced activation in both left and right middle frontal gyri, left and right inferior frontal gyri, and left fusiform gyrus. Dyslexic readers demonstrated increased activation in right occipital cortex. Thus, in a pattern similar to that of dyslexic English readers, dyslexic Chinese children exhibit reduced activation in left occipito-temporal regions (fusiform gyrus). However, in contrast to dyslexic American children, no differences were observed in parietotemporal regions.

Magnetoencephalography and Event Related Potentials Using Electroencephalography

Within brain imaging, multimodal imaging techniques are increasingly being employed in studies of reading and dyslexia. Although considerable evidence has emerged using fMRI and PET to examine the different cortical systems used in reading, both fMRI and PET have a fundamental limitation in terms of the chronometry, the time course in milliseconds (ms) of the activations of systems used for reading. Critical components of the reading process occur within 100–500 ms after presentation of the stimulus, but the response of fMRI and PET signals is in the order of seconds. Fortunately, two technologies—magnetic source imaging using magnetoencephalography (MEG) and event related-potentials

(ERPs) using high-density electroencephalography—provide the tools to begin to resolve the chronometric properties of cognitive processes. Although MEG and ERP signals are able to capture the time course of cognitive processes in brain, they have only moderate spatial resolution. Combining the chronometry provided by MEG and ERP with the superior spatial resolution of fMRI helps improve the source localization accuracy of MEG (Ahlfors et al., 1999) while adding a dynamic dimension of the time course of the response of the cortical systems to print.

Although MEG and EEG both measure changes in postsynaptic neural currents, the magnetic field (MEG), unlike electrical potentials (EEG), is minimally affected by the conductivity of the skull and scalp. This simplifies the deduction of the current sources from the measured field distribution in MEG compared to EEG, which is especially important when it comes to resolving spatiotemporally overlapping subprocesses in reading (Hämäläinen, Hari, Ilmoniemi, Knuutila, & Lounasmaa, 1993).

MEG and ERP Using Words or Pseudowords: Selected Studies

By way of introduction, the signals detected by MEG and ERP are usually referred to as either positive (P) or negative (N) and a time in milliseconds. The time refers to the maximal signal obtained following presentation of a stimulus. For example, N400 refers to a signal that is negative in direction and approximately 400 ms following a stimulus.

Using MEG, Salmelin and colleagues (Salmelin, Service, Kiesila, Uutela, & Salonen, 1996) found that dyslexic adults did not elicit a left occipitotemporal response within the first 200 ms after a written word was presented, whereas fluent readers had a strong transient response at 120 ms post stimulus onset. Intracranial recordings using ERP (Nobre, Allison, & McCarthy, 1994) have suggested a preferential response to letter strings in this vicinity in bilateral fusiform gyrus, findings consonant with the fMRI studies of the left occipitotemporal word-form region noted previously. Unlike normal controls in these studies, the dyslexic readers in these studies also failed to show activation in left temporoparietal areas between 200–400 ms. The dyslexic subjects activate inferior frontal regions, around Broca's area, instead, suggestive of their use of covert articulation routines under phonologically demanding conditions to assist with decoding.

In a separate MEG study also involving printed word recognition, dyslexic children 10–17 years of age showed minimal activation in left temporoparietal areas but consistently activated homologous areas in the right hemisphere instead (Simos, Breier, Fletcher, Bergman, & Papanicolaou, 2000; Simos, Breier, Fletcher, Foorman et al., 2000). They also showed strong left inferior temporal activation, unlike the adult dyslexics in Salmelin's studies. Simos and colleagues attribute this difference across studies to the greater inter-subject consistency in children's use of visual cues. They interpret the underactivation of the left-temporoparietal areas as representing a phonological deficit, with the children's use of right hemisphere temporal areas serving as a compensatory mechanism.

Tarkiainen, Helenius, Hansen, Cornelissen, and Salmelin (1999), also using MEG, found only weak or absent letter-string-specific activation in dyslexic adults compared to normal controls in the occipitotemporal junction around 150 ms poststimulus. They hypothesized that the abnormally early activation in temporal parietal areas seen in some poor readers may be a consequence of this missing occipitotemporal activity. That the dyslexic readers in their study also showed little difference between letters and symbols was further evidence of their poor word-form recognition abilities. In a study of orthographic and phonological processing in dyslexics and normal controls using ERP, Meyler and Breznitz (2005) found that processing differences between the groups was greatest for phonological representations, evident in the P2/P3 responses (positive ERP responses 200 and 300 ms, respectively, after the stimulus). Schulte-Korne and colleagues (Schulte-Korne, Deimel, Bartling, & Remschmidt, 2004), using ERP, found significant differences between dyslexic adolescents and matched controls in the form of an attenuated positivity around 600 ms (P600) for the pseudowords, but no such difference in the recognition of graphic materials. They concluded that dyslexic children's impaired recognition memory was specific for linguistic materials. The results are similar to those obtained using ERP by Russeler, Probst, Johannes, and Münte (2003), who found the P600 with words only in normal readers and not in their adult developmental dyslexic group.

Over the years, research in dyslexia has also implicated speech perception abilities. In an MEG study involving perception of synthetic speech, Breier and colleagues (2003) found increased right temporoparietal activation in subjects with dyslexia compared to unimpaired readers. In fact, the relative activation in this area correlated with reduced performance of the subjects on phonological processing measures. Using ERP and fMRI, Georgiewa and colleagues (Georgiewa et al., 2002) found significant differences in the left frontal electrode voltage between 250–500 ms, along with heightened activation in inferior frontal areas in a group of 13-year-old dyslexic boys compared to normal controls. Insofar as inferior frontal areas—more specifically Broca's area—are considered to be involved in phonological coding, group differences here point to difficulties in the phonological domain for the impaired reader. A closer look at phonological processing during spoken word recognition (lexical decision task) in dyslexic and normal readers using ERP, however, has revealed deviant responses in earlier time windows surrounding N1 (negative response 100 ms following a stimulus) and N2 (negative response 200 ms following a stimulus), for the impaired group, but normal N400 responses comparable to controls (Bonte & Blomert, 2004). The authors interpreted this as selective processing anomalies in dyslexic readers at an earlier phonetic/phonological level, with normal processing at a later phonological/ lexical level.

Though some studies have raised the possibility of a general nonlinguistic low-level auditory deficit in dyslexia, the preponderance of evidence indicates that the principal cognitive deficit in dyslexia is at the level of phonology. Several authors have provided a full discussion of this issue (Rosen, 2003; Studdert-Kennedy & Mody, 1995; White et al., 2006).

MEG and ERP Using Sentences

In contrast to the number of MEG and ERP studies that have examined phonological abilities using single-word or pseudoword tasks, studies of reading comprehension in dys-lexia are relatively few in number. Using MEG and the well-established N400 paradigm, Helenius, Salmelin, Service, and Connolly (1999) tested a group of dyslexic adults and normal controls to examine potential differences in the cortical circuitry for reading com-prehension between the groups. The appropriateness of each sentence-final word fell into one of four categories: congruent, incongruent, rare but possible, and incongruent begin-ning with a phonological foil—with a letter that could be the initial sound of a congruent choice. Both groups exhibited larger responses to the incongruent than to the congruent final words; dyslexic readers exhibited significantly weaker N400 responses to the incon-gruent word starting with the phonological foil compared to the incongruent terminal word. This suggests that the dyslexics may have mistaken the former as a right choice due to a tendency to read sublexically (i.e., slowly, letter by letter). Additionally, their delayed and reduced semantic activation did not start until about 300 ms poststimulus, compared to the 200 ms in the unimpaired readers, though some studies have found a larger N400 in dyslexics thought to result from difficulties with integrating the meaning of words within a sentence (Robichon, Besson, & Habib, 2002). The results of Helenius, Tarkiainen,

Cornelissen, Hansen, and Salmelin (1999) resemble those obtained by Brandeis, Vitacco, and Steinhausen (1994), where poor readers also exhibited reduced N400 responses to deviant sentence endings compared to normal controls.

Increasing numbers of studies appear to have found reduced functional asymmetry in dyslexic subjects, evident in the distribution of activation sources on many of the above auditory tasks (Duncan et al., 1994; Heim, Eulitz, & Elbert, 2003a, 2003b; Helenius, Salmelin, Richardson, Leinonen, & Lyytinen, 2002; Taylor & Keenan, 1990). More recently, altered hemispheric lateralization findings in dyslexic children during printed word processing appear to support the hypothesis of a difficulty in manipulating phonological features of letter strings. Penolazzi and colleagues (Penolazzi, Spironelli, Vio, & Angrilli, 2006) found a left lateralized N400 response, believed to reflect phonological processing during reading (Bentin, Mouchetant-Rostaing, Giard, Echallier, & Pernier, 1999), in controls but not in dyslexic readers, who exhibited a more distributed pattern across both hemispheres.

In summary, reading-specific activations in inferior temporal (150–200 ms) and superior temporal (200–400 ms) cortices appear to be strongly lateralized in the left hemisphere. The dyslexic reader shows absent or delayed activation in both these areas, with a tendency to recruit left inferior frontal and right hemisphere temporal areas. Insofar as the development of reading is necessarily preceded by the acquisition of oral language, especially phonological abilities, the absence of an early letter-string specific response in occipitotemporal areas may be a reflection of a poorly established phonological (sound–symbol correspondence) system.

CLINICAL MANIFESTATIONS

Difficulties in decoding and word recognition may vary according to age and developmental level. Reflecting the phonological nature of the basic difficulty in dyslexia, clues in spoken language may be noted early on, even before children are expected to be able to read. Manifestations of the core phonological difficulty may be detected at all ages, including adulthood. Below, the major clinical findings and approaches to diagnosis are discussed (see chapter 19 by Hook & Haynes). It is also important to appreciate that dyslexia may co-occur with attention-deficit/hyperactivity disorder (ADHD). Although this comorbidity has been documented in both referred samples (40% comorbidity) and nonreferred samples (15% comorbidity), the two disorders are distinct and separable.

DIAGNOSIS

The clinician seeks to determine through history, observation, and psychometric assessment, if there are: (1) unexpected difficulties in reading (i.e., difficulties in reading that are unexpected for the person's age, intelligence, or level of education or professional status) and (2) associated linguistic problems at the level of phonological processing. There is no one single test score that is diagnostic for dyslexia, or, conversely, that rules out a diagnosis of dyslexia. (This is an important point, since many standardized testing agencies seem to deny requests for accommodations based on a single test score. Accommodations are discussed more fully below.) As with any other diagnosis, the diagnosis of dyslexia should reflect a thoughtful synthesis of all the clinical data available. Dyslexia is distinguished from other disorders that may prominently feature reading difficulties by the unique, circumscribed nature of the phonological deficit that does not typically intrude into other linguistic or cognitive domains.

In the preschool child, a history of language delay or early signs of phonological difficulties manifest as not attending to the sounds of words (trouble learning nursery rhymes or playing rhyming games with words, confusing words that sound alike, mispronouncing words), trouble learning to recognize and to name the letters of the alphabet, along with a positive family history, represent important risk factors for dyslexia. In the school-aged child, presenting complaints most commonly center about school performance—"she's not doing well in school,"—and often parents (and teachers) do not appreciate that the reason for this is a reading difficulty. A typical picture is that of a child who may have had a delay in producing first words, does not learn letters by kindergarten, has not begun to learn to read by first grade, and has difficulty consistently sounding out words. The child progressively falls behind, with teachers and parents puzzled as to why such an intelligent child, who seems to grasp concepts so easily, may have difficulty learning to read. The reading difficulty is unexpected with respect to the child's ability, age, or grade. Even after acquiring decoding skills, the child typically remains a slow reader. Thus, dyslexic children, often very bright children, may laboriously learn how to read words accurately but do not become fast or automatic readers (see below). A child's difficulties become apparent when he or she is asked to read aloud in class, where mispronunciations, omissions of words that are present, or conversely, inserting words that are not on the page, reading with a lack of prosody, and frequent pauses, hesitations, or loss of place are noted. Difficulties not only involve decoding, but deficits in spelling are also frequently observed. Together, poor spelling and messy handwriting result in difficulties in note-taking in class. As children progress in school, other problems are noted: seeming inability to learn a second language and an avoidance of reading. At all ages, spoken language difficulties are evident—for example, speech that is not fluent and is replete with hesitations, um's, and mispronunciations, difficulties with word retrieval, circumlocutions, and the need for time to summon an oral response. Listening comprehension is typically robust (Bruck, 1992; Bryant, MacLean, Bradley, & Crossland, 1990; Catts, 1989; Gallagher, Frith, & Snowling, 2000; Scarborough, 1990; S. Shaywitz, 2003; S. Shaywitz et al., 1999).

In several studies, older children have been found to improve reading accuracy over time, albeit without commensurate gains in reading fluency (the ability to read words accurately, rapidly, and with good intonation); they remain slow readers (Bruck, 1990, 1998; Lefly & Pennington, 1991; S. Shaywitz, 2003). In particular, the refractory difficulty in being able to read fluently is often the hallmark of dyslexia in even the brightest of older children and adults. For example, in an accomplished adolescent or young adult, dyslexia is often reflected by slowness in reading or choppy reading aloud that is unexpected in relation to the level of education or professional status—for example, graduation from a competitive college or completion of graduate, law, or medical school and a residency. Thus, in bright adolescents and young adults, a history of phonologically based reading difficulties, requirements for extra time on tests, and current slow and effortful reading—signs of a lack of automaticity in reading—are the sine qua non of a diagnosis of dyslexia. As discussed previously, there is strong evidence of a neurobiological basis for this persistence of slow reading, a disruption in the neural circuitry in the word-form area in the back of the left hemisphere. Self-esteem is frequently affected, particularly if the disorder has gone undetected for a long period of time (S. Shaywitz, 2003). In summary, at all ages, a history of difficulties getting to the basic sounds of spoken language, of mispronunciations, of confusing words that sound alike, of difficulties in word retrieval and a lack of glibness, of laborious and slow reading and writing, of poor spelling, of requiring additional time in reading and in taking tests, provide indisputable evidence of a deficiency in phonological processing, which, in turn, serves as the basis for, and the signature of, a reading disability.

ASSESSMENT

Even prior to the time a child is expected to read, his or her readiness may be assessed by measurement of the skills, especially phonological, related to reading success. Following a predictable developmental pathway, children's phonological abilities can be evaluated beginning at about age 4 to 5 years. Such tests are centered on a child's ability to focus on syllables and then, phonemes. In general, as a child develops, he gains the ability to notice and to manipulate smaller and smaller parts of spoken words (Moats, 2000; Snow, Burns, & Griffin, 1998; Torgesen & Mathes, 2000; Uhry, 2005). Tests of phonological capabilities and reading readiness are becoming increasingly available—for example, the Comprehensive Test of Phonological Processing in Reading (CTOPP) (Torgesen et al., 1999); the CTOPP is normed from age 5 through adult.

Reading is assessed by measuring accuracy, fluency, and comprehension. In the school-age child, one important element of the evaluation is how accurately the child can decode words (i.e., read single words). This is measured with standardized tests of single real word and pseudoword reading, such as the Woodcock–Johnson III (WJ–III; Mather & Woodcock, 2001). Because pseudowords are unfamiliar and cannot be memorized, each nonsense word must be sounded out. Tests of nonsense word reading are referred to as *word attack*. Reading (passage) comprehension is also assessed by the Woodcock–Johnson test. Reading fluency, an often overlooked component of reading, is of critical importance, because it allows for the automatic, attention-free recognition of words. Fluency is generally assessed by asking the child to read *aloud* using the Gray Oral Reading Test (GORT-4) (Wiederholt & Bryant, 2001). This test consists of 13 increasingly difficult passages, each followed by five comprehension questions; scores for accuracy, rate, fluency, and comprehension are provided. Such tests of oral reading are particularly helpful in identifying a child who is dyslexic; by its nature, oral reading forces a child to pronounce each word. Listening to a struggling reader attempt to pronounce each word leaves no doubt about the child's reading difficulty. In addition to reading passages aloud, single-word reading efficiency may be assessed using, for example, the Test of Word Reading Efficiency (TOWRE) (Torgesen et al., 1999), a test of speeded oral reading of individual words. Children who struggle with reading often have trouble spelling; spelling may be assessed with the WJ–III spelling test (Mather & Woodcock, 2001).

The role of intelligence testing in dyslexia is controversial. The traditional IQ-achievement discrepancy is referred to as a *wait to fail* model. It typically takes a child three years to develop a large enough discrepancy to qualify for school services, thus delaying early identification and effective reading intervention. On the other hand, measures of intelligence can be helpful as one component of a comprehensive assessment. Very often they reveal areas of strength, particularly in areas of abstract thinking and reasoning, which are very reassuring to parents and, especially, to the child him/herself. They also indicate that the reading difficulty is isolated and not reflective of a general lack of learning ability. It is inappropriate to wait for a large IQ-reading discrepancy before providing a child with reading intervention. If despite good intelligence, motivation, and appropriate reading instruction the clinical picture, including history of spoken language difficulties, difficulties getting to the sounds of written words, problems reading words accurately or fluently, slow reading, trouble spelling words converges with indications of reading and phonological weaknesses in a school-age child, that child should be eligible to receive school-based reading interventions.

Because they are able to read words accurately (albeit very slowly), dyslexic adolescents and young adults may mistakenly be assumed to have *outgrown* their dyslexia (Bruck, 1998; Lefly & Pennington, 1991; S. Shaywitz, 2003). Data from studies of children with dyslexia who have been followed prospectively support the notion that in adolescents the rate of reading as well as facility with spelling may be most useful clinically in differentiating average from poor readers in students in secondary school, college, and even graduate school. It is important to remember that these older dyslexic students may be similar to their unimpaired peers on untimed measures of word recognition yet continue to suffer from the phonological deficit that makes reading less automatic, more effortful, and slow. Thus the most consistent and telling sign of a reading disability in an accomplished young adult is slow and laborious reading and writing.

The failure either to recognize or to measure the lack of automaticity in reading is perhaps the most common error in the diagnosis of dyslexia in older children and in accomplished young adults. Simple word-identification tasks will not detect a dyslexic accomplished enough to be in honors high school classes or to graduate from college and attend law, medical, or any other graduate degree school. Tests relying on the accuracy of word identification alone are inappropriate to use to diagnose dyslexia in accomplished young adults; tests of word identification reveal little or nothing of a person's struggles to read. It is important to recognize that, since they assess reading accuracy but not automaticity (speed), the kinds of reading tests commonly used for school-age children may provide misleading data on bright adolescents and young adults. The most critical tests are those that are timed; they are the most sensitive to a phonological deficit in a bright adult. However, there are very few standardized tests for young adult readers that are administered under timed and untimed conditions; the Nelson–Denny Reading Test (Brown, Fishco, & Hanna, 1993) represents an exception. Any scores obtained on testing must be considered relative to peers with the same degree of education or professional training.

MANAGEMENT

The management of dyslexia demands a life-span perspective. Early on, the focus is on remediation of the reading problem. As a child matures and enters the more time-demanding setting of secondary school, the emphasis shifts to incorporate the important role of providing accommodations. Effective intervention programs provide children with systematic instruction in each of the critical components of reading (see below) and practice that is aligned with that instruction. The goal is for children to develop the skills that will allow them to read and understand the meaning of both familiar and unfamiliar words they may encounter.

For the first time, there is now developing a knowledge base to inform the practice of evidence-based education. In 1998 the US Congress, concerned with what appeared to be an epidemic of poor reading nationally, mandated that a National Reading Panel (NRP) be formed. A major goal was to review the extant literature on teaching reading and to identify which specific methods and approaches are most effective. Based on a prior consensus report from the National Research Council (Snow et al., 1998) and on the results of its own analysis, the NRP reported that there are five critical elements necessary to effectively teach reading: (1) phonemic awareness (the ability to focus on and manipulate phonemes, speech sounds, in spoken syllables and words); (2) phonics (understanding how letters are linked to sounds to form letter–sound correspondences and spelling patterns); (3) fluency; (4) vocabulary; and (5) comprehension strategies. The NRP emphasized that these elements must be taught systematically and explicitly, rather than in a more casual, fragmented or implicit manner. Such systematic phonics instruction is more effective than *whole word* instruction that teaches little or no phonics or teaches phonics haphazardly or in a *by-the-way* approach. The following discussion on management is based on the findings and recommendations of the Report of the National Reading Panel (2000).

Although it is generally recognized that fluency is an important component of skilled reading, it is often neglected in the classroom. The most effective method to build reading fluency is a procedure referred to as repeated oral reading with feedback and guidance. The teacher models reading a passage aloud; the student rereads the passage repeatedly to the teacher, another adult, or a peer, receiving feedback until able to read the passage correctly. The evidence indicates that repeated oral reading has a clear and positive impact on word recognition, fluency, and comprehension at a variety of grade levels, and that it applies to all students—good readers as well as those experiencing reading difficulties. There is less supporting evidence for programs that encourage large amounts of independent or silent reading without any feedback to the student. No doubt there is a correlation between being a good reader and amount of reading experience, but there is a paucity of evidence indicating that, for poor readers, there is a *causal relationship*. In contrast to teaching phonemic awareness, phonics, and fluency, interventions for reading comprehension are not as well established. In large measure this reflects the nature of the very complex processes influencing reading comprehension. The limited evidence indicates that the most effective methods to teach reading comprehension involve teaching vocabulary and strategies that encourage an active interaction between reader and text.

Large-scale studies to date have focused on younger children; as yet, there are sparse data available on the effectiveness of these training programs on older children. The data on younger children are extremely encouraging, indicating that using evidence-based methods can remediate, and may even prevent, reading difficulties in primary-school-aged children (Foorman, Brier, & Fletcher, 2003; S. Shaywitz, 2003; Torgesen et al., 1999). An essential management component of dyslexia in students in secondary school, and especially in college and graduate school, is the provision of accommodations. Such students with a history of childhood dyslexia often present a paradoxical picture: they are similar to their unimpaired peers on untimed measures of word recognition and comprehension, yet they continue to suffer from the phonological deficit that makes reading less automatic, more effortful, and slow. The provision of extra time is an essential accommodation for these readers; it allows them the time to decode each word and to apply their unimpaired higher order cognitive and linguistic skills to the surrounding context to get at the meaning of words that they cannot entirely or rapidly decode. Although this is by far the most common accommodation for people with dyslexia, other helpful accommodations include allowing the use of laptop computers with spellcheckers, tape recorders in the classroom, and recorded books (materials are available from Recording for the Blind and Dyslexic), and providing access to syllabi and lecture notes, tutors to *talk through* and review the content of reading material, alternatives to multiple-choice tests (e.g., reports or tests requiring short written answers), and a separate, quiet room for taking tests (S. Shaywitz, 2003).

It is important to appreciate that phonological difficulties in dyslexia are independent of intelligence: consequently, many highly intelligent boys and girls have reading problems that are often overlooked and even ascribed to a "lack of motivation." In counseling individuals who are dyslexic, practitioners should bear in mind that many outstanding writers, including John Irving and Richard Ford, lawyers such as David Boies, distinguished physicians, including Dr. Delos Cosgrove, innovator in cardiothoracic surgery, and scientists, including at least two Nobel laureates, Niels Bohr in Physics, and Baruj Benacerraf in Physiology or Medicine, were dyslexic (S. Shaywitz, 2003).

People with dyslexia and their families frequently ask about unconventional approaches to the remediation of reading difficulties. In general, there are very few credible data to support the claims made for these treatments (e.g., optometric training, medication for vestibular dysfunction, chiropractic manipulation, dietary supplementation). Finally, professionals interacting with families of dyslexic children should be aware that there is no one "magical" program that remediates reading difficulties: a number of programs following the guidelines provided earlier have proven to be highly effective in teaching struggling children to read. Early intervention is critical. Studies of young first- and second-grade children (Torgesen et al., 2001) have demonstrated improvements in accuracy and fluency, but it has yet to be demonstrated that interventions with older school-age children are able to close the reading gap between struggling readers and their peers.

Future Directions

Recent technological and conceptual advances offer the hope of understanding reading and reading disabilities at a level that could not have been imagined even a decade ago. These advances fall into several domains: neurobiological advances, including multimodal imaging and imaging and analyzing individual subjects as well as groups of subjects; a focus on reading beyond the word level (i.e., studies examining reading fluency and reading comprehension); and extended longitudinal studies of reading from kindergarten through adulthood.

State-of-the-art advanced structural image analysis tools add still another dimension to the understanding of the neurobiology of struggling compared to skilled readers. For example, methods for assessing brain shape, sulcal pattern asymmetries, gray matter distribution, and cortical gray matter asymmetries over the entire cortical surface are currently being applied in studies of children and adults with dyslexia (Fischl et al., 2004; Silani et al., 2005; Sowell et al., 2003). Tracking white matter connectivity using diffusion tensor imaging (DTI) has demonstrated significant relationships between white matter connectivity in the arcuate fasiculus and reading skill (Beaulieu et al., 2005; Deutsch et al., 2005). Combining these technologies now allows the development of a multidimensional neurobiological model specifying both the functional and structural anatomy of skilled and struggling reading. In all imaging modalities, the use of high magnetic field imagers offers the possibility of beginning to generate data that are reliable and valid for individual subjects.

Progress in neuroimaging is not limited to technological advances; the field is now beginning to examine the underlying neural circuitry for more complex, higher order components of reading. To date, most imaging studies of reading in dyslexic compared to nonimpaired readers have used word-level tasks, though clearly the neurobiology of reading will necessarily be incomplete without a proper understanding of reading sentences and comprehension. Studies are currently in progress examining the neural systems for sentence-level tasks in dyslexic and nonimpaired children and adolescents. Though reading can be conceptualized on a number of levels (e.g., concept activation, inference construction; see Rapp & van den Broek, 2005), neurobiologists have conceptualized reading and comprehending sentences as engaging both semantic and syntactic operations: higher order semantic processing is important to determine the right sense or meaning of words; syntax assigns grammatical structure to determine the semantic relations between words, findings reviewed in (Caplan, 2004).

Extended longitudinal studies provide still another increasingly appreciated paradigm in the study of reading and dyslexia. For example, data from the Connecticut Longitudinal Study have been extremely helpful in beginning to understand the long-term outcome of childhood reading disabilities (RD) in a cohort that has been followed longitudinally beginning in kindergarten and extending through the third—and now into the fourth—decade of life. As noted above, fMRI using word-level tasks performed in this group when the participants were in their early 20s have demonstrated at least two types of reading disability, one hypothesized to be primarily genetic in origin, the other predominantly environmentally influenced. Studies are currently underway to examine this group using sentence-level imaging tasks, both fMRI and MEG. Longitudinal studies of younger groups of disabled readers are currently in progress too—for example, studies of children with dyslexia imaged using fMRI employing word-level tasks at 7–10 years of age, who are now being studied in adolescence using sentence-level tasks both with fMRI and MEG. Such studies allow for an examination of prospectively acquired childhood antecedents and outcome. Although there is a consensus that RD persists, there is also often great variability, both in reported outcomes and in the role of specific modulating influences. It is only a long-term longitudinal study that can provide data on outcome, prognosis, and risk factors influencing the expression, persistence, and impact of a disorder—data critical for planning effective identification and intervention/prevention programs. In particular, empiric data identifying specific antecedents as positive or negative prognostic indicators of adolescent outcomes allows policymakers and educators to develop programs for, and to target, those students most at risk for failure as they transition from childhood to adolescence and beyond.

Implications

The integration of neurobiological findings, together with genetic and behavioral data, represent an exciting beginning to achieving the long-held, but elusive goal of linking specific clinical profiles to disruption in specific neural systems, which, in turn, may be linked to and explained by particular genetic anomalies. This would represent a major step forward in providing the most effective reading instruction and intervention informed by knowledge of the underlying molecular and neurobiology. At another level, the examination of response to intervention paradigms will ensure that struggling readers early on receive effective, evidence-based reading instruction and then, if needed, intervention titrated to their needs.

From a somewhat different but complementary perspective, the findings from laboratories around the world, in every language tested, indicating a neural signature for dyslexia—a disruption of posterior reading systems, primarily systems serving skilled, fluent (rapid) reading—have implications for the acceptance of dyslexia as a valid disorder, a necessary condition for its identification and treatment. Simply put, they provide, for the first time, convincing, irrefutable evidence that what has been considered a hidden disability is "real." This demonstration has implications not only for reading instruction, but also for the provision of accommodations, a critical component of management for older children attending postsecondary and graduate programs. Such findings should encourage policymakers to be more willing to allow children and adolescents with dyslexia to receive accommodations—accommodations such as extra time—on high-stakes tests, which would allow dyslexic readers with a disruption in the word-form area influencing rapid, fluent reading, to be on a level playing field with their peers who do not have a reading disability.

As summarized here, the utilization of advances in neuroscience and genetics to inform educational policy and practices provides an exciting example of translational science being used for the public good.

ACKNOWLEDGMENTS

Sally Shaywitz is The Audrey G. Ratner Professor in Learning Development at the Yale University School of Medicine. The work described in this review was supported by grants from the National Institute of Child Health and Human Development (P50 HD25802; RO1 HD046171; R01 HD057655) to Sally Shaywitz and Bennett Shaywitz, from the National Institute of Neurological Disease and Stroke (R01 NS43530) to Jeffrey Gruen, and from the Mental Illness and Neuroscience Discovery (MIND) Institute to Maria Mody. (Portions of this chapter have appeared whole or in part in S. Shaywitz, 1998, 2003; S. Shaywitz, Morris, & Shaywitz, 2008; S. Shaywitz & Shaywitz, 2003, 2005.)

REFERENCES

Ahlfors, S. P., Simpson, G. V., Dale, A. M., Belliveau, J. W., Liu, A. K., Korvenoja, A., et al. (1999). Spatiotemporal activity of a cortical network for processing visual motion revealed by MEG and fMRI. *Journal of Neurophysiology, 82*(5), 2545–2555.

Anderson, A., & Gore, J. (1997). The physical basis of neuroimaging techniques. In M. Lewis & B. Peterson (Eds.), *Child and adolescent psychiatric clinics of North America* (Vol. 6, pp. 213–264). Philadelphia; PA: W. B. Saunders.

Aylward, E., Richards, T., Berninger, V., Nagy, W., Field, K., Grimme, A. et al. (2003). Instructional treatment associated with changes in brain activation in children with dyslexia. *Neurology, 61*, 212–219.

Beaulieu, C., Plewes, C., Paulson, L. A., Roy, D., Snook, L., Concha, L., et al. (2005). Imaging brain connectivity in children with diverse reading ability. *NeuroImage, 25*(4), 1266–1271.

Bentin, S., Mouchetant-Rostaing, Y., Giard, M. H., Echallier, J. F., & Pernier, J. (1999). ERP manifestations of processing printed words at different psycholinguistic levels: Time course and scalp distribution. *Journal of Cognitive Neuroscience, 11*(3), 235–260.

Berlin, R. (1877). *Eine besondere Art der Wortblindheit*. Wiesbaden, Germany: Vogel.

Bonte, M. L., & Blomert, L. (2004). Developmental dyslexia: ERP correlates of anomalous phonological processing during spoken word recognition. *Brain Research. Cognitive Brain Research, 21*(3), 360–376.

Brandeis, D., Vitacco, D., & Steinhausen, H. C. (1994). Mapping brain electric micro-states in dyslexic children during reading. *Acta Paedopsychiatrica, 56*(3), 239–247.

Breier, J. I., Simos, P. G., Fletcher, J. M., Castillo, E. M., Zhang, W., & Papanicolaou, A. C. (2003). Abnormal activation of temporoparietal language areas during phonetic analysis in children with dyslexia. *Neuropsychology, 17*(4), 610–621.

Brown, J. I., Fishco, V. V., & Hanna, G. S. (1993). *Nelson Denny Reading Test—Manual for Scoring and Interpretation (Forms G and H)*. Itasca, IL: Riverside Publishing.

Brown, W. E., Eliez, S., Menon, V., Rumsey, J. M., White, C. D., & Reiss, A. L. (2001). Preliminary evidence of widespread morphological variations of the brain in dyslexia. *Neurology, 56*(6), 781–783.

Bruck, M. (1990). Word-recognition skills of adults with childhood diagnoses of dyslexia. *Developmental Psychology, 26*(3), 439–454.

Bruck, M. (1992). Persistence of dyslexics' phonological awareness deficits. *Developmental Psychology, 28*(5), 874–886.

Bruck, M. (1998). Outcomes of adults with childhood histories of dyslexia. In C. Hulme & R. Joshi (Eds.), *Reading and spelling: Development and disorders* (pp. 179–200). Mahwah, NJ: Lawrence Erlbaum Associates.

Bryant, P. E., MacLean, M., Bradley, L. L., & Crossland, J. (1990). Rhyme and alliteration, phoneme detection, and learning to read. *Developmental Psychology, 26*(3), 429–438.

Caplan, D. (2004). Functional neuroimaging studies of written sentence comprehension. *Scientific Studies of Reading, 8*, 225–240.

Catts, H. (1989). Speech production deficits in developmental dyslexia. *Journal of Speech and Hearing Disorders, 54*, 422–428.

Cohen, L., Jobert, A., Le Bihan, D., & Dehaene, S. (2004). Distinct unimodal and multimodal regions for word processing in the left temporal cortex. *NeuroImage, 23*(4), 1256–1270.

Cope, N., Harold, D., Hill, G., Moskvina, V., Stevenson, J., Holmans, P., et al. (2005). Strong evidence that KIAA0319 on chromosome 6p is a susceptibility gene for developmental dyslexia. *American Journal of Human Genetics, 76*(4), 581–591.

Damasio, A. R., & Damasio, H. (1983). The anatomic basis of pure alexia. *Neurology, 33,* 1573–1583.

DeFries, J. C., Olson, R. K., Pennington, B. F., & Smith, S. D. (1991). Colorado Reading Project: An update. In D. D. Duane & D. B. Gray (Eds.), *The reading brain: The biological basis of dyslexia* (pp. 53–87). Parkton, MD: York Press.

Dehaene, S., Cohen, L., Sigman, M., & Vinckier, F. (2005). The neural code for written words: A proposal. *Trends in Cognitive Sciences, 9*(7), 335–341.

Dejerine, J. (1891). Sur un cas de cécité verbale avec agraphie, suivi d'autopsie. *Comptes Rendu de Société du Biologie, 43,* 197–201.

Deutsch, G., Dougherty, R., Bammer, R., Siok, W., Gabrieli, J., & Wandell, B. (2005). Children's reading performance is correlated with white matter structure measured by diffusion tensor imaging. *Cortex, 41,* 354–363.

Duncan, C. C., Rumsey, J. M., Wilkniss, S. M., Denckla, M. B., Hamburger, S. D., & Odou-Potkin, M. (1994). Developmental dyslexia and attention dysfunction in adults: Brain potential indices of information processing. *Psychophysiology, 31*(4), 386–401.

Eden, G., Jones, K., Cappell, K., Gareau, L., Wood, F., Zeffiro, T., et al. (2004). Neural changes following remediation in adult developmental dyslexia. *Neuron, 44*(3), 411–422.

Eliez, S., Rumsey, J. M., Giedd, J. N., Schmitt, J. E., Patwardhan, A. J., & Reiss, A. L. (2000). Morphological alteration of temporal lobe gray matter in dyslexia: an MRI study. *Journal of Child Psychology and Psychiatry, 41*(5), 637–644.

Felton, R. H., Naylor, C. E., & Wood, F. B. (1990). Neuropsychological profile of adult dyslexics. *Brain and Language, 39,* 485–497.

Ferrer, E., McArdle, J., Shaywitz, B., Holahan, J., Marchione, K., & Shaywitz, S. (2007). Longitudinal models of developmental dynamics between reading and cognition from childhood to adolescence. *Developmental Psychology, 43*(6), 1460–1473.

Fiez, J. A., & Peterson, S. E. (1998). Neuroimaging studies of word reading. *Proceedings of the National Academy of Sciences U.S.A., 95*(3), 914–921.

Fischl, B., van der Kouwe, A., Destrieux, C., Halgren, E., Segonne, F., Salat, D. H., et al. (2004). Automatically parcellating the human cerebral cortex. *Cerebral Cortex, 14*(1), 11–22.

Fletcher, J. M., Shaywitz, S. E., Shankweiler, D. P., Katz, L., Liberman, I. Y., Stuebing, K. K., et al. (1994). Cognitive profiles of reading disability: Comparisons of discrepancy and low achievement definitions. *Journal of Educational Psychology, 86*(1), 6–23.

Foorman, B. R., Brier, J. I., & Fletcher, J. M. (2003). Interventions aimed at improving reading success: An evidence-based approach. *Developmental Neuropsychology, 24,* 613–639.

Frackowiak, R., Friston, K., Frith, C., Dolan, R., Price, C., Zeki, S., et al. (2004). *Human Brain Function* (2nd ed.). San Diego: Academic Press, Elsevier Science.

Francis, D. J., Shaywitz, S. E., Stuebing, K. K., Shaywitz, B. A., & Fletcher, J. M. (1996). Developmental lag versus deficit models of reading disability: A longitudinal, individual growth curves analysis. *Journal of Educational Psychology, 88*(1), 3–17.

Friedman, R. F., Ween, J. E., & Albert, M. L. (1993). Alexia. In K. M. Heilman & E. Valenstein (Eds.), *Clinical neuropsychology* (3rd ed., pp. 37–62). New York: Oxford University Press.

Fuchs, D., Fuchs, L., & Compton, D. (2004). Identifying reading disability by responsiveness-to-instruction: Specifying measures and criteria. *Learning Disability Quarterly, 27*(4), 216–227.

Galaburda, A. M., Menard, M., & Rosen, G. D. (1994). Evidence for aberrant auditory anatomy in developmental dyslexia. *Proceedings of the National Academy of Sciences U.S.A., 91,* 8010–8013.

Galaburda, A. M., Sherman, G. F., Rosen, G. D., Aboitiz, F., & Geschwind, N. (1985). Developmental dyslexia: Four consecutive patients with cortical anomalies. *Annals of Neurology, 18*(2), 222–233.

Gallagher, A., Frith, U., & Snowling, M. (2000). Precursors of literacy-delay among children at genetic risk of dyslexia. *Journal of Child Psychology and Psychiatry, 41*, 203–213.

Georgiewa, P., Rzanny, R., Gaser, C., Gerhard, U. J., Vieweg, U., Freesmeyer, D., et al. (2002). Phonological processing in dyslexic children: A study combining functional imaging and event-related potentials. *Neuroscience Letters, 318*(1), 5–8.

Geschwind, N. (1965). Disconnection syndromes in animals and man. *Brain, 88*, 237–294.

Gilger, J. W., Borecki, I. B., Smith, S. D., DeFries, J. C., & Pennington, B. F. (1996). The etiology of extreme scores for complex phenotypes: An illustration using reading performance. In C. H. Chase, G. D. Rosen, & G. F. Sherman (Eds.), *Developmental dyslexia: Neural, cognitive, and genetic mechanisms* (pp. 63–85). Baltimore: York Press.

Gough, P. B., & Tunmer, W. E. (1986). Decoding, reading, and reading disability. *Remedial and Special Education, 7*, 6–10.

Hämäläinen, M., Hari, R., Ilmoniemi, R. J., Knuutila, J., & Lounasmaa, O. V. (1993). Magnetoencephalography: Theory, instrumentation and application to noninvasive studies of the working human brain. *Reviews in Modern Physics, 65*, 413–497.

Hannula-Jouppi, K., Kaminen-Ahola, N., Taipale, M., Eklund, R., Nopola-Hemmi, J., Kaariainen, H., et al. (2005). The axon guidance receptor gene *ROBO1* is a candidate gene for developmental dyslexia. *PLoS Genetics, 1*(4), e50.

Heim, S., Eulitz, C., & Elbert, T. (2003a). Altered hemispheric asymmetry of auditory N100m in adults with developmental dyslexia. *NeuroReport, 14*(3), 501–504.

Heim, S., Eulitz, C., & Elbert, T. (2003b). Altered hemispheric asymmetry of auditory P100m in dyslexia. *European Journal of Neuroscience, 17*(8), 1715–1722.

Helenius, P., Salmelin, R., Richardson, U., Leinonen, S., & Lyytinen, H. (2002). Abnormal auditory cortical activation in dyslexia 100 msec after speech onset. *Journal of Cognitive Neuroscience, 14*(4), 603–617.

Helenius, P., Salmelin, R., Service, E., & Connolly, J. F. (1999). Semantic cortical activation in dyslexic readers. *Journal of Cognitive Neuroscience, 11*(5), 535–550.

Helenius, P., Tarkiainen, A., Cornelissen, P., Hansen, P. C., & Salmelin, R. (1999). Dissociation of normal feature analysis and deficient processing of letter-strings in dyslexic adults. *Cerebral Cortex, 4*, 476–483.

Hinshelwood, J. (1895). Word-blindness and visual memory. *The Lancet, 2*, 1564–1570.

Hinshelwood J. (1912). The treatment of word-blindness acquired and congenital. *British Medical Journal, 2*, 1033–1035.

Interagency Committee on Learning Disabilities. (1987). *Learning disabilities: A report to the U.S. Congress.* Washington, DC: US Government Printing Office.

Jezzard, P., Matthews, P., & Smith, S. (2001). *Functional MRI: An introduction to methods.* Oxford: Oxford University Press.

Klingberg, T., Hedehus, M., Temple, E., Salz, T., Gabrieli, J., Moseley, M., et al. (2000). Microstructure of temporo-parietal white matter as a basis for reading ability: Evidence from diffusion tensor magnetic resonance imaging. *Neuron, 25*, 493–500.

Lefly, D. L., & Pennington, B. F. (1991). Spelling errors and reading fluency in compensated adult dyslexics. *Annals of Dyslexia, 41*, 143–162.

Liberman, I. Y., & Shankweiler, D. (1991). Phonology and beginning to read: A tutorial. In L. Rieben & C. A. Perfetti (Eds.), *Learning to read: Basic research and its implications.* Hillsdale, NJ: Lawrence Erlbaum Associates.

Liberman, I. Y., Shankweiler, D., & Liberman, A. M. (1989). Phonology and reading disability: Solving the reading puzzle. In D. Shankweiler & I. Y. Liberman (Eds.), *International Academy for Research in Learning Disabilities monograph series* (Vol. 6, pp. 1–33). Ann Arbor, MI: University of Michigan Press.

Livingstone, M. S., Rosen, G. D., Drislane, F. W., & Galaburda, A. M. (1991). Physiological and anatomical evidence for a magnocellular defect in developmental dyslexia. *Proceedings of the National Academy of Sciences U.S.A., 88*(18), 7943–7947.

Logan, G. (1988). Toward an instance theory of automatization. *Psychological Review, 95*, 492–527.

Logan, G. (1997). Automaticity and reading: Perspectives from the instance theory of automatization. *Reading and Writing Quarterly: Overcoming Learning Disabilities, 13,* 123–146.

Lovegrove, W. J., Bowling, A., Badcock, D., & Blackwood, M. (1980). Specific reading disability: Differences in contrast sensitivity as a function of spatial frequency. *Science, 210,* 439–440.

Lyon, G. R., Shaywitz, S. E., & Shaywitz, B. A. (2003). A definition of dyslexia. *Annals of Dyslexia, 53,* 1–14.

Mather, N., & Woodcock, R. W. (2001). *Woodcock–Johnson III Tests of Achievement: Examiner's manual standard and extended batteries.* Itasca, IL: Riverside Publishing.

McCandliss, B., Cohen, L., & Dehaene, S. (2003). The visual word form area: Expertise in reading in the fusiform gyrus. *Trends in Cognitive Sciences, 7*(7), 293–299.

McCrory, E., Mechelli, A., Frith, U., & Price, C. (2005). More than words: A common neural basis for reading and naming deficits in developmental dyslexia? *Brain, 128*(2), 261–267.

McMaster, K., Fuchs, D., Fuchs, L., & Compton, D. (2005). Responding to non-responders: An experimental field trial of identification and intervention methods. *Exceptional Children, 71,* 445–463.

Meng, H., Smith, S. D., Hager, K., Held, M., Liu, J., Olson, R. K., et al. (2005). DCDC2 is associated with reading disability and modulates neuronal development in the brain. *Proceedings of the National Academy of Sciences U.S.A., 102*(47), 17053–17058.

Meyler, A., & Breznitz, Z. (2005). Impaired phonological and orthographic word representations among adult dyslexic readers: Evidence from event-related potentials. *Journal of Genetic Psychology, 166*(2), 215–238.

Moats, L. (2000). *Speech to Print: Language Essentials for Teachers.* Baltimore: Paul H. Brookes.

Mody, M. (2003). Phonological basis in reading disability: A review and analysis of the evidence. *Reading and Writing: An Interdisciplinary Journal, 16,* 21–39.

Morgan, W. P. (1896). A case of congenital word blindness. *British Medical Journal,* 1378.

Morris, R. D., Stuebing, K. K., Fletcher, J. M., Shaywitz, S. E., Lyon, G. R., Shankweiler, D. P., et al. (1998). Subtypes of reading disability: Variability around a phonological core. *Journal of Educational Psychology, 90,* 347–373.

Nakamura, K., Oga, T., Okada, T., Sadato, N., Takayama, Y., Wydell, T., et al. (2005). Hemispheric asymmetry emerges at distinct parts of the occipitotemporal cortex for objects, logograms and phonograms: A functional MRI study. *NeuroImage, 28,* 521–528.

Nicolson, R. I., & Fawcett, A. J. (1990). Automaticity: A new framework for dyslexia research? *Cognition, 35*(2), 159–182.

Nicolson, R. I., Fawcett, A. J., & Dean, P. (2001). Developmental dyslexia: The cerebellar deficit hypothesis. *Trends in Neurosciences, 24*(9), 508–511.

Nobre, A. C., Allison, T., & McCarthy, G. (1994). Word recognition in the human inferior temporal lobe. *Nature, 372*(6503), 260–263.

Olson, R., Forsberg, H., Gayan, J., & DeFries, J. (1999). A behavioral-genetic analysis of reading disabilities and component processes. In R. Klein & P. McMullen (Eds.), *Converging methods for understanding reading and dyslexia* (pp. 133–153). Cambridge, MA: MIT Press.

Paulesu, E., Demonet, J.-F., Fazio, F., McCrory, E., Chanoine, V., Brunswick, N., et al. (2001). Dyslexia: Cultural diversity and biological unity. *Science, 291,* 2165–2167.

Pennington, B. F., & Gilger, J. W. (1996). How is dyslexia transmitted? In C. H. Chase, G. D. Rosen, & G. F. Sherman (Eds.), *Developmental dyslexia: Neural, cognitive, and genetic mechanisms* (pp. 41–61). Baltimore: York Press.

Penolazzi, B., Spironelli, C., Vio, C., & Angrilli, A. (2006). Altered hemispheric asymmetry during word processing in dyslexic children: An event-related potential study. *NeuroReport, 17*(4), 429–433.

Perie, M., Grigg, W., & Donahue, P. (2005). *The nation's report card: Reading 2005.* Washington, DC: Department of Education, National Center for Education Statistics.

Price, C., & Mechelli, A. (2005). Reading and reading disturbance. *Current Opinion in Neurobiology, 15,* 231–238.

Ramus, F., Rosen, S., Dakin, S., Day, B., Castellote, J., White, S., et al. (2003). Theories of developmental dyslexia: insights from a multiple case study of dyslexic adults. *Brain, 126,* 841–865.

Rapp, D., & van den Broek, P. (2005). Dynamic text comprehension. *Current Directions in Psychological Sciences, 14*(5), 276–279.

Report of the National Reading Panel (2000). *Teaching children to read: An evidence based assessment of the scientific research literature on reading and its implications for reading instruction* (Vol. NIH Pub. No. 00–4754). Washington, DC: US Department of Health and Human Services, Public Health Service, National Institutes of Health, National Institute of Child Health and Human Development.

Robichon, F., Besson, M., & Habib, M. (2002). An electrophysiological study of dyslexic and control adults in a sentence reading task. *Biological Psychology, 59*(1), 29–53.

Rosen, S. (2003). Auditory processing in dyslexia and specific language impairment: Is there a deficit? What is its nature? Does it explain anything? *Journal of Phonetics, 31,* 509–527.

Russeler, J., Probst, S., Johannes, S., & Münte, T. (2003). Recognition memory for high- and low-frequency words in adult normal and dyslexic readers: An event-related brain potential study. *Journal of Clinical and Experimental Neuropsychology, 25*(6), 815–829.

Salmelin, R., Service, E., Kiesila, P., Uutela, K., & Salonen, O. (1996). Impaired visual word processing in dyslexia revealed with magnetoencephalography. *Annals of Neurology, 40,* 157–162.

Scarborough, H. S. (1990). Very early language deficits in dyslexic children. *Child Development, 61,* 1728–1743.

Schulte-Korne, G., Deimel, W., Bartling, J., & Remschmidt, H. (2004). Neurophysiological correlates of word recognition in dyslexia. *Journal of Neural Transmission, 111*(7), 971–984.

Schumacheç, J., Anthoni, H., Dahdouh, F., König, I. R., Hillmer, A. M., Kluck, N., et al. (2006). Strong genetic evidence of *DCDC2* as a susceptibility gene for dyslexia. *American Journal of Human Genetics, 78*(1), 52–62.

Shankweiler, D., Crain, S., Katz, L., Fowler, A. E., Liberman, A. M., Brady, S. A., et al. (1995). Cognitive profiles of reading-disabled children: Comparison of language skills in phonology, morphology, and syntax. *Psychological Science, 6*(3), 149–156.

Shankweiler, D., Liberman, I. Y., Mark, L. S., Fowler, C. A., & Fischer, F. W. (1979). The speech code and learning to read. *Journal of Experimental Psychology: Human Learning and Memory, 5*(6), 531–545.

Share, D. L., & Stanovich, K. E. (1995). Cognitive processes in early reading development: Accommodating individual differences into a model of acquisition. *Issues in Education: Contributions from Educational Psychology, 1*(1), 1–57.

Shaywitz, B. A., Fletcher, J. M., Holahan, J. M., Shneider, A. E., Marchione, K. E., Stuebing, K. K., et al. (1995). Interrelationships between reading disability and attention-deficit/hyperactivity disorder. *Child Neuropsychology, 1*(3), 170–186.

Shaywitz, B. A., Holford, T. R., Holahan, J. M., Fletcher, J. M., Stuebing, K. K., Francis, D. J., et al. (1995). A Matthew effect for IQ but not for reading: Results from a longitudinal study. *Reading Research Quarterly, 30*(4), 894–906.

Shaywitz, B., Shaywitz, S., Blachman, B., Pugh, K., Fulbright, R., Skudlarski, P., et al. (2004). Development of left occipito-temporal systems for skilled reading in children after a phonologically based intervention. *Biological Psychiatry, 55,* 926–933.

Shaywitz, B., Shaywitz, S., Pugh, K., Mencl, W., Fulbright, R., Skudlarski, P., et al. (2002). Disruption of posterior brain systems for reading in children with developmental dyslexia. *Biological Psychiatry, 52*(2), 101–110.

Shaywitz, B., Skudlarski, P., Holahan, J., Marchione, K., Constable, R., Fulbright, R., et al. (2007). Age-related changes in reading systems of dyslexic children. *Annals of Neurology, 61,* 363–370.

Shaywitz, S. E. (1996). Dyslexia. *Scientific American, 275*(5), 98–104.

Shaywitz, S. (1998). Current concepts: Dyslexia. *New England Journal of Medicine, 338*(5), 307–312.

Shaywitz, S. (2003). *Overcoming dyslexia: A new and complete science-based program for reading problems at any level.* New York: Alfred A. Knopf.

Shaywitz, S. E., Escobar, M. D., Shaywitz, B. A., Fletcher, J. M., & Makuch, R. (1992). Evidence that dyslexia may represent the lower tail of a normal distribution of reading ability. *New England Journal of Medicine*, 326(3), 145–150.

Shaywitz, S., Fletcher, J., Holahan, J., Shneider, A., Marchione, K., Stuebing, K., et al. (1999). Persistence of dyslexia: the Connecticut Longitudinal Study at adolescence. *Pediatrics.*, 104(6), 1351–1359.

Shaywitz, S., Morris, R., & Shaywitz, B. (2008). The education of dyslexic children from childhood to young adulthood. *Annual Review of Psychology*, 59, 451–475.

Shaywitz, S., & Shaywitz, B. (2003). Dyslexia: Specific reading disability. *Pediatrics in Review*, 24, 147–153.

Shaywitz, S., & Shaywitz, B. (2005). Dyslexia (specific reading disability). *Biological Psychiatry*, 57, 1301–1309.

Shaywitz, S., Shaywitz, B., Fulbright, R., Skudlarski, P., Mencl, W., Constable, R., et al. (2003). Neural systems for compensation and persistence: Young adult outcome of childhood reading disability. *Biological Psychiatry*, 54(1), 25–33.

Shaywitz, S., Shaywitz, B., Pugh, K., Fulbright, R., Constable, R., Mencl, W., et al. (1998). Functional disruption in the organization of the brain for reading in dyslexia. *Proceedings of the National Academy of Sciences U.S.A.*, 95, 2636–2641.

Silani, G., Frith, U., Demonet, J., Fazio, F., Perani, D., Price, C., et al. (2005). Brain abnormalities underlying altered activation in dyslexia: A voxel based morphometry study. *Brain*, 128, 2453–2461.

Simos, P. G., Breier, J. I., Fletcher, J. M., Bergman, E., & Papanicolaou, A. C. (2000). Cerebral mechanisms involved in word reading in dyslexic children: A magnetic source imaging approach. *Cerebral Cortex*, 10(8), 809–816.

Simos, P. G., Breier, J. I., Fletcher, J. M., Foorman, B. R., Bergman, E., Fishbeck, K., et al. (2000). Brain activation profiles in dyslexic children during non-word reading: A magnetic source imaging study. *Neuroscience Letters*, 290(1), 61–65.

Simos, P. G., Fletcher, J. M., Bergman, E., Breier, J. I., Foorman, B. R., Castillo, E. M., et al. (2002). Dyslexia-specific brain activation profile becomes normal following successful remedial training. *Neurology*, 58(8), 1203–1213.

Siok, W. T., Jin, Z., Fletcher, P., & Tan, L. H. (2003). Distinct brain regions associated with syllable and phoneme. *Human Brain Mapping*, 18(3), 201–207.

Siok, W. T., Perfetti, C. A., Jin, Z., & Tan, L. H. (2004). Biological abnormality of impaired reading is constrained by culture. *Nature*, 431(7004), 71–76.

Snow, C. E., Burns, M. S., & Griffin, P. (Eds.). (1998). *Preventing reading difficulties in young children*. Washington, DC: National Academy Press.

Sowell, E. R., Peterson, B. S., Thompson, P. M., Welcome, S. E., Henkenius, A. L., & Toga, A. W. (2003). Mapping cortical change across the human life span. *Nature Neuroscience*, 6(3), 309–315.

Stanovich, K. E., & Siegel, L. S. (1994). Phenotypic performance profile of children with reading disabilities: A regression-based test of the phonological-core variable-difference model. *Journal of Educational Psychology*, 86(1), 24–53.

Stein, J. (2003). Visual motion sensitivity and reading. *Neuropsychologia*, 41(13), 1785–1793.

Stein, J., & Walsh, V. (1997). To see but not to read: The magnocellular theory of dyslexia. *Trends in Neurosciences*, 20(4), 147–152.

Studdert-Kennedy, M., & Mody, M. (1995). Auditory temporal perception deficits in the reading-impaired: A critical review of the evidence. *Psychonomic Bulletin and Review*, 2, 508–514.

Taipale, M., Kaminen, N., Nopola-Hemmi, J., Haltia, T., Myllyluoma, B., Lyytinen, H., et al. (2003). A candidate gene for developmental dyslexia encodes a nuclear tetratricopeptide repeat domain protein dynamically regulated in brain. *Proceedings of the National Academy of Sciences U.S.A.*, 100(20), 11553–11558.

Tallal, P. (1980). Auditory temporal perception, phonics, and reading disabilities in children. *Brain and Language*, 9(2), 182–198.

Tallal, P. (2000). The science of literacy: From the laboratory to the classroom. *Proceedings of the National Academy of Sciences U.S.A.*, 97, 2402–2404.

Tallal, P., Miller, S., & Fitch, R. (1993). Neurobiological basis of speech: A case for the preeminence of temporal processing. *Annals of the New York Academy of Sciences*, 682, 27–47.

Tarkiainen, A., Helenius, P., Hansen, P. C., Cornelissen, P. L., & Salmelin, R. (1999). Dynamics of letter string perception in the human occipitotemporal cortex. *Brain*, *122*(11), 2119–2132.

Taylor, M. J., & Keenan, N. K. (1990). Event-related potentials to visual and language stimuli in normal and dyslexic children. *Psychophysiology*, *27*(3), 318–327.

Temple, E., Deutsch, G., Poldrack, R., Miller, S., Tallal, P., Merzenich, M., et al. (2003). Neural deficits in children with dyslexia ameliorated by behavioral remediation: Evidence from fMRI. *Proceedings of the National Academy of Sciences U.S.A.*, *100*(5), 2860–2865.

Temple, E., Poldrack, R., Protopapas, A., Nagarajan, S., Salz, T., Tallal, P., et al. (2000). Disruption of the neural response to rapid acoustic stimuli in dyslexia: Evidence from functional MRI. *Proceedings of the National Academy of Sciences U.S.A.*, 97, 13907–13912.

Torgesen, J., Alexander, A., Wagner, R., Rashotte, C., Voeller, K., & Conway, T. (2001). Intensive remedial instruction for children with severe reading disabilities: Immediate and long-term outcomes from two instructional approaches. *Journal of Learning Disabilities*, *34*(1), 33–58.

Torgesen, J., & Mathes, P. (2000). *A basic guide to understanding, assessing and teaching phonological awareness*. Austin, TX: PRO-ED.

Torgesen, J. K., & Wagner, R. K. (1995, May). *Alternative diagnostic approaches for specific developmental reading disabilities*. Manuscript prepared for the National Research Council's Board on Testing and Assessment, presented at a workshop on IQ Testing and Educational Decision Making, Washington, DC.

Torgesen, J. K., Wagner, R. K., Rashotte, C. A., Rose, E., Lindamood, P., Conway, T., et al. (1999). Preventing reading failure in young children with phonological processing disabilities. *Journal of Educational Psychology*, 91, 579–593.

Uhry, J. (2005). Phonemic awareness and reading. In J. Birsh (Ed.), *Multisensory teaching of basic language skills* (2nd ed., pp. 83–111). Baltimore: Paul H. Brookes.

Wagner, R., & Torgesen, J. (1987). The nature of phonological processes and its causal role in the acquisition of reading skills. *Psychological Bulletin*, *101*, 192–212.

White, S., Milne, E., Rosen, S., Hansen, P., Swettenham, J., Frith, U., et al. (2006). The role of sensorimotor impairments in dyslexia: A multiple case study of dyslexic children. *Developmental Science*, *9*(3), 237–255 [discussion 265–269].

Wiederholt, J. L., & Bryant, B. R. (2001). *GORT-4 Examiner's Manual*. Austin, TX: PRO-ED.

Woodcock, R. W., & Johnson, M. B. (1989). *Woodcock–Johnson Psycho-Educational Battery–Revised (WJ–R)*. Allen, TX: Developmental Learning Materials.

Part II

Bases of Child Language Disorders

6

Linguistic Bases of Child Language Disorders

IRENA BOTWINIK-ROTEM and NAAMA FRIEDMANN

What is it that people know when they speak and understand sentences in their native language? Linguistics is the science that aims to explore and reveal this knowledge. The prime change that the Chomskyan revolution brought, Generative Linguistics (Chomsky, 1957, 1965, 1981, 1986b, 1995), was to shift the focus from normative sets of rules according to which people should speak to the description of the native speaker's intuitive knowledge of language. The generative linguist conceives of grammar as a set of rules that reflects native speakers' competence to utter or understand sentences in their language. Viewed from this perspective, the linguistic theory seeks to address four major questions (the first three are adapted from Chomsky, 1986b):

1. What constitutes knowledge of language?
2. How is knowledge of language acquired?
3. How is knowledge of language put to use?
4. How does language break down?

KNOWLEDGE OF LANGUAGE

What is meant by "knowledge of language" is not the kind of explicit, conscious knowledge taught in grammar classes at school. Rather, it is the largely unconscious knowledge used by the native speakers of a language to judge, for example, that sentence (1) is a grammatical sentence of English while (2) is not (asterisk, *, is used throughout to indicate ungrammatical sentences); that despite being very similar, (3) is ambiguous (who holds the binoculars?), whereas (4) is not, and that in (5) the pronoun *he* can refer to *Homer*, though the same is impossible in (6). In sentence examples, the intended reference is usually symbolized by a letter or a number subscript index; identical indices indicate coreference. In (5) and (6) the coreference between the pronoun *he* and *Homer* is symbolized by the subscript index $_1$; it is possible in (5) but not in (6).

(1) Lisa is sitting in the garden.
(2) *Lisa are sits the in garden.

(3) Marge saw the girl with the binoculars.
(4) Marge loved the girl with the binoculars.

(5)   When he$_1$ is tired Homer$_1$ takes a nap.
(6)   *He$_1$ thinks that Homer$_1$ is clever.

Given the unconscious nature of the knowledge, it cannot be observed and studied directly. Thus, a person judging (5) correct and (6) incorrect does not know why he does so. It is possible, however, to observe the speakers' *linguistic performance*, the use of this knowledge as exemplified above, to deduce the underlying *linguistic competence*, the knowledge that permits the speakers to perform their linguistic behavior. Performance, by nature, is influenced by various nonlinguistic factors (e.g., fatigue, absent-mindedness, etc.), giving rise to a variety of ungrammatical sentences that do not bear on the linguistic competence (e.g., "I'm curious to say . . . ahm . . . to hear what you say about. . . .").

Clearly, representing knowledge of a particular language as a list of all possible grammatical sentences is both inconceivable and misses the point. The number of grammatical sentences in any human language is infinite (see Chomsky, 1959, 1965). Given the finite capacity of our brains, it would be absurd to claim that human beings are capable of storing all potential sentences of the language, an infinite set. We must assume that a finite system of principles is what enables human beings to construct and interpret an infinite number of sentences. This finite system of principles is what we refer to as the internal grammar of a language, or its knowledge.

Acquiring Knowledge of Language

Another goal of the linguistic theory is to explain how the knowledge of language is achieved; how children acquire their language. The process of language acquisition can be represented roughly as in (7):

(7)   Linguistic data → | Initial state of linguistic knowledge | → Final state of linguistic knowledge

Although it is logically possible to assume that the initial state contains no linguistic knowledge at all (as in the behaviorist tradition, B. F. Skinner, 1957, rooted in the empiricists' view of seventeenth- and eighteenth-century philosophers like John Locke and David Hume), there is ample evidence indicating that this cannot be the case.

The most compelling evidence comes from directly observing the process of language acquisition. For children who do not have a language impairment or hearing impairment, the time course of language acquisition is very similar, regardless of the environmental conditions of a child. Moreover, there are linguistic phenomena attested in the process of language acquisition, regardless of the language acquired. For instance, children acquiring a variety of languages go through a stage where they do not necessarily produce the subject of the sentence. Although there are languages (e.g., Italian, Spanish, etc.) where the subject does not have to be phonetically realized, many other languages (e.g., French, English) do require a subject: see the Italian example in (8) and its English counterpart in (9). The omission of the subjects in the course of language acquisition is attested regardless of the language acquired, suggesting that it is not triggered by the input data.

(8)   a. Lei è malata.
       b. È malata.
(9)   a. She is ill.
       b. *Is ill.

Further support for the claim that children come into the world endowed with some linguistic knowledge is based on the nature of the input available to them: it is partial (including performance mistakes), not presented in any systematic way, and does not include negative evidence (Brown & Hanlon, 1970). Children are not taught what is ungrammatical in their language (this state of affairs is referred to as the Plato's problem of acquisition or the logical problem of acquisition: for extensive discussion see Hornstein & Lightfoot, 1981; Lightfoot, 1982).

Given this, and assuming a no-initial-knowledge hypothesis, one would expect a great variety of mistakes in the course of language acquisition, contrary to what is attested. Children do make mistakes, but to a much lesser extent than would have been expected given the deficiency of the data and lack of negative evidence. Even more significantly, there are mistakes that they simply never make. In (10), for example, the question word refers to the object of the verb *kissed* in the embedded sentence *that Lisa kissed* (symbolized here by an underline, often referred to in the literature as the gap). This embedded sentence complements the verb *say* in (10a), but the noun *the rumor* in (10b). The contrast illustrated in (10) can be stated informally as follows. When a question word corresponds to the underline in a clause complementing the verb (*say*), the sentence is grammatical. If the underline is in the clause complementing the noun (*the rumor*), the sentence is ungrammatical. How can one learn this? Importantly, children do not make errors like (10b), which means that there is no evidence of a stage of not knowing the statement above, preceding a stage of knowing it. Note that (10b) is logically possible, meaning roughly the same as (10a). The only difference between the sentences in (10) is their syntactic structure. This argues directly against the view (developed in the writings of J. Piaget, cf., Piaget & Inhelder, 1969) that the inborn knowledge is of a general, logically based nature rather than being part of a distinct mental system, the language faculty.

(10)   a.   Who did Bart say that Lisa kissed ___ ?
       b.   *Who did Bart spread the rumor that Lisa kissed ___ ?

Another example of nonexistent mistakes has to do with the phenomenon referred to as Subject–Aux(iliary) inversion in English questions (11). Numerous rules are logically possible for deriving the yes/no question (11b) from the declarative sentence (11a). Some are linear (e.g., "Move the second word to the beginning of the sentence" or "Put the first verb at the beginning of the sentence"), and others are hierarchical (such as "Move the main auxiliary verb to the position before the subject."). Importantly, children never consider linear rules, using only the hierarchical ones. For example, if children could assume that a sentence is a linear string of words, they could have used the rule according to which the first *is* encountered is the one that should be inverted. However, Crain (1991, and Crain & Nakayama, 1987) reported that they never do so. In sentences including two instances of the auxiliary verb *is* (12a), children do not even contemplate a linear rule (invert the first *is*) but, rather, use the hierarchical rule, always inverting *is* of the main clause. As a result, they never produce an incorrect inversion (12b), but only the correct one (12c). This indicates that there must be some general knowledge in the initial state of children that constrains the rules they can consider and eliminates the possibility of considering linear rules (see the next section for further discussion).

(11)   a.   John *is* tall
       b.   *Is* John tall?

(12) a. The man who *is* running *is* bald.
      b. *Is the man who ___ running is bald?
      c. Is the man who is running ___ bald?

Finally, one may suggest that children never produce (10b) or (12b) because they never hear such sentences. This kind of argument is clearly invalid, as there are an infinite number of grammatical sentences that a child never hears and yet produces.

There are additional aspects of linguistic competence that do not seem to be learnable from ordinary linguistic data in the child's environment. In other words, native speakers know things that they could not possibly have learned only from language spoken around them. The conclusion to be drawn from this is that the child does not come empty-handed to the task of language acquisition. Put differently, it is clear that the initial state with which the child is born, has an important role to play in language acquisition. Therefore, in order to answer the second question, how is language acquired, we must investigate the nature of this inborn state of linguistic competence.

Being inborn, the linguistic competence of the initial state is common to all human beings. Therefore it has been called "Universal Grammar"—UG for short. To investigate the UG is to define the principles of grammar it includes. Needless to say, UG is not the grammar of any one language. Rather, it can be conceived of as a blueprint underlying any human language. Thus, it should include the principles that are common to all human languages—e.g., some formulation of the principle that underlies the contrast in (10), and of a principle giving rise to the contrast between (5) and (6), which are common to all human languages.

Given that languages differ from each other, the UG should allow for cross-linguistic variation. Importantly, linguistic research conducted in the past 30 years has revealed that the variation attested across languages is, in fact, quite limited and systematic. Languages do not differ from each other infinitely but, rather, only along certain dimensions. For instance, in many languages the verb agrees in number, gender, and person with the subject, in others it can agree with both the subject and the object, but there are no languages where a verb agrees with the adjacent noun that is neither the subject nor the object: see (13) and (14).

(13) *The girlfriends* of my grandfather adore him.
(14) *The girlfriends of *my grandfather* adores him.

The observation that human languages share certain properties, and that they differ from each other in a limited way, gave rise to the so-called Principles and Parameters (P&P) approach to UG (Chomsky, 1981). Principles encode the invariant properties of languages—the universal properties that make the languages similar. For example, the rule that governs the interpretation of pronouns and proper names—see sentences (5) vs. (6)—is a principle: in any given language it governs the interpretation of pronouns and proper names. Parameters are the part of UG that encodes the properties that vary from one language to another.

For instance, languages can vary in word order, in the way they form questions, or, as already mentioned, in the realization of the subject. In English, the object follows the verb (15a), whereas in Japanese it precedes it (15b). The question element in English occurs in sentence-initial position (16), whereas in Japanese and in Israeli and American Sign Languages it does not (16). Italian allows the subjects to be omitted, but English does not—see (17) and (18).

(15) a. John hit Bill.   English
      b. John-ga   Bill-o but-ta   Japanese
          John-subject Bill-object hit (adapted from Kuno, 1973)
(16) a. Why was John fired?   English
      b. John-wa   naze kubi-ni natta no? Japanese
          John-topic why was fired   question marker (Lasnik & Saito, 1984)
(17) a. Lei è malata.
      b. È malata.
(18) a. She is ill.
      b. *Is ill.

Roughly, we can conceive of a parameter as a yes/no question. Thus, the parameter that relates to the appearance of a subject would have the form in (19):

(19)   Can the subject of a sentence be phonetically null? Yes/No

Depending on the particular language, the answer to the question in (19) will vary. If a child is exposed to Italian, the value of (19) will be positive; if the child is exposed to English, the parameter will be set to the negative value. Because under the P&P approach both the principles and the parameters are given by UG, children are innately endowed with them. The task of the child acquiring a language is, thus, to set the parameters to the value expressed by the language of her environment.

To sum up, UG is the human genetic endowment that is responsible for the course of language acquisition. The knowledge the child brings to the task of language acquisition is often called the "language acquisition device" (LAD), which in addition to UG may include procedures for learning (e.g., the subset principle, see Berwick, 1985, statistical computations, etc.). We can, thus, revise the model in (7) as in (20):

(20)   Linguistic data   → | LAD (UG +learning | →   Grammar
            of language X | procedures) | of language X

Another kind of support for the existence of an innate linguistic system can be drawn from the mere observation that the ability to acquire language is a property common to all human beings, and only to them. Given this, it is only natural to assume that the linguistics system, represented in (7) as the "initial state of linguistic knowledge," is, like other cognitive systems (e.g., the visual system), part of the biological endowment of the human species (Chomsky, 1986b). Innate cognitive systems are known to have the so-called critical period. For instance, kittens exposed only to vertical lines in the first three months of their lives fail to see horizontal lines later on in their lives (Blasdel, Mitchell, & Pettigrew, 1977; Hirsch, 1972; Rauschecker & Singer, 1981; Stryker, Sherk, Leventhal, & Hirsch, 1978). Similarly, a child has to be exposed to natural language during early childhood (be it spoken or signed) in order to establish the basis for intact language development. If the linguistic input is nonexistent or impoverished during this critical period for the acquisition of first language, some aspects of language acquisition, such as the acquisition of syntax, become virtually impossible.

It might very well be that there are two types of critical period: one that is responsible for the acquisition of a first language, which is quite short, and one that is relevant for the acquisition of a second language as a native language once one language has been acquired, which might extend over a longer period. Researchers have made various claims regarding the age at which the critical period for second-language acquisition terminates—some referred to 5 or 6 years, and others talked about the beginning of puberty (see Lenneberg, 1967; Johnson & Newport, 1989; but see Hakuta, Bialystok, & Wiley, 2003). The notion of a critical period for the acquisition of a first language is especially important for children with a hearing impairment. Because the exposure to a natural language, be it signed or oral, within the limited time frame of the critical period for first language is a necessary condition for their acquisition of language, early intervention that would allow them to be exposed to language input within the critical period is a determinant of their ability to acquire language (see Friedmann & Szterman, 2006; Yoshinaga-Itano & Apuzzo, 1998a, 1998b).

Finally, the development of creole languages strongly supports the inborn ability to acquire language. In the nineteenth century, people on plantations and in slave colonies developed a rudimentary form of language communication—a pidgin. Once a pidgin has native speakers, the children of the slaves, it develops into a full language, called a creole (Arends, Muysken, & Smith, 1994). Unlike pidgin, which consists mostly of very basic combinations of informative words, creole languages have functional morphemes (e.g., inflection, case) and a much more elaborated structure. The same is true for the development of the various sign languages (see, for example, Sandler, Meir, Padden, & Aronoff, 2005, on the development of grammatical structure in second-generation signers of Al-Sayyid Bedouin Sign Language, and see Jackendoff, 1994).

If children come into the world empty-handed, at least as far as language is concerned, where would this development come from? Let us turn now to the third question.

Putting Knowledge of Language to Use

We use our knowledge of language to make and understand statements, questions, conditionals, and so on. While doing so, we produce strings of sounds associated with meaning, or perceive strings of sounds and associate them with meaning. These strings of sounds include what we call words (or morphemes), assembled into hierarchical structures, sentences (see the following section for a detailed discussion). It is commonly assumed that words, being idiosyncratic pairs of sound and meaning (as observed by de Saussure, 1916/1977), are stored in our mental lexicon. The assignment of an appropriate structure to a set of words—namely the formation of the sentence—is performed by what is called the computational system (CS). The sensory-motor system is responsible for the phonetic realization/perception of the sentence, and the conceptual–intentional system for its meaning. We can represent the way linguistic knowledge is put to use as in (21).

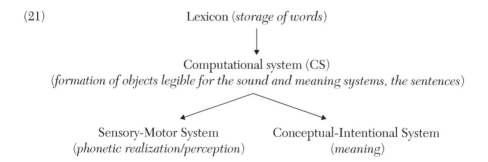

(21)   Lexicon (*storage of words*)

Computational system (CS)
(*formation of objects legible for the sound and meaning systems, the sentences*)

Sensory-Motor System   Conceptual-Intentional System
(*phonetic realization/perception*)   (*meaning*)

Undoubtedly, being able to form sentences in one's language is crucial for the normal use of language. This, however, does not exhaust knowledge of language. In the following subsection we review briefly the components of linguistic knowledge and the research fields concerned with them.

Subfields of Linguistic Research

Our unconscious linguistic knowledge includes the ability to recognize the particular variety of sounds belonging to our language (e.g., /x/ is not a sound used in English, but is in Dutch, Hebrew, or Arabic), as well as the rules underlying the combinations of sounds. For instance, the speakers of English pronounce the final sound in the word *cups* as [s], but in the word *mugs* as [z].

Phonetics and *phonology* are the subfields concerned with the physical and functional properties of sounds, respectively.

The subfields focusing on meaning are *semantics* and *pragmatics*. Semantics is based on the rules of logic defining the assignment of meaning in its narrow sense, and it refers to the assignment of meaning to single words, as well as to the truth conditions at the sentence level. The goal of pragmatics is to specify the rules governing the meaning of the sentences in context (e.g., in a discourse).

(22)   During her summer vacation, Lisa will visit either New York or Tel Aviv.

Given the truth conditions defined formally for the word *or*, (22) is true if one of the following happens:

(i)   Lisa will visit only New York
(ii)   Lisa will visit only Tel Aviv
(iii) Lisa will visit both New York and Tel Aviv

However, in actual conversation, when (22) is uttered, we understand that Lisa will visit only one of the cities mentioned, not both of them. Why and how this happens is addressed by the pragmatic theory of discourse (Grice, 1975).

Syntax is the subfield that examines the formation of sentences across languages, defining the workings of the computational system. In the following sections we focus on syntax, present some central aspects of the syntactic theory, and illustrate their contribution to the research of language acquisition and language impairments.

SENTENCE STRUCTURE

Sentences are produced and perceived as linear strings of words picked up from our mental lexicon. But a closer examination will immediately reveal that the words in a sentence are organized into larger units, referred to as phrases. Consider (23):

(23)   The very talented actress liked the movie with Tim Robbins.

We have a clear intuition that the words *very* and *talented* belong together; *the very talented actress* is a unit, as is *the movie with Tim Robbins*. Compare now (23) with a slightly different (24):

(24)   The very talented actress saw the movie with Tim Robbins.

Sentence (24) is ambiguous. Either the movie is with Tim Robbins, or the actress went with Tim Robbins to see some movie. In the second reading, *with Tim Robbins* is not related to *movie*, but rather directly to the verb *saw*. This fact cannot be expressed by a linear description, as *with Tim Robbins* is not adjacent to the verb. This is exemplified in the structures in (25) and (26), which describe the meaning relations between the parts of the sentence.

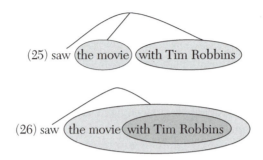

What enables us to interpret (24) in two different ways—to break it into different kinds of phrases—and why this is impossible in (23)? Put differently, what guides the formation of the phrases in a given sentence? In order to answer this question, it is necessary to specify the lexical information associated with words that is relevant for the syntactic component.

Syntactic-Semantic Information in the Lexicon

Categories of words   The lexicon includes words in various categories: the category N(oun) includes words denoting objects or events (e.g., *table, child, Italy, destruction, examination*); members of the category V(erb) denote events and states (e.g., *drink, run, know, love*); words modifying nouns (e.g., *tall, beautiful, red*) belong to the lexical category A(djective), and those modifying verbs and sentences are classified as Adv(erb) (e.g., *happily, peacefully, yesterday, often, fortunately*). These categories (N, A, V, Adv) each include many members and can admit new formations (e.g., *downloadable, emailed, online*, etc.).

There are a limited number of grammatical words of various categories. The grammatical words specify the function or the status of the appropriate lexical categories, and therefore the categories they belong to are referred to as *functional* lexical categories. The category D(eterminer) is composed of definite and indefinite articles (e.g., *the, a*), demonstratives (e.g., *this, these*), and quantifiers (e.g., *some, every, three*)—namely, elements performing some function with respect to Ns. (Pronouns like *he, they, our*, etc. are also analyzed as members of the D category.) Another functional category is I(nflection), which includes auxiliary verbs (*do, is, have*), modals (*can, will, shall*), and the infinitival marker *to*—namely, elements associating the verbs with tense or aspectual specification (e.g., past, future, present, perfective, progressive), and agreement features (Person, Number, and Gender). The category Deg(ree) includes words like *very, too*, and *enough* determining the status of As and Advs. Members of P(reposition), *on, near, before, above, during*, express a relation between two entities—for example, *a book about elephants, drinking before driving* (the classification of P as a functional category is controversial; some linguists view the category P as a lexical category, on a par with N and V, whereas others consider it as being composed of both lexical and functional members). Conj(unction) (*and, or*) combines and groups elements. Members of C(omplementizer), such as *that, whether*, and *if* specify the force of sentences (e.g., declarative, interrogative, subjunctive, etc.). In some linguistic texts, the category I is termed AUX(iliary), and C is COMP. The lexical categories (functional and content) are assumed to be part of our inborn knowledge, the UG. In the process of language acquisition, children learn the words of their language and the category to which these belong.

Thematic Structure and Subcategorization Frames

In addition to their lexical category, the lexical entry of verbs (and certain nouns) includes another kind of information that dictates their incorporation into sentence structure. Specifically, verbs are associated with what is called their *subcategorization frame* and *thematic structure*.

The traditional division of verbs into intransitive, transitive and ditransitive relates to the number of *complements* a verb takes. Some verbs, like *sneeze*, take no complement, as shown in (27). These are the intransitive verbs. Others, the transitive verbs, take one complement, like *found* in example (28), and there are verbs taking two complements, like *gave* in (29), referred to as ditransitive verbs.

		Lexical entries
(27)	Esther sneezed.	*sneeze:* [V] [_]
(28)	Esther found an elephant.	*found:* [V] [_NP]
(29)	Esther gave an apple to the elephant.	*gave:* [V] [_NP PP]

As can be seen in the examples, the lexical entries include, in addition to the lexical category (V, in these cases), the number of phrasal categories that the verb takes as complements, and their type: NP (noun phrase), PP (prepositional phrase), etc. The square brackets include an underscore ("_") that symbolizes the location of the verb and the types of complements that follow it, if any. The information regarding the number of complements and their type is called the *subcategorization frame* of the verb.

There are transitive or ditransitive verbs—like *eat* or *sell*, respectively—that optionally realize (one of) their complements (30). Optional complements are specified in the lexical entry of the verbs in parentheses (e.g., *eat:* [V] [_ (NP)]):

(30)   a. Dan ate (ice cream).
       b. Lisa sold her car (to Bart).

Complements, thus, define the various classes of verbs, and therefore are considered part of the speakers' lexical knowledge of verbs—namely, as part of the verb's lexical entry. However, there are other types of phrases, like those denoting place or time, that can be added freely to (almost) any verb—in square brackets in the examples under (31). Such phrases are termed *adjuncts*, and they are not part of the lexical entry of verbs. Thus, in (31b), for example, "an elephant" is a complement and therefore part of the lexical entry of *found*, whereas "in the kitchen" is an adjunct that can be added to any verb, and therefore there is no need to mention it in the lexical entry of *found*.

(31)   a. Esther sneezed [in the kitchen]/[before breakfast].
       b. Esther found an elephant [in the kitchen]/[before breakfast].
       c. Esther gave an apple to the elephant [in the kitchen]/[before breakfast].

The subcategorization frames of the various verbs are, of course, not accidental. As mentioned, verbs express events. The nature of the event is what determines the necessary number of the participants, as well as their role in the event (Chomsky, 1981). In other words, borrowing the terminology of classical logic, verbs can be characterized by their predicate argument structure (PAS). Intransitive verbs (e.g., *sneeze*) denote events with one participant (the "sneezer") and are referred to as one-place predicates. In the events denoted by the transitive verbs (e.g., *found*), there are two necessary participants (in our case, the "finder," and "the thing being found"), hence these are two-place predicates. Finally, ditransitive verbs like *give* express events with three necessary participants ("the giver," "the thing given," "the recipient"), referred to as three-place predicates. The roles performed by the various participants in an event are called *thematic roles* (also known as theta roles, or θ-roles), and they include the following types: Agent, Cause, Theme, Goal, Experiencer, Location, Source. The necessary participants are usually referred to as the *arguments* of the verb.

Agent is the role of the participant that performs some action or brings about some change consciously (e.g., *Esther* in (32)). A participant serving as the Theme does not perform an action or brings about some change but, rather, undergoes it (e.g., *an elephant*, and *an apple* in (33) and (34), respectively). In an event denoted by a verb of motion or transfer (e.g., *give*), the participant that is the target of the transfer or motion receives the role of a Goal (e.g., *(to) the elephant* in (32)).

(32)   Esther[Agent] sneezed.
(33)   Esther[Agent] found an elephant[Theme].
(34)   Esther[Agent] gave an apple[Theme] to the elephant[Goal].

The verb *loved* in (35) denotes a state, one of whose participants (*Mary*) experiences an emotion (of love), rather than performing some action. This participant's role is that of the Experiencer. In the event expressed by a verb like *put* (36), the locative phrase *on the table* is a necessary participant (**Lisa put the book*), playing the thematic role of Location. (Phrases denoting location are viewed as the verb's complements, rather than adjuncts, only for verbs like *put* or *lived*, for which these phrases are indeed necessary participants in the event.) The verb *bring* exemplifies an event that includes the Source participant (*from the office*) (37). Finally, as shown in (38), the participant bringing about some change does not have to be conscious (*the storm*). Such a participant is termed the Cause, rather than the Agent.

(35)   Mary[Experiencer] loved her dog[Theme].
(36)   Lisa[Agent] put the book[Theme] on the table[Location].
(37)   Homer[Agent] brought a pen[Theme] from the office[Source].
(38)   The storm[Cause] destroyed the town[Theme].

An example of the theta-structure (or *theta-grid*) of the verb *give* is shown in (39):

(39)   *give:* [V] *1* | *2* | *3* (number of necessary arguments/participants)
                Agent | *Theme* | Goal (specification of the thematic roles of the arguments)

The theta-grid of a verb is meant to subsume its subcategorization frame. In most cases this is indeed so—that is, there is no need to specify the phrases of its complements once the theta-grid is given. In the above examples, Theme is realized as a nominal phrase (NP), whereas Goal, Source, and Location are realized as prepositional phrases (PPs). However, this is not always the case. For example, verbs like *trust, depend*, and *claim* assign a Theme. *Trust*, as expected, takes an NP complement (*She trusts Mary*), but *depend* takes a PP complement (*She depends on Mary*), and *claim* takes an embedded sentence (*She claims that Dave plays beautifully*). Note also that the Goal argument of *give* can be an NP—as in

(40)—rather than a PP. Thus, at least for some verbs, the syntactic specification of their complement is necessary, as it is not fully predictable from the thematic role of the relevant argument—as shown in (41) for *give*. It should be pointed out that verbs like *depend on, believe in*, or *look at*, which have an obligatorily prepositional complement, present a further complication. Because the identity of the preposition is verb-specific, it has to be included in some way in the lexical entry of these verbs (for the analysis of such verbs in Hebrew and English see Botwinik-Rotem, 2004).

(40)   Mary[Agent] gave the elephant[Goal] an apple[Theme]
(41)   *give:* [V] *1* | *2* | *3* (number of necessary arguments)
               Agent | *Theme* | *Goal* (specification of the thematic roles of the arguments)
               NP | *NP* | *NP/PP* (realization of the arguments)

Finally, some verbs are associated with more than one theta-grid or subcategorization frame. Take, for instance, a verb like *know*. It can occur with an NP complement (42a), a PP complement (42b), a clausal complement denoting an embedded question (42c), or a clausal propositional (declarative) complement (42d). Assuming that the second thematic role of *know* is invariably Theme, its various syntactic realizations should be specified in the lexical entry of *know*, yielding multiple subcategorization frames. Alternatively, one can hypothesize that the different syntactic realizations indicate that the internal role of this verb is not uniformly Theme (e.g., when it is an NP, the role is Theme, whereas when it is a clause, its role is a Proposition, Grimshaw, 1979, 2005). Consequently, the lexical entry of a verb may include several different theta-grids.

(42)   a. Claudio knew [the answer]. [_NP]
        b. Claudio knew [about the corruption of the government]. [_PP]
        c. Claudio knew [where Broca's area is]. [_CP[Question]]
        d. Claudio knew [that Raffaella loves red clothes]. [_CP[Proposition]]

Predicate Argument Structure: Psychological Reality and Language Disorders

The complexity of the predicate argument structure and of the subcategorization frame has been shown to have an effect on the access to the lexical entry of a verb (Shapiro, Brookins, Gordon, & Nagel, 1991; Shapiro, Gordon, Hack, & Killackey, 1993; Shapiro & Levine, 1990; Shapiro, Zurif, & Grimshaw, 1987, 1989). Shapiro and his colleagues found that the complexity of the argument structure of the verb, defined by the number of thematic options, affects the access to a verb. Namely, the more argument structure options a verb has, the longer it takes to access it in the mental lexicon. This effect was found even when subjects listened to sentences that were structurally biased toward one particular argument structure. For example, even when presented with the sentence *I met the girl that Claudio knew*, in which the verb clearly takes an NP Theme, the subjects still activated all possible argument structure options for *knew* (Shapiro et al., 1989). This occurs regardless of sentence type (Shapiro et al., 1993) and only in the vicinity of the verb (Shapiro & Levine, 1990). Unlike the number of options for complements, the number of complements—0, 1, or 2 complements, see (32)–(34)—did not show an effect on lexical access to the verb. Some adults who have language impairments, such as individuals with Broca's aphasia, appear to have intact predicate argument structure knowledge although their syntactic abilities are impaired. They show the same effect of verb complexity as do typical adults, namely graded response time to verbs as a function of the number of the verbs' complementation options. However, individuals with Wernicke's aphasia do show impairment in predicate argument structure: they do not exhibit the normal predicate argument structure complexity effects in lexical access (Shapiro & Levine, 1990). Data from brain imaging also support the psychological reality of predicate argument structure representation, the complexity of multiple thematic roles, and the relation of predicate argument structure to Wernicke's area. Shetreet, Palti, Friedmann, and Hadar (2007) investigated the patterns of brain activation associated with the increasing number of subcategorization and argument structure options. They reported graded activation in three brain locations as a function of increasing the number of argument structure/ subcategorization options: in the left hemisphere, in left-superior temporal gyrus, a part of Wernicke's area, and in two areas in left-inferior frontal gyrus—in BA 47 and in BA 9— areas that are believed to be involved in semantic memory.

The thematic structure and the subcategorization frame that are specified in the lexical entry of the verb are the basis for the formation of syntactic structures. Specifically, syntactic structures are formed according to the Projection Principle (Chomsky, 1981), which states that the lexical properties of the verb have to be reflected in the sentence structure. A more explicit version of the Projection Principle is the Theta Criterion (Chomsky, 1981) which specifies how this is achieved; the verb assigns all its thematic roles to the appropriate phrases in the sentence, and all the appropriate phrases in the sentence receive thematic roles from the verb.

In the next section we illustrate how the structure of sentences is formed.

The Structure of Sentences

As mentioned, sentences are not just linear strings of words. Rather, they are hierarchically organized combinations of phrases. Consider the simple sentence in (43). As can be seen in the tree diagram in (44), the noun *rain* and the D *the* form a noun phrase (NP) *the rain*. The preposition *about* forms a prepositional phrase (PP), *about the rain*. The noun *song* forms another NP, *a song about the rain*. Phrases can be formed either in combination with additional phrases or by the word itself. Thus, we saw that *rain* can form an NP with the determiner *the*, and *song* can form a noun phrase with the PP *about the rain*. The N *Jane*, on the other hand, forms a noun phrase (NP) by itself (45).

The lexical categories (e.g., N, P, V) that form the phrasal categories (e.g., NP, PP, VP) are referred to as the *heads* of the phrases. They determine the nature of the phrase: a head noun creates a noun phrase; a head verb creates a verb phrase. Put differently, the phrases are *projections* of their heads.

Thus, phrases share the property of being built around a head of the same lexical category. They also have a uniform inner structure, referred to as the X-bar structure exemplified in (46) (Chomsky, 1981, 1986a; Jackendoff, 1977). (X stands for any of the potential heads: N, V, P, A, I, C.) According to the structure in (46), the complements of the head are attached (or merged) to the head, and form with it an intermediate phrasal level, referred to as the *bar*-level (symbolized as N', V', P', etc.)—e.g., the PP *about the rain* in (44) is the complement of the N *song*. Phrases or elements that are not complements of the head are assumed to occupy the *specifier* position (spec, for short), whose attachment to the intermediate level, X', completes the formation of the phrase, XP. For instance, in the nominal phrase *a song about the rain* in (44), the determiner *a* is in the specifier position, creating NP together with the N'. This is a very rough summary of what is known in the literature as the *X-bar theory*, whose origins can be traced to Chomsky (1970). (For a complete description and argumentation of the X-bar theory, see Radford, 1988.)

(43) Jane sang a song about the rain

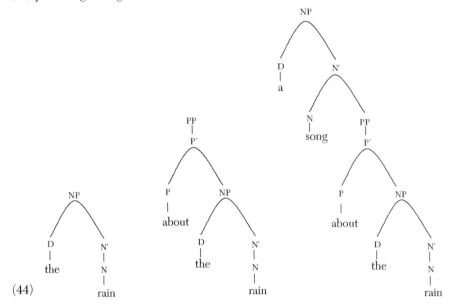

(44)

(45)

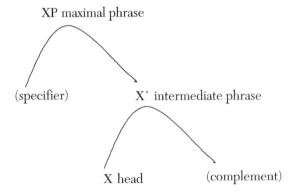

(46) The X-bar scheme for phrases

Although the hierarchical structure of the phrases is assumed to be universal (a principle of UG), the linear ordering between the head and its complement, as well as that between the intermediate level and the specifier position, is language-specific. The latter is viewed as a parametric option (a parameter of UG), giving rise to the various word orders across languages (e.g., "Does the head precede its complement? Yes/No"). For example, in head-initial languages like English, French, or Hebrew, in which the head (here, the verb *ate*) precedes the complement (here, the NP *the apple*), sentences like *John ate an apple* occur, whereas head-final languages like Japanese or German, in which the head follows the complement, have sentences like *John an apple ate*.

Let us now complete the structure of (43), *Jane sang a song about the rain*. Both NPs are the arguments of the verb *sang* (i.e., they realize the necessary participants in the event denoted by the verb). The NP *a song about the rain* is merged as the complement of V and is assigned the thematic role Theme. Arguments that are complements of the verb are referred to as *the internal argument* of the verb. The NP *Jane* is combined with the V' (i.e., it is inserted in spec of VP), it is assigned the thematic role Agent and is referred to as the external argument of the verb. As we will see momentarily, this is not the final position of this NP. Importantly, the association of the verb with its arguments—namely, the assignment of the verb's thematic roles to the relevant syntactic phrases—is what underlies the formation of the VP. Put differently, the assignment of some thematic role can take place only in this very local structural configuration, within the VP. (In head-initial languages the verb precedes its complement, and the internal theta-role is assigned to a position after the verb. In head-final languages, the verb follows its complements; accordingly, the internal theta-role of the verb is assigned to a position before the verb.) For the sake of simplicity, we will not specify the details of every phrase. When the inner structure of some phrase is not relevant, a triangle is used instead of specifying its exact structure—like *the rain* in example (47).

(47) The formation of VP

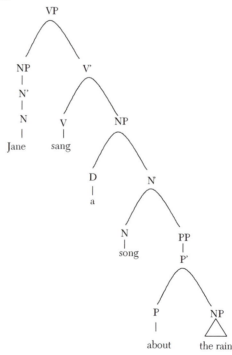

The syntactic tree includes two additional functional layers above the VP layer: the inflectional layer, IP, which is immediately above VP, and the complementizer layer (CP), which is the highest layer in the tree.

The head of the IP, I(nflection), is related to the tense inflection of the verb and its agreement with the subject (in person, gender, and number). It carries the tense of the sentence, either by hosting the modals and auxiliaries (e.g., *will, has*), the particle *to*, or, in sentences like (43) where no overt tense-element is present, the functional head I is assumed to carry abstract tense and agreement features (in our case, [+past], [third person, feminine, singular]).

The specifier of IP is the structural position of the subject of a sentence. To reach this position, the subject moves from its original position within the VP into spec-IP. (The moved element is assumed to leave a trace in its original position. Movement and traces are discussed in the following section.) The claim that the argument serving as the subject of the clause is merged in the VP, rather than being merged directly in the subject position, spec-IP, is known as the *VP-internal subject hypothesis*. (For its motivation and argumentation, see Koopman and Sportiche, 1991.)

(48) The formation of IP   The formation of CP

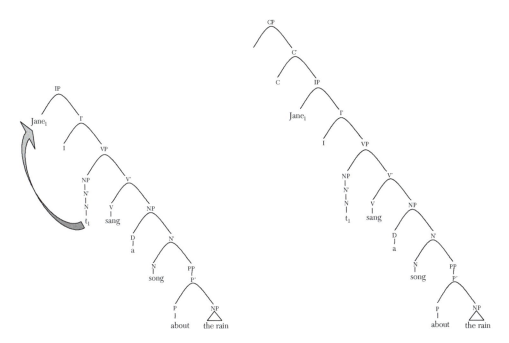

The structure of a sentence is not complete until its force is specified—namely, until it is specified whether it is an interrogative ([+Q(uestion)]) or a declarative ([–Q]) sentence. This function is performed by the functional head C, which, in (48), for instance, endows the IP with the feature [–Q]. C also enables the embedding of the sentence in other sentences. Like the functional head I, C can be realized by overt morphemes, as in embedded English clauses: *John said* that *Lisa won; John asked* whether *Lisa won*. As seen in (48), the combination of the IP with C forms a CP, the phrasal category of what we call a sentence.

The CP plays an important role in various constructions: in addition to embedding markers like *that* and *whether*, it also hosts wh-morphemes in wh-questions (like "*Who* sneezed?"), verbs and auxiliary verbs when they move to the beginning of the sentence ("When *did* Bill sneeze?"), and noun phrases that move to the beginning of the sentence in topicalized sentences (like "*This boy*, the doctor will see right away"), as will be discussed in detail.

The syntactic tree, its hierarchical structure, and the ability to project it all the way up to the functional categories IP and CP are key notions in the explanation of the acquisition of syntax and of generalizations regarding syntactic deficits in individuals with agrammatism and children with hearing impairment. In the realm of language acquisition, a number of researchers—like Lebeaux (1988), Guilfoyle and Noonan (1988), Radford (1990, 1992, 1995), and Platzack (1990)—have argued that the syntactic tree of young children does not include any functional category, and that the tree is actually composed only of VP. Others—like Clahsen (1990/1991), Clahsen, Penke, and Parodi (1993/1994), and Clahsen, Eisenbeiss, and Penke (1996)—suggest a single functional projection (which they term FP) above VP. Yet others suggest that the whole tree, with IP and CP, already exists very early on (Boser, Lust, Santelmann, & Whitman, 1992; Déprez & Pierce, 1993; Poeppel & Wexler, 1993; Weissenborn, 1990). Rizzi (1994) in his truncation hypothesis (also termed the "root infinitive" hypothesis) suggested that children have knowledge of the whole tree, but as they still do not know that it should be obligatorily projected all the way up to CP, they sometimes project the tree only partially.

With respect to syntax in agrammatic aphasia, some researchers suggested that the syntactic tree of individuals with agrammatic aphasia is pruned, and they cannot reach the high nodes of the syntactic tree. This inability to reach the high nodes causes an inability to produce structures that rely on CP such as wh-questions, embedded sentences, and sentences involving movement of the verb to second position (see next section). Some of the patients even fail to reach IP, which causes deficits in the production of tense inflection (see Friedmann, 2001, 2002, 2005, 2006; Friedmann & Grodzinsky, 1997).

Explanations for the deficit in SLI vary (see chapter 1 by Schwartz) but none of the main theories ascribe the deficit to the inability to project the high nodes of the syntactic tree. Leonard (1995, 1998) presented convincing evidence showing that the syntactic tree is present in children with SLI (see also Novogrodsky & Friedmann, 2006 for arguments for intact CP in syntactic SLI). With respect to deaf children, a detailed description of syntactic abilities in deaf children de Villiers, de Villiers, and Hoban (1994) suggested that the central problem of orally trained children with hearing impairment is the functional categories IP and CP.

MOVEMENT

Dislocation of the various syntactic elements (i.e., phrases or heads) is a basic and universal property of human languages (Chomsky, 1986b). Consider the pairs in (49) and (50):

(49) a. John will clean [the orange house]Theme
      b. [*Which house*]Theme will John clean ___ ?
(50) a. John cleaned [*the room*]Theme
      b. [*The room*]Theme was cleaned ___ (by John)

What is common to the constructions in (49b) and (50b) is that the sentence-initial phrases (*which house, the room*) act as the Theme of the verb *clean*, as they do in the corresponding (a) sentences. Given that the verb can assign its thematic roles only within the VP, and that Theme is assigned to the complement of the verb, the question arises as to how the Theme role is associated with the sentence-initial phrases in (49b) and (50)(50b). This led linguists to suggest that the derivation of such sentences involves movement of these phrases from their original theta-position, the complement of V, to another position in the syntactic structure. In what follows, we describe the mechanism that associates the moved phrases with their thematic role, as well as the positions to which they move.

Movement Types

There are several distinct types of syntactic movement. The first classification distinguishes between movement of phrases (e.g., NPs or PPs) and movement of heads (e.g., V or N). The former is called *phrasal movement*, and the latter *head movement*. Phrasal movement can be further classified by the destination of the movement: movement to spec-IP, or movement to spec-CP. In a variety of languages, among them English, the formation of wh-questions, for instance, involves movement of a *wh*-phrase to spec-CP. This position is termed the "nonargument position," and this type of phrasal movement is termed *A′(-movement* (read: *A bar* movement) or *wh*-movement. When phrases move to spec-VP or spec-IP, which are called "argument positions," as is the case in passive sentences, for example, this kind of phrasal movement is referred to as *A(rgument)-movement.*

Head movement occurs in languages where the association of the verb with tense (and agreement) features involves movement of the verb from its base position as the head of the VP (V) to a higher head position, namely, to the functional head I. Verbs raised to I, as well as elements originating in I (e.g., English modals), can move further up to C. In the following subsections we present and discuss briefly the most typical constructions involving these three types of movement.

Phrasal Movement

Constructions Involving A′-Movement A very familiar construction involving A′-movement in a variety of languages is the wh-question. The derivation of such a question is given in (51). Because the thematic role assigned to the *wh*-phrase *which house* is Theme, and since Theme can be assigned only to the complement of the verb, the surface position of the *wh*-phrase is assumed to result from movement of the *wh*-operator from its original position to spec-CP (the dislocation of the modal *will* to the pre-subject position will be addressed in the section on head movement). The position from which movement takes place is marked with *t* (trace) (or viewed as a silent copy of the moved element; Chomsky, 1995). The trace of a moved element and the element itself form a chain. The chain formed by A′-movement is called an A′-chain, and it connects the moved phrase with its original position, allowing it to receive its thematic role. Specifically, the verb assigns the thematic role to the trace of movement, and the trace of movement transfers the thematic role to the moved element (the antecedent) via a chain of movement.

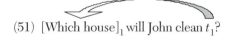

(51) [Which house]$_1$ will John clean t_1?

Note that in English, for example, *wh*-movement is obligatory, and failure to do so results in an ungrammatical sentence (52):

(52) a. *John cleaned which house?
      b. *Will John clean which house?

Another instance of an obligatory A′-movement is illustrated by the relative clause in (53).

(53) I met the boy who Lisa likes

The clause *who Lisa likes* modifies the NP *the boy*. The modified NP is termed the *head of the relative* (not to be confused with the head of a phrase), and the embedded clause is the *relative clause*.

Who in the relative clause is not a question marker (i.e., *who Lisa likes* is not an embedded question)—rather, it is a *relative operator*. Similarly to the movement of the *wh*-phrases in questions, exemplified in (51), the relative operator *who* moves from its original position within the VP to the beginning of the relative clause, spec-CP (54).

(54) I met [$_{NP}$ the boy$_1$] [$_{CP}$ who$_1$ [$_{IP}$ Lisa likes t_1]]

Although the Theme of *likes* (*who*) refers to the same individual as *the boy*, the head of the relative, these are two distinct syntactic entities, each receiving its thematic role from a different verb (*likes* and *met*, respectively). Thus, the coindexing of the head of the relative with the relative operator is means of conveying coreference (identical reference), rather than membership in a chain of movement. (Vergnaud, 1974, and Kayne, 1994, among others, suggest a radically different analysis of relative clauses, according to which it is the relative head itself which moves.)

Relative clauses in English can also have the forms in (55), which do not include a *wh*-phrase and can include the complementizer *that*. These are assumed to involve movement of a phonetically null operator (Op), as shown in (56).

(55) a. I met the boy that Lisa likes ___
     b. I met the boy Lisa likes ___

(56) a. I met the boy$_1$ [Op$_1$ that [$_{IP}$ Lisa likes t$_1$]

     b. I met the boy$_1$ [Op$_1$ [$_{IP}$ Lisa likes t$_1$]

Topicalization, moving of a phrase to the beginning of the clause, is another instance of A′-movement (57).

(57) a. John will clean the orange house tomorrow.
     b. *The orange house*, John will clean tomorrow (and the blue house he will leave for Friday).

Like wh-questions and relative clauses, topicalization involves movement of a phrase to spec-CP. However, topicalization is usually motivated by discourse considerations and is, therefore, not obligatory. Hence, both sentences, with and without the topicalization of the Theme, are grammatical.

A distinction that is important to research in language acquisition and language impairment is the one between subject- and object relative clauses, and between subject- and object questions. Subject relative clauses and questions are created when the subject moves to spec-CP, whereas object relatives and object questions are created by the movement of the object, as seen in (58). For individuals with syntactic deficits (individuals with agrammatism, children with syntactic SLI, and children with hearing impairment), object relatives and object questions are usually more difficult to understand than their subject relative and subject question counterparts (Friedmann & Novogrodsky, 2004; Friedmann

& Shapiro, 2003; Friedmann & Szterman, 2006; Grodzinsky, 2000; Grodzinsky, Piñango, Zurif, & Drai, 1999).

(58) Subject relative: I met the boy who ___ likes Lisa.
      Object relative: I met the boy who Lisa likes ___ .
      Subject question: Who ___ likes Lisa?
      Object question: Who does Lisa like ___ ?

Another classification of relative clauses that was found to affect child language as well as the language of typical adults is the distinction between center-embedding and right-branching relative clause. In sentences like (59) the relative clause is on the right-hand-side, the end of the sentence, whereas in sentence (60) it is embedded in the center of the main clause, between the subject and its predicate (i.e., the main verb). For both children and adults, center-embedded relative clauses are harder to understand than right-branching relatives, and center-embedded relatives are acquired later than are right-branching ones (Correa, 1995; de Villiers, Tager-Flusberg, Hakuta, & Cohen, 1979; Kidd & Bavin, 2002; Sheldon, 1974).

(59) I met the boy that Lisa likes.

(60) The boy that Lisa likes plays the saxophone.

Constructions Involving A-Movement   A-movement is a short movement of a phrase to spec-IP (and possibly also within VP from the complement position to spec-VP). As already mentioned, spec-IP is the position of the subject. Since almost all subjects originate within VP and then move to IP, the derivation of a large variety of clauses involves movement to spec-IP. Apart from this instance of A-movement, there are two additional instances of A-movement: movement of the Theme of unaccusative verbs, and movement of the Theme of passive verbs.

Unaccusative verbs.   Within the realm of intransitive verbs, verbs that take only one NP argument, there are two main subgroups. These include unaccusative verbs like *sank* and *fell*, and unergative verbs like *jumped* and *laughed*. (Reflexive verbs, like *washed* in *Dan washed*, are analyzed as unergatives, see Reinhart & Siloni, 2004.) Both unaccusatives and unergatives take one participant and assign one thematic role. The difference between them relates to the thematic role they assign to their participant. Unaccusative verbs assign Theme, whereas unergatives assign Agent. For example, in *"The leaf fell"*, the *leaf* is not actively responsible for the action of the unaccusative verb *fell* but, rather, undergoes the action (i.e., it has the role of Theme). In contrast, *the bird* in the sentence "*The bird chirped*," which includes an unergative verb, is the Agent.

The difference between these two types of intransitive verbs led researchers to assume different structural analyses for the two types of verbs. The single argument of unaccusatives is base-generated in the object position, after the verb, whereas in unergatives the argument is base-generated before the verb (in spec-VP). Thus, although the sentences *"The leaf fell"* (61) and *"The bird chirped"* (62) both have an NP-V word order, their derivations are different. The NP-V order of (61) is the result of NP-movement from object to the subject position, and it therefore includes a trace in the object position. The NP-V order of (62) involves no movement because the NP is base-generated preverbally.

(61)   fell the leaf

    The leaf$_1$ fell t$_1$

(62)   The bird chirped

This is the "unaccusativity hypothesis" (Levin & Rappaport-Hovav, 1995; Perlmutter, 1978; Perlmutter & Postal, 1984). The term "unaccusative" (which, according to Pullum, 1991, was coined by Pullum and adopted by Perlmutter & Postal) derives from the analysis that although verbs like *fell* have a Theme argument in the object position, they do not assign it accusative case. The moved NP is linked to its initial position via an argument chain (A-chain). Similar to A'-chains, A-chains enable the assignment of thematic roles despite the movement. The verb assigns the thematic role of Theme to the position where the NP was generated (i.e., after the verb), and the role is transferred via the A-chain to the new position, before the verb. In English, sentences with unaccusatives require that the NP argument, which is generated in the object position as the complement of the verb, moves to the subject position. In other languages, like Italian and Hebrew, this movement is optional, and both V-NP and NP-V orders are grammatical with unaccusative verbs.

The unaccusativity hypothesis is also supported by online processing studies. A study that tested the online processing of the moved NP shows that in an English sentence like "The coffee spilled," "the coffee" is first accessed when it is heard at the position before the verb, but then it is also reaccessed after the verb, at the original position of the Theme. In sentences with the same word order (NP-V) but with unergative verbs, no such reaccessing occurs (Friedmann, Taranto, Shapiro, & Swinney, 2008).

Like unaccusatives, the passive construction also involves A-movement of the Theme argument to spec-IP. However, it is rather different and warrants a separate discussion.

Passive verbs.   Passive verbs are derived from their active counterparts, the corresponding transitive verbs. For instance, a transitive verb like *clean*, which assigns Agent and Theme thematic roles (63a), gives rise to the passive *was cleaned* (63b). In the passive construction, the argument bearing the internal thematic role Theme ("the room") appears in the subject position. Because the internal theta-role can be assigned only to the verb's complement, the occurrence of the Theme in the subject position must be the result of movement (63b). The passive verb, unlike its active counterpart, does not assign the external Agent role to the subject position. Note, however, that at the semantic level this role clearly exists and can be realized in a *by*-phrase (63b).

(63) a. John$_{[Agent]}$ cleaned *the room*$_{[Theme]}$.

    b. *The room*$_{1 [Theme]}$ was cleaned t$_1$ (by John).

Head Movement

V to I Movement   As we mentioned in an earlier section, the IP layer is responsible for the tense and agreement inflection of the verb. The head I hosts the appropriate inflectional features. In many richly inflected languages the verb has to move to I in order to collect its inflectional features or to check the features of the I head. This movement, referred to as verb-raising, is reflected in word order changes in certain sentences (see Pollock, 1989, for an extensive discussion and argumentation for verb-raising as pertaining to the different word orders in English and French). For example, in the French sentence (64) the verb precedes the adverb. Importantly, an adverb like *often* resides in a fixed position in the syntactic tree in English and French. It is located above VP—that is, before the VP. Therefore, if the inflected verb in (64) precedes the adverb in French, it indicates that the verb has moved outside the VP, to a position above (and hence before) the adverb, see (65).

(64) Je *mange souvent* de chocolat
      I *eat   often*   of+the chocolate

(65) Je [$_I$ mange [$_{AdvP}$ souvent [$_{VP}$ ___ de chocolat]

(66) I often eat chocolate.

In English the verb follows the adverb (66). This is taken to indicate that the lexical verb in English does not raise overtly to I, and the feature-checking is assumed to be achieved in a different manner. For instance, according to Chomsky (2000, 2001), the checking procedure can be achieved via an operation termed Agree, which allows feature checking to be established without movement. As there are languages like French, involving overt movement of the verb, as well as languages like English, where the lexical verb remains in its base position, the difference between the two kinds of languages is simply one of a parameter: "Does the verb raise overtly to I? Yes/No."

It is customary to split the functional head I into two functional heads, T(ense) and Agr(eement) (referred to in the literature as the "split-Infl hypothesis"). Specifically, instead of assuming that the functional head I carries both the tense and the agreement features of the verb, it is assumed that the tense specification of the verb is associated with the head T, projecting a TP, whereas the agreement features are carried by a distinct functional head Agr that forms an AgrP. As far as verb-movement is concerned, overt verb-raising (as in French, for instance) is movement of the verb from V to both T and Agr. (According to Pollock, 1989, 1993, TP is above AgrP, whereas Belletti, 1990, advocates the order AgrP above TP. Chomsky (1995) dispenses with Agr nodes and suggests that the agreement of the subject is checked in TP.) For reasons of simplicity we will continue assuming that tense and agreement features are carried by a single functional head I.

I to C Movement   A lexical verb raised overtly to I, or an element originating in I (e.g., auxiliary verbs, modals) can move further up to C. Movement of the verb from I to C is obligatory in some languages in question formation, as seen in (67) and (68). Head movement can take place only to the "closest" head position. Thus, it is impossible to move directly from V to C, but it is possible to move from V to I, and from I to C. Given that the verb in English does not raise to I, an English question in which the verb is located in C cannot exist: *Eat you the apples? In other languages, like German and Dutch, the verb in the main clause always has to move to C, and is positioned after the first constituent in the sentence (which is in spec CP). This phenomenon is called "V2" because the verb ends up in second sentential position—see (69) for a German example.

(67) a. John will come.
      b. Will$_v$ John t$_v$ come?

(68) a. John will clean the orange house.
      b. Which house$_1$ will$_v$ John t$_v$ clean t$_1$?
(69)   Gestern tanzte Dani mit Marko.
         Yesterday danced Dani with Marko

In a variety of languages I-to-C movement is not obligatory, occurring mainly when spec CP is filled by an adverb or *wh*-phrase (see, for instance, Shlonsky & Doron, 1992, who term such movement in Hebrew "triggered inversion"). This is illustrated in the Hebrew example in (70), translated into English for simplicity. It has been observed that children acquire V-to-I movement earlier than I-to-C movement (Déprez & Pierce, 1993).

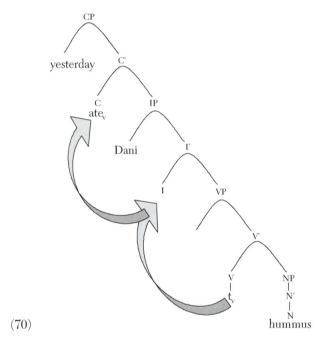

(70)

To summarize this section, elements of a sentence can appear at points in the sentence different from their original position. Analyzing displacement via movement (chain formation) provides an explanation of the association of a moved phrase with the relevant thematic role and accounts for word order alternations within and across languages. Movement also has an important role in explaining a long line of phenomena from language acquisition, language processing, and language disorders.

Syntactic Movement: Psychological Reality and Language Disorders

Many psycholinguistic studies have demonstrated the psychological reality of the trace of syntactic movement, using paradigms such as cross-modal lexical priming (CMLP) to detect the activation of constituents in the sentence during on-line processing. These studies show that in the course of processing of movement-derived sentences, the moved constituent appears to be activated twice in the sentence: once when first encountered and again at the trace, where it is not phonetically present (Love & Swinney, 1996; Nicol & Swinney, 1989; Tanenhaus, Boland, Garnsey, & Carlson, 1989; Zurif, Swinney, Prather, Wingfield, & Brownell, 1995). When the hearer reaches the trace position, the antecedent—the relocated constituent—is reactivated. This finding indicates that the NP is semantically processed in its original position—the trace position. This has been found both for traces of Wh-movement and for traces of A-movement. Another demonstration of the reality of movement traces, in this case its neurological reality, is the finding that sentences that include movement of NPs activate certain areas in the brain, specifically left Broca's and Wernicke's areas (Ben-Shachar, Hendler, Kahn, Ben-Bashat, & Grodzinsky, 2003; Ben-Shachar, Palti, & Grodzinsky, 2004). The trace is, therefore, psychologically real, and its existence, as well as the existence of the chain that connects it to the antecedent, allows for the understanding of "who is doing what to whom" in the sentence.

Movement also plays a key role in the explanation of the order of syntactic acquisition in typically developing children (see Friedmann & Lavi, 2006; Guasti, 2002), as well as syntactic impairments in children (see chapter 1 by Schwartz and chapter 4 by Cleary) and adults. For example, children with hearing impairment show impaired comprehension and production of passive sentences (Power & Quigley, 1973), wh-questions (de Villiers et al., 1994; Geers & Moog, 1978; Quigley, Wilbur, & Montanelli, 1974), topicalization structures (Friedmann & Szterman, 2006), and object relative sentences (see Berent, 1988; de Villiers, 1988; Friedmann & Szterman, 2006; Quigley, Smith, & Wilbur, 1974). The acquisition of passives, wh-questions, topicalized sentences, and relative clauses was reported to be significantly delayed in the language development of children with hearing loss, and in many cases these structures were not mastered even at older ages. These four syntactic structures have a common characteristic that might be the source of the deficit: they all involve phrasal movement.

Similarly, children with SLI who have a syntactic deficit have been reported to have a deficit in the comprehension and production of sentences that are derived by phrasal movement, such as reversible passives in English (Adams, 1990; Bishop, 1979; van der Lely, 1996; van der Lely & Harris, 1990); relative clauses in English, Hebrew, and Greek (Adams, 1990; Friedmann & Novogrodsky, 2004, 2007; Novogrodsky & Friedmann, 2006; Stavrakaki, 2001); and wh-questions (Ebbels & van der Lely, 2001; van der Lely & Battell, 2003).

A deficit in movement is also hypothesized to underlie the comprehension impairment in Broca's agrammatic aphasia (Grodzinsky, 1990, 2000). Individuals with agrammatism show significant difficulties in the comprehension of object relative clauses, object wh-questions, and topicalized structures, all involving A′-movement (Friedmann & Shapiro, 2003; Grodzinsky, 1989, 2000; Grodzinsky, Pierce, & Marakovitz, 1991; Schwartz, Linebarger, Saffran, & Pate, 1987; Schwartz, Saffran, & Marin, 1980; Zurif & Caramazza, 1976; see Grodzinsky et al., 1999, for a review). Structures with V-C movement are also impaired in agrammatism; individuals with agrammatism have difficulties producing and understanding sentences with verbs in C (Friedmann, 2001; Friedmann, Gvion, Biran, & Novogrodsky, 2006; Zuckerman, Bastiaanse, & van Zonneveld, 2001).

Because there is a deficit in syntactic movement in language-impaired populations, syntactic movement is also a crucial notion in treatment of these deficits. Seminal studies by Shapiro and Thompson and their group (Thompson & Shapiro, 1994, 1995; Thompson et al., 1997) indicated that deficits in movement-derived structures can be treated using an intervention program directed at various types of movement, and that the treatment of one structure with a specific type of movement generalizes to other structures derived by the same movement. Treatment using similar principles proved effective also for the syntactic deficit in SLI (Ebbels & van der Lely, 2001; Levy & Friedmann, in press).

To summarize, syntactic movement is not only psychologically real, but more importantly, it is a useful tool in understanding and treating the syntactic impairments in children and adults.

Syntactic movement (i.e., chain formation), thus, is a central mechanism employed by a human language, giving rise to long-distance dependencies. However, not all long-distance dependencies involve movement. Long-distance dependencies that do not involve movement are discussed in the following section.

BINDING

A human language consists of three kinds of nominal expressions (NPs): *R-expressions* (referential NPs), pronouns (pronominal NPs), and anaphors (reflexive and reciprocal NPs).

Referential NPs (R-expressions), which are the vast majority of NPs, refer directly to some individual *in the world* (71). Pronouns can refer to some individual in the world as well (*I, you, we*). However, third person pronouns can, in addition, refer to another *NP in the sentence*. Sentence (72) exemplifies both options: either *him* refers to *John*, symbolized by having the same index, $_i$, as *John*, or it can refer to some other individual in the world, symbolized by having an index distinct from that of the NP *John*. (From now on we will focus only on the reading where the pronoun is coindexed—that is, coreferential—with some NP in a sentence.) Anaphors cannot refer by themselves to an individual in the world. Rather, they have to refer to some *NP in the sentence*, see (73) for a reflexive and (74) for a reciprocal.

(71) John saw the movie.
(72) John$_i$ thinks that Mary likes him$_{i/j}$.
(73) John$_i$ likes himself$_i$.
(74) [John and Mary]$_i$ like each other$_i$.

These NP types have different distribution (i.e., they cannot occur freely in any position in a sentence). We now turn to Conditions A, B, and C of the binding theory (Chomsky, 1981), which are the principles defining the distribution of anaphors, pronouns, and referential NPs, respectively.

Condition A: The Distribution of Anaphors

Compare the grammatical (75) and the ungrammatical (76), both including the reflexive anaphor *himself*. The only difference between them is that in (76) the reflexive anaphor does not occur in the same clause as its *antecedent*, the NP to which it refers (*John*). The antecedent is in the main clause, whereas the anaphor is in the embedded clause.

(75) John$_i$ likes *himself*$_i$.
(76) *John$_i$ thinks [$_{CP}$ that Mary likes *himself*$_i$].
(77) *Himself$_i$ likes John$_i$.

Thus, an anaphor has to occur in the same clause as its antecedent. This, however, is not sufficient, as shown by (77), where both the anaphor (*himself*) and the antecedent (*John*) are clause-mates, and it is still ungrammatical. Sentence (77) differs from the grammatical (75) in the hierarchical relations between the antecedent and the anaphor. In (75), the antecedent is the subject of the sentence and is therefore in the highest clausal position (spec-IP), whereas the anaphor is in the object position (inside the VP). In (77) the hierarchical relation is reversed. The anaphor (*himself*) is higher than the referential NP, it is the subject of the sentence, and the referential NP, the antecedent of the anaphor, is inside the VP.

Based on this, we can define informally the distribution of anaphors: an anaphor has to have an antecedent in the same clause, and the antecedent has to be "higher" in the structure than the anaphor. An anaphor whose antecedent is in the appropriate structural relation and in the same clause is said to be *bound*. Otherwise it is *free*. This holds for reflexive anaphors as well as for reciprocal anaphors. (For the precise formulation of the relevant structural relation, referred to as *c-command*, see Chomsky, 1981.)

Condition A: An anaphor has to be bound in the local domain (roughly, in its clause).

Condition B: The Distribution of Pronouns

Let us now compare the grammatical (78) including a pronoun with the ungrammatical (79), focusing only on the interpretation where the pronoun is coreferential with some other NP. The comparison immediately reveals that a pronoun cannot be bound in the same clause—that is, it cannot have an antecedent in an appropriate structural position as in (79). Being bound by an antecedent in another clause is fine (78). The distribution of the pronouns is, thus, complementary to that of the anaphors (often pronouns and anaphors are said to be in *complementary distribution*). (See Reinhart and Reuland, 1993, for a more precise description regarding the distribution of the pronouns.)

(78)   John$_i$ thinks that Mary likes *him$_i$*.
(79)   *John$_i$ likes *him$_i$*.

Recall that an element which is not bound is free. Consequently, the distribution of pronouns is defined as follows:

Condition B: A pronoun has to be free in its local domain.

Note that the existence of a potential antecedent in the same clause with the pronoun does not necessarily lead to violation of condition B. For example (80), where the antecedent of the pronoun, *John*, is embedded inside the subject of the sentence, *John's mother*, is fine, because here the antecedent of the pronoun is not in the appropriate structural relation to bind the pronoun, and the latter is free, as required by Condition B.

(80)   [John's$_i$ mother]$_j$ likes him$_i$.

Condition C: The Distribution of Referential NPs

As the following examples show, a referential NP (like "John") simply cannot have a binder, in the local domain (81), or outside its local domain (82). It just has to be free (83):

(81)   *He$_i$ likes John$_i$.
(82)   *He$_i$ thinks that Mary likes John$_i$.
(83)   John$_i$ thinks that Mary likes him$_i$.

Condition C: An R-expression has to be free.

Thus, pronouns, anaphors, and referential NPs are governed by different conditions: anaphors must be bound within their domain, pronouns need to be free in their domain, and referential NPs have to be completely free. The differences between these NPs also manifest themselves in language disorders. For example, studies of agrammatic aphasia showed that individuals with agrammatic aphasia have a selective deficit in the interpretation of pronominal dependencies, whereas interpretation of reflexives is unimpaired (see Grodzinsky, Wexler, Chien, Marakovitz, & Solomon, 1993; Ruigendijk, Vasič, & Avrutin, 2006).

To summarize, linguistics has been developed as a description of the internal knowledge of speakers about the rules of their native language. As such, it forms a powerful tool for detailed description, which results in more profound understanding of the process of language acquisition and of the fine line that is drawn between the spared and impaired abilities in language disorders.

REFERENCES

Adams, C. (1990). Syntactic comprehension in children with expressive language impairment. *British Journal of Disorders of Communication*, 25, 149–171.

Arends, J., Muysken, P., & Smith, N. (1994). *Pidgins and creoles: An introduction*. Amsterdam: John Benjamins.

Belletti, A. (1990). *Generalized verb movement: Aspects of verb syntax*. Turin, Italy: Rosenberg & Sellier.

Ben-Shachar, M., Hendler, T., Kahn, I., Ben-Bashat, D., & Grodzinsky, Y. (2003). The neural reality of syntactic transformations: Evidence from fMRI. *Psychological Science*, 14, 433–440.

Ben-Shachar, M., Palti, D., & Grodzinsky, Y. (2004). Neural correlates of syntactic movement: Converging evidence from two fMRI experiments. *NeuroImage*, 21, 1320–1336.

Berent, G. P. (1988). An assessment of syntactic capabilities. In M. Strong (Ed.), *Language learning and deafness* (pp. 133–161). Cambridge, UK: Cambridge University Press.

Berwick, R. (1985). *The acquisition of syntactic knowledge*. Cambridge, MA: MIT Press.

Bishop, D. V. M. (1979). Comprehension in developmental language disorders. *Developmental Medicine and Child Neurology*, 21, 225–238.

Blasdel, G. G., Mitchell D. E., & Pettigrew, J. (1977). A combined physiological and behavioral study of the effect of early visual experience with contours of a single orientation. *Journal of Physiology*, 265, 615–636.

Boser, K., Lust, B., Santelmann, L., & Whitman J. (1992). The syntax of V-2 in early child German grammar: The strong continuity hypothesis. *Proceedings of the Northeast Linguistic Society*, 22.

Botwinik-Rotem, I. (2004). *The category P: Features, projection, interpretation*. Unpublished doctoral dissertation, Tel Aviv University, Tel Aviv.

Brown, R., & Hanlon, C. (1970). Derivational complexity and the order of acquisition in child speech. In J. R. Hayes (Ed.), *Cognition and the development of language*. New York: Wiley.

Chomsky, N. (1957). *Syntactic structures*. Berlin, Germany: Mouton de Gruyter.

Chomsky, N. (1959). [Review of B. F. Skinner *Verbal Behavior*]. *Language*, 35, 26–57.

Chomsky, N. (1965). *Aspects of the theory of syntax*. Cambridge, MA: MIT Press.

Chomsky, N. (1970). Remarks on nominalization. In R. Jacobs & P. Rosenbaum (Eds.), *Readings in English transformational grammar* (pp. 184–221). Waltham, MA: Ginn.

Chomsky, N. (1981). *Lectures on government and binding*. Dordrecht, The Netherlands: Foris.

Chomsky, N. (1986a). *Barriers*. Cambridge, MA: MIT Press.

Chomsky, N. (1986b). *Knowledge of language: Its nature, origin and use*. New York: Praeger.

Chomsky, N. (1995). *The minimalist program*. Cambridge, MA: MIT Press.

Chomsky, N. (2000). Minimalist inquiries. In R. Martin, D. Michaels, & J. Uriagereka (Eds.), *Step by step: Essays on minimalist syntax in honor of Howard Lasnik* (pp. 89–155). Cambridge, MA: MIT Press.

Chomsky, N. (2001). Derivation by phase. In M. Kenstowicz (Ed.), *Ken Hale: A life in linguistics*. *Current Studies in Linguistics 36* (pp. 1–52). Cambridge, MA: MIT Press.

Clahsen, H. (1990/1991). Constraints on parameter setting: A grammatical analysis of some acquisition stages in German child language. *Language Acquisition, 1,* 361–391.

Clahsen, H., Eisenbeiss, S., & Penke, M. (1996). Lexical learning in early syntactic development. In H. Clahsen (Ed.), *Generative perspectives on language acquisition: Empirical findings, theoretical considerations and crosslinguistic comparison* (pp. 129–159). Amsterdam & Philadelphia: Benjamins.

Clahsen, H., Penke, M., & Parodi, T. (1993/1994). Functional categories in early child German. *Language Acquisition, 3,* 395–429.

Correa, L. M. (1995). An alternative assessment of children's comprehension of relative clauses. *Journal of Psycholinguistic Research, 24,* 183–203.

Crain, S. (1991). Language acquisition in the absence of experience. *Behavioral and Brain Sciences, 14,* 597–650.

Crain, S., & Nakayama, M. (1987). Structure dependence in grammar formation. *Language, 63,* 522–543.

Déprez, V., & Pierce, A. (1993). Negation and functional projections in early grammar. *Linguistic Inquiry, 24,* 25–68.

de Villiers, P. A. (1988). Assessing English syntax in hearing-impaired children: Elicited production in pragmatically motivated situations. In R. R. Kretchmer & L. W. Kretchmer (Eds.), *Communication assessment of hearing-impaired children: From conversation to classroom* [Monograph]. *Journal of the Academy of Rehabilitative Audiology, 21*(Suppl.), 41–71.

de Villiers, J., de Villiers, P., & Hoban, E. (1994). The central problem of functional categories in English syntax of oral deaf children. In H. Tager-Flusberg (Ed.), *Constraints on language acquisition: Studies of atypical children* (pp. 9–47). Hillsdale, NJ: Lawrence Erlbaum Associates.

de Villiers, J. G., Tager-Flusberg, H. B., Hakuta, K., & Cohen, M. (1979). Children's comprehension of relative clauses. *Journal of Psycholinguistic Research, 17,* 57–64.

Ebbels, S., & van der Lely, H. K. J. (2001). Metasyntactic therapy using visual coding for children with severe persistent SLI. *International Journal of Language and Communication Disorders, 36*(Suppl.), 345–350.

Friedmann, N. (2001). Agrammatism and the psychological reality of the syntactic tree. *Journal of Psycholinguistic Research, 30,* 71–90.

Friedmann, N. (2002). Question production in agrammatism: The tree pruning hypothesis. *Brain and Language, 80,* 160–187.

Friedmann, N. (2005). Degrees of severity and recovery in agrammatism: Climbing up the syntactic tree. *Aphasiology, 19,* 1037–1051.

Friedmann, N. (2006). Speech production in Broca's agrammatic aphasia: Syntactic tree pruning. In Y. Grodzinsky & K. Amunts (Eds.), *Broca's region* (pp. 63–82). New York: Oxford University Press.

Friedmann, N., & Grodzinsky, Y. (1997). Tense and agreement in agrammatic production: Pruning the syntactic tree. *Brain and Language, 56,* 397–425.

Friedmann, N., Gvion, A., Biran, M., & Novogrodsky, R. (2006). Do people with agrammatic aphasia understand verb movement? *Aphasiology, 20,* 136–153.

Friedmann, N., & Lavi, H. (2006). On the order of acquisition of A-movement, Wh-movement and V-C movement. In A. Belletti, E. Bennati, C. Chesi, E. Di Domenico, & I. Ferrari (Eds.), *Language acquisition and development* (pp. 211–217). Cambridge, UK: Cambridge Scholars Press.

Friedmann, N., & Novogrodsky, R. (2004). The acquisition of relative clause comprehension in Hebrew: A study of SLI and normal development. *Journal of Child Language, 31,* 661–681.

Friedmann, N., & Novogrodsky, R. (2007). Is the movement deficit in syntactic SLI related to traces or to thematic role transfer? *Brain and Language, 101,* 50–63.

Friedmann, N., & Shapiro, L. P. (2003). Agrammatic comprehension of simple active sentences with moved constituents: Hebrew OSV and OVS structures. *Journal of Speech Language and Hearing Research, 46,* 288–297.

Friedmann, N., & Szterman, R. (2006). Syntactic movement in orally-trained children with hearing impairment. *Journal of Deaf Studies and Deaf Education, 11*, 56–75.

Friedmann, N., Taranto, G. Shapiro, L. P., & Swinney, D. (2008). The leaf fell (the leaf): The online processing of unaccusatives. *Linguistic Inquiry, 39*(3).

Geers, A. E., & Moog, J. S. (1978). Syntactic maturity of spontaneous speech and elicited imitation of hearing-impaired children. *Journal of Speech and Hearing Disorders, 43*, 380–391.

Grice, H. P. (1975). Logic and conversation. In P. Cole & J. L. Morgan (Eds.), *Speech acts* (pp. 41–58). New York: Academic Press.

Grimshaw, J. (1979). Complement selection and the lexicon. *Linguistic Inquiry, 10*, 279–326.

Grimshaw, J. (2005). *Words and structure*. Chicago: CSLI/University of Chicago Press.

Grodzinsky, Y. (1989). Agrammatic comprehension of relative clauses. *Brain and Language, 37*, 480–499.

Grodzinsky, Y. (1990). *Theoretical perspectives on language deficits*. Cambridge, MA: MIT Press.

Grodzinsky, Y. (2000). The neurology of syntax: Language use without Broca's area. *Behavioral and Brain Sciences, 23*, 1–71.

Grodzinsky, Y., Pierce, A., & Marakovitz, S. (1991). Neuropsychological reasons for a transformational analysis of verbal passive. *Natural Language and Linguistic Theory, 9*, 431–453.

Grodzinsky, Y., Piñango, M., Zurif, E., & Drai, D. (1999). The critical role of group studies in neuropsychology: Comprehension regularities in Broca's aphasia. *Brain and Language, 67*, 134–147.

Grodzinsky, Y., Wexler, K. Chien, Y.-C., Marakovitz, S., & Solomon, J. (1993). The breakdown of binding relations. *Brain and Language, 45*, 396–422.

Guasti, M. T. (2002). *Language acquisition: The growth of grammar*. Cambridge, MA: MIT Press.

Guilfoyle, E., & Noonan, M. (1988). *Functional categories and language acquisition*. Paper presented at 13th Boston University Conference on Language Development.

Hakuta, K., Bialystok, E., & Wiley, E. (2003). Critical evidence: A test of the critical-period hypothesis for second-language acquisition. *Psychological Science, 14*, 31–38.

Hirsch, H. V. (1972). Visual perception in cats after environmental surgery. *Experimental Brain Research, 15*, 409–223.

Hornstein, N., & Lightfoot, D. (1981). Introduction. In N. Hornstein & D. Lightfoot (Eds.), *Explanation in linguistics: The logical problem of language acquisition*. London & New York: Longman.

Jackendoff, R. (1977). *X'-Syntax: A study of phrase structure*. Cambridge, MA: MIT Press.

Jackendoff, R. (1994). *Patterns in the mind: Language and human nature*. New York: Basic Books.

Johnson, J. S., & Newport, E. L. (1989). Critical period effects in second language learning: The influence of maturational state on the acquisition of English as a second language. *Cognitive Psychology, 21*, 6099.

Kayne, R. (1994). *The antisymmetry of syntax*. Cambridge, MA: MIT Press.

Kidd, E., & Bavin, L. E. (2002). English-speaking children's comprehension of relative clauses: Evidence for general-cognitive and language-specific constraints on development. *Journal of Psycholinguistic Research, 31*, 599–617.

Koopman, H., & Sportiche, D. (1991). The position of subjects. *Lingua, 85*, 211–258.

Kuno, S. (1973). *The structure of the Japanese language*. Cambridge, MA: MIT Press.

Lasnik, H., & Saito, M. (1984). On the nature of proper government. *Linguistic Inquiry, 15*, 235–289.

Lebeaux, D. (1988). *Language acquisition and the form of the grammar*. Unpublished doctoral dissertation, University of Massachusetts.

Lenneberg, E. H. (1967). *Biological foundations of language*. New York: Wiley.

Leonard, L. (1995). Functional categories in the grammars of children with specific language impairment. *Journal of Speech and Hearing Research, 38*, 1270–1283.

Leonard, L. (1998). *Children with specific language impairment*. Cambridge, MA: MIT Press.

Levin, B., & Rappaport-Hovav, M. (1995). *Unaccusativity*. Cambridge, MA: MIT Press.

Levy, H., & Friedmann, N. (in press). Treatment of syntactic movement in syntactic SLI: A case study. *First Language*.

Lightfoot, D. (1982). *The language lottery*. Cambridge, MA: MIT Press.

Love, T., & Swinney, D. (1996). Coreference processing and levels of analysis in object-relative constructions: Demonstration of antecedent reactivation with the cross-modal priming paradigm. *Journal of Psycholinguistic Research, 25,* 5–24.

Nicol, J., & Swinney, D. (1989). The role of structure in coreference assignment during sentence comprehension. *Journal of Psycholinguistics Research, 18,* 5–24.

Novogrodsky, R., & Friedmann, N. (2006). The production of relative clauses in SLI: A window to the nature of the impairment. *Advances in Speech-Language Pathology, 8,* 364–375.

Perlmutter, D. (1978). Impersonal passives and the unaccusative hypothesis. In J. Jaeger et al. (Eds.), *Proceedings of the fourth annual meeting of the Berkeley Linguistic Society* (pp. 159–189). Berkeley: University of California at Berkeley.

Perlmutter, D. M., & Postal, P. M. (1984). The 1-advancement exclusiveness hypothesis. In D. Perlmutter & C. Rosen (Eds.), *Studies in relational grammar 2* (pp. 81–126). Chicago: University of Chicago Press.

Piaget, J., & Inhelder, B. (1969). *The psychology of the child.* New York: Basic Books. (Originally published in French as *La psychologie de l'enfant.* Paris: Presses Universitaires de France, 1966.)

Platzack, C. (1990). A grammar without functional categories: A syntactic study of early Swedish child language. *Working Papers in Scandinavian Syntax, 45,* 13–34.

Poeppel, D., & Wexler, K. (1993). The full competence hypothesis of clause structure in early German. *Language, 69,* 1–33.

Pollock, J.-Y. (1989). Verb movement, universal grammar, and the structure of IP. *Linguistic Inquiry, 20,* 365–424.

Pollock, J. Y. (1993). *Notes on clause structure.* Unpublished manuscript, Université de Picardie, Amiens, France.

Power, D. J., & Quigley, S. P. (1973). Deaf children acquisition of the passive voice. *Journal of Speech and Hearing Research, 16,* 5–11.

Pullum, G. K. (1991). *The great Eskimo hoax and other irreverent essays on the study of language.* Chicago: University of Chicago Press.

Quigley, S. P., Smith, N. L., & Wilbur, R. B. (1974). Comprehension of relativized sentences by deaf students. *Journal of Speech and Hearing Research, 17,* 325–341.

Quigley, S. P., Wilbur, R. B., & Montanelli, D. S. (1974). Question formation in the language of deaf students. *Journal of Speech and Hearing Research, 17,* 699–713.

Radford, A. (1988). *Transformational grammar: A first course.* Cambridge, UK: Cambridge University Press.

Radford, A. (1990). *Syntactic theory and the acquisition of English syntax.* Oxford, UK: Blackwell.

Radford, A. (1992). The acquisition of the morphosyntax of finite verbs in English. In J. M. Meisel (Ed.), *The acquisition of verb placement* (pp. 23–62). Dordrecht, The Netherlands: Kluwer.

Radford, A. (1995). Children: Architects or brickies? In D. MacLaughlin & S. McEwen (Eds.), *Proceedings of the 19th Annual Boston University Conference on Language Development* (Vol. 1., pp. 1–19). Somerville, MA: Cascadilla Press.

Rauschecker, J. P., & Singer W. (1981). The effects of early visual experience on the cat's visual cortex and their possible explanation by Hebb synapses. *Journal of Physiology, 310,* 215–239.

Reinhart, T., & Reuland, E. (1993). Reflexivity. *Linguistic Inquiry, 24,* 657–720.

Reinhart, T., & Siloni, T. (2004). Against the unaccusative analysis of reflexives. In A. Alexiadou, E. Anagnostopoulou, & M. Everaert (Eds.), *The unaccusativity puzzle: Studies on the syntax-lexicon interface.* New York: Oxford University Press.

Rizzi, L. (1994). Some notes on linguistic theory and language development: The case of root infinitives. *Language Acquisition, 3,* 371–393.

Ruigendijk, E., Vasič, N., & Avrutin, S. (2006). Reference assignment: Using language breakdown to choose between theoretical approaches. *Brain and Language, 96,* 302–317.

Sandler, W., Meir, I., Padden, C., & Aronoff, M. (2005). The emergence of grammar: Systematic structure in a new language. *Proceedings of the National Academy of Sciences U.S.A., 102,* 2661–2665.

Saussure, F. de (1977). *Course in general linguistics* (trans. W. Baskin). Glasgow: Fontana/Collins. (Original work published 1916).

Schwartz, M. F., Linebarger, M. C., Saffran, E. M., & Pate, D. C. (1987). Syntactic transparency and sentence interpretation in aphasia. *Language and Cognitive Processes, 2,* 55–113.

Schwartz, M., Saffran, E., & Marin O. (1980). The word-order problem in agrammatism: I. Comprehension. *Brain and Language, 10,* 249–262.

Shapiro, L. P., Brookins, B., Gordon, B., & Nagel, N. (1991). Verb effects during sentence processing. *Journal of Experimental Psychology: Learning, Memory, and Cognition, 17,* 983–996.

Shapiro, L. P., Gordon, B., Hack, N., & Killackey, J. (1993). Verb–argument structure processing in Broca's and Wernicke's aphasia. *Brain and Language, 45,* 423–447.

Shapiro, L. P., & Levine, B. A. (1990). Verb processing during sentence comprehension in aphasia. *Brain and Language, 38,* 21–47.

Shapiro, L. P., Zurif, E., & Grimshaw, J. (1987). Sentence processing and the mental representation of verbs. *Cognition, 27,* 219–246.

Shapiro, L. P., Zurif, E., & Grimshaw, J. (1989). Verb representation and sentence processing: Contextual impenetrability. *Journal of Psycholinguistic Research, 18,* 223–243.

Sheldon, A. (1974). The role of parallel function in the acquisition of relative clauses in English. *Journal of Verbal Learning and Verbal Behavior, 13,* 272–281.

Shetreet, E., Palti, D., Friedmann, N., & Hadar, U. (2007). Cortical representation of verb processing in sentence comprehension: Number of complements, subcategorization, and thematic frames. *Cerebral Cortex, 17*(8), 1958–1969.

Shlonsky, U., & Doron, E. (1992). Verb second in Hebrew. In D. Bates (Ed.), *Proceedings of the West Coast Conference on Formal Linguistics 10* (pp. 431–446). Stanford, CA: Stanford Linguistics Association, Stanford University.

Skinner, B. F. (1957). *Verbal behavior.* New York: Appleton-Century-Crofts.

Stavrakaki, S. (2001). Comprehension of reversible relative clauses in specifically language impaired and normally developing Greek children. *Brain and Language, 77,* 419–431.

Stryker, M. P., Sherk, H., Leventhal, A. G., & Hirsch, H. V. (1978). Physiological consequences for the cat's visual cortex of effectively restricting early visual experience with oriented contours. *Journal of Neurophysiology, 41,* 896–909.

Tanenhaus, M. K., Boland, J., Garnsey, S. M., & Carlson, G. M. (1989). Lexical structure in parsing long-distance dependencies. *Journal of Psycholinguistic Research, 18,* 37–50.

Thompson, C. K., & Shapiro, L. P. (1994). A linguistic specific approach to treatment of sentence production deficits in aphasia. *Clinical Aphasiology, 22,* 307–323.

Thompson, C. K., & Shapiro, L. P. (1995). Training sentence production in agrammatism: Implications for normal and disordered language. *Brain and Language, 50,* 201–224.

Thompson, C. K., Shapiro, L. P., Ballard, K. J., Jacobs, B. J., Schneider, S. S., & Tait, M. E. (1997). Training and generalized production of Wh- and NP-movement structures in agrammatic aphasia. *Journal of Speech, Language, and Hearing Research, 40,* 228–244.

van der Lely, H. K. J. (1996). Specifically language impaired and normally developing children: Verbal passives vs. adjectival passive sentence interpretation. *Lingua, 98,* 243–272.

van der Lely, H. K. J., & Battell, J. (2003). WH-Movement in children with Grammatical-SLI: A test of the RDDR hypothesis. *Language, 79,* 153–179.

van der Lely, H. K. J., & Harris, M. (1990). Comprehension of reversible sentences in specifically language impaired children. *Journal of Speech and Hearing Disorders, 55,* 101–117.

Vergnaud, J.-R. (1974). *French relative clauses.* Unpublished doctoral dissertation, Massachusetts Institute of Technology.

Weissenborn, J. (1990). Functional categories and verb movement: The acquisition of German syntax reconsidered. *Linguistische Berichte, 3,* 190–224.

Yoshinaga-Itano, C., & Apuzzo, M. L. (1998a). Identification of hearing loss after age 18 months is not early enough. *American Annals of the Deaf, 143,* 380–387.

Yoshinaga-Itano, C., & Apuzzo, M. L. (1998b). The development of deaf and hard of hearing children identified early through the high-risk registry. *American Annals of the Deaf, 143,* 416–424.

Zuckerman, S., Bastiaanse, R., & van Zonneveld, R. (2001). Verb movement in acquisition and aphasia: Same problem, different solutions. Evidence from Dutch. *Brain and Language, 77,* 449–458.

Zurif, E., & Caramazza, A. (1976). Psycholinguistic structures in aphasia: Studies in syntax and semantics. In H. Whitaker & H. A. Whitaker (Eds.), *Studies in neurolinguistics* (Vol. 1). New York: Academic Press.

Zurif, E., Swinney, D., Prather, P., Wingfield, A., & Brownell, H. (1995). The allocation of memory resources during sentence comprehension: Evidence from the elderly. *Journal of Psycholinguistic Research, 24,* 165–182.

7

Neurobiology of Child Language Disorders

BAILA TROPPER and RICHARD G. SCHWARTZ

INTRODUCTION

The scientific mapping between brain and language behavior is now proceeding at an exceptionally rapid pace. This venture, though, is far from new; it has deep roots planted in the early nineteenth century (Dax, 1865; Harlow, 1868). In its infancy, research on linking brain and language function was limited to neuroanatomical studies. Early investigations focused on postmortem brains of adults who exhibited language disorders due to acquired brain damage. In recent years, this research has been dramatically expanded within the field of cognitive neuroscience. This branch of study concentrates on the structure and function of the brain underlying cognitive behavior, including perception, attention, memory, executive functions, and language. From among these topics of interest, the study of brain–language relations is the least developed (Brown & Hagoort, 1999). In the area of child language, research concerning brain and language functions is particularly sparse. Even so, there is a growing body of literature on this subject and it appears promising. Yet, we pose the question: *What is the benefit of knowing which brain structures are responsible for typical and atypical language performance?* The present chapter addresses this question by considering a number of critical and multifaceted aspects of neurobiology in normal and disordered child language development.

The study of neurobiology has been propelled by recent technological progress in two areas: imaging the anatomy and ongoing activity of the brain and recording the brain's electrical activity. These advancements have afforded researchers fine-grained online techniques to examine the cortical structures and activities implicated in language processing. In this chapter, we examine studies that have applied these methods in exploring the neurobiology of language. First, we describe research that has employed neuroimaging techniques, including structural and functional magnetic resonance imaging (MRI and fMRI, respectively) and positron emission tomography (PET). We then proceed to discuss studies that have used neurophysiological methods, such as event-related potentials (ERPs).

Our principal goal is to review major findings on the neurobiology of child language disorders. To accomplish this task, we consider studies that have used the aforementioned methods in children from normal and clinical populations. Regrettably, the complete range of developmental language disorders is far too broad to address within the confines of one chapter. We therefore devote the emphasis of our discussion to the relevant issues in *specific language impairment* (SLI). The scope of this review, though, is broadened by considering the neurobiological profile of SLI relative to other child language disorders, among them dyslexia, autism, and Williams syndrome. We conclude by offering suggestions for future research aimed at unveiling the neural correlates of normal and disordered language in children. To begin, a rudimentary background of some essential concepts in neurobiology is provided.

NEUROBIOLOGY PRIMER

At the neurobiological level, the two main categories of interest are brain structure and function. The natural assumption is that these variables bear a one-to-one correspondence but this has yet to be established. There are, in fact, multiple regions that are anatomically but not functionally distinct, at least given our current state of knowledge. The challenge of linking structure and function is complicated by the extensive interconnectedness of the human brain. Because multiple structures typically contribute to a given neural function, it is difficult to identify which brain regions are active in association with particular cognitive processes. Moreover, the structure–function relationship varies across normal individuals because it is determined by factors that differ from person to person. These factors may be categorized as either genetic or environmental. Both types of factors are instrumental in shaping neurobiology, consequently altering cognition. It follows then, that a discussion of neurobiology requires consideration of these influences on neurodevelopment. To abide by the gold standard, we evaluate abnormal neurodevelopment in the context of normal brain development.

NORMAL BRAIN DEVELOPMENT

Genetic and Environmental Effects on Neurodevelopment

Contributions to brain development have traditionally been characterized as either genetic or environmental. Genetic influences are those that involve the innate prespecification of brain structure that is provided by genes. Genes encode structural information to produce proteins that build the central nervous system, including the cortex of the brain. The approximately 10^5 genes possessed by the human are not nearly sufficient to specify the far greater number of neural connections that it accommodates. Therefore, some aspects of brain organization must depend on external factors. Moreover, during early phases of neurodevelopment, any area of cortex can support an assortment of cortical representations, which are manifested as intricate differences in synaptic connections and dendritic branching. External input helps mold the configuration of cortical representations, thereby exploiting the initial plasticity of the cortex. Therefore, in this context, cortical plasticity is a natural and defining aspect of neurodevelopment (De Haan & Johnson, 2003) and the cortex is an outgrowth of a complex interplay between genetic and environmental factors. We follow with a simplified account of this relationship. (The interested reader is referred to chapter 10 by Tomblin for a more comprehensive description of genetics in language development.)

Cortical Differentiation

The growth of the human cortex begins prenatally and continues well into postnatal life. Over this time, the cortex differentiates into areas that support different functions, among them, language processing. It is known that in most normal adults, the same approximate areas of cortex are responsible for specific linguistic functions. This would lead one to assume that the areal differentiation of cortex is genetically predetermined, and it is, but only partially. One prevailing view in cognitive neuroscience is that patterns of gene expression form large-scale areas in the cerebral cortex according to properties that make each area suitable for particular computations. Small-scale regions within these areas develop, or become specialized, through activity-dependent processes that are triggered by environmental experience. The representations that emerge in these smaller-scale regions, however, are not strictly determined by environmental input. They are, rather, constrained by certain architectural properties of the cortex. For example, each lamina, or layer, of the cortex supports specific cell types and patterns of inputs and outputs. Specific connectional and neurochemical features of each large-scale region also limit the representations that emerge within their boundaries (Johnson, 2005). Thus, both genetic and environmental effects are interwoven into the cortical tapestry.

A more specific understanding of genetic–environmental effects on neurodevelopment may be gained by considering the postnatal process of synaptic pruning. Synapses are genetically predetermined but are labile during early stages of development. The labile nature of these connections permits them to either stabilize or regress. Counterintuitively, the selective loss of synapses is actually a gain that occurs through the process of learning because in this context, "to learn is to eliminate" (Changeux, 1985; Changeux, Courrege, & Danchin, 1973). This synaptic loss is enabled by two factors: sensory input (environmental) and spontaneous activity in the neural network (genetic). Both of these factors may affect the activity of postsynaptic cells, resulting in selective synaptic loss that fine-tunes neural connectivity. Thus, environmental input may contribute to genetically programmed processes, leading to synaptic elimination. Consequently, brain anatomy is refined, allowing for increased cognitive capabilities.

Although the aforementioned account of genetic–environmental influences is well grounded, it leaves several questions unanswered. One question that remains is: To what extent are environmental influences constrained by genetic specifications? This question may be best explored in studies of cortical plasticity. The central aim of these studies is to reveal what optimally induces cortical changes to result in improved cognitive capacity. This objective has clear implications for intervention in childhood language disorders. Accordingly, we revisit this topic later in the chapter in remarking on early remediation of language impairment in children. Having provided a basic outline of neurodevelopment, we now focus on the following question: *Where is language processed in the developing brain?*

Language Areas in the Brain

Dividing the brain into areas hinges on the interrelated concepts of *localization* and *specialization*. Here, localization refers to ascribing a particular cognitive function to a specific region of the cerebral cortex. Areas that support particular functions are said to be specialized for those functions. Cortical specialization is a maturational process. During infancy, functional segregation of the cortex is generally poor. For this reason, many areas become partially activated in response to a wide range of sensory information. This has been demonstrated by fMRI studies that have shown a greater degree of brain activation in attention and memory tasks in children, as compared with adults (see Casey, Geidd, & Thomas, 2000, for a review). Over the course of development, the specificity of neural connections increases through processes such as synaptic loss. With changes in intraregional connectivity (large scale), neural activity becomes more narrowed, or finely tuned (small scale), resulting in functional specialization.

The development of functional specialization may enable processing within different areas of the brain to become increasingly segregated. This change, referred to as *parcellation*, may encapsulate, or modularize, information processing streams within their corresponding structures. As a result, there should be less informational exchange, and also less interference, between certain brain regions over the course of neurodevelopment. Presumably, the emergence of partial modularity should increase the efficiency of language processing in the brain (Johnson, 2005). This appealing notion of modularity, though, must be curbed by current knowledge of the interconnected nature of language processing in both the developing and fully developed brain. At this point, there is still strong disagreement over the extent to which language is modular and about whether modularity is the starting point or end product of brain development (Karmiloff-Smith, 1993). Segregating the neuroanatomical landscape according to language functions is misleading because it implies that language is entirely modular. Even so, it is helpful to classify brain regions in relation to their basic language roles if only to provide a framework for understanding the neurobiology of language.

There are several brain areas that have been the historical focus of research in the neurological bases of language. These areas are directly associated with the interrelated tasks of speech perception and production and language comprehension and production. In most individuals, these language functions are dominant, or specialized, in the left hemisphere. In navigating the language areas within this hemisphere, we traverse three anatomical landmarks of the cortex: convolutions, called gyri, depressions between gyri, called sulci, and deeper grooves, called fissures. These landmarks span the four primary lobes of the cerebral cortex, two of which predominate in language: the *frontal* and *temporal lobes* (see Figure 7.1). These two lobes are separated by the lateral sulcus, commonly referred to as the Sylvian fissure. This fissure serves as an inferior boundary for the *frontal lobe* and a medial boundary for the *temporal lobe*. Surrounding the Sylvian fissure are the perisylvian areas of the frontal and temporal lobes that are most crucial for language.

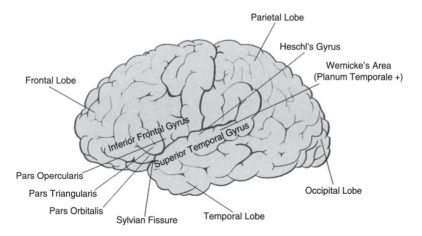

FIGURE 7.1   Primary language-related areas in the left hemisphere of the human brain.

Within the *frontal lobe*, the inferior frontal gyrus includes a critical language region called Broca's area. This area comprises two sections: pars opercularis and pars triangularis, also identified as Brodmann's areas (BA) 44 and 45, respectively. Below BA 45 is another area involved in language functioning, called pars orbitalis (BA 47). Notably, Broca's area lies anterior to the section of the motor strip dedicated to the organs of speech production. Accordingly, this area plays a pivotal role in speech motor planning for the oral production of language.

The *temporal lobe* serves as the station for auditory reception and is thus crucial for receptive language processing. The upper surface of the superior temporal lobe, called Heschl's gyrus, is the site to which all auditory information is projected in the brain. This area comprises part of the superior temporal gyrus, situated along the Sylvian fissure. The area on Heschl's gyrus on the superior portion of the Sylvian fissure is the primary auditory cortex. This area is connected via ascending projections to the medial geniculate nucleus of the thalamus, where auditory information is relayed. The primary auditory cortex is therefore of profound importance for speech perception. Posterior to Heschl's gyrus, on the inferior portion of the Sylvian fissure, is the auditory association area, also called the planum temporale (PT). Encircling the auditory cortex, on the posterior part of the superior temporal gyrus, is Wernicke's area, commonly referred to as BA 22. This area consists of the planum temporale, along with some additional lateral and inferior portions of the superior temporal gyrus. Wernicke's area is most closely associated with the comprehension of spoken language. A neural pathway formed by a fiber bundle, called the arcuate fasciculus, connects Wernicke's area to Broca's area. This connection thus links the primary brain areas involved in the comprehension and generation of language, respectively.

Although descriptions of these primary language areas often seem quite precise, there is substantial uncertainty about their exact locations and boundaries (Uylings, Malofeeva, Bogolepova, Amunts, & Zilles, 1999). Findings of wide interindividual variability suggest the need for further exploration of these language territories. Also, although language is mostly attributed to the perisylvian areas, additional brain regions are of paramount importance in language processes. Other left frontal and temporoparietal areas, as well as areas in the right hemisphere, play important roles in language and related cognitive abilities. Subcortical regions that house structures such as the caudate nucleus (a type of basal ganglion), the cerebellum, and portions of the thalamus are also commonly engaged in language functions.

An account of language areas in the brain gives rise to a fundamental question: *How do we know which brain structures subserve language functions?* The earliest evidence of brain localization for language came from combining clinical and postmortem examinations of language-impaired adults. These studies led investigators to conclude that the primary brain areas for language are those defined above as Broca's and Wernicke's areas. As mentioned, we now know that the initial and long-standing definitions of these areas are not consistent across individuals and that these brain regions are not the sole ones responsible for language. This refinement of our knowledge in neurobiology is owed to several methodological advancements, soon to be discussed. First, though, let us consider how the neurobiological bases of language differ in children with developmental language disorders.

ABNORMAL BRAIN DEVELOPMENT

Like the maturation of other bodily organs, brain development does not always proceed normally. When it does not, there are often adverse consequences on the brain's greatest enterprise—language development. In spite of the great strides made in the study of language acquisition, we still know incredibly little about the neurobiology of developmental language disorders. What we do know is that there are at least some neural correlates of impaired language. We review several of these here, with particular emphasis on those thought to be closely associated with specific language impairment. To begin, let us present a sketch of the distinctive features of this disorder.

SPECIFIC LANGUAGE IMPAIRMENT

Children who fail to acquire language skills age-appropriately, in spite of normal nonverbal intelligence and adequate educational opportunities, fit the diagnostic category of SLI. This disorder is characterized by syntactic and morphological deficits, poor vocabulary, and impaired language comprehension. It is also common to observe poor working memory, attentional deficits, as well as reading problems in individuals with SLI. Notably, there is a great deal of behavioral heterogeneity among affected individuals. Therefore, this inclusive list of deficits lacks the specificity needed to clearly define SLI. This problem is exacerbated by controversy over whether SLI is a disorder specific to language, as its name denotes. By convention, performance on nonlinguistic cognitive tests must be within the average range to meet the criteria for SLI. However, there is bountiful evidence of nonlinguistic deficits in individuals with SLI, observed, for example, in areas of perception, motor abilities, and mental representation (see Leonard, 1998, for a review). These findings have prompted reconsideration of whether language processes play an exclusive role in this disorder.

In the opening chapter of this volume, Schwartz provides a detailed account of the predominant theories of SLI. This account includes proposals of information processing deficits, auditory perceptual deficits, impaired grammatical representations, and abnormal procedural memory in individuals with SLI. The fact that there is a plethora of hypotheses to explain SLI is actually unsurprising, in view of the clinical diversity in this population. Unfortunately, though, this lack of theoretical coherence has wide-ranging repercussions. For researchers, it confounds subject selection, lends to manifold possibilities in data interpretation, and generates piecemeal research that often remains fragmented. For clinicians, the absence of theoretical conformity in defining SLI engenders uncertainty. This may lead to intervention that is more discretionary and less research-based than is desirable. In an effort to resolve this issue, some researchers have asked: *Could knowledge of the neurobiology of SLI demystify this disorder?*

NEUROBIOLOGY OF SPECIFIC LANGUAGE IMPAIRMENT

By definition, SLI is a language disorder that is not accompanied by major signs of neurological impairment, such as focal lesions. However, there must be neurobiological complements to the behavioral differences in this disorder. Linking deviant behavior to deviations in brain structure and function should bring us closer to a coherent account of SLI and other childhood language disorders.

The consensus is that SLI is associated with early neurodevelopmental abnormalities, rather than with acquired insults to the brain. To date, though, the specific origin of these abnormalities has yet to be empirically ascertained. As discussed earlier, neurodevelopment is molded by both genetic and environmental factors. Wide disparities in linguistic input impose relatively minor effects on ultimate linguistic capacity (Bishop, 1997). Therefore, environmental influences are not likely to be the chief culprit in SLI. Instead, it seems that genetic factors impacting upon early stages of neurodevelopment are largely accountable for this disorder. It is thought that developmental language disorders evolve due to genes that prescribe abnormal timing of prenatal neural migration, leading to deviations in the construction of cerebral cortex (Galaburda, Sherman, Rosen, Aboitiz, & Geschwind, 1985). These deviations are thought to compromise patterns of neural connectivity so that the brain is not optimally configured to support language learning from birth. This critical concept is the outgrowth of multiple studies on the neurobiology of language, some of which we present below.

POSTMORTEM STUDIES OF LANGUAGE IMPAIRMENT

Some of the earliest evidence for neurobiological correlates of language was drawn from postmortem studies of adult brains. In a historic study, Geschwind and Levitsky (1968) documented findings of asymmetry in the length of the plana temporale (PT) in a sample of one hundred postmortem adult brains. As described above, the PT is a landmark (not a structure) that is located on the inferior portion of the Sylvian fissure, an area that is critical for receptive language. In this study, leftward asymmetry was observed in 65% of the specimens, whereas PT symmetry was found in 24% of the sample and rightward asymmetry was seen in 11% of the brains examined. This distribution was compared with the patterns of asymmetry in left hemisphere dominance for language, as determined by localization studies. Close similarities between the two distributions were noted. As a result, the structural asymmetries observed in this study were considered possible morphological markers for variations in language functioning. Subsequent findings of similar distributions in children and fetuses bolstered this hypothesis (Chi, Dooling, & Gilles, 1977; Witelson & Pallie, 1973).

Years later, structural asymmetries of the cortex were directly linked to developmental language disorders. Galaburda et al. (1985) reported neuropathological findings in four postmortem brains of adult males who exhibited lifelong reading disability, accompanied by minimally low-average IQ scores. Three of the four individuals also had documented delays in oral language development, which persisted in childhood for at least one member of the group. Autopsy results revealed two main findings. One observation was that all four individuals had symmetrical PT. This symmetry was attributable to a normal-sized left and an abnormally large right PT. As reported by the aforementioned study (Geschwind & Levitsky, 1968), the PT of the left hemisphere is typically larger than that of the right hemisphere. This asymmetry is presumably tied to the critical role of the left hemisphere–PT region in language performance. The second key finding was that all four brains had numerous architectural anomalies in both the right and left hemispheres. For example, all four individuals showed disruptions in laminar structure, called cerebral dysplasias, as well as clusters of malpositioned cells, called cortical ectopias. Notably, some of these anomalies were preponderant in the left hemisphere, surrounding the Sylvian fissure. Recall that the left hemisphere is typically dominant for language and that the areas neighboring the Sylvian fissure (the perisylvian areas) are those conventionally linked with language functioning. The findings by Galaburda et al. thus offered preliminary evidence of a correlation between language-related areas of the brain and developmental reading impairment.

The results of this study also shed light on the *origin* of developmental reading disorders. We know that the observed structural anomalies are rooted in abnormal brain development. Asymmetries of the brain, for example, are established during the third prenatal trimester (Chi et al., 1977). Effects on this period of brain development could thus result in the emergence of atypical PT symmetry. Likewise, the cortical ectopias found in these autopsies arise during prenatal neurodevelopment when clusters of neurons are displaced during neural migration. The course of brain development is also implicated by the bilateral feature of these aberrations. In contrast to localized brain damage that typifies acquired language disorders, the more diffuse brain anomalies in this study concur with the global nature of brain maturation (Plante, 1996).

A methodologically similar study was conducted with three postmortem brains of females who had lifelong reading disability (Humphreys, Kaufmann, & Galaburda, 1990). All three brains were found to have symmetrical PT and cortical ectopias, similar to the male brains discussed above. However, the neuropathological anomalies between the male and female brains of these two studies differed in type, frequency, and distribution, suggesting that cortical structure may vary by gender (Lane, Foundas, & Leonard, 2001).

Findings of atypical symmetry in reading impaired individuals provided the impetus to examine brain structure in related language disorders. To date, we know of only one documented study of the PT in the postmortem brain of a language-impaired child (Cohen, Campbell, & Yaghmai, 1989). This study examined the brain of a 7-year-old girl with a history of language delay and attention-deficit disorder with hyperactivity. Akin to findings for reading impairment (Galaburda et al., 1985), symmetry of the PT was observed in the brain of this language-impaired child.

To recap, early postmortem studies suggest that developmental reading impairment and perhaps language delay are associated with symmetry of the PT. In addition, these studies point to abnormal brain development as the genesis of developmental language disorders. These conclusions are, however, constrained by the limitations inherent in postmortem studies. One drawback of postmortem studies is that they rely on visual inspection and may therefore lend to subjectivity in the analysis and description of findings. Obviously, these investigations are also limited by the small number of specimens included. Of critical import is that research based on postmortem brains of adults can only comment on the *outcome* of language development in adults, not on the *process* of language development in children. Along these lines, it has been well established that autopsy studies of adults with *acquired* language disorders cannot be generalized to normal language populations (Thomas & Karmiloff-Smith, 2002). Finally, we note that both the development and functioning of language involve a dynamic progression of events, which cannot be captured by examination of static postmortem specimens.

Fortunately, the drawbacks of postmortem analysis have been mitigated by technological advances in brain imaging techniques. In the following section, we describe an assortment of studies that have applied these methods to the study of neurobiology in child language disorders. We focus here on the knowledge gleaned from this body of research and refer the reader to chapter 24 by Shafer and Maxfield for a description of some of the methods discussed.

NEUROIMAGING STUDIES OF CHILDHOOD LANGUAGE

Since the 1980s, progress in technology has made us remarkably sophisticated at examining neurobiology. Combined advances in MRI, fMRI, and PET have dramatically enhanced our understanding of brain–language relations. The refinement of MRI, in particular, has facilitated the search for brain correlates of language. This tool allows investigators to measure brain structure within an anatomical region using a method called morphometric analysis. In contrast to autopsy studies, MRI permits the study of live brains and thus confers the benefit of relating neuroanatomical data to behavioral data collected from individuals. In the next section, we review research that has employed MRI in the quest to identify linguistic and nonlinguistic markers in the brains of individuals with SLI. First, the search for linguistic correlates is divided into four sections that discuss brain asymmetry, subcortical structures, gyral morphology, and the relationship between brain structure and language functions in SLI.

Neuroanatomy of SLI: In Search of Linguistic Correlates

Is Brain Asymmetry Typical in SLI?
Using MRI, Plante, Swisher, and Vance (1989) studied a 4.9-year-old pair of dizygotic twins: a male with SLI and a female with no evidence of language impairment. Given the difficulties in using MRI scans to measure the PT, a larger area that includes the PT, the perisylvian area, was measured instead. Typically, this area is larger in the left hemisphere, similar to the normal pattern of leftward PT asymmetry. The male twin with SLI exhibited an atypical configuration: symmetrical perisylvian structures, consistent with the abovementioned findings for individuals with reading disability (Galaburda et al., 1985) and language impairment (Cohen et al., 1989). Interestingly, his nonimpaired twin sister had a right perisylvian area that was larger than the left perisylvian area.

A subsequent MRI study by Plante, Swisher, Vance, and Rapcsak (1991) further investigated perisylvian symmetry in SLI. The perisylvian brain regions of eight males with SLI (ages 4.2–9.6 years) were compared with those of male controls matched for handedness. Most of the SLI subjects (6 out of 8), as compared with only 2 of the 8 control children, deviated from the normal left > right pattern.

A hasty interpretation of the studies by Plante and her colleagues might lead one to conclude that SLI is characterized by atypical patterns of the left–right perisylvian areas. But what of the nonimpaired twin who also showed unusual asymmetry in this region (Plante et al., 1989)? This finding suggests that normally developing siblings of SLI children may also show deviant structural patterns. Plante (1991) probed this supposition by examining the parents and siblings of 4 out of the 8 SLI subjects from the study by Plante et al. (1991). Some of these parents self-reported a history of language problems and several of the siblings were found to have language difficulties at the time of the investigation. Analysis of MRI scans revealed that most parents and siblings of the SLI children had deviant symmetry in the perisylvian region. However, findings of structural configurations did not neatly correspond with the language abilities of the subjects. This factor cast doubt on the behavioral relevance of the observed structural patterns. Moreover, the presence of atypical configurations in nonimpaired individuals indicates that asymmetry of the perisylvian area does not necessarily *cause* language impairment. Thus, at most, the findings of Plante et al. suggest that aberrant asymmetry of the perisylvian area may bear some association with language abilities.

Along with their equivocal findings, these MRI studies of children with SLI and their family members have some significant methodological limitations. For example, the region of interest (ROI) in these studies was liberally defined such that we do not know whether the entire perisylvian area or only a section of it contributed to the observed atypical patterns. We also do not have detailed information on how the groups in Plante's 1991 study were matched. Nonetheless, these investigations are valuable because they expanded the limited database on neuroanatomical correlates of developmental language disorders.

Having designated the perisylvian area as the only ROI, the aforementioned studies (Plante, 1991; Plante et al., 1989, 1991) may have overlooked deviations in other cortical areas in individuals with SLI. Jernigan, Hesselink, Sowell, and Tallal (1991) employed MRI to examine a wider range of cortex in 8–10-year-old children with significant receptive and expressive language delays and severe learning disabilities. Scans of 20 children with this diagnosis were compared with the scans of 12 normally developing controls, matched for age, gender, and handedness. Significant differences in structural symmetry were observed between the groups. The language-learning impaired group exhibited leftward asymmetry of the superior parietal region and rightward asymmetry of the inferior frontal region. Controls, on the other hand, showed reverse patterns of asymmetry. Also reported, were smaller volumes for most of the measured structures in the language-learning impaired subjects. In particular, these subjects demonstrated bilaterally reduced volume in posterior perisylvian regions, which include the planum temporale. Notably, volume was especially reduced in these regions of the left hemisphere in the language-learning impaired subjects. These observations are in line with findings by Plante et al. (1989, 1991) of abnormal configurations of the perisylvian area in children with SLI. A novel observation in this study was that volume was bilaterally reduced in *subcortical* structures, including the caudate nucleus. This finding highlighted the importance of using morphometric analysis to examine deeper structures than those previously associated with developmental language disorders.

Are Subcortical Structures Typical in SLI?   In a case study of a 10-year-old boy with a history of SLI, articulation difficulties, and behavioral problems, Tallal, Jernigan, and Trauner (1994) used MRI to examine subcortical structures. The head of the caudate nucleus was found to be aberrant bilaterally. Notably, though, the child had been severely impaired in expressive language and articulation at 4 years of age, but improved significantly in these areas by age 8. Therefore, relating his neural profile to a discrete diagnosis of SLI seems questionable.

Evidence for an association between subcortical anomalies and language impairment has accumulated from studies of a unique pedigree named the KE family. Among three generations of this family, 15 (6 male, 9 female) of its 37 members have a verbal dyspraxia that is transmitted as an autosomal dominant mutation. Extensive behavioral testing has revealed significantly impaired abilities in affected, relative to unaffected, members in articulation, grammar, semantics, and both verbal and nonverbal IQ. A clear finding is that language production is generally more deficient than language comprehension in the affected group (Belton, Gadian, & Vargha-Khadem, 2003; Vargha-Khadem, Watkins, Alcock, Fletcher, & Passingham, 1995; Vargha-Khadem et al., 1998). Given these deficits and their severity, there is debate as to whether this family can be classified as specifically language-impaired (Bishop, 2003).

Several neuroimaging studies have shown deviations in subcortical structures in impaired members of the KE family. This finding was initially discovered in a functional PET investigation by Vargha-Khadem et al. (1998). The two affected KE members that were studied displayed significantly more activation in the left caudate nucleus than did four normal controls. The structural counterpart of this anomaly was found by comparing affected and unaffected family members using MRI with a method called voxel-based morphometry. This technique is used to detect minor regional differences in gray or white matter. Here, results showed two bilateral subcortical anomalies in affected, but not unaffected, members: less gray matter in the caudate nuclei and more gray matter in the putamen. These findings were replicated in later studies that examined subcortical structures, some of which employed more detailed volumetric analysis (Belton, Salmond, Watkins, Vargha-Khadem, & Gadian, 2003; Liegeois et al., 2003; Watkins et al., 2002).

Two key interpretations have been posited to explain the observed subcortical anomalies in affected family members. One strong proposal is that atypical development of the caudate nucleus is related to deficits in oromotor control and articulation abilities in this family. This suggestion was derived from the significant correlations found between the volume of the nuclei and scores of affected members on a test of oral praxis and a test of nonword repetition (Watkins et al., 2002). This may bear implications for the caudate nuclei abnormalities in language-impaired children that have been reported by Jernigan et al. (1991) and Tallal et al. (1994). It has also been suggested that abnormalities of the caudate nuclei and putamen may be related to the language deficits in affected members. This is based on an extrapolation from the literature on aphasia. Several studies have reported a link between acquired damage to the striatum (caudate nuclei and putamen) and language deficits in adult aphasics that are comparable to those of the KE family (e.g., Pickett, Kuniholm, Protopapas, Friedman, & Lieberman, 1998). However, the developmental nature of the KE family's impairment versus the acquired nature of aphasia limits the explanatory power of this proposal. More conclusive information on brain-language relations in the KE family may be gained by comparing the neural phenotype of affected members with those of other developmental language disorders.

To return to the question of interest, subcortical anomalies have been observed in children with SLI, although these findings require replication. Moreover, preliminary evidence suggests that atypical structure and function of the striatum may be associated with speech and language impairments of a developmental nature. A more definitive interpretation of subcortical anomalies in SLI was recently put forward as part of the "procedural deficit hypothesis" (Ullman & Pierpont, 2005). This hypothesis claims that SLI can be largely accounted for by abnormalities of the brain structures that subserve the procedural memory system, the system that underlies the learning and control of motor and cognitive skills and procedures. These structures are embedded in circuits of frontal cortex and the basal ganglia, both of which have been found deviant in SLI. Although additional data are needed to support this hypothesis, it is valuable because it attempts to bridge the behavioral data on SLI with a neural basis.

The information presented thus far conveys that SLI may be neurobiologically expressed as atypical brain asymmetry and perhaps, as subcortical anomalies. This may not be the full picture, though, because the studies discussed above were limited in their scope of analysis. A more detailed investigation of cortical structure could assess, for example, whether the morphology, or structural form, of gyri differs in SLI.

Is Gyral Morphology Typical in SLI?

This question was addressed by Clark and Plante (1995) in a study examining the inferior frontal gyrus, which includes one of the classical language regions, Broca's area. Upon examination of MRI scans, an additional sulcus was more commonly observed in parents of SLI children with documented language problems, relative to parents without this background and relative to adult controls with normal language functioning.

Jackson and Plante (1997) further examined gyral morpholoy in SLI in an MRI study of 10 affected school-age children, each set of their parents, 10 siblings, as well as 20 adult controls. Among the family members, 15 of the 20 parents and 4 of the 10 siblings demonstrated language deficits, whereas the controls evidenced normal language skills. Analysis of gyral morphology in bilateral posterior perisylvian areas revealed distinct differences between the groups. The typical finding of one gyrus pattern was shown in 75% of the hemispheres in controls but in only 58% of the hemispheres in family members. An intermediate gyrus was observed in 23% of the hemispheres in controls, relative to 41% of the hemispheres in family members. Interestingly, an intermediate gyrus was more commonly shown in the left, rather than right, hemisphere in both groups of subjects. Additionally, no clear correspondence was found between the presence of an intermediate gyrus and language functioning in the family members. This result echoes Plante's (1991) finding of inconsistency between asymmetry in perisylvian areas and language status. Thus, here too, one may question whether the observed differences in brain structure in SLI carry behavioral consequences.

Does Atypical Brain Structure Correlate with Atypical Language Behavior in SLI?   Gauger, Lombardino, and Leonard (1997) searched for a structure–function relationship by acquiring surface area measurements of the classical language regions in children with SLI. High-resolution volumetric MRI scans were used to measure the brains of 11 children with SLI and 19 normal-language controls, matched for age and gender. The planum temporale in Wernicke's area and the pars triangularis in Broca's area were identified as the regions of interest. Quantitative comparisons of these perisylvian areas revealed three group differences: greater rightward asymmetry of the total planum (planum temporale + the posterior ascending ramus, which is the terminal branch of the Sylvian fissure), a significantly smaller left pars triangularis, and narrower right hemispheres in the SLI group. The first two findings contrast with the typical leftward asymmetry of the planum temporale and pars triangularis in normal individuals (Foundas, Leonard, & Heilman, 1995). Given the well-established roles of these areas in language, the present findings for the SLI group were taken as evidence for a correspondence between brain structure and function. This interpretation thus posits that SLI results from neurobiological defects in the perisylvian areas of the brain.

Neuroanatomy of SLI: In Search of Nonlinguistic Correlates

At this point, it is important to recall that SLI children show weaknesses in many tasks that fall outside the domain of language. In view of this factor, we would expect the neurobiology of SLI to reflect not only linguistic limitations, but nonlinguistic deficits as well. A study by Trauner, Wulfeck, Tallal, and Hesselink (2000) tested this assumption. Thirty-five children with SLI and 27 controls with normal language (ages 5–14 years) were assessed via a neurological battery and MRI. Results of the study showed neurological abnormalities (e.g., fine motor impairment) in 70% of the SLI children, as compared with only 22% of the control children.

Similar to the neurological battery, MRI scans also revealed significant group differences. Structural deviations were found in the scans of 12 out of the 35 children with SLI—about one-third of the group—whereas none of the 27 controls showed abnormal scans. Interestingly, the observed abnormalities ranged in type, including ventricular enlargement, central volume loss, and white matter aberrations. This diversity in structural profile demonstrates that children with SLI are neurobiologically heterogeneous. A correlation between these MRI findings and the observed neurological abnormalities would attest to a structure–function relationship for nonlanguage abilities. This association, however, was not borne out. The probability of showing an abnormal MRI scan was apparently no greater if the child had neurological abnormalities than if the child presented as neurologically normal. In spite of this factor, there is a key implication to be drawn from the neurological results. The finding of atypical neurology in many members of the SLI group supports the notion that SLI is not restricted to the sphere of language but is, instead, cognitively pervasive. This conclusion underscores the importance of accounting for nonlinguistic abilities in the neurobiology of SLI.

In pursuit of this goal, Ellis Weismer, Plante, Jones, and Tomblin (2005) recently used functional MRI to examine whether SLI is characterized by a general limitation in processing capacity that affects both linguistic and nonlinguistic performance (Kail, 1994; Leonard, McGregor, & Allen, 1992). To test this claim, verbal working memory was measured in adolescents with SLI and in normal-language controls. Subjects were required to perform a listening span task that involved sentence encoding and recognition of final words from prior groups of sentences. The utility of this task was its ability to provide information about two types of neural systems: those implicated in language processing and those systems involved in more general processing for functions such as working memory and attention.

Neuroimaging revealed several group differences. During encoding, the SLI group showed hypoactivation of two regions implicated in *general* cognitive functions: the left parietal region (PAR), associated with attentional control mechanisms, and the precentral sulcus (PCS), a region associated with memory processes (e.g., Braver et al., 1997; Rypma, Berger, & D'Esposito, 2002; Shaywitz et al., 2001). In the recognition phase, the group with SLI displayed hypoactivation of the insular portion of the inferior frontal gyrus (IFG), which includes Broca's area. Thus, atypical neural activation in the SLI group was observed not only in a language area, but also in regions associated with general cognitive processing. This finding was taken as support for a general processing limitation in adolescents with SLI.

To summarize to this point, neuroimaging studies have revealed differences in brain structure and function in individuals with SLI as compared with normal language controls. Major structural differences in SLI include deviant brain asymmetry in perisylvian areas, reduced volume of cortical and subcortical structures, and aberrant gyral morphology. Functional differences involve abnormal patterns of activation in brain areas associated with both linguistic and nonlinguistic functions. Some of the studies described above considered whether the neurobiology of SLI is concentrated in families. Below, we examine the significance of this inquiry.

Neuroanatomy of SLI: In Search of an Etiology

Earlier in this chapter, we noted that both genetic and environmental factors shape brain development and thus underlie developmental language disorders. Because family members typically share their genes and environment, family studies cater to a vital goal of research in SLI: identification of its etiology. Ultimately, these studies should inform us of the extent to which various genetic and environmental factors place a child at risk for SLI. At this time, though, the evidence accrued mostly pertains to genetic influences, the probable instigators of child language disorders.

Support for genetic contributions to SLI is garnered from at least three types of investigations: twin studies, familial aggregation studies, and pedigree analyses (see Bishop, 2003, for a review). Generally, these investigations involve assessing language status among family members. Some of these studies have focused on examining neurobiology in families with and without a positive history of SLI.

Twin Studies   The principal advantage of twin studies lies in the existence of two types of twins: monozygotic twins (MZ), who are genetically identical and typically share a common environment, and dizygotic twins (DZ), who share an average of 50% of their genes and generally, share a common environment. In theory, there should be higher concordance (shared effects) for MZ twins than for DZ twins if SLI is genetically determined.

Earlier, in reviewing the research of Plante et al. (1989), we discussed the outcomes of an MRI study of 4.9-year-old DZ twins discordant for language status. In a later study, Preis, Engelbrecht, Huang, and Steinmetz (1998) used MRI to examine a pair of 9.2-year-old MZ twin boys concordant for SLI. Results showed bilateral heterotopias (displacements of gray matter from neuronal migration) in the parietotemporal white matter in both twins. The heterotopias were more prominent on the left side in both subjects and were more pronounced in the twin with poorer language abilities. It was therefore concluded that the observed heterotopias were likely to have a causal link with the language impairment in both twins.

Reflecting on these two investigations, it is apparent that twin studies of SLI neurobiology have been limited in their analysis of only one type of twins (MZ or DZ pairs), as well as in their small sample sizes. Future research should capitalize on the potential for twin studies to elucidate the role of genes in the neurobiology of SLI.

Familial Aggregation The hereditary nature of SLI has been corroborated by numerous studies (see Stromswold, 1998, 2000; Tallal et al., 2001; chapter 10 by Tomblin, for reviews), only several of which have examined neurobiological data. In an earlier section, we reviewed two reports of familial aggregation in SLI: deviant asymmetry in the perisylvian region (Plante, 1991) and atypical gyral morphology (Jackson & Plante, 1997).

Hugdahl et al. (2004) followed up on studies of brain *structure* in families with a positive history of SLI by examining brain *function* in such families. Using fMRI, the frontal and temporal lobes of 5 Finnish family members with SLI (1 grandmother, 2 daughters, and 2 grandsons) and 6 normal-language controls were measured to detect changes in neuronal activation. During data acquisition, the participants listened to strings of isolated vowel sounds, pseudowords, and real words. Group differences in activation were observed in both the frontal and the temporal lobes. Within these territories, the SLI family showed reduced activation that was most distinct in two areas: in the dorsal inferior frontal gyrus bordering the premotor area (frontal lobe) and in the medial temporal gyrus bordering the superior temporal sulcus (temporal lobe). These areas are known to be crucial for speech processing and phonological awareness. Thus, a positive family history of SLI was found to co-occur with reduced activation in speech–language areas of the brain. This finding dovetails with those MRI studies that revealed structural abnormalities in the same or approximate regions of the brain.

Evidence for familial concentration, however, does not translate into proof of genetic effects. It is reasonable to surmise that sharing an environment with language-impaired relatives may breed learning of faulty language patterns by genetically intact relatives (Bishop, 2003). These deficient patterns may, in theory, alter the neurobiological substrates of language in individuals with SLI.

Pedigree Analyses Exploring the phenotype of a developmental disorder within an extended family is referred to as pedigree analysis. The most acclaimed one in the relevant literature is by far, the study of the KE family. Above, we described this family as highly heritable for a severe speech and language disorder, which some investigators classify as SLI. Recently, the cause of this disorder was localized to a point mutation of the *FOXP2* gene in affected members (Lai, Fisher, Hurst, Vargha-Khadem, & Monaco, 2001). With this knowledge, researchers have worked toward relating this genetic abnormality to behavioral and neural phenotypes, the latter of which is our present focus (Vargha-Khadem, Gadian, Copp, & Mishkin, 2005).

As would be expected for a neurodevelopmental disorder, the affected members of the KE family have no frank focal lesions on standard neuroradiological measures of MRI. However, using more sensitive methods, structural and functional imaging studies have uncovered multiple brain abnormalities in these individuals. An MRI study (Belton et al., 2003) that used voxel-based morphometry found the following in affected members: levels of gray matter were abnormally low in the inferior frontal gyrus (Broca's area), the precentral gyrus, the temporal pole, the head of the caudate nucleus, and in parts of the ventral cerebellum. Levels of gray matter were abnormally high in the posterior portion of the superior temporal gyrus (Wernicke's area), the angular gyrus, and in the putamen. Note here the prevalence of abnormalities in speech–language areas of the brain.

An fMRI study with two language experiments—one of covert (silent) verb generation and the other of overt (spoken) verb generation and word repetition—also revealed brain anomalies in affected members (Liegeois et al., 2003). In the verb generation tasks, the unaffected group showed a typical left-dominant pattern of activation in Broca's area; in the repetition task, they showed a more bilateral pattern. By contrast, the affected group displayed activation that was more posterior and more widely bilateral in all tasks. More-over, the affected members showed less activation than did the unaffected members in Broca's area, its right homologue, and in the putamen. However, the affected members also displayed overactivation in areas that are not commonly engaged in language, such as the postcentral, posterior parietal, and occipital regions. Three possibilities were put forth to explain this overactivation: the enlisting of compensatory circuits, the use of atypical strategies, and increased cognitive effort or attention.

Together, these results describe the neural phenotype of a speech and language dis-order that is prototypically genetic in nature. Debates persist as to whether this phenotype represents SLI and, if so, whether it can be generalized to all cases of the disorder. Even if the gene-behavior pathway of SLI differs from that of the KE family, as we suspect, this pedigree analysis is helpful for the study of child language disorders. Tracing the effects of the mutated *FOXP2* gene on brain structure and function across development may increase our ability to define the language roles played by particular brain areas at different stages of life.

To conclude this section, neurobiological studies of familial aggregation, the KE pedi-gree, and, to a lesser extent, of twins provide converging evidence for a genetic origin of SLI. Genetic factors are manifested in brain structures that are both language- and nonlan-guage specific. This widespread outcome is consistent with the fact that genes expressed in cortex appear to be expressed throughout most cortical regions (Johnson, 2005). Therefore, early genetic abnormalities may impact multiple areas of the brain, although certain func-tions, such as language, may be differentially vulnerable to these effects. Because genetic outcomes evolve over time, the etiology of SLI will remain obscure until research focuses on the *course* of neurodevelopment as a function of both genes and environment.

The dearth of studies on brain development in SLI is, in part, due to the practical limitations of applying MRI and PET to young, healthy children. Besides, these techniques have poor temporal resolution and are thus of little utility in charting the essential time differences in neural processing across development. Fortunately, though, these inadequa-cies may be surmounted by complementing neuroimaging data with measures of neuro-physiology. Following, is a brief description of these measures, with a synopsis of their main findings for the SLI population (see also chapter 24 by Shafer & Maxfield).

NEUROPHYSIOLOGICAL STUDIES OF CHILDHOOD LANGUAGE

Two methods have been developed to examine *neurophysiology*, or neural activity, in a noninvasive manner. The more common methodology is called electroencephalography (EEG). This technique uses scalp electrodes to record the voltages at the surface of the skull that are generated by neuronal currents in the brain. By time-locking a stimulus to a point in the ongoing EEG and repeating that stimulus, voltage fluctuations that are not tied to the stimulus become eliminated in an averaging process. What remains is the electrical brain activity that is directly related to the specific stimulus, or event, called an *event-related potential* (ERP). The ERP technique offers remarkable temporal precision and is therefore beneficial for examining rapid neural activity, which is common to speech and language processes.

ERPs are displayed as waveforms that are characterized by their *components*. These components represent demarcated scalp distributions of electrical activity that are presumably tied to stimulus variables. The analysis of ERP waveforms involves classification of specific components according to their polarity, the latency of their initial or peak occurrence, and their topographical distribution over the scalp (Otten & Rugg, 2005). There are at least some ERP components that reveal developmental changes in these characteristics from childhood to adulthood (Neville, 1995). In fact, various studies have reported marked developmental changes in ERPs (Albrecht, von Suchodoletz, & Uwer, 2000; Daruna & Rau, 1987; Morr, Shafer, Kreuzer, & Kurtzberg, 2002; Pang & Taylor, 2000; Ponton, Eggermont, Kwong, & Don, 2000; Shafer, Morr, Kreuzer, & Kurtzberg, 2000; Sharma, Kraus, McGee, & Nicol, 1997). Assuming that these changes reflect neurobiological development, ERPs should be particularly useful for examining the maturation of skills in children with and without language impairment (Bishop & McArthur, 2005). ERP studies in the SLI population are relatively sparse but informative. Mirroring our division of neuroimaging data into linguistic and nonlinguistic categories, we present neurophysiological data on children with SLI as follows.

Neurophysiology of SLI: In Search of Linguistic Correlates

Semantic abilities in individuals with SLI have been examined via an ERP component called the N400, a negative-going wave that occurs between 250–500 ms poststimulus onset, peaking at approximately 400 ms (Kutas & Hillyard, 1980). This component is typically observed in the centroparietal region of the brain and has been shown to vary systematically with semantic processing (see Kutas & Federmeier, 2000, for a review). The prevailing belief is that the N400 indexes on-line semantic integration processes, with larger N400s suggestive of more effortful integration (e.g., Holcomb, 1993; but see Besson, Kutas, & Van Petten, 1992; Kellenbach, Wijers, & Mulder, 2000; Kutas & Federmeier, 2000; Kutas & Hillyard, 1989). Neville, Coffey, Holcomb, and Tallal (1993) observed that school-age children with SLI had abnormally large N400 amplitudes in a task of judging the semantic plausibility of sentences with congruent and incongruent word endings. These results contrasted with those of age-matched controls with normal language abilities.

Another ERP study of semantic abilities (Ors et al., 2001) employed a visual semantic priming task in testing parents of children with SLI and parents serving as controls. Despite comparable behavioral performance, the ERPs of fathers (but not of mothers) of SLI children had less differentiated responses between congruent and incongruent sentences as compared with those of controls. Furthermore, the fathers of SLI children displayed larger N400 amplitudes than did the controls. These findings were considered residual markers of language impairment in fathers of children with SLI.

The ERP methodology has also shed light on grammatical skills in children with SLI. In the study by Neville et al. (1993) mentioned above, an SLI subgroup with significant morphosyntactic deficits, as opposed to one with auditory processing problems, did not demonstrate the normal asymmetry of larger N400 amplitudes for closed-class words in the anterior left hemisphere than in the anterior right hemisphere. This finding corresponds with evidence from MRI studies that children with SLI fail to show the typical leftward asymmetry in brain areas associated with language functions (e.g., Gauger et al., 1997; Jernigan et al., 1991; Plante et al., 1991). Also, the ERP differences between subgroups of children with SLI in this study suggest that their behavioral differences in grammatical and auditory processing skills might reflect neurophysiological differences.

Processing in discourse is another language ability that has been examined in individuals with SLI. Shafer, Schwartz, Morr, Kessler, and Kurtzberg (2000) studied the ERP correlates of processing the grammatical function word "the" in story context and followed by nonsense syllables in children with SLI and typical language development (TLD). On both tasks, the SLI group showed reduced activation (indexed by a reduced positivity) at left temporal sites and increased activation at right temporal sites relative to children with TLD. Shafer and her colleagues suggested that children with SLI were compensating for poor processing at a structural level (shown as reduced left hemisphere processing) by depending on discourse information (shown as increased right hemisphere processing). Similar to the aforementioned study, this reversed asymmetry in neurophysiology parallels the deviant asymmetry in neuroanatomy of the perisylvian areas in children with SLI.

In sum, the ERP waveforms of individuals with SLI (and those of their fathers) have shown deviations in linguistic tasks. The differences include abnormally large N400 amplitudes, suggesting excessive effort in semantic integration, and deviant asymmetry in grammatical and discourse processing, which is consistent with anatomical evidence. These preliminary findings suggest that ERPs may enable us to read out a neural code for language abilities in impaired and nonimpaired individuals. This prompts us to ask: *Are there ERP correlates for nonlinguistic abilities in SLI?*

Neurophysiology of SLI: In Search of Nonlinguistic Correlates

One line of ERP research on SLI is concerned with assessing the auditory processing skills of affected individuals. This interest is based on the theory that SLI arises from a nonlinguistic deficit in processing sounds that are presented rapidly (Tallal & Piercy, 1973, 1974). ERP studies of tone detection, frequency discrimination, and automatic discrimination in individuals with SLI have tested the validity of this hypothesis.

The standard ERP waveform in response to a brief auditory stimulus has peaks and troughs that are characterized by their polarity and order. For example, the first positive, first negative, and second positive deflections are labeled P1, N1, and P2, respectively. In general, these early components are highly replicable across sessions within an individual (Halliday, 1982) and have low variability across individuals (e.g., Sandman & Patterson, 2000). Furthermore, these components vary predictably with systematic physical changes in the eliciting stimulus (e.g., frequency), thereby signifying a low-level change in the activation of sensory pathways (see Key, Dove, & Maguire, 2005, for a review).

Studies that have recorded auditory ERPs to tones in language-impaired children have reported mixed findings for the early components. Mason and Mellor (1984) examined responses to a 1000-Hz tone with a duration of 200 ms. No differences were observed between typically developing children and children with SLI in the latency or amplitude of the N1 or P2 responses. There are several investigations, though, that did not replicate these findings. In one case, a group of 5 language-impaired children showed a larger P2 than normally developing peers (Adams, Courchesne, Elmasian, & Lincoln, 1987). A later study (Lincoln, Courchesne, Harms, & Allen, 1995) did not find deviant P2 amplitudes in children with SLI but did observe atypically large amplitudes and long latencies of the N1 in impaired subjects in one of their experiments. Additionally, longer latencies of the N1, P2, and N2 in 20 children with severe language impairment (but with questionable diagnoses), as compared with controls, were reported by Tonnquist-Uhlén (1996). Intriguingly, Neville et al. (1993) found an abnormally small and delayed N1 at right frontal sites in a subset of SLI children who performed poorly on a test of rapid auditory processing.

A number of ERP studies on auditory processing in SLI have focused on frequency discrimination. In two studies of this nature (Bishop & McArthur, 2005; McArthur & Bishop, 2004), the N1-P2-N2 region of average waveforms in children and young adults with SLI was immature relative to age-matched controls with normal language skills. This was the case, however, for several SLI subjects who showed normal performance on a frequency discrimination task.

Automatic discrimination of acoustic stimuli has also been examined in ERP studies of language-impaired individuals. These investigations have focused on a discriminative response called the mismatch negativity (MMN), a sharp negative shift between 100 to 300 ms at frontocentral scalp sites following the onset of an acoustic change. This component is elicited by a stimulus that is "deviant" in a train of "standard" stimuli that are presented frequently. Each new stimulus is compared with a memory trace of preceding auditory information and an MMN occurs if the new stimulus violates the expectation of the auditory cortex. Thus, the MMN indexes the automatic detection of a stimulus change (Näätänen, Gaillard, & Mäntysalo, 1978) and reflects the encoding of a memory trace to a pattern in the environment (Näätänen, Paavilainen, Alho, Reinikainen, & Sams, 1989).

A handful of studies have reported deviant MMNs in children with developmental language disorders (see Leppänen & Lyytinen, 1997, for a review). Kraus et al. (1996) observed smaller MMN amplitudes to synthesized [da] versus [ga] speech sounds with 40-ms transition durations in children with learning problems (learning disability or attention-deficit disorder) relative to children with typical learning skills. Similarly, Uwer, Albrecht, and von Suchodoletz (2002) found smaller MMNs to natural consonant–vowel syllables differing in place of articulation (/ba/, /da/, and /ga/), but not to tones, in children with SLI (also see Shafer, Morr, Datta, Kurtzberg, & Schwartz, 2005). These findings suggest that deviant MMNs in SLI reflect an auditory processing deficit that is specific to speech stimuli.

As noted above, there is inconsistent evidence describing the nature of early components evoked during auditory processing in individuals with SLI. Moreover, the results of various studies do not consistently locate a deficit at the same level of auditory processing. For example, in a study (Ors, Lindgren, Blennow, Nettelbladt, Sahlen, & Rosen, 2002) that involved discrimination of deviant tone and speech stimuli, the N1-P2 components in a group of SLI children matched those of controls. However, the SLI group showed deviations at a later stage of auditory processing: Delayed latencies of the P3 (a positive potential that occurs between 300–800 ms poststimulus onset) to tone and speech stimuli and smaller P3 amplitudes to speech stimuli were observed in the SLI group relative to the controls. In a subsequent study, delayed P3 latencies to speech stimuli were exhibited by parents of children with SLI, as compared with parents serving as controls (Ors, Lindgren, Blennow, & Rosen, 2002). Thus, whereas some results point to a deficit at low levels of cortical processing (indexed by deviant early potentials), others propose a higher-order auditory processing deficit (indexed by deviant P3 responses) in SLI. However, the nature of the children's disorders in these studies differed. The disordered populations included severe language impairments (e.g., Tonnquist-Uhlén, 1996), various learning disabilities (e.g., Kraus et al., 1996), and SLI (e.g., Ors et al., 2002). Thus, it is likely that different auditory processing deficits underlie different types of language/learning impairment.

Overall, then, ERP research suggests that there are neurophysiological correlates of auditory processing deficits in SLI. These markers include waveform differences in the early components, in the MMN response, as well as in the P3. We have yet to determine, though, if these differences support the claim that SLI stems from a global auditory impairment that is not specific to language. Furthermore, it is essential that researchers track the correlates of auditory processing over the course of development, beginning in infants with and without risk for language impairment.

Neurophysiology of SLI: Can ERPs Predict SLI?

Because the ERP method has high temporal resolution, shows maturational changes, and does not require an overt response by the subject, the technique is well suited for studies of child language development. A series of investigations by Molfese and colleagues sparked an interest in using ERPs to predict later developing language abilities (see Molfese, Narter, Van Matre, Ellefson, & Modglin, 2001, for a review). Collectively, these studies showed that electrophysiological recordings at birth could be used to predict later language skills through 5 years of age. Recently, attention has turned toward using this method to identify neurophysiological precursors of language deficits in children.

In a retrospective study, 2.5-year-olds with age-appropriate expressive language skills showed an N400 at 19 months of age; those with poor expressive language skills who were at risk for SLI did not show an N400 at this age (Friedrich & Friederici, 2006). In addition, a study of auditory temporal processing found that 2-month-old infants with a family history of SLI displayed a delayed latency of their positive mismatch response compared to infants without risk (Friedrich, Weber, & Friederici, 2004). This latter finding in infants at risk for SLI appears to match that of newborns at risk for dyslexia: Leppänen, Pihko, Eklund, and Lyytinen (1999) observed delayed and enhanced ERP responses to the short deviant Finnish syllable /ka/, relative to the long standard syllable /ka:/, in a newborn group at risk for dyslexia compared to a not-at-risk control group. Similarities between the infant ERPs of these at-risk groups suggest that SLI and dyslexia may share a neurobiological substrate.

To conclude, the predictive use of ERPs is still at an embryonic stage but research shows its potential for the prognosis of later language skills. If we can identify electrophysiological precursors of language deficits, we may be able to remediate the source of impaired language by providing early intervention. Environmental enrichment might influence brain structure to overcome cortical disruptions, thereby exploiting neural plasticity (Elbert, Heim, & Rockstroh, 2001). Moreover, longitudinal ERP data might allow us to developmentally track the outcomes of intervention and could help us differentiate between the neural profiles of various child language disorders. This latter point brings us to the final section of our chapter.

Neurobiology Within and Between Child Language Disorders

Two key questions in the neurobiological study of language disorders are as follows: Is a given finding of brain structure or function consistent *within* the impaired population? And, is it *specific* to the population of interest? There are, in fact, contradictory results among anatomical and functional studies of SLI. There is also mounting evidence of an overlap between neurobiological features of SLI and other developmental language disorders.

Consider, for example, the phenotypes of SLI and dyslexia. Deficits in auditory and phonological processing are common to both of these disorders (Kamhi & Catts, 1986; Tallal, 2000). Researchers have therefore asked whether the neural profiles of SLI and dyslexia are distinct. Anatomical studies have shown that both disorders are characterized by reduced or reversed asymmetry of the plana temporale (Hynd, Semrud-Clikeman, Lorys, Novey, & Eliopulos, 1990; Kushch et al., 1993; Plante et al., 1991). Several investigations, though, have not replicated this finding and have even reported greater than typical leftward asymmetry in both populations (Leonard et al., 2002; Preis, Jäncke, Schittler, Huang, & Steinmetz, 1998). These inconsistencies may be due to the inclusion of various language and literacy deficits as SLI or dyslexia (Bishop & Snowling, 2004). Functional MRI investigations of SLI and dyslexia have revealed another similarity between the two disorders. Resting levels of brain activity in SLI have shown atypical function of the left hemisphere temporoparietal area (Denays et al., 1989). Dyslexic individuals have likewise shown reduced activity in the left temporoparietal cortex relative to controls (e.g., Paulesu et al., 1996). In spite of these similarities, Leonard et al. (2002) succeeded in identifying three anatomical markers that distinguished groups of children with SLI and reading disability: plana temporale asymmetry, normalized cerebral volume, and surface area of left Heschl's gyrus. These anatomical differences support the view that SLI and dyslexia are qualitatively distinct (Bishop & Snowling, 2004).

A less obvious comparison between the neural profiles of two child language disorders has recently been drawn between SLI and autism. Although diagnoses of SLI and autism are mutually exclusive in the same individual, evidence suggests that a subgroup of autistic children has a language profile that resembles that of SLI (Kjelgaard & Tager-Flusberg, 2001; Roberts, Rice, & Tager-Flusberg, 2000). Accordingly, the expected reversed asymmetry in frontal language cortex in a group of boys with SLI was also found in a group of boys with autism and language impairment, but not in controls (De Fossé et al., 2004). This finding challenges the sharp divide between the neurocognitive phenotypes of SLI and autism. There are, however, multiple neuroanatomical deviations found in autism, implicating the cerebellum, brain stem, thalamus, frontal lobes, and limbic system, that have not been thoroughly examined in SLI (see Filipek, 1999, for a review).

Finally, let us examine the neurobiology of a rare genetic disorder with a unique linguistic profile—namely, Williams syndrome (WS). Interest in WS has largely been driven by the uneven relationship between deficits in several areas of cognition and the relatively preserved linguistic performance in affected individuals. This nonlinearity constitutes the argument for a dissociation between language abilities and other cognitive skills and thus supports the modularity debate (see Stojanovik, Perkins, & Howard, 2004, for a review). Neurobiological evidence from studies of WS, however, weakens this claim. The superior temporal gyrus, which includes the auditory association areas involved in language, was found to be relatively intact in WS. However, deviant asymmetry of the plana temporale has also been observed in this population (Eckert et al., 2006; Galaburda & Bellugi, 2000; Reiss et al., 2000), comparable to findings in individuals with SLI and dyslexia. In addition, ERP responses to auditorily presented words in sentences have revealed two intriguing findings in WS (Mills, Neville, Appelbaum, Prat, & Bellugi, 1997). Individuals with WS showed a greater scalp distribution for the N400 response to semantic anomalies (e.g., "I have five fingers on my *moon*") relative to normal controls. The typical leftward asymmetry for grammatical function words was also lacking in the group with WS. Together, these results add to the accumulating evidence that language functioning in WS is, in fact, abnormal.

Another brain atypicality in WS and other developmental language disorders involves the cerebellum. An abnormal cerebellum has been documented in WS, autism, dyslexia, and fragile X (see Johnson, 2005, for a review). Individuals with WS, for example, show a relative volumetric increase in certain lobules on the cerebellum. In autism, these lobules are relatively smaller than typical (Jernigan & Bellugi, 1994).

Shared brain abnormalities among disorders as diverse as SLI, dyslexia, autism, and WS highlight an important fact: Most neurobiological anomalies in child language disorders are not specific to one disorder (Johnson, 2005). This overlap suggests that the current division of developmental language disorders into discrete categories may not be a reality but a mere convenience for clinicians and scientists. Future research should consider subclassifying language disorders according to a broad range of linguistic and nonlinguistic deficits, allowing for partial overlap between categories. Furthermore, neurobiological similarities across disorders indicate that the quest to discover one particular neural marker for any given impairment is misguided. Instead, a host of studies within and across clinical populations will be needed to construct sets of neural markers that capture the characteristics of each type of child language impairment.

CONCLUSIONS AND FUTURE DIRECTIONS

An array of neuroimaging and neurophysiological techniques has enabled us to study the brain structure and function of child language disorders. In SLI, for example, we now have evidence of abnormal asymmetry in perisylvian areas, subcortical anomalies, atypical gyral morphology, and deviant linguistic and nonlinguistic processing. These findings, however, have not been entirely consistent, which could be due to several factors. Discrepancies among criteria for subject classification, comparison groups, methodological protocols, and anatomical definitions may account for the bulk of this variability. In addition, there is the expected phenotypic heterogeneity that is prevalent in SLI, which is commonly invoked to dismiss unexpected findings. We propose that these heterogeneous data can be more accurately interpreted by subcategorizing SLI into a range of behavioral and neural pheno-types. Also, there are presumably different neurobiological pathways leading to the same behavioral outcome of SLI. Therefore, if we want to draw inferences about cognitive processes from language behavior, matching subjects on the basis of behavioral measures, rather than by neural phenotype, should be reconsidered.

The relevant areas that warrant further research are plentiful. For example, neuro-biological methods require refinement to permit the reliable study of individual data. In addition, the behavioral paradigms used to elicit brain activity should be improved to increase the specificity of processes being measured. Furthermore, results collected by various behavioral and neurobiological methods should be converged to allow comparisons across methodologies. Finally, we propose that longitudinal ERP studies be conducted within and across clinical populations for two key purposes: to establish benchmarks for the prediction of language deficits and to track neurodevelopmental changes in association with intervention.

Overlap in the neurobiological profiles of SLI, dyslexia, autism, and WS underscores the importance of subclassifying these disorders in a manner that acknowledges common-alities between them. Moreover, the goal of neurobiological research should be to identify sets of neural markers that typify distinct subgroups within a given disorder. This novel approach presents a formidable challenge because it opposes traditional research and may require collaboration between laboratories that focus on individual clinical populations. However, it also stands to cultivate our knowledge of child language disorders and the means by which they may be remediated.

NOTES

Preparation of this chapter was supported by a grant from the National Institute on Deafness and Other Communication Disorders, RO1 DC03885 (R. Schwartz, P.I.).

REFERENCES

Adams, J., Courchesne, E., Elmasian, R. O., & Lincoln, A. J. (1987). Increased amplitude of the auditory P2 and P3b components in adolescents with developmental dysphasia. In R. Johnson, R. Parasuraman, & J. W. Rohrbaugh (Eds.), *Current trends in evoked potential research* (pp. 577–583). New York: Elsevier.

Albrecht, R., von Suchodoletz, W., & Uwer, R. (2000). The development of auditory evoked dipole source activity from childhood to adulthood. *Clinical Neurophysiology, 111,* 2268–2276.

Belton, E., Gadian, D. G., & Vargha-Khadem, F. (2003). Evidence for specific motor programming deficit in developmental verbal dyspraxia but not in SLI. *Social Neuroscience Abstract, 196,* 20.

Belton, E., Salmond, C. H., Watkins, K. E., Vargha-Khadem, F., & Gadian, D. G. (2003). Bilateral brain abnormalities associated with dominantly inherited verbal and orofacial dyspraxia. *Human Brain Mapping, 18,* 194–200.

Besson, M., Kutas, M., & Van Petten, C. (1992). An event-related potential (ERP) analysis of semantic congruity and repetition effects in sentences. *Journal of Cognitive Neuroscience, 4,* 132–149.

Bishop, D. V. M. (1997). *Uncommon understanding: Development and disorders of language comprehension in children.* Hove, UK: Psychology Press.

Bishop, D. V. M. (2003). Genetic and environmental risks for specific language impairment in children. *International Journal of Pediatric Otorhinolaryngology, 67,* 143–157.

Bishop, D. V. M., & McArthur, G. M. (2005). Individual differences in auditory processing in specific language impairment: A follow-up study using event-related potentials and behavioural thresholds. *Cortex, 41,* 327–341.

Bishop, D. V. M., & Snowling, M. J. (2004). Developmental dyslexia and specific language impairment: Same or different? *Psychological Bulletin, 130,* 858–886.

Braver, T. S., Cohen, J. D., Nystrom, L. E., Jonides, J., Smith, E. E., & Noll, D. C. (1997). A parametric study of prefrontal cortex involvement in human working memory. *NeuroImage, 5,* 49–62.

Brown, C. M., & Hagoort, P. (Eds.). (1999). *The neurocognition of language.* Oxford, UK: Oxford University Press.

Casey, B. J., Geidd, J. N., & Thomas, K. M. (2000). Structural and functional brain development and its relation to cognitive development. *Biological Psychology, 54,* 241–257.

Changeux, J.-P. (1985). *Neuronal man: The biology of mind.* New York: Pantheon Books.

Changeux, J.-P., Courrege, P., & Danchin, A. (1973). A theory of the epigenisis of neuronal networks by selective stabilization of synapses. *Proceedings of the National Academy of Sciences of the United States of America, 70,* 2974–2978.

Chi, J. G., Dooling, E. C., & Gilles, F. H. (1977). Gyral development of the human brain. *Annals of Neurology, 1,* 86–93.

Clark, M., & Plante, E. (1995). Morphology in the inferior frontal gyrus in developmentally language-disordered adults. Paper presented at the Conference on Cognitive Neuroscience, San Francisco.

Cohen, M., Campbell, R., & Yaghmai, F. (1989). Neuropathological abnormalities in developmental dysphasia. *Annals of Neurology, 25,* 567–570.

Daruna, J. H., & Rau, A. E. (1987). Development of the late components of auditory brain potentials from early childhood to adulthood. *Electroencephalography and Clinical Neurophysiology Supplement, 40,* 590–595.

Dax, M. (1865). Lésions de la moitié gauche de l'encéphale coïncident avec l'oubli des signes de la pensée (lu à Montpellier en 1836). *Bulletin hebdomadaire de médecine et de chirurgie, 2,* 259–262.

De Fossé, L., Hodge, S. M., Makris, N., Kennedy, D. N., Caviness, V. S., McGrath, L., et al. (2004). Language-association cortex asymmetry in autism and specific language impairment. *Annals of Neurology, 56,* 757–766.

De Haan, M., & Johnson, M. H. (2003). Mechanisms and theories of brain development. In M. De Haan & M. H. Johnson (Eds.), *The cognitive neuroscience of development* (pp. 1–18). Hove, UK: Psychology Press.

Denays, R., Tondeur, M., Foulon, M., Verstraeten, F., Ham, H., Piepsz, A., et al. (1989). Regional brain blood flow in congenital dysphasia: Studies with technetium-99m HM-PAO SPECT. *Journal of Nuclear Medicine, 30,* 1825–1829.

Eckert, M. A., Galaburda, A. M., Karchemskiy, A., Liang, A., Thompson, P., Dutton, R. A., et al. (2006). Anomalous sylvian fissure morphology in Williams syndrome. *NeuroImage, 33,* 39–45.

Elbert, T., Heim, S., & Rockstroh, B. (2001). Neural plasticity and development. In C. A. Nelson & M. Luciana (Eds.), *Handbook of developmental cognitive neuroscience* (pp. 191–202). Cambridge, MA: MIT Press.

Ellis Weismer, S., Plante, E., Jones, M., & Tomblin, J. B. (2005). A functional magnetic resonance imaging investigation of verbal working memory in adolescents with specific language impairment. *Journal of Speech, Language, and Hearing Research, 48*, 405–425.

Filipek, P. A. (1999). Neuroimaging in the developmental disorders: The state of the science. *Journal of Child Psychology and Psychiatry and Allied Disciplines, 40*, 113–128.

Foundas, A. L., Leonard, C. M., & Heilman, K. M. (1995). Morphologic cerebral asymmetry and handedness: The pars triangularis and planum temporale. *Archives of Neurology, 52*, 501–508.

Friedrich, M., & Friederici, A. D. (2006). Early N400 development and later language acquisition. *Psychophysiology, 43*, 1–12.

Friedrich, M., Weber, C., & Friederici, A. D. (2004). Electrophysiological evidence for delayed mismatch response in infants at-risk for specific language impairment. *Psychophysiology, 41*, 772–782.

Galaburda, A. M., & Bellugi, U. (2000). Multi-level analysis of cortical neuroanatomy in Williams syndrome. *Journal of Cognitive Neuroscience, 12*(Suppl.), 74–88.

Galaburda, A. M., Sherman, G. F., Rosen, G. D., Aboitiz, F., & Geschwind, N. (1985). Developmental dyslexia: Four consecutive patients with cortical anomalies. *Annals of Neurology, 18*, 222–233.

Gauger, L. M., Lombardino, L. J., & Leonard, C. M. (1997). Brain morphology in children with specific language impairment. *Journal of Speech and Hearing Research, 40*, 1272–1284.

Geschwind, N., & Levitsky, W. (1968). Left–right asymmetry in temporal speech region. *Science, 161*, 187–188.

Halliday, A. M. (1982). *Evoked potentials in clinical testing*. New York: Churchill-Livingstone.

Harlow, J. M. (1868). Recovery from the passage of an iron bar through the head. *Proceedings of the Massachusetts Medical Society, 2*, 327–346. (Original report published in 1848 in a letter to the *Boston Medical and Surgical Journal*, later to become the *New England Journal of Medicine, 39*, 389–392.)

Holcomb, P. J. (1993). Semantic priming and stimulus degradation: Implications for the role of the N400 in language processing. *Psychophysiology, 30*, 47–61.

Hugdahl, K., Gundersen, H., Brekke, C., Thomsen, T., Rimol, L. M., Ersland, L., et al. (2004). fMRI brain activation in a Finnish family with specific language impairment compared with a normal control group. *Journal of Speech, Language, and Hearing Research, 47*, 162–172.

Humphreys, P., Kaufmann, W. E., & Galaburda, A. M. (1990). Developmental dyslexia in women: Neuropathological findings in three patients. *Annals of Neurology, 28*, 727–738.

Hynd, G. W., Semrud-Clikeman, M., Lorys, A. R., Novey, E. S., & Eliopulos, D. (1990). Brain morphology in developmental dyslexia and attention deficit disorder/hyperactivity. *Archives of Neurology, 47*, 919–926.

Jackson, T., & Plante, E. (1997). Gyral morphology in the posterior sylvian region in families affected by developmental language disorders. *Neuropsychology Review, 6*, 81–94.

Jernigan, T. L., & Bellugi, U. (1994). Neuroanatomical distinctions between Williams and Down syndromes. In S. H. Broman & J. Grafman (Eds.), *Atypical cognitive deficits in developmental disorders: Implications for brain function* (pp. 57–66). Hillsdale, NJ: Lawrence Erlbaum Associates.

Jernigan, T. L., Hesselink, J. R., Sowell, E., & Tallal, P. A. (1991). Cerebral structure on magnetic resonance imaging in language and learning-impaired children. *Archives of Neurology, 48*, 539–545.

Johnson, M. H. (2005). *Developmental cognitive neuroscience*. Malden, MA: Blackwell.

Kail, R. (1994). A method for studying the generalized slowing hypothesis in children with specific language impairment. *Journal of Speech and Hearing Research, 37*, 418–421.

Kamhi, A. G., & Catts, H. W. (1986). Toward an understanding of developmental language and reading disorders. *Journal of Speech and Hearing Disorders, 51*, 337–347.

Karmiloff-Smith, A. (1993). *Beyond modularity: A developmental perspective on cognitive science.* Cambridge, MA: MIT Press.

Kellenbach, M. L., Wijers, A. A., & Mulder, G. (2000). Visual semantic features are activated during the processing of concrete words: Event-related potential evidence for perceptual semantic priming. *Brain Research, 10,* 67–75.

Key, A. P. F., Dove, G. O., & Maguire, M. J. (2005). Linking brainwaves to the brain: An ERP primer. *Developmental Neuropsychology, 27,* 183–215.

Kjelgaard, M. M., & Tager-Flusberg, H. (2001). An investigation of language impairment in autism: Implications for genetic subgroups. *Language and Cognitive Processes, 16,* 287–308.

Kraus, N., McGee, T. J., Carrell, T. D., Zecker, S. G., Nicol, T. G., & Koch, D. B. (1996). Auditory neurophysiologic responses and discrimination deficits in children with learning problems. *Science, 273,* 971–973.

Kushch, A., Gross-Glenn, K., Jallad, B., Lubs, H., Rabin, M., Feldman, E., et al. (1993). Temporal lobe surface area measurements on MRI in normal and dyslexic readers. *Neuropsychologia, 31,* 811–821.

Kutas, M., & Federmeier, K. D. (2000). Electrophysiology reveals semantic memory use in language comprehension. *Trends in Cognitive Sciences, 4,* 463–470.

Kutas, M., & Hillyard, S. A. (1980). Reading senseless sentences: Brain potentials reflect semantic incongruity. *Science, 207,* 203–205.

Kutas, M., & Hillyard, S. A. (1989). An electrophysiological probe of incidental semantic association. *Journal of Cognitive Neuroscience, 1,* 38–49.

Lai, C. S. L., Fisher, S. E., Hurst, J. A., Vargha-Khadem, F., & Monaco, A. P. (2001). A forkhead-domain gene is mutated in a severe speech and language disorder. *Nature, 413,* 519–523.

Lane, A. B., Foundas, A. L., & Leonard, C. M. (2001). The evolution of neuroimaging research and developmental language disorders. *Topics in Language Disorders, 21,* 20–41.

Leonard, C. M., Lombardino, L. J., Walsh, K., Eckert, M. A., Mockler, J. L., Rowe, L. A., et al. (2002). Anatomical risk factors that distinguish dyslexia from SLI predict reading skill in normal children. *Journal of Communication Disorders, 35,* 501–531.

Leonard, L. B. (1998). *Children with specific language impairment.* Cambridge, MA: MIT Press.

Leonard, L. B., McGregor, K. K., & Allen, G. D. (1992). Grammatical morphology and speech perception in children with specific language impairment. *Journal of Speech and Hearing Research, 35,* 1076–1085.

Leppänen, P. H. T., & Lyytinen, H. (1997). Auditory event-related potentials in the study of developmental language-related disorders. *Audiology and Neuro-otology, 2,* 308–340.

Leppänen, P. H. T., Pihko, E., Eklund, M., & Lyytinen, H. (1999). Cortical responses of infants with and without a genetic risk for dyslexia: II. Group effects. *NeuroReport, 10,* 969–973.

Liegeois, F., Baldeweg, T., Connelly, A., Gadian, D. G., Mishkin, M., & Vargha-Khadem, F. (2003). Language fMRI abnormalities associated with FOXP2 gene mutation. *Nature Neuroscience, 6,* 1230–1237.

Lincoln, A. J., Courchesne, E., Harms, L., & Allen, M. (1995). Sensory modulation of auditory stimuli in children with autism and receptive developmental language disorder: Event-related brain potential evidence. *Journal of Autism and Developmental Disorders, 25,* 521–539.

Mason, S. M., & Mellor, D. H. (1984). Brain-stem middle latency and late cortical evoked potentials in children with speech and language disorders. *Electroencephalography and Clinical Neurophysiology, 59,* 297–309.

McArthur, G. M., & Bishop, D. V. M. (2004). Which people with specific language impairment have auditory processing deficits? *Cognitive Neuropsychology, 21*(1), 79–94.

Mills, D., Neville, H., Appelbaum, G., Prat, C., & Bellugi, U. (1997). Electrophysiological markers of Williams syndrome. *International Behavioral Neuroscience Society Abstracts, 6,* 59.

Molfese, D. L., Narter, D. B., Van Matre, A. J., Ellefson, M. R., & Modglin, A. (2001). Language development during infancy and early childhood: Electrophysiological correlates. In J. Weissenborn & B. Höhle (Eds.), *Approaches to bootstrapping in early language development* (pp. 181–229). Amsterdam: John Benjamins.

Morr, M. L., Shafer, V. L., Kreuzer, J. A., & Kurtzberg, D. (2002). Maturation of mismatch negativity in typically developing infants and preschool children. *Ear and Hearing, 23*, 118–136.

Näätänen, R., Gaillard, A. W., & Mäntysalo, S. (1978). Early selective attention effect on evoked potential reinterpreted. *Acta Psychologica, 42*, 313–329.

Näätänen, R., Paavilainen, P., Alho, K., Reinikainen, K, & Sams, M. (1989). Do event-related potentials reveal the mechanism of the auditory sensory memory in the human brain? *Neuroscience Letters, 98*, 217–221.

Neville, H. J. (1995). Developmental specificity in neurocognitive development in humans. In M. S. Gazzaniga (Ed.), *The cognitive neurosciences* (pp. 219–231). Cambridge, MA: MIT Press.

Neville, H. J., Coffey, S. A., Holcomb, P. J., & Tallal, P. (1993). The neurobiology of sensory and language processing in language-impaired children. *Journal of Cognitive Neuroscience, 5*, 235–253.

Ors, M., Lindgren, M., Berglund, C., Haegglund, K., Rosen, I., & Blennow, G. (2001). The N400 component in parents of children with specific language impairment. *Brain and Language, 77*, 60–71.

Ors, M., Lindgren, M., Blennow, G., Nettelbladt, U., Sahlen, B., & Rosen, I. (2002). Auditory event-related brain potentials in children with specific language impairment. *European Journal of Paediatric Neurology, 6*, 47–62.

Ors, M., Lindgren, M., Blennow, G., & Rosen, I. (2002). Auditory event-related brain potentials in parents of children with specific language impairment. *European Journal of Paediatric Neurology, 6*, 249–260.

Otten, L. J., & Rugg, M. D. (2005). Interpreting event-related brain potentials. In T. C. Handy (Ed.), *Event-related potentials: A methods handbook*. Cambridge, MA: MIT Press.

Pang, E. W., & Taylor, M. J. (2000). Tracking the development of the N1 from age 3 to adulthood: An examination of speech and nonspeech stimuli. *Clinical Neurophysiology, 111*, 388–397.

Paulesu, E., Frith, U., Snowling, M. J., Gallagher, A., Morton, J., Frackowiak, R. S. J., et al. (1996). Is developmental dyslexia a disconnection syndrome? Evidence from PET scanning. *Brain, 119*, 143–157.

Pickett, E. R., Kuniholm, E., Protopapas, A., Friedman, J., & Lieberman, P. (1998). Selective speech motor, syntax and cognitive deficits associated with bilateral damage to the putamen and the head of the caudate nucleus: A case study. *Neuropsychologia, 36*, 173–188.

Plante, E. (1991). MRI findings in the parents and siblings of speech and language impaired boys. *Brain and Language, 41*, 67–80.

Plante E. (1996). Phenotypic variability in brain-behavior studies of specific language impairment. In M. L. Rice (Ed.), *Toward a genetics of language* (pp. 317–335). Mahwah, NJ: Lawrence Erlbaum Associates.

Plante, E., Swisher, L., & Vance, R. (1989). Anatomical correlates of normal and impaired language in a set of dizygotic twins. *Brain and Language, 37*, 643–655.

Plante, E., Swisher, L., Vance, R., & Rapcsak, S. (1991). MRI findings in boys with specific language impairment. *Brain and Language, 41*, 52–66.

Ponton, C. W., Eggermont, J. J., Kwong, B., & Don, M. (2000). Maturation of human central auditory system activity: Evidence from multi-channel evoked potentials. *Clinical Neurophysiology, 111*, 220–236.

Preis, S., Engelbrecht, V., Huang, Y., & Steinmetz, H. (1998). Focal grey matter heterotopias in monozygotic twins with developmental language disorder. *European Journal of Pediatrics, 157*, 849–852.

Preis, S., Jäncke, L., Schittler, P., Huang, Y., & Steinmetz, H. (1998). Normal intrasylvian anatomical asymmetry in children with developmental language disorder. *Neuropsychologia, 36*, 849–855.

Reiss, A. L., Eliez, S., Schmitt, J. E., Straus, E., Lai, Z., Jones, W., et al. (2000). Neuroanatomy of Williams syndrome: A high-resolution MRI study. *Journal of Cognitive Neuroscience, 12*(Suppl.), 65–73.

Roberts, J., Rice, M., & Tager-Flusberg, H. (2000). Tense marking in children with autism: Further evidence for overlap between autism and SLI. Paper presented at the Symposium on Research in Child Language Disorders, Madison, WI (June).

Rypma, B., Berger, J., & D'Esposito, M. (2002). The influence of working-memory demand and subject performance on prefrontal cortical activity. *Journal of Cognitive Neuroscience, 14*, 721–731.

Sandman, C. A., & Patterson, J. V. (2000). The auditory event-related potential is a stable and reliable measure in elderly subjects over a 3-year period. *Clinical Neurophysiology, 111*, 1427–1437.

Shafer, V. L., Morr, M. L., Datta, H., Kurtzberg, D., & Schwartz, R. G. (2005). Neurophysiological indexes of speech processing deficits in children with specific language impairment. *Journal of Cognitive Neuroscience, 17*, 1168–1180.

Shafer, V. L., Morr, M. L., Kreuzer, J. A., & Kurtzberg, D. (2000). Maturation of mismatch negativity in school-age children. *Ear and Hearing, 21*, 242–251.

Shafer, V. L., Schwartz, R. G., Morr, M. L., Kessler, K. L., & Kurtzberg, D. (2000). Deviant neurophysiological asymmetry in children with language impairment. *NeuroReport, 11*, 3715–3718.

Sharma, A., Kraus, N., McGee, T. J., & Nicol, T. G. (1997). Developmental changes in P1 and N1 central auditory responses elicited by consonant–vowel syllables. *Electroencephalography and Clinical Neurophysiology, 104*, 540–545.

Shaywitz, B. A., Shaywitz, S. E., Pugh, K. R., Fullbright, R. K., Skudlarski, P., Mencl, W. E., et al. (2001). The functional neural architecture of components of attention in language-processing tasks. *NeuroImage, 13*, 601–612.

Stojanovik, V., Perkins, M., & Howard, S. (2004). Williams syndrome and specific language impairment do not support claims for developmental double dissociations and innate modularity. *Journal of Neurolinguistics, 17*, 403–424.

Stromswold, K. (1998). Genetics of spoken language disorders. *Human Biology, 70*, 297–324.

Tallal, P. (2000). Experimental studies of language learning impairments: From research to remediation. In D. V. M. Bishop & L. B. Leonard (Eds.), *Speech and language impairments in children: Causes, characteristics, intervention and outcome* (pp. 131–155). Hove, UK: Psychology Press.

Tallal, P., Hirsch, L. S., Realpe-Bonilla, T., Brzustowicz, L. M., Bartlett, C., & Flax, J. F. (2001). Familial aggregation in specific language impairment. *Journal of Speech, Language, and Hearing Research, 44*, 1172–1182.

Tallal, P., Jernigan, T., & Trauner, D. (1994). Developmental bilateral damage to the head of the caudate nuclei: Implications for speech–language pathology. *Journal of Medical Speech Language Pathology, 2*, 23–28.

Tallal, P., & Piercy, M. (1973). Developmental aphasia: Impaired rate of non-verbal processing as a function of sensory modality. *Neuropsychologia, 11*, 389–398.

Tallal, P., & Piercy, M. (1974). Developmental aphasia: Rate of auditory processing as a selective impairment of consonant perception. *Neuropsychologia, 12*, 83–93.

Thomas, M., & Karmiloff-Smith, A. (2002). Are developmental disorders like cases of adult brain damage? Implications from connectionist modelling. *Behavioral and Brain Sciences, 25*, 727–788.

Tonnquist-Uhlén, I. (1996). Topography of auditory evoked long-latency potentials in children with severe language impairment: The P2 and N2 components. *Ear and Hearing, 17*, 314–326.

Trauner, D., Wulfeck, B., Tallal, P., & Hesselink, J. (2000). Neurological and MRI profiles of children with developmental language impairment. *Developmental Medicine and Child Neurology, 42*, 470–475.

Ullman, M. T., & Pierpont, E. I. (2005). Specific language impairment is not specific to language: The procedural deficit hypothesis. *Cortex, 41*, 399–433.

Uwer, R., Albrecht, R., & von Suchodoletz, W. (2002). Automatic processing of tones and speech stimuli in children with specific language impairment. *Developmental Medicine and Child Neurology, 44*, 527–532.

Uylings, H. B. M., Malofeeva, L. I., Bogolepova, I. N., Amunts, K., & Zilles, K. (1999). Broca's language area from a neuroanatomical and developmental perspective. In C. M. Brown & P. Hagoort (Eds.), *The neurocognition of language* (pp. 319–336). Oxford, UK: Oxford University Press.

Vargha-Khadem, F., Gadian, D. G., Copp, A., & Mishkin, M. (2005). FOXP2 and the neuroanatomy of speech and language. *Nature Reviews Neuroscience, 6,* 131–138.

Vargha-Khadem, F., Watkins, K., Alcock, K. J., Fletcher, P., & Passingham, R. (1995). Praxic and nonverbal cognitive deficits in a large family with a genetically transmitted speech and language disorder. *Proceedings of the National Academy of Sciences of the United States of America, 92,* 930–933.

Vargha-Khadem, F., Watkins, K. E., Price, C. J., Ashburner, J., Alcock, K. J., Connelly, A., et al. (1998). Neural basis of an inherited speech and language disorder. *Proceedings of the National Academy of Sciences of the United States of America, 95,* 12695–12700.

Watkins, K. E., Vargha-Khadem, F., Ashburner, J., Passingham, R. E., Connelly, A., Friston, K., et al. (2002). MRI analysis of an inherited speech and language disorder: Structural brain abnormalities. *Brain, 125,* 465–478.

Witelson, S. F., & Pallie, W. (1973). Left hemisphere specialization for language in the newborn. Neuroanatomic evidence of asymmetry. *Brain, 96,* 641–643.

8

Attention and Memory in Child Language Disorders

RONALD B. GILLAM, JAMES W. MONTGOMERY, and SANDRA L. GILLAM

*L*anguage learning during childhood relies heavily on attention and memory. For example, learning a new word involves focusing attention on something that someone else is saying, listening to and remembering the sequences of sounds that are being said, associating the sequence of sounds with possible meanings that are being expressed, and comparing the sound sequences and potential meanings to prior knowledge (words that already exist in long-term memory). If no match is found, language learners store the new phonological sequence along with additional information about the likely meaning, the event that was occurring when the word was heard, the other words that were spoken at the same time, the order the words were spoken in, and the role that the unknown word may have played in the utterance (subject, verb, object, modifier, etc.). Most children manage this complex task with remarkable ease and agility.

Unfortunately, there are children who have unusual difficulty learning language. Throughout this chapter, we use the term *language disorders* to refer to children who do not profit from their communicative experiences to the same degree that other children do. There are many potential causes of this condition, including cognitive and intellectual disabilities, sensory (hearing or vision) impairments, traumatic brain injury, auditory processing disorders, or language-specific impairments that are related to subtle neurological differences. As our broad review of the literature suggests, it is likely that deficits in attention and memory play a role in language-learning difficulties despite the etiological basis of the problem.

Speech–language pathologists, developmental psychologists, experimental psychologists, and linguists have conducted many experiments to determine whether children with language disorders have difficulty with one or more of the attention and memory mechanisms underlying the language-learning process. Many of these experiments involve relatively simple recall tasks in which children are asked to listen to and repeat words, nonwords, or sentences that have been presented in a variety of ways. The relevance of these memory tasks to language disorders is that they incorporate some of the important cognitive processes that are needed for language development and use, including directing the focus of attention to what others are saying, perceiving speech sounds, encoding or "representing" sounds as phonemes, storing the phonemes in a sequence, relating the sequence of sounds to words that have already been learned, planning a response, and executing a motor pattern. Performance on some memory protocols has been shown to be closely related to children's ability to learn new vocabulary and to read, suggesting that recall tasks tap into important language skills (Gathercole, 2006).

The results of multiple memory experiments have shown that children with language disorders recall significantly less information than do their typically developing age-matched peers, whether the stimuli consist of tones (Marler, Champlin, & Gillam, 2002), phonemes (Tallal & Piercy, 1974), syllables (Stark & Tallal, 1988), numbers (Gillam, Cowan, & Marler, 1998), words (Brock & Jarrold, 2004; Majerus, Van der Linden, Vérane, & Eliez, 2007), nonwords (Campbell, Dollaghan, Needleman, & Janosky, 1997), sentences (Montgomery, 2000a, 2000b), or stories (Gillam & Carlile, 1997; Kaderavek & Sulzby, 2000). There are a number of potential reasons for these memory problems. Studies suggest that children with language disorders may have difficulty focusing attention, representing and storing phonological information, allocating their mental energies to various memory processes, or retaining information over time. We begin this chapter by briefly summarizing a model of attention and memory that relates to language learning. Then we discuss the literature on attention and memory in children and the implications that attention and memory difficulties may have for language development and use.

A MODEL OF ATTENTION AND MEMORY

We suggested earlier that children with language disorders have difficulty remembering and using language. The majority of the memory studies that have been conducted with children have investigated the processes involved in actively representing and storing information (words and nonwords) for short periods while performing some kind of mental operation on that material or some other material. For example, a child might be asked to listen to a sentence, tell whether the sentence is true or false, and then recall the last word in the sentence (Gottardo, Stanovich, & Siegel, 1996). The mental processes that allow an individual to simultaneously store and process verbal information are referred to collectively as *working memory* (Baddeley, 2003a, 2003b; Baddeley & Hitch, 1974). Figure 8.1 illustrates the critical elements of memory and is based on Cowan's (1999) embedded-processes model of information processing. This simplified model accounts for a wide range of neuroimaging and behavioral findings related to attention and memory (Chein, Ravizza, & Fiez, 2003; Cowan, 2001; Cowan et al., 2005) and includes many of the mechanisms and relationships that are important for understanding the role that memory plays in language development and language disorders.

At the center of the model is working memory, which is viewed as the processes involved in activating relevant information from long-term memory and holding that information in a state that is accessible to the focus of attention (Cowan, 2001). Information in long-term memory is brought into working memory when it is activated. This activation is short-lived unless it is brought into the focus of attention. The focus of attention is limited in capacity, so only a small amount of the possible information in memory is readily accessible to the learner at any given time. The central executive (see below for a definition) directs and allocates various processes that are involved in activating memory and focusing attention.

There are a number of processes within working memory that are highly relevant to language learning. According to Baddeley and his colleagues (Baddeley, 2003b; Baddeley, Gathercole, & Papagno, 1998), there is an aspect of working memory, known as the phonological loop, that is highly specialized for retaining verbal information. The phonological loop consists of a phonological store, which holds phonological information for a short period, and a rehearsal process, in which sounds are repeated mentally in order to delay

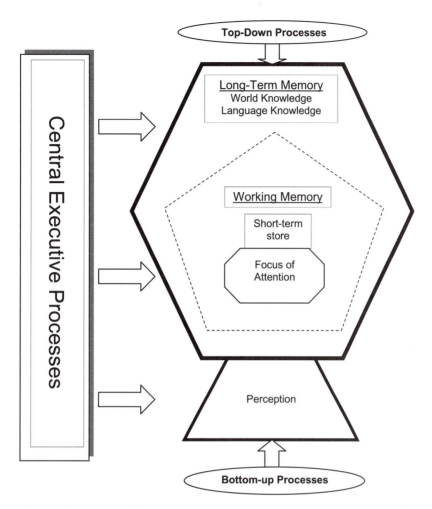

FIGURE 8.1   A simple model of attention and memory.

decay by keeping phonological representations active. The phonological loop's ability to encode, store, and recall sequences of sounds appears to play an important role in language disorders.

Recently, Charles Hulme and his colleagues have argued persuasively for yet another specialized function in working memory, a process that they call redintegration (Brown & Hulme, 1995; Hulme, Newton, Cowan, Stuart, & Brown, 1999). Redintegration is a process that serves to restore sequences of phonological information as they decay. For example, let's assume that you were asked to repeat this list of words: *hippopotamus, piano, motor-cycle, refrigerator, telephone, computer, university.* Even with rehearsal, items in memory will decay. During memory decay, the entire word does not immediately disappear. Rather, parts of a word tend to fade out of the focus of immediate attention. The fourth word in the list might retain only the sounds *refri_tor* in focus. The person faced with this problem could search their long-term memory for all the words that begin with "refri" and end with "tor" and come up with a pretty short list of words that could be used to complete the pattern. Activating "refrigerator" as part of that search process would likely trigger recognition and recall of the entire item. That process is redintegration. Children with language disorders do not have extensive vocabulary knowledge to use in this process, and thus have less efficient redintegrative processes (lexicality effects). As they expend their mental energies on prolonged redintegrative processing, they miss out on learning new vocabulary and concepts

As Gillam and his colleagues (Gillam, Hoffman, Marler, & Wynn-Dancy, 2002) have explained in greater detail elsewhere, there are two ways for information to get into working memory. In bottom-up processing, attention and perception systems deal with information before the mind makes sense of it. In top-down processing, learners use what they already know to create expectancies for what they will likely see and hear. These expectancies influence what is attended to, perceived, and remembered. Most of the time, moment-by-moment attention and perception (bottom-up processing) and expectations based on prior knowledge and experience (top-down processing) work together, simultaneously.

Finally, memory involves a central executive process (see chapter 20 by Windsor & Kohnert), which acts with the learner's motivation and goals to allocate and coordinate mental actions. The central executive determines what cognitive resources are needed to complete a task, applies those resources in some degree, and monitors the outcomes to determine whether other resources or a change in strategy are necessary. For example, children in a classroom are surrounded by multiple sources of information at once. They may focus their mental energies on the child talking next to them, noises out in the hall, posters on the walls, the clock, their growling stomach, thoughts about their dog at home, or (preferably) the teacher. At each moment, children's central executive functions are busy processing all incoming information and internal thought processes and allocating cognitive processes toward one or more of these sources of information in order to reach their goals.

The memory model depicted in Figure 8.1 assumes a general memory capacity that limits the amount of encoding, storage, and retrieval that can be accomplished at any given time. This general capacity is thought to result from the dynamic relationships between information processing functions, language abilities, and knowledge. The capacity limitations that are often discussed in relation to language disorders are understood in this model to be a combination of attention processes, perceptual processes, speed of activation, phonological, lexical, syntactic, and discursive language knowledge, and general knowledge of the topic at hand. Some children may have deficiencies in one or two of these areas, whereas others may have deficiencies in nearly all of these areas. The next sections of this chapter concern four principal aspects of memory that relate to language disorder: attention, phonological memory, central executive processes, and the ability to retain speech and language material over time.

ABILITY TO FOCUS ATTENTION

There is widespread agreement that some children with language disorders exhibit attention problems. For example, Baker and Cantwell (1992) examined the occurrence of speech/language disorders in 65 children aged 6 to 15 years with attention-deficit disorder (ADD). Of these children, 78% had speech articulation disorders; 58% had expressive language disorders; 34% had receptive language disorders; and 69% had language processing (auditory memory, discrimination, or association) disorders. These findings suggest a high degree of overlap between attention deficits and language disorders.

There have been very few attempts to study the role of attention in language disorders directly. Riddle (1992) employed a task in which preschoolers with specific language impairment (SLI) and age controls identified pictures of objects having the same name (e.g., two different looking shoes). A buzzer sounded during some of the picture identification trials. The children's task was to press a button as soon as they heard the buzzer. Although the children with language disorders were highly accurate on the picture task, their responses to the buzzer were slower than those of the controls, suggesting poorer abilities to refocus attention.

Campbell and McNeil (1985) studied the speed of processing in attention more directly. They presented children with language disorders after traumatic brain injury (TBI) with one set of sentences at a slow rate of speed and a second set of sentences at a normal rate of speed. Children exhibited better comprehension of a normal-rate sentence when it was presented immediately after a slowed sentence. Campbell and McNeil hypothesized that the children with language disorders had attention problems that were related to a "limited-capacity" mechanism that could allocate spare attention to the normal sentence only when the first sentence was slowed.

In a similar study, Noterdaeme, Amorosa, Mildenberger, Sitter, and Minow (2001) administered tasks measuring reaction time, attention, and executive functions of children with autism, specific language impairment, and their age-, sex-, and nonverbal-IQ-matched controls. The visual and auditory attention tasks required children to respond only when a specific pattern or tone sequence was presented. Sustained visual and auditory attention tasks required children to indicate when patterns of dots or tones changed. Executive function was measured using tasks requiring children to inhibit responses, shift their attention between different stimuli, and identify symbols embedded in sets of foils. All children performed similarly in terms of reaction times, but children with language disorders were significantly slower and made more errors on the measure of sustained auditory attention, and they made more errors on the selective auditory attention task than did children with autism or controls. The children with autism and language disorders demonstrated significant deficits in executive functions that were not present in the control group.

Given the results reported above, children with language disorders may need longer periods of sustained stimulation or repeated stimulation in order to trigger important attention-focusing mechanisms. Additionally, they may exhibit a limited capacity for sustaining their focus of attention. Children with language disorders may not be able to allocate the specific attention resources that are needed to sustain their focus. Whether children with language disorders have a diminished attention-triggering mechanism, a limited capacity for sustaining the focus of attention, or both, limitations in attention are likely to contribute to their language-learning difficulties. We will return to this issue in greater detail later in the chapter.

REPRESENTING AND STORING PHONOLOGICAL INFORMATION

Learning language involves listening to sequences of speech sounds, storing them while deciding what they mean and how they are used, retaining them, and then retrieving them when they are needed for comprehension or production. Phonological representation refers to the process of mentally representing sequences of phonemes in words. Phonological memory capacity is the amount of phonological information that can be held in the focus of attention at one time (Baddeley, 2003b; Gathercole & Baddeley, 1990; Montgomery, 2004). When good language learners hear a word they do not know, they form well-specified mental representations of sequences of phonemes and remember them while they figure out what the words are and what they mean.

One task that is frequently used to assess phonological representation and phonological capacity is known as nonword repetition. In this task, an examiner presents a multisyllable nonword (e.g. "pembictocade"), and children repeat it back immediately after hearing it (Dollaghan, Biber, & Campbell, 1993; Dollaghan & Campbell, 1998; Gathercole & Baddeley, 1990; Weismer et al., 2000). Successful repetition requires children to invoke a variety of phonological and memory-related processes such as perceiving a sequence of sounds and syllables, mentally encoding them, storing them, retrieving them, and then repeating them back in the same order.

Nonword recall is not a pure test of phonological representation and capacity: previously constructed phonological knowledge also contributes to nonword repetition. Nonwords containing phonemes that appear frequently in a language are repeated more accurately than are nonwords that are comprised of low-frequency phonemes. For example, Edwards, Beckman, and Munson (2004) showed that the relative probability of phoneme co-occurrence is a significant mediator of children's nonword repetition performance. Nonwords that contain phonemes that are likely to occur together in a language are easier to remember than are nonwords containing phoneme sequences that appear less often in a language. Children as young as 2½ years of age have been shown to be sensitive to the phonotactic probability of phoneme sequences during nonword-imitation tasks (Coady & Aslin, 2004). It appears that phonological representation, phonological memory capacity, and prior phonological knowledge are important for language development and use.

IMPLICATIONS FOR LANGUAGE LEARNING AND LANGUAGE DISORDER

Children with language disorders have difficulty learning new words and sentence structures (Fazio, Naremore, & Connell, 1996; Gummersall & Strong, 1999; Oetting, Rice, & Swank, 1995). A number of authors (Adams & Gathercole, 1995; Gathercole & Baddeley, 1990; Montgomery, 1995, 2004) have hypothesized that a deficit in phonological representation and phonological memory contributes to disorders in expressive or receptive language. With respect to expressive language, phonological memory is thought to provide short-term storage for an intended utterance until the motor processes involved in speech production can be executed (Adams & Gathercole, 1995). According to this view, restrictions on the amount of verbal information that can be stored in phonological memory would mean only shorter utterances could be produced. Gathercole and Baddeley (1990) also predicted that impairment in phonological memory should have negative consequences for the acquisition and use of grammatical morphology. Difficulty forming and maintaining phonological representations in phonological memory could lead to problems establishing clear phonological boundaries between word stems and their inflections. With respect to language comprehension, phonological memory constraints could limit the capacity to fully extract and represent the meaning of longer sentences (Montgomery, 2004).

The nature of the relationship between deficiencies in phonological memory and the language problems experienced by children with language disorders is not entirely clear. With respect to receptive language, a number of studies have found positive relationships between lexical comprehension skills, as indexed by a simple picture-pointing task, and phonological memory, as indexed by nonword repetition (e.g., Ellis Weismer, & Thordardottir, 2002; Montgomery, 1995; Norbury, Bishop, & Briscoe, 2002). One of the first studies to assess the relation between phonological memory and sentence comprehension compared children with language disorders with age-matched peers (Montgomery, 1995). Children completed a nonword-repetition task and a sentence comprehension task that included two sentence types: short sentences and long sentences. Both sentence types (matched on syntactic complexity) included simple and complex structures, thus making sentence length the variable of interest. On the nonword-repetition task, children with language disorders performed worse than did controls on the 3- and 4-syllable items. On the comprehension task, the children with language disorders comprehended fewer long sentences than short sentences and fewer long sentences than did the control children. There was a positive correlation between phonological memory and comprehension. Phonological memory was also positively correlated with standardized receptive language performance in children with SLI (Montgomery & Windsor, 2007). Finally, results from a large-scale study by Leonard and colleagues (Leonard et al., 2007) showed that perform-ance on working memory tasks accounted for a large (and significant) amount of variance in the language test scores of 14-year-old children with SLI.

Norbury et al. (2002) explored the intersection of phonological memory and complex grammatical comprehension in children with language disorders. These investigators exam-ined the role of phonological memory (indexed by nonword repetition) on the comprehen-sion of two types of sentences considered to be complex with respect to the process of movement and binding principles (van der Lely, 1996, 1998; van der Lely & Stollwerck, 1997). The complex sentences included passives (*The fish is eaten by the man.*) and sen-tences with pronominal reference (*Mowgli says Baloo Bear is tickling **himself***. *Baloo Bear says Mowgli is tickling **him**.*). Children with language disorders and two control groups were studied. Predictably, the children with language disorders performed significantly worse on the nonword task and on both the passive and pronominal sentences. Correlations between nonword repetition and complex sentence comprehension (in the .20–.40 range) were also significant in the children with language disorders. Such data suggest that the difficulties comprehending complex grammar are related, at least in part, to reduced phonological memory capacity.

LIMITATIONS IN CENTRAL EXECUTIVE FUNCTIONS

There are other aspects of working memory apart from phonological representation and storage that may play a critical role in the development of language abilities and subsequent disorders. Recall from the model of working memory in Figure 8.1 that working memory also includes a central executive component. It should be noted that the central executive is considered by some (e.g., Baddeley, 2003a, 2003b) as an attention supervisory system whose purpose is to coordinate the flow of information by activating and retrieving informa-tion from long memory and regulating the overall processing and storage of information. The central executive includes a resource allocation function that refers to a person's ability to divide attentional resources between two or more different concurrent mental activities. There appear to be limits to the capacity or the mental energy that is available to an individual for use in performing a cognitive task. Developmental research suggests that chil-dren's attentional resource capacity and their ability to allocate these resources effectively improve through adolescence (e.g., Gathercole, 1999; Johnson, 1997).

The central executive component of working memory is thought to be responsible for selective attention, the coordination of performance on two or more separate tasks, and the inhibition of disruptive effects of competing or irrelevant stimuli (Baddeley, 2003a). As such, it would appear to be critical for managing multiple levels of information processing between sensory stimuli and higher order cognitive processes. There have been a few studies that have examined central executive processes in children with language disorders.

Children's executive function abilities are often assessed using dual processing tasks (e.g., listening span task, backwards digit tasks) in which they are asked to engage in simultaneous information processing and storage. For example, the Competing Language Processing Task (CLPT) presents sets of simple sentences ("Pumpkins are *purple*," "Fish can *swim*") and requires comprehension of each sentence (i.e., answer Y/N question) followed by the recall of as many sentence-final words as possible after each set (Gaulin & Campbell, 1994). This task requires children to divide their attentional resources between language processing (i.e., comprehending each sentence) and verbal storage (i.e., remembering words at the end of each sentence in a list). Attentional capacity is assumed to play a key role in working memory functioning (Cowan, 1995, 1999; Engle, Kane, & Tuholski, 1999; Kane, Bleckley, Conway, & Engle, 2001). Some developmental memory researchers (e.g., Barrouillet & Camos, 2001; Gavens & Barrouillet, 2004) have argued that age-related improvement in complex memory performance is primarily attributable to increases in the amount of resources that are available to perform a task (i.e., their cognitive capacity), as opposed to increased efficiency in resource allocation.

Children with language disorders do not perform tasks like the CLPT as well as their nonimpaired peers. Ellis Weismer, Evans, and Hesketh (1999), for example, examined the relation between resource capacity/allocation using the CLPT and performance on standardized nonverbal cognitive and language tests in a group of children with language disorders and age-matched nonimpaired peers. Although both groups had similar comprehension scores (≥ 96% correct), the children with language disorders showed significantly poorer word recall than did the nonimpaired children. The children with language disorders had a 40% recall accuracy score, whereas the nonimpaired children had an accuracy score of 60%. Their performance suggests that they had less overall resource capacity than did their nonimpaired peers, thus leading to their poorer dual task performances (Ellis Weismer et al., 1999). In a more recent study, Mainela-Arnold and Evans (2005), also using the CLPT, reported very similar findings for their children with SLI.

Hoffman and Gillam (2004) used another experimental paradigm to explore the possibility of complex interactions among various information processing factors, including central executive functions, in children with language disorders. Children repeated a series of visually presented digits or pointed to the locations of a series of Xs on grids. In some conditions, they also completed secondary tasks requiring them to identify the color of the stimulus with either a naming or a pointing response. There were six conditions that crossed the primary task (verbal or spatial) with a secondary task (none, verbal, or spatial) under two rates of presentation (fast or slow). A total of 48 children (24 with language disorders and 24 with normal language skills) between the ages of 8:0 and 10:11 participated in the study.

The primary finding was a greater cross-modality effect for the control group than for the group of children with language disorders. Children with language disorders did not appear to benefit from the opportunity to disperse processing across modalities to the same extent that their age-matched peers did. This inability to disperse effective processing across visual and spatial domains resulted in inefficient and ineffective processing of visual information for the group of children with language disorders, particularly in conditions that included a spatial secondary task.

This study brought to light a previously undocumented susceptibility on the part of children with language disorders to nonspecific domain interference. These children had difficulty processing secondary task information that was presented in the opposite domain of that of the primary tasks (i.e., a spatial secondary task paired with a verbal primary task). Thus, children with language disorders have deficits in the central executive function of working memory.

Montgomery (2000a, 2000b) showed that children with SLI could allocate their resources when the task was easy enough. He asked children with SLI and age peers to recall lists of familiar words under three conditions: (1) free recall (requiring no processing), (2) words arranged according to the physical size of the word referents (requiring semantic knowledge of size) and (3) words arranged according to semantic category and word referent size (requiring semantic categorization + semantic knowledge of the size of the word referents within each category). The two groups performed similarly in the first two conditions. Children with SLI had unusual difficulty only when they had to recall lists that were organized according to category and size of the referent; a task requiring a greater number of mental processes. Such findings indicate that children with SLI can allocate their resources to both verbal processing and storage. It is only when the processing demands exceed their overall cognitive capacity that their recall suffers.

We noted previously that children with language disorders have particular difficulty with phonological memory. Some authors have explored the relationship between executive functions and phonological memory in children with language disorders. For example, Marton and Schwartz (2003) asked children with SLI and age-matched children to listen to sentences containing nonwords at the end of short–simple, short–complex, or long–complex sentences. After each sentence children were asked to (1) repeat the nonword (indexing phonological memory) and (2) answer a Y/N question (indexing concurrent language processing). The children with SLI produced significantly fewer nonwords across the sentence types. Although no significant differences emerged within the SLI group for nonword production across the sentence types, there was a strong trend for fewer correct productions as sentences became more complex and lengthy. Children with language impairments also presented significantly poorer comprehension than did their nonimpaired peers, regardless of sentence type. This finding supports the complex connections between language comprehension, memory capacity, and executive processes.

IMPLICATIONS OF CENTRAL EXECUTIVE FUNCTIONS FOR LANGUAGE LEARNING AND LANGUAGE DISORDERS

The potential role of central executive function in language development can readily be hypothesized as follows. During the process of establishing semantic stores in long-term memory, all incoming stimuli could be conceived of as a sensory puzzle that requires analysis, coordination, and interpretation. The central executive regulates the flow of information processing and supports the development of meaning by coordinating selective attention (which would also support the establishment of joint reference between child and caregiver) and the storage of information in long-term memory. Over time, exposure to repetitive combinations of sensory stimuli would establish sensory patterns that the central executive would recognize as being important because they occur frequently and consistently. When this happens, executive processes could regulate the creation of coherent phonological or imagistic representations in long-term memory. The continual coordination of multidomain sensory information would provide the basic framework for cognitive representations, which form the semantic network that is the basis of language development. In this way, adequate central executive function in working memory may be critical to the development of language in young children.

We should mention that executive functions operate at an unconscious level for the very young language learner. Importantly, these basic functions of the central executive component also appear to provide the bedrock foundation for the development of higher order metacognitive skills involved in self-regulation of learning tasks, such as attending selectively, inhibiting actions, restraining and delaying responses, planning, organizing, maintaining, and shifting set. For older children, such executive functions become controlled processes.

Very little is known about the role of the central executive in children's language learning and performance. With respect to auditory sentence comprehension, resource capacity/allocation should be critical, especially for complex sentences. For instance, listeners must be able to allocate sufficient resources to (1) phonological memory, to keep the word sequence in the phonological loop in an active state long enough for it to be processed, (2) the language system, to retrieve appropriate linguistic properties of the input words and to activate appropriate language-processing schemes that generate appropriate linguistic representations of the word sequences (e.g., NP, VP), and (3) retrieval and integration processes responsible for reactivating representations from prior processing that are being temporarily stored in working memory (Just & Carpenter, 1992) and integrating them with newly created representations (e.g., McElree, Foraker, & Dyer, 2003). For those children with reduced attentional resource capacity (i.e., children with SLI or mild intellectual disabilities) comprehension will suffer because they have too few executive resources to devote to the various storage and processing demands of such sentences (Van der Molen, Van Luit, Jongmans, & Van der Molen, 2007).

In two studies Montgomery (2000a, 2000b) explored the influence of resource capacity/allocation on the simple sentence comprehension of a group of children with language disorders and age-matched children. In each study, he used the three-tiered word-recall task (described above) and the comprehension task just described. In both studies, the children with language disorders showed reduced resource capacity (as described above) and the same pattern of comprehension: they comprehended fewer long versus short sentences and fewer sentences than the nonimpaired children. In both studies, however, there was no correlation found between resource capacity and comprehension for either group. The lack of correlation was interpreted to mean that the comprehension of simple grammar by children—even children with SLI—occurs very efficiently and fluidly. Because simple grammar is well within most children's linguistic grasp, very few attentional resources are needed.

Ellis Weismer and colleagues (1999) also examined the relation between resource capacity (using the CLPT) and sentence comprehension in a group of children with language disorders and nonimpaired children. Whereas the nonimpaired children showed a positive relation between CLPT (word recall) and sentence comprehension (score on Test of Auditory Comprehension of Language-R, a measure incorporating both simple and complex structures), no such relation emerged for the children with SLI. These authors suggested that the lack of correlation between the CLPT and language in the children with language disorders might be due to the poorly specified psycholinguistic operations of the comprehension task. A study by Ellis Weismer and Thordardottir (2002) is the only study having assessed the influence of both resource capacity/allocation and phonological memory in the sentence comprehension of children with language disorders and nonimpaired children. After accounting for nonverbal IQ, the most unique variance in children's comprehension was accounted for by resource capacity/allocation, followed by phonological memory. At present, it is unclear to what extent resource capacity/allocation is involved in the sentence comprehension of children with SLI, given that few studies have systematically examined this issue. However, it is very likely that resource capacity/allocation is involved in complex sentence comprehension, given the adult language processing literature (Just & Carpenter, 1992; King & Just, 1991; Miyake, Carpenter, & Just, 1994).

RETAINING INFORMATION OVER TIME

Information in working memory fades away (decays) if it is not acted upon. Rate of memory decay is functionally related to processing speed in that the faster material in phonological memory is processed, the less likely it is to decay (e.g., Gathercole, 1999). Rate of decay is, however, also equally applicable to the rate at which previously processed material being temporarily stored in working memory fades (Towse, Hitch, & Hutton, 1998, 2002). Relatively little is known about temporal decay across development, although Towse et al. (1998) suggest that decay rates decrease with age. Cowan (1997) has suggested that information suspended in children's working memory must be reactivated and enter the focus of processing attention within 2 s–20 s or the material decays.

Relatively little is known about the decay rates of children with language disorders. Gathercole and Baddeley (1990) suggested that speech in phonological memory might fade at a faster rate in children with language disorders than in nonimpaired children. Few empirical studies have addressed this issue. The findings from a suffix effect study by Gillam, Cowan, and Day (1995), however, could be interpreted to suggest that auditory information in phonological memory decays at a faster rate in children with SLI relative to typically developing children, if the input is not processed in a timely fashion.

With respect to decay of material in working memory, results of a study we reviewed earlier (Ellis Weismer et al., 1999) suggest that language material decays more quickly in children with language disorders than in nonimpaired children. Children with language disorders remembered fewer sentence-final words, which presumably were stored in working memory, while they were processing the meaning of each new sentence. This may have happened because the words decayed while children were listening to and processing the subsequent sentences. Interestingly, similar findings were reported by Mainela-Arnold and Evans (2005); however, these authors attributed the poorer recall of children with language disorders to word-frequency effects. Children with language disorders have greater trouble retaining and recalling low-frequency words than high-frequency words. Such findings suggest that the representational strength (i.e., semantic or phonological) of low-frequency words versus high-frequency words is reduced in children with language disorders compared to their typically developing peers, with children with language disorders evidencing reduced representational strength. Reduced representational strength renders low-frequency words more vulnerable to faster decay from phonological memory for children with SLI.

IMPLICATIONS OF RAPID DECAY FOR LANGUAGE LEARNING AND LANGUAGE DISORDER

Unusually rapid memory decay may have two important influences on children's language development. First, it may affect the rate at which lexical material in phonological memory fades. Given that complex input leads to slower processing (King & Just, 1991; Miyake et al., 1994), such material may fade if it is not processed in a timely manner. Thus, children with language disorders may be at greater risk for such material fading because of their slower processing speed. Second, temporal decay should relate to the ability to reactivate, in a timely fashion, those representations that have already been generated and are being held in working memory (Cowan, 1997; Towse et al., 2002). Again, children with language disorders may be at greater risk of such material fading before it can be reactivated and integrated with new information if a disproportionate amount of their attentional resources is being devoted to slower computational processing schemes. More rapid decay should have an amplified effect as sentences become increasingly complex because a greater number of partial analyses must be reactivated over the course of processing a sentence.

SUMMARY

We have reviewed evidence supporting information processing factors that are likely to constrain language processing in children with language disorders. Children with language disorders appear to have limitations that affect attention, speech perception, the adequacy of phonological representations, central executive functions, and/or speed of decay. Regardless of what the primary or secondary limitation might be, it is likely that the language-learning abilities of most children with language disorders are simultaneously constrained by multiple factors that affect information processing.

REFERENCES

Adams, A., & Gathercole, S. (1995). Phonological working memory and speech production in pre-school children. *Journal of Speech and Hearing Research*, 38, 403–414.

Baddeley, A. D. (2003a). Working memory and language: An overview. *Journal of Communication Disorders*, 36, 189–208.

Baddeley, A. D. (2003b). Working memory: Looking back and looking forward. *Nature Reviews*, 4, 828–839.

Baddeley, A. D., Gathercole, S., & Papagno, C. (1998). The phonological loop as a language learning device. *Psychological Review*, 105(1), 158–173.

Baddeley, A. D., & Hitch, G. (1974). Working memory. In G. H. Bower (Ed.), *The psychology of learning and motivation* (Vol. 8, pp. 47–90). New York: Academic Press.

Baker, L., & Cantwell, D. P. (1992). Attention deficit disorder and speech/language disorders. *Comprehensive Mental Health Care*, 2(1), 3–16.

Barrouillet, P., & Camos, V. (2001). Developmental increase in working memory span: Resource sharing or temporal decay? *Journal of Memory and Language*, 45, 1–20.

Brock, J., & Jarrold, C. (2004). Language influences on verbal short-term memory performance in Down Syndrome: Item and order recognition. *Journal of Speech, Language, and Hearing Research*, 47, 1334–1346.

Brown, G. D. A., & Hulme, C. (1995). Modeling item length effects in memory span: No rehearsal needed? *Journal of Memory and Language*, 34(5), 594–621.

Campbell, T., Dollaghan, C., Needleman, H., & Janosky, J. (1997). Reducing bias in language assessment: Processing-dependent measures. *Journal of Speech and Hearing Research*, 40(3), 519–525.

Campbell, T. F., & McNeil, M. R. (1985). Effects of presentation rate and divided attention on auditory comprehension in children with an acquired language impairment. *Journal of Speech and Hearing Research*, 28(4), 513–520.

Chein, J. M., Ravizza, S. M., & Fiez, J. A. (2003). Using neuroimaging to evaluate models of working memory and their implications for language processing. *Journal of Neurolinguistics*, 16, 315–339.

Coady, J., & Aslin, R. (2004). Young children's sensitivity to probabilistic phonotactics in the developing lexicon. *Journal of Experimental Child Psychology*, 89, 183–213.

Cowan, N. (1995). *Attention and memory: An integrated framework*. New York: Oxford University Press.

Cowan, N. (1997). The development of working memory. In N. Cowan & C. Hulme (Eds.), *The development of memory in childhood* (pp. 163–199). Hove, UK: Psychology Press.

Cowan, N. (1999). An embedded-processes model of working memory. In A. Miyake & P. Shah

(Eds.), *Models of working memory: Mechanisms of active maintenance and executive control* (pp. 62–101). New York: Cambridge University Press.

Cowan, N. (2001). The magical number 4 in short-term memory: A reconsideration of mental storage capacity. *Behavioral and Brain Sciences*, 24(1), 87–185.

Cowan, N., Elliott, E. A., Scott, S. J., Morey, C. C., Mattox, S., Hismjatullina, A., et al. (2005). On the capacity of attention: Its estimation and its role in working memory and cognitive aptitudes. *Cognitive Psychology*, 51, 42–100.

Dollaghan, C. A., Biber, M., & Campbell, T. F. (1993). Constituent syllable effects in a nonsense-word repetition task. *Journal of Speech and Hearing Research*, 36(5), 1051–1054.

Dollaghan, C. A., & Campbell, T. F. (1998). Nonword repetition and child language impairment. *Journal of Speech-Language-Hearing Research*, 41, 1136–1146.

Edwards, J., Beckman, M., & Munson, B. (2004). The interaction between vocabulary size and phonotactic probability effects on children's production accuracy and fluency in novel word repetition. *Journal of Speech and Hearing Research*, 47, 421–436.

Ellis Weismer, S., Evans, J., & Hesketh, L. (1999). An examination of verbal working memory capacity in children with specific language impairment. *Journal of Speech, Language, and Hearing Research*, 42, 1249–1260.

Ellis Weismer, S., & Thordardottir, E. (2002). Cognition and language. In P. Accardo, B. Rogers, & A. Capute (Eds.), *Disorders of language development* (pp. 21–37). Timonium, MD: York Press.

Engle, R., Kane, J., & Tuholski, S. (1999). Individual differences in working memory capacity and what they tell us about controlled attention, general fluid intelligence, and functions of the prefrontal cortex. In A. Miyake & P. Shah (Eds.), *Models of working memory: Mechanisms of active maintenance and executive control* (pp. 62–101). Cambridge: Cambridge University Press.

Fazio, B. B., Naremore, R. C., & Connell, P. J. (1996). Tracking children from poverty at risk for specific language impairment: A 3-year longitudinal study. *Journal of Speech and Hearing Research*, 39(3), 611–624.

Gathercole, S. (1999). Cognitive approaches to the development of short-term memory. *Cognitive Science*, 3, 410–419.

Gathercole, S. (2006). Nonword repetition and word learning: The nature of the relationship. *Applied Psycholinguistics*, 27, 513–543.

Gathercole, S. E., & Baddeley, A. D. (1990). Phonological memory deficits in language disordered children: Is there a causal connection? *Journal of Memory and Language*, 29, 336–360.

Gaulin, C., & Campbell, T. (1994). Procedure for assessing verbal working memory in normal school-age children: Some preliminary data. *Perceptual and Motor Skills*, 79, 55–64.

Gavens, N., & Barrouillet, P. (2004). Delays of retention, processing efficiency, and attentional resources in working memory span development. *Journal of Memory and Language*, 51, 644–657.

Gillam, R. B., & Carlile, R. M. (1997). Oral reading and story retelling of students with specific language impairment. *Language, Speech, and Hearing Services in the Schools*, 28(1), 30–42.

Gillam, R., Cowan, N., & Day, L. (1995). Sequential memory in children with and without language impairment. *Journal of Speech and Hearing Research*, 38, 393–402.

Gillam, R. B., Cowan, N., & Marler, J. A. (1998). Information processing by school-age children with specific language impairment: Evidence from a modality effect paradigm. *Journal of Speech, Language, and Hearing Research*, 41(4), 913–926.

Gillam, R. B., Hoffman, L. M., Marler, J. A., & Wynn-Dancy, M. (2002). Sensitivity to increased task demands: Contributions from data-driven and conceptually driven information processing deficits. *Topics in Language Disorders*, 22(3), 30–48.

Gottardo, A., Stanovich, K. E., & Siegel, L. S. (1996). The relationships between phonological sensitivity, syntactic processing, and verbal working memory in the reading performance of third-grade children. *Journal of Experimental Child Psychology*, 63, 563–582.

Gummersall, D. M., & Strong, C. J. (1999). Assessment of complex sentence production in a narrative context. *Language, Speech, and Hearing Services in the Schools*, 30(2), 152–164.

Hoffman, L. M., & Gillam, R. B. (2004). Verbal and spatial information processing constraints in children with specific language impairment. *Journal of Speech, Language, and Hearing Research, 47,* 114–125.

Hulme, C., Newton, P., Cowan, N., Stuart, G., & Brown, G. (1999). Think before you speak: Pauses, memory search, and trace redintegration processes in verbal memory span. *Journal of Experimental Psychology: Learning, Memory, and Cognition, 25*(2), 447–463.

Johnson, M. (1997). *Developmental cognitive neuroscience.* Cambridge, MA: Blackwell.

Just, M., & Carpenter, P. (1992). A capacity theory of comprehension: Individual differences in working memory. *Psychological Review, 99,* 122–149.

Kaderavek, J. N., & Sulzby, E. (2000). Narrative production by children with and without specific language impairment: Oral narratives and emergent readings. *Journal of Speech, Language, and Hearing Research, 43*(1), 34–49.

Kane, M., Bleckley, M., Conway, A., & Engle, R. (2001). A controlled-attention view of working-memory capacity. *Journal of Experimental Psychology: General, 130,* 169–183.

King, J., & Just, M. (1991). Individual differences in syntactic processing: The role of working memory. *Journal of Memory and Language, 30,* 580–602.

Leonard, L., Ellis Weismer, S., Miller, C., Francis, D., Tomblin, J., & Kail, R. (2007). Speed of processing, working memory, and language impairment in children. *Journal of Speech, Language, and Hearing Research, 50,* 408–428.

Mainela-Arnold, E., & Evans, J. (2005). Beyond capacity limitations: Determinants of word-recall performance on verbal working memory span tasks in children with SLI. *Journal of Speech, Language, and Hearing Research, 48,* 897–909.

Majerus, S., Van der Linden, M., Vérane, B., & Eliez, S. (2007). Verbal short term memory in individuals with chromosome 22q11.2 deletion: Specific deficit in serial order retention capacities? *Journal on Mental Retardation, 2,* 79–93.

Marler, J. A., Champlin, C. A., & Gillam, R. B. (2002). Auditory memory for backward masking signals in children with language impairment. *Psychophysiology, 39*(6), 767–780.

Marton, K., & Schwartz, R. (2003). Working memory capacity and language processes in children with specific language impairment. *Journal of Speech, Language, and Hearing Research, 46,* 1138–1153.

McElree, B, Foraker, S., & Dyer, L. (2003). Memory structures that subserve sentence comprehension. *Journal of Memory and Language, 48,* 67–91.

Miyake, A., Carpenter, P., & Just, M. (1994). A capacity approach to syntactic comprehension disorders: Making normal adults perform like aphasic patients. *Cognitive Neuropsychology, 11,* 671–717.

Montgomery, J. (1995). Sentence comprehension in children with specific language impairment: The role of phonological working memory. *Journal of Speech and Hearing Research, 38,* 187–199.

Montgomery, J. (2000a). Relation of working memory to off-line and real-time sentence processing in children with specific language impairment. *Applied Psycholinguistics, 21,* 117–148.

Montgomery, J. (2000b). Verbal working memory and sentence comprehension in children with specific language impairment. *Journal of Speech, Language, and Hearing Research, 43*(2), 293–308.

Montgomery, J. (2004). Sentence comprehension in children with specific language impairment: Effects of input rate and phonological working memory. *International Journal of Language and Communication Disorders, 39,* 115–134.

Montgomery, J., & Windsor, J. (2007). Examining the language performances of children with and without specific language impairment: Contributions of phonological short-term memory and processing speed. *Journal of Speech, Language, and Hearing Research, 50,* 778–797.

Norbury, C., Bishop, D., & Briscoe, J. (2002). Does impaired grammatical comprehension provide evidence of an innate grammar module? *Applied Psycholinguistics, 23,* 247–268.

Noterdaeme, M., Amorosa, H., Mildenberger, K., Sitter, S., & Minow, F. (2001). Evaluation of attention in children with autism and children with a specific language disorder. *European Journal of Child Psychology, 10,* 58–66.

Oetting, J. B., Rice, M. L., & Swank, L. K. (1995). Quick incidental learning (QUIL) of words by school-age children with and without SLI. *Journal of Speech and Hearing Research*, *38*(2), 434–445.

Riddle, L. S. (1992). The attentional capacity of children with specific language impairment (Doctoral dissertation, Indiana University, 1992). *Dissertation Abstracts International*, *53*(6-B).

Stark, R., & Tallal, P. (1988). *Language, speech, and reading disorders in children: Neuropsychological studies*. Boston, MA: Little, Brown, and Company.

Tallal, P., & Piercy, M. (1974). Developmental aphasia: The perception of brief vowels and extended stop consonants. *Neuropsychologia*, *13*, 69–74.

Towse, J., Hitch, G., & Hutton, U. (1998). A reevaluation of working memory capacity in children. *Journal of Memory and Language*, *39*, 195–217.

Towse, J., Hitch, G., & Hutton, U. (2002). On the nature of the relationship between processing activity and item retention in children. *Journal of Experimental Child Psychology*, *82*, 156–184.

van der Lely, H. (1996). Specifically language impaired and normally developing children: Verbal passive vs. adjectival passive sentence interpretation. *Lingua*, *98*, 243–272.

van der Lely, H. (1998). SLI in children: Movement, economy, and deficits in the computational-syntactic system. *Language Acquisition*, *7*, 161–192.

van der Lely, H., & Stollwerck, L. (1997). Binding theory and grammatical specific language impairment in children. *Cognition*, *62*, 245–290.

Van der Molen, M., Van Luit, J., Jongmans, M., Van der Molen, M. (2007). Verbal working memory in children with mild intellectual disabilities. *Journal of Intellectual Disabilities Research*, *51*, 162–169.

Weismer, S. E., Tomblin, J., Zhang, X., Buckwalter, P., Chynoweth, J. G., & Jones, M. (2000). Nonword repetition performance in school-age children with and without language impairment. *Journal of Speech Language, and Hearing Research*, *43*(4), 865–878.

9

Speech Perception and Production in Child Language Disorders

JAN EDWARDS and BENJAMIN MUNSON

INTRODUCTION

*I*f one were to ask a lay person to describe a symptom of a language disorder, the typical answer would probably focus on a phonological error ("wabbit" for *rabbit*); on a problem related to academic performance, such as difficulty in learning to read; or on a specific named disorder that is associated also with deficits in areas other than language, such as autism-spectrum disorder or attention-deficit/hyperactivity disorder. The general public's knowledge of language disorders of an unknown origin is, in general, quite limited. This is true despite the fact that such language impairments are relatively common, with recent prevalence estimates of approximately 7.42% from a population-based sample in the Midwestern United States (Tomblin et al., 1997). Even within the study of functional language impairments, there are great discrepancies in the specific topics that have been studied. Within this research area, a much larger proportion of research has examined morphology, syntax, and academic problems of children with language impairment than has examined these children's speech perception, speech production, and their knowledge of higher-level aspects of the sound structure of language. Yet the latter are arguably the foundations on which knowledge of more abstract aspects of language, such as syntax, is based. Sounds are one of the media through which language is conveyed. Deficits in knowledge of sounds may contribute to, maintain, or even be a causal factor in language impairments. Thus, the topic of this chapter—a review of studies of what children with language impairments know about the knowledge of sounds—is a topic that is both under-studied and poorly understood, as well as being one that can explain much about the nature of a commonly occurring childhood communicative disorder.

There is ample evidence that the task of acquiring knowledge of the sound structure of language is highly protracted and begins quite early in life. Children begin to recognize some familiar words, such as their names, by 4 to 5 months of age (Mandel, Jusczyk, & Pisoni, 1995) and begin to produce words around their first birthday. While most typically developing children produce most or all of the sounds in their native language in a way that listeners perceive to be accurate by about 5 or 6 years of age (Smit, Freilinger, Bernthal, Hand, & Bird, 1990), more subtle measures of speech perception and production suggest that the phonological system is not adult-like until about age 10 or 12 (e.g., Kent & Forner 1980; Goffman, 2004; Hazan & Barrett, 2000; Smith, 1978).

A discussion of the protracted nature of phonological development must begin with a description of phonological *knowledge*. Phonological knowledge is far from monolithic. Knowledge of the sound structure of language includes many different subtypes of knowledge. This includes knowledge of the physical instantiation of phonological categories—*perceptual knowledge* of the acoustic characteristics of speech sounds and their perceptual consequences, and *articulatory knowledge* of the motoric, tactile-kinesthetic, and proprioceptive characteristics of speech sounds. Phonological knowledge also involves more abstract higher-level knowledge of the ways that words can be divided into sounds, and sounds can be combined into meaningful sequences in words. In our previous work (e.g., Munson, Edwards, & Beckman, 2005b), we have referred to this as *higher-level phonological knowledge*. Perceptual, articulatory, and higher-level knowledge all refer to people's knowledge of the way that sounds are used to convey linguistic meaning. One last kind of phonological knowledge, *social-indexical knowledge*, refers to individuals' knowledge of the way that variation in speech production is used to convey social identity and social-group membership.

The different types of phonological knowledge can be illustrated by the knowledge that people have of the sound /r/. People have perceptual knowledge that /r/ is characterized by a low third-formant frequency, as illustrated in studies in which people identify synthetic stimuli varying in third-formant frequency as /r/ if the stimuli have a low F3 and /l/ if the stimuli have a high F3 (e.g., Munson & Nelson, 2005). People also have articulatory knowledge that /r/ can be produced either with a bunched tongue root or with a retroflex movement of the tongue tip, and that different configurations can be used to reduce acoustic variability in this sound (Guenther et al., 1999). People also have higher-level knowledge that /r/ does not occur in any word-initial clusters following /v/, and that /vratʃ/ is not a possible word of English. Finally, people have knowledge of the ways that variation in /r/ production can be used to convey social-group membership. For example, British English speakers presumably have tacit knowledge that labiodental variants of /r/ are more likely to be produced by middle-class women than middle-class men or working-class people (Foulkes & Docherty, 2000). A full characterization of knowledge of /r/ includes all of these different types of knowledge.

This chapter focuses on the development of the first three kinds of phonological knowledge in children with language impairment relative to their typically developing peers, simply because there is little or no research on the acquisition of social-indexical knowledge in children with language impairments relative to their typically developing peers. However, in our conclusions we speculate on how deficits in the acquisition of social-indexical knowledge might interact with the pragmatic problems frequently observed in children with language impairment.

In this chapter, we consider primarily the phonological knowledge of children with language impairments of an unknown origin and, to a lesser extent, of children with a related and sometimes co-occurring disorder, dyslexia (see chapter 5 by Shaywitz et al. and chapter 19 by Hook & Haynes). There are several reasons for this. First, there is a well-established, though small, body of research on phonological acquisition for these children. In contrast, there has been relatively little research on this subject in children with other genetically or neurologically based language impairments, such as autism, Williams syndrome, or fragile X. This discussion will exclude children with broad cognitive deficits, such as developmental disability or Down syndrome. It will also exclude children with hearing impairment. Our motivation for this is twofold. First, the prevalence of many of these disorders is considerably lower than that of specific language impairment. Second, children with language problems associated with cognitive deficits often have concomitant hearing deficits and speech motor deficits, and therefore a discussion of phonological acquisition for these children is considerably more complex. To illustrate, consider two recent findings: Seung and Chapman (2000) found that 11 of their 33 participants with Down syndrome failed a hearing screening but did not differ from the 22 individuals who passed the screening on a psycholinguistic measure closely related to language performance, digit span. Marler, Elfenbein, Ryals, Urban, and Netzloff (2005) found a high rate of sensorineural hearing loss in individuals with Williams syndrome, who are generally characterized as having relatively good language abilities in the absence of low full-scale IQ scores.

In this chapter, we use the term *primary language impairment* (PLI) rather than the more commonly used term *specific language impairment* (SLI) to describe children whose primary problem is with language acquisition and who have age-appropriate nonverbal IQ's, social-emotional skills, and oral-motor ability (following Kohnert & Windsor, 2004; Windsor & Kohnert, 2004). Children with PLI often show deficits in nonlinguistic auditory and visual tasks relative to their typically developing peers (e.g., Kohnert & Windsor, 2004). The word *specific* in the label *specific language impairment* wrongly implies that these children's deficits are specifically limited to tasks involving language (see chapter 1 by Schwartz). Readers should keep in mind that the diagnostic criteria for PLI are identical to those described for SLI: the failure to achieve age-appropriate language skills in the presence of a condition that would otherwise cause a language impairment.

PERCEPTUAL KNOWLEDGE

Speech Perception

In this first section, we focus on speech perception in children with language impairments relative to their typical peers, an area of research that goes back more than 20 years. The interest in speech perception began with the early work of Tallal and colleagues (e.g., Tallal & Piercy, 1973, 1974, 1975; Tallal & Stark, 1981). These researchers found that school-age children with language and/or learning disorders had more difficulty than typically developing age peers in the discrimination of nonspeech tones and in the discrimination of both synthetic speech consonants embedded in CV syllables and in brief synthetic vowels. Crucially, children with language impairment performed more poorly than did their typically developing age peers when the distinction hinged on brief acoustic cues, such as formant transitions, voice onset time, or even steady-state formants for vowels if they were of sufficiently brief duration. This finding has since been replicated by a number of researchers using a variety of experimental paradigms and a variety of stimulus types (e.g., Leonard, McGregor, & Allen, 1992; Tallal & Piercy, 1974, 1975; Tallal & Stark, 1981; Stark & Heinz, 1996; Sussman, 2001). A number of researchers have hypothesized that these observed auditory processing deficits are causally related to language impairment. For example, Leonard et al. (1992) suggested that the difficulty that children with PLI have in learning inflectional morphology might be related to their auditory processing deficit, since the morphemes that are most problematic for children with PLI are those whose acoustic characteristics make them perceptually less salient. In general, these inflectional morphemes can be characterized as having *low phonetic substance* (that is, they are of short duration and low intensity).

This view has been challenged in recent studies. Recent research has suggested that the observed speech perception deficits of children with PLI may have more to do with the nature of the stimulus and the memory demands of the task than with the perception of brief acoustic cues. Coady, Kluender, and Evans (2005) and Coady, Evans, Mainela-Arnold, and Kluender (2007) found that children with PLI performed similarly to typically developing age peers when natural speech rather than synthetic speech was used, when the stimuli were real words rather than nonsense words, and when the memory demands of the task were lessened. This finding is consistent with the claim of Gillam, Hoffman, Marler, and Wynn-Dancy (2002) that the performance of children with PLI is disproportionately affected by task difficulty relative to the performance of chronological-age peers. Nevertheless, this research has served as an impetus to understand how speech perception deficits are related to language impairment, whether these deficits are considered as an underlying cause of the language impairment, as in the work of Tallal and colleagues (e.g., Merzenich, Jenkins, Johnston, Schreiner, Miller, & Tallal, 1996), or as a symptom of a more general processing problem, as in the work of Miller, Kail, Leonard, and Tomblin (2001) and Windsor and Kohnert (2004), among others.

Still other researchers have argued that these studies underestimate the speech perception deficits of children with PLI, because these studies measure speech perception in quiet. A recent study by Ziegler, Pech-Georgel, George, Alario, and Lorenzi (2005) compared speech perception by children with PLI in conditions of steady background noise to ones in which the background noise fluctuated. This methodology is commonly used in studies of auditory perception in individuals with hearing impairment (e.g., Nelson, Jin, Carney, & Nelson, 2004) to examine whether observed speech perception deficits are due to peripheral auditory perception deficits or to more central speech processing problems. The ability to perceive speech better in fluctuating noise as compared to steady-state noise is presumed to reflect intact peripheral auditory processing mechanisms. Ziegler et al. found that children with PLI performed more poorly than did their typically developing peers in both noise types. This was related to severity of language impairment. Both groups perceived speech better in fluctuating than in static noise, suggesting that children with PLI had normal peripheral auditory processing mechanisms and a deficit in ability to associate acoustic signals with phonological categories. More generally, Ziegler et al. criticized previous studies of speech perception in PLI for using optimal listening conditions, which may underestimate the speech-perception deficit of children with PLI.

While some researchers have suggested that differences in speech perception observed in school-age children with language impairment relative to typically developing peers might be a consequence of the language disorder, rather than a cause, recent research suggests that such differences in speech perception are evident as early as the first year of life, even before children begin to produce words. Several recent prospective studies are relevant here. In a longitudinal study of 20 infants, Kuhl, Conboy, Padden, Nelson, & Pruitt (2005), following up on work of Tsao, Liu, and Kuhl (2004), found that expressive vocabulary size in the second year of life was predicted by infant performance on both a native-language and a non-native-language contrast in the first year of life. They found that infants with the largest vocabularies at 24 months were those who had performed best on a native-language contrast and worst on a non-native-language contrast at 7 months. By contrast, the children who had performed best on a non-native-language contrast and worst on a native-language contrast at 7 months had the smallest vocabularies at 24 months. In another prospective study, Benasich and Tallal (2002) examined younger siblings of children with PLI relative to siblings of children with typical language development. Across the two groups of children, they found that performance on a nonspeech auditory discrimination task at 7.5 months predicted subsequent language performance at 16 and 24 months for measures of both language comprehension and production.

Nonspeech Auditory Processing

In addition to differences in speech perception relative to their typically developing peers, recent studies have suggested that children with PLI may differ from their typically developing peers on a range of auditory perception tasks that do not utilize speech signals. The general focus of psychophysical studies since the foundational study of Tallal and Piercy (1973) has been to identify possible difficulties in the perception of acoustic parameters that carry crucial acoustic cues to speech sounds. A finding that children with PLI have difficulty perceiving acoustic parameters in nonspeech stimuli considerably strengthens the hypothesis that general perceptual difficulties may underlie language difficulties.

Wright et al. (1997) examined auditory temporal processing in 8 children with PLI, to examine whether the deficits in rapid auditory processing for speech found by Tallal and colleagues could also be demonstrated for nonspeech stimuli. Wright measured detection thresholds for pure-tone stimuli presented simultaneously with, prior to, or after broadband noise with different spectral characteristics. The crucial condition in this study was the *backward masking* condition. In this condition, a tone is presented immediately prior to an interval of noise. A large, statistically significant group difference was found for detection thresholds in the backward masking condition: the tone needed to be louder in this condition for the PLI children to detect it. This difference was not present when the spectral characteristics of the noise and those of the tone were considerably different. Wright et al. claimed that these findings supported Tallal's earlier conjecture that the perception of brief auditory stimuli is impaired in children with PLI. Wright and Zecker (2004) expanded on this finding with a larger, more heterogeneous group of children, including children with PLI (including the 8 children studied by Wright et al., 1997), children with dyslexia, and children with central auditory processing disorder, as well as age-matched peers with normal language and academic achievement. Again, typically developing children could detect a less-intense tone in the backward-masked condition than the children in any of the other groups. Similar results were found by Bishop, Carlyon, Deeks, and Bishop (1999).

Wright and colleagues' result has been replicated in a number of studies. Marler, Champlin, and Gillam (2002) and Marler and Champlin (2005) further showed that children with PLI have abnormal neurophysiologic responses in the backward-masking condition. Marler, Champlin, and Gillam (2001) examined detection thresholds in backward masking conditions by children with PLI undergoing computer-based auditory training programs (either Fast ForWord or Laureate Learning Systems software) and typically developing controls not receiving treatment. They found no association between participation in these programs and improvement in backward-masking thresholds. Thresholds decreased on successive trials, for both groups of children, suggesting that performance on the backward-masking task is at least partly dependent on task familiarity.

The auditory perception problems of children with PLI may extend beyond temporal perception. McArthur and Bishop (2004) examined frequency discrimination in teenagers and young adults with PLI and peers with typical language achievement. McArthur and Bishop argued that many previous findings regarding the purported auditory temporal processing deficit in children with PLI may be due to their decreased ability to perceive fine differences in frequency. They demonstrated that frequency detection thresholds were lower for people with typical language achievement than for a subgroup of people with PLI who had poor phonemic awareness. In a subsequent study, Bishop and McArthur (2005) showed that some of the children with PLI in the McArthur and Bishop (2004) study had atypical neurophysiologic responses to auditory stimuli, though this did not coincide perfectly with the subset who demonstrated poor frequency discrimination. In follow-up measures taken 18 months later, the frequency discrimination of many of the children with PLI improved, though a large proportion of the group continued to have atypical neurophysiologic responses to stimuli. Bishop, Adams, Nation, and Rosen (2005) examined the perception of brief glide stimuli (i.e., pure tone stimuli that change in frequency). They found that duration and frequency-range thresholds did not differ significantly between the two groups, though they did differ in a linguistic task, perceiving words in noise.

In general, the studies reviewed in this section seem to converge on the notion that at least some children with PLI have deficits in at least some aspects of auditory perception. The interpretation of this finding is qualified, however, by a number of factors. First, not all findings have been replicable across studies, suggesting that small differences in identification criteria used for PLI, or the inclusion of children with a variety of different language impairments (i.e., both PLI and dyslexia) may lead to different results. Second, as discussed by McArthur and Bishop (2004), it is not clear that the tasks that have been used in the classic studies (e.g., Tallal & Piercy, 1973) on the psychophysical abilities measure what they purport to measure. For example, McArthur and Bishop argue that tasks that have been purported to measure temporal-processing abilities may in fact have been measuring frequency perception.

Finally, and perhaps most importantly, there is the possibility that the group differences may reflect task learning rather than psychophysical abilities. Classical research on the psychophysical abilities of adults has examined asymptotic performance on listening tasks. This requires that individual listeners participate in numerous listening sessions to determine threshold performance. The long times required to determine these thresholds in these studies make them inappropriate for children with language impairment, who often show decreased attention. Consequently, thresholds are often determined using procedures that are relatively quick and potentially affected by lapses in attention. The group differences may reflect attention or task learning rather than differences in psychophysical abilities. This possibility is underscored by Marler et al.'s (2001) finding that backward-masked thresholds in children decreased with successive trials. It is possible that, with increased familiarity with a task, the auditory perception of children with PLI may reach levels that are comparable to those of children with typical development. Only one study has examined this possibility systematically. McArthur and Bishop (2004) examined the association between performance on a frequency-detection task and performance on tasks that measure basic-level cognitive processes involved in their task: attention, perception, and temporal-order perception. Though some group differences were found on these measures, McArthur and Bishop argued that "although temporal order and paired association may account for some variance in [frequency detection] thresholds, this amount is too small to explain the poor [frequency detection] thresholds of the [children with PLI demonstrating poor frequency detection]" (p. 537). A challenge for future studies is to further delimit the extent to which group differences in auditory perception are related to task familiarity and other basic-level cognitive processes.

Another challenge for future research is to identify the extent to which individual differences in auditory processing contribute to the heterogeneity in language abilities that is characteristic of the population of children with PLI, beyond what can be predicted by basic-level cognitive processes. Few studies have examined this, and the results of these studies do not find a consistent relationship between psychophysical abilities and language performance, as measured with standardized instruments. For example, Bishop et al. (1999) found that a measure of auditory perception, performance on the *Tallal Auditory Repetition Test*, did not predict scores on a standardized language test as well as did scores on another task, nonword repetition. Much previous research has shown that children with PLI perform more poorly than their typically developing peers on nonword-repetition tasks (e.g., Ellis Weismer et al., 2000). It is well documented that children with PLI very often have lower nonverbal IQ scores than do age- and language-matched peers with typical language development, even when children with scores below a cutoff (i.e., 85) are excluded. As argued by Rosen (2003), these subtle, subclinical differences in nonverbal IQ may account for auditory-processing differences between children with PLI and TD, rather than the differences in language abilities. In short, the findings reviewed in this paragraph support Rosen's (2003) argument that the auditory processing deficits observed in some children with PLI may be co-occurring deficits, rather than a causal deficit.

Relating Speech Perception to Language Skills

Two hallmark symptoms of PLI in English-acquiring preschool children are: (1) vocabulary problems, as exemplified by late talking (a delay in when first words are produced), difficulties with word learning, and a smaller productive vocabulary size than that of typically developing peers at any age (e.g., Dollaghan, 1987; Oetting, Rice, & Swank, 1995); and (2) morphological deficits, as exemplified by a protracted period for morphological acquisition, especially for morphemes related to verb tense (for a summary of this work, see Leonard, 1998). In this section, we consider how these difficulties in word learning and morphological acquisition might be related to early problems in speech perception, such as those observed by Benasich and Tallal (2002), Kuhl et al. (2005), and Tsao et al. (2004).

A large body of research on infant speech perception provides some insight into why early deficits in speech perception might lead to delays in word learning. One of the primary language-learning problems that children must solve in their first year of life is how to pick out words—which they do not yet know—from the continuous stream of speech. This task is made easier by child-directed speech with its larger pitch range, shorter utterances, and simpler syntactic structure, but the problem still remains. Research on speech perception in the first year of life provides much insight into how infants gradually develop the abilities they need in order to delimit words from running speech. By about 9 to 10 months of age, children prefer listening to words with the preferred English strong–weak stress pattern (Jusczyk, Cutler, & Redanz, 1993); they prefer listening to words that contain sequences with permissible phonotactic sequences (Jusczyk, Friederici, Wessels, Svenkerud, & Jusczyk, 1993); and they prefer to listen to sequences with high rather than low phonotactic probabilities (Jusczyk, Luce, & Charles-Luce, 1994). Children are able to exploit these preferences so that they can segment continuous speech into words sometime between 6 and 9 months of age, using phonotactic information (Friederici & Wessels, 1993; Mattys, Jusczyk, Luce, & Morgan, 1999). If children have difficulty with speech perception in their first year of life, then these difficulties might make it more difficult for them to segment out words from running speech, and this difficulty, in turn, could lead to a delay in word learning. There exist any number of deficits in speech perception that might make word learning problematic and relatively few of these deficits have been studied children with PLI. While we know that children with language deficits may have difficulty with distinguishing between minimal pair consonant or vowel segments even as early as 6 months of age (e.g., Leonard et al., 1992; Tallal & Piercy, 1974, 1975; Tallal & Stark, 1981; Stark & Heinz, 1996; Sussman, 2001; Tsao et al., 2004; Kuhl et al., 2005), we know very little about whether children with PLI have other difficulties in speech perception, such as learning which contrasts are relevant in the ambient language (e.g., Werker & Tees, 1984) or determining the statistical patterns in the ambient language so that they can efficiently segment continuous speech into word-sized units (e.g., Saffran, 2001).

Werker, Fennell, Corcoran, and Stager (2002) provide some experimental evidence relevant to the prediction of a relationship between speech perception and word learning.

They examined the auditory word-discrimination skills of children in their second year of life, at a time when there is a wide range in vocabulary size, even for typically developing children. Werker et al. (2002) found that most 14-month-old infants were unable to distinguish between minimal pairs such as /bɪ/ and /dɪ/ in a word-learning task, although they were able to do so in a simpler speech perception task, and in a word-learning task using the phonetically dissimilar nonwords /lɪf/ and /næm/. In contrast, many 17-month-old and most 20-month-old infants could do so. Werker et al. (2002) found that across the whole age range of 14 to 20 months, productive vocabulary size was correlated with the ability to distinguish between minimal pair words on the word-learning task. In addition, they found that infants with a productive vocabulary of at least 25 words or a receptive vocabulary of at least 200 words were successful on this task. Werker and Curtin (2005) interpreted these results within their model of infants' and toddlers' speech perception and word learning (PRIMIR). In the PRIMIR model, there are three multidimensional planes that underlie speech perception and word learning: a general perceptual plane, a word-form plane, and a phoneme plane. Information on the phoneme plane develops gradually, based on regularities that emerge from the multidimensional clusters on the word-form plane. This model predicts an interaction between word learning and phonological development, as observed by Werker et al. (2002). As predicted by the PRIMIR model, children who knew more words have a more highly developed phoneme plane and children with a more highly developed phoneme plane were better word learners.

Research on infant speech perception predicts that children who have perceptual difficulties early on will have difficulty picking words out of running speech and thus will be delayed in word learning. Furthermore, the PRIMIR model predicts that children with delayed word learning will have delayed phonological development as well, because phonological development interacts with word learning. These findings address the first hallmark symptom of PLI—namely, difficulties in word learning.

The second hallmark symptom of PLI in English-speaking children is difficulty in the acquisition of morphology. The deficits in word learning that are observed for English-speaking children with PLI may be related to their deficits in morphological acquisition. There is some evidence that at least some aspects of morphological acquisition are related to vocabulary size. For example, Marchman (1995) found that the best predictor of when English-speaking children begin to overgeneralize the regular past tense (*goed* instead of *went*) is the number of verbs in productive vocabulary. Even for regular morphemes, there is evidence that children need a critical mass of lexical forms to abstract robustly the appropriate allomorphic alternation. The past tense allomorph /ɪd/ is much lower in frequency than the allomorphs /t/ and /d/, and it is the last of the "regular" past tense allomorphs to be acquired (Marchman, Wulfeck, & Ellis Weismer, 1999). Similarly, the plural morpheme /ɪz/ is lower in frequency than its allomorphs /s/ and /z/, and it is the last of the *regular* plural allomorphs to be acquired (Derwing & Baker, 1980). One interpretation of these findings is that children need a "critical mass" of lexical items in order to make a morphological generalization (Marchman & Bates, 1994). Marchman and Bates have simulated these results with a connectionist model in which learning shifts qualitatively from memorization to systematic generalization as a function of vocabulary size. This view of morphological learning predicts that children with smaller vocabularies will have difficulties with the acquisition of morphology, and this is precisely what is observed for English-speaking children with PLI. In short, deficits in building a lexicon may mediate the causal relationship between speech perception deficits and morphological deficits in children with PLI: early speech perception deficits make the task of acquiring words challenging, and the resulting smaller sized vocabulary may limit the robustness of the morphological generalizations that children with PLI can make.

The second area in which speech perception deficits may relate causally to language impairment concerns children with dyslexia. Dyslexia is defined broadly as a deficit in comprehending and producing written language (see chapter 5 by Shaywitz et al.). Like PLI, it is often diagnosed using exclusionary criteria (i.e., poor reading ability in the absence of a deficit that would otherwise compromise reading). It is commonly observed that PLI and dyslexia overlap, though the estimates are higher in clinically referenced samples (e.g., Catts, 1993) than in a population-based sample in the Midwestern United States (Catts, Adlof, Hogan, & Ellis Weismer, 2005). The question of whether children with dyslexia have deficits in speech perception was examined by Manis et al. (1997), who found that children with dyslexia had atypical identification functions for a *bath–path* continuum relative to typically achieving peers. More recently, Joanisse, Manis, Keating, and Seidenberg (2000) found that speech perception deficits occurred in children with dyslexia only if they had a concomitant oral-language impairment. Joanisse et al.'s study provides further evidence for a link between speech perception and language abilities. It further suggests that speech perception deficits in children with dyslexia may be mediated by oral language abilities, rather than being directly attributable to the reading impairment.

ARTICULATORY KNOWLEDGE

The studies reviewed thus far all deal with only one of the four types of phonological knowledge: perceptual knowledge. Another type of phonological knowledge is articulatory knowledge. Relatively few studies have examined speech production directly in children with PLI. Although there is a low comorbidity rate between primary language impairment and phonological disorder (Shriberg, Tomblin, & McSweeny, 1999) at kindergarten entry, the few studies that have been conducted suggest that children with PLI may have speech production deficits relative to their typically developing peers. One example of this is shown by McGregor and Leonard (1994), who showed that children with PLI repeated initial unstressed pronouns and articles less accurately than initial stressed content words. That is, initial syllables were more likely to be deleted in weak–strong sequences like *they RUN* than in strong–strong sequences like *DOGS RUN* (where words in caps indicate stressed words). This is consistent with the behavior of younger, typically developing children (as reviewed in Gerken, 1996) and may indicate that the well-established tendency for children with PLI to omit articles and function-word subjects has a basis in difficulties with speech production rather than in deficits in abstract grammatical knowledge.

Further evidence of speech production deficits in children with PLI comes from studies of articulatory variability. Goffman (1999, 2004) showed that children with language impairments have greater kinematic variability in lip movement than do typically developing age-matched children when producing nonsense sequences. Both groups of children produced greater kinematic variability in weak–strong sequences than in strong–weak ones. This finding was replicated in a recent study by Goffman, Heisler, and Chakraborty (2006), who further showed that these differences occur in different phrase positions. Heisler, Goffman, and Younger (2004) also found that children with PLI show more kinematic variability in word-learning tasks. Crucially, the children with PLI in Goffman's studies did not have frank pronunciation problems: their increased kinematic variability does not appear to be secondary to categorical phonological errors of the type seen in children with articulation and phonological impairments. Goffman's findings suggest that children with PLI have less mature motor control than their typically developing peers.

Finally, some research has shown that children with PLI differ from their TD peers in general motor skills. Bishop (1990) found that children with PLI performed more slowly than did TD children on a timed peg-moving task. Johnston, Stark, Mellits, and Tallal (1981) showed that children with PLI were slower than TD peers in executing rapid finger movements. Together, these findings suggest that the articulatory variability noted by Goffman may relate to a more general motor deficit in children with PLI.

In the PRIMIR model of speech perception and word learning (Werker & Curtin, 2005), higher-level phonological knowledge is highly interrelated with word learning. One prediction that this model makes is that children with smaller vocabularies will have difficulty with higher-level phonological knowledge, such as being able to robustly abstract consonant and vowel categories from their usual consonant–vowel, vowel–consonant, and consonant–consonant contexts. This hypothesis was tested by Munson, Kurtz, and Windsor (2005). They examined nonword repetition in three groups of children. The primary group of interest was a group of 16 school-age children with primary language impairment. These children were compared to two groups of children who were acquiring language typically, a group of children who were matched to the children with PLI on chronological age (CA group) and a group of children who were matched on the basis of an estimate of expressive vocabulary size (the VS group). Munson et al. (2005) examined accuracy of production of high- and low-probability nonwords (i.e., nonwords that contained either all high-frequency or all low-frequency two-phoneme sequences). Previous work (Edwards, Beckman, & Munson, 2004; Munson, Edwards, & Beckman, 2005a) argued that the difference in repetition between high- and low-frequency sequences of phonemes is related to the robustness of children's higher-level phonological knowledge. High-frequency sequences of phonemes, such /mp/, can be repeated accurately by resorting to knowledge in existing lexical items (as in *simple, camper*, etc.). In contrast, low-frequency sequences like /mk/, which occur in no known lexical items, can be repeated accurately only if the child's higher-level phonological knowledge includes knowledge of individual phonemes, like /m/ and /k/, in addition to knowledge of the sound structure of known words.

Analyses of variance showed that all three groups of participants produced the high-probability nonwords more accurately than the low-probability ones. Interestingly, the effect of probability was *larger* for the children with PLI relative to their CA controls and was not significantly different for the children with PLI relative to their VS controls. Thus, Munson et al. (2005) found evidence that children with language impairments have less robust higher-level phonological knowledge than their peers with typical development. These deficits appear to be due entirely to the smaller size of their vocabularies, as shown by the fact that the size of their frequency effect did not differ from that of their VS matches, and by the fact that an estimate of vocabulary size predicted the difference in repetition accuracy between high- and low-probability nonwords. Munson et al. (2005) conjectured that the larger phonotactic-probability effect seen in children with language impairments is related to their word-learning difficulties: children with LI may experience more difficulty than their age peers in learning higher-level phonological knowledge from lexical items. Consequently, the robust *scaffold* that phonological representations serve in word-learning is not available to them, and their subsequent word-learning suffers.

Further evidence for higher-level phonological knowledge deficits can be seen in studies of spoken-word recognition by children with PLI. Dollaghan (1998) examined the ability of children with PLI to recognize spoken words from which acoustic information had been removed. The ability to accurately recognize words with information removed is facilitated if children have higher-level phonological knowledge that words are comprised of strings of phonemes, as this allows them to relate a partial input to a lexical representation in memory (Garlock, Walley, & Metsala, 2001; Walley, 1988). Typically developing children with larger sized lexicons recognize gated words more accurately than did those with smaller sized lexicons (Edwards, Fox, & Rogers, 2002; Munson, 2001). Dollaghan (1998) found that children with PLI did not require more acoustic information than their typically developing peers to recognize familiar words, but they did require significantly more information to recognize unfamiliar words. This finding complements Munson, Kurtz, and Windsor's finding by providing further evidence that children with PLI have a deficit in higher-level knowledge of the phonemic structure of words.

CONCLUSIONS

With the notable exception of work on speech perception in children with PLI, there is a paucity of research on other aspects of phonological knowledge. Even in the area of speech perception, research has focused on whether children with PLI can perceive lower-level phonetic contrasts, rather than on whether they also have difficulty in abstracting higher-level phonological knowledge, such as phonotactic information. In addition, there are relatively few studies on articulatory and higher-level phonological knowledge in children with PLI relative to age controls or vocabulary-size controls. Furthermore, to our knowledge, there is virtually no research on the acquisition of social-indexical knowledge in children with PLI. Social-indexical knowledge refers to knowledge of how linguistic variation is used to convey and perceive membership in different social groups. Social-indexical knowledge encompasses a variety of different factors, including social class, race, gender, and regional dialect. Social-indexical variation can relate to any aspect of linguistic structure, including phonology, syntax, morphology, and the lexicon. Though previous studies have shown the pervasive influence of social-indexical variability on speech production and perception in adults and children (see Foulkes, 2005, for a review), very little research has examined how social-indexical knowledge may be impaired in children with PLI. However, there is some evidence that children with another commonly occurring communication disorder, phonological disorder, have decreased knowledge of social-indexical variability (Nathan & Wells, 2001). It is well established that children with PLI show a host of deficits in social skills and social communication (e.g., Brinton, Fujiki, & McKee, 1998, Brinton, Fujiki, Spencer, & Robinson, 1997; Marton, Abramoff, & Rosenzweig, 2004; see also chapter 15 by Oetting & Hadley). It is possible that a causal or maintaining factor for these concomitant impairments is a decreased ability to perceive and convey social roles and social-group membership through variation in speech production. This is a potentially rich area for future research.

To summarize, while there are many critical gaps in our understanding of phonological knowledge in children with PLI, the research to date suggests that children with PLI have deficits in perceptual knowledge, articulatory knowledge, and higher-level phonological knowledge relative to their typically developing age peers. In this chapter, we have suggested that the observed deficits in perceptual knowledge, in particular, could lead to difficulties with word learning, which, in turn, could lead to difficulties in the acquisition of morphology. Our account of the relationship between speech perception and language acquisition differs from that of others (e.g., Merzenich et al., 1996; Sussman, 2001; Wright et al., 1997). These other accounts have generally proposed a fairly direct link between deficits in speech perception and deficits in language acquisition (for example, children with PLI will have difficulty learning grammatical morphemes if they have difficulty processing rapidly changing temporal information). In contrast, we have proposed that the lexicon plays a crucial role in the acquisition of both phonological knowledge and morphological knowledge. In this account, deficits in speech perception will result in difficulties in word learning, which will, in turn, make the acquisition of robust phonological representations more difficult. This proposal is consistent with theories that posit continuity between processing and knowledge of language (e.g., MacDonald & Christiansen, 2002). Such an account of PLI has many implications, both theoretically and clinically.

ACKNOWLEDGMENTS

The preparation of this chapter was supported by NIH grant R01 DC02932 to Jan Edwards and R03 DC005702 to Benjamin Munson. We especially thank Mary E. Beckman, who has been crucially involved in the development of the model of phonological acquisition described in this chapter.

REFERENCES

Benasich, A. A., & Tallal, P. (2002). Infant discrimination of rapid auditory cues predicts later language impairment. *Behavioural Brain Research*, *136*, 31–49.

Bishop, D. V. M. (1990). Handedness, clumsiness, and developmental language disorders. *Neuropsychologia*, *28*, 681–690.

Bishop, D. V. M., Adams, C., Nation, K., & Rosen, S. (2005). Perception of transient nonspeech stimuli is normal in specific language impairment: Evidence from glide discrimination. *Applied Psycholinguistics*, *26*, 175–194.

Bishop, D. V. M., Bishop, S., Bright, P., James, C., Delaney, T., & Tallal, P. (1999). Different origin of auditory and phonological processing problems in children with language impairment: Evidence from a twin study. *Journal of Speech, Language, and Hearing Research*, *42*, 155–168.

Bishop, D. V. M., Carlyon, R. P., Deeks, J. M., & Bishop, S. J. (1999). Auditory temporal processing impairment: Neither necessary nor sufficient for causing language impairment in children. *Journal of Speech, Language, and Hearing Research*, *42*, 1295–1310.

Bishop, D. V. M., & McArthur, G. (2005). Individual differences in auditory processing in specific language impairment: A follow-up study using event-related potential and behavioural thresholds. *Cortex*, *41*, 327–341.

Brinton, B., Fujiki, M., & McKee, L. (1998). Negotiation skills of children with specific language impairment. *Journal of Speech, Language, and Hearing Research*, *41*, 927–940.

Brinton, B., Fujiki, M., Spencer, C., & Robinson, L. A. (1997). The ability of children with specific language impairment to access and participate in an ongoing interaction. *Journal of Speech, Language, and Hearing Research*, *40*, 1011–1025.

Catts, H. (1993). The relationship between speech-language impairments and reading disabilities. *Journal of Speech and Hearing Research*, *36*, 948–958.

Catts, H., Adlof, S., Hogan, T., & Ellis Weismer, S. (2005). Are specific language impairment and dyslexia distinct disorders? *Journal of Speech, Language, and Hearing Research*, *48*, 1378–1396.

Coady, J. A., Evans, J. L., Mainela-Arnold, E., & Kluender, K. R. (2007). Children with specific language impairments perceive speech most categorically when tokens are natural and meaningful. *Journal of Speech, Language, and Hearing Research*, *50*, 41–57.

Coady, J. A., Kluender, K. R., & Evans, J. L. (2005). Categorical perception of speech by children with specific language impairments. *Journal of Speech, Language, and Hearing Research*, *48*, 944–959.

Derwing, B. L., & Baker, W. J. (1980). Rule learning and the English inflections (with special emphasis on the plural). In G. D. Prideaux, B. L. Derwing, & W. J. Baker (Eds.), *Experimental linguistics: Integration of theories and applications* (pp. 247–272). Ghent, Belgium: E. Sotry-Scientia.

Dollaghan, C. (1987). Fast mapping in normal and language-impaired children. *Journal of Speech and Language Disorders*, *52*, 218–222.

Dollaghan, C. (1998). Spoken word recognition in children with and without specific language impairment. *Applied Psycholinguistics, 19*, 193–207.

Edwards, J., Beckman, M. E., & Munson, B. (2004). The interaction between vocabulary size and phonotactic probability effects on children's production accuracy and fluency in nonword repetition. *Journal of Speech, Language, and Hearing Research, 47*, 421–436.

Edwards, J., Fox, R. A., & Rogers, C. (2002). Final consonant discrimination in children: Effects of phonological disorder, vocabulary size, and phonetic inventory size. *Journal of Speech, Language, and Hearing Research, 45*, 231–242.

Ellis Weismer, S., Tomblin, J., Zhang, X., Buckwalter, P., Chynoweth, J., & Jones, M. (2000). Nonword repetition performance in school-age children with and without language impairment. *Journal of Speech, Language, and Hearing Research, 43*, 865–878.

Foulkes, P. (2005). Sociophonetics. In K. Brown (Ed.), *Encyclopedia of language and linguistics* (2nd ed.). Amsterdam: Elsevier Press.

Foulkes, P., & Docherty, G. (2000). Another chapter in the story of /r/: "labiodental" variants in British English. *Journal of Sociolinguistics, 4*, 30–59.

Friederici, A., & Wessels, J. (1993). Phonotactic knowledge of word boundaries and its use in infant speech perception. *Perception and Psychophysics, 54*, 287–295.

Garlock, V., Walley, A., & Metsala, J. (2001). Age-of-acquisition, word frequency, and neighborhood density effects on spoken word recognition by children and adults. *Journal of Memory and Language, 45*, 468–492.

Gerken, L. A. (1996). Prosodic structure in young children's language production. *Language, 72*, 683–712.

Gillam, R., Hoffman, L., Marler, J., & Wynn-Dancy, M. (2002). Sensitivity to increased task demands: Contributions from data-driven and conceptually driven information processing deficits. *Topics in Language Disorders, 22*, 30–48.

Goffman, L. (1999). Prosodic influences on speech production in children with specific language impairments and speech deficits: Kinematic, acoustic, and transcription evidence. *Journal of Speech, Language, and Hearing Research, 42*, 1499–1517.

Goffman, L. (2004). Kinematic differentiation of prosodic categories in normal and disordered language development. *Journal of Speech, Language, and Hearing Research, 47*, 1088–1102.

Goffman, L., Heisler, L., & Chakraborty, R. (2006). Mapping prosodic structure onto words and phrases in children's and adults' speech production. *Language and Cognitive Processes, 21*, 25–47.

Guenther, F., Espy-Wilson, C., Boyce, S., Matthies, M., Zandipour, J., & Perkell, J. S. (1999). Articulatory tradeoffs reduce acoustic variability during American English /ɹ/ production. *Journal of the Acoustical Society of America, 105*, 2854–2865.

Hazan, V., & Barrett, S. (2000). The development of phonemic categorization in children aged 6–12. *Journal of Phonetics, 28*, 377–396.

Heisler, L., Goffman, L., & Younger, B. (2004). *The influence of word learning on speech production for children with specific language impairment*. Poster presented at the Symposium for Research on Child Language Disorders, Madison, WI.

Joanisse, M., Manis, F., Keating, P., & Seidenberg, M. (2000). Language deficits in dyslexic children: Speech perception, phonology, and morphology. *Journal of Experimental Child Psychology, 77*, 30–60.

Johnston, R. B., Stark, R. E., Mellits, D., & Tallal, P. (1981). Neurological status of language-impaired and normal children. *Annals of Neurology, 10*, 159–163.

Jusczyk, P., Cutler, A., & Redanz, N. (1993). Infants' preference for the predominant stress patterns of English words. *Child Development, 64*, 675–687.

Jusczyk, P., Friederici, A., Wessels, J., Svenkerud, V., & Jusczyk, A. (1993). Infants' sensitivity to the sound patterns of native language words. *Journal of Memory and Language, 32*, 402–420.

Jusczyk, P., Luce, P., & Charles-Luce, J. (1994). Infants' sensitivity to phonotactic patterns in the native language. *Journal of Memory and Language, 33*, 630–645.

Kent, R., & Forner, L. (1980). Speech segment durations in sentence recitations by children and adults. *Journal of Phonetics, 8*, 157–168.

Kohnert, K., & Windsor, J. (2004). The search for common ground: Part 2. Nonlinguistic perform-ance by linguistically diverse learners. *Journal of Speech, Language, and Hearing Research, 47,* 891–903.

Kuhl, P. K., Conboy, B. T., Padden, D., Nelson, T., & Pruitt, J. (2005). Early speech perception and later language development: Implications for the "Critical Period". *Language Learning and Development, 1,* 237–264.

Leonard, L. B. (1998). *Children with specific language impairment.* Cambridge, MA: MIT Press.

Leonard, L. B., McGregor, K. K., & Allen, G. D. (1992). Grammatical morphology and speech perception in children with specific language impairment. *Journal of Speech and Hearing Research, 35,* 1076–1085.

MacDonald, M. C., & Christiansen, M. H. (2002). Reassessing working memory: A comment on Just & Carpenter (1992) and Waters & Caplan (1996). *Psychological Science, 109,* 35–54.

Mandel, D., Jusczyk, P., & Pisoni, D. (1995). Infants' recognition of the sound patterns of their own names. *Psychological. Science, 6,* 315–318.

Manis, F., McBride-Chang, C., Seidenberg, M., Keating, P., Doi, L., Munson, B., & Peterson, A. (1997). Are speech perception deficits associated with developmental dyslexia? *Journal of Experimental Child Psychology, 66,* 211–235.

Marchman, V. (1995). *Lexical development and morphological productivity: Vol. 13. A longitudinal follow-up.* Paper presented at the Biennial Meeting of the Society for Research in Child Development, Indianapolis, IN.

Marchman, V., & Bates, E. (1994). Continuity in lexical and morphological development: A test of the critical mass hypothesis. *Journal of Child Language, 21,* 331–366.

Marchman, V., Wulfeck, B., & Ellis Weismer, S. (1999). Morphological productivity in children with normal language and SLI: A study of the English past tense. *Journal of Speech, Language, and Hearing Research, 42,* 206–219.

Marler, J., & Champlin, C. (2005). Sensory processing of backward-masking signals in children with language-learning impairment as assessed with the auditory brainstem response. *Journal of Speech, Language, and Hearing Research, 48,* 189–203.

Marler, J., Champlin, C., & Gillam, R. (2001). Backward and simultaneous masking measured in children with language-learning impairments who received intervention with Fast ForWord or Laureate Learning Systems software. *American Journal of Speech-Language Pathology, 10,* 258–268.

Marler, J., Champlin, C., & Gillam, R. (2002). Auditory memory for backward masking signals in children with language impairment. *Psychophysiology, 39,* 767–780.

Marler, J., Elfenbein, J., Ryals, B., Urban, Z., & Netzloff, M. (2005). Sensorineural hearing loss in children and young adults with Williams Syndrome. *American Journal of Medical Genetics A, 138,* 318–327.

Marton, K., Abramoff, B., & Rosenzweig, S. (2004). Social cognition and language in children with specific language impairment. *Journal of Communication Disorders, 38,* 143–162.

Mattys, S., Jusczyk, P., Luce, P., & Morgan, J. (1999). Phonotactic and prosodic effects on word segmentation in infants. *Cognitive Psychology, 38,* 465–494.

McArthur, G., & Bishop, D. V. M. (2004). Frequency discrimination deficits in people with spe-cific language impairment: Reliability, validity, and linguistic correlates. *Journal of Speech, Language, and Hearing Research, 47,* 527–541.

McGregor, K., & Leonard, L. B. (1994). Subject pronoun and article omissions in the speech of children with specific language impairment: A phonological interpretation. *Journal of Speech and Hearing Research, 37,* 171–181.

Merzenich, M. M., Jenkins, W., Johnston, P., Schreiner, C., Miller, S., & Tallal, P. (1996). Temporal processing deficits in language-learning impaired children ameliorated by training. *Science, 271,* 77–81.

Miller, C. A., Kail, R., Leonard, L. B., & Tomblin, J. B. (2001). Speed of processing in children with specific language impairment. *Journal of Speech and Hearing Research, 44,* 416–433.

Munson, B. (2001). Relationships between vocabulary size and spoken word recognition in children aged 3–7. *Contemporary Issues in Communication Disorders and Sciences, 28,* 20–29.

Munson, B., Edwards, J., & Beckman, M. E. (2005a). Relationships between nonword repetition accuracy and other measures of linguistic development in children with phonological disorders. *Journal of Speech, Language, and Hearing Research, 48*, 61–78.

Munson, B., Edwards, J., & Beckman, M. E. (2005b). Phonological knowledge in typical and atypical speech-sound development. *Topics in Language Disorders, 25*, 190–206.

Munson, B., Kurtz, B. A., & Windsor, J. (2005). The influence of vocabulary size, phonotactic probability, and wordlikeness on nonword repetitions of children with and without specific language impairment. *Journal of Speech, Language, and Hearing Research, 48*, 1033–1047.

Munson, B., & Nelson, P. B. (2005). Phonetic identification in quiet and in noise by listeners with cochlear implants. *Journal of the Acoustical Society of America, 118*, 2607–2617.

Nathan, L., & Wells, B. (2001). Can children with speech difficulties process an unfamiliar accent? *Applied Psycholinguistics, 22*, 343–361.

Nelson, P. B., Jin, S.-H., Carney, A. E., & Nelson, D. (2004). Understanding speech in modulated interference: Cochlear implant users and normal-hearing listeners. *Journal of the Acoustical Society of America, 113*, 961–968.

Oetting, J., Rice, M., & Swank, L. (1995). Quick incidental learning (QUIL) of words by school-age children with and without PLI. *Journal of Speech, Language, and Hearing Research, 23*, 434–445.

Rosen, S. (2003). Auditory processing in dyslexia and specific language impairment: Is there a deficit? What is its nature? Does it explain anything? *Journal of Phonetics, 31*, 509–527.

Saffran, J. (2001). Words in a sea of sounds: The output of statistical learning. *Cognition, 81*, 149–169.

Seung, H.-K., & Chapman, R. (2000). Digit span in individuals with Down syndrome and in typically developing peers: Temporal aspects. *Journal of Speech, Language, and Hearing Research, 43*, 609–620.

Shriberg, L. D., Tomblin, J. B., & McSweeny, J. L. (1999). Prevalence of speech delay in 6-year-old children and comorbidity with language impairment. *Journal of Speech, Language, and Hearing Research, 42*, 1461–1481.

Smit, A. B., Freilinger, J. J., Bernthal, J. E., Hand, L., & Bird, A. (1990). The Iowa articulation norms project and its Nebraska replication. *Journal of Speech and Hearing Disorders, 55*, 779–798.

Smith, B. (1978). Temporal aspects of English speech production: A developmental perspective. *Journal of Phonetics, 6*, 37–67.

Stark, R. E., & Heinz, J. M. (1996). Vowel perception in children with and without language impairment. *Journal of Speech and Hearing Research, 39*, 860–869.

Sussman, J. E. (2001). Vowel perception by adults and children with normal language and specific language impairment: Based on steady states or transitions? *Journal of the Acoustical Society of America, 109*, 1173–1180.

Tallal, P., & Piercy, M. (1973). Defects of nonverbal auditory perception in children with developmental aphasia. *Nature, 241*, 468–469.

Tallal, P., & Piercy, M. (1974). Developmental aphasia: Rate of auditory processing and selective impairment of consonant perception. *Neuropsychologia, 12*, 83–93.

Tallal, P., & Piercy, M. (1975). Developmental aphasia: The perception of brief vowels and extended stop consonants. *Neuropsychologia, 13*, 69–74.

Tallal, P., & Stark, R. E. (1981). Speech acoustic cue discrimination abilities of normally developing and language impaired children. *Journal of the Acoustical Society of America, 69*, 568–574.

Tomblin, J. B., Records, N. L., Buckwalter, P., Zhang, X., Smith, E., & O'Brien, M. (1997). Prevalence of specific language impairment in kindergarten children. *Journal of Speech, Language, and Hearing Research, 40*, 1245–1260.

Tsao, F.-M., Liu, H.-M., & Kuhl, P. K. (2004). Speech perception in infancy predicts language development in the second year of life: A longitudinal study. *Child Development, 75*, 1067–1084.

Walley, A. C. (1988). Spoken word recognition by young children and adults. *Cognitive Development, 3*, 137–165.

Werker, J. F., & Curtin, S. (2005). PRIMIR: A developmental model of speech processing. *Language Learning and Development, 1*, 197–234.

Werker, J. F., Fennell, C. T., Corcoran, K. M., & Stager, C. L. (2002). Infants' ability to learn phonetically similar words: Effects of age and vocabulary size. *Infancy, 3*, 1–30.

Werker, J. F., & Tees, R. C. (1984). Cross-language speech perception: Evidence for perceptual reorganization during the first year of life. *Infant Behavior and Development, 7*, 49–63.

Windsor, J., & Kohnert, K. (2004). The search for common ground: Part 1. Lexical performance by linguistically diverse learners. *Journal of Speech, Language, and Hearing Research, 47*.

Wright, B., Lombardino, L., King, W., Puranik, C., Leonard, C., & Merzenich, M. (1997). Deficits in auditory temporal and spectral resolution in language-impaired children. *Nature, 387*, 176–178.

Wright, B., & Zecker, S. (2004). Learning problems, delayed development, and puberty. *Proceedings of the National Academy of Sciences U.S.A., 101*, 9942–9946.

Ziegler, J. C., Pech-Georgel, C., George, F., Alario, F.-X., & Lorenzi, C. (2005). Deficits in speech perception predict language learning impairment. *Proceedings of the National Academy of Sciences U.S.A., 102*, 14110–14115.

10

Genetics of Child Language Disorders

J. BRUCE TOMBLIN

Most contemporary views of language development assume that the capacity for language development in humans is, at least in part, dependent upon neural systems that are genetically influenced (Elman et al., 1996; Pinker, 1994). Although speculation regarding the genetic basis of language has a long history, we are only now beginning to find direct evidence of gene(s) that may affect systems necessary for language acquisition and are therefore important to language disorder. This chapter emphasizes the status of research aimed at identifying genes resulting in children with specific language impairment (SLI), because this research allows us to identify genes that may influence the systems that are most specific to language. After discussing this work, I summarize more briefly our knowledge about the genetics of developmental disorders of autism and dyslexia.

BASICS OF GENETICS

The literature on the genetics of developmental language disorder requires a basic familiarity with genetics and some of the terms used to characterize genetic features of DLD (developmental language disorder). Thus, I begin by reviewing some basic concepts and terms in genetics that are relevant to our understanding of the literature in this area. Within the nucleus of each of our cells are structures called chromosomes, consisting of deoxyribonucleic acid (DNA) along with additional proteins. DNA is composed of complementary pairs of four bases (adenine, guanine, cytosine, and thymine). These bases pair up systematically adenine (A) with thymine (T) and guanine (G) with cytosine (C) to form a linear sequence along a sugar phosphate backbone (2′-deoxyribose) forming each chromosome (Figure 10.1). Human cells contain 23 pairs of chromosomes including 2 sex chromosomes (X, Y). The chromosomes are numbered based roughly on their size from 1 (the largest) to 22 (one of the smallest). Each chromosome contains a central hub-like structure called the centromere and extending from the centromere are two arms referred to as the p and q arms, respectively. Each arm ends at a structure called the telomere (Figure 10.2). Each member of the chromosome pair contains genetic information from one parent. The pair of chromosomes contains the individual's genomic information (genotype) for that chromosome. Genomic information on one chromosome is referred to as a haplotype. The location of genetic sequences on chromosomes is referenced to the chromosome number, the arm of the chromosome along with a numbered region based on bands revealed through staining and numbered from the centromere to the telomere. Thus, region 2q11 refers to a region close to the centromere on the q (shorter) arm of chromosome 2.

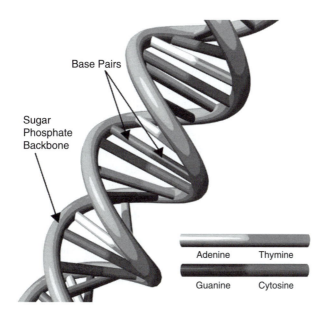

FIGURE 10.1 A segment of DNA showing the arrangement of complementary base pairs arranged along a sugar phosphate backbone.

Our interest in chromosomal maps becomes relevant because genes occupy places or loci on chromosomes, and locating where they are and what they do occupies a large part of molecular genetics. The term *gene* existed long before its biological basis was known. Once biologists learned of Mendel's findings that inheritance of traits was particulate rather than blended, the term gene came to be used to refer to this basic particulate unit of hereditary information. We now know that this information is carried via sequences of DNA, so a gene is a physical structure in a particular region on a chromosome that contains this hereditary information. The information coded by genes usually concerns the structure of proteins;

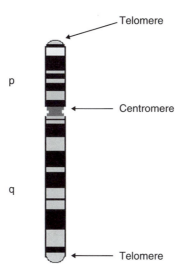

FIGURE 10.2 A schematic diagram of a chromosome showing the two arms labeled *p* and *q*, along with the location of the telomere and centromere. The black and gray bands are the product of staining.

however, recent findings concerning gene expression have begun to place an increased emphasis on genetic coding for RNA as well (Gerstein et al., 2007). Genes and proteins are given the same name, and since these names are often lengthy, they are abbreviated. In reference to genes and proteins in humans, it is common to differentiate between these abbreviations by using italics and upper case for the gene (for example, the Brain Derived Neurotrophic Factor gene is *BDNF*) and nonitalicized capital letters for the protein (BDNF). As shown in Figure 10.3, these blocks of DNA forming genes contain sequences that are described as coding sequences, or exons. Exons contain information about the proteins to be produced by the cell. Interspersed among the exons are sequences that do not code for proteins, called introns. At both ends of the gene are regulatory sequences (promoters and enhancers) that initiate and control the expression of the gene. In between the sequences that comprise genes are sequences of DNA that appear to have no function and are called intergenic DNA. This intergenic DNA and the introns are collectively called noncoding DNA.

The process of making proteins from the genetic information is fairly complex and involves several steps. A key element in this process is a chemical called ribonucleic acid (RNA) that is very similar to DNA. The difference between these two chemicals is that RNA uses a base element uracil (U), in place of the base unit of thymine that forms DNA. RNA provides the means by which the information regarding protein structure is transferred from the chromosome to mechanisms outside the nucleus called ribosomes, which produce proteins. The first step in this process is the creation of an RNA sequence that contains the complementary base units of the DNA in one of the two strands, except where uracil is used in place of thymine. This can be seen in Figure 10.3, where the sequence TAC is transcribed as AUG. This primary RNA transcript contains noncoding intron information as well that is edited out in a translation process to form mRNA, which then moves outside the nucleus, where it is read by the ribosome in order to synthesize the protein. This process is shown in Figure 10.4. The protein products can either go on to aid in the biochemical operations of the cell and thus are called structural proteins, or they can return to the nucleus to interact with the DNA in controlling the transcription of other genes and as such are called transcription factors. Transcription factors are proteins that can bind to DNA at either promoter or enhancer regions. These factors regulate transcription and determine the amount of protein produced by the gene. Later, I discuss the transcription factor called FOXP2, which is associated with speech and language disorders.

The protein structure information contained in the exons uses a code involving base triplets called codons (see Figure 10.3). Each codon encodes the information for a

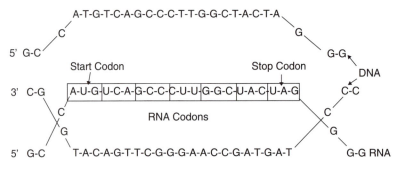

FIGURE 10.3   Transcription of base pair sequence information from a 3′ strand of DNA into a 5′ strand of RNA. The base sequence of the RNA is the same as the 5′ strand, with the exception that uracil is present in the RNA and thymine is present in the DNA. The codon structure of the RNA is shown as blocks of three base pairs.

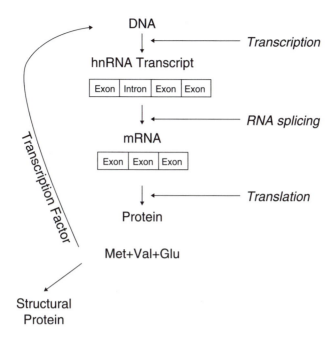

FIGURE 10.4   A schematic of the steps involved in transcribing information from DNA to the sequence of amino acids forming a protein. The product of the transcription of DNA into a heterogeneous nuclear RNA transcript (hnRNA) is shown to include noncoding information in the form of an intron. The hnRNA is converted into mRNA through RNA splicing, during which the noncoding information is deleted—which, along with some additional molecular changes, results in mature mRNA. The mRNA then moves out of the nucleus, where it enters into the process of protein synthesis performed by the ribosomes. The protein product may then be employed by the cell for functional purposes (structural protein) or return to the nucleus and interact with DNA in the form of a transcription factor.

particular amino acid. Proteins are made of amino acid, so a codon sequence spells out the amino acid sequence of a protein. The number of possible triplet "word forms" that can be generated from the four base pairs is 64 (4 base pairs taken to the 3rd power); however, there are only 20 amino acids. It turns out, several different sequences can code for the same amino acid, thus UCG, UCC, UCA, and UCU code for the amino acid serine. Also, some codons serve as controls for transcription rather than coding for amino acids. For instance the sequences UAA, UAG and UGA indicate that transcription should stop at this point so these are called stop codons.

So far, I have characterized genes as if they come in only one flavor, but since biology thrives on variation, this is far from true. Genes come in different varieties. These variations may result in different variations in the protein product, but they do not always do so. Some variations in codons result in the same functional product. The different forms of a given gene that do result in different proteins are called alleles. Thus each allelic variant of a gene will be associated with a different molecular phenotype. A phenotype refers to all the biological properties of the organism, including chemical, structural, and behavioral attributes. Not all phenotypic variations are the result of allelic variations, but all allelic variations will result in phenotypic differences. In fact, because we have two copies of each gene, our phenotype will be the result of the interaction of each allele. If the alleles of a particular gene are the same for an individual, this person is homozygous at this locus. If the person has different alleles of the same gene, then the person is heterozygous at that locus. Alleles do not always have an equal effect on the phenotype. If one allele determines the phenotype when present, it is called a dominant allele. Alleles that have no effect in the presence of the dominant allele are called recessive. Alleles whose effect adds together are said to be additive.

As mentioned earlier, alleles represent variations in gene function. These variations enter into the genome via mutations, which can be of several forms. All forms of mutations involve some alteration in the DNA base pairs of a gene. Some mutations are silent in that they do not result in a different phenotype and thus do not result in a different allele, while other changes can result in phenotypic differences. Some mutations change the characteristics of an exon. If this mutation results in a different amino acid sequence, it is called a missense mutation, since it changes the meaning of the codons. A mutation that results in a stop codon early in the exon sequence will cause the abnormal termination of transcription and is termed a nonsense mutation. This process results in a protein that is shorter than normal and is likely to function differently. Mutations can also involve the addition or deletion of base pairs. These additions or deletions can result in a frameshift of the spelling of the codons so that different amino acids are produced or can again result in a stop codon. Large deletions can involve the elimination of one or more genes, as is found in Williams syndrome, and lengthy increases can result in the disruption of a gene, as in the case of fragile X syndrome.

Most mutations are so small that they cannot be seen by standard microscopy and therefore require molecular methods (e.g., chemical assays) to be identified. Large-scale changes can be seen under a microscope with appropriate cell culturing and either dying or radiographic labeling. These changes can be thought of as involving the chromosome rather than the genes; the study of mutations involving chromosomes is called cytogenetics. Cytogenetic changes of the genome may involve either the loss of a chromosome (monosomy) or the addition of an extra chromosome (usually trisomy). Chromosomes can also involve rearrangements whereby one chromosome breaks at some point and is rejoined in an inverted fashion, thus forming an inversion. Rearrangements can involve pieces of two or more chromosomes breaking and trading places to form novel (derived) chromosomal combinations; this is referred to as a translocation. Finally, as noted earlier, large pieces of DNA can be deleted from a chromosome. In the case of chromosomal arrangements, there may be no functional result so long as the break points do not involve a gene or so long as there is no deletion of all or part of a gene at the breakpoint.

Recall that I said earlier that genes are the basic unit of inheritance. This capacity of inheritance in humans involves the sexual combination and transmission of genetic information from one generation to another. Leaving out many details, the important aspect of this process is that of recombination, which occurs when gametes (sperm and ova) are formed during meiosis. During this process the chromosomes (one from the father and one from the mother) each duplicate themselves, and at one point these duplicated sets of chromosomes pair up to form homologous pairs. Homologous in biology refers to things that are similar because they share a common biologic ancestor. When paired like this, portions of DNA sequences can switch (cross over or recombine) between homologous pairs. Remember that each pair contains DNA from one or the other parent. By allowing this exchange, the resulting chromosome will contain a mixture of paternal and maternal DNA. This is nature's way of shuffling the genetic decks of cards across generations, providing for another way to create variability in organisms beyond mutations. This recombination process has been very useful for genetic research methods, because DNA loci that are located near each other on a chromosome are likely to travel together from one generation to the next. The further apart genes or DNA sequences are on the chromosome, the more likely they will be to be separated through recombination. Thus, the probability of a recombination event separating two loci and the physical distance on a chromosome are related. Thus, the extent to which two loci on a chromosome travel together and hence are near or far from each is termed linkage. Loci that are tightly linked are close to each other; genes that are loosely linked would be far apart on a chromosome. If genes are on different chromosomes, they are not linked at all. Phenotypes can be linked to a locus. In this case, the phenotype is the result of a genotype at a locus. If this phenotype travels through generations with a known DNA marker, the phenotype or disease is linked to the marker locus. Thus, male-pattern baldness is linked to the Y-chromosome in that it travels with the Y-chromosome over generations.

For the time being, this is enough genetics, and we can move on to talking about the genetics of language development and language disorders, beginning with studies of SLI.

NONMOLECULAR EVIDENCE OF GENETIC INFLUENCES ON SLI

The questions asked regarding the genetic basis of any phenotype begin with whether the phenotype is genetically influenced. Initially, we are not likely to look for specific genes influencing the phenotype; rather, we ask if there is indirect evidence of a genetic influence on the phenotype. To answer this question, we can test whether there is covariation between the phenotypic similarity and genetic similarity within sets of individuals who vary in their biological relationship. Therefore, investigators use the natural variation of gene sharing among relatives to be indirect reflections of genetic sources of variance and couple this with variance in phenotypic resemblance. Several types of studies can be conducted to provide converging evidence that genes may influence the phenotype. The study designs differ with respect to the specific family members in the study. Many of these study designs have been used with children with developmental language disorders, and we will therefore discuss the methods in conjunction with the findings for these designs.

Familial Aggregation

If a phenotype is genetically influenced, it should run in biological families. Thus, if we sample a family because a family member (called the index case or proband) has the phenotype (blue eyes or poor language ability), then the close biological relatives of the proband will be more likely to have this trait than would be found in a population of unrelated individuals. For example, if blue eyes are found to occur in 8% of unrelated individuals but in 20% of first-degree family members of blue-eyed probands, and this difference is statistically significant, eye color runs in families. Similarly, if we were to sample probands according their phenotype (blue eyes or brown eyes) and then look at eye color in the first-degree relatives, then we would expect the distribution of eye color in each set of families to differ significantly according to the eye color of the probands if it were genetically influenced. If an association is demonstrated, the phenotype is familial. All phenotypes that are genetically influenced should be familial, but not all familial phenotypes are genetically influenced. Religious beliefs are familial, but certainly are not genetic. Therefore, familiality provides evidence for genetic effects but is by no means conclusive.

Evidence for the familial aggregation of SLI can be found dating back to T. Ingram (1959), who noted that specific disorders of speech and language presented a familial character suggestive of a genetic etiology. Systematic studies directed toward testing such a genetic hypothesis are of more recent origin. Much of this work used a family history method to test whether SLI aggregates in families. Because it is difficult to ask family members to be particularly specific with regard to spoken language, some of these studies asked about speech and reading problems (Beitchman, Hood, & Inglis, 1992; Lewis, Ekelman, & Aram, 1989; Neils & Aram, 1986; Rice, Haney, & Wexler, 1998; Tallal, Ross, & Curtiss, 1989; Tomblin, 1989; van der Lely & Stollwerck, 1996; Whitehurst et al., 1991). Figure 10.5 summarizes the findings of these studies. There is quite a bit of variability in the rates of these disorders, but this might be expected in studies where the phenotype varies. In all cases but the Whitehurst study, the differences between the rates of impairment in the families of the SLI probands were significantly greater than that between the control probands who had normal speech and language. It would appear from these data that having a first-degree relative with a specific speech and language impairment increases by around a factor of 4 your chances of also being affected. A couple of studies have reported the rate of impairment in family members where the determination of SLI was based on testing the family members. Tomblin (1996) reported that 21% of first-degree family members of probands with SLI were also SLI. This study did not include a control group, but if the population prevalence for SLI is around 7% (Tomblin et al., 1997), then SLI is about three times more common in first-degree relatives than would be expected among unrelated individuals. Recently, Tallal and colleagues (Tallal et al., 2001) also tested family members of SLI probands and probands with normal language status. They reported a rate of 31% SLI in the families of the SLI probands and 7.1% in the control families. Thus, SLI in a family increases the risk for SLI in first-degree relatives by a factor of 4.4.

Twin Studies

Although family aggregation studies provide suggestive evidence that genes may play a role in a phenotype, the environment can cause aggregation as well. There is a special type of family relationship—twinning—that provides a means of separating out the environmental and genetic effects. There are two kinds of twins: dizygotic (DZ) twins are genetically like any other sibship in that, on average, they share 50% of their genes, whereas monozygotic (MZ) twins are genetic clones in that they share all their genes. In both cases, twins share the same environment, both *in utero* and to a large extent after birth. This pattern of differential genetic variation between MZ (100%) and DZ (50%) pairs across twin set types and similarity of environmental exposure for both twin types provides a natural experiment.

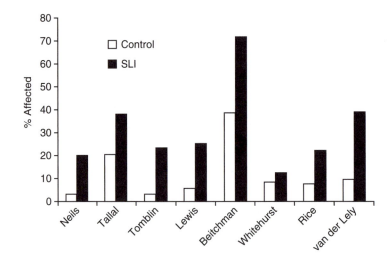

FIGURE 10.5 The rate of language impairment in family members of probands without language impairment contrasted with probands with SLI.

Thus, if a phenotype is genetically influenced, it should be more similar between MZ twins than between DZ twins. If the phenotype being studied is categorical, as in the case of clinical diagnosis (+/− affected), or qualitative (straight vs. curly hair), this between-twin similarity can be represented as concordance. Concordance represents the proportion of twins who have the same phenotype. If a qualitative trait is genetically influenced, the concordance rate in MZ twins should be higher than in DZ twins. When the phenotype is quantitative, the similarity can be represented by regression-based statistics. The magnitude of the difference in phenotypic correlation between twins as a function of twin type is called heritability and provides an index of the proportion of the phenotype variance across individuals that is attributable to genetic factors. For quantitative traits from a broad sample of twins, heritability (h^2) can be represented by doubling the difference between the correlation of MZ twins and DZ twins [$h^2 = 2*(r_{MZ} - r_{DZ})$]. We need to understand that this method represents what is called broad sense heritability, because it represents the total effect of genes on the phenotype, including those instances where alleles have a dominant relationship between each other.

Commonly in SLI research, a quantitative phenotype is used to create an impaired group by selecting individuals at the low end of the distribution of language ability. The standard method for computing heritability based on correlation assumes that the distribution of the phenotype is normal, but cutting off a tail of the distribution violates this assumption. An alternative measure of heritability, called group differences heritability (h^2_g), has been developed for this purpose. In this case, pairs with at least one twin with a score in the tail of the distribution are selected. The twin with a low score is considered the proband. The co-twin is then measured on the phenotype. When this is done across MZ and DZ twins, it is possible to examine whether the DZ co-twins regress toward the general population means to a greater extent than do MZ co-twins. If the trait is heritable, then the MZ co-twins should also have deviant scores that are similar to the MZ proband, whereas the DZ co-twins should be much more like the average individual in the population. Group differences heritability is different from individual differences heritability because the regression in h^2_g concerns a static that applies to the particular group sampled because of scores that fall outside the particular cut-off used.

Twin Studies of SLI   The twin method has been used to test the hypothesis that developmental language disorders are genetically influenced. Concordance rates for SLI were reported in several of these studies. Lewis and Thompson (1992) reported concordance rates of 86% for MZ twins and 48% for DZ twins for a phenotype of clinical identification of speech or language impairment. Bishop, North, and Donlan (1995) reported the results of a twin study of specific speech and language impairments. Using the diagnostic standard of DSM-III-R for SLI, they reported a probandwise concordance of .46 and .70 for the DZ and MZ twins, respectively. Tomblin and Buckwalter (1998) looked at pairs of twins one of whom was a language-impaired proband and found a concordance of .96 for the MZ pairs and .69 for the DZ pairs. Thus, the pattern of higher concordance for MZ than DZ was found, suggesting a genetic influence on SLI.

Some of these studies used quantitative measures of language development, and thus group differences heritability estimates for poor language development could be computed. In one the first of these studies (Bishop et al., 1995), heritability was estimated for the four language measures employed. High h^2_g values in the range of .56 to above 1.0 were obtained for each language measure. These same authors reported a h^2_g of greater than 1.0 for these twins on a nonword-repetition task, suggesting that phonological memory may be strongly genetically influenced. Shortly after this, Tomblin and Buckwalter (1998) reported an h^2_g of .45 for SLI in school-age children, and Dale and colleagues (1998) reported h^2_g

of .73 for delays in vocabulary development of 2-year-olds as a phenotype. The Dale et al. study used children from a large longitudinal study—the Twins Early Development Study (TEDS)—where two indices of environmental effects could be estimated in the twins. In this study the extent to which common environmental experiences contributed to twin resemblance on vocabulary was estimated to be .18, and the unique environmental contributions to vocabulary was .09. Thus, by the end of the 1990s it became clear that the aggregation of developmental language impairments in families was likely to be based in part on genetic factors. The fact that heritability was usually less than 1.0 and that in the TEDS study a direct estimate of shared environment was 0.18 also reminds us that nongenetic factors also are likely to play a role in SLI.

An important by-product of genetic research in general and twin studies in particular is that the manner in which the phenotype is characterized is vital to the success of the research. Therefore, research examining SLI in twins has examined different ways of defining the phenotype. One of these issues pertains to the longstanding question of whether nonverbal skills should be considered in the diagnosis of a language impairment (Cole, Dale, & Mills, 1992; Lahey, 1990). Several studies have examined whether a phenotype that does not require that SLI include some kind of discrepancy between language and performance IQ is more heritable than one that requires such a discrepancy. In general, the results of these studies suggest that higher heritability is found when SLI does not require a performance IQ discrepancy than when the discrepancy is required (Bishop et al., 1995; Eley, Dale, Bishop, Price, & Plomin, 2001; Hayiou-Thomas, Oliver, & Plomin, 2005). Associated with this has been the question of whether the genes responsible for language also affect nonverbal performance. This question has been addressed in different ways in the TEDS study. The general pattern to the findings shows a genetic overlap between language and nonverbal development and deficits (Alarcon, Plomin, Fulker, Corley, & DeFries, 1999; Purcell et al., 2001). This conclusion may need to be qualified on the basis of studies of twins that provided evidence of unique genetic effects on language in twins under 3 years of age (Dale, Dionne, Eley, & Plomin, 2000; Price et al., 2000) and a shift from a unique genetic influence on language at around age 2 to a shared genetic influence on language and nonlanguage development at age 3 (Young, Schmitz, Corley, & Fulker, 2001). Thus, there may be a specific genetic contribution to early stages of language development that diminishes with age.

Another persistent question regarding developmental language disorders concerns whether SLI results from genes that cause poor language performance but do not contribute to individual differences in normal language abilities. This question has been addressed using the TEDS sample. In general the findings show that h^2_g increases as severity of SLI increases, and the heritability of SLI is greater than that found for individual differences in the normal range (Spinath, Price, Dale, & Plomin, 2004; Viding et al., 2004). Bishop (2005) also has reported evidence that a unique gene effect may contribute to the difficulties children with SLI have with obligatory marking of finiteness on main clauses. Thus, it may be that there are genes or mutations of genes the presence of which contributes to SLI. If so, finding these genes could aid in our understanding of SLI.

MOLECULAR GENETIC STUDIES OF SLI

The research from family studies, twin studies, and adoption studies all points to an involvement of genes in SLI. These research methods have one thing in common: none of them actually studied the genotype of the individuals being studied. Instead, the genetic influences in these studies are manipulated indirectly via biological relationships. Advances in molecular genetics have now enabled researchers to directly measure the genotypes of large numbers of individuals and at many locations on the genome. It is now possible to use two alternative approaches to search for genes that are responsible for SLI.

The first approach, referred to as positional cloning, takes advantage of the fact that recombination across generations results in alleles close together that are less likely to be separated by a recombination event than are alleles that are far apart. If a gene influences phenotypic variation, then markers (genes or simply sequences of "noncoding DNA") far apart are going to be less likely to be found traveling across generations together than markers that are close to the gene of interest. If we can find a genetic marker that travels with the phenotype, we can infer that it is close to—linked to—the causal gene and that the causal gene is close to the marker. If we look at enough markers, we can begin to narrow down the location and ultimately locate the gene that is responsible (at least in part) for the phenotype. Positional cloning methods do not require that we have any idea as to what the gene does to produce the disorder. Once identified, the gene can be studied with regard to its protein product, and then its role in the phenotype can be determined.

The alternative molecular genetic strategy is the candidate gene approach. In this case, one begins with an understanding of the nature of the phenotype and the current knowledge about genes and their products. The drugs that are used to treat schizophrenia often target the dopamine receptors. Thus, candidate genes for schizophrenia would be genes involved with the dopaminergic system. A gene involved in this system could be selected and individuals with and without schizophrenia could be genotyped with regard to this gene. If the gene is involved, the distribution of alleles would be different in individuals with and without schizophrenia.

The FOXP2 Gene and SLI

A discussion of the molecular genetics of developmental language disorders needs to begin with one gene, the *FOXP2* gene, which has been associated with developmental speech and language impairment. The discovery of the *FOXP2* gene provides an example of how both positional cloning and candidate gene methods are used to understand a genetically based disorder. Much of what is known about the phenotype of *FOXP2* has come from a three-generation family (KE) consisting of 37 members, 15 of whom had severe speech and language impairment (Vargha-Khadem et al., 1998).

The first published description of affected individuals in the KE family described them as having apraxia of speech and expressive and receptive language problems (Hurst, Baraitser, Auger, Graham, & Norell, 1990). Soon afterward Gopnik and colleagues (Crago & Gopnik, 1994; Gopnik, 1990; Gopnik & Crago, 1991) also described them as having a specific grammatical deficit involving rule-based morphosyntax. Vargha-Khadem et al. (1998) subsequently described these affected individuals as having prominent oral facial apraxia and expressive language impairment. A genome-wide scan of the members of the KE family resulted in a strong linkage signal in the 7q31 region, which was then referred to as the SPCH1 region (Fisher, Vargha-Khadem, Watkins, Monaco, & Pembrey, 1998). The pattern of transmission in this family was consistent with a single gene that was transmitted in a dominant fashion.

Soon after the SPCH1 region had been localized, an independent case with a speech and language disorder who had a balanced translocation in the SPCH1 was found, and markers in the region of this breakpoint were linked to the speech and language affection status of the KE family members (Lai et al., 2000). With the region narrowed, Lai, Fisher, Hurst, Vargha-Khadem, and Monaco (2001) used sequencing methods in this region and found that it contained a gene with a forkhead box binding domain placing it in the family of transcription genes called *FOXP*. Thus, *FOXP2* can be viewed as a gene that produces a protein that functions as a transcription factor. The forkhead box binding domain in the *FOXP2* protein allows this transcription factor to bind to a regulatory site on other genes, which, in turn, produce other proteins. Sequencing of the *FOXP2* gene within the KE family revealed that the 15 affected family members shared a single base-pair substitution mutation in an exon that resulted in an arginine-to-histidine substitution in the protein produced and thus consisted of a misense. This gene is now known to be a transcriptional repressor gene (Li, Weidenfeld, & Morrisey, 2004; Shu, Yang, Zhang, Lu, & Morrisey, 2001) that is expressed in multiple organ systems, including the brain. Studies of *FOXP2* expression in the brain of mouse, rat, and humans show that it is expressed in several brain structures including the cortical plate and basal ganglia, including the striatum, thalamus, inferior olives, and cerebellum (Lai, Gerrelli, Monaco, Fisher, & Copp, 2003; Takahashi, Liu, Hirokawa, & Takahashi, 2003). Studies of the function of the FOXP2 protein that results from the mutation found in the KE family have revealed that this mutation impedes the transport of the FOXP2 protein across the nuclear membrane back into the nucleus, where it should perform its regulatory function, and also limits binding of this protein to DNA target sequences (Vernes et al., 2006). Thus, the mutation results in these individuals having roughly half the amount of functional FOXP2 protein for repression of the target gene expression.

Studies of the behavioral and neurological characteristics of the members of the KE family with the *FOXP2* mutation have shown impairment of the same brain systems where *FOXP2* expression was found. Vargha-Khadem's group (Watkins, Dronkers, & Vargha-Khadem, 2002) compared the affected family members with the unaffected family members with regard to intelligence, language, and limb and oral facial praxis. The affected family members performed more poorly than did the unaffected family members in all but limb praxis. A discriminant analysis indicated that nonword repetition of complex words was the strongest predictor of group membership. Structural brain imaging by this same group (Watkins, Vargha-Khadem, et al., 2002) revealed abnormalities of either elevated or reduced gray matter density in the caudate nucleus, putamen, cerebellum, temporal cortex, inferior frontal gyrus, motor cortex, and the inferior frontal gyrus. Further, several of these regions, particularly the caudate, were shown to be bilaterally abnormal (Belton, Salmond, Watkins, Vargha-Khadem, & Gadian, 2003). Functional imaging showed underactivation of the left (Broca's area) and right inferior frontal gyri and in the putamen. Overactivation during language tasks was also observed in the posterior parietal, occipital, and postcentral regions that are not normally associated with language (Liegeois et al., 2003). The involvement of these brain systems has led Watkins, Dronkers and Vargha-Khadem (2002) to conclude that with regard to *FOXP2*, "the gene product interferes with the normal development of the caudate nucleus (and possibly other components of the motor system) and that this, in turn, impairs procedural learning (p. 463)." In this regard, these authors view the motor impairment as primary and the procedural learning problem as secondary. Ullman (2001) has argued that systems within the cortico-striatal system serve procedural learning, which, in turn, supports grammatical development. Thus, pattern of language impairments in the KE family as well as those with SLI suggest a procedural learning deficit (Ullman & Pierpont, 2005). The procedural memory systems influenced by FOXP2 may be more directly involved in SLI than in the Watkins account.

Soon after the discovery of the *FOXP2* gene, researchers began asking whether this gene can account for speech and language problems in individuals outside the KE family. The research group studying the KE family has not found mutations of *FOXP2* in a large sample of children with SLI (Newbury, Bonora, et al., 2002). Likewise, Meaburn, Dale, Craig, and Plomin (2002) searched for the KE family *FOXP2* mutation in a large twin sample and did not find this particular mutation. Recently, my lab found no evidence of an association between the *FOXP2* markers and SLI, nor did we find evidence of mutations in exon 14 of *FOXP2* in a group of children with SLI (O'Brien, Zhang, Nishimura, Tomblin, & Murray, 2003). Thus, although *FOXP2* appears to affect neural systems important for normal speech and language development, it does not appear to be a very common cause for SLI. MacDermot and colleagues (2005) have cautioned that few of these studies have sequenced all coding regions of *FOXP2*. Mutations in other regions of *FOXP2* may be more common and may contribute to a greater proportion of speech and language disorders than these studies imply.

Although mutations in *FOXP2* may not be the source of many instances of developmental language impairment, at the time of this writing, five unrelated sets (families or individuals) with *FOXP2* abnormalities accompanied by speech and language disorder have been reported. As noted earlier, the first case of an individual outside the KE family was the child whose balanced 5;7 translocation involving a breakpoint in *FOXP2* aided in locating the *FOXP2*. This individual (CS) was described as having a severe oral facial apraxia that also involved speech and language impairment (Lai et al., 2000). There is little information about the characteristics of the breakpoint on chromosome 5, and therefore we cannot be sure whether other genes are involved.

An adult (AA) with a deletion covering the entire region of 7q31 including *FOXP2* and other genes was described by Liegeois and colleagues (2001). AA was described as having severe verbal and orofacial dyspraxia, as well as impairments of expressive vocabulary and grammar. Abnormal fMRI and ERP results were found in verbal tasks. Zeesman and colleagues (2004) recently reported one child with a deletion in the 7q31 region including *FOXP2*. This child was described as having dyspraxia that included an inability to cough, sneeze, or laugh. She was also found to have dysmorphic features and a mild developmental delay. Thus, in the case of AA and Zeesman's patient, the deletions were large enough to have affected genes in addition to *FOXP2*. Therefore, similar to the CS case, some of the phenotype features in these individuals might be due to other gene effects. Recently, my colleagues and I located a mother and daughter (BT) who have a balanced (7;13) translocation with a breakpoint in *FOXP2* (Tomblin, Shriberg, Murray, Patil, & Williams, 2004). Both mother and daughter have low normal nonverbal cognitive ability, but language skills are poorer than nonverbal function and the grammatical abilities of these individuals were found to be particularly affected. Speech production problems characteristic of motor impairments were also found, as was evidence of poor procedural learning. Most recently, MacDermot and colleagues (2005) reported the results of mutational screening of 49 individuals with signs of apraxia of speech. Three instances of point mutations were found, and one of these mutations was also found in a sibling and the mother of the children. These three individuals had noteworthy speech and language problems. Another research group has been recruiting patients with either abnormal *FOXP2* or with developmental verbal apraxia and has reported on 22 of these individuals, 13 of whom the authors describe as having developmental verbal apraxia (DVA; Feuk et al., 2006). Few details were provided regarding the speech and language characteristics of these individuals; however, the DVA status coincides with reports of late talking and articulation disorder. More recently, Lennon and colleagues (Lennon et al., 2007) have also recently reported a case of a child with a deletion in the 7q31 region including *FOXP2* but also including *WNT*—a gene that has been associated with autism. This child demonstrated dysmorphic features and mild-to-moderate mental retardation. Some signs of oral facial motor impairment were noted. These features, along with the language impairment, were interpreted to be evidence of apraxia.

Across these studies, some common phenotypic features can be seen, and these features are similar to those reported for the KE family. In all cases, a motor speech problem is reported. In most cases this problem has been described as apraxia of speech. In the case of the BT family, apraxia is less apparent, and instead the motor impairment may be a dysarthria. In the BT family and the KE family, marked grammatical problems have been described that exceed the expectations based on intelligence. These common features suggest that the genes affected by the FOXP2 transcription factor are responsible for brain systems that affect motor speech and language abilities, with grammar possibly more affected than vocabulary. As more instances of *FOXP2* impairment are found, the details of this phenotype should become clearer.

Positional Cloning Studies for SLI

So far, *FOXP2* represents the singular success case of molecular genetic research into developmental speech and language disorder. Given that there were reasonable doubts as to whether genes with such strong effects on speech and language could be found, we should view this singular result as encouragement to keep looking for more genes associated with language. For one thing, we know that *FOXP2* regulates other genes, and mutations of these genes could be much more common in the populations of language-impaired individuals. One of the principal ways of finding genes that contribute to phenotypes has been the genome-wide linkage study. In such a study, a panel of several thousand genetic markers that have a known location on the genome is used to genotype large numbers of family members in families where developmental language disorder is found. These studies ask whether any of these markers is linked to the language disorder phenotype. In the past three years there have been reports of two genome-wide scans for developmental language disorders. Bartlett and colleagues (Bartlett et al., 2002) reported suggestive linkage of a receptive-language impairment phenotype to a locus on 2p in family members from 5 families originally ascertained for schizophrenia. A linkage of reading to 13q was also reported in this study. The SLI consortium in England (Newbury, Ishikawa-Brush, et al., 2002) performed a genome-wide scan that resulted in loci on chromosome 16q (*SLI1*) and 19q showing linkage to quantitative verbal measures. The language trait linked to chromosome 19q (*SLI2*) was one that represented the children's ability to express words and sentences. The chromosome 16q locus was linked to a measure of phonological working memory requiring remembering and repeating nonsense words. Previous work has shown that phonological memory is a sensitive indicator of SLI and may be an important cognitive skill for language development (Conti-Ramsden & Hesketh, 2003; Dollaghan & Campbell, 1998; Ellis Weismer et al., 2000). Newbury and colleagues reported a replication of the *SLI1* linkage findings for phonological memory, but not for *SLI2* (Newbury et al., 2004). Recently, Monaco (2007) have reanalyzed the data within the SLI consortium using multivariate statistical methods to allow the several language and reading measures to be combined. These results provided further support to the association of *SLI1* to phonological processing, word-reading, and spelling traits. The *SLI2* locus on chromosome 19 was also found to be associated with a general oral language trait. Additionally, this study yielded suggestive evidence of linkage of language to a region on chromosome 10. Thus, two independent genome-wide screens have been performed using language and language-related phenotypes. Neither replicated linkages of the other; however, a within-laboratory replication of *SLI1* has been found, suggesting that this locus contains a gene that influences phonological processing abilities.

Candidate Gene Studies and SLI

In our lab, we used a candidate gene approach to search for possible genes involved with SLI. This method tests for the association between a person having SLI and having a particular allele of a gene. Among the candidate genes studied was the *CFTR* gene that is responsible for cystic fibrosis, and, somewhat surprisingly, an association between *CFTR* and SLI was found (Tomblin, Nishimura, Zhang, & Murray, 1998). *CFTR* was an unlikely gene for SLI, since none of our children had cystic fibrosis. Therefore, the association was probably related to another gene in the region which happens to contain *FOXP2*. Once *FOXP2* was discovered, it became a very good candidate. Thus, we examined *FOXP2* along with additional markers in the same region. As was noted earlier, we did not find that *FOXP2* was associated with SLI, but we did find an association of SLI to two markers flanking *FOXP2* in addition to the *CFTR* association, suggesting that a language-related locus other than *FOXP2* may reside nearby (O'Brien et al., 2003). These findings are of particular interest because the region in which *FOXP2* lies has also been found to be linked to autism in two separate studies (Barrett et al., 1999; International Molecular Genetic Study of Autism Consortium, 1998). This coincidence of SLI and autism at this locus is not altogether surprising. Family members of children with autism show elevated rates of language delay, reading retardation, articulation disorder, and spelling difficulties (Bolton et al., 1994), and there is evidence of greater rates of autism among the siblings of children with developmental language impairment (Tomblin, Hafeman, & O'Brien, 2003). Tyson, McGillivray, Chijiwa, and Rajcan-Separovic (2004) have reported a microdeletion at 7q31.3 in a child with a complex balanced translocation involving chromosomes 5, 6, and 7. This child presented with language impairment and also cleft palate. These authors concluded that their results supported the previous findings (O'Brien et al., 2003) that a gene concerned with language disorders lies in the 7q31.2–31.3 region.

We can conclude at this point that the genetic basis of SLI represents the threshold of genuine insights into the specific genes that influence the individual differences in language ability that mark both normal language development and SLI. If this promise bears fruit, we will be able to use this knowledge to understand the pathways from genes to brain systems and language. As research on the genetics of other forms of developmental language disorders proceeds, we are likely to discover shared and complementary genetic pathways into language systems. With this in mind, I will survey the status of genetic research on dyslexia and autism.

GENETICS OF DYSLEXIA

SLI and dyslexia are both language-based learning disorders that run together in families and are often thought of as the same disorder. Both are conceptually similar in that they refer to poor achievement in the absence of frank sensory or intellectual deficits (see chapter 5 by Shaywitz et al.). Dyslexia has generally been assumed to be a particular subtype of reading disorder, although the degree and manner in which dyslexia has been differentiated from other forms of poor reading has remained a key aspect of research.

Like SLI, dyslexia runs in families. Based on recent family studies, reading disorder or dyslexia is found in approximately 37% of first-degree family members (Wood & Grigorenko, 2001). When contrasted with a prevalence rate of 5–9% in the general population (Shaywitz, Escobar, Shaywitz, Fletcher, & Makuch, 1992), the risk ratio is approximately 5, which is slightly higher than that found for SLI. Several twin studies have been conducted, often with regard to group differences heritability (h^2_g) of poor component reading skills in word reading, decoding of nonwords, or phonological awareness. Gayan and Olson (1999) have noted that studies of the genetic correlation across these traits is high, and thus there are likely to be common genetic roots to these skills; however, there also is evidence for unique genetic contributions to each.

Positional Cloning Studies of Dyslexia

The evidence of familial and heritable qualities of dyslexia resulted in efforts to identify its specific genetic basis using positional cloning methods. This work has had the longest history in studies of the genetics of language-related disorders and as a result has resulted in the largest array of findings. These findings have centered on five primary sites as the result of studies using linkage and association methods; these regions have been labeled *DYXn*, with the *n* value representing the order of their discovery.

DYX1   The first evidence of linkage for dyslexia was reported by Smith and colleagues (1983) to the centromere of chromosome 15. These findings were later replicated by several groups (Bisgaard, Eiberg, Moller, Niebuhr, & Mohr, 1987; Chapman et al., 2004; Grigorenko et al., 1997; Morris et al., 2000), and Taipale and colleagues (2003) identified a gene (*DYX1C1*) in this region that they believe is associated with dyslexia. However, subsequent studies have yet to provide confirmation of the role of *DYX1C1* in dyslexia.

DYX2   More consistent results, particularly for the component skills of nonword reading and phonological awareness, have pointed to a region (6p21; *DYX2*) on chromosome 6 that also contains genes for human leukocyte antigens (HLA) involved with autoimmunity linkage (Cardon et al., 1994; Fisher et al., 1999; Francks et al., 2004; Gayan et al., 1999; Grigorenko et al., 1997; Kaplan et al., 2002; Petryshen, Kaplan, & Field, 1999). Several genes in the *DYX2* region (*VMP, DCDC2, KIAA0319, TTRAP,* and *THEM2*) have been proposed as candidate genes because of the strong linkage evidence to this region (Deffenbacher et al., 2004). Particular support for two of these genes as playing a role in dyslexia has been found. One of these genes is *KIAA0319*, reported on by two studies (Cope, Harold, et al., 2005; Francks et al., 2004). However, two other studies (Meng, Smith, et al., 2005; Schumacher et al., 2006) have not replicated this association. These same studies, though they did not replicate the *KIAA0319* results, did find an association of dyslexia to *DCDC2*, which is in the same *DYX2* region. Both *DCDC2* and *KIAA0319* have been found to disrupt neural migration, and therefore it is possible that both genes play a role in dyslexia.

In addition to these two loci (*DYX1* and *DYX2*), some evidence of linkage of dyslexia to several other regions has been reported on chromosomes: 1 (*DYX8*: Grigorenko et al., 2001; Rabin et al., 1993; Tzenova, Kaplan, Petryshen, & Field, 2004); 2 (2p11; *DYX3*: Fagerheim et al., 1999; Kaminen et al., 2003; Peyrard-Janvid et al., 2004; Raskind et al., 2005;), 3 (3p12: *DYX5*: Nopola-Hemmi et al., 2001), 18 (18p11, DYX6: Fisher et al., 2002). In all but the last two loci (3p12 and 18p11), this linkage has been replicated by at least two research groups, but no region has been replicated by all those performing linkage analyses.

Recent studies have shown that several of these reading loci are also linked to speech sound disorder (*DYX5*: Stein et al., 2004; *DYX1, DYX3*: Smith et al., 2004, 2005). Thus, no gene has been definitively established as having a causal role in dyslexia; however, there is a strong likelihood that in the near future such a gene will emerge from the genetic research.

GENETICS OF AUTISM

Autism is a neurodevelopmental disorder wherein language disorder is a central feature. Individuals with autism have early delays in language development, and even among those who later develop age-appropriate grammar and vocabulary, social use of language is always affected (see chapter 3 by Gerenser). Several studies have shown that family members of children with autism have elevated rates of language impairment (see, e.g., Fombonne, Bolton, Prior, Jordan, & Rutter, 1997; Folstein & Rutter, 1977; Landa et al., 1992; Le Couteur et al., 1996) and, likewise, that children with language impairments have elevated rates of siblings with autism (Tomblin et al., 2003). Tager-Flusberg has recently provided evidence that a subgroup of children with autism may also present features of SLI (De Fosse et al., 2004; Kjelgaard & Tager-Flusberg, 2001; Roberts, Rice, & Tager-Flusberg, 2004). Thus, the etiology of autism may include causal factors that influence particular aspects of language.

During the past several decades a substantial amount of research has addressed the likely genetic bases of autism. Several studies have shown that the risk for autism to siblings of probands with autism is between 2% and 6%, which results in a relative risk ratio of between 50 and 100 (Bolton et al., 1994; Fombonne et al., 1997; Ritvo et al., 1989). Twin studies have found that concordance for autism in MZ twins runs between 60 and 90%, whereas none of the DZ twins were concordant (Bailey et al., 1995; Folstein & Rutter, 1977; Steffenburg et al., 1989). These data from family and twin studies have supported estimates as high as .90 of heritability for autism (Bailey, Phillips, & Rutter, 1996). These epidemiologic findings provide very strong evidence of a genetic basis for autism.

Positional Cloning for Autism

Motivated by the epidemiologic research, there have been several positional cloning studies for autism that have resulted in linkage to several regions across the genome (see Table 10.1). The most widely replicated findings have involved a region on chromosome 7q and 2q. The region on chromosome 7q surrounding *FOXP2* has yielded several positive linkage findings. Of particular interest to those searching for genes affecting language are the findings that in some of these studies the linkage increased as the phenotype was narrowed to emphasize language deficits (Alarcon, Cantor, Liu, Gilliam, & Geschwind, 2002; Alarcon, Yonan, Gilliam, Cantor, & Geschwind, 2005; Wassink et al., 2001). The proximity of these linkage findings to *FOXP2* led several investigators to test for mutations of *FOXP2* in autism. In two cases no association was found (Gauthier et al., 2003; Newbury, Bonora, et al., 2002; Wassink et al., 2002). However, recently Gong and colleagues have reported an association of markers within *FOXP2* to autism in a sample of Chinese individuals of Han decent (Gong et al., 2004). Thus, *FOXP2* may play a role in autism within certain ethnic populations.

TABLE 10.1   Chromosomal regions within which linkage to autism has been reported

	1q	2q	3q	6q	7q	13q	15q	16p	18q	19p
IMGSAC,[a] 1998		x			x			x		x
IMGSAC,[a] 2001		x			x			x		
Philippe et al., 1999		x		x	x			x	x	x
Beck et al., 1999					x	x				
Bass et al., 2000							x			
Auranen et al., 2002	x		x		x					
Shao et al., 2002		x	x		x		x			x
Buxbaum et al., 2001		x								

[a] IMGSAC: International Molecular Genetic Study of Autism Consortium

CANDIDATE GENES FOR AUTISM

In recent years, efforts to identify genes influencing autism have shifted from positional cloning studies such as genome-wide scans to candidate gene studies in which the candidate genes are often those implicated by the genome scans and also are involved in brain function. Mutations in the *WNT2* in the 7q31 region have been associated with autism (Wassink et al., 2001), but McCoy and colleagues (2002) did not replicate these findings. Another gene (*RELN*) is involved in the development of several CNS systems and has been shown to be associated with autism (Persico et al., 2001; Serajee, Zhong, & Huq, 2006; Skaar et al., 2005); however, other studies have not found support for this gene in autism (Bonora et al., 2003; Devlin et al., 2004; Krebs et al., 2002). Two genes in the GABA receptor complex in the 15q region have been found to be associated with autism (e.g., Buxbaum et al., 2002; Cook et al., 1998; Menold et al., 2001); however, other studies (see, e.g., Ma et al., 2005; Maestrini et al., 1999; Martin et al., 2000) have not replicated these findings. Similar mixed findings have been reported for the serotonin transporter gene *5-HTT* (also known as *SLC6A4*), where there have been at least 12 association studies (Freitag, 2007; Santangelo & Tsatsanis, 2005). Finally, the candidate gene *EN2* (engrailed 2) has received both support (Benayed et al., 2005; Gharani, Benayed, Mancuso, Brzustowicz, & Millonig, 2004) and lack of support (Zhong, Serajee, Nabi, & Huq, 2003). At this time, despite very promising evidence of replicated linkage, there appears to be no consensus regarding any particular gene that contributes to autism in the general population (Santangelo & Tsatsanis, 2005); however, several genes continue to be promising. Much of the challenge with regard to work in this area comes from the complexity of the phenotype and the need to establish measurement methods to handle this complexity.

CONCLUSIONS

A quick glance at the reference section of this chapter will show that most of the citations refer to research on the genetics of developmental disorders with a predominant involvement with language that have been conducted within the last 10 to 15 years. The trajectory of this research appears to be ever-increasing. Furthermore, there is substantial overlap across the genetic research on SLI, dyslexia, and autism, at the phenotypic level and at the genotypic level. It is likely that as this work matures, we will begin to discover genes that influence basic neurocognitive systems that, when altered, result in impaired behavioral development, including impaired language. This understanding should result in exciting new insights into fundamental mechanisms and principles governing developmental processes and into more effective modes of clinical management. We are clearly moving from a time when the genetic basis of language was speculation to a time of substantive understanding. Where we will be in even five years is difficult to guess, but we can be quite certain it will be an exciting time.

REFERENCES

Alarcon, M., Cantor, R. M., Liu, J., Gilliam, T. C., & Geschwind, D. H. (2002). Evidence for a language quantitative trait locus on chromosome 7q in multiplex autism families. *American Journal of Human Genetics, 70,* 60–71.

Alarcon, M., Plomin, R., Fulker, D. W., Corley, R., & DeFries, J. C. (1999). Molarity not modularity:

Multivariate genetic analysis of specific cognitive abilities in parents and their 16-year-old children in the Colorado Adoption Project. *Cognitive Development, 14*, 175–193.

Alarcon, M., Yonan, A. L., Gilliam, T. C., Cantor, R. M., & Geschwind, D. H. (2005). Quantitative genome scan and Ordered-Subsets Analysis of autism endophenotypes support language QTLs. *Molecular Psychiatry, 10*, 747–757.

Auranen, M., Vanhala, R., Varilo, T., Ayers, K., Kempas, E., Ylisaukko-Oja, T., et al. (2002). A genome-wide screen for autism-spectrum disorders: Evidence for a major susceptibility locus on chromosome 3q25–27. *American Journal of Human Genetics, 71*, 777–790.

Bailey, A., Le Couteur, A., Gottesman, I., Bolton, P., Simonoff, E., Yuzda, E., et al. (1995). Autism as a strongly genetic disorder: Evidence from a British twin study. *Psychological Medicine, 25*, 63–77.

Bailey, A., Phillips, W., & Rutter, M. (1996). Autism: Towards an integration of clinical, genetic, neuropsychological, and neurobiological perspectives. *Journal of Child Psychology and Psychiatry, 37*, 89–126.

Barrett, S., Beck, J. C., Bernier, R., Bisson, E., Braun, T. A., Casavant, T. L., et al. (1999). An autosomal genomic screen for autism: Collaborative linkage study of autism. *American Journal of Medical Genetics, 88*, 609–615.

Bartlett, C. W., Flax, J. F., Logue, M. W., Vieland, V. J., Bassett, A. S., Tallal, P., et al. (2002). A major susceptibility locus for specific language impairment is located on 13q21. *American Journal of Human Genetics, 71*, 45–55.

Bass, M. P., Menold, M. M., Wolpert, C. M., Donnelly, S. L., Ravan, S. A., Hauser, E. R., et al. (2000). Genetic studies in autistic disorder and chromosome 15. *Neurogenetics, 2*, 219–226.

Beitchman, J. H., Hood, J., & Inglis, A. (1992). Familial transmission of speech and language impairment: A preliminary investigation. *Canadian Journal of Psychiatry, 37*, 151–156.

Belton, E., Salmond, C. H., Watkins, K. E., Vargha-Khadem, F., & Gadian, D. G. (2003). Bilateral brain abnormalities associated with dominantly inherited verbal and orofacial dyspraxia. *Human Brain Mapping, 18*, 194–200.

Benayed, R., Gharani, N., Rossman, I., Mancuso, V., Lazar, G., Kamdar, S., et al. (2005). Support for the homeobox transcription factor gene *ENGRAILED 2* as an autism spectrum disorder susceptibility locus. *American Journal of Human Genetics, 77*, 851–868.

Bisgaard, M. L., Eiberg, H., Moller, N., Niebuhr, E., & Mohr, J. (1987). Dyslexia and chromosome-15 heteromorphism: Negative lod score in a Danish material. *Clinical Genetics, 32*, 118–119.

Bishop, D. (2005). DeFries-Fulker analysis of twin data with skewed distribution: Cautions and recommendations from a study of children's use of verb inflections. *Behavior Genetics, 35*, 479–489.

Bishop, D. V., North, T., & Donlan, C. (1995). Genetic basis of specific language impairment: evidence from a twin study. *Developmental Medicine and Child Neurology, 37*, 56–71.

Bolton, P., Macdonald, H., Pickles, A., Rios, P., Goode, S., Crowson, M., et al. (1994). A case-control family history study of autism. *Journal of Child Psychology and Psychiatry, 35*, 877–900.

Bonora, E., Beyer, K. S., Lamb, J. A., Parr, J. R., Klauck, S. M., Benner, A., et al. (2003). Analysis of reelin as a candidate gene for autism. *Molecular Psychiatry, 8*, 885–892.

Buxbaum, J. D., Silverman, J. M., Smith, C. J., Greenberg, D. A., Kilifarski, M., Reichert, J., et al. (2002). Association between a *GABRB3* polymorphism and autism. *Molecular Psychiatry, 7*, 311–316.

Buxbaum, J. D., Silverman, J. M., Smith, C. J., Kilifarski, M., Reichert, J., Hollander, E., et al. (2001). Evidence for a susceptibility gene for autism on chromosome 2 and for genetic hetero-geneity. *American Journal of Medical Genetics, 68*, 1514–1520.

Cardon, L. R., Smith, S. D., Fulker, D. W., Kimberling, W. J., Pennington, B. F., & DeFries, J. C. (1994). Quantitative trait locus for reading disability on chromosome 6. *Science, 266*, 276–279.

Chapman, N. H., Igo, R. P., Thomson, J. B., Matsushita, M., Brkanac, Z., Holzman, T., et al. (2004). Linkage analyses of four regions previously implicated in dyslexia: Confirmation of a locus on chromosome 15q. *American Journal of Medical Genetics. Part B, Neuropsychiatric Genetics, 131*, 67–75.

Cole, K. N., Dale, P. S., & Mills, P. E. (1992). Stability of the intelligence quotient–language quotient relation: Is discrepancy modeling based on a myth? *American Journal on Mental Retardation*, *97*, 131–143.

Conti-Ramsden, G., & Hesketh, A. (2003). Risk markers for SLI: A study of young language-learning children. *International Journal of Language and Communication Disorders*, *38*, 251–263.

Cook, E. H., Courchesne, R. Y., Cox, N. J., Lord, C., Gonen, D., Guter, S. J., et al. (1998). Linkage-disequilibrium mapping of autistic disorder, with 15q11–13 markers. *American Journal of Human Genetics*, *62*, 1077–1083.

Cope, N., Harold, D., Hill, G., Moskvina, V., Stevenson, J., Holmans, P., et al. (2005). Strong evidence that *KIAA0319* on chromosome 6p is a susceptibility gene for developmental dyslexia. *American Journal of Human Genetics*, *76*, 581–591.

Crago, M. B., & Gopnik, M. (1994). From families to phenotypes: Theoretical and clinical implications of research into the genetic basis of specific language impairment. In R. V. Watkins & M. L. Rice (Eds.), *Specific language impairments in children* (pp. 35–51). Baltimore: Paul H. Brookes.

Dale, P. S., Dionne, G., Eley, T. C., & Plomin, R. (2000). Lexical and grammatical development: A behavioural genetic perspective. *Journal of Child Language*, *27*, 619–642.

Dale, P. S., Simonoff, E., Bishop, D. V. M., Eley, T. C., Oliver, B., Price, T. S., et al. (1998). Genetic influence on language delay in two-year-old children. *Nature Neuroscience*, *1*, 324–328.

Deffenbacher, K. E., Kenyon, J. B., Hoover, D. M., Olson, R. K., Pennington, B. F., DeFries, J. C., et al. (2004). Refinement of the 6p21.3 quantitative trait locus influencing dyslexia: Linkage and association analyses. *Human Genetics*, *115*, 128–138.

De Fosse, L., Hodge, S. M., Makris, N., Kennedy, D. N., Caviness, V. S., McGrath, L., et al. (2004). Language-association cortex asymmetry in autism and specific language impairment. *Annals of Neurology*, *56*, 757–766.

Devlin, B., Bennett, P., Dawson, G., Figlewicz, D. A., Grigorenko, E. L., McMahon, W., et al. (2004). Alleles of a Reelin CGG repeat do not convey liability to autism in a sample from the CPEA network. *American Journal of Medical Genetics. Part B, Neuropsychiatric Genetics*, *126B*, 46–50.

Dollaghan, C., & Campbell, T. F. (1998). Nonword repetition and child language impairment. *Journal of Speech Language and Hearing Research*, *41*, 1136–1146.

Eley, T., Dale, P., Bishop, D. V. M., Price, T. S., & Plomin, R. (2001). Longitudinal analysis of components of cognitive delay: Examining the aetiology of verbal and cognitive delay in preschoolers. *Journal of Educational Psychology*, *93*, 698–707.

Ellis Weismer, S., Tomblin, J. B., Zhang, X. Y., Buckwalter, P., Chynoweth, J. G., & Jones, M. (2000). Nonword repetition performance in school-age children with and without language impairment. *Journal of Speech Language and Hearing Research*, *43*, 865–878.

Elman, J., Bates, E., Johnson, M., Karmiloff-Smith, A., Parisi, D., & Plunkett, K. (1996). *Rethinking innateness: A connectionist perspective on development*. Cambridge, MA: MIT Press.

Fagerheim, T., Raeymaekers, P., Tonnessen, F. E., Pedersen, M., Tranebjarg, L., & Lubs, H. A. (1999). A new gene (*DYX3*) for dyslexia is located on chromosome 2. *Journal of Medical Genetics*, *36*, 664–669.

Feuk, L., Kalervo, A., Lipsanen-Nyman, M., Skaug, J., Nakabayashi, K., Finucane, B., et al. (2006). Absence of a paternally inherited *FOXP2* gene in developmental verbal dyspraxia. *American Journal of Human Genetics*, *79*, 965–972.

Fisher, S. E., Francks, C., Marlow, A. J., MacPhie, I. L., Newbury, D. F., Cardon, L. R., et al. (2002). Independent genome-wide scans identify a chromosome 18 quantitative-trait locus influencing dyslexia. *Nature Genetics*, *30*, 86–91.

Fisher, S. E., Marlow, A. J., Lamb, J., Maestrini, E., Williams, D. F., Richardson, A. J., et al. (1999). A quantitative-trait locus on chromosome 6p influences different aspects of developmental dyslexia. *American Journal of Medical Genetics*, *64*, 146–156.

Fisher, S., Vargha-Khadem, F., Watkins, K., Monaco, A., & Pembrey, M. (1998). Localisation of a gene implicated in a severe speech and language disorder. *Nature Genetics*, *18*, 168–170.

Folstein, S. E., & Rutter, M. (1977). Infantile autism: A genetic study of 21 twin pairs. *Journal of Child Psychology and Psychiatry, 18*, 297–321.

Fombonne, E., Bolton, P., Prior, J., Jordan, H., & Rutter, M. (1997). A family study of autism: Cognitive patterns and levels in parents and siblings. *Journal of Child Psychology and Psychiatry, 38*, 667–683.

Francks, C., Paracchini, S., Smith, S. D., Richardson, A. J., Scerri, T. S., Cardon, L. R., et al. (2004b). A 77-kilobase region of chromosome 6p22.2 is associated with dyslexia in families from the United Kingdom and from the United States. *American Journal of Medical Genetics, 75*, 1046–1058.

Freitag, C. M. (2007). The genetics of autistic disorders and its clinical relevance: A review of the literature. *Molecular Psychiatry, 12*, 2–22.

Gauthier, J., Joober, R., Mottron, L., Laurent, S., Fuchs, M., De Kimpe, V., et al. (2003). Mutation screening of *FOXP2* in individuals diagnosed with autistic disorder. *American Journal of Medical Genetics. Part A, 118A*, 172–175.

Gayan, J., & Olson, R. K. (1999). Reading disability: Evidence for a genetic etiology. *European Child and Adolescent Psychiatry, 8*(Suppl.) 3, 52–55.

Gayan, J., Smith, S. D., Cherny, S. S., Cardon, L. R., Fulker, D. W., Brower, A. M., et al. (1999). Quantitative-trait locus for specific language and reading deficits on chromosome 6p. *American Journal of Human Genetics, 64*, 157–164.

Gerstein, M. B., Bruce, C., Rozowsky, J. S., Zheng, D., Du, J., Korbel, J. O., et al. (2007). What is a gene, post-ENCODE? History and updated definition. *Genome Research, 17*, 669–681.

Gharani, N., Benayed, R., Mancuso, V., Brzustowicz, L. M., & Millonig, J. H. (2004). Association of the homeobox transcription factor, ENGRAILED 2, with autism spectrum disorder. *Molecular Psychiatry, 9*, 540.

Gong, X. H., Jia, M. X., Ruan, Y., Shuang, M., Liu, J., Wu, S. P., et al. (2004). Association between the *FOXP2* gene and autistic disorder in Chinese population. *American Journal of Medical Genetics. Part B, Neuropsychiatric Genetics, 127B*, 113–116.

Gopnik, M. (1990). Feature-blind grammar and dysphasia. *Nature, 344*, 715.

Gopnik, M., & Crago, M. B. (1991). Familial aggregation of a developmental language disorder. *Cognition, 39*, 1–50.

Grigorenko, E. L., Wood, F. B., Meyer, M. S., Hart, L. A., Speed, W. C., Shuster, A., et al. (1997). Susceptibility loci for distinct components of developmental dyslexia on chromosomes 6 and 15. *American Journal of Human Genetics, 60*, 27–39.

Grigorenko, E. L., Wood, F. B., Meyer, M. S., Pauls, J. E. D., Hart, L. A., & Pauls, D. L. (2001). Linkage studies suggest a possible locus for developmental dyslexia on chromosome 1p. *American Journal of Medical Genetics, 105*, 120–129.

Hayiou-Thomas, M. E., Oliver, B., & Plomin, R. (2005). Genetic influences on specific versus nonspecific language impairment in 4-year-old twins. *Journal of Learning Disabilities, 38*, 222–232.

Hurst, J. A., Baraitser, M., Auger, E., Graham, F., & Norell, S. (1990). An extended family with a dominantly inherited speech disorder. *Developmental Medicine and Child Neurology, 32*, 704–717.

Ingram, T. T. S. (1959). Specific developmental disorders of speech in childhood. *Brain, 82*, 450–454.

International Molecular Genetic Study of Autism Consortium (1998). A full genome screen for autism with evidence for linkage to a region on chromosome 7q. *Human Molecular Genetics, 7*, 571–578.

International Molecular Genetic Study of Autism Consortium (2001). A genomewide screen for autism: Strong evidence for linkage to chromosomes 2q, 7q, and 16q. *American Journal of Human Genetics, 69*, 570–581.

Kaminen, N., Hannula-Jouppi, K., Kestila, M., Lahermo, P., Muller, K., Kaaranen, M., et al. (2003). A genome scan for developmental dyslexia confirms linkage to chromosome 2p11 and suggests a new locus on 7q32. *Journal of Medical Genetics, 40*, 340–345.

Kaplan, D. E., Gayan, J., Ahn, J., Won, T. W., Pauls, D., Olson, R. K., et al. (2002). Evidence for linkage and association with reading disability on 6p21.3–22. *American Journal of Human Genetics, 70,* 1287–1298.

Kjelgaard, M., & Tager-Flusberg, H. (2001). An investigation of language impairment in autism: Implications for genetic subgroups. *Language and Cognitive Processes, 16,* 287–308.

Krebs, M. O., Betancur, C., Leroy, S., Bourdel, M. C., Gillberg, C., & Leboyer, M. (2002). Absence of association between a polymorphic GGC repeat in the 5[1] untranslated region of the reelin gene and autism. *Molecular Psychiatry, 7,* 801–804.

Lahey, M. (1990). Who shall be called language disordered? Some reflections and one perspective. *Journal of Speech and Hearing Disorders, 55,* 612–620.

Lai, C. S., Fisher, S. E., Hurst, J. A., Levy, E. R., Hodgson, S., Fox, M., et al. (2000). The *SPCH1* region on human 7q31: Genomic characterization of the critical interval and localization of translocations associated with speech and language disorder. *American Journal of Human Genetics, 67,* 357–368.

Lai, C. S., Fisher, S. E., Hurst, J. A., Vargha-Khadem, F., & Monaco, A. P. (2001). A forkhead-domain gene is mutated in a severe speech and language disorder. *Nature, 413,* 519–523.

Lai, C. S., Gerrelli, D., Monaco, A. P., Fisher, S. E., & Copp, A. J. (2003). *FOXP2* expression during brain development coincides with adult sites of pathology in a severe speech and language disorder. *Brain, 126,* 2455–2462.

Landa, R., Piven, J., Wzorek, M. M., Gayle, J. O., Chase, G. A., & Folstein, S. E. (1992). Social language use in parents of autistic individuals. *Psychological Medicine, 22,* 245–254.

Le Couteur, A., Bailey, A., Goode, S., Pickles, A., Robertson, S., Gottesman, I., et al. (1996). A broader phenotype of autism: The clinical spectrum in twins. *Journal of Child Psychology and Psychiatry, 37,* 785–801.

Lennon, P. A., Cooper, M. L., Peiffer, D. A., Gunderson, K. L., Patel, A., Peters, S., et al. (2007). Deletion of 7q31.1 supports involvement of *FOXP2* in language impairment: clinical report and review. *American Journal of Medical Genetics. Part A, 143,* 791–798.

Lewis, B. A., Ekelman, B. L., & Aram, D. M. (1989). A familial study of severe phonological disorders. *Journal of Speech and Hearing Research, 32,* 713–724.

Lewis, B. A., & Thompson, L. A. (1992). A study of developmental speech and language disorders in twins. *Journal of Speech and Hearing Research, 35,* 1086–1094.

Li, S., Weidenfeld, J., & Morrisey, E. E. (2004). Transcriptional and DNA binding activity of the Foxp1/2/4 family is modulated by heterotypic and homotypic protein interactions. *Molecular and Cellular Biology, 24,* 809–822.

Liegeois, F., Baldeweg, T., Connelly, A., Gadian, D. G., Mishkin, M., & Vargha-Khadem, F. (2003). Language fMRI abnormalities associated with *FOXP2* gene mutation. *Nature Neuroscience, 6,* 1230–1237.

Liegeois, F., Lai, C. S. L., Baldeweg, T., Fisher, S., Monaco, A. P., Connelly, A., et al. (2001). Behavioural and neuroimaging correlates of a chromosome 7q31 deletion containing the *SPCH1* gene [Abstract]. *Abstracts—Society for Neuroscience, 27,* 529.17.

Ma, D. Q., Whitehead, P. L., Menold, M. M., Martin, E. R., Ashley-Koch, A. E., Mei, H., et al. (2005). Identification of significant association and gene–gene interaction of GABA receptor subunit genes in autism. *American Journal of Human Genetics, 77,* 377–388.

MacDermot, K. D., Bonora, E., Sykes, N., Coupe, A. M., Lai, C. S. L., Vernes, S. C., et al. (2005). Identification of FOXP2 truncation as a novel cause of developmental speech and language deficits. *American Journal of Human Genetics, 76,* 1074–1080.

Maestrini, E., Lai, C., Marlow, A., Matthews, N., Wallace, S., Bailey, A., et al. (1999). Serotonin transporter (5-HTT) and gamma-aminobutyric acid receptor subunit beta3 (GABRB3) gene polymorphisms are not associated with autism in the IMGSA families: The International Molecular Genetic Study of Autism Consortium. *American Journal of Medical Genetics, 88,* 492–496.

Martin, E. R., Menold, M. M., Wolpert, C. M., Bass, M. P., Donnelly, S. L., Ravan, S. A., et al. (2000). Analysis of linkage disequilibrium in gamma-aminobutyric acid receptor subunit genes in autistic disorder. *American Journal of Medical Genetics, 96,* 43–48.

McCoy, P. A., Shao, Y., Wolpert, C. M., Donnelly, S. L., Ashley-Koch, A., Abel, H. L., et al. (2002).

No association between the *WNT2* gene and autistic disorder. *American Journal of Medical Genetics, 114,* 106–109.

Meaburn, E., Dale, P. S., Craig, I. W., & Plomin, R. (2002). Language-impaired children: No sign of the *FOXP2* mutation. *NeuroReport, 13,* 1075–1077.

Meng, H. Y., Hager, K., Held, M., Page, G. P., Olson, R. K., Pennington, B. F., et al. (2005). TDT-association analysis of *EKN1* and dyslexia in a Colorado twin cohort. *Human Genetics, 118,* 87–90.

Meng, H. Y., Smith, S. D., Hager, K., Held, M., Liu, J., Olson, R. K., et al. (2005). *DCDC2* is associated with reading disability and modulates neuronal development in the brain. *Proceedings of the National Academy of Sciences U.S.A., 102,* 17053–17058.

Menold, M. M., Shao, Y., Wolpert, C. M., Donnelly, S. L., Raiford, K. L., Martin, E. R., et al. (2001). Association analysis of chromosome 15 GABAA receptor subunit genes in autistic disorder. *Journal of Neurogenetics, 15,* 245–259.

Monaco, A. P. (2007). Multivariate linkage analysis of specific language impairment (SLI). *Annals of Human Genetics, 71,* 1–14.

Morris, D. W., Robinson, L., Turic, D., Duke, M., Webb, V., Milham, C., et al. (2000). Family-based association mapping provides evidence for a gene for reading disability on chromosome 15q. *Human Molecular Genetics, 9,* 843–848.

Neils, J., & Aram, D. M. (1986). Family history of children with developmental language disorders. *Perceptual and Motor Skills, 63,* 655–658.

Newbury, D. F., Bonora, E., Lamb, J. A., Fisher, S. E., Lai, C. S., Baird, G., et al. (2002). *FOXP2* is not a major susceptibility gene for autism or specific language impairment. *American Journal of Human Genetics, 70,* 1318–1327.

Newbury, D. F., Cleak, J. D., Banfield, E., Marlow, A. J., Fisher, S. E., Monaco, A. P., et al. (2004). Highly significant linkage to the *SLI1* locus in an expanded sample of individuals affected by specific language impairment. *American Journal of Human Genetics, 74,* 1225–1238.

Newbury, D. F., Ishikawa-Brush, Y., Marlow, A. J., Fisher, S. E., Monaco, A. P., Stott, C. M., et al. (2002). A genomewide scan identifies two novel loci involved in specific language impairment. *American Journal of Human Genetics, 70,* 384–398.

Nopola-Hemmi, J., Myllyluoma, B., Haltia, T., Taipale, M., Ollikainen, V., Ahonen, T., et al. (2001). A dominant gene for developmental dyslexia on chromosome 3. *Journal of Medical Genetics, 38,* 658–664.

O'Brien, E. K., Zhang, X. Y., Nishimura, C., Tomblin, J. B., & Murray, J. C. (2003). Association of specific language impairment (SLI) to the region of 7q31. *American Journal of Human Genetics, 72,* 1536–1543.

Persico, A. M., D'Agruma, L., Maiorano, N., Totaro, A., Militerni, R., Bravaccio, C., et al. (2001). Reelin gene alleles and haplotypes as a factor predisposing to autistic disorder. *Molecular Psychiatry, 6,* 150–159.

Petryshen, T. L., Kaplan, B. J., & Field, L. L. (1999). Evidence for a susceptibility locus for phonological coding dyslexia on chromosome 6q13–q16.2. *American Journal of Human Genetics, 65,* A32.

Peyrard-Janvid, M., Anthoni, H., Onkamo, P., Lahermo, P., Zucchelli, M., Kaminen, N., et al. (2004). Fine mapping of the 2p11 dyslexia locus and exclusion of *TACR1* as a candidate gene. *Human Genetics, 114,* 510–516.

Philippe, A., Martinez, M., Guilloud-Bataille, M., Gillberg, C., Rastam, M., Sponheim, E. et al. (1999). Genome-wide scan for autism susceptibility genes. *Human Molecular Genetics, 8(5),* 805–812 [erratum: 8(7), 1353].

Pinker, S. (1994). *The language instinct.* New York: William Morrow.

Price, T. S., Eley, T. C., Dale, P. S., Stevenson, J., Saudino, K., & Plomin, R. (2000). Genetic and environmental covariation between verbal and nonverbal cognitive development in infancy. *Child Development, 71,* 948–959.

Purcell, S., Eley, T. C., Dale, P. S., Oliver, B., Petrill, S. A., Price, T. S., et al. (2001). Comorbidity between verbal and non-verbal cognitive delays in 2-yr-olds: A bivariate twin analysis. *Developmental Science, 4,* 195–208.

Rabin, M., Wen, X. L., Hepburn, M., Lubs, H. A., Feldman, E., & Duara, R. (1993). Suggestive linkage of developmental dyslexia to chromosome 1p34–p36 [Letter]. *Lancet, 342,* 178.

Raskind, W. H., Igo, R. P., Chapman, N. H., Berninger, V. W., Thomson, J. B., Matsushita, M., et al. (2005). A genome scan in multigenerational families with dyslexia: Identification of a novel locus on chromosome 2q that contributes to phonological decoding efficiency. *Molecular Psychiatry, 10,* 699–711.

Rice, M. L., Haney, K. R., & Wexler, K. (1998). Family histories of children with SLI who show extended optional infinitives. *Journal of Speech, Language, and Hearing Research, 41,* 419–432.

Ritvo, E. R., Freeman, B. J., Pingree, C., Mason-Brothers, A., Jorde, L., Jenson, W. R., et al. (1989). The UCLA-University of Utah epidemiologic survey of autism: Prevalence. *American Journal of Psychiatry, 146,* 194–199.

Roberts, J. A., Rice, M. L., & Tager-Flusberg, H. (2004). Tense marking in children with autism. *Applied Psycholinguistics, 25,* 429–448.

Santangelo, S. L., & Tsatsanis, K. (2005). What is known about autism: Genes, brain, and behavior. *American Journal of Pharmacogenomics, 5,* 71–92.

Schumacher, J., Anthoni, H., Dahdouh, F., Konig, I. R., Hillmer, A. M., Kluck, N., et al. (2006). Strong genetic evidence of *DCDC2* as a susceptibility gene for dyslexia. *American Journal of Human Genetics, 78,* 52–62.

Serajee, F. J., Zhong, H. L., & Huq, A. H. M. M. (2006). Association of Reelin gene polymorphisms with autism. *Genomics, 87,* 75–83.

Shao, Y., Wolpert, C. M., Raiford, K. L., Menold, M. M., Donnelly, S. L., Ravan, S. A., et al. (2002). Genomic screen and follow-up analysis for autistic disorder. *American Journal of Human Genetics, 114,* 99–105.

Shaywitz, S. E., Escobar, M. D., Shaywitz, B. A., Fletcher, J. M., & Makuch, R. (1992). Evidence that dyslexia may represent the lower tail of a normal distribution of reading ability. *New England Journal of Medicine, 326,* 140–150.

Shu, W., Yang, H., Zhang, L., Lu, M. M., & Morrisey, E. E. (2001). Characterization of a new subfamily of winged-helix/forkhead (*Fox*) genes that are expressed in the lung and act as transcriptional repressors. *Journal of Biological Chemistry, 276,* 27488–27497.

Skaar, D. A., Shao, Y., Haines, J. L., Stenger, J. E., Jaworski, J., Martin, E. R., et al. (2005). Analysis of the *RELN* gene as a genetic risk factor for autism. *Molecular Psychiatry, 10,* 563–571.

Smith, S. D., Deffenbacher, K. E., Boada, R., Raitano, N., Tunick, R., Shriberg, L. D., et al. (2004). Linkage, association and candidategene analyses for reading disability and speech sound disorder. *Behavior Genetics, 34,* 660.

Smith, S. D., Kimberling, W. J., Pennington, B. F., & Lubs, H. A. (1983). Specific reading disability: Identification of an inherited form through linkage analysis. *Science, 219,* 1345–1347.

Smith, S. D., Pennington, B. F., Boada, R., Shriberg, L. D., Tunick, R. A., Boada, R., et al. (2005). Linkage of speech sound disorder to reading disability loci. *Journal of Child Psychology and Psychiatry, 46,* 1057–1066.

Spinath, F. M., Price, T. S., Dale, P. S., & Plomin, R. (2004). The genetic and environmental origins of language disability and ability. *Child Development, 75,* 445–454.

Steffenburg, S., Gillberg, C., Hellgren, L., Andersson, L., Gillberg, I. C., Jakobsson, G., et al. (1989). A twin study of autism in Denmark, Finland, Iceland, Norway and Sweden. *Journal of Child Psychology and Psychiatry, 30,* 405–416.

Stein, C. M., Schick, J. H., Taylor, H. G., Shriberg, L. D., Millard, C., Kundtz-Kluge, A., et al. (2004). Pleiotropic effects of a chromosome 3 locus on speech-sound disorder and reading. *American Journal of Human Genetics, 74,* 283–297.

Taipale, M., Kaminen, N., Nopola-Hemmi, J., Haltia, T., Myllyluoma, B., Lyytinen, H., et al. (2003). A candidate gene for developmental dyslexia encodes a nuclear tetratricopeptide repeat domain protein dynamically regulated in brain. *Proceedings of the National Academy of Sciences U.S.A., 100,* 11553–11558.

Takahashi, K., Liu, F., Hirokawa, K., & Takahashi, H. (2003). Expression of *FOXP2*, a gene involved in speech and language, in the developing and adult striatum. *Journal of Neuroscience Research, 73*, 61–72.

Tallal, P., Hirsch, L. S., Realpe-Bonilla, T., Miller, S., Brzustowicz, L. M., Bartlett, C., et al. (2001). Familial aggregation in specific language impairment. *Journal of Speech Language and Hearing Research, 44*, 1172–1182.

Tallal, P., Ross, R., & Curtiss, S. (1989). Familial aggregation in specific language impairment. *Journal of Speech and Hearing Research, 54*, 167–173.

Tomblin, J. B. (1989). Familial concentration of developmental language impairment. *Journal of Speech and Hearing Disorders, 54*, 287–295.

Tomblin, J. B. (1996). Genetic and environmental contributions to the risk for specific language impairment. In M. L. Rice (Ed.), *Toward a genetics of language* (pp. 191–210). Mahwah, NJ: Lawrence Erlbaum Associates.

Tomblin, J. B., & Buckwalter, P. (1998). The heritability of poor language achievement among twins. *Journal of Speech and Hearing Research, 41*, 188–199.

Tomblin, J. B., Hafeman, L. L., & O'Brien, M. (2003). Autism and autistic behaviors in siblings of children with language impairment. *International Journal of Language and Communication Disorders, 38*, 235–250.

Tomblin, J. B., Nishimura, C., Zhang, X., & Murray, J. (1998). Association of developmental language impairment with loci at 7q31. *American Journal of Human Genetics*, A312.

Tomblin, J. B., Records, N. L., Buckwalter, P., Zhang, X., Smith, E., & O'Brien, M. (1997). The prevalence of specific language impairment in kindergarten children. *Journal of Speech, Language, and Hearing Research, 40*, 1245–1260.

Tomblin, J., Shriberg, L., Murray, J., Patil, S., & Williams, C. (2004). Speech and language characteristics associated with a 7/13 translocation involving *FOXP2*. *American Journal of Medical Genetics. Part B, Neuropsychiatric Genetics, 130B*, 97.

Tyson, C., McGillivray, B., Chijiwa, C., & Rajcan-Separovic, E. (2004). Elucidation of a cryptic interstitial 7q31.3 deletion in a patient with a language disorder and mild mental retardation by array-CGH. *American Journal of Medical Genetics. Part B, 129B*, 254–260.

Tzenova, J., Kaplan, B. J., Petryshen, T. L., & Field, L. L. (2004). Confirmation of a dyslexia susceptibility locus on chromosome 1p34–p36 in a set of 100 Canadian families. *American Journal of Medical Genetics. Part B, Neuropsychiatric Genetics, 127B*, 117–124.

Ullman, M. T. (2001). A neurocognitive perspective on language: The declarative/procedural model. *Nature Reviews Neuroscience, 2*, 717–726.

Ullman, M. T., & Pierpont, E. I. (2005). Specific language impairment is not specific to language: The procedural deficit hypothesis. *Cortex, 41*, 399–433.

van der Lely, H. K., & Stollwerck, L. (1996). A grammatical specific language impairment in children: An autosomal dominant inheritance? *Brain and Language, 52*, 484–504.

Vargha-Khadem, F., Watkins, K. E., Price, C. J., Ashburner, J., Alcock, K. J., Connelly, A., et al. (1998). Neural basis of an inherited speech and language disorder. *Proceedings of the National Academy of Sciences U.S.A., 95*, 12695–12700.

Vernes, S. C., Nicod, J., Elahi, F. M., Coventry, J. A., Kenny, N., Coupe, A. M., et al. (2006). Functional genetic analysis of mutations implicated in a human speech and language disorder. *Human Molecular Genetics, 15*, 3154–3167.

Viding, E., Spinath, F. M., Price, T. S., Bishop, D. V. M., Dale, P. S., & Plomin, R. (2004). Genetic and environmental influence on language impairment in 4-year-old same-sex and opposite-sex twins. *Journal of Child Psychology and Psychiatry, 45*, 315–325.

Wassink, T. H., Piven, J., Vieland, V. J., Huang, J., Swiderski, R. E., Pietila, J., et al. (2001). Evidence supporting *WNT2* as an autism susceptibility gene. *American Journal of Medical Genetics, 105*, 406–413.

Wassink, T. H., Piven, J., Vieland, V. J., Pietila, J., Goedken, R. J., Folstein, S. E., et al. (2002). Evaluation of *FOXP2* as an autism susceptibility gene. *American Journal of Medical Genetics, 114*, 566–569.

Watkins, K. E., Dronkers, N. F., & Vargha-Khadem, F. (2002). Behavioural analysis of an inherited speech and language disorder: Comparison with acquired aphasia. *Brain, 125*, 452–464.

Watkins, K. E., Vargha-Khadem, F., Ashburner, J., Passingham, R. E., Connelly, A., Friston, K. J., et al. (2002). MRI analysis of an inherited speech and language disorder: Structural brain abnormalities. *Brain, 125,* 465–478.

Whitehurst, G. J., Arnold, D. S., Smith, M., Fischel, J. E., Lonigan, C. J., & Valdez-Menchaca, M. C. (1991). Family history in developmental expressive language delay. *Journal of Speech and Hearing Research, 34,* 1150–1157.

Wood, F. B., & Grigorenko, E. L. (2001). Emerging issues in the genetics of dyslexia: A methodological review. *Journal of Learning Disabilities, 34,* 511.

Young, S., Schmitz, S., Corley, R., & Fulker, D. (2001). Language and cognition. In R. N. Emde & J. K. Hewitt (Eds.), *Infancy to early childhood* (pp. 221–240). New York: Oxford University Press.

Zeesman, S., Nowaczyk, M. J. M., Teshima, I., Roberts, W., Cardy, J., Senman, L., et al. (2004). *Speech and language impairment and oromotor dyspraxia due to deletion of 7q31 which involves FOXP2.* Poster presented at the American Human Genetics meeting, Toronto.

Zhong, H., Serajee, F. J., Nabi, R., & Huq, A. H. M. M. (2003). No association between the *EN2* gene and autistic disorder. *Journal of Medical Genetics, 40,* e4.

11

Model-based Approaches to Child Language Disorders

MARC F. JOANISSE

The study of language impairments promises to inform our understanding of the neurocognitive foundations of language by answering a key question: *Do language impairments represent the absence of one or more cognitive modules responsible for language processing?* The idea that the mind is parceled into discrete semi-independent processing mechanisms represents a powerful framework in cognitive psychology (e.g., Fodor, 1983). Consistent with this theory, one could hypothesize that developmental language impairments represent a failure in the development of a subcomponent of language. Disorders that target specific language abilities would seem to constitute evidence for independent (or *domain-specific*) processing modules specialized for language. Such a finding serves to reinforce the theory that language represents a specialized processing modality that is functionally independent from other cognitive capacities such as perception, memory, and learning.

There is an alternative hypothesis, however, which I believe is equally interesting: language disorders might not be due to a domain-specific deficit (van der Lely, 2005) but are, instead, the result of domain-general impairments. As I discuss in this chapter, such hypotheses have been put forward to explain a range of seemingly "specific" language deficits in both developmental and acquired cases. These theories focus on the idea that language disorders can result from an impairment in perception, processing speed, or memory, among others (Gathercole & Baddeley, 1990; Kail, 1994; Tallal, Miller, & Fitch, 1993). Such a hypothesis is compelling because it suggests that difficulties that are domain-general can nevertheless affect different abilities in an *uneven* fashion, such that specific aspects of language processing are disproportionately impaired compared to other capacities. It also serves as a helpful demonstration of how such domain-general mechanisms could play a role in normal language development, which again represents an interesting departure from earlier generative theories of language acquisition.

CONNECTIONIST MODELING

This chapter focuses on how connectionist models have been used to simulate normal and impaired development. The connectionist, or parallel distributed processing (PDP) framework uses computer simulations of artificial neural networks to create models of cognitive processes (Rumelhart, McClelland, & The PDP Research Group, 1986). The key assumptions of the connectionist framework can be summarized as follows (Smolensky, 1999):

1. *Knowledge is encoded as patterns of numerical activity distributed across large numbers of simple processing units.* We assume that knowledge is represented as the activation of many neurons distributed across many brain regions. In connectionist models this is represented as the activation patterns of many simple processing units, which we can call "nodes" or "units." These are functionally similar to neurons but include a range of simplifications that allow us to implement them more easily as computer simulations.

2. *Processing occurs as the transformation of this activity across massively parallel sets of connections.* Mental processes can be described as neurons passing information among themselves across synaptic connections. Connectionist networks capture this through the use of weighted connections that link nodes to each other. The activity of a unit is a direct reflection of the activity of other units in the network that are connected to it, and the strengths of those connections.

3. *Learning occurs through changes to these connections.* A network's behavior is modified by changing the strength (or *weight*) of connections. Three mechanisms influence this: (1) experience; (2) the innate architecture of the system; and (3) the innate learning rule used to modify connections as a function of experience. Thus, much like biological organisms, we assume that how a network learns and behaves is a function of both its inherent structure and the input that is provided to it.

Before the connectionist enterprise came along, the predominant view of cognition was one of a computer analogy, which envisioned the mind as a software program used to perform mental computations, and the brain as the hardware that this program runs on (Block, 1990). This analogy also held that mental representations are symbols, and that mental processes are rule-like operations that are performed on these symbols. This symbolic view has profoundly influenced modern theories of normal and intact language processing. For example, such theories describe our knowledge of language as a set of symbols and rules that operate on them (Chomsky, 1986); learning is seen as the process of acquiring new symbols and rules, and impaired language development is consequently seen as a deficit in specific symbol processing mechanisms (Berwick, 1997).

Connectionism takes a different view of cognition, in which the line between the mind and the brain is blurred. This is because the mechanisms of mental representations, processes, and learning mechanisms are drawn directly from what we know about neural systems (notwithstanding some simplifying assumptions, which I return to later in this chapter). This has a certain reductionist appeal, since it suggests that our mental "software" and neural "hardware" are two in the same. In addition, because this approach is model-based, it also forces researchers to be explicit in specifying the types of processes and knowledge that participate in a cognitive ability such as language learning. This, unfortunately, is also the greatest drawback of connectionism: because the behavior of a model is a direct reflection of how it is implemented, the failure to properly specify the nature of the system can lead to incorrect or inconsistent results (Marcus, 1998). Whether this represents a failure of the connectionist approach as a whole or a local problem with how it is implemented is another matter, however.

Below I discuss connectionist approaches to understanding three types of language processing impairments: reading, grammatical morphology, and syntax. Throughout, I emphasize the similarity in the approaches that have been taken to explaining these disorders within a connectionist framework, how these explanations fit with existing behavioral data, and ways in which this approach can be extended to other types of data or populations.

READING DISORDERS

Perhaps the most closely studied and best understood developmental language disorder is developmental dyslexia (see chapter 5 by Shaywitz et al.). Children with dyslexia have difficulty learning to read in spite of apparently normal sensory, cognitive, neurological, and emotional abilities. The key hallmarks of dyslexia are slow and laborious reading, along with very poor decoding ability (the process of "sounding out" a word using letter-to-sound correspondences). Problems with decoding are best identified using nonwords (e.g., MAVE, STOOK, PLINDER); skilled readers tend to read nonwords effortlessly, whereas dyslexic individuals find them extremely difficult. The prevailing theories of dyslexia have thus focused on the idea that dyslexia represents a disturbance in the ability to learn generalizations about spelling–sound correspondences. One account suggests that children with dyslexia have problems with general phonological processing, and that this deficit contributes directly to their reading difficulties. Consistent with this, dyslexic children have difficulties with rhyme awareness (e.g., judging whether two words rhyme) and phoneme awareness (e.g., deleting a sound from a word, such as saying *split* without the "p" sound) (Goswami, 1999; Wagner, Torgesen, & Rashotte, 1994). In addition, they tend to have poorer than expected categorical perception of speech (Godfrey, Syrdal-Lasky, Millay, & Knox, 1981; Werker & Tees, 1987). The prevailing hypothesis holds that a phonological deficit impairs the ability to accurately acquire letter–sound relationships, which in turn leads to delayed development of fluent reading skills.

One caveat to this is that the direction of causation might not be so straightforward: for instance, reading problems might, instead, be the cause of poor phonological abilities. Studies have also found poorer phonological awareness abilities in normally developing individuals who have never learned to read or who have not been exposed to alphabetic scripts that emphasize letter–sound correspondences (e.g., Morais, Cary, Alegria, & Bertelson, 1979). Thus, perhaps dyslexic individuals are poor at phonology because of their poor reading skills, rather than the other way around.

The second concern with phonology-based theories of dyslexia is the observation that some children with dyslexia have normal decoding and phonological awareness abilities. These children appear, instead, to have problems with reading words with irregular spellings. For instance, although English word pronunciation is typically consistent across words with similar spellings (e.g., SAVE, RAVE, PAVE, GAVE), there are a number of irregular words (or exceptions words) that violate this regularity (e.g., HAVE). As a result, it has been suggested that there are in fact two subtypes of dyslexia: phonological dyslexics who are poor at nonword decoding, and surface dyslexics who have poor irregular word reading (Castles & Coltheart, 1993; Manis, Seidenberg, Doi, McBride-Chang, & Petersen, 1996; Stanovich, Siegel, & Gottardo, 1997). As I discuss below, models of reading have given us some useful ways of thinking about how a complex linguistic task like reading is accomplished, and why reading disorders occur. They also appear to address more specific concerns about the direction of causation of phonological difficulties and subtypes of developmental dyslexia.

Dual-Route Models of Reading and Dyslexia

Reading a word involves two processes: recognizing its sound by translating orthography to phonology, and recognizing its meaning by translating orthography to semantics. Coltheart and colleagues sought to capture this idea within their "dual-route" model of reading (Coltheart, Curtis, Atkins, & Haller, 1993). This model suggests that the two processes in reading occur via discrete processing streams (Figure 11.1, top). The *lexical route* involves a

Coltheart's DRC Model

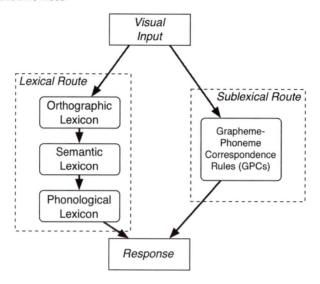

The Seidenberg and McClelland (1989) Model

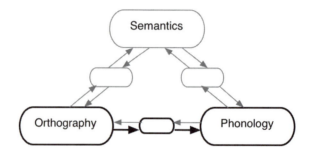

FIGURE 11.1 Models of reading. Top: Coltheart's dual-route model of reading. The model integrates both a lexical route (left) that identifies words holistically, and a sublexical route that decomposes words via grapheme-phoneme correspondence (GPC) rules. Bottom: the Seidenberg and McClelland (1989) connectionist reading model. This model encodes words as patterns of activation across groups of artificial neurons (ellipses) that represent orthographic, phonological and semantic information. Mappings between these codes are accomplished via weighted connections (arrows). Portions in bold represent the usual implementation of the model, as a network that maps orthography to phonology.

holistic lookup process in which a visual word is mapped onto orthographic, semantic, and phonological lexical entries that are organized in a dictionary-like fashion. The *nonlexical route* involves using grapheme-to-phoneme correspondence rules (GPCs) to determine a word's phonological form, which can then be used to access other lexical information indirectly. Recent versions of the dual-route model have modified the way in which lexical and nonlexical information are computed (i.e., the dual-route cascaded model, or DRC, Coltheart, Rastle, Perry, Langdon, & Ziegler, 2001) but maintained the strict division between the two routes. As such, each word must be recognized using one route or the other. This division plays out most strongly with respect to irregular words and nonwords. Because spelling–sound correspondences in irregular words are, by definition, arbitrary, these words must be read via the lexical route. In contrast, nonwords, by definition, do not have lexical representations; they must be read via the nonlexical or GPC route.

The DRC framework models dyslexia as resulting from damage to, or the absence of, a specific component of the model, with subtypes of dyslexia reflecting different types of impaired or absent components. Phonological dyslexia occurs because the nonlexical GPC component of the model is damaged, which impairs the ability to decode nonwords but preserves the ability to read familiar words. In contrast, damage to the lexical route specifically impairs the ability to read irregular words, since they cannot be decoded using GPCs, thereby simulating surface dyslexia (Castles & Coltheart, 1993).

The DRC theory of dyslexia makes two interesting claims about reading impairment. The first is that, because decoding processes in reading are not intrinsically phonological, one need not posit a causal relationship between phonological awareness and reading deficits. Instead, the computational ability that translates orthographic codes to phonological codes is separate from the capacity used for more general phonological processes. Thus, the reading deficit in dyslexia truly is seen as the result of an impairment to reading-specific processing mechanisms. Phonological deficits in dyslexia are seen as either epiphenomenal, or as the result of affected individuals' reading difficulties (rather than the other way around). Likewise, surface dyslexia is conceived as the breakdown of the lexical route, such that the sublexical route is being used to read all words. Finally, the DRC model suggests that, since one complete reading route is spared in either subtype, there should be a strong division in the reading deficits observed in these two forms of dyslexia, such that phonological dyslexics should read irregular words relatively well, and phonological dyslexics should be good nonword readers.

Connectionist Approaches to Reading Impairment

The connectionist theory of word recognition builds on Seidenberg and McClelland's (1989) model of reading (SM89; see Figure 11.1, bottom). This model simulates word reading as taking a word's orthographic form as input (i.e., the orthographic units corresponding to a word's spelling are activated) and computing its phonological and semantic forms. The mappings between orthography, semantics, and phonology are encoded as the weights of connections between units in each of these layers. [Note that additional layers of units, called *hidden layers*, are also used in this network and others like it (Rumelhart et al., 1986). The purpose of these hidden layers is to increase the network's computational capacity by allowing it to encode higher-level mappings between units that are not possible in simpler architectures.] Because of limitations on technology, some earlier implementations of the SM89 model have included only orthography and phonology. This is indicated by the grayed-out portions of the model in Figure 11.1. (A full implementation of this model that includes a semantics layer is presented in Harm & Seidenberg, 2004.)

In the original implementation of the SM89 model, a word's orthography was encoded using *wickelfeatures* (Wickelgren, 1969), where a word is divided into triads of letters, with a single unit assigned for each possible triplet. For instance, the wickelfeatures of the word STOP would be [#ST], [STO], [TOP] and [OP#]. (Note that the "#" symbol here denotes the word boundary. It is used to help the network distinguish triplets that occur at the start and end of a word, vs. the same triplet that occurs midword, such as the [TOP] in *stop* vs. *top*.) The use of wickelfeatures allowed them to uniquely identify the orthographic form of many words using a limited number of units in the model. Phonology was encoded in a similar way, where separate nodes encoded each possible triplet of adjacent phonemes in the training vocabulary (e.g., *make*: [#mA], [mAk], [Ak#]). Their network was able to learn a corpus of English monosyllables, both with regular and irregular spellings, to a good degree of proficiency. In addition, the network's accuracy in producing different forms respected frequency and regularity distinctions known to influence reading times in skilled readers (Jared, 1997). In addition, it was able to generalize what it had learned from the training corpus to novel words, marked by accurate phonological outputs for orthographic forms like NUST. Because the network was able to learn both regular and irregular spellings within a single architecture, there was no need for two distinct routes for reading. Whereas the DRC model computes a word's meaning either via a lexical or sublexical mechanism, the SM89 model uses all connections in parallel to recognize a given word. However, one question is whether the elimination of dissociable routes limits its applicability to dyslexia.

Subsequent models have followed up on this idea. Plaut and colleagues (Plaut, McClelland, Seidenberg, & Patterson, 1996) used an updated network that included enhancements to the network's architecture, training regime, and phonological and orthographic representations. Among other things, they investigated whether "lesions" to a fully trained network would lead to a pattern of impairment consistent with acquired dyslexia following brain damage. Removing either connections between orthography and phonology, or removing some of the hidden units entirely, had a greater impact on the network's ability to recognize irregular compared to regular words, in a way that is very similar to what has been observed in patients with acquired surface dyslexia. In contrast, adding noise to the phonological layer units led to a deficit in reading nonwords, consistent with acquired (*deep*) dyslexia.

More recently, Harm and Seidenberg (1999) tested whether the same logic could be applied to understanding *developmental* dyslexia and whether different subtypes of dyslexia could be induced by impairments to different portions of the model. One interesting finding from their simulations of normal reading development was that the network acquired the reading task much more quickly and accurately when it was given prior experience with phonology. This prior knowledge was provided to the network by pretraining it on a phonological task, in which it learned to encode only the phonological form of English words. This pretraining was intended to reflect the type of phonological knowledge that children acquire before learning to read, such as the features that make up phonemes and the phonological structure of words. In addition, a careful analysis of the network's connection strengths and activation patterns revealed that learning to read resulted in significant changes in how it encoded the phonological forms of words, something that seems consistent with the observation that print exposure can enhance phonological abilities (Morais et al., 1979).

Next, Harm and Seidenberg examined how introducing different types of damage to the network prior to training would simulate developmental dyslexia. Phonological dyslexia was simulated by weakening the network's phonological representations. This was achieved by adding random noise to the units in the phonological layer and severing "cleanup" connections (connections to and from a special type of hidden layer termed a cleanup layer, which the network used to encode higher order phonological information). Such a model showed difficulty encoding and processing phonological information, even before it was trained to read. For instance, it was less accurate at encoding the phonological features of words (marked by "noisier" activation values in the Phonology-layer units). When the phonologically impaired network was trained on the reading task, it demonstrated a general slowing in its ability to recognize all words in the training corpus. However, it was especially poor at nonword reading compared to the intact network.

Surface dyslexia was simulated by reducing the number of hidden units between the orthographic and semantic layers. Hidden units increase a network's computational capacity, in part because the number of connections in a network scales in proportion to the number of hidden units. It was observed that reducing the number of hidden units resulted in generally slower learning, but especially poor performance of exception words, even compared to the phonological dyslexia simulation. (Note that reducing the network's computational capacity should not be construed as simulating a general reduction in cognitive capacity in surface dyslexic children. The authors suggest it could, instead, reflect a reduction in neural capacity in brain regions responsible for learning to map orthographic to phonological information that lead to a general delay in reading acquisition. It is also possible that this deficit is due to environmental factors related to impoverished exposure to print, which would again lead to generally delayed reading skills.) Different types of damage to the SM89 model architecture yield patterns of performance consistent with different subtypes of reading impairment, supporting the theory that a single type of mechanism can be used for reading all word types.

How do the Connectionist and Dual-Route Models Differ?

The DRC model of reading suggests that dyslexia occurs as a result of impairments to one of its routes. The connectionist view of dyslexia differs in several important ways. The first has to do with the extent to which one tends to observe *pure* instances of developmental phonological or surface dyslexia. Studies of dyslexic subtypes have tended to find that a large proportion of children are poor on both nonword and exception-word reading, and very few show a strong deficit on one but not the other (Castles & Coltheart, 1993; Manis et al., 1997; Stanovich et al., 1997). This seems to fit well with Harm and Seidenberg's simulations, which illustrated that such dissociations tend to be partial rather than wholesale. This is because all words are being processed within the same architecture. Differences between phonological and surface dyslexia occur as a result of damage to different subcomponents of the model, which results in different patterns of difficulties. However, all words are impaired to some extent by any damage type. In contrast, the DRC model seems to predict that mixed subtypes will occur as a result of both routes being impaired, with purer subtypes occurring in cases where one route is disproportionately more damaged than the other.

A second point of divergence between dual-route and connectionist models has to do with how they envision the proximal causes of dyslexia. In the dual-route model perspective, dyslexia is seen as a reading-specific disorder that occurs due to damage to one or both of the proposed neurocognitive routes to reading. In contrast, the connectionist model seems to suggest that dyslexia occurs as an epiphenomenon of other types of impairments. This is clearest in the case of phonological dyslexia, where these individuals' deficits are due to a phonological impairment that leads to problems learning spelling–sound correspondences. This view seems much more in keeping with the current view that dyslexia is the result of a phonological processing deficit (Desroches, Joanisse, & Robertson, 2006; Goswami, 1999; Stanovich, 1988; Wagner et al., 1994), rather than the other way around. It also seems consistent with the observation that children with phonological dyslexia have appreciably greater phonological processing problems than do children with surface dyslexia (Joanisse, Manis, Keating, & Seidenberg, 2000; Manis et al., 1996; Stanovich et al., 1997). Note, however, that Castles and Coltheart (2004) dispute the claim that poor phonological ability causes reading deficits. They instead suggest that the reverse is just as likely: phonological problems in these individuals are the result of their impaired reading difficulties. According to this view, children with poor reading abilities have weakened alphabetic knowledge, which in turn leads to poor phonological awareness.

In the case of surface dyslexia, the connectionist theory suggests that this disorder could be the result of a reading delay, due either to endogenous factors such as restricted or delayed processing capacities, or to exogenous factors such as environmental effects leading to impoverished reading experience. Consistent with this, work by Manis and colleagues has found that children with surface dyslexia have nonword- and exception-word-reading abilities that are very similar to younger, typically developing children (Joanisse et al., 2000; Manis et al., 1996). In addition, these studies have observed that surface dyslexic children show slower reaction times on speeded tasks, compared to both phonological dyslexics and typically developing children (Manis et al., 1999). Finally, behavioral genetics data suggest differences in the extent to which heritable and shared environment factors account for reading deficits in surface and phonology dyslexic subtypes (Castles, Datta, Gayan, & Olson, 1999). Phonological dyslexia exhibited very strong heritability with a relatively weaker (but still significant) contribution of environment, whereas the opposite was true in surface dyslexia, where only a relatively weak genetic component was found, with environment playing a much greater role in these individuals. This again seems consistent with Harm and Seidenberg's model, although it also suggests that in both cases there are tradeoffs between endogenous and exogenous risk factors. Because connectionist models address the roles that both types of information play in learning to read, they may play an important role in the exploration of reading disability.

GRAMMATICAL MORPHOLOGY

In this section I discuss impairments to morphology in children and what these deficits tell us about the status of rule-like processes in mental grammars. The focus is on specific language impairment (SLI; see chapter 1 by Schwartz and chapter 15 by Oetting & Hadley), a developmental language impairment that affects multiple aspects of language, while apparently leaving other cognitive abilities intact (Bishop, 1997; Leonard, 1998). Children with SLI have impairments in the development of many areas of language, including phonology, morphology, syntax, and vocabulary, but they apparently do not have nonlinguistic disabilities such as sensory, neural, or pervasive developmental deficits (see chapter 1 by Schwartz). Modular theories of language acquisition suggest that cognitive mechanisms supporting normal language development are independent of those involved in other cognitive processes; the strength of the dissociation between language and nonverbal abilities in children with SLI has thus been taken as strong support for this theory, as it suggests that SLI is caused by a deficit that is specific to the language domain (Pinker, 1991; van der Lely & Ullman, 2001). Thus, domain-specific theories of SLI predict that language deficits in SLI are caused by an underlying deficit specifically involved in language acquisition, such as the acquisition of grammatical rules or the ability to apply innate principles of language (Gopnik & Crago, 1991; Kail, 1994; Rice & Wexler, 1996; van der Lely, 2005). In contrast, domain-general theories suggest that language deficits can occur as a consequence of a nonlinguistic impairment, such as in perception, short-term memory, or processing speed (Gathercole & Baddeley, 1990; Kail, 1994; Leonard, Eyer, Bedore, & Grela, 1997; Tallal, Miller, & Fitch, 1995).

Perhaps the most closely studied aspect of SLI has been the area of English past tense morphology (Gopnik & Goad, 1997; Oetting & Horohov, 1997; Rice & Wexler, 1996; van der Lely, 2005). Past tense in English is usually marked by adding the "-ed" suffix to the ends of verb stems (*talk–talked, glue–glued*; see chapter 15 by Oetting & Hadley). This pattern is usually also applied to new verbs entering English (*downloaded*), and nonce words (*wug–wugged, blick–blicked*) (Berko, 1958). Given this, it is possible to describe past tense formation as following a language-specific grammatical rule, bearing in mind that some English verbs are irregular (e.g., *slept, went, blew*) and do not follow a rule-like pattern, as discussed further below.

Children with SLI have marked difficulty learning morphological patterns such as past tense, both in spontaneous speech samples and in elicitation tasks (e.g., generating a verb's past tense by completing sentences such as *Bobby likes to play. He did that yesterday: he _____*) (Marchman, Wulfeck, & Ellis Weismer, 1999; Oetting & Horohov, 1997; van der Lely & Ullman, 2001; Vargha-Khadem, Watkins, Alcock, Fletcher, & Passingham, 1995). Children with SLI have especially great difficulty with generating nonword past tenses. Unlike familiar past tenses, which could arguably be recalled from memory wholesale, nonword past tenses must be produced by generalization from known forms, either via a rule or through some other type of analogy process. From a domain-specific point of view, one could assume that this difficulty in SLI reflects a problem in mechanisms supporting rule learning. In contrast, domain-general theories suggest that this problem is due to peripheral processing difficulties that interfere with learning past tenses and applying the pattern to novel forms. Finally, the errors that SLI children make are also somewhat distinct from those of typically developing children, as they are less likely to overapply the regular past tense ending to irregulars (e.g., *eated, goed*; Marchman et al., 1999).

As it turns out, the debate about past tense deficits in SLI echoes a broader one in the cognitive science literature concerning how children normally acquire and use the rules of language and how irregular cases are handled. As mentioned earlier, one can conceptualize past tense generation as the process of taking a verb stem ($walk_V$) and using a rule to concatenate the suffix that marks its past tense ($walk_V + ed_{PAST}$). Because the rule acts blindly on any given symbol, it can apply to any form, including a nonword. It has been suggested that this mechanism is insufficient on its own, however, since it cannot be used to generate irregular past tenses like *is–was* and *take–took*. Instead, it has been suggested that a second mechanism is also necessary, one that encodes the past tenses of irregulars in an associative memory system (Pinker, 1991, 1999). Because irregular forms are already marked for past tense, the rule is blocked in these cases.

The connectionist view of past tense is different. It suggests that rules are unnecessary for capturing morphological processes like past tense, and that one can instead implement both regular and irregular past tense learning within a single connectionist mechanism (Rumelhart & McClelland, 1986). In such a model, the mappings between present and past tense forms are encoded within the distributed connection weights. A number of connectionist models of past tense have been developed as part of an ongoing dialogue between dual-mechanism and connectionist proponents (e.g., Daugherty & Seidenberg, 1992; Joanisse & Seidenberg, 1999; MacWhinney & Leinbach, 1991; Plunkett & Marchman, 1993). However, they all capture the same basic assumption that regular and irregular morphological forms can be encoded within a single distributed system. The regular default pattern is learned as a statistical generalization across many different forms, with coarser grained statistics being similarly used to encode idiosyncratic forms (*take–took*). The same process can also capture pools of subregularities among irregulars (*swept, kept, slept; sang, rang, sank*).

Can these theories of past tense help us to understand why children with SLI have difficulty with past tense? Proponents of a dual mechanism model have suggested that affected children have an impaired rule mechanism (Clahsen & Almazan, 1998; Pinker & Ullman, 2002; van der Lely & Ullman, 2001). According to this theory, SLI involves a domain-specific deficit that impairs the cognitive mechanism responsible for encoding grammatical rules. Instead, these children only have access to an associative memory system for learning both regular and irregular past tenses. The prediction of this theory seems to be that children with SLI will tend to have significant problems with regular and nonword forms, since these forms require the use of rules, but they will not have difficulty with irregular forms, since these forms are processed within a separate (and presumably intact) cognitive mechanism.

The connectionist theory takes a different view: that SLI involves a domain-general deficit. Models of past tense deficits in SLI have focused on the idea that these children have perceptual or phonological difficulties that impair the ability to accurately perceive or manipulate phonological information. For example, Hoeffner and McClelland (1993) simulated verb production in a model that took a verb's semantics as an input and output its phonological form. Because present and past tense verbs overlap significantly in their semantic form (i.e., their meanings presumably differ only with respect to "past tense-ness"), similar connections are used for both forms. Similarly, the [PAST TENSE] semantic feature tends to map consistently onto features signaling word-final alveolar stops on the output layer, because all regular past tense forms end in *d* or *t* sounds (as do many irregulars). The reduced salience of word-final stops was simulated by weakening the connections to units that encoded these features. This in itself did not impair the network's ability to learn to produce either past tenses or other words with past-like endings (e.g., *blast, most*). However, when they simulated a speech perception deficit by also weakening inputs to the phonological layer as a whole, the network showed specific deficits in generating past tenses like *walked*. Interestingly, the impaired network was still able to accurately generate other words ending in alveolar stops (e.g., *blast*), because in these cases there was no phonological and semantic competition with an existing present tense form (e.g., **blas*). Thus, this model represents an interesting illustration of how a perceptual deficit can lead to specific problems with morphology rather than weakening representations of all words equally.

More recent work has followed up on this by looking at how a speech perception deficit might impair different types of past tenses, including nonwords, and whether connectionist models can simulate the types of errors that are observed in SLI when such an impairment is implemented (Joanisse, 2000, 2004; Thomas & Karmiloff-Smith, 2003). Joanisse (2000, 2004; Figure 11.2) simulated past tense acquisition as the process of learning to map a word's phonological representation to its semantic form (simulating hearing a verb), as well as the reverse process of mapping semantics to phonology (simulating speaking a verb). The network was trained on a corpus of regular and irregular verbs in their present and past tense forms, where the activation of the [PAST TENSE] unit in the semantic layer signaled

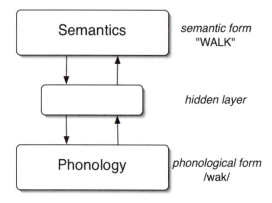

FIGURE 11.2 The Joanisse (2000, 2004) model of past tense. The model encodes a verb's phonological and semantic forms within discrete layers that are connected bidirectionally. A verb is presented with a semantic form as input and provides a phonological form as output, or vice versa, simulating the generation and recognition of present and past tenses.

its tense. In addition to being trained on recognition and production trials, the network was also occasionally given experience with *transformation* trials, in which a present tense phonological form was presented, and the [PAST TENSE] unit was also set to *on*. The network learned to transform the present tense form to its correct past tense, roughly simulating what occurs in a past tense elicitation task.

This network showed several important similarities to normally developing children and adults. When the network was fully trained, it was able to accurately produce, recognize, and transform the verbs in the training corpus at a high degree of proficiency (> 98% correct on all tasks). It was also able to transform a nonword form to its past tense, providing a regular -*ed* ending for this form in nearly every case. Over the course of training, the acquisition of irregular verbs tended to lag behind that of regulars, which is what is typically observed in children (Brown, 1973). Nonword generalization also tended to be acquired later in training than familiar forms, again consistent with what is seen in normal development (Bybee & Slobin, 1982). Finally, during training, the network occasionally produced overregularization errors on irregulars that it had not yet learned correctly (Marcus, Pinker, Ullman, Hollander, Rosen, & Xu, 1992).

Next, an identical model was trained in which a speech perception deficit was implemented by adding small amounts of random noise to the phonological units. This had the effect of causing the network to be slightly less accurate at categorizing phonemes in words. The effect of this impairment was twofold: first, it led to generally slower learning, such that performance on all verb types lagged behind the control simulation and asymptotic performance also never reached the same level of accuracy as the intact network. Second, nonword generalization was especially poor in the impaired model (10–15% correct, depending on the point in training). As it turns out, this pattern of deficit closely resembles what is seen in SLI. A number of studies have found that these children have delayed development of irregular past tenses relative to regulars of a similar frequency, as well as very poor nonword generalization (Robertson, 2003; van der Lely & Ullman, 2001). Third, the network produced fewer overregularization errors and more zero marking errors than did the intact network, which is again consistent with SLI. Overall, then, this model illustrated how a deficit in learning morphology can result from an impairment in perceiving phonological information about words, and that the pattern of deficits that results from this impairment is consistent with what is observed in language-impaired children.

Past Tense Deficits in Other Populations

As with the reading impairment model discussed in the previous section, implementing different types of impairments in the connectionist model of past tense will tend to yield different types of deficits. Specifically, when the network was retrained with a semantic impairment (Joanisse, 2004), a different pattern of impairment was observed. Adding random noise to the network's semantics units during training made it difficult to identify unique word forms, leading to very poor performance on irregulars, while performance on regulars and nonwords was somewhat less impaired. The semantically impaired network also produced many more overregularization errors than the phonologically impaired network. The fact that a semantic deficit leads to a different pattern of errors in the connectionist past tense model suggests that phonology and semantics make different contributions to morphology processing. Phonological information is important in generalizing morphological patterns to nonwords, due to the role that it plays in analyzing the phonological structure of words during learning. For instance, phonology is critical for identifying the phonological overlap between a verb's past and present tense form (i.e., the overlap between *walk–walked, heal–healed,* and *waste–wasted*). It is also used to identify the phonological overlap among past tense forms themselves, such as identifying the phonological features that are shared between *walked, healed*, and *wasted*. This information can apply with minimal recourse to idiosyncratic information such as a word's semantic form, permitting it to be generalized to unfamiliar forms (e.g., *wugged*). Notably however, this information is not as helpful for learning the past tenses of irregulars, where the phonological relationship between present and past tense forms is less consistent. In those cases semantic information becomes critically important, since it is used to uniquely identify a word and the idiosyncratic patterns that are specific to it.

One question that arises from this is whether the pattern of deficit predicted by the semantics-impaired network actually occurs in any known population of children. Nation and colleagues have investigated past tense deficits in children with specific comprehension deficits, or "poor comprehenders" (Nation, Snowling, & Clarke, 2005). These children tend to exhibit very poor language comprehension, especially with respect to reading, even though they have relatively fluent single-word-reading and grammatical abilities. In this study, it was found that poor comprehenders had significant problems with tasks that tap semantic processing, compared to normal controls of the same age. However, their phonological processing abilities were intact. The fact that poor comprehenders have poor semantics seems to predict that they will have problems with irregular past tenses. Consistent with this, they observed a greater proportion of errors on irregular past tenses in poor comprehenders compared to controls, as well as a larger than expected number of overregularization errors.

There is also a growing literature on past tense impairments in Williams syndrome (WS; see also chapter 2 by McDuffie & Abbeduto). WS is a relatively rare developmental disorder that results in a range of cognitive problems, including visuospatial, problem-solving, and numerical deficits (Donnai & Karmiloff-Smith, 2000). In spite of their profound cognitive problems, individuals with WS have relatively good language skills, most famously with respect to their verbal fluency. That said, there is some evidence that these individuals do have language difficulties, especially in the areas of semantics and vocabulary: for instance, affected individuals tend to develop shallower semantic representations of concepts that tend to overemphasize perceptual features while underemphasizing abstract knowledge (Thomas & Karmiloff-Smith, 2003).

There is some question as to how best to characterize the morphological deficits in WS. An earlier study of four individuals with WS found that these individuals had greater difficulties with irregular past tenses compared to regular and nonword items (Clahsen & Almazan, 1998). This pattern of deficit would seem to suggest that affected individuals have difficulty encoding idiosyncratic forms while having a preserved ability to learn rule-like forms. This seems to mesh well with the theory that different processing systems are responsible for learning regular and irregular forms, and that the irregular mechanism can be independently impaired in some individuals (Clahsen & Almazan, 1998). However this characterization has been disputed in a more recent study that involved a larger WS sample and tested these individuals on items more closely matched for factors such as phonological complexity and frequency (Thomas et al., 2001). This study found that individuals with WS had an equal-sized delay on regulars and irregulars, such that they performed slightly worse than did vocabulary-matched controls on both types of past tense. They also showed significantly poorer performance on nonword generalization compared to controls.

Thomas et al. (2001) suggested that this deficit pattern does not correspond to the theory that individuals with WS have a deficit with irregulars, while showing preserved ability to apply rules. They argued instead that it could arise from a more subtle cognitive impairment that affects different aspects of morphological processing to different degrees. This was examined more closely using a connectionist model of past tense (Thomas &

Karmiloff-Smith, 2003). The network architecture they used was similar to the one presented in Figure 11.2, except that it also included two phonological layers, one for input and the other for output. (This simulated the idea that different processing units are used for perceiving and producing a word's phonological form.) They examined a wide array of deficit types in the model in order to more fully flesh out how different patterns of developmental impairment can occur as a result of different underlying deficit types. The manipulations included strengthening and weakening the degree of detail provided by the phonological and semantics layers, slowing the rate at which connection weights could be adjusted during training and adjusting the number of hidden units available to the network. As expected, different impairment types led to different patterns of problems in producing past tenses and different error types such as overgeneralization errors.

Most deficit types resulted in slower general acquisition of past tenses, and typically also impaired the network's ability to fully learn the training vocabulary. With respect to WS, they found that only two specific deficits closely simulated the behavioral pattern observed in affected individuals: reducing the similarity and redundancy of the phonological features being input to the network, and a weakening of the ability of hidden units to integrate phonology and semantics information within the hidden layer. This first deficit is achieved by manipulating the number of units that are being used to uniquely identify phonemes in words in a way that makes it more difficult to specify overlapping features across words that are phonologically similar. The second deficit involved manipulating the activation function of units in the hidden layer such that these units could not respond as effectively to multiple inputs simultaneously. Thomas and Karmiloff-Smith have suggested various ways in which these deficits could map onto the actual cognitive abilities of individuals with WS, but they also acknowledge that this remains an open question. Importantly, their study indicates quite nicely that the past tense deficit in WS is likely to be the result of a relatively general processing impairment—rather than a deficit to a distinct functional module subserving lexical coding, as Clahsen and colleagues have suggested (Clahsen & Almazan, 1998)—and that such a deficit can have nonobvious consequences for the development of morphology. It is also not the case that *any* type of impairment that slows language development will yield precisely the types of difficulties that are observed in impaired individuals.

Also notable is the fact that the Thomas–Karmiloff-Smith model could also simulate past tense deficits in SLI. They observed that weakening the degree to which the network's phonological units could accurately represent phonemes resulted in an SLI-like pattern of deficit. This replicates what was found in the Joanisse (2000, 2004) simulation and again shows that different patterns of developmental deficit can occur as a consequence of subtly different processing impairments.

Summary: Past Tense Deficits

Theories of past tense impairments that build on the symbols-and-rules model of language have suggested that different subtypes of impairment occur due to deficits in different processing modules. In this section I have summarized some of the evidence from the competing Connectionist approach, which suggests that a single neural architecture is responsible for learning both a generalizable morphological rule and also exceptional cases. This approach also suggests that impairments to different aspects of past tense processing can occur due to problems with different aspects of this neural architecture. Given a sufficiently sophisticated model of past tense processing, one can test the nature of behavioral impairments by testing the consequences of fine-grained deficits in the model. Notably, these deficits are seen as domain-general, rather than as impairments in language-specific mechanisms. In the case of SLI, it is hypothesized that a deficit in processing perceptual or phonological information results in a delayed acquisition of past tenses, marked by problems with nonword generalization, and fewer than expected overregularization errors. In contrast, other types of impairments can yield different constellations of deficits, as observed in poor comprehenders and individuals with Williams syndrome. It is argued that there is no need to appeal either to grammatical rules or to a discrete lexicon to explain any of these phenomena.

SYNTACTIC DEFICITS

In addition to morphology deficits, children with SLI also have significant problems processing syntactic relationships in sentences (see chapter 17 by Fletcher). For instance, they have difficulty assigning the correct thematic roles in reversible syntactically complex sentences, such as passives (*The boy is pushed by the girl.*), datives (e.g., *Give the girl the boy.*), and locatives (*The book is on the paper.*) (van der Lely & Harris, 1990). Notably, children with SLI are much better on syntactically similar sentences in which the thematic roles are not reversible: for instance, they are more accurate at choosing the correct meaning of a sentence such as *The ball is thrown by the boy*, or *The cat is on the table*, where the reverse interpretation (a ball throwing a boy, a table on top of a cat) is nonsensical. This would suggest that their difficulty with these sentences is not simply one of lexical semantics or pragmatics. Instead, they appear to have problems understanding how word order specifically modulates a sentence's meaning.

One interesting example of this is the interpretation of bound pronouns by children with SLI. In the sentence *Kathy thinks Marni likes her*, the referent of *her* can be *Kathy*, but it cannot be *Marni*. Likewise, the reflexive pronoun at the end of the sentence *Kathy thinks Marni likes herself* must refer to *Marni* and cannot refer to *Kathy*. The grammatical principles that determine the possible relationships between a pronoun and its referent are known as binding principles (see chapter 6 by Botwinik-Rotem & Friedmann) and are the topic of considerable inquiry in formal linguistics (Chomsky, 1981). Children with SLI perform much more poorly than controls on tests designed to assess this knowledge (van der Lely & Stollwerck, 1997). For instance, they score significantly more poorly than do control children at matching a sentence such as *Peter Pan is tickling him* to a picture that depicts the correct relationship (i.e., Peter Pan tickling another individual vs. Peter Pan tickling himself). In contrast, these same children perform significantly better on control sentences in which semantic information can also be used to resolve pronoun reference. For example, when given the sentence *Peter Pan is tickling her*, they tend not to choose the picture of Peter Pan tickling himself.

Working Memory and Syntax Deficits

It is difficult to imagine how syntactic difficulties such as this one could be related to a domain-general processing deficit. If children have difficulty simply understanding that pronouns refer to other individuals or objects in a given context, they would tend to perform just as poorly in the semantically constrained conditions as in the purely syntactic conditions. Similarly, it could be argued that pronouns and reflexives such as "him", "herself" and "it" are perceptually salient in at least some syntactic contexts. (Note that in some cases such as clitics, the salience of pronouns is reduced; see chapter 13 by Leonard.) In any case, it is unclear that language-impaired children are delayed in their acquisition of pronouns because they are not perceiving them properly. It is still possible that a domain-general processing difficulty might explain these problems, however. In addition to the grammatical and phonological processing difficulties discussed above, children with SLI also appear to have problems with phonological working memory, most notably nonword repetition (Gathercole & Baddeley, 1990; Montgomery, 1995). This task involves repeating nonsense words of different lengths (see chapter 1 by Schwartz and chapter 8 by Botwinik-Rotem & Friedmann). Although children with SLI tend to be as accurate as controls at repeating 1- and 2-syllable nonwords, they are much poorer when the length is increased to 3 and 4 syllables. As such, it appears that their difficulty with this task stems from the ability to maintain these words in working memory for the purpose of then repeating them (Bishop, North, & Donlan, 1996; Gathercole & Baddeley, 1990). One possibility is that limited phonological working memory also weakens sentence comprehension ability on the theory that one must use phonological codes to hold a sentence in memory during syntactic parsing (Just & Carpenter, 1992; MacDonald & Christiansen, 2002).

A Connectionist Model of Pronoun Deficits

Taking this a step further, it is also possible that a phonological working memory deficit could itself be caused by a more basic phonological or perceptual problem, similar to what is suggested in the models of reading and past tense impairments discussed above. According to this account, problems with perceiving or categorizing the phonemes in words can weaken the phonological codes used for holding sentences in memory, which in turn limits the ability to accurately learn and process syntactic relationships within a sentence. This account has previously been disputed by Gathercole and Baddeley (1990), based on their finding that language-impaired children who show working memory problems are nevertheless as accurate as controls at discriminating spoken words and nonwords. However, other studies have identified perceptual deficits in language-impaired children using more sensitive measures of speech perception (Joanisse et al., 2000; Sussman, 1993; Tallal & Piercy, 1974). Such findings suggest that subtle perceptual deficits do tend to occur in SLI.

This theory that a low-level perceptual deficit could lead to problems with sentence comprehension was tested in a connectionist model of sentence comprehension that learned to map a sentence's phonological form to its meaning (Joanisse & Seidenberg, 2003). In this model (Figure 11.3), the input consisted of the phonological forms of each

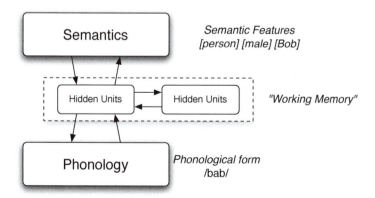

FIGURE 11.3 The Joanisse and Seidenberg (2003) model of sentence comprehension. The model receives the phonological form of each word in a sentence, in sequence, and outputs the semantic form of each word. Pronoun recognition is simulated by generating the semantic form of the pronoun's referent.

word in a sentence presented in sequence, and the output layer encoded a simplified semantic representation of a given word. The network's task was to recognize each word in the sequence (e.g., *Harry danced with Mary*) by activating the correct semantic output. This was complicated somewhat by the fact that some sentences contained bound pronouns and reflexives such as *Harry says Mary danced with her* or *Mary says Harry likes himself*; in these cases the network was also required to output the semantics of the word to which the pronoun or reflexive referred. The dynamic nature of a sentence comprehension task required the network to draw on representations of previous words in a given sequence. To accomplish this, the network had a type of working memory, in the form of two sets of hidden units recurrently interconnected.

The network was trained on a corpus of sentences with and without pronouns. At the end of training it showed good generalization to novel sentences (containing familiar words) and was able to resolve pronouns and reflexives accurately. Next, this network was trained with a simulated perceptual deficit in which random Gaussian noise was added to phonological input units. The speech-impaired network required more time to train, but did eventually acquire the training corpus with a good degree of accuracy. In addition, at the conclusion of training it was able to accurately recognize words in sentences, with one notable exception: the network showed marked difficulty with resolving pronouns and reflexives. In those cases it produced significantly more errors than did the control network. Interestingly, however, these errors were limited to semantically unconstrained cases (*Harry says Bob slapped him/himself*); performance was near ceiling on sentences where semantic information could help resolve pronouns (e.g., *Harry says Mary slapped him/ herself*).

The Joanisse and Seidenberg (2003) model stands as an illustration of how specific syntactic problems can be explained as resulting from a domain-general processing deficit. In the network, a phonological or perceptual deficit (the two were admittedly conflated in this simulation) resulted in a specific problem with syntactic pronoun resolution. Other abilities, such as single-word recognition and the use of semantic context to resolve pronouns mechanisms, remained intact. This deficit seems to closely match what is known about syntax in SLI. The mechanism by which this occurs appears to be a working memory limitation. Even though the impaired and intact networks were architecturally identical, it was hypothesized that a capacity limitation was being induced by weakening the quality of the phonological input the network received. Consequently, it was unable to maintain accurate working memory representations of previous words in a sentence, which limited its ability to learn or use syntactic relationships. The results of the network also suggest that one need not instantiate a domain-specific deficit to explain syntactic problems. For instance, while children with SLI clearly have difficulty with understanding structural complexities in sentences (e.g., pronoun reference, passive voice), this does not require a deficit in core syntax to explain it (van der Lely, 2005).

CHALLENGES FOR MODEL-BASED ACCOUNTS

Simplifying Assumptions

By definition, models are simplifications of an actual system. These *simplifying assumptions* are necessary for implementational reasons having to do with keeping the computational complexity of a model within the parameters of what existing technology permits. They also make it easier to understand and analyze a model's behavior. One consequence of simplifying assumptions is that there is always the risk that they will lead to an inaccurate portrayal of the system that is being simulated. However, just as in any other type of principled scientific simulation, such a breakdown is not an inevitable consequence of model-based approaches to cognition. For instance, implementational constraints related to computer storage space and processor speed have meant that early visual word-recognition models were limited to smaller sets of monosyllabic words. Based on this, these models were not able to handle certain types of words (Besner, Twilley, McCann, & Seergobin, 1990). However, subsequent simulations have indicated that the model does in fact "scale-up" to larger corpora, allowing it to address a broader range of topics (Plaut et al., 1996). Thus, it is important to distinguish between narrow implementational short-comings of a specific *simulation* and more serious theoretical shortcomings of a *model*. I would also argue that, because models are explicit by nature, it is always an empirical question whether simplifying assumptions have hopelessly corrupted a model's generaliz-ability to actual cognitive processes. It is dangerous to assume that a model is intrinsically incompatible with empirical data based on how it has been implemented in a specific instance.

Concerns with the Phonological Deficit Theory

Phonological deficits represent a central theme of the modeling work in phonological dyslexia and SLI. However, there is considerable debate as to whether such a deficit can fully explain the range of problems observed in these children. A central controversy in the literatures on SLI and (to a somewhat lesser extent) dyslexia concerns the extent to which these children also have perceptual deficits (Bishop, Carlyon, Deeks, & Bishop, 1999; Mody, Studdert-Kennedy, & Brady, 1997; Rosen, 2003). There is no doubt that many studies have identified clear perceptual deficits in dyslexia (Chiappe, Chiappe, & Siegel, 2001; Godfrey et al., 1981; Werker & Tees, 1987) and SLI (Sussman, 1993; Tallal et al., 1996; Thibodeau & Sussman, 1979). However, some studies have reported more mixed results—for instance, finding perceptual deficits in only a subset of these impaired children (Joanisse et al., 2000; Rosen & Manganari, 2001). Such findings tend to be problematic for perceptual deficit theories, since they suggest that problems with perception are not a necessary component of broader language disorders. One response to this is that per-ceptual deficits represent a delayed maturation of neural mechanisms supporting sensory processes (Wright et al., 1997). There is some limited support for this theory: in one study, children with SLI who exhibited clear perceptual deficits were retested four years later (Bernstein & Stark, 1985). At that point, many of these same children no longer showed perceptual problems. Notably, however, these children continued to exhibit significant language impairments. This suggests that an early perceptual deficit could interfere with language learning but also be undetectable at a later stage, even while its impact on lan-guage development persists. Similarly, Bishop and McArthur (Bishop & McArthur, 2004) have found that abnormal event-related electroencephalographic responses to auditory stimuli in SLI tend to resemble normal waveforms observed in younger controls. This again seems to support the delayed maturation hypothesis and could explain why it is sometimes difficult to observe perceptual deficits in impaired individuals.

Perhaps questions about perceptual deficits in SLI and dyslexia are moot: speech perception and phonological processing are, after all, independent abilities, and so a per-ceptual deficit might not be a necessary component of a phonological deficit. Some approaches to phonological deficits have not tended to draw a strong distinction between a perceptual and phonological deficit (Tallal et al., 1993). Nevertheless, this distinction could be important for understanding subtle differences between reading and language impair-ments. For instance, there is evidence that many children with phonological dyslexia have very good speech perception abilities, compared to language-impaired children of a similar age (Joanisse et al., 2000). This might mean that, although dyslexia and SLI involve similar problems with phonology, the nature of this deficit is subtly different in the two disorders. Indeed, this could also explain why dyslexia and SLI exist as separate diagnostic categories. Although they involve similar types of problems, subtle differences between the two lead to slightly different types of weaknesses.

Models of reading and language impairments have incorporated simplifying assumptions about phonological representations that make it difficult to study perception and phonology independently from each other. For instance, in the reading, morphology, and syntax models discussed above, the network *perceives* a word by activating its phonological features. There is no discrete mechanism by which auditory information is translated into these features, and thus no straightforward way to simulate more specific perceptual vs. phonological deficits. One possibility is that the phonology/perception distinction is necessary to fully capture the behavioral data. It is possible that future modeling efforts will help uncover these differences and why they occur. For instance, Plaut and Kello (1999) have developed a model of normal phonological development that contains perceptual and articulatory components, as well as an intermediary level that is presumed to represent phonological knowledge. Adapting such a model to the development of higher-level language abilities such as reading and morphosyntax might help shed light on this issue.

CONCLUSION

Language is an enormously complex cognitive ability and one that surely integrates a number of domain-general and domain-specific processes, ranging from low-level sensory abilities (e.g., auditory and visual perception) to higher-level semantic, contextual, and pragmatic knowledge. Thus, it seems reasonable to assume that a deficit at any point in this processing chain can lead to problems with acquiring language. There has been a great deal of interest in whether one can identify deficits that specifically target domain-specific language abilities, since such a finding would attest to the cognitive and neural reality of language-specific processing mechanisms. This modularity hypothesis is an intriguing one and one that has received considerable attention over the past few decades of language research. In this chapter I have suggested that the alternative possibility—that the development of specialized language abilities such as reading, morphology, and syntax depends critically on more basic abilities related to phonology and semantics—is just as interesting. This perspective can be implemented and tested using connectionist models. These models are explicit and testable instantiations of theories of language, and as a result they have the potential to provide us with helpful insights into the cognitive bases of language impairments.

ACKNOWLEDGMENTS

The author was supported by a New Investigator Award from the Canadian Institutes for Health Research and operating grants from the Natural Sciences and Engineering Research Council and the Canadian Language and Literacy Research Network.

REFERENCES

Berko, J. (1958). The child's learning of English morphology. *Word, 14*, 150–177.

Bernstein, L. E., & Stark, R. E. (1985). Speech perception development in language-impaired children: A 4-year follow-up study. *Journal of Speech and Hearing Disorders, 50*, 21–30.

Berwick, R. C. (1997). Syntax facit saltum: Computation and the genotype and phenotype of language. *Journal of Neurolinguistics, 10*(2/3), 231–249.

Besner, D., Twilley, L., McCann, R. S., & Seergobin, K. (1990). On the association between connectionism and data: Are a few words necessary? *Psychological Review, 97*, 432–446.

Bishop, D. V. M. (1997). *Uncommon understanding: Development and disorders of language comprehension in children*. Hove, UK: Psychology Press.

Bishop, D. V. M., Carlyon, R. P., Deeks, J. M., & Bishop, S. J. (1999). Auditory temporal processing impairment: Neither necessary nor sufficient for causing language impairment in children. *Journal of Speech, Language, and Hearing Research, 42*, 1295–1310.

Bishop, D. V. M., & McArthur, G. M. (2004). Immature cortical responses to auditory stimuli in specific language impairment: Evidence from ERPs to rapid tone sequences. *Developmental Science, 7*(4), F11–F18.

Bishop, D. V. M., North, T., & Donlan, C. (1996). Nonword repetition as a behavioral marker for inherited language development: Evidence from a twin study. *Journal of Child Psychology and Psychiatry, 37*, 391–403.

Block, N. (1990). The computer model of the mind. In *Thinking: Vol. 3. An invitation to cognitive science* (pp. 247–289). Cambridge, MA: MIT Press.

Brown, R. (1973). *A first language: The early stages*. Cambridge, MA: Harvard University Press.

Bybee, J., & Slobin, D. (1982). Rules and schemas in the development and use of the English past. *Language, 58*, 265–289.

Castles, A., & Coltheart, M. (1993). Varieties of developmental dyslexia. *Cognition, 47*(2), 149–180.

Castles, A., & Coltheart, M. (2004). Is there a causal link from phonological awareness to success in learning to read? *Cognition, 91*(1), 77–111.

Castles, A., Datta, H., Gayan, J., & Olson, R. K. (1999). Varieties of developmental reading disorder: Genetic and environmental influences. *Journal of Experimental Child Psychology, 72*, 73–94.

Chiappe, P., Chiappe, D. L., & Siegel, L. S. (2001). Speech perception, lexicality, and reading skill. *Journal of Experimental Child Psychology, 80*(1), 58–74.

Chomsky, N. (1981). *Lectures in government and binding*. Dordrecht, The Netherlands: Foris.

Chomsky, N. (1986). *Knowledge of language: Its nature, origin and use*. New York: Praeger.

Clahsen, H., & Almazan, M. (1998). Syntax and morphology in Williams syndrome. *Cognition, 68*, 167–198.

Coltheart, M., Curtis, B., Atkins, P., & Haller, M. (1993). Models of reading aloud: Dual-route and parallel-distributed-processing approaches. *Psychological Review, 100*(4), 589–608.

Coltheart, M., Rastle, K., Perry, C., Langdon, R., & Ziegler, J. (2001). DRC: A dual route cascaded model of visual word recognition and reading aloud. *Psychological Review, 108*(1), 204–256.

Daugherty, K., & Seidenberg, M. S. (1992). Rules or connections? The past tense revisited. In *Proceedings of the Fourteenth Annual Conference of the Cognitive Science Society* (pp. 259–264). Hillsdale, NJ: Lawrence Erlbaum Associates.

Desroches, A. S., Joanisse, M. F., & Robertson, E. K. (2006). Specific phonological impairments in dyslexia revealed by eyetracking. *Cognition, 100*, B32–B42.

Donnai, D., & Karmiloff-Smith, A. (2000). Williams syndrome: From genotype through to the cognitive phenotype. *American Journal of Medical Genetics, 97*, 164–171.

Fodor, J. (1983). *Modularity of mind*. Cambridge, MA: MIT Press.

Gathercole, S. E., & Baddeley, A. D. (1990). Phonological memory deficits in language disordered children: Is there a causal connection? *Journal of Memory and Language, 29*, 336–360.

Godfrey, J. J., Syrdal-Lasky, A. K., Millay, K., & Knox, C. M. (1981). Performance of dyslexic children on speech perception tests. *Journal of Experimental Child Psychology, 32*, 401–424.

Gopnik, M., & Crago, M. (1991). Familial aggregation of a developmental language disorder. *Cognition, 39*, 1–50.

Gopnik, M., & Goad, H. (1997). What underlies inflectional errors in SLI? *Journal of Neuro-linguistics, 10*, 129–137.

Goswami, U. (1999). Causal connections in beginning reading: The importance of rhyme. *Journal of Research in Reading, 22*(3), 217–240.

Harm, M. W., & Seidenberg, M. S. (1999). Phonology, reading acquisition, and dyslexia: Insights from connectionist models. *Psychological Review, 106*(3), 491–528.

Harm, M. W., & Seidenberg, M. S. (2004). Computing the meanings of words in reading: Cooperative division of labor between visual and phonological processes. *Psychological Review, 111*(3), 662–720.

Hoeffner, J. J., & McClelland, J. L. (1993). Can a perceptual processing deficit explain the impairment of inflectional morphology in development dysphasia? A computational investigation. In E. V. Clark (Ed.), *Proceedings of the 25th Annual Child Language Research Forum* (Vol. 25, pp. 38–49). Stanford, CA: Center for the Study of Language and Information.

Jared, D. (1997). Spelling-sound consistency affects the naming of high-frequency words. *Journal of Memory and Language, 36*, 505–529.

Joanisse, M. F. (2000). *Connectionist Phonology*. Unpublished doctoral dissertation, University of Southern California, Los Angeles.

Joanisse, M. F. (2004). Specific language impairments in children: Phonology, semantics and the English past tense. *Current Directions in Psychological Science, 13*(4), 156–160.

Joanisse, M. F., Manis, F. R., Keating, P., & Seidenberg, M. S. (2000). Language deficits in dyslexic children: Speech perception, phonology, and morphology. *Journal of Experimental Child Psychology, 77*(1), 30–60.

Joanisse, M. F., & Seidenberg, M. S. (1999). Impairments in verb morphology after brain injury: A connectionist model. *Proceedings of the National Academy of Sciences U.S.A., 96*(13), 7592–7597.

Joanisse, M. F., & Seidenberg, M. S. (2003). Phonology and syntax in specific language impairment: Evidence from a connectionist model. *Brain and Language, 86*(1), 40–56.

Just, M. A., & Carpenter, P. A. (1992). A capacity theory of comprehension: Individual differences in working memory. *Psychological Review, 99*, 122–149.

Kail, R. (1994). A method for studying the generalized slowing hypothesis in children with specific language impairment. *Journal of Speech, Language, and Hearing Research, 37*(2), 418–421.

Leonard, L. B. (1998). *Children with specific language impairment*. Cambridge, MA: MIT Press.

Leonard, L. B., Eyer, J. A., Bedore, L. M., & Grela, B. G. (1997). Three accounts of the grammatical morpheme difficulties of English-speaking children with Specific Language Impairment. *Journal of Speech, Language, and Hearing Research, 40*, 741–753.

MacDonald, M. C., & Christiansen, M. H. (2002). Reassessing working memory: Comment on Just and Carpenter (1992) and Waters and Caplan (1996). *Psychological Review, 109*(1), 35–54.

MacWhinney, B., & Leinbach, J. (1991). Implementations are not conceptualizations: Revising the verb learning model. *Cognition, 29*, 121–157.

Manis, F. R., McBride-Chang, C., Seidenberg, M. S., Keating, P., Doi, L. M., Munson, B., et al. (1997). Are speech perception deficits associated with developmental dyslexia? *Journal of Experimental Child Psychology, 66*, 211–235.

Manis, F. R., Seidenberg, M. S., Doi, L., McBride-Chang, C., & Petersen, A. (1996). On the basis of two subtypes of developmental dyslexia. *Cognition, 58*, 157–195.

Manis, F. R., Seidenberg, M. S., Stallings, L., Joanisse, M. F., Bailey, C., Freedman, L., et al. (1999). Development of dyslexic subgroups: A one-year follow up. *Annals of Dyslexia, 49*, 105–134.

Marchman, V. A., Wulfeck, B., & Ellis Weismer, S. (1999). Morphological productivity in children with normal language and SLI: A study of the English past tense. *Journal of Speech, Language, and Hearing Research, 42*, 206–219.

Marcus, G. F. (1998). Rethinking eliminative connectionism. *Cognitive Psychology, 37*, 243–282.

Marcus, G. F., Pinker, S., Ullman, M. T., Hollander, M., Rosen, T. J., & Xu, F. (1992). Overregularization in language-acquisition. *Monographs of the Society for Research in Child Development, 57*(4), R5–R165.

Mody, M., Studdert-Kennedy, M., & Brady, S. (1997). Speech perception deficits in poor readers: Auditory processing or phonological coding? *Journal of Experimental Psychology*, *64*, 199–231.

Montgomery, J. W. (1995). Sentence comprehension in children with specific language impairment: The role of phonological working memory. *Journal of Speech and Hearing Research*, *38*, 187–199.

Morais, J., Cary, L., Alegria, J., & Bertelson, P. (1979). Does awareness of speech as a sequence of phones arise spontaneously? *Cognition*, *7*, 323–331.

Nation, K., Snowling, M. J., & Clarke, P. (2005). Production of the English past tense by children with language comprehension impairments. *Journal of Child Language*, *32*(1), 117–137.

Oetting, J. B., & Horohov, J. E. (1997). Past-tense marking by children with and without Specific Language Impairment. *Journal of Speech, Language, and Hearing Research*, *40*, 62–74.

Pinker, S. (1991). Rules of language. *Science*, *253*, 530–535.

Pinker, S. (1999). *Words and rules*. New York: Basic Books.

Pinker, S., & Ullman, M. T. (2002). The past and future of the past tense. *Trends in Cognitive Sciences*, *6*(11), 456–463.

Plaut, D. C., & Kello, C. T. (1999). The emergence of phonology from the interplay of speech comprehension and production: A distributed connectionist approach. In B. MacWhinney (Ed.), *The emergence of language* (pp. 381–415). Mahwah, NJ: Lawrence Erlbaum Associates.

Plaut, D. C., McClelland, J. L., Seidenberg, M. S., & Patterson, K. (1996). Understanding normal and impaired word reading: Computational principles in quasi-regular domains. *Psychological Review*, *103*(1), 56–115.

Plunkett, K., & Marchman, V. (1993). From rote learning to system building: Acquiring verb morphology in children and connectionist nets. *Cognition*, *48*(1), 21–69.

Rice, M. L., & Wexler, K. (1996). A phenotype of specific language impairments: Extended optional infinitives. In M. L. Rice (Ed.), *Toward a genetics of language* (pp. 215–237). Mahwah, NJ: Lawrence Erlbaum Associates.

Robertson, E. K. (2003). *Breadth and basis of overlapping reading and language deficits in dyslexia and specific language impairment*. Unpublished master's thesis, Department of Psychology, University of Western Ontario, Canada.

Rosen, S. (2003). Auditory processing in dyslexia and specific language impairment: Is there a deficit? What is its nature? Does it explain anything? *Journal of Phonetics*, *31*(3–4), 509–527.

Rosen, S., & Manganari, E. (2001). Is there a relationship between speech and nonspeech auditory processing in children with dyslexia? *Journal of Speech, Language, and Hearing Research*, *44*(4), 720–736.

Rumelhart, D., & McClelland, J. L. (1986). On learning the past tenses of English verbs. In D. Rumelhart & J. L. McClelland (Eds.), *Parallel distributed processing: Vol. 2. Psychological and Biological Models*. Cambridge, MA: MIT Press.

Rumelhart, D., McClelland, J. L., & The PDP Research Group. (1986). *Parallel distributed processing: Vol. 1. Foundations*. Cambridge, MA: MIT Press.

Seidenberg, M. S., & McClelland, J. L. (1989). A distributed, developmental model of word recognition and naming. *Psychological Review*, *96*, 523–568.

Smolensky, P. (1999). Grammar-based connectionist approaches to language. *Cognitive Science*, *23*(4), 589–613.

Stanovich, K. E. (1988). The right and wrong places to look for the cognitive locus of reading disability. *Annals of Dyslexia*, *38*, 154–177.

Stanovich, K. E., Siegel, L. S., & Gottardo, A. (1997). Converging evidence for phonological and surface subtypes of reading disability. *Journal of Educational Psychology*, *89*(1), 114–127.

Sussman, J. E. (1993). Perception of formant transition cues to place of articulation in children with language impairments. *Journal of Speech and Hearing Research*, *36*, 1286–1299.

Tallal, P., Miller, S. L., Bedi, G., Vyma, G., Wang, X., Nagarajan, S. S., et al. (1996). Language comprehension in language-learning impaired children improved with acoustically modified speech. *Science*, *272*, 81–84.

Tallal, P., Miller, S., & Fitch, R. H. (1993). Neurobiological basis of speech: A case for the preeminence of temporal processing. *Annals of the New York Academy of Sciences, 682*, 27–47.

Tallal, P., Miller, S., & Fitch, R. H. (1995). Neurobiological basics of speech: A case for the preeminence of temporal processing. *Irish Journal of Psychology, 16*, 194–219.

Tallal, P., & Piercy, M. (1974). Developmental aphasia: Rate of auditory processing and selective impairment of consonant perception. *Neuropsychologia, 12*, 83–94.

Thibodeau, L. M., & Sussman, H. M. (1979). Performance on a test of categorical perception of speech in normal and communication disordered children. *Journal of Phonetics, 7*, 379–391.

Thomas, M. S. C., Grant, J., Barham, Z., Gsödl, M., Laing, E., Lakusta, L., et al. (2001). Past tense formation in Williams syndrome. *Language and Cognitive Processes, 16*, 143–176.

Thomas, M. S. C., & Karmiloff-Smith, A. (2003). Modelling language acquisition in atypical phenotypes. *Psychological Review, 110*(4), 647–682.

van der Lely, H. K. J. (2005). Domain-specific cognitive systems: Insight from grammatical-SLI. *Trends in Cognitive Sciences, 9*(2), 53–59.

van der Lely, H. K. J., & Harris, M. (1990). Comprehension of reversible sentences in specifically language impaired children. *Journal of Speech and Hearing Disorders, 5*, 101–117.

van der Lely, H. K. J., & Stollwerck, L. (1997). Binding theory and grammatical specific language impairment in children. *Cognition, 62*(1), 245–290.

van der Lely, H. K. J., & Ullman, M. T. (2001). Past tense morphology in specifically language impaired and normally developing children. *Language and Cognitive Processes, 16*, 177–217.

Vargha-Khadem, F., Watkins, K., Alcock, K., Fletcher, P., & Passingham, R. (1995). Praxic and nonverbal cognitive deficits in a large family with a genetically transmitted speech and language disorder. *Proceedings of the National Academy of Science U.S.A., 92*, 930–933.

Wagner, R. K., Torgesen, J. K., & Rashotte, C. A. (1994). Development of reading-related phonological processing abilities: New evidence of bi-directional causality from a latent variable longitudinal study. *Developmental Psychology, 30*, 73–87.

Werker, J., & Tees, R. (1987). Speech perception in severely disabled and average reading children. *Canadian Journal of Experimental Psychology, 41*(1), 48–61.

Wickelgren, W. A. (1969). Context sensitive coding, associative memory, and serial order in (speech) behavior. *Psychological Review, 76*(1), 1–15.

Wright, B. A., Lombardino, L. J., King, W. M., Puranik, C. S., Leonard, C. M., & Merzenich, M. M. (1997). Deficits in auditory temporal and spectral resolution in language-impaired Children. *Nature, 387*, 176–178.

Part III

Language Contexts of Child Language Disorders

12

Bilingualism in Child Language Disorders

ELIZABETH D. PEÑA and LISA M. BEDORE

*I*n the United States, an increasing number of children learn language in a bilingual environment. Simultaneous bilinguals are those who are exposed to two languages from birth, or from a very early age (typically before 2 years). Sequential bilinguals learn a second language after they have mastered the first. The majority of these bilingual children are known as early "sequential" bilinguals—learning a home language first—then learning English at the time of initial formal schooling (i.e., preschool or kindergarten). They typically learn a second language after age 2, before mastering their home language. When sequential bilinguals are in the early phase of learning language, it is difficult to differentiate language impairment (LI) from language differences. Until very recently, there have been few systematic studies of LI in bilingual children. Now there is a small, growing database of research that informs practice in this area. In this chapter, we first review some of the prevailing theories about bilingual language acquisition; next we discuss the social factors influencing bilingualism in the United States; then, studies of LI in bilinguals are reviewed with particular attention to similarities and differences in markers of impairment; finally, we discuss current trends and practices in language assessment of bilinguals. For these two latter points we draw on our own research examining language acquisition and LI in Spanish–English bilinguals—one of the largest bilingual populations in the United States.

THEORETICAL PERSPECTIVES ON BILINGUALISM IN CHILDREN

Much of the early research on bilingualism focused on whether the two languages were independent or interdependent (e.g., Genesee, 1978; Volterra & Taeschner, 1978). At present, most scholars agree that bilinguals master the linguistic rule systems for each of their two languages and are able to keep them separate (Genesee, Nicoladis, & Paradis, 1995; Marchman, Martínez-Sussmann, & Dale, 2004; Meisel, 1983). Important current questions are to what extent, in what domains, and at what point in development do the two languages influence each other? The two main hypotheses about bilingual development emphasize independence or interdependence. These hypotheses, in part, reflect the manner in which children become bilingual.

A contemporary statement of the independence hypothesis is De Houwer's (2005) *separate development hypothesis*. This model suggests that when there is bilingual input (defined as a body of dual-language input containing lexical and syntactic input in one language at a time) from birth onwards, children will acquire both of the languages. Because children can form language-specific utterances and development follows the same general patterns and time frame as monolingual development, separate development is assumed. Most of the work evaluating this perspective focuses on morphology (Castro & Gavruseva, 2003; Paradis, Le Corre, & Genesee, 1998) and syntax (Almgren & Barreña, 2001; Flynn, 1996). These domains of study are often integrated with semantics (Álvarez, 2003; Thordardottir, 2005), phonology (Archibald, 1997; Eckman, 2004), and language choice (Pease-Alvarez, 2002; Quay, 1995; Wickström, 2005). From this perspective, linguistic errors are attributed to insufficient input, and it is emphasized that even when speakers produce errors, these errors reflect natural language constraints. Much of the work on the separate development hypothesis focuses on simultaneous bilingual speakers and has not been systematically applied to sequential bilingual learners.

Reflecting an interdependence perspective, some researchers suggest that sequential bilingualism is more interrelated in the early stages of second-language learning because the stronger, established language mediates or guides development in the second language (Meisel, 1983). For example, Gawlitzek-Maiwald and Tracy (1996) propose that the stronger—often the first—language is used to *bootstrap* acquisition of the second language. Thus, learners utilize their knowledge of the structures of the first language as the foundation for the second language. Similarly, the *ivy hypothesis* (Bernardini & Schlyter, 2004) suggests that children use the structure of the stronger language with lexical items from the weaker language when interacting in that language. The weaker language is initially developed via lexical learning. At the same time, languages are not resistant to influences from each other (Grosjean, 1989, 1998). MacWhinney's (2005) *unified model*—based on Bates and MacWhinney's (1987) earlier versions of the competition model—also suggests interdependence between first and second languages but emphasizes the role of learning processes. MacWhinney characterized language learning as competition between cues across arenas (i.e., phonology, lexicon, morphosyntax, and pragmatics). For learners to process information, they must store, chunk, and decode information. Decoding for bilinguals involves language transfer. Children learn their second language through the filter of what they know about their first language. For example, children may retain certain chunks of information or language and associate them based on the language-learning strategies they already have available. Young, early sequential bilinguals can exploit their experience as language learners by using first-language knowledge and rules to learn the second language. But they are limited in their ability to do so because the process of learning the first language is still ongoing when they are introduced to the second language.

Typological differences between language pairs are thought to play a role in the degree to which languages influence each other. From a competition model perspective, children who are exposed to two languages are likely to use high-frequency forms correctly but will make errors on lower frequency forms. Forms that have a high degree of similarity between two languages (e.g., plural -s in English and Spanish) will be mastered sooner. A languages-in-contact perspective (Döpke, 2000) predicts that unambiguously different forms, such as a gender-neutral system of determiners in English, are less likely to be vulnerable to changes. But differences between languages that are more subtle may be more difficult to tease apart. For example, in French and Spanish gender is clearly marked on all determiners (matching the phonological characteristics of the noun) when the noun starts with a consonant (*le toit, el techo* [the roof: masculine] *la pomme, la manzana* [the apple: feminine]: French and Spanish, respectively). But in French if the noun starts with a vowel, the determiner is unmarked for gender (*l'aigle* [the eagle]). In Spanish, if the noun starts with a vowel, the masculine determiner (*el*) is used (e.g., *el águila* [the eagle]) even when the phonological form of the word would otherwise predict the use of a feminine article. Languages with similar features may give rise to more merging of forms, but languages that are more distant in structure will not (Döpke, 2000; Tracy, 1995). This languages-in-contact perspective is consistent with one of interdependence.

From an independence perspective, Hulk and Müller (2000) propose that when language structures overlap but one appears to have more than one interpretation for the same structure (due to the child's language input), there is the potential for mutual influence. For example, a child exposed to languages with optional subject omission or drop (a Romance language) and topic drop (German) will make different assumption about the structure than will a child exposed to a pair of languages that does not permit topic drop (e.g., a Romance language and English). They point out that mutual influence occurs at the intersection between pragmatics and syntax and is a language-internal phenomenon rather than one of language dominance. Another consideration is whether different linguistic domains are differentially influenced by bilingualism. There is evidence that languages influence each other in phonology (Dodd, So, & Li, 1996; Gierut, 1998; Gildersleeve-Neumann, Stubbe Kester, Davis, & Peña, in press), semantics (Ameel, Storms, & Malt, 2005), and syntax (Döpke, 2000; Volterra & Taeschner, 1978). Children must acquire the form of each of their languages, and this has been the area best explained by the independent development models such as the separate development hypothesis. Semantic knowledge is different: children have an underlying set of concepts and may have words for those concepts in one or both of their languages. The argument we will make here is that the independent and interdependent hypotheses are both useful in predicting language development patterns in young sequential bilingual learners. Bilingual children's competence will vary by domain and over time. At some points in time bilinguals will be more like their monolingual peers and at other points in time their mixed knowledge will be more apparent. Rule-based systems are more likely to appear independent, and meaning-based systems are more likely appear to be interdependent.

Configurations of first language (L1) and second language (L2) fluency may reflect the degree to which the two languages are used. Time spent hearing and interacting in one language necessarily influences the time available to hear and interact in the other language. The question of amount of exposure has important implications for examining language abilities of bilinguals and understanding how language impairment may be manifested. With respect to both assessment and intervention, it is important to consider whether both languages should be assessed and how findings in one language or domain might be related to findings in the other language or other domains.

SOCIAL AND LINGUISTIC INFLUENCES ON BILINGUALISM IN THE UNITED STATES

The largest group of bilingual children in the United States is comprised of children of immigrants (Grieco, 2004). Generally, these children are exposed to their parents' language at home and have their first exposure to English by preschool or kindergarten. Bilingualism in this population emerges from the need to communicate in two languages (see Grosjean, 1989, 1998). Variation in the timing, contexts, and amount of exposure to L1 and L2 impacts fluency in each language across contexts. Timing, context, and exposure further guide when and how children learn English as a second language. Timing of English-language exposure may initially be influenced by birth order. First-born children will necessarily learn the language of their parents (Brodie, Steffenson, Vasquez, Levin, & Suro, 2002). Levels of proficiency in each language will influence the extent to which children choose to use each of their languages (Paradis & Nicoladis, 2007). Older children, however, may use English at home with later-born children, thus exposing them to the second language at a younger age (i.e., before school entry). Bilingual and English as a Second Language (ESL) school programs vary in the grade levels at which they are implemented as well as the total amounts of English and other language input that they provide. Social interaction and neighborhood demographics play a part as well. In neighborhoods with high immigrant populations, it is more likely that children will hear their home language spoken by other adults and children in the community, by personnel in retail stores and restaurants, and by medical service providers. These situations provide a variety of contexts in which the child may hear and use the home language as well as how much exposure the child has to it. Parental choice in language use also comes into play. Some parents may choose to maintain the home language deliberately, providing language, literacy, and cultural experiences in the form of after-school programs and weekend schools. Other parents may choose to limit use of the home language and select English-only school programs for their children.

Over time, the configuration of L1 and L2 contexts and degree of exposure to each language changes. As children progress in school, many have increasing exposure to English and to English-speaking peers. The contexts in which bilingual children are exposed to each of their two languages influence the degree of exposure and result in different profiles of knowledge and fluency of L1 and L2 for different children (Pease-Alvarez, 2002; Valdes & Figueroa, 1994; Vasquez, Pease-Alvarez, & Shannon, 1994). Although we might picture all bilinguals as communicating in two languages, it is useful to envision bilingualism as a continuum. Most bilinguals are able to communicate to some degree in each of their languages. At the ends of the continuum, there are individuals who are exposed to bilingual input but use only one language (Valdes & Figueroa, 1994). These individuals are sometimes referred to as *passive bilinguals*. Early sequential bilingual children growing up in the United States present a challenge because, as a group, they tend to begin to be regularly exposed to English before they master their first language. But they begin learning the second language later than the cut-off of about 2 years of age usually established for considering a child to be a simultaneous bilingual. Thus, these children do not fully fit the definition of either sequential or simultaneous bilinguals. At preschool entry, these children have a significant body of first-language knowledge when they start to learn English. As such, predictions about their language knowledge and development may be based on interdependent models. Because second-language learning starts while these children are still acquiring their first language, development may also follow some of the predictions of the independent models. In addition to these social context considerations, linguistic considerations such as typology and domain (as discussed above) may additionally influence the degree of convergence or divergence in a languages-in-contact situation.

LANGUAGE DEVELOPMENT IN BILINGUAL CHILDREN

Children learning language in dual-language environments need to learn and use linguistic forms to meet everyday language-specific discourse demands. Thus, they need to master the phonological patterns, vocabulary, semantics, morphology, syntax, and pragmatics of each language. Research demonstrates that children can separate their languages at the level of speech perception (Bosch & Sebastián-Galles, 2001), speech production (Gildersleeve-Neumann et al., in press), vocabulary (Bedore, Peña, García, & Cortez, 2005; Pearson & Fernández, 1994; Quay, 1995), morphosyntax (De Houwer, 1990), and pragmatics (Genesee, Boivin, & Nicoladis, 1996). Each of these domains of language may, however, allow different degrees of mixing between the two systems. We propose that the intersection of pragmatics with each of these domains serves to constrain or to allow transfer between the two languages. Language transfer may lead to a greater or lesser degree of mixed knowledge, or integration, between the two languages. In the following sections, we discuss vocabulary learning, morphology, syntax, and discourse in greater detail as these are areas that have been studied in bilingual children with LI.

Semantics in Typical Bilingual Children

Vocabulary acquisition in bilinguals has been the focus of study for a number of years, particularly in young bilingual children. Generally, findings indicate that trajectories of word learning in bilinguals are similar to that of monolinguals if words across both languages are counted (Holowka, Brosseau-Lapré, & Petitto, 2002; Patterson, 1998, 2000; Pearson, Fernández, & Oller, 1993, 1995), suggesting mixed knowledge. This has been demonstrated for bilingual toddlers (Conboy & Thal, 2006; Holowka et al., 2002; Patterson, 2000; Pearson et al., 1995), preschoolers (Peña, Bedore, & Zlatic-Guinta, 2002; Thordardottir, 2005; Vermeer, 2001), and school-age children (Umbel, Pearson, Fernández, & Oller, 1992). Even when children are clearly dominant in one language or the other, they often know some items in the weaker language that they do not use in the stronger language (Peña et al., 2002; Umbel et al., 1992). Mixed knowledge occurs because objects and ideas can be encoded in one or both of a bilingual's languages. Bilinguals may therefore exhibit performance differences in comparison to their monolingual peers related to cross-language transfer. Most studies of lexical development demonstrate that word learning is context-specific: children encode items in the language in which they hear and use them (Pearson & Fernández, 1994; Peña et al., 2002). Thus, it is likely that bilinguals and monolinguals have different profiles of word knowledge reflecting language exposure.

Our own findings with Spanish- and/or English-speaking children suggest that early sequential bilingual children lexicalize items specific to language context. We tested bilingual children using a category-generation task in each of their two languages (Peña et al., 2002). Results indicated that bilingual children generated similar numbers of items in each language. Comparisons between the two languages additionally indicated that a large proportion (68.4%) of items was produced in only one language. These results suggest that children who are learning language in bilingual environments may not encode the same items in each of their two languages. Support for this hypothesis was provided by post hoc analysis of the most frequently occurring items in each language. Similarly to previous findings based on monolinguals (Nelson & Nelson, 1990) and bilinguals (Schwanenflugel & Rey, 1986), children were more likely to generate items most familiar to them for a given category. From a pragmatic perspective, for bilinguals, familiarity was further constrained by the linguistic context. For example, they generated *frijoles, arroz,* and *pastel* [*beans, rice,* and *cake*] most frequently when asked to generate foods eaten at a birthday party in Spanish, and *hamburgers, hot dogs,* and *cake* when asked the same question in English.

Two follow-up studies with early sequential bilinguals yielded similar patterns. Peña, Bedore, and Rappazzo (2003) compared three groups of bilingual (Spanish/English) and functionally monolingual (predominantly Spanish-speaking or predominantly English-speaking) 4- to 6-year-old children who completed a battery of semantic tasks (categorization, functions, analogies, comparisons, descriptions, and linguistic concepts). The three language groups had similar total items correct on the semantic battery as a whole, but there were differences in patterns of performance related to task type between languages. For example, English speakers correctly responded to more "linguistic concepts" items than did Spanish speakers. An example of a linguistic concepts item is "*Show me the gift in front of the TV.*" Spanish speakers responded to more "function" items correctly than did English speakers. Function items included such items as "*Which picture shows what a party hat is for*" and "*Show me what you do with a bow.*" Within language, there were small but significant differences between functional monolingual and bilingual children. In addition to differences related to question type, bilingual children may demonstrate different codeswitching (nontarget-language) patterns depending on language context (Bedore et al., 2005). When children in this study did codeswitch, they were more likely to do so from Spanish to English, regardless of language proficiency (13% from Spanish to English, and 3% English to Spanish), perhaps reflecting what they know about the language of schooling. When they provided responses in the nontarget language, they did so to add new information rather than to provide translations of responses they had already given.

Morphology and Syntax in Typical Bilingual Children

In cases where bilingual children are able to communicate in each of their languages (as compared to children who are just beginning to acquire a second language), general indices of syntactic development are comparable to those of monolingual children (see chapter 15 by Oetting & Hadley). For example, children demonstrate mean length of utterance (MLU)—a general index of syntactic complexity—that is within the average range for their monolingual peers. This similarity has been observed for young French–English simultaneous bilinguals at the early stages of word combinations (Paradis & Genesee, 1997), as well as for school-age Spanish–English bilinguals (e.g., Fiestas & Peña, 2004). This similarity also holds for passive bilingual children who have significant exposure (10–30%) to a second language such as Filipino or Spanish but do not actively produce the second language (Lofranco, Peña, & Bedore, 2006; Muñoz, Gillam, Peña, & Gulley-Faehnle, 2003). Japanese-speaking 6- to 10-year-old children acquiring English as a second language demonstrated predicted developmental sequences of syntactic structure from a Universal Grammar perspective (Flynn, 1996). These children produced English modals (e.g., *may, can*) and *do* support for negatives (e.g., he *doesn't* talk loud) with much higher levels of accuracy in comparison to forms such as subject or object gap wh-questions (e.g., *Which girl went to the store? Who did the boy trip?*) or relative clauses (e.g., *I like the picture that the old man painted.*). These findings followed the expected developmental patterns consistent with syntactic complexity or movement.

Consistent with theories of independent development, morphological development also proceeds in developmentally expected ways in bilingual children. French–English simultaneous bilinguals between 2;0 and 3;6 produced very low rates of grammatical errors (0–9%) in their morphologically marked utterances with codeswitches (Paradis, Nicoladis, & Genesee, 2000). Preschool-age Spanish-speaking children acquiring English as a second language produced early emerging morphemes such as the *-ing*, possessive *-s*, or plural *-s* with higher levels of accuracy than later-acquired morphemes, including past tense *-ed* or third person singular present tense *-s* (Bland-Stewart & Fitzgerald, 2001). Verb type influences English monolingual children's use of present and past tense forms. Children are more likely to use past tense *forms* (*-ed* or irregular past) with events or achievement verbs such as *break* or *fly* and the third person singular present tense *-s* with stative verbs such as *like* (e.g., Bloom, Lifter, & Hafitz, 1980). This separation between languages was also observed in a case study of a toddler learning Spanish and English simultaneously in which the child produced more finite forms in Spanish than in English (Castro & Gavruseva, 2003). Of these forms, more of the past-tense examples were used with event verbs and the present-tense forms with stative verbs. Two German speaking children, ages 6;0 and 9;0, who were learning English during a stay in the United States, revealed the same patterns in their L2 acquisition of English (Rohde, 1996).

In spite of these general similarities, some children's productions indicate that knowledge of one language's grammar influences sentence production in the other, as would be predicted by interdependent models. Examples of influenced productions include a young French–English bilingual's use of *"the house of the teddy bear"* instead of the *"teddy bear's house"* (Paradis et al., 2000) or an older Spanish–English bilingual's use of the past progressive (e.g., *"was running"*) in English where she might use an imperfect form (e.g., *"corría,"* [*she used to run*]) in Spanish; and an English monolingual might be expected to use the preterite *"ran"* (unpublished data). An example of an influenced syntactic structure is the use of subject dislocation (e.g., *"The frog, he is escaping from the boat"*) that is observed in the English of Spanish-speaking and in Filipino English. In this example, subject dislocation is carried into English as means of emphasizing the subject. In a story-telling task, a bilingual Spanish–English-speaking child's use of postverbal subject and verb + object configurations was higher in Spanish than in English, as would be predicted by monolingual data (Álvarez, 2003). His use of these forms was higher than expected in English, but lower than expected for Spanish, demonstrating a convergence of these two strategies. Similarly, in a case study, Serratrice, Sorace, and Paoli (2004) reported on subject and object usage in a bilingual Italian–English-speaking child compared to English or Italian monolingual language learners of 1.1–4.8 MLU-words. In both languages, subjects were omitted more often than were objects. Italian-speaking control children omitted subjects more than did English-speaking children. The bilingual child used the null subject form more in Italian than in English, consistent with the monolingual comparison group differences. Relative to his monolingual peers, he used an overt pronominal form more frequently (9% versus 3%) in Italian when the appropriate pragmatic option would have been to use the null subject.

What is notable about these examples is the fact that the resulting forms selected for use are not ungrammatical. Instead, they are forms that might be unexpected, stilted, or low in frequency for a monolingual speaker. The motivation for many of these changes seems to be pragmatic. The speaker has acquired a linguistic distinction in one language (e.g., completed action marked by the preterit in one language vs. imperfect for a continuing action, or the ability to drop the subject once the subject has been established) and then uses his or her morphological or syntactic knowledge to convey that notion in the other language. Influenced utterances of the types described above are used by children who have as little as 10% exposure to a second language (Gregory & Bedore, 2002a).

Children who are exposed to two languages may be more variable in their production of the forms they know. For example, English-dominant children with only 10% exposure to Spanish demonstrated lower than expected accuracy on the third person singular present tense *-s* forms and the past tense *-ed* (Gregory & Bedore, 2002a). Predominantly English-speaking children from Latino backgrounds with exposure to Spanish also produced more ungrammatical utterances than might be expected for their chronological age (Muñoz et al., 2003). At age 4 years, these children produced 58% grammatical utterances and 80% grammatical utterances by age 5 years. By age 5, German–English-learning children produced tense marking correctly 95% of the time in English, their dominant language, but 80–90% correctly in German (Döpke, 2000). Competing input (either from the child's exposure to a second language such as Filipino or Spanish or from the child's exposure to second-language learners) influences children's production of English.

Because the manifestation of these patterns is variable, it may be best to view them as linguistic trade-offs in which the task demand interacts with the speaker's linguistic knowledge in one or both of his or her languages. For example, in a series of narrative samples, several of the Filipino–English-speaking children studied by LoFranco et al. (2006) produced high levels of mazes (up to 60%, with a group average of 25%). This high proportion of mazes was most likely to occur on the first story, when children had to tell a story based on a wordless picture book with no model of the task demands from the examiner. In contrast, Spanish–English bilinguals (4;0–6;0 years) and functionally monolingual Spanish- and English-speaking children produced comparable percentages of mazes in English and Spanish in narratives (Bedore, Fiestas, Peña, & Nagy, 2006). Note, however, that the bilinguals' narratives were slightly less grammatical than those of their functionally monolingual age-matched peers (i.e., 79% vs. 83% for English and 83% vs. 89% for Spanish). Also, more grammatical revisions were produced by the bilingual and functionally monolingual children in Spanish than in English. In Spanish, MLU-words and the number of different words were significantly correlated with the use of grammatical revisions. In English, MLU-words were associated with the repetition of connectors and filled pauses. This pattern suggests a complexity trade-off across languages. In English, children may demonstrate more hesitation phenomena when they attempt to produce longer utterances while they exhibit grammatical revisions under comparable circumstances in Spanish.

There are also trade-offs in the ways that bilingual children achieve linguistic complexity. Fiestas and Peña (2004), for example, observed that early sequential, bilingual (Spanish–English) 5- and 6-year-old children achieved similar measures of productivity (number of C-units, MLU-words, and number of words) and grammaticality on narrative and picture-description tasks. In English, children used a significant proportion (39%) of Spanish-influenced utterances (e.g., word- or phrase-level codeswitches, subject dislocation, use of post noun modifiers with *of*) during the narrative task. English-influenced utterances during production of narratives in Spanish (e.g., noun-modifier reversals, article–noun number agreement) occurred less than 3% of the time. For the picture description task, these differences between languages were significant, but with a much smaller magnitude. The increased use of Spanish-influenced utterances during the more complex story-telling task in English allowed these children to express complex ideas in English, equivalent to the complexity of stories they told in Spanish. On the simpler picture-description task they did not need to use as many influenced utterances in English in order to express their ideas.

Narrative Discourse

Across languages, children with typical development demonstrate highly similar patterns in narrative development. In a comparison of English, German, Spanish, Hebrew, and Turkish, Berman and Slobin (1994) found that younger children told stories with incomplete story structures in comparison to older groups of children. By about 5 years of age, children included information about the characters and story events as well as temporal markers in their stories. By age 9, children provided background and setting information and told complete stories. For bilingual children, the evidence indicates that at a macrolevel, at least in the stronger language, narratives are similar to those of monolinguals. But there may be some influences from both language and culture that do not affect overall meaning.

At the level of discourse, patterns for bilinguals are also similar to reports in other language domains (Fiestas & Peña, 2004; Fusté-Herrmann, Silliman, Bahr, Fasnacht, & Federico, 2006; Gutiérrez-Clellen, 2002), and findings support both independence and interdependence. Bilingual early-school-age children (ages 4;0 to 6;11) produce narratives of equal complexity (Fiestas & Peña, 2004), and school-age children (ages 7;3 to 8;7) have been shown to be equivalent in grammatical accuracy (Gutiérrez-Clellen, 2002) in Spanish and English. In a case study of a simultaneous Spanish–English bilingual child, grammatical knowledge appropriate for story-telling in both languages was observed, indicating independence (Álvarez, 2003). Yet, there were indications of convergence between the two languages consistent with interdependence. For example, the child introduced new information in the postverbal position only slightly (3%) more in Spanish than in English. Differences based on monolingual accounts were expected to be greater (about 14%).

Language-specific demands and proficiency in each language also affect the composition of bilingual children's narratives. Detailed analysis of the story grammar elements (e.g., initiating event, attempt, consequence) indicated that children included *attempts* more often when telling a story in Spanish but used more *consequences* when telling the same story in English (Fiestas & Peña, 2004). The older children in the Gutiérrez-Clellen (2002) study generally recalled more utterances and demonstrated more accurate comprehension in English as compared to Spanish. Individually, some children demonstrated better performance in Spanish than in English. These findings illustrate that both proficiency in each language and task demands impact language performance in different ways for individual children.

When children are bilingual, it is important to know that language performance in each language may not be equivalent, even if they are judged be fluent in both. From these accounts, we know that bilingual children who are developing typically are able to use each language in appropriate ways, and with few errors. Furthermore, the amount of mixing that occurs across the two languages has pragmatic constraints. Language essentially must be understandable to the listener. Switching or mixing at the level of a word may not interfere with meaning, but grammatical violations can change meaning.

Monolingual children as young as 2 years of age seem to have a good understanding of how the language works. When they make errors, communication breakdowns are rare, because the errors do not change the pragmatic intent or global meaning of the child's utterance (Joseph & Pine, 2002; Wexler, 1996). Children with LI, in contrast, have difficulty learning and using language efficiently and effectively and persist in making errors for a longer period of time than their peers (Rice, Wexler, & Hershberger, 1998). Based on the studies reviewed thus far, we see similar patterns of development for typically developing bilingual children, consistent with an independence hypothesis. There is a significant amount of variability in the errors they make, in persistence of errors, and in the other-language influenced forms used, consistent with an interdependence hypothesis. These errors and influenced changes are similar to those made by monolingual children but may differ in frequency. In semantics, children may demonstrate mixed knowledge, selecting an appropriate word from the nontarget language or selecting a closely related word in the target language, demonstrating knowledge constraints in that language. In syntax, children differentiate their two languages from a young age (Nicoladis & Genesee, 1997). The two languages will sometimes have a syntactic-pragmatic influence on each other. This influence may be seen in the forms selected for use that reflect frequency in the other language. In discourse, children are again able to separate their two languages, but there seem to be trade-offs between the number of influenced utterances they use and the amount of complexity. The use of nonstandard and influenced forms allows emerging bilinguals to convey complex ideas in discourse.

How, then, is LI in bilingual children manifested? Do children with LI demonstrate learning patterns that are predicted by hypotheses of independent bilingual language acquisition such as the *separate development hypothesis* (De Houwer, 2005), interdependent models such as the *ivy hypothesis* (Bernardini & Schlyter, 2004), or the unified model proposed by MacWhinney (2005)?

LANGUAGE IMPAIRMENT IN BILINGUALS

SLI is defined as a delay in language development in the absence of frank neurological, cognitive, or physical impairment (see chapter 1 by Schwartz). The incidence of SLI in the mainstream English-speaking US population is 7.4%, according to the most recent epidemiological studies (Tomblin et al., 1997). There are no such studies in bilingual populations because of the lack of typical developmental information, the absence of valid assessment instruments, and the need for studies that focus on the nature of impairment in bilingual children.

It is particularly difficult to identify SLI or LI in bilingual children. Note that in the bilingual literature the term LI is often used. It is often not possible to verify that exclusionary criteria are met due to a lack of valid cognitive measures for bilingual US children (Valencia & Suzuki, 2001). Many of the linguistic errors or changes in language that mark LI in monolinguals are also made by typical children who are learning language in bilingual environments. Therefore, it is important to identify markers that distinguish among typical bilingual learners and bilingual learners with LI. Current studies of language in bilinguals with and without LI inform potential characteristics of LI in bilingual children. Here, we review the available literature in semantics, morphology, syntax, and discourse.

Semantic Performance in Bilingual Children with Language Impairment

Monolingual children with LI typically demonstrate a slower rate of vocabulary acquisition in comparison to their typical age peers during early language learning (Duchan & Erickson, 1976; Gray, 2004) and decreased lexical diversity in their connected speech (Thordardottir & Namazi, 2007). By early school-age these children appear to catch up with their age peers (Hick, Joseph, Conti-Ramsden, Serratrice, & Faragher, 2002; Leonard, Camarata, Rowan, & Chapman, 1982). Typically, their performance on standardized tests of vocabulary is within the normal age range, but below that of their typically developing peers. At school-age children with LI may have word-finding difficulties and naming errors in addition to vocabulary test scores below that of their age peers (Lahey & Edwards, 1999; van der Lely & Howard, 1993; Windsor, 1999).

Available data on semantic performance of bilingual children with LI demonstrate that they make more naming errors and need more processing time to respond in comparison to their typical bilingual peers. Consistent with findings for monolingual children (McGregor, 1997; McGregor, Newman, & Reilly, 2002; McGregor & Windsor, 1996), bilingual children with LI seem to have deficits in retrieval and organizational aspects of semantic use rather than in vocabulary size. Lack of breadth in lexical entries, inadequate or weak links between lexical entries, or limited depth of lexical entries may further compromise performance (Dollaghan, 1992). Peña and Quinn (1997) studied bilingual Puerto Rican and monolingual African American children's performance on picture-naming and description tasks. There were no differences by monolingual/bilingual status, but children with LI scored significantly lower than their age peers on the description task. Kay-Raining Bird and colleagues (Kay-Raining Bird, 2007; Kay-Raining Bird et al., 2005) documented the performance of 8 bilingual children with Down syndrome (DS) relative to developmentally matched children with typical language skills and age-matched monolingual children with DS. In comparison to their developmentally matched bilingual and monolingual peers, children with DS had significantly lower MLUs than their developmentally matched peers and lower expressive Preschool Langu   Scale (PLS) scores than their developmentally matched peers. But, they demonstrat   similar scores on the MacArthur–Bates Communicative Development Inventory (CDI   . subset of French–English bilingual children with DS demonstrated

58% overlap in their French and English vocabularies. This pattern is consistent with values reported elsewhere (e.g., Deuchar & Quay, 2000; Umbel et al., 1992) and suggests that bilingual developmentally delayed children are employing a vocabulary acquisition strategy that is comparable to that employed by other bilinguals while demonstrating reduced lexical entries like that of other children with language impairment.

Bilingual children with LI, like monolingual children (Gray, 2004; Nash & Donaldson, 2005), demonstrate difficulty with learning new words. Word-learning tasks using a dynamic assessment paradigm demonstrate that both monolingual and bilingual children with LI have difficulty learning and using naming strategies (Peña, Iglesias, & Lidz, 2001; Peña, Quinn, & Iglesias, 1992). In these studies, children with and without LI were taught strategies for single-word naming over two sessions. The sessions focused on helping children become aware of single-word picture naming, the importance of using single-word labels, and the use of comparison, categorization, and selection strategies. At posttest, findings demonstrated differential responses to the short-term intervention. Children with LI made virtually no gains, whereas children with typical development made significant gains from pretest to posttest.

Bilingual children with LI appear to have weak semantic representations (Simonsen, 2002), consistent with proposals for monolingual children (Kail, Hale, Leonard, & Nippold, 1984; McGregor & Appel, 2002). The performance of 6-year-old Finnish/Swedish bilinguals with and without LI on the *Word Finding Vocabulary Test* (Renfrew, 1995) was poorer than that of their Swedish monolingual age-matched peers. Within the bilingual group, children with LI scored lower than did typically developing children. Children with LI resorted more often to not responding when they could not name a word, whereas children with typical development used other ways to communicate their knowledge of the word, such as description plus a gesture or using the Finnish translation equivalent in the Swedish condition. Both monolingual and bilingual children with LI made more semantically related errors than did children with typical development.

The above findings for bilingual children are consistent with preliminary findings from our own test development data (Peña, Gutiérrez-Clellen, Iglesias, Goldstein, & Bedore, 2008). We have collected data using the category generation task from 2 children aged 5 years with LI; 5 children 7–9 years in age with LI; 19 children (ages 7–9 years) with typical development (Collings, 2005; Kolanko, 2004); and 44 children (ages 4–6) with typical language development (Peña et al., 2002). In the category generation task (based on Nelson & Nelson, 1990), questions were structured to elicit taxonomic (e.g., animals) and slot-filler (e.g., animals at the zoo or circus) responses. Children with LI generated fewer correct items and made more errors than their age matched peers. The 7- to 9-year-old children in both groups made very few errors overall (LI = 11.13%; NL = 3.80%). Both groups made semantically related and phonologically related errors. Only children with LI made semantically unrelated errors.

Thus far, the limited data available from bilingual children with LI are consistent with findings for monolingual children. Children with LI have semantic systems that are impoverished in their breadth and depth (Dollaghan, 1992; McGregor, 1997; McGregor & Appel, 2002; McGregor & Windsor, 1996). Furthermore, children with LI demonstrate inefficiencies that affect word learning (Gray, 2004; Nash & Donaldson, 2005), retrieval, and lexical organization (Kail et al., 1984; Montgomery, 1999, 2002).

Morphology and Syntax in Bilingual Children with Language Impairment

Bilingual children with LI exhibit morphological error patterns that are analogous to those of monolingual children with LI, and they progress more slowly than do their typically developing peers. Salameh, Håkansson, and Nettelbladt (2004) followed 4- to 7-year-old Swedish–Arabic-learning children with and without LI over a one-year period. The children progressed through five stages of "processability" (Pienemann, 1998), starting with short words and phrases and ultimately moving to lexical morphology (e.g., noun plural or gender), phrasal level structures (e.g., noun phrase agreement), interphrasal structure (e.g., subject verb inversion), and ultimately clausal level structure (e.g., subordinated clauses). At each level of processability, children simplified Swedish and Arabic sentence structures in comparable ways. For example, children omitted auxiliaries or copulas in each language or used present-tense forms in place of past-tense forms. The children with typical development demonstrated knowledge through the most complex—clausal level—structures. In contrast, at the end of the year-long study children with LI tended to perform at the most basic level, using mainly short words and phrases and lexical morphology. Paradis, Crago, Genesee, and Rice (2003) documented performance on tense-bearing (e.g., present and past tense verbs forms) and nontense-bearing morphemes (e.g., articles) produced by English–French balanced bilingual school-age children with LI and their monolingual peers. Consistent with the predictions of the extended optional infinitive hypotheses (e.g., Rice & Wexler, 1996) for monolingual speakers, the bilinguals with LI omitted tense marking in each of their languages. Similarly, school-age Spanish–English sequential bilinguals with LI performed differently than their typically developing peers on tasks requiring them to produce past-tense marking in English (Jacobson & Schwartz, 2005). Typically developing children's production of verb forms demonstrated productive knowledge of the form in question (e.g., correct production or overregularization as in *runned* for *ran*). In contrast, children with LI used the infinitive form (e.g., *run* for *ran*). In Spanish, 4- to 6-year-old bilingual children showed deficits in overall grammaticality including low MLU, verb tense errors, article and clitic errors, and missing grammatical arguments (Gutiérrez-Clellen, Restrepo, & Simón-Cereijido, 2006; Simon-Cereijido & Gutiérrez-Clellen, 2007). This lack of morphological productivity is consistent with observations of the grammatical errors observed in children with SLI who speak English only (e.g., Leonard, Eyer, Bedore, & Grela, 1997; Rice & Wexler, 1996).

Similar syntactic and morphological patterns are seen in case studies of children with LI from other diagnostic categories, including children with DS (Woll & Grove, 1996) and in a polyglot savant (Smith & Tsimpli, 1995). The children with DS were twins who used British sign and English demonstrating poor expressive skills. They had low MLU and omission of grammatical morphemes including present- and past-tense verb forms (Woll & Grove, 1996). Reliance on memorized forms was observed in a case study of a polyglot savant who had basic to communicatively functional language skills in 15–20 languages (Smith & Tsimpli, 1995). He was able to recognize vocabulary and translate passages across languages. A relative weakness was his ability to produce new syntactic structures or judge grammaticality of syntactic structures. These behaviors were highly influenced by his English-language knowledge. Each of these studies illustrates that bilingual children with LI demonstrate skills that reflect the strengths and weaknesses associated with their diagnostic category as well as language input patterns like other bilingual children.

In contrast to the above examples, Restrepo and Kruth (2000) identified error patterns not typically observed in monolingual children with LI in their case study of a 7-year-old sequential bilingual child with a history of language-learning difficulties. This child spoke

Spanish at home until the time of school entry. Her mother reported that in Spanish the child produced words and sentences incorrectly and that she made more such errors than did her younger sibling. She participated in an ESL program from kindergarten through the time of the study. Her progress was compared to that of a classmate who also began to learn English at the time of kindergarten entry. In Spanish, the child with LI produced articles with 6–33% accuracy and produced regular present- and past-tense verbs with 20–50% accuracy. These forms were produced with 80–100% accuracy by her classmate. Her MLU was low, and only 1% of her utterances were complex relative to 30% complex utterances observed in the narrative sample of her classmate. The error types were consistent with observations for Spanish and English monolingual children and are consistent with the findings discussed earlier. This child, however, produced a more limited set of prepositions than is usually observed in second-language learners or in children with LI. For example, the only preposition she produced in English was *on*. Furthermore, she inappropriately used the preposition *con* [with] in contexts that required other prepositions such as *a* [to] or *en* [in/on] or omitted them. Finally, the child with LI demonstrated a decrement in the complexity of her Spanish that was not observed in her typically developing classmate, suggesting that with more of her input shifting to English she had more difficulty maintaining her Spanish skills. The last two findings point to some difficulty integrating input from two languages and are more consistent with predictions from interdependent models.

Cross-Language Narrative Performance in Children with Language Impairment

Most available studies of narrative performance include children with LI who are monolingual English speakers rather than bilingual speakers. Based on these studies, however, it is possible to make some predictions about the kinds of difficulties that bilingual children with LI will have. For the purposes of this chapter, we focus on analyses of narrative structure and organization also referred to as *macrolevel structure*. Children with LI have difficulty taking the listener's perspective and, thus, make assumptions that are inaccurate (Westby, Van Dongen, & Maggart, 1989). Children with LI also have difficulty with the overall organization of the narrative, keeping track of the time elements and cause–effect relationships. Patterns of narrative performance for children with LI include difficulty with use of mental state predicates (Johnston, Miller, & Tallal, 2001), limited use of story structure elements (Merritt & Liles, 1987), difficulty using cohesive devices (Liles, Duffy, Merritt, & Purcell, 1995), and overall organization (Kaderavek & Sulzby, 2000; Merritt & Liles, 1987) when compared to their age-matched peers. Pearce, McCormack, and James (2003) compared children with SLI, LI with low nonverbal IQ, and typical children. Children with SLI told stories that were less complex than those told by typical children. Children with low nonverbal IQs told the simplest stories.

Wagner, Sahlén, and Nettelbladt (1999) studied Swedish children's narratives, comparing 5-year-old children with LI to data from a study of Swedish children with typical development by Nilsson and Vikström (1998). Findings indicated that during story retell and story generation tasks, children with LI had difficulty with episode structure. Typical and low-achieving Spanish-speaking children in the United States performed differently on a narrative task. Children with low achievement used a lower proportion of complex syntax and had increased difficulty in formulation than their typical age peers (Gutiérrez-Clellen, 1998).

At the macrolevel of narrative performance children with LI across English, Swedish, and Spanish have difficulties with organization and formulation of episode structure. Based on these studies of LI as well as cross-linguistic and bilingual studies of narrative development, it is reasonable to expect that bilingual children with LI would have difficulty with overall formulation and with story structure in both of their languages.

In sum, studies of bilingual children who have language impairments (regardless of the cause) demonstrate patterns that are indicative of delayed rather than deviant communication development. Furthermore, the findings are consistent with theories of bilingual and second-language acquisition. For example, consistent with the models focusing on independent development, children who were balanced in their use of both languages demonstrated comparable errors in each of their languages. Independent development was most notable in the case of the French–English bilinguals discussed by Paradis et al. In the study of children with DS (e.g., Kay-Raining Bird et al., 2005) and in the case study of the savant (Smith & Tsimpli, 1995), children demonstrated vocabulary knowledge that appeared to exceed their morphosyntactic knowledge. This finding supports the notion that the establishment of a basic lexicon precedes the development of grammar, as is widely documented in the cross-linguistic monolingual language acquisition literature (Bates, Bretherton, & Snyder, 1991; Caselli & Casadio, 2001; Caselli, Casadio, & Bates, 1999; Fenson et al., 1994; Maital, Dromi, Sagi, & Bornstein, 2000) and more recently with bilinguals (Conboy & Thal, 2006; Marchman et al., 2004). This was most easily observed in the Smith and Tsimpli case study, where translation knowledge facilitated vocabulary development. Reported strengths in memory (leading to cross-language transfer) illustrate the role memory plays in language acquisition. Observation of memory and transfer indicated that the learning processes of MacWhinney's (2005) unified model were at play in that general cognitive mechanisms also predicted language-learning abilities across languages.

IMPLICATIONS FOR ASSESSMENT AND INTERVENTION

Identification of LI in bilinguals, and planning appropriate language intervention for bilingual children is challenging. First, there are no tests that accurately discriminate the performance of bilingual children with and without language impairment. Second, there are limited data on which to base effective interventions for bilingual children. A unique challenge to the needs of bilingual children concerns determination of the most effective language of instruction (for intervention and the classroom) to facilitate language growth and transfer.

Our approach to assessment and intervention combines both interdependence and independence perspectives. An interdependence approach focuses on underlying cognitive linguistic mechanisms (Kohnert & Windsor, 2004; Kohnert, Yim, Nett, Kan, & Duran, 2005), on forms and uses that are common across the language pairs (e.g., gender marking in Catalan and Spanish (Costa, Miozzo, & Caramazza, 1999), and on vocabulary needed in home and school (Peña & Stubbe Kester, 2004). From this viewpoint, children all have the same set of general cognitive tools for learning language (Bates, Devescovi, & D'Amico, 1999; Haywood, Brooks, & Burns, 1992; Kohnert, Bates, & Hernandez, 1999; Magliano, Trabasso, & Graesser, 1999; Naglieri & Das, 1989; Stein & Albro, 1997; Stubbe Kester, Peña, & Gillam, 2001; Tomasello, 2003). Thus, interdependent approaches focus on identification and remediation of inefficient cognitive functions that give rise to difficulty learning and using language. At the same time, there are specific surface structures that must be learned for children to communicate effectively within their social and academic context. An independence approach focuses on specific linguistic structures that might be identified as potential markers of impairment and targets for intervention. The evidence of cross-language influences thus far suggests different degrees of language mixing, dependent on the language domain. The difference in mixing has implications for how language dominance is viewed and assessed and means that there is a role for both interdependence and independence in assessment and treatment of language disorders. We advocate three interrelated principles for the identification and remediation of LI in bilinguals. First, focus on manifestations of difficulty that are consistent with general cognitive functions associated with language impairment. Second, take an interdependent approach that allows for mixed knowledge with a focus on pragmatic use of language. Third, focus on markers of LI that are characteristic of the target language while allowing for changes that arise from languages-in-contact.

Assessment of Language in Bilinguals

Applied to assessment, a focus on underlining cognitive skills associated with LI closely should examine potential difficulties with underlying strategies including attention, memory, storage, processing, organization, retrieval, and self-regulation (Peña, Resendiz, & Gillam, 2007). These cognitive skills may be observed in vocabulary size and retrieval (Kail et al., 1984; Newman & German, 2002; Schiff-Myers & Mikulajova, 1997) as well as in on-line performance of semantic tasks (Chiat & Hunt, 1993; van der Lely & Howard, 1993). Thus, examination of patterns of semantic organization and retrieval is recommended. Children with LI across monolingual and bilingual language environments have difficulty with efficient learning and use of language. Consequently, we would expect them to make more off-target errors in word choice, be less effective in code-switching to add new information, and be less efficient in making conversational repairs.

Assessment strategies such as dynamic assessment focus on underlying cognitive skills (Allal & Ducrey, 2000; Bain & Olswang, 1995; Budoff, 1987; Lidz, 2002; Tzuriel, 2001) and have been applied to assessment of language in areas of vocabulary learning (Peña et al., 2001), categorization (Ukrainetz, Harpell, Walsh, & Coyle, 2000), and narrative development (Gutiérrez-Clellen & Quinn, 1993; Peña et al., 2006) in children from culturally and linguistically diverse backgrounds. Consistent with the notion of examining cognitive skills, findings across a number of studies demonstrate that modifiability measures (e.g., child responsivity and examiner effort) differentiate between children with and without impairment with a high rate of accuracy (about 90%). Follow-up analyses indicate that with preschool children, motivation and persistence were related to language ability (Peña, 2000), and with school-age children, metacognition and flexibility together best differentiated between children with and without LI across African American, Latino American, and European American groups (Peña, Resendiz, & Gillam, 2007). To date, dynamic assessment has not been systematically explored with a large number of bilingual children. Case studies suggest, however, similar findings of change and responsivity for bilingual children with and without LI (Fiestas, Peña, & Gillam, 2006; Gutiérrez-Clellen & Quinn, 1993).

A bilingual or interdependent approach allows for mixed knowledge within and across domains. With respect to dominance, an interdependent approach acknowledges that for children, as well as for adults, dominance at a single point in time may vary, depending on the specific context (Grosjean, 1998). We have found it helpful to use a questionnaire that reports on amount of exposure and use of each language hour-by-hour (Gutiérrez-Clellen & Kreiter, 2003; Restrepo, 1998) in order to have an accurate picture of the percentage of time the child is exposed to and uses L1 and L2. Moreover, this information provides information with respect to communicative demands specific to each language. Children in a bilingual environment may have mixed or distributed knowledge across their two languages and thus may not exhibit all skills subsumed in a given language. This mixed knowledge is apparent in the semantic domain, where children learning language in bilingual environments lexicalize concepts in a distributed manner across two languages (Holowka et al., 2002; Patterson, 1998, 2000; Pearson et al., 1995; Umbel et al., 1992). It may therefore not be appropriate to test only in one of the child's languages or to compare the child to a monolingual standard. Examination of vocabulary size using an approach such as conceptual scoring (Pearson & Fernández, 1994)—scoring each lexicalized concept across languages—is recommended. Our work demonstrates that children's performance across different tasks varies, depending on both language of testing and linguistic status (bilingual vs. monolingual) (Bedore et al., 2005; Peña et al., 2003).

Although semantics allows for mixed use, syntax, morphology, and discourse use are not mixed in the same way. Consistent with the *ivy hypothesis* (Bernardini & Schlyter, 2004), we predict that children with typical development would be most likely to learn vocabulary first in L2, but syntax might be stronger in L1. Children will probably use the main sentence structure of the stronger language but make changes related to the second or weaker language. As they learn more of the second language, they may use more of the words from the second language but may still preserve the word order from the first or stronger language. As they master syntax in L2, they may continue to have difficulties in organization of discourse in L2 and thus demonstrate more intrusions from the other language.

Children with language impairments are likely to use a more restricted repertoire of forms, make more errors, and make errors that change pragmatic meaning or are nonproductive. Typically developing bilingual children are able to tell stories using expected story elements (Fiestas & Peña, 2004). At the individual level, even if children appear to be fluent in both of their languages, they may demonstrate better performance in one language (Gutiérrez-Clellen, 2002). Children who are fluent in the second language but stronger in the primary language may use a higher proportion of influenced utterances in the second language. This higher proportion of influenced utterances may reflect the cognitive demands of narration. Typically developing children, in contrast to those with true language impairment, should be able to use strategies in a way that is pragmatically effective, getting across the main points of the story, albeit with reduced vocabulary and with more influenced utterances.

The contrast in performance between these children with and without LI within bilingual groups, rather than errors or changes relative to English monolingual populations, can help us make diagnostic decisions. Expectations for bilingual children with LI on narrative tasks are similar to those for monolingual children with LI. Bilingual children with LI are also likely have difficulties with organization and complexity of the narrative, while code-switching and influenced utterances should be expected. Our observations of these children are that, regardless of dominance, they display immature story structure with respect to included elements, difficulty formulating the story overall, lack of cohesion, and reduced vocabulary use in their stronger language. These are all potential targets for diagnostic decision-making.

It is important to focus on markers of LI in the target language rather than on changes made due to influence from the other language. We expect bilingual children with LI to make morphosyntactic errors that signal language impairment. In English, for example, errors on third person singular, regular past tense, and copula and auxiliary *to be* forms discriminate between monolingual children with and without LI (Bedore & Leonard, 1998; Rice et al., 1998). With predominantly English-speaking children (exposed to English and Spanish), these errors discriminated the children with 82% accuracy (Gregory & Bedore, 2002b) which is only slightly lower than the 85–100% accuracy reported by Bedore and Leonard (1998). But we would expect that, due to the variability in learning these forms, typically developing bilingual children would have difficulty as well (Gregory & Bedore, 2002b; Paradis, 2005). Thus, differentiation might require adjusted cut-off points, reflecting differences between bilingual children with typical development and those with language impairment. In addition, differentiation might focus on productive use of morphosyntax (Jacobson & Schwartz, 2002).

In the semantic domain, we are currently in the process of examining how children with and without LI performed on the semantic tasks from the Bilingual English–Spanish Assessment (BESA) (Peña et al., 2008). Findings thus far suggest that across Spanish and English there are both similarities and differences in how well different semantic tasks discriminate language impairment. Specifically, consistent with Peña et al. (2003), more function (e.g., *What is a crayon used for?*) items discriminated LI and typical development in Spanish, but more similarities-and-differences (e.g., W*hat is different about these two invitations?*) items discriminated impairment better in English (Bedore, Peña, & Stubbe Kester, 2007).

Given that bilingual children's difficulties are comparable to those of their monolingual peers, it is possible that the clinical markers of LI for monolingual children might characterize the performance of bilingual children with LI. It is important to consider the difficulties that are indicative of impairment in the child's first or stronger language. Thus, a clinician might examine article and clitic difficulties in Spanish or Italian (Bedore & Leonard, 2001, 2005; Leonard, Sabbadini, Leonard, & Volterra, 1987; Restrepo & Gutiérrez-Clellen, 2001), auxiliary, copula and present-tense marking in French (Paradis & Crago, 2000), or perfective and imperfective aspect marking in Chinese (Stokes & Fletcher, 2003), while recognizing that LI influences how children learn their second language as well (Jacobson & Schwartz, 2002). For example, the identified markers of LI in Spanish described above are useful for Spanish-speaking children exposed to English and bilingual children dominant in Spanish (Gutiérrez-Clellen et al., 2006; Simon-Cereijido & Gutiérrez-Clellen, 2007). Note that the decision about the language of evaluation should be made on the basis of domain rather than on the strength of the language as a whole.

Intervention with Bilingual Children with Language Impairment

Children should have the opportunity to use both their languages (Cummins, 1989). Generally, the focus should be on children's learning and using meaningful language rather than correct production of surface forms that might prove difficult during the initial stages of second-language learning. As before, interdependence and independence perspectives can be used in a complementary way to help children meet the daily demands in each of their languages.

A focus on general learning principles needed for language production and use may provide children with basic skills for improving language performance. Cognitive approaches such as those used in mediated learning have been demonstrated to be effective in increasing language performance in the short term in children from culturally diverse backgrounds (Peña & Gillam, 2000; Peña, Gillam, & Resendiz, 2007; Stubbe Kester et al., 2001). For example, in a study following the French- and English-language recovery of a 17-year-old who had undergone a partial left hemispherectomy, Trudeau, Colozzo, Sylvestre, and Ska (2004) hypothesized that bilateral cortical representation of language laid the cognitive foundation for her recovery. Relatively greater improvements in English, however, reflected differences in the amount of input she received in each language.

Helping children to use language in a functional and meaningful way is consistent with this approach. For example, the principles of paying attention to what people say, focusing on meaning, and responding to communicative intent are skills that children will be likely to use across situations and language contexts. A goal for children from bilingual backgrounds might be to improve their vocabulary learning strategies, which would, in turn, lead to being more efficient in the ways that they learn vocabulary in context, such as categorization and notice of similarities and differences (Stubbe Kester et al., 2001; Ukrainetz et al., 2000). Consistent with this approach is support of both the home and school language (Kohnert et al., 2005). Language input can be structured in ways that maximize the likelihood that they will use all of the cues available to derive the meaning of morphological and syntactic structures (Bedore & Leonard, 1995; Peters, 1985). To facilitate bilingual transfer, comparable forms can be modeled in salient positions. For example, to model a plural form, a clinician might use it in sentence-final position where it can be lengthened (*I need two marbles; Necesito dos canicas*).

Approaches that allow for mixed knowledge across two languages may facilitate children's learning of new information. A question that we are frequently asked is whether children with impairment should be limited to one language. Gutiérrez-Clellen (1999) reviewed available studies examining the question of whether instruction in L1 transferred to L2 and vice versa. The bulk of the findings were that bilingual (L1 and L2 together) or primary (L1) instruction was as effective as or slightly more effective than second-language (L2) instruction alone.

Studies of language of intervention for bilingual children with LI are consistent with those for typical bilingual children. These studies demonstrate that instruction in the first or primary language facilitates learning in the second language (when the second language is also taught). For example, Perozzi (1985) explored whether teaching children receptive vocabulary in L1 or L2 first had differential outcomes for L2 learning. Findings for both impaired and typical English-speaking and Spanish-speaking children suggested that teaching L1 receptive vocabulary first had a facilitating effect on learning receptive vocabulary when taught in L2. In a later study, Perozzi and Sanchez (1992) followed up on this question with a larger number of bilingual children. They compared how quickly two groups of bilingual (Spanish–English) children with language delay acquired English prepositions and pronouns comparing language of instruction. In the bilingual condition, children first were instructed in Spanish, then in English. In the monolingual condition, instruction was in English only. The children learned the target words faster in the bilingual condition compared to the English-only condition. These patterns of results have also been found in a study of a child who was an Icelandic–English bilingual. Thordardottir, Ellis Weismer, and Smith (1997) compared a bilingual and monolingual treatment for teaching English vocabulary in a single subject alternating treatment design. In the bilingual treatment, the clinician presented target vocabulary in both languages and responded to and expanded the child's utterances, matching the language the child used. In the monolingual treatment, the clinician presented the child with target vocabulary in English only. Only English responses were responded to and expanded. The child increased production of the target words in both conditions. Follow-up analysis of home versus school words demonstrated an advantage for the bilingual condition for production of home words. Together, these studies indicate that, for children with LI, bilingual approaches have at least the same outcome for learning words in the second language as a monolingual (second-language) approach alone. Furthermore, the first language can facilitate or enhance the rate of learning in the second language (Bernardini & Schlyter, 2004; Miller, Gillam, & Peña, 2001; Perozzi, 1985; Perozzi & Sanchez, 1992). These studies demonstrate that transfer between the two languages can occur, but only when deliberately planned.

For children with cognitive limitations, their cognitive abilities do not restrict bilingual language learning. Rohena, Jitendra, and Browder (2002) studied the effect of using a time delay to teach children to read English sight words varying the language of instruction (in this case English and Spanish). Four Puerto Rican bilingual middle-school children with mental retardation participated. For three of the children, both English and Spanish instruction was equally efficient and effective for teaching the English sight words. For one of the children, the Spanish condition was more efficient and effective for teaching the English sight words. These findings are consistent with those for vocabulary learning in bilingual children with LI.

A question clinicians might ask is whether children need to learn the same vocabulary items in each of their languages. Bilingual children may use vocabulary in context-specific ways. This is reflected in the lack of difference between the conceptual and total score in our own work and in the use of some items from the second language for all of the bilingual children. A specific recommendation that takes mixed knowledge into account is to focus on targets that are related across the two languages while building in strategies for transferring these targets between languages. Similarly, Peña and Stubbe Kester (2004) suggest that targeted vocabulary should be that which is needed for a given situation. Thus, some vocabulary may need to be targeted in both the home and second language, but other words may initially be most needed in only one language. For example, words such as kinship terms may be most functional at home, whereas color, size, and shape words would be most functional at school. Functionally overlapping, commonly used words would provide a basis for transfer across the two languages. This does not mean that the child should not learn home words in the second language or school words in the first language, but that home versus school versus overlapped words would be a starting point for targeting vocabulary teaching. On the basis of the *ivy hypothesis* (Bernardini & Schlyter, 2004), the stronger or home language could be used to support learning the second language. Thus, to begin, intervention would target the stronger language but also help the child build vocabulary in the second language.

Intervention should also focus on language needs that are specific to each language. In the area of morphology and syntax, rules are language-specific: thus, the opportunities for transfer are different for semantics. Children need to master the morphology and syntax of each of the two languages in order to be able to communicate effectively in each. It is also important to focus on structures in each language that are problematic for a particular child, not necessarily those that are simply second-language changes. Potential targets in this domain would be structures that carry meaning and that focus on productive use of morphosyntax. For example, in Spanish articles and clitics are often difficult for children with language impairment, but in English forms related to tense marking are most difficult. These are all meaningful targets because they help the child make reference in discourse. Articles mark new and old information in discourse, and clitic pronouns permit the speaker to pronominalize old information. Tense marking permits the speaker to reference events temporally.

Bilingual children with LI present a unique challenge for researchers in child language and LI as well as for those who provide direct services to this population. Here, we have provided a review of the available research describing the language performance of bilingual children with typical development and children with language impairment. Although their performance is similar in some respects to monolinguals in each of their languages consistent with an independent approach, they also make changes in ways that are predictable from an interdependence perspective. In contrast, bilingual children with language impairments will demonstrate many of the same difficulties as monolingual children with LI in each of their two languages. As a group, they are likely to make more errors and to use their languages in less productive ways. The similarities and differences between bilinguals and monolingual children with and without LI should be taken into consideration when working with these children.

REFERENCES

Allal, L., & Ducrey, G. P. (2000). Assessment of—or in—the zone of proximal development. *Learning and Instruction, 10*(2), 137–152.

Almgren, M., & Barreña, A. (2001). Bilingual acquisition and separation of linguistic codes: Ergativity in Basque versus accusativity in Spanish. In K. E. Nelson, A. Aksu-Koç & C. E. Johnson (Eds.), *Children's language: Interactional contributions to language development* (Vol. 11, pp. 27–48). Mahwah, NJ: Lawrence Erlbaum Associates.

Álvarez, E. (2003). Character introduction in two languages: Its development in the stories of a Spanish–English bilingual child age 6;11–10;11. *Bilingualism: Language and Cognition, 6*(3), 227–243.

Ameel, E., Storms, G., & Malt, B. C. (2005). How bilinguals solve the naming problem. *Journal of Memory and Language, 53*(1), 60–80.

Archibald, J. (1997). The acquisition of English stress by speakers of nonaccentual languages: Lexical storage versus computation of stress. *Linguistics, 35*(1), 167–181.

Bain, B., & Olswang, L. (1995). Examining readiness for learning two-word utterances by children with specific expressive language impairment: Dynamic assessment validation. *American Journal of Speech-Language Pathology, 4*(1), 81–92.

Bates, E., Bretherton, I., & Snyder, L. (1991). *From first words to grammar: Individual differences and dissociable mechanisms.* Cambridge, UK: Cambridge University Press.

Bates, E., Devescovi, A., & D'Amico, S. (1999). Processing complex sentences: A cross-linguistic study. *Language and Cognitive Processes, 14*(1), 69–123.

Bates, E., & MacWhinney, B. (1987). Competition, variation, and language learning. In B. MacWhinney (Ed.), *Mechanisms of language acquisition* (pp. 157–193). Hillsdale, NJ: Lawrence Erlbaum Associates.

Bedore, L. M., Fiestas, C., Peña, E. D., & Nagy, V. (2006). Cross-language comparisons of maze use in Spanish and English in functionally monolingual and bilingual children. *Bilingualism: Language and Cognition, 9*(3), 233–247.

Bedore, L. M., & Leonard, L. B. (1995). Prosodic and syntactic bootstrapping and their clinical applications: A tutorial. *American Journal of Speech Language Pathology, 4*(1), 66–72.

Bedore, L. M., & Leonard, L. B. (1998). Specific language impairment and grammatical morphology: A discriminant function analysis. *Journal of Speech, Language, and Hearing Research, 41*(5), 1185–1192.

Bedore, L. M., & Leonard, L. B. (2001). Grammatical morphology deficits in Spanish-speaking children with specific language impairment. *Journal of Speech, Language, and Hearing Research, 44*, 905–924.

Bedore, L. M., & Leonard, L. B. (2005). Verb inflections and noun phrase morphology in the spontaneous speech of Spanish-speaking children with specific language impairment. *Applied Psycholinguistics, 26*(2), 195–225.

Bedore, L. M., Peña, E. D., García, M., & Cortez, C. (2005). Conceptual versus monolingual scoring: When does it make a difference? *Speech, Language, and Hearing Services in Schools, 36*, 188–200.

Bedore, L. M., Peña, E. D., & Stubbe Kester, E. (2007). *Cross language performance on semantic tasks: Lessons from a test development project.* Manuscript in preparation.

Berman, R. A., & Slobin, D. I. (1994). *Relating events in narrative: A crosslinguistic developmental study.* Hillsdale, NJ: Lawrence Erlbaum Associates.

Bernardini, P., & Schlyter, S. (2004). Growing syntactic structure and code-mixing in the weaker language: The ivy hypothesis. *Bilingualism: Language and Cognition, 7*(1), 49–69.

Bland-Stewart, L. M., & Fitzgerald, S. M. (2001). Use of Brown's 14 grammatical morphemes by bilingual Hispanic preschoolers: A pilot study. *Communication Disorders Quarterly, 22*(4), 171–186.

Bloom, L., Lifter, K., & Hafitz, J   . Semantics of verbs and the development of verb inflection in child language. *Language, 5o*, 386–412.

Bosch, L., & Sebastián-Galles, N. (2001). Evidence of early language discrimination abilities in infants from bilingual environments. *Infancy, 2*(1), 29–49.

Brodie, M., Steffenson, A., Vasquez, J., Levin, R., & Suro, R. (2002). *2002 National Survey of Latinos*. Menlo Park, CA: Henry J. Kaiser Family Foundation and Pew Hispanic Trust.

Budoff, M. (1987). Measures for assessing learning potential. In C. S. Lidz (Ed.), *Dynamic Assessment: An interactional approach to evaluating learning potential* (pp. 173–195). New York: Guilford Press.

Caselli, M. C., & Casadio, P. (2001). Lexical development in English and Italian. In M. Tomasello & E. Bates (Eds.), *Language development: The essential readings*. Oxford: Blackwell.

Caselli, M. C., Casadio, P., & Bates, E. (1999). A comparison of the transition from first words to grammar in English and Italian. *Journal of Child Language, 26*, 69–112.

Castro, D., & Gavruseva, E. (2003). Finiteness and aspect in Spanish/English bilingual acquisition. *First Language, 23*(2), 171–192.

Chiat, S., & Hunt, J. (1993). Connections between phonology and semantics: An exploration of lexical processing in a language-impaired child. *Child Language Teaching and Therapy, 9*(3), 200–213.

Collings, N. (2005). *Category generation performance of Spanish-English bilingual children with and without language*. Unpublished master's thesis, University of Texas at Austin, Austin, TX.

Conboy, B. T., & Thal, D. J. (2006). Ties between the lexicon and grammar: Cross-sectional and longitudinal studies of bilingual toddlers. *Child Development, 77*(3), 712–735.

Costa, A., Miozzo, M., & Caramazza, A. (1999). Lexical selection in bilinguals: Do words in the bilingual's two lexicons compete for selection? *Journal of Memory and Language, 41*, 365–397.

Cummins, J. (1989). A theoretical framework for bilingual special education. *Exceptional Children, 56*(2), 111–119.

De Houwer, A. (1990). *The acquisition of two languages from birth*. Cambridge, UK: Cambridge University Press.

De Houwer, A. (2005). Early bilingual acquisition separate development hypothesis. In J. Kroll & A. De Groot (Eds.), *Handbook of bilingualism* (pp. 30–48). New York: Oxford University Press.

Deuchar, M., & Quay, S. (2000). *Bilingual acquisition: Theoretical implications of a case study*. New York: Oxford University Press.

Dodd, B., So, L., & Li, W. (1996). Symptoms of disorder without impairment. In B. Dodd, R. Campbell, & L. Worrall (Eds.), *Evaluating theories of language: Evidence from disorder* (pp. 119–136). London: Whurr.

Dollaghan, C. (1992). Adult-based models of the lexical long-term store: Issues for language acquisition and disorders. In R. S. Chapman (Ed.), *Processes in language acquisition and disorders* (pp. 141–158). St. Louis: Mosby-Year Book.

Döpke, S. (2000). Generation of and retraction from cross-linguistically motivated structures in bilingual first language acquisition. *Bilingualism: Language and Cognition, 3*(3), 209–226.

Duchan, J. F., & Erickson, J. G. (1976). Normal and retarded children's understanding of semantic relations in different verbal contexts. *Journal of Speech and Hearing Research, 19*(4), 767–776.

Eckman, F. R. (2004). From phonemic differences to constraint rankings: Research on second language phonology. *Studies in Second Language Acquisition 26*(4), 513–549.

Fenson, L., Dale, P. S., Reznick, J. S., Bates, E., Thal, D. J., & Pethick, S. J. (1994). Variability in early communicative development. *Monographs of the Society for Research in Child Development, 59*(5), 1–189.

Fiestas, C. E., & Peña, E. D. (2004). Narrative discourse in bilingual children: Language and task effects. *Language, Speech, and Hearing Services in Schools, 35*(2), 155–168.

Fiestas, C. E., Peña, E. D., & Gillam, R. B. (2006). *Dynamic assessment of narratives: Language of intervention for bilingual children*. Paper presented at the Symposium for Research in Child Language Disorders.

Flynn, S. (1996). A parameter setting approach to second language acquisition. In W. Ritchie & T. H. Bhatia (Eds.), *Handbook of second language acquisition* (pp. 121–158). San Diego: Academic Press.

Fusté-Herrmann, B., Silliman, E. R., Bahr, R. H., Fasnacht, K. S., & Federico, J. E. (2006). Mental state verb production in the oral narratives of English- and Spanish-speaking preadolescents: An exploratory study of lexical diversity and depth. *Learning Disabilities Research and Practice, 21*(1), 44–60.

Gawlitzek-Maiwald, I., & Tracy, R. (1996). Bilingual bootstrapping. *Linguistics, 34*, 901–926.

Genesee, F. (1978). Language processing in bilinguals. *Brain and Language, 5*(1), 1–12.

Genesee, F., Boivin, I., & Nicoladis, E. (1996). Talking with strangers: A study of children's communicative competence. *Applied Psycholinguistics, 17*(4), 427–442.

Genesee, F., Nicoladis, E., & Paradis, J. (1995). Language differentiation in early bilingual development. *Journal of Child Language, 22*, 611–631.

Gierut, J. A. (1998). Treatment efficacy: Functional phonological disorders in children. *Journal of Speech, Language, and Hearing Research, 41*, S85–S100.

Gildersleeve-Neumann, C. E., Stubbe Kester, E., Davis, B., & Peña, E. D. (in press). English speech sound development in preschool-aged children from bilingual English–Spanish environments. *Language, Speech, and Hearing Services in the Schools.*

Gray, S. (2004). Word learning by preschoolers with specific language impairment: Predictors and poor learners. *Journal of Speech, Language, and Hearing Research, 47*(5), 1117–1132.

Gregory, L., & Bedore, L. M. (2002a, July). *English grammatical morphology in children from Spanish-speaking environments: A descriptive analysis.* Paper presented at the International Conference for the Study of Child Language/Symposium for Research on Child Language Disorders, Madison, WI.

Gregory, L., & Bedore, L. M. (2002b, November). *English morphology in children from bilingual Spanish environment.* Paper presented at the American Speech, Language, and Hearing Association, Atlanta, Georgia.

Grieco, E. (2004). *English abilities of the U.S. foreign born-population.* Washington, DC: Migration Policy Institute.

Grosjean, F. (1989). Neurolinguists, Beware! The bilingual is not two monolinguals in one. *Brain and Language, 36*, 3–15.

Grosjean, F. (1998). Studying bilinguals: Methodological and conceptual issues. *Bilingualism: Language and Cognition, 1*, 131–149.

Gutiérrez-Clellen, V. F. (1998). Syntactic skills of Spanish-speaking children with low school achievement. *Language, Speech, and Hearing Services in Schools, 29*(4), 207–215.

Gutiérrez-Clellen, V. F. (1999). Language choice in intervention with bilingual children. *American Journal of Speech Language Pathology, 8*(4), 291–302.

Gutiérrez-Clellen, V. F. (2002). Narratives in two languages: Assessing performance of bilingual children. *Linguistics and Education, 13*(2), 175–197.

Gutiérrez-Clellen, V. F., & Kreiter, J. (2003). Understanding child bilingual acquisition using parent and teacher reports. *Applied Psycholinguistics, 24*(2), 267–288.

Gutiérrez-Clellen, V. F., & Quinn, R. (1993). Assessing narratives of children from diverse cultural/linguistic groups. *Language, Speech, and Hearing Services in the Schools, 24*(1), 2–9.

Gutiérrez-Clellen, V. F., Restrepo, M. A., & Simón-Cereijido, G. (2006). Evaluating the discriminant accuracy of a grammatical measure with Spanish-speaking children. *Journal of Speech, Language, and Hearing Research, 49*(6), 1209–1223.

Haywood, H. C., Brooks, P., & Burns, S. (1992). *Bright start: Cognitive curriculum for young children.* Watertown, MA: Charles Bridge.

Hick, R. F., Joseph, K. L., Conti-Ramsden, G., Serratrice, L., & Faragher, B. (2002). Vocabulary profiles of children with specific language impairment. *Child Language Teaching and Therapy, 18*(2), 165–180.

Holowka, S., Brosseau-Lapré, F., & Petitto, L. A. (2002). Semantic and conceptual knowledge underlying bilingual babies' first signs and words. *Language Learning, 52*, 205–262.

Hulk, A., & Müller, N. (2000). Bilingual first language acquisition at the interface between syntax and pragmatics.. *Bilingualism: Language and Cognition, 3*(3), 227–244.

Jacobson, P., & Schwartz, R. (2002). *Regular and irregular past tense use in early sequential bilingual children with specific language impairment.* Paper presented at the Symposium on Research in Child Language Disorders.

Jacobson, P. F., & Schwartz, R. G. (2005). English past tense use in bilingual children with language impairment. *American Journal of Speech Language Pathology, 14*(4), 313–323.

Johnston, J. R., Miller, J., & Tallal, P. (2001). Use of cognitive state predicates by language-impaired children. *International Journal of Language and Communication Disorders, 36*(3), 349–370.

Joseph, K. L., & Pine, J. M. (2002). Does error-free use of French negation constitute for very early parameter setting? *Journal of Child Language, 29*(1), 71–86.

Kaderavek, J. N., & Sulzby, E. (2000). Narrative production by children with and without specific language impairment: Oral narratives and emergent readings. *Journal of Speech, Language, and Hearing Research, 43*(1), 34–49.

Kail, R., Hale, C. A., Leonard, L. B., & Nippold, M. A. (1984). Lexical storage and retrieval in language-impaired children. *Applied Psycholinguistics, 5*(1), 37–49.

Kay-Raining Bird, E. (2007). The case for bilingualism in children with Down syndrome. In R. Paul (Ed.), *Language disorders from a developmental perspective* (pp. 249–275). Mahwah, NJ: Lawrence Erlbaum Associates.

Kay-Raining Bird, E., Cleave, P., Trudeau, N., Thordardottir, E., Sutton, A., & Thorpe, A. (2005). The language abilities of bilingual children with Down syndrome. *American Journal of Speech-Language Pathology, 14*, 187–199.

Kohnert, K., Bates, E., & Hernandez, A. (1999). Balancing bilinguals: Lexical-semantic production and cognitive processing in children learning Spanish and English. *Journal of Speech, Language, and Hearing Research, 42*(6), 1400–1413.

Kohnert, K., & Windsor, J. (2004). The search for common ground, Part II. Nonlinguistic performance by linguistically diverse learners. *Journal of Speech and Hearing Research, 47*, 891–903.

Kohnert, K., Yim, D., Nett, K., Kan, P. F., & Duran, L. (2005). Intervention with linguistically diverse preschool children: A focus on developing home language(s). *Language, Speech, and Hearing Services in Schools, 36*, 251–263.

Kolanko, H. (2004). *Category generation performance of language impaired and typically developing 7–9 year old bilingual children.* Unpublished master's thesis, University of Texas at Austin, Austin, TX.

Lahey, M., & Edwards, J. (1999). Naming errors of children with specific language impairment. *Journal of Speech, Language, and Hearing Research, 42*(1), 195–205.

Leonard, L. B., Camarata, S., Rowan, L. E., & Chapman, K. (1982). The communicative functions of lexical usage by language impaired children. *Applied Psycholinguistics, 3*(2), 109–125.

Leonard, L. B., Eyer, J. A., Bedore, L. M., & Grela, B. G. (1997). Three accounts of the grammatical morpheme difficulties of English-speaking children with specific language impairment. *Journal of Speech, Language, and Hearing Research, 40*(4), 741–753.

Leonard, L. B., Sabbadini, L., Leonard, J. S., & Volterra, V. (1987). Specific language impairment in children: A cross-linguistic study. *Brain and Language, 32*(2), 233–252.

Lidz, C. S. (2002). Mediated learning experience (MLE) as a basis for an alternative approach to assessment. *School Psychology International, 23*(1), 68–84.

Liles, B. Z., Duffy, R. J., Merritt, D. D., & Purcell, S. L. (1995). The measurement of narrative discourse ability in children with language disorders. *Journal of Speech and Hearing Research, 39*, 185–196.

Lofranco, L., Peña, E. D., & Bedore, L. M. (2006). English language narratives of Filipino children. *Language, Speech, and Hearing Services in the Schools, 37*(1), 28–38.

MacWhinney, B. (2005). A unified model of language acquisition. In J. Kroll & A. DeGroot (Eds.), *Handbook of bilingualism* (pp. 49–67). Oxford: Oxford University Press.

Magliano, J. P., Trabasso, T., & Graesser, A. C. (1999). Strategic processing during comprehension. *Journal of Educational Psychology, 91*(4), 615–629.

Maital, S. L., Dromi, E., Sagi, A., & Bornstein, M. H. (2000). The Hebrew Communicative Development Inventory: Language specific properties and cross-linguistic generalizations. *Journal of Child Language, 27*(1), 43–67.

Marchman, V. A., Martínez-Sussmann, C., & Dale, P. S. (2004). The language-specific nature of grammatical development: Evidence from bilingual language learners. *Developmental Science, 7*, 212–224.

McGregor, K. K. (1997). The nature of word-finding errors of preschoolers with and without word-finding deficits. *Journal of Speech, Language, and Hearing Research, 40,* 1232–1244.

McGregor, K. K., & Appel, A. (2002). On the relation between mental representation and naming in a child with specific language impairment. *Clinical Linguistics and Phonetics, 16*(1), 1–20.

McGregor, K. K., Newman, R. M., & Reilly, R. M. (2002). Semantic representation and naming in children with specific language Impairment. *Journal of Speech, Language, and Hearing Research, 45*(5), 998–1014.

McGregor, K. K., & Windsor, J. (1996). Effects of priming on the naming accuracy of preschoolers with word-finding deficits. *Journal of Speech and Hearing Research, 39*(5), 1048–1058.

Meisel, J. M. (1983). Transfer as a second language strategy. *Language and Communication, 3*(1), 11–46.

Merritt, D. D., & Liles, B. Z. (1987). Story grammar ability in children with and without language disorder: Story generation, story retelling, and story comprehension. *Journal of Speech and Hearing Research, 30,* 539–552.

Miller, L., Gillam, R. B., & Peña, E. D. (2001). *Dynamic assessment and intervention: Improving children's narrative skills.* Austin, TX: PRO-ED.

Montgomery, J. W. (1999). Recognition of gated words by children with specific language impairment: An examination of lexical mapping. *Journal of Speech Language and Hearing Research, 42*(3), 735–743.

Montgomery, J. W. (2002). Examining the nature of lexical processing in children with specific language impairment: Temporal processing or processing capacity deficit? *Applied Psycholinguistics, 23*(3), 447–470.

Muñoz, M. L., Gillam, R. B., Peña, E. D., & Gulley-Faehnle, A. (2003). Measures of language development in fictional narratives of Latino children. *Language, Speech, and Hearing Services in the Schools, 34,* 332–342.

Naglieri, J. A., & Das, J. P. (1989). An exploratory study of planning, attention, simultaneous, and successive cognitive processes. *Journal of School Psychology, 27*(4), 347–364.

Nash, M., & Donaldson, M. L. (2005). Word learning in children with vocabulary deficits. *Journal of Speech, Language, and Hearing Research, 48*(2), 439–458.

Nelson, K., & Nelson, A. P. (1990). Category production in response to script and category cues by kindergarten and second-grade children. *Journal of Applied Psychology, 11,* 431–446.

Newman, R. S., & German, D. J. (2002). Effects of lexical factors on lexical access among typical language-learning children and children with word-finding difficulties. *Language and Speech, 45*(3), 285–317.

Nicoladis, E., & Genesee, F. (1997). Language development in preschool bilingual children. *Journal of Speech-Language Pathology and Audiology, 21*(4), 258–270.

Nilsson, A., & Vikström, L. (1998). *Normalspråkiga Fyra- Och Femåringars Förmåga Att Strukturera Och Förstå Berättelser.* Unpublished master's thesis, Lund University, Lund, Sweden.

Paradis, J. (2005). Grammatical morphology in children learning English as a second language: Implications of similarities with specific language impairment. *Language, Speech, and Hearing Services in the Schools, 36,* 172–187.

Paradis, J., & Crago, M. (2000). Tense and temporality: A comparison between children learning a second language and children with SLI. *Journal of Speech, Language, and Hearing Research, 43,* 834–847.

Paradis, J., Crago, M., Genesee, F., & Rice, M. L. (2003). French–English bilingual children with SLI: How do they compare with their monolingual peers? *Journal of Speech, Language, and Hearing Research, 46*(1), 113.

Paradis, J., & Genesee, F. (1997). On continuity and the emergence of functional categories in bilingual first-language acquisition. *Language Acquisition, 62,* 91–124.

Paradis, J., Le Corre, M., & Genesee, F. (1998). The emergence of tense and agreement in child L2 French. *Second Language Research, 14*(3), 227–256.

Paradis, J., & Nicoladis, E. (2007). The influence of dominance and sociolinguistic context on bilingual preschoolers' language choice. *International Journal of Bilingual Education and Bilingualism, 10*(3), 277–297.

Paradis, J., Nicoladis, E., & Genesee, F. (2000). Early emergence of structural constraints on code-mixing: Evidence from French–English bilingual children. *Bilingualism: Language and Cognition*, 3(3), 245–261.

Patterson, J. L. (1998). Expressive vocabulary development and word combinations of Spanish–English bilingual toddlers. *American Journal of Speech Language Pathology*, 7(4), 46–56.

Patterson, J. L. (2000). Observed and reported expressive vocabulary and word combinations in bilingual toddlers. *Journal of Speech, Language, and Hearing Research*, 43(1), 121–128.

Pearce, W. M., McCormack, P. F., & James, D. G. H. (2003). Exploring the boundaries of SLI: Findings from morphosyntactic and story grammar analyses. *Clinical Linguistics and Phonetics*, 17(4), 325–334.

Pearson, B. Z., & Fernández, S. C. (1994). Patterns of interaction in the lexical growth in two languages of bilingual infants and toddlers. *Language Learning*, 44(4), 617–653.

Pearson, B. Z., Fernández, S., & Oller, D. K. (1993). Lexical development in bilingual infants and toddlers: Comparison to monolingual norms. *Language and Learning*, 43(1), 93–120.

Pearson, B. Z., Fernández, S. C., & Oller, D. K. (1995). Cross-language synonyms in the lexicons of bilingual infants: One language or two? *Journal of Child Language*, 22(2), 345–368.

Pease-Alvarez, L. (2002). Moving beyond linear trajectories of language shift and bilingual language socialization. *Hispanic Journal of Behavioral Sciences*, 24(2), 114–137.

Peña, E. D. (2000). Measurement of modifiability in children from culturally and linguistically diverse backgrounds. *Communication Disorders Quarterly*, 21(2), 87–97.

Peña, E. D., Bedore, L. M., & Rappazzo, C. (2003). Comparison of Spanish, English, and bilingual children's performance across semantic tasks. *Language, Speech, and Hearing Services in the Schools*, 34(1), 5–16.

Peña, E. D., Bedore, L. M., & Zlatic-Guinta, R. (2002). Category-generation performance of bilingual children: The influence of condition, category, and language. *Journal of Speech, Language, and Hearing Research*, 45, 938–947.

Peña, E. D., & Gillam, R. B. (2000). Dynamic assessment of children referred for speech and language evaluations. In C. S. Lidz & J. Elliott (Eds.), *Dynamic assessment: Prevailing models and applications* (Vol. 6). Oxford, UK: Elsevier Science.

Peña, E. D., Gillam, R. B., Malek, M., Ruiz-Felter, R., Resendiz, M., Fiestas, C. E., et al. (2006). Dynamic assessment of school-age children's narrative ability: An experimental investigation of classification accuracy. *Journal of Speech, Language, and Hearing Research*, 49(5), 1037–1057.

Peña, E. D., Resendiz, M. D., & Gillam, R. B. (2008). The role of clinical judgments of modifiability in the diagnosis of language impairment. *Advances in Speech Language Pathology*, 9, 332–345.

Peña, E. D., Gutiérrez-Clellen, V. F., Iglesias, A., Goldstein, B., & Bedore, L. M. (2007). *Bilingual English–Spanish Assessment*. Manuscript in preparation.

Peña, E. D., Iglesias, A., & Lidz, C. S. (2001). Reducing test bias through dynamic assessment of children's word learning ability. *American Journal of Speech-Language Pathology*, 10, 138–154.

Peña, E. D., & Quinn, R. (1997). Task familiarity: Effects on the test performance of Puerto Rican and African American children. *Language, Speech, and Hearing Services in Schools*, 28(4), 323–332.

Peña, E. D., Quinn, R., & Iglesias, A. (1992). The application of dynamic methods to language assessment: A non-biased procedure. *Journal of Special Education*, 26(3), 269–280.

Peña, E. D., & Stubbe Kester, E. (2004). Semantic development in Spanish–English bilinguals: Theory, assessment, and intervention. In B. Goldstein (Ed.), *Bilingual language development and disorders in Spanish-English speakers*. Baltimore: Paul H. Brookes.

Perozzi, J. A. (1985). A pilot study of language facilitation for bilingual, language-handicapped children: Theoretical and intervention implications. *Journal of Speech and Hearing Disorders*, 50(4), 403–406.

Perozzi, J. A., & Sanchez, M. C. (1992). The effect of instruction in L1 on receptive acquisition of L2 for bilingual children with language delay. *Language, Speech, and Hearing Services in Schools*, 23(4), 348–352.

Peters, A. M. (1985). Language segmentation: Operating principles for the perception and analysis of language. In D. Slobin (Ed.), *The crosslinguistic study of language acquisition* (Vol. 2, pp. 1029–1068). Hillsdale, NJ: Lawrence Erlbaum Associates.

Pienemann, M. (1998). Developmental dynamics in L1 and L2 acquisition: Processability theory and generative entrenchment. *Bilingualism: Language and Cognition, 1*(1), 1–20.

Quay, S. (1995). The bilingual lexicon: Implications for studies of language choice. *Journal of Child Language, 22*(2), 369–387.

Renfrew, C. (1995). *Word finding vocabulary test* (4th ed.). Oxford, UK: Winslow Press.

Restrepo, M. A. (1998). Identifiers of predominantly Spanish-speaking children with language impairment. *Journal of Speech, Language, and Hearing Research, 41*(6), 1398–1411.

Restrepo, M. A., & Gutiérrez-Clellen, V. (2001). Article use in Spanish-speaking children with specific language impairment. *Journal of Child Language, 28*(2), 433–452.

Restrepo, M. A., & Kruth, K. (2000). Grammatical characteristics of a Spanish–English bilingual child with specific language impairment. *Communication Disorders Quarterly, 21*(2), 66–76.

Rice, M. L., & Wexler, K. (1996). Toward tense as a clinical marker of specific language impairment in English-speaking children. *Journal of Speech and Hearing Research, 39*(6), 1239–1257.

Rice, M. L., Wexler, K., & Hershberger, S. (1998). Tense over time: The longitudinal course of tense acquisition in children with specific language impairment. *Journal of Speech, Language, and Hearing Research, 41*(6), 1412–1431.

Rohde, A. (1996). The aspect hypothesis and the emergence of tense distinctions in naturalistic L2 acquisition. *Linguistics, 34*, 1115–1137.

Rohena, E. I., Jitendra, A. K., & Browder, D. M. (2002). Comparison of the effects of Spanish and English constant time delay instruction on sight word reading by Hispanic learners with mental retardation. *Journal of Special Education, 36*(3), 169–184.

Salameh, E.-K., Håkansson, G., & Nettelbladt, U. (2004). Developmental perspectives on bilingual Swedish-Arabic children with and without language impairment: A longitudinal study. *International Journal of Language and Communication Disorders, 39*(1), 65–91.

Schiff-Myers, N., & Mikulajova, M. (1997). Word-finding problems in children with language disorders: Assessment and intervention. *Issues in Special Education and Rehabilitation, 12*(1), 5–19.

Schwanenflugel, P. J., & Rey, M. (1986). The relationship between category typicality and concept familiarity: Evidence from Spanish- and English-speaking monolinguals. *Memory and Cognition, 14*, 150–163.

Serratrice, L., Sorace, A., & Paoli, S. (2004). Crosslinguistic influence at the syntax-pragmatics interface: Subjects and objects in English–Italian bilingual and monolingual acquisition. *Bilingualism: Language and Cognition, 7*(3), 183–205.

Simon-Cereijido, G., & Gutiérrez-Clellen, V. F. (2007). Spontaneous language markers of Spanish language impairment. *Applied Psycholinguistics, 28*(2), 317–339.

Simonsen, A. (2002). Naming amongst 6 year old children. In *Working Papers* (Vol. 50, pp. 79–84). Lund, Sweden: Department of Linguistics, Lund University.

Smith, N. V., & Tsimpli, I.-M. (1995). *The mind of a savant: Language learning and modularity*: Blackwell.

Stein, N. L., & Albro, E. R. (1997). Building complexity and coherence: Children's use of goal-structured knowledge in telling stories. In M. Bamberg (Ed.), *Narrative Development: Six Approaches* (pp. 5–44). Hillsdale, NJ: Lawrence Erlbaum Associates.

Stokes, S. F., & Fletcher, P. (2003). Aspectual forms in Cantonese children with specific language impairment. *Linguistics, 41*(2), 381–405.

Stubbe Kester, E., Peña, E. D., & Gillam, R. B. (2001). Outcomes of dynamic assessment with culturally and linguistically diverse students: A comparison of three teaching methods. *Journal of Cognitive Education and Psychology, 2*, 42–59.

Thordardottir, E. T. (2005). Early lexical and syntactic development in Quebec French and English: Implications for cross-linguistic and bilingual assessment. *International Journal of Language and Communication Disorders, 40*(3), 244–276.

Thordardottir, E. T., Ellis Weismer, S., & Smith, M. E. (1997). Vocabulary learning in bilingual and monolingual clinical intervention. *Child Language Teaching and Therapy, 13*(3), 215–227.

Thordardottir, E. T., & Namazi, M. (2007). Specific language impairment in French-speaking children: Beyond grammatical morphology. *Journal of Speech, Language, and Hearing Research, 50*(3), 698–715.

Tomasello, M. (2003). *Constructing a language: A usage-based theory of language acquisition.* Cambridge, MA: Harvard University Press.

Tomblin, J. B., Records, N. L., Buckwalter, P., Zhang, X., Smith, E., & O'Brien, M. (1997). Prevalence of specific language impairment in kindergarten children. *Journal of Speech, Language, and Hearing Research, 40*, 1245–1260.

Tracy, R. (1995). *Child language in contact: Bilingual language acquisition (English/German) in early childhood.* Unpublished doctoral dissertation, University of Tübingen, Tübingen, Germany.

Trudeau, N., Colozzo, P., Sylvestre, V., & Ska, B. (2004). Language following functional left hemispherectomy in a bilingual teenager. *Brain and Cognition, 53*, 384–388.

Tzuriel, D. (2001). *Dynamic assessment of young children.* New York: Kluwer Academic/Plenum.

Ukrainetz, T. A., Harpell, S., Walsh, C., & Coyle, C. (2000). A preliminary investigation of dynamic assessment with native American kindergartners. *Language, Speech, and Hearing Services in the Schools, 31*(2), 142–154.

Umbel, V., Pearson, B. Z., Fernández, M. C., & Oller, D. K. (1992). Measuring bilingual children's receptive vocabularies. *Child Development, 63*, 1012–1020.

Valdes, G., & Figueroa, R. (1994). *Bilingualism and testing: A special case of bias.* Norwood, NJ: Ablex.

Valencia, R., & Suzuki, L. (2001). *Intelligence testing and minority students: Foundations, performance factors, and assessment issues.* Thousand Oaks, CA: Sage.

van der Lely, H. K. J., & Howard, D. (1993). Children with specific language impairment: Linguistic impairment or short-term memory deficit? *Journal of Speech and Hearing Research, 36*(6), 1193–1207.

Vasquez, O. A., Pease-Alvarez, L., & Shannon, S. M. (1994). *Pushing boundaries: Language and culture in a Mexicano community.* Cambridge, UK: Cambridge University Press.

Vermeer, A. (2001). Breadth and depth of vocabulary in relation to L1/L2 acquisition and frequency of input. *Applied Psycholinguistics, 22*(2), 217–234.

Volterra, V., & Taeschner, T. (1978). The acquisition and development of language by bilingual children. *Journal of Child Language, 5*(2), 311–326.

Wagner, C. R., Sahlén, B., & Nettelbladt, U. (1999). What's the story? Narration and comprehension in Swedish preschool children with language impairment. *Child Language Teaching and Therapy, 15*(2), 113–137.

Westby, C., Van Dongen, R., & Maggart, Z. (1989). Assessing narrative competence. *Seminars in Speech and Language, 10*, 63–75.

Wexler, K. (1996). The development of inflection in a biologically based theory of language acquisition. In M. L. Rice (Ed.), *Towards a genetics of language.* Hillsdale, NJ: Lawrence Erlbaum Associates.

Wickström, B.-A. (2005). Can bilingualism be dynamically stable? A simple model of language choice. *Rationality and Society, 17*(1), 81–115.

Windsor, J. (1999). Effect of semantic inconsistency on sentence grammaticality judgements for children with and without language-learning disabilities. *Language Testing, 16*(3), 293–313.

Woll, B., & Grove, N. (1996). On language deficits and modality in children with Down syndrome: A case study of twins bilingual in BSL and English. *Journal of Deaf Studies and Deaf Education, 1*(4), 271.

13

Cross-Linguistic Studies of Child Language Disorders

LAURENCE B. LEONARD

INTRODUCTION

As noted in chapter 1 (Schwartz), children with specific language impairment (SLI) exhibit significant deficits in their language ability, yet do not display the symptoms associated with other clinical populations. These children earn age-appropriate scores on nonverbal tests of intelligence, they pass screening tests for hearing acuity and oral-motor structure and function, and they do not show clear evidence of neurological disease or impairment. The term "specific language impairment" is not the clinical label always adopted; other terms still in use include "developmental dysphasia" and the more general term "language impairment." However, regardless of the term, the existence of language disorders without accompanying deficits in other areas has been widely recognized by researchers and clinicians alike. Not surprisingly, this kind of disorder has been reported in many different languages. Yet, despite the apparently universal nature of this disorder, there are striking differences in how SLI manifests itself across languages.

In this chapter, we review some of these systematic differences across groups of languages, discuss the explanations offered thus far, and propose some modifications of these explanations that might lead toward a more complete account of this disorder. Initially, we focus on the common SLI grammatical profile for English, placing emphasis on grammatical morphology. We then turn to the grammatical profile reflected in other Germanic languages (German, Dutch, Swedish), followed by the profile seen in "null-subject" languages (Italian, Spanish). In the review of each type of language, we consider how three types of accounts of grammatical deficits in SLI would attempt to explain the particular profile observed. These accounts can be roughly categorized as: (1) those that highlight the processing demands that particular language typologies may place on children; (2) those that put a premium on the phonological and prosodic requirements of the languages; and (3) those that assume a constraint in the underlying grammar.

THE SLI GRAMMATICAL PROFILE FOR ENGLISH

Probably the best-documented problem in English-speaking children with SLI is an especially serious deficit in the use of grammatical morphemes that mark tense and agreement (see chapter 15 by Oetting & Hadley). These morphemes include the inflections, past tense -*ed*, third person singular -*s*, and the copula and auxiliary forms of *be* (*is, are, am, was, were*). As a group, children with SLI make less use of these morphemes than do young typically developing children matched for mean length of utterance (MLU) (e.g., Johnston & Kamhi, 1984; Leonard, Eyer, Bedore, & Grela, 1997; Oetting & Horohov, 1997; Rice & Wexler, 1996). These limitations can continue into the early elementary-school grades (Marchman, Wulfeck, & Ellis Weismer, 1999; Norbury, Bishop, & Briscoe, 2001; Rice, Wexler, & Hershberger, 1998). Studies of individual children (e.g., van der Lely, 1997) have reported serious problems with these morphemes at even later ages. Composite measures of tense and agreement morphemes show good sensitivity and specificity in distinguishing children with SLI from their typically developing peers (Bedore & Leonard, 1998; Rice, 1998).

The differences between English-speaking children with SLI, younger typically developing children matched for MLU (TD-MLU children), and typically developing children matched for age (TD-A children) are differences in degree of use. It is rarely the case that children with SLI fail to use these forms altogether. Furthermore, when these morphemes are used, they are nearly always applied in the appropriate contexts. Productions such as *They runs fast* are rare. In addition, occasional overgeneralizations are seen in the speech of these children, such as *throwed* for *threw* (see review in Leonard, 1998). Such findings suggest that in spite of their limited use of tense and agreement morphemes in obligatory contexts, children with SLI possess knowledge of their grammatical function and where not to use them.

Tense and agreement morphemes are not the only elements of grammatical morphology that have been studied in the speech of English-speaking children with SLI. Differences favoring TD-MLU (and TD-A) children have also been found for possessive 's (e.g., *Kate's car*), the infinitival complementizer *to* (e.g., *They like to eat grapes*), and nonthematic *of* (e.g., *cup of tea*) (e.g., Leonard, 1995; Owen & Leonard, 2006). There has been somewhat mixed evidence for three other morpheme types. Initial reports suggested that children with SLI are less proficient than TD-MLU children in the use of noun plural inflections (Leonard, Bortolini, Caselli, McGregor, & Sabbadini, 1992; Leonard et al., 1997; Rice & Oetting, 1993), but other studies report either no group differences or group differences with percentages sufficiently high for the SLI group not to be considered clinically significant (Oetting & Rice, 1993; Rice & Wexler, 1996). McGregor and Leonard (1994) and Rice and Wexler (1996) found lower degrees of article use by children with SLI than by TD-MLU children, but Leonard et al. (1992) found only a nonsignificant trend favoring TD-MLU children.

The third morpheme type yielding slightly mixed findings is the passive participle -*ed* (e.g., *Tarzan got pushed by Buzz Lightyear*). Whereas two studies found less consistent use of this inflection by children with SLI than by TD-MLU children (Leonard, Deevy, Miller, Rauf, et al., 2003; Leonard, Wong, Deevy, Stokes, & Fletcher, 2006), one study found no group difference (Redmond, 2003). However, the studies do agree in finding greater use of the participle -*ed* than the past tense -*ed*.

Typology-Related Accounts and the English SLI Data

Some accounts assume that the extraordinary difficulty with grammatical morphology is the result of an interaction between a more general limitation in language-learning ability and the properties of the particular system of grammar that must be learned. These accounts differ somewhat in whether they assume that the operative factor is the status of bare stems in the language, the number of inflections in the language (Leonard, Sabbadini, Leonard,

& Volterra, 1987), or the cues to grammatical function that the grammatical morphemes provide (Lindner & Johnston, 1992). In English, bare stems are frequent, inflections are sparse, and grammatical morphemes provide relatively few cues to roles such as subject and object. For example, from the verb *like* in *like to eat ice cream* it is not clear whether the subject is the first or second person (*I* or *you*) or singular or plural (*I* or *we*).

A necessary assumption of each variant of these typology-related accounts is that children with SLI have a limited processing capacity. The typology of English is assumed to place significant processing demands on the learning of grammatical morphology. Faced with a limited processing capacity, children with SLI must devote their limited resources to the more prevalent structural information conveyed by word order. Fewer resources remain for the learning of grammatical morphology, requiring more encounters with grammatical morphemes before they can be learned.

It should be noted that typology-related accounts predict problems with grammatical morphology that extend beyond those that express tense and agreement. This has been both a strength and a weakness for these types of accounts. On the one hand, studies have shown that English-speaking children with SLI make less use of morphemes such as possessive *'s* and the infinitival complementizer *to* than do younger TD children, and these morphemes are not tied to agreement or tense. On the other hand, as noted above, tense and agreement morphemes are especially vulnerable in the speech of children with SLI, and typology-related accounts provide no basis for distinguishing them from other morphemes that are at risk given the typology of English and the assumption of a limitation in processing capacity in children with SLI.

Phonology/Prosody Accounts and the English SLI Data

Other accounts of the difficulties with grammatical morphology hold that the phonotactic or prosodic demands of grammatical morphemes are especially troublesome for children with SLI. For example, Marshall and van der Lely (2006) found that English-speaking children with SLI had greater difficulty with past tense *-ed* inflections that form word-final consonant clusters that do not exist in monomorphemic words (e.g., *rushed*) than with past tense *-ed* inflections that form word-final consonant clusters that do exist in monomorphemic words as well as in past tense forms (e.g., *crossed*; note the existence of words such as *cost, frost, last, test*). This difference was not found in the productions of the TD children in the comparison groups, who performed at a significantly higher level on both types of past tense forms. Such a finding suggests that the past tense use of children with SLI may benefit from the practice gained in the production of word-final consonant clusters when grammatical morpheme use is not involved.

Difficulties with grammatical morphology are not limited to inflections: they are also seen in function words. McGregor and Leonard (1994) found that English-speaking children with SLI had more difficulty than typically developing children in producing function words (e.g., articles) that took the form of weak, nonfinal monosyllables. Bortolini and Leonard (1996) extended this finding to uncontractible copula forms. They found that children with SLI differed most from younger TD-MLU controls in their use of these nonfinal weak-syllable function words, but they differed as well even in their ability to use nonfinal weak syllables in monomorphemic words (e.g., the first syllable of *banana*). Such a finding suggests that prosodic factors pose problems for children with SLI that are then exacerbated when the prosodically challenging elements have morpheme status.

As was the case for typology-related accounts, the reach of phonology/prosody accounts extends beyond morphemes that mark tense and agreement, including function words such as articles and the infinitival complementizer *to*, and inflections such as noun plural *-s* and possessive 's. For both articles and noun plurals, the evidence of special difficulties has been quite mixed. On the other hand, a morpheme that should pose no special phonological/prosodic challenge is the word-final syllabic progressive inflection, -ing. This morpheme seems to be used by children with SLI with a fair degree of proficiency (e.g., Leonard, Deevy, Miller, Charest, et al., 2003).

Checking Constraints and the English SLI Data

Some attempts to explain the tense and agreement morpheme limitations seen in SLI make use of the minimalist framework of Chomsky (1995) as a foundation. One such account is the extended unique checking constraint (EUCC) account of Wexler (1998, 2003), an important elaboration of the extended optional infinitive approach (e.g., Rice & Wexler, 1996) and the agreement/tense omission model (Wexler, Schütze, & Rice, 1998). Wexler proposed that children with SLI go through a protracted period during which a determiner (D) feature in a determiner phrase (DP) can only check the noninterpretable D feature of one functional category. For English, this means that the subject DP can check the D feature at tense (TNS) only or at Subject Agreement (AGRS) only.

This constraint has major implications for grammatical morphemes that express tense and agreement. For example, the morphemes third person singular -s and the copula and auxiliary forms is/are/am/was/were mark both tense and agreement. Therefore, when checking occurs at only one of these functional categories (TNS or AGRS), the remaining category is not projected, and the use of the morpheme is blocked. Less obviously, past tense -ed use can also be adversely affected. Use of this inflection will not be blocked if checking occurs at TNS only. However, checking might, instead, occur at AGRS only. In this instance, TNS will not be projected, and past tense -ed will not be used. An example of an utterance of this type would be Yesterday she walk all the way home, where the nominative case pronoun she is assumed to result from checking at AGRS and the absence of -ed is taken to mean that checking did not occur at TNS.

The appearance of the bare stem form walk in the above example should not be interpreted as a failed attempt to include the -ed inflection. Rather, Wexler made the assumption than when the checking constraint applies and the inflection cannot be expressed, a nonfinite form is used in its place. Thus, walk is comparable to the nonfinite verb walk in the adult utterance We saw the girl walk all the way home. For contexts requiring a copula or auxiliary be form, application of the constraint results in the absence of the tense/agreement morpheme. Here, again, there are parallels in the adult grammar, as can be seen by comparing the (constraint-driven) utterance The boy running and the adult production We saw the boy running.

THE SLI GRAMMATICAL PROFILE FOR OTHER GERMANIC LANGUAGES

In languages such as German and Dutch, verb inflections that mark tense and agreement are more abundant than is the case for English. For example, whereas English has only one inflection in the present-tense paradigm (third person singular), German possesses an inflection for each person and number combination (e.g., lerne: "I learn", lernst: "you learn"], lernt: "he/she learns"). Yet differences between children with SLI and their younger MLU-matched compatriots are nevertheless observed in these languages (e.g., Bartke, 1994; de Jong, 1999; Rice, Noll, & Grimm, 1997). When children fail to use tense and agreement inflections, they are quite likely to use nonfinite forms such as infinitives in their place. Unlike English, in these languages infinitives have overt inflections (e.g., German "to learn" is *lernen*, not the bare stem *lern*). However, in both German and Dutch, bare stems are also produced at times in contexts requiring a tense and agreement inflection (e.g., de Jong, 1999; Rice et al., 1997; Roberts & Leonard, 1997).

Languages such as German and Dutch are viewed as *verb-second* languages. In these languages, the verb expressing agreement and/or tense must appear as the second constituent in the sentence. For utterances with sentence-initial subjects, the word order matches that of English, as in *die Frau fand die Kinder*: "The woman found the children." However, when a constituent other than the subject appears in sentence-initial position, the finite verb rather than the subject appears next, as in *gestern fand die Frau die Kinder*, which has the meaning of "Yesterday the woman found the children" but is literally translated as "Yesterday found the woman the children." Children with SLI sometimes fail to use the proper verb-second word order. (As we shall see, this difficulty may not be independent of their problems with tense and agreement morphology.)

In German and Dutch, when children use nonfinite verbs in place of verbs with tense and agreement inflections, they often produce them in sentence-final position. Indeed, sentence-final position is the usual position for nonfinite verb forms, as in the German utterance *Chris kann das kochen*: "Chris can that cook" (= "Chris can cook that") where *kochen* is the infinitive "to cook." However, children with SLI may produce the infinitival form in sentence-final position even when an auxiliary such as "can" is not included, as in *Chris das kochen*: "Chris that cook" (= "Chris cook that").

Although all Germanic languages show evidence of word order errors by children with SLI, there appear to be cross-linguistic differences. For example, Rice et al. (1997) found that German-speaking children with SLI used finite verb forms in (appropriate) second position in 74% of their sentences on average, whereas Leonard, Hansson, Nettelbladt, and Deevy (2005) found that Swedish-speaking children with SLI of the same age used finite verb forms in second position in 93% of their sentences. Swedish differs from German and Dutch in that nonfinite forms such as infinitives immediately follow the finite verb; they are not placed in sentence-final position. Thus, the utterance "You must buy milk" is *Du måste köpa mjölk*, reflecting the same word order as in English, whereas in German the infinitive "buy" would appear in sentence-final position. However, this difference between Swedish on the one hand and German and Dutch on the other does not change the verb-second property of Swedish. As in these other Germanic languages, if a Swedish speaker chose for pragmatic reasons to begin the sentence with "milk," the finite verb must appear in second position, in front of the subject, as in *Mjölk måste du köpa*: "Milk must you buy." The figure of 93% correct use given for the Leonard et al. (2005) study above was, in fact, based only on utterances that had a nonsubject in sentence-initial position. In each of these utterances, the child had to deviate from the usual subject–verb–object order of Swedish.

Typology-Related Accounts and the SLI Data for Other Germanic Languages

Although children with SLI in languages such as German, Dutch, and Swedish are less proficient than MLU controls in the use of tense and agreement morphemes, the differences do not appear to be of the same magnitude as is found in English. Furthermore, the percentages of use by children with SLI in these languages are notably higher than those seen for English-speaking children with SLI. For example, Leonard and Deevy (2006) reviewed several studies of English-, German-, and Dutch-speaking children with SLI of comparable age and overall severity of language disorder. They found that the children produced present third person singular inflections in an average of 34%, 50%, and 61% of obligatory contexts, respectively. In a direct comparison between English- and German-speaking children with SLI, Roberts and Leonard (1997) found significantly higher percentages of use of the present third person singular inflection by the German-speaking children. Leonard et al. (2005) directly compared English- and Swedish-speaking children with SLI according to their use of past tense inflections. In both languages, these inflections mark tense but not agreement. The differences were significant and favored the Swedish-speaking children (86% versus 53% use in obligatory contexts). Typology-related accounts offer a plausible reason for the higher percentages for German, Dutch, and Swedish than for English: Inflections are greater in number in these languages than in English, and bare stems are much less frequent.

Word order errors are rare in English but, as noted earlier, they are clearly evident in the speech of children with SLI in verb-second languages. Typology-related accounts make the assumption that children with SLI operate with limited processing capacities. Unlike the case for English, children with SLI learning German, Dutch, and Swedish must attend to the verb-second requirements. Such word order information might compete with grammatical morpheme information for dominance as cues to sentence interpretation and use, resulting in occasional errors in both domains.

Phonology/Prosody Accounts and the SLI Data for Other Germanic Languages

Studies of children with SLI in Germanic languages have not placed emphasis on possible prosodic influences on the use of grammatical morphology. Nevertheless, phonology/prosody accounts might well be applied to these languages. The clearest cases of difficulty with tense and agreement inflections occur with those inflections that involve word-final consonants or consonant clusters (e.g., Dutch -*t*, German -*st*, -*t*). In German, the copula and auxiliary forms used in the present perfect—the most common means of referring to past events (e.g., *er ist gegangen*: "he has gone")—are weak monosyllables, and these are deleted to a greater extent by children with SLI than by younger TD children (e.g., Rice et al., 1997; Roberts & Leonard, 1997).

Definite articles are also omitted quite frequently by German-speaking children with SLI (Roberts & Leonard, 1997), and these, too, are weak monosyllabic forms. Hansson, Nettelbladt, and Leonard (2003) attempted to separate the effects of prosody in children's article use from any effects that might be attributable to the particular grammatical function of these morphemes. These investigators examined the article use of children with SLI who were acquiring Swedish. In this language, indefinite articles are preverbal monosyllabic function words (e.g., *en bil*: "a car", *ett hus*: "a house"), but definite forms often take the form of a syllabic suffix (e.g., *bilen*: "the car," *huset*: "the house"). Hansson et al. found that Swedish-speaking children with SLI used definite suffixes as accurately as do TD same-age peers, but they used indefinite articles less accurately than either younger TD-MLU children or TD-A peers. Because these two morpheme types differ in definiteness as well as in prosody, these investigators also examined the children's use of definite forms in constructions with an adjective preceding the noun. Such constructions require an article in preadjective position, for both definite and indefinite reference (e.g., *den svarta katten*: "the black cat"). The children with SLI produced definite as well as indefinite articles in fewer obligatory contexts than did either TD-MLU or TD-A children. These findings suggest that the prosodic position of a definite form probably has a bearing on these children's production success, independent of grammatical function.

Checking Constraints and the SLI Data for Other Germanic Languages

According to Wexler (1998, 2003), the grammars of languages such as German and Dutch render them vulnerable to the same kind of inconsistent expression of tense and agreement by children with SLI as is seen in English. In both of these languages, for example, present tense inflections also mark agreement. Therefore, checking only at TNS or at AGRS will prevent the use of the inflection. Because children presumably select a nonfinite form in place of the finite form in such instances, an infinitive can result (e.g., *lernen*: "to learn" in place of *lernt*: "learns"). It is not clear how this type of account can explain the appearance of bare stems in finite verb contexts, yet such errors also occur in these languages.

Children with SLI acquiring Swedish show greater use of present and past tense inflections than do their German- and Dutch-speaking counterparts. Within the checking constraint framework, this difference has a ready explanation. In Swedish, neither present tense inflections nor past tense inflections express agreement. Thus, the same present tense inflection *-er* is used for "I play" (*jag leker*) and "she plays" (*hon leker*); similarly, the same past tense inflection *-te* is used for "I played" (*jag lekte*) and "she played" (*hon lekte*). If checking occurs at TNS only, the inflection used for "she plays," for example, will not be blocked, whereas the corresponding inflection in German will be blocked, as this inflection marks agreement as well as tense.

The same factor might also account for why Swedish-speaking children with SLI have more success with verb-second use than do children with SLI who are acquiring German or Dutch. In the linguistic framework employed by Wexler (1998, 2003), the structure assumed for Swedish is shown in Figure 13.1.

As a verb-second language, Swedish involves the movement of the finite verb to the Complementizer (C) position. The presence of lexical material in the Specifier (Spec)

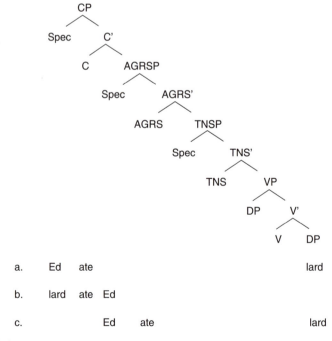

FIGURE 13.1   The structure assumed for Swedish in Wexler's (1998, 2003) linguistic framework.

position of the Complementizer Phrase (CP) seems to be the necessary condition for movement of the finite verb to C. In fact, Wexler (1998) treats this as the "verb-second parameter" that he assumes is correctly set from an early age. Thus, if the verb is not finite, it will not move to C. Given these assumptions, subject-initial sentences have two possible representations. If the subject appears in the Spec position of CP, as in (a) of Figure 13.1, the verb will move to C. On the other hand, the subject might appear in the Spec position of AGRSP, as in (c) of Figure 13.1, in which case the verb will appear in AGRS. If a constituent other than the subject appears in the Spec position of CP, as in (b) of Figure 13.1, the verb will move to C and the subject will remain in the Spec position of AGRSP.

Recall that, in Swedish, nonfinite verb forms immediately follow the finite verb (the equivalent of "You must buy milk"): they do not appear in sentence-final position, as in German and Dutch (the equivalent of "You must milk buy"). If checking occurs only at AGRS (and not at TNS), the child will produce a nonfinite verb form such as an infinitive. However, the only utterances containing such nonadult-like nonfinite forms will be subject-initial sentences with the subject presumably in the Spec position of AGRSP (TNS will not be projected in this instance). Sentences with lexical material in the Spec position of CP will not have a nonfinite verb in C, given the early, correct setting of the verb-second parameter. Put differently, for any sentence with lexical material in the Spec position of CP without an available finite verb, the derivation will crash—that is, the sentence will not be permitted by the child's grammar. Thus, in principle at least, word order errors should not be seen in the speech of Swedish-speaking children with SLI. In contrast, in German or Dutch, when the checking constraint applies, the subject will appear in a lower position, followed by the object, with the nonfinite verb in sentence-final position. This will constitute a word order error (subject–object–verb instead of subject–verb–object).

The checking constraint approach might also offer an explanation for why Swedish-speaking children with SLI show higher percentages of past tense inflections than do children with SLI who are acquiring English. At first blush, the percentages of past tense inflection use might be expected to be the same in the two languages, given that in both English and Swedish, these inflections mark tense but not agreement. Thus, in each language, checking at TNS only should permit use of the past tense inflection, and checking at AGRS only should block use of this inflection. However, Leonard et al. (2005) have proposed that Wexler's (1998) assumption of the children's correct setting of the verb-second parameter should result in different levels of success for Swedish and English. Assume that, in both languages, checking is equally likely at TNS only and at AGRS only. English is not a verb-second language, and thus the verb-second parameter is not applicable. All instances of checking at AGRS only can result in a sentence with a nonfinite verb. However, in Swedish, checking at AGRS only will result in a sentence with a nonfinite verb only if there is no lexical material in the Spec position of CP, as in when the subject is in sentence-initial position and occupies the Spec position of AGRSP. This is because the derivation will crash for instances in which lexical material occupies the Spec position of CP with checking at AGRS only, because only finite verbs can move to C. In contrast, if checking occurs at TNS only, the finite verb is not blocked (as the inflection marks tense only), and sentences of the type shown in (a), (b), and (c) of Figure 13.1 are possible. It would seem, then, that the proportion of cases in which a nonfinite form can emerge in a past tense context is smaller in Swedish than in English.

THE SLI GRAMMATICAL PROFILE FOR NULL-SUBJECT LANGUAGES

In recent years, children with SLI who speak languages such as Italian and Spanish have been the focus of increasing investigative attention. In these languages, the subject of the sentence can be omitted when either the physical context or the discourse context makes the referent of the subject quite clear. Thus, for example, in Italian, *corrono*: "[they] run" would be a very natural response when asked "Tell me about the boys in this picture." In such null-subject languages, the verb inflection paradigms are rich. In fact, in Italian and Spanish, bare stems do not appear. It is therefore more accurate to say that a stem appears with a variety of inflections than to say that inflections are actually added to the stems. Although the most frequent word order in these languages is subject–verb–object, their rich verb morphology permits considerable variation in word order as a function of pragmatic context.

The evidence from Italian and Spanish differs markedly from that from English and other Germanic languages. Relatively few differences are found between children with SLI and younger TD children matched for MLU, and for many tense and agreement inflections, the children with SLI are as proficient as their TD same-age peers (Bedore & Leonard, 2001, 2005; Bortolini, Caselli, & Leonard, 1997). When errors do occur, they rarely take the form of infinitives. Instead, children with SLI produce substitute inflections that usually differ from the appropriate inflections by only one feature. For example, the most likely substitute for a third person plural inflection is the third person singular inflection; the most likely replacement for a first person plural inflection is the first person singular inflection (Bortolini et al., 1997).

One tense and agreement inflection that has consistently produced differences between SLI and TD-MLU groups is the third person plural inflection of Italian (e.g., *dormono*: "[they] sleep"). This inflection seems to be especially difficult for children with SLI. The corresponding morpheme in Spanish (e.g., *duermen*: "[they] sleep") is also somewhat difficult for Spanish-speaking children with SLI, yet they do not differ from TD-MLU children in their success in supplying this inflection in appropriate contexts.

The advantage that null-subject languages hold for inflections does not apply to function words. Italian- and Spanish-speaking children with SLI make use of several different types of function words with significantly lower percentages than younger TD-MLU children. For Italian, differences of this type have been documented for definite articles, direct object clitics, and certain auxiliary verbs (Bortolini & Leonard, 1996; Bortolini et al., 1997; Leonard & Bortolini, 1998; Leonard et al., 1992). For Spanish, differences of this type have been documented for definite articles and direct object clitics (Bedore & Leonard, 2001, 2005; Restrepo & Gutierrez-Clellan, 2001). Some studies on Spanish have employed only comparisons between SLI and TD-A groups; in these studies, children with SLI have made less use of these forms than did their same-age peers (Eng & O'Connor, 2000; Jacobson & Schwartz, 2002).

Although Italian and Spanish have produced similar function-word differences between children with SLI and their typically developing peers, the results for the two languages are not identical. In Italian, omissions of function words predominate; substitution errors are relatively infrequent. Those substitutions that do occur are based on rather predictable factors. For example, most masculine singular nouns in Italian require the definite article *il* (e.g., *il gatto*: "the cat," *il cane*: "the dog"). However, when the word immediately following the article begins with [z], or an [s]-cluster, the masculine singular article *lo* must be used (e.g., *lo zaino*: "the backpack," *lo studente*: "the student"). Children sometimes produce the more frequent masculine singular *il* in place of *lo*—an error probably related to their lack of understanding of the phonotactic rules dictating use of *lo*. Apart from errors of this type, substitutions are quite rare, and omissions are the typical form of error, even when the omitted element has semantic substance. For example, in tasks requiring children to complete a sentence with the direct object clitic followed by the finite verb, children with SLI often provide the finite verb without the clitic. Such a production lacks an obligatory element of the sentence, the direct object. An example from Leonard et al. (1992) is shown in (1).

(1)   Examiner: Qui la ragazza prende il piatto, e qui . . .
                           Here the girl takes the plate, and here . . .
       Appropriate response: (*lo* lava)
                                              ([she] washes *it*)
       Child's response: (lava)
                                              ([she] washes)

In Spanish, omissions of function words are also made significantly more frequently by children with SLI than by TD-MLU children. However, in this language, substitutions are also rather frequent, in contrast with the case for Italian. Analyses of the substitution errors for both definite articles and direct object clitics reveal that singular forms are somewhat more likely to replace plural forms than the reverse. In addition, errors might be best characterized as "near-miss" errors, because the substitute form often differs from the appropriate form by only one feature. For example, feminine plural definite articles are more likely to replace masculine plural articles than masculine singular articles. When masculine singular articles are replaced, the substitute is usually a feminine singular article (Bedore & Leonard, 2005).

Typology-Related Accounts and the SLI Data for Null-Subject Languages

According to accounts that assume an interaction between language-learning ability and language typology, Italian- and Spanish-speaking children with SLI should devote their limited resources to inflectional morphology. In these languages, subjects are often absent, word order can vary, and verb inflections can provide essential cues to the identity of the subject. For example, the inflected Italian verb form *corro* makes it clear that the subject is first person singular ("[I] run") whereas the verb form *corri* is unmistakable in having a second person singular subject ("[you] run"). Similarly, from a verb form such as *prendo*, it is clear that the subject is first person singular, whether the direct object follows the verb, as in *prendo la rivista*: "[I] take the magazine", or precedes it, as in *la rivista prendo*: "the magazine [I] take".

According to typology-related accounts, the allocation of resources toward inflectional morphology would be expected to narrow the differences between Italian- and Spanish-speaking children with SLI and their typically developing peers, because this area of grammar plays such a central role in these languages. The available evidence for inflections certainly supports this view. Considering how weak inflectional morphology is in English-speaking children with SLI—especially with regard to tense and agreement inflections—the finding of few, if any, group differences in Italian and Spanish is striking.

However, it is equally clear that typology-related accounts offer no insight into the difficulty that children with SLI experience with function words. For example, in both Italian and Spanish, articles contain information not only about definiteness, but also about the number and gender of the nouns with which they are associated. From this perspective, they contain considerably more grammatical information than articles in English. Yet, not only are articles more difficult for children with SLI than for TD-MLU children in these languages, their percentages of use by children with SLI are no higher than for English-speaking children with SLI (e.g., Bortolini, Leonard, & Caselli, 1998).

Phonology/Prosody Accounts and the SLI Data for Null-Subject Languages

In Italian and Spanish, present tense and agreement inflections are usually word-final syllables (e.g., Italian *dormo*: "[I] sleep," *dorme*: "[he/she] sleeps") or word-final two-syllable inflections with stress on the first of these syllables (e.g., Spanish *corremos*: "[we] run"). In (Mexican) Spanish, the preterite is the most frequent means of expressing past tense, and monosyllabic inflections in the preterite place primary stress on the final syllable (the inflection), not on the penultimate syllable (e.g., *corrí*: "[I] ran"). It can be seen, then, that in each of these cases the tense and agreement inflection is syllabic and appears in stressed or word-final position—precisely the prosodic properties that should render them less problematic for children with SLI. The findings of similar production levels by children with SLI and MLU-matched TD children seem consistent with this expectation.

Recall that one of the Italian tense and agreement inflections, present third person plural, has been the exception to the usual pattern. This inflection is less likely to be produced by children with SLI than by TD children matched for MLU. It is perhaps no coincidence that this inflection is also an exception to the typical prosodic pattern of Italian. Verbs inflected for third person plural carry stress on the initial syllable (e.g., the first syllable of *dormono* "[they] sleep"), resulting in an inflection consisting of two consecutive weak syllables. It should also be pointed out that there are a handful of verbs with short stems whose third person plural forms consist of only two syllables (e.g., *fanno*: "[they] do/make," *danno*: "[they] give"). Therefore, these forms have a strong syllable–weak syllable pattern, in keeping with the penultimate stress pattern of Italian. These forms are not problematic for children with SLI (Leonard et al., 1992). Because the verbs of this type are frequently used in Italian, we cannot be certain that children's relative success with them is not simply a function of extended practice. Nevertheless, the collective evidence from Italian and Spanish inflections is consistent with a phonological/prosodic view.

Whereas typology-related accounts provide no insight into the function word difficulties of Italian- and Spanish-speaking children with SLI, phonology/prosody accounts do offer a possible explanation. In studies on Italian, all of the function words that have produced differences favoring TD-MLU and TD-A children over children with SLI have been weak monosyllables in nonfinal position. The great majority of errors by the children with SLI have been omissions. Included among the function words yielding group differences are the Italian auxiliary forms *è* and *ha* (e.g. *è andata*: "[she] has gone" produced as *andata*: "[she] gone"; *ha mangiato*: "[he] has eaten" produced as *mangiato*: "[he] eaten"). It should be noted that these data come from spontaneous speech samples (e.g., Leonard & Bortolini, 1998) and obligatory contexts for multisyllabic auxiliary forms (e.g., *abbiamo mangiato*: "[we] have eaten") have been relatively infrequent. Nevertheless, based on the limited number of contexts identified, multisyllabic auxiliary forms do not appear to show group differences between children with SLI and TD-MLU children.

Italian direct object clitics are also weak monosyllables. When assessed in their most frequent, preverbal position, as shown earlier in (1), these morphemes also reveal lower percentages of use by children with SLI than by TD-MLU children. When these morphemes have been studied in their less frequent postverbal position (e.g., *lo* in *ha smesso di farlo*: "[she] has stopped doing *it*"), children with SLI have been as proficient as TD-MLU children. This combination of findings suggests that when clitics appear in nonfinal position, they are more vulnerable to omission by children with SLI.

As noted earlier, definite articles are also omitted more often by Italian-speaking SLI groups than by TD-MLU groups. These morphemes are weak monosyllables that can never appear in final position.

The data for Spanish are generally consistent with the data for Italian. Definite articles and direct object clitics are weak monosyllabic forms appearing in nonfinal position that are more difficult for Spanish-speaking children with SLI than for TD-MLU children. Omissions are more likely to be seen in the SLI data than in the TD-MLU data. However, one finding is not handled well by phonology/prosody accounts: Substitution errors are as prevalent as omission errors. An example of a clitic substitution error from Bedore and Leonard (2001) is shown in (2).

(2)   Examiner: *El niño compra el halado y luego . . .*
                   The boy buys the ice cream, and then . . .
   Appropriate response: (*lo* come)
                           ([he] eats *it* [masculine singular])
   Child's response: (*la* come)
                           ([he] eats *it* [feminine singular])

Why would errors of this type (a feminine singular clitic replacing a masculine singular clitic) occur if the children's chief difficulty was the production of morphemes that take the form of nonfinal weak syllables? The only explanation that would be compatible with a phonology/prosody account would be that the prosodic characteristics of Spanish are not, in fact, comparable to those of Italian, at least with respect to nonfinal weak syllables. Indeed, there is reason to suspect that there are differences between the two languages. Unlike Italian, Spanish is traditionally classified as a syllable-timed language, and the duration differences between stressed and unstressed syllables in Spanish are smaller than those seen in other languages studied (Delattre, 1966). As a result, the durations of the syllables represented in definite articles and direct object clitics are not as short relative to phonetically similar stressed syllables as they are in other languages, including Italian (Farnetani & Kori, 1982).

In addition, Gennari and Demuth (1997) have proposed that unstressed monosyllabic morphemes such as definite articles and direct object clitics are attached to a higher node of the prosodic phrase than the comparable morphemes in other languages. This higher attachment might make these morphemes less vulnerable to the omission of nonfinal weak syllables. This proposal warrants consideration, especially considering that nonfinal weak syllables that are in monomorphemic words (e.g., the first syllable of *banana*) are not omitted as often as are monosyllabic morphemes such as articles. These two types of nonfinal weak syllables occupy different locations in prosodic structure. It is not implausible, then, that the same morpheme type (e.g., definite articles) could show cross-linguistic differences in degree of omission if its placement in prosodic structure differed across the languages. Of course, such an explanation can only serve as a possible reason for the differences between Spanish and Italian in degree of omission. It sheds no light on the finding that Spanish-speaking children with SLI produce more substitution errors than do Spanish-speaking TD-MLU children.

Checking Constraints and the SLI Profile for Null-Subject Languages

A major reason for Wexler's (1998, 2003) EUCC proposal was that the extended optional infinitive account and the agreement-tense omission model do not capture the fact that children acquiring null-subject languages do not exhibit the difficulty with tense and agreement inflections that is seen in languages such as English and German. Rather than assuming that children with SLI differ across languages, Wexler assumed that the same constraint, the EUCC, manifests itself differently in different languages. Specifically, he assumes that in null-subject languages such as Italian and Spanish, only TNS carries a noninterpretable D feature; AGRS has no noninterpretable D feature to check. Checking, then, is limited to the D feature in TNS, and such checking at a single functional category obeys the EUCC. Thus, the use of tense and agreement inflections in these languages should not be adversely affected. Given the findings of very few differences between SLI and TD-MLU groups in the use of tense and agreement inflections in these null-subject languages, the EUCC account seems to hold considerable promise.

This account also provides a possible explanation for some of the difficulties with function words seen in null-subject languages. Wexler (1998, 2003) assumes that in languages such as Italian and Spanish, a functional category *auxiliary* (AUX) exists, which has a noninterpretable D feature. Thus, utterances employing the present perfect (commonly used in Italian in past contexts) such as *Anna ha visto Gina*: "Anna has seen Gina" requires checking of the D feature, first at AUX, and then at TNS. Such checking at two functional categories violates the EUCC and should result in an utterance that lacks the auxiliary (*Anna visto Gina*: "Anna seen Gina"). Given that auxiliaries such as *è* and *ha* are frequently omitted by Italian-speaking children with SLI, Wexler's account seems very plausible. Two-syllable auxiliaries appear less prone to omission, though the evidence in this case is limited to small samples from spontaneous speech.

The difficulty with clitics experienced by Italian- and Spanish-speaking children with SLI might also be handled by this checking constraint account. Wexler (1998, 2003) assumes that direct object clitics originate inside the VP, either as the clitic itself or as a phonetically null noun phrase. This element is assumed to have a D feature. Presumably, the clitic first passes through an intermediate position, the functional category Object Agreement, where it must be checked for accusative case, and then proceeds to the functional category Clitic, to occupy its preverbal position. According to Wexler, these movements can be viewed as checking the D feature twice, which runs counter to the EUCC. Consequently, the utterance might be produced without the clitic, as shown in the earlier example (1). This account does not address the clitic substitution errors seen in Spanish but does provide a possible explanation for the omissions that occur in both Spanish and Italian. Problems with other types of function words, such as articles, do not seem to be addressed by the EUCC.

SUMMARY

Each of the accounts explored in this chapter—those based on typology, those that emphasize phonology/prosody, and those that rely on an assumption of constraints on checking—can offer a sensible explanation for a significant portion of the findings across the languages covered. At the same time, it should be clear that none of these approaches is wholly successful: often some area of difficulty attested in SLI seems to fall outside the scope of the account. For example, typology-related accounts provide a reasonable explanation for many cross-linguistic differences, but they have no provisions for predicting that function words will be problematic even in languages where these morphemes convey several grammatical features (e.g., articles that mark number and gender) and can represent obligatory arguments of the sentence (e.g., clitics that serve as direct objects). Phonology/prosody accounts offer a reason for difficulties with function words as well as consonantal inflections but do not explain why inflections that mark tense and agreement seem to be the most difficult of all. Checking constraint accounts can handle an impressive range of grammatical phenomena, including inconsistent use of tense and agreement inflections in some but not other languages, and verb-second word order errors. However, it is not clear why tense and agreement inflections will be used more by German- and Dutch-speaking children with SLI than by children with SLI who are acquiring English.

In this chapter, only particular types of languages have been discussed. It is virtually certain that any revisions of the above accounts based on further study of the languages covered here will not be the last of the modifications required. Many other types of languages are now receiving investigative attention, and some are the focus of relatively intense study, including languages as varied as French (e.g., Thordardottir & Namazi, 2007; Paradis & Crago, 2001; Paradis, Crago, & Genesee, 2003), Hebrew (Dromi, Leonard, Adam, & Zadunaisky-Ehrlich, 1999; Dromi, Leonard, & Shteiman, 1993), and Cantonese (e.g., Fletcher, Leonard, Stokes, & Wong, 2005; Wong, Leonard, Fletcher, & Stokes, 2004). Studies of bilingual children with SLI are also beginning to appear (e.g., Paradis, 2007). It remains to be seen whether the current accounts of grammatical deficits in SLI will be able to accommodate the SLI profiles that emerge from these additional languages. However, it is clear that future research on these languages will move us toward a greater understanding of this perplexing disorder.

REFERENCES

Bartke, S. (1994). *Dissociations in SLI children's inflectional morphology: New evidence from agreement inflections and noun plurals in German.* Paper presented at the Meeting of the European Group for Child Language Disorders, Garderen, The Netherlands.

Bedore, L., & Leonard, L. (1998). Specific language impairment and grammatical morphology: A discriminant function analysis. *Journal of Speech, Language, and Hearing Research, 41,* 1185–1192.

Bedore, L., & Leonard, L. (2001). Grammatical morphology deficits in Spanish-speaking children with specific language impairment. *Journal of Speech, Language, and Hearing Research, 44,* 905–924.

Bedore, L., & Leonard, L. (2005). Verb inflections and noun phrase morphology in the spontaneous speech of Spanish-speaking children with specific language impairment. *Applied Psycholinguistics, 26,* 195–225.

Bortolini, U., Caselli, M. C., & Leonard, L. (1997). Grammatical deficits in Italian-speaking children with specific language impairment. *Journal of Speech, Language, and Hearing Research, 40,* 809–820.

Bortolini, U., & Leonard, L. (1996). Phonology and grammatical morphology in specific language impairment: Accounting for individual variation in English and Italian. *Applied Psycholinguistics, 17,* 85–104.

Bortolini, U., Leonard, L., & Caselli, M. C. (1998). Specific language impairment in Italian and English: Evaluating alternative accounts of grammatical deficits. *Language and Cognitive Processes, 13,* 1–20.

Chomsky, N. (1995). *The minimalist program.* Cambridge, MA: MIT Press.

de Jong, J. (1999). Specific language impairment in Dutch: Inflectional morphology and argument structure. *Groningen Dissertations in Linguistics, 28.*

Delattre, P. (1966). A comparison of syllable length conditioning among languages. *International Review of Applied Linguistics in Language Teaching, 4,* 183–198.

Dromi, E., Leonard, L., Adam, G., & Zadunaisky-Ehrlich, S. (1999). Verb agreement morphology in Hebrew-speaking children with specific language impairment. *Journal of Speech, Language, and Hearing Research, 42,* 1414–1431.

Dromi, E., Leonard, L., & Shteiman, M. (1993). The grammatical morphology of Hebrew-speaking children with specific language impairment: Some competing hypotheses. *Journal of Speech and Hearing Research*, 36, 760–771.

Eng, N., & O'Connor, B. (2000). Acquisition of definite article + noun agreement of Spanish–English bilingual children with specific language impairment. *Communication Disorders Quarterly*, 21, 114–124.

Farnetani, E., & Kori, S. (1982). Lexical stress in spoken sentences: A study on duration and vowel formant pattern. *Quaderni del Centro di Studio per le Ricerche di Fonetica*, 1, 104–133.

Fletcher, P., Leonard, L., Stokes, S., & Wong, A. M.-Y. (2005). The expression of aspect in Cantonese-speaking children with specific language impairment. *Journal of Speech, Language, and Hearing Research*, 48, 621–634.

Gennari, S., & Demuth, K. (1997). Syllable omission in the acquisition of Spanish. In E. Hughes, M. Hughes, & A. Greenhill (Eds.), *Proceedings of the 21st Annual Boston University Conference on Language Development* (Vol. 1, pp. 182–193). Somerville, MA: Cascadilla Press.

Hansson, K., Nettelbladt, U., & Leonard, L. (2003). Indefinite articles and definite forms in Swedish children with specific language impairment. *First Language*, 23, 343–362.

Jacobson, P., & Schwartz, R. (2002). Morphology in incipient bilingual Spanish-speaking preschool children with specific language impairment. *Applied Psycholinguistics*, 23, 23–41.

Johnston, J., & Kamhi, A. (1984). Syntactic and semantic aspects of the utterances of language-impaired children: The same can be less. *Merrill-Palmer Quarterly*, 30, 65–85.

Leonard, L. (1995). Functional categories in the grammars of children with specific language impairment. *Journal of Speech and Hearing Research*, 38, 1270–1283.

Leonard, L. (1998). *Children with specific language impairment*. Cambridge, MA: MIT Press.

Leonard, L., & Bortolini, U. (1998). Grammatical morphology and the role of weak syllables in the speech of Italian-speaking children with specific language impairment. *Journal of Speech, Language, and Hearing Research*, 41, 1363–1374.

Leonard, L., Bortolini, U., Caselli, M. C., McGregor, K., & Sabbadini, L. (1992). Morphological deficits in children with specific language impairment: The status of features in the underlying grammar. *Language Acquisition*, 2, 151–179.

Leonard, L., & Deevy, P. (2006). Cognitive and linguistic issues in the study of children with specific language impairment. In M. Traxler & M. Gernsbacher (Eds.), *Handbook of psycholinguistics* (pp. 1143–1171). London: Academic Press.

Leonard, L., Deevy, P., Miller, C., Charest, M., Kurtz, R., & Rauf, L. (2003). The use of grammatical morphemes reflecting aspect and modality by children with specific language impairment. *Journal of Child Language*, 30, 769–795.

Leonard, L., Deevy, P., Miller, C., Rauf, L., Charest, M., & Kurtz, R. (2003). Surface forms and grammatical functions: Past tense and passive participle use by children with specific language impairment. *Journal of Speech, Language, and Hearing Research*, 46, 43–55.

Leonard, L., Eyer, J., Bedore, L., & Grela, B. (1997). Three accounts of the grammatical morpheme difficulties of English-speaking children with specific language impairment. *Journal of Speech, Language, and Hearing Research*, 40, 741–753.

Leonard, L., Hansson, K., Nettelbladt, U., & Deevy, P. (2005). Specific language impairment in children: A comparison of English and Swedish. *Language Acquisition*, 12, 219–246.

Leonard, L., Sabbadini, L., Leonard, J., & Volterra, V. (1987). Specific language impairment in children: A cross-linguistic study. *Brain and Language*, 32, 233–252.

Leonard, L., Wong, A. M.-Y., Deevy, P., Stokes, S., & Fletcher, P. (2006). The production of passives by children with specific language impairment acquiring English or Cantonese. *Applied Psycholinguistics*, 27, 267–299.

Lindner, K., & Johnston, J. (1992). Grammatical morphology in language-impaired children acquiring English or German as their first language: A functional perspective. *Applied Psycholinguistics*, 13, 115–129.

Marchman, V., Wulfeck, B., & Ellis Weismer, S. (1999). Morphological productivity in children with normal language and SLI: A study of the English past tense. *Journal of Speech, Language, and Hearing Research, 42,* 206–219.

Marshall, C., & van der Lely, H. (2006). A challenge to current models of past tense inflection: The impact of phonotactics. *Cognition, 100,* 302–320.

McGregor, K., & Leonard, L. (1994). Subject pronoun and article omissions in the speech of children with specific language impairment: A phonological interpretation. *Journal of Speech and Hearing Research, 37,* 171–181.

Norbury, C. F., Bishop, D. V. M., & Briscoe, J. (2001). Production of English finite verb morphology: A comparison of SLI and mild–moderate hearing impairment. *Journal of Speech, Language, and Hearing Research, 44,* 165–178.

Oetting, J., & Horohov, J. (1997). Past tense marking by children with and without specific language impairment. *Journal of Speech, Language, and Hearing Research, 40,* 62–74.

Oetting, J., & Rice, M. (1993). Plural acquisition in children with specific language impairment. *Journal of Speech and Hearing Research, 36,* 1241–1253.

Owen, A., & Leonard, L. (2006). The production of finite and nonfinite complement clauses by children with specific language impairment and their typically developing peers. *Journal of Speech, Language, and Hearing Research, 49,* 548–571.

Paradis, J. (2007). Bilingual children with specific language impairment: Theoretical and applied issues. *Applied Psycholinguistics, 28,* 551–564.

Paradis, J., & Crago, M. (2001). The morphosyntax of specific language impairment in French: An extended optional default account. *Language Acquisition, 9,* 269–300.

Paradis, J., Crago, M., & Genesee, F. (2003). Object clitics as a clinical marker of SLI in French: Evidence from French–English bilingual children. In B. Beachley, A. Brown, & F. Conlin (Eds.), *Proceedings of the 27th Annual Boston University Conference on Language Development* (Vol. 2, pp. 638–649). Somerville, MA: Cascadilla Press.

Redmond, S. (2003). Children's productions of the affix *-ed* in past tense and past participle contexts. *Journal of Speech, Language, and Hearing Research, 46,* 1095–1109.

Restrepo, M. A., & Gutierrez-Clellan, V. (2001). Article use in Spanish-speaking children with SLI. *Journal of Child Language, 28,* 433–452.

Rice, M. (1998). In search of a grammatical marker of language impairment in children. *Division One Newsletter, American Speech, Language, and Hearing Association, 5,* 3–7.

Rice, M., Noll, K. R., & Grimm, H. (1997). An extended optional infinitive stage in German-speaking children with specific language impairment. *Language Acquisition, 6,* 255–295.

Rice, M., & Oetting, J. (1993). Morphological deficits in children with SLI: Evaluation of number marking and agreement. *Journal of Speech and Hearing Research, 36,* 1249–1257.

Rice, M., & Wexler, K. (1996). Toward tense as a clinical marker of specific language impairment in English-speaking children. *Journal of Speech, Language, and Hearing Research, 39,* 1239–1257.

Rice, M., Wexler, K., & Hershberger, S. (1998). Tense over time: The longitudinal course of tense acquisition in children with specific language impairment. *Journal of Speech, Language, and Hearing Research, 41,* 1412–1431.

Roberts, S. S., & Leonard, L. (1997). Grammatical deficits in German and English: A cross-linguistic study of children with specific language impairment. *First Language, 17,* 131–150.

Thordardottir, E. & Namazi, M. (2007). Specific language impairment in French-speaking children: Beyond grammatical morphology. *Journal of Speech, Language, and Hearing Research, 50,* 698–715.

van der Lely, H. (1997). Language and cognitive development in a grammatical SLI boy: Modularity and innateness. *Journal of Neurolinguistics, 10,* 75–107.

Wexler, K. (1998). Very early parameter setting and the unique checking constraint. *Lingua, 106,* 23–79.

Wexler, K. (2003). Lenneberg's dream: Learning, normal language development, and specific language impairment: In Y. Levy & J. Schaeffer (Eds.), *Language competence across populations: Toward a definition of specific language impairment* (pp. 11–61). Mahwah, NJ: Lawrence Erlbaum Associates.

Wexler, K., Schütze, C., & Rice, M. (1998). Subject case in children with SLI and unaffected controls: Evidence for the Arg/Tns omission model. *Language Acquisition, 7,* 317–344.

Wong, A. M.-Y., Leonard, L., Fletcher, P., & Stokes, S. (2004). Questions without movement: A study of Cantonese-speaking children with and without specific language impairment. *Journal of Speech, Language, and Hearing Research, 47,* 1440–1453.

14

Language Variation in Child Language Disorders

JULIE A. WASHINGTON

M ainstream American English (MAE, also called Standard American English or SAE) is regarded as the standard of language use for American English speakers. The syntactic, semantic, and phonological rules of MAE, for both writing and speaking, have been the focus of countless trade books, textbooks, and research studies. These rules are thus well understood for adults and to a slightly lesser extent for children as well. It is important to realize from the outset, however, that despite all of the attention to this standard, in purely linguistic terms there is no single, standard variety of English (Wolfram, Temple Adger, & Christian, 1999). Rather, there is a form of English that has been defined *socially* to be the "correct" form of English by individuals from a particular social and economic group (Wolfram et al., 1999). It is the linguistic system supported by *this* power group that is regarded as mainstream.

Patterns of use of American English vary widely for individuals from different socioeconomic backgrounds, geographic regions, and who differ ethnically or culturally. The term *dialect* often is used to index these widely varying differences from the linguistic *standard*. This use of the term dialect regards all variations from this mainstream standard as *nonstandard* or *nonmainstream*. Unfortunately, there is frequently an undeserved, negative connotation attached to these differences and the terminology used to index them (Wolfram et al., 1999). The term dialect is used here to refer to *language variations* and *linguistic diversity* demonstrated by individuals from different cultural, racial, or ethnic backgrounds. In addition, African American English (AAE), a major dialect of American English, is highlighted. The current state of our knowledge regarding dialectal variations, as well as the impact of these variations on the study of childhood language impairments, is the major focus of this chapter.

Linguistic diversity has significant implications for anyone interested in speech and language development and disorders (Craig & Washington, 2006; Taylor, 1993; Washington, 1996). The clinical and educational implications of this diversity are of particular concern because of the potential skewing of language outcomes (Battle, 1993; Stockman, 2000; Taylor, 1993; Washington, 1996). Although the *specific* influence of linguistic variation on outcomes may be debated, it is largely agreed that the presence of this variation can complicate assessment (including identification and diagnosis) and treatment of childhood language impairments with minority children. Communication impairments are more prevalent among minorities than in the majority population (Battle, 1993; Tomblin et al.,

1997), and these students comprise a significant, albeit disproportionate, percentage of students enrolled on speech and language caseloads nationwide (NCES, 2003). These facts require that the potential impact of linguistic variation be considered when assessment and treatment plans are formulated and when research is conducted.

Linguistic variation also impacts the conduct of research in important ways. Research implications, however, have received much less attention in speech–language pathology than have the implications of language variation in the clinical domain. In cross-cultural psychology, there is ongoing debate about the importance of considering cultural influences in the design of research studies. This debate centers largely around whether or not it is valid to use universal approaches to the study of human behavior, versus adoption of approaches that are designed to be sensitive to the specific influence of culture on methods, analyses, and outcomes (Berry, 1999; Helfrich, 1999; Niblo & Jackson, 2004). The former framework is believed to enhance the ability to make comparisons across investigations by maintaining uniformity, whereas the latter is believed to provide outcomes that are much more sensitive to cultural variations in performance, resulting in more valid outcomes (Wong & Rowley, 2001). Both perspectives are examined later in this chapter.

DIALECTAL VARIATION

Linguistic variation among speakers is impacted by a variety of factors, including geographic region, racial/ethnic group membership, age, and social class. Within individual speakers from ethnic minority groups, linguistic variations may be influenced by more than one of these factors. For example, a low-income African American speaker from the southern United States may have dialectal variants evident in her speech that reflect ethnicity, geography, and socioeconomic status. Across dialect speakers, the linguistic community, as well as the social and interactive context, are important influences on dialect use. Although dialectologists are reluctant to count dialects given the ambiguity inherent in determining discrete dialectal boundaries (W. Wolfram, personal communication, 2005), dialects of English are increasing and changing with the increase in the linguistic diversity of the people and communities in the United States (Labov, 2001).

The rapid growth of minority communities and in the dialects that develop within and across these communities has contributed to the ambiguity reported for dialectal boundaries. It is well documented that languages and dialects grow and change when they come into contact with other languages and dialects (Holm, 2004; Winford, 2003; Wolfram & Schilling-Estes, 1998). Changes in the patterns of migration and cross-cultural community settlement, particularly in urban communities, has resulted in creative uses of language that have often been needed to bridge differences in language usage by groups residing in close physical proximity to each other. *Language contact* influences both the form and the use of language as members of different language or dialect communities borrow from each other. This mixing of languages is a rule-governed process that can affect the vocabulary or the structure of the languages involved, sometimes resulting in the creation of new languages or dialects altogether (Holm, 2004; Winford, 2003). Wolfram and Schilling-Estes (1998) cite the influence of the French language on the English used by the Creole people of New Orleans as an example of linguistic borrowing and mixing.

The adoption of language forms by one group from another is not, typically, a deliberate act. Rather, the process frequently occurs naturally over time with consistent interaction between groups. Speakers are typically unaware that these changes have occurred. In the case of young minority children acquiring language, a more active process is frequently underway that involves construction of a new language system from the input provided in the child's changing environment (Lanza, 2004). In this case, *language mixing* refers not to the subtle, gradual process of combining languages that is described for adults: rather, for children, language contact is more likely to involve active acquisition of a home or community language system, while also acquiring the code used by language users outside the child's immediate community, most often in school. For bilingual children learning two languages simultaneously, this often involves mixing languages at the word or utterance levels in the process of acquiring both languages (Lanza, 2004). For bidialectal children, early contact with the dialect of the majority community will require development of code-switching skills in order to be successful in mainstream social and academic contexts. These early contacts enrich the child's language in development but also result in complications as the child gets older and must successfully learn the rules for code-switching in order to succeed in school and beyond (Craig & Washington, 2006).

COMMUNICATION IMPAIRMENTS IN MINORITY POPULATIONS

Among preschool-aged children speech and language impairment is the most frequently reported disability category for all racial/ethnic groups except American Indian/Alaska Native, for whom developmental delay was the most frequently reported disability category (U.S. Department of Education, 2002). Speech- and language-impaired children account for nearly half of all preschool children served under the Individuals with Disabilities Education Act (IDEA). The incidence of all major disability categories, including speech and language impairment, is relatively equal across ethnic/racial groups at this young age.

For 6- to 21-year-olds, four disability categories (specific learning disabilities, speech or language impairments, mental retardation, and emotional disturbance) account for the majority of students served under IDEA (US Department of Education, 2002). The racial/ethnic make up of students in this age group for 2000–2001, the most recent year for which these data were available, was as follows: Caucasian students, 62.3% of students served; African American, 19.8%; Hispanic, 14.5%; Asian/Pacific Islander, 1.5%; and American Indian/Alaska Native, 1.5% of students served (US Department of Education, 2002; NCES, 2003). When compared with the average percentages for all students with disabilities, the percentages of African American students receiving services for mental retardation or emotional disturbance were higher than for their White peers. Although African American children and adults represent 12% of the general population (U.S. Census Bureau, 2005), African American children represent 20% of the national special education enrollment (NCES, 2005). The higher rate of qualification for services in the areas of mental retardation and emotional disabilities is particularly troublesome, as there is no medical evidence to suggest that African Americans are at higher risk or incidence for these disability types. In the case of mental retardation, the Diagnostic and Statistical Manual of Mental Disorders–IV–TR (DSM–IV–TR) (American Psychiatric Association, 2000) reports that approximately 1% of individuals in a typical population will be mentally retarded. In many school districts nationally, the incidence is more than twice this estimate for African American students (Conahan & Vaira, 2005).

Empirical investigations of the prevalence of language impairments in African American children suggest that the incidence may in fact be higher in this population than in majority language speakers. Specific language impairment (SLI), in particular, has been examined for its prevalence in African American children, and results suggest that a higher rate of language impairment among African Americans compared to White Americans may, in fact, exist. Tomblin et al. (1997) examined the prevalence of SLI in a sample of 7,218 Midwestern kindergartners assessed using a variety of speech and language instruments.

Their outcomes indicated that the prevalence of SLI was 7.4% in the general population of kindergartners overall. Native American and African American children presented the highest rates of SLI: approximately 12% and 11% of children screened, respectively. These rates were significantly higher than those for the general population. The authors cautioned that these higher prevalence estimates may have been influenced by the use of assessment instruments not sensitive to linguistic differences or may have been confounded by the socioeconomic status (SES) of the parents.

In an investigation focused entirely on African American children, Washington and Craig (2004) screened a sample of 196 children between 3 and 5 years of age. Following the methodology of Tomblin and colleagues (1997), children who failed the screening were administered a larger assessment battery. The outcomes of this assessment revealed an 18% failure rate for this small urban population. In contrast, examination of the prevalence rates for African American children from a small college town, matched with the urban sample for SES and maternal education, revealed a prevalence estimate (7%) that was similar to the general rate reported by Tomblin using the same screening and assessment battery.

The Washington and Craig assessment was designed specifically to avoid the cultural biases often identified for assessments developed for use with majority children. Specifically, each assessment was developed and items were tested with typically developing African American children, and local norms were established. In addition, vocabulary and morpho-syntactic structure of nonstandardized assessments were carefully examined and controlled in an effort to control for the impact of dialectal variations and poor world knowledge associated with poverty on children's linguistic performance. In addition, standardized assessments were administered and the outcomes examined prior to being included in the screening protocol in order to ensure that each was appropriate for use with African American children who were dialect speakers.

Examination of the sensitivity and specificity of the assessment protocol indicated that the battery was both valid and reliable for use with African American children from pre-school through fifth grade (Craig & Washington, 2000, 2006). The disparate findings within these two samples of African American children, as evidenced by the high rate of failure in the urban sample compared to the suburban one, suggests that these prevalence estimates likely represent valid indicators of the differences in the incidence of language impairments for African American children, depending upon the community in which they reside. Interestingly, the African American sample included in the Tomblin et al. (1997) investigation was an urban sample as well. Unfortunately, no nonurban sample of African American children was available for comparison. Data with larger samples are needed to verify these community outcomes.

Assessment Implications

The role of standardized language assessment in the overrepresentation of minority children on special education caseloads, and particularly in the area of speech and language impairment, has been an area of significant focus in child language research for many years (Battle, 1993; Campbell, Dollaghan, Needleman, & Janosky, 1997; Craig & Washington, 2006; Peña, Iglesias, & Lidz, 2001; Seymour, Bland-Stewart, & Green, 1998; Washington, 1996). Dialectal variations such as AAE impact morphological, syntactic, semantic, and phonological aspects of language in predictable ways that have been well documented. When the linguistic forms impacted by the dialect of minority children are the same ones as those used to diagnose language impairment, the dialect speaker is in danger of being falsely identified as language-impaired.

In recent years, a number of influential investigations have been undertaken that have focused on development of unbiased assessment procedures for use with African American children in particular, and minority language speakers in general. Seymour, Bland-Stewart, and Green (1998) provided a useful framework for characterization of investigations that seek to differentiate deficits and disorders in AAE speakers using a *contrastive* versus *noncontrastive* feature distinction. Briefly, contrastive forms are those in the AAE speakers' repertoire that characterize AAE but are not shared with MAE. Conversely, noncontrastive features are those aspects of the linguistic system that are shared by AAE and MAE speakers.

1 a. She know____ we ____ leaving now.
1 b. She knows we are leaving now.
1 c. She knows ____are leaving now.

In 1a the third person *–s* form of the verb *know* and the copula form *are* have been omitted. These omissions are characteristic of AAE but would not be produced by a MAE speaker. The omission of these forms in AAE is optional, meaning that in some linguistic contexts they will be deleted, whereas in other contexts they might be included. Accordingly, Example 1b may be spoken by either an AAE or an MAE speaker. The final example, 1c, involves omission of the pronoun *we*. Pronominal omissions do not characterize either AAE or MAE. Example 1a represents a *contrastive* utterance, whereas 1b and 1c are both examples of *noncontrastive* productions.

The inclusion and exclusion criteria that characterize production and comprehension of contrastive forms of AAE are not well understood, although new data are emerging (Coles-White, 2004; Johnson, 2006). Accordingly, most investigations have focused on unbiased assessment of African American children's noncontrastive language forms. In addition, a third group of studies—those focused on the cultural fairness of standardized language measures—has also made important contributions to this body of work.

Although it was not uncommon in early studies to focus on the contrasts between MAE and AAE (McDavid & McDavid, 1971; Wolfram, 1971), only a few recent investigations have examined *contrastive* forms of AAE. These more recent studies investigated the qualitative and quantitative differences between AAE forms and the linguistic forms that both characterize specific language impairment and overlap with AAE.

In particular, Oetting and her colleagues (Oetting, Cantrell, & Horohov, 1999; Oetting & McDonald, 2001, 2002) have compared African American English in Southern speakers (SAAE) and Southern White English (SWE), with encouraging results. Oetting and McDonald (2001) examined nonmainstream dialect use in a sample of 93 4- to 6-year-old children, 40 of whom used SAAE and 53 who were speakers of SWE. Of these, 16 of the SAAE speakers and 15 of the SWE speakers had been previously diagnosed as SLI. Although the characteristics of AAE and SLI have been reported to overlap to a great extent, Oetting and McDonald found that it was possible to distinguish the children with SLI who used SAAE from their normally developing peers who were also dialect speakers. Discriminant function analyses revealed that although the dialectal forms characterizing SAAE and the linguistic characteristics of SLI appeared to be quite similar on the surface, the frequency of use of selected forms (e.g., question formation, zero marking of irregular third person forms, and weak tense marking in obligatory contexts) reliably differentiated the two groups.

In a follow-up investigation, Oetting and McDonald (2002) extended this work by identifying three methods that could be used reliably to classify nonmainstream dialect use (in this case SAAE and SWE) in young children. Specifically, listener judgments, token-based counts of nonmainstream pattern use, and typed-based counts were examined. Outcomes confirmed that whereas type and token counts were accurate and very useful for researchers interested in morphosyntax, listener judgments resulted in accurate classification of dialect speakers 90% of the time. It was recommended that listener judgments be considered in future research as a quick, valid, and reliable way to classify speakers.

The knowledge gained from the comparisons in these two studies has been critical both for distinguishing those characteristics of the Southern AAE-speaking child's speech from the regional dialect and for distinguishing typical patterns of SAAE usage from patterns that are characteristic of African American children with SLI. These investigations have revealed significant differences in the distributional properties of targeted linguistic forms used by normally developing speakers of SAAE and speakers with SLI. These outcomes are promising for researchers interested in AAE speakers in other dialect regions as well. Because AAE shares its roots with the SWE dialect (McDavid & McDavid, 1971; Wolfram, 1971), there will be no other region in the country for which the regional dialect will overlap to the extent evident for SAAE and SWE, and most of the characteristics of SAAE are shared by AAE speakers in other geographic regions. Accordingly, future investigations should examine whether Oetting and McDonald's findings extend to all speakers of AAE, regardless of dialect region.

The work of Washington and Craig has focused on *noncontrastive* aspects of the African American child's linguistic system. Specifically, major language-developmental processes that are important regardless of ethnic group membership, such as comprehension of wh-questions (Craig, Washington, & Thompson-Porter, 1998), passive sentence comprehension (Craig et al., 1998), vocabulary development (Washington & Craig, 1994, 1999), and development of complex syntax have been the focus (Craig & Washington, 1994). This work has been important for developing expectations for language use by African American children who are AAE speakers without relying upon our knowledge of AAE rules—an ongoing area of study, with much work to be completed. Using this noncontrastive approach, normative expectations for development of language skills have been established for African American children from preschool through fifth grade in the linguistic domains mentioned above (Craig & Washington, 2006).

For example, wh-question comprehension and formation has proven promising for identification of language deficits in African American children (Craig et al., 1998; Oetting & McDonald, 2002). Craig et al. (1998) described a task designed in their laboratory to assess comprehension of wh-questions of increasing cognitive and linguistic complexity. Subsequent investigations have confirmed that African American children from impoverished language backgrounds and those with language deficits experience difficulty with development of this important linguistic skill (Craig & Washington, 2006). A cross-sectional investigation of wh-question comprehension skills at preschool age and in later elementary school also demonstrated that these skills were predictive of later literacy skill development as well (Craig, Connor, & Washington, 2003).

Oetting and McDonald (2002) also found that question formulation distinguished SAAE speakers with SLI from their typically developing peers. Specifically, the rate of noninversion of wh-questions was higher for the children with language impairments than for the normal-language controls. Combined with the findings of Washington and Craig, these outcomes suggest that both comprehension and expression of wh-questions may be an important noncontrastive language skill to consider in future studies of African American children who use AAE.

Another major noncontrastive language skill that has received considerable interest across disciplines for its ability to predict both language and literacy skill growth is vocabulary use and development (Champion, Hyter, McCabe, & Bland-Stewart, 2003; Hart &

Risley, 1995; Scarborough, 1991; Washington & Craig, 1994, 1999). Vocabulary skills have consistently been identified as an area of developmental concern for children from impoverished backgrounds, and African American children are disproportionately poor. In their now landmark investigation, Hart and Risley (1995) demonstrated that low-SES children who begin life with poor vocabulary skills face a monumental task as they try to develop those skills and keep up with their peers whose vocabularies may be much richer.

Although some nonstandardized methods of vocabulary assessment have been utilized to measure young children's vocabularies (e.g., type–token ratios and number of different words), standardized assessment of these skills is more typical. Unfortunately, there is considerable controversy regarding whether or not standardized vocabulary testing under-estimates the skills of African American children by introducing bias into the outcomes.

Champion et al. (2003) examined the performance of 49 3- to 5-year-old children on the Peabody Picture Vocabulary Test-III (Dunn & Dunn, 1997), a widely used test of receptive vocabulary. Their low SES subjects produced an overall mean score that was close to one standard deviation ($M = 86.84$, $SD = 10.96$) below the published mean for this instrument. An item analysis revealed no systematic item-level bias. Rather, it appeared that the low group mean was an accurate reflection of the poor vocabulary skills of the low-SES participants. Washington and Craig (1999) presented similar findings from administration of the PPVT-III to 59 at-risk preschoolers from both middle- and low-SES homes. The group mean for these participants was 91 ($SD = 11$). Despite performance below the published mean, the scores of these preschoolers distributed normally. Thus, the PPVT-III appeared to be appropriate for use with these children, and their vocabulary skills were clearly below average.

Standardized assessments continue to be scrutinized by researchers because of concerns that the normative samples for these instruments often do not include enough children from major minority groups to ensure unbiased, representative speech and language measurements. Indeed, it is standardized assessments that are implicated most often when discussing overrepresentation on special education caseloads. Thomas-Tate, Washington, and Edwards (2004) examined the performances of low-income African American first graders on the Test of Phonological Awareness (TOPA; Torgesen & Bryant, 1994). Like the outcomes reported above for the PPVT-III, the overall group mean was significantly below the published mean for the instrument. More importantly, the participants' performance was not normally distributed but was negatively skewed, and all scored within normal limits on a test of basic reading skills. Based upon these outcomes, the TOPA was not recommended for use with African American children.

Peña et al. (2001) compared dynamic assessment in which a test–retest and learning component are added to a static assessment procedure, in this case the Expressive One Word Picture Vocabulary Test–Revised (EOWPT–R; Gardner, 1990). Performance improved significantly using dynamic assessment compared to the static procedure. Washington and Craig (2004) reported similar outcomes for African American boys who failed a brief screening protocol and then exhibited language skills well within normal limits when a longer, more dynamic assessment was administered.

Although it has been demonstrated that many of these static standardized assessments may not reflect the best performance of children who are culturally and linguistically different (Peña et al., 2001; Thomas-Tate et al., 2004), they continue to be the standard for special education placement nationwide. Consequently, we must be able to rely upon them to validly and reliably identify dialect speakers who should receive language intervention and not identify those who do not.

In an important investigation designed to reduce bias in assessment with African American children, Campbell et al. (1997) and Dollaghan and Campbell (1998) proposed processing dependent measures, in this case nonword repetition (NWR), as a promising alternative to knowledge-dependent assessments. Their outcomes using this noncontrastive approach to language assessment revealed high sensitivity and specificity for NWR as a measure for distinguishing African American children with dialects from those who have language impairments. The authors suggested further that because the assessment procedures rely upon processing rather than specific knowledge, they should be fair for use with African American children who are frequently impoverished and, thus, may be disadvantaged on knowledge-based assessments.

Research Implications

The presence of cultural linguistic differences in a child's language system presents a challenge for the researcher interested in examining and describing the child's language skills as well. Sensitivity to both the language differences and the sociocultural context within which those language differences exist and thrive is paramount. It is easy to interpret the behaviors of minority populations in the context of majority viewpoints and behaviors, but these interpretations almost always result in underrepresentation (and sometimes devaluation) of the skills of the minority child or adult (Wong & Rowley, 2001). Inappropriate comparisons to a control group that differs in key ways (e.g., culture and socioeconomic status) from the minority participant can lead to outcomes that misrepresent these participants as deficient.

How best to approach this issue is far from agreed-upon in the research community. Whereas it is important to value the differences presented by individual cultural groups, for generalization purposes there is also inherent value in pursuing linguistic universals that can be applied cross-culturally. Pike (1967) referred to this important distinction as *etic* and *emic* approaches to the study of human behavior and viewed them as complementary. *Etic* refers to the study of language using universally accepted methodologies and analysis, and *emic* approaches encourage the study of individual languages in their own right from inside the system.

Bloom and Lahey (1976) discussed the importance of adopting an *etic to emic to etic* approach to the study of child language. When beginning to study a population, use of an established, a priori schema may be necessary as a starting point (etic). However, it is important in this view that the researcher progress from etic to emic, such that a progression toward understanding the child's behaviors in their own right without the adult model as an overlay is the goal. Finally, the return to etic recognizes the importance of interpreting emically derived outcomes in the context of the etic in order to allow generalization to a larger group of children.

Berry (1999) further subdivided these methods into *imposed etic, parallel emic*, and *derived etic*. Similar to the view espoused by Pike, the *imposed etic* phase of research is regarded by Berry to be a necessary first step. The researcher in this phase approaches the research with his/her own scientifically and culturally derived assumptions guiding the process. Although this is not ideal, in the absence of guidance in the extant literature, sometimes there are few alternatives. Indeed, it is often the case with research involving diverse cultural groups that, at the outset, there may be little published research available to guide questions and methods. Thus, the researcher must rely upon established methods that were likely developed for individuals from the majority culture. The alternative would be a pure emic approach in which there are no preconceptions, no hypotheses, no procedures to be followed, and no foreknowledge, just general knowledge of the subject matter to be investigated (Ho, 1988). Not surprisingly, few investigators adopt this approach.

The second step, in Berry's scheme, the *parallel emic*, involves investigation of cultural phenomena from *inside the system*. Effective research at this phase requires the conduct of research from an insider's perspective, often including identification of informants, consultants or research participants who are members of the cultural group of interest (Wong & Rowley, 2001). For example, Peña et al. (2001) used parent reports about the language skills of their bilingual child participants to aid in the interpretation of the children's behavior.

The third, and final phase, the *derived etic*, brings this process full circle. After extensive investigation using emic approaches, the derived outcomes are used in a comparative process that is designed to lead to the universals that have been central to etically focused investigations. This final phase permits valid empirically driven cross-cultural comparisons.

This model is particularly useful when thinking about methodologies that can be applied to the study of cultural linguistic differences. In our own work, we have applied this model by avoiding the use of Caucasian American control groups to represent the standard by which African American children's language is interpreted (Washington & Craig, 1992, 1994, 1998, 1999). Instead, the importance of the emic is recognized by focusing on and developing a within-group understanding of the linguistic skills of African American children. This approach has been successful for advancing our knowledge of African American children and their families.

There are research questions for which use of comparison groups that differ linguistically and culturally is entirely appropriate. For example, Oetting and McDonald (2002) sought to understand the similarities and differences between SAAE and SWE. The absence of a Caucasian American group for comparison would not have allowed this important question to be addressed. Thus, the use of a comparison group was necessary to advance our knowledge and has been used successfully by these researchers to answer important questions about language impairment as well.

The research implications of the *etic to emic to etic* model are significant. The model offers a way to examine childhood dialects and their implications in a manner that is child-centered and culturally sensitive. Frequently with minority groups there is little information available at the outset to guide the researcher, and an *etic* approach to the question is a wise way to begin. This is the *imposed etic* phase described by Berry (1999). Washington and Craig (1994) began the examination of dialectal variations in preschool children by starting with a list of AAE features provided by linguists interested in adult behavior. Progression to the *emic* required stepping away from this adult-influenced list and searching for any features that might be child-specific, as well as the social status variables that influence these features for children.

The United States is a highly diverse country that is becoming more diverse each year. In order to avoid the development of separate expectations, assessments, and goals for each of the groups that we are charged to serve and seek to study, it will be important for dialect researchers to move toward the final *derived etic* phase and attempt to interpret these within-group observations in a larger context that will allow generation of hypotheses and development of theories regarding home and community dialect development that can be generalized to larger groups of children.

Intervention Implications

There is a paucity of information available that focuses specifically on intervention with children who speak cultural dialects. One limiting factor is the absence of information on typical language development for children whose home and school languages differ (Kohnert, Yim, Nett, Kan and Duran, 2005). This is also true for children who are bidialectal: information regarding the development of the home and school dialects for these children is just beginning to emerge. In the absence of this information, establishing language targets for intervention research is particularly challenging. In their work with African American children, Craig and Washington have provided developmental expectations for noncontrastive language skills (Craig & Washington, 2002; Craig, Washington, & Thompson, 2005) and for changes in the use of the child's home dialect over time (Craig & Washington, 2004). This foundational work should allow the development of intervention studies.

Kohnert et al. (2005) focused their intervention program on maintaining the home language for their bilingual participants. In clinical disciplines such as speech and language pathology, it is important to affirm the child's own language or dialect system and not make the child's cultural language system the focus of intervention efforts. In fact, the American Speech-Language-Hearing Association (ASHA) has issued a position paper (1998) and several fact sheets designed to provide guidance to clinicians working with individuals who use cultural dialects. These documents focus on the importance of honoring the child's home linguistic system and not treating dialect differences like disorders, as well as presenting guidelines for delivery of culturally sensitive clinical services.

In disciplines and programs focused on linguistics and education rather than clinical concerns, the African American child's own dialectal variations have been the focus of academic teaching. There is longstanding concern about the impact of AAE on the African American child's development of literacy skills, and urban school districts are responding by focusing on the teaching of "academic language skills." For example, in the Los Angeles Unified School District (LAUSD), the *Academic English Mastery Program* makes a distinction between students that it terms Standard English Learners (SELs) and English Language Learners (ELLs). SELs are students for whom MAE is not their native home language, and ELLs are students for whom English is not the native home language (http://iss.lausd.net/aemp/faq.html.; accessed January 24, 2005). Accordingly, this program provides a Mainstream English Language Development program (MELD) that provides daily instruction in MAE for SELs, and an English Language Development program (ELD) for ELLs that provides similar instruction in English. Craig and Washington (2004) found that African American students who had not mastered academic English did, in fact, fall behind their peers who learned to code switch to the use of academic English. By fourth grade these students were more than one grade level behind. The LAUSD program and others like it acknowledge the difficulty that dialectal variations can create for children learning to read MAE texts, and they attempt to address this issue by focusing on language differences in the academic context, being careful not to denigrate, rather to honor, the home language.

SUMMARY

Dialects are, it seems, rapidly becoming the rule in the United States rather than the exception. This is particularly true in urban contexts. This change in the linguistic landscape of our communities may necessitate that we rethink our service delivery model in schools and clinics that serve children who come from culturally and linguistically diverse backgrounds. In school settings, the majority of these children will enter preschool or kindergarten with a linguistic code that differs significantly from the code that they will encounter in the school context (Delpit, 1996). The impact of these code differences on academic performance have been well documented (Craig & Washington, 2006; Delpit, 2001) and are believed to contribute in significant ways to the achievement gap in American schools (Phillips, Crouse, & Ralph, 1998). Current approaches to reading require that students be able to *break the code* in order to master phonological, lexical, and structural aspects of reading. Ignoring the impact of the code that the students bring to school on the job ahead of them as they learn the code of the classroom and the code of literacy could very well undermine the goal of the 2001 No Child Left Behind Act that every child will be a reader by the end of third grade.

The impact on research warrants some consideration as well. So little is currently known about the home and school language development of African American children who use dialect and of bilingual speakers who are entering school with a home language that is different from the school's that our attempts to move beyond assessment to service and intervention is somewhat hampered. Notable are the efforts of Seymour and colleagues to develop an assessment instrument for use with child dialect speakers that is designed to inform intervention efforts directly (Seymour, Roeper, & de Villiers, 2004). Although there is a great deal of important work being accomplished in the area of child language and child language disorders, the focus on dialect and minority groups is not keeping pace. This is of grave concern, as we are aware that the need for this information is growing annually as the country becomes more ethnically diverse. It will be important as we chart our research agendas for the future to consider the needs of this rapidly growing segment of the population and what it will mean for us as language researchers. Furthermore, examining our current methodologies and adapting them to maximize the cultural relevance and generalizability will be critical as well.

REFERENCES

American Psychiatric Association. (2000). *Diagnostic and statistical manual of mental disorders* (4th ed.–text revision). Washington, DC: Author.

American Speech-Language-Hearing Association. (1998). *Students and professionals who speak English with accents and nonstandard dialects: Issues and recommendations* [Technical report]. Rockville, MD: Author.

Battle, D. E. (Ed.). (1993). *Communication disorders in multicultural populations*. Boston: Andover Medical.

Berry, J. W. (1999). Emics and etics: A symbiotic conception. *Culture and Psychology*, 5, 165–171.

Bloom, L., & Lahey, M. (1976). *Language development and language disorders*. New York: Wiley.

Campbell, T. F., Dollaghan, C., Needleman, H., & Janosky, J. (1997). Reducing bias in language assessment: Processing-dependent measures. *Journal of Speech, Language, and Hearing Research*, 40, 519–525.

Champion, T., Hyter, Y., McCabe, A., & Bland-Stewart, L. (2003). "A matter of vocabulary": Performances of low-income African American Head Start children on the Peabody Picture Vocabulary Test III. *Communication Disorders Quarterly*, 24 (3), 121–127

Coles-White, D. J. (2004). Negative concord in child African American English: Implications for specific language impairment. *Journal of Speech, Language, and Hearing Research*, 47, 212–222.

Conahan, F., & Vaira, P. (2005, 26 June). Tackling the last bastion of over-representation of African American students in Charles County schools: Achieving parity among students served under eligibility code 01, mental retardation. *In Motion Magazine*.

Craig, H., Connor, C., & Washington, J. (2003). Early positive predictors of later reading comprehension for African American students: A preliminary investigation. *Language, Speech, and Hearing Services in Schools*, 34, 31–34.

Craig, H. K., & Washington, J. A. (1994). The complex syntax skills of poor, urban, African American preschoolers at school entry. *Language, Speech, and Hearing Services in Schools*, 25, 181–190.

Craig, H. K., & Washington, J. A. (2000). An assessment battery for identifying language impairments in African American children. *Journal of Speech, Language, and Hearing Research, 43,* 366–379.

Craig, H. K., & Washington, J. A. (2002). Oral language expectations for African American preschoolers and kindergartners. *American Journal of Speech-Language Pathology, 11,* 59–70.

Craig, H. K., & Washington, J. A. (2004). Grade-related changes in the production of African American English. *Journal of Speech, Language, and Hearing Research, 47*(2), 450–463.

Craig, H. K., & Washington, J. A. (2006). *Malik goes to school: Examining the language skills of African American students from preschool–5th grade.* Mahwah, NJ: Lawrence Erlbaum Associates.

Craig, H. K., Washington, J. A., & Thompson, C. A. (2005). Oral language expectations for African American children: Grades 1–5. *American Journal of Speech-Language Pathology, 14,* 119–130.

Craig, H. K., Washington, J. A., & Thompson-Porter, C. (1998). Performances of young African American children on two comprehension tasks. *Journal of Speech, Language, and Hearing Research, 41,* 445–457.

Delpit, L. (1996). *Other people's children: Cultural conflict in the classroom.* New York: New Press.

Delpit, L. (2001). The politics of teaching literate discourse. In E. Cushman, E. R. Kintgen, B. M. Kroll, & M. Rose (Eds.), *Literacy: A critical sourcebook* (pp. 545–554). Boston: Bedford/St. Martin's.

Dollaghan, C. A., & Campbell, T. F. (1998). Nonword repetition and child language impairment. *Journal of Speech, Language, and Hearing Research, 41,* 1136–1146.

Dunn, L., & Dunn, L. (1997). *Peabody Picture Vocabulary Test* (3rd ed.). Circle Pines, MN: American Guidance Service.

Gardner, M. F. (1990). *Expressive One Word Picture Vocabulary Test–Revised.* Novato, CA: Academic Therapy.

Hart, B., & Risley, T. R. (1995). *Meaningful differences in the everyday experience of young American children.* Baltimore: Paul H. Brookes.

Helfrich, H. (1999). Beyond the dilemma of cross-cultural psychology: Resolving the tension between etic and emic approaches. *Culture and Psychology, 5,* 131–153.

Ho, D. Y.-F. (1988). Asian psychology: A dialogue on indigenization and beyond. In A. C. Paranjpe, D. Y.-F. Ho, & R. W. Rieber (Eds.), *Asian contributions in psychology* (pp. 53–77). New York: Praeger.

Holm, J. (2004). *Languages in contact: The partial restructuring of vernaculars.* Cambridge, UK: Cambridge University Press.

Johnson, V. (2006). Comprehension of third person singular /s/ in aae-speaking children. *Language, Speech, and Hearing Services in Schools, 36,* 116–124.

Kohnert, K., Yim, D., Nett, K., Kan, P., & Duran, L. (2005). Intervention with linguistically diverse preschool children: A focus on developing home language(s). *Language, Speech, and Hearing Services in Schools, 36,* 251–263.

Labov, W. (Ed.). (2001). *Principles of linguistic change: Social factors* (Vol. 2). Malden, MA: Blackwell.

Lanza, E. (2004). *Language mixing in infant bilingualism: A sociolinguistic perspective.* Oxford, UK: Oxford University Press.

McDavid, R. I., & McDavid, V. G. (1971). The relationship of the speech of American negroes to the speech of whites. In W. Wolfram & N. H. Clarke (Eds.), *Black–white speech relationships.* Arlington, VA: Center for Applied Linguistics.

NCES. (2003). *Status and trends in the education of American Indians and Alaska natives.* Washington, DC: National Center for Education Statistics, Institute of Education Sciences, U.S. Department of Education.

Niblo, D. M., & Jackson, M. S. (2004). Model for combining qualitative emic approach with the quantitative derive etic approach. *Australian Psychologist, 39*(2), 127–133.

Oetting, J. B., Cantrell, J. P., & Horohov, J. E. (1999). A study of specific language impairment (SLI) in the context of nonstandard dialect. *Clinical Linguistics and Phonetics, 13,* 25–44.

Oetting, J. B., & McDonald, J. L. (2001). Nonmainstream dialect use and specific language impairment. *Journal of Speech, Language, and Hearing Research, 44*, 207–223.

Oetting, J. B., & McDonald, J. L. (2002). Methods for characterizing participants' nonmainstream dialect use in child language research. *Journal of Speech, Language, and Hearing Research, 45*, 505–518.

Peña, E., Iglesias, A., & Lidz, C. S. (2001). Reducing test bias through dynamic assessment of children's word learning ability. *American Journal of Speech-Language Pathology, 10*, 138–154.

Phillips, M., Crouse, J., & Ralph, J. (1998). Does the black–white test score gap widen after children enter school. In C. Jencks & M. Phillips (Eds.), *The black–white test score gap* (pp. 229–272). Washington, DC: Brookings Institution Press.

Pike, K. L. (1967). Etic and emic standpoints for the description of behavior. In D. C. Hildum (Ed.), *Language and thought: An enduring problem in psychology* (pp. 32–39). Princeton, NJ: Van Nostrand.

Scarborough, H. S. (1991). Very early language deficits in dyslexic children. *Annual Progress in Child Psychiatry and Child Development*, 204–227.

Seymour, H. N., Bland-Stewart, L., & Green, L. (1998). Difference versus deficit in child African American English. *Language, Speech, and Hearing Services in Schools, 29*(2), 96–108.

Seymour, H. N., Roeper, T. W., & de Villiers, J. (2004). *Diagnostic evaluation of language variation*. San Antonio, TX: Harcourt Assessment.

Stockman, I. J. (2000). The new Peabody Picture Vocabulary Test–III: An illusion of unbiased assessment? *Language, Speech, and Hearing Services in Schools, 31*, 340–353.

Taylor, O. L. (1993). Foreword. In D. E. Battle (Ed.), *Communication disorders in multicultural populations* (pp. xii–xiii). Andover, ME: Andover Medical

Thomas-Tate, S., Washington, J. A., & Edwards, J. (2004). Standardized assessment of phonological awareness skills in low-income African American first graders. *American Journal of Speech-Language Pathology, 13*(2), 143–149.

Tomblin, J. B., Records, N. L., Buckwalter, P., Zhang, X., Smith, E., & O'Brien, M. (1997). Prevalence of specific language impairment in kindergarten children. *Journal of Speech, Language, and Hearing Research, 40*, 1245–1260.

Torgesen, J. K., & Bryant, B. R. (1994). *Test of Phonological Awareness* (TOPA). Austin, TX: PRO-ED.

U.S. Census Bureau (2005). *National population estimates: Characteristics*. Washington, DC: Author.

U.S. Department of Education. (2002). *Twenty-fourth annual report to Congress on the implementation of the Individuals with Disabilities Education Act, Part II. Student characteristics* (pp. II-1–II-44). Washington, DC: Author.

Washington. J. (1996). Issues in assessing language skills in African American children. In A. G. Kahmi, K. G. Pollock, & J. L. Harris (Eds.), *Communication development and disorders in African American children: Research, assessment and intervention* (pp. 35–54). Mahwah, NJ: Lawrence Erlbaum Associates.

Washington, J. A., & Craig, H. K. (1992). Performances of low-income African American preschool and kindergarten children on the Peabody Picture Vocabulary Test–Revised. *Language, Speech, and Hearing Services in Schools, 23*, 329–333.

Washington, J. A., & Craig, H. K. (1994). Dialectal forms during discourse of urban, African American preschoolers living in poverty. *Journal of Speech and Hearing Research, 37*, 816–823.

Washington, J. A., & Craig, H. K. (1998). Socioeconomic status and gender influences on children's dialectal variations. *Journal of Speech and Hearing Research, 41*(3), 618–626.

Washington, J. A., & Craig, H. K. (1999). Performances of at-risk African American preschoolers on the Peabody Picture Vocabulary Test–III. *Language, Speech, and Hearing Services in Schools, 30*, 75–82.

Washington, J. A., & Craig, H. K. (2004). A language screening protocol for use with young African American children in urban settings. *American Journal of Speech–Language Pathology, 13*, 329–340.

Winford, D. (2003). *An introduction to contact linguistics (language in society)*. Malden, MA: Blackwell Publishing.

Wolfram, W. (1971). Black–white speech differences revisited. In W. Wolfram & N. H. Clarke (Eds.), *Black–white speech relationships*. Arlington, VA: Center for Applied Linguistics.

Wolfram, W., & Schilling-Estes, N. (Eds.). (1998). *American English* (Vol. 24). Malden, MA: Blackwell.

Wolfram, W., Temple Adger, C., & Christian, D. (1999). *Dialects in schools and communities*. Mahwah, NJ: Lawrence Erlbaum Associates.

Wong, C. A., & Rowley, S. J. (2001). The schooling of ethnic minority children: Commentary. *Educational Psychologist, 36*(1), 57–66.

Part IV

Deficits, Assessment, and Intervention in Child Language Disorders

15

Morphosyntax in Child Language Disorders

JANNA B. OETTING and PAMELA A. HADLEY

*T*he morphological deficits of children with specific language impairment (SLI) have been extensively documented, and there is a growing literature base of comparative studies investigating the structural systems of children with other developmental disabilities. Much of this work has been grounded in methods and constructs first developed by Brown (1973). These include the use of spontaneous language samples as a method of data collection and mean length of utterance (MLU), Brown's 14 morphemes, and 90% mastery as constructs by which to assess a child's morphological profile. In the current chapter, we review these studies as they relate to the broad categories of deficits, assessment tools, and intervention methods. Although our review is limited to studies of English-speaking children, we try to present the work in a way that highlights a number of scientific advances that have been made over the last 30 years (for crosscultural/crosslinguistic studies, see chapter 12 by Peña & Bedore and chapter 13 by Leonard).

Some of the advances have been empirical in nature. Researchers have identified limits to the use of Brown's approach as it has been applied to clinical populations (for MLU, see DeThorne, Johnson, & Loeb, 2005; Eisenberg, Fersko, & Lundgren, 2001; Johnston, 2001; Klee, Stokes, Wong, Fletcher, & Gavin, 2004; for Brown's 14 morphemes, see Balason & Dollaghan, 2002; for percentage use, see Hadley & Short, 2005; Oetting & McDonald, 2001). Since the 1970s, researchers have also developed new methods to study children's morphological systems. These include productivity probes, grammatical judgment tasks, and experimental tasks involving primed/unprimed elicitation. These new methods are now often used in tandem with, or as a replacement for, language sample analyses.

Other advances have been theoretical in nature. Under the influence of generative linguistic theory, scholars now recognize a distinction between the emergence of structures associated with lexical and functional categories (Chomsky, 1995). Lexical categories are characterized as Noun, Verb, Adjective, and Preposition—those categories associated with both syntactic and semantic information. In contrast, functional categories do not contain semantic information; they are purely responsible for realizing grammatical features such as tense, agreement, definiteness, and so forth. From this categorical perspective, the surface forms once studied as distinct elements of morphology and syntax are unified (hence our use of the term morphosyntax as opposed to morphology).

Initial investigations of children's morphosyntactic deficits examined the status of functional categories in the grammar (Eyer & Leonard, 1995; Leonard, 1995; for current work see Hegarty, 2005), but more recent investigations have focused most explicitly on children's use of functional morphemes that mark finiteness (i.e., tense and/or agreement). Figure 15.1 organizes the morphemes originally studied by Brown within this framework.

MORPHOSYNTACTIC DEFICITS ACROSS POPULATIONS

Specific Language Impairment

By definition, children with SLI present delayed language growth in the absence of other developmental conditions. During the early preschool years, a lower than expected MLU with limited use of grammatical morphology is a salient indicator of delayed growth. Young preschoolers with SLI often produce a number of morphemes at rates that are lower than those of age-matched and language-matched controls. These morphemes cut across lexical and functional categories; however, group differences are most consistent and dramatic for functional morphemes that mark finiteness, especially when children's MLUs are above 3.50 and language matching is incorporated into a study (for data supporting this claim and for a detailed discussion of language-matching, see Leonard, 1998; for more current work, see Bedore & Leonard, 1998; Leonard, Miller, & Gerber, 1999; and for studies involving MLUs below 3.0, see Beverly & Williams, 2004; Ingram & Morehead, 2002; Paul & Alforde, 1993).

By age 5, and up to at least age 8, difficulties with finite verb morphology become even more pronounced for children with SLI (Bishop, 1994; Conti-Ramsden, 2003; Krantz & Leonard, 2007; Leonard et al., 2003; Leonard, Bortolini, Caselli, McGregor, & Sabbadini, 1992; Oetting & Horohov, 1997; Owen & Leonard, 2006; Marchman, Wulfeck, & Ellis

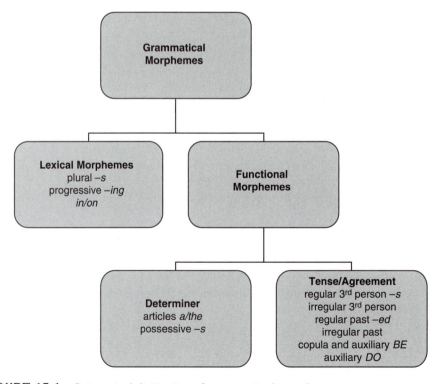

FIGURE 15.1 Categorical distinction of grammatical morphemes.

Weismer, 1999; Redmond, 2003; Rice & Wexler, 1996; Rice, Wexler, & Cleave, 1995; Rice, Wexler, & Hershberger, 1998). For example, within the Rice and Wexler (1996) study, children with SLI produced lower rates of finite verb morphemes when compared to both age and language-matched controls, with effect sizes ranging from .40 to .52. Moreover, using a composite measure of finite marking and 80% as a clinical cutoff, over 97% of the children were correctly classified as either SLI or typically developing.

Conti-Ramsden (2003) and Oetting and McDonald (2001) found complementary findings with children in this same age range. In Conti-Ramsden's study, children produced a British dialect of English, and measures included productivity probes of past tense and plural and two probes unrelated to morphosyntax (i.e., probes of nonword repetition and digit recall). For all tasks, children with SLI earned lower scores than did controls, but the children's past tense scores, together with their nonword repetition scores, yielded the highest level of diagnostic accuracy (sensitivity = .81; specificity = .91). The children's marking of past tense alone yielded sensitivity and specificity rates of .81.

In Oetting and McDonald's study, children produced a rural variety of either Southern White English or Southern African American English, and measures included frequency counts of 35 different morphosyntactic patterns within language samples. Although all 35 patterns were entered into the analysis, patterns related to finite verb morphology best separated the groups according to language ability. For Southern White English speakers, children with and without SLI were distinguished with 91% accuracy by the rate at which they produced unmarked forms of irregular past, irregular third, auxiliary *do*, and omissions of auxiliary *do* and infinitive *to*. For Southern African American English speakers, those with and without SLI were distinguished with 82% accuracy by the rate at which they produced unmarked forms of irregular past, irregular third, and Wh-noninversion (see chapter 14 by Washington; for other vernacular dialect studies showing finite verb morphology deficits in children with SLI, see Oetting, Cantrell, & Horohov, 1999; Oetting & Garrity, 2006; Ross, Oetting, & Stapleton, 2004; but also see Seymour, Bland-Stewart, & Green, 1998).

After age 8, it is more difficult to distinguish children with and without SLI using finite verb morphology, as evidenced by Conti-Ramsden, Botting, and Faragher's (2001) study of 11-year-olds. Measures were from probes and included regular and irregular marking of past tense, regular third person marking, sentence imitation, and nonword repetition. Again on all four tasks, children with SLI scored lower than did controls. Using the 16th percentile as a clinical cutoff, all four measures also showed fair-to-good specificity at .87 or higher. Only sentence imitation, however, demonstrated good sensitivity at .90. For the two finite verb morphemes, sensitivity was too low at this age to be clinically useful (past tense = .74, third person = .63), and adjusting the cutoff downward also did not improve the results (for additional studies of older children, see Betz, 2005; Mackie & Dockrell, 2004; Windsor, Scott, & Street, 2000).

The nature of children's difficulties with finite verb morphology has been studied longitudinally with a clinical sample and a large epidemiologically ascertained sample (Rice, 2004; Rice, Tomblin, Hoffman, Richman, & Marquis, 2004; Rice, Wexler, Marquis, & Hershberger, 2000; Rice, Wexler, & Redmond, 1999; Rice, Wexler, & Hershberger, 1998). Results indicate that the acquisition of these morphemes by children with SLI lags behind, and is not predicted by, their general delays in vocabulary and MLU or by IQ and maternal education. Nevertheless, children with SLI present growth trajectories for individual finite morphemes that are similar to each other and in parallel to those observed for typically developing controls. For both groups, a combination of linear and quadratic growth (showing early linear growth followed by deceleration) occurs even though rates of marking by those with SLI are protracted.

Children's difficulties with finite verb morphology have not been found to be strongly related to children's scores on tasks involving nonword repetition (Bishop, Adams, & Norbury, 2006), sentence imitation (Conti-Ramsden et al., 2001), and perception of natural speech stimuli (Evans, Viele, Kass, & Tang, 2002, see also van der Lely, Rosen, & Adlard, 2004). There is also evidence from a pedigree analysis and a twin study that this area of language may be heritable and that a single major gene may be implicated (Bishop, 2005; Bishop et al., 2006; Rice, Haney, & Wexler, 1998).

Children's difficulties with finite verb morphology primarily involve errors of omission (e.g., *He walking* and *Everyday she dance*). Errors of commission, such as *He am walking* and *I dances*, are rare and comparable in frequency to rates produced by language-matched controls (rates range from 0% to 9%, depending upon study; see Cleave & Rice, 1997; Eadie, Fey, Douglas, & Parsons, 2002; Leonard et al., 1992; Rice et al., 1995; but also see Pine, Joseph, & Conti-Ramsden, 2004, regarding interpretations of error-free productions). What are not included in these counts of errors are overregularizations of regular affixes (e.g., *he felled, two mices, got hanged up*). Children with SLI do overregularize past, plural, and passive participle markers, but the frequency at which they make these errors does not typically exceed that of controls (Leonard, Eyer, Bedore, & Grela, 1997; Leonard et al., 2003; Marchman et al., 1999; Oetting & Horohov, 1997; Oetting & Rice, 1993). Arguably, these types of errors also involve the surface realization of the marked form (regular vs. irregular) rather than a misapplication of a marker (for data and discussion of overregularization as morphophonological rather than morphosyntactic, see Redmond & Rice, 2001; Rice et al., 2000).

When children with SLI omit finite verb morphemes (e.g., *he falling*), they are also less able than age-matched controls—and often language-matched controls—to detect errors involving these same types of utterances during grammatical judgment tasks. At the same time, children with SLI can detect errors of commission (i.e., *he am falling*), overregularization (i.e., *he felled*), irregularization (i.e., *leck* for *looked*), and other types of omission errors (i.e., *he is walk* where the progressive *-ing* is omitted). Direct evidence for this claim can be found in studies by Montgomery and Leonard (1998), Redmond and Rice (2001), Rice et al. (1999, 2000), and van der Lely and Ullman (1996). These findings have helped rule out production constraints as a causal mechanism to explain children's protracted development of finite verb morphology (for other grammatical judgment studies, see Bishop, 1994; Kahmi & Catts, 1986; Wulfeck, 1993). That children with SLI are better able to complete grammatical judgment tasks with some types of errors than with others also suggests that results from these tasks cannot be explained by a more general deficit in metalinguistic development.

Although children with SLI omit finite verb morphemes for a longer period than do age- and language-matched controls, other aspects of their morphological systems appear intact. Oetting and Rice (1993) and Oetting and Horohov (1997) demonstrated this with regular and irregular markers of plural and past tense. In the former, children were asked to produce novel noun compounds with regular and irregular plurals (i.e., *he is a X-eater* with targets such as *mice* and *dogs*), and in the latter, they were asked to produce past tense expressions for pairs of homophonous verbs where one item in the pair depicted an action that could be described with an irregular past tense form (e.g., *meet–met*) whereas the other was a newly created action that required a child to express past using a verb that had been derived from a noun (*meat–meated*). For reasons that are not critical to the presentation here, typically developing children and adults produce past and plural irregular forms differently than do regulars within these tasks. For example, irregular nouns can be expressed in the singular or plural form within compounds (e.g., *mouse-eater* and *mice-eater*), but nouns taking regular plural markers are only felicitous in the singular form (*dog-eater* but not *dogs-eater*). On these tasks, children with SLI perform like controls because their responses show clear distinctions between items requiring regular and irregular markings (for similar findings, see Grela, Synder, & Hiramatsu, 2005; Jacobson & Schwartz, 2005).

There are also other ways in which the morphosyntactic systems of children with SLI are robust. For example, Hadley and Rice (1996) showed that children with SLI understand the distributive properties of auxiliary and main verb BE and DO forms as well as the properties of subject–verb agreement from the earliest appearance of these forms. Cleave and Rice (1997) also noted parallel findings between children with and without SLI for BE forms relative to grammatical function (auxiliary vs. copula) and contractibility (both phonetic, as in *she's* vs. *Bess is*, and syntactic, as in *she is* vs. *is she*). Finally, Ogiela, Casby, and Schmitt (2005) examined the types of verbs and verb predicates that children with SLI produce with present progressive *-ing*, regular and irregular past, and third person singular *-s*. Consistent with patterns reported for typically developing children, those with SLI produced *-ing* most frequently with activity predicates, regular and irregular past forms most frequently with event predicates, and third person forms most frequently with state and activity predicates combined.

Children with SLI present difficulties with other morphosyntactic structures that are not necessarily related to markers of finiteness, but the nature and the scope of these difficulties are not yet fully known. For example, investigations of the passive participle (i.e., *the football was kicked*) have yielded mixed findings. Redmond (2003) and Smith-Locke (1993) found children with SLI to mark participles at rates that were comparable to language-matched controls, but Leonard et al. (2003) found group differences favoring controls. In all three studies, however, children with SLI produced greater rates of marking for participles than for the past tense. Mixed findings have also been reported for articles and plurals (Beastrum & Rice, 1986; Eadie et al., 2002; Leonard et al., 1997; McGregor & Leonard, 1994; Oetting & Rice, 1993; Rice & Oetting, 1993; Rice & Wexler, 1996).

Findings have been more consistent for subject case marking of pronouns, with group differences favoring language-matched controls reported in multiple studies (Loeb, 1994; Loeb & Leonard, 1988, 1991; Loeb & Mikesic, 1992; but also see Moore, 1995). Across comparative studies, variability is also generally greater for children with SLI. Nevertheless, the nature of children's difficulties with this structure remains elusive because errors are not apparent for all children and error rates differ across forms such as *he* versus *she* (Pine et al., 2004; Pine, Rowland, Lieven, & Theakston, 2005; Rispoli, 1998, 1999; Schütze, 1999; Wexler, Schütze, & Rice, 1998).

For other structures, weaknesses by children with SLI have been documented, but replication of the findings is still needed. The dative preposition *to* (i.e., *to the girl*) is one of these structures. Grela, Rashiti, and Soares (2004) examined children's use of this structure along with their use of locative prepositions *in* and *on* (i.e., *in the box*). Group differences favoring the controls were found for the dative structure but not for the locatives, and incorrect responses were errors of commission rather than omission. Other structures that have been flagged as problematic, but for which there are limited data from children with SLI, include nonthematic *of*, infinitival complementizer *to*, modals *could* and *should*, and possessive *-'s* (Eyer & Leonard, 1995; Leonard, 1995; Leonard et al., 1992, 1997).

In some, but not all, cases the morphosyntactic skills of children with SLI have also been shown to be more affected by experimental manipulations of stimuli than those of language-matched controls. For example, Redmond and Rice (2001) found that children with SLI were less able than controls to make grammatical judgments when sentences involved complex syntax (i.e., *he made the robot fall/fell/falled of a block*), even though they performed similarly to the controls when the stimuli involved simple syntax (i.e., *the space robot fall/fell/felled off a block*). Although manipulations involving the allomorphic characteristics of affixes (e.g., *-t* vs. *-d* of past tense and *-s* vs. *-z* vs. *-əz* of plurals) affect children with and without SLI similarly, the inflectional frequency of word roots (frequent vs. infrequent) and the phonotactic properties of the resulting affixed clusters (whether or not the cluster is legal in the final positions of monomorphemic words) do not (Marshall, 2004; Oetting & Horohov, 1997; Oetting & Rice, 1993; van der Lely & Ullman, 1996; and for age-controls, see Marchman et al., 1999). For both of these latter cases, marking by children with SLI differs as a function of the manipulation, whereas marking by controls is not.

Findings have also been mixed for structural priming. Leonard et al. (2000) found that structural priming affected the auxiliary *be* productions of children with SLI to a greater extent than those of language-matched controls, but this finding was not replicated by Leonard et al. (2002). Other manipulations involving sentence length and argument structure complexity have not led to significant group-by-condition interactions when language matching has been employed (Grela & Leonard, 2000). However, when these authors examined differences between two of their argument structure conditions (intransitive vs. ditransitive), effect sizes for the children with SLI were twice as large as those of the language-matches (SLI: $d = .66$ vs. MLU-matched: $d = .25$).

Williams Syndrome

Children with Williams syndrome (WS) present difficulties with morphosyntax even though the language profiles of these children are often described as precocious in light of their general cognitive deficits and their severe weaknesses in visual–spatial, number concept, and motor skill learning (Bromberg, Ullman, Marcus, Kelly, & Coppolla, 1994; Karmiloff-Smith et al., 1997; Mervis, 2003; Mervis, Morris, Bertrand, & Robinson, 1999; see also chapter 2 by McDuffie & Abbeduto). Emerging findings indicate that these children's morphosyntactic difficulties differ from those documented for SLI (Clahsen & Almazan, 1998, 2001; Clahsen & Temple, 2003; Krause & Penke, 2002; Niedeggen-Bartke, 2001; Levy, 2002; Levy & Herman, 2003; Rice, 1999; Thomas et al., 2001; Volterra, Caselli, Capirci, Tonucci, & Vicari, 2003; Zukowski, 2005). Children with WS mark many finite verb morphemes (i.e., regular past, third person singular, and copular and auxiliary *be*) at rates commensurate to those of mental-age-matched controls, and their correct use of these structures can be close to ceiling levels by 7 years of age. Children with WS also do not seem to have difficulties with regular plural marking, prepositions *in* and *on*, and adjectival *-er* or the use of various regular affixes on nonce words that exceed their general delays in language and cognition.

For children with WS, however, use of irregular morphosyntax (and use of other types of constructions that require access to the mental lexicon) often lags behind that of mental-age-matched controls. The nature of this difficulty within the WS profile is currently the center of debate. Data collected by Clahsen and colleagues show children with WS producing rates of overregularization that are higher than mental-age controls in a variety of tasks that require irregular productions (Clahsen & Almazan, 1998, 2001; Clahsen & Temple, 2003). In sharp contrast, other data (Zukowski, 2005) show children with WS having rates of overregularization that are less than those of mental-age-matched controls. Moreover, when Zukowski provided prompting to highlight the contrasting nature of the referents used in the experiment (e.g., the singular versus plural nature of the stimuli), the children with WS increased their rate of correct irregular productions to a level that was comparable to that of the controls. Reconciling the findings of these studies is complicated by the fact that the control groups performed very differently across the studies.

Like other children with developmental disorders, the most common type of morphosyntactic error children with WS make involves omissions. Nevertheless, Volterra et al. (2003) showed that children with WS are 10 times more likely than controls to add morphemes to sentences when they are asked to repeat them (e.g., on a task with 51 sentences, 6 children with WS made 44 of these errors; controls made 3), and often these added morphemes are relics from previous utterances within the stimuli. On these tasks, children with WS also make some substitutions and word order errors that disrupt the meaning of the sentence, whereas these types of errors are rarely made by controls. Some have suggested that the unique morphosyntactic profile of WS (and the specific error patterns observed during elicitation tasks) is directly related to these children's particular strengths in, or particular dependency upon, short-term phonological memory for learning language (Lukács, Racsmány & Pléh, 2001; Robinson, Mervis & Robinson, 2003; but also see Brock, 2007).

Down Syndrome

The morphosyntactic deficits of children with Down syndrome (DS) have been characterized as similar to those with SLI because children with DS have more difficulties with this area of language than is expected given their chronological age, nonverbal mental age, vocabulary ability, and MLU; their grammatical errors also primarily involve omissions (Abbeduto & Murphy, 2004; Chapman, Schwartz & Kay-Raining Bird, 1991; Chapman, Seung, Schwartz, & Kay-Raining Bird, 1998; Eadie et al., 2002; Laws & Bishop, 2003; Rutter & Buckly, 1994; Thordardottir, Chapman, & Wagner, 2002; Volterra et al., 2003; see also chapter 2 by McDuffie & Abbeduto). However, some differences in the morphosyntactic profiles of DS and SLI have been noted. Children with DS present a wider spread between their scores on vocabulary and morphosyntactic tests as compared to children with SLI (Laws & Bishop, 2003). Children with DS also have better morphosyntactic skills when tested in comprehension than production (Chapman et al., 1998, 2000). This incongruence has not been documented in the same way for children with SLI (but see Laws & Bishop, 2003, for data showing a comprehension–production gap in both DS and SLI when vocabulary and morphosyntactic measures are combined).

Importantly, the specific nature of the DS morphosyntactic profile is still not well understood, and the study of DS is complicated by these children's severe deficits in auditory working memory, decreased rates of intelligibility, and fluctuating hearing loss (cf. Chapman & Hesketh, 2000). Nevertheless, the expressive grammatical deficits of DS appear more expansive than those of SLI, with omissions of modals, articles, prepositions, pronouns, conjunctions, adverbial adjuncts, progressive *-ing*, possessive *-'s*, and regular plural co-occurring with omissions of finite verb morphemes (Chapman et al., 1998). In morpheme elicitation tasks (Laws & Bishop, 2003), children with DS are also more likely than children with SLI to refuse to reply or to respond with a word that did not require a target affix (DS = 30% vs. SLI = 7%). When these errors were excluded, the children with DS produced higher rates of past tense marking than did children with SLI. In contrast, another study (Eadie et al., 2002) revealed that children with DS and children with SLI omitted a number of morphemes at rates that were higher than those of controls; however, the DS and SLI groups were indistinguishable from one another. Findings from these three studies are difficult to reconcile because of differences in the matching criteria (mental age vs. MLU) and the age of the children studied (in Chapman et al., age range = 5–20 years; in Laws & Bishop, age range = 10–19 years; in Eadie et al., age = 7 years). Type of task (elicitation vs.

language sample), type of language sampling context (narrative vs. conversational), and type of analysis (parametric vs. nonparametric) also varied across these studies.

Autism

The morphosyntactic profiles of children with autism are highly variable (see chapter 3 by Gerenser), with some children showing relatively intact systems, others showing delays and/or weaknesses relative to their general level of language ability, and still others presenting limits in language that are so severe as to preclude even cursory study of this area (Tager-Flusberg, 2004). Of the studies that have examined morphosyntax (e.g., Bartolucci & Albers, 1974; Bartolucci, Pierce, & Streiner, 1980; Botting & Conti-Ramsden, 2003; Howlin, 1984; Kjelgaard & Tager-Flusberg, 2001; Roberts, Rice, & Tager-Flusberg, 2004), research by Botting and Conti-Ramsden and by Tager-Flusberg and colleagues aligns most closely with other studies that have been completed on children with SLI. The study conducted by Roberts et al. included 62 children with autism who were verbal and the target morphemes were three markers of finiteness (i.e., regular third person and regular and irregular past tense). The children's use of these structures was examined as a function of subgroups (Group 1 = vocabulary score above −1 SD of normative mean; Group 2 = vocabulary score between −1 and −2 SD; Group 3 = vocabulary score below −2 SD) and scoring method (all errors considered vs. exclusion of idiosyncratic errors such as no responses, no verb responses, echolalic responses, and creative verb responses). Three findings from this study are relevant here.

First, finite marking differed across the three groups. Those with vocabulary scores in the normal range (Group 1) had relatively high rates of correct use, especially when idiosyncratic responses were excluded from the calculations (rates 81–86%), whereas rates of marking by the children with very low vocabulary scores (Group 3) were much lower (65–68%). Rates of use for Group 2 fell in the middle and are harder to interpret. When all errors were considered, their rates of use were lower, but not significantly different from those in Group 1. When idiosyncratic errors were removed, their rate of correct marking for third person was low (69%), but for past tense it was relatively high and similar to that of Group 1 (86%).

Second, although the children with autism produced a number of error types not seen in children with SLI, morpheme omissions were common. In addition, overregularizations of regular affixes were very rare (averaged <1%). Others who have reported similar findings regarding morpheme omissions and overregularizations include Bartolucci et al. (1980), Howlin (1984), and Tager-Flusberg (1989). Finally, the three subgroups of children with autism also differed in nonword repetition scores. The rates of correct morpheme production were found to be moderately correlated with this measure, although the relationship weakened when vocabulary scores were partialed out (for details regarding group data, see Kjelgaard & Tager-Flusberg, 2001).

Findings from the above studies have been interpreted by Tager-Flusberg and others as indicating overlapping profiles between children with SLI and some children with autism. Family pedigree studies and genetic linkage and association studies also support the notion of overlapping profiles between these two conditions (cf. Tomblin, Hafeman, & O'Brien, 2003). Nevertheless, the study of morphosyntax in children with autism is complicated by a number of issues. Two of these issues relate to the semantic–pragmatic difficulties of children with autism and their tendency to perseverate and to produce echolalia (Tager-Flusberg, 2000). Both of these issues make it difficult to interpret morphosyntactic data from experimental tasks. Another issue relates to developmental changes in the relation between the language skills and nonverbal cognitive skills of children with autism (Joseph,

Tager-Flusberg, & Lord, 2002). Unlike children with Down syndrome, however, the articulation skills of children with autism who are verbal appear relatively intact and do not seem to serve as a barrier to the study of these children's morphosyntactic difficulties (Tager-Flusberg, 2004).

Other Childhood Developmental Disabilities

The search for clinical markers and precise behavioral descriptions (i.e., phenotypes) of different types of childhood developmental disabilities has led to a number of other cross-etiology comparisons in the area of morphosyntax. These studies have included children with mild to moderate sensorineural hearing loss (Norbury, Bishop, & Briscoe, 2001; see also chapter 4 by Cleary), severe speech and physical impairments (Redmond & Johnston, 2001), attention-deficit/hyperactivity disorder (ADHD; Redmond, 2004, 2005), and co-existing deficits in nonverbal intelligence and language impairment (Rice et al., 2004). Emerging findings from these studies suggest that these groups do not have morphosyntactic profiles that mirror those of SLI, WS, DS, or autism. Nevertheless, difficulties with finite verb morphology (specifically past tense and third person) were found for a subset of children with hearing impairments. Low scores on three standardized language tests, but not degree of hearing loss, age of receiving hearing aids, nonword repetition scores, or nonverbal IQ, were directly related to this subgroup's difficulty with finite verb morphology.

ASSESSMENT OF MORPHOSYNTACTIC DEFICITS

Documentation of the morphosyntactic deficits of children plays an important role in assessment, because grammatical ability is essential for effective spoken and written forms of communication. As shown in the deficits section, fine-grained analyses of morphological productivity and error patterns may eventually help professionals to differentially diagnose and explain different types of morphosyntactic profiles in children. These profiles may or may not cut across etiologies.

Norm-Referenced Tests

Standardized tests have long been used as a time-efficient means for assessing morphosyntax. Examples of norm-referenced tools used in research and clinical practice include receptive tools such as the Test of Auditory Comprehension of Language–3 (Carrow-Woolfolk, 1999) and the Test for Reception of Grammar–2 (Bishop, 2003), expressive tools such as the Structured Photographic Expressive Language tests (SPELT, Preschool–2; Dawson et al., 2005; SPELT–3; Dawson, Stout, & Eyer, 2003), and subtests of omnibus tests such as the Clinical Evaluation of Language Fundamentals–4 (Semel, Wiig, & Secord, 2003) and Test of Language Development, Primary–3 (Newcomer & Hammill, 1997). Typically, drawings or photographs and questions or cloze prompts are used to assess children's production of morphosyntactic structures (e.g., *The girl spilled the juice. Then what did she do? She_____*; Dawson et al., 2005). Although such tasks are generally viewed as measures of expressive morphosyntax, children with stronger receptive abilities may be better able to use the structured prompts to supply target responses (Perona, Plante, & Vance, 2005).

A central assumption of norm-referenced test interpretation is that children with language impairments will demonstrate below-average performance. Yet in a comprehensive, empirical review of commercially available test manuals, Spaulding, Plante, and Farinella (2006) documented the inadequacy of this assumption for accurate identification of children with language impairments. Many tests failed to reveal large group differences between children with and without language impairments; however, tests of morphosyntax were generally most robust. Given the limited sensitivity of many existing tools, Plante and her colleagues have argued for the use of data-driven, alternative cutoff points that discriminate maximally between children with language impairments and those with typically developing language (Perona et al., 2005; Plante & Vance, 1994, 1995; Spaulding et al., 2006). For example, in a recent study exploring the diagnostic accuracy of the Structured Photographic Expressive Language Test–Third Edition (SPELT–3; Dawson et al., 2003), Perona et al. (2005) demonstrated that a standard score cutoff of 95 provided the best classification accuracy, identifying 92% of the children with SLI as affected and 100% of the typically developing children as unaffected. By contrast, use of a more traditional standard score cutoff of 85 reduced the test's sensitivity to unacceptably low levels (i.e., 72%). (For additional studies that have explored empirically derived cutoffs, see Oetting, Cleveland, & Cope, 2008.)

Although the establishment of data-driven cutoffs provides an empirically derived solution to the problem of underidentification, clinicians should also ask why a test has poor sensitivity in the first place. Underidentification is more likely for children with relatively selective impairments, such as children with SLI as compared to children with more global developmental disabilities. To improve identification for children with more selective impairments, content validity should be examined. Sound content validity depends upon sufficient opportunities to measure a particular construct (i.e., content coverage) while avoiding extraneous items unrelated to the construct (i.e., content relevance; McCauley, 2001). On many tools, only a few items may assess structures known to be especially difficult (i.e., finite verb morphology), which are then collapsed with other structures not known to be diagnostically sensitive (e.g., progressive -*ing*, plural -*s*) to derive total scores. Table 15.1 illustrates a content analysis of the items contained on the SPELT: Preschool–2

TABLE 15.1   Item analysis by categorical distinction

Category	Structure	SPELT–P2 Items	SPELT–3 Items
Lexical	Prepositions	1	1, 2, 3, 4
	Plural -*s*	3, 4, 5	5, 6, 7
	Progressive -*ing*	7, 11, 25	8
Functional	Articles	2	—
Nontense/agreement	Possessive -'*s*	8	29, 30
	Possessive Pronoun	9	31, 32, 33, 34
Functional	Third Sing Present -*s*	19, 20	9, 24, 25, 26
Finite Verb	Past regular	14, 15	11, 16
Morphology	Past irregular	26, 27	14, 23
	Copula	16, 17, 18	20, 21, 22, 50
	Auxiliary BE	6, 10, 24	13, 15, 17, 18, 19
	Modal will	—	10, 12
	Tense + nondeclarative syntactic contexts	22, 23, 33, 34, 35, 36, 37	38, 39, 42, 43, 44, 45, 46, 47, 49
Complex Syntax	Infinitival to	31, 32	24, 25, 26, 49
	Dependent clauses	21, 30, 38, 39, 40	28, 51, 52, 53, 35, 36, 37, 49
Other		12, 13, 28, 29	27, 40, 41, 48

(Dawson et al., 2005) and SPELT–3 (Dawson et al., 2003). As can be seen on both versions, children's overall performance on these tests will be heavily influenced by their proficiency with finite verb morphology. However, the way in which these structures are collapsed with less diagnostically sensitive structures may provide some explanation for this tool's limited sensitivity as documented by Perona et al. (2005).

Criterion-Referenced Tools

Although it is possible to identify broad deficits in morphosyntactic abilities using norm-referenced tools, these tools were not designed to provide descriptive characterizations of children's progress toward mastery of individual structures or composite constructs such as finite verb morphology. To establish preintervention abilities and measure progress over time, criterion-referenced approaches are necessary (McCauley, 2001). Criterion-referenced tools are designed to differentiate individuals who have mastered a particular body of knowledge or set of skills from those who have not. To do so, items included on criterion-referenced tools are focused explicitly on the knowledge/skill set of interest. Performance is judged relative to a predetermined criterion level or a cut-off score, not in relationship to the performance of other individuals. Ideally, criterion levels are established empirically, although sometimes they may be based upon expert review of existing literature.

Given that typically developing children master nearly all elements of morphosyntax before kindergarten entry, criterion-referenced approaches provide an appropriate means of assessing progress in morphosyntactic development during the preschool years and beyond. An innovative approach to criterion-referenced assessment is reflected in the Rice–Wexler Test of Early Grammatical Impairment (TEGI; Rice & Wexler, 2001). The TEGI is a standardized, criterion-referenced tool made up of several elicitation probes designed to assess production of regular past tense, irregular past tense, third person singular, auxiliary and copula *BE* in questions and statements, and auxiliary *DO* in questions. Multiple opportunities are provided to estimate children's progress toward mastery for each structure as well as for a combined tense composite. Empirically derived cut-off scores are provided for children, ages 3;0–8;11, along with full documentation of the associated levels of sensitivity and specificity for alternative cut-off values. School-age children with performance levels below the criterion have not mastered this knowledge. For preschool children, performance below the criterion indicates those who are unlikely to master tense by kindergarten entry. Thus, the TEGI can be used to identify deficits in finite verb morphology as well as to document progress toward mastery over time.

The TEGI also provides a unique format for eliciting grammaticality judgments from children. In this task, children are asked to judge the statements of two robots who sometimes say things "right" and sometimes say things that are "not so good." This format reveals whether or not children will accept omissions or errors on morphosyntactic structures as permissible. This focus differs considerably from the format of other receptive measures of grammar that determine whether children are able to match morphosyntactic structures to events in the world from a set of contrasting pictures (e.g., Show me "The boy climbed the tree.").

Training items ask children to judge the use of two lexical morphemes, plural -*s* and progressive -*ing*, each used correctly and incorrectly on five occasions. Only if children are able to complete the judgment task with the lexical morphemes do they proceed to items designed to assess knowledge of obligatory tense morpheme use and subject–verb agreement in simple clauses. Children with selective deficits would be expected to perform poorly on items where tense is omitted, but they would be expected to make more accurate judgments on items involving subject–verb agreement errors and omission of progressive *-ing*. In contrast, poor performance across all three judgment probes would indicate more general limitations in grammatical development or metalinguistic ability (cf. Rice & Wexler, 2001).

Language Samples

Despite its time-consuming nature, language sampling remains the mainstay of authentic, ecologically valid assessment. Certainly, if children do not possess the knowledge to perform well on structured tasks, deficits are also likely in discourse. However, other children may have sufficient knowledge for constructing adult-like sentences in structured probes, yet be unable to deploy this knowledge rapidly and automatically in spontaneous speech (Lahey, 1990).

Eisenberg et al. (2001) discussed important considerations for gathering valid language samples and computing MLU. They also reviewed existing reliability and validity studies to provide empirically sound guidelines for interpreting MLU. Beyond these considerations, clinicians need to think consciously about creating opportunities for children to use morphosyntactic structures of particular interest while gathering language samples, otherwise too few obligatory contexts will be available for analysis (Balason & Dollaghan, 2002). To elicit production of past tense verb forms, opportunities to relate past events are critical, and to elicit question and negative forms, planned probes and false assertions should be used strategically (see Cleave & Fey, 1997; Cleave & Rice, 1997). For samples collected as part of parent–child interaction, it may be helpful to suggest ways of talking about the toys rather than what the parent or child is doing. This reduces the number of sentences with first and second person subjects (i.e., *I'm . . . you're . . .*) where finite verb morphology may not be fully analyzed. Discussion about the toys should also create more opportunities to assess the productivity of subject–verb agreement on copula, auxiliary, and/or third person verb forms (e.g., *The baby is tired. She needs a nap*).

Interpretation of MLU provides only a first step for subsequent examination of morphosyntactic abilities. MLU often overestimates children's grammatical complexity in samples of children with developmental language disorders (Scarborough, Rescorla, Tager-Flusberg, Fowler, & Sudhalter, 1991). If MLU is very low relative to age expectations, children's morphosyntactic abilities are likely to be poor relative to age expectations as well (Eisenberg et al., 2001). In other words, MLU has very good positive predictive value. A clinician can be relatively confident of language-impaired status when a positive result (i.e., very low MLU) is observed. In contrast, MLU has relatively poor negative predictive value. Thus, when a negative result is obtained (i.e., age-appropriate MLU), a clinician cannot be confident of a child's typical language status.

For children with MLUs under 3.00, it is most appropriate to focus analyses upon the *emergence* and *productivity* of morphosyntactic structures (cf. Miller & Deevy, 2003; Miller & Leonard, 1998; Hadley, 1998; Scarborough, 1990). Recently, Hadley and Short (2005) developed several cumulative measures of tense onset for use with younger children at risk for SLI. Two measures focused upon the emergence of structures (i.e., the initial appearance or first use of a form in children's spontaneous speech), and two measures focused upon varying degrees of productivity (i.e., the use of tense morphemes in two to five sufficiently different contexts). Hadley and Short demonstrated that a cumulative productivity score reflecting up to five sufficiently different uses of five tense morphemes (i.e., third person singular present, past tense, copula BE, auxiliary BE, and auxiliary DO) was moderately correlated with a conservative measure of tense mastery. However, fair differentiation of children at risk for SLI from those with low average language abilities was observed for the measure of tense onset (i.e., sensitivity = 79%, specificity = 83%), whereas overlapping distributions resulted for the measure of tense mastery. Interestingly, the children at risk for SLI were more likely to demonstrate higher levels of mastery despite more limited productivity. Thus, analyses focused upon the *mastery* of structures within obligatory contexts should be reserved until there is sufficient evidence that the structures are instantiated as distinct entries in the mental lexicon and are fully productive, typically characteristic of MLUs well beyond 3.00.

The use of MLU referencing can be used to recognize more pronounced deficits in morphosyntax. Goffman and Leonard (2000) provide a detailed discussion of this procedure, illustrating longitudinal change for children with SLI on a composite measure of finite verb morphology relative to expectations for MLU. As expected, pronounced weakness in mastery of finite verb morphology, exceeding expectations based on MLU, was a hallmark characteristic of the children with SLI. More recently, Hadley and Holt (2006) examined evidence for individual differences in tense onset between the ages of 2 and 3. This study revealed robust individual differences in the linear growth of tense morpheme productivity at 30 months of age, even after average levels of MLU and MLU growth were controlled (i.e., MLU-referenced in a statistical sense). Further research is needed to determine whether individual differences in the rate of tense onset will explain the pronounced deficits observed in tense mastery, relative to MLU expectations, among older children with SLI at later stages of grammatical development.

Parent Report Tools

Although parent report tools have been most widely developed and used to assess young children's vocabulary knowledge (see chapter 16 by McGregor), this methodology holds promise for assessing early grammatical abilities as well. To date, only two studies have examined the validity of parent report for assessing early syntax, in general (Dale, 1991; Thal, O'Hanlon, Clemmons, & Fralin, 1999), and only one has focused upon the emergence of finite verb morphology, in particular (Bryant, 2003). All three studies have used the MacArthur–Bates Communicative Development Inventories (CDI; Fenson et al., 2003). The CDI: Words and Sentences (CDI:WS) includes a section designed to evaluate emerging grammatical complexity for children 16–30 months of age. A similar section can be found on the CDI: Level 3 (Dale, 2001) for children 30–37 months of age.

To explore the validity of parent report for assessing tense onset, Bryant (2003) examined the two different reporting formats on the CDI:WS for obtaining information about finite verb morphology. As part of the Helping Verb section, parents reported on the presence/absence of tense morphemes in their children's spontaneous speech. Of particular interest were *am, are, did/did ya, do, does, is, was, were*. As part of the Complexity section, parents were asked to mark one of two sentence pairs that sounds MOST like the way their child talks (e.g., *Baby crying* versus *Baby is crying*). Six items focused on past tense *-ed*, copula BE, auxiliary BE, and auxiliary DO. Parent report for these items was then compared to the children's frequency and productivity of these forms in spontaneous language samples. In general, parents were better reporters when sentence contexts were provided. The reporting format for the Helping Verb section proved more difficult for parents. When these forms were marked, they were associated with the emergence of *main verb* forms of BE and DO, but without any evidence for the emergence of *auxiliary* BE or DO in the children's language samples. Based on these findings, Bryant (2003) and Hadley (2006) recommended a subset of six items on the Complexity section to determine emergence of past tense *-ed*, auxiliary BE, and auxiliary DO and five word forms from the Helping Verbs section (i.e., *is, am, are, was, were*) to provide evidence for copula BE. With further development and refinement, parent report tools are likely to provide a valid means of assessing the emergence of specific morphosyntactic structures with children under age 3 as well.

INTERVENTION FOR MORPHOSYNTACTIC DEFICITS

Given the numerous deficits children with developmental language disorders experience, clinicians must consider the extent to which morphosyntax is a priority for a given child. Such targets are likely to be of low priority until children demonstrate social engagement, participate easily in the event structure of everyday activities, and are familiar with the concepts and vocabulary associated with those events. Once these prerequisites are in place and children are producing basic sentence structures, morphosyntactic intervention objectives may be appropriate. Yet intervention focused on morphosyntax should remain consistent with Fey, Long, and Finestack's (2003) first principle of grammar facilitation. Grammar interventions should be designed to improve children's abilities to participate fully in activities of daily living and to communicate more effectively within those situations. The priority placed upon morphosyntax may also be influenced by a child's anticipated future needs for literacy and participation within an academically oriented curriculum. However, when grammar is targeted within a functional communication context, clinicians will be addressing communicative effectiveness simultaneously (Bunce & Watkins, 1995; Johnston, 1985; Rice, 1991).

Over two decades ago, Johnston (1985) claimed that language intervention should use "focused linguistic input, to narrow the child's search for order, and simplify his rule formation task" (p. 130). Today, evidence documenting the effectiveness of this principle has mounted (e.g., Fey, Cleave, & Long, 1997; Fey, Cleave, Long, & Hughes, 1993; Tyler, Lewis, Haskill, & Tolbert, 2002, 2003). Across studies, the interventions have varied in their intensity and duration. Most programs have been implemented by clinicians, although Fey and his colleagues have examined the effectiveness of a parent-implemented program as well. Fey et al. (1993) found no difference in the average gains between parent- and clinician-implemented programs; however, more consistent results were observed in the clinician-implemented program. Most intervention packages have used focused stimula-tion. In this approach, specific intervention targets are selected, and then a high density of target forms is produced in a variety of discourse-appropriate contexts. Opportunities are also created for children to encourage them to produce the target by manipulating the nonlinguistic environment or discourse context (for a detailed description of programs and techniques, see Cleave & Fey, 1997). Other studies have explicitly compared the relative efficiency of specific techniques. For example, conversational recasting has been identified as a more efficient technique than imitation for promoting generalization to spontaneous speech (Camarata, Nelson, & Camarata, 1994; Nelson, Camarata, Welsh, Butkovsky, & Camarata, 1996; see also chapter 23 by Fey & Finestack), at least when these techniques are used in isolation. However, the use of imitation, when used to contrast grammatical forms or to practice accessing the phonological form of a target morpheme, remains an issue worthy of further investigation (cf. Fey et al., 2003). Future research is also needed to examine the most efficient goal-attack strategies, especially for children with many areas of language deficits. Tyler and her colleagues (Tyler et al., 2003) revealed that greater morphosyntactic gains were observed for children with co-occurring phonological and morphosyntactic deficits when intervention targets alternated between these two domains from week to week as opposed to targeting these areas sequentially in 12-week blocks or simultaneously for 24 weeks.

Yet to implement focused stimulation procedures, practicing clinicians are still faced with the daunting task of selecting and prioritizing morphosyntactic targets. Several important questions remain to be fully evaluated. For example, is there an ideal time to initiate intervention on morphosyntactic targets? Which targets should be selected? How should they be prioritized? If a structure is prioritized in treatment, will a child's acquisition of this structure facilitate the acquisition of related structures? Although answers to these questions are far from certain, some implications for the design of intervention can be drawn from the existing intervention literature and from descriptive studies of morphosyntactic development in typical and atypical populations.

As more is learned about the nature of morphosyntactic growth trajectories, interventionists may be better able to time interventions to children's underlying biological propensities for language learning (Rice, 2004). In the meantime, intervention objectives and techniques can be better matched to the morphosyntactic tasks of early grammatical development. That is, for children with MLUs under 3.00 who have just begun to produce simple sentences, intervention should focus upon the emergence and productivity of structures within a system rather than upon the use or mastery of a single form. In a recent longitudinal study of slow-developing language learners, Hadley and Short (2005) documented a consistent order of emergence among three tense morphemes: copula BE, third person singular, and auxiliary BE. Moreover, the full set emerged across the paradigm before strong productivity of the earliest emerging form was apparent. Importantly, these morphemes reflect a system of contrasts for marking tense across different predicate types. To facilitate emergence of such grammatical contrasts, simple contrasts between predicate and verbal states might be emphasized initially (e.g., *The baby is hungry. She needs milk*) followed by contrasts between states and actions (e.g., *The baby is drinking.*). Use of grammatical contrasts have been used to teach novel derivational morphemes in short-term learning paradigms (e.g., Connell, 1987; Kiernan & Snow, 1999; Swisher, Restrepo, Plante, & Lowell, 1995; Swisher & Snow, 1994) as well as in more naturalistic settings (i.e., focused contrasts, Bunce & Watkins, 1995). After productive use of contrasting target morphemes is apparent, intervention can then shift toward mastery of given structures. By this time, MLUs are likely to be nearing 3.00.

As treatment goals shift toward mastery, clinicians may eliminate concerns about *which* morphosyntactic structures to prioritize by applying a cyclical goal attack strategy (cf. Cleave & Fey, 1997; Tyler et al., 2003). Given what is known about children's difficulties with finite verb morphology, a treatment objective could be to increase the obligatory marking of finiteness. With this goal, different surface structures that mark finiteness could be targeted for a set period of time (e.g., 60 minutes). Evidence for the psychological reality of underlying grammatical features has been demonstrated through a recent intervention study by Leonard, Camarata, Brown, and Camarata (2004). In this study, children received intervention on either third person singular present tense or forms of auxiliary BE. Children in each group showed significantly greater use of their targeted morphemes as well as cross-morpheme generalization to the other form. However, cross-morpheme generalization to past tense -*ed* (which shares tense but not agreement features with the other morphemes) was not observed. Thus, the use of cyclical goal attack strategies for targets sharing grammatical features would reflect an appreciation for the gradual nature of language development, the way in which related structures share similar growth trajectories (Rice et al., 1998), and the need to target multiple morphemes within these systems until more is understood about the nature of cross-morpheme generalization patterns (Leonard et al., 2004).

The facilitation of morphosyntax also requires clinicians to be knowledgeable about the developmental relationships between the acquisition of morphosyntax, semantic representation, and discourse. To begin, detection of morphosyntactic forms and analysis of their function will be simplified when the content words in the sentence are already known. Modeling and production practice with grammatical contrasts appear to be helpful; however, explicit metalinguistic instruction on the rules governing the use of bound morphemes is not effective (Connell, 1987; Swisher et al., 1995). Clinicians must also know the semantic contexts in which a particular morphosyntactic form is most likely to appear (Johnson & Fey, 2006; Ogiela et al., 2005). Typically developing children produce past *-ed* morphology with greater accuracy in accomplishment predicates compared to activities, particularly for verbs with more phonologically complex codas (Johnson & Fey, 2006; Johnson & Morris, 2007). Therefore, when targeting past tense morphology, clinicians can assist children by selecting verbs with phonologically simple codas (e.g., *showed*) and targeting these in semantically facilitating contexts with clear results or endpoints (e.g., *He showed me the picture*). Similarly, clinicians must know the discourse contexts in which forms are felicitous. If a clinician intends to target third person singular present, it is crucial to recognize that the simple present is only marked on state verbs (e.g., *goes, fits, needs, wants*). When this morpheme marks action verbs, its use reflects habitual aspect rather than simple present (e.g., *She rides the bus to school* [*every day*] vs. *She is riding the bus to school* [*right now*]). Thus, the more clinicians know about the controlling environments for specific morphosyntactic structures, the more they will be able to manipulate the language-learning task at hand to meet the needs of children.

CONCLUSIONS

Several large-scale cross-sectional and longitudinal investigations have characterized the morphosyntactic deficits of children with SLI. More recently, cross-population comparison studies have begun to appear in the literature. Although preliminary, findings from these studies suggest that there are both similarities and differences in the manifestation of morphosyntactic deficits as well as subsets of children across clinical populations who present with nearly identical difficulties. Additional research is needed to explain the patterns of relative strengths, weaknesses, and error types observed across these different groups of language learners. The study of children's morphosyntactic deficits has also led to several assessment approaches that can be used to improve the identification of children with morphosyntactic deficits in different clinical populations. Future research is needed to refine assessment tools for use with younger children in particular. Finally, several comprehensive treatment programs have been developed to facilitate children's development of morphosyntax. Future research is needed to determine the optimal timing, intensity, and duration of these interventions to maximize children's successful participation in their social and academic settings.

ACKNOWLEDGEMENTS

The authors would like to thank Matthew Rispoli, April Garrity, and Sonja Pruitt for help with the literature review and for numerous discussions about morphosyntax. Appreciation is also extended to Michael Hegarty for his expertise in linguistic theory and to Andrea Zukowski for her expertise on Williams syndrome.

REFERENCES

Abbeduto, L., & Murphy, M. M. (2004). Language, social cognition, maladaptive behavior, and communication in Down syndrome and Fragile X syndrome. In M. L. Rice & S. F. Warren (Eds.), *Developmental language disorders: From phenotypes to etiologies* (pp. 77–98). Mahwah, NJ: Lawrence Erlbaum Associates.

Balason, D. V., & Dollaghan, C. A. (2002). Grammatical morpheme production in 4-year-old children. *Journal of Speech, Language, and Hearing Research, 45,* 961–969.

Bartolucci, G., & Albers, R. J. (1974). Deictic categories in the language of autistic children. *Journal of Autism and Childhood Schizophrenia, 4,* 131–141.

Bartolucci, G., Pierce, S. J., & Streiner, D. (1980). Cross-sectional studies of grammatical morphemes in autistic and mentally retarded children. *Journal of Autism and Developmental Disorders, 10,* 39–49.

Beastrum, S., & Rice, M. L. (1986). *Comprehension and production of the articles* a *and* the. Paper presented at the convention of the American Speech-Language-Hearing Association, Detroit, MI.

Bedore, L., & Leonard, L. B. (1998). Specific language impairment and grammatical morphology: A discriminant function analysis. *Journal of Speech, Language, and Hearing Research, 41,* 1185–1192.

Betz, S. K. (2005). *Language based event-related potentials in children with and without specific language impairment.* Unpublished dissertation, University of Kansas, TX.

Beverly, B. L., & Williams, C. C. (2004). Present tense Be use in young children with specific language impairment: Less is more. *Journal of Speech, Language, and Hearing Research, 47,* 944–956.

Bishop, D. V. M. (1994). Grammatical errors in specific language impairment: Competence or performance limitations? *Applied Psycholinguisics, 15,* 507–550.

Bishop, D. (2003). *Test for Reception of Grammar–2.* San Antonio, TX: Harcourt Assessment.

Bishop, D. V. M. (2005). DeFries-Fulker analysis of twin data with skewed distributions: Cautions and recommendations from a study of children's use of verb inflections. *Behavior Genetics, 35,* 479–490.

Bishop, D. V. M., Adams, C. V., & Norbury, C. F. (2006). Distinct genetic influences on grammar and phonological short-term memory deficits: Evidence from 6-year-old twins. *Genes, Brain and Behavior, 5,* 168–169.

Botting, N., & Conti-Ramsden, G. (2003). Autism, primary pragmatic difficulties, and specific language impairment: Can we distinguish them using psycholinguistic markers? *Developmental Medicine and Child Neurology, 45,* 515–524.

Brock, J. (2007). Language abilities in Williams syndrome: A critical review. *Development and Psychopathology, 19,* 97–127.

Bromberg, H., Ullman, M., Marcus, G., Kelly, K., & Coppolla, M. (1994). *A dissociation of memory and grammar: Evidence from Williams syndrome.* Paper presented at the Boston University Conference on Language Development, Boston, MA.

Brown, R. (1973). *A first language.* Cambridge, MA: Harvard University Press.

Bryant, C. (2003). *Assessing the emergence of tense markers in young children: Is parent report valid?* Unpublished master's thesis, Northern Illinois University, DeKalb.

Bunce, B., & Watkins, R. (1995). Language intervention in a preschool classroom: Implementing a language-focused curriculum. In M. Rice & K. Wilcox (Eds.), *Building a language-focused curriculum for the preschool classroom: Vol. 1. A foundation for lifelong learning* (pp. 39–72). Baltimore: Paul H. Brookes.

Camarata, S., Nelson, K., & Camarata, M. (1994). Comparison of conversational recasting and imitative procedures for training grammatical structures in children with specific language impairment. *Journal of Speech and Hearing Research, 37,* 1414–1423.

Carrow-Woolfolk, E. (1999). *Test of Auditory Comprehension of Language* (3rd ed.). Austin, TX: PRO-ED.

Chapman, R. S., & Hesketh, L. J. (2000). Behavioral phenotype of individuals with Down syndrome. *Mental Retardation and Developmental Disabilities, 6,* 84–95.

Chapman, R. S., Schwartz, S. E., & Kay-Raining Bird, E. (1991). Language skills of children and adolescents with Down syndrome: I. *Journal of Speech, Language, and Hearing Research*, *34*, 1106–1120.

Chapman, R. S., Seung, H. K., Schwartz, S. E., & Kay-Raining Bird, E. (1998). Language skills of children and adolescents with Down syndrome: II. Production deficits. *Journal of Speech, Language, and Hearing Research*, *41*, 861–873.

Chapman, R. S., Seung, H. K., Schwartz, S. E., & Kay-Raining Bird, E. (2000). Predicting language production in children with Down syndrome: The role of comprehension. *Journal of Speech, Language, and Hearing Research*, *43*, 340–350.

Chomsky, N. (1995). *The minimalist program*. Cambridge, MA: MIT Press.

Clahsen, H., & Almazan, M. (1998). Syntax and morphology in Williams syndrome. *Cognition*, *68*, 167–198.

Clahsen, H., & Almazan, M. (2001). Compounding and inflection in language impairment: Evidence from Williams syndrome (and SLI). *Lingua*, *111*, 729–757.

Clahsen, H., & Temple, C. (2003). Words and rules in children with Williams syndrome. In Y. Levey & J. Schaeffer (Eds.), *Language competence across populations* (pp. 323–352). Hillsdale, NJ: Lawrence Erlbaum Associates.

Cleave, P., & Fey, M. (1997). Two approaches to the facilitation of grammar in children with language impairments: Rationale and description. *American Journal of Speech-Language Pathology*, *6*(1), 22–32.

Cleave, P. L., & Rice, M. (1997). An examination of the morpheme BE in children with specific language impairment: The role of contractibility and grammatical form class. *Journal of Speech, Language, and Hearing Research*, *40*, 480–492.

Connell, P. (1987). Teaching language rules as solutions to language problems: A baseball analogy. *Language, Speech, and Hearing Services*, *18*, 194–205.

Conti-Ramsden, G. (2003). Processing and linguistic markers in young children with specific language impairment (SLI). *Journal of Speech, Language, and Hearing Research*, *46*, 1029–1037.

Conti-Ramsden, G., Botting, N., & Faragher, B. (2001). Psychological markers for specific language impairment (SLI). *Journal of Child Psychology and Psychiatry*, *42*, 741–748.

Dale, P. S. (1991). The validity of a parent report measure of vocabulary and syntax at 24 months. *Journal of Speech and Hearing Research*, *34*, 565–571.

Dale, P. S. (2001). *The MacArthur Communicative Development Inventory: Level III*. University of Missouri, Columbia.

Dawson, J., Stout, C., & Eyer, J. (2003). *Structured Photographic Expressive Language Test* (3rd ed.). DeKalb, IL: Janelle.

Dawson, J., Stout, C., Eyer, J., Tattersall, P., Fonkalsrud, J., & Croley, K. (2005). *Structured Photographic Expressive Language Test, Preschool* (2nd ed.). DeKalb, IL: Janelle.

DeThorne, L. S., Johnson, B. W., & Loeb, J. W. (2005). A closer look at MLU: What does it really measure? *Clinical Linguistics and Phonetics*, *19*, 635–648.

Eadie, P. A., Fey, M. E., Douglas, J. M., & Parsons, C. L. (2002). Profiles of grammatical morphology and sentence imitation in children with specific language impairment and Down syndrome. *Journal of Speech, Language, and Hearing Research*, *45*, 720–732.

Eisenberg, S. L., Fersko, T. M., & Lundgren, C. (2001). The use of MLU for identifying language impairment in preschool children: A review. *American Journal of Speech-Language Pathology*, *10*, 323–342.

Evans, J., Viele, K., Kass, R., & Tang, F. (2002). Grammatical morphology and perception of synthetic and natural speech in children with specific language impairments. *Journal of Speech, Language, and Hearing Research*, *45*, 494–504.

Eyer, J., & Leonard, L. (1995). Functional categories and specific language impairment: A case study. *Language Acquisition*, *4*, 177–203.

Fenson, L., Dale, P., Reznick, J., Thal, D., Bates, E., Hartung, J., Pethick, S., & Reilly, J. (2003). *MacArthur-Bates Communicative Developmental Inventories*. Baltimore: Paul H. Brookes.

Fey, M., Cleave, P., & Long, S. (1997). Two models of grammar facilitation in children with language impairments: Phase 2. *Journal of Speech and Hearing Research*, *40*, 5–19.

Fey, M., Cleave, P., Long, S., & Hughes, D. (1993). Two approaches to the facilitation of grammar in children with language impairment: An experimental evaluation. *Journal of Speech and Hearing Research*, *36*, 141–157.

Fey, M., Long, S., & Finestack, L. (2003). Ten principles of grammar facilitation for children with specific language impairments. *American Journal of Speech-Language Pathology*, *12*, 3–15.

Goffman, L., & Leonard, J. (2000). Growth of language skills in preschool children with specific language impairment: Implications for assessment and intervention. *American Journal of Speech-Language Pathology*, *9*, 151–165.

Grela, B., & Leonard, L. B. (2000). The influence of argument-structure complexity on the use of auxiliary verbs by children with SLI. *Journal of Speech, Language, and Hearing Research*, *43*, 1115–1125.

Grela, B., Rashiti, L., & Soares, M. (2004). Dative prepositions in children with specific language impairment. *Applied Psycholinguistics*, *25*, 467–480.

Grela, B., Synder, W., & Hiramatsu, K. (2005). The production of novel root compounds in children with specific language impairment. *Clinical Linguistics and Phonetics*, *19*, 701–715.

Hadley, P. A. (1998). Early verb-related vulnerability among children with specific language impairment. *Journal of Speech, Language, and Hearing Research*, *41*, 1384–1397.

Hadley, P. A. (2006). Assessing the emergence of grammar in toddlers at-risk for specific language impairment. *Seminars in Speech and Language*, *27*, 173–186.

Hadley, P. A., & Holt, J. (2006). Individual differences in the onset of tense marking: A growth curve analysis. *Journal of Speech, Language, and Hearing Research*, *49*, 984–1000.

Hadley, P. A., & Rice, M. L. (1996). Emergent uses of BE and DO: Evidence from children with specific language impairment. *Language Acquisition*, *5*, 209–243.

Hadley, P. A., & Short, H. (2005). The onset of tense marking in children at-risk for specific language impairment. *Journal of Speech, Language, and Hearing Research*, *48*, 1344–1362.

Hegarty, M. (2005). *Feature-based functional categories: The structure, acquisition, and specific impairment of functional systems*. Berlin: Mouton de Gruyter.

Howlin, P. (1984). The acquisition of grammatical morphemes in autistic children: A critique and replication of the findings of Bartolucci, Pierce, and Streiner, 1980. *Journal of Autism and Developmental Disorders*, *14*, 127–136.

Ingram, D., & Morehead, D. (2002). Morehead & Ingram (1972) revisited. *Journal of Speech, Language, and Hearing Research*, *45*, 559–563.

Jacobson, P., & Schwartz, R. (2005). English past tense use in bilingual children with language impairment. *American Journal of Speech Language Pathology*, *14*, 313–323.

Johnson, B., & Fey, M. (2006). Interaction of lexical and grammatical aspect in toddlers' language. *Journal of Child Language*, *33*, 419–435.

Johnson, B., & Morris, S. (2007). Clinical implications of the effects of lexical aspect and phonology on children's production of the regular past tense. *Child Language Teaching and Therapy*, *23*, 287–306.

Johnston, J. R. (1985). Fit, focus, and functionality: An essay on early language intervention. *Child Language Teaching and Therapy*, *1*, 125–134.

Johnston, J. (2001). An alternate MLU calculation: Magnitude and variability of effects. *Journal of Speech, Language, and Hearing Research*, *44*, 156–164.

Joseph, R. M., Tager-Flusberg, H., & Lord, C. (2002). Cognitive profiles and social-communicative functioning in children with autism spectrum disorder. *Journal of Child Psychology and Psychiatry and Allied Disciplines*, *43*, 807–821.

Kamhi, A. G., & Catts, H. W. (1986). Toward an understanding of developmental language and reading disorders. *Journal of Speech and Hearing Research*, *51*, 337–347.

Karmiloff-Smith, A., Grant, J., Berthoud, I., Davies, M., Howlin, P., & Udwin, O. (1997). Language and Williams syndrome: How intact is intact? *Child Development*, *68*, 246–262.

Kiernan, B., & Snow, D. (1999). Bound-morpheme generalization by children with SLI: Is there a functional relationship with accuracy of response to training targets? *Journal of Speech, Language, and Hearing Research*, *42*, 649–662.

Kjelgaard, M. M., & Tager-Flusberg, H. (2001). An investigation of language impairment in autism: Implications for genetic subgroups. *Language and Cognitive Processes, 16*, 287–308.

Klee, T., Stokes, S. F., Wong, A. M., Fletcher, P., & Gavin, W. J. (2004). Utterance length and lexical diversity in Cantonese-speaking children with and without specific language impairment. *Journal of Speech, Language, and Hearing Research, 47*, 1396–1410.

Krantz, L. R., & Leonard, L. (2007). The effect of temporal adverbs on past tense production. *Journal of Speech, Language, and Hearing Research, 50*, 137–148.

Krause, M., & Penke, M. (2002). Inflectional morphology in German Williams syndrome. *Brain and Cognition, 48*, 410–413.

Lahey, M. (1990). Who shall be called language disordered? Some reflections and one perspective. *Journal of Speech and Hearing Disorders, 55*, 612–620.

Laws, G., & Bishop, D. V. M. (2003). A comparison of language abilities in adolescents with Down syndrome and children with specific language impairment. *Journal of Speech, Language, and Hearing Research, 46*, 1324–1339.

Leonard, L. B. (1995). Functional categories in the grammars of children with specific language impairment. *Journal of Speech and Hearing Research, 38*, 1270–1283.

Leonard, L. B. (1998). *Children with specific language impairment*. Cambridge, MA: MIT Press.

Leonard, L. B., Bortolini, U., Caselli, M. C., McGregor, K. K., & Sabbadini, L. (1992). Morphological deficits in children with specific language impairment: The status of features in the underlying grammar. *Language Acquisition, 2*, 151–179.

Leonard, L., Camarata, S., Brown, B., & Camarata, M. (2004). Tense and agreement in the speech of children with specific language impairment: Patterns of generalization through intervention. *Journal of Speech, Language, and Hearing Research, 47*, 1363–1379.

Leonard, L. B., Deevy, P., Miller, C. A., Rauf, L., Charest, M., & Kurtz, R. (2003). Surface forms and grammatical functions: Past tense and passive participle use by children with specific language impairment. *Journal of Speech, Language, and Hearing Research, 46*, 43–55.

Leonard, L. B., Eyer, J., Bedore, L., & Grela, B. (1997). Three accounts of the grammatical morpheme difficulties of English-speaking children with specific language impairment. *Journal of Speech, Language, and Hearing Research, 40*, 741–752.

Leonard, L. B., Miller, C. A., Deevy, P., Rauf, L., Gerber, E., & Charest, M. (2002). Production operations and the use of nonfinite verbs by children with specific language impairment. *Journal of Speech, Language, and Hearing Research, 45*, 744–758.

Leonard, L. B., Miller, C. A., & Gerber, E. (1999). Grammatical morphology and the lexicon in children with specific language impairment. *Journal of Speech, Language, and Hearing Research, 40*, 741–752.

Leonard, L. B., Miller, C. A., Grela, B., Holland, A. L., Geber, E., & Petucci, M. (2000). Production operations contribute to the grammatical morpheme limitations of children with specific language impairment. *Journal of Memory and Language, 43*, 362–378.

Levy, Y. (2002). Longitudinal study of language acquisition in two children with Williams Syndrome. In B. Skarabela, S. Fish, & A. Do (Eds.), *Proceedings of the 26th Boston University Conference on Child Language Development* (pp. 348–358), Somerville, MA: Cascadilla Press.

Levy, Y., & Herman, S. (2003). Morphological abilities of Hebrew-speaking adolescents with Williams syndrome, *Developmental Neuropsychology, 23* (1&2), 59–83.

Loeb, D. F. (1994). *Pronoun case errors of children with and without specific language impairment: Evidence from a longitudinal elicited imitation task*. Paper presented at the Stanford Child Language Research Forum. Stanford, CA.

Loeb, D. F., & Leonard, L. (1988). Specific language impairment and parameter theory. *Clinical Linguistics and Phonetics, 2*, 317–327.

Loeb, D. F., & Leonard, L. (1991). Subject case marking and verb morphology in normally developing and specifically impaired children. *Journal of Speech and Hearing Research, 34*, 340–346.

Loeb, D. F., & Mikesic, E. (1992). Pronominal acquisition in language-impaired and normally developing children. *Kansas University Working Papers in Language Development, 6*, 285–303.

Lukács, Á., Racsmány, C., & Pléh, C. (2001). Vocabulary and morphological patterns in Hungarian children with Williams syndrome: A preliminary report. *Acta Linguistica Hungarica, 48* (1–3), 243–269.

Mackie, C., & Dockrell, J. (2004). The nature of written language deficits in children with SLI. *Journal of Speech, Language, and Hearing Research, 47*, 1469–1483.

Marchman, V., Wulfeck, B., & Ellis Weismer, S. (1999). Morphological productivity in children with normal language and SLI: A study of past tense. *Journal of Speech, Language, and Hearing Research, 40*, 165–178.

Marshall, C. (2004). *The morpho-phonological interface in specific language impairment.* Unpublished doctoral dissertation. University College London, UK.

McCauley, R. (2001). *Assessment of Language Disorders in Children.* Mahwah, NJ: Lawrence Erlbaum Associates.

McGregor, K., & Leonard, L. B. (1994). Subject pronoun and article omissions in the speech of children with specific language impairment: A phonological interpretation. *Journal of Speech and Hearing Research, 37*, 171–181.

Mervis, C. B. (2003). Williams syndrome: Fifteen years of psychological research. *Developmental Neuropsychology, 23* (1&2), 1–12.

Mervis, C. B., Morris, C., Bertrand, J., & Robinson, B. (1999). Williams syndrome: Findings from an integrated program of research. In H. Tager-Flusberg (Ed.), *Neurodevelopmental disorders* (pp. 65–110). Cambridge, MA: MIT Press.

Miller, C., & Deevy, P. (2003). A method for examining productivity of grammatical morphology in children with and without specific language impairment. *Journal of Speech, Language, and Hearing Research, 46*, 1154–1165.

Miller, C., & Leonard, L. B. (1998). Deficits in finite verb morphology: Some assumptions in recent accounts of specific language impairment. *Journal of Speech, Language, and Hearing Research, 41*, 701–707.

Montgomery, J., & Leonard, L. B. (1998). Real-time inflectional processing by children with specific language impairment: Effects of phonetic substance. *Journal of Speech, Language, and Hearing Research, 41*, 1432–1443.

Moore, M. (1995). Error analysis of pronouns by normal and language-impaired children. *Journal of Communication Disorders, 28*, 57–72.

Nelson, K., Camarata, S., Welsh, J., Butkovsky, L., & Camarata, M. (1996). Effects of imitative and conversational recasting treatment on the acquisition of grammar in children with specific language impairment and younger language-normal children. *Journal of Speech, Language, and Hearing Research, 39*, 850–859.

Newcomer, P. L., & Hammill, D. D. (1997). *Test of Language Development, Primary* (3rd ed.). Austin, TX: PRO-ED.

Niedeggen-Bartke, S. (2001). *The default-rule, sub-regularities, and irregulars in the morphology of German Williams syndrome.* Paper presented at the 25th Annual Boston University Conference on Language Development, Boston, MA.

Norbury, C. F., Bishop, D. V. M., & Briscoe, J. (2001). Production of English finite verb morphology: A comparison of SLI and mild-moderate hearing impairment. *Journal of Speech, Language, and Hearing Research, 44*, 165–178.

Oetting, J. B., Cantrell, J. P., & Horohov, J. E. (1999). A study of specific language impairment (SLI) in the context of nonstandard dialect. *Clinical Linguistics and Phonetics, 13*, 25–44.

Oetting, J. B., Cleveland, L. H., & Cope, R. (2008). Empirically-derived combinations of tools and clinical cutoffs: An illustrative case with a sample of culturally/linguistically diverse children. *Language, Speech, and Hearing Services in Schools, 39*, 44–53.

Oetting, J. B., & Garrity, A. W. (2006). Variation within dialects: A case of Cajun/Creole influence within child SAAE and SWE. *Journal of Speech, Language, and Hearing Research, 49*, 16–26.

Oetting, J. B., & Horohov, J. E. (1997). Past tense marking by children with and without specific language impairment. *Journal of Speech and Hearing Research, 40*, 62–74.

Oetting, J. B., & McDonald, J. L. (2001). Nonmainstream dialect use and specific language impairment. *Journal of Speech, Language, and Hearing Research, 44*, 207–223.

Oetting, J. B., & Rice, M. (1993). Plural acquisition in children with specific language impairment. *Journal of Speech and Hearing Research, 36*, 1236–1248.

Ogiela, D. A., Casby, M., & Schmitt, C. (2005). Event realization and default aspect: Evidence from children with specific language impairment. In A. Brugos, M. R. Clark-Cotton, & S. Ha (Eds.), *Proceedings of the 29th Annual Boston University Conference in Language Development* (pp. 424–435). Somerville, MA: Cascadilla Press.

Owen, A. J., & Leonard, L. B. (2006). The production of finite and nonfinite complement clauses by children with specific language impairment and their typically developing peers. *Journal of Speech, Language, and Hearing Research, 49*, 548–571.

Paul, R., & Alford, S. (1993). Grammatical morpheme acquisition in 4-year-olds with normal, impaired, and late-developing language. *Journal of Speech and Hearing Research, 36*, 1271–1275.

Perona, K., Plante, E., & Vance, R. (2005). Diagnostic accuracy of the Structured Photographic Expressive Language Test (3rd ed., SPELT–3). *Language, Speech, and Hearing Services in Schools, 36*, 103–115.

Pine, J., Joseph, K., & Conti-Ramsden, G. (2004). Do data from children with specific language impairment support the agreement/tense omission model? *Journal of Speech, Language, and Hearing Research, 47*, 913–923.

Pine, J., Rowland, C., Lieven, E., & Theakston, A. (2005). Testing the agreement/tense omission model: Why the data on children's use of non-nominative 3psg subjects count against ATOM. *Journal of Child Language, 32*, 269–289.

Plante, E., & Vance, R. (1994). Selection of preschool language tests: A data-based approach. *Language, Speech, and Hearing Services in Schools, 25*, 15–24.

Plante, E., & Vance, R. (1995). Diagnostic accuracy of two tests of preschool language. *American Journal of Speech-Language Pathology, 4*, 70–76.

Redmond, S. M. (2003). Children's productions of the affix -ed in past tense and past participle contexts. *Journal of Speech, Language, and Hearing Research, 46*, 1095–1109.

Redmond, S. M. (2004). Conversational profiles of children with ADHD, SLI, and typical development. *Clinical Linguistics and Phonetics, 18*(2), 107–125.

Redmond, S. M. (2005). Differentiating SLI from ADHD children using sentence recall and production of past tense morphology. *Clinical Linguistics and Phonetics, 19*(2), 109–127.

Redmond, S. M., & Johnston, S. S. (2001). Evaluating the morphological competence of children with severe speech and physical impairments. *Journal of Speech, Language, and Hearing Research, 44*, 1362–1375.

Redmond, S. M., & Rice, M. L. (2001). Detection of irregular verb violations by children with and without SLI. *Journal of Speech, Language, and Hearing Research, 44*, 655–669.

Rice, M. L. (1991). Children with specific language impairment: Toward a model of teachability. In N. A. Krasnegor, D. M. Rumbaugh, R. L. Schiefelbusch, & M. Studdert-Kennedy (Eds.), *Biological and behavioral determinants of language development* (pp. 447–480). Hillsdale, NJ: Lawrence Erlbaum Associates.

Rice, M. L. (1999). Specific grammatical limitations in children with specific language impairment. In H. Tager-Flusberg (Ed.), *Neurodevelopmental disorders* (pp. 331–360). Cambridge, MA: MIT Press.

Rice, M. L. (2004). Growth models of developmental language disorders. In M. L. Rice & S. F. Warren (Eds.), *Developmental language disorders: From phenotypes to etiologies.* (pp. 207–240). Mahwah, NJ: Lawrence Erlbaum Associates.

Rice, M. L., Haney, K. R., & Wexler, K. (1998). Family histories of children with SLI who show extended optional infinitives. *Journal of Speech, Language, and Hearing Research, 41*, 419–432.

Rice, M. L., & Oetting, J. B. (1993). Morphological deficits of children with SLI: Evaluation of number marking and agreement. *Journal of Speech and Hearing Research, 36*, 1249–1257.

Rice, M. L., Tomblin, J. B., Hoffman, L., Richman, W. A., & Marquis, J. (2004). Grammatical tense deficits in children with SLI and nonspecific language impairment: Relationships with nonverbal IQ over time. *Journal of Speech, Language, and Hearing Research, 47*, 816–834.

Rice, M. L., & Wexler, K. (1996). Toward tense as a clinical marker of specific language impairment in English-speaking children. *Journal of Speech and Hearing Research*, *39*, 1239–1257.

Rice, M. L., & Wexler, K. (2001). *Rice/Wexler Test of Early Grammatical Impairment*. San Antonio, TX: Psychological Corporation.

Rice, M. L., Wexler, K., & Cleave, P. L. (1995). Specific language impairment as a period of extended optional infinitive. *Journal of Speech and Hearing Research*, *38*, 850–863.

Rice, M. L., Wexler, K., & Hershberger, S. (1998). Tense over time: The longitudinal course of tense acquisition in children with specific language impairment. *Journal of Speech, Language, and Hearing Research*, *41*, 1412–1431.

Rice, M. L, Wexler, K., Marquis, J., & Hershberger, S. (2000). Acquisition of irregular past tense by children with SLI. *Journal of Speech, Language, and Hearing Research*, *43*, 1126–1145.

Rice, M. L., Wexler, K., & Redmond, S. M. (1999). Grammatical judgments of an extended optional infinitive grammar: Evidence from English-speaking children with specific language impairment. *Journal of Speech, Language, and Hearing Research*, *42*, 943–961.

Rispoli, M. (1998). Me or my: Two different patterns of pronoun case errors. *Journal of Speech, Language, and Hearing Research*, *41*, 385–393.

Rispoli, M. (1999). A developmental psycholinguistic approach to pronoun case error: A reply to Schütze. *Journal of Speech, Language, and Hearing Research*, *42*, 1020–1022.

Roberts, J., Rice, M., & Tager-Flusberg, H. (2004). Tense marking in children with autism, *Applied Psycholinguistics*, *25*, 429–448.

Robinson, B. F., Mervis, C. B., & Robinson, B. W. (2003). The roles of verbal short-term memory and working memory in the acquisition of grammar by children with Williams syndrome. *Developmental Neuropsychology*, *23* (1&2), 13–31.

Ross, S, Oetting, J. B., & Stapleton, B. (2004). Preterite Had + V-ed: A developmental narrative discourse structure in AAE. *American Speech*, *79*, 167–193.

Rutter, T., & Buckley, S. (1994). The acquisition of grammatical morphemes in children with Down syndrome. *Down Syndrome: Research and Practice*, *2*, 76–82.

Scarborough, H. (1990). Index of Productive Syntax. *Applied Psycholinguistics*, *11*, 1–22.

Scarborough, H., Rescorla, L., Tager-Flusberg, H., Fowler, A., & Sudhalter, V. (1991). The relation of utterance length to grammatical complexity in normal and language-disordered groups. *Applied Psycholinguistics*, *12*, 23–45.

Schütze, C. T. (1999). Explaining patterns of pronoun case error: Response to Rispoli. *Journal of Speech, Language, and Hearing Research*, *42*, 1016–1020.

Semel, E., Wiig, E. H., & Secord, W. A. (2003) *Clinical Evaluation of Language Fundamentals* (4th. ed.). San Antonio, TX: Psychological Corporation.

Seymour, H., Bland-Steward, L., & Green, L. (1998). Difference versus deficit in child African American English. *Language, Speech, and Hearing Services in the Schools*, *29*, 96–108.

Smith-Locke, K. M. (1993). Morphological analysis and the acquisition of morphology and syntax in specifically language impaired children. *Haskins Laboratories Status Report on Speech Research*, *114*, 113–138.

Spaulding, T., Plante, E., & Farinella, K. (2006). Eligibility criteria for language impairment: Is the low end of normal always appropriate? *Language, Speech, and Hearing Services in the Schools*, *37*, 61–72.

Swisher, L., Restrepo, M. A., Plante, E., & Lowell, S. (1995). Effect of implicit and explicit "rule" presentation on bound-morpheme generalization in specific language impairment. *Journal of Speech, Language, and Hearing Research*, *38*, 168–173.

Swisher, L., & Snow, D. (1994). Learning and generalization components of morphological acquisition by children with specific language impairment: Is there a functional relation? *Journal of Speech, Language, and Hearing Research*, *37*, 1406–1413.

Tager-Flusberg, H. (1989). A psycholinguistic perspective on language development in autistic children. In G. Dawson (Ed.). *Autism: New directions in diagnosis, nature and treatment* (pp. 92–115). New York: Guilford Press.

Tager-Flusberg, H. (2000). The challenge of studying language development in autism. In L. Menn

& N. Bernstein Ratner (Eds.), *Methods for studying language production* (pp. 313–332). Mahwah, NJ: Lawrence Erlbaum Associates.

Tager-Flusberg, H. (2004). Do autism and specific language impairment represent overlapping language disorders? In M. L. Rice & S. F. Warren (Eds.), *Developmental language disorders: From phenotype to etiologies.* Mahwah, NJ: Lawrence Erlbaum Associates.

Thal, D. J., O'Hanlon, L., Clemmons, M., & Fralin, L. (1999). Validity of parent report measure of vocabulary and syntax for preschool children with language impairment. *Journal of Speech, Language, and Hearing Research, 42,* 482–496.

Thomas, M., Grant, J., Barham, Z., Gsodl, M., Laing, E., & Lakusta, L. (2001). Past tense formation in Williams syndrome. *Language and Cognitive Processes, 16,* 143–176.

Thordardottir, E. T., Chapman, R. S., & Wagner, L. (2002). Complex sentence production by adolescents with Down syndrome. *Applied Psycholinguistics, 23,* 163–183.

Tomblin, J. B., Hafeman, L., & O'Brien, M. (2003). Autism and autism risk in siblings of children with specific language impairment. *International Journal of Language and Communication Disorders, 38,* 235–250.

Tyler, A., Lewis, K., Haskill, A., & Tolbert, L. (2002). Efficacy and cross-domain effects of a morpho-syntax and a phonology intervention. *Language, Speech, and Hearing Services in Schools, 33,* 52–66.

Tyler, A., Lewis, K., Haskill, A., & Tolbert, L. (2003). Outcomes of different speech and language goal attack strategies. *Journal of Speech, Language, and Hearing Research, 46,* 1077–1094.

van der Lely, H. K. J., Rosen, S., & Adlard, A. (2004). Grammatical language impairment and the specificity of cognitive domains: Relations between auditory and language abilities, *Cognition, 94,* 167–183.

van der Lely, H. K. J., & Ullman, M. (1996). The computation and representation of past tense morphology in specifically language impaired and normally developing children. In A. Stringfellow, D. Cahana-Amitay, E. Hughes, & A. Zukowski (Eds.), *Proceedings of the 20th annual Boston University Conference on Child Language Development* (pp. 804–815). Somerville, MA: Cascadilla Press.

Volterra, V., Caselli, M. C., Caprici, O., Tonucci, F., & Vicari, S. (2003). Early linguistic abilities of Italian children with Williams syndrome. *Developmental Neuropsychology, 23* (1&2), 33–58.

Wexler, K., Schütze, C., & Rice, M. (1998). Subject case in children with SLI and unaffected controls: Evidence for the agr/tns omission model. *Language Acquisition: A Journal of Developmental Linguistics, 7,* 317–344.

Windsor, J., Scott, C. M., & Street, C. K. (2000). Verb and noun morphology in the spoken and written language of children with language learning disabilities. *Journal of Speech, Language, and Hearing Research, 43,* 1322–1336.

Wulfeck, B. B. (1993). A reaction time study of grammaticality judgments in children. *Journal of Speech and Hearing Research, 36,* 1208–1215.

Zukowski, A. (2005). Knowledge of constraints on compounding in children and adolescents with Williams syndrome. *Journal of Speech, Language, and Hearing Research, 48,* 79–92.

16

Semantics in Child Language Disorders

KARLA K. McGREGOR

*C*hildren with deficits in semantics have difficulty understanding and conveying the meanings of words, sentences, and extended discourse. The nature of these deficits varies from population to population and, of course, from child to child. This chapter is an overview of semantic deficits that characterize selected pediatric populations as well as state-of-the-art assessments and interventions for addressing these deficits.

SEMANTIC DEFICITS ACROSS POPULATIONS

Specific Language Impairment

Often the first sign of specific language impairment (SLI) is late onset of first words (for a more detailed discussion of SLI see chapter 1 by Schwartz). As a group, children with SLI begin expressing meaning with conventional words 11 months later than do typical children (Trauner, Wulfeck, Tallal, & Hesselink, 1995). Receptive vocabulary may be delayed as well, and late talkers who exhibit receptive delays are more likely to be diagnosed with SLI during the preschool years than their late-talking peers with intact receptive abilities (Thal, Reilly, Seibert, Jeffries, & Fenson, 2004). Children with SLI continue to exhibit delays in receptive vocabulary (Bishop, 1997; Clarke & Leonard, 1996) and expressive vocabulary (Leonard, Miller, & Gerber, 1999; Thal, O'Hanlon, Clemmons, & Fralin, 1999; Watkins, Kelly, Harbers, & Hollis, 1995) throughout the preschool period.

During the school years, the vocabulary deficits of children affected by SLI may become more marked (Haynes, 1992; Stothard, Snowling, Bishop, Chipchase, & Kaplan, 1998). Characteristics may include word-finding problems (Dockrell, Messer, George, & Wilson, 1998; Lahey & Edwards, 1999; Leonard, Nippold, Kail, & Hale, 1983), sparse lexical semantic representations (McGregor & Appel, 2002; McGregor, Newman, Reilly, & Capone, 2002; Munro & Lee, 2005), and sparse semantic category knowledge (Kail & Leonard, 1986). Comprehending the meaning of connected speech may be problematic as well. For example, when asked to identify agents in NVN, NNV, and VNN constructions, the comprehension strategies applied by school-aged children with SLI were easily disrupted by increases in external processing demands (Evans, 2002). Schoolchildren with SLI have difficulty comprehending the meaning of stories, whether the meanings are explicit or implicit and whether the stories are presently verbally or nonverbally (Bishop & Adams, 1992). Adolescents with SLI continue to present with difficulties in communicating meanings especially via figurative language and extended discourse (Norbury, 2004; Rinaldi, 2000).

Semantic deficits of children with SLI may stem from a number of causes. First, these children have poor working memory (Bishop, North, & Donlan, 1995; Dollaghan & Campbell, 1998; Gathercole & Baddeley, 1990; Montgomery, 1995). Given that mapping words to meanings requires holding novel word forms in short term memory while hypothesizing the meaning of the word from contextual cues, this limitation could reduce successful word mappings. Gathercole and Baddeley (1989) found scores on the Children's Nonword Repetition Test, a measure of working memory, to account for significant variation in receptive vocabulary growth over a two-year period. More direct evidence for a causal role of working memory limitations in the semantic deficits associated with SLI was provided by Gathercole and Baddeley in 1990. They found children with SLI to lag 20 months behind typical children in receptive vocabulary development but four years behind these same children in working memory performance, leading them to conclude that the word-learning lag was a consequence of the extraordinary memory deficit.

We can look to the grammar for another potential source of the semantic deficit. The grammatical impairment that is considered a hallmark of SLI (Leonard, 1998) may have knock-on effects on the semantic system. Children who are developing normally use syntactic cues such as word order, function words, and inflections to *bootstrap* the semantics of words. For example, one can infer from a sentence like "the girl *glimmed* some *pov*" that *glim* is an action that is carried out on objects and that *pov* is an object of a particular kind, a substance. Given the grammatical impairments of children with SLI, they should be less able to make such inferences. Indeed syntactic bootstrapping limitations among children with SLI are well documented (Eyer et al., 2002; O'Hara & Johnston, 1997; Rice, Cleave, & Oetting, 2000; Shulman & Guberman, 2007; van der Lely, 1994). Syntactic bootstrapping is thought to play a more important role in verb learning than in noun learning (Gentner & Boroditski, 2001; Gillette, Gleitman, Gleitman, & Lederer, 1999; Gleitman, 1990), therefore the syntactic bootstrapping limitations of children with SLI may be one basis for their problems with verbs (Conti-Ramsden & Jones, 1997; Fletcher & Peters, 1984; Loeb, Pye, Redmond, & Richardson, 1996; Oetting, Rice, & Swank, 1995; Watkins, Rice, & Moltz, 1993; Windfuhr, Faragher, & Conti-Ramsden, 2002). Mental state predicates may present challenges for similar reasons (Johnston, Miller, & Tallal, 2001).

Developmental Delay

Children with developmental delays present with language impairment secondary to mental retardation; however, their semantic systems are not necessarily commensurate with their level of mental retardation (see chapter 2 by McDuffie & Abbeduto for additional information about developmental delays). Scores on intelligence tests account for only 29% of the variability in vocabulary scores earned by children and adolescents with mental retardation of mixed etiology (Facon, Facon-Bollengier, & Grubar, 2002). Furthermore, the relationship between intelligence and semantic development depends on which aspects of semantic development are being measured. For example, the mental age scores of schoolchildren with mild mental retardation correlate more strongly with their knowledge of relational labels (e.g., size, direction, quantity, time) than with their knowledge of labels for objects and events (Fazio, Johnston, & Brandl, 1993). Finally, the relation between mental age and semantic development varies with etiology. Children with Down syndrome (DS) and Williams syndrome (WS) will be compared to illustrate this point.

In some respects, children with DS present profiles of overall language development that parallel those of children with SLI (see Laws & Bishop, 2004 for a review); in particular, semantic development is generally stronger than grammatical development but is still delayed relative to nonverbal mental age (Kumin, 1996). Like children with SLI, children with DS may experience semantic deficits because of limitations in working memory (Chapman, 1995; Hick, Botting, & Conti-Ramsden, 2005; Jarrold & Baddeley, 1997; Kay-Raining Bird & Chapman, 1994; Mervis, 1990; Wang & Bellugi, 1994).

Hick et al. (2005) compared the vocabulary development, on both receptive and expressive levels, of children with DS or SLI and their normally developing peers over the course of a year, beginning when participants in all three groups presented with nonverbal mental ages between 42 and 60 months. The DS and SLI groups had similar vocabulary scores at the final test, and both groups were significantly lower than their normal peers. However, their patterns of vocabulary growth varied over the course of the year. The children with DS began at a higher level, but their vocabulary growth plateaued, whereas the children with SLI made slow but steady progress. Miller (1995) reported deficits in the rate of vocabulary learning in children with DS relative to mental-age peers, with these deficits increasing with age, again suggesting a plateau.

In contrast to children with DS, the receptive vocabularies of children with WS are higher than mental age expectations (and sometimes higher than chronological age expectations as well) (Brock, 2007). This observation must be qualified in several ways. First, superior lexical skills are not yet apparent in younger children affected by WS (Thal, Bates, & Bellugi, 1989); in fact, emergence of first words is late and generally commensurate with mental age (Mervis, Robinson, Rowe, Becerra, & Klein-Tasman, 2003). Second, a number of studies have revealed qualitative differences in semantic knowledge among children with WS. For example, they demonstrate less sophisticated underlying semantic structures as compared to receptive vocabulary-matched peers with moderate learning difficulties (Jarrold, Hartley, Phillips, & Baddeley, 2000) and their ability to define words, retrieve words for naming, and identify names in contexts that require fine-grained semantic knowledge are weaker than those of their typically developing mental-age peers (Brock, 2007). Finally, children with WS do not abide by the same word-learning heuristics as normally developing children, indicating atypical developmental pathways (Laing et al., 2002; Stevens & Karmiloff-Smith, 1997).

In summary, it is difficult to characterize semantic deficits associated with developmental delay. Degree of mental retardation accounts for the deficit to some extent but patterns of deficit vary with etiology and with the aspect of semantic development under consideration.

Autism Spectrum Disorders

Children with autism spectrum disorders (ASD) are a heterogeneous group with language abilities that range from normal to nonverbal (for additional information on autism see chapter 3 by Gerenser). Semantic development is a concern for many of these children. Among those who are verbal, loss of meaningful words in the expressive vocabulary is a unique, but not universal, symptom of ASD during the second year of life (Lord, Shulman, & DiLavore, 2004), thus the potential usefulness of word-learning abnormalities as a clinical warning sign of autism.

Among children with ASD, the frequency of social bids toward communicative partners (e.g., verbal imitation and use of gesture to initiate joint attention) is positively associated with expressive vocabulary growth (Smith, Mirenda, & Zaidman-Zait, 2007). Because most children with ASD find it challenging to attend to and process social information, they may miss important cues to word meaning. For example, children with ASD are less able than their peers with developmental delays to infer an intended referent from a speaker's eyegaze (Baron-Cohen, Baldwin, & Crowson, 1997). Perhaps the mismappings that result from the inability to fully utilize social cues to meaning explain, in part, the use of neologisms and idiosyncratic words on the part of speakers with ASD (Volden & Lord, 1991).

For children with ASD, deficits in social cognition disrupt development of theory of mind (Baron-Cohen, Tager-Flusberg, & Cohen, 1993). Theory of mind refers to the awareness that others have mental and emotional states and that these states may differ from one's own or from reality. Theory of mind deficits are reflected in the difficulty that children with ASD have in comprehending and using mental state terms such as "imagine" and "pretend" (Baron-Cohen, 1991; Baron-Cohen et al., 1994). Theory of mind deficits also lead to problems sustaining conversations and constructing coherent narratives (Bruner & Feldman, 1993).

Recent research reveals the existence of a subgroup of children particularly relevant to discussions of semantics and ASD. These children have a profile of language deficits similar to those of children with SLI (Kjelgaard & Tager-Flusberg, 2001; Tager-Flusberg & Joseph, 2003). This profile includes some weaknesses in semantic processing. For example, Norbury (2005) compared two groups of 9- to 17-year-olds with ASD, one group with low verbal performance and one with verbal abilities in the normal range, with a group of children with SLI and a group of normally developing age mates. These groups participated in tasks requiring word-to-picture matching for words with both dominant meanings (e.g., *bank* to mean a place to keep money) and secondary meanings (e.g. *bank* to mean the edge of a river). The children with ASD and low verbal abilities performed like the children with SLI. These children were less able than the other two groups to identify secondary word meanings correctly and were less efficient in using semantic context to facilitate this identification. Another similarity emerges by comparing the work of Tager-Flusberg (1985) and McGregor and Waxman (1998). These investigators found typical organization of the semantic lexicons of children with ASD and SLI, respectively, but in both cases lexicons that were less developed and more prone to error. A final similarity is that children with ASD and those with SLI have difficulty using sentences and discourse to aid interpretation of meaning (López & Leekam, 2003; Montgomery, 1995; Norbury, 2004). Despite these overlapping profiles, the similarities between children with SLI and children with ASD plus low verbal abilities are not without limit. Of the two, children with SLI are poorer at using syntax to bootstrap the referents of new words (Shulman & Guberman, 2007).

Hearing Impairment

Children with hearing impairment (HI) face some obvious challenges in learning language via audition (for a more detailed summary of hearing impairment see chapter 4 by Cleary). There is an inverse relationship between severity of HI and receptive vocabulary as measured by the Peabody Picture Vocabulary Test (PPVT-III) (Dunn, Dunn, & Williams, 1997). On average, 7- and 8-year-olds with mild impairments earned a standard score of 89.3 on the PPVT-III; whereas, at the highest severity level, those with profound impairments earned a standard score of 62.7 (Wake, Poulakis, Hughes, Carey-Sargeant, & Rickards, 2005). In contrast, age at enrollment in intervention, but not severity of loss, predicted outcomes on the PPVT (Dunn & Dunn, 1965) or PPVT–R (Dunn & Dunn, 1981) among a group of 5-year-olds with congenital HI. Children who were enrolled in intervention by 11 months of age demonstrated significantly better vocabulary than did later-enrolled children (Moeller, 2000). Furthermore, the scores of the early intervention recipients were similar to those of their normal hearing age mates. Family involvement also played an important role in outcome.

Older children with HI, those already receiving intervention, continue to struggle with word learning. Stelmachowicz, Pittman, Hoover, and Lewis (2004) compared schoolchildren with mild–moderate HI to their normal hearing age mates in a task that involved exposure to eight novel words in an animated story and a posttest of their learning that measured comprehension via word-to-picture matching. The children with HI identified fewer referents on the posttest. Significant predictors of performance were existing vocabulary knowledge, hearing status, dB level at which the words were presented, and number of exposures to the target words in the story. The number of words to be learned probably influenced outcomes as well. Consider, for example, the findings of Gilbertson and Kamhi (1995). These investigators studied children with mild–moderate HI and younger normal-hearing peers who were matched on the basis of receptive vocabulary knowledge. These children were presented with four novel words in the context of a hiding game. The two groups performed similarly when learning was measured as the ability to comprehend the new words (word-to-referent matching), but the HI group required more exposures to the words before they could recall the words for production. Therefore, whereas word-learning problems associated with HI were evident in comprehension when eight new words were presented (Stelmachowicz et al., 2004), they were evident in production but not comprehension when four new words were presented (Gilbertson & Kamhi, 1995). Finally, recent data indicate that the word-learning problems experienced by children with HI are not as severe, on average, as those associated with SLI. In a word-learning task modeled after Gilbertson and Kamhi (1995), children with mild–moderate HI performed better than did their peers with SLI (Hansson, Forsberg, Löfqvist, Mäki-Torkko, & Sahlén, 2004).

Beyond hearing the words, why might children with HI have any difficulties with word learning? One hypothesis is that, because of limited acuity, their language development slows, and, without the foundation of a strong linguistic system, bootstrapping and integration of new words into the semantic lexicon is difficult. This hypothesis is supported indirectly by the variables that are reported to predict word learning in children with HI. These variables include the status of the existing vocabulary as measured by receptive vocabulary tests (Gilbertson & Kamhi, 1995; Stelmachowicz et al., 2004) and the status of verbal working memory (Gilbertson & Kamhi, 1995; Hansson et al., 2004).

Semantic deficits associated with HI are not limited to the lexicon—rather, several studies reveal broader deficits. As a group, children with HI are late to produce two-term semantic relations (Kiese-Himmel & Ohlwein, 2003). Older children with HI. The processing of the semantic dimensions of spoken words in a different way from their normally hearing peers (Jerger & Stout, 1993). Adolescents with HI have great difficulty applying top-down, contextual strategies to pull meaning from written text (Banks et al., 1989), especially when those meanings are implicit (Doran & Anderson, 2003). Finally, children and adolescents with HI demonstrate delays in theory of mind. Children ranging from 6 to 18 years (mean age = 15.28 years), with hearing losses ranging from mild to profound, comprehended emotion labels at a level comparable to that of their much younger hearing peers (mean age = 8.77 years) matched on verbal ability (Dyck, Farrugia, Shochet, & Holmes-Brown, 2004). Depressed language levels and reduced exposure to talking about mental states may limit access to such labels (Peterson & Siegal, 2000).

Reading Impairment

By definition, children with dyslexia (for more information on dyslexia see chapter 5 by Shaywitz et al.) do not have semantic deficits: rather, their reading problems involve difficulty decoding print, and that difficulty is generally attributed to deficits in phonological processing (e.g., Shankweiler et al., 1995). However, there are important reasons to pay attention to semantics when considering children with reading impairments (see review in McGregor, 2004). First, not all children with reading impairments have dyslexia. A subgroup of reading-impaired children is composed of "poor comprehenders." Unlike children with dyslexia, these children can decode print, but they have difficulty attaching meaning to it (Nation & Snowling, 1998; Oakhill, 1982; Stothard & Hulme, 1995). These children are particularly challenged when they must depend on semantic context for correct interpretation, as required for low-frequency exception words (Nation & Snowling, 1998). Their semantic deficits extend to oral language as well. Nation and Snowling (1998) found these children to be weaker than normal age-mates on both receptive and expressive subtests of the Test of Word Knowledge (Wiig & Secord, 1992). In addition, on probes of oral language ability, they were poorer at synonym judgment (e.g., fast–quick) but not rhyme judgment (e.g., joke–coke) and poorer at semantic fluency (e.g., say all of the animals you can think of) but not rhyme fluency (e.g., say all the rhymes you can think of for the word "plate"). Though these children can learn orally presented word forms as well as their normal age-mates, they are particularly weak in learning the meanings of those words (Nation, Snowling, & Clarke, 2007).

A second population of impaired readers is also relevant to discussions of semantics. Children with hyperlexia decode print at grade levels above their general functioning; however, this skill is sharply dissociated from their ability to attach meaning to print (Nation, 1999; Silberberg & Silberberg, 1967). Children with hyperlexia typically have receptive and expressive oral language deficits as well. These deficits include problems with single-word meanings (Aram, Rose, & Horwitz, 1984) and meanings expressed by sentences and narrative discourse (Snowling & Frith, 1986). These children may learn to read words before they can speak them (Elliot & Needleman, 1976). Unlike children with dyslexia, children with hyperlexia typically have some degree of mental retardation (Nation, 1999). They also have opposite strengths and weakness: as compared to children with dyslexia, their decoding is superior but their comprehension is much poorer (Snowling, 1987).

A third reason to focus on semantics and reading impairment is that people who have difficulty reading read more slowly, less often, and with less enjoyment, thereby limiting important opportunities for word learning throughout the life span. These missed opportunities tend to exacerbate any existing deficiencies in the semantic system, creating a downward spiral of skills relative to developmental expectations, a phenomenon dubbed the *Matthew effect* (Stanovich, 1986). Evidence for the reading–semantics connection is that, among children (Cunningham & Stanovich, 1991; Echols, Stanovich, West, & Zehr, 1996) and adults (Stanovich & Cunningham, 1992), exposure to print accounts for significant variance in vocabulary size, even when age, IQ, reading comprehension, and phonological decoding skills are factored out. More direct evidence of Matthew effects is that the size of vocabulary gaps between good and poor readers grows over time (Serniclaes, Sprenger-Charolles, Carré, & Demonet, 2001; White, Graves, & Slater, 1990; but see Bast & Reitsma, 1998). Matthew effects are generally thought of in connection with reading impairment; however, children from each of the populations considered in this chapter may be prone to these effects. In particular, slow reading development is frequently associated with SLI (Catts, 1993; Catts, Fey, Zhang, & Tomblin, 1999; Stothard et al., 1998) and HI (Conrad, 1977; DiFrancesca, 1972; Holt, Traxler, & Allen, 1997). Furthermore, a number of children with ASD exhibit hyperlexia (Burd & Kerbeshian, 1985; Grigorenko et al., 2002; Whitehouse & Harris, 1984).

Summary

Semantic deficits are characteristic of a variety of developmental language disorders. Regardless of diagnosis, some symptoms are common. These include slow word learning, difficulties with semantic content that relies upon theory of mind, problems using nonliteral and secondary meanings, and limitations in use of sentence and discourse contexts to infer meaning. Despite commonalities across diagnostic groups, the nature and severity of semantic deficits will vary greatly from child to child. Therefore, careful assessment will be necessary to guide clinical management.

ASSESSMENT

Assessment of semantics is trickier than it may first appear. Beyond the very earliest stages of semantic development, the vocabulary is too large to measure in its entirety. Also, because children find themselves in very different learning contexts, vocabulary is extremely individual in its content. The child with a bedtime prayer ritual has a meaning attached to the word *pray*; the child whose parents are dairy farmers knows the difference between *calf, cow*, and *bull*. Furthermore, though we can determine that a child does or does not know a given word, it is more difficult to determine the depth of knowledge for any given word. The dairy farmers' child is certainly not alone in knowing the meaning of *cow* at a young age, but she may well have a deeper knowledge of *cow* than the child of the accountant who lives down the street. Finally, meaning is not conveyed by single words alone but by combinations of those words into phrases, sentences, and textual discourse. Measuring semantic development at each of these levels is important, but it is also difficult, as the complete disentangling of semantic and grammatical contributions to any observed deficits may not be possible. The following sections summarize the primary approaches to assessment of semantics and the best uses of each approach are emphasized.

Parent Report

For the child who is very young or very low functioning, parent report can be a valid, reliable, and efficient means of determining the approximate size of the lexicon. In the last decade or so, checklists (e.g., Fenson et al., 1993; Rescorla, 1989) have largely replaced diary methods as a means of gathering parents' reports of their children's vocabulary knowledge. Checklists are preferred to diaries because they are more efficient, involving a one-time tally as opposed to daily notes, and more reliable, involving a recognition format rather than free recall.

The MacArthur–Bates Communicative Development Inventory (MBCDI; Fenson et al., 1993) is a widely used checklist. The Words and Gestures form of the MBCDI assesses the receptive and expressive vocabulary of children functioning between 8 and 16 months of age by asking parents to endorse object, action, and description words that their child understands and says. The Words and Sentences form of the MBCDI is a 680-word checklist designed to assess the expressive vocabularies of children functioning in the 16–30-month age range. A large literature supports the reliability and validity of the MBCDI (see Fenson et al., 2007, for a review).

The MBCDI allows an estimation of vocabulary size and comparison to normative expectations via percentile and age equivalency scores. Normative data are also available for a number of different language communities (Fenson et al., 2007), including deaf and hard-of-hearing children who use English (Mayne, Yoshinaga-Itano, Sedey, & Carey, 2000a, 2000b) and ASL (Anderson & Reilly, 2002). A unique aspect of the MBCDI is that it includes normative data for individual words—that is, one can determine at what age the majority of children in the normative sample were reported to know *tickle*, for example (Dale & Fenson, 1996). Therefore the MBCDI may be effective not only as an assessment instrument, but also as one means of selecting appropriate vocabulary to target in early intervention. Finally, several recent or pending improvements to the MBCDI stand to increase its clinical utility. These include a short form for maximum efficiency in educational settings, a specialized form that is maximally sensitive to the performance of lower functioning children, and a database on MBCDI performance from a number of clinical populations, including children with DS, cleft palate, and drug exposure (Fenson et al., 2007).

Standardized Tests

To measure receptive or expressive semantics at the word, phrase, sentence, or text levels in the older or higher-functioning child, standardized tests are a frequently employed option. A sample of standardized tests designed in part or full to measure semantics appears in Table 16.1, together with target ages. Most of these tests estimate the child's semantic knowledge and compare that knowledge to that of the normative sample via standard scores, percentiles, and age-equivalencies. These tests do not attempt to document the entire semantic system as this becomes an impossible goal once vocabulary size increases beyond roughly 500 or 600 words and word combining is well underway (Fenson et al., 1994). Rather, these tests estimate receptive or expressive development by sampling performance on what is meant to be a representative subset of the system. They do so efficiently and they are widely used; however, some caution is warranted.

First, tests should be selected carefully. Because semantic knowledge is heavily influenced by cultural experiences, cultural bias may lead to an underestimation of a child's developmental level. No standardized test is perfect in this regard, but some are better than others (see Washington & Craig, 1999). Second, because only a subsample of age-appropriate words and phrases can be included in any one test, these tests are not particularly helpful in guiding selection of intervention goals. Third, empirical results do not support the use of standardized vocabulary tests for screening or diagnosis of primary language disorders (Gray, Plante, Vance, & Henrichsen, 1999). Finally, the clinician should be cognizant that a majority of tests approach the measurement of word knowledge in a binary fashion: the child gets the item right or wrong. Therefore, most standardized tests do not measure depth of semantic knowledge.

Probes

Nonstandardized probes offer solutions to the limitations of standardized tests. Take for example, their limitations in measuring depth, as opposed to breadth, of semantic knowledge. The sensitivity of tests to depth of knowledge may be improved by presenting target words in forced-choice formats with a large number of close semantic (and phonological) distractors (Chiat, 2000). Parsons, Law, and Gascoigne (2005) employed this method successfully as a means of goal selection in a case study of two children with SLI. Another approach is illustrated by McGregor and her colleagues (2002), who asked children to draw and to define objects that they could and could not name. Both the drawings and the definitions were rated for the amount of information they contained, not just whether they were accurate or inaccurate, thereby yielding an estimate of depth of knowledge. The drawing and defining ratings correlated with each other, and both ratings were lower for misnamed objects than for correctly named objects. These findings suggest the validity of the probes as a means of exploring depth of word knowledge. These are only two examples. Miller and Paul (1995) provide a variety of suggestions for additional probes of extant semantic knowledge for all levels of language learners.

TABLE 16.1 Some standardized tests that measure semantic development

Test	Receptive/ Expressive	Age
Adolescent Language Screening Test (ALST; Morgan & Guilford, 1984)	receptive, expressive	11;0–17;11
Bankson Language Test (BLT–2; Bankson, 1990)	receptive, expressive	3;0–6;11
Carolina Picture Vocabulary Test (CPVT; Layton & Holmes, 1985)	receptive	4;0–11;5
Clinical Evaluation of Language Fundamentals (CELF–4; Semel, Wiig, & Secord, 2003)	receptive, expressive	5;0–21;0
Clinical Evaluation of Language Fundamentals: Preschool–2 (CELF: P–2; Wiig, Secord, & Semel, 2005)	receptive, expressive	3;0–6;11
Comprehensive Assessment of Spoken Language (CASL; Carrow-Woolfolk, 1999a)	expressive	3;0–21;11
Comprehensive Receptive and Expressive Vocabulary Test (CREVT–2; Wallace & Hammill, 2002)	receptive, expressive	4;0–89;0
Developmental Indicators for the Assessment of Learning (DIAL–3; Mardell-Czudnowski & Goldenberg, 1998)	receptive, expressive	3;0–6;11
Expressive One Word Picture Vocabulary Test (EOWPVT; Brownell, 2000a)	expressive	2;0–18;11
Expressive Vocabulary Test (EVT–2; Williams, 2007)	expressive	2;6–90 +
Oral and Written Language Scales (OWLS; Carrow-Woolfolk, 1996)	receptive, expressive	5;0–21;11
Peabody Picture Vocabulary Test (PPVT–4; Dunn & Dunn, 2007)	receptive	2;6–90 +
Preschool Language Assessment Instrument (PLAI–2; Blank, Rose, & Berlin, 2003)	receptive, expressive	3;0–5;11
Preschool Language Scale (PLS–4; Zimmerman, Steiner, & Pond, 2002)	receptive, expressive	Birth–6;11
Receptive-Expressive Emergent Language Test (REEL–3; Bzoch, League, & Brown, 2003)	receptive, expressive	Birth–3;0
Receptive One Word Picture Vocabulary Test (ROWPVT–2000; Brownell, 2000b)	receptive	2;0–18;11
Reynell Developmental Language Scales (RDLS–III; Edwards et al., 1997)	receptive, expressive	1;3–7;6
Rossetti Infant-Toddler Language Scale (RITLS; Rosetti, 2006)	receptive, expressive	Birth–3;0
Test of Adolescent and Adult Language (TOAL–4; Hammill, Brown, Larsen, & Wiederholt, 2007)	receptive, expressive	12;0–24;11
Test of Adolescent/Adult Word Finding (TAWF; German, 1990)	expressive	12;0–80;0
Test of Auditory Comprehension of Language (TACL–3; Carrow-Woolfolk, 1999b)	receptive	3;0–9;11
Test of Early Language Development (TELD–3; Hresko, Reid, & Hammill, 1999)	receptive, expressive	2;0–7;0
Test of Language Development: Intermediate (TOLD: I–3; Hammill, & Newcomer, 1997a)	receptive, expressive	8;0–12;11
Test of Language Development: Primary (TOLD: 3P; Hammill, & Newcomer, 1997b)	receptive, expressive	4;0–8;11
Test of Semantic Skills: Intermediate (TOSS: I; Bowers, Huisingh, LoGuidice, & Orman, 2004a)	receptive, expressive	9;0–13;11
Test of Semantic Skills: Primary (TOSS: P; Huisingh, Bowers, LoGuidice, & Orman, 2004)	receptive, expressive	4;0–8;11
Test of Word Finding (TWF–2; German, 2000)	expressive	4;0–12;11
Test of Word Knowledge (ToWK; Wiig & Secord, 1992)	receptive, expressive	5;0–17;11
WORD Test–2: Elementary (Bowers, Huisingh, LoGiudice, & Orman, 2004b)	expressive	6;0–11;11
WORD Test–2: Adolescent (Huisingh, Bowers, LoGiudice, & Orman, 2005)	expressive	12;0–17;11

Probes may also be designed to measure the child's ability to learn new semantic information. As an example of such a dynamic assessment, consider Lederberg, Prezbindowski, and Spencer (2000), who observed children with HI during a rapid word-learning task and a novel mapping task. In the rapid word-learning task, the examiner pointed to a new object while naming it three times. The novel mapping task was similar, except that the examiner did not point out the object; instead, the child had to infer that the new name must refer to the new object, because the other objects in the environment had familiar names. The child passed either task if he or she could later identify the object in an array upon hearing its name and could also identify a new example of the object (i.e., one that was of a different color or size than the trained object). Performance on these tasks was indicative of the child's extant vocabulary development. Those with the largest vocabularies passed both tasks; those with moderately sized vocabularies passed the rapid word-learning but not the novel mapping task; and those with the smallest vocabularies passed neither task. Dynamic word learning also reflects extant vocabulary knowledge among hearing children (McGregor, Sheng, & Smith, 2005).

Dynamic assessments may be particularly useful when determining whether a child's poor vocabulary development is the result of a true impairment or of an environmental difference. Because vocabulary learning is highly dependent upon input and children from impoverished families are exposed to less input (Hart & Risley, 1995), standardized tests tend to overidentify these children (Dollaghan et al., 1999; Whitehurst, 1997). Graham (2005) compared children from lower and higher socioeconomic backgrounds on depth of word knowledge via a definition probe. The children from the lower SES families displayed shallower word knowledge. However, they fared well on a dynamic assessment involving novel word mapping, suggesting that the problem was one of exposure rather than impairment.

Language Samples

Language samples should not be ignored as a source of data on semantic development. One widely used and easily calculated measure is the number of different words (NDW) in the sample. NDW in a 50- or 100-utterance sample reliably differentiates children with SLI from their normally developing age-mates (Klee, 1992; Watkins et al., 1995). Furthermore, NDW reflects vocabulary breadth. For example, the number of different words (signs) produced by 4-year-olds who were deaf correlated with their receptive vocabulary scores on standardized measures (Everhart, 1993). Finally, NDW is readily interpretable as norms are available for children ages 3–13 (Miller & Chapman, 2000; Miller & Leadholm, 1992).

One limitation of NDW is that it is not independent of utterance length or total sample length; therefore it reflects not only lexical diversity but also grammatical ability and overall volubility. An alternative measure, D, is less vulnerable to sample size variations and is, therefore, a purer measure of lexical diversity (Owen & Leonard, 2002). Essentially, the D procedure involves multiple calculations of word type-to-word token ratios based on random samples of 35–50 tokens from a given language transcript (McKee, Malvern, & Richards, 2000). D calculations may be accomplished with VOCD, a program option within CLAN software (MacWhinney, 2000). D scores distinguish younger from older language learners (Owen & Leonard, 2002) and correlate positively with scores on expressive vocabulary tests (Silverman & Ratner, 2002). Moreover, a combination of D, MLU, and age accurately differentiates children with SLI from those with normal language development (Klee, Stokes, Wong, Fletcher, & Gavin, 2004).

Language samples can aid in the identification of word-finding deficits. Circumlocutions, reformulations, nonspecific words, and wrong word usages may be relevant signs (German & Simon, 1991). The rate of circumlocutions and reformulations can be interpreted in comparison to normative expectations if these are coded as mazes in the Systematic Analysis of Language Transcripts and the corresponding database is used for the normative comparison (Miller & Chapman, 2000).

Finally, language samples can be used to monitor generalization of treatment effects, especially when collected in contexts that are apt to elicit relevant targets. For example, asking the child to compare and contrast may elicit description words; asking for a fictional story may elicit temporal conjunctions; and asking for a summary of a chapter from a science book may elicit relevant academic vocabulary.

One caution about the use of language samples should be noted. The lexical semantic development of very young or low-functioning children may be underestimated by language samples because their word productions occur infrequently and may be highly context-dependent (Fenson et al., 1994). In these cases, parent report is a better alternative.

Summary

The breadth and depth of semantic development may be measured at varying levels of complexity, word, phrase, sentence, or text, and with a variety of tools, parent reports, standardized tests, and probes. Choosing the correct levels and the correct battery of measures will be a highly individual decision; however, the recommendations set forth by Watkins and DeThorne (2000) are generally applicable: (1) "Integrate multiple types of assessment tools in the evaluation of vocabulary abilities," (2) "Use measures with demonstrated validity for appropriate purposes," (3) "Recognize that vocabulary comprehension and production are heavily dependent on life experience," and (4) "Incorporate word-learning measures in vocabulary assessment practices" (Watkins & DeThorne, 2000, pp. 240–242).

INTERVENTION

Goals

Semantic interventions may be focused on development of the single-word lexicon or the integration of words into meaningful phrases, sentences, and text. At the most general level, goals may involve increasing the breadth or depth of the semantic lexicon. To achieve increased breadth, the child will learn new words and idiomatic phrases or, perhaps, less common or less literal meanings of old words. Also, for the higher functioning child, learning to create new meanings via word formation (i.e., compounding and derivation) or word combination (e.g., sentence construction and text building) may be an appropriate way to expand breadth of the semantic system. To increase depth, the child will enrich understanding of old words and phrases, perhaps by learning new semantic relationships between these words, relationships that might include coordination (e.g., *beetle, cricket*); collocation (e.g., *butter, knife*); superordination (e.g., *tool, compass*); synonymy (e.g., *thirsty, dehydrated*); or antonymy (e.g., *starving, satiated*).

Functionality is key in selecting target content. For example, the target vocabulary for children who are not yet communicating with conventional words or other symbols often includes names of important people (e.g., *mama, papa*) and favorite objects (e.g., *juice, bear*) as well as ways to express needs and desires (e.g., *help, more*). Functionality continues to guide goal selection for older, more sophisticated children. For example, a focus on vocabulary associated with academic themes or social situations may be functional for the adolescent with semantic deficits.

Finally, goals may focus on strategies in addition to content. When children are able to reflect on language, they are ready to learn strategies. These may be *learning to learn* strategies such as techniques for inferring meaning from context or *learning to remember* strategies such as mnemonics for word or meaning recall.

Techniques

Successful interventions for addressing semantic goals provide opportunities for the child to participate as an active learner in meaningful, interesting contexts that involve multiple exposures to the target content. This section is an overview of training and intervention research that illustrates the effectiveness of these general principles and points to more specific techniques for facilitating semantic development.

Some investigators have taken a didactic approach to semantic intervention, others a more incidental approach. Either of these (and their combination) can be effective. Consider, for example, the work of Yoder, Kaiser, Alpert, and Fischer (1993), who taught preschoolers with developmental delays new object labels in play contexts using a milieu method (Kaiser, Hendrickson, & Alpert, 1991). Milieu teaching is didactic. In this case, it involved asking the child to imitate the name of a new object and then answer a question that obligated an additional production of the name. Correct names were expanded into longer utterances by the teacher and rewarded by access to the object. Importantly, this didactic approach did not ignore the child's interest. The teaching took place in a motivating play context. Furthermore, half of the words were taught at moments when the child expressed interest in the objects, and half were taught at moments when the child's attention had to be directed to the object. Word learning occurred in both conditions, but more often in the condition that respected the child's interests.

Gray and her colleagues (Gray, 2003, 2004; Kiernan & Gray, 1998) have completed a series of studies with the general aim of determining how best to facilitate word learning among children affected by SLI. Their approach involves use of a didactic "supported-learning context" in which the instructor provides repeated models of new words in daily sessions, prompts the child to produce the words, and provides feedback to the child about accuracy of these productions during interactive play with toys. In such supported learning contexts, children with SLI do acquire new words. However, normally developing age-mates, the comparison group in these studies, typically learn to comprehend and to produce significantly more words and to achieve this learning in fewer trials. Presenting phonological cues (i.e., initial sound, syllable, or rhyme) or semantic cues (i.e., category, function, physical features) immediately after new words were modeled to the child with SLI enhanced their expressive learning and receptive learning, respectively (Gray, 2005). This finding illustrates the importance of direct teaching of semantic (or phonological) content.

In a series of studies, Rice and her colleagues (Oetting et al., 1995; Rice, Buhr, & Nemeth, 1990; Rice, Oetting, Marquis, Bode, & Pae, 1994) have examined the ability of children with SLI to learn words incidentally from cartoon-like narratives. An important difference between this approach and that of Gray is that there was no direct tutelage. Children with SLI did learn new words incidentally, but learning was more limited than that of age-matched peers. Increasing the numbers of exposures to words (from 3 to 10) enhanced the learning of the children with SLI to age-appropriate levels when learning was tested immediately after exposure to the narratives; however, this boost to learning was not retained when tested again a few days later (Rice et al., 1994).

Nash and Donaldson (2005) compared the word learning of children with SLI in didactic contexts (like those used by Gray) and incidental contexts (like those used by Rice). The two contexts were equally useful for teaching the word form, but the didactic context better promoted semantic learning. Specifically, the children with SLI—as well as their normally developing peers—demonstrated superior learning in the didactic context when learning was measured by recognition or production of correct word definitions. This is consistent with findings that direct definition instruction results in more words learned than incidental learning contexts (Baumann & Kameenui, 1991).

That is not to say that drill on definitions is the preferred method of didactic instruction. Adolescents with language-learning disabilities comprehended scientific text better when science vocabulary instruction focused on superordination (e.g., organizing target words into a semantic hierarchy) and collocation (e.g., using target words to answer cloze sentences) than on definitions (Bos & Anders, 1990). Similar semantic mapping activities may be modified for younger children. For example, semantic relations between target words may be emphasized via activities such as *which of these things belong together*, *odd-man out*, and quiz games with semantic clues (see Norbury & Chiat, 2000, Appendix 2, p. 162).

Given the size of the lexicon and the vast number of possible meaningful relations expressed by combinations of lexical items, didactic instruction of content alone is, arguably, a losing battle. Therefore, content goals may be supplemented by didactic instruction of compensatory strategies to aid future independent learning. A widely applied strategy is the keyword method. In this approach, the child is taught to construct a visual image that links the target word or phrase with a familiar similar-sounding word. For example, when learning the word *empirical*, the child could retrieve *peer* because of the similar word form, and then recall an image of a scientist peering at her data. The keyword method has demonstrated utility in both first- and second-language word learning (see reviews in Baumann & Kameenui, 1991; and Pressley, Levin, & Delaney, 1982) and is superior to other methods that involve rehearsal of definitions (Mastropieri, Scruggs, and Fulk, 1990) and exposure to words in meaningful sentence contexts (Condus, Marshall, & Miller, 1986). It has been used with children who have language-learning disabilities (Condus et al., 1986; Mastropieri et al., 1990), developmental delays (Scruggs, Mastropieri, & Levin, 1985), and behavioral disorders (Mastropieri, Emerick, & Scruggs, 1988). Logically this strategy will be most useful for children whose problems involve memory limitations in linking words to meanings.

The single best way to remediate semantic deficits may be to teach the child to be a successful and avid reader (Nagy, Herman, & Anderson, 1985). Although this is not possible for all children affected by pediatric language disorders, reading does figure prominently as a context for intervention in the semantic domain (see review in Kaderavek & Justice, 2002). Because written text is thematic, new words and concepts are naturally introduced together with related words and concepts, aiding both inferences about meaning and integration into the child's existing semantic network. Joint book reading (i.e., child and caregiver reading together) promotes word learning (e.g., Dale, Crain-Thoreson, Notari-Syverson, & Cole, 1996) and increases word combinations (e.g., Yoder, Spruytenburg, Edwards, & Davies, 1995) among children affected by language disorders.

The child who actively participates during joint book reading learns more words than does the child who participates passively (Ewers & Brownson, 1999). One method for stimulating the child's active role is termed dialogic reading (Whitehurst et al., 1988). In dialogic reading, the caregiver scaffolds the child's experience with storybooks so that the child eventually becomes the storyteller. The caregiver administers a sequence of techniques known as PEER beginning with a *prompt* for the child to say something about a book, followed by an *evaluation* of the child's comment and an *expansion* of the comment, and ending with a request to the child for *repetition* to ensure comprehension and aid learning. In other words, dialogic reading provides a didactic scaffold for the already rich incidental learning opportunities provided by storybooks. As an example of its effectiveness, consider that children with HI whose parents received 20 minutes of PEER training and storybooks supplemented with prompt questions made significantly greater gains on the PPVT-III (Dunn et al., 1997) after eight weeks of twice-weekly story reading than did children of untrained parents who used the same storybooks on the same time schedule (Fung, Chow, & McBride-Chang, 2005). Dialogic reading techniques implemented in day-care classrooms have also been successful in improving the vocabulary of hearing children from impoverished families (Hargrave & Sénéchal, 2000; Whitehurst et al., 1994).

Summary

There is a wide variety of interventions for enhancing semantic development, and this chapter includes only a small sample of the possibilities. Nonetheless, some themes emerged. Whether didactic or incidental teaching is employed, frequent exposure to targets in meaningful contexts is important. Those contexts may involve play, storybooks, or structured games and activities, depending on which of these maintains the child's interest and promotes active participation. Interventions that introduce or enhance semantic content as well as those that focus on strategies for learning and communicating meaning may be valuable.

CONCLUSIONS

Efforts to enhance a child's communication of meaning are no less than efforts to enhance a child's life. The status of the semantic system, particularly the lexicon, is a strong predictor of academic and social success (e.g., Gertner, Rice, & Hadley, 1994; Walker, Greenwood, Hart, & Carta, 1994). Fortunately, the semantic system is plastic and capable of change throughout the lifespan (Neville & Bruer, 2001). Therefore, enhancing the semantic development of children affected by developmental language disorders is not only a valuable goal but an attainable one. Continued attention to this goal in the home, the classroom, the clinic, and the laboratory is essential.

Future work on semantic deficits associated with developmental language disorders will build on our current knowledge base. This chapter, a broad overview of the extant literature, elaborates seven themes from this knowledge base: (1) Semantic deficits are characteristic of a variety of developmental language disorders; (2) these deficits may affect comprehension or expression of meaning at the word, phrase, sentence, or text levels; (3) assessment tools that aid in identification of semantic deficits include parent report surveys, standardized tests, nonstandardized probes of static or dynamic knowledge, and language samples; (4) increased breadth and depth of semantic content as well as strategies for learning, remembering, and using such content are useful goal areas; (5) some helpful components of semantic interventions include repeated exposure to targets, meaningful contexts, and active engagement on the part of the learner; (6) both incidental and didactic interventions can stimulate semantic development, though for some goals, didactic approaches may be more effective; and (7) reading provides excellent opportunities for incidental learning and a context to support didactic interactions.

ACKNOWLEDGMENTS

I thank Richard Schwartz for giving me the opportunity to synthesize this information, Ellen Marschner and Amanda Murphy for their assistance with Table 16.1, Christen Conrad for careful proofreading, Aicha Rochdi and Sung Hee Lee for fruitful discussions of the literature, and the National Institutes of Health for supporting my research via NIH-NIDCD R01 DC003698.

REFERENCES

Anderson, D., & Reilly, J. S. (2002). The MacArthur Communicative Development Inventory: Normative data for American Sign Language. *Journal of Deaf Studies and Deaf Education, 7*, 83–106.

Aram, D. M., Rose, D. F., & Horwitz, S. J. (1984). Hyperlexia: Developmental reading without meaning. In R. Malatesha & H. A. Whitaker (Eds.), *Dyslexia: A global issue* (pp. 517–531). The Hague: Martinus Nijhoff.

Banks, J., Fraser, R., Fyfe, J., Grant, C., Gray, M., MacAuley, M., & Williams, S. (1989). Teaching deaf children to read: A pilot study of a method. *Journal of the British Association of Teachers of the Deaf, 13*, 129–141.

Bankson, N. W. (1990). *Bankson Language Test* (2nd ed.). Austin, TX: PRO-ED.

Baron-Cohen, S. (1991, March). The development of a theory of mind in autism: Deviance and delay? *Psychiatric Clinics of North America, 14*, 33–51.

Baron-Cohen, S., Baldwin, D. A., & Crowson, M. (1997). Do children with autism use the speaker's direction of gaze strategy to crack the code of language? *Child Development, 68*, 48–57.

Baron-Cohen, S., Ring, H., Moriarty, J., Schmitz, B., Costa, D., & Ell, P. (1994). Recognition of mental state terms: Clinical findings in children with autism and a functional neuroimaging study of normal adults. *British Journal of Psychiatry, 165*, 640–649.

Baron-Cohen, S., Tager-Flusberg, H., & Cohen, D. J. (1993). *Understanding other minds: Perspectives from autism*. Oxford, UK: Oxford University Press.

Bast, J., & Reitsma, P. (1998). Analyzing the development of individual differences in terms of Matthew effects in reading: Results from a Dutch longitudinal study. *Development Psychology, 34*, 1373–1399.

Baumann, J. F., & Kameenui, E. J. (1991). Research on vocabulary instruction: Ode to Voltaire. In J. Flood, J. J. D. Lapp, & J. R. Squire (Eds.), *Handbook of research on teaching the English language arts* (pp. 604–632). New York: Macmillan.

Bishop, D. V. M. (1997). *Uncommon understanding: Development and disorders of language comprehension in children*. Hove, UK: Psychology Press.

Bishop, D. V. M., & Adams, C. (1992). Comprehension problems in children with specific language impairment: literal and inferential meaning. *Journal of Speech and Hearing Research, 35*, 119–129.

Bishop, D. V. M., North, T., & Donlan, C. (1995). Genetic basis of specific language impairment: Evidence from a twin study. *Developmental Medicine and Child Neurology, 37*, 56–71.

Blank, M., Rose, S. A., & Berlin, L. J. (2003). *Preschool Language Assessment Instrument* (2nd ed.). Austin, TX: PRO-ED.

Bos, D. S., & Anders, P. L. (1990). Effects of interactive vocabulary instruction on the vocabulary learning and reading comprehension of junior-high learning disabled students. *Learning Disability Quarterly, 13*, 31–42.

Bowers, L., Huisingh, R., LoGuidice, C., & Orman, J. (2004a). *Test of Semantic Skills—Intermediate* Austin, TX: PRO-ED.

Bowers, L., Huisingh, R., LoGiudice, C., & Orman, J. (2004b). *WORD Test 2—Elementary*. East Moline, IL: LinguiSystems.

Brock, J. (2007). Language abilities in Williams syndrome: A critical review. *Development and Psychopathology, 19*, 97–127.

Brownell, R. (2000a). *Expressive One Word Picture Vocabulary Test*. Novato, CA: Academic Therapy.

Brownell, R. (2000b). *Receptive One Word Picture Vocabulary Test (ROWPVT–2000)*. Novato, CA: Academic Therapy.

Bruner, J., & Feldman, C. (1993). Theories of mind and the problem of autism. In S. Baron-Cohen, H. Tager-Flusberg, & D. Cohen (Eds.), *Understanding Other Minds: Perspectives from Autism* (pp. 267–291). Oxford, UK: Oxford University Press.

Burd, L., & Kerbeshian, J. (1985). Inquiry into the incidence of hyperlexia in a statewide population of children with pervasive developmental disorder. *Psychological Reports, 57*, 236–238.

Bzoch, K. R., League, R., & Brown, V. L. (2003). *Receptive–Expressive Emergent Language Test* (3rd ed.). Austin, TX: PRO-ED.

Carrow-Woolfolk, E. (1996). *Oral and Written Language Scales*. Bloomington, MN: Pearson.

Carrow-Woolfolk, E. (1999a). *Comprehensive Assessment of Spoken Language*. Bloomington, MN: Pearson.

Carrow-Woolfolk, E. (1999b). *Test of Auditory Comprehension of Language* (3rd ed.). Austin, TX: PRO-ED.

Catts, H. W. (1993). The relationship between speech-language impairments and reading disabilities. *Journal of Speech and Hearing Research, 36*, 948–958.

Catts, H. W., Fey, M. E., Zhang, X., & Tomblin, J. B. (1999). Language basis of reading and reading disabilities: Evidence from a longitudinal investigation. *Scientific Studies of Reading, 3*, 331–362.

Chapman, R. S. (1995). Language development in children and adolescents with Down syndrome. In P. Fletcher & B. MacWhinney (Eds.), *Handbook of child language* (pp. 641–663). Oxford, UK: Blackwell.

Chiat, S. (2000). *Understanding children with language problems*. Cambridge, UK: Cambridge University Press.

Clarke, M., & Leonard, L. (1996). Lexical comprehension and grammatical deficits in children with specific language impairment. *Journal of Communication Disorders, 29*, 95–105.

Condus, M. M., Marshall, K. J., & Miller, S. R. (1986). Effects of the keyword mnemonic strategy on vocabulary acquisition and maintenance by learning disabled children. *Journal of Learning Disabilities, 19*, 609–613.

Conrad, R. (1977). The reading ability of deaf school-leavers. *British Journal of Educational Psychology, 47*, 138–148.

Conti-Ramsden, G., & Jones, M. (1997). Verb use in specific language impairment. *Journal of Speech, Language, and Hearing Research, 40*, 1298–1313.

Cunningham, A. E., & Stanovich, K. E. (1991). Tracking the unique effects of print exposure in children: Associations with vocabulary, general knowledge, and spelling. *Journal of Educational Psychology, 83*, 264–274.

Dale, P. S., Crain-Thoreson, C., Notari-Syverson, A., & Cole, K. I. (1996). Parent–child book reading as an intervention technique for young children with language delays. *Topics in Early Childhood Special Education, 16*, 213–235.

Dale, P. S., & Fenson, L. (1996). Lexical development norms for young children. *Behavior Research Methods, Instruments, and Computers, 28*, 125–127.

DiFrancesca, S. (1972). *Academic achievement test results of a national testing program for hearing-impaired students* (Spring, Series D., No. 9). Washington, DC: Gallaudet College, Office of Demographic Studies.

Dockrell, J. E., Messer, D., George, R., & Wilson, G. (1998). Children with word finding difficulties: Prevalence, presentation, and naming problems. *International Journal of Language and Communication Disorders, 33*, 445–454.

Dollaghan, C., & Campbell, T. (1998). Nonword repetition and child language impairment. *Journal of Speech, Language, and Hearing Research, 41*, 1136–1146.

Dollaghan, C. A., Campbell, T. F., Paradise, J. L., Feldman, H. M., Janosky, J. E., Pitcairn, D. N., & Kurs-Lasky, M. (1999). Maternal education and measures of early speech and language. *Journal of Speech, Language, and Hearing Research, 42*, 1432–1443.

Doran, J., & Anderson, A. (2003). Inferencing skills of adolescent readers who are hearing impaired. *Journal of Research in Reading, 26*, 256–266.

Dunn, L., & Dunn, L. (1965). *Peabody Picture Vocabulary Test*. Circle Pines, MN: American Guidance Service.

Dunn, L., & Dunn, L. (1981). *Peabody Picture Vocabulary Test–Revised (PPVT–R)*. Circle Pines, MN: American Guidance Service.

Dunn L., Dunn L., & Williams K. T. (1997). *Peabody Picture Vocabulary Test* (3rd ed.). Circle Pines, MN: American Guidance Service.

Dunn, L. M., & Dunn, D. M. (2007). *Peabody Picture Vocabulary Test* (4th ed.). Bloomington, MN: Pearson.

Dyck, M. J., Farrugia, C., Shochet, I. M., & Holmes-Brown, M. (2004). Emotion recognition/understanding ability in hearing- or vision-impaired children: Do sounds, sights, or words make the difference? *Journal of Child Psychology and Psychiatry, 45*, 789–800.

Echols, L., Stanovich, K., West, R., & Zehr, K. (1996). Using children's literacy activities to predict growth in verbal cognitive skills: a longitudinal investigation. *Journal of Educational Psychology, 88*, 296–304.

Edwards, S., Fletcher, P., Garman, M., Hughes, A., Letts, C., & Sinka, I. (1997). *Reynell Developmental Language Scales–III*. London, UK: Nelson.

Elliot, E., & Needleman, R. (1976). The syndrome of hyperlexia. *Brain and Language, 3*, 339–349.

Evans, J. L. (2002). Variability in comprehension strategy use in children with SLI: A dynamical systems account. *International Journal of Language and Communication Disorders, 37*, 95–117.

Everhart, V. (1993). *The development of sign language use in deaf preschoolers and their hearing mothers*. Dallas, TX: University of Texas.

Ewers, C., & Brownson, S. (1999). Kindergarteners' vocabulary acquisition as a function of active vs. passive storybook reading, prior vocabulary, and working memory. *Journal of Reading Psychology, 20*, 11–20.

Eyer, J. A., Leonard, L. B., Bedore, L. M., McGregor, K. K., Anderson, B., & Viescas, R. (2002). Fast mapping of verbs by children with specific language impairment. *Clinical Linguistics and Phonetics, 16*, 59–77.

Facon, B., Facon-Bollengier, T., & Grubar, J. C. (2002). Chronological age, receptive vocabulary, and syntax comprehension in children and adolescents with mental retardation. *American Journal on Mental Retardation, 107*, 91–98.

Fazio, B. B., Johnston, J. R., & Brandl, L. (1993). Relation between mental age and vocabulary development among children with mild mental retardation. *American Journal of Mental Retardation, 97*, 541–546.

Fenson, L., Dale, P. S., Reznick, J. S., Bates, E., Hartung, J. P., Pethick, S., & Reilly, J. S. (1993). *MacArthur Communicative Development Inventories: User's guide and technical manual*. San Diego, CA: Singular Publishing Group.

Fenson, L., Dale, P. S., Reznick, J. S., Bates, E., Thal, D., & Pethick, S. J. (1994). Variability in early communicative development. *Monographs of the Society for Research in Child Development, 59*(5, Serial No. 242).

Fenson, L., Marchman, V. A., Thal, D., Dale, P. S., Bates, E., & Reznick, J. S. (2007). *The MacArthur-Bates Communicative Development Inventories: User's guide and technical manual* (2nd ed.). Baltimore: Paul H. Brookes.

Fletcher, P., & Peters, J. (1984). Characterizing language impairment in children: An exploratory study. *Language Testing, 1*, 33–49.

Fung, P. C., Chow, B. W. Y., & McBride-Chang, C. (2005). The impact of a dialogic reading program on deaf and hard-of-hearing kindergarten and early primary school-aged students in Hong Kong. *Journal of Deaf Studies and Deaf Education, 10*, 82–95.

Gathercole, S. E., & Baddeley, A. D. (1989). Evaluation of the role of phonological STM in the development of vocabulary in children: A longitudinal study. *Journal of Memory and Language, 28*, 200–213.

Gathercole, S. E., & Baddeley, A. D. (1990). Phonological memory deficits in language disordered children: Is there a causal connection. *Journal of Memory and Language, 29*, 336–360.

Gentner, D., & Boroditski, L. (2001). Individuation, relativity, and early word learning. In M. Bowerman & S. Levinson (Eds.), *Language acquisition and conceptual development* (pp. 215–256). New York: Cambridge University Press.

German, D. J. (1990). *Test of Adolescent/Adult Word Finding.* Austin, TX: ProEd.

German, D. J. (2000). *Test of Word Finding* (2nd ed.). Austin, TX: PRO-ED.

German, D. J., & Simon, E. (1991). Analysis of children's word-finding skills in discourse. *Journal of Speech and Hearing Research, 34,* 309–316.

Gertner, B. L., Rice, M. L., & Hadley, P. A. (1994). Influence of communicative competence on peer preferences in a preschool classroom. *Journal of Speech and Hearing Research, 37,* 913–923.

Gilbertson, M., & Kamhi, A. G. (1995). Novel word learning in children with hearing impairment. *Journal of Speech and Hearing Research, 38,* 630–642.

Gillette, J., Gleitman, H., Gleitman, L., & Lederer, A. (1999). Human simulations of vocabulary learning. *Cognition, 73,* 135–176.

Gleitman, L. (1990). The structural sources of verb meanings. *Language Acquisition, 1,* 3–55.

Graham, A. M. (2005). *Socioeconomic environment influences lexical knowledge.* Paper presented at the Convention of the American Speech, Language, Hearing Association, San Diego, CA.

Gray, S. (2003). Word-learning by preschoolers with specific language impairment: What predicts success? *Journal of Speech, Language, and Hearing Research, 46,* 56–67.

Gray, S. (2004). Word learning by preschoolers with specific language impairment: Predictors and poor learners. *Journal of Speech, Language, and Hearing Research, 47,* 1117–1132.

Gray, S. (2005). Word learning by preschoolers with specific language impairment: Effect of phonological or semantic cues. *Journal of Speech, Language, and Hearing Research, 48,* 1452–1467.

Gray, S., Plante, E., Vance, R., & Henrichsen, M. (1999). The diagnostic accuracy of four vocabulary tests administered to preschool-age children. *Language, Speech, and Hearing Services in Schools, 30,* 196–206.

Grigorenko, E. L., Klin, A., Pauls, D. L., Senft, R., Hooper, C., & Volkmar, F. (2002). A descriptive study of hyperlexia in a clinically referred sample of children with developmental delays. *Journal of Autism and Developmental Disorders, 32,* 3–12.

Hammill, D. D., & Newcomer, P. L. (1997a). *Test of Language Development—Intermediate* (3rd ed.). Austin, TX: PRO-ED.

Hammill, D. D., & Newcomer, P. L. (1997b). *Test of Language Development—Primary* (3rd ed.). Austin, TX: PRO-ED.

Hammill, D. D., Brown, V. L., Larsen, S. C., & Wiederholt, J. L. (2007). *Test of Adolescent and Adult Language* (4th ed.). Austin, TX: PRO-ED.

Hansson, K., Forsberg, J., Löfqvist, A., Mäki-Torkko, E., & Sahlén B. (2004). Working memory and novel word learning in children with hearing impairment and children with specific language impairment. *International Journal of Language and Communication Disorders, 39,* 401–422.

Hargrave, A. C., & Sénéchal, M. (2000). A book reading intervention with preschool children who have limited vocabularies: The benefits of regular reading and dialogic reading. *Early Childhood Research Quarterly, 15,* 75–90.

Hart, B., & Risley, T. R. (1995). *Meaningful differences in the everyday experience of young American children* Baltimore: Paul H. Brookes.

Haynes, C. (1992). Vocabulary deficit-one problem or many? *Child Language Teaching and Therapy, 8,* 1–17.

Hick, R. F., Botting, N., & Conti-Ramsden, G. (2005). Short-term memory and vocabulary development in children with Down syndrome and children with specific language impairment. *Developmental Medicine and Child Neurology, 47,* 532–538.

Holt, J. A., Traxler, C. B., & Allen, R. E. (1997). *Interpreting the scores: A user's guide to the 9th edition Stanford Achievement Test for educators of deaf and heard-of-hearing students.* Washington, DC: Gallaudet Research Institute.

Hresko, W. P., Reid, K., & Hammill, D. D. (1999). *Test of Early Language Development* (3rd ed.). Austin, TX: PRO-ED.

Huisingh, R., Bowers, L., LoGuidice, C., & Orman, J. (2004). *Test of Semantic Skills—Primary.* East Moline, IL: LinguiSystems.

Huisingh, R., Bowers, L., LoGiudice, C., & Orman, J. (2005). *WORD Test 2—Adolescent*. East Moline, IL: LinguiSystems.

Jarrold, C., & Baddeley, A. D. (1997). Short-term memory for verbal and visuo-spatial information in Down's syndrome. *Cognitive Neuropsychiatry, 2,* 101–122.

Jarrold, C., Hartley, S. J., Phillips. C., & Baddeley, A. D. (2000). Word fluency in Williams syndrome: Evidence for unusual semantic organization? *Cognitive Neuropsychiatry, 5,* 293–319.

Jerger, S., & Stout, G. (1993). Auditory stroop effects in children with hearing impairment. *Journal of Speech and Hearing Research, 36,* 1083–1096.

Johnston, J. R., Miller, J., & Tallal, P. (2001). Use of cognitive state predicates by language impaired children. *International Journal of Language and Communication Disorders, 36,* 349–370.

Kaderavek, J., & Justice, L. M. (2002). Shared storybook reading as an intervention context: Practices and potential pitfalls. *American Journal of Speech-Language Pathology, 11,* 395–406.

Kail, R., & Leonard, L. B. (1986). Word-finding abilities in language-impaired children. *ASHA Monographs, 25.*

Kaiser, A. P., Hendrickson, J. M., & Alpert, C. L. (1991). Milieu language teaching: A second look. *Advances in Mental Retardation and Developmental Disabilities, 4,* 63–92.

Kay-Raining Bird, E., & Chapman, R. S. (1994). Sequential recall in individuals with Down syndrome. *Journal of Speech and Hearing Research, 37,* 1369–1380.

Kiernan, B., & Gray, S. (1998). Word learning in a supported-learning context by preschool children with specific language impairment. *Journal of Speech, Language, and Hearing Research, 41,* 161–171.

Kiese-Himmel, C., & Ohlwein, S. (2003). Characteristics of children with permanent mild hearing impairment. *Folia Phoniatrica et Logopaedica, 55,* 70–79.

Kjelgaard, M. M., & Tager-Flusberg, H. (2001). An investigation of language impairment in autism: Implications for genetic subgroups. *Language and Cognitive Processes, 16,* 287–308.

Klee, T. (1992). Developmental and diagnostic characteristics of quantitative measures of children's language production. *Topics in Language Disorders, 12,* 28–41.

Klee, T., Stokes, S. F., Wong, A., Fletcher, P., & Gavin, W. J. (2004). Utterance length and lexical diversity in Cantonese-speaking children with and without specific language impairment. *Journal of Speech, Language, and Hearing Research, 47,* 1396–1410.

Kumin, L. (1996). Speech and language skills in children with Down syndrome. *Mental Retardation and Developmental Disabilities Research Reviews, 2,* 109–115.

Lahey, M., & Edwards, J. (1999). Naming errors of children with specific language impairment. *Journal of Speech, Language, and Hearing Research, 42,* 195–205.

Laing, E., Butterworth, G., Ansari, D., Gsödl, M., Longhi, E., Panagiotaki, G., et al. (2002). Atypical development of language and social communication in toddlers with Williams syndrome. *Developmental Science, 5,* 233–246.

Laws, G., & Bishop, D. V. M. (2004). Verbal deficits in Down's syndrome and specific language impairment: A comparison. *International Journal of Language and Communication Disorders, 39,* 423–451.

Layton, T. L., & Holmes, D. W. (1985). *Carolina Picture Vocabulary Test*. Austin, TX: PRO-ED.

Lederberg, A. R., Prezbindowski, A. K., & Spencer, P. E. (2000). Word learning skills of deaf preschoolers: The development of novel mapping and rapid word learning strategies. *Child Development, 53,* 1055–1065.

Leonard, L. B. (1998). *Children with specific language impairment*. Cambridge, MA: MIT Press.

Leonard, L., Miller, C., & Gerber, E. (1999). Grammatical morphology and the lexicon in children with specific language impairment. *Journal of Speech, Language, and Hearing Research, 42,* 678–689.

Leonard, L., Nippold, M., Kail, R., & Hale, C. (1983). Picture naming in language impaired children. *Journal of Speech and Hearing Research, 26,* 609–615.

Loeb, D. F., Pye, C., Redmond, S., & Richardson, L. (1996). Eliciting verbs from children with specific language impairment. *American Journal of Speech-Language Pathology, 5,* 17–30.

López, B., & Leekam, S. R. (2003). Do children with autism fail to process information in context? *Journal of Child Psychology and Psychiatry, 44,* 285–300.

Lord, C., Shulman, C., & DiLavore, P. (2004). Regression and word loss in autistic spectrum disorders. *Journal of Child Psychology and Psychiatry, 45*, 936–955.

MacWhinney, B. (2000). *The CHILDES project: Tools for analyzing talk* (3rd ed.). Mahwah, NJ: Lawrence Erlbaum Associates.

Mardell-Czudnowski, C., & Goldenberg, D. S. (1998). *Developmental Indicators for the Assessment of Learning* (3rd ed.). Bloomington, MN: Pearson.

Mastropieri, M. A., Emerick, K., & Scruggs, T. E. (1988). Mnemonic instruction of science concepts. *Behavioral Disorders, 14*, 48–56.

Mastropieri, M. A., Scruggs, T. E., & Fulk, B. J. (1990). Teaching abstract vocabulary with the keyword method: Effects on recall and comprehension. *Journal of Learning Disabilities, 23*, 92–107.

Mayne, A. M., Yoshinaga-Itano, C., Sedey, A. L., & Carey, A. (2000a). Expressive vocabulary development of infants and toddlers who are deaf or hard of hearing. *Volta Review, 100*, 1–28.

Mayne, A. M., Yoshinaga-Itano, C., Sedey, A. L., & Carey, A. (2000b). Receptive vocabulary development of infants and toddlers who are deaf or hard of hearing. *Volta Review, 100*, 29–52.

McGregor, K. K. (2004). Developmental dependencies between lexical semantics and reading. In C. A. Stone, E. R. Silliman, B. J. Ehren, & K. Apel (Eds.), *Handbook of language and literacy* (pp. 302–317). New York: Guilford Press.

McGregor, K. K., & Appel, A. (2002). On the relation between mental representation and naming in a child with specific language impairment. *Clinical Linguistics and Phonetics, 16*, 1–20.

McGregor, K. K., Newman, R. M., Reilly, R., & Capone, N. C. (2002). Semantic representation and naming in children with specific language impairment. *Journal of Speech, Language, and Hearing Research, 45*, 998–1014.

McGregor, K. K., Sheng, L., & Smith, B. (2005). The precocious two-year-old: Status of the lexicon and links to the grammar. *Journal of Child Language, 32*, 563–585.

McGregor, K. K., & Waxman, S. R. (1998). Object naming at multiple hierarchical levels: A comparison of preschoolers with and without word-finding deficits. *Journal of Child Language, 25*, 419–430.

McKee, G., Malvern, D., & Richards, B. (2000). Measuring vocabulary diversity using dedicated software. *Literary and Linguistics Computing, 15*, 323–337.

Mervis, C. (1990). Early conceptual development of children with Down syndrome. In: D. Cicchetti & M. Beeghly (Eds.), *Children with Down syndrome: a developmental perspective* (pp. 252–301). Cambridge, UK: Cambridge University Press.

Mervis, C. B., Robinson, B. F., Rowe, M. L., Becerra, A. M., & Klein-Tasman, B. P. (2003). Language abilities of individuals with Williams syndrome. *International Review of Research in Mental Retardation. 27*, 35–81.

Miller, J. F. (1995). Individual differences in vocabulary acquisition in children with Down syndrome. *Progress in Clinical and Biological Research, 393*, 93–103.

Miller, J. F., & Chapman, R. S. (2000). *Systematic Analysis of Language Transcripts, Version 6.1*. Madison, WI: Language Analysis Laboratory, Waisman Center, University of Wisconsin.

Miller, J. F., & Leadholm, B. (1992). *Language sample analysis guide: The Wisconsin guide for the identification and description of language impairment in children*. Madison, WI: Wisconsin Department of Public Instruction.

Miller, J. F., & Paul, R. (1995). *The clinical assessment of language comprehension*. Baltimore: Paul H. Brookes.

Moeller, M. P. (2000). Early intervention and language development in children who are deaf and hard of hearing. *Pediatrics, 106*, 43–51.

Morgan, D. L., & Guilford, A. M. (1984). *Adolescent Language Screening Test*. Austin, TX: PRO-ED.

Montgomery, J. W. (1995). Sentence comprehension in children with specific language impairment: The role of phonological working memory. *Journal of Speech and Hearing Research, 38*, 187–199.

Munro, N., & Lee, K. (2005, July). *Fast mapping and lexical learning: Expressive and receptive profiles of children with language impairment and their typically developing peers*. Paper presented at the meeting of the International Association for the Study of Child Language, Berlin, Germany.

Nagy, W. E., Herman, P. A., & Anderson, R. (1985). Learning words from context. *Reading Research Quarterly, 19*, 304–330.

Nash, M., & Donaldson, M. L. (2005). Word learning in children with vocabulary deficits. *Journal of Speech, Language, and Hearing Research, 48*, 439–458.

Nation, K. (1999). Reading skills in hyperlexia: A developmental perspective. *Psychological Bulletin, 125*, 338–355.

Nation, K., & Snowling, M. J. (1998). Semantic processing and the development of word recognition skills: Evidence from children with reading comprehension difficulties. *Journal of Memory and Language, 39*, 85–101.

Nation, K., Snowling, M. J., & Clarke, P. (2007). Dissecting the relationship between language skills and learning to read: Semantic and phonological contributions to new vocabulary learning in children with poor reading comprehension. *Advances in Speech-Language Pathology, 9*, 131–139.

Neville, H. J., & Bruer, J. T. (2001). Language processing: How experience affects brain organization. In D. B. Bailey, Jr., J. T. Bruer, F. J. Symons, & J. W. Lichtman (Eds.), *Critical thinking about critical periods* (pp. 151–172). Baltimore: Paul H. Brookes.

Norbury, C. F. (2004). Factors supporting idiom comprehension in children with communication disorders. *Journal of Speech, Language, and Hearing Research, 47*, 1179–1193.

Norbury, C. F. (2005). Barking up the wrong tree? Lexical ambiguity resolution in children with language impairments and autistic spectrum disorders. *Journal of Experimental Child Psychology, 90*, 142–171.

Norbury, C. F., & Chiat, S. (2000). Semantic intervention to support word recognition: A single-case study. *Child Language Teaching and Therapy, 16*, 141–163.

Oakhill, J. (1982). Constructive processes in skilled and less-skilled comprehenders' memory for sentences. *British Journal of Psychology, 73*, 13–20.

Oetting, J., Rice, M., & Swank, L. (1995). Quick incidental learning (QUIL) of words by school-age children with and without SLI. *Journal of Speech and Hearing Research, 38*, 434–445.

O'Hara, M., & Johnston, J. (1997). Syntactic bootstrapping in children with specific language impairment. *European Journal of Disorder of Communication, 32*, 147–164.

Owen, A. J., & Leonard, L. B. (2002). Lexical diversity in the spontaneous speech of children with specific language impairment: Application of D. *Journal of Speech, Language, and Hearing Research, 45*, 927–937.

Parsons, S., Law, J., & Gascoigne, M. (2005). Teaching receptive vocabulary to children with specific language impairment: A curriculum-based approach. *Child Language Teaching and Therapy, 21*, 39–59.

Peterson, C. C., & Siegal, M. (2000). Insights into theory of mind from deafness and autism. *Mind and Language, 15*, 123–145.

Pressley, M., Levin, J. R., & Delaney, H. D. (1982). The mnemonic keyword method. *Review of Educational Research, 52*, 61–69.

Rescorla, L. (1989). The Language Development Survey: A screening tool for delayed expressive language in toddlers. *Journal of Speech and Hearing Disorders, 54*, 587–599.

Rice, M. L., Buhr, J., & Nemeth, M. (1990). Fast mapping word-learning abilities of language-delayed preschoolers. *Journal of Speech and Hearing Disorders, 55*, 33–42.

Rice, M. L., Cleave, P. L., & Oetting, J. B. (2000). The use of syntactic cues in lexical acquisition by children with SLI. *Journal of Speech, Language, and Hearing Research, 43*, 582–594.

Rice, M., Oetting, J., Marquis, J., Bode, J., & Pae, S. (1994). Frequency of input effects on word comprehension of children with specific language impairment. *Journal of Speech and Hearing Research, 37*, 106–122.

Rinaldi, W. (2000). Pragmatic comprehension in secondary school-aged students with specific developmental language disorder. *International Journal of Language and Communication Disorders, 35*, 1–29.

Rosetti, L. (2006). *Rossetti Infant–Toddler Language Scale*. East Moline, IL: LinguiSystems.

Scruggs, T. E., Mastropieri, M. A., & Levin, J. R. (1985). Vocabulary acquisition by mentally retarded students under direct and mnemonic instruction. *American Journal of Mental Deficiency, 89,* 546–551.

Semel, E., Wiig, E. H., & Secord, W. (2003). *Clinical Evaluation of Language Fundamentals* (4th ed.). San Antonio, TX: Harcourt Assessment.

Serniclaes, W., Sprenger-Charolles, L., Carré, R., & Demonet, J. F. (2001). Perceptual discrimination of speech sounds in developmental dyslexia. *Journal of Speech, Language, and Hearing Research, 44,* 384–399.

Shankweiler, D., Crain, S., Katz, L., Fowler, A. E., Liberman, A. M., Brady, S. A., et al. (1995). Cognitive profiles of reading disabled children: Comparison of language skills in phonology, morphology, and syntax. *Psychological Science, 6,* 149–156.

Shulman, C., & Guberman, A. (2007). Acquisition of verb meaning through syntactic cues: A comparison of children with autism, children with specific language impairment (SLI) and children with typical language development (TLD). *Journal of Child Language, 34,* 411–423.

Silberberg, N., & Silberberg, M. C. (1967). Hyperlexia: Specific word recognition skills in young children. *Exceptional Children, 34,* 41–42.

Silverman, S., & Ratner, N. B. (2002). Measuring lexical diversity in children who stutter: Application of vocd. *Journal of Fluency Disorders, 27,* 289–304.

Smith, V., Mirenda, P., & Zaidman-Zait, A. (2007). Predictors of expressive vocabulary growth in children with autism. *Journal of Speech, Language, and Hearing Research, 50,* 149–160.

Snowling, M. (1987). *Dyslexia: A cognitive developmental perspective.* Oxford, UK: Blackwell.

Snowling, M., & Frith, U. (1986). Comprehension in "hyperlexic" children. *Journal of Experimental Psychology, 42,* 392–415.

Stanovich, K. E. (1986). Matthew effects in reading: Some consequences of individual differences in the acquisition of literacy. *Reading Research Quarterly, 21,* 360–407.

Stanovich, K. E., & Cunningham, A. E. (1992). Studying the consequences of literacy within a literate society: The cognitive correlates of print exposure. *Memory and Cognition, 20,* 51–68.

Stelmachowicz, P. G., Pittman, A. L., Hoover, B. M., & Lewis, D. E. (2004). Novel-word learning in children with normal hearing and hearing loss. *Ear and Hearing, 25,* 47–56.

Stevens, T., & Karmiloff-Smith, A. (1997). Word learning in a special population: Do individuals with Williams syndrome obey lexical constraints? *Journal of Child Language, 24,* 737–765.

Stothard, S. E., & Hulme, C. A. (1995). Comparison of phonological skills in children with reading comprehension difficulties and children with decoding difficulties. *Journal of Child Psychology and Psychiatry, 36,* 399–408.

Stothard, S. E., Snowling, M. J., Bishop, D. V. M., Chipchase, B. B., & Kaplan, C. A. (1998). Language impaired preschoolers: A follow-up into adolescence. *Journal of Speech, Language, and Hearing Research, 41,* 407–418.

Tager-Flusberg, H. (1985). The conceptual basis for referential word meaning in children with autism. *Child Development, 56,* 1167–1178.

Tager-Flusberg, H., & Joseph, R. M. (2003). Identifying neurocognitive phenotypes in autism. *Philosophical Transactions of the Royal Society of London, 358,* 303–314.

Thal, D., Bates, E., & Bellugi, U. (1989). Language and cognition in two children with Williams syndrome. *Journal of Speech and Hearing Research, 32,* 489–500.

Thal, D., O'Hanlon, L., Clemmons, M., & Fralin, L. (1999). Validity of a parent report measure of vocabulary and syntax for preschool children with language impairment. *Journal of Speech, Language, and Hearing Research, 42,* 482–496.

Thal, D. J., Reilly, J., Seibert, L., Jeffries, R., & Fenson, J. (2004). Language development in children at risk for language impairment: Cross-population comparisons. *Brain and Language, 88,* 167–179.

Trauner, D., Wulfeck, B., Tallal, P., & Hesselink, J. (1995). *Neurologic and MRI profiles of language impaired children* (Technical Report, Publication No. CND-9513). San Diego, CA: Center for Research in Language, UCSD.

van der Lely, H. (1994). Canonical linking rules: Forward versus reverse linking in normally developing and specifically language-impaired children. *Cognition, 51,* 29–72.

Volden, J., & Lord, C. (1991). Neologisms and idiosyncratic language in autistic speakers. *Journal of Autism and Developmental Disorders*, *21*, 109–130.

Wake, M., Poulakis, Z., Hughes, E. K., Carey-Sargeant, C., & Rickards, F. W. (2005). Hearing impairment: A population study of age at diagnosis, severity, and language outcomes at 7–8 years. *Archives of Disease in Childhood*, *90*, 238–244.

Walker, D., Greenwood, C., Hart, B., & Carta, J. (1994). Prediction of school outcomes based on early language production and socioeconomic factors. *Child Development*, *65*, 606–621.

Wallace, G., & Hammill, D. D. (2002). *Comprehensive Receptive and Expressive Vocabulary Test* (2nd ed.). Austin, TX: PRO-ED.

Wang, P. P., & Bellugi, U. (1994). Evidence from two genetic syndromes for a dissociation between verbal and visual-spatial short-term memory. *Journal of Clinical and Experimental Neuropsychology*, *16*, 317–322.

Washington, J., & Craig, H. (1999). Performance of at-risk, African American preschoolers on the Peabody Picture Vocabulary Test–III. *Language, Speech, and Hearing Services in Schools*, *30*, 75–82.

Watkins, R. V., & DeThorne, L. S. (2000). Assessing children's vocabulary skills: From word knowledge to word-learning potential. *Seminars in Speech and Language*, *21*, 235–245.

Watkins, R. V., Kelly, D. J., Harbers, H. M., & Hollis, W. (1995). Measuring children's lexical diversity: Differentiating typical and impaired language learners. *Journal of Speech, Language, and Hearing Research*, *38*, 1349–1355.

Watkins, R., Rice, M., & Moltz, C. (1993). Verb use by language-impaired and normally developing children. *First Language*, *13*, 133–144.

White, T., Graves, M., & Slater, W. (1990). Growth of reading vocabulary in diverse elementary schools: Decoding and word meaning. *Journal of Educational Psychology*, *82*, 281–290.

Whitehouse, D., & Harris, J. (1984). Hyperlexia in infantile autism. *Journal of Autism and Developmental Disorders*, *14*, 281–289.

Whitehurst, G. J. (1997). Language processes in context: Language learning in children reared in poverty. In L. B. Adamson, & M. S. Romski (Eds.), *Research on communication and language disorders: Contribution to theories of language development* (pp. 233–266). Baltimore: Paul H. Brookes.

Whitehurst, G. J., Arnold, D. S., Epstein, J. N., Angell, A. L., Smith, M., & Fishcel, J. E. (1994). A picture book reading intervention in day care and home for children from low-income families. *Developmental Psychology*, *30*, 679–689.

Whitehurst, G. J., Falco, F. L., Lonigan, C. J., Fischel, J. E., DeBaryshe, B. D., Valdez Menchaca, M. C., et al. (1988). Accelerating language development through picture book reading. *Developmental Psychology*, *24*, 552–559.

Wiig, E. H., & Secord, W. (1992). *Test of Word Knowledge*. San Antonio, TX: Psychological Corporation.

Wiig, E. H., Secord, W., & Semel, E. (2005). *Clinical Evaluation of Language Fundamentals: Preschool–2*. San Antonio, TX: Harcourt Assessment.

Williams, K. T. (2007). *Expressive Vocabulary Test* (2nd ed.). Bloomington, MN: Pearson.

Windfuhr, K. L., Faragher, B., & Conti-Ramsden, G. (2002). Lexical learning skills in young children with specific language impairment (SLI). *International Journal of Language and Communication Disorders*, *37*, 415–432.

Yoder, P. J., Kaiser, A. P., Alpert, C., & Fischer, R. (1993). Following the child's lead when teaching nouns to preschoolers with mental retardation. *Journal of Speech and Hearing Research*, *36*, 158–167.

Yoder, P., Spruytenburg, H., Edwards, A., & Davies, B. (1995). Effect of verbal routine contexts and expansions on gains in the mean length of utterance in children with developmental delays. *Language, Speech, and Hearing Services in Schools*, *26*, 21–32.

Zimmerman, I. L., Steiner, V. G., & Pond, R. E. (2002). *Preschool Language Scale* (4th ed.). San Antonio, TX: Harcourt Assessment.

17

Syntax in Child Language Disorders

PAUL FLETCHER

*P*honology and inflectional morphology in English present the analyst with relatively constrained systems within which impairment can be defined. This is not true of syntax, although definitions of this level can be beguilingly straightforward. Trask (1993, p. 273) provides this succinct description: "[t]he branch of grammar dealing with the organization of words into larger structures, particularly into sentences." Such a broad sweep is necessary to embrace structures from simple noun phrases to sentences with recursion, but it underplays the complexity of the problem space. It also misses the psychological dimension resulting from Chomsky's view of grammar (Chomsky, 1965) as the description both of a language, and of the linguistic knowledge of the native speaker (see chapter 6 by Botwinik-Rotem & Friedmann). As inflectional morphology—a paradigmatic dimension of sentence structure—is addressed elsewhere in this volume (see chapter 15 by Oetting & Hadley), I consider exclusively the syntagmatic—linear—dimension that Trask's definition encapsulates. To address the intrinsic complexity of syntax, linguists have developed distinct theoretical approaches and a variety of descriptive frameworks. In facing the considerable problems posed by the nature of the system and linguists' solutions to dealing with it, those working in language impairment have adopted different strategies. They have focused the spotlight of a particular theory, usually Chomskyan, onto their data, or they have applied a descriptive framework to one subarea of syntax, or to the profiling of the full range of individuals' syntactic abilities and deficits. In this light it is perhaps not surprising that, in contrast to phonology and inflectional morphology, no coherent picture of syntactic impairment in English-speaking children emerges. After three decades of research, we have a reasonable grasp of what phonological impairment looks like. And there is ample evidence that tense and agreement inflections in English pose a particular problem for children with language impairment. So far, comparable clarity is not available for syntax. In what follows we review work on syntactic impairment primarily in children with specific language impairment, but also in those with other developmental disabilities.

SPECIFIC LANGUAGE IMPAIRMENT

A Chomskyan Perspective

The major part of research on syntactic impairment has been on children with specific language impairment (SLI). A comprehensive treatment of syntactic problems in children with SLI, inspired by Chomskyan theory, is the computational grammatical complexity hypothesis (CGC), previously known as the representation deficit for dependent relations, developed by van der Lely and colleagues (e.g., van der Lely, 2003, 2004, 2005). There are other approaches to the explanation of SLI that take their genesis from Chomskyan theory, such as the grammatical agreement deficit (GAD) account (Clahsen, Bartke, & Göllner, 1997); the extended optional infinitive (EOI) hypothesis (Rice & Wexler, 1996; Rice, Wexler, & Cleave, 1995); the extended unique checking constraint (EUCC) (Wexler, 1998); and the agreement/tense omission hypothesis (ATOM) (Wexler, Schütze, & Rice, 1998). Restricted as they are to tense, especially past tense, and to agreement relationships, it is not easy to see how these accounts could extend to the full range of syntactic limitations found in children with SLI. The CGC, however, promises to go further, predicting "a pervasive deficit in grammatical components determined by structural complexity" (van der Lely, 2005, p. 55). An impaired individual's limitations will be especially apparent in nonlocal dependencies in syntactic structures. A dependency is any relation between two positions in a sentence where "the presence, absence or form of an element in one position is correlated with the presence, absence or form of an element in another position" (Trask, 1993, p. 77). Subject–verb agreement in English would be an example of a nonlocal dependency. The subject noun form that governs the choice of marking on the verb may not be adjacent to the verb. Compare *the boys in the band keep time well* and *the boy in the band keeps time well*. In both examples, it is the subject noun that determines whether the verb is marked for agreement (*boys . . . keep*) or not (*boy . . . keeps*). Another example of a nonlocal dependency would be the kind of pronominal reference to be seen in a sentence like *Kevin said Michael had injured himself*, where a competent English speaker knows that the reflexive pronoun *himself* is bound to (refers to) *Michael* rather than *Kevin*. Other structures in which nonlocal dependencies can be identified are wh-questions, relative clauses, and passive sentences (see chapter 6 by Botwinik-Rotem & Friedmann and below). The CGC predicts problems for individuals with SLI in any of these areas, and there is evidence in support of these predictions. Van der Lely and colleagues have identified deficits in a group of individuals referred to as Grammatical (G)-SLI in wh-questions (van der Lely & Battell, 2003), in passives (van der Lely, 1996), and in the assignment of appropriate reference to pronouns (van der Lely & Stollwerck, 1997).

The CGC, like the EOI and GAD, is a domain-specific hypothesis. In line with the theoretical linguistic perspective it springs from, which sees syntax as a genetically endowed, specialized cognitive system, the CGC predicts that deficits linked to nonlocal dependencies are internal to that system and cannot be attributed to such factors as perceptual deficiencies or working memory limitations. In light of evidence that specific language impairment may be linked to such factors (e.g., Bishop & McArthur, 2005; Gathercole & Baddeley, 1990; Newbury, Bishop, & Monaco, 2005; Ziegler, Pech-Georgel, George, Alario, & Lorenzi, 2005), it is important for the CGC theory that empirical findings identify children with the expected syntactic difficulties but without processing deficits. A group of children with a "relatively rare form of SLI" (van der Lely, 2005, p. 53), (G)-SLI provide this confirmation. These individuals present with computational grammatical deficits of the predicted types, but intact sensory and nonverbal abilities.

An explanatory account of SLI such as the CGC has the considerable advantage that it can call on an explicit and internally coherent linguistic theory. By exploiting a particular feature of the syntactic framework arising from the linguistic theory, namely nonlocal dependencies, it can link apparently disparate phenomena such as agreement, pronominal reference, and wh-questions. It would appear however, that the numbers of children with SLI who can be designated G-SLI is a very small percentage of a larger SLI population that has syntactic deficits but may also have concomitant difficulties in other areas (Bishop, Bright, James, Bishop, & van der Lely, 2000). The focus on the cluster of nonlocal dependencies relevant to the CGC can draw our attention away from a wider range of syntactic deficits in the SLI population generally, which we need to be aware of for assessment and intervention purposes.

We have, for example, become increasingly aware that verb argument structure is both a significant underpinning for the child's learning of the simple sentence (Pinker, 1989), and a source of difficulty for children with language impairment (e.g., Chiat, 2000; Ingham, Fletcher, Schelletter, & Sinka, 1998; O'Hara & Johnston, 1997). Beyond the simple sentence, in the grammatical developments Brown (1973) identifies as criterial of his Stages IV and V, embedding and coordination, difficulties also arise. These areas have also been identified as problematic for children with language impairment (e.g., Hesketh, 2004; Marinellie, 2004; Schuele & Nicholls, 2000). If we are to assess systematically and structure intervention efficiently, we need to widen the scope of inquiry, in order to identify appropriate target forms in areas of simple sentence construction, and in complex sentences.

The Simple Sentence: Verbs and Argument Structure

Central to the organization of the simple sentence is the main or lexical verb. Sentences have to have verbs, and verbs have arguments—noun phrases (NP) or sometimes prepositional phrases (PP)—that they mandate. A distinction is made between *internal* arguments and *external* arguments. Internal arguments are those that are within the verb phrase (VP) and are subcategorized for by the verb. So the verbs *move* and *give* differ in their internal arguments, with *move* requiring only a single NP (*move the cupboard*), while *give* requires either an NP + PP sequence or NP + NP (*give the bone to the dog/give the dog the bone*). The subject NP, obligatory in most English sentences, is an external argument. If a child understands that subjects are obligatory and is aware of the internal argument requirements for a particular verb, then the basic syntactic structure of the simple sentence falls out automatically. Furthermore, as Pinker (1989, pp. 179ff.) points out, children can be guided to internal argument structure by a verb's semantics. The semantics of *put*, for instance, entails something located and a location, which are expressed respectively in an NP and a PP. The syntax-enabling potential of verb semantics has come to be known as *semantic bootstrapping*. This intimate relationship between lexis and simple sentences implies that deficiencies in verb learning in children with LI will have syntactic consequences. There is ample indication of problems with the learning of verbs, and with argument structure, in children with language impairment. This evidence is reviewed in detail by Leonard and Deevy (2004). Some representative examples will suffice here.

First, experimental evidence suggests that children with LI are not as adept as age controls in fast-mapping names for actions, and they have problems retaining information about verbs that they have initially acquired after a limited number of exposures (Rice, Oetting, Marquis, Bode, & Pae, 1994). Chiat (2000) suggested why verbs present a particular challenge for inefficient language learners. Verbs rarely occur in isolation, and they typically receive less stress than the words around them, which may affect the integrity or specificity of verbs' phonological representations and hence their identification and recognition (see also Leonard & Deevy, 2004, p. 223). Further problems may result from limited understanding of the perspectives verbs impose on the events they characterize, especially as these events are often of relatively brief duration.

There are also reports of difficulties with both internal and external arguments in children with language impairment. Fletcher (1991) reported errors of omission of internal arguments (e.g., *he puts webs*), and also incorrect ordering of arguments (e.g., *my mum was take me a picture*) in a group of 15 school-age children with SLI. Thordardottir, Elin, and Ellis Weismer (2002), in a study of argument structure use in spontaneous language samples, reported that children with SLI use fewer argument types, argument structure types, and verb alternations than do age-matched controls. The issue of alternations was also explored in a video elicitation task (King, Schelletter, Sinka, Fletcher, & Ingham, 1995). Their method exploited the alternating argument structures available with certain verbs to compare children with SLI and younger typically developing children matched on vocabulary test scores. Included in the set of verbs used were those permitting causative-inchoative and locative alternations (Levin, 1993). The video scenes were designed to elicit one of the possible argument frames for a word. So for the causative-inchoative pair *the boy was bouncing the ball/the ball was bouncing*, the scene for the first item in the pair showed the agent, the boy, setting off the bouncing of the theme, the ball, across a patio. In the second scene the boy was edited out of the scene, and just the bouncing ball is visible. In contrast to the younger typically developing children, across all alternations the children with SLI tended to prefer one description for both scenes. In the causative-inchoative case, the preferred version was the one with agent as subject and the theme as direct object, as in the first example of the pair above. In a study that expressly addressed external arguments, children with SLI were more likely to omit subject arguments as internal argument structure complexity increased (Grela, 2000).

The Simple Sentence: Other Features

Working out the argument structure potential of lexical verbs is a significant part of early language learning, but it does not guarantee all aspects of the syntactic structure of simple sentences. The child has also to come to grips with what Brown (1973) referred to as the modalities of the simple sentence, including interrogatives, verb premodification, and pre- and postmodification in noun phrases. The research that is available on these topics indicates that children with language impairment present with deficits in all of these areas. Problems with the syntactic organization of interrogatives, attributed to difficulties with wh-movement, are found by van der Lely and Battell (2003) in a group of G-SLI children. In another study of children with SLI, not restricted to the grammatical subtype, Deevy and Leonard (2004) attributed the difficulties these children have with the comprehension of wh-questions, which are more marked in longer sentences, to processing difficulties rather than a particular grammatical operation. There are two major types of wh-questions, referred to as subject and object questions. In subject questions, such as *Who ate my porridge?* the wh-word is the subject of the main verb and is in the syntactic position relative to that verb that it would have in any English sentence. In object questions, such as *What did Goldilocks eat?*, the wh-word is the direct object of the verb but has been "moved" to the initial position in the sentence. Understanding this syntactic relationship appears to present a problem for G-SLI children (van der Lely & Battell, 2003). In the study by Deevy and Leonard (2004), the group of children with SLI that they tested did show more problems with wh-questions than a group of typically developing (TD) children, but only in one of their experimental conditions. Deevy and Leonard (2004) manipulated the length of the questions subjects were required to understand. Children with SLI performed as well as TD children on short questions, whether subject or object type. However, they were less accurate on long object questions than on long subject questions, and less accurate on long object questions than the TD group. These results suggest that for children with SLI who do not fall into the restricted G-SLI set, demands on processing abilities are a significant part of their syntactic problems.

English has a complex system of lexical verb premodification, with a possible maximal expansion consisting of modal + perfect + progressive—for example, *might have been* in *Mummy might have been shopping*. There is ample evidence for the omission of single auxiliaries in children with SLI (Leonard, 1998, pp. 59ff.), especially in progressive (*be + ing*) constructions. Information on modals is however, sparse. Leonard et al. (2003) found that a group of children with SLI used *can* (in its ability sense) in a lower percentage of likely contexts than a group of age controls. In another study that compared children with SLI with age peers and younger typically developing children (YTD), the group with SLI had significantly less control of *could*, in its ability in the past meaning, than the comparison groups, though they were as proficient with *can* as the YTD children (Leonard, Wong, Deevy, Stokes, & Fletcher, 2007). We do not have studies of other modals (*must, shall, should, will, would, may, might*). Nor do we have any sense, in typically developing children or those with language impairment, how the complex sequencing of pre-main verb modification in English unfolds.

English noun phrase structure also presents a test for the learner. An example, from Huddleston and Pullum's (2003, p. 332) comprehensive treatment of the grammar of English, with extensive pre- and postmodification of the head noun, underlines the extent of the challenge: ***even all the preposterous salary from Lloyds*** *that Bill gets*. It is true that this is not a sentence that would be expected from a child, but analogous structures, using noun pre- and postmodification to specify a referent or referents for a hearer, would be expected at least in the early school years (e.g., ***all the boys in the class*** *I like*). Again, little is known of the acquisition of control of the syntax of noun phrases of this degree of complexity by typically developing children or of any lack of control by children who have difficulty learning language. There is some evidence, from a study by Gavin, Klee, and Membrino (1993), that noun phrase expansion, the degree of modification included in noun phrases, is a discriminator between typically developing children and those with SLI.

Combining Sentences: Typically Developing Children   In addition to the syntactic structure of simple sentences, somewhat later in their development children also have to master the devices in the language for combining sentences. There are two main types of linkage (Clark, 2003, p. 245). One, referred to as coordination, using conjunctions like *and* or *but*, links two or more sentences that are not syntactically dependent on one another. The second, subordination, does have one sentence syntactically dependent on the other. The subordinate structure is said to be *embedded* in the main sentence. This can be because it fills one of the grammatical roles in the matrix clause (*Mummy thinks **I've been naughty***); or because it acts as a postmodifier, a relative clause, in a noun phrase, as in (*Esme broke the toy **Gran gave me***); or because it operates as an adverbial modifier of a verb phrase (*I had a lot of hair **when I was a baby***). These devices permit the child to: "convey more complex information in a single utterance and to produce coherent sequences of utterances when . . . recounting an adventure, telling a joke, or explaining how a toy came to be broken" (Clark, 2003, p. 245).

As the child gets older and her experience expands, and particularly when she gets to school, increasing control of complex syntax is necessary to meet the linguistic demands placed on her. For the typically developing child, the journey towards mastery of complex syntax begins relatively early. The precursors of most coordinate and subordinate structures are seen in the third year of life (Clark, 2003, pp. 245ff.). Sentences linked with *and* are perhaps the earliest to appear. Of the subordinate structures, relative clauses are reported for some children soon after the second birthday. However, many of these early relative clauses lack relative pronouns. This tendency to omit grammatical markers of subordination is also seen in other prototype structures. Certain complement-taking verbs such as *want* require the verb in the complement structure to be preceded by *to: I want that man to go now*. The earliest attempts at such structures tend to omit *to*. Other subordinating constructions do not omit the linking forms but are initially restricted in the range of forms they can deal with. Typically developing preschool children begin to express temporal and causal relations in their third year, most commonly with *when* as the subordinator for the former and *'cause* for the latter. Conditional constructions can also appear in the second half of the third year, as this example (Clark, 2003, p. 267) demonstrates: *If I get my graham cracker in the water, it'll get all soapy*.

Combining Sentences: Children with Language Impairment

In a cross-sectional study of 65 children with language impairment aged 6–11 years, Hesketh (2004) used subtests from a standardized procedure, Assessment of Comprehension and Expression 6–11 (Adams, Cooke, Crutchley, Hesketh, & Reeves, 2001), to elicit complex sentences. The main aim of the study was to compare the relative effectiveness of structured elicitation and a narrative task in drawing target structures out of children, but the study allows some general conclusions about the availability of complex sentences to these children. First, many—but not all—of the children were using the constructions of interest. Approximate percentage values for these constructions were as follows: coordination, 75%; relative clause, 75%; subordination (verb complement, temporal or causal linkage) 65%; conditional, 45%. Hesketh (2004, p. 170) provided values for both structured elicitation and narrative. The percentages quoted are for whichever value is the higher. Second, via the structured elicitation procedure, a developmental progression between 6 and 11 years was apparent, at least for subordinate constructions and conditionals. Finally, there is some indication in examples quoted in the study of the omission of obligatory grammatical markers.

A useful complement to this large sample cross-sectional study is a longitudinal case study of MM, a boy with SLI, between the ages of 3;3 and 7;10 (Schuele & Dykes, 2005), in which a dozen samples of conversational speech were analysed. The MLU range from the first to the last sample was 1.91 to 5.46. There is little evidence of the availability of complex constructions until sample 6 (age 4;8, MLU 3.12), when coordinating and subordinating conjunctions appear. Sample 8 (age 5;9, MLU 4.27) sees sentential verb complements, relative clauses, and conditionals. The percentage of complex sentence use increased from LS6 onwards, with 31% of utterances in Sample 12 consisting of complex constructions. The data from MM confirm the persistence of grammatical marker omissions within these complex constructions as they develop. For example, the obligatory relative marker in subject relative clauses (e.g., *that* in *I was scared of the boy that chased us*) was omitted in every instance, over a long period. A "subject" relative is one where the matrix sentence noun, which is postmodified, functions as the subject noun of the relative clause, as in the example above. For subject relatives, a grammatical marker *who* or *that* is obligatory. In object relatives, those in which the modified matrix noun functions as the object of the relative clause, as in *I was scared of the boy (that) you chased*, the relative marker is optional and is often omitted. This vulnerability of obligatory markers in subject relatives was confirmed by Schuele and Tolbert (2001). They compared a group of children with SLI between 5 and 7 years, and a younger typically developing group aged 3–5 years. The younger typically developing children never omitted the marker from subject relatives, but the children with SLI left them out of 63% of the time (see also Schuele & Nicholls, 2000).

As Schuele and Dykes (2005) pointed out, our information on the acquisition of complex constructions by children with SLI is still quite limited in comparison to our knowledge of morphosyntactic development. As with other areas of the grammar, the course of complex sentence development in children with language impairment starts later than it does in typically developing age peers. This is particularly apparent in a longitudinal study of a child with SLI (Schuele & Dykes, 2005), where the fifth year, rather than the third year, sees these constructions emerge. A majority of school-age children with language impairment appear to be able produce a range of complex constructions (Marinellie, 2004). However, these children tend to omit obligatory grammatical markers. This was reported by Schuele and Dykes (2005) in their longitudinal study, for infinitival *to* (see also

Eisenberg, 2003), wh-pronouns in embedded clauses, and subject relative markers. Specific examples of subject relative marker omissions appeared in a study of three children with SLI in one family by Schuele and Nicholls (2000):

She's got all the dishes __ need to be washed
And the man __ owns it, he said
We got one girl __ have a birthday in March

Problems with relative clauses are also reported for languages other than English. Omission of relative markers is reported for children with SLI in Swedish (Håkansson & Hansson, 2000). Difficulties with object relatives emerge in both comprehension and production for Hebrew-speaking children with SLI (Friedmann & Novogrodsky, 2004; Novogrodsky & Friedmann, 2006). In the profile of delay and deficit they reveal, these findings on complex sentences mirror the results from extensive studies of grammatical morphology in children with SLI. These children are slower to acquire elements of the inflectional system, they find the development of the system more problematic than younger typically developing children, but the errors they do make are similar to those found in typical developers. We do not find children with language impairment constructing deviant grammars of the inflectional system, and this also appears to be true of the syntax of complex sentences.

From a descriptive or assessment perspective, the term complex sentence is a useful catch-all for the set of syntactic devices English provides for linking simple sentences, but for effective assessment and intervention the distinct functions of the forms we have discussed have to be recognized, in addition to their syntactic requirements. We can see this in relation to two types of subordination described as embedding, verb complementation and relative clauses. Main verbs in the former, like *know, believe* (*I know **she's coming***; *Freya thinks **she's a princess***) reflect the speaker's attitude to the content expressed in the complement clause (Clark, 2003, p. 255), where *attitude* is a cover term for the degree of commitment the speaker has to the propositional content of the embedded clause. A verb such as *know* is interpreted by the hearer as entailing that the proposition is true, whereas from *think* the hearer infers only that the speaker believes it to be true. Children have to learn to select the verb appropriate to the attitude they wish to express and to formulate the content of the embedded sentence. Relative clauses are also embeddings of one sentence into another, though their insertion point is within a noun phrase. The role of relative clauses is the same as that of nonclausal noun postmodification, namely to further specify the head noun. By providing further information about the head noun, relative clauses help to restrict possible referent identifications the hearer could make. For another type of subordination involving temporal linkage, the child's central task is to learn the semantics of the various linking words—*when, after, before, while*—and how they relate to the events described in the two sentences being linked. For sentences linked by *while*, for example, the time of the event described in the sentence preceding *while* has to co-occur with, or occur within, the timespan of the event described in the sentence following it: *Nero was fiddling while Rome burned; Mind the baby while I go to the shop.* Understanding the semantics of the relevant connectives and of the relationship of the events being linked is also crucial for complex sentences characterizing causal relationships. Donaldson, Reid, and Murray (2007) found that 5- to 7-year-old children with language impairment have "marked and extensive problems" using sentences with connectives *because* and *so*. Intervention that seeks to develop complex sentences will inevitably pay close attention to the formal demands of these structures but, equally, has to recognize that their successful deployment mandates a clear understanding of their informational function.

Other childhood developmental disabilities

Other developmental disabilities that have attracted the attention of researchers in relation to syntactic impairment are Williams syndrome, Down syndrome, and autism (see chapter 2 by McDuffie & Abbeduto and chapter 3 by Gerenser). We will deal with these in turn, and also note studies that have made comparisons between any of these groups.

Williams syndrome (WS) is a rare, genetically based developmental disorder. Stromme, Bjornstad, and Ramstad (2002) give a prevalence estimate of 1 in 7,500 live births, based on data from Norway. Despite its rarity, the condition has played an important role in theoretical debate about the relationship between language and cognition—a debate that is important for our understanding of normal language development and hence of language impairment. The significance lies in the apparent dissociation between language abilities in individuals with WS and their severe cognitive deficits (Mervis, 2003). Initial reports, in particular Bellugi, Sabo, and Vaid (1988), indicated intact language ability in the context of severe mental retardation. Individuals with WS "were able to produce and comprehend complex grammatical constructions such as reversible passives, conditionals . . . yet are unable to conserve quantity or number" (Mervis, 2003, p. 2). Such observations appear to support the claims of those who argue for modularity in cognitive organization. Extensive research since the initial reports has however, refined the initial view of a dislocation between linguistic and cognitive abilities. A number of later studies have indicated that individuals with WS have syntactic abilities not inconsistent with their mental age (MA). As Karmiloff-Smith (1998, p. 395) points out, fluent language in an adult with WS and an IQ of 51 might lead us to infer a syntactic module developing independently of other cognitive faculties. But the same linguistic fluency in the context of this individual's MA of 7 years alters our view. We would expect individuals with MAs at this level to have acquired most of the syntactic structures of English.

A study by Grant, Valian, and Karmiloff-Smith (2002) addressed the relations among chronological age, mental age, and syntactic ability in this syndrome. A group of 14 individuals with WS (ages 8;1–30;9 mean = 17;11), took part in an imitation task designed around relative clauses. The mean vocabulary mental age of the WS group (derived from the British Picture Vocabulary Scales: Dunn, Dunn, & Whetton, 1982) was 8;9 years. Their performance was compared with three groups of typically developing children aged 5, 6, and 7 years. There were no differences among the groups on subject relatives, but on object relatives the WS group performed similarly to the 5-year-olds. Both groups were significantly different from the 6- and 7-year-olds. These results underline the considerable delay in syntactic abilities identifiable in older children and adults with WS. They also indicate some delay relative to mental age. Further analysis of the WS group results provides two points worth noting. First, the patterning of their responses across different types of relative clauses is similar to that of all typically developing children. So, for example, all groups found subject relatives easier than object relatives. Second, the WS group found those relative clauses that contained an overt marker of the relativization easier to deal with. In object relatives it is possible to say either *the cat chased the dog that you scared* or, omitting the relative marker, *the cat chased the dog you scared*. This is interpreted by Grant et al. (2002, p. 414) as indicating that "older children and adults with WS may be unable to extract meaning from syntactically complex sentences without a great deal of syntactic support."

An alternative view comes from researchers who, from a Chomskyan perspective, emphasize the sparing of syntax and rule-governed morphology in WS, relative to cognitive abilities. Clahsen and Almazan (1998), tested four individuals with WS, aged 11;2–15;4, whose MAs ranged from 5;4 to 7;6, on a range of syntactic and morphological tasks (for the morphology findings see chapter 15 by Oetting & Hadley). The syntactic tasks included comprehension of passives, using a procedure adapted from van der Lely (1996), and interpretation of pronominal reference, using materials from van der Lely and Stollwerck (1997). Data from the control groups for each of these studies was used to compare with the WS group. In both tasks, the WS group performed at ceiling, and their performance was superior to that of the control groups. The authors concluded that grammatical mechanisms involved in these structures appear to be intact in individuals with WS. In a review of research on WS, Karmiloff-Smith and Mills (2006) concede that while it is possible that WS syntax is intact, the claim is unlikely, for several reasons, including the relative clause performance of the subjects studied by Grant et al. (2002). They also reported problems that French- and Italian-speaking WS children have with gender concord—an area of the grammar acquired easily by very young children. Clearly, the line under this debate is not yet drawn.

Down syndrome (DS) is also a genetically based disorder, resulting from a third copy of chromosome 21 (see chapter 2 by McDuffie & Abbeduto). Syntax has been identified as an area of deficit in individuals with DS. However, Abbeduto and Chapman (2005) claimed that the deficit is more marked in production than comprehension, "until late adolescence, when losses in syntax comprehension are encountered" (Abbeduto & Chapman, 2005, p. 59). Children with DS evidence very slow expressive development. Throughout childhood, delays in expressive language, relative to receptive language and to nonverbal cognition, are identified, in vocabulary, and in utterance length, and in complexity (Abbeduto & Chapman, 2005, p. 55). While these deficits persist into adolescence, syntactic progress does continue to be made. This is evidenced in a study by Thordardottir, Chapman, and Wagner (2002). They compared a group of 24 adolescents with DS, mean age 16.5, to an MLU-matched control group of much younger typically developing children (average age 3;1 years). All the individuals involved produced a 12-minute narrative sample, which was scrutinized for the use of complex sentences. Coordinated sentences, and both types of embedded sentences discussed above, verb complements, and relative clauses appear in the samples from both DS and controls, and there are no significant differences between the groups for proportion of complex sentences, or for diversity of complex sentence types. While acknowledging the absence of difference between the groups, Thordardottir et al. (2002) drew attention to the high degree of variability in the DS group. Individual differences in developmental rate are also found in DS individuals. Chapman, Hesketh, and Kistler (2002) obtained a variety of measures from a group of 31 individuals with DS whose ages ranged between 5 and 20 years, at four time intervals over six years. They identified visual and auditory working memory, along with chronological age, as the best predictors of receptive syntactic ability.

Comparisons have been made between individuals with DS and those with other developmental disabilities. Laws and Bishop (2003) compared adolescents with DS with children with SLI matched for nonverbal cognitive ability. They found that the linguistic profiles of the two groups were similar, with receptive language superior to expressive, and grammar lagging behind vocabulary in both comprehension and production. In a study comparing adolescents with DS and WS, however, Ring and Clahsen (2005) did find differences in syntactic ability in tasks involving the interpretation of passive structures and of syntactic binding of reflexive and nonreflexive pronoun reference. The WS group performed no differently from controls matched for mental age on both passive structures and structures involving the interpretation of reflexive pronouns (assigning the correct referent in sentences such as *Is Mowgli tickling himself?*). The DS children were significantly poorer than the WS children on passives. They were as capable as the WS group and the controls in understanding nonreflexive pronouns (identifying the referent of *her* in *Is Minnie the*

Minx tickling her?). But their success rate on reflexive pronouns (as in *Is Minnie the Minx tickling herself?*) was significantly lower than the WS and control groups.

The issue of individual variability in linguistic ability, apparent in DS, arises again in autism. Communication impairment is one of the defining features of this condition (Baird, Cass, & Slonims, 2003), but the linguistic abilities of individuals with autism span a considerable range "from a delay in the development of expressive language to a total lack of expressive language, from problems with initiating or sustaining a conversation to use of stereotyped, repetitive and idiosyncratic language" (Gernsbacher, Geye, & Ellis Weismer, 2005, p. 73).

Some detail on this variability comes from a study of 89 children who met the DSM-IV criteria for autism, by Kjelgaard and Tager-Flusberg (2001). Using a battery of standardized tests to explore phonological, lexical, and grammatical abilities, they found that while more than 90% of children were able to complete the phonological and vocabulary tests, only about half were able to complete the CELF (Semel, Wiig, & Secord, 1995). The CELF explores receptive and expressive language skills in the areas of morphology, syntax, semantics, and working memory for language. Of the 44 children who were able to complete the CELF, 10 were designated as linguistically normal, with standard scores above 85; a further 13, with standard scores between 70 and 84, were labelled borderline. And the remainder (*N* = 21), with standard scores of 70 or less (i.e., two standard deviations or more below the mean), were considered impaired. A profile of poorer grammatical than lexical ability in the borderline and impaired individuals leads Kjelgaard and Tager-Flusberg (2001) to compare the performance of this subset of their sample to the phenotype of SLI (Tager-Flusberg & Cooper, 1999). The possible overlap between autism and SLI, and between autism and pragmatic language impairment (PLI) is discussed in some detail by Gernsbacher et al. (2005, pp. 83ff.; see also Botting & Conti-Ramsden, 2003).

ASSESSMENT OF SYNTACTIC IMPAIRMENT

Standardized Tests

Many of the tests referred to in chapter 15 (Oetting & Hadley) for the identification of language impairment have syntactic content and are viable for screening or initial identification purposes, to identify children who may be language-impaired and who may have syntactic problems. Standardized procedures do include some of the structures identified above as relevant to syntactic impairment, as can be seen from two language assessment procedures widely used in the United Kingdom and elsewhere, the Test for Reception of Grammar 2 (TROG 2; Bishop, 2003) and the Reynell Developmental Language Scales–III (RDLS–III; Edwards et al., 1997). As its name indicates, the TROG, normed on 750 4- to 14-year-olds in the United Kingdom, provides information on comprehension only. The test is organized into 20 blocks, each containing four items devoted to the same structure. Structures addressed include relative clauses, reversible passives, and pronominal reference. RDLS-III is normed on 1,074 children between the ages of 1;6 and 7 years in the United Kingdom and the Republic of Ireland. It has separate assessments of comprehension and expressive language. The comprehension scale contains examples of relative clauses and short passives (i.e., passive structures lacking an agent phrase such as *the sheep was pushed*). The expressive scale includes a section requiring the child to imitate relative clauses and subordinate structures linked by *after, though*, and *while*.

There are however, inherent limitations to the use of available tests for diagnostic purposes, relating primarily to their content validity. Time constraints preclude an adequate sampling of the full range of syntactic structures in the language, and methodological difficulties mean that some central areas of syntax are difficult to address. For example, it is not straightforward in comprehension procedures, which require an unequivocal behavioural response to pictures or the manipulation of toys, to construct stimuli to investigate the child's understanding of the full range of modal verbs. Interrogative structures and complex sentences other than relative clauses tend not to be included in expressive language tests. For the exploration of the full range of structures in expressive syntactic impairment, language samples have been an important source of information. And for the in-depth investigation of particular syntactic structures, especially but not exclusively in comprehension, researchers have developed specific probes.

Language Sampling and Other Methods

It is now hard to imagine the study of language development in children without conversational language samples. The detailed longitudinal samples described in Brown (1973) were the forerunners of other corpora from English-speaking children, both typical and atypical developers, and then from children learning languages other than English. Since Brown's time, the development of large computer databases and of computational procedures for sample analysis procedures has greatly facilitated child language research in both typically and atypically developing children. Brown's samples, and many of the corpora collected since, are available in the Child Language Data Exchange System (CHILDES) at the system's website: www.psy.cmu.edu. The CHILDES system incorporates a standard transcriptional format (CHAT), and a series of programs (CLAN) for automatic analysis of language samples. Full details are available in MacWhinney (2000), which is downloadable from the website. The CLAN programs include, among an extensive set, procedures for calculating MLU and for assigning parts of speech to a corpus, as well as a flexible coding facility whereby analysts can devise their own codes relevant to specific areas of interest and then compute frequencies. A measure recently added to the CLAN suite, VOCD, developed by Malvern and colleagues (Malvern, Richards, Chipere, & Durán, 2004) provides an estimate of lexical diversity in a language sample. An alternative computer-based procedure, Systematic Analysis of Language Transcripts (SALT), has a wide range of automatically derivable measures in English and Spanish (Miller & Iglesias, 2006). The standard measures for English include MLU, lists and frequencies of bound morphemes, frequencies for elements of particular grammatical classes (e.g., question words, auxiliaries), and measures of fluency and rate. Measures derived from samples can be compared to those derived from a reference database of close to 400 children between 3 and 13 years in age.

Language samples are readily available in clinical contexts, and Brown (1973) had demonstrated the potential offered by conversational samples for information on a child's language status. From this example followed the development of profiling procedures designed to extract from language samples information on syntax and morphology, which would assist the clinician in assessment and remediation (e.g., Crystal, Fletcher, & Garman, 1989; Leadholm & Miller, 1992; Miller, 1981). The procedure developed by Crystal et al. (1989), the Language Assessment, Intervention and Screening Procedure (LARSP), was an attempt to codify the major features of syntactic development in English from the onset of single words through to the development of complex subordinate structures, covering the age-range from around 18 months to 4;6 years. Applied to a language sample from a child in the clinic, a LARSP profile identifies areas of syntactic strength and weakness relative to the normal developmental course. The LARSP procedure has been computerized (Long, Fey, & Channell, 2004).

LARSP and other profiling procedures are essentially qualitative analyses. Indices designed to quantify developmental change via language samples, and so identify syntactic deficits, have also been developed. These include developmental sentence scoring (DSS; Lee, 1974) and the index of productive syntax (IPSyn; Scarborough, 1990). These systems give scores for the occurrence of specific structures and aggregate these scores into a total that can then be compared to a norm. IPSyn works off a sample of 100 child utterances, which are examined for 56 specific language structures (for example, auxiliaries, modals, specific types of subordinate clauses). The scores for individual structures (a range of 0–2 for each structure) are then added to provide an overall total, with a maximum of 112. The automatic measurement of IPSyn has been discussed by Sagae, Lavie, and MacWhinney (2005).

Though language samples have an advantage in terms of their ecological validity, as evidence of the child's ability to produce and respond to syntactic structures in real time and in naturalistic situations, they do have limitations in their reliability. Factors such as interviewer ability, topic choice, length of time involved, and the child's own performance on the day can conspire to deliver a less than optimal profile of the child's syntactic repertoire from a specific language sample. Transcriptional choices can also influence reliability, especially in relation to comparisons between samples from the same child or different children. An important issue here is segmentation—the demarcation of units upon which syntactic analysis is conducted. Unless a principled and consistent approach to utterance segmentation is adopted, particularly with data from school-age children who may be using more complex utterances, reliability can be compromised (for discussion see Fletcher & Garman, 1995; Scott & Stokes, 1995).

In exploring comprehension, or in investigating structures in a child's expressive language that may rarely occur in language samples, researchers have had recourse to specific probes. There are many examples of ingenious procedures in the literature, including in papers cited in this chapter. Here, one example each for receptive and expressive language will suffice. For comprehension, a developmentally graduated series of procedures is described in detail in Miller and Paul (1995). The structures addressed range from the comprehension of two- and three-word instructions, through word order comprehension in reversible active sentences, to the comprehension of different question types and the making of inferences in discourse. For several of the procedures, alternative methods are provided. So for comprehension of locative prepositions, three tasks are provided: a search task, in which the child has to find an object; a placement task, where the response involves placing an object in accordance with an instruction; and a body placement task, where the child locates herself according to an instruction.

The two techniques Novogrodsky and Friedmann (2006) provide for the elicitation of relative clauses can serve to exemplify expressive probes. Their first approach is purely verbal. The individual being tested is given a scenario and then asked a question: "There are two children. One gives a present, the other child receives a present. Which child would you rather be? Start with *I would rather be* . . . or *The child* . . ." The expected answer (the antecedent is the subject of relative clause) is either *I would rather be the child that receives the present*, or *The child that receives the present*. The alternative technique relies on the use of pictures. The individual being tested sees two scenes, one in which a child is washing a giraffe, and the other in which a giraffe is washing a child. The picture is described, and a question asked: "Here are two girls. In one picture the girl is washing the giraffe, in the other picture the giraffe is washing the girl. Which girl is this (pointing to the picture of the giraffe washing the girl)? Start with *This is the girl*. . . ." In this instance it is the object relative (the antecedent is the object of the relative clause) that is the desired response: *This is the girl that the giraffe is washing*.

INTERVENTION

In a systematic review of 25 studies (Law, Garrett, & Nye, 2003), the findings on the effectiveness of intervention (see also chapter 23 by Fey and Finestack) on the expressive syntax of children with language impairment were mixed, with some studies showing positive outcomes and others not. Also, no significant differences in outcome were found between clinician-administered intervention and that supplied by trained parents, or between intervention supplied to individuals and that supplied to groups. Because of the terms of the systematic review, the studies analyzed were only those which could be considered as randomized controlled trials (RCTs). Although studies of intervention are limited, compared to those that explore the nature and extent of syntactic impairment, there is a body of research other than RCTs that is informative about potentially effective remediation methods. Fey and Proctor-Williams (2000) examined the evidence from this research in relation to three procedures designed to introduce and entrench target structures in the syntactic repertoires of children with language impairment. The first of these, recasting, resembles the natural reformulations adults provide for typically developing children (Chouinard & Clark, 2003, p. 639):

> Parent: What did you do
> Child: I go to school
> Parent: You went to school with your brother

Fey and Proctor-Williams (2000) defined recastings as "adult responses that immediately follow the child's utterance and share referential contexts, referents and major lexical items with that utterance, while maintaining the child's original meaning." At the same time, the recasting modifies one or more syntactic elements from the child's original utterance. The major advantage of recasts compared to other methods of intervention such as elicited imitation or modelling is that these responses can be fed naturally into a conversation a clinician is having with a child. Fey and Proctor-Williams (2000) reported results from a study of parent-directed intervention that shows that the frequency of recasts does have an effect on the ability of children with SLI to use target forms. Elicited imitation and modelling can also be effective, as studies cited Fey and Proctor-Williams (2000) demonstrate. As its label indicates, imitation as a technique requires the child to directly repeat a stimulus utterance that focuses on a syntactic element or elements of interest. In modelling, the child is presented with a series of examples of a target syntactic structure, perhaps as many as 20, and then the child has to respond in a guided conversation using the structure just modelled.

As Oetting and Hadley (chapter 15) point out in relation to morphology, selecting an intervention procedure is relatively straightforward by comparison with identifying a target structure, or achieving a prioritization of target structures. This is an even greater problem in syntax, given the overall complexity of the system. In the main, what guidance is available recommends using the normal development course as the template for advancement (Crystal et al., 1989; Miller, 1981). However, the level of abstraction at which even detailed assessment procedures such as LARSP identify targets can be misleading. The abstraction built into a syntactic assessment procedure by a type label such as S(ubject)V(erb)O(bject) can obscure the requirement for a clinician to carefully consider the choice of lexical verb realizations for this structure in intervention, if this is designated as a target because an individual's language samples lack transitive sentences.

Recent developments in research on typical language development (e.g., Tomasello, 2000, 2003) argue for an approach to assessment and intervention that is lexically informed.

A basic tenet of the construction grammar approach of Tomasello and colleagues is that the language children initially produce is not organized in terms of abstract linguistic categories such as N, VP, or SVO but is "almost totally concrete" (Tomasello, 2000, p. 2), and progress to abstract categories is gradual. Evidence for this view of the extended development of a verb-general transitive construction, for instance, comes from two directions. Experimental studies revealed that it is only by about 4 years of age that the majority of typically developing children demonstrate the ability to use a novel verb in a transitive frame (Tomasello, 2003, p. 130). And longitudinal studies of speech samples from children between 1 and 3 years of age have indicated a selectivity of construction types for particular verbs and little evidence that children knew how to reliably mark subjects and objects syntactically via pronoun case (Tomasello, 2000, p. 3). By contrast, there are two recent experimental studies, based on children's comprehension, that suggest earlier abstraction of syntactic representations receptively. In a study involving 21- and 25-month old typically developing children, Gertner, Fisher, and Eisengart (2006) found that their subjects could use word order appropriately to extend their knowledge of English word order to novel verbs. Also, Fernandes, Marcus, Di Nubila, and Vouloumanos (2006) reported a study in which children aged 27–35 months mapped an event onto transitive and intransitive sentence frames. Both studies point to a more abstract receptive competence for simple sentence structures than is apparent in research based on children's production. But in relation to children with SLI, who are likely to be at least two years behind their peers in their capacity for abstraction, it would be reasonable to make minimal assumptions about their facility for detecting general syntactic patterns, to initially assess their competence for simple sentence structures from a lexical perspective (see Fletcher, Stokes, & Wong, 2005, pp. 47ff. for further discussion), and to build well-motivated lexical choice into intervention materials.

CONCLUSION

There is still much to learn about syntactic impairment in children with developmental disabilities. There are areas of sentence syntax that are relatively unexplored, such as noun modification, preverb modification, and complex sentences other than those involving relative clauses and the clausal complements of verbs. And we know little about growth trajectories for syntax in any of the disabilities reviewed. This will be important not only for tracing the natural history of syntactic structure change in clinical populations, but also for gaining insight into the variability inherent in these populations. As we have seen at points in this chapter, and as Garman, James, and Stojanovik (2005) emphasized, variability within groups of children with impairment is high, and its significance not well understood. As they argued, future research that delivers both detailed case studies and longitudinal information would have the potential to advance our knowledge of the constraints on syntactic learning in special populations.

REFERENCES

Abbeduto, L., & Chapman, R. (2005). Language development in Down syndrome and fragile X syndrome. In P. Fletcher & J. Miller (Eds.), *Developmental theory and language disorders* (pp. 53–72). Amsterdam: John Benjamins.

Adams, C., Cooke, R., Crutchley, A., Hesketh, A., & Reeves, D. (2001). *Assessment of Comprehension and Expression 6–11*. Windsor, ON, Canada: NFER-Nelson.

Baird, G., Cass, H., & Slonims, V. (2003). Clinical review: Diagnosis of autism. *British Medical Journal, 327,* 488–493.

Bellugi, U., Sabo, H., & Vaid, J. (1988). Dissociation between language and cognitive functions in Williams syndrome. In D. Bishop & K. Mogford (Eds.), *Language development in exceptional circumstances* (pp. 177–189). London: Churchill-Livingstone.

Bishop, D. (2003). *Test for Reception of Grammar–2.* San Antonio, TX: Harcourt Assessment, Inc.

Bishop, D. V. M., Bright, P., James, C., Bishop, S. J., & van der Lely, H. K. J. (2000). Grammatical SLI: A distinct subtype of developmental language impairment? *Applied Psycholinguistics, 21,* 159–181.

Bishop, D. V. M., & McArthur, G. M. (2005). Individual differences in auditory processing in specific language impairment: A follow-up study using event-related potentials and behavioural thresholds. *Cortex, 41,* 327–341.

Botting, N., & Conti-Ramsden, G. (2003). Autism, primary pragmatic difficulties and specific language impairment: Can we distinguish them using psycholinguistic markers? *Developmental Medicine and Child Neurology, 45,* 515–524.

Brown, R. (1973). *A first language: The early stages.* London: George Allen & Unwin.

Chapman, R., Hesketh, L., & Kistler, D. (2002). Predicting longitudinal change in language production and comprehension in individuals with Down syndrome. *Journal of Speech, Language, and Hearing Research, 45,* 902–915.

Chiat, S. (2000). *Understanding children with language problems.* Cambridge, UK: Cambridge University Press.

Chomsky, N. (1965). *Aspects of the theory of syntax.* Cambridge, MA: MIT Press.

Chouinard, M., & Clark, E. (2003). Adult reformulations of child errors as negative evidence. *Journal of Child Language, 30,* 637–669.

Clahsen, H., & Almazan, M. (1998). Syntax and morphology in children with Williams syndrome. *Cognition, 68,* 167–198.

Clahsen, H., Bartke, S., & Göllner, S. (1997). Formal features in impaired grammars: A comparison of English and German SLI children. *Journal of Neurolinguistics, 10,* 151–171.

Clark, E. (2003). *First language acquisition.* Cambridge, UK: Cambridge University Press.

Crystal, D., Fletcher, P., & Garman, M. (1989). *The grammatical analysis of language disability* (2nd ed.). London: Cole & Whurr.

Deevy, P., & Leonard, L. (2004). The comprehension of wh-questions in children with specific language impairment. *Journal of Speech, Language, and Hearing Research, 47,* 802–815.

Donaldson, M., Reid, J., & Murray, C. (2007). Causal sentence production in children with language impairments. *International Journal of Language and Communication Disorders, 42,* 155–186.

Dunn, L. M., Dunn, L. M., & Whetton, C. (1982). *British Picture Vocabulary Scale.* Windsor, ON, Canada: NFER-Nelson.

Edwards, S., Fletcher, P., Garman, M, Hughes, A. Letts, C., & Sinka, I. (1997). *The Reynell Developmental Language Scales–III: The University of Reading Edition.* Windsor, ON, Canada: NFER-Nelson.

Eisenberg, S. (2003). Production of infinitival object complements in the conversational speech of 5-year-old children with language-impairment. *First Language, 23,* 327–341.

Fernandes, K., Marcus, G., Di Nubila, J., & Vouloumanos, A. (2006). From semantics to syntax and back again: Argument structure in the third year of life. *Cognition, 100,* 10–20.

Fey, M., & Proctor-Williams, K. (2000). Recasting, elicited imitation and modelling in grammar intervention for children with specific language impairments. In D. V. M. Bishop &. L. B. Leonard (Eds.), *Speech and language impairments in children: Causes, characteristics, intervention and outcome* (pp. 177–194). Hove, UK: Psychology Press.

Fletcher, P. (1991). Evidence from syntax for language impairment. In J. Miller (Ed.), *Research on child language disorders: A decade of progress* (pp. 169–187). Austin, TX: PRO-ED.

Fletcher, P., & Garman, M. (1995). Transcription, segmentation and analysis: Corpora from the language-impaired. In G. Leech, G. Myers, & J. Thomas (Eds.), *Spoken English on computer* (pp. 116–127). Harlow, UK: Longman.

Fletcher, P., Stokes, S., & Wong, A. (2005). Constructions and language development: Implications for language impairment. In P. Fletcher & J. Miller (Eds.), *Developmental theory and language disorders* (pp. 35–51). Amsterdam: John Benjamins.

Friedmann, N., & Novogrodsky, R. (2004). The acquisition of relative clause comprehension in Hebrew: A study of SLI and normal development. *Journal of Child Language*, *31*, 661–681.

Garman, M., James, D., & Stojanovik, V. (2005). Developmental theory and language disorders: A thematic summary. In P. Fletcher & J. Miller (Eds.), *Developmental theory and language disorders* (pp. 147–164). Amsterdam: John Benjamins.

Gathercole, S., & Baddeley, A. (1990). Phonological memory deficits in language disordered children: Is there a causal connection? *Journal of Memory and Language*, *2*, 103–127.

Gavin, W. J., Klee, T., & Membrino, I. (1993). Differentiating specific language impairment from normal grammatical development using grammatical analysis. *Clinical Linguistics and Phonetics*, *7*, 191–206.

Gernsbacher, M., Geye, H., & Ellis Weismer, S. (2005). The role of language and communication impairments within autism. In P. Fletcher & J. Miller (Eds.), *Developmental theory and language disorders* (pp. 73–93). Amsterdam: John Benjamins

Gertner, Y., Fisher, C., & Eisengart, J. (2006). Learning words and rules: Abstract knowledge of word order in early sentence comprehension. *Psychological Science*, *17*, 684–691.

Grant, J., Valian, V., & Karmiloff-Smith, A. (2002). A study of relative clauses in Williams syndrome. *Journal of Child Language*, *29*, 403–416.

Grela, B. (2000). The omission of subject arguments in children with specific language impairment. *Clinical Linguistics and Phonetics*, *17*, 153–169.

Håkansson, G., & Hansson, K. (2000). Comprehension and production of relative clauses: A comparison between Swedish impaired and unimpaired children. *Journal of Child Language*, *27*, 313–333.

Hesketh, A. (2004). Grammatical performance of children with language disorder on structured elicitation and narrative tasks. *Clinical Linguistics and Phonetics*, *18*, 161–182.

Huddleston, R., & Pullum, G. (2003). *The Cambridge grammar of the English language*. Cambridge, UK: Cambridge University Press.

Ingham, R., Fletcher, P., Schelletter, C., & Sinka, I. (1998). Resultative VPs and specific language impairment. *Language Acquisition*, *7*, 87–111.

Karmiloff-Smith, A. (1998). Development itself is the key to understanding developmental disorders. *Trends in Cognitive Sciences*, *2*, 389–398.

Karmiloff-Smith, A., & Mills, D. L. (2006). Williams syndrome. In K. Brown (Ed.), *Encyclopedia of language and linguistics* (2nd ed., pp. 585–589). Oxford, UK: Elsevier.

King, G., Schelletter, C, Sinka, I., Fletcher, P., & Ingham, R. (1995). Are English-speaking SLI children with morpho-syntactic deficits impaired in their use of locative-contact and causative alternations? *Reading Working Papers in Linguistics*, *2*, 45–65.

Kjelgaard, M., & Tager-Flusberg, H. (2001). An investigation of language impairment in autism: Implications for genetic sub-groups. *Language and Cognitive Processes*, *16*, 289–308.

Law, J., Garrett, Z., & Nye, C. (2003). Speech and language therapy interventions for children with primary speech and language delay or disorder. *Cochrane Database of Systematic Reviews* (Issue 3).

Laws, G., & Bishop, D. (2003). A comparison of language abilities in adolescents with Down syndrome and children with specific language impairment. *Journal of Speech, Language, and Hearing Research*, *46*, 1324–1339.

Leadholm, B., & Miller, J. (1992). *Language sample analysis guide: The Wisconsin guide for the identification and description of language impairment in children*. Madison, WI: Wisconsin Department of Public Instruction.

Lee, L. (1974). *Developmental sentence analysis*. Evanston, IL: Northwestern University Press.

Leonard, L. B. (1998). *Children with specific language impairment*. Cambridge, MA: MIT Press.

Leonard, L. B., & Deevy, P. (2004). Lexical deficits in specific language impairment. In L. Verhoeven

& H. van Balkom (Eds.), *Classification of developmental language disorders: Theoretical issues and clinical implications* (pp. 209–233). Mahwah, NJ: Lawrence Erlbaum Associates.

Leonard, L. B., Deevy, P., Miller, C., Charest, M., Kurtz, R., & Rauf, L. (2003). The use of grammatical morphemes reflecting aspect and modality by children with specific language impairment. *Journal of Child Language, 30,* 769–795.

Leonard, L. B., Wong, A. M.-Y., Deevy, P., Stokes, S., & Fletcher, P. (2007). Modal verbs with and without tense: A study of English- and Cantonese-speaking children with specific language impairment. *International Journal of Language and Communication Disorders, 42,* 209–228.

Levin, B. (1993). *English verb classes and alternations.* Chicago: University of Chicago Press.

Long, S., Fey, M., & Channell, R. (2004). *Computerized Profiling* (Version 9.6.0). Cleveland, OH: Case Western Reserve University.

MacWhinney, B. (2000). *The CHILDES project: Tools for analyzing talk* (3rd ed.). Mahwah, NJ: Lawrence Erlbaum Associates

Malvern, D. D., Richards, B. J., Chipere, N., & Durán, P. (2004). *Lexical diversity and language development: Quantification and assessment.* Basingstoke, UK: Palgrave Macmillan.

Marinellie, S. (2004). Complex syntax used by school-age children with specific language impairment (SLI) in child-adult conversation. *Journal of Communication Disorders, 37,* 517–533.

Mervis, C. (2003). Williams syndrome: 15 years of psychological research. *Developmental Neuropsychology, 23,* 1–12.

Miller, J. (1981). *Assessing language production in children: Experimental procedures.* Baltimore: University Park Press.

Miller, J., & Iglesias, A. (2006). *Systematic Analysis of Language Transcripts (SALT), English and Spanish* (Version 9) [Computer Software]. Madison, WI: Language Analysis Laboratory, University of Wisconsin-Madison.

Miller, J., & Paul, R. (1995). *The clinical assessment of language comprehension.* Baltimore: Paul H. Brookes.

Newbury, D., Bishop, D. V., & Monaco, A. (2005). Genetic influences on language impairment and phonological short-term memory. *Trends in Cognitive Sciences, 9,* 527–534.

Novogrodsky, R., & Friedmann, N. (2006). The production of relative clauses in syntactic SLI: A window on the impairment. *Advances in Speech-Language Pathology, 8,* 364–375.

O'Hara, M., & Johnston, J. (1997). Syntactic bootstrapping in children with specific language impairment. *European Journal of Disorders of Communication, 32,* 189–205.

Pinker, S. (1989). *Learnability and cognition: The acquisition of argument structure.* Cambridge, MA: MIT Press.

Rice, M. L., Oetting, J., Marquis, J., Bode, J., & Pae, S. (1994). Frequency of input effects on word comprehension of children with specific language impairment. *Journal of Speech and Hearing Research, 37,* 106–122.

Rice, M. L., & Wexler, K. (1996). Toward tense as a clinical marker of specific language impairment in English-speaking children. *Journal of Speech and Hearing Research, 39,* 1239–1257.

Rice, M. L., Wexler, K., & Cleave, P. (1995). Specific language impairment as a period of Extended Optional Infinitive. *Journal of Speech and Hearing Research, 38,* 850–863.

Ring, M., & Clahsen, H. (2005). Distinct patterns of language impairment in Down's syndrome and Williams syndrome: The case of syntactic chains. *Journal of Neurolinguistics, 18,* 479–501.

Sagae, K., Lavie, A., & MacWhinney, B. (2005). Automatic measurement of syntactic development in child language. In *Proceedings of the 42nd Meeting of the Association for Computational Linguistics, Ann Arbor, MI* (pp. 197–204). Morristown, NJ: Association for Computational Linguistics. Automatic measurement of syntactic development in child language

Scarborough, H. (1990). Index of Productive Syntax. *Applied Psycholinguistics, 11,* 1–22.

Schuele, C., & Dykes, J. (2005). Complex syntax acquisition: A longitudinal case study of a child with specific language impairment. *Clinical Linguistics and Phonetics, 19,* 295–318.

Schuele, C., & Nicholls, L. (2000). Relative clauses: Evidence of continued linguistic vulnerability in children with specific language impairment. *Clinical Linguistics and Phonetics, 14,* 563–585.

Schuele, C., & Tolbert, L. (2001). Omissions of obligatory relative markers in children with specific language impairment. *Clinical Linguistics and Phonetics, 15,* 257–274.

Scott, C., & Stokes, S. L. (1995). Measures of syntax in school-age children and adolescents. *Language, Speech, and Hearing Services in Schools, 26*, 309–319.

Semel, E., Wiig, E., & Secord, W. (1995). *Clinical evaluation of language fundamentals* (3rd ed.). San Antonio, TX: Psychological Corporation.

Stromme, P., Bjornstad, P. G., & Ramstad, K. (2002). Prevalence estimation of Williams syndrome. *Journal of Child Neurology, 17*, 269–271.

Tager-Flusberg, H., & Cooper, J. (1999). Present and future possibilities for defining a phenotype for specific language impairment. *Journal of Speech, Language, and Hearing Research, 42*, 1275–1278.

Thordardottir, E., Chapman, R., & Wagner, L. (2002). Complex sentence production by adolescents with Down syndrome. *Applied Psycholinguistics, 23*, 163–183.

Thordardottir, E., Elin, T., & Ellis Weismer, S. (2002). Verb argument structure weakness in specific language impairment in relation to age and utterance length. *Clinical Linguistics and Phonetics, 16*, 233–250.

Tomasello, M. (2000). Acquiring syntax is not what you think. In D. V. M. Bishop & L. B. Leonard (Eds.), *Speech and language impairments in children: Causes, characteristics, intervention and outcome* (pp. 1–15). Hove, UK: Psychology Press.

Tomasello, M. (2003). *Constructing a language: A usage-based theory of language acquisition.* Cambridge, MA: Harvard University Press.

Trask, R. L. (1993). *A dictionary of grammatical terms in linguistics.* London: Routledge.

van der Lely, H. K. (1996). Specifically language impaired and normally developing children: Verbal passive vs. adjectival passive interpretation. *Lingua, 98*, 243–272.

van der Lely, H. K. (2003). Do heterogeneous SLI deficits need heterogeneous theories? SLI subgroups, G-SLI and the RDDR hypothesis. In Yonata Levy & Jeannette Schaeffer (Eds.), *Towards a definition of specific language impairment* (pp. 109–134). Mahwah, NJ: Lawrence Erlbaum Associates.

van der Lely, H. K. (2004). Evidence for and implications of a domain-specific grammatical deficit. In Lyle Jenkins (Ed.), *The genetics of language* (pp. 117–145). Oxford, UK: Elsevier.

van der Lely, H. K. (2005). Domain-specific cognitive systems: Insight from grammatical specific language impairment. *Trends in Cognitive Sciences, 9*, 53–59.

van der Lely, H., & Battell, J. (2003). Wh-movement in children with grammatical SLI: A test of the RDDR hypothesis. *Language, 79*, 153–181.

van der Lely, H. K., & Stollwerck, L. (1997). Binding theory and specific language impairment in children. *Cognition, 62*, 245–290.

Wexler, K. (1998). Very early parameter setting and the unique checking constraint: A new explanation of the optional infinitive stage. *Lingua, 106*, 23–79.

Wexler, K., Schütze, C., & Rice, M. (1998). Subject case in children with SLI and unaffected controls: Evidence for the Agr/Tns omission model. *Language Acquisition, 7*, 317–344.

Ziegler, J., Pech-Georgel, C., George, F., Alario, F.-X., & Lorenzi, C. (2005). Deficits in speech perception predict language impairment. *Proceedings of the National Academy of Sciences U.S.A., 102*(39), 14110–14115.

18

Pragmatics and Social Communication in Child Language Disorders

MARTIN FUJIKI and BONNIE BRINTON

We introduce Devon and Brad, two 11-year-old boys, and invite them to sit at a table where there are some toys. The boys talk together for a few minutes, and then we bring in 12-year-old Norris. "Devon and Brad," we say, "This is Norris. Norris, this is Devon and Brad." Norris sits down in the empty chair between the other two boys. Devon says, "Hi." Norris does not respond. Devon pulls several pieces of a wooden dinosaur skeleton out of a box. Norris also pulls out some pieces. Devon and Brad begin to assemble the skeleton body, talking about the various pieces and their placement. Norris remains silent and works alone on some segments of the dinosaur tail. About 5 minutes into the interaction, Devon hands Norris a vertebra, saying, "Here's another one of those pieces." Norris takes the piece and looks at it. Seven minutes into the interaction, Devon reaches across Norris and picks up a piece of the skeleton. For 13 more minutes, Devon and Brad talk and work together. Norris sits between them, silently manipulating the tailpieces.

A clinician is talking with 7-year-old Cody. The clinician comments, "Last night I went to McDonald's. I got a shake. I spilled it all over my pants!" Cody laughs and replies, "I watch Ren and Stimpy and this guy was mad and know what? Yeah and it and Ren and Stimpy was in the dungeon . . ."

Six-year-old Kari is playing with Rose and Edie. Kari suggests they play school and announces that she is the teacher. She begins to question the others about the story of the three pigs. Then Kari asks, "Which ah lights are hanging above the wall?" Rose and Edie look up at the ceiling, puzzled. Edie asks, "Lights hanging above the wall?" Kari picks up an imaginary cell phone, "Yeah? Hello? Hello. Nothing good about it. This is Mrs. Kinner's class and we're talking about." Kari turns to Rose and Edie and stage whispers, "everybody in their seats and you can color." She turns back to the imaginary phone, "You guys uhm have a nice dinner, yeah, and we're gonna stay in their seats . . ."

Each of the case excerpts above illustrates a pragmatic problem. Although clinicians working with children with language impairment (LI) have long been concerned with the social ramifications of impaired communication, the pragmatic aspects of LI did not become a topic of general concern across categories of impairment until the 1970s (Bricker, 1993). The resulting innovations in language assessment and intervention have been called the "pragmatics revolution" (Duchan, 1984). Since the 1970s, pragmatics has been an important consideration in the assessment and treatment of children with LI.

DEFINING PRAGMATICS

The Traditional Formalist View of Pragmatics

Defining pragmatics is both a relatively simple and a dauntingly difficult task. Pragmatics is traditionally viewed as one of three major components of language, the other two being linguistic form and meaning. Within this framework, pragmatics is defined as the use of language in social contexts (e.g., Berko Gleason, 2005). Pragmatics is thus considered to be a domain of linguistic behavior similar to phonology, semantics, or syntax. One may describe pragmatic behaviors and the rules for their application in much the same way as one might describe syntactic or semantic forms and rules (Craig, 1995; McTear & Conti-Ramsden, 1992). Some behaviors typically considered within the realm of pragmatics include conveying communicative intent, managing conversations, adjusting contributions to conversations according to shared information, using grammatical forms within the context of shared meaning (e.g., knowledge of deictic forms), formulating various types of narratives, and understanding rules for linguistic politeness.

Defining pragmatics as the use of language in social contexts is not as straightforward as it might initially seem, however. An examination of pragmatic behaviors quickly extends into areas traditionally outside the realm of linguistics, such as social psychology and cultural anthropology (Ninio & Snow, 1996). By way of illustration, consider a behavior that falls squarely within the domain of pragmatics: topic manipulation in conversation. Successful speakers introduce, maintain, change, reintroduce, and close topics, and one may formulate rules that describe a speaker's behavior in performing these actions. Successful topic manipulation, however, involves other skills, such as reading the social and emotional cues of others. It also requires broad knowledge of social norms (e.g., taboo topics) and specific knowledge of one's conversational partner (e.g., shared background information, interest in a topic, etc.). It becomes extremely difficult to draw a clean line between pragmatics and the domains represented by these additional skills and knowledge bases.

From a formalist perspective, pragmatic impairments are considered in relation to the child's strengths and limitations in syntax and semantics (Craig, 1995). For example, to be characterized as a pragmatic deficit, Cody's failure to maintain the topic introduced by his clinician would have to exist in the face of relatively strong structural and lexical skills. If Cody also had serious syntactic and semantic deficits, it would be difficult to determine if he lacked the pragmatic knowledge to maintain the topic, or if he did not have the language structure or vocabulary to do so. This approach to characterizing the pragmatic problems of children with language difficulties has been applied to different categories of disability with varying success. For example, it is generally accepted that many children with autism have difficulty with pragmatics that extends beyond their structural limitations. In contrast, opinions regarding children with specific language impairment (SLI) are more varied.

Functionalist Views of Pragmatics

An alternative view considers pragmatics as the central force underlying other aspects of language. From this functionalist perspective, syntax and semantics exist only for their contribution to the successful communication of messages in a social context (Givon, 1985; Ninio & Snow, 1999). Pragmatics thus provides an organizational structure for the other aspects of language, rather than being one of several equal components. Thus, as Ninio and Snow wrote, "the proper concern of pragmatics is the description of phenomena related to the use of meaningful linguistic forms for communicative purposes" (p. 348). In addition to obscuring the distinction between form, meaning, and use, this view has important implications for language intervention. A functionalist approach emphasizes the import-ance of the intervention environment and the selection of more holistic communication targets. The clinician must employ interactive methods that place intervention in a real communicative context (for examples of a functionalist view of LI, see Craig, 1995; van Balkom & Verhoeven, 2004).

Social Communication

Although it may be important to delineate areas of study clearly, clinicians are often faced with clients who present deficits that cross domains of behavior in complex ways. It has become increasingly necessary to consider a wider view of pragmatics that reaches into realms beyond language structure. Building on the functionalist position, a more expanded view of pragmatics leads to social communication.

Social communication has been defined as "The intersection of language and social behaviors observed during peer interactions . . . that is, the verbal and nonverbal behaviors children display as they approach peers, maintain conversations, and resolve conflicts dur-ing peer interactions" (Timler, Olswang, & Coggins, 2005, p. 171). Adams (2005) argued that although pragmatics and social communication are often used as if they were one and the same, pragmatics is only one of four aspects contributing to social communication. Adams suggested that social communication skills develop from the "synergistic emer-gence of social interaction, social cognition, pragmatics (verbal and nonverbal aspects) and language processing (receptive and expressive)" (Adams, 2005, p. 182). In Adams's frame-work, the term pragmatics refers to the ways in which context influences linguistic form.

Approaching children with LI from a social communication perspective removes the focus from specific speech and language behaviors and places it on social interaction. This broader focus allows consideration and integration of a wider range of behaviors than are considered in traditional language intervention. For example, Timler et al. (2005) discussed interventions for successful peer group entry and sustained cooperative play. These inter-ventions involved behaviors traditionally considered as pragmatic, such as increased con-versational responsiveness. They also focused on behaviors outside these boundaries. For example, with respect to group entry, children were taught to approach the ongoing inter-action and to engage in behavior similar to that of the peers the child wished to join. The ultimate goal of intervention was not to teach specific behaviors or skills but to improve interactional abilities.

In truth, it is difficult to consider pragmatic behaviors as they are used in actual inter-actions without considering cognitive and social cognitive factors. Although we focus much of the following discussion on pragmatic behaviors, it is important to remember that these behaviors must ultimately be viewed in the wider context of social communication.

THE NATURE OF PRAGMATIC PROBLEMS IN CHILDREN WITH LI

Considerable research has examined the nature of pragmatic problems in children with language difficulties. Most of this work has been category-specific, concentrating on describing the pragmatic abilities of children with autism spectrum disorders (ASD), SLI, mental retardation, and other disabilities (Adams, 2005). A good deal of this research has focused on individual pragmatic skills, often assessing performance in relation to other linguistic abilities. A review of the pragmatic difficulties of children across diagnostic categories is beyond the scope of this chapter. We do, however, focus on children with autism and SLI to illustrate the nature of the pragmatic difficulties associated with each diagnostic category (for more information see chapter 2 by Gerenser and chapter 1 by Schwartz).

Children with Autism

Pragmatic language problems are a defining characteristic of autism. Children with autism use a restricted range of speech acts, have difficulty estimating the presuppositional knowledge of listeners, have problems understanding nonliteral forms, and exhibit a range of difficulties in conversational interactions (Tager-Flusberg, 2004). Many of these impairments may be traced back to two basic aspects of development: the capacity for joint attention to objects and events with other persons (Mundy & Burnette, 2005; Wetherby, 2006), and the ability to understand the symbolic function of language (Wetherby, 2006).

Children with autism may not produce the same range of communicative intentions as typical children. The intentions that prove most difficult are those that involve joint attention skills. For example, although they are capable of directing the behavior of others, children with autism may not do so for purposes of gaining attention to share feelings or experiences (Wetherby, Prizant, & Schuler, 2000). Rather, the development of joint attention and requesting appear to be disassociated (Travis & Sigman, 2001). Although some of these children produce request forms relatively early in development, they do so without using the eye contact and gaze alternation basic to joint attending. Hale and Tager-Flusberg (2005) speculated that problems with joint attention may be a forerunner to the difficulties in discourse interaction and theory of mind that are so often associated with autism.

Another pragmatic problem associated with autism stems from difficulty using symbols. For example, a child who has difficulty using symbols may show an overreliance on reenactment strategies. A reenactment strategy "involves the linear repetition of a single event or sequence of events in anticipation of an associated outcome" (Wetherby et al., 2000, p. 114). One well-known illustration is Kanner's (1946) report of a child who said, "Don't throw the dog off of the balcony" to self-regulate behavior. This usage was inappropriately extended from a prior context in which the child's mother had told him to stop throwing a stuffed animal off the hotel balcony (cited by Fay & Schuler, 1980).

A second category of problematic behavior related to the symbolic function of language is the inappropriate use of challenging behaviors to communicate intention. Maladaptive behavior such as head banging may be communicative, perhaps indicating a desire to avoid a particular task or situation (Wetherby et al., 2000). There is considerable evidence that providing a more appropriate means of communicating can result in a decrease in the challenging behavior in question, not only in children with ASD, but in children with a range of disabilities (Carr et al., 1994; Halle, Ostrosky, & Hemmeter, 2006).

The influence of the emphasis on pragmatics can be seen in the communicative programs designed for children with autism. In the 1960s, interventions involving highly operant approaches with discrete trial teaching formats dominated the therapy landscape. Social context was not an important consideration, and the same procedures were used to teach a wide range of skills. Such methods, however, often produced behaviors that could not be used in spontaneous, creative ways to communicate, and learned skills often failed to generalize beyond the contexts in which they were trained (Prizant, Wetherby, & Rydell, 2000). Although these methods are still widely used today, it is generally acknowledged that they must be supplemented with more naturalistic intervention procedures to achieve full functionality (Rogers, 2006).

The following principles, described in greater detail by Prizant et al. (2000), emerged from the general interest in pragmatics in the late 1970s and are foundational to many treatment programs currently used for children with autism.

1. Social context is important, and naturally occurring social interactions with people in the child's environment should be highlighted in intervention.
2. The child is an active participant in the learning process.
3. The role and impact of the caregiver on language development is important and should be highlighted in intervention (e.g., providing facilitating contexts, supporting interactions through scaffolding, adjusting interactional style to the child's level, etc.).
4. Intervention should consist of an individualized treatment program based on the child's profile of strengths and limitations.
5. Intervention should focus immediately on functional communication, rather than on teaching phonemes, words, sentences, or other behaviors in limited social contexts in the hope that these isolated targets will ultimately be used to communicate.

Some treatment frameworks, such as milieu teaching, blend these pragmatic principles with operant procedures (Kaiser, Yoder, & Keetz, 1992; Warren et al., 2006). In these approaches, clinicians create salient communicative contexts and also take advantage of spontaneously occurring interactions. Clinicians focus on child initiation by prompting and reinforcing attempts to communicate with an emphasis on meaningful exchanges (Rogers, 2006).

Pragmatic principles are at the core of developmental sociopragmatic interventions that emphasize meaningful exchanges in natural, communicative contexts (e.g., Prizant, Wetherby, Rubin, Laurent, & Rydell, 2005). The clinician interacts in a facilitative manner, focusing on objects and events that capture the child's attention or interest. The child's attempts to communicate are accepted in a way that emphasizes the meaning being communicated rather than language form. Additionally, attention is also given to appropriate means of emotional expression and social control (Prizant et al. 2000).

Children with SLI

One's view of the pragmatic abilities of children with SLI depends on how one conceptualizes SLI and pragmatic impairment. As noted, from a traditional modular approach, pragmatic deficits are identified in relation to strengths or deficits in form and meaning. When considered in this context, the evidence for pragmatic problems is equivocal. In some comparisons, children with SLI have performed similarly to their language-age-matched peers (e.g., Fey & Leonard, 1984; Leonard, 1986). In studies revealing differences, children with SLI have generally demonstrated the same basic pragmatic functions as their typical peers, although they perform them in less appropriate or efficient ways (e.g., Brinton, Fujiki, & Sonnenberg, 1988; Conti-Ramsden & Friel-Patti, 1983). Some interpret these findings to indicate that pragmatic deficits stem from limitations in structural skills rather than from a lack of pragmatic knowledge (see Craig, 1995; for discussion).

Evidence suggests, however, that some children with SLI have pragmatic problems that do not stem directly from difficulties with linguistic form or meaning. One source of evidence for this conclusion comes from detailed analyses of conversational behavior Bishop (2000). For example, Bishop, Chan, Adams, Hartley, and Weir (2000) examined the ability of children with SLI (age 6–8 years) and their typical chronological-age- and language-age-matched peers to respond to conversational bids (e.g., requests for information) from an adult. The group with SLI was composed of two subgroups: children with traditional SLI and those with pragmatic difficulties. Both subgroups with SLI provided fewer adequate responses than did the control groups. Children with SLI in the pragmatic subgroup were more likely than children in either of the typical control groups to give no response to an adult bid. This finding is notable because nonverbal responses were considered as acceptable. Thus, the failure to respond was not directly linked to structural language limitations (see Brinton, Fujiki, & Powell, 1997 for a second example).

Another indication that children with SLI have pragmatic difficulties that are not motivated by problems in other aspects of language can be found in taxonomies that group these children by specific type of impairment (Bishop, 2000). Both Bishop and Rosenbloom (1987) and Conti-Ramsden, Crutchley, and Botting (1997) described a subtype of children whose impairments are primarily pragmatic. Originally identified as "semantic pragmatic deficit syndrome," this category has since been relabeled as "pragmatic language impairment" (PLI). These children have problems that include nonresponsiveness to questions in conversation, difficulty interacting on a shared topic, and problems assessing the background knowledge of conversational partners. At the same time, they have relatively good structural skills and may even be overly verbose.

There is evidence, then, that at least some children with a traditional diagnosis of SLI have pragmatic difficulties that are not related to their structural language problems. It might be asked if such children are simply misclassified, and whether they might fit better under the label of high-level autism (Shields, Varley, Broks, & Simpson, 1996). Many children characterized as having PLI, however, do not meet the diagnostic criteria for ASD (Bishop & Norbury, 2002). Given the recently highlighted similarities between autism and SLI (e.g., Tager-Flusberg, 2004), it may be more productive to view structurally based SLI and ASD as two ends of a continuum on which many combinations of pragmatic and structural language deficits may occur (Bishop, 2003a).

In conclusion, pragmatic impairment may be found in a range of individuals with language problems. We have focused on two of these groups: individuals with autism and those with SLI. For children with autism, pragmatic problems constitute a central component of the impairment. For children with SLI, the situation is more varied. It does appear to be the case, however, that at least some children wearing a diagnostic label of SLI have pragmatic difficulties that cannot be attributed solely to structural problems. Others may have pragmatic problems associated with their structural deficits. It is also important to recognize that even LI that does not involve pragmatic behaviors is likely to have implications for social communication. To be most productive, interventions should go beyond improving specific skills to facilitate the use of language in social interactions.

ASSESSMENT OF PRAGMATICS

Pragmatic principles have had an important impact on language assessment. As clinicians and researchers, we now have a better understanding of how contextual variables may influence interactions. This knowledge, in turn, has impacted the assessment of the syntactic and semantic aspects of language. Pragmatic principles have also led to the development of methods that seek to assess children's linguistic knowledge in ecologically valid learning contexts (e.g., dynamic assessment, in which the clinician strives to determine the amount of support the child needs to learn language behaviors). In addition, assessment has been extended to include pragmatic behaviors, per se.

The assessment of pragmatic skills can be beneficial for at least two reasons. First, it provides a unique view of social and cognitive functioning that cannot be examined without considering language (Adams, 2002). Second, it can guide social communication interventions for individuals with a range of diagnoses, including ASD, SLI, PLI, and hyperactivity disorder. Adams notes that examiners must structure their assessment to identify the underlying problems that are the basis for pragmatic failure. The assessment process must be guided by a strong theoretical base that allows the formulation of hypotheses regarding the underpinnings of pragmatic problems. Because pragmatic problems may stem from a variety of interrelated factors, forming a hypothesis may demand consideration of linguistic, social, cognitive, and emotional competence. We focus our discussion on the evaluation of some basic pragmatic behaviors and their impact, but it is often necessary for an educational team to extend assessments into other developmental domains.

Begin with a General Overview

In approaching the assessment of pragmatics, it is useful to get a general idea of a child's functioning in order to determine the focus of further assessment. Some children with language problems do quite well in social communication. Others may struggle, however, and thus require more careful assessment. Identifying children who need further attention promotes efficient use of clinical resources. Two approaches used to do this are standardized testing and teacher/parent interview.

Standardized Tests

Standardized tests are time-efficient and may be effective at separating typically developing children from children with disabilities. Unfortunately, pragmatic skills do not lend themselves to standardized assessment formats. Pragmatic behaviors, by definition, are influenced by contextual and social variables. Formal tests attempt to neutralize these factors by standardizing context to allow reliable comparisons of performance to a normative standard. There are tests, however, as well as subscales contained within tests, that are designed to examine aspects of pragmatic knowledge. These tests allow comparisons of performance on the tasks involved and may separate children with varying levels of ability. The skills needed to complete these tasks often extend beyond the boundaries of pragmatics, however (see Adams, 2002, for review). The extent to which these measures actually examine pragmatic skills, as they are used in real interactions, is unknown.

There are some standardized measures, however, that are helpful in highlighting areas of pragmatics that require a closer look. These measures incorporate methods that sample behavior across multiple contexts. For example, the *Communication and Symbolic Behavior Scales Developmental Profile* (Wetherby & Prizant, 2001) uses a combination of parent report, naturalistic observation, and probes inserted into interactions to assess a range of communicative behaviors, including the general areas of communicative intent, reciprocity, and social affective signaling. Norms are provided for the age range of 9 months to 2 years.

Teacher and Caretaker Interviews

Interviewing teachers and caretakers can provide an indication of the need for an assessment of pragmatics. Teachers and parents often have vague or specific worries about a child's ability to use language in social contexts. Children who have difficulties with pragmatics sometimes fit poorly into classroom and neighborhood activities. They may not be well integrated into work or play, and they may have trouble making friends. Asking teachers and parents about the way that a child interacts with peers will often reveal concerns that suggest that further assessment is warranted.

Rating scales organize information from those familiar with the child and assist in determining if there is a problem. These scales provide a list of critical behaviors that are rated as to their occurrence and/or frequency, thus taking advantage of the insights of informants who have observed the individual over a period of time in a variety of contexts. Additionally, they allow the clinician to gather data on persons who may not be able to provide reliable information about themselves, such as those who are too young, unaware, or unwilling to do so. On the negative side, it must be remembered that these measures do not sample actual behaviors. Rating scales may also be subject to rater biases and various sources of error, such as setting variance (Merrell, 2003).

With the above caveats in mind, rating scales may provide a useful way of screening for pragmatic problems. Several scales have been developed that quickly document the existence of "red flags" that suggest certain problems (e.g., Brinton & Fujiki, 1994). Another measure, the pragmatic protocol (Prutting & Kirchner, 1987), combines the rating scale format with observational methods. Based on 15 minutes of observation, the examiner rates 30 different pragmatic behaviors as appropriate, inappropriate, or no opportunity to observe.

The *Children's Communication Checklist-2* (CCC-2, Bishop, 2003b) is a rating scale developed for the assessment of pragmatic language impairment that includes normative data. The CCC-2 is made up of 10 scales, 5 of which focus on pragmatic behaviors. Normative data are provided for ages 4;0–16;11 years. By summing various scale scores, a general communication composite may be obtained, which is highly effective at identifying children with language difficulties. A social interaction deviance composite score may also be calculated. This score can be used to characterize the skills of children whose pragmatic skills are impaired relative to other language areas.

Rating scales can provide a general characterization of a child's pragmatic abilities and, to some extent, of their social communication. These scales will suggest areas that warrant consideration and focus. For example, consider the children mentioned at the beginning of the chapter. A profile of Norris may describe a child who is reticent in interactions and is often excluded from play and ignored by peers. Cody's profile may suggest that he seeks interaction but is sometimes nonresponsive. Kari's profile may indicate that she is disruptive to group activity and avoided by her peers. At this point, it becomes important to conduct a more detailed evaluation to describe specific behaviors and their impact on the social worlds of these children.

Narrowing the Focus: Pinpointing and Describing Behavior

Once data from interviews, rating scales, and similar sources are obtained, assessment can be further narrowed to pinpoint and describe behaviors that appear to be problematic. In addition to weaknesses, it is also important to consider behaviors that are more robust, because these strengths may be useful to exploit when facilitating new behaviors. The most widely accepted means of describing pragmatic behaviors is to observe real interactions in which these behaviors occur. Several analyses and procedures have been suggested (e.g., Adams, 2002; Brinton & Fujiki, 1989; Coggins & Olswang, 2007).

Observation and analysis of real interactional contexts are time-consuming and difficult processes that are not always practical in clinical practice, however. Several tools have been developed to make gathering and analyzing information from spontaneous interactions more feasible. Rice, Sell, and Hadley (1990) described a real-time (i.e., the observation and analysis are conducted as the examiner watches children interact) analysis system, the Social Interactive Coding System (SICS). The SICS was designed to capture initiations and responses by speaker, addressee, level of play, and nature of the interaction. Damico (1992) also presented a real-time coding system, the Systematic Observation of Communicative Interaction (SOCI). The SOCI was designed to describe the interactional behaviors of individuals 6 years of age and older. Using the SOCI, the observer codes the illocutionary act performed, its appropriateness, and problematic verbal and nonverbal behaviors that occur. Olswang, Coggins, and Svensson (2007) developed the Social Communication Coding System (SCCS) to focus on dimensions rather than discrete behaviors. A child's classroom interactions are coded into dimensions of hostile/coercive, prosocial/engaged, assertive, passive/disengaged, adult seeking, and irrelevant behavior. Using a hand-held computer to record data, the examiner is able to capture information regarding occurrence, frequency, and duration of each dimension. Using these types of tools, the clinician may gain a sense of a child's interactional abilities in a time-efficient manner.

Another way of making pragmatic assessment more time-efficient is to insert a probe or use a script within an otherwise naturalistic interaction. Brinton et al. (1997) provided an example of a probe, designed to examine the topic manipulation skills of 6- and 7-year-old children. Within the context of a naturalistic interaction, the examiner introduces topics labeled as either verbal or object-verbal. Verbal topics consist of an utterance such as, "I like to watch TV. Yesterday I saw a really scary show." Object-verbal topics consist of a spoken statement, paired with an object (e.g., "I got this for my birthday. I don't know how it works." The examiner then places a toy camera on the table). After making the statement, the examiner pauses to allow the child to respond. The examiner acknowledges the child's utterances, or makes brief comments (e.g., "OK") to encourage the child to keep talking. This procedure has been used to identify patterns of topic maintenance that distinguished children with SLI from their typical language-age and chronological-age-matched peers. Such probes can reveal patterns of behavior that may be difficult to examine in completely naturalistic contexts. It should be noted, however, that these probes typically only show behavior in a limited context. It is important to integrate this information with other data to obtain a more holistic picture of the child's performance.

A second way of assessing pragmatic behaviors in a spontaneous sample is to use a scripted protocol designed to elicit specific information. Creaghead (1984) presented an example of this strategy—"the peanut butter protocol." As the child enters the room, the examiner notes whether the child produces a greeting. Before the child arrives, the examiner places cookies and crackers in a glass jar within the child's view but out of reach. The examiner notes whether or not the child requests the cookies and crackers. The examiner then hands the child the jar, which has a tightly closed lid, and observes whether the child asks for help opening the jar. The interaction continues in this manner, as the examiner follows a set of scripted probes designed to assess expression of a range of speech acts.

In utilizing various analysis systems and probes, one must maintain a delicate balance of holistic and narrow viewpoints. Because social interactions are so complex, it is necessary to focus on those behaviors that initial overviews have suggested are most important. At the same time, it is wise to maintain a wide-enough view to allow consideration of behaviors that may occur outside the narrow focus. For example, in the midst of an observation structured to illustrate cooperative work in a triad, we once observed a child's behavior break down dramatically in response to a time limit imposed on the task. It was important to consider this behavior in addition to the various cooperative bids the child had demonstrated. As with all assessments, the value lies in the synthesis of the information obtained and the clinical decisions that follow.

Synthesizing the Data   Because assessing pragmatic behaviors demands so much time, thought, and effort, it is important to maximize the clinically important information gleaned from evaluations. As observations and analyses are conducted, it is helpful to consider the functional significance of behaviors. Given the context of the home, the classroom, and the community, what are the aspects of the child's pragmatic behavior that enhance or limit social communication? Important considerations include the consistency of the behaviors, the effectiveness of any compensatory behaviors, and the impact of the behaviors on peer relationships and learning opportunities. For example, Norris' difficulty joining social interactions prevents his access to many learning contexts in his classroom. Cody's nonresponsive bids exclude him from peer conversation. Kari's tendency to control interactions limits her ability to establish and maintain friendships. When pragmatic difficulties are judged to limit the child's ability to participate in academic, social, and other life contexts, intervention may be warranted.

INTERVENTION

As indicated earlier, the idea that language behaviors may be best facilitated within contexts that mirror real communicative interactions has permeated even fairly structured behavioral paradigms. Language behaviors that are not necessarily pragmatic are facilitated within tasks that are pragmatic in nature. These more naturalistic contexts are designed to engage and motivate children, to highlight specific language targets within communicative tasks, and to encourage generalization.

Many clinicians and researchers have gone a step further, however, designing treatment approaches that focus on aspects of social communication as primary intervention targets (e.g., Hadley & Schuele, 1998; Timler et al., 2005). A range of potential behaviors might be targeted in treatment depending on one's view of pragmatics in the communication system. From a modular view of pragmatics, it would make sense to target pragmatic behaviors that lag behind other components of the child's linguistic system. For example, for a child who has the necessary structural abilities, a behavior such as responding to questions in conversation might be facilitated.

The point of intervention might be viewed differently from a functionalist perspective. If pragmatics is viewed as a central motivating force underlying language, the range of treatment targets is dramatically increased. The desired outcomes of treatment are expanded as well, with the ultimate objective being improved social communication. For example, children who have difficulty with syntactic-pragmatic behaviors such as responding to questions or structural discourse features such as taking turns in conversation may also be withdrawn (Fujiki, Brinton, Morgan, & Hart, 1999). If this is the case, facilitating specific pragmatic behaviors may also demand consideration of aspects of social and emotional functioning. The ultimate goal of treatment would not be just enhanced conversational patterns, but also improved social competence.

Facilitating Appropriate Social Goals

When conceptualizing intervention paradigms for facilitating social communication in children with LI, it is important to consider children's underlying social goals. In other words, what do these children want to get out of interaction? If children do not have positive social goals, it may be ineffective to encourage them to be more active or responsive in conversation (Taylor & Asher, 1984). For example, Kari gravitates to other children and is anxious to "play" with them. She has little notion of reciprocal relationships, however, and does not seem interested in exchanges that she cannot control. Norris, on the other hand, shies away from other children and seems to have little understanding that interacting with other children can be rewarding. Both Norris and Kari need to learn that interacting with peers in a reciprocal fashion can be enjoyable and can enhance relationships. It is important to remember that many children with social communication problems come to treatment with social expectations different from those of their typically developing peers. They may have little experience with felicitous exchanges with peers or with high-quality friendships. Their interactions may have been unsatisfying at best and victimizing at worst. Their social goals in specific situations may be to escape or to aggress. They may need to adopt more positive social goals to motivate the acquisition of social communication or pragmatic behaviors.

Unfortunately, it is both unwise and impractical to address social goals explicitly in treatment (Taylor & Asher, 1984). It is impossible to force a child toward social goals such as enjoying interactions with peers, being likeable, and making friends. It is feasible to facilitate such goals indirectly, however. Within the regular course of treatment, it is possible to illustrate that felicitous interactions with others are desirable. For example, in a social communication treatment program for first graders with LI, we found it helpful to take every opportunity to point out that "it is fun to play with other people," and that children playing or working cooperatively were enjoying themselves. ("Look at those kids. They're playing together. They are cooperating. Look at their faces. They are smiling and laughing. They are having fun.") As children experience more felicitous interchanges with peers, they may see new possibilities in social interaction and become more likely to adopt positive social goals (Brinton & Fujiki, 2006). Consideration of a child's personal social goals should remain a backdrop of treatment over the long term because these goals will motivate a child's progress in intervention (Brinton, Fujiki, & Robinson, 2005).

Intervention Principles

In planning direct intervention with social communication skills, there are at least six principles to be considered to maximize the effectiveness of treatment programs.

Principle 1   The language demands of instruction need to be adjusted to accommodate the abilities of individual children. There are many treatment programs designed to facilitate specific social behaviors and skills (e.g., Merrell, Carrizales, & Feuerborn, 2004). These programs can provide a rich resource of tasks and ideas for enhancing social communication behaviors. Many of these programs and tasks are heavily language-based; tasks are presented and explained using language. Because language is the major medium through which social communication behaviors are displayed, there is no getting around the verbal nature of treatment tasks. It is important, therefore, to ensure that the language of instruction is accessible to an individual child. For example, explanations and instruction must be presented in a way that the child can readily understand. In addition, the language requirements of the social behaviors to be facilitated must be within the child's behavioral repertoire.

Principle 2   The more complex the range of application for a behavior, the more intense and comprehensive the instruction needs to be. For purposes of this discussion, the range of application refers to the variety of contexts in which a behavior may be used. With syntactic and semantic targets, the range of application can usually be described fairly clearly. For example, regular past tense is generally transparent, and its use can be predicted. With social communication behaviors, the range of application is extremely complex and depends on linguistic, social, and world knowledge. Consider a seemingly straightforward behavior such as responding to product questions. How much information does one give to whom ("How much money does your mom make?")? When is it acceptable, or even advisable, to avoid responding directly ("When will your parents be home?")? How does one adjust the response, depending on one's relationship with the conversational partner ("What do you want for your birthday?")? Treatment needs to be designed to help children understand the impact of social communication behaviors in an almost limitless variety of contexts. The demanding nature of this type of treatment leads to the third principle.

Principle 3   Facilitating social communication behaviors requires considerable time and effort. There are many social skill programs designed for children with a range of disabilities, and results of treatment studies have not always been impressive (La Greca, 1993). It is our experience that treatment paradigms frequently underestimate the amount of time and commitment required to facilitate the acquisition of social communication behaviors in a way to produce positive social outcomes. For many children, treatment must continue over an extended period and requires a significant commitment of clinical resources (Brinton, Robinson, & Fujiki, 2004).

Principle 4   Treatment tasks can be effectively embedded within existing communicative contexts that are important to the child. In describing an intervention hierarchy for facilitating social behaviors, including social communication behaviors, Brown, Odom, and Conroy (2001) suggested that some children may benefit from incidental teaching conducted within other preschool or school activities, but other children may require more direct, individualized attention. When working with children with ASD or SLI, facilitating social communication behaviors most often involves some direct small-group or individual instruction. Even so, the tasks in which behaviors are highlighted should be part of the regular communicative world of the child and should involve interaction with family members and peers. Home or classroom routines provide powerful contexts to support social communication behaviors. For instance, a common classroom activity, such as show and tell, can be carefully designed to facilitate appropriate introduction of shared referents in topic initiation, maintaining topics, or responding to listener bids. A family task such as preparing salads for family members can be structured to highlight making requests for information ("What kind of dressing do you want?"), listening to others' contributions in conversation, and acting on the responses of conversational partners.

Principle 5   Language and social behaviors can be facilitated simultaneously within the same treatment program. Children with language problems frequently need intervention to target specific aspects of language structure and content as well as social skills. Tasks and activities that are designed to stimulate social communication can stimulate specific language forms at the same time. For example, the acquisition of new vocabulary items and responding to listener bids in conversation can be targeted in the same tasks and activities. For older children, facilitating social communication can involve tasks that combine literacy and positive social behaviors. For example, using a restaurant script in which a child must take an order could be structured to focus on listening and responding to another child's order, reading the menu, and writing down the order.

Principle 6   Teamwork is essential to the clinical process. Social communication behaviors require a child to integrate many kinds of knowledge in a wide variety of interactional contexts. It is vital to work with parents, other caretakers, siblings, teachers, and other professionals to choose treatment objectives, design treatment tasks, and implement treatment procedures in contexts that permeate the child's social world.

Focusing Intervention

Assessment may reveal that a child has multiple clinical needs, and it is sometimes difficult to choose specific behaviors to target. Because clinical resources are generally limited, it is important to focus them wisely. We recommend prioritizing behaviors that are essential to interpersonal communication, especially with peers. For some children who are low-functioning, these behaviors might be as basic as establishing joint attention with a conversational partner. For children who are more mature, it is helpful to consider basic conversational parameters such as responsiveness. Within these parameters, intervention can be geared to the child's interactional pattern and personal temperament.

Entering Interaction   In order to be involved in social communication, children have to engage with others. Typically developing children employ many strategies to interact with others, but some reticent children, like Norris, find it very difficult to join others in work or play. Children like Kari may be eager to join in ongoing interactions, but their strategies are ineffective and disruptive (e.g., barging into the middle of a game). For children like Norris and Kari, it may be helpful to facilitate basic skills that allow access to ongoing work or play. Preliminary treatment programs have identified and targeted a number of important behaviors that are associated with gaining access to ongoing interaction. For example, Timler et al. (2005) employed a sequence of behaviors that included approaching peers at play, watching what peers are doing, engaging in that activity, and making a statement about that play ("tell an idea" p. 176). Brinton and Fujiki (2006) taught similar steps to enter play using cue cards depicting "walk" (approach the play), "watch" (watch what peers are doing), "talk" (say something nice about the play) and "play" (engage in the same activity). In these programs, the behaviors are taught, practiced, and then reviewed in group sessions. Direct instruction was followed by hints and prompts in naturalistic contexts such as recess or free play ("Steven and David are having fun together. Go play with them—you know what to do."). Subsequent review can underscore successful attempts ("I saw you play with Steven and David at recess. That looked like fun").

Becoming Part of an Interaction   Once children gain access to interaction, they need to integrate themselves within the ensuing interaction. Children with LI may not understand the need to become a part of the work or play, and they may sit quietly, pursue an activity of their own, or actually wander off. These children need to learn prosocial strategies and approaches to integrate themselves within a dyad or group. There are many appropriate ways to contribute to interaction, and targeted strategies and approaches must be geared to the temperament of the individual child. Kari and Cody, for instance, may choose to assume more active roles in conversation than will Norris. The amount of these children's conversation is not the most important element ensuring their place in the interaction. Rather, the key to their felicitous integration within groups is their responsiveness to others. Responsiveness can be demonstrated in many ways, especially through various aspects of turn exchange and topic manipulation.

Most children know a great deal about turn-taking in conversation before they acquire their first words. Children who struggle with social communication may lag well behind their typically developing peers in terms of their understanding how turn exchange can be manipulated to relate to others in interaction. For example, Kari wants the conversational floor; she has little interest in reciprocity. Norris does not know what to do with the floor, and Cody knows just enough to wait for a turn to talk about something he is interested in. These children need guidance to build conversations around a responsive exchange of contributions. They need to understand that all participants need a place in conversation, and turn exchange helps assure that place. For some children, it may be helpful to use an analogy such as throwing a ball back and forth among players (Brinton et al., 2004). Both throwing and catching the ball are part of the game.

Turn exchange is a basic aspect of conversation, but the topical content within turns may be even more important. Many children with LI have trouble initiating and maintaining topics in a responsive manner. These children may need to learn specific strategies such as introducing referents in a way to establish shared information, responding to requests for repair in topic initiation, and choosing topics that others might find of interest. It is also very important to facilitate maintenance of topics introduced by others, a difficult task for some children with language problems (Brinton et al., 1997). It is important that structure and function interact to produce the desired social communicative end.

It is possible to facilitate a number of behaviors that support children in maintaining topics of interest to others. Treatment programs that encourage cooperative work or play behaviors tend to capitalize on responsive patterns of topic manipulation as a means to effect integration into group activities (Adams, 2005; Timler et al., 2005). Intervention may also target other topic-maintaining behaviors, such as the production of validating comments, which are defined as positive comments that concern the current actions and verbal contributions of others (e.g., "You almost made it," "Good throw"). Facilitating these comments helps children to focus on the contributions of others and to gear their own conversational bids to the work or play at hand (Brinton & Fujiki, 2006). For more mature children, it may be possible to instruct responsive topic manipulation by facilitating specific conversational bids such as asking a question, listening to the response, and commenting on that response (Brinton et al., 2004). In any event, when facilitating responsive patterns of topic manipulation, it is important to help children process linguistic information, consider shared knowledge, think about contextual information, and read the emotional cues of their partners.

Documenting Change

Because social communication is so complex, it may be challenging to select intervention targets that can be captured in tidy goals with clear behavioral objectives. It is entirely possible, however, to select meaningful goals that are associated with positive social outcomes. Important social communication behaviors can be observed and described in semi-structured and naturalistic activities. Analysis systems can be tailored to characterize a child's progress on specific targets, and changes can be documented. Here again, teamwork is vital to observing behaviors by a variety of individuals in a variety of ecologically valid contexts.

CONCLUSION

Research and practice in pragmatics has helped to define language intervention over the course of the last 30 years. Whether viewed as a component of language or as the underlying motivation for language, pragmatics has pushed intervention toward naturalistic and communicative contexts and approaches. Focusing on pragmatic aspects of language has broadened the scope of clinical practice, since it is difficult to consider pragmatic behaviors without placing them within the wider context of social communication. Pragmatic behaviors have social roots and ramifications, and pragmatic and social skills frequently overlap. Understanding the complex range of application of pragmatic behaviors requires linguistic, cognitive, social, and emotional knowledge.

Pragmatic language behaviors constitute important intervention targets for children who struggle with social communication. Treatment should focus on those behaviors that support positive interpersonal relationships and provide access to learning contexts. In the course of treatment, it is important to help children establish appropriate prosocial goals through implicit teaching. Specific pragmatic behaviors to realize those goals can be enhanced through direct instruction.

Facilitating social communication requires a serious commitment of clinical time and resources and may branch beyond the typical clinical practice of speech-language pathology. Teaming with parents, other caregivers, family members, and other professionals is essential to design assessment and intervention approaches that will provide children with the language, cognitive, emotional, and social knowledge necessary to navigate their social world.

REFERENCES

Adams, C. (2002). Practitioner review: The assessment of language pragmatics. *Journal of Child Psychology and Psychiatry, 43*, 973–987.

Adams, C. (2005). Social communication intervention for school-age children: Rationale and description. *Seminars in Speech and Language, 26*, 181–188.

Berko Gleason, J. (2005). *The development of language* (6th ed.). Needham Heights, MA: Allyn & Bacon.

Bishop, D. V. M. (2000). Pragmatic language impairment: A correlate of SLI, a distinct subgroup, or part of the autistic continuum? In D. V. M. Bishop & L. B. Leonard (Eds.), *Speech and language impairments in children: Causes, characteristics, intervention, and outcome.* Philadelphia: Taylor & Francis.

Bishop, D. V. M. (2003a). Autism and specific language impairment: Categorical distinction or continuum? *Novartis Foundation Symposium, 251*, 213–234.

Bishop, D. V. M. (2003b). *The Children's Communication Checklist* (2nd ed.). London: Harcourt Assessment.

Bishop, D. V. M., Chan, J., Adams, C., Hartley, J., & Weir, F. (2000). Conversational responsiveness in specific language impairment: Evidence of disproportionate pragmatic difficulties in a subset of children. *Development and Psychopathology, 12*, 177–199.

Bishop, D. V. M., & Norbury, C. F. (2002). Exploring the borderlands of autistic disorder and specific language impairment: A study using standardized diagnostic instruments. *Journal of Child Psychology and Psychiatry and Allied Disciplines, 43*, 917–929.

Bishop, D. V. M., & Rosenbloom, L. (1987). Classification of childhood language disorders. In: W. Yule & M. Rutter (Eds.), *Language development and disorders* (pp. 16–41). London: MacKeith Press.

Bricker, D. (1993). Then, now, and the path between: A brief history of language intervention. In A. P. Kaiser & D. B. Gray (Eds.), *Enhancing children's communication: Research foundations for intervention* (pp. 11–31). Baltimore: Paul H. Brookes.

Brinton, B., & Fujiki, M. (1989). *Conversational management with language-impaired children.* Rockville, MD: Aspen.

Brinton, B., & Fujiki, M. (1994). Ways to teach conversation. In J. Duchan, L. Hewitt, & R. Sonnenmeier (Eds.), *Pragmatics: From theory to practice* (pp. 59–71). Englewood Cliffs, NJ: Prentice-Hall.

Brinton, B., & Fujiki, M. (2006). Improving peer interaction and learning in cooperative learning groups. In T. A. Ukrainetz (Ed.), *Contextualized language intervention: Scaffolding K-12 literacy achievement* (pp. 289–318). Eau Claire, WI: Thinking Publications.

Brinton, B., Fujiki, M., & Powell, J. M. (1997). The ability of children with language impairment to manipulate topic in a structured task. *Language, Speech, and Hearing Services in Schools, 28*, 3–11.

Brinton, B., Fujiki, M., & Robinson, L. A. (2005). Life on a tricycle: A case study of language impairment from four to nineteen. *Topics in Language Disorders, 25*, 338–352.

Brinton, B., Fujiki, M., & Sonnenberg, E. A. (1988). Responses to requests for clarification by linguistically normal and language-impaired children in conversation. *Journal of Speech and Hearing Disorders, 53*, 383–391.

Brinton, B., Robinson, L. A., & Fujiki, M. (2004). Description of a program for social language intervention: "If you can have a conversation, you can have a relationship." *Language, Speech, and Hearing Services in Schools, 35,* 283–290.

Brown, W. H., Odom, S. L., & Conroy, M. A. (2001). An intervention hierarchy for promoting young children's peer interactions in natural environments. *Topics in Early Childhood Special Education, 21,* 162–175.

Carr, E. G., & Durand, V. M. (1985). The social-communicative basis of severe behavior problems in children. In S. Reiss & R. R. Bootzin (Eds.), *Theoretical issues in behavior therapy* (pp. 219–254). New York: Academic Press.

Carr, E. G., Levin, L., McConnachie, G., Carlson, J. L., Kemp, D. C., & Smith, C. E. (1994). *Communication-based intervention for problem behavior.* Baltimore: Paul H. Brookes.

Coggins, T. E., & Olswang, L. B. (2007, June). *Conducting research in disorders of social communication: Theory to practice in clinical research.* Symposium on Research in Child Language Disorders, Madison, WI.

Conti-Ramsden, G., Crutchley, A., & Botting, N. (1997). The extent to which psychometric tests differentiate subgroups of children with SLI. *Journal of Speech, Language, and Hearing Research, 40,* 765–777.

Conti-Ramsden, G., & Friel-Patti, S. (1983). Mothers' discourse adjustments to language-impaired and non-language-impaired children. *Journal of Speech and Hearing Disorders, 48,* 360–367.

Craig, H. K. (1995). Pragmatic impairments. In P. Fletcher & B. MacWhinney (Eds.), *The handbook of child language* (pp. 623–640). Cambridge, MA: Blackwell.

Creaghead, N. (1984). Strategies for evaluating and targeting pragmatic behaviors in young children. *Seminars in Speech and Language, 5,* 241–251.

Damico, J. S. (1992). Systematic observation of communicative interaction: A valid and practical descriptive assessment technique. *Best Practices in School Speech/Language Pathology: Descriptive/Nonstandardized Language Assessment, 2,* 133–143.

Duchan, J. (1984). Language assessment: The pragmatics revolution. In R. Naremore (Ed.), *Language science.* San Diego, CA: College-Hill Press.

Fay, W. H., & Schuler, A. L. (1980). *Emerging language in autistic children.* Baltimore: University Park Press.

Fey, M. E., & Leonard, L. B. (1984). Partner age as a variable in the conversational performance of specifically language-impaired and normal-language children. *Journal of Speech and Hearing Research, 27,* 413–423.

Fujiki, M., Brinton, B., Morgan, M., & Hart, C. H. (1999). Withdrawn and sociable behavior of children with specific language impairment. *Language, Speech, and Hearing Services in Schools, 30,* 183–195.

Givon, T. (1985). Language, function and typology. *Journal of Literary Semantics, 14,* 83–97.

Hadley, P. A., & Schuele, C. M. (1998). Facilitating peer interaction: Socially relevant objectives for preschool language intervention. *American Journal of Speech-Language Pathology, 7,* 25–36.

Hale, C. M., & Tager-Flusberg, H. (2005). Social communication in children with autism. *Autism, 9,* 157–178.

Halle, J. W., Ostrosky, M. M., & Hemmeter, M. L. (2006). Functional Communication Training: A strategy for ameliorating challenging behavior. In R. J. McCauley & M. E. Fey (Eds.), *Treatment of language disorders in children* (pp. 509–545). Baltimore: Paul H. Brookes.

Kaiser, A. P., Yoder, P. J., & Keetz, A. (1992). Evaluating milieu teaching. In S. Warren & J. Reichle (Eds.), *Communication and language intervention series: Vol. 1. Causes and effects in communication and language intervention* (pp. 9–47). Baltimore: Paul H. Brookes.

Kanner, L. (1946). Irrelevant and metaphorical language of early infantile autism. *American Journal of Psychiatry, 103,* 242–246.

La Greca, A. M. (1993). Social skills training with children: Where do we go from here? *Journal of Clinical Child Psychology, 22,* 288–298.

Leonard, L. B. (1986). Conversational replies of children with specific language impairment. *Journal of Speech and Hearing Research, 29,* 114–119.

McTear, M., & Conti-Ramsden, G. (1992). *Pragmatic disability in children*. San Diego, CA: Singular Publishing Group.

Merrell, K. W. (2003). *Behavioral, social, and emotional assessment of children and adolescents* (2nd ed.). Mahwah, NJ: Lawrence Erlbaum Associates.

Merrell, K. W., Carrizales, D., & Feuerborn, L. (2004). *Strong kids: A social-emotional learning curriculum for students in Grades 4–8*. Eugene, OR: University of Oregon, Oregon Resiliency Project.

Mundy, P., & Burnette, C. (2005). Joint attention and neurodevelopmental models of autism. In F. R. Volkmar, R. Paul, A. Klin, & D. Cohen (Eds.), *Handbook of autism and pervasive developmental disorders: Vol. 1. Diagnosis, development, neurobiology, and behavior* (3rd ed., pp. 650–681). Hoboken, NJ: John Wiley & Sons.

Ninio, A., & Snow, C. (1996). *Pragmatic development*. Boulder, CO: Westview Press.

Ninio, A., & Snow, C. (1999). The development of pragmatics: Learning to use language appropriately. In T. Bhatia & W. Ritchie (Eds.), *Handbook of language acquisition* (pp. 347–383). New York: Academic Press.

Olswang, L. B., Coggins, T. E., & Svensson, L. (2007). Assessing social communication in the classroom. *Topics in Language Disorders*, 27(2), 111–127.

Prizant, B. M., Wetherby, A. M., Rubin, E., Laurent, A., & Rydell, P. (2005). *The SCERTS model: A comprehensive educational approach for children with autism spectrum disorders: Vol. 1. Assessment*. Baltimore: Paul H. Brookes.

Prizant, B. M., Wetherby, A. M., & Rydell, P. (2000). Communication intervention issues for young children with autism spectrum disorders. In A. M. Wetherby & B. M. Prizant (Eds.), *Autism spectrum disorders: A transactional developmental perspective* (pp. 193–224). Baltimore: Paul H. Brookes.

Prutting, C. A., & Kirchner, D. M. (1987). A clinical appraisal of the pragmatic aspects of language. *Journal of Speech and Hearing Disorders*, 52, 105–119.

Rice, M., Sell, M. A., & Hadley, P. A. (1990). The Social Interactive Coding System: An on-line, clinically relevant descriptive tool. *Language, Speech, and Hearing Services in Schools*, 21, 2–14.

Rogers, S. J. (2006). Evidence-based interventions for language development in young children with autism. In T. Charman & W. Stone (Eds.), *Social and communication development in Autism Spectrum Disorders* (pp. 143–179). New York: Guilford Press.

Shields, J., Varley, R., Broks, P., & Simpson, A. (1996). Social cognition in developmental language disorders and high-level autism. *Developmental Medicine and Child Neurology*, 38, 487–495.

Tager-Flusberg, H. (2004). Do autism and specific language impairment represent overlapping language disorders? In M. Rice & S. Warren (Eds.), *Developmental language disorders: From phenotypes to etiologies* (pp. 31–52). Mahwah, NJ: Lawrence Erlbaum Associates.

Taylor, A. R., & Asher, S. (1984). Children's goals in social competence: Individual differences in a game playing context. In T. Field, J. L. Roopnarine, & M. Segal (Eds.), *Friendship in normal and handicapped children* (pp. 53–78). Norwood, NJ: Ablex.

Timler, G. R., Olswang, L. B., & Coggins, T. E. (2005). Social communication interventions for preschoolers: Targeting peer interactions during peer group entry and cooperative play. *Seminars in Speech and Language*, 26, 170–180.

Travis, L. L., & Sigman, M. (2001). Communicative intentions and symbols in autism: Examining a case of altered development. In J. A. Burack, T. Charman, N. Yirmiya, & P. R. Zelazo (Eds.), *The development of autism: Perspectives from theory and research* (pp. 279–308). Mahwah, NJ: Lawrence Erlbaum Associates.

van Balkom, H., & Verhoeven, L. (2004). Pragmatic disability in children with specific language impairments. In L. Verhoeven & H. van Balkom (Eds.), *Classification of developmental language disorders: Theoretical issues and clinical implications* (pp. 283–305). Mahwah, NJ: Lawrence Erlbaum Associates.

Warren, S., Bredin-Oja, S. L., Fairchild Escalante, M., Finestack, L. H., Fey, M. E., & Brady, N. C. (2006). Responsivity education/prelinguistic milieu teaching. In R. J. McCauley & M. E. Fey (Eds.), *Treatment of language disorders in children* (pp. 47–75). Baltimore: Paul H. Brookes.

Wetherby, A. M. (2006). Understanding and measuring social communication in children with Autism Spectrum Disorders. In T. Charman & W. Stone (Eds.), *Social and communication development in Autism Spectrum Disorders* (pp. 3–34). New York: Guilford Press.

Wetherby, A. M., & Prizant, B. M. (2001). *Communication and Symbolic Behavior Scales Developmental Profile*. Baltimore: Paul H Brookes.

Wetherby, A. M., Prizant, B. M., & Schuler, A. L. (2000). Understanding the nature of communication and language impairments. In A. M. Wetherby & B. M. Prizant (Eds.), *Autism spectrum disorders: A transactional developmental perspective* (pp. 109–141). Baltimore: Paul H. Brookes.

19

Reading and Writing in Child Language Disorders

PAMELA E. HOOK and CHARLES W. HAYNES

The National Institutes of Health have recognized that high illiteracy rates are a national health care crisis that needs immediate attention. Approximately 10–15% of school age children have a learning disability, and, of these, around 70% display disabilities specific to the literacy skills of reading and writing. Given the magnitude of this challenge, there is a critical need for practitioners to understand and effectively diagnose and treat reading and related language-learning difficulties. This chapter provides an overview of the processing skills and deficits associated with reading and writing difficulties and outlines principles and methods related to assessment and intervention.

PROCESSES INVOLVED IN READING AND WRITING

A complex reciprocal relationship exists between spoken and written language. In fact, approximately two thirds of children with oral language difficulties also have problems in the areas of reading and writing (Stackhouse & Wells, 1997; Tallal, 1988). Two separate, but highly interrelated components interact in the acquisition of reading and writing skills. The first is code-related and primarily affects word identification and spelling, whereas the second is content-related and influences primarily comprehension and written expression. Even mild difficulties in word identification can reduce the speed of reading, draw attention away from the underlying meaning, and create the need to reread selections to grasp the meaning (Lyon, 1995; Torgesen, Rashotte, & Alexander, 2001). Similarly, difficulties in spelling or handwriting (transcription) interfere with efficient and coherent written formulation (McCutchen, 1995). These basic relationships between word identification/spelling and comprehension/written expression are illustrated in Figure 19.1, *Processes involved in reading and writing*.

Although all aspects of spoken language influence reading and writing, certain components are more directly related to word identification and spelling, whereas others are more directly related to reading comprehension and writing. As is illustrated in Figure 19.1, aspects of *phonological* processing, specifically the development of phonemic awareness, are more directly related to the acquisition of skills related to word identification and spelling, whereas *morphology, syntax, semantics, discourse*, and *pragmatics* are more directly related to reading comprehension and written expression. In addition to phonological processing, word identification involves *orthographic* processing (the abilities involved in

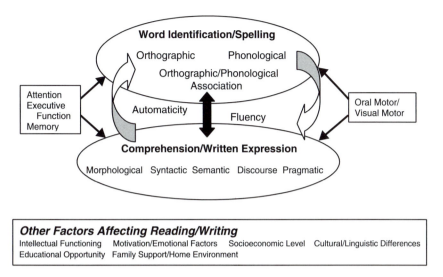

FIGURE 19.1   Processes involved in reading/writing.

identifying specific patterns of letters). To read a word, these two kinds of processing interact to create orthographic/phonological associations for accessing lexical information in long-term memory storage (Adams, 1990). Additionally, automatic retrieval of the phonological representation that corresponds to a specific orthographic representation is crucial for fluent reading. Weaknesses in any of these systems will affect acquisition of efficient and effective reading and writing.

On the left and right in Figure 19.1 are other intrinsic factors that affect reading and writing development: these include attention, executive function, and memory, as well as visual-motor and oral-motor skills. As indicated at the bottom of Figure 19.1, intellectual functioning as well as emotional and motivational factors also play important roles. Additionally, it is critical to examine extrinsic factors such as socioeconomic, cultural, and linguistic differences, the school environment, educational opportunities, family support, and the home environment. (For more in-depth discussions of these influences, see chapter 12 by Peña & Bedore, chapter 13 by Leonard, and chapter 14 by Washington.)

In addition to the acquisition of spoken language skills, the development of reading and writing requires metalinguistic abilities or the capacity to analyze linguistic rules and apply them in novel contexts. In fact, reading can be viewed as inherently metalinguistic in nature; it requires an awareness of the structure of the language across all areas: phonology, morphology, syntax, semantics, discourse, and pragmatics. This kind of awareness is not necessary for the acquisition of spoken language skills (Catts & Kamhi, 1999). The metalinguistic nature of reading acquisition can create confusion in diagnosis, when some children with reading problems display no overt deficits in their spontaneous oral language yet struggle with metalinguistic tasks such as breaking words apart at the level of the phoneme, applying morphological rules in decontextualized situations such as, "Here is a wug. Now there is another one. There are two _____." (from Jean Berko's *Wug Test*, 1958), understanding multiple meanings of words, or drawing inferences. Difficulty with developing an awareness of the rules that govern the structure of language has important implications for all aspects of reading, including word identification, fluent reading with appropriate phrasing, and higher order thinking skills necessary for comprehension. For these reasons, most children who struggle with reading and writing need to be taught linguistic rules explicitly.

DISORDERS OF READING AND WRITING

Definitions/Characteristics

There are various reasons why students may experience difficulties with reading and writing, but most revolve around issues related to the spoken language system. Reading problems primarily related to word identification are often associated with a diagnosis of dyslexia. In contrast, reading comprehension issues related to more broadly based language comprehension difficulties are often associated with diagnoses of specific language impairment (SLI) or language-learning disability (LLD). Consistent with our thinking here, Bishop and Snowling (2004) argued that, although both categories of impairment (dyslexia and SLI/LLD) involve language-processing disorders that affect reading, they should remain distinct. As illustrated in Figure 19.1, all of the components of language interact to affect reading; difficulties in specific areas of language will interfere with reading in different ways.

The International Dyslexia Association defines dyslexia as:

> a specific learning disability that is neurobiological in origin. It is characterized by difficulties with accurate and/or fluent word recognition and by poor spelling and decoding abilities. These difficulties typically result from a deficit in the phonological component of language that is often unexpected in relation to other cognitive abilities and the provision of effective classroom instruction. (Lyon, Shaywitz, & Shaywitz, 2003, p. 2)

This definition highlights the importance of difficulties in automatic word recognition and stresses the importance of underlying phonological processing abilities. In fact, phonological processing, particularly phonemic awareness, is central to most word-identification difficulties, and a core phonological processing deficit has been posited as the most salient problem associated with word-identification deficits (Brady, 1997; Share & Stanovich, 1995; Torgesen, 1997). Problems with "reading comprehension and reduced reading experience that can impede growth of vocabulary and background knowledge" are considered secondary (Lyon et al., 2003, p. 2). (For an in-depth discussion of the typology and definition of dyslexia, see chapter 5 by Shaywitz et al.)

Children with SLI may be identified on the basis of late onset and delayed development of morphosyntactic, semantic, phonological, or pragmatic skills relative to other areas of development. They are generally identified between the ages of 3 and 5 during preschool (Tager-Flusberg & Cooper, 1999, p. 1276). Catts and Kahmi (1999) define students with LLD as possibly having deficits in "vocabulary, morphology, syntax, and/or text-level processing . . ." (p. 65) and estimate that up to 50% of poor readers have language deficits that go beyond phonological processing. The distinction between these diagnostic categories is unclear: SLI is often associated with preschool children, whereas LLD with school age. Regardless, children identified as SLI or LLD typically show significant difficulties with reading comprehension. The above diagnostic categories can overlap: students with SLI/LLD may also share characteristics of dyslexia (i.e., phonological processing problems that interfere with word identification) and students with dyslexia can display weaknesses in language areas in addition to phonology (see chapter 1 by Schwartz, chapter 9 by Edwards & Munson, and chapter 20 by Windsor & Kohnert).

Other types of language-related reading difficulties are found in children who have more limited intellectual potential or who have not had environmental opportunities to learn standard English. The first group, often categorized as *garden variety* poor readers, may have difficulties in the same areas of language as children with dyslexia or SLI/LLD, but they also have generally low cognitive abilities. Children with limited knowledge of standard English may speak a nonstandard dialect or speak English as an additional language (English language learners: ELL) or may come from a linguistically impoverished environment and have never been exposed to adequate language input. These additional language related factors may complicate diagnosis and intervention (see chapter 12 by Peña & Bedore and chapter 14 by Washington).

SKILLS LINKED TO PROCESSING DEFICITS

Phonemic Awareness

Acquisition of reading skills requires the development of phonemic awareness—the awareness of the sound structure of language at the single phoneme level. This skill is critical for learning how speech sounds map onto print. It involves the ability to segment, blend, and manipulate those sounds. Phonemic awareness falls under the larger umbrella of phonological awareness, which also includes word, rhyme, and syllable awareness. The development of these phonological awareness skills follows a continuum that begins in the preschool years and is usually accomplished by age 8. It starts with a sense of rhyme and moves forward with an awareness of syllables in words, beginning and ending sounds, and then individual sounds within words. Ultimately, around third grade, children learn to manipulate sounds in word games such as *Pig Latin*.

A strong relationship exists between early phonemic awareness and later reading success (Adams, 1990; Snow, Burns, & Griffin, 1998). Preschool and kindergarten phonemic awareness abilities are highly predictive of children's word-identification performance at the end of first grade (Adams, Foorman, Lundberg, & Beeler, 1996; Ball & Blachman, 1991; Juel, 1991). In fact, the explicit awareness of the sound structure of language has been found to be the most accurate predictor of early reading achievement cited in the research literature. Although many children develop phonemic awareness naturally, roughly 25% of middle-class first graders and substantially more of those who come from less literacy-rich backgrounds need direct instructional support (Adams, 1990).

Orthographic Processing

A second component of word recognition involves orthographic processing or the ability to recognize and retrieve underlying representations of letter sequences or patterns. Orthography is defined as the total writing system of a language and also refers to the spelling patterns that correspond to spoken words. Although controversy exists concerning the exact role of orthographic processing in reading disabilities, there is evidence that it is an important component, albeit secondary in importance to phonological processing (Badian, 1997, 2005; Share & Stanovich, 1995).

Reading and spelling of words may be particularly difficult in English because the manner in which sounds map onto print is often ambiguous (in contrast with more transparent languages such as Spanish or Italian). In English, there are around 44 phonemes and only 26 letters, with sound/symbol correspondences for vowel sounds being particularly complex. Despite this complexity, up to 84% of English is regular for reading if students know enough about the structure of the orthographic system. Given the nature of English orthography, which includes many complex spelling patterns, the ability to form strong orthographic representations is critical for accurate and automatic word identification and particularly for spelling.

Rapid Serial Naming

In addition to difficulties in phonemic awareness and orthographic processing, rapid serial naming plays a significant and independent role in the acquisition of word-identification skills (Wolf, 1997). The deficit involves difficulty with the rapid repeated naming of a small set of familiar words such as names for common objects, colors, numbers, or letters in response to visual stimuli. Difficulties in rapid naming have been found to directly affect automaticity both in earlier stages of reading, when students are memorizing sound/symbol associations, as well as at later stages, when fluent text-level reading is important for comprehension (Wolf & Bowers, 1999).

Phonological and Verbal Working Memory

The term phonological memory span refers to the capacity to hold speech information temporarily (see chapter 8 by Gillam, Montgomery, & Laing). Digit span tasks assess phonological memory span and are highly predictive of word-identification skills (Hulme, 1988). Verbal working memory is associated with phonological span and refers to the ability to manipulate speech information held in temporary store (Baddeley, 1986; Torgesen, 1996). Nonword-repetition tasks tap into phonological working memory and predict both word identification and syntactic comprehension (Caplan & Waters, 1999; Snowling, 2000).

Double or Triple Deficits

Wolf and Bowers (1999) hypothesize that there are actually three subgroups of children with word-identification difficulties: (1) those with phonological processing deficits, (2) those with rapid automatic naming deficits, and (3) those with both phonological processing deficits and automatic naming deficits. Children in this last group (those with a "double deficit) have the most serious difficulties in acquiring effective word-recognition skills (Manis & Freedman, 2001). (For a review of current research on the double deficit hypothesis, see Vukovic & Siegel, 2006.) Badian (1997, 2005) has suggested a *triple deficit* hypothesis that incorporates orthographic processing deficits as an important third component for many children. The more severe the difficulties in each of these areas and the more areas that are affected, the more intensive the intervention needs to be.

Links among Phonemic Awareness, Phonics, and Orthographic Reading

As illustrated in Figure 19.2, there is an interaction between the development of phonemic awareness and phonic word-attack strategies (Ehri, 1998; Share & Stanovich, 1995). With the development of a strong base in phonemic awareness (base of lower triangle), children are then able to acquire phonic word-attack strategies more easily (middle diamond); this in turn increases their phonemic awareness. Additionally, this strong base in phonemic awareness and related phonics skills is important to the development of automatic word identification through orthographic reading (upper triangle). Frith (1985) has developed a theory of reading/spelling development that highlights the changing importance of phonological and orthographic processing skills as children move through the steps involved in the acquisition of automatic word identification and spelling.

Of course, all of these word-identification skills influence and are facilitated by the processes involved in comprehension. Once students have achieved fluency, they are no longer *learning to read* but are ready to shift to an emphasis on *reading to learn*, usually around the fourth grade (Chall, 1983). The type of text shifts from being primarily narrative to expository, and the language complexity of the written material begins to increase

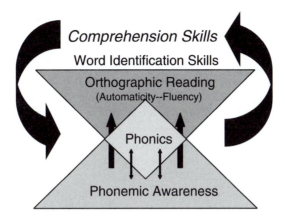

FIGURE 19.2 Development of orthographic reading skills.

dramatically (including vocabulary level, sentence complexity, and text structure). The importance of background knowledge for comprehension also increases. Fluent reading at this point is essential. As children move up through middle school, high school, and beyond, there is increasing emphasis on higher order thinking skills, comparing and contrasting viewpoints, and constructing knowledge. (For a complete discussion of stage theory of reading acquisition, see Chall, 1983, or Ehri, 1994.)

Automaticity and Fluency

Some researchers and practitioners do not differentiate between automaticity and fluency; they define them as the fast and accurate identification of words either at the single word or text level (for a discussion of this issue, see Torgesen, 1996). A broad, more inclusive definition of fluency will be used here with the assumption that developing automatic application of appropriate phrasing and prosodic features is important for comprehension and should be directly addressed, particularly with children who do not do this naturally. Automaticity is therefore defined as fast, accurate, and effortless word identification at the single-word level. Fluency, in contrast, involves not only automatic word identification, but also the application of appropriate prosodic features (rhythm, intonation) and syntactic chunking at the phrase, sentence, and text levels. Thus, fluent reading incorporates elements from syntax, morphology, semantics, discourse, and pragmatics. These relationships are illustrated in Figure 19.1. Wood, Flowers, and Grigorenko (2001) emphasized that fluency also involves anticipation of what will come next in the text and that speeded practice alone is not sufficient for achieving fluent reading. Anticipation facilitates reaction time and is particularly important for comprehension.

PROCESSES IN READING COMPREHENSION/ WRITTEN EXPRESSION

Reading comprehension is a complex cognitive linguistic process that involves multiple levels of processing, particularly in the higher grades. All components of language (phonology, morphology, syntax, semantics, discourse structure, and pragmatics) are involved, as well as attention, executive function, and memory skills (see Figure 19.1). Given these relationships, it is not surprising that oral language comprehension was found to be the best predictor of reading comprehension in typically developing third-grade students (Spear-Swerling, 2006). Although the development of these components in spoken language is necessary for effective reading, it is not sufficient; one must also develop metalinguistic knowledge of the rules governing these systems. Fluent readers do not use context to help decode words, but struggling readers must often rely on the syntactic and semantic cues provided by context (Share & Stanovich, 1995). However, the ability to recognize the morphological structure of language is often weaker in children who struggle with reading (Carlisle, 2004), as is the syntactic complexity of their spoken and written language (Scott & Windsor, 2000). Thus, if these systems themselves or the metalinguistic abilities related to them are weak, the application of context strategies can be difficult and may need to be taught explicitly.

The semantic system is, of course, heavily involved in reading and writing, both of which require active construction of meaning. In addition to vocabulary acquisition, an awareness of the rules governing meaning in different contexts and understanding relationships between words becomes increasingly important as children progress through school. There is an increased need for higher order cognitive linguistic skills such as categorization, getting the main idea, drawing inferences and conclusions, and making predictions.

Pragmatics, or the rules for how language is used in a social context, plays a significant role in written language acquisition related to identifying the author's intent as well as understanding different purposes for reading and writing reflected in different genres (see chapter 18 by Fujiki & Brinton). It also includes aspects of language such as intonation and prosody. As noted above, fluent reading requires the application of appropriate phrasing and stress to text, which proves to be quite difficult for struggling or beginning readers. These prosodic features must be superimposed on the text by the reader (again, a metalinguistic activity), which is not the case in spoken language interactions. Clues to correct phrasing and intonation are often found in small visual signals such as commas, periods, and question marks, which tend to elude struggling readers.

ASSESSMENT

There are four general types of assessment that serve different purposes: *screening, diagnostic, progress monitoring,* and *outcomes*. Although many tests can serve more than one purpose, the goal is to find the most effective and efficient battery. A screening identifies children who are at risk for failure and need additional assessment; it also allows for the implementation of extra instructional supports (see response to intervention, Tiers 2 and 3, later in this chapter). In-depth diagnostic assessment is used to determine at-risk students' specific patterns of strengths and weaknesses and their instructional needs. These tests are often individually administered and require lengthy testing sessions.

Progress monitoring assessments should occur throughout the year to ensure that adequate progress in reading growth is being achieved. This type of evaluation is also called *formative* or *dynamic* assessment. These tests are often criterion-referenced (more directly related to the actual material being taught) or based on a specified benchmark (expected level of performance); they can be utilized to determine whether or not intervention techniques are effective or need to be modified. Progress data is critical for determining a student's response to intervention (see below). Outcomes assessment, the fourth type of assessment, is summative in nature and is designed to evaluate overall reading/writing achievement. Students are often compared to a standard to determine overall progress in comparison to other students in the same grade. Outcomes measures are often group-administered, norm-referenced achievement tests or high stakes tests designed at the state level.

Areas of Assessment for In-depth Diagnostic Testing

Assessment should aid in the development of curricula and intervention strategies; it is important, therefore to evaluate skills in critical areas related to listening, speaking, reading, and writing. An in-depth assessment should answer three basic questions:

1. What are the student's underlying spoken language skills?
2. What are the student's reading and writing skills, and how do they compare to the underlying spoken language skills?
3. What are the student's underlying processing skills and how are they affecting acquisition of reading and writing?

All of this information needs to be combined with general developmental, cognitive, medical, behavioral, social, and cultural factors to create a complete profile for the individual student.

Underlying Spoken Language   Within the area of *spoken language*, it is helpful to have some measure of vocabulary knowledge in that it is highly related to reading comprehension, particularly in the upper grades. If weaknesses in other components of the spoken system are suspected, it is useful to assess morphological and syntactic performance and to examine the semantic system by assessing higher order thinking skills (analogies, main idea, inferences, drawing conclusions, predicting, etc.). Some spoken language issues can be subtle and require examination of metalinguistic skills involved in comprehension of metaphors, jokes, riddles, or the application of syntax knowledge to a new situation.

Reading and Writing   In the area of *reading*, it is important to consider both the *accuracy* and the *speed* with which each task can be accomplished, as well as the effects of *meaning* and *context* on performance. Students who struggle primarily with word identification (e.g., often individuals with dyslexia) frequently read more effectively when meaning is available, as in sentence or paragraph reading, and time is unlimited. In contrast, students with underlying comprehension difficulties may be overwhelmed by the complexity of the language and may not necessarily benefit from extended time (e.g., often individuals diagnosed as SLI or LLD). A comparison of performance on real words versus nonwords and isolated words versus reading in context both in *timed* and *untimed* environments allows one to determine whether there are differences between accuracy and automaticity/fluency. Similarly, timed reading comprehension should be compared to untimed to help determine if the difficulty in comprehension is primarily related to lack of automatic word identification or a more fundamental language comprehension disorder.

Because of their varying requirements, oral reading can also differ substantially from silent reading; some children understand better when allowed to read silently, whereas others, often younger or more severely impaired, benefit from reading orally. It is therefore important to consider the effects of different modes of assessment on performance. In addition, for reading comprehension, some tests use paragraph-level input and questions given in a multiple choice format, while others involve a cloze procedure (filling in a missing word from a sentence or paragraph). Still others ask for an open-ended response, such as retelling. These response formats place differing demands on word retrieval and language formulation.

When evaluating writing, it is important to examine functions related to planning, translating, and reviewing (Hayes & Flower, 1980). This allows one to determine the extent to which problems in mechanics (spelling, handwriting, and punctuation) interfere with production and the extent to which language formulation and organization may be factors. Automatic mechanics are critical for adequate engagement of attention and executive function capabilities necessary for planning and editing (see McCutchen, 1995, for an excellent discussion of the factors involved in writing and how they relate to executive function as well as to automaticity and fluency). Obtaining a written language sample (two for the older student: one narrative and one expository) is essential and will demonstrate the student's ability to perform the most complex of language tasks. These samples can be analyzed for phonological, orthographic, syntactic, semantic, and discourse structure skills.

Underlying Processing—The Why?   In addition to obtaining basic knowledge of their spoken and written language skills, it is important to determine a struggling student's strengths and weaknesses in phonological awareness, phonological working memory, rapid serial naming, and orthographic processing. These processing skills link directly to word identification as well as to automaticity, fluency, and comprehension. Tests of processing skills are typically administered individually and therefore take more time than group assessments. Commonly used tests of phonological processing measure aspects of phonological awareness skills such as rhyming, segmenting, blending, and manipulating sounds, often with real and pseudoword stimuli. (e.g., The Phonological Awareness Test—Robertson & Salter, 1997; and the Comprehensive Test of Phonological Processing—Wagner, Torgesen, & Rashotte, 1999). Elision tasks, which involve removing one or more phonemes from a word and determining what the new word will be (e.g., "Say brought without the /r/." *bought*), are commonly used because of their high correlation with word-identification performance. For phonological memory, tasks of digit repetition (forward and backward) or nonword repetition are common. Standard batteries for rapid serial naming usually involve the timed repetition of six to eight randomly mixed numbers, letters, objects, or colors. Numbers and letters are the most highly related to word identification, but objects and colors can offer helpful information for younger, preliterate children and nonreaders.

Although there are many tools for assessing phonological skills (awareness, memory, and rapid naming), there are fewer tests to assess orthographic skills. Olson, Forsberg, Wise and Rack (1994) have developed an experimental task that has been used to assess orthographic recognition; it involves choosing the correctly spelled word in a pair (e.g., take/taik; trowsers/trousers; aplause/applause). This task taps into orthographic memory and can be used for informal analysis but is not currently standardized. Another task (e.g., Test of Silent Word Reading Fluency: Mather, Hammill, Allen, & Roberts, 2004) assesses some aspects of orthographic processing by asking students to draw lines between words where spaces have been omitted (e.g., *eachmuchthreezooapplefarfly*). Divisions between words are often marked by orthographic patterns that are not present or are infrequent in English (e.g., *hm* [*eachmuch*] and *hp* [*epochpreclude*]). However, items increase in difficulty as the student moves through the test, and vocabulary knowledge becomes a significant factor for older children.

If time constraints prevent individual testing, a group spelling test can serve as a window into phonological awareness and orthographic knowledge. Analysis of errors may indicate a phonological awareness problem and will suggest the degree to which a student has mastered the orthographic patterns of English. For example, a student who spells *switch* as *wathch* has difficulties with phonological awareness, often confusing the order of sounds, substituting sounds, and omitting sounds, whereas a student who spells *throat* as *throte* clearly has trouble with ambiguous words, indicating weaknesses in orthographic memory. Errors such as *smug* for *smudge* or *traped* for *trapped* indicate a weakness in orthographic memory as well as a lack of ability to apply orthographic rules and generalizations to rule-based words. Once spelling samples have been analyzed, further individual testing may be employed with students who exhibit difficulties.

Patterns of Performance A well-integrated assessment will link the patterns in the test data so that reading and writing abilities are considered in the context of the broader language system. For example, a problem in reading comprehension could be due to various factors, ranging from word-identification difficulties, to metalinguistic problems, to overt problems in one or more of the spoken language components. Figure 19.1 can be used to guide analyses of spoken-written language performance. For example, weak word identification combined with strong underlying listening skills may explain unexpectedly strong reading comprehension scores because the student uses strengths in aspects of language more related to comprehension to compensate. Alternatively, poor receptive and expressive spoken language in combination with strong word identification may explain poor reading comprehension. Reading comprehension problems could, of course, be related to a combination of the above factors, as well as to deficits in executive function, attention difficulties, or first-language differences.

INTERVENTION

Over the last almost 50 years, there has been considerable debate over how reading should be taught. An important aspect of the discussion concerns whether or not there should be primarily a meaning emphasis (top-down) or a code emphasis (bottom-up) for teaching beginning or struggling readers. Reviews of the research on reading acquisition have consistently suggested that a code emphasis is more successful for teaching beginning reading skills (Adams, 1990; Chall, 1996; National Institute of Child Heath and Human Development, 2000; Snow et al., 1998). This is not to imply, however, that meaning-based approaches are not important; in general, a relatively "balanced approach" is desirable and the weighting of the "balance" should be determined by the children's individual needs. The National Research Council (Snow et al., 1998) identified three "stumbling blocks" to becoming a skilled reader: failure to grasp the alphabetic principle resulting in inaccurate word recognition, failure to acquire comprehension skills and strategies, and inadequate motivation (pp. 315–316). The Council concluded that instructional approaches that are more explicit have the strongest impact on the reading growth of children at risk for reading disabilities.

Other important issues in reading instruction for at-risk populations involve the timing and the intensity of intervention. There is strong converging evidence supporting the view that early intervention geared toward the prevention of reading failure is critical (Snow et al., 1998; Torgesen, 1997). In a study of third- through fifth-grade children, Torgesen and colleagues (Torgesen, Wagner, & Rashotte, 1997) found that children who receive intensive appropriate intervention often catch up in the areas of word attack, text reading accuracy, and reading comprehension, but not in the area of fluency. Preventative (early intervention) studies were found to produce better outcomes for fluency than remediation studies (Torgesen et al., 2001). In addition, because of the need for more explicit, direct instruction, struggling readers need a more intense kind of instruction, often in small groups over a longer period of time (Torgesen et al., 2001).

Thus, when developing intervention programs, the intensity of instruction should differ, depending on the student's responsiveness to different levels of intervention. Berninger and colleagues have proposed a 3-tiered response to intervention (RTI) model, which conceptualizes intervention as layered over time and gauged to the child's level of need (Berninger, Stage, Smith, & Hildebrand, 2001). Tier 1 instruction comprises research-based instruction for all children during the literacy block within the regular education classroom. According to the National Reading Panel (National Institute of Child Heath and Human Development, 2000), this instruction should include a core curriculum that systematically introduces phonemic awareness, phonics, fluency, vocabulary, and comprehension. Students who fail to progress adequately in Tier 1 move to Tier 2 instruction, which emphasizes small group supplemental instruction within the classroom. Students for whom Tier 2 instruction is insufficient are, in turn, referred for Tier 3 intervention. Teaching in Tier 3 is intensive and strategic and is provided by a professional who is qualified to deliver special instruction in reading. At each level, periodic benchmark testing is employed to determine whether or not a child should remain at their current level or move to a more or less intensive level of instruction (see also Vaughn, 2003). The RTI model also has diagnostic implications and has been incorporated into the Individuals with Disabilities Education Act (IDEA, 2004, 614b), as a means of identifying students with specific learning disability without the use of a discrepancy model (http://idea.ed.gov/explore/search). (See Fuchs & Fuchs, 2006, for an in-depth discussion.)

The most commonly used intensive Tier 3 types of instruction developed for struggling readers and writers are often referred to as multisensory structured language approaches (MSL). These approaches share the following characteristics:

- explicit presentation of concepts;
- structured and sequential order of presentation;
- multisensory stimulation (visual, auditory and tactile/kinesthetic modalities);
- intensive review and practice.

Many MSL approaches also incorporate mnemonics to aide recall of the arbitrary, non-meaningful letter symbols as well as the structure of other aspects of language (e.g., narrative and expository structure). The focus of these programs is on developing an awareness of the rule structure of the various components of language: phonological, morphological, syntactic, semantic, discourse, and pragmatic (metalinguistic awareness). Instruction is highly scaffolded in the beginning with a gradual release of this external structure as the student takes on more responsibility until they can ultimately perform independently. Although these programs often contain a multisensory component, the relative value of this component is underresearched. However, after careful examination of the issues, Moats and Farrell (2005) conclude:

> Conceptions of memory organization, neural activation patterns in language processing, and the importance of metacognition are consistent with the efficacy of multisensory techniques. . . . Most likely, it is not simply the multimodal nature of such practice that explains its power but the mediating effect of various sensory and motor experiences on attention and recall. (p. 34)

To examine the efficacy of phonemic awareness training and phonics instruction on word recognition, fluency, and reading comprehension for all children and for children with reading disabilities, the National Reading Panel conducted a large meta-analysis and computed effect sizes (.20 = small effect; .50 = moderate effect; .80 = large effect) based on the results of studies that met their criteria for being empirically sound (National Institute of Child Heath and Human Development, 2000). In the area of word recognition, their findings were consistent with Ball and Blachman (1991) in that they found a stronger effect size for phonemic awareness with letters than for phonemes only (.67 vs. .38). The effect of systematic phonics for all children was larger in kindergarten and first grade than in Grades 2–6 (.54 vs. .27). However, for children with reading disabilities, the effect size was larger than for typically developing children and continued from kindergarten through Grade 6 (.74). Thus, phonics instruction is important for developing word-recognition skills in the early grades for all children and remains important for struggling readers throughout elementary school. Approaches to improving reading fluency have often involved repeated readings of the same material with corrective feedback as well as increased raw amounts of reading through incentives for silent reading of more books. Guided repeated reading resulted in moderate effects on accuracy, speed, and comprehension (.55, .44 and .35, respectively). The effects on general reading abilities for average readers were moderate (.49) for kindergarten through fourth grade and for children with reading disabilities the effect (.47) remained through Grade 12. The implications of this analysis are that guided, repeated reading is proven to enhance reading accuracy, speed, and comprehension in reading-disabled children and in children overall. The National Reading Panel found no empirical support for improving reading fluency by simply increasing children's amount of reading.

Word Identification and Spelling

As noted above, English orthography is semi-alphabetic in nature, and thus emphasis must be placed on developing strong orthographic representations. The orthographic structure of English can be divided into four categories: (1) regular for reading and for spelling (e.g., *dig, sprint*)—unambiguous spelling-to sound-relationship; (2) regular for reading but ambiguous for spelling (e.g., *boat*—could be *bote*, *plain*—could be *plane*); (3) rule- or generalization-based (e.g., *planning*—doubling rule; *back, badge, batch*—based on -ck, -tch, -dge generalization); and (4) irregular (e.g., *beauty*)—note, that most of this word is regular (only *eau* is irregular). Students must learn to recognize and recall all four types of words automatically in order to be effective readers and spellers; thus, techniques for developing strong orthographic representations for each type of word are essential.

Phonological Awareness: A Foundation Skill   There are compelling reasons to teach phonological awareness skills to children acquiring reading skills. A number of researchers have investigated the efficacy of training phonological awareness on the acquisition of literacy skills in children (for recent meta-analyses, see Bus & van IJzendoorn, 1999; Ehri, et al., 2001). The ability to read and spell words that are regular depends on students' development of phonemic awareness. In the 1970s Elkonin (1973) devised what is now a classic and representative technique for developing phonological awareness that specifically addresses segmentation and blending skills. It first utilizes tokens representing sounds and then moves to letters representing those sounds. The student segments the word or word part into sounds (phonemes) while moving one token down to a segmented line or series of boxes for each sound in the word. The activity can be systematically adjusted to represent words of increasing phonemic complexity (VC, CVC, CCVC, CCVCC, and CCCVC) depending on an individual student's abilities. It employs all the aspects of multisensory structured language techniques: explicit training of segmentation and blending, systematic and sequenced instruction, ample opportunity for practice, and multisensory delivery (involving motor movement as well as visual and auditory processing).

Orthography   As previously discussed, research indicates that intervention training methods that combine phonemic awareness with direct instruction in how sounds map onto letters (phonics) are more effective at improving word-recognition skills than phonemic awareness instruction alone (Ball & Blachman, 1991; Bus & van IJzendoorn, 1999; Lundberg, Frost, & Petersen, 1988; National Institute of Child Heath and Human Development, 2000). The segmenting techniques discussed above are excellent for bridging between phonemic awareness and phonics instruction as one moves from the use of tokens to the use of letters.

The order in which sound–symbol correspondences should be taught varies from one program to another; regardless, a structured sequence is essential. Many programs teach high-frequency letters that are not visually or auditorily similar first in order to avoid unnecessary confusions (e.g., *s, t, m* will be easier than *b, d, p* in that they are visually and auditorily distinct). However, some programs choose a sequence based on how sounds are produced in the mouth and therefore would present *p/b* and *t/d* early on, because the sounds that these letters represent vary in only one aspect, voicing. Thus, it is not a particular sequence that is necessary but, instead, a consistent structured sequence. A common technique employed by MSL programs is the use of tactile kinesthetic cues to aid in recall of sound/symbol correspondences. These programs often use techniques such as tracing on a rough surface or sky writing to help solidify the associations between the auditory, visual, and tactile–kinesthetic modalities (see Gillingham & Stillman, 1997 for an in-depth discussion of this approach). Tactile-kinesthetic cues from the articulators also help students to create strong metalinguistic awareness of the phonological structure of spoken language— see *LiPs* (Lindamood & Lindamood, 1998); *Lively Letters* (Telian, 2001); and *Reading by the Rules* (Weiss-Kapp, 2005). For example, these programs organize sounds into "minimal pairs" based on similarities in articulation and varying only in voicing (e.g., /p/-/b/, /d/-/t/, or /k/-/g/). Mnemonics such as a key word with a picture or stories help children to remember sound/symbol correspondences (Telian, 2001; Weiss-Kapp, 2005).

In addition to learning sound/symbol correspondence, students need to recognize the orthographic patterns of letters within a syllable that govern pronunciation; to accomplish this end, many MSL programs teach six syllable types: closed (*not*), open (*no*), silent e (*note*), vowel combination (*moat*), r controlled (*part*), and consonant-le (*noble*) (see Moats, 2000, for an in-depth discussion of these syllable types). This is the first step in moving from the application of phonic word-attack strategies to becoming an orthographic or automatic reader. For example, if asked to read the pseudo-word *nim*, the majority of people use a short sound for the /i/. It is the consonant following the single vowel in a closed syllable such as *nim* that signals the short sound of *i*. Although good readers may not be consciously aware of these aspects of English orthography, they have intuited the "rules" often through analogy to words (e.g., for the syllable *nim*, they would associate it with the real word "him" or with the first syllable in *nimble*). Because they have adequate phonological awareness and orthographic memory, they are able to invoke these associations automatically, with little or no conscious effort. While younger students may continue to work on one-syllable words, older students may be ready to move on to strategies for syllable division. *Visually* recognizing two vowel–consonant patterns that allow them to determine where to divide words (VCCV and VCV) will help in deciphering them. Most MSL programs have systematic instruction in these as well as more complex rules for syllable division.

Morphological Structure   Application of phonic word attack strategies is heavily dependent on awareness of the structure of language at the level of phonology and the syllable. However, for multisyllable words of more than two syllables, awareness of the morphological structure of language has proven to be helpful. This involves understanding prefixes, stems, and suffixes and the rules that govern their pronunciation within words. Although there are extremely large numbers of syllables, there are a finite number of prefixes, stems, and suffixes, which recur in many words (e.g., **ex**port, **im**port, **re**port; and **re**peat, **re**flect, **re**tract). They also have meaning ("ex" means "out of" and "port" means "to carry"); thus, the task of creating orthographic representations to aid decoding is simplified, and the study of morphology can also be used to enhance vocabulary knowledge.

Many programs categorize English words based on their origin—Anglo-Saxon, Latin, or Greek. Anglo-Saxon-based words tend to be of higher frequency and deal with everyday life (*boat, home, rain*), whereas Latin-based words are often associated with government or law (*constitution, transportation, structure*) and Greek with math, science, and the theater (*biology, parallel, proscenium*). There are also many interesting accent placement rules that can open the door to many otherwise inaccessible words (for a systematic sequence and scripted lesson plans for teaching structural analysis see Henry, 2003; for a thorough treatment of accent placement see *Solving Language Difficulties*, Steere, Peck, & Kahn, 1988).

Spelling When dealing with words that are regular for spelling, reading and spelling can progress in parallel. But once the other word types are introduced, reading can progress more quickly than spelling, particularly for ambiguous (*rain, light*) or irregular (*friend*) words. The latter kinds of words place much more strain on orthographic memory as well as lexical association because there are no rules governing their spelling. In order to know if the spelling is *pain* or *pane*, one must memorize the orthographic pattern in relationship to its meaning. Typical MSL strategies for increasing orthographic memory are tracing or writing while naming letters; or fading of letter cues while copying, simultaneously naming letters, and then ultimately writing from memory.

One way to work on ambiguous words has been to combine theory and practice from associative verbal learning strategies with visualizing and verbalizing techniques (Bell, 1997). This strategy capitalizes on the often stronger ability of the student with learning disabilities to remember meaningful information (concept images) than to recall arbitrary nonmeaningful letter strings (symbol images). When utilizing this visual associative spelling technique, students semantically associate words with similar orthographic patterns (*ai* words: *sail, pail, tail, mail,* etc.); they form a meaningful visual image in their heads and describe the image verbally. This image enables them to recall the correct spelling of a set of orthographically similar words linked through that image (Hook & Telian, 1996). Drawing pictures to illustrate these associations may also be helpful (Fischer, 1999).

Many English words follow orthographic rules that revolve around the vowel sounds, particularly short vowels. The spelling of words such as *chatting, stitch, lodge,* and *smack* involves the application of rules or generalizations related to single-syllable words with short vowels (i.e., these words contain an extra consonant after the single short vowel). Armed with the four most common spelling rules—the *f-l-s-z* rule (*muff, tell*), the doubling rule (*running*), the drop *e* rule (*skating*), the change *y* rule (*candies*)—and a handful of generalizations, students can learn to spell a large number of words that would otherwise elude them. Most of the MSL programs have systematic presentations of these orthographic rules.

Developing Automaticity

Most students who learn through systematic teaching techniques to apply phonic word-attack strategies and later structural analysis can become quite accurate in their reading. However, because of difficulties in forming strong orthographic representations, many have trouble moving to automatic orthographic reading for words in isolation or in text. They remain slow and laborious in their word identification, thus continuing to have comprehension problems, particularly in timed situations. As a result, many older students and adults who have seemingly compensated for their reading difficulties often require extended time when taking tests.

Approaches have been developed that use a variety of strategies to strengthen orthographic representations for automatic reading (see Hook & Jones, 2002). Extensive opportunity for repeated practice in pattern recognition is often necessary. The use of speed drills consisting of lists of six to eight isolated words with contrasting vowel sounds is common (e.g., *rid, ride, hid, hide, kit, kite*) (Fischer, 1999). Individual goals are established, and the number of words read correctly within a minute is recorded in successive sessions. Speed drills can also be used for irregular words (*from, of, come, some, one*) as well as multisyllable words that incorporate higher-level concepts of structural analysis (prefix, stem and suffix).

Developing Fluency: Phrasing and Chunking Text

Although speed and accuracy are the most important factors at the single-word level, the additional application of intonation and stress through syntactic chunking is considered critical for developing fluency at the text level. Increased speed is therefore not necessarily the sole aim and, in fact, one must often caution students to slow down and monitor for meaning, particularly in the beginning. Although periodic timing of the reading of connected text is important for monitoring progress in developing fluency, equally important is the focus on applying prosodic features and chunking. Reading with natural prosody has been found to be most strongly facilitated by repeated readings of text printed with spaces between phrases and ends of lines at clause boundaries, thus, providing visible support for sentence structure (LeVasseur, Macaruso, & Shankweiler, 2007). The incorporation of a multisensory component of scooping (drawing an arc) under predetermined syntactic chunks may benefit some students.

Repeated readings of the same text has been found to be effective in increasing reading rate, with three or four readings of the text as the optimum number (Meyer & Felton, 1999; National Institute of Child Heath and Human Development, 2000). However, research on repeated readings of paragraphs has indicated that generalization may be limited somewhat to the specific words being practiced (Rashotte & Torgesen, 1985). It is therefore recommended that high-frequency words be included in the texts to provide as many exposures as possible to these types of words. Whether or not decodable text is used, teachers should choose text for fluency practice that students are able to read with around 95% accuracy.

Developing Anticipatory Set

As noted above, in addition to repeated readings and other sorts of speeded practice, being able to anticipate what will come next in the text enhances fluency; this, in turn, enhances comprehension (Wood, Flowers, & Grigorenko, 2001). The use of a cloze procedure where a word must be determined through the use of context, with or without first letter cues, can be helpful in developing a conscious use of syntactic and semantic cues. Activation of prior knowledge and reviewing what will be happening in the story can be instrumental in helping students predict text content. Summarizing the story and discussing the characters or previewing the pictures to get ideas of what the story may be about may also serve to improve anticipatory set and thus enhance fluency. Other commonly used strategies such as reviewing the vocabulary and comprehension questions before reading the passage may also be helpful in this regard.

Comprehension and Written Expression

Many traditional approaches to reading comprehension involve practice rather than the acquisition of strategies for understanding text. They are often composed of a series of paragraphs with questions following that tap into key comprehension skills (i.e., getting the facts, getting the main idea, drawing inferences, drawing conclusions, predicting outcomes, and determining vocabulary meaning from context). Extra practice can be helpful for some students, but most students with language disorders will need to be systematically taught strategies for comprehending text. Many of these strategy-based approaches are also multisensory and use manipulatives to reinforce concepts.

Intervention in the area of reading comprehension and written expression requires that one determine in which areas the student struggles: morphology, syntax, semantics, discourse structure, or pragmatics. If understanding the rules that govern the morphological structure of language is an issue, direct instruction in this area is necessary. For example, these difficulties can be apparent in oral reading where students tend to omit endings, or in writing when a child spells *shopping* as *shopen* versus *shoping*—neither is correct, but the second implies an awareness of morphological endings. Systematic teaching of prefixes, roots, and suffixes can substantially increase a student's awareness of morphological rules, as can direct instruction in monitoring the correctness of written text.

For students with weaknesses in syntax, explicit teaching of sentence structure will enhance comprehension as well as production. Solid understanding of sentence structure will also improve the student's ability to develop syntactic chunking for fluency. Approaches that emphasize the core of a sentence (subject and predicate) and how that core can be systematically expanded through answering such questions as *when, where, how long*, and *why* by the identification of signal words can improve a student's awareness of syntactic structure at the phrase and sentence levels. Often work on writing at the sentence level will reinforce these same concepts. For example, *Framing Your Thoughts* (Enfield & Green, 1997) combines explicit teaching of sentence structure through reading and writing by giving students extensive opportunities to analyze sentences in written text and to produce sentences in writing. Unfortunately, work at the sentence level is often omitted from reading comprehension and writing programs.

The area of semantics includes different levels of comprehension: literal, inferential, and applied. It incorporates vocabulary, categorical thinking, and higher order thinking skills required for deeper comprehension of text-based material. As with all instruction for struggling readers, it is important that these skills be taught explicitly. For vocabulary, it is critical to choose appropriate words for instruction as well as expose the student to many personally meaningful activities to enhance acquisition. Isabel Beck has developed a three-tier model to guide educators in the choice of words. Tier 1 words are those from everyday life and typically do not need to be taught (e.g., *baby, happy, talk*), while Tier 3 words are low-frequency and domain-specific words (e.g., *isotope, lathe, peninsula*). She stresses the need to focus on Tier 2 words, which are high frequency for mature language learners and occur in many domains (e.g., *coincidence, absurd, industrious*). These words are useful and can be worked with in a variety of ways so students can build rich representations for them and easily connect to other words and concepts. *Bringing Words to Life* (Beck, McKeowin, & Kucan, 2002) provides an in-depth discussion of this model as well as suggestions for how activities should be structured.

Another important aid to comprehension is the use of visualizing strategies that involve students creating a mental image of what they are reading. For example, *Visualizing and Verbalizing* (Bell, 1991) incorporates a structured and sequential program that combines creating visual images with verbalization to enhance listening, speaking, reading, and writing skills. Through a questioning technique, students create a picture of what they are reading in their heads and then describe their visualization. This approach is designed to improve integration of information as well as memory for what was read, both of which are common problems for children who struggle with listening and reading comprehension. It systematically teaches children to identify facts, get the main idea, draw inferences and conclusions, predict, extend, evaluate, and summarize.

Understanding discourse structure (narrative and expository) is also important for reading comprehension and written formulation. Narratives often have a predictable structure (main character, setting, kick-off event, attempts at resolution, and resolution) that can be taught through the use of manipulatives. The use of icons to represent each element of the structure and systematic practice retelling stories using these icons forms the basis for several approaches (see *The Story-Grammar Marker*, Moreau, 1994, and *Story Form*, Enfield & Greene, 1994). These types of programs also extend this structure into summarizing and creating narratives in written form.

Careful teaching of the structure of expository paragraphs and attention to the prerequisites for writing at the paragraph level can enhance students' comprehension and written expression. Common expository paragraph types include, but are not limited to: descriptive, enumerative, sequential/process, and comparison/contrast. When introducing a given paragraph structure, it is helpful to teach first the key sentence type(s) at the core of that paragraph. For example, for a student to write a comparison paragraph, it is helpful for them to first master sentences signaling comparison. Similarly, descriptive paragraph writing can be enhanced by teaching adjective types (e.g., color, composition, inner feelings, age) and adjective stacking (Jennings & Haynes, 2002).

In addition to language disorders, many students with reading difficulties have related problems with executive function including planning, organization, attention, inhibition, and working memory (Denckla, 1996). Techniques have been developed to aid students in their approach to reading tasks by providing them with strategies for *before, during* and *after* reading. Focus on developing intentionality in the reader is a frequent component of these strategies.

A common before and after reading activity is the use of the *KWL* chart, where a student works with the teacher to: (1) activate background knowledge: *K* = what they already *know* about the topic; (2) create a specific reason for reading: *W* = what they *want* to know; and (3) relate the information that they read with what they knew before and what they wanted to know: L = what they have *learned* after they read. Self-questioning strategies such as reciprocal teaching (Brown & Palincsar, 1987) are good during reading activities in that the student is taught to ask themselves questions as they read to clarify information and direct their thinking. A program that systematically incorporates metacognitive strategies into the daily lesson for reading comprehension is *Developing Metacognitive Skills: Vocabulary and Comprehension* developed by the Neuhaus Education Center (Carreker, 2004). This program incorporates multisensory activities as well as color coding to teach comprehension strategies.

Even more emphasis must be placed on developing abilities related to executive function for writing. (For an in-depth discussion of the processes involved in writing—long term memory, planning, translating, and reviewing—see MacArthur, Graham, & Fitzgerald, 2006, and McCutcheon, 1995.) To address these needs, Singer and Bashir (2004) developed an instruction and intervention approach to teaching expository writing called *EmPOWER*™ specifically designed for students who exhibit language-learning disabilities and executive function disorders as well as general education students who struggle with self-regulating their writing. *EmPOWER™* represents a six-stage writing process: *E*valuate, *M*ake a *P*lan, *O*rganize, *W*ork, *E*valuate, *R*ework. Specific strategies are taught explicitly to support the numerous cognitive and linguistic subprocesses of writing.

CONCLUSIONS

Given the direct relationships between spoken and written language, it is critical that professionals working with students who struggle to acquire these basic communication skills have sufficient knowledge in both areas. With prevention of problems in reading and writing through early identification and appropriate intervention as a goal, it is imperative that the students who are likely to struggle be identified early. Careful assessment of spoken and written language skills will enhance our ability to identify and address areas of need. The patterns of strengths and weaknesses in language skills and processing abilities of students who struggle with the acquisition of reading and writing vary enormously. It is these patterns, however, that determine the kind of intervention that is necessary. The application of the RTI model and the implementation of appropriate instruction in the regular classroom should reduce the number of children who need intensive work, thus allowing professionals to carefully tailor instruction to individual student needs.

REFERENCES

Adams, M. (1990). *Beginning to read: Thinking and learning about print*. Cambridge, MA: MIT Press.

Adams, M., Foorman, B., Lundberg, I, & Beeler, T. (1996). *Phonemic awareness in young children*. Baltimore: Paul H. Brookes.

Baddeley, A. D. (1986). *Working memory*. Oxford, UK: Oxford University Press.

Badian, N. (1997). Dyslexia and the double deficit hypothesis. *Annals of Dyslexia, 47*, 69–88.

Badian, N. (2005). Does a visual-orthographic deficit contribute to reading disability? *Annals of Dyslexia, 55*, 28–52.

Ball, E., & Blachman, B. (1991). Does phoneme awareness training in kindergarten make a difference in early word recognition and developmental spelling? *Reading Research Quarterly, 24*, 49–66.

Beck, I., McKeowin, M., & Kucan, L. (2002). *Bringing words to life*. New York: Guilford Press.

Bell, N. (1991). *Visualizing and verbalizing for language comprehension and thinking*. Paso Robles, CA: Academy of Reading.

Bell, N. (1997). *Seeing stars*. San Luis Obispo, CA: Gander Educational.

Berko, J. (1958). The child's learning of English morphology. *Word, 14*, 150–177.

Berninger, V., Stage, S., Smith, D., & Hildebrand, D. (2001). Assessment for reading and writing intervention: A 3-tier model for prevention and intervention. In J. Andrews, D. Saklofske, & H. Janzen (Eds.), *Ability, achievement, and behavior assessment: A practical handbook* (pp. 195–223). New York: Academic Press.

Bishop, D., & Snowling, M. (2004). Developmental dyslexia and specific language impairment: Same or different? *Psychological Bulletin, 30*(6), 858–886.

Brady, S. (1997). Ability to encode phonological representations: An underlying difficulty of poor readers. In B. Blachman (Ed.), *Foundations of reading acquisition and dyslexia* (pp. 21–47). Mahwah, NJ: Lawrence Erlbaum Associates.

Brown, A. L., & Palincsar, A. S. (1987). Reciprocal teaching of comprehension strategies: A natural history of one program for enhancing learning. In J. D. Day & J. G. Borkowski (Eds.), *Intelligence and exceptionality: New directions for theory, assessment, and instructional practice* (pp. 81–132). Norwood, NJ: Ablex.

Bus, A. G., & van IJzendoorn, M. H. (1999). Phonological awareness and early reading: A meta-analysis of experimental training studies. *Journal of Educational Psychology, 91,* 403–414.

Caplan, D., & Waters, G. (1999). Verbal working memory and sentence comprehension. *Behavioral and Brain Sciences, 22,* 77–94.

Carlisle, J. (2004). Morphological processes that influence learning to read. In A. Stone, E. Silliman, B. Ehren, & K. Apel (Eds.), *Handbook of language and literacy: Development and disorders* (pp. 318–339). New York: Guilford Press.

Carreker, S. (2004). *Developing meta-cognitive skills: Vocabulary and comprehension.* Houston, TX: Neuhaus Education Center.

Catts, H., & Kamhi, A. (1999). *Language and reading disabilities.* Boston: Allyn & Bacon.

Chall, J. (1983). *Stages of reading development.* New York: McGraw-Hill.

Chall, J. (1996). *Learning to read: The great debate.* New York: McGraw-Hill.

Denckla, M. B. (1996). A theory and model of executive function: A neuropsychological perspective. In G. R. Lyon & N. A. Krasnegor (Eds.), *Attention, memory and executive function* (pp. 263–278). Baltimore: Paul H. Brookes.

Ehri, L. (1994). Development of the ability to read words: Update. In R. Ruddell, M. Ruddell, & H. Singer (Eds.), *Theoretical models and processes of reading* (pp. 323–358). Newark, DE: International Reading Association.

Ehri, L. (1998). Grapheme–phoneme knowledge is essential for learning to read words in English. In J. Metsala & L. Ehri (Eds.), *Word recognition in beginning reading* (pp. 3–40). Hillsdale, NJ: Lawrence Erlbaum Associates.

Ehri, L., Nunes, S., Willows, D., Schuster, B., Yaghoub-Zadeh, Z., & Shanahan, T. (2001). Phonemic awareness instruction helps children learn to read: Evidence from the National Reading Panel's meta-analysis. *Reading Research Quarterly, 36,* 250–287.

Elkonin, D. B. (1973). U.S.S.R. In I. Downing (Ed.), *Comparative reading* (pp. 551–580). New York: Macmillan.

Enfield, M., & Greene, V. (1994). *Story form.* Bloomington, MN: Language Circle/Project Read.

Enfield, M., & Greene, V. (1997). *Framing your thoughts.* Bloomington, MN: Language Circle/ Project Read.

Fischer, P. E. (1999). *Concept phonics.* Farmington, ME: Oxton House.

Frith, U. (1985). Beneath the surface of developmental dyslexia. In L. Patterson, J. Marshall, & M. Coltheart (Eds.), *Surface dyslexia* (pp. 301–303). London: Lawrence Erlbaum Associates.

Fuchs, D., & Fuchs, L. (2006). Introduction to Response to Intervention: What, why, and how valid is it? *Reading Research Quarterly, 41,* 93–99.

Gillingham, A., & Stillman, B. (1997). *The Gillingham manual: Remedial training for children with specific disability in reading, writing, and penmanship* (8th ed.). Cambridge, MA: Educators Publishing Service.

Hayes, J., & Flower, L. (1980). Identifying the organization of writing processes. In L. W. Gregg & E. R. Steinberg (Eds.), *Cognitive processes in writing* (pp. 3–30). Hillsdale, NJ: Lawrence Erlbaum Associates.

Henry, M. (2003). *Unlocking literacy: Effective decoding and spelling instruction.* Baltimore: Paul H. Brookes.

Hook, P., & Jones, S. (2002). The importance of automaticity and fluency for efficient reading comprehension. *Perspectives, The International Dyslexia Association, 28*(1), 9–14.

Hook, P., & Telian, N. (1996). *A maze of arbitrary symbols? Find the way through meaning/imagery.* Poster session presented at the 47th Annual Conference of the Orton Dyslexia Society, Boston.

Hulme, C. (1988). Short term memory development and learning to read. In M. Gruneberg, O. Moerris, & R. Sykes, *Practical aspects of memory: Current research and issues: Vol. 2. Clinical and educational implications* (pp. 234–271). Chichester, UK: Wiley.

Jennings, T., & Haynes, C. (2002). *From talking to writing: Strategies for scaffolding expository expression.* Prides Crossing, MA: Landmark School.

Juel, C. (1991). Beginning reading. In R. Barr, M. Kamil, P. Mosenthal, & P. Pearson (Eds.), *Handbook of reading research* (Vol. 2, pp. 759–788). Mahwah, NJ: Lawrence Erlbaum Associates.

LeVasseur, V., Macaruso, P., & Shankweiler, D. (2007, May). Promoting gains in reading fluency: A comparison of three approaches [Electronic version]. *Reading and Writing*, doi:10.1007/ s11145–007–9070–1

Lindamood, P., & Lindamood, P. (1998). *The Lindamood phoneme sequencing program for reading, spelling and speech (LiPS)*. Austin, TX: PRO-ED.

Lundberg, I., Frost, J., & Petersen, O. (1988). Effects of an extensive program for stimulating phonological awareness in preschool children. *Reading Research Quarterly, 23*, 263–284.

Lyon, G. (1995). Towards a definition of dyslexia. *Annals of Dyslexia, 45*: 3–27.

Lyon, G., Shaywitz, S., & Shaywitz, B. (2003). A definition of dyslexia. *Annals of Dyslexia, 53*: 1–14.

MacArthur, C., Graham, S., & Fitzgerald, J. (2006). *Handbook of writing research*. New York: Guilford Press.

Manis, F., & Freedman, L. (2001). The relationship of naming speed to multiple reading measures in disabled and normal readers. In M. Wolf (Ed.), *Dyslexia, fluency and the brain* (pp. 65–92). Timonium, MD: York Press.

Mather, N., Hammill, D., Allen, E., & Roberts, R. (2004). *TOSWRF: Test of Silent Word Reading Fluency: Examiner's manual*. Austin, TX: PRO-ED.

McCutchen, D. (1995). Cognitive processes in children's writing development and individual differences. *Issues in Education: Contributions from Educational Psychology, 1*(2): 123–160.

Meyer, M., & Felton, R. (1999). Repeated reading to enhance fluency: Old approaches and new directions. *Annals of Dyslexia, 49*, 283–306.

Moats, L. (2000). *Speech to print: Language essential for teachers*. Baltimore: Paul H. Brookes.

Moats, L., & Farrell, M. (2005). Multisensory structured language education. In J. Birsh (Ed.), *Multisensory teaching of basic language skills* (2nd ed., pp. 23–42). Baltimore: Paul H. Brookes.

Moreau, M. (1994). *The story-grammar marker*. Springfield, MA: MindWing Concepts.

National Institute of Child Heath and Human Development. (2000). *Report of the National Reading Panel. Teaching children to read: An evidence-based assessment of the scientific research literature on reading and its implications for reading instruction: Reports of the sub-groups* (NIH Publication No. 00–4754). Washington, DC: US Government Printing Office. Also available from http://www.nichd.nih.gov/publications/nrp/report.htm

Olson, R., Forsberg, H., Wise, B., & Rack, J. (1994). Measurement of word recognition, orthographic and phonological skills. In R. Lyon (Ed.), *Frames of reference for the assessment of learning disabilities* (pp. 269–277). Baltimore: Paul H. Brookes.

Rashotte, C. A., & Torgesen, J. K. (1985). Repeated reading and reading fluency in learning disabled children. *Reading Research Quarterly, 20*, 180–188.

Robertson, C., & Salter, W. (1997). *The Phonological Awareness Test*. East Moline, IL: LinguiSystems.

Scott, C., & Windsor, J. (2000). General language performance measures in spoken and written narrative and expository discourse in school-age children with language learning disabilities. *Journal of Speech, Language, and Hearing Research, 43*, 324–339.

Share, D., & Stanovich, K. (1995). Cognitive processes in early reading development: Accommodating individual differences into a model of acquisition. *Issues in Education: Contributions from Educational Psychology, 1*(1), 1–57.

Singer, B. D., & Bashir, A. S. (2004). EmPOWER: A strategy for teaching students with language learning disabilities how to write expository text. In E. R. Silliman & L. Wilkinson (Eds.), *Language and literacy learning* (pp. 239–272). New York: Guilford Press.

Snow, C. E., Burns, M. S., & Griffin, P. (Eds.). (1998). *Preventing reading difficulties in young children*. Washington, DC: National Academy Press.

Snowling, M. (2000). *Dyslexia*. Oxford, UK: Blackwell.

Spear-Swerling, L. (2006). Children's reading comprehension and oral reading fluency in easy text. *Reading and Writing, 19*, 199–220.

Stackhouse, J., & Wells, B. (1997). How do speech and language problems affect literacy development? In C. Hulme & M. Snowling (Eds.), *Dyslexia: Biology, cognition, and intervention* (pp. 182–211). London: Whurr.

Steere, A., Peck, C., & Kahn, L. (1988). *Solving language difficulties*. Cambridge, MA: Educators Publishing Service.

Tager-Flusberg, H., & Cooper, J. (1999). Present and future possibilities for defining a phenotype for specific language impairment. *Journal of Speech, Language, and Hearing Research, 42*, 1275–1278.

Tallal, P. (1988). Developmental language disorders. In J. F. Kavanaugh & T. J. Truss, Jr. (Eds.), *Learning disabilities: Proceedings of the national conference* (pp. 181–272). Parkton, MD: York Press.

Telian, N. (2001). *Lively letters*. Stoughton, MA: Telian-Cas Learning Concepts.

Torgesen, J. (1996). A model of memory from an information processing perspective. In R. Lyon & N. Krasnegor (Eds.), *Attention, memory, and executive function*. Baltimore: Paul H. Brookes.

Torgesen, J. (1997). The prevention and remediation of reading disabilities: Evaluating what we know from research. *Journal of Academic Language Therapy, 1*, 11–47.

Torgesen, J., Alexander, A., Wagner, R., Rashotte, C., Voeller, K., Conway, T., & Rose, E. (2001). Intensive remedial instruction for children with severe reading disabilities: Immediate and long-term outcomes from two instructional approaches. *Journal of Learning Disabilities, 34*, 33–58.

Torgesen, J., Rashotte, C., & Alexander, A. (2001). Principles of fluency instruction in reading: Relationships with established empirical outcomes. In M. Wolf (Ed.), *Dyslexia, fluency, and the brain* (pp. 333–355). Timonium, MD: York Press.

Torgesen, J., Wagner, R., & Rashotte, C. (1997). The prevention and remediation of severe reading disabilities: Keeping the end in mind. *Scientific Studies of Reading, 1*, 217–234.

Vaughn, S. (2003, December). *How many tiers are needed for response to intervention to achieve acceptable prevention outcomes?* Paper presented at the Responsiveness-to-Intervention Symposium, National Research Center on Learning Disabilities, Kansas City, MO. Retrieved August 22, 2005, from http://www.nrcld.org/symposium2003/vaughn/vaughn1.html

Vukovic, C., & Siegel, L. (2006). The double-deficit hypothesis: A comprehensive analysis of the evidence. *Journal of Learning Disabilities, 39*, 25–47.

Wagner, R., Torgesen, J., & Rashotte, C. (1999). *Comprehensive Test of Phonological Processing*. Austin, TX: PRO-ED.

Weiss-Kapp, S. (2005), *WKRP: Reading by the rules*. Arlington, MA: Dearborn Academy.

Wolf, M. (1997). A provisional integrative account of phonological and naming-speed deficits in dyslexia: Implications for diagnosis and intervention. In B. Blachman (Ed.), *Foundations of reading acquisition and dyslexia: Implications for early intervention* (pp. 67–92). Mahwah, NJ: Lawrence Erlbaum Associates.

Wolf, M., & Bowers, P. (1999). The double-deficit hypothesis for the developmental dyslexias. *Journal of Educational Psychology, 91*, 415–438.

Wood, F., Flowers, L., & Grigorenko, E. (2001). On the functional neuroanatomy of fluency or why walking is just as important to reading as talking is. In M. Wolf (Ed.), *Dyslexia, fluency, and the brain* (pp. 235–244). Timonium, MD: York Press.

20

Processing Speed, Attention, and Perception in Child Language Disorders

JENNIFER WINDSOR and KATHRYN KOHNERT

*I*n the last decade, increasing emphasis has been placed on the underlying cognitive functions that accompany or cause child language disorders. This is true for language disorders that are secondary to known genetic syndromes and other conditions, as well as for language disorders resulting from complex genetic interactions and/or occurring in the absence of frank neurological dysfunction. Child language disorders typically are part of a broader, often variable behavioral phenotype. Our focus in this chapter is on the cognitive functions associated particularly with the language abilities of children with language disorders, and not the broader phenotypes. We first review the cognitive constructs that have received substantial research attention and that appear to interact in fundamental ways in language. In the second section we discuss three cognitive constructs of key interest: processing speed, attention, and perception. The third section highlights major methodological issues that have influenced understanding of these constructs. We consider assessment and intervention implications in the final section.

COGNITIVE CONSTRUCTS IN RESEARCH ON CHILD LANGUAGE DISORDERS

As in many disciplines, understanding of cognitive function and language performance is often confounded by an abundance of concepts, terms, definitions, methods, and theories. Current ideas about child language disorders tend to be more prototypical than precise and reflect different theoretical orientations, the child language disorders of interest, and the specific anatomical or functional components of the brain thought to be involved. As examples, processing speed deficits have been studied in specific or primary language impairment (SLI), reading disability, attention-deficit disorder, and autism (Catts, Gillispie, Leonard, Kail, & Miller, 2002; Welsh, Ahn, & Placantonakis, 2005; Willcutt, Pennington, Olson, Chhabildas, & Hulslander, 2005; Windsor, Milbrath, Carney, & Rakowski, 2001). Deficits in executive function and other aspects of attention, perceptual deficits for rapid stimuli, and deficits in other aspects of auditory and visual perception have been studied in many of the same groups (Cornish et al., 2004; Luna, Doll, Hegedus, Minshew, & Sweeney, 2007; Nigg, 2005; Rosen, 2003; Szelag, Kowalska, Galkowski, & Pöppel, 2004; see chapter 9 by Edwards & Munson). The constructs of phonological and visuospatial short-term memory and working memory have been of interest in Down syndrome, Williams syndrome,

SLI, and reading disability (Chapman & Hesketh, 2000; Hoffman & Gillam, 2004; Nichols et al., 2004; Vellutino, Fletcher, Snowling, & Scanlon, 2004). Finally, phonological processing (coding or representation) has been articulated as a central neuropsychological deficit in some groups, especially children with reading disability (Vellutino et al., 2004).

The same constructs also have been applied to typical language development. Processing speed has received extensive attention in the research on healthy aging (Span, Ridderinkhof, & van der Molen, 2004). Attention in the form of executive control and interference or response inhibition has been of interest in bilingual and monolingual language development and adult language performance (Hernandez, Martinez, & Kohnert, 2000; Kenmotsu, Villalobos, Gaffrey, Courchesne, & Müller, 2005; Kohnert, Bates, & Hernandez, 1999). Processing speed and working memory have been of interest in reading in a second language; and speech perception has been investigated in first and second language acquisition for children and adults (Manis, Lindsey, & Bailey, 2004; Nenonen, Shestakova, Huotilainen, & Näätänen, 2005; Tsao, Liu, & Kuhl, 2004).

How do these or other constructs inform theory and practice in child language disorders? We propose that the three constructs of processing speed, attention, and perception have potential to move basic and applied research forward. Our emphasis on these constructs is built on two recent observations in the literature. First, there appears to be an overarching qualitative similarity among child language disorders, at least for certain disorder subtypes at certain points in development (Bates, 2004, though see Rice, Warren, & Betz, 2005). Also, different clinical subgroups often are comorbid or show overlapping performance (Bishop & Snowling, 2004; Cohen et al., 2000; Miller, Kail, Leonard, & Tomblin, 2001; Pickles et al., 2000; Rice & Warren, 2004; Tager-Flusberg, 2004). Thus, we may gain deeper insights into language disorders by examining those cognitive constructs that are relevant across the full range of variation in language performance rather than investigating constructs that are relevant to specific languages or specific clinical groups.

The second observation is that we may better understand the nature and cause(s) of child language disorders from this type of bottom-up approach of identifying disturbances in basic cognitive functions than we will from a top-down approach of examining language performance (Müllen, 2005). Language performance is a highly complex and relatively later-occurring developmental phenomenon that is influenced heavily by exposure and experience as well as by any underlying disorder. Difficulties in relying on language-based performance measures alone to inform our knowledge of language disorders have become obvious with cross-linguistic and bilingual research. For instance, although there presumably are different reasons for the groups' performances, monolingual English-speaking children with SLI have been found to make the same kinds of morphosyntactic errors and to show overlapping performance in picture naming and listening span tasks as typical children learning English as a second language (Kohnert, Windsor, & Yim, 2006; Paradis, Crago, Genesee, & Rice, 2003; Windsor & Kohnert, 2004).

PROCESSING SPEED, ATTENTION, AND PERCEPTION AS COGNITIVE CONSTRUCTS

Processing speed, attention, and perception fit well as potential bottom-up explanatory mechanisms across a breadth of child language disorders. Processing speed and attention may well be key determinants of cognitive-linguistic development and breakdown across the lifespan. These two constructs draw from distinct, usually nonoverlapping research perspectives and literatures. Although working memory also has received a great deal of attention in the literature on child language disorders (see chapter 8 by Gillam et al.), this construct appears to overlap substantially with attention and processing speed (described below). The third construct of interest, perception, is also correlated with cognitive development. However; the core, independent construct of preattentional perception has yet to be a strong focus of interest in child language disorders. Brief definitions, neurological correlates, and studies of each construct as an index of cognitive–linguistic development and disorders are outlined in the following sections. Although there is an emerging body of research on the cognitive abilities of typical and language-disordered bilingual populations, especially from attentional control or working memory perspectives (Bialystok & Martin, 2004; D'Angiulli, Siegel, & Serra, 2001; Kohnert et al., 1999; Swanson, Saez, Gerber, & Leafstedt, 2004), the historical focus of research has been on monolingual populations.

Processing Speed

Several researchers have argued that information processing speed is a central functional basis of cognition. When cognitive function in a given time is of interest, processing speed is conceived of as processing efficiency or rate (Kail & Salthouse, 1994; Salthouse, 1996). If there is a specific brain morphology or neurophysiology that underlies processing speed, it has yet to be isolated in a reliable way. However, the working assumption is that the construct of processing speed relies on neural processing speed (Jensen, 1993), including excitatory and inhibitory synaptic transmission of cortical and subcortical neuronal circuitry. Neural speed may be a function of specific cell and chemical receptor type. For example, speed of Purkinje cell synaptic transmission in the cerebellum may be tied to precision of motor coordination (Barski et al., 2003). It also has been suggested that there is an upper limit on the frequency of electrical oscillation or rhythm in the brain that constrains neural speed (Grushin & Reggia, 2005; Rypma, Berger, Genova, Rebbechi, & D'Esposito, 2005). For at least one child language disorder, it has been proposed that a breakdown in processing speed may be tied intimately to underlying neural transmission. Welsh et al. (2005) suggested that there is a neural speed asynchrony in the inferior olive of the brainstem for individuals with autism (see chapter 7 by Tropper & Schwartz). The asynchrony results in aberrant rhythmic output to the cerebellum and thus leads to a deficit in using the rapid temporal cues underlying language.

The main empirical evidence for the primacy of processing speed in cognitive development is that processing speed measures covary robustly with chronological age in samples of typical children as well as children with language disorders such as SLI and learning disabilities (Kail, 1991; Weiler, Forbes, Kirkwood, & Waber, 2003; Windsor et al., 2001). Moreover, much of the association between chronological age and individual differences in measures of other cognitive constructs, such as executive function and proactive interference in recall, phonological short-term memory span, working memory capacity, and possibly inhibition of attention appears to be mediated by or directly co-occurring with the relation between age and processing speed (Bayliss, Jarrold, Baddeley, Gunn, & Leigh, 2005; Kail, 2002).

Much of the research on processing speed has focused on the specific nature of speed constraints. Specifically, it has been argued that if there is an overall upper limit on speed of neural transmission, then processing speed is best viewed as a finite cognitive resource. Also, if different neurons are associated with different transmission speeds, there may not be a single processing speed that drives complex language behavior. There is a longstanding debate about whether variation in language performance across development is best explained by general (shared) limitations on processing speed or limitations on only certain aspects of the cognitive architecture (Kail & Miller, 2006; Span et al., 2004).

For child language disorders, this debate has been of particular interest in SLI. Kail

(1994) demonstrated that the average group reaction time (RT) of children with SLI was slower than that of typical chronological-age peers in a range of cognitive tasks. An ordinary least squares regression technique showed that the SLI group RT was slowed by a constant proportion across tasks. For tasks that took shorter or longer to complete, the average SLI RT was slowed by the same proportion relative to the average RT of the typical group. This finding suggested that, rather than the specific content or nature of individual tasks being responsible for the slower RT, there was a general underlying factor that slowed all cognitive operations to the same extent. The most likely candidate as the general cognitive factor was a limit on speed of neural transmission. The finding of proportional slowing was replicated by Windsor and Hwang (1999) and by Miller et al. (2001). However, an important caveat to these findings is that the results from all three studies may well be inflated or artificial, with ordinary least squares regression not being suitable for these types of group data.

Using the more appropriate technique of hierarchical linear modeling, Windsor et al. (2001) showed that the RT of SLI groups relative to typical groups was not slower by a constant factor. Instead, the extent of slowing varied widely across different study comparisons. This result indicates that children with SLI may be more or less vulnerable to specific linguistic, higher-level nonlinguistic, and/or perceptual-motor processing demands. For example, as suggested by Montgomery (2005), children with SLI may have particular difficulty with speed of lexical access and integration rather than with speed of acoustic-phonetic processing. Although there has been continued research in SLI (e.g., Schul, Stiles, Wulfeck, & Townsend, 2004), the exact role of general and process-specific constraints on processing speed in SLI remains an open question. It is plausible that both types of mechanisms play a role, with neither mechanism necessarily excluding the presence of the other (Windsor, 2002). What does seem clear is that the group results mask important heterogeneity within SLI samples. Although many children with SLI show a slower RT than typical peers, a substantial minority have an equivalent RT to typical peers (Miller et al., 2001; Windsor & Hwang, 1999). Substantive within-group variability in processing speed also has been documented for other groups of children with learning and attention disorders (Calhoun & Mayes, 2005). Of particular interest, an important processing speed marker in clinical groups may be greater variability in processing speed within a given task for individual children (Kalff et al., 2005; Willcutt et al., 2005).

Attention

Another cognitive construct that has been proposed as a central basis of human cognition is attention. Attention often is seen as an overarching function with three independent subset functions: alerting, orienting, and executive control (Posner & Rothbart, 2007; Rueda et al., 2004). Respectively, these refer to achieving an alert state, selecting information from the input, and resolving conflicting responses or ignoring irrelevant stimuli (Fan, McCandliss, Sommer, Raz, & Posner, 2002). Many terms are used in research on attention, such as self-regulation, vigilance, and effortful and strategic control as well as selected, focused, directed, and divided attention and scope of attention (Berger & Posner, 2000; Cowan et al., 2005; Jones, Rothbart, & Posner, 2003). Activation, inhibition, and cognitive control and flexibility of these various attentional functions have been explored in a range of typical and disordered populations across the lifespan (Kohnert, 2002; Murray, Holland, & Beeson, 1998).

As for processing speed, the specific biological correlate(s) of attention have yet to be resolved. Rather than neural speed, the magnitude of neural processing in certain parts of the brain has been of interest in research on attention. For example, the parietal cortex and other subcortical areas appear to be implicated in attention alertness and orienting. The anterior cingulate gyrus and supplemental motor area of the frontal lobe are implicated in divided attention and executive control. Activation of the lateral prefrontal cortex also has been found in executive control tasks (Kerns et al., 2004; Loose, Kaufman, Auer, & Lange, 2003; Posner, 1992).

Attention and attentional biases develop gradually in the first year of life; and development continues through childhood. Development of attention appears to be nonlinear during maturation, perhaps corresponding to spurts in brain development. For instance, children may show rapid early growth in focused attention with other periods of rapid growth in the early school years. Similarly, children's development of attention-shifting has been found to develop in phases or steps (Klimkeit, Mattingley, Sheppard, Farrow, & Bradshaw, 2004). However, measures of attention do covary with mental age for typically developing children and children with language disorders within certain age periods (Davis & Anderson, 2001). Researchers have described a maturational lag or deficit in various aspects of attention across clinical groups—for example, difficulty in disengaging attention for children with autism (Landry & Bryson, 2004). Children with Down syndrome appear to show voluntary orienting consistent with developmental level (Goldman, Flanagan, Shulman, Enns, & Burack, 2005). Children with fragile X have been found to show perseveration errors that lower their accuracy in selected attention tasks, but their RTs also seem to be the same as those of mental-age peers (Scerif, Cornish, Wilding, Driver, & Karmiloff-Smith, 2004).

The focus on attention as a key cognitive construct draws on much the same arguments raised for processing speed—that of being linked to development and covarying or predicting performance on other cognitive constructs. To the extent that attention has been incorporated in working memory models, it has traditionally been assumed to be a finite or limited-capacity resource. Although it remains controversial, the notion of a global workspace in which attention brings conscious, intentional behavior into focus reframes the idea of capacity (Barrs, 2002). Specifically, it has been claimed that there is a large amount of ongoing unconscious neuronal activity, and that unspecialized neurons are activated or otherwise brought into play through conscious attention to a specific task or goal. Conscious attention then facilitates learning across domains.

Perception

Exposure to more or less salient stimuli lies at the core of the construct of perception. It has been argued that cognition is inherently perceptual, and hypothesized that perception rests on two components (Barsalou, 1999): one an unconscious, preattentive, or baseline neural state that is sensitive to stimulus type and frequency, the other a conscious experience of, or selected attention to perceived internal or external entities or events. The first component of preattention is considered preprocessing of information that is necessary for later attentional processing. For example, automatically segmenting a visual field into possible objects/nonobjects would be a preattentional prerequisite for a visual object search task (Treisman, Vieira, & Hayes, 1992). The second component of conscious attention clearly links the constructs of perception and attention, as well as linking social context and experience with cognitive development. Perception develops very early, but extends beyond infancy in its attentional component. There is an increasing specificity in perception with development; infants move from global perception to perception of more nested or embedded relationships (Bahrick, 2001). In early infancy, multimodal or redundant input may be most salient perceptually and thus learned better than other input. Cross-modal perception develops in infancy for typically developing children but appears to be delayed for infants with developmental disabilities (Ermolaeva, 2001).

There are identified brain correlates of perception; the brain is activated by different properties of perceived events. For example, Eimer and Schröger (1998) found that perception of transient auditory and visual stimuli during spatial attention tasks evoked separate patterns of electrical activity. Fugelsang, Roser, Corballis, Gazzaniga, and Dunbar (2005) showed that the right prefrontal and parietal lobes are activated during spatial processing of contiguous visual events and that the right prefrontal and temporal lobes are activated during temporal processing of the same events. In these two examples, both hypothesized components of perception, preattention and ongoing attention, are involved.

Several studies have investigated preattentive or automatic perception using components of event-related potentials (ERPs), including the mismatch negativity component (MMN) (Friedrich, Weber, & Friederici, 2004; Stevens, Sanders, & Neville, 2006; see chapter 7 by Tropper & Schwartz). The very quick MMN response to an unmatched stimulus in a stream of like stimuli is thought to capture preattentive processing, although it remains controversial whether MMN captures *only* preattentive perception. As an example of this research, Shafer, Morr, Datta, Kurtzberg, and Schwartz (2005) found that unlike age-peers, only a small number of individual school-age children with SLI showed the MMN effect during either passive or attention-demanding exposure to brief vowels. The authors interpreted their overall negative findings as indicating that, among other factors, automaticity may play a role in poor speech perception for some children with SLI.

Most of the research on the perception of children with language disorders has focused on perception during tasks in which attention is involved. For instance, the Tallal repetition task, in which children replicate two-tone sequences, has been described as a measure of low-level auditory temporal processing (Tallal, 1980). However, this task has attentional and other cognitive-decision demands (Bishop, Carlyon, Deeks, & Bishop, 1999; Heath & Hogben, 2004). Other tasks, such as discrimination of upward and downward frequency glides (Bishop, Adams, Nation, & Rosen, 2005), may be very useful to identify whether children with language disorders have acoustic or speech perception difficulties. However, these types of tasks also do not focus on preattentional perception. Almost by definition, all behavioral measures of language involve attention.

Processing Speed, Attention, and Perception as Integrated Constructs

Overlaps among the Constructs of Working Memory, Attention, and Processing Speed Although it is very difficult to isolate reliably, the unconscious or automatic detection of the perceptual properties of stimuli is separable from perception that occurs during tasks in which conscious attention is engaged. However, the constructs of attention, processing speed, and the particular construct of working memory (i.e., short-term memory and a finite attentional component) are much more difficult to differentiate clearly. Certain types of conscious attention overlap with or have been considered to be an integral part of working memory (Cowan et al., 2005; Gruber & Goschke, 2004). This is especially apparent in examinations of child language disorders within Baddeley's (2003) model of working memory (Montgomery, 2002 provides a review of research on SLI; also see chapter 8 by Gillam et al.). This model includes a phonological memory component as well as a resource-limited central executive that functions as an overall attentional controller. Processing speed also appears to play an integrated role in working memory and has been suggested as a key determinant of both short-term memory span and working memory capacity (Ferguson & Bowey, 2005; Fry & Hale, 2000; Kail & Salthouse, 1994). Some research has called into question the notion of working memory as an independent cognitive construct. Using a developmental model focusing on activation and inhibition of limited-capacity mental attention operators, Pascual-Leone and colleagues argued that the specific construct of working memory serves no additional explanatory role (Johnson, Im-Bolter, & Pascual-Leone, 2003; Pascual-Leone, 2000). Also, MacDonald and Christiansen (2002) considered that factors such as phonological coding and processing speed interacting with experience were sufficient to explain individual variation in adult language comprehension, without utilizing the additional construct of working memory. Because of these overlaps, we have not considered working memory as a core cognitive construct that is as useful as processing speed and attention in conceptualizing child language disorders from a bottom-up perspective. Recent research by Leonard et al. (2007) and Montgomery and Windsor (2007) with children who have SLI suggests that processing speed and working memory are related but statistically separable concepts in this population. Additional research clearly is necessary to determine how best to operationally define processing speed and working memory and to clarify the unique contributions of these constructs.

Overlaps between the Constructs of Attention and Processing Speed   If working memory performance may be explained adequately by the combined effects of attention and processing speed, attention and processing speed may be different aspects of a single construct. Depending on the task measure, the constructs of processing speed and attention may be difficult to disentangle, as may the underlying variables of neural speed and magnitude. For at least some researchers, processing speed or efficiency appears to be an inherent part of attention (Cicerone, 1997). Arguably, these constructs are interrelated at the neuronal level. However, different measures have directed researchers to different conceptual constructs. Neuroimaging techniques (e.g., functional magnetic resonance imaging, fMRI) focus on the extent of activation in certain brain areas, as in the study of attention. Electrophysiological techniques (e.g., ERP) focus on brain timing, as in the study of processing speed. Gazzaley, Cooney, McEvoy, Knight, and D'Esposito (2005) suggested that both the speed and the magnitude of neural activity are modulated by top-down directed attention. Specifically, using fMRI and ERP, these authors showed that neural speed and magnitude in the visual association cortex of the occipital lobe could be enhanced or suppressed in active processing relative to a passive baseline level of the perceptual influence of a visual stimulus.

Measuring the Role of Processing Speed, Attention, and Perception in Child Language Disorders

It is not yet fully understood how slowed or asynchronous neural processing speed, attention, or perception are involved directly in the complex and experience-dependent language and associated nonlinguistic breakdowns seen in child language disorders. Given the apparent stability and predictive ability of all three constructs as indices of cognitive development, they seem to be excellent candidates to reveal the underlying nature of language development and disorders. However, there is a range of methodological issues that influence current understanding of these constructs. Although neurophysiological and neuroimaging studies of child language disorders are becoming more frequent, these techniques still are in their relative infancy. For instance, one technological problem is the difficulty in accurately applying many newer techniques to study early development (Müllen, 2005). Most of our information currently comes from well-established behavioral measures. Behavioral measures are very important in better defining the phenotypes associated with child language disorders. However, these measures are not free from interpretive difficulties.

RT is a very common behavioral measure that has been used in studies of processing speed, attention, and perception. There is consistent evidence that monolingual English-speaking children with language disorders show a slower RT than their peers. Children with SLI and children with mild developmental delay show slower RT than typical age peers across many perceptual-motor, nonlinguistic-cognitive, and language tasks (Miller et al., 2001). Good readers show faster RT than do poor readers across the same range of tasks (Catts et al., 2002). Children with SLI show slower RT than age peers with focal brain lesions in grammatical judgments; and adolescents with autism are slower than typical age peers in simple perceptual-motor and attention-orienting RT tasks (Townsend, Harris, & Courchesne, 1996; Wulfeck, Bates, Krupa-Kwiatkowski, & Saltzman, 2004). There are fewer RT data on children with autism and language disorders secondary to conditions such as Down syndrome and fragile X, perhaps because RT is more difficult to measure reliably in these populations.

Although these results may provide insight about language performance, what they convey about underlying cognitive function should be considered carefully. One problem is that inferences about cognitive constructs often are made on the basis of single RT tasks containing a relatively small or unrepresentative number of stimulus items. Performance on any single behavioral measure could reflect several underlying constructs, not just the construct of targeted interest. Moreover, when single RT measures from timed tasks are correlated, any significant correlation may suggest nothing more than that the measures share a general component related to rapid execution rather than any deeper relation (Savage & Frederickson, 2005). A second problem is that RT and other behavioral tasks vary considerably in the demands they place on motor, perceptual, and elementary and higher-level cognitive processing. RT has sometimes been considered synonymous with processing speed; these two constructs need to be disambiguated better in the study of child language disorders. Tasks that carry a minimal cognitive load (e.g., making a timed response to identify one of two pure tones, very easy visual matching, or search tasks) should reflect neural processing speed better than either purely perceptual-motor tasks or higher-level cognitive tasks. In particular, RT performance on any complex language or nonlinguistic task will be influenced by experiential variables such as native language, acquired knowledge, world experience, and so on in addition to underlying cognitive function (Birren & Fisher, 1995; Salthouse, 1993).

RT and other behavioral measures can be influenced by variation in language experience in addition to a diagnosis of a language disorder. Examples of the importance of this come from our research with typically developing monolingual English-speaking children, monolingual English-speaking children with SLI, and typically developing proficient bilingual Spanish–English speakers. As noted earlier, the proficient bilingual children tend to show overlapping RT or accuracy with monolingual children who have SLI in performing several language tasks. These include group results from conventional picture naming and word-recognition tasks as well as overall sensitivity and specificity measures from nonword-repetition and listening span tasks (Kohnert et al., 2006; Windsor & Kohnert, 2004). Finally, it is important to remember that aspects of electrophysiological and other measures also may be influenced by experience. ERP does, however, provide better temporal correspondence to underlying neurological processes than RT and provides ways to explore qualitative differences in waveforms among clinical groups (Aydelott, Kutas, & Federmeier, 2005).

ASSESSMENT AND INTERVENTION IMPLICATIONS FOR RESEARCH NEEDS

The overall weight of evidence suggests that the observable language deficits in child language disorders are part of a broader cognitive profile(s) that include deficits in processing speed and attention, and perhaps in preattentive perception. These deficits may be most visible in the area of language, but are not restricted to the language domain. Thus, it seems reasonable that assessment and intervention methods that focus directly on processing speed, attention, or perception of linguistic and, in some cases, nonlinguistic information may have a role in assessment and intervention. This perspective is consistent with interactive processing theories of first- and second-language acquisition that highlight interactions between general cognitive mechanisms and language (Kohnert, 2004a, 2007).

Assessment

Children can be vulnerable to below-average language performance relative to age peers as a result of deficits in underlying cognitive functions or due to factors related to varying experiences with spoken or written language. Many speech-language pathologists and other educators provide services to children in both situations. For example, services may be provided to enrich the vocabulary of children who are considered at risk for academic delays due to limited home literacy as well as of children with poor vocabulary skills associated with developmental deficits in attention and language. However, if the goal is to identify children who are at risk for deficits in spoken language or reading performance because of cognitive constraints, then assessment tools that deemphasize the role of experience are needed. Because experience interacts with cognitive functioning in multiple ways beginning early in development, we cannot create a truly experience-independent behavioral task. We can, however, create tasks that take into account children's current state of accumulated language and other cognitive knowledge. With an increasingly culturally and linguistically diverse population in the United States and in other countries, there is a clear need to determine the role of experience in distinguishing language disorders from differences and to provide appropriate services to all children with language disorders (Kan & Kohnert, 2005; Kohnert, 2007; Kohnert, Kennedy, Glaze, Kan, & Carney, 2003).

As noted previously, evidence suggests that even very subtle language variation, such as that shown by highly sophisticated bilingual children in one or more of their languages, can affect performance on language measures. One immediate implication of these findings is that language processing measures such as nonword repetition, which have been proposed as nonbiased assessment measures, may in fact not reduce the role of language experience adequately to be valid measures of language ability. Although performance on a nonword-repetition task may be sufficient to identify English-only speaking children as showing either typical development or SLI, likelihood ratios indicate that the task has low specificity with bilingual children (Kohnert et al., 2006). This finding reminds us that we can emphasize the role of processing over experience in assessment measures, but we may not completely separate language processing from language knowledge and experience.

There may, however, be ways to create language measures that further reduce experiential bias to assess underlying integrity of cognitive-linguistic processing. For instance, conventional word-recognition tasks may or may not separate monolingual English-speaking children with SLI from age-peers (see Kohnert et al., 2004). However, Kohnert et al. (2004) found that a word-recognition RT task that substantially reduced the role of lexical experience successfully separated a group of children with SLI from typical monolingual English age-peers. The task also successfully separated children with more severe SLI from children with less severe SLI. Using Spanish–English cognates, this task highlighted the role of phonology rather than an accumulated English vocabulary in word recognition. Specifically, monolingual English-speaking children with SLI performed as well as age-peers in identifying that the Spanish word *bebe* conveyed the same concept as the English word *baby*, presumably because there was strong cross-linguistic phonological overlap in the two words. However, the children with SLI were substantially outperformed by age-peers in identifying that the minimally phonologically overlapping Spanish word *cuna* conveyed the same concept as the English word *crib*. We have not yet assessed children with different language experiences using cognates, but this example suggests that there may be creative ways to develop specific language processing tasks to deemphasize acquired language knowledge and experience.

A more productive avenue to develop less biased assessment tools may be to exploit the broader nonlinguistic profile accompanying a range of child language disorders. Although we do not yet know which nonlinguistic tasks most heavily emphasize processing speed or attention, the extant literature indicates that both constructs are implicated in the overall profile of child language disorders. It remains an open question whether attention and processing speed are causally related to language disorders. This issue aside, experience-independent nonlinguistic tasks may provide simple and reliable screening measures to complement existing language-based measures. For example, Kohnert and Windsor (2004) showed that monolingual-English speakers with SLI were substantially slower than typical monolingual English-speaking and bilingual Spanish-English age-peers on a visual detection task implemented as a choice RT task. Windsor and Kohnert (in press) showed that accuracy on an auditory serial memory task and the Tallal repetition task also clearly separated a subset of the same group of monolingual children with SLI from typical bilingual and monolingual peers. These tasks may be useful candidates for further development. We may be able to identify children with language disorders from diverse linguistic backgrounds through their performance on elementary perceptual-motor and higher-level nonlinguistic tasks that stress processing speed or attention in systematic ways. As with any assessment tools, sensitivity and specificity measures will be important rather than a heavy reliance on group results.

Intervention

Intervention studies are critical to advance our understanding of the nature of child language disorders as well as to help individual children. Robust evidence for a direct relation between cognitive function and attained language abilities would be to demonstrate through systematic training that increases in processing speed, attention, or perception lead to improved language performance (cf. Hayiou-Thomas, Bishop, & Plunkett, 2004). Here we focus on general implications for intervention, based on existing evidence, as well as possible directions for future research.

Interventions that focus on increasing a child's efficiency in processing linguistic information are already an essential tool in the clinical kit of many speech-language pathologists. For instance, clinicians may focus a child's attention on the contrastive use of linguistic units, such as *is/are* for treatment of tense/agreement errors in English (Leonard, Camarata, Brown, & Camarata, 2004). Attention to linguistic detail under increasing processing demands also can be incorporated into the treatment hierarchy. For example, children may first be trained to attend to minimal linguistic pairs or specific morphosyntactic targets in quiet, with or without amplification from an auditory trainer. Once targeted skills are mastered under optimal conditions, processing demands might be gradually increased, either by degrading the auditory signal by increasing background noise or increasing the rate of presentation for these now familiar linguistic forms. Because this type of information processing approach may be incorporated into multifaceted intervention packages or programs, it will be important to identify the specific treatment components that are efficacious in these larger programs (Gillam, Hoffman, Marler, & Wynn-Darcy, 2002).

Speed of language processing can be facilitated through guided, thematic repetition of language targets, gradually increasing the task demands by imposing time constraints or adding extraneous stimuli. Other explicit techniques that may facilitate the speed of language use include verbal rehearsal, chunking, and prediction that could be incorporated into narrative or schema-based activities. If only certain aspects of language processing are vulnerable in child language disorders, that is, if the slowing is process-specific, then those are the aspects that would be the key intervention targets (Windsor, 2002). For some bilingual children with language disorders, explicitly training perception and attention to meaningful cross-linguistic correspondences may be an effective intervention strategy (Kohnert, 2004a).

Interventions that emphasize processing speed, attention, or perception of nonlinguistic stimuli are less common intervention strategies. However, a general cognitive approach leaves open the possibility that, in some cases, intervention to strengthen general underlying cognitive processing mechanisms may lead to gains in overall language ability. Depending on the child's specific profile of cognitive-linguistic strengths and weaknesses, activities incorporating nonlinguistic information that target perception and attention might include visual or auditory attention tasks such as search games requiring the child to find target objects, numbers, letters, or shapes among distractors of varying complexity (Kohnert & Derr, 2004). For some children, tasks that focus on perception, attention, and processing of information in all forms, including nonverbal or nonlinguistic, may be a preliminary step to more language-specific training, or such tasks may form one component of a broader intervention program. As with language-based processing interventions, the long-range goal of nonlinguistic interventions is to increase communicative competency.

Finally, a potential advantage to a general cognitive approach as one component in a broader intervention program is that it may provide a foothold from which monolingual clinicians can facilitate broad gains across both languages in bilingual clients. Kohnert (2004b) reported on a nonlinguistic intervention designed to facilitate naming and other language skills in both the first (Spanish) and second (English) languages of an adult bilingual with transcortical motor aphasia. Intervention activities included card-sorting tasks to target perception and categorization skills; written single-digit computations; visual number and letter searches to facilitate sustained and alternating attention; and several higher-level attention tasks. No direct intervention was provided for Spanish- or English-language skills. Pre- and postintervention comparisons showed improvement on four of five language measures in Spanish. In English, there were gains on all five language measures following this cognitive intervention. This type of intervention may also be applicable to school-age children with language disorders.

There are a number of challenges to be met in order to translate research findings on processing speed, attention, and perception into clinical and educational settings. For example, it remains unclear whether all processing speed tasks assess the same underlying construct. In the same vein, it is difficult to disambiguate different aspects of attention. Separating the role of perceptual-motor speed from other aspects of cognitive function also remains challenging (Feldmann, Kelly, & Diehl, 2004). Despite these significant challenges, an approach that focuses on the fundamental cognitive functions underlying child language disorders may point us in new directions in the development of assessment and intervention techniques.

ACKNOWLEDGMENT

We thank Dr. Yang Zhang at the University of Minnesota for his very helpful comments on an earlier version of the manuscript.

REFERENCES

Aydelott, J., Kutas, M., & Federmeier, K. (2005). Perceptual and attentional factors in language comprehension: A domain-general approach. In M. Tomasello & D. Slobin (Eds.), *Beyond nature-nurture: Essays in honor of Elizabeth Bates* (pp. 281–314). Mahwah, NJ: Lawrence Erlbaum Associates.

Baddeley, A. (2003). Working memory and language: An overview. *Journal of Communication Disorders, 36,* 189–208.

Bahrick, L. (2001). Increasing specificity in perceptual development: Infants' detection of nested levels of multimodal stimulation. *Journal of Experimental Child Psychology, 79,* 253–270.

Barrs, B. (2002). The conscious access hypothesis: Origins and recent evidence. *Trends in Cognitive Sciences, 6,* 47–52.

Barsalou, L. (1999). Perceptual symbol systems. *Behavioral and Brain Sciences, 22,* 577–660.

Barski, L., Hartmann, J., Rose, C., Hoebeek, F. Mori, K., Noll-Hussong, M., de Zeeuw, C., Konnerth, A., & Meyer, M. (2003). Calbindin in cerebellar purkinje cells is a critical determinant of the precision of motor control. *Journal of Neuroscience, 23,* 3469–3477.

Bates, E. (2004). Explaining and interpreting deficits in language development across clinical groups: Where do we go from here? *Brain and Language, 88,* 248–253.

Bayliss, D., Jarrold, C., Baddeley, A., Gunn, D., & Leigh, E. (2005). Mapping the developmental constraints on working memory span. *Developmental Psychology, 41,* 579–597.

Berger, A., & Posner, M. (2000). Pathologies of brain attentional networks. *Neuroscience and Biobehavioral Reviews, 24,* 3–5.

Bialystok, E., & Martin, M. (2004). Attention and inhibition in bilingual children: Evidence from the dimensional change card sort task. *Developmental Science, 7,* 325–339.

Birren, J., & Fisher, L. (1995). Aging and speed of behavior: Possible consequences for psychological functioning. *Annual Review of Psychology, 46,* 329–353.

Bishop, D., Adams, C., Nation, K., & Rosen, S. (2005). Perception of transient nonspeech stimuli is normal in specific language impairment: Evidence from glide discrimination. *Applied Psycholinguistics, 26,* 175–194.

Bishop, D., Carlyon, R., Deeks, J., & Bishop, S. (1999). Auditory temporal processing impairment: Neither necessary nor sufficient for causing language impairment in children. *Journal of Speech, Language, and Hearing Research, 42,* 1295–1310.

Bishop, D., & Snowling, M. (2004). Developmental dyslexia and specific language impairment: Same or different? *Psychological Bulletin, 130,* 858–886.

Calhoun, S., & Mayes, S. (2005). Processing speed in children with clinical disorders. *Psychology in the Schools, 42,* 333–343.

Catts, H., Gillispie, M., Leonard, L., Kail, R., & Miller, C. (2002). The role of speed of processing, rapid naming, and phonological awareness in reading achievement. *Journal of Learning Disabilities, 35,* 510–525.

Chapman, R., & Hesketh, L. (2000). Behavioral phenotype of individuals with Down syndrome. *Mental Retardation and Developmental Disabilities Research Reviews, 6,* 84–95.

Cicerone, K. (1997). Clinical sensitivity of four measures of attention to mild traumatic brain injury. *The Clinical Neuropsychologist, 11,* 266–272.

Cohen, N., Vallance, D., Barwick, M., Im, N., Menna, R., Horodezky, N., & Isaacson, L. (2000). The interface between ADHD and language impairment: An examination of language, achievement, and cognitive processing. *Journal of Child Psychology and Psychiatry, 41,* 353–362.

Cornish, K., Turk, J., Wilding, J., Sudhalter, V., Munir, F., Kooy, F., & Hagerman, R. (2004). Annotation:

Deconstructing the attention deficit in fragile X syndrome: A neuropsychological approach. *Journal of Child Psychology and Psychiatry, 45,* 1042–1053.

Cowan, N., Elliott, E., Saults, J., Morey, C., Mattox, S., Hismjatullina, A., & Conway, A. (2005). On the capacity of attention: Its estimation and its role in working memory and cognitive aptitudes. *Cognitive Psychology, 51,* 42–100.

D'Angiulli, A., Siegel, L., & Serra, E. (2001). The development of reading in English and Italian in bilingual children. *Applied Psycholinguistics, 22,* 479–507.

Davis, H., & Anderson, M. (2001). Developmental and individual differences in fluid intelligence: Evidence against the unidimensional hypothesis. *British Journal of Developmental Psychology, 19,* 181–206.

Eimer, M., & Schröger, E. (1998). ERP effects of intermodal attention and cross-modal links in spatial attention. *Psychophysiology, 35,* 313–327.

Ermolaeva, V. (2001). The role of cross-modal perception in the development of the attention process and uncovering of its deficits in the first year of life. *Human Physiology, 27,* 306–311.

Fan, J., McCandliss, B., Sommer, T., Raz, A., & Posner, M. (2002). Testing the efficiency and independence of attentional networks. *Journal of Cognitive Neuroscience, 14,* 340–347.

Feldmann, G., Kelly, R., & Diehl, V. (2004). An interpretative analysis of five commonly used processing speed measures. *Journal of Psychoeducational Assessment, 22,* 151–163.

Ferguson, A., & Bowey, J. (2005). Global processing speed as a mediator of developmental changes in children's auditory memory span. *Journal of Experimental Child Psychology, 91,* 89–112.

Friedrich, M., Weber, C., & Friederici, A. (2004). Electrophysiological evidence for delayed mismatch response in infants at-risk for specific language impairment. *Psychophysiology, 41,* 772–782.

Fry, A., & Hale, S. (2000). Relationships among processing speed, working memory, and fluid intelligence in children. *Biological Psychology, 54,* 1–34.

Fugelsang, J., Roser, M., Corballis, P., Gazzaniga, M., & Dunbar, K. (2005). Brain mechanisms underlying perceptual causality. *Cognitive Brain Research, 24,* 41–47.

Gazzaley, A., Cooney, J., McEvoy, K., Knight, R., & D'Esposito, M. (2005). Top-down enhancement and suppression of the magnitude and speed of neural activity. *Journal of Cognitive Neuroscience, 17,* 501–517.

Gillam, R., Hoffman, L., Marler, J., & Wynn-Darcy, M. (2002). Sensitivity to increased task demands: Contributions from data-driven and conceptually driven information processing deficits. *Topics in Language Disorders, 22,* 30–48.

Goldman, K., Flanagan, T., Shulman, C., Enns, J., & Burack, J. (2005). Voluntary orienting among children and adolescents with Down syndrome and MA-matched typically developing children. *American Journal on Mental Retardation, 110,* 157–163.

Gruber, O., & Goschke, T. (2004). Executive control emerging from dynamic interactions between brain systems mediating language, working memory and attentional processes. *Acta Psychologica, 115,* 105–121.

Grushin, A., & Reggia, J. (2005). Evolving processing speed asymmetries and hemispheric interactions in a neural network model. *Neurocomputing: An International Journal, 65–66,* 47–53.

Hayiou-Thomas, M., Bishop, D., & Plunkett, K. (2004). Simulating SLI: General cognitive processing stressors can produce a specific linguistic profile. *Journal of Speech, Language, and Hearing Research, 47,* 1347–1362.

Heath, S., & Hogben, J. (2004). The reliability and validity of tasks measuring perception of rapid sequences in children with dyslexia. *Journal of Child Psychology and Psychiatry, 45,* 1275–1287.

Hernandez, A., Martinez, A., & Kohnert, K. (2000). In search of the language switch: An fMRI study of picture naming in Spanish–English bilinguals. *Brain and Language, 73,* 421–431.

Hoffman, L., & Gillam, R. (2004). Verbal and spatial information processing constraints in children with specific language impairment. *Journal of Speech, Language, and Hearing Research, 47,* 114–125.

Jensen, A. (1993). Why is reaction time correlated with psychometric g? *Current Directions on Psychological Science, 2,* 53–56.

Johnson, J., Im-Bolter, N., & Pascual-Leone, J. (2003). Development of mental attention in gifted and mainstream children: The role of mental capacity, inhibition, and speed of processing. *Child Development, 74*, 1594–1614.

Jones, L., Rothbart, M., & Posner, M. (2003). Development of executive attention in preschool children. *Developmental Science, 6*, 498–504.

Kail, R. (1991). Processing time declines exponentially during childhood and adolescence. *Developmental Psychology, 27*, 259–266.

Kail, R. (1994). A method for studying the generalized slowing hypothesis in children with specific language impairment. *Journal of Speech and Hearing Research, 37*, 418–421.

Kail, R. (2002). Developmental change in proactive interference. *Child Development, 73*, 1703–1714.

Kail, R., & Miller, C. (2006). Developmental change in processing speed: Domain specificity and stability during childhood and adolescence. *Journal of Cognition and Development, 7*, 119–137.

Kail, R., & Salthouse, T. (1994). Processing speed as a mental capacity. *Acta Psychologica, 86*, 199–225.

Kalff, A., De Sonneville, L., Hurks, P., Hendricksen, J., Kroes, M., Feron, F., Steyaert, J., Van Zeben, T., Vles, J., & Jolles, J. (2005). Speed, speed variability, and accuracy of information processing in 5- to 6-year-old children at risk of ADHD. *Journal of the International Neuropsychological Society, 11*, 173–183.

Kan, P., & Kohnert, K. (2005). Preschoolers learning Hmong and English: Lexical-semantic skills in L1 and L2. *Journal of Speech, Language, and Hearing Research, 48*, 1–12.

Kenmotsu, N., Villalobos, M., Gaffrey, M., Courchesne, E., & Müller, R. (2005). Activity and functional connectivity of inferior cortex associated with response conflict. *Cognitive Brain Research, 24*, 335–342.

Kerns, J., Cohen, J., MacDonald, A., Cho, R., Stenger, V., & Carter, C. (2004). Anterior cingulated conflict monitoring and adjustments in control. *Science, 303*, 1023–1026.

Klimkeit, E., Mattingley, J., Sheppard, D., Farrow, M., & Bradshaw, J. (2004). Examining the development of attention and executive functions in children with a novel paradigm. *Child Neuropsychology, 10*, 201–211.

Kohnert, K. (2002). Picture naming in early sequential bilinguals: A 1-year follow-up. *Journal of Speech, Language, and Hearing Research, 45*, 759–771.

Kohnert, K. (2004a). Children learning a second language: Processing skills in early sequential bilinguals. In B. Goldstein (Ed.), *Bilingual language development and disorders in Spanish–English speakers* (pp. 53–76). Baltimore: Paul H. Brookes.

Kohnert, K. (2004b). Cognitive and cognate treatments for bilingual aphasia: A case study. *Brain and Language 91*, 294–302.

Kohnert, K. (2007). *Language disorders in bilingual children and adults*. San Diego, CA: Plural Publishing.

Kohnert, K., Bates, E., & Hernandez, A. E. (1999). Balancing bilinguals: Lexical-semantic production and cognitive processing in children learning Spanish and English. *Journal of Speech, Language, and Hearing Research, 42*, 1400–1413.

Kohnert, K., & Derr, A. (2004). Language intervention with bilingual children. In B. Goldstein (Ed.), *Bilingual language development and disorders in Spanish–English speakers* (pp. 315–343). Baltimore: Paul H. Brookes.

Kohnert, K., Kennedy, M., Glaze, L., Kan, P. F., & Carney, E. (2003). Breadth and depth of diversity in Minnesota: Challenges to clinical competency. *American Journal of Speech-Language Pathology, 12*, 259–272.

Kohnert, K., & Windsor, J. (2004). The search for common ground: Part II. Nonlinguistic performance by linguistically diverse learners. *Journal of Speech, Language, and Hearing Research, 47*, 891–903.

Kohnert, K., Windsor, J., & Miller, R. (2004). Crossing borders: Recognition of Spanish words by English-speaking children with and without language impairment. *Applied Psycholinguistics, 25*, 543–564.

Kohnert., K., Windsor, J., & Yim, D. (2006). Do language-based processing tasks separate children with primary language impairment from typical bilinguals? *Learning Disabilities Research and Practice, 21*, 19–29.

Landry, R., & Bryson, S. (2004). Impaired disengagement of attention in young children with autism. *Journal of Child Psychology and Psychiatry, 45*, 1115–1122.

Leonard, L., Camarata, S., Brown, B., & Camarata, M. (2004). Tense and agreement in the speech of children with specific language impairment: Patterns of generalization through intervention. *Journal of Speech, Language, and Hearing Research, 47*, 1363–1379.

Leonard, L., Ellis Weismer, S., Miller, C., Francis, D., Tomblin, J. B., & Kail, R. (2007). Speed of processing, working memory, and language impairment in children. *Journal of Speech, Language, and Hearing Research, 50*, 408–428.

Loose, R., Kaufmann, C., Auer, D., & Lange, K. (2003). Human prefrontal and sensory cortical activity during divided attention tasks. *Human Brain Mapping, 18*, 249–259.

Luna, B., Doll, S., Hegedus, S., Minshew, N., & Sweeney, J. (2007). Maturation of executive function in autism. *Biological Psychiatry, 61*, 474–481.

MacDonald, M., & Christiansen, M. (2002). Reassessing working memory: Comment on Just & Carpenter (1992) and Waters & Caplan (1996). *Psychological Review, 109*, 35–54.

Manis, F., Lindsey, K., & Bailey, C. (2004). Development of reading in grades K-2 in Spanish-speaking English-language learners. *Learning Disabilities Research and Practice, 19*, 214–224.

Miller, C., Kail, R., Leonard, L., & Tomblin, J. B. (2001). Speed of processing in children with specific language impairment. *Journal of Speech, Language, and Hearing Research, 44*, 416–433.

Montgomery, J. (2002). Understanding the language difficulties of children with specific language impairments: Does verbal working memory matter? *American Journal of Speech-Language Pathology, 11*, 77–91.

Montgomery, J. (2005). Effects of input rate and age on the real-time language processing of children with specific language impairment. *International Journal of Language and Communication Disorders, 1*, 177–188.

Montgomery, J., & Windsor, J. (2007). Examining the language performances of children with and without language impairment: Contributions of phonological short-term memory and speed of processing. *Journal of Speech, Language, and Hearing Research, 50*, 778–797.

Müllen, R. (2005). Neurocognitive studies of language impairments: The bottom-up approach. *Applied Psycholinguistics, 26*, 65–78.

Murray, L., Holland, A., & Beeson, P. (1998). Spoken language of individuals with mild fluent aphasia under focused and divided attention conditions. *Journal of Speech, Language, and Hearing Research, 41*, 213–227.

Nenonen, A., Shestakova, A., Huotilainen, M., & Näätänen, R. (2005). Speech-sound duration processing in a second language is specific to phonetic categories. *Brain and Language, 92*, 26–32.

Nichols, S., Jones, W., Roman, M., Wulfeck, B., Delis, D., Reilly, J., & Bellugi, U. (2004). Mechanisms of verbal memory impairment in four neurodevelopmental disorders. *Brain and Language, 88*, 180–189.

Nigg, J. (2005). Neuropsychologic theory and findings in attention-deficit/hyperactivity disorder: The state of the field and salient challenges for the coming decade. *Biological Psychiatry, 57*, 1424–1435.

Paradis, J., Crago, M., Genesee, F., & Rice, M. (2003). French–English bilingual children with SLI: How do they compare with their monolingual peers? *Journal of Speech, Language, and Hearing Research, 46*, 113–127.

Pascual-Leone, J. (2000). Reflections on working memory: Are the two models complementary? *Journal of Experimental Child Psychology, 77*, 138–154.

Pickles, A., Starr, E., Kazak, S., Bolton, P., Papanikolaou, K., Bailey, A., Goodman, R., & Rutter, M. (2000). Variable expression of the autism broader phenotype: Findings from extended pedigrees. *Journal of Child Psychology and Psychiatry, 41*, 491–502.

Posner, M. (1992). Attention as a cognitive and neural system. *Current Directions in Psychological Science, 1*, 11–14.

Posner, M., & Rothbart, M. (2007). Research on attention networks as a model for the integration of psychological science. *Annual Review of Psychology, 58,* 1–23.

Rice, M., & Warren, S. (Eds.). (2004). *Developmental language disorders: From phenotypes to etiologies.* Mahwah, NJ: Lawrence Erlbaum Associates.

Rice, M., Warren, S., & Betz. S. (2005). Language symptoms of developmental language disorders: An overview of autism, Down syndrome, Fragile X, specific language impairment, and Williams syndrome. *Applied Psycholinguistics, 26,* 7–27.

Rosen, S. (2003). Auditory processing in dyslexia and specific language impairment: Is there a deficit? Does it explain anything? *Journal of Phonetics, 31,* 509–527.

Rueda, M., Fan, J., McCandliss, B., Halparin, J., Druber, D., Lercari, L., & Posner, M. (2004). Development of attentional networks in childhood. *Neuropsychologia, 42,* 1029–1040.

Rypma, B., Berger, J., Genova, H., Rebbechi, D., & D'Esposito, M. (2005). Dissociating age-related changes in cognitive strategy and neural efficiency using event-related fMRI. *Cortex, 41,* 582–594.

Salthouse, T. (1993). Speed and knowledge as determinants of adult age differences in verbal tasks. *Journal of Gerontology: Psychological Sciences, 48,* P29–36.

Salthouse, T. (1996). The processing-speed theory of adult age differences in cognition. *Psychological Review, 103,* 403–428.

Savage, R., & Frederickson, N. (2005). Evidence of a highly specific relationship between rapid automatic naming of digits and text-reading speed. *Brain and Language, 93,* 152–159.

Scerif, G., Cornish, K., Wilding, J., Driver, J., & Karmiloff-Smith, A. (2004). Visual search in typically developing toddlers and toddlers with Fragile X or Williams syndrome. *Developmental Science, 7,* 116–130.

Schul, R., Stiles, J., Wulfeck, B., & Townsend, J. (2004). How "generalized" is the "slowed processing" in SLI? The case of visuospatial attentional orienting. *Neuropsychologia, 42,* 661–671.

Shafer, V., Morr, M., Datta, H., Kurtzberg, D., & Schwartz, R. (2005). Neurophysiological indexes of speech processing deficits in children with specific language impairment. *Journal of Cognitive Neuroscience, 17,* 1168–1180.

Span, M., Ridderinkhof, K., & van der Molen, M. (2004). Age-related changes in the efficiency of cognitive processing across the life span. *Acta Psychologica, 117,* 155–183.

Stevens, C., Sanders, L., & Neville, H. (2006). Neurophysiological evidence for selective auditory attention deficits in children with specific language impairment. *Brain Research, 1111,* 143–152.

Swanson, H., Saez, L., Gerber, M., & Leafstedt, J. (2004). Literacy and cognitive functioning in bilingual and nonbilingual children at or not at risk for reading disabilities. *Journal of Educational Psychology, 96,* 3–18.

Szelag, E., Kowalska, J., Galkowski, T., & Pöppel, E. (2004). Temporal processing deficits in high-functioning children with autism. *British Journal of Psychology, 95,* 269–282.

Tager-Flusberg, H. (2004). Do autism and specific language impairment represent overlapping language disorders? In M. Rice & S. Warren (Eds.), *Developmental language disorders: From phenotypes to etiologies* (pp. 31–52). Mahwah, NJ: Lawrence Erlbaum Associates.

Tallal, P. (1980). Auditory temporal perception, phonics, and reading disabilities in children. *Brain and Language, 9,* 182–198.

Townsend, J., Harris, N., & Courchesne, E. (1996). Visual attention abnormalities in autism: Delayed orienting to location. *Journal of the International Neuropsychological Society, 2,* 541–550.

Treisman, A., Vieira, A., & Hayes, A. (1992). Automaticity and preattentive processing. *The American Journal of Psychology, 105,* 341–362.

Tsao, F., Liu, H., & Kuhl, P. (2004). Speech perception in infancy predicts language development in the second year of life: A longitudinal study. *Child Development, 75,* 1067–1084.

Vellutino, F., Fletcher, J., Snowling, M., & Scanlon, D. (2004). Specific reading disability (dyslexia): What have we learned in the past four decades? *Journal of Child Psychology and Psychiatry, 45,* 2–40.

Weiler, M., Forbes, P., Kirkwood, M., & Waber, D. (2003). The developmental course of processing speed in children with and without learning disabilities. *Journal of Experimental Child Psychology, 85,* 178–194.

Welsh, J., Ahn, E., & Placantonakis, D. (2005). Is autism due to brain desynchronization? *International Journal of Developmental Neuroscience, 23,* 253–263.

Willcutt, E., Pennington, B., Olson, R., Chhabildas, N., & Hulslander, J. (2005). Neuropsychological analyses of comorbidity between reading disability and attention deficit hyperactivity disorder: In search of the common deficit. *Developmental Neuropsychology, 27,* 35–78.

Windsor, J. (2002). Contrasting general and process-specific slowing in language impairment. *Topics in Language Disorders, 22,* 49–61.

Windsor, J., & Hwang, M. (1999). Testing the generalized slowing hypothesis in specific language impairment. *Journal of Speech, Language, and Hearing Research, 42,* 1205–1218.

Windsor J., & Kohnert, K. (2004). The search for common ground: Part I. Lexical performance by linguistically diverse learners. *Journal of Speech, Language, and Hearing Research, 47,* 877–890.

Windsor, J., & Kohnert, K. (in press). Processing measures of cognitive-linguistic interactions for children with language impairment and reading disabilities. In M. Mody & E. Silliman (Eds.), *Language impairment and reading disability: Brain, behavior, and experience.* New York: Guilford Press.

Windsor, J., Milbrath, R., Carney, E., & Rakowski, S. (2001). General slowing in language impairment: Methodological considerations in testing the hypothesis. *Journal of Speech, Language, and Hearing Research, 44,* 446–461.

Wulfeck, B., Bates, E., Krupa-Kwiatkowski, M., & Saltzman, D. (2004). Grammaticality sensitivity in children with early focal brain injury and children with specific language impairment. *Brain and Language, 88,* 215–228.

Part V

Research Methods in Child Language Disorders

21

Language Production Approaches to Child Language Disorders

LIAT SEIGER-GARDNER

*L*anguage production limitations in children with language deficits are manifested in all areas of language: form (phonology, syntax, and morphology), content (semantics), and use (pragmatics). In the last two decades, the focus of research has been the underlying mechanisms involved in language production that may be inadequate or inefficient in children with expressive language impairments and may contribute to their limited expressive language abilities. In this chapter I review the off-line and on-line methodologies, techniques, and procedures used in clinical and theoretical research to investigate the various aspects of child expressive language impairments and the underlying mechanisms that are postulated to subserve the expressive language skills. This chapter addresses the use of online procedures in the investigations of child language production, their constraints as well as their potential application to research on child language impairment.

Research exploring the underlying mechanisms involved in language production in child language impairment is determined by the methodologies used in the investigations. To date, direct observations of processes involved in language production are very sparse and are limited to the application of electrophysiological and fMRI measurements. Most research methods involve indirect observational measures that inherently affect the investigation. Various aspects of these measures interact with the process being investigated, influencing their natural occurrence and making it difficult to make clear inferences about the investigated process itself.

Methods used in research to examine the expressive language abilities in children with language impairments can be one of two types: off-line methods and on-line methods. Off-line methods, such as naming tasks, sentence completion tasks, and discourse-narrative tasks, measure effects at the end-points of a process. They examine the end-products of a process and use these end products to infer about the process as it occurs. Because these methods are affected by memory and attentional demands (see chapter 8 by Gillam et al. and chapter 20 by Windsor & Kohnert), the end-products may be the result of the interaction between various factors and not merely the result of the process investigated. Whereas off-line methods probe the linguistic system more globally, on-line methods examine the linguistic system more locally, tapping into the elements of the process as they unfold over time. These methods provide more fine-grained information about the ongoing process at different points in time.

To date, most research studies on language production in child language impairment have used off-line methodologies. The use of on-line measures is very limited. In the following section I review the most common off-line tasks used in research to investigate the processes involved in language production in children with language impairment as well as the few research studies that used on-line measures in their investigations. I discuss the potentials and advantages of using on-line measures in future research on language production in children.

OFF-LINE MEASURES OF LANGUAGE PRODUCTION

Picture Naming (Confrontation Naming)

Naming is a complex process that involves the identification of an object, the activation of the object's name in the mental lexicon, and the generation of a response. It is a fundamental ability that children use very early in development to communicate (Johnson, Paivio, & Clark, 1996). They become more proficient in naming pictures and objects as they develop, evidenced by an increase in the speed of naming (Kail, 1991, 1992; Kail & Hall, 1994) and a decline in the number of errors produced while in the process of naming (Jaeger, 1992, 2005; Stemberger, 1989; Wijnen, 1992). Picture-naming is the most commonly used task in research as well as in clinic to assess the semantic, phonological, and articulatory abilities of children with language impairment; it is an integral part of every speech and language evaluation.

The naming task has been most frequently used with children with word-finding difficulties, also called naming deficits, to evaluate the nature of the underling semantic and phonological representations of lexical items. The investigations centered on finding the underlying cause of the naming deficit, whether in the representations of words or in the retrieval of the semantic or phonological features of words from the lexicon. A picture-naming task was used by Leonard, Nippold, Kail, and Hale (1983) to examine the effect of word frequency (i.e., low- versus high-frequency words) on the ability of children with language impairment to name pictures. A total of 64 pictured-objects of high and low frequency were shown to the children, and they were asked to name the pictures as quickly as possible. Children with language impairment were overall slower in naming pictures compared to their age-matched controls; however, they showed similar pattern of response to that of their age-matched peers, with high-frequency words being named more rapidly than low-frequency words. It suggested a similar lexical organization for children with and without language impairment. In a similar study (Swan & Goswami, 1997), a picture-naming task was administered to children with dyslexia to examine the effects of word length (defined by the number of syllables) and word frequency (i.e., low versus high) on their naming abilities. A total of 40 pictures, half with short and half with long names, were presented to the children. Half of the names in each length category were high-frequency words and half were low-frequency words. Children with dyslexia, overall, named fewer pictures than did their age-matched and reading age-matched controls. Their naming deficit was most evident in naming pictures with long names and low frequency. Their naming errors were frequently phonologically similar to the target words. Based on these results, the authors concluded that the picture-naming deficits in children with dyslexia are due in part to difficulties in specifying and retrieving the phonological counterparts of words.

Variations of the simple naming task, where pictured objects are presented to children and they are asked to name them, are common in research and are used to target specific information. For example, in a study by McGregor and Waxman (1998), children with word-finding difficulties were asked to name pictured objects at multiple levels of noun hierarchy (i.e., superordinate, coordinate, and subordinate). Contrast questions were used in conjunction with the pictures to elicit the targeted level of noun hierarchy; thus, for a picture of a *rose* the child was asked if it was an animal in order to elicit the superordinate level name of *plants*. The child was asked if it was a tree to elicit the coordinate level name of *flower*, and lastly the child was asked if it was a dandelion, in order to elicit the subordinate level name of *rose*. The results of this study revealed insufficient depth and breadth of the semantic lexicon in children with word-finding difficulties. Follow-up questions in conjunction with picture-naming task were used in a study examining the effects of different lexical factors (i.e., word frequency, age of acquisition, lexical neighborhood, and stress pattern) on the ability of children with language impairment to name pictures (Newman & German, 2002). Participants were asked to name verb and noun depicted pictures following questions that were aimed to elicit the targeted word, such as "what is she doing?" or "these are all. . . ." High-frequency words from low-density neighborhoods that were acquired early in life and contained the typical stress pattern of the English language were easier to retrieve. Although the effect of age-of-acquisition decreased with maturation for typically developing children, it continued to play a major role in the ability of children with word-finding difficulty to retrieve words.

Another variation to the simple naming task is the application of the tip-of-the-tongue (TOT) paradigm (Faust, Dimitrovsky, & Davidi, 1997; Faust, Dimitrovsky, & Shacht, 2003; Faust & Sharfstein-Friedman, 2003). In this paradigm, a simple confrontation-naming task is administered to participants who are asked to name the pictures as quickly as they can. If a participant fails to name a picture, the examiner inquires whether the participant felt that he knew the name of the picture but could not retrieve it at that moment (i.e., a TOT response). The examiner then asks the participant to provide information about the object (semantics) or about the name of the object (phonology). If the participant responds with a *don't know* response, the examiner goes to the next trial. This paradigm permits the assessment of the partial semantic and phonological lexical knowledge that children with word-finding difficulties have access to even in the absence of full access to target words. The application of this paradigm in the investigation of naming difficulties in children with language impairment (Faust et al., 1997) and children and adolescents with dyslexia (Faust & Sharfstein-Friedman, 2003; Faust et al., 2003) attributed the naming deficits to problems in access and retrieval of phonological information during naming. Children with language impairment and dyslexia provided less valid and more invalid phonological information about words while in the TOT state.

Another task that has been widely used and has been considered the gold standard of naming tests in clinical practice and in research is the rapid automatic naming (RAN) task (Catts, Gillispie, Leonard, Kail, & Miller, 2002; Compton, Olson, DeFries, & Pennington, 2002; Katz, Curtiss, & Tallal, 1992; Manis, Doi, & Bhadha, 2000; Manis, Seidenberg, & Doi, 1999; Misra, Katzir, Wolf, & Poldrack, 2004; Schatschneider, Carlson, Francis, Foorman, & Fletcher, 2002; Waber, Wolff, Forbes, & Weiler, 2000). The traditional RAN task requires rapid naming of a visual array of 50 stimuli, consisting of 5 high-frequency stimuli that are presented 10 times in random order in 5 rows (Denckla & Rudel, 1976). Scores on the RAN task are based on the amount of time required to correctly name all 50 stimuli. The types of stimuli that can be presented in the RAN task are letters, pictured objects, colors, and numbers. The most common ones are the RAN letters and RAN pictures. The RAN letters task was found to correlate with reading ability and, thus, to successfully predict performance on reading measures (Misra et al., 2004). The task was a strong predictor of first- and second-graders' performance on three tasks (i.e., orthographic choice, word-likeness judgment, and exception word pronunciation) in which orthographic information is key (Manis et al., 1999). The RAN pictures task, however, was a reliable predictor of reading ability only up to kindergarten years but not thereafter (Misra et al., 2004). A variation of the RAN is the rapid alternating stimulus (RAS) task. The RAS includes either two sets of letters and numbers or three sets of letters, numbers, and colors. The first includes 10 high-frequency stimuli (5 letters and 5 numbers) and the latter includes 15 high-frequency stimuli (5 letters, 5 numbers, and 5 colors) that are randomly repeated in an array of five rows for a total of 50 stimuli. Wolf (1986) found that performance on the RAS distinguished the poor readers from their typically developing peers. She suggested that early RAS performance is a great predictor of later reading abilities, particularly at the single-word-reading level.

Conversations, narrations, and discourse, unlike confrontation naming, provide contextual cues that facilitate word retrieval. Children with language impairment manifest word-finding difficulties, not only in single-word-naming tasks, but also in discourse (German & Simon, 1991), suggesting that they may not be able to utilize contextual primes to aid word retrieval during naming. A new priming variant was added to the simple confrontation-naming task in a study by McGregor and Windsor (1996). The influence of primes on word retrieval in children with word-finding difficulties was examined by asking children to name 40 pictured objects once under primed condition and once under unprimed condition (McGregor & Windsor, 1996). The primed condition included semantic primes embedded in a carrier phrase (e.g., *this man likes to go walking*) that primed simple (e.g., *cane*) or compound (e.g., *walking stick*) nouns and served as a partial lexical prime only to the compound nouns. Although the children with word-finding difficulties were able to use the primes to ease retrieval, evidenced by decreased error rate and increased use of compound nouns, they did not benefit as much from the primes as their typically developing peers. The primes did not fully compensate for the word-finding difficulties these children exhibited, as evidenced by the constant gap between the mean error rates of the two groups under the primed condition; children with language impairment produced significantly more errors than their typically developing peers.

Finally, picture-naming tasks have been used in efficacy studies as an assessment tool to measure the naming abilities of children with word-finding difficulties (McGregor, 1994; McGregor & Leonard, 1989; Wright, 1993) and children with phonological disorders (Saben & Ingram, 1991) pre- and posttreatment. The naming task was administered to children before and after treatment and in some cases also periodically during the treatment phase in order to assess treatment success. The application of the picture-naming task is not restricted to off-line methodologies, as described above. It is one of the most common tasks used in research employing on-line methodologies, which are reviewed later in the chapter.

Verbal Fluency Tasks

Verbal fluency tasks are commonly used in research in aging adults and adults with aphasia, Alzheimer's disease, schizophrenia, and other clinical populations (Bozikas, Kosmidis, & Karavatos, 2005; Diaz, Sailor, Cheung, & Kuslansky, 2004; Rogers, Ivanoiu, Patterson, & Hodges, 2006; Troyer, Moscovitch, & Winocur, 1997). The most common verbal fluency tasks are letter fluency and semantic fluency. Letter fluency requires the participant to retrieve as many words as possible beginning with certain letters (e.g., *F, A,* and *S*) under a time constraint (e.g., 60 s). This task (Sauzeon, Lestage, Raboutet, N'Kaoua, & Claverie, 2004) has been modified for younger, preliterate children as a phonological fluency task requiring the production of words beginning with certain sounds (e.g., /f/, /s/, /a/). Semantic fluency task requires the participant to retrieve as many words as possible from a specific semantic category (e.g., animals, fruits, supermarket) under a time constraint of usually 60 seconds.

Verbal fluency reveals the phonological and semantic representations of words, requiring categorical knowledge (Diaz et al., 2004; Sauzeon et al., 2004) and a degree of phonological awareness (Diaz et al., 2004; Sauzeon et al., 2004; Weckerly, Wulfeck, & Reilly, 2001). It also taps retrieval processes such as switching and clustering that aid in the retrieval of more lexical items. The switching strategy involves the retrieval of different phonological and semantic subcategories and reflects the ability to shift from one to the other; the clustering strategy involves the retrieval of lexical items within the same phonological or semantic category and reflects the category size. Adequate verbal fluency requires both intact semantic memory storage and an efficient retrieval mechanism (Troyer et al., 1997).

To date, only a small number of developmental studies have been reported (Kave, 2006; Koren, Kofman, & Berger, 2005; Matute, Rosselli, Ardila, & Morales, 2004; Riva, Nichelli, & Devoti, 2000; Sauzeon et al., 2004) and even fewer have included clinical populations such as children with attention-deficit/hyperactivity disorder (ADHD) (Hurks et al., 2004) and children with specific language impairment (Weckerly et al., 2001).

Nonword and Sentence Repetition

The nonword-repetition task has been recommended as a nonbiased, processing-dependent measure of language performance in children (Campbell, Dollaghan, Needleman, & Janosky, 1997). It is frequently used as a measure of phonological short-term memory in children with and without language impairments (Gathercole & Baddeley, 1990, 1995). The nonword-repetition task involves the perception and temporary storage of sequences of sounds, the construction of the sequences' phonological representations, and their production. The difficulties children with language impairment exhibit in repeating nonsense words and recalling lists of real words suggest imprecise phonological representations, limited phonological storage capacity, or rapid decay of phonological traces in phonological working memory (Gathercole & Baddeley, 1990; Montgomery, 1995). Dollaghan and Campbell (1998) designed a nonword-repetition task that consisted of 16 nonwords, 4 at each syllable length (i.e., one, two, three, and four syllables). All nonwords' initial and final phonemes were consonants, and they contained no consonant clusters. A total of 20 children with language impairment performed less accurately than did 20 age-matched controls, particularly for the three- and four-syllable-level nonwords. The authors concluded that this is an unbiased tool that accurately distinguishes children with and without language impairment. These findings were confirmed in a longitudinal, epidemiological investigation of specific language impairment (SLI) (Weismer, Tomblin, Zhang, Buckwalter, Chynoweth, & Jones, 2000).

Preschoolers with SLI exhibited similar deficits on the Children's Test of Nonword Repetition (CNRep; developed by Gathercole, Willis, Baddeley, & Emslie, 1994). The CNRep includes 40 target items, ranging from two to five syllables. The CNRep scores were found to be highly sensitive in discriminating between children with language impairment and children with typical language development (Gray, 2003).

The nonword-repetition task was used in another study to examine working memory capacity and its relation to language comprehension in children with SLI (Marton & Schwartz, 2003). A total of 24 nonwords (free of lexicality and phoneme predictability) were constructed such that they varied in syllable length (two, three, and four syllables). The poor performance of children with SLI on nonword repetition across tasks, especially as syllable length increased, suggests limitations in simultaneous processing rather than deficits in phonological encoding and decoding (see chapter 9 by Edwards & Munson). In contrast, nonword repetition appears to be a reliable measure of phonological working memory in children with Down syndrome (Laws, 1998); performance on the CNRep (Gathercole et al., 1994) was highly correlated in these children with language-based memory measures (i.e., auditory digit span, word span, sentence repetition, and fluency) and language measures (i.e., receptive vocabulary, language comprehension, and reading).

Sentence repetition, also referred to as sentence imitation or sentence recall, is commonly part of many clinical standardized tests, such as the Clinical Evaluation of Language Fundamentals (CELF) (Semel, Wiig, & Secord, 2003) and the Test of Language Development (TOLD) (Newcomer & Hammill, 1997). Sentence repetition tasks entail the processing and production of phonological information but also involve syntactic and semantic information. A degree of semantic knowledge is needed in order for the child to be able to process, comprehend, and repeat the sentence heard (Conti-Ramsden, Botting, & Faragher, 2001). The performance of children with language impairment may vary on nonword and sentence tasks depending on the child's deficits. Children exhibiting specific difficulties in encoding, processing, or holding phonological information in short-term memory may have more difficulty performing on the nonword-repetition task than on the sentence repetition task. The contextual information provided in sentences may serve as scaffolding for easier retrieval. However, children exhibiting morphosyntactic deficits may have no difficulties performing on the nonword-repetition task but have great difficulty repeating sentences that increase in syntactic complexity.

Sentence repetition performance was also found to be a clinical marker for children with SLI. In two different studies, Conti-Ramsden and her colleagues (2001) found sentence repetition performance to be the best indicator (very high sensitivity and specificity) of SLI compared to other linguistic tasks, such as nonword repetition and tense marking (Conti-Ramsden et al., 2001). The sentence repetition task is also thought to be sensitive in discriminating children with SLI from children with other language disorders such as autism spectrum disorders (ASD) (Botting & Conti-Ramsden, 2003), and it is sensitive in identifying Cantonese-speaking children with SLI (Stokes, Wong, Fletcher, & Leonard, 2006).

A hybrid of nonword-repetition and sentence repetition tasks was used by Marton and Schwartz (2003) to examine the effects of syntactic complexity and sentence length on working memory in children with SLI. Three types of sentences were used: simple short sentences, complex short sentences, and complex long sentences. At the end of each sentence there was a nonword (two to four syllables in length), which the children were asked to repeat after listening to the whole sentence. As hypothesized, children's performance decreased as the length of the nonwords and the sentences increased, and the complexity of the sentences increased as well. Administering the same tasks to Hungarian (a language with complex morphology and no fixed word order) children with and without SLI revealed that the memory capacity deficit common to SLI across languages was due to linguistic complexity rather than sentence length or syntactic complexity exclusively (Marton, Schwartz, Farkas, & Katsnelson, 2006).

Sentence and Story Completion Tasks

Obligatory context probes, also called cloze procedures—such as the Illinois Test of Psycholinguistic Abilities (ITPA) Morphological Closure (Hammill, Mather, & Roberts, 2001)— are the most commonly used tasks in research to assess the use of morphological markers in children with language impairment (Bedore & Leonard, 2001; Bortolini & Caselli, 1997; Grela & Leonard, 2000; Leonard, Dromi, Adam, & Zadunaisky-Ehrlich, 2000; Leonard & Eyer, 1997; Leonard et al., 2003; Marchman et al., 1999; Rice, Wexler, & Hershberger, 1998; Rice, Wexler, Marquis, & Hershberger, 2000). Obligatory contexts include tasks such as sentence completion, where the child is required to complete a sentence using a target morpheme. For example, *"Here is one bird and here are two (bird**s**)"* could be used to target the noun plural, and *"This is the girl's dress and this is the ____ (boy**'s** hat)"* could be used to target the possessive /s/ morpheme. The obligatory context can be in the form of sentence completion or in the form of a question such as *"The girl got up in the morning, looked in the mirror, and then what did she do? She comb**ed** her hair* for regular past tense" (Leonard & Eyer, 1997). All the obligatory contexts are accompanied by pictures that illustrate for the child the context of the appropriate response.

Another type of obligatory context is a story-completion task. A story completion task was used to examine the ability of children with language impairment to produce sentences of varying complexity that contained intransitive, transitive, and ditransitive verbs (Grela & Leonard, 2000). They examined the influence of argument structure complexity on the omission of auxiliary *be* verbs. The children listened to short stories that were animated by the examiner using figures and objects, each targeting a specific type of verb. Their task was to complete the story by describing the final action performed by the figures using the verb that the examiner provided. A similar task was used in another study examining the use of tense and finiteness in children with language impairment (Leonard, Dromi, et al., 2000). During the story, the children were asked to complete the examiner's sentences with the appropriate verbs, altering the tense or finiteness of the verb in the preceding sentence.

Tasks involving structural priming have been used in several studies to examine morphosyntax in children with language impairment (Bedore & Leonard, 2001; Bortolini & Caselli, 1997; Leonard, Miller, et al., 2000; Leonard et al., 2002; Rice et al., 2000). Structural priming is the tendency to use the same syntactic configuration or structure as that of a previously heard sentence (Bock & Griffin, 2000; Chang, Dell, Bock, & Griffin, 2000). For example, with a picture intended to target the auxiliary *are*, the examiner produces the sentence "the boys are washing the car" as a prime and asks "what's going on now?" The child is expected to respond with a sentence that incorporates the auxiliary *is* or *are* (Leonard et al., 2002). Structural priming appears to increase the efficiency of sentence formulation in children (Leonard, Miller, et al., 2000; Leonard et al., 2002) as well as in adults (Bock & Griffin, 2000). Children with SLI were able to use structural priming to formulate sentences with the auxiliary forms *is* and *are* that are typically omitted in their spontaneous language production (Leonard, Miller, et al., 2000; Leonard et al., 2002).

Spontaneous Language Samples and Elicited Productions

Spontaneous language sampling (see chapter 17 by Fletcher) is a commonly used tool in clinical practice to assess a child's strengths and weaknesses in all language areas: syntax and morphosyntax (e.g., calculating MLU, examining the length and complexity of utterances), phonology (e.g., phonetic inventory, syllable structure complexity, and phonological processes), semantics (e.g., vocabulary size), and pragmatics (e.g., cohesive ties, story grammar). It is also used to assess the effects of intervention programs on the language abilities of children with language impairment by comparing the language samples pre- and postintervention (Windfuhr, Faragher, & Conti-Ramsden, 2002).

Spontaneous language samples are frequently used to document the phonological profiles of young children with and without language impairment (Leonard, 1982; Paul & Jennings, 1992; Rescorla & Bernstein-Ratner, 1996; Roberts, Rescorla, Giroux, & Stevens, 1998; Schwartz, Leonard, Folger, & Wilcox, 1980; Shriberg & Kwiatkowski, 1994; Whitehurst, Smith, Fischel, Arnold, & Lonigan, 1991). Lexical diversity, measured by the number of different words, the number of total words produced, and the type–token-ratio

(TTR: ratio of number of different words to number of total words) can also be assessed in the spontaneous language samples of children (Owen & Leonard, 2002; Watkins & Kelly, 1995) as well as story grammar (Roth & Spekman, 1986). Spontaneous language samples can also serve as the basis for assessing morphosyntactic abilities (Bedore & Leonard, 1998; Beverly & Williams, 2004; Hewitt, Hammer, Yont, & Tomblin, 2005; Leonard & Eyer, 1997; Marinellie, 2004; Oetting & Horohov, 1997; Rescorla, Dahlsgaard, & Roberts, 2000; Rice & Oetting, 1993; Rice & Wexler, 1996; Rice et al., 1998). For example, spontaneous language samples were used to assess the concurrent validity and temporal stability of the MLU index in children aged 3–10, with and without SLI (Rice, Redmond, & Hoffman, 2006).

A variant of a spontaneous language sample is a conversational sample (Johnston, Miller, Curtiss, & Tallal, 1993). For example, samples consisting of answers to a series of questions about life experiences (e.g., daily routines, birthdays) were elicited from children (2;6 to 7;8) with and without SLI. This variant was adopted in this study deliberately to examine the effects of adults' questions on children's MLUs. Adults' questions increased the frequency of ellipsis and, thus, reduced MLU, particularly for children with SLI.

Elicited Narratives and Story Retelling

A widely used clinical and research technique for evaluating discourse is narrative analysis. In narratives, all language components come together to form a cohesive, well-formulated, meaningful story. Thus, the analysis of narratives provides information about grammatical skills and the ability of children to formulate sentences (Gillam & Johnston, 1992; Liles & Duffy, 1995; Paul & Smith, 1993; Scott & Windsor, 2000; Thordardottir & Weismer, 2002), to use cohesive devices relating meanings across sentences (Gillam & Johnston, 1992; Hesketh, 2004; Liles, 1985a, 1985b; Liles & Duffy, 1995; Paul & Smith, 1993; Purcell & Liles, 1992; Ripich & Griffith, 1988; van der Lely, 1997), and to organize the story content in a meaningful way (Gillam & Johnston, 1992; Liles, 1987; Liles & Duffy, 1995; Merritt & Liles, 1989; Paul & Smith, 1993; Ripich & Griffith, 1988; Scott & Windsor, 2000). In addition, similar to typical language samples, it provides information about the degree of language productivity (Liles, 1985a, 1985b; Merritt & Liles, 1987, 1989).

Procedures used to elicit narratives from children are *story generation*, in which children are instructed to compose stories from sequencing cards or wordless books, and *story retelling*, in which children listen to stories narrated by the experimenter and are asked to retell the stories back to the experimenter. Both procedures require the children to produce stories that will be composed of well-formed, well-organized, coherent sentences. However, they differ in that the story generation procedure requires children to self-conceptualize the story plot, whereas the story retelling procedure requires children to understand the plot narrated by the experimenter (Merritt & Liles, 1989).

ON-LINE MEASURES OF LANGUAGE PRODUCTION

As mentioned earlier in the chapter, off-line measures can be viewed as macrolevel measures compared to on-line measures that allow for a microlevel examination of a linguistic process. This difference was illustrated by Shapiro, Swinney, and Borsky (1998), describing the challenges a clinician might face in developing an intervention program for a client with word-finding difficulties. Multiple factors may affect or cause word-finding difficulties. Knowing which factor underlies the deficit can facilitate the delivery of the right treatment. For example, a breakdown at the semantic level of processing versus a breakdown at the phonological level of processing might merit a different treatment approach, focusing on different areas of language. An online task that examines the timing and nature of different processing levels (i.e., phonology or semantics) of lexical access during naming may be more advantageous for developing a focused remedial program.

Picture–Word Interference Paradigm

One of the most common online tasks used in research on language production is the Picture–Word Interference (PWI) paradigm. This paradigm has been widely used to evaluate lexical access during language production in adults (Alario, Segui, & Ferrand, 2000; Cutting & Ferreira, 1999; Jescheniak & Schriefers, 1998; La Heij, Dirkx, & Kramer, 1990; Levelt et al., 1991; Peterson & Savoy, 1998; Schriefers, Meyer, & Levelt, 1990). This paradigm provides information about the timing at which specific lexical information (i.e., semantic, phonological, or morphosyntactic) becomes available during word production. This technique has only recently been applied to children with language impairment (Seiger, 2005; Seiger-Gardner & Brooks, in press; Seiger-Gardner & Schwartz, in press) and to children with hearing impairments (Jerger, Lai, & Marchman, 2002a, 2002b).

In this paradigm, participants are presented with pictures of common objects and are instructed to name them as quickly as they can. Interfering stimuli (words or pictures) are presented either auditorily or visually at different points in time relative to the presentation of the pictures, also called stimulus onset asynchrony (SOA); thus, the interfering stimuli can precede the onset of the pictures, appear simultaneously with the pictures, or follow the onset of the pictures (see Figure 21.1). Participants are instructed to ignore the interfering stimuli and to concentrate on naming the pictures. Depending on the focus of the investigation, the interfering stimuli vary in their relationship to the target pictures. For example, the interfering stimuli may be auditorily presented words related in meaning or in phonological form to the target pictures. To measure the effects of the interfering stimuli on the naming process, response latencies under the related interfering stimulus conditions (i.e., semantic and phonological) are compared to the response latencies under the unrelated condition. In adults (Schriefers et al., 1990) and typically developing children (Brooks & McWhinney, 2000; Jerger, Martin, & Damian, 2002; Seiger, 2005; Seiger-Gardner & Schwartz, 2008), semantically related information, such as words that belong to

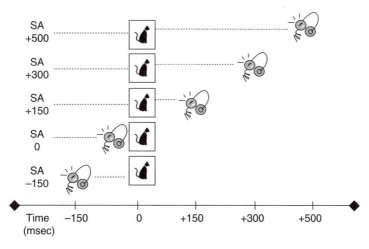

FIGURE 21.1 Schematic of the cross-modal PWI paradigm in the study (Seiger, 2005; Seiger-Gardner & Schwartz, 2008).

the same superordinate category (i.e., coordinates, *plane–bike*), presented early in the word-production process, delay the availability of semantic information of the target word, therefore inhibiting word production. The semantically related words serve as competitors to the target items, hindering their quick retrieval. Phonologically related information, such as words that share onset consonant(s) (e.g., *cat–car*), presented later in the process of word production, speed up the availability of phonological information of the target word, facilitating word production. The phonological features shared by the targets and the distractor-words become activated as soon as the words are presented, contributing to a faster retrieval of the target items (Jescheniak & Schriefers, 1998; Schriefers et al., 1990; Seiger-Gardner & Brooks, in press). These effects suggest that semantic information becomes available for retrieval during word production prior to the availability of phonological information. They are the core assumptions of most of the current models of lexical access that view lexical access as a two-stage process (Dell & O'Seaghdha, 1992; Levelt, 1992).

Theories of lexical access differ in their assumptions regarding the temporal interplay between the two levels of processing: cascading of activation versus discrete nonoverlapping stages and forward versus backward activation. The discrete two-stage model assumes a modular system with two serially ordered, nonoverlapping, independent stages that operate on different inputs (Levelt et al., 1991; Schriefers et al., 1990). Thus, only semantic information is processed during semantic processing and only phonological information is processed during phonological encoding. In contrast, the interactive models, the spreading activation model (Dell, 1986) and the cascaded processing model (Cutting & Ferreira, 1999; Jescheniak, & Schriefers, 1998; Peterson & Savoy, 1998), view the system of lexical access in a more continuous way. They view the production system as "globally modular but locally interactive" (Dell & O'Seaghdha, 1991, p. 604); activation is predominantly semantic during semantic processing and predominantly phonological during phonological encoding. However, some activation of phonological properties takes place during semantic processing and some activation of semantic properties takes place during phonological encoding; activation cascades between the two levels.

Recent studies in adults using the PWI paradigm indicated early activation of the phonological properties of words while semantic information had been processed (Cutting & Ferreira, 1999; Griffin & Bock, 1998; Jescheniak & Schriefers, 1997, 1998; Peterson & Savoy, 1998). Distractors that were phonologically related (e.g., *soda* and *count*) to target pictures and their synonyms (e.g., *sofa* and *couch*, respectively), revealed phonological facilitation effects for both distractors (e.g., *soda* and *count*) early on in the process of lexical access (Jescheniak & Schriefers, 1997, 1998; Peterson & Savoy, 1998). Thus, the phonological forms of both target items (e.g., *sofa* and *couch*) were activated early on in the process, while the semantic properties of the lexical items were being specified. Similar results were revealed for children (Jescheniak, Hahne, Hoffman, & Wagner, 2006). The two interactive models diverge in their assumptions regarding the flow of activation. The spreading activation model assumes bidirectional flow of activation; activation can flow forward, from the semantic level to the phonological level, and backward (Dell, 1988). In contrast, the cascaded processing model assumes unidirectional activation; thus, activation can flow only forward.

The PWI paradigm has only recently been applied to typically developing children, examining the development progression of lexicalization (Brooks & MacWhinney, 2000; Jerger et al., 2002; Jescheniak et al., 2006; Seiger, 2005; Seiger, Brooks, Sailor, & Bruening, 2005; Seiger-Gardner & Brooks, in press; Seiger-Gardner & Schwartz, in press). Jerger and her colleagues (2002) investigated the stages of picture naming in children 5–7 years of age and in teenagers. Semantic and phonologically related auditory distractors were used at three SOAs (i.e., −150, 0, and +150) to infer the time course of lexical access in children. The results from the children supported a nondiscrete time course of lexical access, revealing early activation of both phonological and semantic information. Information processing in children appeared to be more interactive than in adults, revealing periods of time where semantic and phonological information was processed simultaneously (Jerger et al., 2002). Hanauer and Brooks (2005) found cross-modal semantic inhibition effect in children ages 3–7 when semantically related interfering words were paired with pictures that were presented 500 ms after the offset of the interfering word. This early semantic inhibition effect was attributed to the children's inefficient suppression mechanism.

Phonological processing during language production has been further examined in children aged 4;11–11;9 (Brooks & MacWhinney, 2000). All children named pictures faster in the presence of phonological distractor words that shared the onset consonant(s) with the target pictures. When the phonologically related distractors rhymed with the target pictures, only the youngest group revealed faster response times. It suggested that the lexicon of children undergo a developmental shift from a rhyme-based structure to an onset-based structure, as in adults. The same methodology was used in another study examining phonological processing in children with SLI (Seiger-Gardner & Brooks, in press). In the SLI group, onset-related distractors led to slower RTs compared with unrelated distractors (i.e., inhibition) when presented before the picture, and faster RTs (i.e., facilitation) when presented after the picture. No effects (inhibition or facilitation) were observed in the rhyme-related condition. The authors concluded that the priming effects from onset-related distractors and the lack of effects from rhyme-related distractors in SLI support *just in time* incremental processing, similar to that observed in children with typical language development. However, the early observed phonological inhibition effect in the SLI group suggests that children with SLI experience phonological interference from members of a lexical cohort while accessing words.

Semantic-phonological mediated priming was used by Jescheniak and his colleagues (2006) to examine the cascade of activation during lexical access in children. Semantic–phonological-mediated priming refers to the priming effects revealed in the presence of distractors that are phonologically related to a semantic category coordinate of the target picture. Its presence suggests the activation of the phonological properties of lexical competitors. Distractors in this study were either phonologically related (*cap*) to the target pictures (*cat*) or were phonologically related in a mediated fashion (*doll*) to semantic coordinates (*dog*) of the target pictures. Phonological facilitation effects were found in the late stimulus asynchronies from the phonologically related distractors (*cap–cat*), but an interference effect was found from the mediated semantic–phonologically related distractors (*doll–cat*).

The PWI paradigm was used for the first time with children with language impairment in a study investigating the locus of breakdown in the lexical system of children with language impairment that cause word-finding difficulties (Seiger, 2005; Seiger-Gardner & Schwartz, in press). Word-finding difficulties are the most frequently observed lexical limitation in school-aged children with language impairment (Faust, Dimitrovsky, & Davidi, 1997; German 1979, 1984, 1987; Leonard et al., 1983; McGregor & Leonard, 1989; Nippold, 1992; Wiig & Becker-Caplan, 1984). Semantic or phonological deficits have been postulated to underlie word-finding difficulties. Despite a focus on finding the locus of breakdown in the lexical system of these children, most studies have used offline techniques (e.g., analysis of naming errors), and even the addition of reaction time measures did not provide information about the subprocesses involved in the process of word-finding. The PWI paradigm in Seiger (2005; Seiger-Gardner & Schwartz, in press) permitted an examination of the mechanisms underlying word-finding difficulties in children with language impairments. In this study, school-aged children ages 8;0–10;0 with and without SLI were asked to name black-and-white line drawings quickly and accurately while ignoring auditorily presented distractor-words. The distractor-words were either semantically (coordinates: *lion–pig*) or phonologically (share the onset consonant/s: *lion–lips*) related to the target pictures, or were unrelated in either form or meaning to the target pictures (*lion–boat*). The presentation of the distractor-words was manipulated in time relative to the presentation of the pictures such that they appeared 150 ms before the pictures, with the pictures or 150, 300, or 500 ms after the pictures (see Figure 21.1). Children with SLI exhibited lingering semantic interference effects, as indicated by longer response latencies in the presence of semantically related distractor words compared with unrelated distractor words. These effects were not seen in their typically developing peers. Phonological priming effects (i.e., shorter response latencies in the presence of phonologically related words) were apparent in children with SLI, suggesting that phonologically related words were used as primes to facilitate lexical access during word production, similar to typically developing children and normal adults. The use of the PWI paradigm provided a temporal picture of lexical access in children with SLI, tracking moment-by-moment the processes involved in lexicalization. It enabled the researchers to ascribe the locus of lexical breakdown that causes word-finding difficulties to the lexical-semantic level.

Two other studies that utilized the cross-modal paradigm investigated the lexical abilities of children with and without hearing loss (Jerger et al., 2002a, 2002b). In the first study, semantically related (e.g., *hot dog–pizza*) and unrelated (e.g., *dress–pizza*) auditory distractors were presented at different points in time relative to the presentation of the pictures. Interference effects in the presence of semantically related distractors were observed in both groups of participants, suggesting similar lexical semantic representations in children with and without hearing loss. A delay in the time course of semantic interference effect in some children with hearing loss suggested different semantic processing, attributable to the early childhood hearing loss. In the second study, phonologically related and unrelated nonsense-syllable distractors were compared to the unrelated condition (i.e., vowel nucleus verbal baseline). The nonsense-syllable distractors were of two types: matching in place of articulation and voicing to the target picture (e.g., /ti/–*teeth*) or incongruent, conflicting in voicing and place (e.g., /bi/–*teeth*) or in voicing (e.g., /di/–*teeth*) or place (e.g., /pi/–*teeth*) with the target picture. For children with and without hearing loss, naming latencies in the presence of the congruent distractors were shorter relative to the unrelated condition, but longer in the presence of the incongruent distractors. As a group, the children with hearing loss seemed to have similar fine-grained phonological representations to those of children with normal hearing. However, when phoneme discrimination skills were assessed, the children with hearing loss and poor auditory perceptual skills exhibited no effects in the presence of the incongruent distractors compared to their typically developing peers. Thus, the authors concluded that children with hearing loss and poor auditory perceptual skills may have more holistic and less specified phonological representations compared to their typically developing peers and children with hearing loss with good auditory perceptual skills. This online task permitted a direct examination of auditory perceptual abilities while processing phonological information for production.

As mentioned earlier, the use of online tasks in the investigation of language production in children with language impairment is very limited. The PWI task is potentially a powerful tool that can be used in research to investigate the different levels of language processing involved in production operations. It has some significant advantages: it allows for a temporal ongoing investigation of a linguistic process on a moment-by-moment basis; it is sensitive to automatic processing, where the participant is not consciously involved in the analysis of the distractors; and it is finely tuned to processes that involve the integration of inputs from different sources and the interaction between the different levels of processing involved in an operation. Furthermore, because the picture to be named and the distractor are separable stimuli, the PWI paradigm allows the experimenter to vary systematically the timing of the distractor stimulus relative to the time of presentation of the picture in order to identify the timing of specific information availability or its time course. This method has significant implications for clinical practice. It has the potential to provide specific information about the mechanisms underlying the deficits observed in these children. Focused remedial programs can then be developed to address the specific deficits. Furthermore, the PWI paradigm has the potential of becoming an integral part of the battery of language tests used to assess on-line language abilities of children with language impairments.

Electrophysiological Measures

Many of the linguistic processes involved in language production are temporally short-lived and, thus, difficult to examine given the current methods. Event-related potentials (ERPs) are ideal for the examination of these temporally transient processes because of their millisecond-to-millisecond temporal resolution. This method allows an ongoing recording of information throughout the entire time course of the linguistic processes being investigated. Research employing electrophysiological techniques (see chapter 24 by Shafer & Maxfield) use scalp-recorded brain potentials to record the temporal course of information processing.

Electrophysiological studies in adults have provided more specific information about the time course of lexical access during word production, particularly about the relative timing of semantic processing and phonological encoding during word production (Schmitt, Münte, & Kutas, 2000; van Turennout, Hagoort, & Brown, 1997, 1998). The go/no-go paradigm was used to distinguish the influence of semantic information from that of phonological information on response preparation. Participants were asked to classify a picture along semantic (animate/inanimate) and phonological (word-final or initial phoneme) dimensions. Depending on the outcome of the semantic and phonological classifications, a left-hand response, a right-hand response, or no response was given.

Two ERP components were used in the investigations—the Lateralized Readiness Potential (LRP) and N200. N200 is elicited when a potential response is withheld or inhibited. In a go/no-go paradigm, the N200 is elicited when the participant does not give a response. The presence of the N200 implies that the information, which determines whether or not a response should be provided, must have been processed. Thus, the N200 provides an estimate of the timing at which specific information has been encoded. In the case where the semantic classification determines the response side and the phonological classification determines the go/no-go decision, the N200 provides information about the availability of phonological information; when the semantic and phonological decisions are reversed, such that the phonological decision determines the response side and the semantic decision determines the go/no-go execution, the N200 provides information about the availability of semantic information. A comparison between the onset and peak latencies of the N200 under the two conditions provides information about the type of information (semantic or phonological) that becomes available first.

The LRP is a slow negative-going potential that starts to develop prior to the execution of a voluntary movement and reaches its maximum just after the movement onset. The LRP permits the investigation of motor-related brain activities before an overt response is executed. More importantly, it reveals motor activation, or response preparation, even in the absence of an overt response (Schmitt et al., 2000). It is important to note that the LRP does not indicate when information is available but, rather, when it is used to prepare or influences a response (van Turennout, Hagoort, & Brown, 1997). In the case where the semantic classification determines the response side and the phonological classification determines the go/no-go decision, an LRP effect is expected to initially develop on both go and no-go trials at about the same latency. After some time, response preparation on no-go trials is expected to decrease because of the completion of the phonological decision, and the LRP is expected to return to the baseline. In the case where the semantic and phono-logical classifications are reversed such that semantic information determines the go/no-go and the phonological classification determines the response side, it is expected that the go/no-go decision can be made before information about the response hand becomes available. Therefore, the presence of an LRP is expected only for go trials. These outcomes are obviously expected only under the assumption that semantic information becomes available before phonological information. This assumption was confirmed by the avail-ability of semantic information approximately 90 ms prior to phonological information for word production in the measurements of both ERP components (N200 and the LRP) (Schmitt et al., 2000; van Turennout et al., 1997).

One of the challenges in using electrophysiological measures in the investigation of language production operations is the presence of the muscle or movement artifacts during the electroencephalogram (EEG) recordings. The muscle artifact occurs due to jaw move-ment during speech, which can mask the smaller amplitude waveforms that reflect specific linguistic processes. Thus, in studies on language production that apply electrophysiological measures, the participants are asked to produce the verbal response after a poststimulus delay to avoid the muscle artifact (Greenham & Stelmack, 2001; Greenham, Stelmack, & van der Vlugt, 2003; Jescheniak et al., 2002). The measurement of production before the actual production occurs raises some concerns regarding the extent to which the ERPs reflect production operations per se and not some planning processes. In an ERP study investigating the time course of lexical access during word production in adults (van Turennnout et al., 1997), subjects named pictures aloud only on filler trials that were embedded within the experiment. On the target trials they named the pictures aloud only after a button press response (i.e., after a delay following the offset of the picture stimulus). The authors argued that because the participants were instructed to name the pictures aloud on all trials, regardless of whether or not it was after a button-press response, their subjects were in the mode of language production, and the ERPs reflected production operations rather than planning processes.

A similar approach was employed in a study that adapted the behavioral PWI paradigm to examine the activation of semantic and phonological information during speech produc-tion using ERPs (Jescheniak et al., 2002). While participants prepared the production of a depicted object's name, they heard an auditory distractor word that was either related in form or in meaning to the target, or unrelated. In order to avoid the movement artifact, Participants were asked to overtly name the pictures only after receiving a visual cue. The effects of semantic and phonological distractors compared to unrelated distractors on the N400 component were examined. As expected, the N400 was attenuated when the target words were paired with the related primes (phonological and semantic) compared to when paired with the unrelated primes.

The use of ERPs to examine language production in children with and without lan-guage impairments has been quite limited. In a study examining the role of attention in naming of pictures and printed words by children and adults (Greenham & Stelmack, 2001), the morphology of the ERP waveforms that children develop while selectively attending to and naming words or pictures was described. A negative waveform that develops at about 450 ms (N450) over anterior scalp regions seemed to be sensitive to variations in semantic processing. An earlier negative waveform at about 280 ms (N280) that develops over anterior sites, when the task involves superimposed arrays of pictures and words, appeared to index an early stage of attention processing.

In a study of developmental learning disabilities (Greenham et al., 2003), children with reading and spelling difficulties were expected to exhibit a normal N450 when naming pictures, but a reduced N450 when naming words. Children were tested under three conditions: attend-word condition, attend-picture condition, and a control condition. In the attend-word condition, they were presented with picture–word pairs and were instructed to attend to and to name the words and ignore the pictures and, in the attend-picture condition, they were instructed to attend to and name the pictures and ignore the words. In the control condition, children were presented with the individual words and pictures and were instructed to name them. The 180 word–picture pairs consisted of 60 congruent stimuli (a picture of a doll and the word DOLL), 60 semantically associated stimuli (a picture of a nest and the word BIRD), and 60 incongruent stimuli (a picture of a dog and the word POTATO). As expected, children with reading and spelling difficulties exhibited a smaller N450 than did their typically developing peers under the control condition when naming individually presented words, but not when naming individually presented pictures. It suggests that children with learning disabilities exhibit specific difficulties in processing linguistic information. Although there were no differences in the amplitude of the N450 for pictures, these children exhibited behavioral word-finding deficits. The authors concluded that the word-finding deficit might influence and be reflected in a later stage of processing, during the generation or production of the naming response, rather than at the stage reflected by the N450. There was a similar response pattern for the attending conditions, with a reduced N450 for words and not for pictures, suggesting that the word-finding difficulties in these children are due to a linguistic rather than an attentional deficit.

More recently, language production research in adults extended the investigation beyond processing during production operations, moving toward localization of these operations using functional magnetic resonance imaging (fMRI). Neuroimaging studies can provide information about the neuroanatomical organization of the lexical system that may refine the theoretical models of language production (de Zubicaray, Wilson, McMahon, & Muthiah, 2001). For example, Kemeny and colleagues (2006) introduced a latency component into a conventional naming paradigm, delaying the production response, in order to dissociate the processes involved in lexical selection and articulation. There was activation in the left hemisphere perisylvian areas during early lexical access and activation of the motor and auditory areas during overt articulation.

Another fMRI study examined the neural responses of adults associated with the semantic interference (SI) effect in a PWI task (de Zubicaray et al., 2001). Overt vocalization of picture names occurred in the absence of scanner noise, allowing reaction time data to be collected. Activation of both the left midsection of the middle temporal gyrus (MTG) and the left posterior superior temporal gyrus (STG) suggested that the SI effect occurs both in the conceptual and phonological levels of lexical access. This result supports the interactive models of lexical access that postulate bidirectional flow of activation between the different levels of processing. In a similar investigation, the neural correlates of grammatical gender selection in German were investigated during overt picture naming using fMRI techniques (Heim, Opitz, & Friederici, 2002). Subjects named black-and-white line drawings of real objects. Compared to simply naming a picture, the production of the definite determiner of the picture name, which required the participant to access the gender marker for that name, resulted in marked activation of a single region in the superior portion of Broca's area.

Magnetoencephalography (MEG) has also been used to examine lexical production. In this case a simple naming task was used to examine the dissociation between noun and verb representations (Soros, Cornelissen, Laine, & Salmelin, 2003). The naming performance of 10 healthy adults was compared with that of an anomic patient who exhibited superior verb naming (compared to nouns). The task involved the presentation of a prompt word that indicated to the subject whether to name the action or the object in a line drawing. Marked differences between action and object naming were apparent in the left hemisphere of the anomic patient but not in that of the healthy adults. The recovery process from a disruption in the normal language network (i.e., aphasia) may lead to a reorganization of brain functions, and, thus, to dissociation between the neural correlates associated with verb and noun production.

CONCLUSION

The use of on-line behavioral techniques (e.g., picture–word interference paradigm), electrophysiological measures, and imaging techniques (fMRI and MEG) to investigate language production in children is still in its infancy. These measures provide fine-grained, in-depth information about the processes involved in language production operations. This information will lead to a better understanding of atypical language processing and the development of advanced remedial programs that will better serve children with language impairments.

REFERENCES

Alario, F. X., Segui, J., & Ferrand, L. (2000). Semantic and associative priming in picture naming. *Quarterly Journal of Experimental Psychology, 53*, 741–764.

Bedore, L. M., & Leonard, L. B. (1998). Specific language impairment and grammatical morphology: A discriminant function analysis. *Journal of Speech, Language, and Hearing Research, 41*, 1185–1192.

Bedore, L. M., & Leonard, L. B. (2001). Grammatical morphology deficits in Spanish-speaking children with specific language impairment. *Journal of Speech, Language, and Hearing Research, 44*, 905–924.

Beverly, B. L., & Williams, C. C. (2004). Present tense *be* use in young children with specific language impairment: Less is more. *Journal of Speech, Language, and Hearing Research, 47*, 944–956.

Bock, K., & Griffin, Z. M. (2000). The persistence of structural priming: Transient activation or implicit learning? *Journal of Experimental Psychology: General, 129*, 177–192.

Bortolini, U., & Caselli, M. C. (1997). Grammatical deficits in Italian-speaking children with specific language impairment. *Journal of Speech, Language, and Hearing Research, 40*, 809–821.

Botting, N., & Conti-Ramsden, G. (2003). Autism, primary pragmatic difficulties, and specific language impairment: Can we distinguish them using psycholinguistic markers? *Developmental Medicine and Child Neurology, 45*, 515–524.

Bozikas, V. P., Kosmidis, M. H., & Karavatos, A. (2005). Disproportionate impairment in semantic verbal fluency in schizophrenia: Differential deficit in clustering. *Schizophrenia Research, 74*, 51–59.

Brooks, J. P., & MacWhinney, B. (2000). Phonological priming in children's picture naming. *Journal of Child Language, 27*, 335–366.

Campbell, T. F., Dollaghan, C., Needleman, H., & Janosky, J. (1997). Reducing bias in language assessment: Processing-dependant measures. *Journal of Speech, Language, and Hearing Research, 40*, 519–525.

Catts, H. W., Gillispie, M., Leonard, L. B., Kail, R. V., & Miller, C. A. (2002). The role of speed of processing, rapid naming, and phonological awareness in reading achievement. *Journal of Learning Disabilities, 35*, 509–524.

Chang, F., Dell, G. S., Bock, K., & Griffin, Z. M. (2000). Structural priming as implicit learning: A comparison of models of sentence production. *Journal of Psycholinguistic Research, 29*, 217–229.

Compton, D. L., Olson, R. K., DeFries, J. C., & Pennington, B. F. (2002). Comparing the relationships among two different versions of alphanumeric rapid automatized naming and word level reading skills. *Scientific Studies of Reading, 6*, 343–368.

Conti-Ramsden, G., Botting, N., & Faragher, B. (2001). Psycholinguistic markers for specific language impairment (SLI). *Journal of Child Psychology and Psychiatry, 42*, 741–748.

Cutting, J. C., & Ferreira, V. S. (1999). Semantic and phonological information flow in the production lexicon. *Journal of Experimental Psychology: Learning, Memory, and Cognition, 25*(2), 318–344.

Dell, G. S. (1986). A spreading activation theory of retrieval in sentence production. *Psychological Review, 93*, 283–321.

Dell, G. S. (1988). The retrieval of phonological forms in production: Tests of predictions from a connectionist model. *Journal of Memory and Language, 27*, 124–142.

Dell, G. S., & O'Seaghdha, G. P. (1991). Mediated and convergent lexical priming in language production: A comment on Levelt et al. (1991). *Psychological Review, 98*, 604–614.

Dell, G. S., & O'Seaghdha, G. P. (1992). Stages of lexical access in language production. *Cognition, 42*, 287–314.

Denckla, M., & Rudel, R. G. (1976). Rapid "automatized" naming (R.A.N): Dyslexia differentiated from other learning disabilities. *Neuropsychologia, 14*, 471–479.

de Zubicaray, G. I., Wilson, S. J., McMahon, K. L., & Muthiah, S. (2001). The semantic interference effect in the picture-word paradigm: An event-related fMRI study employing overt responses. *Human Brain Mapping, 14*, 218–227.

Diaz, M., Sailor, K., Cheung, D., & Kuslansky, G. (2004). Category size effects in semantic and letter fluency in Alzheimer's patients. *Brain and Language, 89*, 108–114.

Dollaghan. C., & Campbell, T. F. (1998). Nonword repetition and child language impairment. *Journal of Speech, Language, and Hearing Research, 41*, 1136–1146.

Faust, M., Dimitrovsky, L., & Davidi, S. (1997). Naming difficulties in language-disabled children: Preliminary findings with the application of the Tip-of-the-Tongue paradigm. *Journal of Speech, Language, and Hearing Research, 40*, 1026–1036.

Faust, M., Dimitrovsky, L., & Shacht, T. (2003). Naming difficulties in children with dyslexia: Application of the tip-of-the-tongue paradigm. *Journal of Learning Disabilities, 36*, 203–215.

Faust, M., & Sharfstein-Friedman, S. (2003). Naming difficulties in adolescents with dyslexia: Application of the tip-of-the-tongue paradigm. *Brain and Cognition, 53*, 211–217.

Gathercole, S., & Baddeley, A. (1990). Phonological memory deficits in language disordered children: Is there a causal connection? *Journal of Memory and Language, 29*, 336–360.

Gathercole, S. E., & Baddeley, A. D. (1995). Short-term memory may yet be deficient in children with language impairments: A comment on van der Lely & Howard (1993). *Journal of Speech, Language, and Hearing Sciences, 38*, 463–472.

Gathercole, S. E., Willis, C. S., Baddeley, A. D., & Emslie, H. (1994). The children's test of nonword repetition: A test of phonological working memory. *Memory, 2*, 103–127.

German, J. D. (1979). Word-finding skills in children with learning disabilities. *Journal of Learning Disabilities, 12*, 43–48.

German, J. D. (1984). Diagnosis of word-finding disorders in children with learning disabilities. *Journal of Learning Disabilities, 17*, 353–359.

German, J. D. (1987). Spontaneous language profiles of children with word-finding problems. *Language, Speech, and Hearing Services in Schools, 8*, 217–230.

German, J. D., & Simon, E. (1991). Analysis of children's word-finding skills in discourse. *Journal of Speech and Hearing Research, 34,* 309–316.

Gillam, R. B., & Johnston, J. R. (1992). Spoken written language relationships in language/learning-impaired and normally achieving school-age children. *Journal of Speech and Hearing Research, 35,* 1303–1315.

Gray, S. (2003). Diagnostic accuracy and test-retest reliability of nonword repetition and digit span tasks administered to preschool children with specific language impairment. *Journal of Communication Disorders, 36,* 129–151.

Greenham, S. L., & Stelmack, R. M. (2001). Event-related potentials and picture-word naming: Effects of attention and semantic relation for children and adults. *Developmental Neuropsychology, 20,* 619–639.

Greenham, S. L., Stelmack, R. M., & van der Vlugt, H. (2003). Learning disability subtypes and the role of attention during the naming of pictures and words: An event-related potential analysis. *Developmental Neuropsychology, 23,* 339–358.

Grela, B. G., & Leonard, L. B. (2000). The influence of argument-structure complexity on the use of auxiliary verbs by children with SLI. *Journal of Speech, Language, and Hearing Research, 43,* 1115–1125.

Griffin, Z. M., & Bock, K. (1998). Constraint, word frequency, and the relationship between lexical processing levels in spoken word production. *Journal of Memory and Language, 38,* 313–338.

Hammill, D. D., Mather, N., & Roberts, R. (2001). *Illinois Test of Psycholinguistic Abilities.* Austin, TX: PRO-ED.

Hanauer, J. B., & Brooks, P. J. (2005). Contributions of response set and semantic relatedness to cross-modal Stroop-like picture-word interference in children and adults. *Journal of Experimental Child Psychology, 90,* 21–27.

Heim, S., Opitz, B., & Friederici, A. D. (2002). Broca's area in the human brain is involved in the selection of grammatical gender for language production: Evidence from event-related functional magnetic resonance imaging. *Neuroscience Letters, 328,* 101–104.

Hesketh, A. (2004). Grammatical performance of children with language disorder on structured elicitation and narrative tasks. *Clinical Linguistics and Phonetics, 18,* 161–182.

Hewitt, L. E., Hammer, C. S., Yont, K. M., & Tomblin, J. B. (2005). Language sampling for kindergarten children with and without SLI: Mean length of utterance, IPSYN, and NDW. *Journal of Communication Disorders, 38,* 197–213.

Hurks, P. P., Hendriksen, J. G., Vles, J. S., Kalff, A. C., Feron, F. J., Kroes, M., et al. (2004). Verbal fluency over time as a measure of automatic and controlled processing in children with ADHD. *Brain and Cognition, 55,* 535–544.

Jaeger, J. J. (1992). "Not by the chair of my hinny hin hin": Some general properties of slips of the tongue in young children. *Journal of Child Language, 19,* 335–366.

Jaeger, J. J. (2005). *Kid's slips: What young children's slips of the tongue reveal about language development.* Mahwah, NJ: Lawrence Erlbaum Associates.

Jerger, S., Lai, L., & Marchman, V. A. (2002a). Picture naming by children with hearing loss: I. Effect of semantically related auditory distractors. *Journal of American Academy of Audiology, 13,* 463–477.

Jerger, S., Lai, L., & Marchman, V. A. (2002b). Picture naming by children with hearing loss: II. Effect of phonologically related auditory distractors. *Journal of American Academy of Audiology, 13,* 478–492.

Jerger, S., Martin, R. C., & Damian, M. F. (2002). Semantic and phonological influences on picture naming by children and teenagers. *Journal of Memory and Language, 47,* 229–249.

Jescheniak, J. D., Hahne, A., Hoffman, S., & Wagner, V. (2006). Phonological activation of category coordinates during speech planning is observable in children but not in adults: Evidence for cascaded processing. *Journal of Experimental Psychology: Learning Memory and Cognition, 32,* 373–386.

Jescheniak, J. D., & Schriefers, H. (1997). Lexical access in speech production: Serial or cascaded processing? *Language and Cognitive Processes, 12,* 847–852.

Jescheniak, J. D., & Schriefers, H. (1998). Discrete serial versus cascaded processing in lexical access in speech production: Further evidence from the coactivation of near-synonyms. *Journal of Experimental Psychology: Learning, Memory, and Cognition, 24*(5), 1256–1274.

Jescheniak, J. D., Schriefers, H., Garrett, M. F., & Friederici, A. D. (2002). Exploring the activation of semantics and phonological codes during speech planning with event-related brain potentials. *Journal of Cognitive Neuroscience, 44*, 951–964.

Johnson, C. J., Paivio, A., & Clark, J. M. (1996). Cognitive components of picture naming. *Psychological Bulletin, 120*, 113–139.

Johnston, J. R., Miller, J. F., Curtiss, S., & Tallal, P. (1993). Conversations with children who are language impaired. *Journal of Speech and Hearing Research, 36*, 973–978.

Kail, R. (1991). Processing time declines exponentially during childhood and adolescence. *Developmental Psychology, 27*, 259–266.

Kail, R. (1992). Processing speed, speech rate, and memory. *Developmental Psychology, 28*, 899–904.

Kail, R., & Hall, L. K. (1994). Processing speed, naming speed, and reading. *Developmental Psychology, 30*, 949–954.

Katz, W. F., Curtiss, S., & Tallal, P. (1992). Rapid automatized naming and gestures by normal and language-impaired children. *Brain and Language, 43*, 623–641.

Kave, G. (2006). The development of naming and word fluency: Evidence from Hebrew-speaking children between ages 8 and 17. *Developmental Neuropsychology, 29*, 493–508.

Kemeny, S., Xu, J., Park, G. H., Hosey, L. A., Wettig, C. M., & Braun, A. R. (2006). Temporal dissociation of early lexical access and articulation using a delayed naming task: An FMRI study. *Cerebral Cortex, 16*, 587–595.

Koren, R., Kofman, O., & Berger, A. (2005). Analysis of word clustering in verbal fluency of school-aged children. *Archives of Clinical Neuropsychology, 20*, 1087–1104.

La Heij, W., Dirkx, J., & Kramer, P. (1990). Categorical interference and associative priming in picture naming. *British Journal of Psychology, 81*, 511–525.

Laws, G. (1998). The use of nonword repetition as a test of phonological memory in children with Down syndrome. *Journal of Child Psychology and Psychiatry, 38*, 1119–1130.

Leonard, L. B. (1982). Phonological deficits in children with developmental language impairment. *Brain and Language, 16*, 73–86.

Leonard, L. B., Deevy, P., Miller, C. A., Rauf, L., Charest, M., & Kurtz, R. (2003). Surface forms and grammatical functions: Past tense and passive participle use by children with specific language impairment. *Journal of Speech, Language, and Hearing Research, 46*, 43–55.

Leonard, L. B., Dromi, E., Adam, G., & Zadunaisky-Ehrlich, S. (2000). Tense and finiteness in the speech of children with specific language impairment acquiring Hebrew. *International Journal of Language and Communication Disorders, 35*, 319–335.

Leonard, L. B., & Eyer, J. A. (1997). Three accounts of the grammatical morpheme difficulties of English-speaking children with specific language impairment. *Journal of Speech, Language, and Hearing Research, 40*, 741–753.

Leonard, L. B., Miller, C. A., Deevy, P., Rauf, L., Gerber, E., & Charest, M. (2002). Production operations and the use of nonfinite verbs by children with specific language impairment. *Journal of Speech, Language, and Hearing Sciences, 45*, 744–758.

Leonard, L. B., Miller, C., Grela, B., Holland, A., Gerber, E., & Petucci, M. (2000). Production operations contribute to the grammatical morpheme limitations of children with specific language impairment. *Journal of Memory and Language, 43*, 362–378.

Leonard, L. B., Nippold, M. A., Kail, R., & Hale, C. A. (1983). Picture naming in language-impaired children. *Journal of Speech and Hearing Research, 26*, 609–615.

Levelt, W. J. M. (1992). Accessing words in speech production: Stages, processes and representations. *Cognition, 42*, 1–22.

Levelt, W. J. M., Schriefers, H., Vorberg, D., Meyer, A. S., Pechmann, T., & Havinga, J. (1991). The time course of lexical access in speech production: A study of picture naming. *Psychological Review, 98*, 122–142.

Liles, B. Z. (1985a). Cohesion in the narratives of normal and language-disordered children. *Journal of Speech and Hearing Research, 28*, 123–133.

Liles, B. Z. (1985b). Production and comprehension of narrative discourse in normal and language disordered children. *Journal of Communication Disorders, 18,* 409–427.

Liles, B. Z. (1987). Episode organization and cohesive conjunctives in narratives of children with and without language disorder. *Journal of Speech and Hearing Research, 30,* 185–196.

Liles, B. Z., & Duffy, R. J. (1995). Measurement of narrative discourse ability in children with language disorders. *Journal of Speech and Hearing Research, 38,* 415–426.

Manis, F. R., Doi, L. M., & Bhadha, B. (2000). Naming speed, phonological awareness, and orthographic knowledge in second graders. *Journal of Learning Disabilities, 33,* 325–333, 374.

Manis, F. R., Seidenberg, M. S., & Doi, L. M. (1999). See Dick RAN: Rapid naming and the longitudinal prediction of reading subskills in first and second graders. *Scientific Studies of Reading, 3,* 129–157.

Marchman, V. A., Wulfeck, B., & Weismer, S. E. (1999). Morphological productivity in children with normal language and SLI: A study of the English past tense. *Journal of Speech, Language, and Hearing Research, 42,* 206–219.

Marinellie, S. A. (2004). Complex syntax used by school-age children with specific language impairment (SLI) in child-adult conversation. *Journal of Communication Disorders, 37,* 517–533.

Marton, K., & Schwartz, R. G. (2003). Working memory capacity and language processes in children with specific language impairment. *Journal of Speech, Language, and Hearing Research, 46,* 1138–1153.

Marton, K., Schwartz, R. G., Farkas, L., & Katsnelson, V. (2006). Verbal working memory and executive functions in Hungarian children with specific language impairment: A cross-linguistic analysis. *International Journal of Language and Communication Disorders, 41*(6), 653–673.

Matute, E., Rosselli, M., Ardila, A., & Morales, G. (2004). Verbal and nonverbal fluency in Spanish-speaking children. *Developmental Neuropsychology, 26,* 647–660.

McGregor, K. K. (1994). Use of phonological information in a word-finding treatment for children. *Journal of Speech, Language, and Hearing Research, 37,* 1381–1396.

McGregor, K. K., & Leonard, L. B. (1989). Facilitating word-finding skills of language-impaired children. *Journal of Speech and Hearing Disorders, 54,* 141–147.

McGregor, K. K., & Waxman, S. R. (1998). Object naming at multiple hierarchical levels: A comparison of preschoolers with and without word-finding deficits. *Journal of Child Language, 25,* 419–430.

McGregor, K. K., & Windsor, J. (1996). Effects of priming on the naming accuracy of preschoolers with word-finding deficits. *Journal of Speech, Language, and Hearing Research, 39,* 1048–1063.

Merritt, D. D., & Liles, B. Z. (1987). Story grammar ability in children with and without language disorder: Story generation, story retelling, and story comprehension. *Journal of Speech and Hearing Research, 30,* 539–552.

Merritt, D. D., & Liles, B. Z. (1989). Narrative analysis: Clinical applications of story generation and story retelling. *Journal of Speech and Hearing Disorders, 54,* 438–447.

Misra, M., Katzir, T., Wolf, M., & Poldrack, R. A. (2004). Neural systems for rapid automatized naming in skilled readers: Unraveling the RAN-reading relationship. *Scientific Studies of Reading, 8,* 241–256.

Montgomery, J. W. (1995). Sentence comprehension in children with specific language impairment: The role of phonological working memory. *Journal of Speech, Language, and Hearing Research, 38,* 187–199.

Newcomer, P. L., & Hammill, D. D. (1997). *Test of Language Development–Primary* (3rd ed.). Austin, TX: PRO-ED.

Newman, R. S., & German, D. J. (2002). Effects of lexical factors on lexical access among typical language-learning children and children with word-finding difficulties. *Language and Speech, 45,* 285–317.

Nippold, M. A. (1992). The nature of normal and disordered word finding in children and adolescents. *Topics in Language Disorders, 13,* 1–14.

Oetting, J. B., & Horohov, J. E. (1997). Past-tense marking by children with and without specific language impairment. *Journal of Speech, Language, and Hearing Research*, 40, 62–74.

Owen, A. J., & Leonard, L. B. (2002). Lexical diversity in the spontaneous speech of children with specific language impairment: Application of D. *Journal of Speech, Language, and Hearing Research*, 45, 927–937.

Paul, R., & Jennings, P. (1992). Phonological behavior in toddlers with slow expressive language development. *Journal of Speech and Hearing Research*, 35, 99–107.

Paul, R., & Smith, R. L. (1993). Narrative skills in 4-year-olds with normal, impaired, and late-developing language. *Journal of Speech and Hearing Research*, 36, 592–598.

Peterson, R. R., & Savoy, P. (1998). Lexical selection and phonological encoding during language production: Evidence for cascaded processing. *Journal of Experimental Psychology: Learning, Memory, and Cognition*, 24, 539–557.

Purcell, S. L., & Liles, B. Z. (1992). Cohesion repairs in the narratives of normal-language and language-disordered school-age children. *Journal of Speech and Hearing Research*, 35, 354–362.

Rescorla, L., & Bernstein-Ratner, N. (1996). Phonetic profiles of toddlers with specific expressive language impairment (SLI-E). *Journal of Speech Hearing Research*, 39, 153–165.

Rescorla, L., Dahlsgaard, K., & Roberts, J. (2000). Late-talking toddlers: MLU and IPSyn outcomes at 3;0 and 4;0. *Journal of Child Language*, 27, 643–664.

Rice, M. L., & Oetting, J. B. (1993). Morphological deficits of children with SLI: Evaluation of number marking and agreement. *Journal of Speech and Hearing Research*, 36, 1249–1257.

Rice, M. L., Redmond, S. M., & Hoffman, L. (2006). Mean length of utterance in children with specific language impairment and in younger control children shows concurrent validity and stable and parallel growth trajectories. *Journal of Speech, Language, and Hearing, Research*, 49, 793–808.

Rice, M. L., & Wexler, K. (1996). Toward tense as a clinical marker of specific language impairment in English-speaking children. *Journal of Speech and Hearing Research*, 39 1239–1266.

Rice, M. L., Wexler, K., & Hershberger, S. (1998). Tense over time: The longitudinal course of tense acquisition in children with specific language impairment. *Journal of Speech, Language, and Hearing Research*, 41, 1412–1431.

Rice, M. L., Wexler, K., Marquis, J., & Hershberger, S. (2000). Acquisition of irregular past tense by children with specific language impairment. *Journal of Speech, Language, and Hearing Research*, 43, 1126–1145.

Ripich, D. N., & Griffith, P. L. (1988). Narrative abilities of children with learning disabilities and nondisabled children: Story structure, cohesion, and propositions. *Journal of Learning Disabilities*, 21, 163–173.

Riva, D., Nichelli, F., & Devoti., M. (2000). Developmental aspects of verbal fluency and confrontation naming in children. *Brain and Language*, 71, 267–284.

Roberts, J., Rescorla, L., Giroux, J., & Stevens, L. (1998). Phonological skills of children with specific expressive language impairment (SLI-E): Outcome at age 3. *Journal of Speech, Language, and Hearing Research*, 41, 374–387.

Rogers, T. T., Ivanoiu, A., Patterson, K., & Hodges, J. R. (2006). Semantic memory in Alzheimer's disease and the frontotemporal dementias: A longitudinal study of 236 patients. *Neuropsychology*, 20, 319–335.

Roth, F. P., & Spekman, N. J. (1986). Narrative discourse: Spontaneously generated stories of learning-disabled and normally achieving students. *Journal of Speech and Hearing Disorders*, 51, 8–23.

Saben, C. B., & Ingram, J. C. (1991). The effects of minimal pairs treatment on the speech-sound production of two children with phonologic disorders. *Journal of Speech and Hearing Research*, 34, 1023–1040.

Sauzeon, H., Lestage, P., Raboutet, C., N'Kaoua, B., & Claverie, B. (2004). Verbal fluency output in children aged 7–16 as a function of the production criterion: Qualitative analysis of clustering, switching processes, and semantic network exploitation. *Brain and Language*, 89, 192–202.

Schatschneider, C., Carlson, C. D., Francis, D. J., Foorman, B. R., & Fletcher, J. M. (2002). Relationship of rapid automatized naming and phonological awareness in early reading development: Implications for the double-deficit hypothesis. *Journal of Learning Disabilities*, *35*, 245–256.

Schmitt, B. M., Münte, T. F., & Kutas, M. (2000). Electrophysiological estimates of the time course of semantic and phonological encoding during implicit picture naming. *Psychophysiology*, *37*, 473–484.

Schriefers, H., Meyer, A. S., & Levelt, W. J. M. (1990). Exploring the time course of lexical access in language production: Picture-word interference studies. *Journal of Memory and Language*, *29*, 86–102.

Schwartz, R. G., Leonard, L. B., Folger, M. K., & Wilcox, M. J. (1980). Early phonological behavior in normal-speaking and language disordered children: Evidence for a synergistic view of linguistic disorders. *Journal of Speech and Hearing Disorders*, *45*, 357–377.

Scott, C. M., & Windsor, J. (2000). General language performance measures in spoken and written narrative and expository discourse of school-age children with language learning disabilities. *Journal of Speech, Language, and Hearing Research*, *43*, 324–339.

Seiger, L. (2005). Lexical access in school-aged children with and without specific language impairment. *Dissertation Abstracts International*, *65* (12), 6341. (UMI No. 3159256)

Seiger, L., Brooks P., Sailor, K., & Bruening, P. (2005). *Semantic processing during language production in typically developing children.* Poster session presented at the 10th International Congress for the Study of Child Language, Berlin, Germany.

Seiger-Gardner, L., & Brooks, P. (in press). Phonological processing of onset and rhyme-related distractors in children with specific language impairment. *Journal of Speech, Language, and Hearing Research.*

Seiger-Gardner, L., & Schwartz, R. G. (in press). Lexical access during word production in children with and without SLI: A cross-modal picture-word interference study. *International Journal of Language and Communication Disorders.*

Semel, E., Wiig, E. H., & Secord, W. A. (2003). *Clinical Evaluation of Language Fundamentals, CELF–4.* San Antonio, TX: Psychological Corporation.

Shapiro, L., Swinney, D., & Borsky, S. (1998). Online examination of language performance in normal and neurologically impaired adults. *American Journal of Speech-Language Pathology*, *7*, 49–60.

Shriberg, L. D., & Kwiatkowski, J. (1994). Developmental phonological disorders, I: A clinical profile. *Journal of Speech and Hearing Research*, *37*, 1100–1126.

Soros, P., Cornelissen, K., Laine, M., & Salmelin, R. (2003). Naming actions and objects: Cortical dynamics in healthy adults and in an anomic patient with a dissociation in action/object naming. *NeuroImage*, *19*, 1787–1801.

Stemberger, J. P. (1989). Speech errors in early child language production. *Journal of Memory and Language*, *28*, 164–188.

Stokes, S. F., Wong, A. M.-Y., Fletcher, P., & Leonard, L. B. (2006). Nonword repetition and sentence repetition as clinical markers of specific language impairment: The case of Cantonese. *Journal of Speech, Language, and Hearing Research*, *49*, 219–236.

Swan, D., & Goswami, U. (1997). Picture naming deficits in developmental dyslexia: The phonological representation hypothesis. *Brain and Language*, *56*, 334–353.

Thordardottir, E. T., & Weismer, S. E. (2002). Verb argument structure weakness in specific language impairment in relation to age and utterance length. *Clinical Linguistics and Phonetics*, *16*, 233–250.

Troyer, A. K., Moscovitch, M., & Winocur, G. (1997). Clustering and switching as two components of verbal fluency: Evidence from younger and older healthy adults. *Neuropsychology*, *11*, 138–146.

van der Lely, H. (1997). Narrative discourse in grammatical specific language impaired children: A modular language deficit? *Journal of Child Language*, *24*, 221–256.

van Turennout, M., Hagoort, P., & Brown, M. C. (1997). Electrophysiological evidence on the time course of semantic and phonological processes in speech production. *Journal of Experimental Psychology: Learning, Memory, and Cognition*, *23*, 787–806.

van Turennout, M., Hagoort, P., & Brown, M. C. (1998). Brain activity during speaking: From syntax to phonology in 40 milliseconds. *Science, 280,* 572–574.

Waber, D. P., Wolff, P. H., Forbes, P. W., & Weiler, M. D. (2000). Rapid automatized naming in children referred for evaluation of heterogeneous learning problems: How specific are naming speed deficits to reading disability? *Child Neuropsychology, 6,* 251–261.

Watkins, R. V., & Kelly, D. J. (1995). Measuring children's lexical diversity: Differentiating typical and impaired language learners. *Journal of Speech, Language, and Hearing Research, 38,* 1349–1359.

Weckerly, J., Wulfeck, B., & Reilly, J. (2001). Verbal fluency deficits in children with specific language impairment: Slow rapid naming or slow to name? *Child Neuropsychology, 7,* 142–152.

Weismer, S. E., Tomblin, J. B., Zhang, X., Buckwalter, P., Chynoweth, J. G., & Jones, M. (2000). Nonword repetition performance in school-age children with and without language impairment. *Journal of Speech, Language, and Hearing Research, 43,* 865–878.

Whitehurst, G. J., Smith, M., Fischel, J. E., Arnold, D. S., & Lonigan, C. J. (1991). The continuity of babble and speech in children with specific expressive language delay. *Journal of Speech, Language, and Hearing Research, 34,* 1121–1129.

Wiig, E. H., & Becker-Caplan, L. (1984). Linguistic retrieval strategies and word finding difficulties among children with language disabilities. *Topics in Language Disorders, 4,* 1–18.

Wijnen, F. (1992). Incidental word and sound errors in young speakers. *Journal of Memory and Language, 31,* 734–755.

Windfuhr, K. L., Faragher, B., & Conti-Ramsden, G. (2002). Lexical learning skills in young children with specific language impairment (SLI). *Journal of Speech, Language, and Hearing Research, 37,* 415–432.

Wolf, M. (1986). Rapid alternating stimulus naming in the developmental dyslexias. *Brain and Language, 27,* 360–379.

Wright, S. H. (1993). Teaching word-finding strategies to severely language-impaired children. *European Journal of Disorders of Communication, 28,* 165–175.

22

Language Comprehension Approaches to Child Language Disorders

PATRICIA DEEVY

INTRODUCTION

*H*istorically, language comprehension has been studied less extensively in children than language production. Although production offers explicit data for analysis, comprehension can only be measured indirectly, making it a more challenging object of study. As described in this chapter, we measure comprehension by observing behavior in response to language; this response can be as overt as acting out the meaning of a sentence with toys or as subtle as shifting eye gaze to a named object. In adults, we can assume that the methods we use isolate language comprehension to a large extent; in children, it is unclear that this assumption is warranted. In drawing conclusions about comprehension in children, as measured behaviorally, we must consider the nature of their developing cognitive and linguistic systems and how these contribute to observed performance. Increasingly, researchers are trying new methods that circumvent some of the difficulties of testing comprehension in young children and thereby provide better insight into children's knowledge and receptive processing of language.

Studies of comprehension in language-disordered children have also been done much less frequently than studies of language production. A distinction has traditionally been made between children who have both expressive and receptive delays and those who have only expressive delays. Careful testing, however, has shown that most children with specific language impairment (SLI) have at least some comprehension difficulties and that children differ only in the degree to which both receptive and expressive language is affected rather than falling into strict subtypes (Bishop, 1997). Many of the methods discussed here have been or are beginning to be used to study language in atypical populations, particularly children with SLI. Before introducing specific methods, we review relevant concepts and outline some general considerations in testing comprehension in children with language disorders.

Competence and Performance

The distinction between competence and performance is useful when thinking about the goals of any comprehension experiment. Linguistic competence is a speaker's implicit knowledge of the rules of his or her language. Language knowledge is organized at many levels, each of which constitutes a level of receptive processing. For spoken language, these levels include auditory processing of the acoustic waveform, phonetic feature extraction, phonological analysis, word recognition and retrieval, syntactic parsing, semantic interpretation, use of inference from linguistic and nonlinguistic context, and interpretation of social context (Bishop, 1997). Linguistic performance is the use of this knowledge to produce and comprehend language. Although competence in adults is thought to be relatively stable and constant, performance is affected by transitory states (e.g., fatigue) and inherent cognitive constraints (e.g., limitations in short-term memory). By testing adults' receptive processing as it happens in real time, it has been shown that comprehension is very fast, automatic, and incremental. Interpretation begins as soon as linguistic information is available. For example, as the initial sounds of a word are processed, a set of possible candidates are accessed in the lexicon; as more information is processed, this set is incrementally narrowed down.

For children, the division between language knowledge and language processing is not as clear. It is even less clear for children with language disorders. Probing grammatical knowledge with comprehension tasks can be difficult because immature memory, attention, and behavior can obscure the child's knowledge. In addition, some aspects of grammatical knowledge may not be stable during development, as reflected, for example, in variable production of grammatical morphemes. Many of the methods reviewed in this chapter reflect attempts to circumvent these limitations as much as possible in order to get a clear picture of children's competence. Methods for testing the processing of stable aspects of children's grammatical knowledge are just beginning to provide hints at how children's performance systems are similar to and different from adults'.

OFF-LINE AND ON-LINE COMPREHENSION TASKS

The methods reviewed in this chapter are categorized as either off-line or on-line. As described earlier, language processing is immediate and incremental. On-line methods are those that try to measure the intermediate stages of receptive processing as it happens in real time. Off-line methods are those that measure the output of all stages of receptive processing. Typically, the subject does not respond until after the stimulus is presented in its entirety, and this response is not timed. As such, off-line measures do not provide insight into the many intermediate steps in comprehension that led up to a response. The difference between final and intermediate stages of comprehension can be seen in the processing of temporarily ambiguous sentences, such as *The police shot the man with a knife*. On-line studies have demonstrated processing difficulty at *a knife*. Setting aside the reasons for this difficulty, it is clear that when first encountered, the immediate preference is to treat *with* as introducing an instrument of *shoot*, not as a modifier of *man*; on the instrument reading, *a knife* is unexpected. However, the correct interpretation is available upon reflection, as the final product of processing the sentence.

In terms of their application, off-line tasks are best thought of as methods for testing linguistic competence; they are used to establish what a child knows about language. On-line tasks are used to test processing of aspects of language for which competence is established in the group tested. When this is not clear (e.g., when testing young typical or atypical children), studies will include an off-line test of the knowledge being tested on-line.

GENERAL METHODOLOGICAL CONSIDERATIONS

Before reviewing individual tasks, we consider some aspects of research design that apply generally to studies testing comprehension in children with atypical language. The most basic question is, of course, which task to use. This requires, at minimum, consideration of the group's ability level, the researcher's resources, and the potential of the method to address the research question in an interesting way. The following methodological considerations will help to inform these decisions.

Comparison Groups

A comparison group provides a point of reference in a study of children with language impairment. Although a group matched for chronological age may be adequate, it is often desirable to include a group that matches on some aspect(s) of comprehension ability, as determined by a standardized test. The reasoning is as follows: language-impaired children are likely to perform more poorly than same-age peers on most language measures, so the comparison may not reveal anything interesting about the status of a given ability relative to other comprehension abilities (Leonard, 1998). Depending on the choice of matching criterion, this comprehension-matched group may be one to two years younger than the impaired group, so it is important to determine whether this younger group will be able to complete the task successfully.

The choice of matching criterion can reflect an approach that is more or less conservative, depending on how much overlap there is between the types of structures and abilities targeted by the standardized test used for matching and those targeted by the experiment. If there is significant overlap, it is possible that no differences between groups will be found in the experiment because they are so closely matched on the ability tested by it. For example, when testing children's sentence comprehension, one could match using raw scores from a test of receptive syntax or from a test of receptive vocabulary. Obviously, the former is more conservative and the latter is less so, in the sense just described. A compromise is to use a receptive test that probes a range of comprehension skills, including, but not limited to, the one to be studied. Besides being an appropriate measure of comprehension, this test must be standardized for the entire age range of the children participating in the study. The Peabody Picture Vocabulary Test–III (PPVT–III) (Dunn & Dunn, 1997) is an excellent choice for matching on receptive vocabulary; it is carefully normed on a very wide age range (2–90 years old). The Test of Auditory Comprehension of Language–3 (TACL–3; Carrow-Woolfolk, 1999) includes subtests of vocabulary, grammatical morphology, and sentence structure and can be used with children aged 3–10. The Test for Reception of Grammar–2 (TROG–2; Bishop, 2003) targets grammatical morphology and sentence structure and is standardized for ages 4–16. Although it was standardized in the United Kingdom, there do not appear to be any dialect-sensitive items in the test, and it has been used by both British and American researchers.

Additional Design Considerations

All methods of testing comprehension are intended to provide insight into the knowledge and processes that underlie children's language comprehension. However, other factors also play a role. As will be seen below, all tasks make demands on the child's nonlinguistic abilities; and children vary in their individual abilities. When testing a clinical population, there may be known or suspected nonlinguistic weaknesses that could affect performance. For example, children with SLI may have weaknesses in auditory perception, motor ability, memory, and attention. Although the group may be defined as having SLI by a common profile of diagnostic test scores, these weaknesses may create even more heterogeneity in performance than would be found in a young typically developing group. On-line studies measuring reaction time are especially sensitive to these differences. For this reason, within-subjects designs are strongly suggested (McKee, 1996). Another suggestion is to include an adequate number of trials per condition, keeping in mind that more trials may be lost in the impaired or young language-matched group than anticipated due to immature attention or behavior. Consideration of the following points may help to control for or help to isolate the source of performance differences.

Studies for which reaction time (RT) is the dependent variable should include some sort of response baseline. For example, if a button press is used to measure RT, all children could complete a task in which they repeatedly press a button in response to a tone; this provides a baseline measure of motor response to an auditory signal, independent of language processing. Each child's mean baseline RT can be included as a covariate in the analysis of RTs, eliminating it as a confounding factor. Working memory and attention measures administered at the time of the experiment may also be informative in interpreting the results.

Stimuli

Visual stimuli, where used, must be carefully controlled. Target and distractor stimuli should differ from each other minimally, so that one is not chosen on the basis of visual interest alone. When using pictures as the visual stimuli, it may be necessary to use a professional illustrator to achieve consistency and quality. Cautions about balancing the content of target and distractor also apply to videos, as detailed by Hirsh-Pasek and Golinkoff (1996). Depending on the type of linguistic stimuli being tested, one could also use a commercially available set of pictures such as Snodgrass and Vanderwart (1980). This set includes 260 pictures of common nouns that were standardized for adults for a variety of properties including name agreement, familiarity, and visual complexity. They have since been normed for 5- to 7-year-old children for name agreement, familiarity, and complexity (Cycowicz, Friedman, & Rothstein, 1997).

In constructing the linguistic stimuli for sentence-comprehension tasks, the content of the stimuli must be controlled in terms of the real-world plausibility of the sentences in each condition since young children may base their response on plausibility instead of linguistic structure. One should also take into consideration the frequency of the words used. Word frequency provides an index of word familiarity and, consequently, of the ease of lexical access in auditory comprehension. If comprehension of a particular sentence structure is of interest, controlling for the familiarity of individual words across items can help to ensure consistency in the difficulty of the sentences and allow you to better isolate syntax as the variable of interest. If receptive processing of individual words is the focus of the study, then, clearly, frequency must be controlled, as it is the main determinant of speed of lexical access. Word frequencies for young school-aged children can be obtained through the corpus of Moe, Hopkins, and Rush (1982); for older school-aged children, see Carroll, Davies, and Richman (1971). Another way to ensure familiarity to young children is to draw vocabulary from an early expressive vocabulary checklist such as Rescorla (1989) or the MacArthur–Bates Communicative Development Inventory (CDI; Fenson et al., 1993).

The linguistic stimuli in comprehension tasks should be recorded for presentation, rather than presented live-voice. This guarantees that presentation across children and across clinical groups does not vary in speed or intonation in a way that would differentially affect comprehension. Even very young children are comfortable with viewing pictures on a computer screen and responding to linguistic stimuli presented over the computer's speakers.

A final consideration in most comprehension tasks is the control of context. If context is not provided (i.e., sentences are presented in isolation) or it is not carefully controlled, a child may be confused or make assumptions that could affect his or her responses in ways not anticipated by the researcher. Although children have some ability to use context in interpreting sentences, they may not be as proficient as adults at accommodation in the absence of context (Crain & Thornton, 1998).

General Procedures

As with any experimental task with children, careful piloting with the intended age group and population is very important. Pilot performance can reveal whether the task is too difficult and whether there are obvious biases in response or other unforeseen problems. This is particularly important for on-line tasks that have not often been used with children. Along the same lines, adequate practice should be provided before presenting the target items. Given the smaller number of children included in studies of clinical populations, it is important that data are not wasted because the child did not understand the task. Finally, the experimenter should be aware of any possibility for unconsciously cueing the child about an answer. The experimenter should continue to look down or at the child's face, not at the visual stimuli, in case the child would pick up on that cue.

OFF-LINE METHODS

The methods reviewed below have been designed primarily to explore sentence-level syntactic and semantic knowledge in children learning their first language(s). Where appropriate, examples will be given showing how the technique could be used to test comprehension of individual words or discourses.

Picture Selection

The picture selection task has been used to test a variety of language abilities with a variety of populations. In this type of task, the child is simply presented with an array of pictures and must choose the one that illustrates the meaning of a word or sentence. The nontarget pictures in the array (called distractors or foils) are chosen to provide alternatives to the correct picture that could plausibly tempt the child; they can also provide information about the nature of the child's grammar when he answers incorrectly.

This task is attractive as a test of comprehension in children because it is simple to administer; it can be done relatively quickly and does not require special facilities other than a quiet room. Also, because it does not require a complex response from the child, such as formulating a verbal response or acting out the meaning of the sentence, it can be used with very young children, and with a variety of clinical groups. This wide applicability makes it useful in comparing performance across ages and groups (Blockberger & Johnston, 2003; Gerken & McIntosh, 1993; van der Lely, 1996).

These advantages require some qualification. There are limits on the range of events that can be depicted in a static, two-dimensional format. For example, suppose we wanted to ask whether children know the meaning of tense marking on the auxiliary in sentences like *she is dancing* and *she was dancing*. There is no direct way to depict the past-tense version of the sentence in a single picture. In many more cases, an event is too abstract or a construction too complex to profitably test with sets of drawings. In addition, young children may have difficulty interpreting drawings if they are not yet familiar with conventions such as shading to indicate depth or lines to indicate motion (Cocking & McHale, 1981). Finally, Shorr and Dale (1984) showed that children differ in their approach to this task: some respond slowly and only after studying the pictures, and others are more impulsive. Obviously, impulsive children may do more poorly when tested with this task, even though they may have the same grammatical knowledge.

The picture selection task has been used to test children's comprehension at many levels of linguistic structure. To test for comprehension of phonological distinctions, Velleman (1988) had preschoolers respond to minimal pairs (*fox/box*) by pointing to the corresponding picture. To test the word-learning abilities of children with SLI and typical language development, Oetting, Rice, and Swank (1995) showed children videos with a narration using the novel words. Later, comprehension was tested using a picture selection task. Deevy and Leonard (2004) investigated the role of processing limitations in the comprehension of wh-questions, varying syntactic complexity and length. Children indicated comprehension of questions (e.g., *Who is washing the [happy brown] dog?*) by pointing to the correct character in a picture that shows someone washing the dog and someone being washed by the dog. Picture selection has also been used to test children for comprehension of passive sentences, relative clauses, pronouns, and reflexives (for a review, see O'Grady, 1997).

In developing the task for an experiment, pictures must be created that represent the targeted linguistic structure and the distractors. At least one distractor must differ from the test sentence only by the grammatical feature tested. For example, for a sentence like *the turtle was covered by the frog*, the focus of testing could be the child's comprehension of word order or of past tense. Each requires a different critical distractor. Testing word order would require a distractor in which the turtle covers the frog; testing tense would require a distractor showing an uncovered turtle about to be covered by a frog. Although it is possible to use one distractor in a picture selection task, two or three is ideal. Assuming that each distractor represents an equally plausible alternative, the level of chance performance is reduced from 50% with one distractor to 25% with three distractors. However, depending on the complexity of the linguistic stimulus and pictures and on the age of the child, four pictures may be too many to reasonably expect the child to carefully consider while at the same time remembering the sentence.

Finally, in presenting the stimuli, the pictures should be presented before the target word or sentence (assuming that it is the child's grammatical knowledge, not processing ability, that is being tested). A procedure in which the sentence is presented before the pictures are seen may place an undue burden on verbal working memory, placing children with language disorders at a disadvantage that is unrelated to linguistic knowledge.

Act-out

As an off-line method for testing comprehension, the act-out task has a more limited applicability than picture selection. It has been used to test sentence-level comprehension, in structures in which the referent of a noun phrase or pronoun is of interest (for references, see Goodluck, 1996). It has also been used to evaluate children's knowledge of relative clauses (Hamburger & Crain, 1982; Tavakolian, 1981) and the role of syntactic knowledge in learning verb meanings (Akhtar & Tomasello, 1997; Naigles, Gleitman, & Gleitman, 1993). In all cases, children were asked to demonstrate their understanding of the test sentence by acting out the sentence with toys.

The act-out task can be illustrated with an example from Tavakolian (1981). She tested preschoolers' comprehension of a variety of relative clause types including the following: *the dog pushed the sheep that jumped over the pig*. For each test sentence, children were given three toys (e.g., dog, sheep, and pig) with which to act out their understanding. Typical prompts in act-out tasks include "do what I say," "show me . . ." or "[puppet name] wants you to. . . ." In this study, rather than act out the correct meaning of the relative clause sentence, many children had the dog push the sheep and then jump over the pig. This was consistent with Tavakolian's claim that young children treat the second verb phrase in this sentence as conjoined with the first rather than modifying *the sheep*.

This task is of interest because it is not a forced-choice method; thus, it may reveal that the child has assigned an interpretation not anticipated by the experimenter. In addition, the act-out task is inexpensive to assemble and is appealing to children. Although it has been used with children under three to test for comprehension of fairly simple linguistic stimuli (Akhtar & Tomasello, 1997; Naigles et al., 1993), it is not an ideal task for children this young because they may not be as consistently willing or able to comply with instructions to act out what is heard. Even for older children, the task can be cognitively demanding in that it requires them to assign a syntactic representation to the sentence they heard, extract its meaning, and then plan and carry out a response based on this analysis.

Although the task's open-ended nature is its main advantage, it can also be a disadvantage when interpreting the results, as detailed by Goodluck (1996). When children respond to a sentence in a nonadult fashion, one cannot necessarily conclude that they have a grammar that differs from that of the adult. Instead, it may be that they mentally recoded the sentence to a simpler or more familiar one before acting it out. On the other hand, even when they do respond in an adult fashion, we cannot rule out the possibility that their grammar allows some nonadult reading(s) as well; this is because the task only reveals the reading a child chooses to act out. Crain and Thornton (1998) point out that the conclusions that can be made about a child's linguistic competence on the basis of a behavioral test of comprehension are always limited in this way. For example, a sentence that is unambiguous in adult grammar might allow two meanings in the grammar of the child. Although the child shows comprehension of the adult meaning, his grammar may differ from the adult's by also allowing an alternative. This would not be revealed in a task that did not probe specifically for this alternative meaning.

Response biases can also muddy the waters in interpreting results in the act-out task. For example, the *bird-in-the-hand* strategy may have been responsible for the response to the relative clause sentence observed by Tavakolian. Children had a tendency to act out the second clause (*that jumped over the pig*) with *the dog* as subject because it was already *in hand*, having just been used in performing the action of the main verb. A bias may also develop due to the particular items tested in a study. Goodluck (1996) gives an example from her own work on the reference of a null subject (i.e., the "jumper") in sentences like: *Before _ jumping up and down, the girl kisses the boy*. Goodluck found that in one experiment with children, they preferred to associate the empty position with a referent outside the sentence and in another they preferred a referent inside the sentence. A bias may have been established in the first study by the presence of other sentences in the experiment for which children preferred a sentence-external referent (i.e., for the pronoun in *For him to hug the tiger would upset the horse*).

These difficulties should be kept in mind when planning an act-out task. Although the task apparently has not been used with language-disordered groups, there is no obvious reason why it could not be used in this way. As always, when a method is being used with a new population, it would be best to test structures for which there is a track record of getting interesting and interpretable results from children with typical language development at a similar language level.

Truth-Value Judgments

The truth-value judgment task has been used primarily to probe knowledge of sentence-level syntactic and semantic constraints in children with typical language development. In brief, the child watches as an experimenter describes a scenario and acts it out with toys. The child must then decide whether a target sentence is a true or false statement about the scene just witnessed. Crucially, the test sentence can only be judged to be true or false on the basis of grammatical knowledge; the child must be able to construct a representation of the sentence on the basis of this knowledge and compare its meaning to the facts of the scenario in order to compute a truth value. Although this process sounds complex, it reflects the kind of interpretation in context that a language user does routinely. The task is less demanding than a grammaticality judgment task which requires the child to think metalinguistically about the sentence, considering its form rather than, and possibly independent of, its meaning (e.g., detecting the error in *Whenever she's in New York, Sally visit the museums*).

Crain and Thornton (1998) described how this task could be used to test children's interpretation of pronouns. An example of a target sentence is given in (1) (elements that share the same index are interpreted as coreferring). A grammatical constraint prohibits the indexing in (1a) while allowing (1b) (i.e., *He* cannot refer to *the Troll*, only to some other character).

(1)   a. He_i said that the $Troll_i$ is the best jumper.
     b. He_j said that the $Troll_i$ is the best jumper.

In order to test whether children know this constraint, a scenario is set up in which both of these readings are raised as possibilities, but the grammatical one turns out to be untrue. For example, the scenario for (1) involves a jumping competition with a judge and three competitors (Cookie Monster, Grover, and the Troll). The judge considers the Troll's performance, admiring his ability, but ultimately deems Grover the best jumper. The Troll states that the decision is unfair, given his superior jumping. Next, the puppet attempts to describe the situation, stating the test sentence: "I know one thing that happened. *He said that the Troll is the best jumper.*" This sentence is true on the reading (1a) in which *he* refers to the Troll, but not true on reading (1b) in which *he* refers to another character. Thus, if children know the grammatical constraint, they will reject the puppet's statement.

The context presented with these sentences is a very important aspect of the method. By explicitly providing options for interpreting the sentence, it can be determined whether the child accepts a reading that was conceptually possible but excluded by the grammatical constraint. The fact that the child must show knowledge of the constraint by rejecting the puppet's sentence makes it a more conservative test of children's knowledge, in part because subjects are biased to say "yes."

As detailed in Crain and Thornton (1998), there are several advantages to using this task. First, by acting out the scenario with toys, it is possible to depict events that pictures could not show. They also believe that toys are more interesting to children than pictures and thus hold their attention better. The toys also provide an immediate physical record of the participants and events, reducing demands on memory. Task demands are generally reduced because the child must simply understand the scenario and the target sentence and choose a binary response rather than having to formulate a more complex response or interpret the sentence and then reconstruct it with toys. Ideally, this task will provide an opportunity to isolate and observe the child's linguistic knowledge, relatively unhindered by immature nonlinguistic abilities.

This task has not often been used to test children with language impairment. Schulz and Wittek (2003) used it to test German-speaking children with SLI (aged 4;3–6;3) for comprehension of aspectual properties of verbs. The fact that the task is designed to minimize nonlinguistic demands makes it ideal for use with this population; in fact, it has been used with typically developing children as young as 2 (Crain & McKee, 1985). Unlike a grammaticality judgment, a truth-value judgment does not rely on metalinguistic skills, which may be weak in children with SLI; this judgment is strictly based on interpretation. However, processing deficits could still obscure grammatical knowledge in this task if the scenarios are too long or complex.

One last comment about this task addresses the nature of the true/false judgment response. Most researchers have the child indicate his or her judgment by *rewarding* or *punishing* the puppet who states the target sentence. If the puppet's statement is *good* or *right*, the child feeds the puppet a cookie; if it is *silly* or *wrong*, the puppet is fed a rag. This makes the task appealing and makes both types of response more likely. Still, when children have only two possible responses, they may perseverate on one. Training on the task using simple examples may prevent this or at least alert the experimenter when a child is not consistently basing responses on the test sentence.

Intermodal Preferential Looking

The development of the intermodal preferential looking paradigm (IPLP) was a major step forward in testing comprehension in infants and toddlers. In this task, eye gaze is measured as the child views two video monitors (showing either objects or events) and listens to a word or sentence that describes one of the videos but not the other. The total time spent looking at the screen that matches the audio compared to the screen that does not match provides the measure of comprehension. It is considered an off-line measure for our purposes because cumulative looking time indicates the child's overall preference; thus, it does not provide information about intermediate stages of receptive processing. The main advantage of using eye gaze is that it does not require the child to respond overtly; it requires only attention to the stimuli. Also, it allows presentation of events that could not be clearly depicted in pictures. Below, we discuss how the method has been used to measure on-line processing.

Golinkoff, Hirsh-Pasek, Cauley, and Gordon (1987) first used the IPLP to test 14- and 18-month-olds for comprehension of familiar nouns and word combinations, respectively. They reasoned that if toddlers looked longer at a video image of a shoe when hearing *shoe* than at an image of a boat, then the basis of this preference could only be their comprehension of the linguistic stimulus (assuming that other factors were controlled). Because this study established that comprehension could be reliably measured with the IPLP, others have used it to test hypotheses about word learning in 1- to 2-year-olds (Hollich et al., 2000), comprehension of constituent structure in 14-month-olds (Hirsh-Pasek & Golinkoff, 1996), verb argument structure in 2-year-olds (Hirsh-Pasek & Golinkoff, 1996; Naigles, 1990), pronouns and reflexives in 3-year-olds (Hirsh-Pasek, Golinkoff, Hermon, & Kaufman, 1995), and abstract knowledge of word order in 21- and 25-month-olds (Gertner, Fisher, & Eisengart, 2006).

A typical IPLP experiment is set up as follows (see Figure 22.1). The child sits in front of two adjacent monitors on a caregiver's lap. A speaker located between the two screens plays the linguistic stimuli. A light above the speaker is used to attract the child's attention

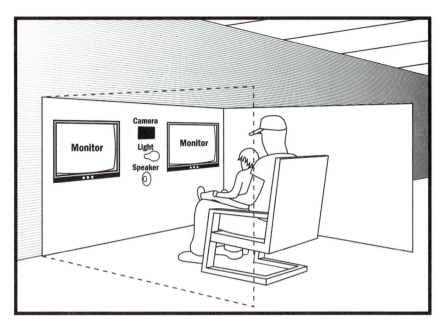

FIGURE 22.1 Illustration of the intermodal preferential looking paradigm (IPLP) procedure.

to the midline. The child's looks to the two screens and to midline are recorded by a video camera above the speaker. The pattern and timing of the child's eye gaze are later coded by an experimenter who is blind to the linguistic condition. To guard against cueing, the caregiver cannot see or hear the stimuli.

During the experiment, the child is first familiarized to the scenes, viewing them one at a time. Next, the two videos are presented simultaneously with a neutral linguistic stimulus (*"What do you see?"*). In the analysis phase, the experimenter can use the measurements from this trial to establish whether or not the child had a bias to look at one video more that the other in the absence of linguistic information to guide him. During the actual experimental trials, the child hears the (recorded) linguistic stimulus and then is shown both videos. Typically, four to six cycles of test trials are completed with each child, each testing a different token of the structure of interest.

There are several considerations in using this technique. Obviously, more time and money must be invested in setting up a laboratory, creating stimuli, and analyzing results than is the case for the previously discussed methods. Another limitation is that the method can only be used in group designs with infants and toddlers; it has not yet been shown to be statistically reliable in the study of individual performance. Bates (1993) argued that due to the limited number of trials that can be completed with these young children, and given binomial probabilities, performance must be perfect to reach significance (in this case, longer looking times to the correct video on six out of six trials). Although effects are significant at the group level, individual children do not perform this consistently in the task; children's bias to look at the target is at 66% on average (four out of six trials).

In part because of the potential of this technique to help identify early symptoms of language disorders, there is great interest in improving reliability at the individual level. Current efforts in this direction include increasing the number of trials that can be completed by testing a child in multiple sessions, finding ways to design stimuli that will hold children's attention across more trials, and finding measures that are more informative than total looking time (e.g., Schafer & Plunkett, 1998, have used longest look to target in an ILPL study of novel word learning).

One reason to be optimistic about the value of the IPLP for studying language comprehension at the individual level comes from a recent study using the head-turn preference procedure (another method of testing sensitivity to linguistic stimuli in infants). Newman, Ratner, Jusczyk, Jusczyk, and Dow (2006) conducted a retrospective study of children who had participated as infants in language perception studies (for a prospective study, see also Kuhl, Conboy, Padden, Nelson, & Pruitt, 2005). They found that children who had shown the pattern of response indicating that they could segment running speech as infants had a larger expressive vocabulary at 24 months and scored higher at around 4½ years of age on measures of vocabulary and syntax than did children who had failed to make the discrimination as infants. Although the method used by Newman et al. differs from the IPLP, it is subject to the same kinds of problems that lead to variable data in other infant behavioral studies; still, they were able to find relationships between early and later performance, suggesting that what is found at the individual level in infant studies truly reflects ability.

Because the IPLP is designed to minimize task demands for subjects, it could be useful in testing impaired populations. At this point, it is known to be reliable and informative for children 3 years old and younger; for syndromes that allow very early identification, it should be possible to use this method to test receptive language abilities in this age range. For example, it has been used in a study of 2- to 3-year-old children with autistic spectrum disorder (ASD; Swenson, Kelley, Fein, & Naigles, 2007). Like the comparison group of typically developing 21-month-old language matches, the ASD group showed comprehension in advance of production of subject–verb–object word order and a bias to interpret novel words as nouns. This suggests that, although delayed, the process of language acquisition in the ASD group had similarities to that of the typical group. This method could also have utility in testing comprehension in late talkers. Because not all late talkers go on to show language impairment, this technique might reveal how early comprehension ability contributes to outcome. However, to use the IPLP prospectively in this way would require data that are reliable at the individual level.

The ILPL has also been used to examine language development in young children with cochlear implants (Houston, Ying, Pisoni, & Kirk, 2001) and in children with otitis media with effusion (OME) (Petinou, Schwartz, Gravel, & Raphael, 2001). As this method does not require the child to follow verbal directions, it is ideal for assessing very early stages of language development in children with a history of hearing loss. For example, Houston et al. were able to assess the pre-word-learning skills of earlier (7–15-month-old) and later (16–25-month-old) implanted children. Petinou et al. examined the effects of OME in 26–28-month-olds on perception of /s/ and /z/ in phonological and morphophonological contexts.

Use of this method with older language-impaired children has been reported, although no research has yet been published (Finneran, Hollich, Seidl, & Leonard, 2005; Lum & Bavin, 1999). Both studies tested 4- to 6-year-old children on comprehension of sentences, comparing them to comprehension matches and age matches, respectively. Both found that typically developing matches looked longer at the target in conditions that were predicted to be easier (based on syntactic complexity) than they did in difficult conditions; children with SLI spent significantly less time looking at the target overall and showed no effect of condition. Further research may reveal whether these children's looking patterns reflect a lack of grammatical knowledge, some type of linguistic processing deficit, or a deficit in coordinating attentional resources.

Although the IPLP, as discussed here, does not provide information about on-line processing, it does have the potential to do so. For example, Fernald, Pinto, Swingley, Weinberg, and McRoberts (1998) examined 15-, 18-, and 24-month-olds' processing of individual words by analyzing the timing of their shift in eye gaze to a target picture relative to the presentation of the auditory stimulus. Where it is possible to time-lock shifts in looking to particular aspects of the verbal stimuli, this method may prove useful in testing comprehension on-line and with a wider age range.

ON-LINE METHODS

Lexical Priming

Lexical priming is an experimental paradigm that exploits a type of phenomenon, also called priming, wherein there is "an improvement in performance on a cognitive task, relative to an appropriate baseline, as a function of context or prior experience" (McNamara & Holbrook, 2003). In the case of lexical priming, accessing a word in memory is faster when a semantically or phonologically related word has recently been accessed, compared to when an unrelated word has been accessed. For example, when presented with a series of words, adults will respond faster to a target word like *nurse* when it has been preceded by *doctor* (semantic prime) or *purse* (phonological prime) than when it has been preceded by *table* (unrelated). Although the lexical priming task does not test comprehension of word meaning, it allows the experimenter to probe receptive processing of known words (i.e., retrieval) and to make inferences about the nature of the representations and how the stored meanings of words are organized.

Lexical priming effects are commonly described within a spreading activation model. In this model, words or concepts are represented by nodes that are organized according to relatedness. When a word is accessed, the activation level of its node is raised; this activation then spreads to neighboring (related) words. When one of these related words subsequently must be accessed, as in the priming task, its retrieval is facilitated by the residual activation.

In a lexical priming task with adults, either both primes and targets are presented visually, as written words (intramodal priming), or the prime word is presented auditorily and a written word is used to elicit the target (cross-modal priming). Many lexical priming studies with school-aged children also use written words as primes and targets, but these are typically concerned with the development of reading skills. Studies concerned with language processing in younger children use pictures instead of words as the visual stimuli in intramodal and cross-modal priming. In order to measure the speed of lexical access of the target, the child can simply name the target picture or make a lexical decision. The latter is the more difficult task, requiring the child to make a categorical decision about some property of the picture stimulus (e.g., Is it alive or not alive?). Older children, like adults, may make a decision about the status of a spoken or written word (i.e., Is it a word in English or not?). Examples of studies using this method with children are given below.

Nation and Snowling (1999) used lexical priming to study the semantic representations of words in children who show poor comprehension both in reading and in listening. Prime and target words were presented auditorily and the children (mean age 10.7 years) performed a lexical decision task. In a variation on the normal procedure, children made a lexical decision to all words—primes and targets—rather than just targets. Although this may have reduced the magnitude of the priming effect, it was meant to ensure that children attended to all of the prime words. They manipulated the type of semantic relation between prime–target pairs (category-related vs. functionally related) as well as whether the pairs were associated or not. For example, *brother–sister* and *cow–goat* both share a superordinate category, but only the first pair is also associated. Similarly, *beach–sand* and *circus–lion* are functionally related, but only the first pair is associated. Priming effects were found for both groups in all conditions with one exception: the poor comprehenders did not show priming in the nonassociated category-related pairs (*cow–goat*). Functionally related pairs and highly associated category coordinates co-occur in the real world, while the organization of semantic memory around category relations is known to be later developing, requiring the abstraction of semantic properties. This study suggests that poor comprehenders are delayed relative to age matches in their development of the more abstract semantic network.

McGregor and Windsor (1996) used a naming task in a priming study of preschoolers with word-finding deficits. Rather than measuring latency to name, they examined accuracy and error patterns. They found that the disordered group benefited from primes, but they benefited less than the typical age-matched group did. Based on models of the adult lexicon, they considered as explanations the possibility that the links among lexical entries were deficient or that the lexical entries themselves were deficient in terms of the richness of semantic detail that was stored.

The lexical priming studies reviewed here were all intramodal. However, cross-modal priming has also been used with adults to investigate the nature of lexical processing. In cross-modal studies, the priming stimulus is auditory, and the target is a written word. For example, Sonnenstuhl, Eisenbeiss, and Clahsen (1999) investigated the processing of morphologically complex words in German, asking whether regularly inflected words are analyzed into their component parts or, like irregulars, are stored whole. Subjects heard a regularly (e.g., geöffnet, *opened*) or irregularly (geschlafen, *slept*) inflected verb participle as prime and saw a morphologically related, written word (öffne, *open* and schlafe, *sleep*) as the target. Response times to targets differed such that the regulars produced more priming than irregulars. The authors argue that this is because the regular form is decomposed during processing, priming the lexical material common to the inflected form and its related form.

Another variation on this task that has been used extensively with adults is cross-modal lexical priming in the context of a sentence rather than in the context of single preceding word. Adults sit in front of a computer monitor, listening to an ongoing sentence. At the critical point, a word appears on the screen to which they respond with a lexical decision. Latency to respond to the target word indicates how accessible the concept represented by that word is at that particular point in the sentence. This technique has been used to ask questions about how contextual and lexical information interact on-line. For example, can sentence context determine in advance which meaning of an ambiguous word is accessed when it is encountered? Or does lexical access happen independently, with both meanings of the word accessed immediately and one disposed of at a later point? (For a summary of this research, see Simpson, 1994.)

Although cross-modal lexical priming has not been used with children to ask these particular kinds of questions, it has been used, in adapted form, to study the on-line comprehension of referentially dependent elements such as pronouns, reflexives, and traces of movement. In a study with adults, for example, the subject would hear the sentence in (2); immediately after *him* the word *skier* or *doctor* would appear as a visual target for lexical decision.

(2) The skier_i said that   the doctor for the team would blame
    antecedent   *nonantecedent*
    him_i *****SKIER***** for the recent injury.
    pronoun word prime

If adults use their syntactic knowledge to interpret the pronoun, they would refer back to *skier* upon hearing the pronoun, but not *doctor* (although *doctor* was more recently heard). The finding that *skier* is primed, but *doctor* is not, is argued to result from the listener's automatic activation of the antecedent at the pronoun as part of on-line interpretation. In addition, while priming for *skier* occurs immediately after the pronoun, priming does not occur when *skier* is probed at an earlier point in the sentence. This effect has been found for adults for many types of referential dependencies. In the next section, extensions of the use of this the paradigm to children's comprehension are reviewed.

Cross-Modal Picture Priming

The cross-modal lexical priming paradigm described above has been adapted to explore on-line comprehension in children. In cross-modal picture priming (CMPP) studies, children listen to sentences for comprehension (i.e., they are required to answer comprehension questions periodically). During the sentence, a picture target is presented on a screen for which the child must make a categorical decision (e.g., Is it or is it not alive? Is it edible or not edible?), pressing a response button as fast as possible. The secondary task does not depend on reading skills or the ability to make a metalinguistic decision; consequently, it has proven successful in experiments with typically developing children as young as 4 years old (Love, 2007; McKee, Nicol, & McDaniel, 1993; Roberts, Marinis, Felser, & Clahsen, 2007; Swinney & Prather, 1989).

In the McKee et al. study, processing of pronouns and reflexives was investigated in children between ages 4;1 and 6;4. This study sought to determine if children, like adults, use their knowledge of grammar on-line to access potential antecedents in the sentence. Specifically, does the reflexive *himself* in (3) immediately trigger activation of its antecedent *leopard*?

(3) The alligator knows that   the leopard with green eyes is patting
                             antecedent
    himself   *****leopard***** on the head with a soft pillow.
    reflexive   *picture prime*

According to the logic of the experiment, in order to interpret the reflexive, its antecedent (*leopard*) must be accessed. Reaccessing *leopard* at *himself* heightens the activation of *leopard*. If children do access antecedents on-line, they should show priming effects to the target picture (*leopard*) immediately following *himself*. Like adult controls in the study, the children responded faster to the picture prime *leopard* in the reflexive condition than in a pronoun or control condition—for example, where *himself* in (3) is replaced with *him* or *the nurse* for which leopard is not the antecedent. This shows that they did apply their grammatical knowledge immediately to interpret the reflexive.

Two recently reported studies used CMPP in studies of language-impaired children. Girbau and Schwartz (2005) tested Spanish-speaking children with SLI (8- to 11 years old) and age-matched peers in a paradigm similar to that of McKee et al. In a sentence with the same structure as that in (3), pronouns instead of reflexives were probed. Again, only one of the two possible antecedents was grammatical (the first subject noun). Typically developing children showed more priming after the pronoun for a picture of this noun than for a picture of the nonantecedent or a control. Children with SLI showed priming for both the antecedent and nonantecedent nouns in the sentence. The authors speculated that children with SLI may resolve the interpretation of the pronoun at a point later in the sentence than did the typical children or that an inability to inhibit irrelevant information hurt performance.

Marinis and van der Lely (2007) investigated the processing of wh-questions in 10- to 17-year-olds with a severe and persistent form of SLI. In this study, children heard a statement followed by a wh-question (4). A picture prime could appear at one of three positions during the question. If children, like adults, use syntactic structure to interpret the question, priming for the referent of *who* (i.e., *the rabbit*) is expected only at point [3] (at the object of the preposition), because this is the syntactic location at which *who* can be interpreted. Typically developing age and comprehension matches, like adults in other studies, showed activation for the prime *rabbit* at point [3]. Children with SLI showed priming only at point [1], suggesting that they use lexical-thematic rather than syntactic information to interpret these questions.

(4) Balloo gives a long carrot to the rabbit$_i$.
   Who$_i$ did Balloo give the long carrot to t$_i$ at the farm?
   $\qquad\qquad\uparrow\qquad\quad\uparrow\qquad\qquad\uparrow$
   $\qquad\qquad$[1]$\qquad\;\;$[2]$\qquad\quad\;$[3]

Although it has been used with children as young as 4, this task is complex, requiring children to do two tasks at the same time—comprehend the sentence and make a timed judgment to the picture prime. For this reason, McKee et al. found a lot of variability in reaction times. Preschoolers with language impairment probably could not do this task. McKee et al.'s study tried to offset these risks with extensive piloting, extensive training of the child subjects, careful selection of stimuli, and a relatively large number of trials.

Word Monitoring

The word-monitoring task was first used to test on-line comprehension processes in children by Tyler and Marslen-Wilson (1981). More recently, it has been used extensively by Montgomery and colleagues to study language processing in children with SLI (Montgomery, 2000; Montgomery, Scudder, & Moore, 1990; Stark & Montgomery, 1995). As in the CMPP task, children are required to listen to a sentence for comprehension and perform a secondary task. Before they hear the sentence, they are given a target word and instructed that when they hear it in the sentence, they must respond as quickly as possible by pressing a button. The speed of response to the target reflects the ease with which it could be processed; if it follows some sort of violation (e.g., phonological, morphological), response time is longer. The degree to which response is slowed relative to control conditions indicates whether the violation was noticed and to what extent the correct information was "necessary for the listener to develop the appropriate representation" of the unfolding sentence (Tyler, 1992, p. 6).

A study by Montgomery and Leonard (1998) illustrates the use of this method. They compared sensitivity to grammatical morphemes of low (third singular -*s*, past tense -*ed*) and high (progressive -*ing*) phonetic substance in a group of children with SLI (mean age 8;6), age matches, and younger comprehension matches (mean age 6;8). The children monitored sentences for familiar nouns; the position of the target noun was systematically varied so as to prevent subjects from predicting when it would appear. Preceding the target nouns—italicized in (5)—were verbs that either included or incorrectly omitted the grammatical inflection of interest. The typically developing groups showed sensitivity to all morphemes by responding more slowly after incorrect than after correct forms. The children with SLI showed this pattern only for *-ing*, indicating a lack of sensitivity to the morphemes of low phonetic substance.

(5) a. Everyday he races home and eat**s** *cookies* before dinner.
     b. She always gets up early and eat_ *breakfast* before she watches cartoons.

The cautions mentioned above for the CMPP task also apply to the word-monitoring task. In all cases, this task has been used with school-aged children with language impairment. The youngest typical children were 5 years old. More variable reaction times and an inability to consistently perform the secondary task make it difficult for preschool language-impaired children. In addition, it has been claimed that the task is an indirect measure of receptive processing for which the underlying source(s) of effects may be hard to determine. Trueswell, Sekerina, Hill, and Logrip (1999) used the findings in Tyler and Marslen-Wilson's (1981) study to illustrate this point. In that study, children showed increasingly longer RTs to a probe word in three kinds of sentences: a normal one, a syntactically sound but semantically anomalous one, and one that was both syntactically and semantically anomalous. Tyler and Marslen-Wilson interpreted this as supporting the view that children, like adults, use linguistic and nonlinguistic information to build a representation of meaning on-line; when these sources of information are not available, processing is disrupted. Trueswell et al. (1999) pointed out that rather than reflecting disruption of presumed syntactic and semantic processes, the effect could reflect children's (and adults') sensitivity to distributional information in language; as words become less predictable, RT to the word probe slows.

Self-Paced Listening

Two recent studies employed self-paced listening to study sentence comprehension in school-aged children with typical language development (Booth, MacWhinney, & Harasaki, 2000; Felser, Marinis, & Clahsen, 2003). In a self-paced listening task, sentences are partitioned into "windows" containing a whole phrase or an individual word. Subjects listen to these sentences through headphones, advancing the audio region by region by pressing a computer key. The time spent listening to each region before advancing is recorded by the computer. The sentence stimuli are designed so that a critical region can be compared across sentence conditions; relative slowing in a region in a given condition is interpreted as processing difficulty. Comprehension questions are presented after all experimental sentences.

Both Felser et al. and Booth et al. were interested in testing children's processing of relative clauses. Felser et al. tested sentences like that in (6), evaluating 6- to 7½-year-old children's preferences for interpreting the relative clause as a modifier of *nurse* vs. *pupil*. By manipulating agreement on the verb, they could indicate which of the nouns was modified by the relative clause (in this case, *the nurse*) and then measure listening times to the region containing the agreeing verb. For example, if children use a general strategy of associating the relative clause to the first noun (*nurse*), the *who were* continuation should be slower than the *who was* continuation. In addition to analysis of listening times to critical regions, they assessed accuracy of answers to comprehension questions (e.g., *who was feeling tired?*) as well as the relationship between memory span and interpretation preferences.

6.   The doctor recognized the nurse of the pupils *who was feeling very tired.*

In this, as in other on-line comprehension methods, trials are not included in the analysis if the comprehension question is not answered correctly. Given complex sentences like those tested here, this can mean exclusion of many trials. For children whose overall response accuracy is low, it is hard to know whether they really comprehend the remaining sentences. This is an issue that these authors address and one that should be kept in mind in attempting to use it with language-impaired children.

Monitoring Eye Movements

The development of new technology has opened the door in recent years to the use of eye movements as a measure of on-line comprehension in children. A miniaturized eye-tracking system is attached to a visor and worn by children while they view pictures, a video screen, or an array of objects and respond to spoken instructions. This newer equipment allows for children's eye movements to be tracked without requiring them to sit still. Using this technique with adults, it has been shown that eye movements are tightly time-locked to the speech input—that is, adults look immediately to objects as they are mentioned (Tanenhaus, Spivey-Knowlton, Eberhard, & Sedivy, 1995). Several studies have now reported on aspects of children's comprehension including the use of context to resolve syntactic ambiguity (Trueswell et al., 1999), the resolution of pronoun reference (Sekerina, Stromswold, & Hestvik, 2004), and the use of verb-specific information in sentence comprehension (Nation, Marshall, & Altmann, 2003).

The first published study of children's comprehension using the head-mounted eye-tracker was reported by Trueswell et al. (1999). Figure 22.2 illustrates the equipment and method used in the study. Two miniature video cameras and a dichroic mirror are attached to a visor, which is worn by the child. A beam of infrared light illuminates the eye, which is then recorded by an infrared-sensitive camera from the reflection on the inner side of the mirror; this provides information about the location of the pupil. The second camera records what the subject is looking at, as reflected on the outer side of the mirror. A computer analyzing the ongoing eye movement information plots the eye position and superimposes it on the image of the scene. The video record of the child's eye movements across the scene, along with the spoken stimuli, provide the raw data for analysis. Analysis is done on the proportion of fixations to particular objects in the scene as a function of the timing of the spoken stimulus.

Trueswell and his colleagues were interested in typically developing children's on-line sentence processing generally and, in particular, in their ability to use context to interpret ambiguous sentences. They constructed two kinds of scenes with toys and two ways of instructing the children (aged 4;8–5;10) to manipulate the toys. For example, there were two kinds of context including a frog sitting on a napkin, an empty napkin, an empty box, and either a frog or a horse sitting on nothing (see Figure 22.2). Subjects heard the sentence *"put the frog on the napkin in the box."* This instruction was temporarily ambiguous, as the prepositional phrase (PP) *on the napkin* could refer to a location of or destination for the frog. Eye movements during the words *on the napkin* were of interest. At this point, when there was no second frog in the context, both children and adults were more likely to look to the empty napkin, indicating a preference for the "destination" reading of the PP. However, when there was a second frog in the context, adults looked at the two

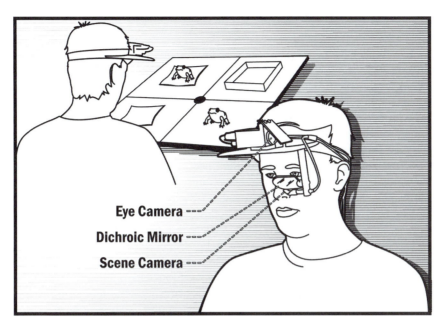

FIGURE 22.2   Illustration of the head-mounted eye-tracker and an example scene from the study by Trueswell et al. (1999).

frogs. The presence of the second frog overrode their preference to treat the PP as a destination; instead, they interpreted it as a location, providing information relevant for determining the reference of *the frog* (i.e., the one on the napkin, not the other one). Children looked at the empty napkin regardless of the presence of the second frog and often moved the frog from one napkin to the other and then into the box, indicating that they held fast to the destination meaning, never considering how meaning and context might interact. Thus, children's actions showed that they often chose the wrong reading of the PP, and their eye movements to the objects in the scene showed that they did not consult context in a way that would have helped. In contrast, adults' eye movements showed that they did use context on-line.

One study has tested a clinical population using eye movements. Nation et al. (2003) examined the spoken-language-processing abilities of children whose reading comprehension was poor (and who also had significantly weaker spoken language abilities). Although they found no differences between groups in their eye movements in response to the language manipulation, the authors reported general differences in the eye movements of the group with poor reading and language skills. They made a greater number of movements to the target in all conditions than did the skilled group, and these were of shorter duration. Nation et al. suggested two possible explanations for the difference. Given that the less skilled comprehenders also had weaker verbal memory skills, it is possible that the more frequent eye movements reflected an attempt by these children to refresh memory traces. A second possibility is that this group was less able to suppress irrelevant information, leading to more eye movements to the distractor pictures. This explanation is consistent with the children's poorer performance on an attention measure. Although more needs to be known about the relationship between eye movements and coordination of attention and memory in children, this method clearly holds promise as a method for studying language processing in language-impaired populations.

Neuroimaging Methods

In addition to the behavioral methods discussed in the preceding sections, there is increasing interest in the use of electrophysiological (EEG and MEG) and hemodynamic (fMRI and PET) methods to study language organization and processing in children in typical and atypical populations. These methods are discussed in depth in chapter 24 of this volume (Shafer & Maxfield) but are described briefly here in the context of testing comprehension of words and sentences.

Functional magnetic resonance imaging (fMRI) and positron emission tomography (PET) track local changes in blood flow in the brain in response to neural activity. As such, these are particularly useful in localizing different aspects of language processing. Electroencephalography (EEG) and magnetoencephalography (MEG) track changes in voltage and magnetic fields (respectively) associated with neural activity. When the EEG is averaged over many related trials, a waveform that is time-locked to stimulus presentation emerges; this measure is called the event-related potential (ERP). Determining the source of measurements taken at the scalp is not straightforward, because the EEG can be affected by intervening tissue and bone; thus ERP provides tentative information about localization and lateralization of language function. However, the temporal resolution of the ERP is excellent, providing timing information in milliseconds. Because MEG is not affected by intervening structure to the same degree as EEG is, it provides better spatial resolution, but it is still not as good as that of fMRI or PET. Of the two electrophysiological measures, EEG has proven to be a better match for use with children than MEG, primarily for technical reasons (for discussion, see Phillips, 2005). The focus here is thus on the use of ERPs to study language comprehension in children.

As described in the introduction to this chapter, comprehension is fast, automatic, incremental, and involves a multileveled analysis of the input. The ERP waveform varies in response to stimuli in polarity, latency, amplitude, and distribution over the scalp, providing a rich and sensitive measure that is highly suitable to investigating the processes that underlie language comprehension. Because of the high temporal resolution, ERPs can register very fast changes in neural response. Because ERPs can be recorded during passive listening, the brain's automatic response to language can be observed without the demands of an explicit task, avoiding some of the problems of behavioral methods and making it attractive for testing children and impaired populations.

Research using ERPs with adults has established signature waveforms that are associated with different aspects of language processing, including the N400 and the P600. The N400 is a negative voltage shift that reaches its peak amplitude at about 400 ms poststimulus and is believed to index semantic processing. It was first observed in response to a semantically incongruous continuation of a sentence (e.g., *He spread the warm bread with* **socks**), but its amplitude and distribution can be modulated by priming and degree of incongruity (for review, see Coch, Maron, Wolf, & Holcomb, 2002). Thus, "its amplitude reflects the effort for integrating a potentially meaningful stimulus into the current semantic context" (Friedrich & Friederici, 2006). Studies with normally developing children have shown an adult-like N400 response to incongruity in sentence contexts in children ranging in age from 5 to 15 with either latency (Hahne, Eckstein, & Friederici, 2004) or both amplitude and latency (Holcomb, Coffey, & Neville, 1992) decreasing with age. Studies have also tested single-word comprehension in children as young as 14 months old (Friedrich & Friederici, 2005) by presenting pictures of known words along with matching or mismatching spoken words. The ERP beginning at 400 ms was more negative for the nonmatching than matching word; on average, the difference became significant later and lasted longer than that of the adult comparison group, suggesting slower lexical—semantic processes in children.

The P600 is a positive voltage shift that reaches its peak latency at around 600 ms poststimulus and is believed to index later-stage syntactic processing. Like the N400, the P600 has primarily been demonstrated in response to anomaly, including ungrammaticality (e.g., *The spoiled child are throwing the toy on the ground*) and unexpected continuations (e.g., *The stockbroker persuaded **to** sell the stock called his lawyer* is less expected than *persuaded **him** to sell . . .*). Ongoing work is attempting to specify more precisely what this component reflects. Another marker of syntactic anomaly, the early left anterior negativity (ELAN), has been associated with the initial stages of processing a syntactic structure. Studies have sought to establish whether children show the same patterns and whether these change across time. Friederici and Hahne (2001) tested 7- to 8-year-olds and 6- to 13-year-olds (Hahne et al., 2004) by having them listen and make grammaticality judgments to German sentences that were correct or that included a semantic or syntactic violation. While adult controls showed a biphasic ERP pattern with an ELAN followed by a P600, only the oldest children (13-year-olds) showed the same. The P600 peaked later and lasted longer in the youngest children; latency decreased with age. The ELAN was not found in 6-year-olds and was not identifiably adult-like in 7- to 10-year-olds. Recent work has investigated the ELAN/P600 pattern in children across the 2–4 age range (Oberecker & Friederici, 2006; Oberecker, Friedrich, & Friederici, 2005; Silva-Pereyra, Klarman, Jo-Fu, & Kuhl, 2005; Silva-Pereyra, Rivera-Gaxiola, & Kuhl, 2005). Clearly, the electrophysiological characteristics of processing at this age differ from older children and adults; more research is needed to establish how the profile changes over time and whether there is a developmental relationship between early and later ERP profiles.

To date, very little work has been published on the use of ERPs to study higher-level receptive processing in children with language disorders (see chapter 7 by Tropper & Schwartz). The work that does exist highlights the kinds of questions that can be addressed with this method. First, Neville, Coffey, Holcomb, and Tallal (1993) compared 8- to 10-year-old typical and language-disordered children, addressing the question of whether neurophysiological differences underlie the language differences in the two groups. They measured ERPs to open and closed class words and to semantically anomalous and congruent sentence-final words. Sentences were presented visually, one word at a time. Whereas typical children and adults show a larger N400 over the left hemisphere for closed class words, a subset of the SLI children who had particularly poor grammatical skills showed a symmetrical response. Also, the N400 to semantic anomaly was larger and significantly later in the SLI group. Because the children were also poor readers, the increased difficulty in lexical integration that was indexed by the larger N400 may be partially due to reading ability. Recent unpublished studies have examined differences in the N400 to semantic anomaly in sentence contexts and in the P600 to syntactic errors (Betz & Rice, 2005; van der Lely & Fonteneau, 2006; Weber-Fox et al., 2005).

The method of measuring ERPs during comprehension can also be used to look for early neural precursors of language impairment. Friedrich and Friederici (2006) did a retrospective study in which children who had participated in a lexical processing study at 19 months (described above) were given a language test at 30 months. On the basis of their expressive language scores, they were assigned to control and at risk groups. The control group, but not the at-risk group, showed the N400 to nonmatching words at 19 months, indicating that delays in semantic processing existed a year before expressive delays were detected.

ERPs will no doubt contribute greatly to the understanding of receptive processing in language-disordered children. However, certain obstacles to this research must be overcome, as detailed by Phillips (2005). First, there is a need for more basic research with unimpaired children in order to reliably establish what is normal in terms of ERP profiles. Second, there is a need for detailed models of the temporal characteristics of processing in children with language disorders from which testable hypotheses can be derived; without these, it is difficult to interpret the large amount of detailed data generated by the method. Third, better signal-to-noise ratios are needed. In order to get a reliable ERP, many trials must be completed; especially when testing sentence-length stimuli, the time required to complete the experiment may be prohibitive for very young or disordered populations.

CONCLUSION

This chapter describes the methods available for testing general comprehension of words and sentences in children and for testing the nature of real-time receptive processing of known words and structures. The list encompasses basic tried-and-true techniques that are common in research and in clinical practice (e.g., picture selection and act-out) as well as very new and sophisticated techniques (e.g., eye-tracking and neuroimaging). It is of value to researchers and clinicians to be familiar with these methods and the findings generated by them. Taken together, results obtained using a range of different methods can provide complementary or converging evidence for a particular model of language development and disorders, or they may reveal discrepancies that point toward important new lines of questioning. In addition, knowing more about the strengths and weaknesses of each method allows one to better understand and assess the significance of reported findings.

Testing comprehension in children with atypical language can present challenges that either do not exist or that are at least more manageable when testing typically developing children. For example, there is increased likelihood with a disordered population that nonlinguistic deficits will interfere with linguistic performance. Teasing apart these factors appears to be the greatest challenge facing many studies of comprehension, in particular on-line behavioral studies. However, interest in language development in disordered populations motivates a great deal of interesting and innovative research; this research will pay dividends in terms of our progress in understanding language development, and cognitive development more generally.

ACKNOWLEDGMENTS

The writing of this chapter was supported by Research Grant R01 00458 from the National Institute on Deafness and Other Communication Disorders. Thanks also to George Hollich, Laurence Leonard, and Chris-Weber Fox for helpful discussion and comments.

REFERENCES

Akhtar, N., & Tomasello, M. (1997). Young children's productivity with word order and verb morphology. *Developmental Psychology*, 33, 952–965.

Bates, E. (1993). Comprehension and production in early language development. *Monographs of the Society for Research in Child Development*, 58(3–4), 222–242.

Betz, S., & Rice, M. (2005). *ERP measures of syntactic and semantic processing in children with and without SLI*. Paper presented at the 27th annual Boston University Conference on Language Development, Boston, MA.

Bishop, D. V. M. (1997). *Uncommon understanding: Development and disorders of language comprehension in children*. Hove, UK: Psychology Press.

Bishop, D. V. M. (2003). *Test for Reception of Grammar, Version 2*. London: Psychological Corporation.

Blockberger, S., & Johnston, J. (2003). Grammatical morphology acquisition by children with complex communication needs. *Augmentative and Alternative Communication, 19*(4), 207–221.

Booth, J., MacWhinney, B., & Harasaki, Y. (2000). Developmental differences in visual and auditory processing of complex sentences. *Child Development, 71*(4), 981–1003.

Carroll, J. B., Davies, P., & Richman, B. (1971). *The American Heritage word frequency book*. Boston, MA: Houghton Mifflin.

Carrow-Woolfolk, E. (1999). *Test for Auditory Comprehension of Grammar* (3rd ed.). Austin, TX: PRO-ED.

Coch, D., Maron, L., Wolf, M., & Holcomb, P. (2002). Word and picture processing in children: An event-related potential study. *Developmental Neuropsychology, 22*(1), 373–406.

Cocking, R., & McHale, S. (1981). A comparative study of the use of pictures and objects in assessing children's receptive and productive language. *Journal of Child Language, 8*, 1–13.

Crain, S., & McKee, C. (1985). The acquisition of structural restrictions on anaphora. In S. Berman, J.-W. Choe, & J. McDonough (Eds.), *Proceedings of NELS 16*. Amherst, MA: GLSA, University of Massachusetts.

Crain, S., & Thornton, R. (1998). *Investigations in universal grammar*. Cambridge, MA: MIT Press.

Cycowicz, Y., Friedman, D., & Rothstein, M. (1997). Picture naming by young children: Norms for name agreement, familiarity, and visual complexity. *Journal of Experimental Child Psychology, 65*, 171–237.

Deevy, P., & Leonard L. B. (2004). Comprehension of Wh-questions in children with specific language impairment. *Journal of Speech, Language, and Hearing Research, 47*(4), 802–815.

Dunn, L. M., & Dunn, L. M. (1997). *Peabody Picture Vocabulary Test* (3rd ed.). Circle Pines, MN: American Guidance Service.

Felser, C., Marinis, T., & Clahsen, H. (2003). Children's processing of ambiguous sentences: A study of relative clause attachment. *Language Acquisition, 11*(3), 127–163.

Fenson, L., Dale, P., Reznick, S., Thal, D., Bates, E., Hartung, J., et al. (1993). *MacArthur Communicative Development Inventories*. San Diego, CA: Singular Publishing Group.

Fernald, A., Pinto, J., Swingley, D., Weinberg, A., & McRoberts, G. (1998). Rapid gains in speed of verbal processing by infants in the 2nd year. *Psychological Science, 9*(3), 228–231.

Finneran, D., Hollich, G., Seidl, A., & Leonard, L. (2005). *Preferential looking tests of Wh-questions in children with specific language impairment*. Poster presented at the meeting of the Society for Research on Child Development, Atlanta, GA.

Friedrich, M., & Friederici, A. (2005). Lexical priming and semantic integration reflected in the ERP of 14-month-olds. *NeuroReport, 16*, 653–656.

Friedrich, M., & Friederici, A. (2006). Early N400 development and later language acquisition. *Psychophysiology, 43*, 1–12,

Friederici, A., & Hahne, A. (2001). Development patterns in brain activity reflecting semantic and syntactic processes. In J. Weissenborn & B. Hohle (Eds.), *Approaches to Bootstrapping* (Vol. 2, pp. 231–246). Philadelphia: John Benjamins.

Gerken, L. A., & McIntosh, B. (1993). Interplay of function morphemes and prosody in early language. *Developmental Psychology, 29*(3), 448–457.

Gertner, Y., Fisher, C., & Eisengart, J. (2006). Learning words and rules: Abstract knowledge of word order in early sentence comprehension. *Psychological Science, 17*(8), 684–691.

Girbau, D., & Schwartz, R. (2005). *Pronoun processing in Spanish-speaking children with SLI: Gender and number agreement*. Poster presented at the Symposium on Research on Child Language Disorders, Madison, WI.

Golinkoff, R. M., Hirsh-Pasek, K., Cauley, K. M., & Gordon, L. (1987). The eyes have it: Lexical and syntactic comprehension in a new paradigm. *Journal of Child Language, 14*, 23–45.

Goodluck, H. (1996). The act-out task. In D. McDaniel, C. McKee, & H. S. Cairns (Eds.), *Methods for assessing children's syntax* (pp. 147–162). Cambridge, MA: MIT Press.

Hahne, A., Eckstein, K., & Friederici, A. (2004). Brain signatures of syntactic and semantic processes during children's language development. *Journal of Cognitive Neuroscience, 17*(7), 1302–1318.

Hamburger, H., & Crain, S. (1982). Relative acquisition In S. Kuczaj (Ed.), *Language development: Syntax and semantics* (pp. 245–274). Hillsdale, NJ: Lawrence Erlbaum Associates.

Hirsh-Pasek, K., & Golinkoff, R. M. (1996). *The origins of grammar.* Cambridge, MA: MIT Press.

Hirsh-Pasek, K., Golinkoff, R. M., Hermon, G., & Kaufman, D. (1995). *Evidence from comprehension for the early knowledge of pronouns.* Paper presented at the 26th Annual Child Language Research Forum, Stanford, CA.

Holcomb, P., Coffey, S., & Neville, H. (1992). The effects of context on visual and auditory sentence processing: A developmental analysis using event-related brain potentials. *Developmental Neuropsychology, 8*, 203–241.

Hollich, G., Hirsh-Pasek, K., Golinkoff, R., Brand, R., Brown, E., Chung, H. L., et al. (2000). Breaking the language barrier: An emergentist coalition model for the origins of word learning. *Monographs of the Society for Research in Child Development, 65*(3).

Houston, D., Ying, E., Pisoni, D., Kirk, K. (2001). Development of pre-word-learning skills in infants with cochlear implants. *Volta Review, 103*(4), 303–326.

Kuhl, P., Conboy, B., Padden, D., Nelson, T., & Pruitt, J. (2005). Early speech perception and later language development: Implications for the "Critical Period." *Language Learning and Development, 1*(3&4), 237–264.

Leonard, L. (1998). *Children with specific language impairment.* Cambridge, MA: MIT Press.

Love, T. (2007). The processing of non-canonically ordered constituents in long distance dependencies by pre-school children: A real-time investigation. *Journal of Psycholinguistic Research, 36*(3), 191–206,

Lum, J., & Bavin, E. (1999). *Comprehension deficits in children with specific language impairment: Evidence for an inter-modal experiment.* Poster presented at the Symposium on Research on Child Language Disorders, Madison, WI.

Marinis, T., & van der Lely, H. (2007). On-line processing of wh-questions in children with G-SLI and typically developing children. *International Journal of Language and Communication Disorders, 42*, 557–582.

McGregor, K., & Windsor, J. (1996). Effects of priming on the naming accuracy of preschoolers with word-finding deficits. *Journal of Speech and Hearing Research, 39*, 1048–1058,

McKee, C. (1996). On-line methods. In D. McDaniel, C. McKee, & H. S. Cairns (Eds.), *Methods for assessing children's syntax.* Cambridge, MA: MIT Press.

McKee, C., Nicol, J., & McDaniel, D. (1993). Children's application of binding during sentence processing. *Language and Cognitive Processes, 8*(3), 265–290.

McNamara, T., & Holbrook, J. (2003). Semantic memory and priming. In I. B. Weiner (Series Ed.), A. F. Healy, & R. W. Proctor (Vol. Eds.), *Handbook of psychology: Vol. 4. Experimental psychology* (pp. 447–474). New York: Wiley.

Moe, A., Hopkins, C., & Rush, T. (1982). *The vocabulary of first-grade children.* Springfield, IL: Charles C. Thomas.

Montgomery, J. (2000). Relation of working memory to off-line and real-time sentence processing in children with specific language impairment. *Applied Psycholinguistics, 21*, 117–148.

Montgomery, J., & Leonard, L. (1998). Real-time inflectional processing by children with specific language impairment: Effects of phonetic substance *Journal of Speech, Language, and Hearing Research, 41*, 1432–1443.

Montgomery, J., Scudder, R., & Moore, C. (1990). Language-impaired children's real time comprehension of spoken language. *Applied Psycholinguistics, 11*, 273–290.

Naigles, L. (1990). Children use syntax to learn verb meanings. *Journal of Child Language, 17*, 357–374.

Naigles, L., Gleitman, H., & Gleitman, L. (1993). Children acquire word meaning components from syntactic evidence. In E. Dromi (Ed.), *Language and cognition: A developmental perspective.* Norwood, NJ: Ablex.

Nation, K., Marshall, C., & Altmann, G. (2003). Investigating individual differences in children's real-time sentence comprehension using language-mediated eye movements. *Journal of Experimental Child Psychology, 86,* 314–329.

Nation, K., & Snowling, M. (1999). Developmental differences in sensitivity to semantic relations among good and poor comprehenders: Evidence from semantic priming. *Cognition, 70*(1), B1–B13.

Neville, H., Coffey, S., Holcomb, P., & Tallal, P. (1993). The neurobiology of sensory and language processing in language-impaired children. *Journal of Cognitive Neuroscience, 5,* 235–253.

Newman, R., Ratner, N., Jusczyk, A., Jusczyk, P., & Dow, K. (2006). Infants' early ability to segment the conversational speech signal predicts later language development: A retrospective analysis. *Developmental Psychology, 42*(4), 643–655.

Oberecker, R., & Friederici, A. (2006). Syntactic event-related potential components of 24-month-olds' sentence comprehension. *NeuroReport, 17*(10), 1017–1021.

Oberecker, R., Friedrich, M., & Friederici, A. (2005). Neural correlates of syntactic processing in two-year-olds. *Journal of Cognitive Neuroscience, 17*(10), 1667–1678.

Oetting, J., Rice, M., & Swank, K. (1995). Quick incidental learning (QUIL) of words by school-age children with and without SLI. *Journal of Speech and Hearing Research, 38*(2), 434–445.

O'Grady, W. (1997). *Syntactic development.* Chicago: University of Chicago Press.

Petinou, K., Schwartz, R., Gravel, J., & Raphael, L. (2001). A preliminary account of phonological and morphological perception in young children with and without otitis media. *International Journal of Language and Communication Disorders, 36*(1), 21–42.

Phillips, C. (2005). Electrophysiology in the study of developmental language impairments: Prospects and challenges for a top-down approach. *Applied Linguistics, 26,* 79–96.

Rescorla, L. (1989). The Language Development Survey: A screening tool for delayed language in toddlers. *Journal of Speech and Hearing Disorders, 54*(4), 587–599.

Roberts, L., Marinis, T., Felser, C., & Clahsen, H. (2007). Antecedent priming at trace positions in children's sentence processing. *Journal of Psycholinguistic Research, 36*(2), 175–188.

Schafer, G., & Plunkett, K. (1998). Rapid word learning by fifteen-month-olds under tightly controlled conditions. *Child Development, 40*(2), 309–320.

Schulz, P., & Wittek, A. (2003). Opening doors and sweeping floors: What children with specific language impairment know about telic and atelic verbs. In B. Beachley, A. Brown, & F. Conlin (Eds.), *Proceedings of the 27th annual Boston University Conference on Language Development* (pp. 727–738). Somerville, MA: Cascadilla Press.

Sekerina, I., Stromswold, K., & Hestvik, A. (2004). How do adults and children process referentially ambiguous pronouns? *Journal of Child Language, 31*(1), 123–152.

Shorr, D., & Dale, P. (1984). Reflectivity bias in picture-pointing grammatical comprehension tasks. *Journal of Speech and Hearing Research, 27,* 549–556.

Silva-Pereyra, J., Klarman, L., Jo-Fu, L., & Kuhl, P. (2005). Sentence processing in 30-month-old children: An event-related potential study. *Cognitive Neuroscience and Neuropsychology, 16*(6), 645–648.

Silva-Pereyra, J., Rivera-Gaxiola, M., & Kuhl, P. (2005). An event-related potential study of sentence comprehension in preschoolers: Semantic and morphosyntactic processing. *Cognitive Brain Research, 23,* 247–258.

Simpson, G. (1994). Context and the processing of ambiguous words. In M. Gernsbacher (Ed.), *Handbook of psycholinguistics.* New York: Academic Press.

Snodgrass, J. G., & Vanderwart, M. (1980). A standardized set of 260 pictures: Norms for name agreement, image agreement, familiarity, and visual complexity. *Journal of Experimental Psychology: Human Learning and Memory, 6,* 174–215.

Sonnenstuhl, I., Eisenbeiss, S., & Clahsen, H. (1999). Morphological priming in the German mental lexicon. *Cognition, 72*(3), 203–236.

Stark, R., & Montgomery, J. (1995). Sentence processing in language-impaired children under conditions of filtering and time compression. *Applied Psycholinguistics, 16,* 137–154.

Swenson, L., Kelley, E., Fein, D., & Naigles, L. (2007). Processes of language acquisition in children with autism: Evidence from preferential looking. *Child Development, 78*(2), 542–557.

Swinney, D., & Prather, P. (1989). On the comprehension of lexical ambiguity by young children: Investigations into the development of mental modularity. In D. S. Gorfein (Ed.), *Resolving semantic ambiguity*. Berlin: Springer-Verlag.

Tanenhaus, M., Spivey-Knowlton, M., Eberhard, K., & Sedivy, J. (1995). Integration of visual and linguistic information in spoken language comprehension. *Science, 268*, 1632–1634.

Tavakolian, S. (1981). The conjoined-clause analysis of relative clauses. In S. Tavakolian (Ed.), *Language acquisition and linguistic theory* (pp. 167–187). Cambridge, MA: MIT Press.

Trueswell, J., Sekerina, I., Hill, N., & Logrip, L. (1999). The kindergarden-path effect: Studying on-line sentence processing in young children. *Cognition, 73*, 89–134.

Tyler, L. (1992). *Spoken language comprehension* Cambridge, MA: MIT Press.

Tyler, L., & Marslen-Wilson, W. (1981). Children's processing of spoken language. *Journal of Verbal Learning and Verbal Behavior, 20*(4), 400–416.

van der Lely, H. (1996). Specifically language impaired and normally developing children: Verbal passive vs. adjectival passive sentence interpretation. *Lingua, 98*(4), 243–272.

van der Lely, H., & Fonteneau, E. (2006, March). *ERP investigations in typically developing and language-impaired children reveal a domain-specific neural correlate for syntactic dependencies*. Paper presented at the On-line methods in children's language processing conference, CUNY Graduate Center, New York.

Velleman, S. (1988). The role of linguistic perception in later phonological development. *Applied Psycholinguistics, 9*(3), 221–236.

Weber-Fox, C., Spruill, J. E., Fick, W., Hampton, A., Cochran, E., Leonard, L., & Tomblin, B. (2005). *Linguistic and non-linguistic auditory processing in adolescents with specific language impairment (SLI): An ERP study*. Poster session presented at the annual meeting of the Cognitive Neuroscience Society, New York.

23

Research and Development in Child Language Intervention: A Five-Phase Model

MARC E. FEY and LIZBETH H. FINESTACK

A casual observer assigned to evaluate the history of intervention research in children's language disorders might well determine that the modus operandi has been "All researchers to themselves!" There clearly are pockets of investigations that reflect thematic, programmatic research targeting specific intervention methods and strategies across studies and even across laboratories (see especially studies on *milieu* approaches to early intervention, Hancock & Kaiser, 2006; Warren et al., 2006), but it is far more common to find strands of research that, if in any sense complete, still are left unreplicated, with key methodological, empirical, theoretical, and consequently, clinical issues inadequately addressed. Law, Garrett, and Nye's (2004) recent meta-analysis of randomized controlled trials (RCTs) evaluating speech and language interventions for children with primary speech and language disorders is an excellent illustration of this point. Although hundreds of published studies of language intervention are available, these investigators found only 25 RCTs that met their criteria for inclusion. Most importantly, only 13 of these, carried out over a 25-year period, dealt with issues similar enough to allow for combination into some form of subanalysis (e.g., expressive phonology, expressive vocabulary, receptive syntax).

There are many reasons for this apparent lack of direction found in studies over the past 30–40 years in this area. Some of the leading candidates include (1) the complex, abstract nature of language, yielding a huge number of possible intervention goals that vary greatly in their breadth and surface-level accessibility; (2) the multidimensionality and sheer complexity of the interventions, which make it difficult and costly to ensure treatment fidelity, to establish and sustain appropriate controls, and to apply crucial methodological rigor; (3) the lack of agreement regarding appropriate outcome measures; (4) until the last 15 years or so, the lack of funding sources capable of supporting major efforts to develop and evaluate language intervention approaches; and (5) the limited promise of economic return following successful completion of the evaluative process.

In our view, however, the single most important reason for the lack of clear streams of language intervention research documenting the effectiveness of intervention strategies is the failure of the discipline to adopt a systematic framework for evaluating existing interventions and developing treatment innovations. As Robey and Schultz (1998), Robey (2004), and Pring (2004) have noted, other clinical professions have adopted a four- or five-phase approach for examining the outcomes of clinical procedures. By and large, studies in earlier phases involve fewer participants and address many key issues other than intervention effectiveness. In and of themselves, they represent relatively low levels of evidence in support of a treatment. These earlier phases of research are essential, however, because they address key early intervention questions at relatively low cost. Each earlier phase serves as logical and empirical motivation for more time-consuming and costly research at subsequent phases. In most cases, studies at later phases are justified only when they have been given direction and support by research in earlier phases. New treatments cannot be approved and applied clinically unless they have passed through such a recognized system of development.

If such a model were firmly in place in the study of child language intervention, researchers would have a set of expectations for what must happen in the development of a new treatment; they would be guided, if not forced, to proceed systematically through each evaluative step. Thus, key methodological, empirical, theoretical, and clinical issues would be systematically and adequately addressed by intervention researchers. Moreover, investigators would be expected to publish their findings from each phase of their research program to publicly document the systematic development of their clinical innovations.

In this chapter on child language intervention research, we begin by defining some terms that are often misunderstood but are essential to our proposal for a phased system for developing and evaluating intervention approaches. Next, we present a model of the structure of language intervention approaches. The details of this framework are beyond the scope of this chapter and have been discussed elsewhere (McCauley & Fey, 2006). Nevertheless, the framework enables us to illustrate the complexity of language intervention, the potential for asking an enormous range of important intervention research questions, and many of the problems researchers have in addressing even a small fraction of these questions in a scientifically appropriate manner. Finally, we present our own vision of a five-phase system for developing language interventions with children, which is based loosely on systems used in other clinical professions (Piantadosi, 1997; Pring, 2004; Robey & Schultz, 1998). Our contention is that adoption of such a system is essential to the growth of language intervention science and to the development of an evidence base suitable for guiding clinicians in making crucial treatment decisions (Fey & Justice, 2007; Justice & Fey, 2004).

DEFINING SOME BASIC TERMS

Most health professionals have adopted a common set of terms that are essential in discussions of efforts to study the effects and values of clinical interventions. The meanings of these terms are highly specialized, however, and may be interpreted differently in broader intervention contexts. In this section, we present a small subset of these terms to add clarity to the rest of our presentation.

Efficacy and Effectiveness

In colloquial usage, efficacy and effectiveness may be considered to be synonyms. For example, The *American Heritage Dictionary* (2000) defines efficacy as "Power or capacity to produce a desired effect; effectiveness." In clinical research, however, there is an important distinction between these terms. Efficacy studies evaluate hypothesized causal relationships between treatments and outcomes under ideal, laboratory conditions. Thus, they place a premium on *internal* validity and replicability. The principle purpose of any efficacy study is to provide a relatively bias- and subjectivity-free demonstration of a causal relationship between an intervention and an outcome. In contrast, effectiveness studies evaluate the effects of efficacious treatments across broader, more typical populations and under broader, more typical clinical conditions. Thus, for studies of effectiveness, there is a premium on *external* validity and generalizability to real-world clinical applications.

Because of the fundamental differences between efficacy and effectiveness, studies of effectiveness logically follow studies of efficacy in the development of a treatment. That is, studies of a treatment in real-world contexts should be carried out only when it has already been shown to be causally related to desirable outcomes in efficacy experiments (Pring, 2004; Robey, 2004; Robey & Schultz, 1998).

Clinical Trials

The term *clinical trials* is used in different ways by different investigators. For example, Robey (2004) and others apply the term only to randomized experimental trials that compare the outcomes of a target treatment with a comparison treatment and/or no-treatment controls. The website on clinical trials provided by the US National Institutes of Health, the National Library of Medicine, and others (http://www.clinicaltrials.gov/ct2/info/glossary) takes a more general approach, however: "A clinical trial is a research study to answer specific questions about vaccines or new therapies or new ways of using known treatments. . . . Carefully conducted clinical trials are the fastest and safest way to find treatments that work in people" (National Institutes of Health, 2007). What all definitions have in common is that clinical trials are research investigations structured into ordered phases ultimately to determine the safety and effectiveness of clinical treatments in humans. In this chapter, we use the term *clinical trials* to refer to all studies in which the investigator controls the administration of one or more variables with the expressed intent of improving language performance and/or language-learning ability among children with language disorders. By this definition, even some pre-efficacy studies may be considered clinical trials.

Developmental Phases of Clinical Trials

Clinical trials are usually arranged into four or five phases. In drug testing, four phases, labeled simply I, II, III, and IV, are generally acknowledged (National Institutes of Health, 2007; Piantadosi, 1997). In other health and applied health disciplines (e.g., oncology, studies of prevention, surgical trials, studies of medical devices), a fifth phase or subphase has been adopted (Piantadosi, 1997; Robey, 2004; Robey & Schultz, 1998). The goals and types of studies representing each phase differ somewhat across these systems. In each case, however, there is an acknowledged pattern of development, with early studies addressing questions and issues that are fundamental to the later developmental phases.

An examination of the phases associated with drug studies can provide a better sense of this developmental process. In many *early development*—or Phase I—studies, specialized research designs are implemented to study appropriate doses of the treatment and, more generally, to track the body's reaction (e.g., cell absorption, metabolism) to a new drug or vaccine. *Middle development*—or Phase II—studies typically involve efforts to evaluate the side effects of fixed doses presumed to be tolerable based on the findings of early development studies. They also evaluate the feasibility of administering the intervention and estimate its cost. More importantly, middle development studies provide the first real indications of the efficacy of an intervention. Evidence of efficacy at this phase is preliminary at best, however, because the limitations in numbers of participants and study design render these studies inadequate for determining cause–effect relationships between the treatment and the outcomes measured.

Comparative treatment efficacy studies (Piantadosi, 1997)—or Phase III studies—involve direct comparisons of outcomes associated with the target intervention and other treatments and/or no-treatment controls. Phase III studies typically are true experiments with randomized assignment of subjects and definitive outcome measures. They may involve hundreds or thousands of participants in multiple clinical sites and are fully powered to find even very small effects when such effects are deemed clinically important.

Late development—or Phase IV—studies usually are carried out after a new drug is taken to market. They often involve thousands of participants so that long-term side effects (e.g., increased incidence of heart attack or premature death) and benefits can be determined, and optimal applications can be identified.

From the outset, it seems clear that any plan for the phased development of language intervention approaches must differ in many ways from that for the study of drugs or vaccines. For example, although we believe that there *is* potential for language intervention to be harmful to children and their families, these risks are clearly different in magnitude and type from those of pharmacologic treatments. Thus, early development—or Phase I—studies must look different for language intervention development than for development of a new drug. Similarly, although there is a tremendous need for evaluations of the long-term benefits of language intervention, there is little need for the long-term surveillance for side effects and toxicity that often characterizes Phase IV studies (and often requires huge participant samples).

THE STRUCTURE OF LANGUAGE INTERVENTION

In this section, we present an intervention model that highlights the complexity of language intervention as well as the variables that may be systematically controlled or carefully studied by intervention researchers (see Figure 23.1). McCauley and Fey (2006, ch. 1) adapted this model from Fey (1986, 1990). In general, it reflects the types of factors that must be considered and decisions that must be made in any comprehensive language intervention program. The examples provided in the boxes for Intermediate and Specific Goals apply to the specific case of grammar facilitation. The available options within each component include, but are not limited to, those represented in the figure.

In planning a comprehensive language intervention, a practicing clinician needs to consider issues related to each component of the language intervention model, including: specific characteristics of the child; a hierarchically ordered set of goals designed to meet the child's needs; the intervention agent and context; treatment intensity, including frequency and length of sessions; procedures; goal attack strategies; activities; and outcome measures. In general, the goals reflect the content of the intervention and are selected on the basis of an evaluation of the child's language performance. The procedures represent the active ingredients of the intervention approach—that is, the mechanisms presumed to inform or teach children, thus leading them to new levels of knowledge and performance. The outcomes reflect the variables for measuring change in the child's performance and knowledge. All of the other components refer to options for delivery of the procedures to the child. Because procedures are of the greatest theoretical interest, child language researchers have often been most concerned with testing the efficacy of a procedure with limited variation in other treatment components. Ultimately, however, the effectiveness of an intervention will depend on the interactive effects of decisions made for *each* of the intervention components shown in Figure 23.1. Therefore, an assessment of the effectiveness of an intervention must include a phase during which the effects of options in other treatment components are carefully evaluated.

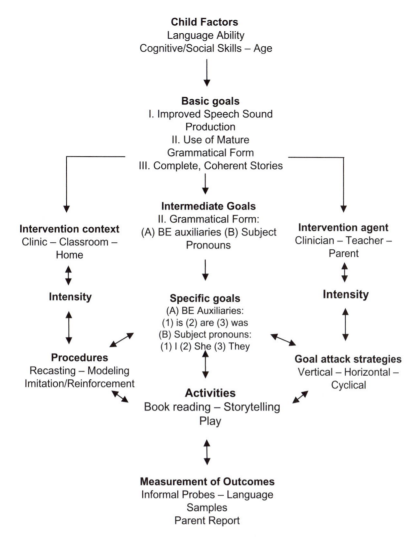

Child Factors
Language Ability
Cognitive/Social Skills – Age

Basic goals
I. Improved Speech Sound
Production
II. Use of Mature
Grammatical Form
III. Complete, Coherent Stories

Intermediate Goals
II. Grammatical Form:
(A) BE auxiliaries (B) Subject
Pronouns

Intervention context
Clinic – Classroom –
Home

Intervention agent
Clinician – Teacher –
Parent

Intensity

Intensity

Specific goals
(A) BE Auxiliaries:
(1) is (2) are (3) was
(B) Subject pronouns:
(1) I (2) She (3) They

Procedures
Recasting – Modeling
Imitation/Reinforcement

Goal attack strategies
Vertical – Horizontal –
Cyclical

Activities
Book reading – Storytelling
Play

Measurement of Outcomes
Informal Probes – Language
Samples
Parent Report

FIGURE 23.1   A framework for children's language intervention with examples from a program for a child with an impairment of expressive grammar. (Adapted from McCauley & Fey (2006). *Treatment of language disorders in children*. Baltimore: Paul H. Brookes, by permission.)

To understand how each of these variables contributes on its own and in combination with other variables to intervention success or failure, a plan is needed to study language intervention innovations from their pretrial beginnings to their implementation by practicing clinicians in typical clinical contexts working under typical clinical conditions. We present such a plan for development in the next section.

A FIVE-PHASE PLAN FOR THE STUDY OF LANGUAGE INTERVENTION EFFECTIVENESS

Figure 23.2 presents a schematic of our proposed five-phase sequence to evaluate intervention effectiveness in children's language disorders. Although there are research designs

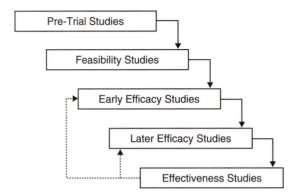

FIGURE 23.2   A five-phase plan for studying the effectiveness of language intervention.

that typify each phase, the crucial distinguishing characteristics are the research questions addressed by studies at each phase and the existing state of knowledge at the time of the study. It is possible, for example, for a study with a research design more characteristic of a feasibility study to serve the role of an effectiveness study. This could occur, however, only when the essential information on efficacy is already available to the investigator. Furthermore, it should be the case that studies at later efficacy and effectiveness phases generate new hypotheses that then are best examined in early and later efficacy trials.

To enhance user-friendliness, we have assigned descriptive labels rather than numbers to each phase. In the sections that follow, we describe the phases and provide examples of studies that exemplify the types of studies appropriate for each. All of our sample studies come from research focusing on the language intervention procedure of recasting. Although there are many different conceptualizations of recasts (Fey, Krulik, Loeb, & Proctor Williams, 1999), generally they are defined as adult responses that follow child utterances, maintain the child's basic meaning, and add grammatical (and sometimes semantic) information that may or may not correct an error in the child's production. For example, if the child says, "Daddy driving," while pushing a truck, an adult might respond with the recast, "Yeah, Daddy is driving." This recast corrects the child's utterance by filling in crucial grammatical detail and is often called an expansion. Other recasts may add semantic as well as grammatical information (e.g., *Daddy is driving a truck [to the store]*) or change the modality of the child's sentence (e.g., *Is daddy driving [a truck]?*). We chose to focus on studies investigating recasts mainly because there are many studies in this area that exemplify the qualities of each of our proposed intervention phases. However, we could have just as easily selected an alternative intervention procedure such as focused stimulation (Ellis Weismer & Robertson, 2006), milieu teaching (Hancock & Kaiser, 2006), or Fast ForWord (Agocs, Burns, DeLey, Miller, & Calhoun, 2006) or a line of research focusing on a particular population, such as children with Down syndrome, to illustrate the intervention phases.

Pretrial Studies

Clinical trials in medicine are virtually always preceded by a substantial period of bench research during which biological models are developed and then tested on animals. Because we are dealing with language, animal models for our interventions are generally unavailable. Still, the seeds of most intervention approaches have been sown in programs of basic research in which the investigator asks questions, such as:

- How can we best measure language growth?
- What relationships exist between the form, content, and use of language throughout development?
- What factors are associated with faster language development among children developing typically and those with language disorders?
- What distinguishes children with typical language from children with language disorders?

The designs of these studies are often observational or correlational. They may be experimental evaluations of language facilitation mechanisms, however, when they are applied to children developing typically. Such studies are not considered clinical trials because the investigator does not exert control over any intervention mechanisms that are hypothesized to affect development among children with language disorders. In fact, investigators in these studies may have no clinical interests at all at the time of the study. Nevertheless, these studies serve to generate hypotheses about clinical interventions, and it is likely that intervention researchers will continue to derive most of their best intervention ideas from the vast body of basic research on children's language development. We believe this connection with basic research is appropriate and important, so we acknowledge this as the first phase of intervention development.

Because pretrial studies are not clinical trials, their strengths as contributions to intervention science must be measured by the strength of the underlying theories or hypotheses they develop, and the implications they have for developing intervention procedures, identifying and structuring goals, and determining the intensities of intervention procedures likely to be needed to ensure efficacy. These studies also provide information on the reliability and validity of dependent variables that could ultimately serve as endpoints for clinical trials.

Nelson (1977) marks one of the earliest attempts to demonstrate quasi-experimentally the teaching potential of recasts of children's spontaneous utterances. The participants were twelve children with typical language and MLUs between 3 and 4 morphemes. The investigator assigned the children to treatment groups to ensure that three children in each group used no examples of what are described as complex verbs or questions and three other children lacked only certain types of these forms. The children then attended five 1-hour play sessions over a two-month period, during which the examiner recast child utterances with extremely high rates of complex question forms for one group and equally high rates of complex verb forms for the other group. All children in the group receiving complex verb recasts used those forms spontaneously at the end of the intervention period, but only one demonstrated use of complex questions. In contrast, all six children in the complex question intervention used complex questions in the final two sessions, whereas only one used a complex verb.

Despite its methodological weaknesses, many of which are explicitly acknowledged by the author, this study does demonstrate a relationship between very high recast rates on particular grammatical forms not attested in the children's grammars and the subsequent spontaneous use of those forms by children with typical language development. This study is a good example of an instance in which a theoretically driven attempt to account for variability in typical development could serve as the beginning of development of a clinical language intervention approach.

Nelson et al. (1984) used a correlational design to examine the potential effects of different types of recasts under naturalistic conditions on the grammatical development of children with typical language. Simple recasts were those that modified or corrected only a single constituent in the child's utterance. Complex recasts included adult responses that modified or corrected multiple constituents from the child's utterance. The investigators observed that the mothers' use of simple recasts at 22 months was significantly correlated with the children's measures of auxiliary use and utterance length 5 months later. In contrast, mothers' early use of complex recasts was negatively correlated with children's auxiliary use and utterance length at the later test point. These findings suggest that certain types of recasts may be more efficacious than others. This general possibility has been suggested in numerous other pretrial studies (Farrar, 1990; Fey et al., 1999; Saxton, 1997, 2000; Saxton, Kulcsar, Marshall, & Rupra, 1998) but generally has not been evaluated in clinical trials (cf. Fey & Loeb, 2002).

Feasibility Studies

Based on clinical experience and information from pretrial research, clinical investigators are in a position to develop hypotheses about language intervention strategies. Feasibility research includes the first (albeit nondefinitive) tests of such hypotheses. The principle purpose of these studies, though, has less to do with measuring treatment outcomes than with evaluating the clinical viability of an untested intervention component or package. The following questions are characteristic of feasibility studies.

- How frequently and over how long a period is intervention likely to be necessary to achieve a measurable effect?
- Do the children (and parents) enjoy and/or will they tolerate the approach and the intensity of treatment anticipated to be needed?
- Do the children stay engaged in the activities planned?
- Do the activities lend themselves to the frequent administration of intervention procedures?
- How much time is required to train intervention agents to administer the intervention?
- What outcome measures (or endpoints) are most useful clinically and/or most sensitive to the intervention?
- Do the hypothesized intervention mechanisms *appear* to have the predicted effects?

Based on the definition provided earlier, feasibility studies *are* clinical trials, but they are designed to be exploratory and preliminary with respect to intervention outcomes. They should serve primarily to determine whether and how more rigorous and costly studies should be done with children with language disorders. If experiments are conducted at this phase, they are likely to involve typical children in efforts to determine reasonable treatment intensities or to develop the types of activities that children might enjoy or at least tolerate as the procedures are implemented. Such studies are relatively inexpensive, because it is easier to recruit typical children than children with language disorders. Studies involving children with language disorders may be pre–post investigations of small groups or even case studies, typically involving more than a single subject (i.e., case series). Even if they do involve a control group or within-subject controls, the relatively small numbers of subjects included in feasibility studies limits their statistical power to detect meaningful intervention effects.

Feasibility studies will meet many researchers' definitions of pilot research, and many will suggest that this research should not be published. We believe, on the contrary, that even though these studies provide only very weak evidence of intervention efficacy, publication of feasibility research is pivotal to the development of a strong research base that is capable of supporting evidence-based practice in children's language disorders. There are several reasons for taking such a position. First, the information gleaned from feasibility studies is crucial for the development of more labor-intensive and expensive efficacy trials. Second, publication of this work will encourage early discussions across research laboratories regarding conceptual characteristics and possible improvements in the intervention, appropriate outcome measures, and research design. Third, if feasibility studies are viewed as potentially publishable, investigators will not have to wait possibly years before their work has any promise for publication. Therefore, it will be more reasonable for young investigators interested in moving through the academic ranks to think about developing lines of intervention research. Finally, researchers will be less likely to skip studies of feasibility only to jump prematurely to experimental tests of their intervention ideas. These efforts can be wasteful of time and money (e.g., Sorensen & Fey, 1992) and should be discouraged.

Clearly, not all reports of feasibility investigations are worthy of publication. Perhaps the most essential key to publication should be the strength of the theoretical or empirical motivation for the intervention approach. Producers of feasibility reports should be responsible for utilizing pretrial research to explain why their treatment might reasonably be expected to work. When they cannot, publication may not be warranted.

There are methodological features as well that should render reports of feasibility studies more adequate for publication. First, the intervention should be carefully described, and measures of treatment fidelity should be reported, to ensure that the intervention being tested actually was reliably delivered. Second, the reliability of outcome measures must be reported. Finally, even when the measured outcomes are highly positive, feasibility study reports should be free of efficacy claims. When they are, this substantiates the investigator's claim that the study was designed to assess feasibility rather than efficacy. Positive outcomes provide the motivation for the next level of testing, early efficacy.

Although many language intervention studies fit the general characteristics of the feasibility phase, the only study of which we are aware that was planned and reported as a test of feasibility is the investigation of Swanson, Fey, Mills, and Hood (2005). Although recasts were a part of the procedural complex in this study, they are far from the predominant procedure in this study, so we provide no further details on the study here.

A good example of a feasibility study in the literature on recasts that was not necessarily designed as such was reported by McLean and Vincent (1984). In this study, five 2- to 4-year-old children with developmental delay received expansions of target early word combinations (e.g., *mommy laugh; eat the cookie*) during play for 20 minutes, four times weekly, for four weeks. The children showed noteworthy gains during the play treatment sessions in their spontaneous use of targeted semantic relations after only one week. These improvements were maintained in only three of the five children, however, when they were reevaluated 3 to 8 weeks after the end of the intervention in a new context. Taken on their own, these results provide very limited evidence of efficacy of the expansion treatment. Because no controls were implemented, observed gains could have been the result of any number of uncontrolled variables, including measurement error. As an efficacy study, then, this report is weak. On the other hand, the results reported in this study provide compelling evidence that this relatively simple intervention *may be* efficacious, thus, clearing the way for additional tests on children with developmental disabilities. Just as importantly, McLean and Vincent found that they could train university students to use the expansion intervention in a preschool environment after a single 20-minute session. This is precisely the type of information needed to continue development of an intervention, and it should have motivated continued study by the investigators as well as by teams of investigators in other laboratories.

Early Efficacy Studies

The closest analog for early efficacy studies in medicine can be found in oncology at what is sometimes referred to as Phase IIb. Studies at this phase involve comparisons of treatments or of treatments and no-treatment controls using surrogate endpoints (Piantadosi, 1997). These comparative treatment designs may be either quasi-experimental, in which participants are assigned to treatment or no-treatment control groups based on convenience, or experimental, in which treatment (or goal) assignments are made at random. Regardless of the design used, early efficacy studies are intended to address the basic question, "Is there a cause–effect relationship between the treatment variable and the target outcome?"

Because they are the first studies capable of determining efficacy, a number of steps are taken to minimize the costs of early efficacy trials. These steps tend to increase the power of the studies, but they also minimize their generalizability. For example, the intervention typically focuses on a single or a small set of complementary intervention procedures and targets a single goal or a contrastive pair of goals (e.g., the auxiliaries *is* and *are* or the pronouns *he* and *him*) in a very limited context. Under these conditions, higher doses of the circumscribed treatment procedures can be directed toward the child's use of intervention targets, and the child's attention is not divided between multiple intervention goals. Surrogate endpoints are the rule in these studies rather than the exception. Examples of such endpoints include use of a target form in response to pictures, consistent imitation of sentences containing target forms, spontaneous use of target forms in the therapy context and/or with the clinician, and many other possibilities. The combined effects of these methods ensure that, if the intervention has effects, they will be manifested quickly, leaving little time for control participants or control behaviors (e.g., in within-subject trials) to show gains due to influences outside the intervention context. Reports of early efficacy studies can be strengthened by careful attention to (1) description of the treatment, (2) measurement of treatment fidelity, (3) reliability of outcome measures, and (4) internal validity.

As we have already indicated, many studies of language intervention fit into the category of early efficacy studies. This is especially true in the case of studies of the effects of sentence recasts. Here, we briefly summarize two such studies already in the literature to illustrate the category and to demonstrate its breadth.

Camarata and Nelson (1992) used a within-subjects experimental design to compare the outcomes associated with recasts with those associated with a didactic imitation-based treatment in four participants with specific language impairment (SLI). Each child was assigned one or two pairs of developmentally equivalent intermediate grammatical goals (e.g., wh-questions, relative clauses, auxiliary verbs). Then, the members of each pair were assigned randomly to be treated during play sessions using recasts or during didactic treatment sessions, using imitation and response feedback. Children were seen twice weekly in 30-minute sessions, half of which were devoted to recasts and half of which utilized the imitation treatment. Analysis of the results following 16 weeks of treatment indicated that the children made their first spontaneous use of targets earlier for goals treated using recasts than they did for goals treated using imitation. They also made more frequent spontaneous uses of their recast than their imitated target forms in interactions with the clinician. Despite the inclusion of only four subjects and a surrogate endpoint, the within-subject controls employed in this study demonstrated the efficacy of recasts, this time involving children with SLI.

Camarata, Nelson, and Camarata (1994) followed the Camarata and Nelson (1992) study with a much larger investigation, which included 21 children with SLI. Although a broader range of grammatical goals was included, this study had essentially the same design as the earlier study and yielded virtually identical results. More importantly, the study used the same surrogate endpoints, rather than adopting a measure such as frequency of use of targets in nontreatment contexts with an individual other than the clinician. For this reason, we regard this study as a high-quality early efficacy study that strengthens the case for the efficacy of recast interventions on children's grammatical performance.

An excellent final example of early efficacy studies involving sentence recasts that employs yet another experimental design was reported by Scherer and Olswang (1989). This study included five 4-year-old males with autism who had begun the process of combining words into two-word utterances but were not yet using semantic relations involving location (e.g., *kitty bed*), possession (e.g., *daddy hat*), or attribution (e.g., *funny girl*). In each session, the clinician presented the child with 10 objects or object groups. The clinician first manipulated an object to depict the target semantic relationship. If the child labeled the object, the clinician expanded the child's utterance to include the target relation. If the child failed to label the object, the clinician solicited a label and then expanded it to the target relation. If the child imitated the expansion, the clinician proceeded with relevant conversation. Otherwise the child was allowed to play with the objects before the clinician introduced another trial.

Each subject served as his own control in this study involving multiple baselines across behaviors. The results were very consistent and compelling. Without treatment, none of the children used the target semantic relations. Once treatment began, they began immediately to imitate the target semantic relations spontaneously. Then, as treatment continued, imitations decreased, and spontaneous use of target utterances increased. For each child, as a new relation was treated and intervention on the original goal was stopped, spontaneous performance on the previous target relation remained high and spontaneous use of the new target began slowly to increase. As further display of efficacy, three of the five children were observed during maintenance testing to produce novel examples of the target relations with words not introduced in treatment.

With the exception of the Camarata et al. (1994) study, each of these and other studies that we might have included as examples have small sample sizes, and, without exception, each utilizes outcome variables that are far from clinically definitive. In a phased plan for evaluating treatment efficacy, however, these types of studies have an important place. If studies of this type do not reveal signs of efficacy, investigators would need to make significant changes in the administration of the treatment (e.g., Yoder, Spruytenburg, Edwards, & Davies, 1995) or give it up altogether. Where effects are demonstrated, however, investigators are in an excellent position to pursue later efficacy studies and to seek funding to support them.

Later Efficacy Studies

Similar to early efficacy studies, later efficacy studies involve direct comparisons of the target intervention to an alternative intervention or a no-treatment condition to answer the question, "Is there a cause–effect relationship between the treatment variable and the target outcome?" However, later efficacy studies address this question under more generalizable conditions. For example, studies in this phase should test a coherent set of intervention components that have already been tested in relative isolation in the early efficacy phase. The treatment outcome measures should always be definite endpoints that are clinically meaningful indications of performance, reflecting marked improvements on target (and possibly related nontarget) behaviors with individuals who were not involved in the intervention and in contexts unlike those used in the treatment. The strongest later efficacy studies compare the new target intervention with standard intervention practices.

One investigation on recasting that we conceive as a later efficacy study was reported by

Nelson, Camarata, Welsh, Butkovsky, and Camarata (1996). Seven children with SLI and seven children with typical language development, whose language skills were commensurate with those of the children with SLI, were included in the study. The investigators selected three intermediate (morpho-)syntactic goals that were absent from the children's expressive repertoires and randomly assigned them to a recast, imitation, or no-treatment condition. Three additional goals that the children had partially mastered were also identified but not treated. This feature allowed the investigators to consider a second question: "Do goals that are already partially mastered need to be treated directly in intervention?"

The recasting and imitation procedures used were similar to those employed in previous investigations carried out by this research group (Camarata & Nelson 1992; Camarata et al., 1994). Each child participated in two 50-minute sessions per week for 12 weeks with a clinician as the intervention agent. Like the studies of Camarata and colleagues, the outcome measures in this study included both elicited and generalized spontaneous productions occurring during clinical treatment sessions. Unlike the earlier studies, however, these investigators added as an outcome the number of spontaneous uses of grammatical targets during conversations between the children and their mothers at home.

The results indicated that the imitation approach led to greater gains than were observed for no treatment and that the recast intervention was more beneficial than was imitation. This finding held for both the children with SLI and the children with typical language development. Moreover, analyses of the use of target forms in the homes revealed that all of the children were more likely to produce forms taught using the recast procedure than forms taught using imitation. Furthermore, children showed significant gains in their spontaneous use of untargeted, partially mastered forms.

In this study, as well as previous studies conducted by Camarata and his colleagues (Camarata & Nelson, 1992; Camarata et al., 1994), a cause–effect relationship between recasting and language learning clearly is demonstrated. Unlike the previous early efficacy studies, however, this study included a generalization outcome measure outside the clinical treatment sessions with an individual who did not participate in the intervention. The investigators also addressed a critical issue in the selection of treatment targets: whether partially mastered forms need to be treated directly to show significant development. The addition of these features to the previous protocols makes this study more meaningful to clinicians and reflects an appropriate developmental shift from early to later efficacy concerns.

Fey and Loeb (2002) produced a study that serves as an example of how the results of a series of clinical trials can lead to more specific questions that themselves can be answered with efficacy trials (see Figure 23.2). A reasonably large body of studies, many of which have been summarized in this chapter, has provided evidence that recasts can facilitate grammatical development among children with language disorders. Recasts can vary considerably, however, in the manner and extent to which they differ from the child's platform utterance. For example, they may be simple, adding limited information to the child's utterance or complex, modifying multiple elements of the child's utterance. They may correct the child's utterance, as in expansions, or not, as when an appropriate child noun phrase is augmented by a recast containing a relative clause. They may also change the modality of the child's utterance; for example, from declarative to interrogative. The recasts used in the Fey and Loeb study presented target auxiliary verbs in yes–no interrogative recasts (e.g., *Is daddy driving? Will daddy drive?*). This study included 16 children with SLI and 18 younger language-matched children with typical language development. All of the children were using subject–verb–object sentences, but none was producing auxiliary verbs. The investigators randomly assigned the children to either an auxiliary verb enrichment intervention or a control play condition. Children's utterances in the enrichment intervention were recast by a clinician with a yes–no interrogative containing either *is* or *will* in the sentence-initial position. Children assigned to the control group engaged in play with the clinician. During the play sessions, the clinicians limited their use of questions and provided no question recasts that began with *is* or *will*. Regardless of group assignment, each child received three 30-minute sessions per week for 8 weeks.

As an outcome measure, Fey and Loeb (2002) sampled the children's use of targeted and nontargeted auxiliaries in spontaneous language during play interactions with a parent and with an unfamiliar examiner over an 8-month period. The dependent variable was the sampling session at which each child had produced four unique instances of the target auxiliaries (*is* and *will*) and four exemplars of the broader *BE* and modal auxiliary categories (e.g., *am, are, was* and *can, may, should*). The results of this study provided no evidence that interrogative recasts facilitate the acquisition of auxiliaries among children not already using auxiliaries. The authors speculated that interrogative recasts may be too complex in comparison to the child's utterance to facilitate children's initial productions of auxiliaries (see our previous discussion of Nelson et al., 1984). It may be that recasts need to differ only in small ways from the child's utterance, or they may need to correct the grammatical form of the child's utterance to enable the child to utilize the grammatical information they contain (Saxton, 1997, 2000). These hypotheses are themselves amenable to additional efficacy trials.

Later efficacy studies provide clear evidence of a target intervention's efficacy under ideal laboratory conditions. As with studies representing other investigative phases, later efficacy studies should be published and archived for researchers and clinicians to use as experimental evidence to support further investigations and clinical practice. Although later efficacy studies may guide clinical practice, it is important to note that later efficacy studies are limited in their scope and are not the final level of evidence needed to support clinical practice (Pring, 2004). That is, later efficacy studies are limited to laboratory conditions and do not inform researchers and clinicians of treatment effects in everyday clinical settings. The highest level of evidence that both researchers and clinicians should seek are studies of intervention effectiveness.

Effectiveness Studies

The effectiveness phase of intervention effectiveness evaluation is reached only after satisfactory demonstrations of efficacy. The primary focus of effectiveness studies should be on examination of outcomes of the efficacious intervention procedures under typical clinical contexts. In the area of child language disorders, there are many prototypical questions associated with studies at this phase:

- Are effects similar to those found in later efficacy studies observed:
  - with different and more heterogeneous (sub)populations?
  - when other interventions addressing other basic goals (and, thus, more intermediate and specific goals) are added to address children's more comprehensive needs?
  - using different service delivery options (e.g., different intervention agents and contexts, treatment intensities, goal attack strategies)?
  - with unplanned variations in the protocol (e.g., variable parent cooperation, numerous child or clinician absences)?
  - using more functional outcome measures than those that often characterize efficacy studies?
- What are the differences in costs of programs?
- Are the benefits worth the costs?

Participants in effectiveness studies may have a wider range of disabilities characteristic of more typical clients (e.g., borderline or lower intelligence, physical and sensory disabilities, behavior problems). Therefore, compared to efficacy research, the clinical approaches studied in effectiveness studies are likely to be broader in scope, requiring more than a single basic goal and, possibly, different types of intervention representing each. Furthermore, effectiveness research must involve careful consideration of who will perform the treatment, where it will be presented, how each of the goals will be addressed (or attacked), and how intensively the treatment can realistically be presented (see Figure 23.1). In fact, whereas efficacy studies focus primarily on documenting the effects of clinical procedures, effectiveness experiments often identify other components (e.g., intervention agent, context, intensity, goal attack strategy) of intervention as independent variables (see Tyler, Lewis, Haskill, & Tolbert, 2003).

Clinicians in effectiveness studies should not be "cherry-picked" and should represent ordinary clinicians, parents, or paraprofessionals working in typical contexts. Although they may be essential to efficacy evaluations, no special incentives should be used to ensure family and child adherence to the intervention protocol in effectiveness studies. This naturally will lead to greater variance in service delivery and, in all likelihood, outcomes. Endpoints should be functional measures of language use in meaningful contexts, such as academic performance, social or adaptive performance, or measures of quality of life, including parental stress, social development, and emotional well-being (e.g., Robertson & Weismer, 1999; Wake, Hughes, Poulakis, Collins, & Rickards, 2004) rather than measures of specific behavioral symptoms in limited contexts.

From the standpoint of research design, studies of effectiveness may be fully powered, randomized controlled trials, as if they were later efficacy trials performed "in the field" rather than in the laboratory (Piantadosi, 1997). The grammar facilitation studies of Fey and colleagues (Fey, Cleave, Long, & Hughes, 1993; Fey et al., 1994) are reasonably good examples of this type of study. The Fey et al. (1993) study was a 4½-month evaluation of two versions of a focused stimulation approach based largely, but not entirely, on the use of recasts that targeted expressive grammatical skills of children with expressive language problems. Most of children also had speech problems, and seven had performance IQs that were in the borderline range, between 70 and 85. The primary basic goal was to achieve broad gains in expressive grammatical complexity during meaningful conversations, although it was hypothesized that the grammar intervention would also have an impact on the children's phonological productions (Fey et al., 1994).

Several features of this study make it a useful, if somewhat less than prototypical, example of a randomized effectiveness trial. First and foremost, even in 1993, recasting had a history of positive outcomes in pretrial, feasibility, and efficacy studies. Second, not all of the children were specifically language-impaired, and most had speech as well as grammatical production problems. This made the sample more representative of clinical populations than is frequently the case in efficacy studies. Third, the goals of the intervention were not simply improved production of specific (e.g., *is, are, was*) or intermediate (e.g., BE auxiliaries) grammatical goals, but broadly improved expressive grammatical abilities. This was reflected in the primary outcome measure, the developmental sentence score (DSS) (Lee, 1974). DSS is a general measure of complexity of children's spontaneous sentences, which in this study were collected during play interactions with the children's mothers. Fourth, the primary questions addressed were characteristic of effectiveness studies.

- Is there a meaningful effect on children's grammatical expression when the intervention is packaged in a conventional manner with a clinician as intervention agent?

- Is there a meaningful effect when the intervention is packaged into a less costly program with several different features, including parents as primary intervention agents?
- Is one intervention package more effective than the other?
- Is grammar facilitation, using recasts and other focused stimulation techniques, effective when it is used to attack specific goals in a cyclical manner rather than using more conventional horizontal or vertical strategies?
- Does the grammatical intervention provided either by parents or clinicians yield changes in the children's phonological production (Fey et al., 1994)?

Fifth, the intensity of the treatments was dictated by consideration of what clinicians might view as practical or tolerable. Thus, children in the clinician-administered treatment were seen in two one-hour small-group sessions and one one-hour individual session each week for 4½ months. The parent intervention was developed to take approximately half as much of the clinician's time over the same 4½-month treatment period. Finally, the study was a randomized controlled trial. The 30 participants were randomly assigned to receive one of the two recast-based, focused stimulation treatment packages or to receive no treatment.

The only design feature of the Fey et al. (1993) study that limited its status as an assessment of effectiveness was that the same clinician, working in the same university clinic, was responsible for all clinician-administered intervention and parent education sessions. This limits the generalizability of the study outcomes to the broader community of clinicians, many of whom may be more or less skilled than the one used in the study.

The Fey et al. (1993) study yielded several important conclusions. Both interventions led to significant improvements in the children's grammatical production. Neither approach was significantly more effective than the other, although children's responses to the clinician-administered treatment were less variable than those to the parent intervention. Because recasts were not the only procedures used, their specific contributions to the intervention effects cannot be determined. Based on previous studies of recast efficacy, however, it is reasonable to assume that recasts were important contributors to the treatment's success.

In addition to these primary outcomes, Fey et al. (1993) demonstrated the viability of the cyclical goal attack strategy in grammar facilitation, although its specific role in the positive treatment outcomes must await further testing through early and later efficacy trials (see Figure 23.2). Furthermore, using data from the Fey et al. (1993) study, Fey et al. (1994) observed that despite its effectiveness in facilitating grammatical expression, the grammar facilitation approach had no effect on the children's speech sound production. This suggests that other studies are needed to evaluate ways to treat both phonological and grammatical problems when they co-occur in children with language-learning problems (e.g., Tyler et al., 2003).

Given the costs of randomized controlled effectiveness trials and the length of time necessary to complete them, we believe that the answers to many effectiveness questions can be obtained satisfactorily using nonexperimental pre–post designs, quasi-experimental designs with historical controls, or even case series, much as is the case for feasibility studies. The principal difference between these studies and studies characteristic of feasibility or early efficacy studies will be the point at which each lies in the path of treatment development; either before or after successful efficacy trials. Gillon (2005) provides an excellent example of a nonexperimental trial planned as a follow-up to a collection of later efficacy studies. She recognized that there is a significant body of evidence from efficacy trials demonstrating a direct relationship between efforts to teach phonemic awareness to school-aged children with reading problems and both improved phonemic awareness and improved reading (Ehri, 2004). What she wanted to determine was whether her intervention could bring about significant improvements in the phonemic awareness of preschool children. Gillon's 3- and 4-year-old participants were not only younger than participants typical of previous efficacy trials, they also had clinically significant speech disorders. The results of this study provide compelling support for efforts to train phoneme awareness in young children with speech disorders. This is in part because of the large effects observed, but it is also and just as significantly because the evidence from randomized controlled trials had already established the causal relationship between techniques like those used by Gillon and improvements in phonemic awareness.

We are aware of no published examples of child language effectiveness trials with designs characteristic of the feasibility phase. Consider, however, the study of McLean and Vincent (1984), summarized earlier as a feasibility study. Had this study been planned after 1996, a point by which most of the studies on recasting reviewed in this chapter had already been reported, it could well have served purposes characteristic of the effectiveness phase. For example, most clinical studies of recasts have included children with relatively specific language disorders. McLean and Vincent included children with general developmental delay, however. Therefore, they might have asked their study questions somewhat differently from an effectiveness perspective.

- Given that recasts have been shown to facilitate development of later developing grammatical forms among children with SLI, will a recast intervention targeting semantic relations be similarly effective with 2- to 4-year-old children with developmental delay?
- Can paraprofessionals be trained to implement the recast intervention during play with children with developmental delay? How much training is necessary?
- What is the impact of the addition of this treatment on delivery of other needed services for these children and on their daily routines?

On its own, the pre–post design of McLean and Vincent (1984) is no more suitable for answering the efficacy question after 1996 than it was in 1984. The body of evidence documenting the effects of recasting, however, makes it far more reasonable after 1996 to attribute the positive gains made by the children in the study of McLean and Vincent to the treatment than it was in 1984. These results should pave the way for clinicians to implement the approach in their typical clinical settings for children with developmental delay.

Effectiveness studies of this sort would not be limited to the *testing* of clinical hypotheses in clinical settings. They are even better suited to *generate* hypotheses that could then be tested in efficacy trials. For example, McLean and Vincent found that only three of their five participants maintained their gains 3 to 8 weeks after treatment was discontinued. The researchers could have examined carefully whether any factors appeared to distinguish between the children who maintained their gains and those who did not. They could then have hypothesized adaptations in their approach that might lead to more consistent and larger effects. These hypotheses could then be tested in subsequent early or later efficacy trials (see Figure 23.2).

CONCLUSION

Language intervention researchers and clinicians may not share our view of the most appropriate progression for developing language intervention approaches. Even if they do, there is a great deal of room for disagreement as to the phase that a particular investigation best represents.

Notwithstanding these differences of opinion, we believe that there can be little doubt that codification of a multiphase model, such as the adaptation presented in this chapter, would have many positive ramifications for researchers and clinicians in speech-language pathology. First, adoption of such a model would clarify the importance of and need for intervention studies that are nonexperimental in addressing both feasibility and effectiveness issues. Second, the model would highlight the need for short-term clinical experiments that address early efficacy questions concerning individual intervention components, using surrogate endpoints, even though the outcomes of these studies cannot readily be generalized to the clinic. Third, if the need for feasibility and early efficacy studies is taken seriously, and young investigators have some assurance that well-executed studies of these types have some certainty of publication, they are more likely to get involved early in their careers, directing their talents toward intervention effectiveness concerns. This would dramatically increase the number of child language intervention research programs across the globe. Fourth, the trend for researchers to carry out and report early efficacy studies and then discontinue their research would necessarily be replaced by their continued efforts to produce more generalizable later efficacy and effectiveness trials. Finally, a multiphase model for child language treatment research would stress the importance of methodological rigor and better research at *every* phase of investigation, including early feasibility studies and nonexperimental studies of effectiveness, as well as single-subject experiments and fully powered randomized control trials of effectiveness.

REFERENCES

Agocs, M. M., Burns, M., DeLey, L. E., Miller, S. L., & Calhoun, B. M. (2006). Fast ForWord. In R. J. McCauley & M. E. Fey (Eds.), *Treatment of language disorders in children*. Baltimore, MD: Paul H. Brookes.

The American Heritage dictionary of the English language (4th ed.). (2000). New York: Houghton Mifflin.

Camarata, S. M., & Nelson, K. E. (1992). Treatment efficiency as a function of target selection in the remediation of child language disorders. *Clinical Linguistics and Phonetics, 6*, 167–178.

Camarata, S. M., Nelson, K. E., & Camarata, M. N. (1994). Comparison of conversational-recasting and imitative procedures for training grammatical structures in children with specific language impairment. *Journal of Speech and Hearing Research, 37*(6), 1414–1423.

Ehri, L. C. (2004). Teaching phonemic awareness and phonics: An explanation of the National Reading Panel meta-analyses. In P. McCardle & V. Chhabra (Eds.), *The voice of evidence in reading research* (pp. 153–186). Baltimore: Paul H. Brookes.

Ellis Weismer, S., & Robertson, S. (2006). Focused stimulation approach to language intervention. In R. J. McCauley & M. E. Fey (Eds.), *Treatment of language disorders in children*. Baltimore: Paul H. Brookes.

Farrar, M. J. (1990). Discourse and the acquisition of grammatical morphemes. *Journal of Child Language, 17*(3), 607–624.

Fey, M. E. (1986). *Language intervention with young children*. Austin, TX: PRO-ED.

Fey, M. E. (1990). *Understanding and narrowing the gap between treatment research and clinical practice with language-impaired children* (Vol. 20). Rockville, MD: American Speech-Language-Hearing Association.

Fey, M. E., Cleave, P. L., Long, S. H., & Hughes, D. L. (1993). Two approaches to the facilitation of grammar in children with language impairment: An experimental evaluation. *Journal of Speech and Hearing Research, 36*(1), 141–157.

Fey, M. E., Cleave, P. L., Ravida, A. I., Long, S. H., Dejmal, A. R., & Easton, D. (1994). Effects of grammar facilitation on the phonological performance of children with speech and language impairments. *Journal of Speech and Hearing Research, 37*(3), 594–607.

Fey, M. E., & Justice, L. M. (2007). Evidence-based decision making in communication intervention. In R. Paul & P. W. Cascella (Eds.), *Introduction to clinical methods in communication disorders* (2nd ed., pp. 179–202). Baltimore: Paul H. Brookes.

Fey, M. E., Krulik, T. E., Loeb, D. F., & Proctor Williams, K. (1999). Sentence recast use by parents of children with typical language and children with specific language impairment. *American Journal of Speech-Language Pathology, 8*(3), 273–286.

Fey, M. E., & Loeb, D. F. (2002). An evaluation of the facilitative effects of inverted yes–no questions on the acquisition of auxiliary verbs. *Journal of Speech, Language, and Hearing Research, 45*(1), 160–174.

Gillon, G. T. (2005). Facilitating phoneme awareness development in 3- and 4-year-old children with speech impairment. *Language, Speech, and Hearing Services in Schools, 36*, 308–324.

Hancock, T. B., & Kaiser, A. P. (2006). Enhanced milieu teaching. In R. J. McCauley & M. E. Fey (Eds.), *Treatment of language disorders in children*. Baltimore: Paul H. Brookes.

Justice, L. M., & Fey, M. E. (2004). Evidence-based practice in schools: Integrating craft and theory with science and data. *ASHA Leader, 9*(17), 4–5.

Law, J., Garrett, Z., & Nye, C. (2004). The efficacy of treatment for children with developmental speech and language delay/disorder: A meta-analysis. *Journal of Speech, Language, and Hearing Research 47*, 924–943.

Lee, L. L. (1974). *Developmental sentence analysis*. Evanston, IL: Northwestern University Press.

McCauley, R. J., & Fey, M. E. (2006). *Treatment of language disorders in children*. Baltimore: Paul H. Brookes.

McLean, M., & Vincent, L. (1984). The use of expansions as a language intervention technique in the natural environment. *Journal of the Division for Early Childhood* (Fall), 57–66.

Nelson, K. E. (1977). Facilitating children's syntax acquisition. *Developmental Psychology, 13*, 101–107.

Nelson, K. E., Camarata, S. M., Welsh, J., Butkovsky, L., & Camarata, M. (1996). Effects of imitative and conversational recasting treatment on the acquisition of grammar in children with specific language impairment and younger language-normal children. *Journal of Speech and Hearing Research, 39*(4), 850–859.

Nelson, K. E., Denninger, M., Bonvillian, J. D., Kaplan, B. J., & Baker, N. (1984). Maternal input adjustments and non-adjustments as related to children's linguistic advances and to language acquisition theories. In A. D. Pellegrini & T. D. Yawkey (Eds.), *The development of oral and written languages: Readings in developmental and applied linguistics* (pp. 31–56). Norwood, NJ: Ablex.

Piantadosi, S. (1997). *Clinical trials: A methodologic perspective*. New York: Wiley-Interscience.

Pring, T. (2004). Ask a silly question: Two decades of troublesome trials. *International Journal of Language and Communication Disorders, 39*(3), 285–302.

Robertson, S. B., & Weismer, S. E. (1999). Effects of treatment on linguistic and social skills in toddlers with delayed language development. *Journal of Speech, Language, and Hearing Research, 42*(5), 1234–1248.

Robey, R. R. (2004). A five-phase model for clinical-outcome research. *Journal of Communication Disorders, 37*(5), 401–411.

Robey, R. R., & Schultz, M. C. (1998). A model for conducting clinical-outcome research: An adaptation of the standard protocol for use in aphasiology. *Aphasiology 12*(9), 787–810.

Saxton, M. (1997). The contrast theory of negative input. *Journal of Child Language, 24*(1), 139–161.

Saxton, M. (2000). Negative evidence and negative feedback: Immediate effects on the grammaticality of child speech. *First Language, 20*(60, Pt. 3), 221–252.

Saxton, M., Kulcsar, B., Marshall, G., & Rupra, M. (1998). Longer-term effects of corrective input: An experimental approach. *Journal of Child Language, 25*(3), 701–721.

Scherer, N. J., & Olswang, L. B. (1989). Using structured discourse as a language intervention technique with autistic children. *Journal of Speech and Hearing Disorders, 54* (3), 383–394.

Sorensen, P., & Fey, M. E. (1992). Informativeness as a clinical principle: What's really new? *Language, Speech, and Hearing Services in Schools, 23*(4), 320–328.

Swanson, L. A., Fey, M. E., Mills, C. E., & Hood, L. S. (2005). Use of narrative-based language intervention with children who have specific language impairment. *American Journal of Speech-Language Pathology, 14*(2), 131–143.

Tyler, A. A., Lewis, K. E., Haskill, A., & Tolbert, L. C. (2003). Outcomes of different speech and language goal attack strategies. *Journal of Speech, Language, and Hearing Research, 46*(5), 1077–1094.

U.S. National Institutes of Health (2007, September). *ClinicalTrials.gov.* Retrieved February 18, 2008, from http://www.clinicaltrials.gov/ct2/info/glossary

Wake, M., Hughes, E. K., Poulakis, Z., Collins, C., & Rickards, F. W. (2004). Outcomes of children with mild-profound congenital hearing loss at 7 to 8 years: A population study. *Ear and Hearing, 25*(1), 1–8.

Warren, S. F., Bredin-Oja, S. L., Fairchild, M., Finestack, L. H., Fey, M. E., & Brady, N. C. (2006). Responsivity education/Prelinguistic milieu teaching. In R. J. McCauley & M. E. Fey (Eds.), *Treatment of language disorders in children.* Baltimore: Paul H. Brookes.

Yoder, P. J., Spruytenburg, H., Edwards, A., & Davies, B. (1995). Effect of verbal routine contexts and expansions on gains in the mean length of utterance in children with developmental delays. *Language, Speech, and Hearing Services in Schools, 26*(1), 21–32.

24

Neuroscience Approaches to Child Language Disorders

VALERIE L. SHAFER and NATHAN D. MAXFIELD

INTRODUCTION

To date, behavioral research has been our primary means of learning about childhood language disorders. As part of this approach, researchers have assembled detailed profiles of the speech and language behaviors exhibited by children with specific language impairment, autism-spectrum disorder, dyslexia, and other language disorders. Although certainly useful, this approach has provided limited insight into the causes of such disorders. This is because language performance is inherently rooted in cognition, and descriptions of behavior do not fully capture the cognitive processing activities that drive language performance. Researchers are now beginning to turn to neurobiological science, a method with good construct validity for uncovering these processes. The aim of this chapter is to provide an overview of some of the more relevant neurobiological methods that are currently in use.

Understanding the role of brain function in typical, as well as atypical, language development is important for addressing the causes of a disorder, because it provides a basis for observing where, in the physical system, known processing activities deviate from normal, and how such deviations might ultimately contribute to atypical language development and behavior.

Our understanding of brain structure and function derives from a number of different methods. To a great extent, our knowledge of how the brain works at a micro level (i.e., cellular level) derives from methods using autopsied brain tissue or other highly invasive techniques (e.g., cortically implanted electrodes). Similarly, our knowledge of structure and function at the macro level (i.e., gross neural structure-language function relationships) for much of the twentieth century derived from examination of clinical cases, such as people with aphasia, whose brains were also examined invasively, albeit postmortem. Today, a number of neuroscience methods allow for the examination of brain structure and function, with minimal risk, in living participants (in vivo). These latter methods, which also focus on the identification of macro systems underlying language performance, are likely to be the most used for the study of developmental language disorders in the next few decades. Even so, it is important to examine brain structure and function at the micro level and the methods used to uncover this knowledge, because a real and useful understanding of findings from macrolevel imaging studies requires us to relate these results to function and structure at the micro level, as is illustrated in this chapter.

In this chapter, we first describe some important basic principles of neurobiology at the level of the neuron that are necessary to understand what neuroscience methods are measuring. This section also includes a brief discussion of the methods that have been used to derive this knowledge. The second part of the chapter describes the most popular methods that have been used for studying higher-level brain function and that may be used, or in some cases have already been used, in the study of language development and disorders. In the final section, we discuss some factors that should be considered in interpreting data from these neurobiological methods.

BASIC PRINCIPLES OF NEUROBIOLOGY

In recent years, considerable advances have been made in our understanding of the neurobiology of speech and language in the adult. The study of language-supporting neural structures suggests that the language system consists of many interconnected *functional modules*. As discussed below, each module is composed of cells, cell assemblies, and cell assembly networks that contribute to language processing in specialized ways (see Bookheimer, 2002). This view extends our prior understanding of language processing and organization, which was largely based on investigations of language breakdown (e.g., aphasia) that were interpreted as pointing to somewhat localized, language-specific processing regions in the brain. Current research on typical language-brain function is focused on precisely identifying the locations and architecture of language-supporting modules. Understanding how these modules contribute to language processing, and how their dysfunction might contribute to language disorder, requires knowledge of a number of basic principles of neuroscience, which are discussed below.

In this section, we first describe several of the methods that have been used to understand the function and structure at the micro level. This is followed by a description of micro level structure and function.

Neuroscience Methods for Studying Microstructure

Much of our knowledge of the function and structure of the brain at the cellular level comes from research on nonhuman animals. In this research the electro-chemical properties and structural and biochemical organization (cytoarchitechtonics) of brain cells are examined using samples of brain tissue from dead specimens or invasive experiments, typically using living nonhuman animals (Kolb & Wishaw, 1996).

The principal method for identifying structural organization of brain cells consists of using selective stains on dissected brain tissue that will allow researchers to identify types of structures, such as cell type (e.g., size, shape) and distribution of cells, along with their connectivity. Brodmann's areas (e.g., primary auditory cortex is Brodmann's Area 41) are the result of these investigations. Methods used to study the biochemical activity of brain cells include determining the function of a neurotransmitter (e.g., excitatory), demonstrating that stimulation leads to release of the neurotransmitter, identifying the biochemical structure of the neurotransmitter, and experimentally demonstrating its function. Methods for studying the electrical activity of brain cells include testing the electrical properties of brain structure after dissection (e.g., conductivity of dissected axons) or using electrodes implanted in the brain tissue of live animals to examine the physiology of clusters of brain cells.

These methods have been instrumental in determining the basic principles of how the brain functions and is organized (see Kolb & Wishaw, 1996); these are described below.

Neural Circuitry

The brain stores and communicates information by transmitting electrochemical signals between neurons. The neuron has three major parts: a cell body, an axon, and numerous dendrites. The cell body is responsible for metabolic functions. The axon conducts information (or electrical activity) away from the cell body, whereas dendrites gather information from other neurons. The neural impulse sent down an axon terminates at a synapse and causes chemical agents, called neurotransmitters, to be released in a cleft between the synapse and the membrane of another neuron (often on a dendrite). The type of transmitter determines whether the synapse is excitatory or inhibitory. Receptors on the postsynaptic membrane are sensitive to particular transmitters. These chemical messages can lead to changes in the electrical potential of the receiving neuron. Sufficient change in potential can lead to depolarization and excitation (firing), or hyperpolarization and inhibition of firing.

A neural circuit is made up of axonal connections between thousands of neurons. Within a circuit, neurons fire synchronously to particular stimulus properties or processing demands (Hebb, 1949; see Vaughan & Kurtzberg, 1992). Intracranial recordings have revealed that neurons operate in clusters, or cell assemblies (Engel, Moll, & Fried, 2005). Groups of tens of thousands of neurons, spaced closely together in a radius equal to that of a pencil eraser, can become excited or inhibited all at once in response to stimulation (Calvin, 1975). Furthermore, different neural circuits, or cell assemblies, can be linked together to accomplish more complex processing tasks. Specific patterns of excitation and inhibition across cell assemblies have been traced to specific complex processing tasks.

Neural Circuitry for Learning and Memory

Language processing, similar to other functions, requires the learning and storing of information in memory. The manner in which this learning occurs at a neurophysiological level has been called Hebbian learning. Learning is seen as the strengthening or weakening of synaptic connections between neurons through repeated stimulation of connections to create a circuit (e.g., Hebb, 1949; Vaughan & Kurtzberg, 1992). There is some biological determination of circuits, but maintenance of a circuit, even one that is prewired, often requires stimulation, and further tuning and strengthening of the circuit can occur with stimulation. These changes can lead to the creation of novel neural circuits, or to the linking of a number of circuits into higher order circuits.

Memory at higher levels of the nervous system is often the result of synaptic modifications. Brain circuits that function in memory for a stimulus or task also participate in the learning of this information. Memory for information may be seen as patterned electrochemical activity across neurons responding to some event or task, with the pattern of activation established during the Hebbian learning process described above. Humans have evolved specialized neural subsystems, including limbic structures, hippocampus, and basal ganglia, that support learning and memory (e.g., by acting as sophisticated association areas, or relay stations, that connect different parts of the brain). Attentional systems (including the cingulated gyrus and basal ganglia structures) also play an important role in language learning and processing (see Koch, 2004). These systems all play a major role in learning and memory for language information (Squire & Kandel, 1999).

Structure of Neocortex

The cortex in primary sensory regions (e.g., visual, auditory) is dominated by a layer of granular neurons that receives sensory information from the periphery, whereas cortex in primary motor regions is dominated by a layer of granular neurons that sends motor commands to the peripheral muscular system. In contrast, cortex in association regions (e.g., cerebellum) is dominated by layers of neurons that both send and receive information to and from other cortical areas. Differences in brain tissues can be identified at the cortical level fairly easily, because neurons are organized in four to six layers, with motor output to the muscles (efferent) originating at Layer V, sensory inputs from the periphery (afferent) terminating at Layer IV, and axonal connections between neurons in different brain regions (i.e., cortico-cortical) generally originating and terminating in Layers II and III. Layer I (closest to the scalp), called the molecular layer, largely contains dendrites of neurons in deeper layers and axons synapsing on these dendrites, or axons with targets in other layers passing through this layer. Layer VI, called the fusiform layer, consists of a mixture of dendrites from cell bodies in Layers II (external granular layer) and IV (internal granular layer). Different types of neurons are often found in different layers. For example, pyramidal neurons, which are larger than other neuron types, send (efferent) projections to more distal sites and are more abundant in Layer V than in Layers II and III (Kandel, Schwartz, & Jessell, 2000; Kolb & Wishaw, 1996). It is noteworthy that allocortex, an evolutionarily older region of the brain covering many of the limbic structures (e.g., cingulated gyrus, hippocampus, parahippocampal gyrus), is comprised of just three layers of neurons, many of which communicate with prefrontal cortex via the thalamus.

In summary, this section describes some basic principles of the nervous system, which are necessary for understanding neuroscience methods used to study developmental language disorders and to interpret results from these investigations.

IN VIVO BRAIN IMAGING

The most exciting and potentially profitable neuroscience methods are those that are minimally invasive and allow the investigation of structure and function in healthy participants. The most commonly used methods are described in this section, along with examples of how they have been or could be applied to the study of developmental disorders.

Structural Imaging

The volume of particular brain regions can be measured in vivo using brain imaging methods such as computerized tomography (CT) scans and magnetic resonance imaging (MRI). MRI is the currently favored method, because it provides high resolution. Specifically, MRI is sensitive to the density of hydrogen atoms in tissue. These atoms normally exhibit random orientation but line up roughly in parallel with respect to the force lines of a strong magnetic field. Radio waves are passed across the atoms, which then emit detectable signals that can be used to reconstruct their density. Unique radio frequency pulses are delivered to different loci in the brain. Thus, the precise location of the returning signal measured by the magnet's coils is known via its frequency. The intensity of the signal is used to reconstruct the tissue density at the different loci (Papanicalaou, 1998).

The utility of this method for studying developmental disorders is illustrated by the following research. Anatomical studies have previously suggested that typical adults show a hemispheric asymmetry for language-processing regions. For example, the planum temporale is larger in the left than the right hemisphere in most right-handed individuals (for review, Kolb & Wishaw, 1996). The left planum temporale is believed to play a special role in speech and language processing (Scott & Wise, 2004). A number of investigations have suggested abnormalities in size or in asymmetry of language-related regions in children with developmental language disorders (De Fosse et al., 2004; Leonard et al., 2002; Plante, 1991). For example, Gauger and colleagues found a significantly smaller pars triangularis in the left hemisphere for children with SLI (Gauger, Lombardino, & Leonard, 1997). At the same time, gross anatomical measures do not provide information about how deviant findings are related to function. Also, as with any measure, arbitrary measurement decisions can lead to different results. For example, some studies have measured the entire volume of the planum temporale, whereas others have divided it into two portions.

In summary, methods for imaging brain structure in vivo have provided valuable information and should continue to be used. These methods, however, are more powerful when used in conjunction with neuroimaging studies of function.

IN VIVO METHODS FOR IDENTIFYING FUNCTION

A number of other brain-imaging methods are available for investigating how the brain's neural circuitry functions in order to drive language performance. Functional brain imaging methods that are seeing increased use are electrophysiology, magnetoencephalography, functional magnetic resonance imaging, and positron emission tomography. Each of these methods is described below, along with current or proposed ways of using each method to investigate childhood language disorders.

Electrophysiology

Electrophysiology is the brain imaging method most commonly used with pediatric populations, primarily because it is easy to use with children and is relatively inexpensive; for these reasons, we present more detailed information on this method. Electrophysiological methods exploit the phenomenon that neuronal firing leads to changes in the electrical potential (specifically, postsynaptic excitatory and inhibitory potentials) of the extracellular solution. In many regions of neocortex, adjacent neurons are arranged in parallel, so that the axons of the neurons are mainly aligned on one end, while inputs into the dendrites are mainly aligned on the other end. This arrangement leads to the circuit behaving like a dipolar current source when the neurons in a neural circuit or cell assembly fire in synchrony (For a neurophysics explanation, see Nunez & Srinivasan, 2006). Thus, on one end (e.g., negative end), ions of the opposite polarity will be attracted, and this perturbation will propagate to the scalp, while on the other end the opposite pattern will be found. Of critical importance, these perturbations propagate (volume conduct) to the surface of the scalp, where they can be recorded and, ultimately, amplified and measured. ERP research in animal models using intracortical electrodes has been able to pinpoint sources of dipolar volume-conducted activity seen at the scalp to discrete cortical layers. For example, in response to visual stimuli by primates, a scalp-recorded negativity peaking at 40 ms is found to reflect excitation in cortical Layer IV in visual cortex. These data demonstrate that, at least for sensory and cognitive processes shared by humans and animals, there is the possibility of explaining scalp-recorded ERP components in terms of their neural correlates (Vaughan & Kurtzberg, 1992).

Different methods of signal processing have been developed to isolate the electrical patterns related to a single event of interest. The most common method involves averaging portions of the EEG that are time-locked to a repeated event. The goal is to decrease the contribution from processes that are not time-locked to this event (e.g., background noise), while increasing the contribution from event-generated, time-locked fluctuations elicited from a neural source(s) that is too small to resolve in the unprocessed EEG. This method is called averaged evoked potentials (AEPs) or averaged event-related potentials (ERPs) (see Luck, 2005 for an excellent introduction to ERP methods). Figure 24.1 illustrates how noise approaches zero with averaging, leaving potential fluctuations time-locked to the stimulus.

Electrophysiological measures provide high-temporal resolution, making them suitable for addressing questions regarding the relative time-course and speed of cognitive processing. It should be noted, however, that the change in electrical activity found in some brain regions (e.g., sulci) cannot be measured at the scalp, because the orientation of neurons are such that the activity cancels out (Nunez & Srinivasan, 2006).

The principal ERP components that have been used to study speech and language development primarily fall into the class of components that are called endogenous (or cognitive) potentials, although exogenous (obligatory components) can be used to rule out lower-level sensory or motor deficits. Endogenous potentials are dependent on the nature of the processing task. In contrast, exogenous potentials are elicited or evoked by the physical characteristics of the stimulus. The P1 (50–100 ms) and N1 (80–140 ms) ERP components are considered exogenous, and each component's amplitude, latency, and topography is largely determined by the physical characteristics of a stimulus. Although

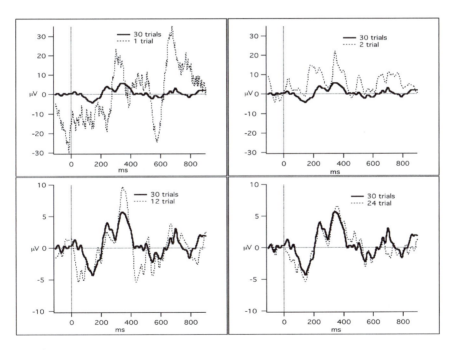

FIGURE 24.1   The graphs illustrate how noise approaches zero with averaging, leaving potential fluctuations time-locked to the stimulus. The top left graph displays one epoch (trial) of the EEG versus 30 epochs, all time-locked to the onset of consonant–vowel–consonant (CVC) words. The top right, bottom left, and bottom right display 2, 12, and 24 trials, respectively, compared to 30 trials. The activity in the prestimulus baseline (−100 to 0 ms) diminishes as more trials are added; the series of peaks between 0 and 400 ms become more distinct, and less variability is seen with additional trials. Amplitude (in microvolts) is plotted on a finer scale for the bottom graphs.

these components do not reflect higher level language processing, they can be useful for assessing the presence of a sensory processing disorder. Figure 24.2a shows that latency and amplitude of the P1 and N1 reflect the physical differences between stimuli, in this case a vowel versus a CVC syllable. Endogenous components used to study speech and language include mismatch negativity (MMN) for examining phonetic and phonological discrimination, N400 for examining lexical access and semantic/pragmatic integration, (early) left anterior negativity ([e]LAN) for examining morphosyntactic processing, and P600 for examining late syntactic processes related to reevaluating and/or repairing sentence structure (see Friederici, 2002; Shafer & Garrido-Nag, 2007). Several studies have also used the N2 and lateralized readiness potential (LRP) to examine access of linguistic information in production (Schmitt, Münte, & Kutas, 2000; van Turennout, Hagoort, & Brown, 1998). Most of these endogenous components are elicited by some *deviant* form and are best observed by subtracting the ERP to the control from that of the deviant, as demonstrated for the N400 in Figure 24.2b. Each component also has a specific topography. For example, MMN shows negativity at frontocentral sites and positivity at inferior sites, as shown in

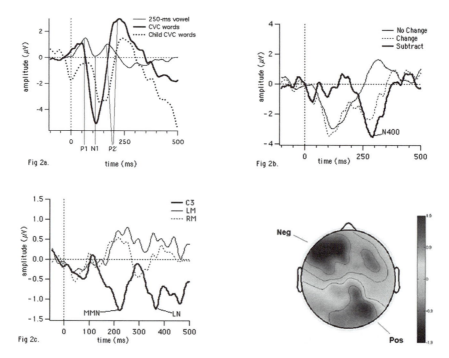

FIGURE 24.2 ERPs typically recorded in speech and language studies show at the vertex (CZ) referenced to the nose. (a) P1, N1 and P2 latencies are determined primarily by the physical properties of the stimulus. The amplitude of these components is dependent on stimulus intensity and on interstimulus interval (ISI). The 250-ms stimulus was presented with a shorter ISI (350 ms) compared to the CVC words (1,500 ms) and thus shows greater amplitude attenuation. Child N1 and P2 peaks to the CVC words occur approximately 30 ms later than the adult peaks. (b) The subtraction of the second word of a pair of words differing in consonant onset (*bad–gad*) from the second word of a pair with no change (*gad–gad*) is a useful way to identify a component peak, in this case a phonological N400 at site PZ (see Shafer, Schwartz, & Kessler, 2003). (c) The time course of the topography of MMN is illustrated by graphing a left superior central site (C3) against left and right inferior mastoid sites (LM and RM) (see Shafer, Morr, Datta, Kurtzberg, & Schwartz, 2005). (d) The early left anterior negativity (LAN) shown in a contour maps for one time-point at all sites (see Hestvik, Maxfield, Schwartz, & Shafer, 2007).

Figure 24.2c, and eLAN shows left inferior anterior negativity and right posterior positivity, as seen in 24.2d.

In terms of testing children, electrophysiology is relatively tolerant of movement, which is difficult to control in young children. It is also more acceptable to parents because it is noninvasive. Figure 24.3 shows a child, wearing a 65-electrode Geodesic net, who has comfortably sat through a 30-minute speech perception study. Few investigations have examined speech processing in children using ERPs, but more recently laboratories are beginning to do this. Children even as young as 2 years of age exhibit speech- and language-related ERP components; however, there are also striking differences between child and adult data, in particular later latencies (see Figure 24.2a), and sometimes an additional component that does not appear to be directly related to an adult component, such as the positive mismatch response (MMR) found in infants (see Shafer & Garrido-Nag, 2007).

ERPs have been used in even fewer investigations of developmental language disorders (see chapter 7 by Tropper & Schwartz). These studies, however, illustrate the value of using ERPs in the study of developmental language disorders. For example, Shafer and colleagues found that children with SLI had a reduced-amplitude left hemisphere and increased-amplitude right hemisphere response at temporal electrode sites compared to children with typical language (Shafer, Schwartz, Morr, Kessler, & Kurtzberg, 2000). This finding was interpreted as deficient processing in left hemisphere cortex. There is also interest in determining whether some ERP measure will be able to provide early identification of children at risk for developmental language disorders. There is evidence that certain ERP components are deviant in infants with familial risk for SLI (e.g., Benasich, et al., 2006), or dyslexia (Leppänen, Pihko, Eklund, & Lyytinen, 1999). We have found that the Ta component elicited to auditory information and measured at temporal sites (particularly

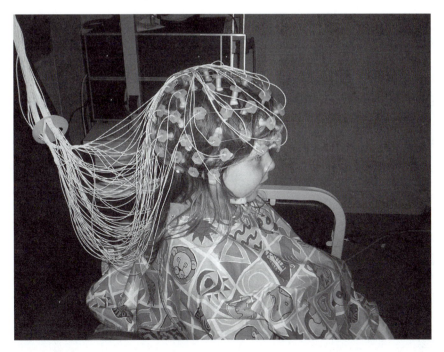

FIGURE 24.3 A 4-year-old child wearing a 65-electrode Geodesic net. Application of the net and checking contact impedances takes between 10 and 20 minutes. In this study the child then listens to speech sounds for 20 to 30 minutes while watching a movie with the sound muted.

for the right site) shows good sensitivity (.82) and specificity (.80) in a sample of 33 typical and 22 language-impaired 7- to 10-year-old children irrespective of stimulus type (vowels, CV or CVC syllables; Shafer, Schwartz, & Ponton, 2007). As of yet, it is unknown which ERP measure(s) from infants will be most predictive of language outcome.

Magnetoencephalography (MEG)

MEG is not typically used with pediatric populations because it requires the participant to remain stationary. However, it offers a unique picture of brain function, and thus the effort needed to study children using MEG is worth while. MEG complements the ERP method in that it can better index neural activity in cortical sulci than EEG, which is more sensitive to activity along gyral surfaces. MEG also provides good temporal resolution, similar to ERPs. Figure 24.4 shows a child who has successfully participated in an MEG study examining language processing.

MEG is a measure of the magnetic fields at the scalp surface, which arise from electromagnetic source currents. The magnetic field is perpendicular to the source current, and its direction is such that if the thumb of the right hand points in the direction of the source current flow, the direction of the magnetic field is that of the curled fingers. These magnetic fields are not distorted by passing through tissue and bone to reach the head surface, which, in principle, allows for more accurate source localization than ERPs (see Nunez & Srinivasan, 2006, pp. 84–90). The magnetic fields measured in MEG are primarily source activity from dendritic currents, because activity at synaptic and axon terminals cancel out. MEG is poor at detecting deep sources and sources oriented perpendicularly to the scalp (i.e., on the surface of gyri), because the magnetic fields are too weak at the locations where they emerge from the head (Nunez & Srinivasan, 2006; Papanicalaou, 1998).

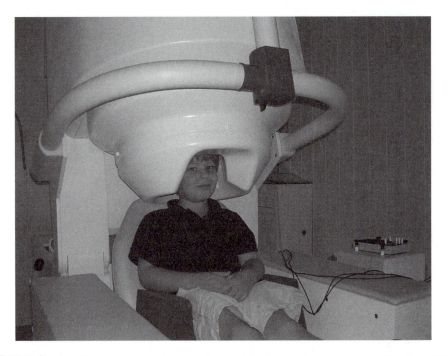

FIGURE 24.4 The magnetometers are housed in the container surrounding the child's head. (Image courtesy of Jeffrey David Lewine, PhD, Director, MEG Program, Hoglund Brain Imaging Center).

The magnetic fields are recorded by instruments called magnetometers, which are arranged such that they surround the head. A magnetometer consists of a loop of wire placed parallel to the surface of the head. Magnetic field (or flux) lines pass through the loop and induce a current that is proportional to the density of the flux strength. The intensity of these currents is so small that the instruments need to be cooled to 4 degrees Kelvin to make them superconductive. This necessity leads to MEG experiments being considerably more expensive than those using the EEG. The intensity of the recorded signal is proportional to the distance from the source and to the orientation of the flux lines. Lines that are closer to perpendicular induce greater current than do those that approach parallel. This knowledge makes it possible to infer the source of a signal, although the inference is never certain because researchers typically do not know how many sources contributed to the signal (as is discussed further under interpretation of neuroimaging data).

MEG has been used in a few pediatric studies of older children with various disorders (e.g., Paul, Bott, Heim, Eulitz, & Elbert, 2006). For example, Lewine and colleagues (2005) used MEG to show that some children with regressive autism spectrum disorders have multifocal epileptiform activity, including the same perisylvian regions that underlie the language breakdown in Landau–Kleffner syndrome. They also found that MEG showed greater sensitivity to this deviant activity than did EEG (Lewine et al., 2005). This study illustrates the utility of MEG for examining childhood behavioral disorders, since the behavioral manifestation of seizures had not been observed for half of the children with autism.

Functional MRI

FMRI takes advantage of the fact that oxygenated and de-oxygenated blood have different magnetic properties. Increased metabolic activity of a brain region requires more glucose and oxygen and thus more blood flow. This increased blood flow delivers greater amounts of oxygenated blood to the activated area of brain tissue. Even though the trigger for this increased blood flow is depletion of oxygen, the measurable difference in metabolism is observed following this depletion as an increase in the amount of oxygenated compared to de-oxygenated blood, leading to a more homogenous magnetic field and, thus, to greater signal intensity. FMRI, which involves measuring these magnetic fields with a magnet, can provide fairly precise localization, on the order of millimeters, but has relatively poor temporal resolution, given that the increase in blood flow occurs 5–8 s following the event (Bookheimer, 2000; Papanicalaou, 1998).

Using fMRI with children is challenging for several reasons. As with MEG, participants must remain still while in the magnet, or else the spatial resolution is compromised. The environment of the magnet can also be frightening. Both of these requirements have led to researchers developing techniques to train children to hold still in the magnet and to acclimatize them to the magnet environment (Bookheimer, 2000; Seyffert & Castellanos, 2005). Even so, it is unlikely that good fMRI data will be collected from nonclinical child groups under the age or 4 years, because toddlers are often unwilling to cooperate and are incapable of remaining still (while awake) for the necessary length of time needed to collect fMRI. Despite the difficulties in performing these studies with pediatric populations, there have been a few recent studies examining developmental language disorders. For example, children with SLI were found to show less activation than controls in brain regions typically activated in attention, memory, and language processes using verbal working memory tasks (Weismer, Plante, Jones, & Tomblin, 2005).

Positron Emission Tomography (PET)

PET works by detecting photons that are emitted during the process of decay of a radioactive substance with a relatively short half-life, such as Oxygen-15 (^{15}O). When the radioactive substance decays, it emits its excess positive charge (positron). After traveling a short distance (generally less than 2 mm), the positron collides with an electron to produce two photons that travel in opposite directions with equal velocity. The detectors record the time and location of each photon, and an image is reconstructed by calculating the most probable origin of the collisions. The radioactive substances (radioisotopes) are made by bombarding stable atoms with protons. The extra positive charges are unstable and will be emitted over time, and each radioisotope has a characteristic half-life. This half-life, or time a substance takes to lose half of its excess charge, determines the temporal resolution of the PET images, with short half-lives resulting in better resolution. The radioisotope is typically injected intravenously into the participant for rapid uptake by brain structures. FMRI, described above, provides better spatial resolution than does PET, but it is limited to measuring oxygenation. In contrast, PET can be used to create images of how different regions use various substances in the brain, such as neurotransmitters and glucose, in addition to oxygen (Papanicalaou, 1998).

Because of its invasive nature, PET is rarely used to examine healthy pediatric populations. Even so, its use in studies of disorders can provide information regarding brain function that could inform our understanding of language disorders. PET imaging has primarily been used with children only in clinical cases that might require some surgery, such as epilepsy (Juhasz & Chugani, 2003). However, certain types of epilepsy (e.g., Landau-Kleffner) lead to language impairment, and thus PET imaging can provide useful information on the role of substances, such as neurotransmitters, in this type of disorder.

INTERPRETATION OF IMAGING DATA

In interpreting brain images, it is necessary to consider a number of factors. Images of brain structure and function constructed from these various methods represent different aspects of the actual processes and structures. The relationship between the representations and the reality of these functions and structures is dependent on what is being measured (e.g., electrical current, blood flow), the nature of the recording instruments, and the choice of techniques for constructing the images. These factors are discussed below.

Activation

Functional images are typically described as representing brain activation. This activation, however, can be the result of neural signaling or changes in metabolism (Papanicalaou, 1998). EEG and MEG measure aspects of neural signaling, whereas fMRI measures aspects of metabolism. PET reflects aspects of neural signaling when neurotransmitters are tagged and aspects of metabolism when oxygen or glucose is tagged. The spatial and temporal resolutions of neural activation are limited by what aspect of function is measured. For example, the spatial extent of activation of neural tissue is delimited more precisely by neurotransmitter release. In contrast, increases in oxygen consumption would lead to increases in oxygen in the activated neural tissue and in the neighboring blood vessels. The spatial extent of activation of neural tissue in this latter case can only be estimated from the metabolic activation, because the relationship between extent of neural activation and blood supply is not precisely known. In addition, the temporal interval of activation of neural tissue is precisely delimited by changes in electrical potential but is less precise for changes in metabolism.

These factors impose a lower limit on the spatial and temporal resolution of neural activation as measured by a particular method. Thus, improvements in the resolution of the instrumentation or analysis techniques do not necessarily lead to improvement in resolution of neural activation. For example, an instrument with spatial resolution of 1 mm that measures increases in blood flow provides high resolution for the blood flow changes itself, but the spatial resolution for neural activation is poorer than this because the relationship between the spatial extent of increases in blood flow and that of neural activation is unknown and probably not equivalent.

An issue of interpretation specifically affecting fMRI is that fMRI signal intensity is a relative measure rather than being a direct measure of blood flow, because a number of variables, other than blood flow, can affect the intensity. For this reason, interpretation of fMRI data requires comparison of signal intensity across at least two conditions. Bookheimer (2000) pointed out that this factor leads to challenges in pediatric research. In particular, it is important to equate performance on control tasks between groups. Otherwise, apparent differences in the experimental variable could, rather, be due to differences in performance on the control task. An example of this problem is the following: Increases in blood flow are often related to increases in the rate or effort of task performance. However, less brain activation in children than adults on a particular task could be due to worse performance, in the sense that they do not increase their rate of performance on a difficult task and, rather, stop performing. Alternatively, decreased brain activity could be due to greater ease in performance. This example suggests that it is important to have a measure of behavioral performance to help interpret the results, because an increase in errors along with a decrease in brain activation would indicate decreased effort in doing a task. It is also possible that differences in task difficulty may lead to the use of additional brain regions in performing a task. Thus, finding an additional area of activation in an impaired versus a control group may indicate the recruitment of additional areas in performance of a difficult task rather than a deviant pattern of processing (Bookheimer, 2000). These potential confounds apply, to different degrees, to all studies comparing groups differing on some dimension.

Instrumentation

The instruments also impose limitations on spatial and temporal resolution. Spatial resolution is limited by the number of detectors and the size of detectors. For example, older PET instruments had fewer and larger detectors and thus poorer spatial resolution than do newer instruments. Electrophysiology has improved the spatial resolution dramatically in the past decade by increasing the number of electrode scalp sites, and most current systems record from a minimum of 64 sites.

Spatial resolution is also limited by the distance of the recording instruments from the source for EEG, MEG, and PET because the signal becomes distorted with increasing distance from the source, for several different reasons. In the case of EEG, the distortion is due to conductivity of different tissues and to the summation at the scalp of electrical activity from an unknown number of sources. MEG signals do not suffer from distortions in traveling through tissue, but the number of sources contributing to the signal is typically unknown, as with EEG (Nunez & Srinivasan, 2006). Spatial resolution of PET is a function of the distance a positron travels before a collision, which releases positrons. Also, photons are increasingly likely to be deflected when the source is in deep brain structures, because they must travel through a greater extent of tissue. In contrast, identifying the location of source signals using MRI and fMRI is precise, because a unique code for position is provided in terms of signal frequency. Thus, in this latter case, spatial resolution of metabolic activation is limited only by the size of the pixel that can be measured by the instrument (Papanicalaou, 1998).

The temporal resolution of the instruments is determined by the sampling rate and can be quite high (on the order of a millisecond) in the case of EEG and MEG. The temporal resolution of PET is limited by the half-life of the chosen isotope. Specifically, to determine whether there is increased activation, the instrument needs a sufficient number of photon pairs. An isotope with a shorter half-life leads to a greater number of photons emitted per unit of time and, thus, to better temporal resolution than an isotope with a longer half-life.

Analysis

Each method presents unique challenges in developing analysis techniques that will provide the most valid and reliable representation of a particular function or structure. One challenge facing the construction of PET images is in developing methods for estimating sources, given that there is noise in the data from deflections of photons and from erroneously pairing two photons that do not derive from the same positron source. A second challenge, which is a concern for fMRI as well, is determining what level of activation above the baseline noise should be considered to be significant. The choice to use a more restrictive significance level will lead to a smaller area showing significant activation. Thus, the wrong decision can lead to erroneous interpretation of the data.

The major analysis challenge facing EEG and MEG is determining the number of sources or components contributing to the electromagnetic signals recorded at the surface. Sources are locations of the neural activation. Components reflect neural activation that covaries. Using a known set of source signals and their strength and direction, it is possible to predict the surface distribution of electrical potential or magnetic flux. However, any given surface distribution can be generated by multiple solutions. Thus, it is impossible to determine the location, direction, and strength of the sources of the scalp distribution without having some a priori information. Unfortunately, in research with humans it is unlikely that we will have prior knowledge of all the sources contributing to a signal or their signal strength and direction. Even so, researchers have developed methods that can be used to make intelligent guesses about the number or sources, location of sources, direction of signals, temporal properties of components, and strength of components. These methods are only beginning to be widely used, since the advent of multichannel recordings. Techniques such as principal components analysis (PCA) and independent components analysis (ICA) have been used to identify combinations of electrodes (spatial mode) or time-points (temporal mode) at which similar EEG/ERP or MEG variance was recorded (e.g., Hyvarinen, Karhunen, & Oja, 2001; Makeig, Jung, Bell, Ghahramani, & Sejnowski, 1997; Spencer, Dien, & Donchin, 2001). Dipole source modeling estimates the location, direction, and strength of sources by finding the best fit of the data (e.g., Scherg, Vajsar, & Picton, 1989). This method requires using a priori knowledge of where sources are likely to be to arrive at a reasonable model. Figure 24.5. shows the results of a dipole analysis of the child P100 component to a speech sound plotted on a standardized MRI. Global Field Power is used to calculate the peak and temporal extent of variance across scalp sites (Lehmann & Skrandies, 1980). This method is useful for determining timing of peak activation. Detailed descriptions of these different methods are beyond the scope of this chapter, but it will be necessary to have some understanding of these to evaluate their validity (for an introduction, see Luck, 2005; for advanced reading, Nunez & Srinivasan, 2006).

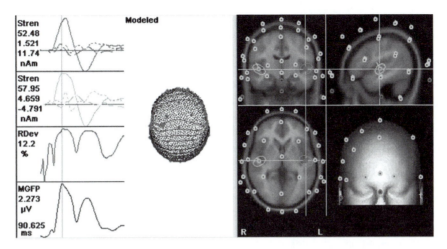

FIGURE 24.5 Results of a dipole analysis of the child P100 component to a speech sound plotted on a standardized MRI (courtesy of Curtis Ponton).

Convergence of Methods

Each of the neuroscience methods described above has different strengths and limitations. Thus, the most powerful approach to studying the neurobiological basis of developmental language disorders is to make use of all of these methods. Having results from several different methods point to a common finding can only strengthen confidence in that finding. For example, the finding that children with SLI have structurally deviant left hemisphere regions in a study using MRI (Gauger et al., 1997) and that such children have functionally deviant left temporal activity in a study using ERPs (Shafer et al., 2000) considerably strengthens the claim that left hemisphere dysfunction is a factor in SLI.

It will also be important to tie the results from neuroimaging studies to the micro level of brain structure and function. Several examples of why this can be informative follow.

Evidence from structural cytoarchitectonics can help to interpret findings from ERP investigations. For example, structural cytoarchitectonics has been used to examine maturational changes. Specifically, researchers have shown that primary cortical regions, which are dominated by Layer IV or Layer V, mature earlier than association cortex, which is dominated by Layers II and III (Huttenlocher & Dabholkar, 1997). The deficits found in developmental language disorders have not been investigated in terms of deviancy or differences at this cellular level. However, there are studies relating changes in neurophysiological measures to maturation of cortical layers, which illustrate the importance of this knowledge. Specifically, Tonnquist-Uhlen, Ponton, Eggermont, Kwong, and Don (2003) suggest that the predominance of a positive component (P1) and absent negative component (N1) around 100 ms in the child auditory evoked potential (AEP) reflects early maturation of Layer IV in the superior temporal plane of secondary auditory cortex (seen as P1) and immaturity of Layers II and III in primary and secondary cortex (resulting in absent N1). The Ta and Tb AEP components recorded at temporal sites (approximately 1 cm above the ear) reflect activation of cells in early maturing Layer IV of secondary auditory cortex on the lateral surface (Tonnquist-Uhlen et al., 2003). P1 and Ta/Tb index parallel streams of input from the thalamus to auditory cortex. In our recent research, we have found a small subset of children with SLI have delayed P1 latencies (Shafer, Ponton, Datta, Morr, & Schwartz, 2007), but a larger proportion have reduced amplitude

Ta components across four different experiments of children with SLI (Shafer, Schwartz, & Ponton, 2008). Our knowledge of the cortical source of Ta and the structural design of this cortical region allows us to speculate that deviant processing is occurring in Layer IV on the lateral surface of secondary auditory cortex and that, possibly, maturation of Layer IV in auditory cortex is particularly delayed or deviant. Thus, relating these different research findings allows development of novel hypotheses and research directions.

It will also be important to relate neuroimaging findings to the underlying bio-chemistry. As discussed above, we pointed out the deviant AEPs seen at temporal electrode sites in children with SLI might indicate deficits in Layer IV of lateral secondary auditory cortex. To understand why these AEP components are abnormal, we ultimately need to go further and determine whether the deviance is due to structural deficits, such as a reduced number of neurons in Layer IV or a delay in myelination of axons, or is due to biochemical deficits, such as reduced levels of some neurotransmitter or abnormality of receptor cells for a particular neurotransmitter.

A few investigations of childhood cognitive disorders suggesting abnormalities related to biochemistry illustrate the importance of examining language disorders in these terms. Researchers have argued that the neurotransmitter serotonin plays a role in cortical abnormalities that underlie autism and epilepsy (Chugani, 2004). This type of knowledge provides the impetus for investigating possible reasons for abnormal amounts or uptake of neurotransmitters, such as inadequate diet, genetics, and so on. In another example, learning-disabled children seem to have significant differences in the levels of a number of different elements (e.g., manganese, lead; Kolb & Wishaw, 1996), and these elements can affect neurotransmitters or be the by-product of abnormal biochemistry.

CONCLUSIONS

Neurobiological methods are beginning to provide valuable information regarding devel-opmental language disorders. The value of this research is greatly increased if we have information from multiple methods, because each method measures different aspects of function and structure and provides different levels of spatial and temporal resolution. A continuing challenge for research in this area is in developing methods that can be used with young children and infants. Despite the difficulties in this endeavor, the information that will result from these studies makes this challenge worth meeting.

REFERENCES

Benasich, A. A, Choudhury, N., Friedman, J. T., Realpe-Bonilla, T., Chojnowska, C., & Gou, Z. (2006). The infant as a prelinguistic model for language learning impairments: Predicting from event-related potentials to behavior. *Neuropsychologia. 44*(3), 396–411.

Bookheimer, S. Y. (2000). Methodological issues in pediatric neuroimaging. *Mental Retardation and Developmental Disabilities Research Reviews, 6*, 161–165.

Bookheimer, S. (2002). Functional MRI of language: New approaches to understanding the cortical organization of semantic priming. *Annual Review of Neuroscience, 22*, 151–188.

Calvin, W. H. (1975). Generation of spike trains in CNS neurons. *Brain Research, 84*, 1–22.

Chugani, D. D. (2004). Serotonin in autism and pediatric epilepsies. *Mental Retardation and Devel-opmental Disabilities Research Review, 10*(2), 112–116.

De Fosse, L., Hodge, S. M., Makris, N., Kennedy, D. N., Caviness, V. S. Jr, McGrath, L., et al. (2004). Language-association cortex asymmetry in autism and specific language impairment. *Annals of Neurology, 56*(6), 755–756.

Engel, A. K., Moll, C. K. E., & Fried, I. (2005). Invasive recordings from the human brain: Clinical insights and beyond. *Nature Reviews Neuroscience, 6*, 35–47.

Friederici, A. D. (2002). Towards a neural basis of auditory sentence processing. *Trends in Cognitive Sciences, 6*, 78–84.

Gauger, L., Lombardino, L. J., & Leonard, C. M. (1997). Brain morphology in children with specific language impairment. *Journal of Speech, Language, and Hearing Research, 40*, 1272–1284.

Hebb, D. (1949). *The organization of behavior: A neurophysiological theory.* New York: Wiley.

Hestvik, A., Maxfield, N., Schwartz, R. G., & Shafer, V. L. (2007). Brain responses to ungrammatically filled gaps. *Brain and Language, 100*(3), 301–316.

Huttenlocher, P. R., & Dabholkar, A. S. (1997). Regional differences in synaptogenesis in human cerebral cortex. *Journal of Comparative Neurology, 387*, 167–178.

Hyvarinen, A., Karhunen, J., & Oja, E. (2001). *Independent component analysis.* New York: Wiley.

Juhasz, C., & Chugani, H. T. (2003). Imaging the epileptic brain with positron emission tomography. *Neuroimaging Clinics of North America, 13*(4), 705–716.

Kandel, E., Schwartz, J., & Jessell, T. (2000). *Principles of neural science.* New York: Heinemann, Harvard University Press.

Koch, C. (2004). *The quest for consciousness: A neurobiological approach.* Englewood, CO: Roberts.

Kolb, B., & Wishaw, I. Q. (1996). *Fundamentals of human neuropsychology.* New York: Freeman.

Lehmann, D., & Skrandies, W. (1980). Reference-free identification of components of checkerboard-evoded multichannel potential fields. *Electroencephalography and Clinical Neurophysiology, 48*, 609–621.

Leonard, C. M., Lombardino, L. J., Walsh, K., Eckert, M. A., Mockler, J. L., Rowe, L. A., et al. (2002). Anatomical risk factors that distinguish dyslexia from SLI predict reading skill in normal children. *Journal of Communication Disorders. 35*(6), 501–531.

Leppänen, P., Pihko, E., Eklund, K. M., & Lyytinen, H. (1999). Cortical responses of infants with and without a genetic risk for dyslexia, II: Group effects. *NeuroReport, 10*, 969–973.

Lewine, J. D., Andrews, R., Chez, M., Patil, A. A., Devinsky, O., Smith, M., et al. (2005). Magnetoencephalographic patterns of epileptiform activity in children with regressive autism spectrum disorders. *Pediatrics, 104*, 405–418.

Luck, S. J. (2005). *An introduction to the event-related potential technique.* Cambridge, MA: MIT Press.

Makeig, S., Jung, T.-P., Bell, D., Ghahramani, D., & Sejnowski, T. (1997). Blind separation of auditory event-related responses into independent components. *Proceedings of the National Academy of Sciences, U.S.A., 94*: 10979–10984.

Nunez, P. L., & Srinivasan, R. (2006). *Electric fields of the brain: The neurophysics of EEG* (2nd ed.). Oxford: Oxford University Press.

Papanicalaou, A. C. (1998). *Fundamentals of functional brain imaging. A guide to the methods and their applications to psychology and behavioral neuroscience.* Lisse, The Netherlands: Swets & Zeitlinger.

Paul, I., Bott, C., Heim, S., Eulitz, C., & Elbert, T. (2006). Reduced hemispheric asymmetry of the auditory N260m in dyslexia. *Neuropsychologia, 44*, 785–794.

Plante, E. (1991). MRI findings in the parents and siblings of specifically language-impaired boys. *Brain and Language, 41*(1), 67–80.

Scherg, M., Vajsar J., & Picton, T. W. (1989). A source analysis of the late human auditory evoked potentials. *Journal of Cognitive Neuroscience, 1*, 336–355.

Schmitt, B. M., Münte, T. F., & Kutas, M. (2000). Electrophysiological estimates of the time course of semantic and phonological encoding during implicit picture naming. *Psychophysiology, 37*, 473–484.

Scott, S., & Wise, R. (2004). The functional neuroanatomy of prelexical processing in speech perception. *Cognition, 92*, 1–2, 13–45.

Seyffert, M., & Castellanos, F. X. (2005). Functional MRI in pediatric neurobehavioral disorders. *International Review of Neurobiology, 67*, 239–284.

Shafer, V. L., & Garrido-Nag, K. (2007). The neurodevelopmental bases of language. In M. Shatz & E. Hoff (Eds.), *The handbook of language development* (pp. 21–45). Oxford: Blackwell.

Shafer, V. L, Morr, M. L., Datta, H., Kurtzberg, D., & Schwartz, R. G. (2005). Neurophysiological indices of speech processing deficits in children with specific language impairment. *Journal of Cognitive Neurosciences, 17*, 1168–1180.

Shafer, V. L., Ponton, C., Datta, H., Morr, M. L., & Schwartz, R. G. (2007). Neurophysiological indices of attention to speech in children with SLI. *Clinical Neurophysiology, 118*, 1230–1243.

Shafer, V. L., Schwartz, R. G., Morr, M. L., Kessler, K. L., & Kurtzberg, D. (2000). Deviant neurophysiological asymmetry in children with language impairment. *NeuroReport, 11*, 3715–3718.

Shafer, V. L., Schwartz, R. G., & Ponton, C. (2008). *Evidence of deficient central auditory processing in children with specific language impairment: The T-complex.* Manuscript in preparation.

Shafer, V. L., Ponton, C., Datta, H., Morr, M. L. & Schwartz, R. G. (2007). Neurophysiological indices of attention to speech in children with SLI. *Clinical Neurophysiology, 118*, 1230–1243.

Shafer, V. L., Schwartz, R. G., & Kessler, K. L. (2003). ERP indices of phonological and lexical processing in children and adults. *Proceedings of the 27th Annual Boston University Conference on Language Development* (pp. 751–761). Somerville, MA: Cascadilla Press.

Spencer, K. M., Dien, J., & Donchin, E. (2001). Spatiotemporal analysis of the late ERP responses to deviant stimuli. *Psychophysiology, 38*(2), 343–358.

Squire, L., & Kandel, E. (1999). *Memory: From mind and molecules.* New York: Scientific American Library.

Tonnquist-Uhlen, I., Ponton, C. W., Eggermont, J. J., Kwong, B., & Don, M. (2003). Maturation of human central auditory system activity: The T-complex. *Clinical Neurophysiology, 114*(4), 685–701.

van Turennout, M., Hagoort, P., & Brown, C. M. (1998). Brain activity during speaking: From syntax to phonology in 40 milliseconds. *Science, 280*, 572–574.

Vaughan, H., & Kurtzberg, D. (1992). Electrophysiologic indices of human brain maturation and cognitive development. In: M. R. Gunnar & C. A. Nelson (Eds.), *Developmental behavioral neuroscience.* Hillsdale, NJ: Lawrence Erlbaum Associates.

Weismer, S. E., Plante, E., Jones, M., & Tomblin, J. B. (2005). A functional magnetic resonance imaging investigation of verbal working memory in adolescents with specific language impairment. *Journal of Speech, Language, and Hearing Research, 48*(2), 405–425.

Author Index

Subject Index

Page entries in **bold** refer to figures and tables.
Page entries for headings with subheadings refer to general aspects of that topic.